# CITIES OF THE UNITED STATES

ISSN 0899-6075

# CITIES OF THE UNITED STATES

## FIFTH EDITION

A Compilation of Current Information on
Economic, Cultural, Geographic, and Social Conditions

In Four Volumes

### Volume 1:
## The South

Alabama
Arkansas
Delaware
Florida
Georgia
Kentucky
Louisiana
Maryland
Mississippi
North Carolina
Oklahoma
South Carolina
Tennessee
Texas
Virginia
Washington, D.C.
West Virginia

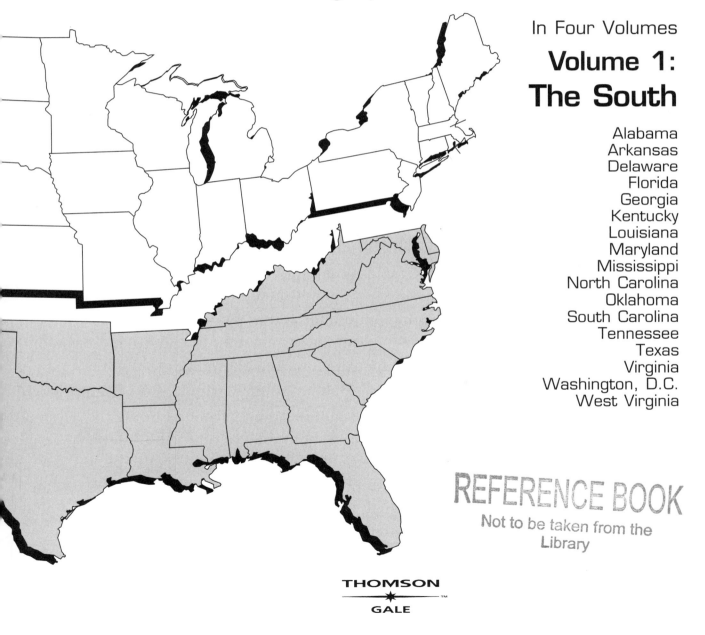

THOMSON

GALE

Detroit • New York • San Francisco • San Diego • New Haven, Conn. • Waterville, Maine • London • Munich

# THOMSON
★
## GALE

### Cities of the United States, Fifth Edition

**Project Editors**
Lisa C. DeShantz-Cook, Jacqueline K. Mueckenheim, Kristy Swartout

**Editorial Support Services**
Luann Brennan, Grant Eldridge, Wayne D. Fong

**Imaging and Multimedia**
Leitha Etheridge-Sims, Lezlie Light, Jillean McCommons, Dan Newell, Christine O'Bryan

**Rights and Acquisitions**
Edna M. Hedblad, Shalice Shah-Caldwell, Kim Smilay

**Product Design**
Jennifer Wahi

**Composition and Electronic Prepress**
Evi Seoud

**Manufacturing**
Rita Wimberley

**LIBRARY OF CONGRESS CATALOGING-IN-PUBLICATION DATA**

ISBN 0-7876-7369-2 (set)
ISBN 0-7876-7370-6 (v.1)
ISBN 0-7876-7371-4 (v.2)
ISBN 0-7876-7372-2 (v.3)
ISBN 0-7876-7373-0 (v.4)
ISSN 0899-6075

This title is also available as an e-book.
ISBN 1-4144-0600-2 (set)
Contact your Thomson Gale sales representative for ordering information.

Printed in the United States of America
10 9 8 7 6 5 4 3 2 1

# Volume 1—The South

# Contents

# Volume 2—The West

# Contents

# Volume 3—The Midwest

# Contents

# Volume 4—The Northeast
# Contents

# INTRODUCTION

*Cities of the United States (CUS)* provides a one-stop source for all the vital information you need on 189 of America's top cities—those fastest-growing, as well as those with a particular historical, political, industrial, and/or commercial significance. Spanning the entire country, from Anaheim to Virginia Beach, each geographically-arranged volume of *CUS* brings together a wide range of comprehensive data. The volumes include: *The South; The West; The Midwest;* and *The Northeast.*

Within each volume, the city-specific profiles organize pertinent facts, data, and figures related to demographic, economic, cultural, geographic, social, and recreational conditions. Assembling a myriad of sources, *CUS* offers researchers, travelers, students, and media professionals a convenient resource for discovering each city's past, present, and future.

For this completely updated fifth edition, eleven new cities have been added, providing even greater access to the country's growing urban centers. The new city profiles include:

- Akron, OH

- Aurora, IL

- Casper, WY

- El Paso, TX

- Fort Smith, AR

- Henderson, NV

- Huntington, WV

- Mesa, AZ

- Nampa, ID

- Overland Park, KS

- Warwick, RI

## Key Features Unlock Vital Information

*Cities of the United States* offers a range of key features, allowing easy access to targeted information. Features include:

- Section headings—Comprehensive categories, which include **History, Geography and Climate, Population Profile, Municipal Government, Economy, Education, Research, Health Care, Recreation, Convention Facilities, Transportation,** and **Communications** (including city web sites), make it easy for you to locate answers to your specific questions.

- Combined facts and analysis—Fact-packed charts and detailed descriptions bring you the statistics and the rest of the story.

- "In Brief" fact sheets—One-page "at a glance" overviews provide the essential facts for each state and each city profiled.

- Economic information—Detailed updates about such topics as incentive programs, development projects, and largest employers help you rate the business climate using criteria that matter to you.

- Directory information—Contact information at the end of many entry sections provides addresses, phone numbers, and email addresses for organizations, agencies, and institutions you may need to contact.

- Detailed maps—City landmarks, mileage scales, and regional insets allow you to locate many of the points of interest described in main city entries, as well as provide a greater perspective on the city in which you are interested.

- Selected bibliography listings—Historical accounts, biographical works, and other print resources suggest titles to read if you wish to learn more about a particular city.

- Web sites for vital city resources—Access points to URLs for information-rich sources, such as city government, visitors and convention bureaus, economic development agencies, libraries, schools, and newspapers provide researchers an opportunity to explore cities in more detail.

- Enlightening illustrations—Numerous photographs highlight points of interest to you.

- Handy indexing—A referencing guide not only to main city entries, but also to the hundreds of people and place names that fall within those main entries, leading you directly to the information you seek.

## Designed For a Variety of Users

Whether you are a researcher, traveler, or executive on the move, *CUS* serves your needs. This is the reference long sought by a variety of users:

- Business people, market researchers, and other decision-makers will find the current data that helps them stay informed.

- People vacationing, conventioneering, or relocating will consult this source for questions they have about what's new, unique, or significant about where they are going.

- Students, media professionals, and researchers will discover their background work already completed.

## Hurricanes of 2005 and Their Impact on the United States

The powerful hurricanes of 2005—Hurricane Katrina on August 29 followed by Hurricane Rita on September 24—devastated the Gulf Coast region of the United States. From Alabama to the shores of Texas, these two hurricanes had profound impact—from the loss of lives to the loss of infrastructure (utilities, roads, commerce), industry, and manufacturing. Cities directly hit by these hurricanes, such as New Orleans, Louisiana and Biloxi, Mississippi, will undergo recovery efforts for years to come, and it is unknown at the time of publication of *Cities of the United States,* 5th edition just how long and how far-reaching that recovery will be.

It is also important to note that not only are the cities hit directly by these hurricanes affected; cities that have offered refuge to evacuees and contributed greatly to the relief efforts will continue to be affected as they work to aid the recovery efforts, putting their own development initiatives on hold. Cities such as Mobile, Alabama; Baton Rouge, Louisiana; and Jackson, Mississippi will also continue to experience the effects of these unprecedented natural disasters.

The essays profiled herein for the states of Alabama, Louisiana, Mississippi, and Texas were updated prior to August 2005 and reflect information that was then current.

## Definitions of Key Statistical Resources

Following are explanations of key resources used for statistical data:

*ACCRA (The Council for Community Economic Research; formerly the American Chamber of Commerce Researchers Association):* The Cost of Living Index, produced quarterly, provides a useful and reasonably accurate measure of living cost differences among urban areas. Items on which the Index is based have been carefully chosen to reflect the different categories of consumer expenditures, such as groceries, housing, utilities, transportation, health care, and miscellaneous goods and services; taxes are excluded. Weights assigned to relative costs are based on government survey data on expenditure patterns for midmanagement households (typically the average professional worker's home, new construction with 2,400 square feet of living space). All items are priced in each place at a specified time and according to standardized specifications. Information regarding ACCRA and the Cost of Living Index can be found at www.accra.org. Please note that the ACCRA Cost of Living Index and ACCRA housing price information are reprinted by permission of ACCRA.

*Metropolitan Statistical Area (MSA)*: The U.S. Office of Management and Budget (OMB) provides that each Metropolitan Statistical Area must include (a) at least one city with 50,000 or more inhabitants, or (b) a U.S. Census Bureau-defined urbanized area (of at least 50,000 inhabitants) and a total metropolitan population of at least 100,000 (75,000 in New England). The term was adopted in 1983. The term "metropolitan area" (MA) became effective in 1990. During the 2000 Census, the MSA standards were revised, establishing Core Based Statistical Areas (CBSAs). CBSAs may be either Metropolitan Statistical Areas or Micropolitan Statistical Areas. It is important to note that standards, and therefore content of 1990 Census MSAs, are not identical to 2000 Census MSA standards. Additional information regarding MSAs can be found at http://census.state.nc.us/glossary/msa.html.

*FBI Crime Index Total:* The total number of index offenses reported to the FBI during the year through its Uniform Crime Reporting Program. The FBI receives monthly and annual reports from law enforcement agencies throughout the country. City police, sheriffs, and state police file reports on the number of index offenses that become known to them. The FBI Crime Index offenses are: murder and non-negligent manslaughter; forcible rape; robbery; aggravated assault; burglary; larceny; motor vehicle theft; and arson.

*Estimates of population:* Between decennial censuses, the U.S. Bureau of the Census publishes estimates of the population using the decennial census data as benchmarks and data available from various agencies, both state and federal, including births and deaths, and school statistics, among other data.

## Method of Compilation

The editors of *Cities of the United States* consulted numerous sources to secure the kinds of data most valuable to you. Each entry gathers together economic information culled in part from the U.S. Department of Labor/Bureau of Labor Statistics and state departments of labor and commerce, population figures derived from the U.S. Department of Commerce/Bureau of the Census and from city and state agencies, educational and municipal government data supplied by local authorities and historical narrative based on a variety of accounts. Along with material supplied by chambers of commerce, convention and visitors bureaus, and other local sources, background information was drawn from periodicals and books chosen for their timeliness and accuracy. Through print resources, web sites, email contact, and/or phone calls with agency representatives, the information reflects current conditions.

## Acknowledgments

The editors are grateful for the assistance provided by dozens of helpful chambers of commerce and convention and visitors bureau professionals, as well as municipal, library, and school employees for their invaluable generosity and expertise.

## Comments and Suggestions Welcome

If you have questions, concerns, or comments about *Cities of the United States*, please contact the Project Editors:

*Cities of the United States*
Thomson Gale
27500 Drake Road
Farmington Hills, MI 48331
Phone: (248)699-4253
Toll-free: (800)347-GALE
Fax: (248)699-8075
URL: http://www.gale.com

# Map Credits

Regional and city maps for *Cities of the United States,* 5th edition, were created by Teresa San Clementi and XNR Productions Inc.

✳ ✳ ✳ ✳

# Photo Credits—Volume 1

**Photographs appearing in *Cities of the United States,* 5th edition, Volume 1—*The South* were received from the following sources:**

## ALABAMA:
*Birmingham*—1996, photograph. Birmingham Area Chamber of Commerce. Reproduced by permission: p. 5; showing Statue of Martin Luther King, photograph. Birmingham Area Chamber of Commerce. Reproduced by permission: p. 13
*Mobile*—photograph. Courtesy of Mobile Bay Convention & Visitors Bureau. Reproduced by permission: p. 19; showing the Battleship *U.S.S. Alabama*, photograph. Reproduced by permission of Bill Tunnell: p. 27
*Montgomery*—showing State Capitol, photograph. Courtesy of the Montgomery Area Chamber of Commerce. Reproduced by permission: p. 31; showing first White House of Confederacy, photograph by James Blank. © James Blank. Reproduced by permission: p. 40

## ARKANSAS:
*Fort Smith*—showing historic homes in Fort Smith, photograph. Fort Smith Convention & Visitors Bureau. Reproduced by permission: p. 49; showing historical landmark, photograph. Fort Smith Convention & Visitors Bureau. Reproduced by permission: p. 58
*Little Rock*—photograph: p. 61

## DELAWARE:
*Dover*—photograph. Kent County Convention & Visitors Bureau. Reproduced by permission: p. 77; showing Loockerman Street, photograph. Kent County Convention & Visitors Bureau. Reproduced by permission: p. 82
*Wilmington*—photograph. © Kevin Fleming/Corbis: p. 89; showing Old Town Hall, photograph: p. 98

## FLORIDA:
*Jacksonville*—St. John's River, Jacksonville, Florida, photograph by James Blank. © James Blank. Reproduced by permission: p. 107; showing St. Augustine Lighthouse, photograph by James Blank. © James Blank. Reproduced by permission: p. 116
*Miami*—photograph. © Alan Schein/Corbis: p. 121
*Orlando*—photograph by James Blank. © James Blank. Reproduced by permission: p. 137; showing entrance to Epcot Center, photograph by James Blank. © James Blank. Reproduced by permission: p. 146
*St. Petersburg*—photograph by James Blank. © James Blank. Reproduced by permission: p. 151; photograph by James Blank. © James Blank. Reproduced by permission: p. 160
*Tallahassee*—showing old and new State Capitols, photograph. Tallahassee Area Convention and Visitors Bureau. Reproduced by permission: p. 165; showing road to old State Capitol, photograph. © Nik Wheeler/Corbis: p. 172
*Tampa*—photograph. Courtesy of Tampa Bay Convention and Visitors Bureau. Reproduced by permission: p. 177; showing the University of Tampa campus, photograph by James Blank. © James Blank. Reproduced by permission: p. 185

## GEORGIA:
*Atlanta*—photograph by James Blank. © James Blank. Reproduced by permission: p. 193; showing historic Swan House, photograph by James Blank. © James Blank. Reproduced by permission: p. 201
*Marietta*—photograph. Marietta Welcome Center & Visitors Bureau. Reproduced by permission: p. 207; showing Welcome Center, photograph. Marietta Welcome Center. Reproduced by permission: p. 215
*Savannah*—photograph. Courtesy of the Georgia Department of Economic Development. Reproduced by permission: p. 219; showing Historical Gaston House, photograph by James Blank. © James Blank. Reproduced by permission: p. 227

**KENTUCKY:**
*Frankfort*—showing State Capitol, photograph by James Blank. © James Blank. Reproduced by permission: p. 235; showing Liberty Hall, photograph by James Blank. © James Blank. Reproduced by permission: p. 243
*Lexington*—photograph by James Blank. © James Blank. Reproduced by permission: p. 247; showing Memorial Hall at the University of Kentucky, photograph by James Blank. © James Blank. Reproduced by permission: p. 255
*Louisville*—showing skyline along Ohio River, photograph by James Blank. © James Blank. Reproduced by permission: p. 261; showing Churchill Downs, photograph. Louisville Convention and Visitors Bureau. Reproduced by permission: p. 270

**LOUISIANA:**
*Baton Rouge*—photograph. Baton Rouge Area Convention & Visitors Bureau. Reproduced by permission: p. 277; showing Old State Capitol, photograph. Baton Rouge Area Convention & Visitors Bureau. Reproduced by permission: p. 284
*New Orleans*—photograph by James Blank. © James Blank. Reproduced by permission: p. 289; showing French Quarter, photograph by James Blank. © James Blank. Reproduced by permission: p. 298

**MARYLAND:**
*Annapolis*—photograph by Bohdan Romaniuk. Reproduced by permission: p. 307; showing U.S. Naval Academy, photograph by James Blank. © James Blank. Reproduced by permission: p. 315
*Baltimore*—showing Inner Harbor: p. 319; showing Washington Monument, photograph by James Blank. © James Blank. Reproduced by permission: p. 327

**MISSISSIPPI:**
*Biloxi*—photograph by James Blank. © James Blank. Reproduced by permission: p. 337; photograph. Mississippi Gulf Coast Convention and Visitors Bureau. Reproduced by permission: p. 345
*Jackson*—photograph by Gil Ford Photography. Reproduced by permission: p. 349; showing State Capitol, photograph by James Blank. © James Blank. Reproduced by permission: p. 356

**NORTH CAROLINA:**
*Charlotte*—photograph. © Richard Cummins/Corbis: p. 363
*Greensboro*—photograph by Robert Calvin. Greensboro Area Convention & Visitors Bureau. Reproduced by permission: p. 375; showing Tannenbaum Park, photograph. Greensboro Area Convention & Visitors Bureau. Reproduced by permission: p. 384
*Raleigh*—photograph. © Joseph Sohm; ChromoSohm/Corbis: p. 389; showing State Capitol, photograph by Peter Damroth. Reproduced by permission: p. 397

**OKLAHOMA:**
*Oklahoma City*—photograph by James Blank. © James Blank. Reproduced by permission: p. 405; showing "End of the Trail" by James Earle Fraser, sculpture in the National Cowboy Hall of Fame, photograph. Oklahoma City Convention & Visitors Bureau. Reproduced by permission: p. 413
*Tulsa*—photograph. Metro Tulsa Chamber of Commerce. Reproduced by permission: p. 419; showing River Parks Amphitheatre, photograph. Metro Tulsa Chamber of Commerce. Reproduced by permission: p. 427

**SOUTH CAROLINA:**
*Charleston*—photograph by James Blank. © James Blank. Reproduced by permission: p. 435; showing Magnolia Plantation and Gardens, photograph. Charleston Trident Convention & Visitors Bureau. Reproduced by permission: p. 444
*Columbia*—photograph. Columbia Metropolitan Convention and Visitors Bureau. Reproduced by permission of Sam Holland: p. 451; State Capitol, photograph by Alt Lee, Inc. Courtesy of the Columbia Metropolitan Convention and Visitors Bureau and Alt Lee, Inc. Reproduced by permission: p. 460

**TENNESSEE:**
*Chattanooga*—showing Lookout Mountain, photograph. © Charles E. Rotkin/Corbis: p. 467
*Knoxville*—photograph. © Raymond Gehman/Corbis: p. 481
*Memphis*—photograph. © Raymond Gehman/Corbis: p. 495
*Nashville*—showing Bicentennial Mall, photograph. © 1999 Gary Layda: p. 509; showing Belle Meade Mansion, photograph. © Robin Hood: p. 519

**TEXAS:**

*Austin*—photograph. Austin Convention & Visitors Bureau. Reproduced by permission: p. 527; showing State Capitol, photograph. Austin Convention & Visitors Bureau. Reproduced by permission: p. 535

*Dallas*—photograph by James Blank. © James Blank. Reproduced by permission: p. 539; showing State Fair Park, photograph by James Blank. © James Blank. Reproduced by permission: p. 547

*El Paso*—photograph by James Blank. © James Blank. Reproduced by permission: p. 553; showing Hueco Tanks State Park, photograph. © David Muench/Corbis: p. 562

*Fort Worth*—photograph by James Blank. © James Blank. Reproduced by permission: p. 567; showing stockyards, photograph. © Joseph Sohm; ChromoSohm Inc./Corbis: p. 575

*Houston*—showing Convention Center, photograph by James Blank. © James Blank. Reproduced by permission: p. 579; showing San Jacinto Memorial, photograph. Courtesy of the Greater Houston Convention and Visitors Bureau. Reproduced by permission: p. 588

*San Antonio*—showing Arneson River Theater along Paseo Del Rio River, photograph by James Blank. © James Blank. Reproduced by permission: p. 593; San Jose Mission, San Antonio, Texas, photograph by James Blank. © James Blank. Reproduced by permission: p. 602

**VIRGINIA:**

*Norfolk*—photograph. Courtesy of Norfolk Convention and Visitors Bureau. Reproduced by permission: p. 611

*Richmond*—photograph. Metropolitan Richmond Convention & Visitors Bureau. Reproduced by permission: p. 625; showing Jefferson Davis Monument, photograph. Metropolitan Richmond Convention & Visitors Bureau. Reproduced by permission: p. 634

*Virginia Beach*—January 9, 2003, photograph by Jay Bernas. AP/Wide World Photos. Reproduced by permission: p. 641; photograph by James Blank. © James Blank. Reproduced by permission: p. 649

**WASHINGTON, D.C.:**

*Washington, D.C.*—showing the National Mall, photograph. Washington, D.C. Convention and Visitors Association. Reproduced by permission: p. 653; showing Capitol, photograph by James Blank. © James Blank. Reproduced by permission: p. 661

**WEST VIRGINIA:**

*Charleston*—photograph by Steve Shaluta, Jr. © West Virginia Division of Tourism. Reproduced by permission: p. 669; showing State Capitol, photograph. © Richard T. Nowitz/Corbis: p. 677

*Huntington*—photograph by David Fatellah. Cabell: p. 681

# CITIES OF THE UNITED STATES

# ALABAMA

# The State in Brief

**Nickname:** Heart of Dixie; Camellia State
**Motto:** We dare defend our rights

**Flower:** Camellia
**Bird:** Yellowhammer

**Area:** 50,744 square miles (2000; U.S. rank: 30th)
**Elevation:** Ranges from sea level to 2,407 feet
**Climate:** Subtropical and humid; summers are long and hot, winters mild, rainfall abundant

**Admitted to Union:** December 14, 1819
**Capital:** Montgomery
**Head Official:** Governor Bob Riley (R) (until 2006)

## Population
**1980:** 3,894,000
**1990:** 4,040,587
**2000:** 4,447,100
**2003 estimate:** 4,500,752
**Percent change, 1990–2000:** 10.1%
**Percent change, 2000–2003:** 1.2%
**U.S. rank in 2003:** 23rd
**Percent of residents born in state:** 73.4% (2000)
**Density:** 87.6 people per square mile (2000)
**2002 FBI Crime Index Total:** 200,331

## Racial and Ethnic Characteristics (2000)
**White:** 3,162,808
**Black or African American:** 1,155,930
**American Indian and Alaska Native:** 22,430
**Asian:** 31,346
**Native Hawaiian and Pacific Islander:** 1,409
**Hispanic or Latino (may be of any race):** 75,830
**Other:** 28,998

## Age Characteristics (2000)
**Population under 5 years old:** 295,992
**Population 5 to 19 years old:** 960,177
**Percent of population 65 years and over:** 13.0%
**Median age:** 35.8 years (2000)

## Vital Statistics
**Total number of births (2003):** 59,356
**Total number of deaths (2003):** 46,598 (infant deaths, 519)
**AIDS cases reported through 2003:** 7,607

## Economy
**Major industries:** Paper products, agriculture, chemicals, textiles, lumber, wood, metals, electronics, automobiles, food processing
**Unemployment rate:** 5.2% (November 2004)
**Per capita income:** $26,276 (2003; U.S. rank: 42nd)
**Median household income:** $37,419 (3-year average, 2001-2003)
**Percentage of persons below poverty level:** 15.1% (3-year average, 2001-2003)
**Income tax rate:** Ranges from 2.0 to 5.0%
**Sales tax rate:** 4.0%

# Birmingham

## The City in Brief

**Founded:** 1871 (chartered 1864)

**Head Official:** Mayor Bernard Kincaid (since 2000)

**City Population**
1980: 284,413
1990: 265,347
2000: 242,820
2003 estimate: 236,620
Percent change, 1990–2000: –8.7%
U.S. rank in 1980: 50th
U.S. rank in 1990: 60th (State rank: 1st)
U.S. rank in 2000: 82nd (State rank: 1st)

**Metropolitan Area Population**
1980: 815,000
1990: 839,945
2000: 921,106
Percent change, 1990–2000: 9.6%

**U.S. rank in 1980:** 42nd
**U.S. rank in 1990:** Not reported
**U.S. rank in 2000:** 54th

**Area:** 151.95 square miles (2000)
**Elevation:** Average 620 feet above sea level
**Average Annual Temperature:** 62.5° F
**Average Annual Precipitation:** 52.16 inches of rain; 2.1 inches of snow

**Major Economic Sectors:** services, wholesale and retail trade, government
**Unemployment rate:** 4.3% (November 2004)
**Per Capita Income:** $15,663 (2000)

**2002 FBI Crime Index Total:** 21,265

**Major Colleges and Universities:** University of Alabama at Birmingham; Samford University; Birmingham-Southern College; Miles College

**Daily Newspaper:** *Birmingham Post-Herald; Birmingham News*

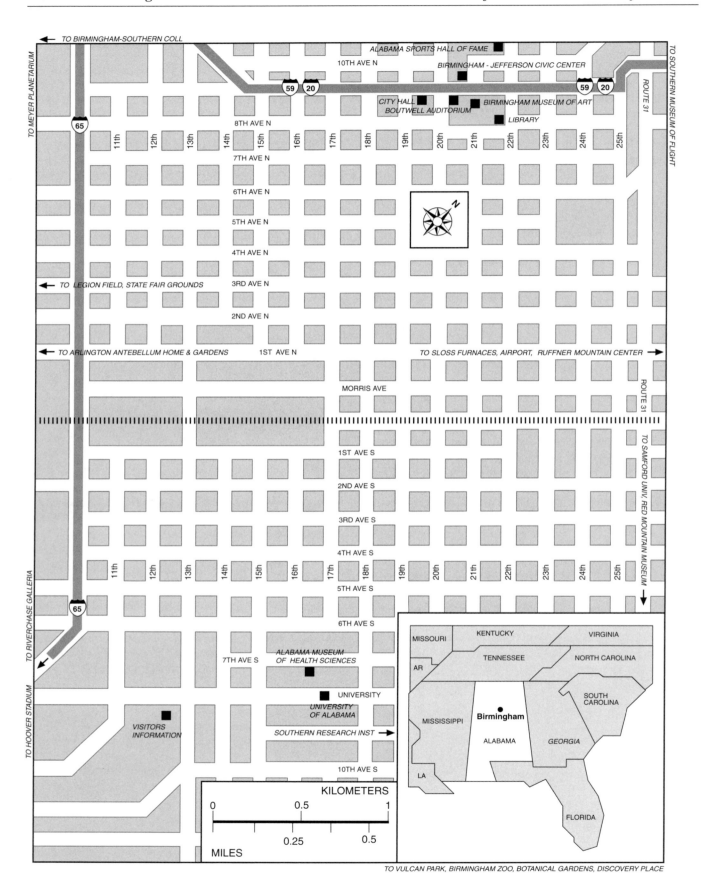

# Introduction

Modern Birmingham calls itself the "Magic City," but this young city, which was founded after the Civil War, has seen its days of adversity. Early in its history it suffered from epidemics, crime, and violence. It failed badly in two depressions and saw, in its darkest days, violent racial confrontations. After years of hard work on race relations, Birmingham gradually moved to such a state of racial equality that it was designated an "All America City" for its progress. The Birmingham Civil Rights Institute, located near the downtown statue of Dr. Martin Luther King, Jr., works to educate about the community and beyond in lessons on race relations. In other ways, Birmingham has done much to distance itself from the past and move forward. One of Birmingham's darkest chapters came to a close in 2002 when jurors delivered a guilty verdict in the case of the 1963 church bombing that killed four African American girls. Once dubbed the "Pittsburgh of the South," the city now employs the majority of its workers in service jobs. The arts continue to flourish, the city's medical research and treatment facilities are world class, and Birmingham is the second largest financial and banking area in the Southeast. Residents attend plays, concerts, and sports events in one of the finest facilities in the country, and they shop, eat, and relax in one of the Southeast's largest enclosed malls, the sparkling Riverchase Galleria. At the heart of the new Birmingham stands the city's symbol, a statue of Vulcan, Roman god of fire and the forge. To many, Birmingham seems to have been magically forged anew.

# Geography and Climate

Located 300 miles north of the Gulf of Mexico in north central Alabama, Birmingham lies in the Jones Valley between a ridge of hills running from northeast to southwest and the Red Mountain Range, which runs in roughly the same direction. A hilly city, Birmingham stretches for about 15 miles along the valley. The hills northeast and north of the city are the foothills of the Appalachian Mountains. During the winter, Birmingham experiences rather low minimum temperatures. Occasional very low temperatures prevent the growth of some vegetation that might usually be expected in a subtropical climate. Snow accumulation, however, is seldom heavy enough to cause problems. In summer, days are very warm; from April through October the daily highs are usually above 75° F, with lows seldom falling below 50° F. Most of the summer precipitation comes in the form of thunderstorms, especially in the month of July.

**Area:** 151.95 square miles (2000)

**Elevation:** Averages 620 feet above sea level

**Average Temperatures:** January, 42.0° F; July, 80.0° F; annual average, 62.5° F

**Average Annual Precipitation:** 52.16 inches of rain; 2.1 inches of snow

# History

### Steel-Making Potential Spurs Growth

The Cherokee, Choctaw, and Chickasaw tribes hunted in the Jones Valley long before the first white man set foot there. The natives found a valley teeming with game and strikingly marked with giant outcroppings of red rock. John Jones and a group of pioneers came to the area in 1815 and established the village of Jonesboro, and in 1819 Jefferson County was formed. Over the next few decades the population of the area gradually increased, and the abundant red rock was found to be high-grade iron ore. By the time of the Civil War, two ore-reducing furnaces were operating for the Confederacy. They were destroyed by Wilson's Raiders in 1865, and development of the valley was virtually halted until 1871, when the Elyton Land Company, realizing the tremendous potential of the valley rich in not only iron ore, but also coal and limestone—the essential ingredients in steel making—founded and incorporated a city to be built at the junction of two major railroads. Thus Birmingham, named for the steel-producing city in England, came into being.

With the expansion of the railroads, what had once been farms and woods became a boomtown, its population growing from 1,200 people in 1871 to 4,000 people in 1873. By 1875, however, after a cholera epidemic and other setbacks, the city's population had dropped back to 1,200 people. Birmingham expanded again in 1880 when the Pratt mining operation began making coke. Two coke furnaces went into blast that year, and by 1885, the population was 25,000 people. Birmingham was growing, and it was beginning to experience some big-city problems, such as crime and disease (particularly typhoid, dysentery, and tuberculosis). The 1890s marked the founding of Birmingham-Southern College, the Mercy Home, and St. Vincent's Hospital, but it was also a decade torn by violence stemming from dangerous mine and foundry conditions and conflicts between union organizers and mine owners.

After January 1, 1900, when the first commercial shipment of steel was made, rolling mills and other factories producing finished steel products began operating in Birmingham. Labor troubles continued in the new century, and the city was plagued with corrupt government officials, vice, and gambling. But Birmingham was growing in positive ways as well. A new model town of Corey, planned by U.S. Steel, was developed by private business, and eight suburbs were incorporated into the city, doubling its population. In October 1921, the city celebrated its fiftieth birthday with four days of festivities, including a visit by U.S. President Warren G. Harding and his wife. On a crest of prosperity that followed World War I, new apartment buildings, hotels, business facilities, and homes went up in Birmingham. During the 1920s, however, the secret white-supremacist organization, the Ku Klux Klan, gained considerable influence in the city; harassment, floggings, and unexplained violence against African Americans were unofficially tolerated by local authorities. As a one-industry town, Birmingham was devastated when the Great Depression of the 1930s reduced demand for iron and steel products; it was quickly deemed ''the hardest hit city in the nation'' by President Hoover's administration.

Birmingham was slow to recover from the Depression, although the federal government poured more than $350 million into the area in an attempt to stimulate the economy. The Works Progress Administration (WPA) tended to Birmingham's streets and parks, and among its projects was the restoration of the city's statue of Vulcan, the Roman god of the forge. The statue was removed from the fairgrounds and placed atop a pedestal on Red Mountain, where it still stands today. Gradually the city began to recover, and by the time World War II was declared in Europe, Birmingham's manufacturing plants were busy preparing for an all-out war effort.

**City Meets Post-War Challenges**

Following World War II, the economy of Birmingham continued to flourish, and to help fill the need for economic diversification, two important institutions were brought to the city: the Medical School of the University of Alabama at Birmingham and the Alabama Research Institute, now called the Southern Research Institute and known worldwide for its research in industrial and medical fields. A development committee attracted more than one hundred new industries to the Birmingham area in the decade following World War II. In spite of such diversification, however, Birmingham was still hard hit by the recession in 1957, and by 1960 the city was again struggling with unemployment. Along with economic woes, Birmingham was embroiled in civil rights conflicts in the 1950s and 1960s as it sought to avoid forced integration of public transport and facilities. In 1963 civil rights advocate Martin Luther King, Jr. began leading peaceful demonstrations in Birmingham. African American children joining in the protests were arrested by the thousands, and photographs from Birmingham of demonstrators being hosed down by police and attacked by police dogs were published worldwide. State police were eventually called in to help restore order. Tensions over the proposed full-scale integration of city classrooms erupted in

more violence when a bomb exploded in the basement of a church, killing four young girls who were changing into their choir robes. Birmingham and the nation were shocked by the event, which convinced the city of the need for change and signaled the end of racial violence.

In the 1970s Birmingham was once again booming, as residential areas spread south and east, millions of feet of warehouse space were constructed, new shopping malls sprang up, and the downtown area was revitalized. The 1979 election of an African American educator as mayor ushered in a new era of racial harmony.

Today's Birmingham, with nearly one million residents in the metropolitan area, is the largest city in Alabama. It has become a worldwide center for health care and boasts a large regional presence in finance, education, research, engineering, transportation and distribution. The early part of the new century saw the city as a booming technological center, with a growing number of people employed in technology jobs. Its symphony, ballet, orchestra, and outstanding schools make it a leader in the arts. And, above all, Birmingham's residents have made integration work—in employment, education, recreation, and health care.

*Historical Information:* Birmingham Historical Society, One Sloss Quarters, Birmingham, AL 35222; telephone (205)251-1880

# *Population Profile*

**Metropolitan Area Residents**
*1980:* 815,000
*1990:* 839,945
*2000:* 921,106
*Percent change, 1990–2000:* 9.6%
*U.S. rank in 1980:* 42nd
*U.S. rank in 1990:* Not reported
*U.S. rank in 2000:* 54th

**City Residents**
*1980:* 284,413
*1990:* 265,347
*2000:* 242,820
*2003 estimate:* 236,620
*Percent change, 1990–2000:* -8.7%
*U.S. rank in 1980:* 50th
*U.S. rank in 1990:* 60th (State rank: 1st)
*U.S. rank in 2000:* 82nd

*Density:* 1,619.7 people per square mile (in 2000, based on 2000 land area)

*Racial and ethnic characteristics* (2000)
White: 58,457
Black: 178,372
American Indian and Alaska Native: 422
Asian: 1,942
Native Hawaiian and Pacific Islander: 87
Hispanic or Latino (may be of any race): 3,764
Other: 1,513

*Percent of residents born in state:* 82.7% (2000)

*Age characteristics* (2000)
Population under 5 years old: 16,564
Population 5 to 9 years old: 17,349
Population 10 to 14 years old: 16,967
Population 15 to 19 years old: 17,325
Population 20 to 24 years old: 19,511
Population 25 to 34 years old: 36,196
Population 35 to 44 years old: 36,628
Population 45 to 54 years old: 31,407
Population 55 to 59 years old: 9,675
Population 60 to 64 years old: 8,516
Population 65 to 74 years old: 16,388
Population 75 to 84 years old: 11,661
Population 85 years and older: 4,633
Median age: 34.3 years

*Births* (2001)
Total number: 4,122

*Deaths* (2001)
Total number: 3,060 (of which, 68 were infants under the age of 1 year)

*Money income* (1999)
Per capita income: $15,663
Median household income: $26,735
Total households: 98,748

*Number of households with income of . . .*
less than $10,000: 19,813
$10,000 to $14,999: 9,591
$15,000 to $24,999: 17,047
$25,000 to $34,999: 14,679
$35,000 to $49,999: 15,339
$50,000 to $74,999: 13,022
$75,000 to $99,999: 4,796
$100,000 to $149,999: 2,831
$150,000 to $199,999: 637
$200,000 or more: 993

*Percent of families below poverty level:* 20.9% (52.1% of which were female householder families with related children under 5 years)

*2002 FBI Crime Index Total:* 21,265

# Municipal Government

Birmingham operates under a mayor-council form of government. The mayor is elected at large every four years; the nine council members are also elected at large, but on a staggered basis in odd-numbered years. Birmingham was one of the nation's first cities to participate in an innovative program whereby citizens serve on boards, make economic decisions, and undertake various neighborhood projects. The Birmingham City Council is divided into nine committees, with three Council Members on each committee. Committee chairpersons are assigned by the president of the council. Each committee is responsible for hearing items that fall under its jurisdiction and then making recommendations to the council as a whole.

**Head Official:** Mayor Bernard Kincaid (D) (since 1999; current term expires 2006)

**Total Number of City Employees:** 4,992 (2005)

*City Information:* City Hall, 710 N. 20th St., Birmingham, AL 35203; telephone (205)254-2000

# Economy

## Major Industries and Commercial Activity

For many years Birmingham was a one-industry town, dependent on the iron and steel industry. Today, though, Birmingham's economy relies more heavily on the medical industry as well as trade, finance, research and government. The major industrial investments in Birmingham have been in automotive components manufacturing and distribution, machinery, and the metals industries. At the base of the expanding telecommunications industry is one of two regional corporate headquarters of BellSouth Telephone Company. Birmingham is headquarters for the engineering and technical services of several power companies, including Alabama Power Company, ENERGEN Corporation, and SONAT. Metro Birmingham is a leading retail and wholesale trade center for Alabama and parts of Florida, Georgia, Tennessee, and Mississippi. According to the Alabama Department of Industrial Relations, projections for the fastest-growing occupations in Birmingham through 2012 include jobs in medical services. A mecca for health care and medical research, Birmingham boasts the University of Alabama Medical Center, known throughout the world for its research on the treatment of cardiovascular disease, diabetes, cancer, AIDS, and arthritis. Birmingham's Southern Research Institute, the largest nonprofit independent research laboratory in the southeast, has gained national prominence.

With a plethora of Birmingham businesses working in international trade and warehousing and with the city's nearby waterways, Birmingham is a major distribution center. The city's proximity to the Warrior-Tombigbee River System, which connects to the Tennessee-Tombigbee Waterway, enables Birmingham to be a major shipper of general commodities. Birmingham has also experienced significant growth as a transportation hub because of its central southeast location, and the fact that it is served by eight airlines, five air cargo services, approximately 100 truck lines, four railroads, and more than ten barge lines. Multimillion-dollar runway and cargo facility expansions at Birmingham International Airport took place in 2004 as part of the city's efforts to encourage further growth in the transportation and distribution industries.

*Items and goods produced:* cast iron pipe, transportation equipment (automotive, rail, and aircraft equipment), fabricated metal products, electronics, plastic products, office furniture, containers, paper products, and fire extinguishers

### Incentive Programs—New and Existing Companies

The City of Birmingham Office of Economic Development (OED) provides a wide variety of federal, state and locally-sponsored programs and activities, including financial assistance, employment and training, business assistance and retention programs, and site specific targeted economic development initiatives.

*Local programs*—The Birmingham Business Resource Center (BBRC) is a one-stop center for small business finance and related technical assistance. BBRC is sponsored by the City of Birmingham and area banks. It brings together in one location a number of small business loan programs previously offered by the Office of Economic Development and area banks.

*State programs*—Alabama boasts a progressive state business environment as demonstrated by its comprehensive right-to-work laws, one-stop environmental permitting, and a positive state and local government attitude toward new and expanding business. Tax rates are competitive; for example, employers who provide or sponsor an approved basic skills education program qualify to receive a 20 percent credit on state corporate income tax liability. The Alabama Enterprise Zone Program helps attract new business to Alabama with tax breaks to those operating in the designated 10,000-acre industrial area. Information about these incentives is available through the Alabama Development Office.

*Job training programs*—In April 2001 Jefferson State Community College unveiled its new manufacturing center, where students learn vocational skills including industrial maintenance, automation, computer aided drafting and drawing, machining and telecommunications. The manufacturing program's goal is to train workers who can be productive as soon as they are hired. Rather than instruct students by theory, the school asked area manufacturers to detail their needs. Top business executives in Alabama applaud the state's Industrial Development Training Program, which does everything from advertising, to processing job applications, to training and delivering employees.

### Development Projects

After considerable renovations in 2000, the upgraded Birmingham-Jefferson Civic Center opened as the newly named Birmingham-Jefferson Convention Complex. The upgraded complex hosts a variety of events in its many venues, which include the ample exhibition hall and meeting rooms, a 19,000 seat sports and performance arena, a theater and an adjoining hotel. Developers and city agencies are looking toward major revitalization efforts in downtown Birmingham. The city's skyline changed when work was completed in 2002 on the $27 million, 11-story Concord Center office building, the first new multi-tenant office building downtown in 11 years. Operation New Birmingham (ONB), a non-profit organization, is supported by the City of Birmingham and by contributions from businesses, individuals and Jefferson county, works with developers to revitalize the downtown business district. Among ONB's projects are renovations, completed in 2004, of several downtown buildings into retail and loft space. In 2005, plans include a $34 million new construction that will house the Birmingham District of the Federal Bureau of Investigations. The Park Place/Metropolitan Gardens Redevelopment will replace a deteriorating low-income housing project with 663 mixed-housing units in a six-block community. The city's largest planned downtown residential project, the Railroad Reservation Lofts, is a $22 million, nine-story structure that is slated for completion in 2007. The planned project will offer commercial space, apartments and condominiums.

In private developments, so many auto-related companies have located in greater Birmingham that residents call the area "little Detroit." A half hour southwest of Birmingham, in the tiny town of Vance in Tuscaloosa County, a new road called Mercedes Drive leads to the first Mercedes-Benz (a division of Daimler-Chrysler) auto plant ever built in North America. The Mercedes-Benz Vance plant, built in 1993, is also the first Mercedes-Benz passenger-car assembly plant outside Germany. Alabama offered $80 million in incentives to entice Mercedes-Benz to set up shop in the state; by 2000 Mercedes had invested $380 million in Alabama. In 2001 Mercedes-Benz began construction on a $600 million expansion that is estimated to double production, with an expected completion date of 2005. State investments in auto production have led several auto service production plants to open shop in other areas of the state, namely Hyundai in Montgomery and Honda in Lincoln.

In other private developments, one of downtown Birmingham's largest and most conspicuous vacant building received a $30 million face-lift from Bayer Properties, which finished conversion in 2003 of the eight-story 1908 Pizitz department store building to Class A office space with a ground-floor retail component. In 2002, American Cast Iron Pipe Co. (ACIPCO) prepared for stricter pollution regulations with an $80 million expansion at its North Birmingham plant. The company added 61,000 square feet of space to add a state-of-the-art, electrically-fired furnace.

There is also plenty of activity going on at the University of Alabama at Birmingham (UAB). In 1998, Alabama health officials endorsed a 5-year, $578 million expansion of UAB's University Hospital complex. In late 2004, the new 885,000 square foot, 11-story hospital opened with 37 operating suites, 4 intensive care units, 96 private patient rooms and an emergency unit the size of a football field. In April 2002, UAB broke ground on a new 300,000-square-foot, 12-story Shelby Interdisciplinary Biomedical Research Building, which will house four distinct research programs. Due to be completed in 2005, the new facility is expected to generate $100 million in annual grants and employ 1,400 people. Oxmoor Valley research park was created by a partnership of UAB and the city of Birmingham, and houses the university's Office for the Advancement of Developing Industries Technology Center (OADI). Since UAB became an autonomous campus, it has spent about $800 million on new construction and has built about 100 buildings in an 82-block area.

*Economic Development Information:* City of Birmingham Office of Economic Development, 710 20th Street North, Birmingham, AL 35203; telephone (205)254-2799; fax (205)254-7741; email cmsmith@earthlink.net. BBRC, 110 12th Street North, Birmingham, AL 35203; telephone (205)250-6380; fax (205)250-6384; email info@bbrc.biz. Alabama Development Office, Neal Wade, Director, 401 Adams Avenue, Suite 670, Montgomery, AL 36130-4106; telephone (800)248-0033; email idinfo@www.ado.state.al .us. Alabama Department Of Industrial Relations, Phyllis Kennedy, Director, 649 Monroe Street, Montgomery, AL 36131; telephone (334)242-8859; fax (334)242-2543; email LMI@dir.state.al.us. Operation New Birmingham, 505 20th Street North, Suite 150, Birmingham, AL, 35203; telephone (205)324-8797; fax (205)324-8799.

## Commercial Shipping

Born at the junction of two railroads, and always an important transportation center, Birmingham today is served by an outstanding network of highways, extensive rail track, air-cargo facilities, and nearby navigable waterways. The CSX

and Burlington Northern Santa Fe railroad systems haul freight to and from the metropolitan area, where a multimodal system is located. More than 100 truck lines, many with nationwide service, and five air-cargo firms move goods and products for Birmingham companies. Birmingham's Airport Industrial Park is designated as a Foreign Trade Zone, a major asset in attracting additional business to the area. General commodities are transported economically on barges along the nearby Warrior-Tombigbee River System and the Tennessee-Tombigbee Waterway to other inland cities and through the Port of Mobile to foreign countries.

## Labor Force and Employment Outlook

Birmingham's transformed economy is now less dependent on cyclical manufacturing and mining sectors and more on health and financial services. Birmingham is the state's center for advanced technology and there are more engineers per capita living in the local area than in any other southeastern city.

Birmingham, like other Alabama cities, enjoys a good reputation in Asia. Local analysts predict that the region will continue to be a magnet for overseas capital.

The following is a summary of data regarding the Birmingham metropolitan area labor force, 2003 annual averages.

*Size of nonagricultural labor force:* 474,500

*Number of workers employed in . . .*
 *construction and mining:* 32,300
 *manufacturing:* 40,400
 *trade, transportation and utilities:* 102,200
 *information:* 13,700
 *financial activities:* 39,100
 *professional and business services:* 59,700
 *educational and health services:* 54,400
 *leisure and hospitality:* 37,200
 *other services:* 23,100
 *government:* 72,000

*Average hourly earnings of production workers employed in manufacturing:* $14.56

*Unemployment rate:* 4.6% (October 2004)

| *Largest county employers* | *Number of employees* |
|---|---|
| University of Alabama at Birmingham | 16,271 |
| U.S. Government | 9,690 |
| BellSouth | 7,500 |
| State of Alabama | 6,784 |
| Baptist Health Systems | 6,000 |
| Bruno's Incorporated | 5,374 |
| Jefferson County Board of Education | 5,000 |
| Birmingham Public Schools | 4,555 |

| Largest county employers | Number of employees |
|---|---|
| City of Birmingham | 4,500 |
| Walmart | 4,320 |
| Jefferson County Government | 4,191 |

## Cost of Living

Birmingham's cost of living, as well as its housing prices, are slightly below the national average.

The following is a summary of data regarding several key cost of living factors for the Birmingham area.

*2004 (3rd Quarter) ACCRA Cost of Living Index:* not reported (U.S. average = 100.0)

*2004 (3rd Quarter) ACCRA Average House Price:* not reported

*State income tax rate:* Ranges from 2.0% to 5.0%

*State sales tax rate:* 4.0%

*Local income tax rate:* 1.00% (occupational)

*Local sales tax rate:* 6.0 to 9.0%

*Property tax rate:* $18.70 per $1,000 assessed value (2004)

*Economic Information:* Metropolitan Development Board, 2027 First Avenue North, Suite 1300, Birmingham, AL 35203; telephone (205)328-3047; fax (205)328-3073. Office of Economic Development, City of Birmingham, 710 North 20th Street, Birmingham, AL 35203; telephone (205)254-2799. State of Alabama, Department of Industrial Relations, 649 Monroe Street, Montgomery, AL 36131

# Education and Research

## Elementary and Secondary Schools

The Birmingham public schools offer the Education Program for the Individual Child (EPIC schools) with a population of 50 percent typical children and 50 percent children with developmental challenges; or 50 percent African American students and 50 percent white students; or 50 percent girls and 50 percent boys. EPIC schools aim to foster the individual student's sense of self-worth by helping students to communicate and understand one another. Seventeen public school systems serve the five-county Birmingham area. Fourteen of the seventeen systems rank above the national average on Scholastic Aptitude Test scores. Birmingham is the home of the Alabama School of Fine Arts, one of only a few such schools in the country to offer intensive study in both academic areas and the arts for

grades seven through twelve. Mikhail Baryshnikov ranks the ballet school as one of the top three in the country.

The following is a summary of data regarding the Birmingham public schools as of the 2002–2003 school year.

*Total enrollment:* 36,133

*Number of facilities*
  *elementary schools:* 52
  *junior high/middle schools:* 18
  *senior high schools:* 12
  *other:* 10

*Student/teacher ratio:* 15.6:1 (2005)

*Teacher salaries (2004-05)*
  *minimum:* $30,387
  *maximum:* $67,496

*Funding per pupil:* $8,778

## Colleges and Universities

Eleven major institutions of higher learning are located in metropolitan Birmingham. They offer undergraduate and graduate degrees in such fields as engineering, business, education, medicine, nursing, pharmacy, religion, law, music, and liberal arts. The largest is the University of Alabama at Birmingham (UAB), with 16,000 students. UAB is ranked as one of the finest medical centers in the world. According to *The New York Times,* UAB plays a major role in the life of the city. It provides assistance to ninety public schools and research information to numerous developing local businesses. Other Birmingham schools include Samford University, a private institution affiliated with the Baptist State Convention; Birmingham-Southern College, a four-year liberal arts school affiliated with the Methodist Church; Miles College; Bessemer State Technical College; Jefferson State Community College; University of Montevallo; Virginia College at Birmingham; Herzing College; Lawson State Community College; and ITT Technical Institute.

## Libraries and Research Centers

In addition to 21 Birmingham Public Library locations, the Jefferson County Library System has 19 municipal libraries. The system numbers more than 1.5 million items in its collection and circulates almost 4 million items per year, including books, magazines, and recordings. More than 20 other libraries serve Birmingham; some of them are affiliated with educational institutions, while others are associated with religious groups or research centers. Their collections focus on such areas of interest as botany and horticulture, art, law, religion, regional history, engineering, genealogy, energy, science, medicine, and business.

**Martin Luther King, Jr., is honored in a Birmingham sculpture. The city was a center for the civil rights movement during the 1960s.**

In keeping with its status as a medical center for the southeast, Birmingham is home to a large number of health care research centers, most of which are supported by the University of Alabama at Birmingham (UAB). UAB, with its affiliate Southern Research Institute, receives more than $460 million in grant and contract money. Major projects center on aging, heart disease, human genetics, and immunological and other diseases. UAB is a designated center for AIDS research, and its Spinal Cord Injury Care System is one of the few in the nation. The Southern Research Institute is nationally recognized for its virus studies and cancer research and industrial research programs. Area research centers are active in other fields as well, including computers, education, labor, urban affairs, metallurgy, and electronics.

***Public Library Information:*** Birmingham Public Library, 2100 Park Place, Birmingham, AL 35203; telephone (205)226-3610

# Health Care

Internationally known as a medical center, Birmingham is a leader in the prevention and treatment of illness. The University of Alabama at Birmingham (UAB) is a leader in research and education. Its Comprehensive Cancer Center, one of 41 in the country and the only one in a five-state area, is ranked as expert.

Many of the 17 hospitals in the area offer specialized care while providing a total of more than 6,000 beds. Health care institutions other than those affiliated with the University of Alabama include hospitals operated by the Baptist and Methodist churches and others. UAB's specialty hospitals include the Spain Rehabilitation Center and the Callahan Eye Foundation Hospital. UAB's $125-million Kirklin outpatient superclinic houses 32 outpatient facilities and more than 60 physicians.

# Recreation

## Sightseeing

Visitors to Birmingham will enjoy the variety of parks throughout the city, including the 90-acre Highland Park with its modern sports complex and golf course; Roebuck Park, known for its beautiful golf course and wooded grounds; Avondale, with an amphitheater, duck pond, and formal rose garden; East Lake, with more than 50 acres of fresh water; and Magnolia, known for its flowing fountains. Birmingham's

Vulcan Park features a towering statue of Vulcan, the Roman god of fire and the forge, the city's symbol. Said to be the largest iron figure ever cast, it rises 55 feet above its pedestal to reach a total of 179 feet. This monument, a tribute to the iron industry in Birmingham, is unique in that it honors an industry rather than a person or event. A glass enclosed elevator takes visitors to the statue's climate controlled observation deck for an aerial view of the city.

One of the largest zoos in the Southeast, the Birmingham Zoo exhibits mammals, birds, and reptiles in near-natural surroundings within a 100-acre compound. Rare species such as Siberian tigers, white rhinoceroses, gorillas, and polar bears join exhibits of specimens from nations around the globe. The Social Animals Building is the latest example of a leading-edge zoo concept that groups animals in exhibits according to lifestyle characteristics rather than species. In 2005, the zoo will celebrate its 50th year with the addition of a $15 million exhibit devoted to the urban, rural and wild animals and environment of Alabama. Across the street from the zoo are Birmingham's internationally known Botanical Gardens, which offer the visitor both indoor and outdoor plant displays of common and rare plants. Among its more than 67 acres of flowers and plants from all over the world are an authentic Japanese garden and a rose garden featuring more than two thousand blooming plants.

Birmingham's early history is preserved at the Arlington Antebellum Home and Gardens, a Greek Revival mansion built between 1845 and 1850, now restored to its original splendor and filled with period pieces. The home also hosts craft demonstrations and a variety of social functions.

At Ruffner Mountain Nature Center, a 1,000-acre nature preserve just five miles from the heart of the city center, 11 miles of hiking trails allow visitors to explore the nation's largest urban wilderness. The environmental education center offers a variety of changing exhibits and a gift shop. Free admission and free and fee-based programs are available for all ages. Thirty minutes south of the city, Oak Mountain State Park is Alabama's largest state park and offers 10,000 acres of mountains, forest land and lakes with space for camping, hiking biking, fishing and horseback riding.

## Arts and Culture

Birmingham is fast becoming a leading center for the arts in the Southeast, providing superb facilities, emphasizing arts education, and showcasing numerous performances and exhibits. The pride of Birmingham is the Birmingham-Jefferson Convention Complex, which occupies a seven-square-block area in the heart of the city. Presenting more than 600 events a year, the complex hosts meetings, conventions, sporting events, ballets, operas, plays, concerts, shows, and lectures. The complex's concert hall, called one of the finest facilities in the world, seats 3,000 people in an acoustically superior auditorium. Its theater seats more than 1,000 people and features a stage that can change from a proscenium opening to three other forms, depending on the performance. The theater plays host to the Alabama Symphony Orchestra, which showcases both classical and pops performances. For young people interested in drama, the Birmingham Children's Theatre, which performs at the theater, has gained a national reputation.

The non-profit Birmingham Music Cooperative is comprised of four member organizations and is dedicated to scheduling, fundraising, education, community outreach and marketing efforts on behalf of its members, who include: the Birmingham Art Music Alliance, which features new music by local composers, community members, students and professionals; the Birmingham Chamber Music Society, which performs in and around Birmingham; the Birmingham Music Club, which offers specialty performances by world-class performers and a strong outreach program; and Opera Birmingham, which stages full operas and recitals. The Birmingham Metropolitan Orchestra made its debut in 1996.

Birmingham is home to the Alabama Ballet, which performs on tour and in the city. The Alabama School of Fine Arts is famous for the quality of its young dancers. Southern Danceworks operates as Alabama's only modern dance company. The Birmingham Repertory Theatre, the Birmingham Festival Theatre, and the Terrific New Theatre (TNT) also stage dramatic offerings. The Alabama Jazz Hall of Fame has a permanent home downtown in the Art Deco Carver Theatre and jazz is also performed by the Birmingham Heritage Band. The Alabama Theatre, a restored 1920s movie palace with a classic Wurlitzer organ, features concerts, plays, and recitals.

The University of Alabama at Birmingham hosts many cultural events; the city expanded its offerings in 1997 when the $17 million Alys Robinson Stephens Performing Arts Center opened its doors. That facility is part of a complex that includes a recital hall, a ''black box'' theater for student productions, and the Sirote Theater, where performances of the Alabama Shakespeare Festival are scheduled.

Birmingham's museums and galleries reflect its history, as well as the diverse interests of its residents. Located in the expanded Convention Complex, The Alabama Sports Hall of Fame Museum displays a host of articles relating to the sports history of the state, including plaques, trophies, uniforms, recordings, and films. Memorabilia such as Coach Paul ''Bear'' Bryant's cap and Pat Sullivan's Heisman trophy are housed in the museum.

The Birmingham Museum of Art celebrated a 50-year anniversary in 2001 and holds a collection of 21,000 works of art. Said to be the largest municipally supported museum in the South, the Museum features paintings and sculptures from many cultures and periods, including Pre-Colombian, Indian, and African. It is also noted for its collections of Wedgwood ceramics, Remington bronzes, and Oriental Art. The BMA completed a $17 million renovation in 1992; additions included a sculpture garden, 7,000 more feet of gallery space, a 350-seat auditorium, and a restaurant.

The Birmingham Civil Rights Institute houses exhibits that depict historical events pertaining to race relations from post-World War I to the present. The institute promotes research and discussion through its education program services. It was constructed across from the Sixteenth Street Baptist Church, where it is the focal point of a Civil Rights District that includes the church, an African American commercial neighborhood, the Fourth Avenue Business District, the Alabama Jazz Hall of Fame, and Kelly Ingram Park, site of many 1960s civil rights marches.

Among Birmingham's other museums are the Alabama Museum of the Health Sciences, which contains items relating to the history of medicine; the Southern Museum of Flight, whose holdings include replicas of monoplanes and other items relating to the history of flight in Alabama; Meyer Planetarium, which gives programs on the stars and constellations; Bessemer Hall of History, which displays pioneer items, fossils, Civil War artifacts, and other unusual exhibits such as Adolph Hitler's typewriter; and the Sloss Furnaces National Historical Landmark, a combination museum and park where visitors can examine two blast furnaces and observe iron-making technology. The McWane Center in downtown Birmingham promotes scientific exploration for all ages. The 180,000 square foot Center features an IMAX Dome Theater, hands-on exhibits, educational programming and permanent and traveling exhibits.

**Festivals and Holidays**

Each April, the world-famous Birmingham International Festival, Birmingham's largest festival, salutes a different foreign country. During three days of activities devoted to film, dance, sculpture, music, fashion, food, and fun, more than 250,000 people attend events sponsored by civic organizations, schools, churches, museums, and ethnic groups. The International Festival runs in conjunction with the city's annual Magic City Art Connection, featuring more than 200 juried art exhibitors. Also in spring, the Birmingham International Educational Film Festival features outstanding educational films. June's City Stages Festival fills Linn Park with three days of performances by more than fifty top jazz, blues, rock and gospel musical acts. Birmingham Jam, held in the fall at Sloss Furnaces, brings jazz, blues, and gospel groups from around the country for three days of quality performances.

The young and growing Sidewalk Moving Picture Festival in September offers four days of independent film viewing at venues in Birmingham's downtown theater district. At the Bluff Park Arts and Crafts Show each October, browsers can see and buy arts and crafts items and enjoy a barbecue. Fall is the season for the Alabama State Fair, held at the State Fairgrounds in Birmingham. Demonstrations, exhibitions, contests, and entertainment are presented along with items for display and for sale. Other major celebrations include the Greek Food Festival, Oktoberfest, the Juneteenth Culture Fest and the Lebanese Food and Cultural Festival.

### Sports for the Spectator

Often called "The Football Capital of the South," Birmingham enjoys a rich sports history. The legendary Paul "Bear" Bryant and Ralph "Shug" Jordan both coached football teams for many years at Birmingham's Legion Field Stadium, where the University of Alabama's Crimson Tide played its games to capacity crowds. In 2004, structural issues to Legion Fields upper deck seating forced the Tide to move most of their games to the Bryant-Denny Stadium. Legion Field hosts the Magic City Classic, the annual clash between Alabama State and Alabama A & M, and is home to the university's Division IA football team. Baseball fans go to Hoover Metropolitan Stadium from April to September to watch the Birmingham Barons, a Double A farm club of the Chicago White Sox. The Barons' former home and oldest American ballpark, Rickwood Field, is enjoying restoration and offers visitors a glimpse into history with tours and games. Greyhounds race at the Birmingham Race Course, a track set on a 330-acre wooded site. The grandstand can accommodate 20,000 spectators who may also enjoy the clubhouse and private facilities. The University of Alabama at Birmingham Blazers play at UAB Arena and the Birmingham-Jefferson Convention Complex. The Birmingham-Jefferson Convention Complex regularly hosts prestigious national basketball events and championships and is home to the Birmingham Steeldogs football team. Greystone Country Club hosts the Bruno's Memorial Classic Senior PGA tournament each May. It has become one of the most popular venues on the Senior Tour.

### Sports for the Participant

The Birmingham Park and Recreation Board operates 127 public recreational facilities, which host 2 public golf courses, 16 swimming pools, more than 120 tennis courts, and 23 softball fields. Suburban communities also boast fine recreational opportunities. Marathoners can test their endurance in the annual Mercedes Marathon, or the city's 10K Vulcan Run. A massive theme park in nearby Bessemer called VisionLand includes water sports, rides, auto racing, and skeet shooting. The Barber Vintage Motorsports Park opened in 2003. The $54 million racing facility and museum houses the Porsche Driving Experience school and hosts a variety of motorcycle and auto racing events. Built

into the landscape, the state-of-the-art racetrack has no grandstands, with seating built into the surrounding hillside and offering good viewing vantage points from most locations. The Museum showcases nearly 900 motorcycles and 45 cars, most from businessman George W. Barber Jr.'s own collection.

Birmingham is famous for its beautiful golf courses. Its Oxmoor Valley Golf Course is one stop on the Robert Trent Jones Golf Trail, the largest golf course construction project ever attempted with a total of 378 holes over 18 courses throughout the state. According to *Golf* magazine, the course is "Alabama's equivalent of Disney World."

### Shopping and Dining

The most recent center to open is Colonial Promenade Tutwiler Farm shopping center, whose tenants will include Home Depot, SuperTarget, and Books-A-Million. The new Watermark Place Outlet Center features more than 30 outlet stores. The Summit, with just under 80 shops opened in November 1997 and includes stores never before seen in the state, including Williams-Sonoma. One of the most exciting shopping centers in the Southeast is the Riverchase Galleria, located at the interchange of I-459 and U.S. 31, thirteen miles south of downtown Birmingham and in the center of the Riverchase community. The mall boasts the luxurious Wynfrey Hotel, an office tower, a ten-foot statue of blue herons in flight, the largest skylight in the country, and more than 200 stores. Five Points South is an entertainment and shopping area on the south side that offers unique restaurants, bars and specialty shops; it is the scene of a variety of festivals. The sights, sounds, and scents of an old-fashioned farmer's market are available at two Birmingham locations, the Jefferson County Truck Growers Association and Pepper Place Market. The Jefferson County market is open daily, year-round. The Pepper Place Market in the Lakeview Design District operates on Saturdays and offers fresh vegetables and flowers, baked goods, local organic produce and cooking demonstrations by area chefs.

Magic City residents are proud of their tradition of sumptuous dining coupled with southern hospitality. More than 600 restaurants dot the Birmingham area, from fast-food outlets to establishments specializing in ethnic cuisine and those featuring traditional southern barbecue: meat cooked slowly over coals and basted with savory sauce.

***Visitor Information:*** Greater Birmingham Convention and Visitors Bureau, 2200 Ninth Avenue North, Birmingham, AL 35203; telephone (205)458-8000. Visitor Information Centers are located on the lower level of the Birmingham International Airport, telephone (205)458-8002, and at 1201 University Boulevard, telephone (205)458-8001. For information on University of Alabama events, call 934-0553. For weather information, call (205)945-7000.

# Convention Facilities

The Birmingham-Jefferson Convention Complex completed a $140 million expansion in 2000, creating even more versatile convention facilities. Located on seven square blocks in downtown Birmingham, the center is only ten minutes from the airport. Its facilities include the Exhibition Hall, covering 220,000 square feet and featuring 74 meeting rooms to accommodate up to 1,200 participants; the 3,000-seat Concert Hall, one of the most acoustically effective structures in the country; the 1,000-seat Theatre, with a moveable stage that can be adjusted to suit differing performance requirements; and the Arena, which seats 19,000 people, making it one of the largest such facilities in the southeast. Within the Complex, the ten-story Medical Forum building contains classrooms, meeting space, commercial office suites and an auditorium. The Complex also features retail operations including the Alabama Sports Hall of Fame, and adjoining 770-room Sheraton Birmingham hotel.

The newly renovated art deco Boutwell Municipal Auditorium offers a main arena seating capacity of 5,700 people and an exhibition hall capacity of 1,000. About 20 minutes from the airport, the Bessemer Civic Center has a main hall that seats 1,600 people and additional meeting rooms for up to 300 people. Arthur's Conference Center is an elegant new facility with 1,560 square feet of meeting/banquet space that can be broken down into three smaller rooms. With a total of more than 14,000 hotel and motel rooms in the metropolitan area, many of them having gone through renovations in the 1990s and in the early part of the new century, Birmingham is ready to accommodate large and small groups.

***Convention Information:*** Greater Birmingham Convention and Visitors Bureau, 2200 North Avenue North, Birmingham, AL 35203; telephone (800)458-8085

# Transportation

## Approaching the City

Eight commercial airlines operating at Birmingham International Airport offer 154 daily flights to and from 25 non-stop destinations and 35 direct flight destinations. The airport is only ten minutes from downtown. It recently completed a $43 million runway expansion, and added 400,000 square feet to its air cargo facility space. Four interstate highways bring motorists into Birmingham: Interstates 20 or 59 from the northeast or southwest; Interstate 65 from north or south; and Interstate 459, which loops to the southeast of the city. U.S. Highway 280 enters from the southeast, U.S. 31 from the north, U.S. 78 from the northwest, and U.S. 11 from the southwest and northeast. Amtrak offers daily passenger service to Birmingham from Mobile, New Orleans, and New York. Greyhound serves Birmingham out of a downtown terminal.

## Traveling in the City

A hilly city, Birmingham lies in a valley running from northeast to southwest. The roads are laid out in a grid pattern; those that run roughly east to west are designated as numbered avenues, while those that run north to south are designated as numbered streets. The Birmingham-Jefferson County Transit Authority provides public transportation within the city of Birmingham. Nicknamed MAX—for Metro Area Express—the bus system provides regular city bus service and, in the downtown area, trolley-like vehicles called DART that carry passengers from location to location throughout the central business district.

# Communications

## Newspapers and Magazines

Birmingham is one of the few American cities that still have separately-owned competing daily newspapers. Birmingham's major daily newspaper is the *Birmingham Post-Herald* (afternoons). The *Birmingham News* publishes an afternoon edition and a combined edition with the *Post-Herald* on Saturdays. Other newspapers appeal to African Americans, college students, and various religious groups. Also published in Birmingham are the regional magazine *Southern Living,* a monthly focusing on homes, cuisine, gardens, and recreation; and *Cooking Light,* the country's number one healthy lifestyle magazine. Nearly twenty other magazines are published here.

## Television and Radio

Birmingham is served by eight television stations, of which four are affiliated with the major commercial networks and one with public broadcasting. Additional stations are available via cable. The city's 19AM and 16 FM radio stations broadcast a wide range of programs, from gospel, country/western, and inspirational to big band, classical, and rock.

***Media Information:*** *Birmingham Post-Herald,* 2200 4th Avenue North, Birmingham, AL 35203; telephone (205)325-2344. *Birmingham News,* PO Box 2553, Birmingham, AL 35202; telephone (205)325-2444

## Birmingham Online

Alabama Bureau of Tourism and Travel. Available www.touralabama.org

Alabama Development Office. Available www.ado.state.al.us

Alabama Live (entertainment listings and more). Available www.al.com

Birmingham News. Available www.al.com/news

Birmingham Post-Herald. Available www.postherald.com

Birmingham Public Library. Available www.bham.lib.al.us

Birmingham Public Schools. Available www.bhm.k12.al.us

City of Birmingham Home Page. Available www.informationbirmingham.com

City of Birmingham Office of Economic Development. Available www.informationbirmingham.com/economic.htm

Greater Birmingham Convention and Visitors Bureau. Available www.bcvb.org

Information about development opportunities, events, and amenities in City Center. Available www.yourcitycenter.com

Online CityGuide. Available www.onlinecityguide.com/al/birmingham

## Selected Bibliography

Dunnavant, Keith, *Coach: The Life of Paul ''Bear'' Bryant* (New York: Simon & Schuster, 1996)

Hemphill, Paul, *Leaving Birmingham: Notes of a Native Son* (Tuscaloosa: University of Alabama Press, 2000)

Jefferson County Historical Commission, ed., *Birmingham and Jefferson County Alabama* (Charleston, S.C.: Arcadia Publishing, 1998)

# Mobile

## The City in Brief

**Founded:** 1702 (incorporated 1819)

**Head Official:** Mayor Michael C. Dow (N-P) (since 1989)

**City Population**
   **1980:** 200,452
   **1990:** 199,973
   **2000:** 198,915
   **2003 estimate:** 193,464
   **Percent change, 1990–2000:** −.3%
   **U.S. rank in 1980:** 72nd
   **U.S. rank in 1990:** 79th
   **U.S. rank in 2000:** 105th (State rank: 3rd)

**Metropolitan Area Population**
   **1980:** 444,000
   **1990:** 476,923
   **2000:** 540,258
   **Percent change, 1990–2000:** 13.3%
   **U.S. rank in 1980:** 74th
   **U.S. rank in 1990:** Not reported
   **U.S. rank in 2000:** 78th

**Area:** 118 square miles (2000)
**Elevation:** 211 feet above sea level
**Average Annual Temperature:** 68° F
**Average Annual Precipitation:** 66 inches

**Major Economic Sectors:** Wholesale and retail trade, services, government
**Unemployment rate:** 6.0% (November 2004)
**Per Capita Income:** $18,072 (1999)

**2002 FBI Crime Index Total:** 17,949

**Major Colleges and Universities:** University of South Alabama, University of Mobile, Spring Hill College

**Daily Newspaper:** *The Mobile Register*

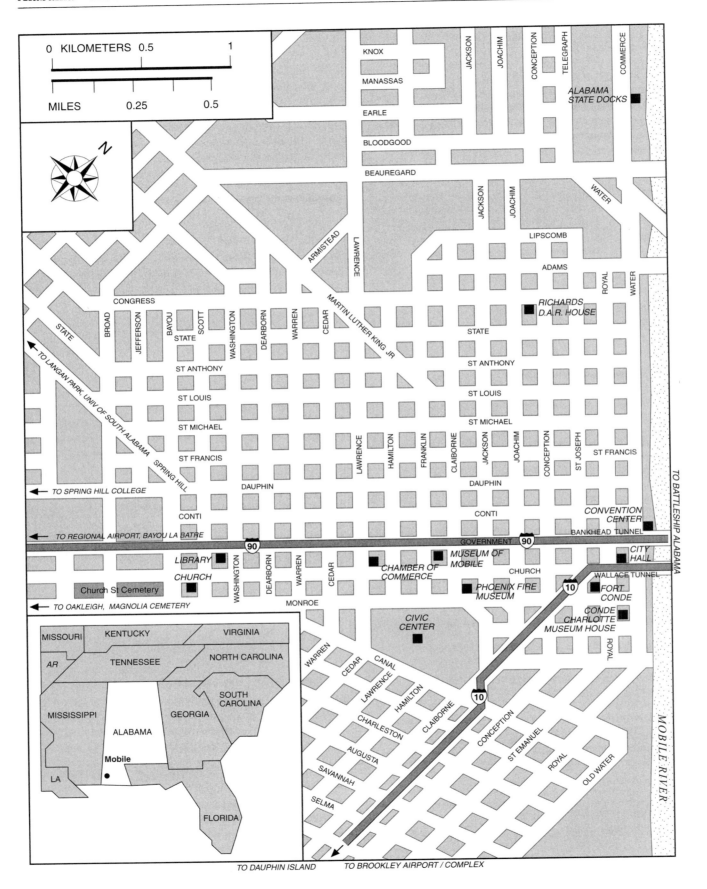

# Introduction

Mobile, Alabama's oldest and third largest city, is also the state's only seaport, serving as a major industrial, shipping, and shipbuilding center. Located on the Mobile River at the head of the Gulf of Mexico's Mobile Bay, it was an important maritime site during the Civil War and both world wars. The area that is now Mobile was France's first Gulf Coast settlement, and except for St. Augustine, Florida, it is the oldest Latin town east of Mexico. Also settled by Spanish and British populations during its colorful early years, Mobile has preserved its historic sites and architecture, as well as its Creole culture and traditions, and so retains much of the rich heritage of the American South while remaining substantially different from inland communities. *Money* magazine consistently rates Mobile in the top 100 best metropolitan areas in which to live in the United States. In the 1990s the city underwent a $168 million revitalization of its waterfront and downtown areas. Today's Mobile, while steeped in the heritage of a genuinely Southern past, continues to move forward as a truly modern city.

# Geography and Climate

Mobile is located at the mouth of the Mobile River in southwest Alabama and stands at the head of Mobile Bay, 31 miles inland from where the bay meets the Gulf of Mexico.

Mobile is one of the nation's wettest cities. Rainfall occurs fairly evenly throughout the year. Summers are hot and muggy; winters are mild. Mobile averages only nineteen days each year at or below freezing temperatures. Average annual snowfall is less than half an inch.

The city is occasionally threatened by hurricanes from the Gulf of Mexico and the West Indies. In 2004, hurricane Ivan wreaked havoc on Mobile and surrounding areas.

**Area:** 118.0 square miles (2000)

**Elevation:** 211 feet above sea level

**Average Temperatures:** January, 51° F; July, 82° F; average annual temperature, 68° F

**Average Annual Precipitation:** 66 inches

# History

### French Establish First Settlement

Represented on maps as early as 1507, the Gulf of Mexico inlet now known as Mobile Bay was navigated by European seafarers in 1519 when ships under the command of Spanish Admiral Alonso Alvaraz de Pineda sought a safe harbor in which to undertake repairs. The bay area was not really explored, however, until 1558. It was included in the vast region that was claimed for France's King Louis XIV and was named Louisiana by French explorer Robert Cavelier de La Salle in 1682. France authorized two brothers, Pierre Le Moyne d'Iberville and Jean Baptiste Le Moyne de Bienville, to explore territories in Louisiana, and they arrived at the gulf inlet that is now called Mobile Bay in 1699. The area was subsequently considered crucial to establishing French occupation of Louisiana and the brothers were ordered to colonize the region, which was inhabited by the Mobile, or Maubila, tribe. In 1702 Bienville established Fort Louis de la Mobile—named to honor France's king and to acknowledge the native tribe—at Twenty Seven Mile Bluff on the banks of the Mobile River, just north of present-day Mobile. It was the first French town in the gulf region.

The settlement, which consisted of the log fort, Creole houses, a church, a hospital, a marketplace with shops, and a well, served as the capital of the vast Louisiana Territory. Women joined the community in 1704. When river flooding forced the colony to abandon Fort Louis de la Mobile in 1711, the settlement's four hundred inhabitants moved downstream to a new site protected by a wooden fort at the river's mouth on Mobile Bay. During this era, pelts, furs, wax, and tallow were transported down river to where the bay meets the gulf for transfer to ocean-going vessels. This settlement retained the name Mobile and remained the capital of the Louisiana Territory until New Orleans assumed that title in 1720. That same year Mobile renamed its fort Fort Conde. A brick structure later replaced the original fort.

### Mobile Becomes Part of the United States

Mobile continued to serve as an important center for diplomatic dealings with the neighboring tribal inhabitants. France ceded its territory east of the Mississippi River to Britain in 1763, and that year, taking possession of Fort Conde, the British renamed it Fort Charlotte. Two years later Mobile was the site of the Great Choctaw-Chickasaw Congress held among tribal leaders and British officials.

When Spain, at war with Britain, captured Mobile in 1779, the area traded in cotton and indigo and supported sawmills and brickyards. After two decades of Spanish rule, the region was returned to France, who sold the Louisiana Territory to the United States in 1803. It was not until after the War of 1812, however, that U.S. influence began to be felt in the region. The Bank of Mobile was established in 1818, Mobile was incorporated as a city shortly after Alabama attained statehood in 1819, and Fort Charlotte was dismantled in 1820.

### Explosion Destroys City

Mobile's population by 1822 had reached nearly 3,000 people, a figure that subsequently quadrupled in less than two decades. As steamboats made upstream transportation possible, Mobile served as an important port for distributing goods brought in by ocean-going vessels as well as for exporting cotton and lumber. By the 1850s Mobile was the South's second largest cotton port, following New Orleans. Although tested by fires and yellow fever epidemics, Mobile's prosperity by mid-century was secure. In 1861, recognizing the nation's deep political and social division, Alabama seceded from the United States as the Republic of Alabama, and joined other southern states to form the Confederacy.

Mobile was particularly valuable to the South because of its location on the Gulf of Mexico. The city maintained trade with Europe and the West Indies while constructing the first submarine used in warfare. But in 1864 during the Battle of Mobile Bay, Union forces, urged on by Admiral David Farragut's famous rallying cry, "Damn the torpedoes, full speed ahead!," defeated Confederate troops and captured southern strongholds around Mobile. Still, Mobile was the only major southern port unoccupied by Yankee troops during the Civil War. At the war's end a tremendous ammunitions explosion in Mobile left massive destruction. The Battle of Mobile rendered the navies of the world obsolete as the era of the wooden ship had ended.

### Mobile Emerges Triumphant

The city's post-Civil War recovery was aided by port-related activity; the shipping channel was deepened and shipbuilding increased. In the 1870s, Mobile began to serve as a major center for the importation of Brazilian coffee. Railroad expansion also contributed to Mobile's emergence as a major distribution center. At the beginning of the twentieth century, the city's port underwent further development and modernization, and in the 1920s the Alabama State Docks were conceived and realized as a means of providing and maintaining adequate port facilities. Mobile's shipbuilding contributed to the war efforts during World War I, and in the 1940s the city's shipyards were packed with shifts of workers welding hulls for World War II naval operations.

While Mobile found itself weathering the violent racial tensions that swept the nation in the 1960s, the city was and is often the site of damaging tropical storms. Mobile sustained heavy losses after hurricane Camille hit the Gulf Coast in 1969, destroying a total of $1.5 billion worth of property along the coast and claiming 250 lives in Mobile. Ten years later hurricane Frederic was especially brutal for the city, with property damage in Mobile mounting to $1 billion. In 2004, hurricane Ivan attacked the Gulf Coast, leaving Mobile another hefty bill.

An economically diverse community, Mobile now counts oil and gas reserves, discovered in the 1970s, among its economic resources. The city continues to benefit from port activities and is also a center for manufacturing. The area produces chemicals, steel, wood pulp and paper products, furniture, rayon fibers, and clothing, and is a growing center for medical care, research, and education. Tourists and conventioneers enjoy the city's Creole charm and nearby coastal beaches. Mobile's long-term French and Spanish heritage make it unique in Alabama and places the city among the elite urban centers of the South. In 2002, Mobile celebrated its 300th birthday with events around the city.

***Historical Information:*** Historic Mobile Preservation Society, 300 Oakleigh Place, Mobile, AL 36606; telephone (251)432-6161. Bienville Historical Society, The Center for Gulf Studies Library, 606 Government Street, Mobile, AL 36602; telephone (205)457-5242

# *Population Profile*

### Metropolitan Area Residents
*1980:* 444,000
*1990:* 476,923
*2000:* 540,258
*Percent change, 1990–2000:* 13.3%
*U.S. rank in 1980:* 74th
*U.S. rank in 1990:* Not reported
*U.S. rank in 2000:* 78th

### City Residents
*1980:* 200,452
*1990:* 199,973
*2000:* 198,915
*2003 estimate:* 193,464
*Percent change, 1990–2000:* − .3%
*U.S. rank in 1980:* 72nd
*U.S. rank in 1990:* 79th (State rank: 2nd)
*U.S. rank in 2000:* 105th (State rank: 3rd)

*Density:* 1,687.1 people per square mile (2000)

*Racial and ethnic characteristics* (2000)
    White: 100,251

Black or African American: 92,068
American Indian and Alaska Native: 487
Asian: 3,022
Native Hawaiian and Pacific Islander: 52
Hispanic or Latino (may be of any race): 2,828
Other: 1,046

*Percent of residents born in state:* 72.7% (2000)

*Age characteristics* (2000)
Population under 5 years old: 14,480
Population 5 to 9 years old: 15,100
Population 10 to 14 years old: 14,495
Population 15 to 19 years old: 14,754
Population 20 to 24 years old: 15,387
Population 25 to 34 years old: 27,076
Population 35 to 44 years old: 28,613
Population 45 to 54 years old: 25,207
Population 55 to 59 years old: 8,830
Population 60 to 64 years old: 7,700
Population 65 to 74 years old: 13,778
Population 75 to 84 years old: 9,968
Population 85 years and older: 3,527
Median age: 34.3 years

*Births* (2002)
Total number: 5,830

*Deaths* (2002)
Total number: 3,929 (of which, 60 were infants under the age of 1 year)

*Money income* (1999)
Per capita income: $18,072
Median household income: $31,445
Total households: 78,548

*Number of households with income of . . .*
less than $10,000: 13,142
$10,000 to $14,999: 7,145
$15,000 to $24,999: 12,026
$25,000 to $34,999: 10,400
$35,000 to $49,999: 12,155
$50,000 to $74,999: 12,450
$75,000 to $99,999: 5,211
$100,000 to $149,999: 3,597
$150,000 to $199,999: 1,055
$200,000 or more: 1,367

*Percent of families below poverty level:* 17.9% (63.3% of which were female householder families with related children under 5 years)

*2002 FBI Crime Index Total:* 17,949

# Municipal Government

Mobile has a mayor/council form of government made up of seven council members plus the mayor who are elected for four-year terms.

**Head Official:** Mayor Michael C. Dow (N-P) (since October 1989; current term expires 2005)

**Total Number of City Employees:** 2,450 (2005)

*City Information:* City of Mobile, PO Box 1827, Mobile, AL, 36633-1827; telephone (251)208-7209

# Economy

## Major Industries and Commercial Activity

Benefiting from abundant natural resources, a diversified work force, and a prime location, Mobile enjoyed steady economic expansion throughout the twentieth century. Since 1990 the city has had its healthiest economy in decades, based on factors such as tax revenue, Port of Mobile tonnage, total employment, and residential sales.

Medicine and research, aerospace, retail trade, services, construction, and manufacturing are among Mobile's major businesses. From 1993 to 2003, 87 new companies were created and 399 existing companies were expanded, resulting in 13,983 new jobs. The city's fastest-growing jobs are those in tourism and services.

Austal USA, a joint venture between its parent company in Australia and Mobile's Bender Shipbuilding and Repair Company, will bring 600 new jobs to the area in 2005 and 2006. Austal USA broke ground in early 2005 on a new shipbuilding facility created for design and construction of a new U.S. Navy ship. Also in early 2005 construction began on a new aircraft facility adjacent to the Mobile Regional Airport. EADS CASA North America will occupy the 13,000 square foot center when it relocates its aircraft service and support operation from Chantilly, Virginia to Mobile. An April 2004 article in the *Mobile Register* quoted Carl Ferguson, director of the University of Alabama's Center for Business and Economic Research, as saying that Mobile added 1,700 new jobs from February 2003 to February 2004. The same article offers that the 2004 opening of Carnival Cruise Lines' Mobile operation will not only create direct jobs, but will create more jobs in the port area by spurring new restaurants, shops, and tourist attractions.

*Items and goods produced:* wood pulp and paper, aircraft engines, aluminum, chemicals and paints, cement, apparel, pumps, batteries, ship-related items, rayon fibers, bakery products

## Incentive Programs—New and Existing Companies

*Local programs*—The Mobile Chamber of Commerce serves as a regional economic development agency, coordinating with city, county and private partners. According to the Chamber, both local and state incentives are available to help firms reduce initial capital costs, develop a labor force, and lessen long term tax burdens.

*State programs*—Alabama boasts a progressive state business environment as demonstrated by its comprehensive right-to-work laws, one-stop environmental permitting, and a positive state and local government attitude toward new and expanding business. Tax rates are competitive; for example, employers who provide or sponsor an approved basic skills education program qualify to receive a 20 percent credit on state corporate income tax liability. Parts of Mobile have been designated as part of the Alabama Enterprise Zone Program, which helps attract new business to Alabama with tax breaks to those operating within the zone. Information about these incentives and Alabama's state-of-the art industrial training programs is available through the Alabama Development Office.

*Job training programs*—Top business executives in Alabama applaud the state's Industrial Development Training Program, which supports local businesses by doing everything from advertising, to processing job applications, to training and delivering employees. In Mobile, the Center for Workforce Development (CWD) was launched in January 2000 in response to business community needs for better-trained workers. The CWD's purpose is to form strategic alliances in workforce development with area business, education, and community leaders. These alliances are designed to foster improvements in the quality of Mobile's workforce and ensure that the region remains competitive in a global economy.

## Development Projects

The Museum of Mobile expanded in 2000 and moved next door to the Exploreum in the Southern Market/Old City Hall on Royal Street. After massive renovations in the late 1990s and early in the new century, the city of Mobile's waterfront and downtown areas were rebuilt into a venue of cultural, tourist, and entertainment outlets named Mobile Landing. In addition to a host of new restaurants, a waterfront and concert park and the Gulf Coast Exploreum Science Center and IMAX Theater have sprung up. In 2004, Carnival Cruise Lines opened for business with a one-year contract to sail its massive cruise ship, the 1,452-passenger Holiday, out of Mobile Bay. The ship leaves the new $20 million Mobile

Alabama Cruise Terminal on four- and five-night cruises to Mexico and is expected to help boost what is already a $500 million tourism industry. The Maritime Center, slated to open in May 2006, will offer interactive exhibits, programs, and ferry rides.

In 2000 the Mobile Public Library began work on a multimillion-dollar expansion. Plans were underway in 2004 for expanding the Main Library from 20,000 to more than 63,000 square feet at a projected cost of $7.5 million. By that year, construction had begun on the 58,457 square foot West Regional Library on Grelot Road at a projected cost of $10.8 million, and the new Toulminville Branch opened after construction was completed at a cost of $2 million.

In 2005, funding was still being secured and plans were underway for the University of South Alabama's $100-million USA Cancer Research Institute (USACRI). The 100,000 square foot center will focus on both research and treatment, and is expected to be completed in 2006.

In private investments, in 2001 Ipsco Inc. completed construction of a new plate mill in Mobile County. The steel mill, which cost $425 million to build, generates 1.25 million tons of steel annually and employs 450 people. The company selected Mobile County because of its highly skilled workforce, competitive power rates, good tax practices, and transportation logistics.

***Economic Development Information:*** Mobile Area Chamber of Commerce, 451 Government Street, Mobile, AL 36652; telephone (251)433-6951; fax (251)432-1143; email info@mobilechamber.org. Alabama Development Office, Neal Wade, Director, 401 Adams Avenue, 6th Floor, Montgomery, AL 36130; telephone (800)248-0033; email adoinfo@www.ado.state.al.us

## Commercial Shipping

Mobile, long recognized as a prime port location, experienced a period of strong growth in the 1990s that continued into the new century. The Port of Mobile is one of the largest deepwater ports in the United States, served by more than 130 steamship lines providing substantial shipping capabilities connected to 376 inland dock facilities. Mobile also boasts two huge ship repair businesses and numerous barge repair companies; more than 300 private firms work to support the maritime industry in Mobile. Mobile's importance as the center of a far-reaching distribution network is further enhanced by the Brookley Complex, a designated Foreign Trade Zone. The 1,700-acre trade and industrial complex is operated by the Mobile Airport Authority and provides connections to air, rail, waterway, and interstate transportation. Sixty-five motor freight lines are certified to transport interstate shipments to and from the Mobile area.

## Labor Force and Employment Outlook

Alabama is a right-to-work state and ranks below half the states in its percentage of nonagricultural union membership. Employment opportunities are plentiful and diverse in Mobile. In the 10-year span from 1993 to 2003, nearly 14,000 new jobs were created by new or expanding companies in the Mobile area.

The following is a summary of data regarding the Mobile metropolitan area labor force, 2003 annual averages.

*Size of nonagricultural labor force:* 224,400

*Number of workers employed in . . .*
　*construction and mining:* 15,600
　*manufacturing:* 20,500
　*trade, transportation and utilities:* 49,900
　*information:* 3,000
　*financial activities:* 12,300
　*professional and business services:* 25,900
　*educational and health services:* 54,400
　*leisure and hospitality:* 22,900
　*other services:* 12,600
　*government:* 36,000

*Average hourly earnings of production workers employed in manufacturing:* $14.75

*Unemployment rate:* 6.0% (November 2004)

| Largest employers | Number of employees |
|---|---|
| Mobile County School System | 7,187 |
| Univ. of South Alabama and USA Health System | 4,972 |
| Mobile Infirmary Medical Center | 3,500 |
| City of Mobile | 2,466 |
| Providence Hospital | 2,307 |
| County of Mobile | 1,700 |
| ST Mobile Aerospace Engineering | 1,500 |
| Springhill Memorial Hospital | 1,400 |
| Winn Dixie Food Stores | 1,052 |

## Cost of Living

The following is a summary of data regarding several key cost of living factors for the Mobile area.

*2004 (3rd Quarter) ACCRA Average House Price:* $213,394

*2004 (3rd Quarter) ACCRA Cost of Living Index:* 88.3 (U.S. average = 100.0)

*State income tax rate:* Ranges from 2.0% to 5.0%

*State sales tax rate:* 4.0%

*Local income tax rate:* None

*Local sales tax rate:* 4.0% (city); 1.0% (county)

*Property tax rate:* $56.50 total for city, county, and state per $1000 assessed valuation; assessment rate, 10% for residential, 20% for commercial (2005)

*Economic Information:* Mobile Area Chamber of Commerce, 451 Government Street, PO Box 2187, Mobile, AL 36652; telephone (251)433-6951; Fax (251)432-1143; e-mail info@mobilechamber.org.

# Education and Research

## Elementary and Secondary Schools

The Mobile County Public School System is the oldest in the state and encompasses five separate school districts. The system educates 65,000 students and employs more than 7,000 people. The school system completed the largest building program in its history with the opening of Spencer Elementary School in the fall of 1999. Spencer Elementary was the last project in the Phase I Building Program that consisted of one high school, two middle schools, five elementary schools, and six additions to existing elementary schools. The school system then began another aggressive building program that includes several new elementary schools. In 2001, voters passed a bond to increase funding for the school system.; currently the systems' budget exceeds $400 million yearly.

The school system, the Mobile Chamber of Commerce, and area businesses and training organizations work together to provide vocational training for Mobile students. Programs include Family and Consumer Sciences Education; Health Science; Agriscience and Technology; Business/Marketing Education; Career/Technical Cooperative Education; Career Technology; and the School-to-Work program. One of the few of its kind, the Environmental Studies Center offers more than 500 acres of woodlands and teaches students and the community about the natural environment.

The following is a summary of data regarding Mobile's public schools as of the 2002–2003 fiscal year.

*Total enrollment:* 65,000

*Number of facilities*
　*elementary schools:* 55
　*middle schools:* 16
　*senior high schools:* 14
　*other:* 15 magnet, vocational and other

*Student/teacher ratio:* 16:1

*Teacher salaries (2004-05)*
   *minimum:* $29,538
   *maximum:* $48,832

*Funding per pupil:* $3,955

In addition to the many parochial and private schools in Mobile county, the Alabama School of Mathematics and Science is a residential high school educating sophomores, juniors, and seniors in advanced studies of math, science, and technology.

*Public Schools Information:* Mobile County Schools, PO Box 1327, Mobile, AL 36633; telephone (251)221-4000

### Colleges and Universities

Two private institutions and one state-supported school offer college degrees in the Mobile area. The University of South Alabama is a state school that offers bachelor's and master's degrees and enrolls more than 13,000 students. The University of Mobile, a private institution, is affiliated with the Southern Baptist Church. Spring Hill College is a private Catholic institution. Mobile is also served by three technical and trade schools, including an aviation school; a branch of Montgomery's Faulkner University offering 2-year degrees; and four campuses of Bishop State Community College.

### Libraries and Research Centers

The Mobile Public Library maintains seven branches, bookmobiles, and a collection of more than 400,000 volumes, as well as CDs, films, and tapes. In 2005 major renovations were underway of the library's main branch, bringing about a temporary location move to the Mobile Civic Center's Expo Hall. Much of the material in the library's special collections focuses on regional history. The system's specialized libraries in the area maintain holdings on fine arts, banking and finance, law, sports, and health sciences.

Research centers in the Mobile area include mineralization and primate research laboratories at the University of South Alabama, which also supports a Center for Business and Economic Research. On nearby Dauphin Island, 22 Alabama universities and colleges maintain a Sea Lab research complex for marine studies. Paper and pollution are among the subjects studied at the Erling Riis Research Laboratory. When completed in 2006, the University of South Alabama's new USA Cancer Research Institute (USACRI) is expected to serve an estimated 2.5 million people in 42 Gulf Coast counties of Alabama, Mississippi, and Florida.

*Public Library Information:* Mobile Public Library, 700 Government St., Mobile, AL 36602-1403; telephone (251)208-7106

# Health Care

Mobile offers a full range of basic and specialty health care in five general hospitals, a women's and children's hospital, both a public and a private mental health hospital, a rehabilitation hospital, outpatient surgery centers, and more than 850 physicians and 175 dentists. A designated regional trauma center, the University of South Alabama Medical Center has a Level I Trauma Center, an emergency helicopter, the region's only burn center, and a cancer center. The University also boasts the USA Children's and Women's Hospital, with sophisticated facilities and services, and Knollwood Park Hospital; the institution also provides instruction through its colleges of medicine, nursing, and allied health professions. The Mobile Infirmary Medical Center is the state's largest not-for-profit hospital and includes cardiac and cancer services plus a 50-bed rehabilitation hospital. Mobile's other hospitals include Providence Hospital, Springhill Medical Center, Thomas Hospital, and Mercy Medical.

# Recreation

### Sightseeing

Visitors to Mobile may want to stop at the Fort Conde Welcome Center at 150 Royal Street in the Church Street East district. Built between 1724 and 1735, the brick fort was demolished 100 years later. The site was discovered during freeway excavations in the 1970s, and using original plans archived in France, the city undertook a partial reconstruction of the fort, which was dedicated in 1976. Today, a video presentation about Mobile and interactive video screens offer a glimpse of the many sightseeing opportunities that abound in this historic city. Visitors may tour Fort Conde accompanied by costumed guides who will fire period muskets and cannons.

Mobile's colorful heritage has also been preserved in other historic districts. Near Fort Conde, the Conde Charlotte Museum has been furnished in the various styles of Mobile's past eras. Among other historic sites in the Church Street East district are the Bishop Portier House, a Creole cottage from the 1830s, and townhouses dating from the 1850s and 1860s. The Oakleigh Garden historic district, a group of nineteenth-century Gulf Coast and Victorian cottages, centers around Oakleigh, an 1830s residence on 3.5 acres enhanced by azaleas and moss-covered oak trees. The nearby Cox-Deasy house, a good example of Creole Cottage Style, can also be toured.

Seven miles from Mobile Bay, near Spring Hill College, the Spring Hill historic district features mansions dating from the 1850s. The 1855 Bragg Mitchell Mansion on Spring Hill

**Tours of the *USS Alabama* are offered at Battleship Memorial Park.**

Avenue is a handsome antebellum mansion open to the public. The nine-block area known as De Tonti Square historic district consists of elegant townhouses, built in a variety of styles between 1840 and 1900, which are illuminated by the neighborhood's antique gas lights. The 1860 Italianate Richards-DAR House is splendidly furnished and boasts iron lace porches and beautiful gardens. Included on the National Register of Historic Places are Mobile's Church Street Graveyard and Magnolia Cemetery, which contain headstones and funerary monuments from the earliest days of the area's history.

At Mobile's Battleship Alabama Memorial Park, the USS *Alabama,* the World War II submarine USS *Drum,* and the Aircraft Pavilion can be toured. The park also features a nature observatory. The Mobile Botanical Gardens, adjacent to Langan Municipal Park, presents 100 acres of azaleas, camellias, magnolias, roses, and other native and exotic plants. Twenty miles south of Mobile, the 900-acre Bellingrath Gardens estate dazzles sightseers with 65 acres of landscaped flowers, trees, shrubs, and flowering bushes surrounding a luxurious home; 200 species of birds frequent the gardens. Bayou La Batre, a fishing and shipbuilding community near Mobile, affords visitors many sightseeing opportunities, especially during the festivities connected with the annual blessing of the fleet. When Dauphin Island, two miles off the coast of Mobile County where Mobile Bay meets the Gulf of Mexico, was discovered by the Le Moyne brothers in 1699, it was found to be the site of burial grounds termed Indian shell mounds. The island also features Fort Gaines and lovely gulf beaches. Fort Morgan on the tip of Gulf Shores Island is another remaining Confederate fort.

## Arts and Culture

Among the community theater groups in Mobile are the Mobile Theatre Guild, the Joe Jefferson Players, and the Chickasaw Civic Theatre. Children's theater is presented by Mobile's Youth Theatre at the Playhouse in the Park. Mobile's colleges and universities also mount stage productions. Mobile audiences enjoy music performed during annual visits of the Alabama Symphony Orchestra and the New Orleans Symphony Orchestra. The Mobile Chamber Music Society and the Mobile Symphony also sponsor concerts. The Mobile Symphony Youth Orchestra completed its first season in 2000-2001 under the auspices of the Mobile Symphony. The following year, a new acoustical shell created a new listening experience for symphony-goers. Mobile Symphony and Mobile Opera jointly purchased a building to be used for rehearsals, teaching studios, and administrative offices; renovations were completed in 2002, and the center opened as the Josephine Larkins Music Center. During warm weather in downtown Mobile a weekly concert series entertains at lunch time on Bienville Square, while pops concerts can be heard in the city's parks. The renovated 1,900-seat Saenger Theatre

offers up theater and musical productions. The Mobile Ballet brings exciting dance presentations to the area; its dance school educates residents from toddlers to pre-professionals. The Alabama Contemporary Dance Company trains local dancers and brings contemporary dance to the city.

Mobile's municipal museum system maintains three facilities: the Museum of Mobile, Carlen House, and the Phoenix Fire House Museum. The Museum of Mobile moved to the Old City Hall in fall 2000, where it showcases furniture, silver, arms, ship models, documents, and historical records; its former location will serve as a new Mardi Gras Museum. Carlen House is a Creole cottage where period crafts such as spinning, weaving, and quilting are demonstrated. The Phoenix Fire House Museum is devoted to the city's fire fighting history.

The Mobile Museum of Art is located west of downtown and houses a collection of more than 6,000 pieces spanning more than 2,000 years of culture, including paintings, prints, sculpture, lithographs, silver, quilts, porcelain, seventeenth- and eighteenth-century southern furnishings, and African art. The museum reopened in 2002 after undergoing an expansion costing $15 million, which brought the gallery's exhibition space to 95,000 square feet.

At the University of South Alabama the Museum Gallery Complex consists of Toulon House, a former plantation home built in 1828; Seamen's Bethel, built in 1860 and now serving as a theater; and the Isaac Max Townhouse, dating from 1870.

The Gulf Coast Exploreum Science Center and IMAX Dome Theater features exhibits that let visitors explore aquatic life and human science, and games and puzzles that demonstrate scientific concepts and stimulate problem-solving skills.

## Festivals and Holidays

Rooted in ancient Grecian and Roman celebrations and adapted to fit the Christian Church's calendar, Mardi Gras is an outpouring of revelry that precedes the penitential Lenten period observed for 40 days prior to Easter. Mardi Gras practices are thought to have been brought to the first Mobile settlement by its French colonists around 1700, and were later enhanced with traditions added by Spanish and subsequent settlers. Resumed after the Civil War, Mobile's Mardi Gras today is observed with two weeks of balls, floats and parades, costumes, music from bands and minstrels, and pageantry. Mardis Gras is celebrated in Mobile with a variety of citywide events.

Also in late winter, Mobile celebrates its Azalea Trail Festival, when 37 miles of azalea shrubs in bloom throughout Mobile are marked out on two driving routes that afford trail followers a spectacular floral display. The festival also includes a 10-kilometer footrace, a historic homes tour, and other events. Spring events in Mobile include the Festival of Flowers on the campus of Spring Hill College, and the Blakeley Battle Festival reenactment commemorating the last major Civil War land battle. In June, 52 contestants in the America's Junior Miss program compete in Mobile for college scholarships and other prizes.

Proximity to the Gulf of Mexico inspires summer events in and around Mobile. Among these is the Blessing of the Fleet in neighboring Bayou La Batre, where fishing boats are decorated for a water parade, arts and crafts are displayed, live crabs are raced, and seafood and gumbo are served in abundance. During the Alabama Deep Sea Fishing Rodeo held for a weekend on nearby Dauphin Island, anglers test their skills against each other and such prize fish as shark and blue marlin. In September the Fall Outdoor Arts and Crafts Fair also includes music, food, and games.

October's National Shrimp Festival in Gulf Shores promises seafood contests, a parade, an arts and crafts show, dancing, fireworks, boat racing, and a ten-kilometer footrace. Also in October, the Greater Gulf State Fair features exhibits of commercial, cultural, leisure, military, and agricultural interest. October 2005's BayFest Festival expected a draw of 200,000 for its annual 3-day continuous-music festival. The Mobile International Festival in November showcases food and customs of more than 30 countries. Seasonal celebrations at Mobile's historic locations in December are followed by festivities surrounding January's Senior Bowl, a yearly football event that draws national attention.

### Sports for the Spectator

Sports enthusiasts can view a wide range of sporting events in the Mobile area, which annually hosts the Alabama-Mississippi All Star Classic high school football competition. Collegiate sports played in Mobile include baseball, basketball, and wrestling. Ladd-Peebles Stadium hosts the annual GMAC Bowl, started in 1999.

Each January the nation's top-ranking college seniors meet in the city to play football in the prestigious Senior Bowl. The post-season competition, televised nationally, showcases upcoming talent and attracts scouts, coaches, and management representing professional football. Stock car racing and dog racing at Mobile Greyhound Park are also on view in the Mobile area. Mobile's AA baseball team, the Mobile BayBears, entertain fans at the Hank Aaron Stadium.

### Sports for the Participant

The city of Mobile maintains 85 facilities that provide a variety of sports activities and opportunities. Langan Park's 700 acres surrounding a 40-acre lake offer golf, tennis, baseball, bicycling, paddle boating, and picnicking. Bowling

alleys, skating rinks, swimming pools, and many tennis and basketball courts throughout Mobile add to the city's active life. Mobile's Magnolia Grove Golf Course is a stop on the Robert Trent Jones Golf Trail, the largest golf course construction project ever attempted with a total of 378 holes over 18 courses throughout the state.

Mobile's residents and visitors can engage in many activities on or in adjacent water bodies. The city's proximity to the Gulf of Mexico is appreciated by bird watchers, who have an opportunity to view many migratory species crossing the gulf, as well as an abundance of local species. Sailing, wind surfing, canoeing, kayaking, water-skiing, swimming, and scuba diving are common on the area's rivers, on Mobile Bay, and on the Gulf of Mexico. The Gulf Yachting Association sponsors a variety of racing events around the Gulf Coast. At nearby Gulf State Park, 6,150 acres of park land include a 2 mile stretch of sandy beach, a beach front lodge, cabins, a campground, a swimming pool, two freshwater lakes for skiing, canoeing, sailing, and fishing, and facilities for tennis, cycling, and golf. Among the Gulf area's other sites for sporting activities are Dauphin Island and Pleasure Island.

Fishing and hunting are also popular pursuits in the Mobile area. Freshwater fishing on such waterways as Dog River, Mobile River, the Tennessee-Tombigbee system, and the Tensaw River yield catches of bream, bass, and perch. Saltwater fishing from piers or banks on the Mobile Bay or the gulf brings in trout, flounder, and Spanish mackerel. Deep-sea fishing can be chartered in the Mobile area, yielding land sharks, snapper, amberjack, and sailfish. Hunters in the Mobile area bag waterfowl and game such as deer and wild turkey.

### Shopping and Dining

Shopping venues in the Mobile area range from regional malls to specialty boutiques. A district of shops surrounds restored Fort Conde, and recent developments to the downtown waterfront area have brought about new entertainment, restaurant and shopping options. The Bel Air shopping mall also features a food court offering a variety of ethnic and American foods. Mobile restaurants take full advantage of the area's abundant seafood, including gulf and bay shrimp, oysters, soft-shell crab, blue crab, red snapper, flounder, mullet, and trout. Among Mobile's other regional specialties are Creole and Cajun menus, Caribbean dishes such as West Indies salad, and traditional Southern fare such as catfish and barbecue. Ethnic dining is also available at establishments featuring European, Oriental, and Mexican menus.

***Visitor Information:*** Mobile Area Chamber of Commerce, 451 Government Street, Mobile AL 36652; telephone (800)422-6951 or (251)433-6951. Mobile Bay Convention and Visitors Bureau, PO Box 204, Mobile AL 36601; telephone (800)5-MOBILE or (251)208-2000

# Convention Facilities

Downtown Mobile boasts the 400,000-square-foot Mobile Civic Center Complex, which features a 10,000-seat arena and 80,000 square feet of exhibit space. There are also a 28,000-square-foot exposition hall, a 1,950-seat theater, and ample meeting rooms.

Part of the downtown revitalization program is the Mobile Convention Center, a $50 million facility that opened in 1993. The center offers 100,000 square feet of exhibit space, 50,000 square feet of meeting and banquet space, and a 52,000-square-foot area for registration and receptions. The center is adjacent to the Adam's Mark Hotel. Among Mobile's other convention facilities are a dozen hotels, with meeting rooms for groups of 100 to 5,000 people.

*Convention Information:* Mobile Bay Convention and Visitors Bureau, PO Box 204, Mobile AL 36601; telephone (800)5-MOBILE or (251)208-2000

# Transportation

## Approaching the City

The Mobile Regional Airport is located approximately 14 miles from downtown Mobile. Air travelers are served by Delta, Northwest Airlines, Continental Express, and U.S. Airways. The Downtown Airport at Brookley is a 1,700-acre transportation terminal favored by private and corporate planes for its proximity to downtown Mobile, which is only four minutes away by car. Motorists may reach Mobile via two interstate highways, I-10 and I-65, and by U.S. highways 31, 43, 45, 90, and 98. A $100 million interstate spur completed in 1995 connects I-65 and I-10 in downtown Mobile. In addition, several state roads head into the city. Amtrak provides passenger rail service between Mobile and New Orleans, Atlanta, and New York.

## Traveling in the City

The Mobile Metro Transit Authority operates more than twenty local bus routes to serve the area's transit needs. The Transit Authority also operates an electric-run trolley through downtown Mobile, Monday through Friday. The LoDa moda! makes 22 stops to downtown businesses, parks, hotels, and city buildings, and is free of charge.

# Communications

## Newspapers and Magazines

Mobile's largest-circulation newspaper is *The Mobile Register,* Alabama's oldest newspaper, dating back to 1813. *The Mobile Press* combines with the Register on weekends and prints as *The Mobile Press Register.* Two African-American-oriented newspapers, the *Mobile Beacon* and *The New Times,* are published in Mobile. Other publications focus on industry, education, and Christian themes.

## Television and Radio

Mobile is served by five local television stations and receives broadcasts from other stations originating in Pensacola, Florida, and Huntsville, Alabama. Mobile's 6 AM radio stations broadcast a range of rock and roll, contemporary, and country and western music as well as religious and news programming. The city's 8 FM radio stations program classical, jazz, popular, easy listening, urban, and progressive music.

*Media Information:* The Mobile Register, 304 Government Street, PO Box 2488, Mobile, AL 36630; telephone (251)219-5400

## Mobile Online

Alabama Bureau of Tourism and Travel. Available www .touralabama.org

Alabama Development Office. Available www.ado.state.al .us

City of Mobile home page. Available www.cityofmobile.org

Mobile Bay Convention and Visitor's Bureau. Available www.mobile.org

Mobile Chamber of Commerce. Available www.mobile chamber.com

Mobile County Public Schools. Available www.mcpss.com

Mobile Museum of Art. Available www.mobilemuseumofart .com

Mobile Public Library. Available www.mplonline.org

*Mobile Register.* Available www.al.com/mobileregister

## Selected Bibliography

Bergeron, Arthur W., Jr., *Confederate Mobile* (Jackson, MS: University Press of Mississippi, 1991)

Pride, Richard A., *The Confession of Dorothy Danner: Telling a Life.* (Nashville: Vanderbilt University Press, 1995)

# Montgomery

## The City in Brief

**Founded:** 1819 (incorporated 1819)

**Head Official:** Mayor Bobby N. Bright (since 1999)

**City Population**
1980: 177,857
1990: 187,106
2000: 201,568
2003 estimate: 200,123
Percent change, 1990–2000: 5.6%
U.S. rank in 2000: 100th (State rank: 2nd)

**Metropolitan Area Population (MSA)**
1980: 272,631
1990: 292,517
2000: 333,055
Percent change, 1990–2000: 13.9%

U.S. rank in 1990: 120th
U.S. rank in 2000: 121st (MSA)

**Area:** 155 square miles (2000)
**Elevation:** 221 feet above sea level
**Average Annual Temperature:** 67.2° F
**Average Annual Precipitation:** 44.5 inches

**Major Economic Sectors:** Services, government, trade
**Unemployment rate:** 5.1% (November 2004)
**Per Capita Income:** $19,385 (1999)

**2002 FBI Crime Index Total:** 17,617

**Major Colleges and Universities:** Alabama State University, Auburn University at Montgomery, Faulkner University, Southern Christian University, Troy State University Montgomery, Community College of the Air Force

**Daily Newspaper:** *The Montgomery Advertiser, The Montgomery Independent*

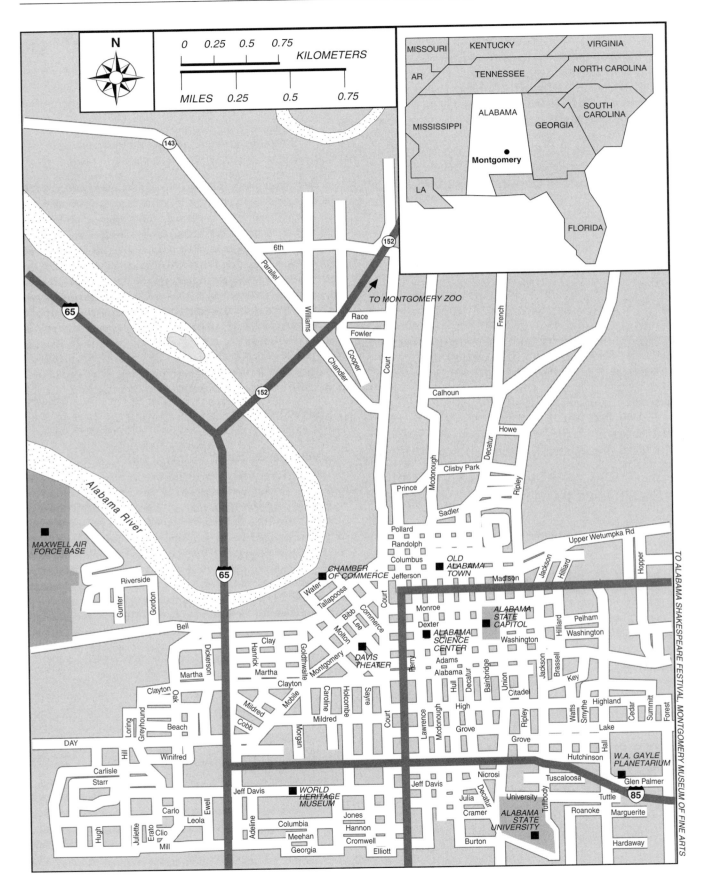

# Introduction

As the home of a fine art museum and highly respected Shakespeare Festival, the city of Montgomery combines a small town feel with an aura of cultural sophistication. Blessed with beautiful parks and gardens as well as a rich historical legacy, the city is both a tourist attraction and the administrative site of the Alabama state government.

# Geography and Climate

Montgomery, located in the state's south-central region, lies on the south bank of the Alabama River in a gently rolling area with fertile soil. The city is 100 miles south of Birmingham and 172 miles southwest of Atlanta, Georgia.

No topographical feature of the Montgomery area appreciably influences the local climate. Generally the days from June through September show little change, with frequent afternoon rain showers that soon dissipate. Beginning in late August, the weather gets drier until the period of December through April, when there are great differences from day to day in the amount and intensity of rainfall. Droughts sometimes occur in spring, late summer, and early autumn. The occurrence of snow is a rarity.

**Area:** 155 square miles (2000)

**Elevation:** 221 feet above sea level

**Average Temperatures:** January, 49.4° F; July, 83.6° F; annual average, 67.2° F

**Average Annual Precipitation:** 44.5 inches

# History

### Early Days in Montgomery

Many centuries before Montgomery was founded, the land on which it sits was the site of two Indian towns called Ikanatchati and Towasa. Numerous mounds and burials sites have been uncovered there, proving it to have been an area thickly settled by ancestors of the Creek people, the Alibamu Indians, from whom the state took its name.

The first Europeans to visit the region were Hernando De Soto and his fellow Spanish explorers, who passed through the region in 1540. The first white inhabitant of the area was James McQueen, a Scottish trader, who arrived in 1716. The area remained sparsely inhabited until 1814, when Arthur Moore and his companions built cabins on local riverbanks. Three years later, the land was put up for sale and purchased by two groups of speculators.

General John Scott led a group of Georgians who built the town of Alabama but abandoned it when a second group of poor New Englanders founded a nearby town they called Philadelphia. Scott and his companions then built a new town they called East Alabama. Both groups began their settlements to make riches on future growth of the area.

The rivalry between the two groups was finally settled in December 1819, when they merged the towns under the name Montgomery, Incorporated. The name was chosen to honor General Richard Montgomery, who had died in the Revolutionary War. Eleven days after Montgomery's founding, Alabama was admitted as a state. Three years earlier, Montgomery County had been named in honor of a local man, Major Lemuel P. Montgomery, who later lost his life when serving with U.S. President Andrew Jackson during a war with the Creek Indians.

### Lafayette's Visit a Local Highlight

The year 1821 was an important one for Montgomery as the first steamboats reached the city, which was the northernmost point up the Missouri River to which large vessels from Mobile could travel. That same year a stage line began to carry passengers eastward, and the newspaper the Montgomery *Republican* was founded.

From Montgomery's earliest days, cotton production was its most important local industry, with the first commercial cotton gin having been installed in the area at the beginning of the nineteenth century. Montgomery soon became an important port for shipping cotton from the region. Although the town was still small, it had two general stores whose owners accepted payment in "either cotton or cash." The town also boasted a private school, a dancing school, a court whose docket showed more than one hundred cases, and a lively social calendar for the wealthier residents.

A grand ball held during the 1825 visit of distinguished Frenchman the Marquis de LaFayette was the highlight of the town's early history. About that time, the State Bank was founded, and real estate companies began to flourish as new settlers moved to the area.

### Montgomery Becomes State Capital

In 1834, the state of Alabama voted to establish the Montgomery Railroad Company and build a rail route to West Point, Georgia. In time it became an important link in service between New York City and New Orleans. By 1840, Montgomery had a population of 2,179 residents.

On January 30, 1846, the Alabama legislature announced that it had voted to remove the capital city from Tuscaloosa to Montgomery. The first legislative session in the new capital met in December 1847. In time, a Capitol building was erected under the direction of a Philadelphia, Pennsylvania architect. The original structure burnt down in 1849 but was rebuilt in 1851 following the original plans.

### Secession and Its Consequences

By the time of the Civil War, Alabamians were among the Southerners with the strongest anti-Northern sentiments. Their slave-based economy was made up of the triad of wealthy white planters, working class whites, and a large group of African American slaves who served at the whims of their masters. The wealthy planters were adamant about protecting the entrenched socio-economic structure and their accumulated wealth.

As the whites' fears of change accelerated, it did not take long for the movement for secession from the Union to strengthen, and a Secession Convention met in Montgomery on January 6, 1861. On February 4, representatives of six seceding states assembled in Montgomery, which they chose to serve as the provisional capital of the Confederate States of America. Five days later, Jefferson Davis was unanimously chosen to serve as President of the Confederacy. A torchlight parade held on March 4 culminated in his inauguration. At that time, the population of the city stood at more than 8,850 citizens.

Montgomery's stint as capital of the Confederacy was short lived, however, when it became apparent that Virginia was to be the site of much of the early fighting. It then became necessary to shorten the line of communication between military headquarters and the field officers. At the first Montgomery meeting of the Provisional Congress, the representatives decided that the capital should be moved to Richmond, Virginia, within two months.

Dedication to the Confederate cause remained strong, even when General James Wilson's federal raiders entered Montgomery in April 1865. Upon their arrival, local citizens burned more than 100,000 bales of cotton to prevent their falling into Union hands. In response, Union troops burned the local small arms factories, the railroad cars, and five steamboats.

### Troubled Times Improve

The Reconstruction period following the end of the Civil War in 1865 was a time of hardships. Much of the wealth of local citizens had been wiped out, articles of common use were scarce, stores lay empty, and the means of traveling by steamer and railroad had been destroyed.

A slow and painful economic and social recovery took place. By 1880, the population had grown to 16,713 people and railroad expansion had helped local conditions to improve.

Montgomery's geographic location and proximity to the most productive agricultural regions of the South, as well as the fact that it was the state capital, soon brought about the re-connection of the city with other areas of the state and nation via roads and railway routes. By 1885, an intra-city electric trolley car system had been constructed.

In 1890, industrialists and financiers began to visit Montgomery in search of business sites. The first large lumber mill had been opened and the local population stood at 21,883. In time, local textile and garment factories, cotton processing plants, and fertilizer plants were established.

### First Half of Twentieth Century Brings Industrial Growth

The years between 1900 and 1940 saw steady industrial progress and a local population growth from more than 30,000 to about 78,000 residents. Montgomery remained a focal point for cotton farmers, and livestock and dairy production became vital industries. In 1910, flight pioneers Orville and Wilbur Wright built an airfield in the city and opened a school of aviation. Later, during mid-century, Montgomery became a center for packing plants, furniture, construction, and chemical and food production.

During the 1940s, Southern African American citizens began to show their dissatisfaction with the restrictive "Jim Crow" laws allowing discrimination, including the restriction of their voting rights. By the mid-1950s, the call for African American voter registration had greatly increased.

### Desegregation and the Civil Rights Movement

In 1955 Montgomery saw a simple but historical event that was to influence the history of the United States. That year, a Montgomery woman named Rosa Parks was arrested for not yielding her bus seat to a white man. For the 381 days that followed, Montgomery African Americans boycotted the city's buses, making way for the December 1956 U.S. Supreme Court order for the desegregation of Montgomery buses.

The 1960s were a period of great upheaval in the United States and in the city of Montgomery. Supporters of the civil rights movement from the North and other areas of the South began coming to the city to support efforts by African Americans to gain their civil rights, and Montgomery became the virtual headquarters of the civil rights movement. Groups of African American and white people, known as Freedom Riders, rode buses together throughout the south as a way to protest segregation. On May 20, 1961, when a number of Freedom Riders arrived at the Montgomery bus station, they were beaten by local Ku Klux Klansmen, who were later tried and sentenced for their crimes.

In 1962, George Corley Wallace won the governorship of Alabama after a campaign based on his support for segregation. Standing on the state's Capitol steps, he made a famous speech championing segregation. The next year, Dr. Martin Luther King, Jr. came to Montgomery and preached against segregation.

In 1965, King led 25,000 demonstrators on a four-day march from Selma, Alabama to Montgomery to seek voting rights for African Americans. When the 600 civil rights marchers reached the Edmund Pettus Bridge shortly after the walk began, they were attacked by local lawmen carrying clubs and using tear gas. The march continued only after a federal judge granted the protestors a court order protecting their right to march from Selma to Montgomery. Nearly 3,200 marchers set out for Montgomery, walking 12 miles a day and sleeping in fields. By the time they reached the capitol, their numbers had swelled to 25,000 people. Less than five months after the march, President Lyndon B. Johnson signed the Voting Rights Act of 1965, which represented a major victory for civil rights advocates.

In 1971, attorney Morris Dees founded the Southern Poverty Law Center in the city of Montgomery. The center promoted tolerance and took up the cause of poor people and minorities. It also helped to sponsor the building of the local civil rights memorial. In 1991 a U.S. federal district judge furthered civil rights efforts when he ordered Alabama State University and other state institutions to hire more minority faculty and staff and to make changes in their financial and admission policies.

The last decades of the 1900s brought many changes to the city of Montgomery. A new spirit of cooperation grew between its African American and white citizens and new industries grew, especially in the area of high technology. In addition, the establishment of Maxwell-Gunter Air Force Base further strengthened the local economy. By 1999, a wealth of new construction and the addition of Overlook Park where once a parking lot stood marked the beginning of an extensive downtown renaissance. The Montgomery of the new century is boosted by a burgeoning tourism industry based on the city's plethora of Civil War and Civil Rights historical sites.

**Historical Information:** Montgomery County Historical Society, PO Box 1829, Montgomery, AL 36102; telephone (334)264-1837. Alabama Department of Archives and History Museum, 624 Washington Ave., Montgomery, AL 36130; telephone (334)242-4435; email Mark.Palmer @archives.alabama.gov

# Population Profile

## Metropolitan Area Residents
*1980:* 272,631

*1990:* 292,517
*2000:* 333,055
*Percent change, 1990–2000:* 13.9%
*U.S. rank in 1990:* 120th (MSA)
*U.S. rank in 2000:* 121st (MSA)

## City Residents
*1980:* 177,857
*1990:* 187,106
*2000:* 201,568
*2003 estimate:* 200,123
*Percent change, 1990–2000:* 5.6%
*U.S. rank in 2000:* 100th (State rank: 2nd)

*Density:* 1,297.3 people per square mile (2000)

*Racial and ethnic characteristics* (2000)
   White: 96,085
   Black or African American: 100,048
   American Indian and Alaska Native: 500
   Asian: 2,146
   Native Hawaiian and Pacific Islander: 71
   Hispanic or Latino (may be of any race): 2,484
   Other: 748

*Percent of residents born in state:* 71.5% (2000)

*Age characteristics* (2000)
   Population under 5 years old: 14,259
   Population 5 to 9 years old: 14,912
   Population 10 to 14 years old: 14,729
   Population 15 to 19 years old: 15,465
   Population 20 to 24 years old: 17,365
   Population 25 to 34 years old: 29,703
   Population 35 to 44 years old: 30,331
   Population 45 to 54 years old: 25,398
   Population 55 to 59 years old: 8,649
   Population 60 to 64 years old: 6,957
   Population 65 to 74 years old: 12,376
   Population 75 to 84 years old: 8,415
   Population 85 years and older: 3,009
   Median age: 32.9 years

*Births* (2002)
   Total number: 3,338

*Deaths* (2002)
   Total number: 2,124 (of which, 39 were infants under the age of 1 year)

*Money income* (1999)
   Per capita income: $19.385
   Median household income: $35,627
   Total households: 78,436

*Number of households with income of . . .*
  less than $10,000: 10,255
  $10,000 to $14,999: 5,798
  $15,000 to $24,999: 11,337
  $25,000 to $34,999: 11,130
  $35,000 to $49,999: 12,837
  $50,000 to $74,999: 13,295
  $75,000 to $99,999: 6,261
  $100,000 to $149,999: 4,997
  $150,000 to $199,999: 1,229
  $200,000 or more: 1,297

*Percent of families below poverty level:* 13.9% (54.6% of which were female householder families with related children under 5 years)

*2002 FBI Crime Index Total:* 17,617

# Municipal Government

Montgomery's municipal affairs are managed by a nine-member city council and a mayor, all elected for four-year terms.

**Head Official:** Mayor Bobby N. Bright (since 1999; current term expires 2007)

**Total Number of City Employees:** 2,900 (2000)

*City Information:* Mayor's Office, City of Montgomery, PO Box 1111, Montgomery, AL 36101; telephone (334)241-2000; email mayor@ci.montgomery.al.us

# Economy

## Major Industries and Commercial Activity

Government at the local, state, and federal levels plays a major role in Montgomery's economy. It makes up one-fourth of the work force and lends a strong stability to the local economy. The local colleges and universities make an important contribution to the economy, as does the major military presence of Maxwell Gunter Air Force Base. The relatively new addition of automotive companies to central Alabama has created new opportunities for workers and suppliers.

Montgomery's location in the center of a zone of rich black soil that stretches across Alabama makes it an important processing and shipping center for cotton, dairy, and other farm products. The city also boasts a large livestock market. The city's role as a regional trade center is firmly estab-

lished, and it serves as a wholesaling and distribution gateway to the entire southeast.

Among the variety of Montgomery's industries are metal fabrication, food processing, lumber processing, and furniture production. Sand, gravel, grain, and chemicals are transported north and south via barge from the Montgomery region.

More than 135 information technology (IT) companies were based in Montgomery in 2005. The IT industry in Montgomery has an estimated $1 billion per year economic impact and accounts for approximately 14,000 workers in private, federal and state sectors. In addition, the tourism industry, which annually pours more than $350 million into the local economy, employed more than 11,000 people.

*Items and goods produced:* food, lumber, furniture, metal products, textiles, brick, glass, printing/publishing, plastics, software engineering products

## Incentive Programs—New and Existing Companies

*Local programs*—The Montgomery Area Center for Entrepreneurial Development provides help to small businesses with everything from startup and counseling to nonconventional financing, training, recognition, and networking. An offshoot of the Montgomery Area Chamber of Commerce, the center also provides affordable space at below-market rates for startup entrepreneurs. Manufacturing/distribution projects may receive exemptions for up to 10 years from *ad valorem* taxes other than those levied for educational purposes.

*State programs*—The City of Montgomery is an Urban Enterprise Zone, which results in state tax and nontax incentives that are some of the best in the United States. Montgomery has been designated as a general purpose foreign trade zone, which provides payment deferrals or cancellation for businesses in the zone. New or expanding businesses may also qualify for grants of money for carrying out site improvements.

Alabama offers a full gamut of financial incentives aimed at promoting economic growth. These include payroll tax breaks, industrial revenue bonds for land, building, and equipment for new and expanding plants. The Alabama Economic Development Loan Program can be used to purchase land, buildings, machinery, and equipment. There are also three revolving loan funds. Business loan guarantees are available to firms that create or retain permanent jobs. The Capital Investment Tax Credit program is available to new and expanding businesses involved in manufacturing, warehousing, research, and computer services. Other innovative programs include the State Industrial Site Preparation Grant Program and the Public Works and Development Facilities Grant Program.

*Job training programs*—The Alabama Industrial Development Training (AIDT) program provides a total delivery system for screening and selecting trainees and for designing and implementing training for any new or expanding manufacturer in the state of Alabama. The program provides a full range of customized technical training programs that are free to employers and trainees. Thirty-six mobile training units go directly to the employer site to provide classroom and hands-on training. The program's AIDT project supports the development and enhancement of the city's professional Information Technology community as well as its aerospace, chemical industry, and other area manufacturers. The Workforce Investment Act helps defer the costs of hiring and training new employees for private businesses.

## Development Projects

In 2005, plans were underway for a major overhauling of the Montgomery Riverfront district. The City of Montgomery, the Montgomery Riverfront Development Foundation, and the Montgomery Area Chamber of Commerce had formed an alliance and were working together towards this end. The riverfront plan consists of a $29 million upgrade of the current civic center and a new $53 million hotel in the heart of the district. Those efforts will join the new amphitheatre, stadium, and riverwalk, and combine with an already thriving entertainment district. In addition, the city's revitalization efforts will include a new intermodal transportation center at Union Center. The center, funded in part by federal money to the tune of $8.1 million, will serve as a hub for the transportation system and the downtown trolley system.

In 2004 construction of four new shopping centers began under the development of Aronov Realty Management. Each new center is to be anchored by a Publix grocery store. The four centers will offer 500,000 square feet of retail and business space. In 2004 the Headquarters Standards Systems Group (SSG) broke ground at Maxwell Airforce Base, Gunter Annex. SSG's new $12.6 million 51,450-square-foot Integrated Operational Support Facility is expected to be completed in 2006.

Also in 2004 plastics manufacturer Webster Industries expanded, opening a second operating facility and adding 300 new jobs. Production at Hyundai Motor Manufacturing Alabama is expected to begin in spring 2005. Hyundai's Montgomery plant will occupy 1,720 acres and pump out an estimated 300,000 vehicles and engines, as well as bring 2,000 jobs to the state.

***Economic Development Information:*** Montgomery Community Development Department, PO Box 1111, Montgomery AL 36101; telephone (334)241-2996. Montgomery Area Chamber of Commerce, 41 Commerce Street, PO Box 79, Montgomery, AL 36101; telephone (334)834-5200

## Commercial Shipping

Montgomery is served by 48 motor freight carriers. The Norfolk Southern Company and CSX railroads provide transport opportunities for many local industries. The Alabama River provides a nine-foot channel for barges to cross into the Gulf of Mexico through the port of Mobile. Alabama State Docks in Mobile, accessible via waterway from Montgomery, offer 1000-ton capacity facilities inside a protected barge-turning basin. Barge transportation to the Great Lakes is available through the Tennessee-Tombigbee Waterway.

## Labor Force and Employment Outlook

In 2000 a corporate research group that specializes in the study of job creation named Montgomery as one of the nation's top 25 small metropolitan area "hot spots" for entrepreneurial growth. Montgomery's job growth today relies on the city's burgeoning tourism industry as well as its resident air force base, universities, and information technology industry.

The following is a summary of data regarding the Montgomery metropolitan area labor force, 2003 annual averages.

*Size of nonagricultural labor force:* 163,300

*Number of workers employed in . . .*
   *construction and mining:* 8,500
   *manufacturing:* 15,900
   *trade, transportation and utilities:* 30,400
   *information:* 2,600
   *financial activities:* 10,400
   *professional and business services:* 17,200
   *educational and health services:* 17,800
   *leisure and hospitality:* 13,600
   *other services:* 8,200
   *government:* 38,300

*Average hourly earnings of production workers employed in manufacturing:* $13.56 (statewide)

*Unemployment rate:* 5.1% (November 2004)

| *Largest employers* | *Number of employees* |
|---|---|
| Maxwell-Gunter Air Force Base | 12,700 |
| State of Alabama | 9,500 |
| Baptist Health | 4,300 |
| Montgomery Public Schools | 3,700 |
| ALFA Insurance Companies | 2,568 |
| City of Montgomery | 2,500 |
| Jackson Hospital & Clinic | 1,300 |
| Rheem Manufacturing Co. | 1,150 |

## Cost of Living

The following is a summary of data regarding several key cost of living factors for the Montgomery area.

*2004 (3rd Quarter) ACCRA Average House Price:* $241,263

*2004 (3rd Quarter) ACCRA Cost of Living Index:* 94.3 (U.S. Average = 100.0)

*State income tax rate:* 2.0 to 5.0%

*State sales tax rate:* 4.0%

*Local income tax rate:* None

*Local sales tax rate:* 3.5% city, 2.5% county

*Property tax rate:* $3.45 per $100 of assessed value

*Economic Information:* Montgomery Area Chamber of Commerce, 41 Commerce Street, PO Box 79, Montgomery, AL 36101; telephone (334)834-5200

# Education and Research

## Elementary and Secondary Schools

Montgomery's school system includes nine magnet schools with specialized programs each with its own focus, including arts, technology, math, science, international studies, and advanced academics. The schools offer gifted and special education programs as well as a Career Tech program. The Partners In Education (PIE) program is a joint venture of the Montgomery Public Schools, the Montgomery Area Chamber of Commerce, Junior League of Montgomery, and the Volunteer and Information Center. PIE's 500 partners, consisting of local businesses and organizations, encourage improvement in the school system through partnerships, materials, and donations. The Children's Center of Montgomery is a non-profit organization serving Montgomery's severely disabled and special needs children. The Center is funded in part by the County Board of Education and the State Department of Education, among others. The late 1990s saw the opening of several new schools and a number of additions to existing schools. Brewbaker Technology Magnet High School is designed to expose students to career opportunities in such diverse technical fields as graphics design, pre-engineering, building sciences, e-commerce, medicine, and computer information systems.

The following is a summary of data regarding the Montgomery public school system as of the 2004–2005 school year.

*Total enrollment:* 33,000

*Number of facilities*
  *elementary schools:* 36
  *junior high/middle schools:* 11

*senior high schools:* 7
*other:* 6

*Student/teacher ratio:* 15.4 (2002-2003)

*Teacher salaries*
  *minimum:* $29,538
  *maximum:* $44,936

*Funding per pupil:* $5,728 (2000-2001)

Montgomery also has 37 private and religious schools, pre-kindergarten and early education centers.

*Public Schools Information:* Montgomery Public Schools, 307 S. Decatur St., Montgomery, AL 36104; telephone (334)223-6700

## Colleges and Universities

Montgomery is home to a variety of institutions of higher learning. Alabama State University offers programs in health information management and occupational therapy, and master's degree programs in a variety of education fields and accounting. It has recently expanded to include a graduate program in physical therapy as well as a doctoral program in environmental biology and education.

Auburn University Montgomery is known for its Center for Government and Public Affairs and its Center for Business and Economic Development. Faulkner University offers such programs as the Alabama Christian College of Arts and Sciences, the Harris College of Business and Education, and the Jones School of Law. Its program at the Cloverdale Center for Family Strengths reflects the school's emphasis on family stability through training, counseling, and research. Huntingdon College students participate in the Huntingdon Plan, which encompasses many areas including global awareness, critical thinking, strong writing, and hands-on learning as well as Judeo-Christian heritage and values.

John M. Patterson State Technical College offers varied programs in technical, industrial, and service professions. South College Montgomery, a branch of Savannah, Georgia's South College, offers associate degrees in business and computer- related fields. Montgomery is also home to Southern Christian University, which educates Protestant ministers. Trenholm State Technical College provides training in programs such as auto body repair, childcare, broadcasting technology, and other trades. Adult students who work during the day are the special focus of Troy State University Montgomery. Students there earn associate, undergraduate, or graduate degrees while attending school exclusively at night and on the weekends. Troy State programs focus on business, education, the arts, history, sciences, and social science; its graduate programs offer degrees in education, counseling, and business.

Thousands of military students come to Maxwell-Gunter Air Force Base to study at the Air War College and the Air Command and Staff College and at the Squadron Officer College. The College for Enlisted Professional Military Education (CEPME) at Maxwell's Gunter Annex oversees and standardizes all Air Force educational programs.

### Libraries and Research Centers

Montgomery has a variety of public and private libraries. Montgomery City-County Public Library has 600,000 volumes with a circulation of more than one-half million items. The facility has ten branches and a bookmobile. The Alabama Supreme Court & State Law Library has 200,000 volumes on Alabama law and history. Maxwell-Gunter Air Force Base is home to the Air University Library, one of the largest federal libraries outside Washington D.C., and the largest military academic library in the world.

College libraries include the 258,000-volume Alabama State University Library, which has special collections on accounting and allied health; the Auburn University Montgomery (AUM) library, with 270,000 titles; and the Huntingdon College Library, which has more than 225,000 holdings, and subject interests in business education, ethnic studies, and gerontology. Faulkner University Library's collection houses 100,000 volumes in its Gus Nichols Main Library; the George H. Jones, Jr. Law Library serves the needs of the University's law school students. Troy State University Montgomery Library is housed on the 2nd and 3rd floors of the Rosa Parks Library and Museum building. Opened in 2000, the new structure was built on the site where Mrs. Parks boarded the bus on which she refused to give up her seat.

Baptist Medical Center, Central Alabama Veterans Health Care System, and Jackson Hospital & Clinic maintain medical libraries. Other libraries in the city include the Montgomery County Law Library, the Montgomery Museum of Fine Arts Library, the U.S. Environmental Protection Agency, and Validata Computer and Research Corporation. Auburn University research centers in Montgomery include the Center for Demographic and Cultural Research.

***Public Library Information:*** Montgomery City-County Public Library, 245 High St., PO Box 1950, Montgomery, AL 36102; telephone (334)240-4300

# Health Care

The Baptist Health network operates not-for-profit clinics and hospitals throughout Montgomery. Baptist Medical Center East is a 150-bed full-service hospital that offers a wide variety of services, such as emergency care, obstetrics, surgical services, laser surgery, nuclear medicine, outpatient addictive disease care, and wellness programs. Baptist Medical Center South, with 454 beds, is known for its Center for Advanced Surgery and regional Neonatal Intensive Care Unit. Baptist Health also operates three PriMed clinics throughout Montgomery which are open every day for illnesses and minor emergencies, and the free-standing Montgomery Surgical Center.

Jackson Hospital has 379 beds and 30 long-term acute care beds, and encompasses a 13-city-block area. It features a Diabetes Center, Wound Treatment Center, a Women's Health unit specializing in breast biopsies, a Sleep Disorders Center, and a specialized Cardiac Care center with new open heart surgical suites. The oncology unit treats cancer patients and the obstetrics unit offers labor, delivery, recovery, and postpartum care in special suites.

# Recreation

### Sightseeing

The Visitor Center, located in historic Union Station at Riverfront Park, offers maps and brochures for visitors to use in touring the city. Many of Montgomery's most important tourist sites are located in the city's downtown and are within walking distance of one another. The Alabama State Capitol, built in 1850–1851, is a National Historic Landmark and has been restored to its original design. At this site Jefferson Davis was sworn in as President of the Confederacy and Martin Luther King, Jr. culminated the historic march through downtown Montgomery by asking for equality for all Americans.

The Civil Rights Memorial lists the key events in the American civil rights movement, including the names of forty men, women, and children who were killed during the struggle. Nearby is Dexter Avenue King Memorial Baptist Church where Dr. Martin Luther King, Jr. issued many of his pleas for freedom. The church also served as the center of the famous 1955 bus boycott.

Montgomery is also the home of the First White House of the Confederacy, where President Jefferson Davis and his family resided. The Alabama Judicial Building houses the state Supreme Court, the courts of Criminal and Civil Appeals, and the state law library. In nearby Wetumpka, at the site of Fort Toulouse in 165-acre Jackson Park is the William Bartram Arboretum, a museum, historic buildings, and an Indian mound dating back thousands of years.

Old Alabama Town is a collection of restored homes and buildings from the 19th and early 20th centuries, set in the

A museum today, the First White House of the Confederacy contains artifacts and exhibits about the Confederacy and its president, Jefferson Davis.

heart of Montgomery's historic downtown. The site features a walking tour, live demonstrations, and a gift shop. Another popular tourist stop is the U.S. Air Force Heritage Museum, which houses the Air Force Enlisted Heritage Hall. The museum, on the grounds of Maxwell-Gunter Air Force Base, highlights important achievements of enlisted soldiers and the airplanes they used, as well as vintage military uniforms, historical photos, and paintings. The Air Force Base occupies the site where in 1910 Wilbur and Orville Wright operated the world's first flight training school. Tours of the stainless steel Monument to Powered Flight are conducted there daily and visitors have the opportunity to see vintage aircraft.

The Alabama Science Center encourages hands-on learning through touch-screen interactive computer programs and video presentations.

Renowned country singer Hank Williams, Sr. is a son of Montgomery. The museum that bears his name features his 1952 Cadillac and other items such as his clothing, piano, and band members' possessions. A life-sized statue of the beloved singer stands across the street from the old city auditorium where many of his performances and his funeral took place.

Rosa L. Parks, the African American heroine who was the catalyst for the 1955 Montgomery bus boycott, is honored at Troy State University Montgomery's Rosa Parks Library and Museum, which opened in 2000. The 55,000-square-foot structure was built on the site where Mrs. Parks boarded the bus on which she refused to yield her seat. The interpretive museum is housed in the 7,000 square foot first floor of the three-story building, which also houses the Troy State University Library. Permanent exhibits commemorating the civil rights movement are displayed, including a replica of the bus, original historical documents on loan from the City of Montgomery, and various sculptures. The Museum also contains a 2,200 square foot, 103-seat multimedia auditorium.

The Alabama Cattleman's Association MOOseum tells the story of the agricultural history of the state, focusing on the history of the cattle industry from the explorations of DeSoto to the present day.

Visitors are alerted to ''expect the unexpected'' at the 40-acre Montgomery Zoo, which displays more than 700 animals from five continents living in a ''barrier free'' setting lush with vegetation and crashing waterfalls. One of the largest planetariums in the Southeast, the W.A. Gayle Planetarium allows 230 visitors to view the sun, moon, planets, and stars projected on a 50-foot domed ceiling. Laser Lights are a highlight of the facility, which is set in beautiful Oak Park.

Teague House offers visitors a chance to observe one of the south's finest examples of late Greek Revival architecture, while the Murphy House antebellum mansion, which now houses the Montgomery Waterworks Board, is open for free

tours. The stern-wheel riverboat *Betsy Ann* provides nautical tours of the city from its berth in historic Riverfront Park.

**Arts and Culture**

The 150-acre Wynton M. Blount Cultural Park plays host to two Montgomery Gems: The Montgomery Museum of Fine Arts and the Alabama Shakespeare Festival. The Montgomery Museum of Fine Arts' noted Blount Collection includes works by John Singer Sargent and Edward Hopper and spans 200 years of American art. The museum also displays collections of European art and offers an educational gallery called ARTWORKS, through which patrons can use their five senses to learn about works in the permanent collection and art in general. The acclaimed Alabama Shakespeare Festival makes its home at the Carolyn Blount Theatre in the Cultural Park. The complex includes two separate theaters, a 750-seat Festival Stage, and the 225-seat Octagon Theatre. The Shakespeare Festival attracts more than 300,000 visitors annually. The park's Shakespeare Gardens hosts many events, including acoustic music concerts, lectures, and theatrical productions. The grounds are festooned with numerous lush plantings and an Elizabethan herb garden. Blount Cultural Park is a $21.5 million facility representing the largest single gift in the history of American arts philanthropy.

The Alabama Artists Gallery features the work of the state's artists.

The F. Scott and Zelda Fitzgerald Museum is located in a former home of F. Scott Fitzgerald, the author of *The Great Gatsby* and other American classics. It houses a large collection of photos, possessions, partial manuscripts, and original correspondence between Fitzgerald and his wife Zelda, a fine artist.

Troy State University's Davis Theatre for the Performing Arts, which opened in 1930, is a renovated former movie palace that now hosts professional musicals, drama, chamber music, symphony concerts, dance, and other performances. It is home to the Montgomery Symphony Orchestra and the Montgomery Ballet. Faulkner University's Dinner Theatre holds claim to Montgomery's only dinner theater venue.

The Montgomery Symphony Orchestra began in 1976 as a community orchestra with 30 musicians. Now, with 75 musicians and a full-time maestro, the symphony performs 7 concerts per season and oversees a variety of educational programs as well as the Montgomery Youth Orchestra. The Montgomery Ballet professional dance company and school features performances of classics throughout the year. Two of the Ballet's annual traditions are *The Spring Gala* and *Ballet and the Beasts,* a free performance at the Montgomery Zoo.

The 34,406-square-foot Armory Learning Arts Center, a one-time National Guard Armory that underwent complete renovation in 1983, brings art, music, dance, and gymnastic instruction to the community. The Center is the permanent home of the Alabama Dance Theatre, which presents both contemporary and classical dance performances, and twice a year presents major productions at the Davis Theatre. The company offers a free performance each summer at the Armory Center. The Capri Theatre features art, foreign, and classic films.

## Festivals and Holidays

Autumn is the season for many annual events on Montgomery's calendar. September brings the annual *Ballet & the Beasts* at Montgomery Zoo, the Alabama Jazz and Blues Federation River Jam, the annual Storytelling Festival, and the Alabama Highland Games.

October's calendar features the 10-day Alabama National Fair at Garrett Coliseum. Also in October, residents have enjoyed the Festival in the Riverfront Park (formerly the Festival in the Park) in downtown Montgomery since 1972. The festival features arts and crafts exhibitors, children's activities, food, and a 5-kilometer run/walk. November brings the Turkey Day Classic at Crampton Bowl, where Alabama State University takes a stand against its biggest rival, Tuskegee University. Events kick off with the Turkey Day Classic Parade down Dexter Avenue.

January brings the Fitzgerald Museum Gala & Auction, and DESTA, a festival that highlights African-American arts and culture. March brings the annual Miss Rodeo Alabama pageant during the week-long Southeastern Livestock Exposition Rodeo, and the Junior League Rummage Sale. The Jubilee City Fest is a three-day music, arts, and food festival held near the State Capitol building in May.

Culture blossoms in the summer air with July's free Montgomery Ballet Performance on the Green at Wynton M. Blount Cultural Park and the free Day of Late Summer performance by Alabama Dance Theatre. The Montgomery Symphony Orchestra bids summer adieu with the ''Broadway Under the Stars'' free performance at the Alabama Shakespeare Festival grounds.

## Sports for the Spectator

As the home of Alabama State University, Auburn University Montgomery, Troy State College, and other colleges, Montgomery offers a variety of football and baseball games and other college sports for fans to watch. The Montgomery Biscuits AA Southern League baseball team (Tampa Bay Devil Rays affiliate) makes their home at Montgomery's new (2004) Riverwalk Stadium, at the corner of Coosa and Tallapoosa Streets. Victoryland Greyhound Park offers daily races witnessed by up to 4,000 people per day. Mont-

gomery Motorsports Park offers year-round drag racing and weekly events.

## Sports for the Participant

Montgomery has 19 city parks that cover more than 400 acres. Among the most popular are Buddy Watson Park, Oak Park, Riverfront Park, Overlook Park, Vaughn Road Park, and Woodmere Park. Tennis and softball facilities dot the parks, and arts, crafts, and fitness programming is available at The Armory on Madison Avenue. The 26,000 square foot Therapeutic Center on Augusta Street features a gymnasium, indoor and outdoor swimming pools, a weight room, game room, locker rooms, meeting rooms, a kitchen, and tennis courts. Lagoon Park Golf Course offers year-round opportunity to play on a 6,773 yard par 72 championship course.

## Shopping and Dining

The Shoppes at EastChase opened in 2002 with an open-air ''main street'' concept and feature fountains, street lamps, lush landscaping, and upscale tenants. Montgomery Mall is anchored by JCPenney and Parisian and features more than 100 other tenants. Eastdale Mall, with 80 stores, is the site of Dillards, Sears, Parisian, and JCPenney department stores. Festival Plaza offers 110,000 square feet of shopping and entertainment. Cloverland Shopping Center features everyday necessities, and Eastbrook Flea Market and Antique Mall offers something a little different for the antique and bargain shopper. The Mulberry Shopping District features unique boutiques, antique shops, galleries, and restaurants. Fresh fruits, vegetables, and home-cooked specialties are for sale year-round at the State Farmers Market; the Montgomery Curb Market and Fairview Farmers Market are open seasonally.

Tourist-friendly Montgomery offers restaurants featuring a variety of cuisines from country to Cajun, Mexican, and Thai. Specialties include down-home Southern fare and just-caught seafood from the Gulf of Mexico. Others choices include Indian restaurants, an Australian steakhouse, Italian, Chinese, and the Farmers Market Café, which features fresh fruits and vegetables.

*Visitor Information:* Montgomery Area Visitor Center, 300 Water Street., Montgomery, AL 36104; telephone (334)262-0013; email tourism@montgomerychamber.com

# Convention Facilities

Montgomery offers a variety of sites for conferences and conventions. The Montgomery Civic Center features a main exhibition hall measuring 200 by 300 feet, with an acoustical ceiling 35 feet high. Telescopic risers and chairs in the arena are used to provide seating for up to 8,000 people. The center's 16 carpeted meeting rooms seat from 45 to 1,600 guests, and the catering kitchen can serve up to 4,000 people. By the beginning of 2005, the Center was in the midst of construction, creating expanded offerings in its new Convention Center with an attached four-star hotel. Garrett Coliseum, offers 31,000 square feet of meeting space and contains seating for 13,500, with an arena, barns, and parking facilities for 5,000 people.

The Embassy Suites Hotel, next to the Civic Center, offers 15,000 square feet of meeting space and can seat up to 900 people. The Governor's House Hotel & Conference Center features more than 18,000 square feet of meeting and banquet space. The Holiday Inn East Holidome has 5,300 square feet of meeting space and 5 meeting rooms. The Holiday Inn Hotel and Suites Downtown offers 10 meeting rooms and can accommodate up to 750 people.

*Convention Information:* Montgomery Area Chamber of Commerce, 41 Commerce Street, PO Box 79, Montgomery, AL 36101; telephone (334)834-5200; email macoc @montgomerychamber.com. Montgomery Area Visitor Center, 300 Water Street, Montgomery, AL 36104; telephone (334)261-1100 or (800)240-9452; email tourism @montgomerychamber.com

# Transportation

## Approaching the City

Montgomery Regional Airport, located six miles southwest of the city, supports civilian use and provides facilities for the Alabama Army and Air National Guard. Air carriers serving Montgomery include Delta, Northwest Airlink, US Airways Express, and beginning in 2005, Continental Express. Daily flights travel to and from Atlanta, Dallas-Ft. Worth, Houston, and Charlotte.

Interstate Highway I-65, which runs north and south, and I-85, which runs east and west, intersect in Montgomery. The two highways lead to Atlanta, Birmingham, Mobile, Huntsville, and Nashville. Bus service to other parts of the region and the country is provided by Greyhound and Capital Trailways.

## Traveling in the City

Montgomery is served by U.S. Highways 31, 80, 82, 231, and 331, all of which are connected by a four-lane perimeter road surrounding the city. Major east-west streets include Fairview Avenue, Madison Avenue, and South Boulevard,

while important north-south streets are Union and Perry streets and Norman Bridge Road.

The Montgomery Area Transit System (MATS) is the local bus line with 15 fixed service routes throughout Montgomery. MATS also provides a demand response service that allows riders to specify pickup and drop-off locations, and the Lightning Route, a turn of the century replica trolley that circulates the historic downtown district.

# Communications

## Newspapers and Magazines

The *Montgomery Advertiser* is the city's only daily newspaper. The *The Montgomery Independent* is published weekly. Several magazines focusing on hunting, fishing, farming, and agriculture are published in Montgomery. *Alabama Living* features stories of interest to rural and city-dwelling residents.

## Television and Radio

The six local television stations include four network stations, a public television station, and an independent station. The five local FM radio stations offer jazz, country, religious, adult contemporary, and Top 40 formats. The two local AM radio stations feature religious and sports programming.

*Media Information:* The *Montgomery Advertiser*, 200 Washington St., Montgomery, AL 36104; telephone (334)262-1611. *The Montgomery Independent*, 1810 W. Fifth St., Montgomery, AL 36106; telephone (334)265-7320

## Montgomery Online

Alabama Shakespeare Festival. Available www.asf.net

City of Montgomery. Available www.montgomery.al.us

City of Montgomery Parks and Recreation. Available http:// parks.ci.montgomery.al.us

Maxwell-Gunter Air Force Base. Available www.au.af.mil

Montgomery Area Chamber of Commerce. Available www .montgomerychamber.com

Montgomery Area Visitor Center. Available www.visiting montgomery.com

Montgomery Biscuits baseball. Available www.biscuits baseball.com

Montgomery City-County Public Library. Available www .montgomery.al.us/city/library

Montgomery Public School System. Available www.mccpl .lib.al.us

Online Montgomery. Available www.onlinemontgomery .com

## Selected Bibliography

Burns, Stewart, ed. *Daybreak of Freedom: The Montgomery Bus Boycott* (Chapel Hill, NC: University of North Carolina Press, 1997)

Lewis, Wendy I. and Marty Ellis. *Montgomery: At the Forefront of a New Century.* (Community, 1996)

Parks, Rosa, *Quiet Strength: The Faith, Hope, and the Heart of a Woman Who Changed a Nation* (Grand Rapids, MI: Zondervan Publishing House, 1994)

Rogers, William Warren, *Confederate Home Front: Montgomery During the Civil War* (Tuscaloosa, AL: University of Alabama Press, 1999)

# ARKANSAS

# The State in Brief

**Nickname:** Land of Opportunity
**Motto:** *Regnat populus* (The people rule)

**Flower:** Apple blossom
**Bird:** Mockingbird

**Area:** 53,179 square miles (2000; U.S. rank: 29th)
**Elevation:** Ranges from 55 feet to 2,753 feet above sea level
**Climate:** Long hot summers, mild winters, ample rainfall

**Admitted to Union:** June 15, 1836
**Capital:** Little Rock
**Head Official:** Governor Michael D. Huckabee (R) (until 2007)

**Population**
  **1980:** 2,286,000
  **1990:** 2,350,725
  **2000:** 2,673,398
  **2003 estimate:** 2,725,714
  **Percent change, 1990–2000:** 13.7%
  **Percent change, 2000–2003:** 2.0%
  **U.S. rank in 2003:** 32nd
  **Percent of residents born in state:** 63.9% (2000)
  **Density:** 51.3 people per square mile (2000)
  **2002 FBI Crime Index Total:** 112,672

**Racial and Ethnic Characteristics** (2000)
  **White:** 2,138,598
  **Black or African American:** 418,950
  **American Indian and Alaska Native:** 17,808
  **Asian:** 20,220
  **Native Hawaiian and Pacific Islander:** 1,668
  **Hispanic or Latino (may be of any race):** 86,866
  **Other:** 40,412

**Age Characteristics** (2000)
  **Population under 5 years old:** 181,585
  **Population 5 to 19 years old:** 578,924
  **Percent 65 years and over:** 14.0%
  **Median age:** 35.3 years (2000)

**Vital Statistics**
  **Total number of births (2002):** 37,437
  **Total number of deaths (2001):** 27,124 (infant deaths, 307)
  **AIDS cases reported through 2003:** 3,581

**Economy**
  **Major industries:** Food products, agriculture, tourism, manufacturing
  **Unemployment rate:** 5.6% (November 2004)
  **Per capita income:** $24,296 (2003; U.S. rank: 50th)
  **Median household income:** $33,259 (3-year average, 2001-2003)
  **Percentage of persons below poverty level:** 18.5% (3-year average, 2001-2003)
  **State income tax rate:** Ranges from 1.0% to 7.0%
  **State sales tax rate:** 5.125%

# Fort Smith

## *The City in Brief*

**Founded:** 1817

**Head Official:** Mayor C. Ray Baker, Jr. (unaffiliated) (since 1991)

**City Population**
  1980: 72,734
  1990: 73,511
  2000: 80,268
  2003 estimate: 81,562
  Percent change, 1990–2000: 9.2%
  U.S. rank in 2000: 363

**Metropolitan Area Population**
  1980: 203,511
  1990: 175,911
  2000: 207,290
  Percent change, 1990–2000: 17.8%
  U.S. rank in 2000: 162nd

**Area:** 52.94 square miles (2000)
**Elevation:** 463 feet above sea level
**Average Annual Temperature:** 61° F
**Average Annual Precipitation:** 40.9 total inches of precipitation; 6.2 inches of snow

**Major Economic Sectors:** Manufacturing, trade, transportation, utilities, education, health services, government
**Unemployment rate:** 4.5% (November 2004)
**Per Capita Income:** $18,994 (2000)

**2002 FBI Crime Index Total:** 7,498

**Major Colleges and Universities:** University of Arkansas at Fort Smith, Webster University, John Brown University

**Daily Newspaper:** *The Times Record*

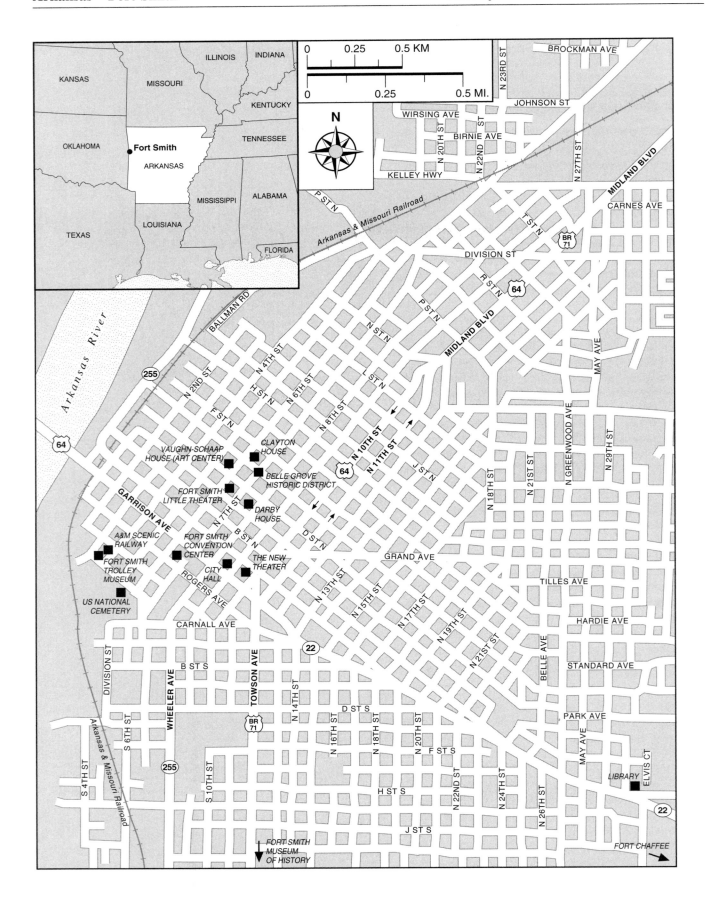

# Introduction

Located on the Arkansas River where the state of Arkansas meets Oklahoma, Fort Smith is the western gateway to Arkansas. The former military fort was situated with great purpose in 1817 to separate warring native tribes, and its location continues to serve Fort Smith today as a manufacturing and tourism destination. The Arkansas River Valley separates the Ozark Plateau from the Ouachita Mountains, giving Fort Smith visitors and residents a smorgasbord of outdoor activities in which to participate. Fort Smith is known as the Wild West town of Arkansas, capitalizing on its history as a frontier military installation and the site of "Hanging" Judge Parker's notorious courtroom. During and just after the Civil War, former slaves and refugees from repressive regimes found a temporary home in Fort Smith and nearby Fort Chaffee in anticipation of a more democratic style of life. Today, Fort Smith remains a gateway to and from the west as a mecca for manufacturing businesses and as a burgeoning tourist destination on its own merits.

# Geography and Climate

Fort Smith is located on the Arkansas-Oklahoma border, where it is bisected by the Arkansas River and sandwiched between the Ouachita and Ozark national forests. Built on the flats left by the meandering river, the city is level and green but enjoys easy access to mountains. Fort Smith sees the sun more than 200 days out of the year and experiences temperate weather during most months. The winters are generally mild, with less than seven inches of snow on average, while the summers are warm and often humid. Fort Smith sits at the edge of the reputed "Tornado Alley," and in spring of 1996 its downtown was devastated by a class F2 (on the Fujita scale based on damage, with F1 being lowest to F5 being highest) twister.

**Area:** 52.94 square miles (2000)

**Elevation:** Approximately 463 feet above sea level

**Average Temperatures:** January, 36.1° F; July, 81.5° F; annual average, 61° F

**Average Annual Precipitation:** 40.9 total inches of precipitation; 6.2 inches of snow

# History

**The Fort That Wouldn't Die**

The groundwork for Fort Smith's role in U.S. and Arkansas history was laid early and deep, as the native tribes that originally peopled the area during the Stone Age established communities in what later became valued and contested lands. Early inhabitants of western Arkansas have been characterized as "bluff dwellers" whose civilization dates back to 10,000 BC. The bluff dweller culture was absorbed into that of invading tribes, and by the time that Spanish explorer Hernando de Soto ventured into Arkansas in 1541, the most numerous Arkansas residents were of the Quapaw tribe.

Other explorers followed, claiming the land in the name of their sponsoring country; in 1682, French explorer Robert cavelier de La Salle claimed the area for France as part of the Louisiana Territory. In Arkansas and back east, relocation of native peoples soon began as early European settlers required more land on which to live, hunt, and farm. The later 1700s saw an increasing mix of native tribes west of the Mississippi, not all of who were on friendly terms. Closer proximity naturally resulted in heightened tensions and conflicts, endangering not just the tribe members themselves but also the increasing population of fur traders and pioneers who were employing the Arkansas River Valley as a funnel into the southwest. After Arkansas became an official part of the United States as the District of Arkansas in 1803, the federal government perceived a need to intervene in intertribal hostilities on the western edge of the burgeoning country. A new fort was established in 1817 on the banks of the Arkansas River where it meets the Poteau River, on a promontory of bluffs called Belle Point; the fort was named for General Thomas Smith of the federal garrison in St. Louis. For the next seven years, Fort Smith military personnel arbitrated clashes between the Osage and Cherokee tribes, negotiated treaties, and also patrolled the borders of the United States that were contested by Spain.

The military presence in Arkansas allowed for an influx of settlers from the east, and a community began to grow up around Fort Smith. New businesses catered to the soldiers with a drive to keep the installation occupied and thriving. Military forts of the time typically had a relatively brief lifespan as the western boundary of the United States continued to edge toward the Pacific. Indeed, the troops encamped at Fort Smith were relocated further west in 1924; the fort retained its utility by serving as the headquarters for the Western Choctaw Agency and also as the hub of enforcement for prohibition activities in that area. Location played a major role in Fort Smith's continued viability; the Arkansas River Valley provided easy access to the west where the fort and its surrounding community became the meeting point for many primary roads. The federal government and its military more and more viewed Fort Smith as a strategic site based on access and the fact that it was near but not encroaching a newly established Choctaw reservation in what had come to be known as Indian Territory. A new Fort Smith garrison was constructed in 1938, bringing with it an official town of the same name.

### Fort Smith: A Stop on the "Trail of Tears"

The history of Fort Smith is inextricably interwoven with that of native peoples in the United States, from the fort's time as a peacekeeping entity to the part it played in the forced relocation of thousands of native tribes west of the Mississippi River. During Thomas Jefferson's tenure as president, American citizens began to wish for more land and less conflict with the previous inhabitants of the eastern area. Jefferson's proposed solution was to relocate eastern native tribes to a buffer zone between U.S. territory holdings and land claimed by European countries. Between 1816 and 1840, a number of eastern tribes ceded their land to the United States and voluntarily headed west to what is now Oklahoma. In 1830, President Andrew Jackson put into effect further plans for the relocation of eastern native peoples; the result was an exodus of more than 100,000 native men, women and children on an arduous route that took them halfway across the country. There were several points of debarkation and several western routes used, but the "Trail of Tears" ultimately passed right through the gateway community of Fort Smith. Military installations in the area assisted tribe members in rejoining their own communities or held them temporarily while land assignments were made.

Fort Smith had come full circle. Its troops were once again in the position of keeping watch on a forced collective of age-old foes and allies in a relatively concentrated area, more for purposes of protecting pioneers and California-bound prospectors of European descent than for protecting and preserving the tribes themselves. But then came a new kind of war.

### Citizen Against Citizen: The Civil War at Fort Smith

In 1860, the state of Arkansas had achieved a population of 435,450 people, 111,115 of whom were slaves of African descent and 11,481 of whom were slave owners of primarily European background. It appeared inevitable that when the Confederacy voted to secede from the Union in April 1861, Arkansas would be on board with the Confederates; however, while more than 60,000 Arkansas residents joined rebel troops, at least 9,000 Anglos and more than 5,000 African Americans fought on the side of the Union in this conflict that divided communities and families. Fort Smith was no exception—it began its participation in the war as a Confederate military installation and supply depot until September 1, 1863, when Union troops took the post.

Fort Smith's strategic location on intersecting rivers and roads made it both a valuable staging area as a Union outpost and a continuing target for the Confederate faithful holed up in the surrounding mountains and in Indian Territory. The garrison became, not for the last time in history, a refuge for besieged citizens aligned with the Union and suffered through much deprivation when supply sources were ambushed by rebel troops. In 1865, Confederate leadership officially turned Arkansas, Texas and Indian Territory over to the Union, and the Fort Smith Confederates returned home to begin the work of rebuilding for the community's future.

### Reconstruction, Retribution and Reconciliation

Post-Civil War Reconstruction returned some of the states in the Union to a military form of government; consequently, Fort Smith became an outpost in the subdistrict of Arkansas, charged with enforcement of Reconstruction regulations and registration of freedmen. As a community, Fort Smith's function began to evolve from military to administration of frontier justice, as a succession of tough judges presided on the bench and attempted to impose order on the populace. Judge Isaac Parker, the infamous "hanging judge," meted out sentences over a 21-year period, ordering hundreds of defendants to jail and 160 men to "hang by the neck until you are dead, dead, dead!"

In 1896, Fort Smith ceased operations as a military outpost and the community's focus became that of municipal growth while sustaining the city's formative history. Reverberations from the Civil War continued as, in 1891, Jim Crow legislation was passed segregating rail stations and keeping the population divided literally and figuratively, until the issue of integration came to a head in 1957. In the interim, Arkansas weathered the Great Depression, accompanied as it was by crop-killing drought and the departure of many citizens from Fort Smith and Arkansas in general for what appeared to be greener pastures.

As the country began to rebound, Fort Smith established its identity as an industrial hub seated fortuitously at the nexus of two rivers leading to the Mississippi and an abundance of roadways radiating off across the country. The former military installation briefly served as a relocation camp for Japanese and German U.S. citizens during World War II, but in 1975 and 1980 also provided shelter and transition for Vietnamese and Cuban refugees seeking asylum in the United States. Fort Smith's public school system now proudly embraces the diversity of its students even as the city embraces its history; adaptability and survival may be the best descriptors for the former Wild West town.

***Historical Information:*** Fort Smith Historical Society, PO Box 3676, Fort Smith, AR 72913; telephone (479)478-6323

# Population Profile

**Metropolitan Area Residents (MSA)**
*1980:* 203,511
*1990:* 175,911
*2000:* 207,290
*Percent change, 1990–2000:* 17.8%
*U.S. rank in 2000:* 162nd

**City Residents**
*1980:* 72,734
*1990:* 73,511
*2000:* 80,268
*2003 estimate:* 81,562
*Percent change, 1990–2000:* 9.2%
*U.S. rank in 2000:* 363rd

*Density:* 1,594.2 people per square mile (2000)

*Racial and ethnic characteristics* (2000)
White: 63,868
Black or African American: 7,548
American Indian and Alaska Native: 2,541
Asian: 4,101
Native Hawaiian and Other Pacific Islander: 105
Hispanic or Latino (may be of any race): 7,048
Other: 4,040

*Percent of residents born in state:* 56.1%

*Age characteristics* (2000)
Population under 5 years old: 6,083
Population 5 to 9 years old: 5,581
Population 10 to 14 years old: 5,363
Population 15 to 19 years old: 5,586
Population 20 to 24 years old: 5,681
Population 25 to 34 years old: 11,454
Population 35 to 44 years old: 12,040
Population 45 to 54 years old: 10,513
Population 55 to 59 years old: 3,884
Population 60 to 64 years old: 3,082
Population 65 to 74 years old: 5,376
Population 75 to 84 years old: 4,113
Population 85 years and over: 1,512
Median age: 35.3

*Births* (Sebastian County; 2001)
Total number: 1,827

*Deaths* (Sebastian County; 2001)
Total number: 1,134

*Money income* (1999)
Per capita income: $18,994
Median household income: $32,157

Total households: 32,398

*Number of households with income of . . .*
less than $10,000: 4,095
$10,000 to $14,999: 2,887
$15,000 to $24,999: 5,374
$25,000 to $34,999: 5,092
$35,000 to $49,999: 5,054
$50,000 to $74,999: 5,233
$75,000 to $99,999: 2,092
$100,000 to $149,999: 1,537
$150,000 to $199,999: 405
$200,000 or more: 676

*Percent of families below poverty level:* 12.1% (59.7% of which were female householder families with related children under 5 years

*2002 FBI Crime Index Total:* 7,498

# Municipal Government

Fort Smith operates under a city administrator form of government in which the governing body is composed of a mayor and seven board directors. Four of the directors represent wards of the City of Fort Smith, while the mayor and the other three directors are elected by the broader population of the city. Terms of service are four years in duration, with off-set elections. The Board of Directors is chaired by the mayor and oversees matters of policy and budget. The board employs a city administrator to oversee daily operations for the city.

**Head Official:** Mayor C. Ray Baker, Jr. (unaffiliated) (since 1991; current term expires 2006)

**Total Number of City Employees:** 850 (2005)

*City Information:* City of Fort Smith, 623 Garrison Avenue, Fort Smith, AR 72901; mailing address PO Box 1908, Fort Smith, AR 72902; telephone (479)785-2801

# Economy

## Major Industries and Commercial Activity

Fort Smith is the manufacturing hub of Arkansas, with more goods produced in that vicinity than anywhere else in the state. National and international companies such as Weyerhauser, Gerber Foods, Whirlpool Corporation and Rheem Air Conditioning Products have facilities in Fort Smith and employ thousands of area workers to generate wood and paper products, food products, air conditioning system components and appliances. Recreation and tourism, particularly structured around the unique history of Fort Smith, is a growing industry with a workforce that is growing apace.

*Items and goods produced:* air conditioning systems, food products, appliances, paper products, wood products, composite building materials

### Incentive Programs—New and Existing Companies

*Local programs*—In conjunction with the Arkansas Department of Economic Development, Fort Smith offers a variety of investment and job creation incentives designed to attract and retain thriving businesses.

*State programs*—Arkansas' incentive plan was updated in 2003; counties are divided into four tiers based on rates in the areas of poverty, unemployment, per capita income and population growth. More lucrative incentives are offered for businesses that choose to locate in underserved counties.

Start-up businesses can take advantage of several incentive packages, including Advantage Arkansas (an income tax credit program), Tax Back (refunds of sales and use taxes), and InvestArk (a sales and use tax credit program). Businesses in highly competitive categories such as manufacturing, agriculture and information technology may be eligible for incentive programs such as Create Rebate (payroll rebates) and the ArkPlus income tax credit program.

The State of Arkansas additionally provides specialized incentive programs to encourage development of specific components of a business (child care facilities, customized training, recycling) or to recruit particular industries to the area (motion picture companies, tourism businesses).

*Job training programs*—The Arkansas Construction Education Foundation Training Program offers classroom and real-world experience through apprenticeship programs in Fort Smith and three other Arkansas locations. The University of Arkansas Fort Smith's Center for Business and Professional Development partners with local companies to develop skills of employees.

### Development Projects

With Community Development Block Grant (CDBG) funding, the City of Fort Smith is implementing a 5-year strategic action plan to address affordable housing issues, increase resources for the homeless, and attract corporate expansion and relocations in the metropolitan area to increase employment opportunities for mid- and low-income community members. A number of the plan's strategies seek to increase the income of workers in relation to their rental or mortgage burden, with tactics to include promotion of General Educa-

tion Development (GED) programs that serve adults, encouragement of higher education for workers, and provision of quality childcare services that will allow parents to work outside of the home.

Downtown Fort Smith has experienced a renaissance in response to a growing tourism and convention market. The Fort Smith Downtown Development association has thrown considerable energy into recruiting businesses into the area and into increased valuation of properties, including $55 million in improvements to the Fort Smith Convention Center, the Riverfront Development and Garrison Street. Building on the draw of Fort Smith's history, the municipal government has agreed to restore brick streets in the Belle Grove Historic District in downtown.

Nearby Fort Chaffee is undergoing change at the start of the new century as well. The Fort Chaffee Redevelopment Authority, created in 1997 after the base was closed in 1995, is in the process of creating residential, commercial and industrial resources on 7,000 acres of former military land. The new Chaffee Crossing will preserve the local history of the fort while offering modern facilities, parks, homes and business opportunities. Some office and warehouse buildings are already available for leasing; the remainder of the project is still undergoing development.

***Economic Development Information:*** Fort Smith Regional Chamber of Commerce, PO Box 1668, Fort Smith, AR 72902; telephone 479-783-6118; email info@fortsmith chamber.com

### Commercial Shipping

Sited at the confluence of the Arkansas and Poteau Rivers, the Port of Fort Smith is experiencing growth in tonnage, primarily composed of steel and scrap metal, passing through its terminal and on through the Mississippi River system. The port is served by the Arkansas-Missouri Railroad and a variety of trucking companies. In general, local trucking companies have seen continued demand for service as they transport general commodities throughout the United States. Air freight services are also available through local companies and the Fort Smith Regional Airport, which serves an eight-county area.

### Labor Force and Employment Outlook

With a strong base of manufacturing and the recent addition of a major medical center, Fort Smith is experiencing an upswing in employment, as evidenced by decreased layoffs compared to years previous. From 1990 to 2001, the Fort Smith metropolitan area demonstrated a 26.2% growth in nonfarm employment, compared to a rate of 25.2% for the state of Arkansas. Mainstay local manufacturers such as Gerber Foods, Weyerhauser, Rheem Air Conditioning and

Whirlpool Corporation all provide products for which there appears to be relatively stable demand, thereby minimizing employment fluctuations. Growing areas of employment include health services, as well as leisure and hospitality. With a growing and involved local university, Fort Smith is seeing increasing support for professional and business service professions. According to the U.S. Department of Labor, a long term shift from goods-producing employment to service-producing activities is expected.

The following is a summary of data regarding the Fort Smith metropolitan area labor force, 2003 annual averages.

*Size of nonagricultural labor force:* 99,700

*Number of workers employed in . . .*
  *natural resources and mining:* 1,000
  *construction:* 4,500
  *manufacturing:* 25,400
  *trade, transportation and public utilities:* 19,700
  *information:* 1,600
  *financial activities:* 3,600
  *professional and business services:* 9,700
  *educational and health services:* 12,800
  *leisure and hospitality:* 7,200
  *other services:* 2,800
  *government:* 11,400

*Average hourly earnings of production workers employed in manufacturing:* $13.73

*Unemployment rate:* 4.5% (November 2004)

| *Largest employers* | *Number of employees* |
|---|---|
| Whirlpool Corporation | 4,500 |
| Sparks Regional Medical center | 2,180 |
| Rheem Air Conditioning Products | 1,592 |
| City of Fort Smith | 850 |
| University of Arkansas at Fort Smith | 807 |
| Gerber Products | 600 |
| Owens-Corning (Composite Materials Division) | not reported |
| Planters Peanuts Company | not reported |

**Cost of Living**

*2004 (3rd Quarter) ACCRA Cost of Living Index:* 85.7

*2004 (3rd Quarter) ACCRA Average House Price:* $205,946

*State income tax rate:* Ranges from 1% on the first $3,999 of net taxable income to 7% on amounts over $27,500

*State sales tax rate:* 6%

*Local income tax rate:* 1.5%

*Local sales tax rate:* 2% on taxable goods and services

*Property tax rate:* Assessed valuation is equal to 20% of the market value of property

**Economic information:** Fort Smith Regional Chamber of Commerce, PO Box 1668, Fort Smith, AR 72902; telephone (479)783-6118; email info@fortsmithchamber.com

# Education and Research

**Elementary and Secondary Schools**

The Fort Smith Public Schools (FSPS) offers education services to students within the city's municipal boundaries, with students from outside the area eligible to apply to the School of Choice program. The student population increased slightly during the 2003-2004 school year, with the most marked growth in non-English speaking and economically disadvantaged students. Fort Smith Public Schools celebrates its diversity, noting that 20 languages are spoken by FSPS students. The school system demonstrates gains on all categories of the Arkansas End of Course tests, which determine student mastery of essential academic skills and knowledge in areas of core knowledge.

Eight Fort Smith elementary schools and all of its secondary schools were designated as Arkansas Schools of Excellence for the 2003-2004 school year; two high schools were selected as National Schools of Excellence. The school district has created discipline-specific task forces to support curriculum development in math, science, literacy and social sciences. Other facilities in the school district include an adult education center, a parent resource center, an alternative learning center, and a professional development and technology center.

Recent legislation passed by the Arkansas General Assembly promises to have a significant impact on the Fort Smith Public School System, including increases in funding available for education of students from lower-income families and students with limited backgrounds in English language, a higher minimum teacher's salary, and additional financial support for early childhood programs.

The following is a summary of data regarding Fort Smith Public Schools as of the 2003-2004 school year.

*Total enrollment:* 12,871

*Number of facilities*
  *elementary schools:* 19
  *junior high/middle schools:* 4
  *high schools:* 2
  *other:* 4

*Student/teacher ratio:* 16:1

*Teacher salaries*
    *minimum:* $29,750
    *maximum:* $56,545

*Funding per pupil:* $6,863

Preschool, Headstart and specialized programs are offered privately or through religious institutions.

***Public Schools Information:*** Fort Smith Public Schools, 3105 Jenny Lind, PO Box 1948, Fort Smith, AR 72902-1948; telephone (479)785-2501

### Colleges and Universities

Institutions of higher education in Fort Smith offer a full array of academic opportunities including associate degrees, bachelor degrees, and master's degrees through the University of Arkansas at Fort Smith, the University Center at Westark and the Business and Industrial Institute. Advanced degrees are also available through John Brown University and Webster University. The University of Arkansas at Fort Smith (UA Fort Smith) is the fifth largest institution of higher education in the state, with an enrollment of 6,406 reported for fall 2003. UA Fort Smith offers a range of educational degree programs, including technical certifications, certificates of proficiency, associate degrees, bachelor degrees and master's degrees. UA Fort Smith students are able to tap into the resources of other University of Arkansas campuses via the University Center; an active and involved Business and Professional Institute at the University offers training and continuing education programs to area businesses and community agencies. Health Sciences is also an education concentration that makes UA Fort Smith remarkable; between Business and Health Sciences students, UA Fort Smith provides the state of Arkansas with the bulk of its technical and health care workers.

John Brown University (JBU), a private Christian institution, maintains an educational outreach center in Fort Smith. Total enrollment for JBU in 2004 was 1,947; students were offered 51 undergraduate majors and 6 graduate programs. Two endowed, associated centers located at JBU indicate the university's commitment to graduating civically engaged students: The Soderquist Center for Leadership & Ethics and the Center for Marriage and Family Studies.

Webster University has played a unique role in the local community. Located on the grounds of nearby decommissioned Fort Chaffee in 1989, the University originally provided graduate level classes to military personnel through the Joint Readiness Training Center. In 1991, Webster University made a commitment to stay in Fort Smith but has now focused on master's degree programming in Human Resource Management and Business Administration.

### Libraries and Research Centers

Having the University of Arkansas as a community partner allows Fort Smith residents to take advantage of its Boreham Library, with access to thousands of books, periodicals and databases; the Health Sciences program at UA Fort Smith also maintains a specialized library that benefits not only its students but residents working in the healthcare sector.

The Fort Smith Public Libraries system is comprised of one main library and three branch libraries, supplemented by a bookmobile program. In February of 2001, the main library's new building was featured on the cover of an architectural edition of *Library Journal.* The library also hosts a specialized section for genealogical research. A law library is available at the Sebastian County Courthouse facility in Fort Smith. The Fort Smith Historical Society produces a journal and maintains archives of historical information regarding the city and its environs.

***Public Library Information:*** Fort Smith Public Library, 3201 Rogers Ave., Fort Smith, AR 72903; telephone (479)783-0229

# Health Care

The greater Fort Smith Arkansas-Oklahoma metropolitan area of 11 counties is served by 5 hospitals and 23 clinics, with outpatient and specialty services being provided by 591 organizations and individuals in private practice. The primary provider of healthcare services locally is Sparks Regional Medical Center, established in Arkansas in 1887. Sparks offers a range of outpatient and inpatient services, from preventive programs for diabetes and heart disease to rehabilitation for post-operative patients. The hospital's oncology unit is supported by a local cancer care house for the comfort and convenience of cancer patients and their families. Saint Edward Mercy Medical Center, an affiliate of the Sisters of Mercy healthcare network, has served the Fort Smith community since 1905, providing acute care medical intervention to the metropolitan area. Specialties of the medical center include behavioral services, a hospice program, and the Mercy Northside Clinic, which provides affordable healthcare and bilingual staff to an underserved segment of the Fort Smith population. Vista Health of Fort Smith, originally part of the Saint Edward Mercy system, now acts as a stand-alone not-for-profit behavioral health provider of inpatient and outpatient services to adults, adolescents and children. Sixteen local organizations and individuals provide alternative health care services to the metropolitan community.

Fort Smith and greater Sebastian County are in the process of mobilizing a Hometown Health Initiative under the auspices of the Arkansas Department of Health. The Initiative encourages communities to actively participate in large-scale prevention and health improvement.

# Recreation

### Sightseeing

The best way to get to know the city is to begin at the Fort Smith National Historical Site on the grounds of the old military installation. Here visitors can trace the history of the area from Wild West fort to "Trail of Tears" waystation, to frontier justice courtroom. Fort Smith then continues its transformation, becoming a World War II relocation facility and then a refugee camp, to its preservation in 1961 as a National Historical Site and its current status as modern city. Located at 4th Street and Garrison Avenue, the urban park consists of maintained trails that lead guests past and through the remains of the two forts, a reconstruction of Judge Parker's infamous gallows and a portion of the "Trail of Tears" along the Arkansas River. The Visitor Center at the Historical Site features displays that reflect on the fort's history from 1817 to 1871. The "Living the Legacy" educational program is a curriculum designed for grades two through five that makes history come alive. The nearby Fort Smith Museum of History makes a convenient and logical follow-up stop.

The history tour of Fort Smith continues in the downtown area with the Belle Grove Historic District, a 22-square-block area that was added to the National Register of Historic Places in the early 1970s. Within the vicinity of 5th, H, 8th, and C Streets are 22 houses, some up to 150 years old, that have been restored along with the brick-paved streets. The area contains a number of notable residences such as the Darby House, the Vaughn-Schaap House and the Clayton House. No visit to downtown Fort Smith would be complete without a stop at Miss Laura's Visitor Center, allegedly the only former house of prostitution on the National Register of Historic Places. From there it's a short distance to The Hangman's House, the former residence of George Maledon, who carried out executions for Judge Isaac Parker for a number of years.

Tourists interested in transportation will enjoy both the Fort Smith Air Museum and the Fort Smith Trolley Museum. The Fort Smith Air Museum is located at the Fort Smith Regional Airport Terminal; visitors can take a self-guided tour at no cost, viewing displays that detail military, agricultural and commercial aviation history. Back in the downtown area, travelers who enjoy a leisurely pace can ride the restored 1926 trolley that makes a circuit from Garrison Street

to the Fort Smith National Cemetery. On its route, the trolley will stop at the Trolley Museum, containing transportation-related artifacts.

The U.S. National Cemetery in Fort Smith, served by the trolley and within walking distance of downtown, provides its own silent commentary on the history of Fort Smith, with 10,000 gravesites dating from the establishment of the original fort. Confederate and Union soldiers both rest at this site, and visitors can view the repositories of men hung at the order of Judge Isaac Parker as well as the grave of the infamous judge himself. Judge Parker's hanging legacy continues at the Oak Cemetery, which is also the final resting place of a number of deputy U.S. Marshalls who worked with the judge.

### Arts and Culture

The Fort Smith Art Center, housed in the Vaughn-Schaap House in the Belle Grove Historic District, is an architectural work of art and a rare example of Victorian Second Empire buildings in Fort Smith. Displays inside the Center include a permanent contemporary art show featuring local artists and monthly exhibits in a variety of media featuring local and national artists. Art classes and an art camp are also offered through the Fort Smith Art Center.

The Western Arkansas Ballet Company not only offers lavish productions of well-known ballets but also operates a ballet academy and summer ballet instruction for local children and adults. Productions are often performed in conjunction with performing arts departments of the Fort Smith Public Schools system or the University of Arkansas at Fort Smith. In 2005, the Fort Smith Symphony began its 81st season as a professional orchestra performing classical and popular music throughout the region.

Theater fans can take in a performance of "The Medicine Show on Hanging Day" at Miss Laura's Visitor Center, featuring Miss Laura and Hanging Judge Parker as characters. A more mainstream option might be provided by the all-volunteer Fort Smith Little Theater, which debuted in 1948. The players produce and perform an eclectic assortment of comedies, dramas and musicals year-round.

The University of Arkansas at Fort Smith hosts a variety of cultural events throughout the year, including performances of vocal and instrumental music, operas, and plays throughout the year.

*Arts and Culture Information:* Fort Smith Convention & Visitors Bureau, 2 North B, Fort Smith, AR 72901; telephone (800)637-1477 or (479)783-8888

### Festivals and Holidays

Each May, Memorial Day weekend is kicked off in Fort Smith with a PRCA (Professional Rodeo Cowboys Associa-

**Fort Smith is home to numerous historical landmarks.**

tion) Rodeo parade that leads up to the Old Fort Days Rodeo and Barrel-Racing Futurity. Rated as one of the best rodeo events in the country, the event runs for ten days and provides a large pay-off for entrants in the Wild West contests. A natural follow-up is the Old Fort Riverfest in June, a three-day festival of music, food, and art for the entire family. The Arkansas-Oklahoma State Fair in late September offers a similar flavor of down-home fun seasoned with history.

Celebrating the Scottish heritage of western Arkansas is the focus of the Scottish Border Games and Gathering held each fall; authentic Scottish foods, music and competitions are offered during the three-day fair. Another eclectic offering is the Riverfront Blues Festival, where for two days soulful music can be heard wafting over the Arkansas River.

The calendar year winds up with Frontier Fest, held in late October and celebrating the long and varied history of Fort Smith, and the Arkansas Trail of Holiday Lights displayed in December.

### Sports for the Spectator

The University of Arkansas at Fort Smith athletic department houses a baseball team, women's and men's basketball programs and a women's volleyball squad, all of which play at the top of Division I in the National Junior College Athletic Association.

### Sports for the Participant

The Arkansas River is fed by smaller tributaries that are ideal for canoeing, kayaking and whitewater rafting. Enthusiasts recommend the Mulberry River, the White River, Lee Creek, the Fourche River, and the slightly more distant Buffalo River. Abundant water in rivers and lakes makes the Fort Smith area an angler's paradise; top spots for fishing include the rivers, Lake Fort Smith, Blue Mountain Lake, Lake Shepherd Springs and a wealth of small bayous known only to the locals.

Fort Smith is close enough for a day-trip to a variety of state parks with extensive trail systems. After a scenic drive south from Fort Smith, Queen Wilhelmina State Park offers a selection of trails with a variety of difficulty ratings. Nearby Blue Lake Mountain Trail is a beautiful and easy hike for trekkers of any ability. On Highway 10 to the east of Fort Smith, the Mount Magazine Trail is a bit more challenging with a pay-off of breathtaking views. Mount Magazine State Park also offers more than 100 rock climbing routes that range from easy to a 5.10 difficulty rating. The state parks include camping accommodations, as do the national forests in the Arkansas River Valley; the Ozark and Ouachita Mountain ranges are close enough for driving tours, overnight or multi-day camping outings.

With more than 200 days of sunshine and temperate weather throughout much of the year, Fort Smith golf courses are always open for business. The public course at Ben Geren Park has 27 holes, and there is a public 9-hole course at the Fort Smith Country Club. Private 18-hole golf courses include Hardscrabble and Fianna Hills.

### Shopping and Dining

The Historic Belle Grove District in downtown Fort Smith is home to specialty and antique stores, and is a central location for souvenir shopping. Central Mall Fort Smith, located at 5111 Rogers Avenue, houses stores selling a wide variety of wares including shoes, jewelry, clothing, books, cards and foods. The Brunwick Place farmers' market is held from spring through fall.

Fort Smith visitors and residents can choose from approximately 300 restaurants featuring a broad selection of ethnicities and tastes. Southern food and barbecue joints hold down a corner of the market, with more global fare represented by a menu of Mexican, Italian, Chinese and Thai eateries. Dining in Fort Smith covers all bases, from drive-through chain restaurants, to eat-with-your-fingers rib shacks, to fine bistro victuals. Lattes, espressos, mochas and the occasional plain black coffee are served at local coffee shops and some restaurants.

***Visitor Information:*** Fort Smith Convention & Visitors Bureau, 2 North B, Fort Smith, AR 72901; telephone (800)637-1477 or (479)783-8888

# Convention Facilities

Central to the Belle Grove Historic District, the U.S. National Cemetery, the Riverfront Park, and other downtown attractions is the Fort Smith Convention Center. The facility was completed in 2001 and features 40,000 feet of open space that can be subdivided, 8 conference rooms, theater-style seating for up to 5,200 people, banquet-style seating for 2,700 people, room for 231 exhibit booths, and a performing arts theater that can seat up to 1,331 in the audience.

Slightly north and east of the downtown Fort Smith area is Kay Rodgers Park, which annually hosts the Arkansas-Oklahoma State Fair and the Old Fort Rodeo and Barrel Racing Futurity. Kay Rodgers Park is home to the Expo Center, with 24,000 feet of meeting and exhibition space, and the Harper Arena. The Harper Arena is a covered open-air stadium that can seat 7,000 to 14,000 attendees for a variety of events. Barns and a smaller arena are also available. Plentiful parking accommodates RVs and smaller vehicles.

Meeting rooms and pavilions can be reserved through the Parks and Recreation Department of the City of Fort Smith.

# Transportation

### Approaching the City

The Fort Smith Regional Airport is located just outside the city limits to the south, at 6700 McKennon Blvd., and is served by American and Northwest Airlines. In 2002, the airport completed a new terminal complex with improved accommodations for waiting passengers. This effort was to be followed in 2004 by the construction of two new jet bridges that would allow passengers to avoid inclement weather when boarding planes. Car rental services are available at the airport terminal, which is also the site of an aviation museum.

Vehicle traffic enters and exits Fort Smith via a network of interstate, national and state highways, including Interstates 40 and 540, State highway 22, and U.S. Highways 71 and 64. Greyhound Bus service operates a terminal in Fort Smith, which is located at 116 N. 6th St.

Aside from rail service linked to the Port of Fort Smith, there is no passenger train route through the vicinity.

### Traveling in the City

Streets in the downtown area of Fort Smith are laid out in a grid pattern with somewhat of a northeastern orientation. U.S. Highway 64 and State Highway 22 intersect in the heart of Fort Smith, while Interstate 540 provides a bypass around the downtown area. The Fort Smith Transit Department provides daytime and nighttime bus service to most parts of the city, and specialized services are available for community members and visitors with disabilities. The Fort Smith Trolley offers limited transportation between some downtown attractions.

# Communications

### Newspapers and Magazines

The city of Fort Smith's local daily paper, the *Times Record* is circulated throughout the Fort Smith metropolitan area and Sebastian County. A magazine detailing local events, *Entertainment Fort Smith*, is also published locally.

### Television and Radio

Fort Smith is served by seven television stations, with four representing the major networks, one Fox affiliate, one UPN affiliate and independent station KFSM-TV. Approximately 33 radio stations broadcast in the Fort Smith metro area, running the gamut from alternative rock to talk radio.

*Media Information:* Times Record, 3600 Wheeler Avenue, Fort Smith, AR 72901; telephone (479)785-7700

### Fort Smith Online

City of Fort Smith. Available www.fsark.com

Fort Smith Convention and Visitors Bureau. Available www .fortsmith.org

Fort Smith National Historical Site. Available www.nps .gov/fosm

Fort Smith Public Library. Available www.fspl.lib.ar.us

Fort Smith Public Schools. Available www.fssc.k12.ar.us

Fort Smith Regional Chamber of Commerce. Available www.fschamber.com

*Times Record.* Available www.swtimes.com

Western Arkansas Planning and Development District. Available www.wapdd.org

### Selected Bibliography

Bears, Edwin C. and Arrell M. Gibson, *Fort Smith: Little Gibraltar on the Arkansas, Second Edition* University of Oklahoma Press, 1979

# Little Rock

## *The City in Brief*

**Founded:** 1820 (incorporated 1835)

**Head Official:** Mayor Jim Dailey (NP) (since 1995; current term expires in 2006)

**City Population**
    1980: 158,915
    1990: 175,727
    2000: 183,133
    2003 estimate: 184,053
    Percent change, 1990–2000: 4.2%
    U.S. rank in 1990: 96th (State rank: 1st)
    U.S. rank in 2000: 128th (State rank: 1st)

**Metropolitan Area Population**
    1980: 474,484
    1990: 513,026
    2000: 583,845

    Percent change, 1990–2000: 13.8%
    U.S. rank in 1990: 71st
    U.S. rank in 2000: 73rd

**Area:** 116 square miles (2000)
**Elevation:** Ranges from 300 feet to 630 feet above sea level
**Average Annual Temperature:** 62.1° F
**Average Annual Precipitation:** 45.73 inches of rain; 5.2 inches of snow

**Major Economic Sectors:** services, wholesale and retail trade, government
**Unemployment rate:** 4.3% (November 2004)
**Per Capita Income:** $23,209 (1999)

**2002 FBI Crime Index Total:** 20,680

**Major Colleges and Universities:** University of Arkansas at Little Rock, Arkansas Baptist College, Philander Smith College, Webster University

**Daily Newspaper:** *Arkansas Democrat-Gazette*

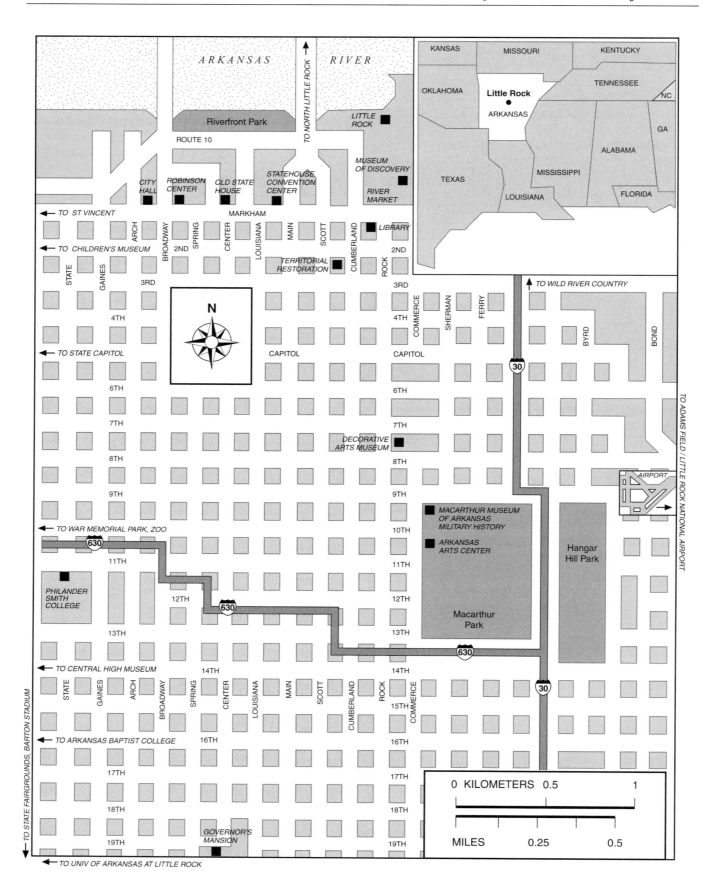

# Introduction

Located in the geographic center of Arkansas, Little Rock is also the state's undisputed historic, cultural, and economic hub. The capital since 1821 (when Arkansas was still just a territory) and the seat of Pulaski County, Little Rock now finds itself to be a key link between markets in the southwest and the southeast. The network of federal and state highways that pass through or near the city have brought it within 500 miles of ten major economic centers, and business and government leaders have worked to take advantage of this situation by bolstering the area's industrial base, expanding port facilities, and encouraging financial institutions to establish offices.

In other ways, too, Little Rock serves as a bridge between the "Old South" and the "New South." Nicknamed "The City of Roses" for its many gardens, Little Rock combines an old-fashioned, small-town ambience with a modern dynamism that often turns to Dallas or Houston for inspiration. Historic sites documenting more than 150 years of Arkansas life are carefully preserved next to sparkling new skyscrapers. Little Rock is a city that honors its past while welcoming the future.

# Geography and Climate

Centrally located on the Arkansas River on the dividing line between the Ouachita Mountains to the west and the flat lowlands of the Mississippi River valley to the east, Little Rock experiences all of the air mass types common to North America. Winters are mild, but periods of cold weather can occur when arctic air moves in from the north. The city's proximity to the Gulf of Mexico results in summers that are often hot and humid. Precipitation is evenly distributed throughout the year, with the heaviest rain falling during the winter and early spring. Snowfall is almost nonexistent, but freezing rain is a possibility when cold air flow from the north meets up with the moist Gulf air.

**Area:** 116 square miles (2000)

**Elevation:** Ranges from 300 feet to 630 feet above sea level

**Average Temperatures:** January, 40.1° F; July, 82.4° F; annual average, 62.1° F

**Average Annual Precipitation:** 45.73 inches of rain; 5.2 inches of snow

# History

**Little Rock Named Territorial Capitol**

The earliest inhabitants of the area that is now Little Rock were Stone Age people who—despite their lack of sophisticated tools, wagons, and domesticated animals—constructed huge earthen mounds that are still in existence. (Some of the most significant ones in the state are located just a short distance down the Arkansas River from Little Rock.) Used as public meeting places, living quarters, and burial chambers, these mounds have yielded numerous examples of pottery and other artifacts. Historians believe that the mound-builders' culture was eventually absorbed into that of more advanced and aggressive invaders.

In 1541, when Spain's Hernando de Soto became the first European to explore the territory, he and his party encountered a group of Indians who called themselves Quapaws or "downstream" people, a reference to the fact that they had migrated down the Mississippi River from Sioux lands in Missouri. It was estimated that approximately 7,000 Quapaws were then scattered throughout the region; by the time the French explorer Robert Cavelier de La Salle claimed it as part of the Louisiana Territory in 1682, this number had dwindled to about 1,300 people, primarily due to disease and war.

The naming of Little Rock is said to have occurred in 1722 when another French explorer, Bernard de la Harpe, was leading a party up the Arkansas River from New Orleans and came upon two rock outcroppings, one large, one small, on opposite sides of the river. Local Indians had long used both rocks as landmarks; de la Harpe presumably decided on the name "little rock" as a means of distinguishing the smaller outcropping from the larger bluff upstream, which he christened "French Rock."

Throughout the years when control of the region alternated between the Spanish and the French, few permanent settlements were established. Thus, at the time of the Louisiana Purchase in 1803, Arkansas was virtually uninhabited. Once the territory became part of the United States, however, increasing numbers of Americans were willing to move west of the Mississippi. The first white settler near the "little rock" is believed to have been William Lewis, a hunter. In July 1812 he built a small hut and planted a few pumpkin seeds so that he could file a homestead claim. In 1819 a land speculator from St. Louis named William Russell bought Lewis' claim, and by May 1820, he had staked out a town site. Later that same year, members of a rival faction laid out a second town site that they named Arkopolis. In 1821 Russell's Little Rock settlement was chosen as the capital of Arkansas Territory. When tensions between the two opposing groups touched off fears that the capital would be moved elsewhere, the speculators resolved their differences amicably, and the site was authoritatively named Little Rock.

### Civil War Divides Citizens

Little Rock grew rather slowly after that, though remained a boisterous frontier village for many years; it was officially chartered in 1831 and reincorporated in 1835. The 1830s also marked the beginning of cotton cultivation on a major scale, and it soon became the area's chief cash crop. Little Rock saw its importance as a distribution center increase as southbound steamboats loaded with cotton bales passed northbound boats carrying clothing, tools, and molasses from New Orleans.

A slave state with a large rural population of small farmers, Arkansas was drawn into national politics when it seceded from the Union in 1861 and then began serving as a supply center for the Confederate Army. The state's sympathies were not entirely with the South, however; many citizens had opposed secession, particularly those in the northern counties. When Little Rock was captured in 1863 and made headquarters for Union troops, the occupation was exceptional in its orderliness and cordiality.

### Conservatives Rule for a Century

The postwar Reconstruction period in Arkansas was marked by financial ruin and political upheaval. Attempts to create a northern-style industrial economy failed, largely because the demands placed on the agrarian society were too great. Furthermore, disagreements between Republican liberals (who controlled the state government through a system of executive patronage) and mostly Democratic conservatives crippled efforts to establish a more progressive regime. The conflict came to a head in 1874 with the so-called Brooks-Baxter War, when two rival politicians claimed the governorship of Arkansas. A legal battle ensued, and eventually the state constitution was rewritten to impose severe limits on the chief executive's power. Arkansas then entered a phase of conservative rule that endured for nearly a century.

After the turmoil of the Reconstruction period ended, Little Rock slowly began to broaden its economic base, especially in the areas of commerce and industry. The 1880s saw a great expansion in the state's railroad system, and the city's population soared to 25,874 people by 1890 (up from 12,000 people in 1870). During World War I, Little Rock became an army induction and training center with the opening of nearby Camp Pike, which was reactivated (as Camp Robinson) during World War II and again provided an influx of money and jobs in Little Rock.

In 1957 world attention was drawn to the Arkansas capital when Governor Orval E. Faubus and the Arkansas National Guard forcibly tried to prevent the integration of Little Rock Central High School. President Dwight D. Eisenhower responded by sending U.S. troops to the city with orders to enforce the integration and protect the students. The incident left its mark, however; business and industrial developers were reluctant to locate to an area linked so closely in the public's mind with racism and segregation.

The 1960s brought sweeping changes to the South, and today's Little Rock has for the most part abandoned the attitudes of the "Old South" to embrace a lifestyle compatible with that of the Sunbelt. The area's good climate and abundance of water and energy make it increasingly attractive to industry, and the 1970s and 1980s saw it recovering some of the ground it lost in earlier years, as evidenced by employment and industrial growth. In a state known as the "Land of Opportunity," Little Rock continues to be the centerpiece of progress and development.

### A Presidential City

The election of progressive Arkansas Governor Bill Clinton to the U.S. presidency in 1992 placed a new focus on the city. The nation began associating Little Rock with the birthplace of its president rather than a center of racial strife. President Clinton facilitated this new focus, accepting the presidency on the steps of the Old State House in 1992, and celebrating his reelection in 1996 on its balcony. Even after his terms expired, he continued the momentum of this presidential connection. In November 2004 the William J. Clinton Presidential Center opened its doors, drawing the spotlight of national and international attention and tourism to Little Rock for years to come.

***Historical Information:*** Arkansas History Commission, One Capitol Mall, Little Rock, AR 72201; telephone (501)682-6900

## *Population Profile*

### Metropolitan Area Residents
*1980:* 474,484
*1990:* 513,026
*2000:* 583,845
*Percent change, 1990–2000:* 13.8%
*U.S. rank in 1990:* 71st
*U.S. rank in 2000:* 73rd

### City Residents
*1980:* 158,915
*1990:* 175,727
*2000:* 183,133
*2003 estimate:* 184,053

*Percent change, 1990–2000:* 4.2%
*U.S. rank in 1990:* 96th (State rank: 1st)
*U.S. rank in 2000:* 128th (State rank: 1st)

*Density:* 1,576 people per square mile (2000)

*Racial and ethnic characteristics* (2000)
  White: 100,848
  Black or African American: 74,003
  American Indian and Alaska Native: 500
  Asian: 3,032
  Native Hawaiian and Pacific Islander: 64
  Hispanic or Latino (may be of any race): 4,889
  Other: 2,348

*Percent of residents born in state:* 68% (2000)

*Age characteristics* (2000)
  Population under 5 years old: 12,989
  Population 5 to 9 years old: 12,599
  Population 10 to 14 years old: 12,254
  Population 15 to 19 years old: 12,093
  Population 20 to 24 years old: 13,560
  Population 25 to 34 years old: 29,463
  Population 35 to 44 years old: 28,547
  Population 45 to 54 years old: 25,852
  Population 55 to 59 years old: 8,180
  Population 60 to 64 years old: 6,269
  Population 65 to 74 years old: 10,484
  Population 75 to 84 years old: 7,891
  Population 85 years and older: 2,952
  Median age: 34.5 years

*Births* (Pulaski County, 2001)
  Total number: 8,345

*Deaths* (Pulaski County, 2001)
  Total number: 3,331 (of which, 62 were infants under
    the age of one year)

*Money income* (1999)
  Per capita income: $23,209
  Median household income: $37,572
  Total households: 84,793

*Number of households with income of . . .*
  less than $10,000: 8,416
  $10,000 to $14,999: 5,267
  $15,000 to $24,999: 11,626
  $25,000 to $34,999: 10,820
  $35,000 to $49,999: 12,567
  $50,000 to $74,999: 13,184
  $75,000 to $99,999: 6,683
  $100,000 to $149,999: 4,992
  $150,000 to $199,999: 1,721
  $200,000 or more: 2,245

*Percent of families below poverty level:* 11.1% (48.3% of
  which were female householder families with related
  children under 5 years)

*2002 FBI Crime Index Total:* 20,680

# Municipal Government

Little Rock operates under a city manager/board of directors form of government. An 11-member board of directors—elected on a non-partisan basis for staggered four-year terms—employs the manager to supervise the daily operations of the city. In 1995 Little Rock installed its first elected mayor, who also serves on the board of directors. The following year Little Rock decentralized many of its city services in an effort to make them more responsive to residents' needs. A newly formed ward system placed planning and development responsibilities in the hands of neighborhood organizations.

The city appointed its first African American police chief in 2000. Chief Lawrence Johnson had a difficult tenure, however. According to *The New York Times,* the Fraternal Order of Police accused Johnson of being unresponsive to the needs of officers and of showing favoritism toward African American officers. He, in turn, criticized city leaders for a lack of support for the department and the community. On January 1, 2005, Johnson stepped down from his position, stating that his decision was part of his plan to retire after five years and not an outcome of his frustration with officials.

**Head Officials:** Mayor Jim Dailey (NP) (since 1995) and
  City Manager Bruce Moore

**Total Number of City Employees:** 2,058 (2003)

*City Information:* Little Rock City Hall, 500 West Markham, Little Rock, AR 72201; telephone (501)371-4510; email slangley@littlerock.state.ar.us

# Economy

## Major Industries and Commercial Activity

As the largest city in a primarily rural and agricultural state, Little Rock is the center of economic activity in Arkansas. For decades, cotton and then rice, soybeans, and other crops were the area's main source of income. Their cultivation and distribution monopolized the labor pool and available capital and made it virtually impossible for industry to gain a foothold, even in Little Rock. During the 1950s and 1960s, however, the Arkansas Industrial Development Corp., headed by Winthrop Rockefeller, who later served as governor, began an aggressive campaign to attract manufacturers to the state. Although few firms established large operations, hundreds of companies moved in and set up small factories employing fewer than 1,000 people.

Local, state, and federal government have been Little Rock's major employers for many years. Medical facilities, banks, and other service industries are also important to the economy, and their presence has in turn attracted to the area other companies that offer a variety of support services, especially those that are computer-related.

Revitalization of downtown Little Rock has fueled its attraction to major corporations in a variety of industries, particularly manufacturing, transportation, and service. The city manager's office reports that Little Rock was one of the nation's 15 most aggressive development markets in the early part of the new century; it has doubled in the past 20 years and is expected to double again over the next 20 years.

Aviation is among the most dynamic industries in Little Rock. Aircraft and spacecraft are Arkansas' largest export, the revenue of which has grown from $35 million in 2000 to $441 million in 2002, according to the Arkansas Department of Economic Development. In Little Rock itself, several aircraft companies bolster the local economy. Central Flying Service Inc. is one of the nation's largest fixed-base operations, and Dassault Aviation SA's primary service and completion center for its Falcon jets is located in Little Rock. Additionally, Raytheon Aircraft announced in 2002 an expansion of its Little Rock plant, which will add 350 new jobs over five years.

Biotechnology is an emerging industry in Little Rock. The University of Arkansas for Medical Sciences is the cornerstone for medical biotechnology research in Arkansas. The facility not only conducts research and development, it offers a business incubator program to support start-up biotechnology companies. Moreover, the stock of Cytomedix Inc., which manufactures wound-healing therapy in Little Rock, more than doubled in the year 2004 to $2.55 per share.

Agriculture maintains a firm hold on the economy of Little Rock and Arkansas as a whole. About one-fourth of all jobs in the state involve agriculture to some degree. Soybeans, rice, timber, and poultry continue to be the primary agricultural enterprises in the state.

Because of its strategic location, Little Rock has long served as a center for trade. The Little Rock Port Industrial Park offers some of the finest facilities on the Arkansas River, enabling the city to promote itself not only as a distribution center for the state's agricultural products, but also for its increasing number of manufactured goods.

*Items and goods produced:* Metals, soybeans, rice, chemicals, textiles, paper products, timber, and aircraft

## Incentive Programs—New and Existing Companies

*Local programs*—The basic method of financing new and expanding industry in the region is through the use of Act 9 Industrial Revenue Bonds issued at the municipal and county levels. Up to $6 million of an Act 9 issue can be guaranteed under state insurance guarantee programs.

*State programs*— The Arkansas Science and Technology Authority, located in Little Rock, was established in 1983 to promote scientific research, technology development, and business innovation in the state. To this end, it provides financial support for the transfer and development of innovative technology to an enterprise based in Arkansas. The Authority currently offers three programs: the Applied Research Grant Program, the Seed Capital Investment Program, and the Technology Development Program.

The Small Business Loan Program was founded in 1999 to stimulate economic growth by providing up to 50 percent of a small business loan to qualified applicants. This financing, administered by the Arkansas Department of Economic Development, can be used as working capital, to purchase machinery and equipment, and to construct or renovate commercial real estate.

There are several special industrial location incentives offered by the State of Arkansas. Two of the major programs are the Arkansas Enterprise Zone Program and Arkansas Workers' Compensation, legislation passed in 1993 that makes workers' compensation insurance more affordable for employers. The Chamber of Commerce has information about the many other incentives offered by the state of Arkansas, which include corporate income tax credits, sales and use tax refunds, and the payment in lieu of taxes program.

*Job training programs*—The Business and Industry Training Program sponsored by the Arkansas Department of Economic Development designs customized training programs to meet the specific needs of particular industries. Its emphasis is three-fold: recruiting workers, pre-employment training, and on-the-job training.

## Development Projects

Eleven counties, including Pulaski, united in 2003 to form the Central Arkansas Economic Development Alliance (CAEDA) to promote the region as an attractive location to new businesses. Funded by both private-sector companies and individual economic development agencies, CAEDA markets the region's workforce, low cost of doing business, central U.S. location, and transportation infrastructure.

Commercial development was also boosted by the passage of Arkansas' Tax Increment Financing (TIF) law in 2004. This tax incentive tool enables local governments to develop and improve infrastructure using future tax dollars instead of relying solely on funding by private developers. Intended to bolster the redevelopment of blighted areas, TIF has been embraced by even the most economically vibrant cities throughout the state.

In early 2002 Pulaski County received the long-sought designation as an Urban Empowerment Zone by the U.S. Department of Housing and Urban Development. In a program that extends through 2009, this designation will entitle Pulaski County to a portion of the $17- to $22-billion national package to foster growth and revitalization in distressed communities.

The efforts have already produced results in Little Rock, as evidenced by the establishment or expansion of large-scale business in the early 2000s. In late 2003 ground was broken in the River Market District for a new International Center for Heifer International, an organization that assists small-scale farmers worldwide in an effort to combat hunger, alleviate poverty, and restore the environment. The $23 million First Security Center is a 14-story building occupied by First Security Bank, a 120-room hotel by Marriott Courtyard, as well as luxury condominiums. Raytheon Aircraft announced in 2002 the expansion of its plant in Little Rock, adding 350 jobs to the area. In a $6 billion deal that will add 4,000 new employees and make it the nation's fifth-largest wireless company, ALLTEL Corp. announced its acquisition of Western Wireless Corp. in January 2005.

***Economic Development Information:*** Little Rock Regional Chamber of Commerce, 1 Chamber Plaza, Little Rock, AR 72201; telephone (501)374-2001; email chamber@littlerock chamber. Arkansas Department of Economic Development, One Capitol Mall, Little Rock, AR 72201; telephone (501)682-1121; toll-free 1-800-ARKANSAS; fax (501)682-7394; email info@1800arkansas.com

## Commercial Shipping

With its central location and accessibility to the Arkansas River, Little Rock is one of the major transportation centers of the South. The city's main asset is its port. The development of the Arkansas River into a year-round barge navigation route has meant that a city as far west as Tulsa, Oklahoma has access to the Mississippi River, which in turn provides access to global markets through the international port at New Orleans, Louisiana. Consequently, a variety of products pass through the port, including forest products, bagged goods, steel coils and pipes, aluminum products, and such bulk products as rice, clay, bauxite, rock, fertilizer, and cement. Little Rock Port Terminal has a cargo lift capacity of 50 tons and bulk handling capacity of 200 tons/hour

inbound and 350 tons/hour outbound. It also offers 157,000 square feet of warehouse space and 45,000 square feet of outside storage area.

The Little Rock Port Authority Railroad, operating on 12.2 miles of track, connects with the Union Pacific Railroad and the Burlington Northern Santa Fe Railway. Each year it switches approximately 5,500 railroad cars, and services 60 percent of all cargo handled through the river terminal.

Little Rock Port Industrial Park is designated as a Foreign Trade Zone, enabling goods to be stored or processed without payment of customs duty until they are moved out of the zone and into normal domestic channels. Services in the Foreign Trade Zone are offered through 14 contract carrier barge lines, and include barge, rail, and truck terminals, as well as warehouse space and material handling equipment. Little Rock is also a U.S. Customs Port of Entry for both freight and passengers.

More than 60 franchised motor carriers in the metropolitan area provide regular service to points in each of the 48 contiguous states; ten major cities are within a day's drive. Air freight service, ranging from small package expediting to international freight forwarding, is readily available at Little Rock National Airport, where airlines and air cargo carriers processed more than 19 million pounds of freight and 14 million pounds of mail in 2001.

## Labor Force and Employment Outlook

The civilian labor force in the Little Rock area is drawn from four counties. Arkansas has been a right-to-work state since 1944, and state law makes violence in connection with a labor dispute a felony. According to *The New York Times,* state and local economic development efforts, including tax incentives promoting international trade and improved job training, have helped the area to outpace neighboring states in terms of growth in employment, growth in manufacturing jobs, and income growth in recent years.

Two of the fastest growing industries for employment in Arkansas are agriculture and trucking. About one-fourth of all jobs in the state revolve around agriculture or agriculture-related processing, and the Arkansas Department of Economic Development predicts a future shortage of qualified work force in that area. Likewise, trucking—the state's fifth-largest industry—is expected to experience an increase of available jobs through 2010. Some of the nation's largest trucking companies are headquartered in Arkansas and operate throughout the state. In addition, corporations that own and operate private fleets expect to be seeking truck drivers and related personnel. Little Rock is home to two such companies, Entergy Inc. and Quality Foods Inc.

The following is a summary of data regarding the Little Rock-North Little Rock metropolitan area labor force, 2003 annual averages.

*Size of nonagricultural labor force:* 317,100

*Number of workers employed in . . .*
*construction and mining:* 17,100
*manufacturing:* 24,700
*trade, transportation, and utilities:* 67,000
*information:* 9,400
*financial activities:* 19,400
*professional and business services:* 39,600
*educational and health services:* 40,700
*leisure and hospitality:* 24,600
*other services:* 12,000
*government:* 62,700

*Average hourly earnings of production workers employed in manufacturing:* $13.81

*Unemployment rate:* 4.3% (November 2004)

| Major employers | Number of employees |
|---|---|
| State of Arkansas | 28,100 |
| Federal Government | 9,400 |
| Pulaski County Public School Districts | 8,868 |
| Baptist Health | 7,000 |
| Little Rock Air Force Base | 5,445 |
| University of Arkansas for Medical Sciences | 5,392 |
| Ryerson-Tull AFCO Metals | 5,051 |
| St. Vincent Infirmary Medical Center | 4,200 |
| ALLTEL Corp. | 4,000 |
| Timex Corp. | 3,873 |

### Cost of Living

The following is a summary of data regarding several key cost of living factors for the Little Rock area.

*2004 (3rd Quarter) ACCRA Cost of Living Index:* 92.1 (U.S. average = 100.0)

*2004 (3rd Quarter) ACCRA Average House Price:* $204,003

*State income tax rate:* Ranges from 1.0% on the first $2,999 of net taxable income to 7.0% on amounts over $25,000

*State sales tax rate:* 6%

*County sales tax rate:* 0.0051%

*Local income tax rate:* None

*Local sales tax rate:* 0.005%

*Property tax rate:* $69 per $1000 of assessed valuation (2001) (assessed valuation = 20% of market value)

*Economic Information:* Little Rock Regional Chamber of Commerce, 1 Chamber Plaza, Little Rock, AR 72201; telephone (501)374-2001; email chamber@littlerockchamber. Arkansas Department of Economic Development, One Capitol Mall, Little Rock, AR 72201; telephone (501)682-1121; toll-free 1-800-ARKANSAS; fax (501)682-7394; email info@1800arkansas.com

# Education and Research

### Elementary and Secondary Schools

The Little Rock School District provides education to students within the city boundaries, as well as to students who live outside the city who opt to transfer to one of the magnet or interdistrict schools. Local schools are recognized for their multicultural diversity and high academic standards. The McClellan High School business education program was named best in the nation during the 1995–1996 school year. Nearly two dozen magnet and incentive schools offer students focused academic programs in such disciplines as art, math/science, communications, and international studies.

In 2002, after more than 40 years of court-supervised desegregation monitoring, Little Rock was found to have met the terms of a 1998 plan to improve performance of minority students. Two years later, however, this ruling was reversed, citing inadequate measurement of such progress. Little Rock's efforts will remain under court supervision until at least 2006.

The following is a summary of data regarding Little Rock's public schools as of the 2003–2004 school year.

*Total enrollment:* 25,491

*Number of facilities*
*elementary schools:* 34
*junior high/middle schools:* 8
*senior high schools:* 6
*other:* the Alternative Learning Center serves grades 6 through 12, and the Accelerated Learning Center provides education for students in grades 9 through 12

*Student/teacher ratio:* 14.6:1

*Teacher salaries*
*average:* $39,531 (2000–2001)

*Funding per pupil:* $7,189 (2000–2001)

A number of private and parochial schools also offer programs from pre-kindergarten through high school. In addition, the city is home to two special facilities, the Arkansas School for the Blind and the Arkansas School for the Deaf.

***Public Schools Information:*** Little Rock School District, 810 W. Markham Street, Little Rock, AR 72201; telephone (501)447-1000

## Colleges and Universities

Little Rock has two universities and two colleges that offer a variety of two- and four-year programs as well as advanced study in such areas as medicine, engineering, law, and social work. The University of Arkansas at Little Rock is by far the largest institution of higher learning in the city, enrolling more than 11,000 students. A branch of the main campus in Fayetteville, the Little Rock facility offers more than 90 degree programs ranging from associate to doctoral. Medicine, nursing, health-related professions, and pharmacy are taught on a separate campus in town, the University of Arkansas for Medical Sciences. The university's William H. Bowen School of Law is located within walking distance from the judicial hub of downtown Little Rock.

Philander Smith College is a private four-year liberal arts college that is the state's only institution affiliated with United Negro College Fund. Philander Smith was founded in 1877 and was one of the Southwest's first African American colleges.

Arkansas Baptist College, founded in 1884 as the Minister's Institute, offers degrees in social sciences, business administration, theology, and liberal arts.

Webster University, established in Little Rock in 1986, offers master's degrees in business administration, international business, management, computer resources management, health services management, and human resources development.

Little Rock area residents also attend institutions in neighboring communities, including the University of Central Arkansas, Central Baptist College, Hendrix College, Shorter College, and Pulaski Technical College.

***Higher Education Information:*** University of Arkansas at Little Rock, 2801 S. University Ave., Little Rock, AR 72204-1099; telephone (501)569-3000

## Libraries and Research Centers

The Central Arkansas Library System (CALS) serves Pulaski County and neighboring Perry County (with the exception of North Little Rock). In 1997 the main branch spent $12.5 million to renovate a warehouse, and relocated into the River Market District of downtown Little Rock. That same year, the Richard C. Butler Center for Arkansas Studies was established within CALS to promote the study of Arkansas history though online resources and lesson plans for teachers. Additionally, there are 11 branches throughout the area, housing a total of more than one-half million volumes.

Approximately two dozen special libraries also operate in Little Rock, most of them serving very specific medical or business needs. Other libraries offering specialized collections are the Arkansas Arts Center/Elizabeth Prewitt Taylor Memorial Library, which specializes in art, drama, and early American jazz; the Arkansas State University/Dean B. Ellis Library, which houses the Lois Lenski Collection, Arkansas Authors of Children's Books Collections, and the Cass S. Hough Aeronautical Collection; and the Arkansas Territorial Restoration Library, which features material on state and local history, decorative arts, conservation, and historic preservation.

The American Native Press Archives at the University of Arkansas at Little Rock, established in 1983 as a clearinghouse for information on American Indian and Alaska Native newspapers and periodicals, has evolved into one of the world's largest repositories of Native thought. A joint effort of the Department of English and the Ottenheimer Library, it now serves to collect and archive the products and materials of the Native press, to collect and document the works of Native writers, and to construct bibliographies of Native writing and publishing. The Archives, located in the Sequoyah Research Center, also serves as repository for the archives of the Native American Journalists Association and the Wordcraft Circle of Native Writers and Storytellers.

In addition to the academic libraries of colleges and universities in the area, Little Rock is home to such special libraries as those operated by the Arkansas Geological Commission, the Arkansas History Commission and State Archives, and the Arkansas Supreme Court. It is also the seat of the Arkansas State Library, which serves as the information center for the state's libraries.

***Library Information:*** Central Arkansas Library System, 100 Rock Street, Little Rock, AR 72201; telephone (501)918-3000

# Health Care

Medical facilities in the Greater Little Rock area provide comprehensive, quality service for more than two million people in the metropolitan area and the state. Little Rock itself has 650 physicians and surgeons in 11 hospitals and 70 clinics, with bed space for more than 5,000 patients. The largest among these is Baptist Medical Center, which houses cardiac and cancer units and the state's only rehabilitation institute. St. Vincent's Health System, founded in 1888, is one of the city's oldest healthcare institutions. Its network includes an infirmary medical center, a doctors' hospital, a North Little Rock medical center, a rehabilitation hospital, and various medical clinics and free community clinics. The city's third largest facility is the University of Arkansas for Medical Sciences (UAMS), the state's only comprehensive academic health center. Founded in 1879 as a proprietary medical school by a group of eight physicians with 22 students, the institution is affiliated with the Arkansas Children's Hospital and the Central Arkansas Veterans Healthcare System. The geriatrics clinical care program of UAMS was ranked 32nd in the nation by *U.S. News & World Report* (July 12, 2004).

# Recreation

## Sightseeing

A good place to begin a tour of Little Rock is Riverfront Park, located directly on the riverfront in the center of the city. The park is the site of numerous fairs and festivals during the year, and it also offers the visitor a place to relax or stroll along the promenade and read about the area's early history in an open-air pavilion. The "little rock," or *Le Petite Roche,* that gave the city its name is visible at the north end of Rock Street, which is adjacent to Riverfront Park.

Within walking distance of Riverfront Park is the Old State House, the original Arkansas state capitol building. This antebellum Greek Revival structure now houses a museum of Arkansas history that features changing exhibits of Victorian decorative arts and costumes, six period rooms, and items of state historical interest.

Also within walking distance of the park is the Arkansas Territorial Restoration, a complex of more than a dozen antebellum buildings, some of which are on their original sites. Five homes (now museums) are of particular interest: Noland House, Woodruff House, Conway House, Hinderliter Tavern, and a log house.

Many fine examples of antebellum and Victorian architecture are also on display in the Quapaw Quarter, the oldest part of Little Rock. A number of the homes have been restored and are listed in the National Register of Historic Places. Some were built prior to the Civil War. The Villa Marre, a nineteenth century Italianate Victorian home decorated with period furnishings, was featured in the television series *Designing Women* (1986-1993). Visitors can drive or walk through this nine-square-mile area.

West of the downtown area is the Arkansas State Capitol, begun in 1899 and finished sixteen years later. The nation's only scaled replica of the National Capitol in Washington, D.C., it is made of white limestone and marble, and features a chandelier and six solid brass doors purchased from Tiffany's in New York City in 1908. South of downtown is the Governor's Mansion, a brick Georgian building completed in 1950 from materials gathered from older state properties. A double iron filigree gate taken from the Confederate Soldiers' Home opens onto a circular drive fronting the mansion, which is surrounded by eight acres of lawn and gardens.

The Little Rock Zoo offers visitors the opportunity to observe more than 725 mammals, birds, reptiles, amphibians, and fish. The zoo's Children's Farm offers visitors a hands-on opportunity to interact with and learn about animals. The zoo participates in a variety of conservation efforts around the globe.

The Aerospace Education Center features aviation and aerospace exhibits, the state's only IMAX theater, and exhibits of American and Russian space exploration.

Little Rock Central High School was designated a National Historic Site in 1998. Located at the intersection of Daisy L. Gatson Bates Drive and Park Street, the school commemorates the desegregation movement in the United States, particularly the nine African American students, known as the "Little Rock Nine," who were escorted into the school by federal troops in 1957. Across the street, a visitor's center is located in a former Mobil gasoline station.

*Sightseeing Information:* Little Rock Convention & Visitors Bureau, Markham and Broadway, PO Box 3232, Little Rock, AR 72203; telephone (501)376-4781; toll-free 1-800-844-4781

## Arts and Culture

Robinson Center, located in the downtown area in Statehouse Plaza, is Little Rock's major performing arts facility. For more than forty years, major Broadway shows, musical events, and ballets have been staged at Robinson Center. It is also the home of Ballet Arkansas, the Arkansas Symphony Orchestra, and Celebrity Attractions, a professional organization that offers a subscription season from September through May.

The Arkansas Arts Center is also an important location on the Little Rock arts scene. Based at the center is the Children's Theatre, where live performances are staged and where young people can receive theater training. The Arts Center houses six permanent galleries, a museum gift shop, and a restaurant. Classes in painting, drawing, photography, and dance are also offered.

Other theatrical organizations in Little Rock are the Arkansas Repertory Theater, which brings eight professional shows to town from September through June; Wildwood Park for the Performing Arts, which offers opera, cabaret, chamber performances and festivals throughout the year; and Murry's Dinner Playhouse, presenting popular plays year-round.

Little Rock's museums and galleries offer visitors a view of Arkansas history and native crafts. At the Museum of Discovery, an interactive children's museum, visitors can learn about the region's first inhabitants, the Arkansas Indians; they can also explore the Worlds of the Forests, take a journey through science, or even build a robot. This museum is located in the River Market District's Museum Center, which was redesigned in 1998 to include several restaurants.

The Historic Arkansas Museum is the state's largest historic museum, and houses paintings, textiles, glassware, and other objects created by Arkansas artists over the past 200 years. Other historical museums are the MacArthur Museum of Arkansas Military History; the Old State House Museum; and Ernie's Museum of Black Arkansans, the state's first African American history museum.

Elsewhere in the city is the Decorative Arts Museum, which houses exhibits of contemporary and historic objects, including ceramics, glass, textiles, crafts, and Oriental works of art.

The University of Arkansas at Little Rock features a fine arts museum and a planetarium that are open to the public. The museum has changing exhibits of paintings, sculpture, graphics, arts and crafts, and photography, while the planetarium stages shows that cover astronomy, history, and science fiction.

The William J. Clinton Presidential Center opened its doors in November 2004. This $165-million center, the 11th in the Presidential Library system, is an archive, library, and museum housing millions of documents and artifacts relating to his administration. Sitting on 26 acres of park alongside the Arkansas River in downtown Little Rock, the center is also Clinton's post-presidency office, and is expected to serve as a gathering place for world leaders.

***Arts and Culture Information:*** Little Rock Convention & Visitors Bureau, Markham and Broadway, PO Box 3232, Little Rock, AR 72203; telephone (501)376-4781; toll-free 1-800-844-4781. William J. Clinton Presidential Center, 1200 President Clinton Ave., Little Rock, AR 72201

## Festivals and Holidays

Riverfest, celebrated in Riverfront Park every Memorial Day weekend, is Little Rock's biggest annual event. More than 225,000 people attended the festivities in 2004, walking through the park, sampling ethnic foods, and admiring the arts and crafts on display. There are also performances by musicians, including major stars, along with impromptu shows by jugglers, mimes, and magicians.

Also important to Little Rock is the Arkansas State Fair, held for eleven days in late September through early October. Attended by 400,000 visitors, it features typical state fair events such as livestock judging and auctions, home arts competitions, rodeos, musical performances, motor sports, talent contests, and carnival rides, games, and amusements.

Martin Luther King Jr. is honored every January with a parade, as is St. Patrick in March. The Quapaw Quarter Spring Tour of Historic Homes takes place each May, the same month that offers the Annual Territorial Fair at Historic Arkansas Museum, the Greek Food Festival, and the Annual Jamfest Heritage Festival. Music dominates the scene during June's Wildwood Festival of Music and Arts and the July 4th Pops on the River, an event of the Arkansas Symphony Orchestra. Each year the Museum of Discovery sponsors the Dino Dash and Discovery Fest. The city hosts the Arkansas Arts Crafts & Design Fair in November. December features an annual Christmas Frolic and Open House at Historic Arkansas Museum.

***Festivals Information:*** Little Rock Convention & Visitors Bureau, Markham and Broadway, PO Box 3232, Little Rock, AR 72203; telephone (501)376-4781; toll-free 1-800-844-4781

## Sports for the Spectator

North Little Rock's ALLTEL Arena, an $80 million facility, opened with an Arkansas RiverBlades ice hockey game on October 28, 1999. ALLTEL Arena is also home to the University of Arkansas basketball team as well as the Arkansas Rim-Rockers, the state's first professional basketball team, which was born into the American Basketball Association in January 2004.

Also in North Little Rock, construction is expected to begin in 2005 on an 11-acre ballpark stadium and complex for the Arkansas Travelers, a farm club of baseball's St. Louis Cardinals, who play from April to August.

## Sports for the Participant

Located as it is on the Arkansas River, Little Rock offers anglers some of the best fishing of any city in America. Not far from the metropolitan area are many lakes, streams, and several state and national parks that also attract fans of sailing and other water sports.

For those who prefer to stay within the city, Little Rock has 56 public parks and nearly 200 recreation facilities, some featuring such amenities as swimming pools, tennis courts, playgrounds, golf courses, and softball fields. Little Rock's best-known park is Riverfront Park, which boasts an amphitheater on the riverbank and an open-air pavilion as well as fountains and tree-lined walkways. War Memorial Park, one of the city's oldest, features a zoo, a fitness center, the 8,000-seat Ray Winder Field, and the 53,000-seat War Memorial Stadium.

## Shopping and Dining

No single area in Little Rock is the main shopping district; centers are scattered throughout the city. The River Market District offers a Farmer's Market plus restaurants and groceries in a scenic setting on the Arkansas River. Two of the area's largest shopping centers, Park Plaza and University Mall, are located in trendy West Little Rock, where the area's newest shops and restaurants are springing up. McCain Mall, the largest shopping center in the state, is across the Arkansas River in neighboring North Little Rock.

The offerings of Little Rock's more than 300 restaurants range from down-home southern cooking (including ribs) to continental-style haute cuisine. Seafood and catfish abound at restaurants along the river, and ethnic specialties are available at a number of establishments in the metropolitan area.

*Visitor Information:* Little Rock Convention & Visitors Bureau, Markham and Broadway, PO Box 3232, Little Rock, AR 72203; telephone (501)376-4781; toll-free 1-800-844-4781

# Convention Facilities

With the development of Statehouse Plaza and its complex of meeting facilities and hotels, Little Rock has made a special effort to attract convention business. Situated along the Arkansas River, Statehouse Plaza is an eight-square-block area in downtown Little Rock that includes the Statehouse Convention Center and University Conference Center, Robinson Center, and several major hotels, including the Peabody, Capital, and Double Tree.

The Statehouse Convention Center features the Governor's Exhibition Hall, which has nearly 83,000 square feet of space that can be divided into four rooms or left as one large room. The Wally Allen Ballroom was created in a 1999 expansion that added more than 18,000 square feet of space. Other rooms are available for a variety of events. Atop the Center is the Peabody Little Rock Hotel, product of a $40 million reconstruction of the former Excelsior Hotel that was completed in January 2002. The Peabody has approximately 40,000 square feet of meeting and exhibit space, with an additional 19,000 square feet in the Peabody Conference Center.

Adjacent to the Statehouse Convention Center is the University Conference Center, which has 50,000 square feet of space, more than 13,000 square feet of which is designed specifically for meetings. Of additional interest are satellite down-links that allow for regional, national, or international teleconferences.

Down the street from these two facilities is the Robinson Center, which has a 14,867-square-foot exhibition hall that can hold 800 people in the main room, with additional exhibition space and seating in other exhibition and meeting rooms. Adjacent to this complex is the Doubletree Hotel, which emerged from a 1996 renovation of the former Camelot Hotel with 287 rooms and 13 suites.

Additional meeting rooms in the Statehouse Plaza area are available at the Arkansas Bar Center and the Old State House. Other area hotels and motels also provide meeting facilities for smaller groups.

*Convention Information:* Little Rock Convention & Visitors Bureau, Markham and Broadway, PO Box 3232, Little Rock, AR 72203; telephone (501)376-4781; toll-free 1-800-844-4781

# Transportation

## Approaching the City

The Little Rock National Airport is located within the city limits and is only three miles from downtown, thus making it one of the most convenient urban airports in the country. It is served by American Eagle, Comair, Continental Express, Delta, Delta Connection, Northwest, Northwest Airlink, Southwest, and US Airways Express. The airport handles about 2.1 million passengers each year and has facilities for private planes and corporate aircraft. Each day more than 120 flights arrive or depart, among them regional jets to and from Cincinnati, a service it launched in 1997. A parking deck was added in 2001, and a $3 million renovation of the baggage claim wing went underway in 2003.

For those approaching the city by car, access is made easy by the network of U.S. and state highways that intersect the metropolitan area. Additionally, five Interstate highways—30, 40, 430, 440, and 630—facilitate Little Rock travelers.

Amtrak provides daily passenger service from Little Rock's restored Union Station to Chicago, St. Louis, Dallas, Fort Worth, Austin, and San Antonio; connections to El Paso, Tucson, and Los Angeles are available three times a week. The city is also served by Greyhound buses.

## Traveling in the City

Little Rock is laid out in a basic grid pattern with streets numbered consecutively from the river to the edge of town. Two major expressways, I-630 and I-30, bisect the city;

freeway traffic is usually heavy. Bus service is provided by the municipally owned and operated Central Arkansas Transit (CAT).

Reborn after 57 years, Little Rock's streetcars began rolling again in November 2004. The River Rail Electric Streetcar system runs along a 2.5-mile track that links the major attractions between Little Rock and North Little Rock. Destinations include the ALLTEL Arena, the Statehouse Convention Center, River Market, Discovery Museum, and the Robinson Auditorium Concert Hall.

# Communications

## Newspapers and Magazines

Little Rock has one major daily newspaper, the *Arkansas Democrat-Gazette,* a morning paper that is circulated statewide. The weekly publication *Arkansas Times* is a general lifestyle newspaper aiming to educate readers about life in Arkansas, and the *Arkansas Business News* serves readers on a weekly basis. Several magazines are also based in the city; most serve specific business or religious interests.

## Television and Radio

Seven television stations—five network affiliates, one public, and one independent—broadcast from Little Rock. Twenty radio stations serve listeners in the area with a wide variety of formats.

*Media Information: Arkansas Democrat-Gazette,* 121 E. Capitol Ave., Little Rock, AR 72201; telephone (501)378-3400

## Little Rock Online

*Arkansas Democrat-Gazette.* Available www.ardemgaz.com

Arkansas Department of Economic Development. Available www.1800arkansas.com

Arkansas History Commission. Available www.ark-ives.com

Little Rock City Hall. Available www.accesslittlerock.org

Little Rock Convention & Visitors Bureau. Available www.littlerock.com

Little Rock Regional Chamber of Commerce. Available www.littlerockchamber.com

Little Rock School District. Available www.lrsd.org

University of Arkansas at Little Rock. Available www.ualr.edu

William J. Clinton Presidential Center. Available www.clintonpresidentialcenter.org

## Selected Bibliography

Beals, Melba, *Warriors Don't Cry: A Searing Memoir of the Battle to Integrate Little Rock's Central High* (New York: Pocket Books, 1995)

Kirk, John A., *Redefining the Color Line: Black Activism in Little Rock, Arkansas, 1940–1970* (Gainesville, FL: University Press of Florida, 2002)

Worthen, Bill, *Little Rock: One from the Heart*, Urban Tapestry Series(Memphis, TN: Towery Publishing, 1996)

# DELAWARE

# The State in Brief

**Nickname:** First State; Diamond State
**Motto:** Liberty and independence

**Flower:** Peach blossom
**Bird:** Blue hen chicken

**Area:** 2,489 square miles (2000; U.S. rank: 49th)
**Elevation:** Ranges from sea level to 440 feet above sea level
**Climate:** Temperate, with mild winters and hot summers

**Admitted to Union:** December 7, 1787
**Capital:** Dover
**Head Official:** Governor Ruth Ann Minner (D) (until 2009)

**Population**
   **1980:** 594,000
   **1990:** 666,000
   **2000:** 783,600
   **2003 estimate:** 817,491
   **Percent change, 1990–2000:** 17.6%
   **Percent change, 2000–2003:** 4.3%
   **U.S. rank in 2003:** 45th
   **Percent of residents born in state:** 48.3% (2000)
   **Density:** 401.1 people per square mile (in 2000, based on 2000 land area)
   **2002 FBI Crime Index Total:** 31,803

**Racial and Ethnic Characteristics** (2000)
   **White:** 584,773
   **Black or African American:** 150,666
   **American Indian and Alaska Native:** 2,731
   **Asian:** 16,259
   **Native Hawaiian and Pacific Islander:** 283
   **Hispanic or Latino (may be of any race):** 37,277
   **Other:** 15,855

**Age Characteristics** (2000)
   **Population under 5 years old:** 51,531
   **Population 5 to 19 years old:** 166,719
   **Percent of population 65 years and over:** 13%
   **Median age:** 36 years (2000)

**Vital Statistics**
   **Total number of births (2003):** 12,120
   **Total number of deaths (2002):** 6,860 (infant deaths, 96)
   **AIDS cases reported through 2003:** 3,231

**Economy**
   **Major industries:** Chemicals, agriculture, food products, paper products, printing and publishing, rubber and plastic products
   **Unemployment rate:** 4.0% (November 2004)
   **Per capita income:** $33,321 (2003; U.S. rank: 12th)
   **Median household income:** $50,451 (3-year average, 2001-2003)
   **Percentage of persons below poverty level:** 7.7% (3-year average, 2001-2003)
   **Income tax rate:** Ranges from 2.2% to 5.95%
   **Sales tax rate:** None

# Dover

## The City in Brief

**Founded:** 1683; incorporated 1829

**Head Official:** Mayor Stephen R. Speed (N-P) (since 2001)

**City Population**
　**1980:** 23,507
　**1990:** 27,630
　**2000:** 32,135
　**2003 estimate:** 32,808
　**Percent change, 1990–2000:** 16.30%
　**U.S. rank in 1990:** 1,160th (State rank: 2nd)
　**U.S. rank in 2000:** Not reported (State rank: 2nd)

**Metropolitan Area Population**
　**1980:** 98,219 (Kent County)
　**1990:** 110,993 (Kent County became an MSA in 1990)
　**2000:** 126,697 (MSA)

**Percent change, 1990–2000:** 14.15%
**U.S. rank in 2000:** 225th

**Area:** 22.7 square miles (2000)
**Elevation:** 36 feet above sea level
**Average Annual Temperature:** 55° F
**Average Annual Precipitation:** 44.14 inches

**Major Economic Sectors:** services, trade, manufacturing, military
**Unemployment rate:** 2.7% (November 2004)
**Per Capita Income:** $19,445 (1999)

**2002 FBI Crime Index Total:** 1,923

**Major Colleges and Universities:** University of Delaware, Delaware State University, Wesley College, Delaware Technical and Community College, Wilmington College—Kent County

**Daily Newspaper:** *Delaware State News, News Journal*

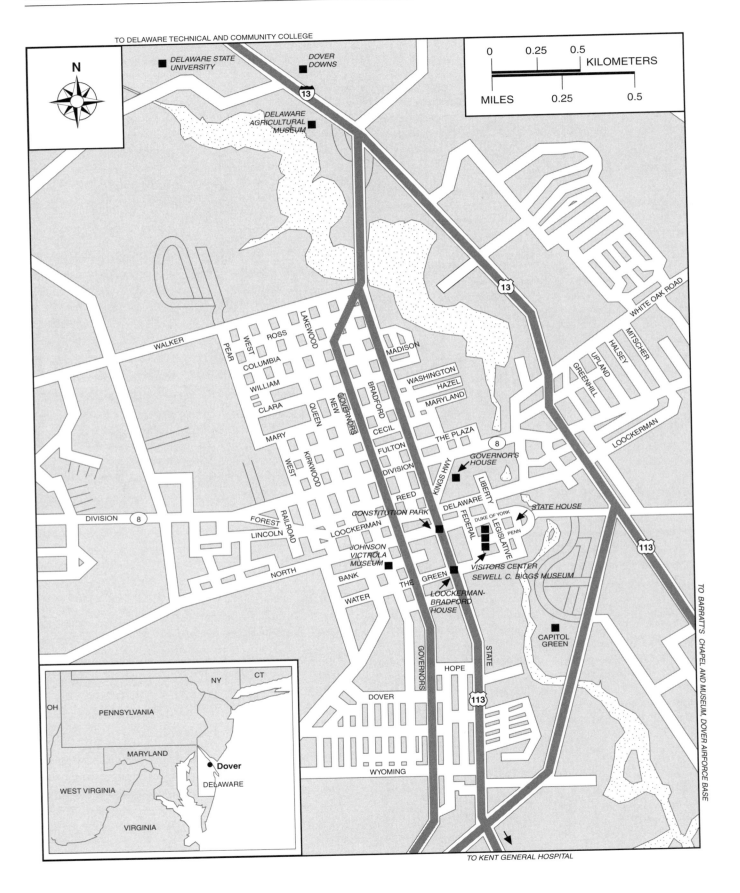

TO DELAWARE TECHNICAL AND COMMUNITY COLLEGE

N

DELAWARE STATE UNIVERSITY

DOVER DOWNS

0   0.25   0.5
KILOMETERS

MILES   0.25   0.5

13

DELAWARE AGRICULTURAL MUSEUM

13

WHITE OAK ROAD

WALKER

PEAR   WEST   ROSS   LAKEWOOD

MADISON

MITSCHER   HALSEY   UPLAND

COLUMBIA

WASHINGTON

GREENHILL

WILLIAM   BRADFORD

HAZEL

LOOCKERMAN

CLARA   QUEEN   NEW   GOVERNORS   CECIL   MARYLAND

MARY

FULTON   THE PLAZA

8

KIRKWOOD   WEST   DIVISION   KINGS HWY   GOVERNOR'S HOUSE

LIBERTY   STATE HOUSE

DIVISION   8   REED   DELAWARE   DUKE OF YORK   PENN

CONSTITUTION PARK   FEDERAL   LEGISLATIVE

FOREST   RAILROAD

LINCOLN   LOOCKERMAN

JOHNSON VICTROLA MUSEUM   VISITORS CENTER   SEWELL C. BIGGS MUSEUM

NORTH

BANK   THE GREEN   LOOCKERMAN-BRADFORD HOUSE

WATER

CAPITOL GREEN

GOVERNORS   HOPE   STATE

113

DOVER   113

WYOMING

TO KENT GENERAL HOSPITAL

TO BARRATT'S CHAPEL AND MUSEUM, DOVER AIRFORCE BASE

OH   NY   CT

PENNSYLVANIA

MARYLAND

WEST VIRGINIA   • **Dover**   DELAWARE

VIRGINIA

# Introduction

Dover is the capital of Delaware and the seat of Kent County. The city, which dates back to the 1600s, is acclaimed for its lovely tree-lined streets, preserved town green, and impressive Georgian and Victorian architecture. Long a center of government, business, and agriculture, Dover has become a tourist mecca as visitors come to enjoy the city's historical offerings, tax-free shopping, and the excitement of slots, NASCAR racing, and harness racing that takes place at Dover Downs. The city was named after Dover in England and is the site of Dover Air Force Base, which houses the world's largest air cargo planes.

# Geography and Climate

Dover is located in central Delaware on the Delmarva peninsula and on the St. Jones River. It is approximately 40 miles south of Wilmington. The rather flat area has a moderate climate with four distinct seasons. Summer has many warm days with hot, humid periods and mild nights. Surface winds generally blow from the northwest except in June when southerly winds prevail. From May through September winds blow from the southwest.

**Area:** 22.7 square miles (2000)

**Elevation:** 36 feet above sea level

**Average Annual Temperature:** 55° F

**Average Annual Precipitation:** 44.14 inches

# History

### Dover Becomes State Capital

At the time of the arrival of the first white men, the Lenape Indians lived along the banks of the Delaware River. The land where Dover now stands was part of a much larger grant called Zwaanendael (Valley of the Swans), where a group of Dutch patrons attempting to colonize it were killed by the local tribe in 1631. William Penn chartered Kent County, and Penn ordered his surveyors to lay out a town in 1683. In 1697, a court house was built at the site, but it was not until 1717 that Dover was plotted around a central green. By that time, most of the Native Americans had been forced to relocate elsewhere. Craftsmen and artisans such as cabinet makers, shoemakers, carpenters, tailors, and hatters shared the green with government officials and residents, as well as several inns and taverns. An Act of Assembly in 1742 provided for the establishment of a market square, and the 1751 census estimated the population of Kent County to be 1,320 families. In 1777, Dover became the capital of Delaware, largely because it was deemed safer from attack than the old capital, New Castle. Ten years later, in a Dover tavern, a Delaware convention ratified the Federal Constitution. Because it was the first to ratify, Delaware became known as "the first state" and enjoys the highest level of seniority at ceremonial events.

From the 1720s to the 1770s the construction of many fine homes took place throughout Dover and the surrounding countryside, many of which still survive today. During the Revolutionary War, the famous Delaware militia marched to join Washington's main army. It earned the nickname "Blue Hens Chickens" because of the spirited fighting cocks that Delaware men carried with them to war. The city of Dover was incorporated in 1829, and it has remained one of the nation's smallest state capitals.

During the eighteenth century, Kent County was an important agricultural area, providing grain, fruit, and vegetables to the Continental army. However, worn out by generations of poor farming practices, Kent County's soil became far less productive during the Federal period. By the time of the Civil War, the soil had recovered and agriculture became stronger than ever. Farmers introduced fertilizer and employed scientific methods to graft peach trees. The extension of the Delaware Railroad line to Dover in 1856 enabled Kent County farmers to reach a national market. Just the year before, two men by the names of Richardson and Roberts had opened a canning company to process local products, and other canneries soon followed. Eventually, canning became Dover and Kent County's principal industry.

During the Civil War period in the mid-nineteenth century, every possible attitude toward the Confederate conflict had adherents in Dover, from those who passionately supported the federal government, to those who were willing to fight to maintain the Southern way of life. Federal troops entered the area during the 1862 and 1864 elections to guard the polls from violence.

### A Century of Development

During the post Civil-War era, Dover continued to grow, and electricity was introduced to the city. A building boom added the Post Office, a Roman Catholic Church, and a new Kent County Court House. The year 1873 marked the opening of the Wilmington Conference Academy, now Wesley College. The next year Thomas Coke, D.D., founded a new American religion and Dover became known as the "Cradle of Methodism in America."

In 1933, Capitol Square was laid out and the Legislative Hall became the home of the State's General Assembly. The creation of the capitol complex, paid for out of lottery funds, along with the expansion of City Plaza, lent a handsome setting for Dover's Georgian and Victorian architecture.

The first non-agricultural major industry to locate in Dover was International Latex, now known as Playtex, which opened its first operation in 1937 and continues to be an important employer in the community. Among the products assembled at this location, the biggest operation of all of Playtex's North American sites, are tampons, latex gloves, and disposable baby bottles and liners. Today Dover is a pleasant community; it was chosen by *Employment Review* magazine in May 2000 as one of the best small cities to live and work for job seekers looking for a much quieter lifestyle than can be found in the larger cities that usually appear on such lists. The magazine referred to Dover as a city that has ''displayed incredible employment potential, a top-notch quality of life, outstanding educational standards, [and] opportunities for companies interested in relocating.''

Dover has created a unique balance between maintaining its small-town feel and economic prosperity. This is illustrated by the continuing population and job growth despite the country's economic recession with Dover Air Force Base providing great stability as the top employer along with prominent manufacturers such as Playtex. NASCAR racing and slots gambling at Dover Downs make the area a hotbed of tourist activity while a 19,000 square foot recreation center was proposed in 2004 that will serve as a huge draw for residents and visitors.

*Historical Information:* Delaware Public Archives, 121 Duke of York St., Dover, DE 19901; telephone (302)744-5000; email archives@state.de.us.

# Population Profile

## Metropolitan Area Residents
*1980:* 98,219 (Kent County)
*1990:* 110,993 (MSA)
*2000:* 126,697 (MSA)
*Percent change, 1990–2000:* 14.15%
*U.S. rank in 2000:* 225th

## City Residents
*1980:* 23,507
*1990:* 27,630
*2000:* 32,135 (of which, 17,013 were females and 15,122 were males)
*2003 estimate:* 32,808

*Percent change, 1990–2000:* 16.30%
*U.S. rank in 1990:* 1,160 (State rank: 2nd)
*U.S. rank in 2000:* Not reported (State rank: 2nd)

*Density:* 1,435.0 people per square mile (2000)

*Racial and ethnic characteristics* (2000)
White: 17,655
Black or African American: 11,961
American Indian and Alaska Native: 146
Asian: 1,016
Native Hawaiian and Pacific Islander: 12
Hispanic or Latino (may be of any race): 1,327
Other: 503

*Percent of residents born in state:* 38.8% (2000)

*Age characteristics* (2000)
Population under 5 years old: 2,146
Population 5 to 9 years old: 2,118
Population 10 to 14 years old: 2,133
Population 15 to 19 years old: 2,958
Population 20 to 24 years old: 3,259
Population 25 to 34 years old: 4,396
Population 35 to 44 years old: 4,564
Population 45 to 54 years old: 3,707
Population 55 to 59 years old: 1,432
Population 60 to 64 years old: 1,138
Population 65 to 74 years old: 2,143
Population 75 to 84 years old: 1,518
Population 85 years and older: 623
Median age: 32.9 years

*Births* (2002, Kent County)
Total number: 1,902

*Deaths* (2002, Kent County)
Total number: 1,113 (of which, 27 were infants under the age of 1 year)

*Money income* (1999)
Per capita income: $19,445
Median household income: $38,669
Total number of households: 12,460

*Number of households with income of . . .*
less than $10,000: 1,272
$10,000 to $14,999: 984
$15,000 to $24,999: 1,836
$25,000 to $34,999: 1,550
$35,000 to $49,999: 2,191
$50,000 to $74,999: 2,319
$75,000 to $99,999: 1,203
$100,000 to $149,999: 829
$150,000 to $199,999: 192
$200,000 or more: 84

*Percent of families below poverty level:* 11.5% (45.4% of which were female householder families with related children under 5 years; 1999)

*2002 FBI Crime Index Total:* 1,923

# Municipal Government

Dover operates with a council-manager form of government. The mayor and nine council members serve two-year terms.

**Head Official:** Mayor Stephen R. Speed (N-P) (since 2001; current term expires 2006)

**Total Number of City Employees:** 378 (2004)

*City Information:* City of Dover, 15 East Loockerman Street, PO Box 475, Dover, DE 19903; telephone (302)736-7004

# Economy

### Major Industries and Commercial Activity

Dover, the second largest city in the state, is a center of government, commerce, and industry for Central Delaware. Long involved in agricultural trade, the city is home to Kraft Foods and Procter & Gamble facilities. Kraft produces gelatin, puddings desserts, rice, and other food items at its 121-acre site. Procter & Gamble's Dover plant produces disposable wet wipe paper products at a 546,000 square foot site it acquired in 1996. Mrs. K's Salsa distributes home-style salsa in the area as well as shipping it nationwide. Since the early 1980s, the number of farms in the area has decreased including a drop from 767 in 1997 to 721 in 2002, according to the most recent Census of Agriculture report from the National Agricultural Statistics Service. Further, the number of acres under cultivation, which had remained relatively stable despite the loss of farms, also suffered a decline of about 10,000 acres from 1997 to 2002 (about 185,000 acres). Field crops in Kent County have a market value of approximately $54 million (from $62.6 million in 1997), and the once-growing broiler chicken industry witnessed a reduction in farms down from 133 in 1997 to 121 in 2002.

Playtex Apparel, Inc. and Playtex Products, Inc. manufacture and distribute intimate apparel as well as personal care items. Foods and food items produced in Dover include soft drinks, dairy products, corn, wheat, fruits and vegetables, and dry and canned goods. Major manufacturers include PPG Industries, which produces paint products; Eagle Group, a leading maker of metal files and storage cabinets and related items; Hirsch Industries, a leading manufacturer of consumer durables such as file cabinets; Reichold Inc., a producer of coatings, polyesters, emulsions, and adhesives; and Sunroc Corporation, which produces water coolers and drinking fountains. Refrigerators, brick, aerospace equipment, synthetic polymers and adhesives, and chemicals are also made in Dover.

Dover Air Force Base has a substantial economic impact on the local economy totaling more than $331 million per year. The base operates the largest aerial port facility on the East Coast, and serves as a focal point for military cargo movement to Europe and the Middle East. Its mechanized-computerized cargo handling arrangement makes possible the processing of up to 1,200 tons of cargo during a 24-hour period. The air base's military and civilian payroll of nearly $170 million is mostly pumped back into the local economy.

Tourism is a growing industry in Dover and Kent County. Because dollars often go a lot further in Dover due to the absence of sales tax, visitors from nearby states such as New York and New Jersey have been coming more often and staying longer in recent years. The addition of slot machines at the horse racing tracks in Dover, Harrington, and Wilmington brings in even more visitors. Ticket sales at the local NASCAR races, as well as related industries such as the restaurants and hotel/motel businesses, have a $47 million impact on Dover's economy.

*Items and goods produced:* foodstuffs, paper products, latex paint, beverages, home appliances, textiles, foundry works, and feed

### Incentive Programs—New and Existing Companies

The Central Delaware Economic Development Council assists companies with basic information, building and site selection, and dealing with local and state government agencies.

*State programs*—The state of Delaware has no general sales tax, no unitary tax, no fixtures tax, and no personal property or inventory tax. The Small Business Administration Section 504 Program offers long-term fixed assets financing at fixed rates for projects with an average net income of less than $2.5 million, which typically involve 50 percent funding from a private lender, 40 percent from the Delaware Development Corporation, and 10 percent from the business. The Delaware Economic Development Office offers assistance in loan packaging by utilizing existing state and federal programs, including Industrial Revenue Bond Financing, various bridge grants and loans, and Small Business Administration Assistance.

The state of Delaware has created incentives for financial institutions through the passage of the Financial Center

**The Loockerman Business District in Dover.**

Development Act in 1981, by which banks in certain circumstances receive a declining rate of taxation; the Consumer Credit Bank Act in the early 1980s, which gives financial benefits to smaller banks locating operations in the state; and the International Banking Act.

*Local programs*—In 1999 Kent County implemented a development incentive fund and also provides a 10-year property tax incentive program available for targeted industries. The Central Delaware Chamber of Commerce offers existing businesses consulting assistance and counseling services by retired executives.

*Job training programs*—The Delaware Economic Development Office custom designs and operates training programs on a shared or no-cost basis to be determined individually. Delaware Technical & Community College provides start-up and upgrading programs tailored to the needs of new and existing industries through its IT Learning Center.

## Development Projects

According to local analysts, Dover's recent population growth is caused by local business expansion and the growth of Dover Air Force Base. The construction of Kent County's Aeropark, an 115-acre industrial park adjacent to the base, began in the mid-1990s to house Sunroc, a water cooler manufacturer. The Aeropark project was greatly enhanced by the Air Force's granting of two military runways to accommodate Aeropark businesses. However, the civilian air terminal has been indefinitely shut down due to security concerns following the September 11, 2001 terrorist attacks.

Retail firms in the area are also expanding, as evidenced by the addition in the 1990s of new shopping centers and megastores such as Wal-Mart, Sam's Club, and Lowe's. The Dover Mall underwent a $500,000 renovation that was completed in 1997 and includes over 100 different retail shops including Sears, Old Navy, and JC Penney. The proliferation of newer chain eateries is represented by Applebee's, Red Lobster, Olive Garden, and Boston Market restaurants. There also has been a mushrooming of housing developments in West Dover, including such complexes as the Carlisle Villages, the Greens, and The Village of Westover. The introduction of slot machine gambling in 1995 prompted the Dover Downs facility to undergo expansions that concluded in March 2004 increasing the size to 91,000 square feet with 2,500 machines.

***Economic Development Information:*** Central Delaware Economic Development Council, 435 N. Dupont Hwy, PO Box 576, Dover, DE 19901; telephone (302) 678-0892; fax (302)678-0189; email director@cdedc.org. Delaware Economic Development Office, 99 Kings Hwy., Dover, DE 19901; telephone (302) 739-4271; fax (302) 739-5749.

## Commercial Shipping

Dover has four motor freight carriers and is served by Conrail. The Port of Wilmington, 40 miles north, provides direct access to I-495, and both Conrail and CSX railroads serve the terminal with rail sidings viable at most warehouse facilities at the port. In the late 1990s, the port expanded its docking area to handle both larger ships and a greater number of ships.

## Labor Force and Employment Outlook

Kent County boasts an available and trainable labor force and a pool of skilled labor with an excellent work ethic. Between 1970 and 2000, the county's labor force more than doubled while the number of new companies increased by more than 10 percent in a decade. In November 2004 the Milken Institute, a nonpartisan and nonprofit research organization, ranked Dover as fourth on their ''Best Performing Cities: Small Cities List'' which marked an improvement from the 29th position it occupied in 2003. The institute attributed this to the opening of a Wal-Mart distribution center, in addition to which the Dover Air Force Base's future appears stable. Also, a study by the American City Business Journals in 2004 named the Dover metropolitan area as the ''Hottest Market in the East for Job Creation'' and second in the nation only behind Las Vegas. In 2004 Delaware's economy marked its return to the Corporation for Enterprise Development's (CFED) ratings list that grades the best states in the nation on a variety of economic factors. Compared to other states, Delaware is among the top five in the nation, earning As and Bs in the major grading categories by the nationally-recognized economic research organization. For seven consecutive years prior to 2000, personal and business taxes were cut in Delaware.

The 1999 purchase by the city of Dover of 385-plus acres, known as the Garrison Oak Technology Park, provides Kent County with the potential for significant future job growth in manufacturing, research and development, and high-technology industry. In addition, the proposed High-Technology Business Incubator, to be located at Delaware State University, will provide additional future job and company growth potential although construction was delayed until 2005 due to economic concerns after a 2002 groundbreaking.

The following is a summary of data regarding the Dover metropolitan area labor force, 2003 annual averages.

*Size of nonagricultural labor force:* 58,700

*Number of workers employed in . . .*
  *construction and mining:* 3,000
  *manufacturing:* 4,900
  *trade, transportation, and utilities:* 10,800

*information:* 700

*financial activities:* 2,600

*professional and business services:* 3,700

*educational and health services:* 7,100

*leisure and hospitality:* 6,700

*other services:* 2,200

*government:* 17,200

*Average hourly earnings of production workers employed in manufacturing:* $16.90

*Unemployment rate:* 2.7% (November 2004)

| *Largest employers* | *Number of employees* |
|---|---|
| Dover Air Force Base | 8,595 total: |
|  | 5,715 (military) |
|  | 1,090 (civilian) |
|  | 1,790 (reserves) |
| Bayhealth Medical Center (includes Kent General Hospital and Milford Memorial Hospital) | 2,527 |
| Dover Downs | 1,200 |
| Delaware State University | 1,150 |
| Playtex Products, Inc. | 1,105 |
| Capital School District | 809 |
| Kraft Foods | 621 |
| Bank of America | 600 |
| Aetna U.S. Healthcare | 525 |
| City of Dover | 375 |
| Procter and Gamble | 327 |

## Cost of Living

As of 2000, Dover had a cost of living slightly above the national average, but the local tax burden is competitive with most other states.

The following is a summary of data regarding several key cost of living factors for the Dover area.

*1999 (4th Quarter) ACCRA Average House Price:* $141,874

*2000 (4th Quarter) ACCRA Cost of Living Index:* 104.2 (U.S. average = 100.0)

*State income tax rate:* Ranges from 2.2% to 5.95%

*State sales tax rate:* None

*Local income tax rate:* None

*Local sales tax rate:* None

*Property tax rate:* $0.41 per $100.00 of assessed fair market value

***Economic Information:*** Central Delaware Chamber of Commerce, 435 N. Dupont Hwy, Dover, DE 19901; telephone (302) 678-0892; fax (302)678-0189; email info@cdcc.net.

# Education and Research

## Elementary and Secondary Schools

In 1995 the Capital School District received one of 17 national Challenge Grants from the U.S. Department of Education in the programs's inaugural year. The $5.5 million grant spanned five years and supported technology at school and in the home. The district offers a computer training laboratory in each school, gifted programs in elementary and secondary schools, language arts and mathematics programs, and a school with multiage grouping. Dover High School offers a Technical Preparation program. The schools also conduct a curriculum in which members of the community serve as writing coaches. Handicapped children are served by the Kent County Community School.

The following is a summary of data regarding the Capital School District as of the 2003–2004 school year.

*Total enrollment:* 5,909

*Number of facilities*
  *elementary schools:* 7
  *middle schools:* 2
  *senior high schools:* 1
  *other:* 1 (Kent County Community School)

*Student/teacher ratio:* 15.2:1

*Teacher salaries*
  *average:* $49,989

*Funding per pupil:* $8,922 (2003)

***Public Schools Information:*** Superintendent's Office, Capital School District, 945 Forest St., Dover, DE 19904-3498; telephone (302)672-1500; fax (302)672-1714

## Colleges and Universities

Delaware State University, with about 3,178 students, is the state's historically African American institution of higher learning. The university has three undergraduate schools, a college, and a graduate school offering master's degrees in seven areas. Founded in 1873, Wesley College has 30 bachelor's degree programs and four associates degrees along with four master's programs. It is affiliated with the United Methodist Church. Bachelor's and master's degree programs are available through Wilmington College, which has sites at Dover Air Force Base and just north of Dover Downs. More than 42,500 students each year enroll in diversified technical associate degree programs, diploma programs, and certificate and special interest programs offered at the Delaware Technical and Community College's four locations. Three thousand students attend the Dover campus each semester; the other campuses are in Georgetown, Stanton, and Wilmington. The University of Delaware maintains a campus that includes an associates degree art program.

## Libraries and Research Centers

The Dover Public Library, which underwent renovations in 2002 and 2003, has more than 97,000 volumes, 350 magazine subscriptions, and 12 newspapers and services about 500 patrons daily in its 17,500 square foot facility. The library also contains films, records, audiocassettes, and videocassettes. Services include reference materials and aids, book talks, and seasonal and children's programs.

The Dover Air Force Base maintains a library containing nearly 30,000 volumes focusing on the United States Air Force and various military topics, with special collections on Transition Assistance. Besides being the site of the Delaware Division of Libraries State Library, Dover is home to the state's Department of Transportation Library, the Delaware State Archives, and libraries of the Delaware Department of Public Instruction, the Delaware State House Museum, the Legislative Council Library, and the State's Law Library. The State Library of Delaware provides special services to people who are blind, physically handicapped, or homebound. Both local colleges and the local hospital also have library facilities.

Founded in the 1950s, the National Council on Agricultural Life and Labor Research Fund (NCALL Research) provides housing counseling services along with studies on safe and sanitary rural housing, particularly for farm workers.

The St. Jones Estuarine Research Reserve offers group tours and free general admission to its environmental research center that features a variety of programs and nature trails along with canoe and boat trips as it strives to promote the general public's knowledge of estuaries.

*Public Library Information:* Dover Public Library, 45 S. State St., Dover, DE 19901-3526; telephone (302)736-7030; fax (302)736-5087

*Research Information:* Delaware National Estuarine Research Reserve, 818 Kitts Hummock Rd., Dover, DE 19901; telephone (302)739-3436

# Health Care

The medical needs of Dover's residents are met at the city's Kent General Hospital, a 231-bed facility. The hospital offers a variety of services including in-patient and outpatient care, neonatal special care, coronary care, same-day surgery, a modern imaging department, respiratory care and neurodiagnostics, and a 24-hour emergency department.

# Recreation

## Sightseeing

A good place to begin exploring Dover is the Delaware State Visitor Center on Federal Street in the downtown area, which offers maps, brochures, and information. The center also features changing exhibits about the area. Many historic structures are clustered downtown around the Green, with buildings ranging from those built in Colonial times to the Victorian period. Once the site of early fairs and markets, today the Green hosts political rallies, public events, and civic celebrations. Although the building itself was demolished in 1830, visitors can still visit the Golden Fleece Tavern site where Delaware representatives ratified the U.S. Constitution.

At one end of the Green stands the Old State House, where the General Assembly met from 1777 until 1934, which was restored in 1976. That body now meets in the Legislative Hall, which displays paintings of former governors and war heroes. Nearby are the Colonel John Haslett Armory and the refurbished Richardson & Robbins canning plant, which now houses the Department of Natural Resources and other state offices. At Christ's Church there is a monument to Caesar Rodney (1729–84), signer of the Declaration of Independence, an esteemed patriot and local leader. Perhaps the quaintest building on the Green is the tiny Old Post Office, believed to be the city's first.

Thousands of people each year travel to the Air Mobility Command Museum at Dover Air Force Base, which houses a growing collection of vintage planes and artifacts that reflect the evolution, history, and varied missions of military airlift and tanker aircraft. Special emphasis is placed on the history of Dover AFB since its beginnings in 1941. Housed in a restored World War II hangar that was once the home of the Army Air Force Rocket Test Center, the museum is a registered National Historic Site. There is a large outside airpark, a commemorative garden, and an excellent spot to watch airfield operations.

The history of 200 years of farm life is exhibited at the Delaware Agricultural Museum and Village, which opened in 1980 and features 10,000 objects, and a re-created nineteenth-century village.

Nipper, the famous RCA Victor canine symbol, is the star of the Johnson Victrola Museum, which traces the history of the Victor Talking Machine Company, now known as RCA. The museum is a replica of a 1920s Victrola dealer's store.

## Arts and Culture

Dover has a number of interesting historical and art museums. The Hall of Records, which houses the Division of Historical and Cultural Affairs, contains the Royal Charter that Charles II gave to the Duke of York for the land that is now Delaware. The Meeting House Galleries I (also known as the Delaware Archaeology Museum) and II (Delaware Museum of Small Town Life) offer an archaeological exhibit, especially focusing on Native Americans, and a Main Street exhibit on typical small town life.

Originally founded in 1904, the 600-seat Schwartz Center for the Arts is the home of the Dover Symphony and presents comedy shows, music, dance, live theater, and film festivals. Originally named The Dover Opera House, the building was renamed The Capital Theater in 1923. After decades of success, it fell into disrepair and the building was closed in 1982. Spurred on by a statewide fundraising effort, the dilapidated facility was revived in October 2001 after an $8.3 million restoration. In 2004 a community partnership was formed with nearby Wilmington's Grand Opera House, local universities, and other arts organizations to maximize usage of the center.

Theater and dance troupes are among the entertainment at the Delaware State University Education and Humanities Theatre along with an art gallery on the campus grounds. On a smaller scale, the Wesley College Chapel plays host to a wide array of performances.

The Sewell Biggs Museum of Art, which opened in 1993 and was founded by Sewell C. Biggs, features 14 galleries of decorative arts. The Dover Art League's Art Center offers classes, a series of exhibits, and a children's summer arts camp.

*Arts and Culture Information:* Greater Dover Arts Council, PO Box 475, Dover, DE 19903-0475; telephone (302)736-7050

## Festivals and Holidays

A festive parade and dancing around the maypole mark the opening of the Old Dover Days, a celebration with music, arts and crafts, and a showcase of local homes and gardens that takes place over the first weekend in May. June brings a variety of music at the June Jam and the Annual Spring and Summer Performing Arts Series on the Green along with the African American Heritage Festival at Mirror Lake. A fireworks display at the Capitol Square tops off the annual Fourth of July Celebration, and later in the month the Delaware State Fair spotlights top-name music stars, auto racing, a rodeo, and demolition derbies. Fairgoers flock to the animal and agricultural exhibits and the gigantic midway offering amusement rides and name entertainment.

Each October the Dover Arts Council sponsors Capitol City Arts Tour and Pumpkin Glow. The month is further enlivened by the Governor's Annual Fall Festival at Woodburn. The holiday season is welcomed by the Delaware Hospice Festival of Trees, the Caroling on the Green event, and the Governor's Annual Christmas Open House at Woodburn. Downtown Dover's First Night New Year's Eve Celebration rings in the new year. February's Winter Festival takes place at the Delaware State University and March brings the Governor's Annual Easter Egg Hunt.

## Sports for the Spectator

Dover does not field any teams in major league sports but it does offer the excitement of racing. Dover Downs is said to be the only facility in the country that accommodates both horse racing and auto racing, on two separate tracks. Each sport attracts nearly a third of a million fans to the track annually. The first weekend in June is the time for the MBNA 200 NASCAR Busch Series and MBNA 400 Nextel Cup Series. September brings the Dover 200 NASCAR Busch Series and MBNA 400 NASCAR Nextel Cup races. Live harness racing is presented during the winter months.

## Sports for the Participant

Dover's Silver Lake, one of four lakes in Kent County, offers picnicking, boating, and fishing on 182 acres. The city has 25 other parks that provide a variety of features including historic monuments, children's playground equipment, and fishing piers. Short drives to Delaware Bay and the Atlantic Ocean provide opportunities for swimming, water skiing, and other water-related activities. Public golf courses are available and tennis courts can be found at school and college grounds.

Schutte Park, one of the city's more recently opened parks, is located on the west side of town and takes up 57 acres to house its softball/baseball and hockey/soccer fields along with ample space for picnic pavilion rentals. The Parks and Recreation Department is seeking to expand next to this land with a site proposed in 2004 named ''Westside Recreation Center'' on more than 19,000 square feet and at a projected cost exceeding $2.3 million.

About 10 miles north of Dover is the Bombay Hook National Wildlife Refuge in Smyrna where visitors can view migratory shorebirds and waterfowl via hiking and driving tours of the 16,000 acres of marshes, ponds, fields, and forest.

*Sports Information:* Parks and Recreation Office, PO Box 475, Dover, DE 19903-0475; telephone (302)736-7050; email parks@cityofdover.com

**Shopping and Dining**

Tax-free shopping attracts people from all over the region to Dover's stores. Main Street Dover boasts many specialty shops located in unique buildings. Curbside horses and buggies from nearby Amish towns are a common site at the legendary Spence's Bazaar on New Street, where bargain hunters peruse everything from housewares to antique furniture. The Dover Mall, with nearly 100 stores, is anchored by Boscov's, Sears, Strawbridge's, and JC Penney.

With approximately 220 eateries, Kent County has claimed to have the highest amount of restaurants per capita in the United States. Dover and the surrounding area boast a wide variety of dining establishments, featuring everything from traditional Southern fare to foods of many nations including Thai, Chinese, Indian, Mongolian, Mexican, and Italian. Seafood places and casual American eateries also abound. A variety of fine dining can be found as well.

***Visitor Information:*** Kent County Convention & Visitors Bureau, 435 N. DuPont Hwy., Dover, DE 19901; telephone (302)734-1736 or (800)233-KENT; fax (302)734-0167.

# Convention Facilities

The Dover Sheraton Conference Center is the primary conference site in the city. The center offers 21,000 square feet of exhibition space, a ballroom that can accommodate 1,500 for dinner, and 22 meeting rooms, as well as 156 hotel rooms. An 18,000 square foot ballroom is available at the Dover Downs Hotel & Conference Center that can be divided into three separate areas if needed for events such as stand-up receptions, sit-down dinners, and tradeshows. Further, the hotel provides six corporate meeting rooms and three smaller hospitality suites. Military and veterans groups can reserve meeting rooms for 30 to 200 people at the Air Mobility Command Museum on Dover Air Force Base.

***Convention Information:*** Kent County Convention & Visitors Bureau, 435 N. DuPont Hwy., Dover, DE 19901; telephone (302)734-1736 or (800)233-KENT; fax (302)734-0167. Air Mobility Command Museum, 1301 Heritage Rd., Dover AFB, DE, 19902-5301, telephone (302)677-5938; fax (302)677-5940. Dover Downs Hotel & Conference Center, 1131 N. DuPont Hwy., Dover, DE, 19901; telephone (302)674-4600 or (800)711-5882. Sheraton Dover Hotel, 1570 N. DuPont Hwy., Dover, DE 19901; telephone (302)678-8500; fax (302)678-9073; email sherdov @sheratondover.com.

# Transportation

**Approaching the City**

For many years, metropolitan Dover was a bottleneck, especially on the weekends, with visitors traveling to and from the Atlantic beaches. Relief arrived with the opening of a $100 million bypass around the city on Route 1. Carolina Trailways offers bus service to the city. The closest Amtrak rail service is available at Wilmington and the major airport close to Dover is at Philadelphia.

**Traveling in the City**

U.S. highways 13 and 113 run north and south in Dover and connect to Delaware Route 1, and state highway 8 is the main east-and-west passage. Central Delaware Transit offers a state-run, fixed-route bus system that operates around the city. Historic attractions around the Green are accessible on foot.

# Communications

**Newspapers and Magazines**

Dover's daily newspaper is the *Delaware State News,* published Monday through Sunday. Wilmington's *The News Journal* is also read in Dover. The *Dover Post* is its weekly shopper.

**Television and Radio**

One television station (WBOC-TV), one AM station (WDOV-AM), and one FM station (WDSD-FM) broadcast out of Dover.

***Media Information:*** *Delaware State News,* PO Box 737, Dover, DE 19903; telephone (302)674-3600.

**Dover Online**

Capital School District profile. Available issm.doe.state.de .us/profiles/Reports/PDF/2004/13/13_Profile.PDF

Central Delaware Chamber of Commerce. Available www .cdcc.net

Central Delaware Economic Development Council. Available www.cdedc.org

City of Dover home page. Available www.cityofdover.com

Delaware Economic Development Office. Available www .state.de.us/dedo

Delaware Online. Available www.delawareonline.com

Dover Air Force Base. Available www.public.dover.amc.af .mil

Dover Post. Available www.doverpost.com

The Historical Society of Delaware. Available www.hsd.org

Kent County Convention and Visitors Bureau. Available www.visitdover.com

School district statistics. Available www.doe.state.de.us/ edstats/Menu/EdStats.htm

State of Delaware, Department of Transportation. Available www.deldot.net/index.shtml

University of Delaware. Available www.udel.edu

WDOV-AM radio home page. Available www.wdov.com

WDSD-FM radio home page. Available www.wdsd.com

Welcome to Dover. Available www.state.de.us/facts/ history/dover.htm

## Selected Bibliography

Jackson, James B, *The Golden Fleece Tavern: The Birthplace of the First State* (Dover, DE: Friends of Old Dover, 1987)

Walls, Bruce, *Tales of Old Dover* (Decatur, IL: Spectator Books, 1977)

# Wilmington

## *The City in Brief*

**Founded:** 1638 (chartered 1739)

**Head Official:** Mayor James M. Baker (D) (since 2001)

**City Population**
  **1980:** 70,195
  **1990:** 71,529
  **2000:** 72,664
  **2003 estimate:** 72,051
  **Percent change, 1990–2000:** 1.5%
  **U.S. rank in 1990:** 311th (state rank: 1st)
  **U.S. rank in 2000:** 417th (state rank: 1st)

**Metropolitan Area Population**
  **1990:** 5,892,937 (CMSA)
  **2000:** 6,188,464 (CMSA)

  **Percent change, 1990–2000:** 5%
  **U.S. rank in 1990:** 5th (CMSA)
  **U.S. rank in 2000:** 6th (CMSA)

**Area:** 10.8 square miles (2000)
**Elevation:** Approximately 74 feet above sea level
**Average Annual Temperature:** 54.0° F
**Average Annual Precipitation:** 40.25 inches; 19.9 inches of snow

**Major Economic Sectors:** services, manufacturing, wholesale and retail trade
**Unemployment rate:** 4.0% (November 2004)
**Per Capita Income:** $20,236 (1999)

**2002 FBI Crime Index Total:** not reported

**Major Colleges and Universities:** University of Delaware, Widener University

**Daily Newspaper:** *The News-Journal*

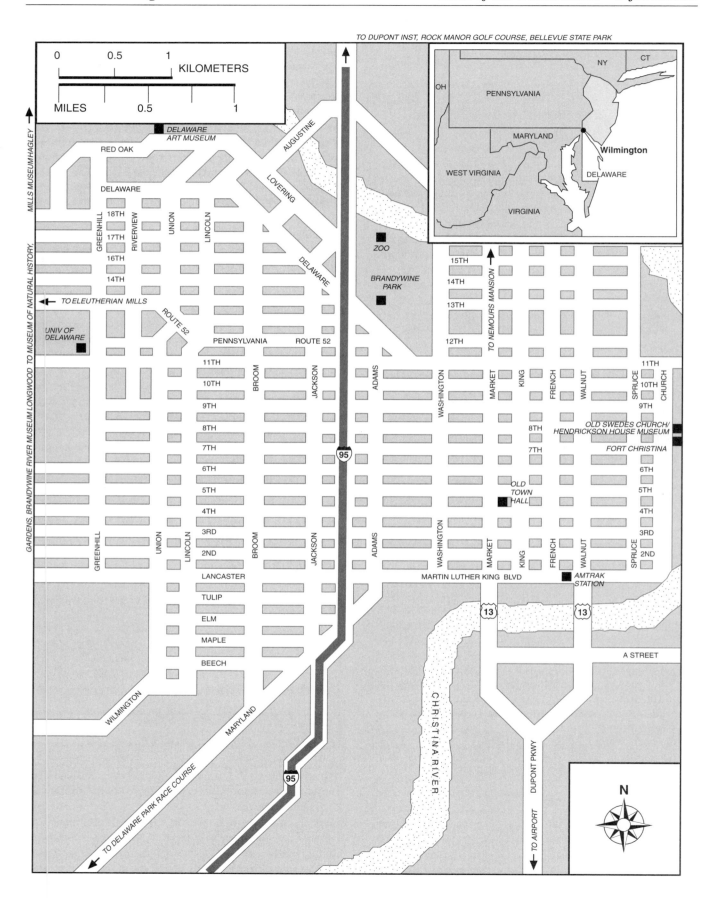

# Introduction

After years of living in Philadelphia's shadow, Wilmington has emerged as a national banking center. Beginning with the du Pont family enterprises, the city has been a leading industrial and shipping hub since the nineteenth century. Today its diversified labor force, low corporate tax burden, economic incentives for new and expanding companies, and teamwork between the public and private sectors make it extremely attractive to new businesses. Although situated in the most densely populated area of the northeast, Wilmington is a very livable city. Because of its small size, it enjoys the advantages of a large metropolitan area while escaping the disadvantages, such as traffic congestion, noise pollution, and smog. City residents profit from a comparatively low cost of living and cultural perquisites inherent in an area that boasts two of the country's top museums and bills itself as the "Corporate Capital of the World."

# Geography and Climate

Wilmington is located in the northeast corner of Delaware, on the western bank of the Delaware River where the Christina River joins Brandywine Creek. The city is part of the Atlantic Coastal Plain, which combines flat, low land at sea level with gentle, rolling hills that extend northward into Pennsylvania. The Delaware River forms the city's eastern border with the Atlantic Ocean beyond; Chesapeake Bay lies to the southwest. These large water masses determine the city's climate. Summers are warm and humid, and winters are generally mild. During the summer relative humidity is about 75 percent, and fog is frequent throughout the year. Average annual snowfall is 19.9 inches, but the snow never stays on the ground for more than a few days. Most winter precipitation falls as rain or sleet. Rainfall is heaviest in summer when it comes in the form of thunderstorms. Hurricanes moving northward along the Atlantic Coast occasionally cause heavy rainfall, but winds seldom reach hurricane force in Wilmington. Strong easterly and southeasterly winds sometimes cause high tides in the Delaware River, resulting in flooding of lowlands and damage to riverfront properties.

**Area:** 10.8 square miles (2000)

**Elevation:** Approximately 74 feet above sea level

**Average Temperatures:** January, 32.0° F; July, 76.0° F; annual average, 54.0° F

**Average Annual Precipitation:** 40.25 inches; 19.9 inches of snow

# History

Lenni-Lenape Indians lived in the Wilmington area long before Europeans and Africans arrived on Delaware's shores. "Lenni" means pure or original, and "Lenape" means the people. Their control extended north into Pennsylvania and south to the Potomac; their customs and traditions resembled those of their neighbors, the Nanticokes and the Powhatans of Virginia. European settlers first encountered this tribe of "peacemakers" in the early seventeenth century.

**Various Countries Possess Early Colony**

Wilmington was the first permanent Old World settlement in the entire Delaware Valley. In March 1638, a Swedish expedition led by Peter Minuit entered Delaware Bay. They sailed up the river and entered the Minquas Kill (today's Christina River). Going 2 miles inland, they cast anchor opposite a natural stone wharf. Here at "The Rocks"—which are still visible today at the foot of Seventh Street—Minuit stepped ashore and made a treaty with the Lenni-Lenapes. The land he purchased was dubbed New Sweden, and Swedish soldiers soon began constructing a fort they named after their queen, Christina. Inside the fort they built the first log cabins in America. Before the ship left in June, the 24 original Swedes, Finns, Dutch, and German settlers were joined by Anthoni, "The Black Swede," a freedman from the Caribbean. All 25 were alive and well two years later when the ship returned. In all, Sweden sent 12 expeditions to the new world, but the fledgling colony received little support from Queen Christina and in 1656 was overtaken by the Dutch. Peter Stuyvesant, the Governor of New Amsterdam, laid siege to the tiny colony and ultimately the Swedes surrendered.

In 1664, as a result of a war between Holland and England, the colony along the Delaware was brought under English rule. Then, in 1681, William Penn received a grant from England's King Charles II for the largest tract ever given a commoner. "Penn's Woods," or Pennsylvania, was intended to be a haven for members of the Society of Friends, or Quakers. For the next fifty years, Penn and Lord Baltimore would vie for ownership of the three counties of New Castle, Kent, and Sussex. As Pennsylvania added western counties, Delaware demanded home rule, and in 1704 the counties were granted their own assembly with Pennsylvania and Delaware sharing the same crown-appointed governor.

Around 1730, a large tract of land in what is now Wilmington was deeded to a man named Thomas Willing, who called the tiny settlement Willingtown. Willingtown was a farming community of 15 to 20 houses when prosperous

Quakers began to arrive in 1735. Immediately they began investing in property and, simultaneously, the town began to grow. At this time there was no formal government; therefore, decisions were made by consent of all the towns-people. Then, in 1739, England's King George II granted a charter addressed to "the People of Wilmington;" the king is thought to have arbitrarily named the town after his friend Spencer Compton, Earl of Wilmington. The first election held under the borough charter took place on September 8, 1740. This same year the first vessel built for foreign trade, the *Wilmington,* sailed for Jamaica. A brisk shipping trade continued to benefit local merchants despite wars and privateers. Industries such as brick-making, pottery, tanning, and flour-milling (at mills along the Brandywine) began to flourish.

## Wilmington in Revolutionary Times

The summer of 1777 found the community of Wilmington in the center of the struggle for American independence from England. George Washington established Revolutionary army headquarters in Wilmington, as did General Anthony Wayne. After the British took Wilmington, following the Battle of Brandywine, the town became a British camp. The Presbyterian Meeting House was used as a prison, and residents' houses were requisitioned to care for the wounded. Wilmingtonians did not see the last of British troops until the end of October 1777. An economic slump followed the war, but soon Wilmington had a fleet of ships engaged in coastal, as well as European, trade. Many Irish passed through the Port of Wilmington at this time, as well as French refugees from Santo Domingo. Scarcely had these immigrants settled when hundreds more poured in from Philadelphia, where yellow fever was rampant. Until the epidemic, Wilmington merchants had depended on Philadelphia banks for financial support. Suddenly isolated from their neighbor, they realized the need for economic self-sufficiency and founded the Bank of Delaware in 1795.

## Economic Development Marks Nineteenth Century

Between the close of the Revolution and the War of 1812, Wilmington's population increased to 5,000, the town spread westward, and streets were widened to accommodate the flow of traffic. Five turnpikes built between 1808 and 1815 greatly increased Wilmington's trade. Steamboats ran regularly between the town and Philadelphia, as did stage-coaches carrying passengers and freight. One of the earliest railroads in the United States, the Newcastle & Frenchtown Railway, opened in 1831, and soon after came the Wilmington & Susquehanna. By 1831 Wilmington's population had grown so large that leading citizens petitioned the legislature to incorporate the town as a city. The charter was granted in 1832, and city officials were elected.

From 1832 until the Civil War, new enterprises sprang up on the shores of the Christina River, supplementing those already prospering along the Brandywine. Shipbuilding, paper milling, and the manufacture of machine tools, iron, railroad cars, and cotton joined the earlier industries of flour milling and leather tanning.

## Wilmington in the Twentieth Century

World War I kept all available industrial plants working full time; blast furnaces and shipyards operated round-the-clock. The conflict brought immense trade to E. I. du Pont de Nemours and Company, which had been producing gun powder in the area since 1802. After the war du Pont moved away from explosives to manufacture materials such as Nylon, Dacron, Orlon, and Cellophane. When other chemical companies moved into the region, Wilmington became known as "The Chemical Capital of the World." This industrial expansion brought great wealth to the area, and in the decades following World War II, a large increase in population.

Like many American cities, Wilmington has seen a steady flow of residents leave the city for the suburbs. The exodus of the middle class left the city to the urban poor, particularly to blacks and the elderly, creating new problems. Racial violence that broke out in the wake of Martin Luther King's assassination on April 4, 1968, required heavy patrol by the National Guard for many months. Today Wilmington is dealing successfully with the problem of urban safety. Teamwork by government and business leaders has focused on making public transit and the entire downtown area once again attractive to residents and visitors. The revitalization of downtown buildings and new housing construction and the redevelopment of the Christina Riverfront continue to be priorities for the city and state governments. The revitalization of the central business area continues to stimulate increased interest in Wilmington. Revitalization efforts include many new restaurants plus the construction of a new live performance theater, a baseball stadium, the First USA Riverfront Arts Center in 1998, a 1.7-mile Riverwalk and the Shipyard Shops along the riverfront, and the 2003 installation of a steel-rail trolley connecting the riverfront with the business area. Other cultural developments include a recent $12 million expansion of the Grand Opera House on Market Street, a $25 million expansion of the Delaware Art Museum on Grand Kentmere Parkway, and construction of Theatre N at Nemours, the first movie theater in the city since 1982.

Since the mid-1990s more than $1 billion, much of it in private funds, has been invested in major downtown redevelopment projects. The MBNA complex, after moving to downtown Wilmington in 1993 and undertaking a $32 million renovation of the former Daniel L. Herrmann Courthouse, now consists of seven buildings. In 2002 the huge former Delaware Trust Building, which had been destroyed by fire, was converted to the Residences at Rodney Square, a 278 unit luxury apartment complex.

Mayor James M. Baker, who took office in 2001, has seen positive developments in the city's ongoing fight with crime and blight. Overall crime rates have dropped, and the city has enforced stricter registration fees and building code violations on owners of vacant properties to encourage property rehabilitation.

***Historical Information:*** Historical Society of Delaware Library, 505 Market Street Mall, Wilmington DE 19801; telephone (302)655-7171

# Population Profile

## Metropolitan Area Residents
*1990:* 5,892,937(CMSA)
*2000:* 6,188,463 (CMSA)
*Percent change, 1990–2000:* 14.2%
*U.S. rank in 1990:* 5th (CMSA)
*U.S. rank in 2000:* 6th (CMSA)

## City Residents
*1980:* 70,195
*1990:* 71,529
*2000:* 72,664
*2003 estimate:* 72,051
*Percent change, 1990–2000:* 1.5%
*U.S. rank in 1990:* 311th (state rank: 1st)
*U.S. rank in 2000:* 417th (state rank: 1st)

*Density:* 6,698 people per square mile (2000)

*Racial and ethnic characteristics* (2000)
   White: 25,811
   Black or African American: 41,001
   American Indian and Alaska Native: 185
   Asian: 473
   Native Hawaiian and Pacific Islander: 20
   Hispanic or Latino (may be of any race): 7,148
   Other: 3,750

*Percent of residents born in state:* 58.1% (2000)

*Age characteristics* (2000)
   Population under 5 years old: 4,953
   Population 5 to 9 years old: 5,424
   Population 10 to 14 years old: 5,308
   Population 15 to 19 years old: 5,105
   Population 20 to 24 years old: 5,121
   Population 25 to 34 years old: 11,906

Population 35 to 44 years old: 11,349
Population 45 to 54 years old: 8,861
Population 55 to 59 years old: 3,080
Population 60 to 64 years old: 2,434
Population 65 to 74 years old: 4,401
Population 75 to 84 years old: 3,411
Population 85 years and older: 1,311
Median age: 33.7 years

*Births* (2002)
   Total number: 1,254

*Deaths* (2000)
   Total number: 779

*Money income* (1999)
   Per capita income: $20,236
   Median household income: $35,116
   Total households: 28,661

*Number of households with income of . . .*
   less than $10,000: 4,444
   $10,000 to $14,999: 2,132
   $15,000 to $24,999: 3,886
   $25,000 to $34,999: 3,825
   $35,000 to $49,999: 4,610
   $50,000 to $74,999: 4,605
   $75,000 to $99,999: 2,373
   $100,000 to $149,999: 1,792
   $150,000 to $199,999: 390
   $200,000 or more: 604

*Percent of families below poverty level:* 16.8% (43.1% of which were female householder families with related children under 5 years)

*2002 FBI Crime Index Total:* not reported

# Municipal Government

Wilmington, the New Castle County seat, has a mayor-council form of government. Elected to a four-year term, the mayor is the city's chief administrator. Like the mayor, Wilmington's thirteen city council members are elected for four-year terms every presidential election year.

**Head Official:** Mayor James M. Baker (D) (since January 2001; current term expires November 2008)

**Total Number of City Employees:** 1,192 (2005)

***City Information:*** City of Wilmington, 800 French St., Wilmington, DE 19801; telephone (302)571-4100

# *Economy*

## Major Industries and Commercial Activity

Companies working in service industries such as health care, banking, trade, and manufacturing remain Wilmington's largest employers. The Wilmington/Newark metropolitan area is home to some of the world's most prominent technology companies, including DuPont, AstraZeneca, W.L. Gore and Associates, Hercules, Inc., and Andersen Consulting. The Delaware Technology Park in Newark is host to more than 49 technology-driven businesses. Delaware is a national corporate center, and more than half of the *Fortune 500* charter their operations in the city because of the state's favorable corporate franchise tax laws and nationally recognized Court of Chancery.

More than 60 banks—state, national and regional—are located in Wilmington. MBNA Bank is the area's largest employer with more than 11,000 workers. American Life Insurance Company's world headquarters is an impressive anchor in the city's developing Christina Gateway, a commercial center encompassing the eastern sector to the waterfront. Chase Manhattan has invested millions of dollars in downtown offices, as have PNC, First Union, Wilmington Trust, First USA, and Beneficial National Bank. Manufacturers Hanover has relocated a portion of its domestic lending operation to the city as well.

Other large manufacturing companies with operations in the Wilmington region include Daimler-Chrysler, Ciba-Geigy (pharmaceuticals), and Dade Behring (medical apparatus manufacturers).

*Items and goods produced:* chemicals, medical apparatus, mineral products, pharmaceuticals, aerospace products, automobiles

## Incentive Programs—New and Existing Companies

*Local programs*—Wilmington provides strong incentives to businesses thinking of establishing operations in the city. Among the city incentives are: Christina Gateway Tax Incentive Program; Real Property Tax Exemption Program; Head Tax, which allows any new or relocating business in the city that brings over 100 new employees to obtain a waiver to the City's Head tax, a $6.00 fee per employee the city charges for upkeep of the city's infrastructure, police and other city services; Enterprise Zone; Blue Collar Tax Program, which provides that any business that creates blue-collar jobs in the city is eligible for a $250.00 state tax credit per $100 million invested; and incentives for locating in brownfields.

*State programs*—Delaware corporations have always benefited from the absence of either sales or inventory tax, and there are tax credits on corporate income and gross receipts tax reductions for new or expanding key industries. State incentive programs include Industrial Revenue Bond Financing; the Delaware Innovation Fund, developed to support the creation and development of new high growth, technology based firms, and high quality jobs in Delaware; and The Delaware Access Program, developed to assist banks in making high-risk business loans.

*Job training programs*—When the labor market cannot respond to an employer's needs, or when additional skills are necessary because of a particular business situation, the Delaware Economic Development Office has access to recognized educational resources that can provide skill training designed to the company's specifications. Training contracts may be arranged with colleges, vocational schools, specialized training centers, and independent agencies that provide business, industrial, and service-related instruction.

## Development Projects

In his 2000 message to the city, Mayor Sills reported the following developments in Wilmington: "Through initiatives like Wilmington Renaissance, major corporations have expanded their business operations in the city, largely by shifting thousands of employees and new jobs to Wilmington from suburban locations. . . [In recent years] we have also brought in more than $10 million in private and government funds for key neighborhood development projects." Wilmington Renaissance is a nonpartisan, nonprofit organization that works to expand downtown employment and downtown living through partnerships with the mayor, city council, state and county officials, and agencies supporting development in Wilmington's downtown. A major recent project that has come out of the collaboration is a retail and residential project in the city's historic Ships Tavern District. The $24 million development, completed in the fall of 2004, brought more than 80 apartments and 18 retail shops to a city block that holds more than a dozen historically significant buildings. Originally constructed in the 18th and 19th centuries, the three- and four-story buildings had mostly been sitting vacant or used as warehouse space for more than two decades.

Mayor James M. Baker also announced plans to begin construction in March 2005 on a new 150,000-square-foot office and retail complex at the site of the former Wilmington Dry Goods in downtown Wilmington. Called the Renaissance Centre, the $50 million project would house more than 550 employees and is expected to be completed by 2007. The city also came to an agreement that would allow the Brandywine Realty Trust Corp. to develop a piece of prime downtown property with a proposed 22-story, 500,000-square-foot office complex near 2nd and King Street.

*Economic Development Information:* Delaware Economic Development Office, 820 N. French Street, Wilmington, DE

19901; telephone (302)577-8477. New Castle County Chamber of Commerce, County Commerce Office Park, Suite 201, 630 Churchman's Road, Newark, DE; telephone (302)737-4345

## Commercial Shipping

The flow of goods in and out of Wilmington is facilitated by its network of interstate highways and air and rail freight service. The city also boasts one of the busiest ports in the world. Perhaps the city's greatest economic asset, the state-owned Port of Wilmington lies at the mouth of the Christina River, only 65 miles from Atlantic Ocean shipping lanes. Incoming cargo, such as fresh fruit, concentrated juice, frozen meat, vehicles, lumber, and steel can be dispatched directly from ships to freight cars, trucks, and lighter carriers, saving handling costs and speeding delivery. The port has been designated a Free Trade Zone, offering customs benefits that are attractive to international trade. The full-service, deep-water port handles more than 400 vessels and nearly 5 million tons of cargo yearly, and its discharging facilities include two 46-ton container cranes that can handle 35 containers an hour.

The interstate highways that pass through Wilmington give truckers direct access to one-third of the nation's consumers; more than 60 common and contract carriers operate in the metropolitan area. Wilmington is also served by the main-line of Norfolk Southern System, with excellent direct freight service to major markets.

The New Castle County Airport offers worldwide cargo services with an unusually fast and efficient ground delivery system. Repair and maintenance services, leasing and storage facilities for commercial and corporate aircraft are also available. Also within a short commute of Wilmington are both Philadelphia International Airport and Dover Air Force Base. Additionally the smaller public-use airports of New Garden, Brandywine, and Spitfire are within 20 miles of downtown Wilmington.

## Labor Force and Employment Outlook

Wilmington offers businesses a diverse labor force with a good mixture of blue- and white-collar workers. *Forbes* magazine rated the Wilmington-Newark and Dover metropolitan areas among the nation's "Best Places for Business and Careers" in the May 2000 edition.

The following is a summary of data regarding the Wilmington-Newark metropolitan area labor force, 2003 annual averages.

*Size of nonagricultural labor force:* 318,500

*Number of workers employed in . . .*
  *construction and mining:* 18,100
  *manufacturing:* 23,400

*trade, transportation and utilities:* 58,500
*information:* 6,500
*financial activities:* 39,500
*professional and business services:* 52,800
*educational and health services:* 38,300
*leisure and hospitality:* 26,000
*other services:* 13,500
*government:* 41,900

*Average hourly earnings of production workers employed in manufacturing:* $21.76

*Unemployment rate:* 4.0% (November 2004)

| *Largest employers* (2004; New Castle County, including Wilmington) | *Number of employees* |
|---|---|
| MBNA Corp. | 11,000 |
| EI DuPont de Nemours Co. | 9,600 |
| Christina Care Health Services | 6,500 |
| Alfred I. DuPont Institute (Medical Campus) | 2,800 |
| Astra-Zeneca | 2,400 |

## Cost of Living

In comparison with other eastern seaboard cities such as Philadelphia and New York, Wilmington boasts of relatively low living costs, particularly those associated with housing.

The following is a summary of data regarding several key cost of living factors for the Wilmington area.

*2004 (3rd Quarter) ACCRA Cost of Living Index:* 105.4 (U.S. average = 100.0)

*2004 (3rd Quarter) ACCRA Average House Price:* $247,820

*State income tax rate:* Ranges from 2.2% to 5.95%

*State sales tax rate:* None

*Local income tax rate:* 1.42%

*Local sales tax rate:* None

*Property tax rate:* $1.3348 per $100 of assessed valuation (assessed valuation = 100% of fair market value)

**Economic Information:** City of Wilmington Department of Commerce, City-County Building, 800 French St., Wilmington, DE 19801-3537; telephone (302)571-4169

# Education and Research

## Elementary and Secondary Schools

In 1976 the New Castle County School District was reorganized and divided into four separate districts: Brandywine,

Red Clay Consolidated, Christina (the largest), and Colonial. Each district encompasses some part of Wilmington along with other suburban communities, and each elects a seven-member board of education to govern its elementary and secondary schools. The New Castle County Vo-Tech School District provides vocational training for area students. The Christina School District offers special programs for gifted students, fine arts classes in all secondary schools, special education, including the Delaware Autistic Program, and the State's school for visually-impaired and hearing-impaired persons.

In addition to the public school system, there are seven private and parochial high schools and 10 private and parochial primary and middle schools that vary from college preparatory to religious training.

The following is a summary of data regarding Wilmington's Christina school district as of the 2002–2003 school year.

*Total enrollment:* 19,605

*Number of facilities*
  *elementary schools:* 20
  *junior high/middle schools:* 3
  *senior high schools:* 3
  *other:* 2 (Delaware Autism Program; Delaware School for the Deaf

*Student/teacher ratio:* 15:1

*Teacher salaries (2004)*
  *minimum:* $32,559
  *maximum:* $71,295

*Funding per pupil:* $9,373

The other Wilmington districts are as follows: Brandywine district (10,102 students in 18 buildings); Christina district (19,000 students in 28 buildings); Red Clay Consolidated district (16,000 students in 23 buildings); and New Castle County VoTech (3,300 students in 3 buildings).

### Colleges and Universities

Since the late 1990s five additional post-secondary institutions have established operations in downtown Wilmington. Much of this growth in post-secondary education in Wilmington was the result of an aggressive recruitment strategy by the Wilmington Renaissance Corporation, which called for the creation of a university campus district near Market Street. Together these efforts brought an additional 7,195 students to downtown Wilmington. Both Delaware State University and Drexel University have recently opened satellite campuses on Market Street. In addition, the Delaware College of Art and Design, Delaware's only professional art and design school, opened in 1997; and Springfield College also launched a center for human services near downtown.

Other major accredited institutions in the Wilmington metropolitan region include the University of Delaware (Newark, DE); West Chester University of Pennsylvania (West Chester, PA); Widener University, with its Delaware Law School, the state's only law school (Chester, PA and downtown Wilmington campus); and Wilmington College and Golden-Beacom College (both in Wilmington).

### Libraries and Research Centers

The Wilmington Institute Free Library system, consisting of the Wilmington, North Wilmington, Woodlawn, and La Biblioteca del Pueblo libraries, serves a population of 400,000 people and continues to expand in size, services offered, and collection of materials. Founded in 1788, the library houses more than 320,000 volumes, as well as a special collection of Delawareana, film and record collections, and an African American Collection of books, videos, and audio cassettes. Other public libraries include the Concord Pike, Kirkwood Highway, and Elsemere Public libraries.

Wilmington is also home to numerous special libraries. Among them are the Delaware Academy of Medicine's Lewis B. Flinn Library, devoted to consumer health; Delaware Art Museum Library; School of Law Library at Widener University; E. I. du Pont de Nemours and Company Law Library; Hagley Museum and Library; and the Historical Society of Delaware Library. Research centers located in Wilmington include the Delaware Biotechnology Institute, a public-private partnership doing scientific research that is helping to develop Delaware's growing life sciences industry. In addition, five state-sponsored Advanced Technology Centers provide research and development in the areas of laser optics, semiconductors, and advanced materials. Alfred I. du Pont Institute of the Nemours Foundation performs research in pediatric orthopedics, cytogenetics, and microbial genetics. Delaware All-Sports Research performs and publishes research in sports medicine.

***Public Library Information:*** Wilmington Institute Free Library, 10th and Market Streets, Wilmington, DE 19801; telephone (302)571-7400

# Health Care

Two of Delaware's largest medical facilities, Christina Care Health System and the Alfred I. du Pont Institute, are located in Wilmington. Christina Care comprises Christina Hospital, Eugene du Pont Preventive Medicine and Rehabilitation Institute, Riverside Long-term & Extended Care, and Wilmington Hospital. The center is a teaching hospital affiliated with Thomas Jefferson University, the University of Delaware, and Delaware Technical and Community College. Since 1940, the

Alfred I. du Pont Institute has treated children who suffer from crippling diseases. Today it is a multispecialty pediatric center researching problems in neurology, genetics, developmental medicine, plastic surgery and sports medicine. The institute also works with the Nemours Health Clinic to provide health services to the elderly.

Wilmington's other medical facilities include St. Francis Hospital and The Veteran's Administration Medical Center.

# Recreation

### Sightseeing

From the eighteenth-century homes in Wilmington Square to the country estates along the Brandywine, Wilmington's attractions are rich in history. Prominent among them is the legacy of one family. The du Ponts, who did so much to shape the city's economy, have also had a pervasive influence on its cultural life.

One of the du Pont's greatest contributions is Nemours Mansion and Gardens, the 300-acre estate of Alfred I. du Pont, who designed the mansion in the style of a Louis XVI chateau and filled it with European art works. Its 77 rooms are furnished with antique furniture, oriental rugs, tapestries, and outstanding paintings dating to the fifteenth century. Outside, formal gardens extend a third of a mile from the main vista of the mansion. Ten miles north is Longwood Gardens, the 1,050-acre horticultural masterpiece of Pierre Samuel du Pont. In spring, summer, and fall, visitors enjoy more than 350 acres of outdoor gardens, fountain displays, fireworks, theatrical productions, and concerts. During the winter months the main attraction is a group of heated conservatories that shelter many rare and exotic plants. Gardening enthusiasts can also experience naturalistic garden designs and native plants at their best at the Mt. Cuba Center, the former estate of Mr. and Mrs. Lammot Copeland du Pont, in nearby Greenville.

Historic Wilmington can be glimpsed at several locations in the area. Fort Christina State Park is the site of the original fort the Swedes built when they landed in 1638. Today visitors see a monument to that expedition by Swedish sculptor Carl Milles and the kind of log cabin that would have been built by an early settler. Next to the park is the Tall Ship *Kalmar Nyckel,* a full-size recreation of the ornate, armed ship that brought the early settlers here. The 139-foot ship is Delaware's sea- going Ambassador of Good Will. Erected in 1698, Holy Trinity Church (also known as Old Swedes Church) is the oldest church in the United States that stands as originally built and is still used for regular worship. Once of Swedish Lutheran affiliation, it has been used for Episcopal

services since 1791. Formerly the center of Wilmington's social and political life, Old Town Hall (1798) serves as a museum, while a beautiful Art Deco building across the street houses the Historical Society of Delaware's Museum offices and Research Library. Visitors can view exhibits pertaining to Delaware history at the Delaware History Museum, part of the complex. For military history buffs, the Air Mobility Command Museum, located in Hangar 1301 on Dover Air Force Base in Dover, Delaware, houses some of the most unique and distinguished military flying machines of the past 50 + years. The Grand Opera House is one of the finest examples of cast-iron architecture in America. Built in 1871, the meticulously restored theater serves as Delaware's Center for the Performing Arts. Rockwood, built in 1851 by Quaker merchant Joseph Shipley, serves as an outstanding example of rural Gothic architecture; the English-style country house and gardens are now administered by New Castle County's Department of Parks and Recreation. The mansion's furnishings include decorative arts and archives from the seventeenth to the early twentieth centuries. At Wilmington Square are four beautiful eighteenth-century houses, moved to the site in 1976, which are now used for meeting and office space by the Historical Society of Delaware.

Wilmington residents enjoy a total of more than 550 acres of park land, almost 200 acres of which comprise Brandywine Park. Designed by Frederick Law Olmsted, who created New York City's Central Park, Brandywine provides a setting of natural beauty only ten minutes from downtown Wilmington. Brandywine Zoo houses many exotic species of animals from North and South America and Africa. A focal point of Wilmington's waterfront attractions is the Port of Wilmington at the end of Christina and Terminal avenues. Visitors are invited to witness the day-to-day operations of one of the nation's busiest ports. Approximately four miles upstream, running from the Amtrak Station to the Shipyard Shops/Frawley Stadium/Bank One Riverfront Arts Center, is the Riverwalk with many Christina River attractions. The Christina Riverboat Company offers lunch, dinner, moonlight, and specialty cruises on a three-mile boat ride down the Christina Riverfront.

### Arts and Culture

The cultural tastes of Wilmington's benefactors are reflected in sites throughout the area, while widespread patronage sustains local artists and arts organizations. The Delaware State Arts Council, headquartered in Wilmington, is the mentor to many of the city's cultural groups. It directly supports monthly exhibitions of the visual arts and publishes a *Directory of Visual Artists.*

Theater, dance, and music productions figure prominently in the city's cultural life. Highlighting Wilmington's downtown renewal efforts is the 1,100-seat Grand Opera House,

**Wilmington's Old Town Hall, home to the Historical Society of Delaware's Museum and Library.**

home of the Delaware Symphony and OperaDelaware. Delaware's professional symphony orchestra performs more than 40 classical, pops, and chamber concerts each year, as well as touring engagements. One of the city's oldest arts companies, OperaDelaware performs two annual fully-staged productions with complete orchestra plus a Family Opera Theater production each spring. The Opera House also hosts stand-up comedians, jazz concerts, and world culture events on its 100-event annual schedule. The 400-seat Delaware Theatre Company offers a series of plays in its Christina riverfront location from November to April. Six professional first-run Broadway shows and an acclaimed Children's series are staged regularly from September to May at the 1,200-seat DuPont Theater (formerly the Playhouse Theatre) in the Hotel du Pont. The DuPont Theater is also the setting each December for a lavish production of the ''Nutcracker Ballet'' performed by the Wilmington Academy of the Dance. Other theater groups include the Wilmington Drama League, the New Candlelight Theater in Arden, and Three Little Bakers Dinner Theatre.

Like so many other attractions in the area, several of Wilmington's major museums and galleries are linked to the du Pont family. Henry Francis du Pont spent a lifetime collecting the finest American furniture and decorative arts made or used between 1640 and 1840. At Winterthur Museum, the furniture of Duncan Phyfe, the silver of Paul Revere, and room furnishings from all over the eastern seaboard are displayed in 200 period settings, from a New England kitchen to a Georgia Empire-style dining room. Three new galleries have been built adjacent to the existing museum. Surrounding the museum are 200 landscaped acres, reminiscent of an eighteenth-century English park, and Chandler Woods.

Eleuthere I. du Pont, discovering that high-quality black powder (gunpowder) was a scarce commodity in eighteenth-century America, began an industry that grew into one of the world's largest corporations. At Hagley Museum on the Brandywine the life of the nineteenth-century mill worker has been recreated. As visitors stroll along the banks of the river, they see a restored operating wooden water wheel, turbine-powered roll wheels, a vintage steam engine, a stone quarry, a machine shop, and a hydroelectric plant. Overlooking the powder yards is Eleutherian Mills, the Georgian-style country home built by E. I. du Pont in 1803. The Hagley Library is one of the finest repositories of industrial and manufacturing history in the United States.

The Delaware Museum of Natural History reflects the interests of its founder, John du Pont. Visitors encounter examples of Delaware flora and fauna. They can also walk across Australia's Great Barrier Reef, view an African waterhole, and enter the Hall of Birds, which features a 27-pound bird egg. In addition, the museum houses one of the world's finest shell collections, a scale model of the International Space Station, and a permanent dinosaur exhibit.

The Wilmington area's other museums include the Brandywine River Museum, which houses three generations of Wyeth family paintings as well as works by Howard Pyle, Maxfield Parrish, and many other American artists. The Rockwood Museum, a nineteenth-century country estate, features decorative arts from the seventeenth through nineteenth centuries, and the George Reed II House & Garden in Historic New Castle is a fine example of Georigan architecture. The First USA Riverfront Arts Center opened in 1998 as a major part of the redevelopment of the Christina Riverfront. This 25,000-square-foot exhibition center's first exhibition was Nicholas & Alexandra: The Last Imperial Family of Czarist Russia. The exhibit attracted more than 500,000 people during its six-month run. Other attractions include the Biggs Museum of American Art in Dover, the 33,000 square-foot Delaware Center for Contemporary Art in Wilmington, and the Delaware Center for Horticulture on DuPont Street.

The Delaware Art Museum closed in the fall of 2004 to begin a $25 million expansion, which will update the facility with a new facade, additional exhibit and conference space, outdoor gardens for sculptural displays, and improved handicap access. A world-class institution, the Museum hosts a 12,000 piece collection of traditional and contemporary paintings, sculpture, photography, and crafts that represent some of the finest American art from 1840 to the present, and includes the largest collection of Pre-Raphaelite paintings outside the United Kingdom. The expansion and renovation was due to be completed in spring 2005.

**Festivals and Holidays**

Ethnic festivals dot the city's calendar, beginning with the Irish Worker's Festival in April. In May, residents celebrate the Jewish Festival, as well as the annual Wilmington Flower Market week-long celebration, followed in June by Greek Days and the one-day annual Polish Festival (celebrating it's 50th year in 2006). June is also the month when thousands flock to Wilmington's Little Italy (the area surrounding St. Anthony of Padua Church) for the annual Italian Festival. In July, Rockwood Museum's Old-Fashioned Ice Cream Festival is a family favorite. In fall comes the Brandywine Arts Festival, when more than 250 artists from around the country exhibit their works along the riverbank. Visitors can find paintings, sculpture, jewelry, and crafts, or partake in an afternoon auction each day of the festival while they enjoy the scenic beauty of Brandywine Park. Many local museums host special Christmas events, including a Christmas at Rockwood, a Yuletide Tour at Winterthur, and a holiday Candlelight Tour at Hagley Mills Museum.

## Sports for the Spectator

The Wilmington Blue Rocks, a Class A minor league team affiliated with the 2004 World Champion Boston Red Sox, plays at the 6,532 seat Daniels S. Frawley Stadium on Madison Street. Racing enthusiasts in Wilmington enjoy the Delaware Park Race Track and Slots Casino, which hosts daytime thoroughbred racing from April to September at one of the nation's most picturesque sporting facilities. A different kind of racing draws Wilmingtonians to the Winterthur Point-to-Point on the first Sunday in May. Five amateur steeplechases are the main event, preceded by pony races and a parade of horse-drawn coaches and carriages. Every June, the du Pont Country Club welcomes the world's best women golfers for the LPGA McDonald's Championship. The First Union Cycling includes Wilmington in its Mid-Atlantic series of venues in May. The massively popular NASCAR auto racing circuit makes two stops annually at the Dover International Speedway. Blue Diamond Park in New Castle features Motocross, BMX, and ATV racing.

## Sports for the Participant

Wilmington residents have easy access to more than 4,500 acres of county park land. Those who prefer to ride their own horses are invited to try the equestrian trails at Bellevue State Park on the former estate of William du Pont. The park's nearly 300 acres offer bridle trails, indoor and outdoor equestrian tracks, a fishing pond, a fitness track, and the Bellevue Tennis Center. Public golf courses include Rock Manor Golf Course, Three Little Bakers Country Club, Frog Hollow Golf Course, Ed Oliver Golf Club, and the private Delaware National Country Club. Delaware's largest freshwater marsh is in Brandywine State Park, making it a favorite with birdwatchers. Avid fishermen reel in crappie, bluegill, and rock bass here. The park offers 12 miles of hiking and equestrian trails, as well as canoeing on Brandywine Creek. Rolling meadows and woodlands also make this a winter favorite for cross-country skiers. Wilmington has three YMCAs and a downtown racquetball facility.

## Shopping and Dining

Because there is no sales tax in Delaware, retailing is strong in Wilmington. The enclaves of Trolley Square, Historic New Castle, Hockessin, Little Italy, Newark, Centreville, and Kennett Square in PA, offer one-of-a-kind shops and boutiques. Market Street Mall offers specialty shops, restaurants, and cafes in the heart of Wilmington's central business district. Christina Mall (south of Wilmington, along I-95), features 4 major anchor stores and more than 130 shops. Concord Mall, on Concord Pike, has more than 80 specialty shops. The 200,000-square-foot Riverfront Wilmington's Shipyard Shops outlets offer daily discounts. Four art galleries featuring hand-made crafts and fine art from around the country are within a half-hour drive of each

other: The Andre Harvey Studio, Creations Fine Woodworking Gallery, Helen May Glickstein Gallery, and Sommerville Manning Gallery.

Fine dining is the norm for Wilmington's upscale population. City restaurants feature everything from Chesapeake Bay blue crabs to Japanese tempura. Many of the area's colonial inns and taverns are still serving guests. Fresh seafood and steaks are the norm at the waterside restaurants along Riverfront Wilmington. Mediterranean and Italian fare can be found at Wilmington's Little Italy neighborhood. Trolley Square has sidewalk cafes, cozy bistros, and lively pubs. For a taste of history, visitors and locals go to the colonial taverns in nearby historic New Castle.

*Visitor Information:* Wilmington Convention and Visitors Bureau, 100 West 10th Street, Suite 20, Wilmington, DE 19801; telephone (302)652-4088; fax (302)652-4726

# Convention Facilities

The Wilmington area offers meeting planners more than 4,000 rooms plus meeting facilities that range from intimate country getaways to large world-class conference centers accommodating 1,000 people in a single room. The area's largest event and convention venue is the Bank One Center on the Riverfront, which offers more than 60,000 square feet of exhibit and meeting space, including an additional 45,000 square feet new in 2005. Convenient to major airports, hotels, I-95, and Amtrak, the center has boardrooms, meeting rooms, ballrooms, state-of-the-art audio-visual, and more than 2,400 parking spaces.

New Castle County convention bureau officials boast of more than 40 hotels that specialize in medium-size and small conferences and meetings plus 400 restaurants—all set in the beautiful Brandywine Valley with its vistas made famous by three generations of Wyeths. One of the larger venues is Clayton Hall Conference Center at the University of Delaware, which offers state-of-the-art amenities accommodating intimate gatherings to 1,500-person conclaves. The Chadds Ford Ramada Inn & Conference Center in nearby Glenn Mills, Pennsylvania, offers almost 15,000 square feet made up of 13 well-lit meeting/banquet rooms, including a state-of-the-art auditorium with built-in AV and seating for up to 200 people. The Hotel du Pont is a historic property that includes 30 meeting rooms, five in the self-contained Executive Conference Center, and 11 rooms in a state-of-the-art High Tech Conference Center. Also located within the Hotel du Pont is the multipurpose 1,200-seat Du Pont Theater, available for meetings. Both the Embassy Suites Hotel and the Radisson Hotel and Suites Wilmington offer meeting space in the

Greater Wilmington Area. Unique meeting sites in Wilmington include the Delaware Art Museum, Delaware Museum of Natural History, and The Grand Opera House.

***Convention Information:*** Wilmington Convention and Visitors Bureau, 100 West 10th Street, Suite 20, Wilmington, DE 19801; telephone (302)652-4088; fax (302)652-4726

# Transportation

## Approaching the City

More than 580 flights arrive daily at the Philadelphia International Airport, making Wilmington (25 minutes away) easy to reach by plane. Door-to-door limousine service is available to all parts of the city.

Located in the middle of the heavily traveled northeast corridor, Wilmington is also convenient to reach by car. Interstate 95, the major north-south route from Maine to Florida, cuts through the western portion of the city. The Wilmington Bypass, I-495, connects I-95 with downtown and offers easy access to the Port of Wilmington. Travelers arriving on the New Jersey Turnpike from points north cross the Delaware River and enter Wilmington on I-295. In addition to the interstate highway system, U.S. routes 13, 40, 41, and 202 allow access to the city. With the completion of limited access Delaware-1, central and south Delaware to the Maryland border are now connected to Interstate 95.

Wilmington's Amtrak Station provides passenger service with connections to all major points. Travelers arriving from New York, Philadelphia, Baltimore, or Washington, D.C. can take the high speed Acela Express rapid metroliner as well as conventional Amtrak and SEPTA (commuter) trains. The station is a five-minute walk to downtown stores and hotels, and has facilities for both long-term and short-term parking. Currently more than 80 trains daily stop at the Amtrak Station.

## Traveling in the City

Because of Wilmington's small size, residents enjoy minimal levels of traffic congestion, noise pollution, and smog. If they choose, they can drive from the heart of downtown to the open spaces of the "chateau country" in fifteen minutes. A number of well-traveled routes carry commuters to the central business district from the densely populated suburbs. Well over 10,000 parking spaces in the downtown area allow for easy access to offices, restaurants, shops, and entertainment centers. To promote individual and business use of carpooling, vanpooling and bus service, Delaware's Commuter Service Administration has developed a free, computerized matching service including auto-geo coding for more than 17,000 streets in New Castle County.

Another alternative for city residents is public transportation. The Delaware Authority for Regional Transit (DART) operates 63 bus routes serving northern Delaware, including Wilmington and Newark. The Delaware Authority for Specialized Transit (DAST) provides lift-equipped buses for the elderly and the handicapped. Engineering studies for running trolleys down Market Street to connect the Brandywine River to the Amtrak station and the Shipyard Shops are underway.

# Communications

## Newspapers and Magazines

One Wilmington-based daily newspaper, *The News Journal,* serves the state of Delaware. Other Wilmington publications include: *Delaware Today,* a general-interest monthly magazine; *Big Shout Magazine,* featuring entertainment information; *The Dialog,* published by the Catholic Press of Wilmington; *Delaware Medical Journal*; and *Out & About,* an entertainment monthly.

## Television and Radio

Two television stations originate in Wilmington, one of which is an educational affiliate of the Public Broadcasting System. Comcast Cable provides cable television service to greater Wilmington. Wilmington viewers receive most programs from stations located in Philadelphia and other cities in Pennsylvania and New Jersey. The same is true of radio broadcasts; the city is home to four AM stations and three FM stations, but is considered part of a market that also encompasses eastern Pennsylvania (including Philadelphia) and northern New Jersey.

***Media Information:*** *The News Journal,* 950 West Basin Road, New Castle, DE 19720; telephone (302)324-2500 or (800)235-9100

## Wilmington Online

Brandywine School District. Available www.bsd.k12.de.us

Christina School District. Available www.christina.k12.de.us

City of Wilmington home page. Available www.ci.wilmington.de.us

Delaware Office of Economic Development. Available www.state.de.us/dedo

Delaware Online. Available www.delawareonline.com

New Castle County Economic Development Council. Available http://www.nccedc.com

New Castle County Online. Available www.newcastle comag.com

New Castle County VoTech. Available www.k12.de.us/ nccvotech

Red Clay Consolidated School District. Available www .redclay.k12.de.us

School district statistics. Available www.doe.state.de.us/ edstats/Menu/EdStats.htm

Wilmington Convention and Visitors Bureau. Available www.wilmcvb.org

Wilmington Public Library. Available www.wilmlib.org

## Selected Bibliography

Hoffecker, Carol E., *Corporate Capital: Wilmington in the Twentieth Century.* (Philadelphia: Temple University Press, 1983)

Lincoln, Anna T., *Wilmington, Delaware: Three Centuries under Four Flags, 1609-1937*(Kennikat Press, 1977)

Thompson, Priscilla, and Sally O'Byrne, *Wilmington's Waterfront* (Charleston, S.C.: Arcadia Publishing, 1999)

# FLORIDA

# The State in Brief

**Nickname:** Sunshine State
**Motto:** In God we trust

**Flower:** Orange blossom
**Bird:** Mockingbird

**Area:** 65,754.59 square miles (2000; U.S. rank: 22nd)
**Elevation:** Ranges from sea level to 345 feet above sea level
**Climate:** Humid with abundant sunshine; ranges from subtropical to tropical

**Admitted to Union:** March 3, 1845
**Capital:** Tallahassee
**Head Official:** Governor John Ellis Bush (R) (until 2007)

## Population
    **1980:** 9,746,000
    **1990:** 12,938,000
    **2000:** 15,982,378
    **2004 estimate:** 17,397,161
    **Percent change, 1990–2000:** 23.5%
    **U.S. rank in 2004:** 4th
    **Percent of residents born in state:** 32.7% (2000)
    **Density:** 296.4 people per square mile (2000)
    **2002 FBI Crime Index Total:** 905,957

## Racial and Ethnic Characteristics (2000)
    **White:** 12,465,029
    **Black or African American:** 2,335,505
    **American Indian and Alaska Native:** 53,541
    **Asian:** 266,256
    **Native Hawaiian and Pacific Islander:** 8,625
    **Hispanic or Latino (may be of any race):** 2,682,715
    **Other:** 477,107

## Age Characteristics (2000)
    **Population under 5 years old:** 945,823
    **Population 5 to 19 years old:** 3,102,809
    **Percent of population 65 years and over:** 17.6%
    **Median age:** 38.7 years (2000)

## Vital Statistics
    **Total number of births (2003):** 212,144
    **Total number of deaths (2003):** 168,598 (infant deaths, 1,576)
    **AIDS cases reported through 2003:** 43,223

## Economy
    **Major industries:** Agriculture, tourism, manufacturing, services, trade, government
    **Unemployment rate:** 4.5% (December 2004)
    **Per capita income:** $29,972 (2003; U.S. rank: 25th)
    **Median household income:** $29,294 (3-year average, 2001-2003)
    **Percentage of persons below poverty level:** 14.9% (3-year average, 2001-2003)
    **Income tax rate:** None
    **Sales tax rate:** 6.0% on most items

# Jacksonville

## The City in Brief

**Founded:** 1816 (incorporated 1832)

**Head Official:** Mayor John Peyton (R) (since 2003)

**City Population**
    **1980:** 540,920
    **1990:** 635,230
    **2000:** 735,617
    **2003 estimate:** 773,781
    **Percent change, 1990–2000:** 15.8%
    **U.S. rank in 1980:** 53rd
    **U.S. rank in 1990:** 15th (State rank: 1st)
    **U.S. rank in 2000:** 20th (State rank: 1st)

**Metropolitan Area Population**
    **1980:** 722,000
    **1990:** 906,727
    **2000:** 1,100,491

    **Percent change, 1990–2000:** 21.3%
    **U.S. rank in 1980:** 50th
    **U.S. rank in 1990:** 47th
    **U.S. rank in 2000:** 45th

**Area:** 758 square miles (2000)
**Elevation:** ranges from sea level to 71 feet
**Average Annual Temperature:** 68.0° F
**Average Annual Precipitation:** 51.3 inches

**Major Economic Sectors:** finance, insurance, government, manufacturing, wholesale and retail trade
**Unemployment rate:** 4.2% (December 2004)
**Per Capita Income:** $20,337 (1999)

**2002 FBI Crime Index Total:** 51,021

**Major Colleges and Universities:** University of North Florida, Jacksonville University, Florida Community College at Jacksonville

**Daily Newspaper:** *Florida Times-Union*

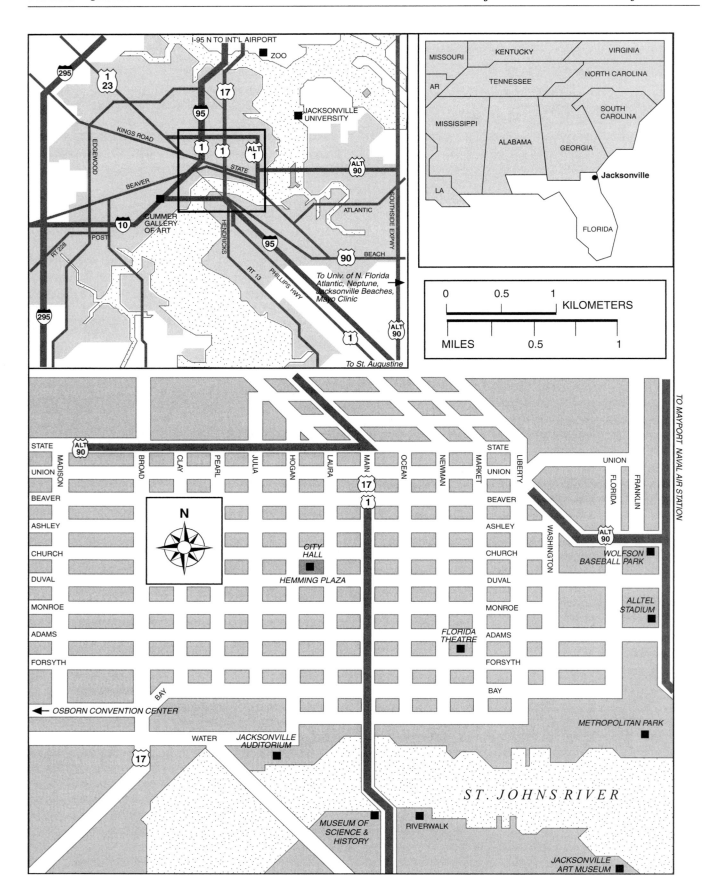

# Introduction

Jacksonville is a cosmopolitan riverside city that is one of the largest cities in area in the United Sates. In addition to the miles of beautiful sea coastline nearby, tourists are drawn to this rapidly growing city by its sunny climate, recreational activities, culture, and a bustling downtown, as well as sites such as a restored Civil War fortress, America's oldest city (which is nearby), and the rich African American cultural heritage evident in many of its historical sites. With its variety of naval facilities that remain a major employer, Jacksonville is one of the most requested U.S. Navy duty stations.

Within comfortable driving distance from many large southeastern metro areas, Jacksonville is a major transportation and distribution center. Developments in the late twentieth and early twenty-first centuries attest to the success of the city's efforts to diversify and revitalize the downtown area, which had stagnated. City leaders successfully attracted new companies and retained existing businesses, and by 2004 Jacksonville was home to three *Fortune 500* companies. Only 12 years after winning an NFL franchise, the Jacksonville Jaguars, the city hosted Super Bowl XXXIX in 2005.

Jacksonville consistently appears at the top of rankings in terms of quality of life and business. In March 2004 *Inc.* magazine named Jacksonville one of the top 10 large U.S. cities for doing business. *Money* magazine placed the city in the number three spot in its ''Best Places to Retire'' ranking in July 2004. And in the February 2005 issue of *Men's Fitness,* Jacksonville was ranked as one of the top 20 fittest cities in the nation.

# Geography and Climate

Jacksonville is located in the northeast corner of Florida on the banks of the St. Johns River, adjacent to the Atlantic Ocean. The city has four distinct seasons: cool in spring and fall, mild in winter, and warm in summer with plenty of sunshine year round. There was only one serious hurricane in the twentieth century (Hurricane Dora in 1964) as natural phenomena form a weather shield for the area.

**Area:** 758 square miles (2000)

**Elevation:** Ranges from sea level to 71 feet

**Average Temperatures:** January, 53.5° F; July 81° F; annual average, 68.0° F

**Average Annual Precipitation:** 51.3 inches

# History

### Town Founded on River Site

Historians hold that the Timucua tribe lived on the site of today's Jacksonville since before the year 2000 B.C. The first documented European visitors to the area were a group of French Huguenots, led by Rene de Laudonniere, who sailed into the mouth of the St. Johns River in 1562. They soon founded Fort Caroline (on the river north of the present downtown), which was captured by the Spanish during a bloody massacre in 1565. The Florida region became a territory of the United States in 1821, following a 300-year period of battles between Spain, France, and Great Britain. That same year Georgia plantation owner Isaiah D. Hart moved to the narrowest spot of the St. Johns River known as ''Cowford,'' where cows were transported by ferry across the river. On this site in 1822 Hart laid out the plans for the town of Jacksonville, which he named after General Andrew Jackson, provisional governor of the Florida Territory who later became president. The small community of 100 people was chartered as a town and elected its first mayor in 1832. In 1845 Florida became a state. By 1859, when Jacksonville was chartered as a city, it had become the state's major port, exporting both timber goods and cotton.

### Jacksonville During the Latter Nineteenth Century

Jacksonville was not part of the Confederacy during the time of the Civil War (1861–1865); however, both sides fought for the land and the Union Army occupied the city on four different occasions. Following the battle of Olustee, which took place in the city, wounded Union soldiers were brought to Jacksonville's homes and churches, some of which were converted to military hospitals. Union forces destroyed the city but it was quickly rebuilt.

During the second half of the nineteenth century, Jacksonville had a population of about 7,500 permanent residents and drew more than 75,000 tourists annually. Jacksonville began to grow and prosper during the 1870s with the development of its lumber and shipping industries. Like many other east Florida coastal areas, Jacksonville's beach communities became established with the development of the railway system. A group of Jacksonville businessmen united in the late 1800s to construct a rail system that ended at the beach east of town. In time deluxe hotels were built, beach property was sold, and in 1888 the first direct railroad service between the city and the North was established. That same year, 427 people were killed by a yellow fever epidemic that assailed the city.

### Fire Causes Large-Scale Destruction

By 1900 the city had a population approaching 30,000 people. The new century dawned with the Great Fire of 1901 when embers from a stove ignited materials at the Cleveland Fiber Factory. Before it was extinguished, the fire had destroyed nearly 2,400 buildings, decimated 146 city blocks, killed 7 people, left 10,000 people homeless, and destroyed $15 million worth of property. Fortunately, the city was once again quickly rebuilt and the population grew to more than 91,000 people by 1920.

## Briefly a Film Center; Industry Revives

Jacksonville was an important site for the early development of the film industry, and Florida's first motion picture studios opened there in 1908. The warm weather year round and the low cost of labor and housing boosted this development, which continued until the early 1920s, when the industry moved to California.

The population of Jacksonville stood at more than 173,000 people by 1940. Mayport Naval Base and two naval air stations were built in the city during the Second World War (1941–1945). Suburban sprawl during the 1950s resulted in a loss of population for the city, while the county population grew. In 1968 the city and Duval County consolidated, and Jacksonville grew in the rankings of U.S. cities by size from sixty-first to twenty-second.

In the period of the 1960s and 1970s local focus was directed toward industrial diversification and development of the city's port facilities. Redevelopment efforts transformed the downtown area, and new service industries, especially finance and insurance, were booming as the city entered the twenty-first century.

Jacksonville expanded into a new direction when it was awarded a team franchise by the National Football League in 1993. The Jacksonville Jaguars draw thousands of fans to the downtown area on a regular basis, adding lifeblood to the local businesses. This newfound football momentum sharply increased when the city hosted Super Bowl XXXIX in February 2005, the smallest market ever to do so. ''I hope this will be an experience that will introduce the city to the world,'' said Mayor John Peyton in the *Los Angeles Times*.

**Historical Information:** Jacksonville Historical Society, 317 A. Philip Randolph Blvd., Jacksonville, FL 32202; telephone (904)665-0064; fax (904)665-0069

# Population Profile

## Metropolitan Area Residents
*1980:* 722,000
*1990:* 906,727
*2000:* 1,100,491

*Percent change, 1990–2000:* 21.3%
*U.S. rank in 1980:* 50th
*U.S. rank in 1990:* 47th
*U.S. rank in 2000:* 45th

## City Residents
*1980:* 540,920
*1990:* 635,230
*2000:* 735,617
*2003 estimate:* 773,781
*Percent change, 1990–2000:* 15.8%
*U.S. rank in 1980:* 53rd
*U.S. rank in 1990:* 15th (State rank: 1st)
*U.S. rank in 2000:* 20th (State rank: 1st)

*Density:* 970.9 people per square mile (based on 2000 land area)

*Racial and ethnic characteristics* (2000)
  White: 474,307
  Black or African American: 213,514
  American Indian and Alaska Native: 2,474
  Asian: 20,427
  Native Hawaiian and Pacific Islander: 448
  Hispanic or Latino (may be of any race): 30,594
  Other: 9,816

*Percent of residents born in state:* 49.2% (2000)

*Age characteristics* (2000)
  Population under 5 years old: 53,938
  Population 5 to 9 years old: 55,679
  Population 10 to 14 years old: 55,311
  Population 15 to 19 years old: 51,816
  Population 20 to 24 years old: 50,844
  Population 25 to 34 years old: 114,352
  Population 35 to 44 years old: 123,558
  Population 45 to 54 years old: 96,664
  Population 55 to 59 years old: 32,580
  Population 60 to 64 years old: 24,960
  Population 65 to 74 years old: 40,738
  Population 75 to 84 years old: 26,678
  Population 85 years and older: 8,499
  Median age: 33.8 years

*Births* (Duval County, 2003)
  Total number: 12,421

*Deaths* (Duval County, 2003)
  Total number: 6,838 (of which, 130 were infants under the age of 1 year)

*Money income* (1999)
  Per capita income: $20,337
  Median household income: $40,316
  Total households: 308,736

*Number of households with income of . . .*
    less than $10,000: 27,216
    $10,000 to $14,999: 16,735
    $15,000 to $24,999: 38,253
    $25,000 to $34,999: 40,276
    $35,000 to $49,999: 52,391
    $50,000 to $74,999: 57,369
    $75,000 to $99,999: 26,044
    $100,000 to $149,999: 17,492
    $150,000 to $199,999: 4,010
    $200,000 or more: 4,875

*Percent of families below poverty level:* 9.4% (43.9% of which were female householder families with related children under 5 years)

*2002 FBI Crime Index Total:* 51,021

# Municipal Government

The city of Jacksonville and Duval County voted in 1968 to establish a consolidated government designed to use all community resources in solving problems that affect the entire county area. The city's strong-mayor form of government is divided into 14 districts of nearly equal population, each of which is represented by a council member. Five additional council members represent the entire community as a whole. These 19 council members are the legislative body of Jacksonville, and are elected to four-year terms.

**Head Official:** Mayor John Peyton (R) (since 2003; current term expires June 2007)

**Total Number of City Employees:** 8,019 (2004)

*City Information:* City of Jacksonville, 117 W. Duval St., Jacksonville, FL 32202; telephone (904)630-CITY

# Economy

## Major Industries and Commercial Activity

With its diverse economic base, young, energetic population, and high quality of life, Jacksonville experienced substantial growth during the latter decades of the twentieth century and into the twenty-first.

The city is a transportation hub, with a 38-foot deepwater port that ranks with New York as the top two vehicle-handling ports in the nation. It is served by four airports, three seaports, a highway system that links the city to three major interstates, and a rail system served by three railroads—CSX, Norfolk Southern, and Florida East Coast.

The automotive parts and accessories industry is attracted by this logistics network, as well as the fact that less than two percent of the city's manufacturing industry is unionized. Jacksonville was selected as the site of Southeast Toyota, the largest distributor in the United States, and of a distribution center for General Motors Corp. that serves Georgia, South Carolina, and Florida.

Pulp and paper mills play substantial roles in the local economy, and Georgia Pacific Corp. and Smurfit-Stone Container Corp. are two of the area's largest manufacturers. Construction equipment and building materials is another key segment of the Jacksonville economy, with Ring Power Corp., U.S. Gypsum, and Florida Rock Industries Inc. among the top employers in the region. Other large manufacturers are Northrop Grumman Corp. (aircraft), Anheuser-Busch Companies Inc. (beer), Vistakon (optical products), Swisher International Inc. (cigars and smokeless tobacco), Medtronic Xomed (surgical products), and Dura Automotive Systems Inc. (automotive components).

Three important naval air stations within the city limits and Kings Bay Submarine Base nearby give Jacksonville one of the largest military presences in the country, topped only by Norfolk, Virginia, and San Diego, California. The total economic impact of the bases in the community is about $6.1 billion annually.

Aviation is a natural fit to Jacksonville. Of the 6,000 naval personnel that exit the military every year in Jacksonville, over 80 percent remain in northeast Florida, supplying the area with a rich resource of aviation skills and related technical experience. Additionally, more than 15,000 students enroll in aviation-related programs in the Jacksonville area. One such program is Florida Community College of Jacksonville's Aviation Center of Excellence, located at the Cecil Commerce Center, which is also home to one of four airports in Jacksonville. The city was experiencing a boom in the aviation industry in the early 2000s. Flightstar Aircraft Services Inc. began operations in Jacksonville in 2000, Kaman Aerospace Corp. launched business there three years later, and Embraer broke ground in 2004 on a facility to accommodate work on a $879 million Army contract to assemble surveillance aircraft.

Import-export operations are a vital segment of Florida's economy, and Jacksonville is a major center for that activity. World Trade Center Jacksonville, one of six trade centers in the state, assists Florida companies to enter or expand into overseas markets. Along with an international trade library housing 2,500 volumes and 700 periodicals, it provides basic and intensive research, offers monthly seminars on various trade topics, and permits use of its boardroom and several meeting rooms at no charge. Jacksonville is also a pilot city for TradeRoots, an initiative of the U.S. Chamber of Commerce and the National Chamber Foundation, that studies the benefits that trade brings to local communities. The Jacksonville Port Authority manages the Free Trade Zone, an area in which goods arriving from a foreign country are temporarily exempt from import duties unless and until they are permanently delivered to the U.S. The city is home to Foreign Trade Zone #64 and there are designated customs facilities at the Jacksonville International Airport. The city's top exports are building materials, medical/health and beauty products, transportation equipment, food and restaurant equipment, construction equipment, packaging, generators, and chemicals.

Jacksonville, once abandoned by the motion picture and television industry, is experiencing a renaissance. The Jacksonville Film and Television Office was formed to attract film and video production to the area and helps streamline the production process. As a result, numerous motion pictures, television movies, commercials, and videos were produced in Jacksonville in recent years. Each movie or television series filmed there can add millions of dollars to the local economy, through housing, hiring of a local labor crew, catering, special heavy equipment rental, and expenses. The city was the filming location for the 2004 remake of the film *The Manchurian Candidate*. The Jacksonville Economic Development Commission reports that the industry had an economic impact of more than $99 million in fiscal year 2002/2003.

*Items and goods produced:* aircraft, machinery, paper and paper products, building products, beer, soft drinks, tobacco, and optical and surgical products

## Incentive Programs—New and Existing Companies

*Local programs*—Cornerstone is the economic development initiative of the Jacksonville Regional Chamber of Commerce. It is led by a group of companies and individuals who provide the leadership and resources to foster business expansion and relocation in Jacksonville. Investment dollars are channeled into business recruitment, existing business services, education and workforce preparation, and special economic initiatives.

Several incentive programs are managed at the local level. Portions of downtown Jacksonville are part of either the Empowerment Zone or the Enterprise Zone, each of which offers tax or wage credits to businesses based on the number of new jobs created. The Northwest Jacksonville Area Fund makes available grants or loans for infrastructure improvements, facade renovation, and purchase of land or buildings. The Qualified Target Industry Tax Refund is extended to companies that are on the list of industries identified by the city as desirable additions to the local economy. Similarly,

Targeted Economic Development Area Special Funds are designed to induce the location of high economic value projects to critical areas of Jacksonville. Lastly, Industrial Development Revenue Bonds afford manufacturing companies access to low-interest, tax-exempt loans.

The Chamber of Commerce maintains close relationships with the City of Jacksonville, the Jacksonville Economic Development Commission, the Jacksonville Port Authority, and the 4,000 local businesses that are Chamber members and Cornerstone investors. The businesses that have located or expanded in Jacksonville cite the many city and state incentives that are available, the support of city and business leaders, and the fact that the consolidated city-county government allows for faster permitting and less bureaucratic red tape overall.

*State programs*—Enterprise Florida is a partnership between Florida's government and business leaders and is the principal economic development organization for the state of Florida. Enterprise Florida's mission is to increase economic opportunities for all Floridians by supporting the creation of quality jobs, a well-trained workforce, and globally competitive businesses. It pursues this mission in cooperation with its statewide network of economic development partners.

Among the incentive programs managed at the state level is the Economic Development Transportation Fund, which provides up to $2 million to fund the cost of transportation projects such as access roads and road widening required for the establishment, expansion, or retention of businesses in Florida. The Brownfield Bonus Program, which is available to most of downtown Jacksonville, extends a bonus for each new job created. The state also offers various sales and use tax exemptions for machinery and equipment purchase, electric energy, research and development, and other aspects of doing business in the area.

*Job training programs*—The Workforce Development Board (WDB), commonly known as Jobs & Education Partnership, is a part of Enterprise Florida. WDB provides policy, planning, and oversight for job training programs funded under the federal Workforce Investment Act, along with vocational training, adult education, employment placement, and other workforce programs administered by a variety of state and local agencies. Regional Workforce Development Boards operate under charters approved by the Workforce Development Board. The 24 regional boards have primary responsibility for direct services through a state-wide network of One-Stop Career systems.

State and local workforce development efforts are concentrated on three broad initiatives. First Jobs/First Wages focuses on preparing workers for entry-level employment including the School-to-Work and WAGES programs. High

Skill/High Wages targets the higher skills needs of employers and trains workers for advancement through such programs as Performance Based Incentive Funding, Occupational Forecasting Conference/Targeted Occupations, Quick Response Training, and Incumbent Worker Training. One-Stop Career Centers are the central elements of the One-Stop system that provide integrated services to employers, workers, and jobseekers.

## Development Projects

The Better Jacksonville Plan was approved by voters in 2000. This plan increased the sales tax by a half-cent to raise $2.25 billion over 30 years to fund road improvements, environmental clean-up and conservation, the Northwest Jacksonville Economic Development Fund, and the construction of new public facilities downtown. It also enabled the establishment of Cecil Commerce Center, a mixed-use industrial/business park located about 20 minutes from downtown Jacksonville. Approximately 4,800 acres are available for light industrial expansion, with another 800 set aside for heavy industrial use. Also zoned for commercial, recreational, and aviation use, Cecil Commerce Center provides the setting to attract more distribution, manufacturing, and aviation economic activities to the city.

Also established in 2000 was Downtown Vision, Inc. (DVI), a not-for-profit organization designed to bolster the downtown community and promote it as an ideal venue for business and tourism. Its initiatives include programs to make the downtown area clean and safe, to market the area through television programs, radio spots, and publications, to tackle transportation and parking issues, and retain and attract business. In 2003 DVI launched a Downtown Image campaign that included a new logo and tagline: Downtown Jacksonville—Not Your Ordinary Neighborhood.

Cornerstone, the city's economic development initiative, reported that 60,000 new jobs were created by companies expanding or relocating to Jacksonville between 1999 and 2004. CSX Corp. and Fidelity National Financial, Inc. relocated their corporate headquarters to the city in 2003, joining Winn-Dixie Stores, Inc. in the ranks of *Fortune 500* companies headquartered in Jacksonville. Cingular Wireless also added 400 new jobs to the area that year. Major expansions and relocations the following year include Washington Mutual, which created 725 new jobs, and State Farm, Option One, and Wal-Mart Distribution, each of which added 300 new jobs. It's no wonder that *Expansion Management* magazine rated Jacksonville in the top 10 "Hottest Cities in America" for each of the six years the list has been published, of which Jacksonville was ranked number one three times.

*Economic Development Information:* Jacksonville Regional Chamber of Commerce, 3 Independent Dr., Jacksonville, FL 32202; telephone (904)366-6680; fax (904)353-

6343. Enterprise Florida, 390 N. Orange Ave., Ste. 1300, Orlando, FL 32801; telephone (407)316-4600; fax (407)316-4599. Downtown Vision, Inc., 214 N. Hogan St., Ste. 120, Jacksonville, FL 32202; telephone (904)634-0303; fax (904)634-8988.

## Commercial Shipping

The hub of seven major highways—I-10, I-95, I-295, and U.S. Highways 1, 17, 90, and 301—Jacksonville has a straight shipping line to the Midwest, West, and Northeast. It is served by more than 100 trucking lines, three major railroads, and Jacksonville International Airport. As the largest deepwater port in the South Atlantic, Jacksonville is the leading U.S. port for automobile imports.

## Labor Force and Employment Outlook

Jacksonville is an attractive site for expanding companies, in part because of its abundance of workers due to in-migration, natural growth, a strong military presence, and the area's educational institutions. The metropolitan area population, which topped 1.1 million in 2000, is significantly younger than all major Florida cities, with a median age of under 34 years old.

Relocating businesses are drawn to the area's quality of life, its sunshine, and its sports, recreational, and cultural opportunities, as well as the region's emphasis on well-planned growth. Between 1999 and 2004, approximately 60,000 new jobs were created by companies expanding or relocating to Jacksonville. In its September 2003 issue, *Business 2.0* magazine reported the 10-year projected job growth rate for the city to be 24.8 percent.

The following is a summary of data regarding the Jacksonville metropolitan area labor force, 2003 annual averages.

*Size of nonagricultural labor force:* 559,700

*Number of workers employed in . . .*
　　*manufacturing:* 33,000
　　*trade, transportation and utilities:* 124,200
　　*information:* 12,500
　　*financial activities:* 57,300
　　*professional and business services:* 84,600
　　*educational and health services:* 64,100
　　*leisure and hospitality:* 52,100
　　*other services:* 25,600
　　*government:* 69,700

*Average hourly earnings of production workers employed in manufacturing:* $14.09 (2003 statewide average)

*Unemployment rate:* 4.2% (December 2004)

*Largest employers*
*(Duval County)*            *Number of employees*

| | |
|---|---|
| Naval Air Station | 19,537 |
| Naval Station Mayport | 15,293 |
| Duval County Public Schools | 15,000 |
| City of Jacksonville | 8,019 |
| Winn-Dixie Stores, Inc. | 7,238 |
| Blue Cross Blue Shield of Florida, Inc. | 7,000 |
| Publix Distribution Center | 6,615 |
| Baptist Health System | 5,600 |
| CSX Corp. | 4,400 |
| Citibank | 4,000 |
| Bank of America Corp. | 4,000 |

## Cost of Living

Jacksonville ranks lowest among the five major metropolitan statistical areas in Florida and lower than many comparable cities nationwide in terms of cost of living. Housing costs are among the least expensive in Florida among cities with populations over 500,000.

The following is a summary of data regarding several key cost of living factors for the Jacksonville area.

*2004 (3rd Quarter) ACCRA Average House Price:* $225,636

*2004 (3rd Quarter) ACCRA Cost of Living Index:* 92.2 (U.S. average = 100.0)

*State income tax rate:* None for personal income; 5.5 percent of state's portion of federal taxable income for corporations

*State sales tax rate:* 6.0%

*Local income tax rate:* None

*Local sales tax rate:* 1.0%

*Property tax rate:* $19.3913 per $1,000 (2004)

**Economic Information:** Jacksonville Regional Chamber of Commerce, 3 Independent Dr., Jacksonville, FL 32202; telephone (904)366-6680

# Education and Research

## Elementary and Secondary Schools

Duval County Public Schools, the 20th largest school system in the nation, serves about 127,500 students. The system is run by a seven-member Board of Education, who are elected for four-years terms, and who appoint the superintendent. A magnet school program permits students to choose to attend specialized schools in such areas as language, arts, or mathematics. The Duval County Public Schools enforce a mandatory uniform policy for elementary and middle school students throughout the district.

The following is a summary of data regarding the Duval County public schools as of the 2004–2005 school year.

*Total enrollment:* approximately 127,500

*Number of facilities*
   *elementary schools:* 104
   *junior high/middle schools:* 25
   *senior high schools:* 17
   *other:* 3 exceptional student centers, 5 special schools, 2 academies of technology, and 7 charter schools

*Student/teacher ratio:* 17:1

*Teacher salaries*
   *minimum:* $31,000
   *maximum:* $60,489

*Funding per pupil:* $5,672

There are 103 private schools in the Jacksonville area, with an enrollment of more than 15,000 students. Included are boarding schools and day schools, both coeducational and single sex. Many of these schools are church-related and some are for students with special needs.

**Public Schools Information:** Duval County Public Schools, 1701 Prudential Dr., Jacksonville, FL 32207; telephone (904)390-2126

## Colleges and Universities

Nine institutions of higher learning serve the Jacksonville area. In addition, several satellite campuses, such as the Columbia College Navy Campus, established at naval bases also serve the civilian population. The University of North Florida, a state school, enrolls more than 12,000 students, and the privately run Jacksonville University has 2,100 students. The University of Florida in nearby Gainesville has 16 colleges and four schools. Florida Community College at Jacksonville has a student population of 41,000 full-time and part-time students, making it one of the largest such institutions in the country. Other higher education facilities include historically African American Edward Waters College; Jones College, specializing in business and computers; and St. Johns River and Lake City community colleges. There are five vocational/technical schools, including Florida Technical College and ITT Technical Institute.

The Florida Coastal School of Law and satellite campuses of Webster, Embry-Riddle Aeronautical, Central Michigan, Southern Illinois, and Florida A&M universities, and of St. Leo and Columbia colleges also serve Jacksonville-area students.

## Libraries and Research Centers

The Jacksonville Public Libraries include the main library, 20 branches, and one bookmobile. The library has nearly 2 million volumes and subscribes to more than 2,400 periodicals. Special collections are devoted to Floridiana, music, and genealogy. There are at least 19 other libraries in the city. Some are affiliated with higher educational institutions, while others are associated with religious groups, research centers, or the U.S. Navy. Their collections focus on such areas as art, science, health care delivery, law, business, education, and liberal arts.

The Center for Local Government Administration, First Coast Technology Park, Center for Public Leadership, and the Institute of Police Technology and Management are associated with the University of North Florida. Jacksonville State University conducts research on mathematics and on business and economics.

***Public Library Information:*** Jacksonville Public Libraries, 122 North Ocean Street, Jacksonville, FL 32202-3374; telephone (904)630-2665

# Health Care

Jacksonville's health care system has an approximately $2.5 billion annual impact on the local economy. There are more than 2,300 physicians in the area, 19 clinics, and 5 major general hospitals: University Medical Center, Baptist Medical Center, St. Luke's Hospital, St. Vincent's Medical Center, and Columbia Memorial Hospital.

Jacksonville is home to a branch of the renowned Mayo Clinic, which provides medical diagnosis, treatment, and surgery in more than 50 specialties. Opened in 1986, the Jacksonville facility was the first extension of Mayo Clinic of Rochester, Minnesota. Between 1986 and 2003, its 316 staff physicians and scientists treated approximately 665,000 patients. In 2002 the clinic opened the doors of the Griffin Cancer Research Building, its first facility devoted primarily to cancer research. Patients of the Mayo Clinic who need hospitalization are admitted to nearby St. Luke's Hospital, a 289-bed facility that affiliated with Mayo Clinic in 1987.

Also affiliated with the Mayo Clinic of Jacksonville is the Nemours Children's Clinic, an ambulatory care center that provides subspecialty services for children with complex medical or surgical problems. Sixty pediatric specialists treat 38,000 children each year. The clinic, located on south bank of the St. Johns River, is connected to the Wolfson Children's Hospital.

# Recreation

## Sightseeing

The hub of Florida's First Coast has much to offer visitors with its theaters, museums, art galleries, riverboat cruises, beautiful fountains, outstanding musical events, and historic sites.

Jacksonville's miles of beautiful wide beach area has three main sections: Atlantic Beach, Neptune Beach, and Jacksonville Beach. The Jacksonville Beach Pier is a place known for fishing and people-watching; and artifacts, paintings, and lighthouse models are the focus at the American Lighthouse Museum in Jacksonville Beach. The beach's Seawalk Pavilion features music concerts at its 2,000-seat open air auditorium. The Pablo Historical Park, a few blocks off the beach, preserves the area's railroad history with a nineteenth-century station master's house, a railroad depot, and a 1911 steam locomotive. The nostalgic autoferry Jean Ribault carries visitors to the nearby fishing village of Mayport, home of a large commercial shrimp fleet, as well as to historic Fort George Island. Mayport Naval Air Station, one of the nation's largest navy ship facilities, is located in this charming community. Favorite beach area recreation and camping sites are the Kathryn Abbey Hanna State Park with 450 acres of picnic areas, salt and freshwater fishing, and Little Talbot Island State Park beach and campground.

Jacksonville's beautiful downtown area, which has seen more than a billion dollars in restoration, is centered around the shores of the St. Johns River. On the north bank of the river is Jacksonville Landing, a festive marketplace featuring fine dining, boutiques, and an open courtyard that frequently offers entertainment. Located at the landing is the Jacksonville Maritime Museum, which contains artifacts embracing all facets of the maritime scene from historical to technical. Across the river on the Southbank is the Riverwalk. Its wooden boardwalk, lined with shops, restaurants, and outdoor vendors, extends for more than a mile along the river, allowing visitors a wonderful view of the city's skyline. At the end of the Riverwalk is Friendship Park, the site of one of the tallest fountains in the world. Water taxis offer an enjoyable way to cross the St. Johns River.

The Jacksonville Zoological Gardens, located on the city's north side, consists of 89 acres and houses more than 1,000 animals. An African veldt (an open grazing area typical of southern Africa) has been recreated and visitors can experience it firsthand on a wood boardwalk. The Okavango Village is a replica of an African riverfront village that features a dock, wildlife exhibits, a petting zoo and a river shuttle back and forth from downtown. Tours that display all the steps of the beer-making process are available at the Anheuser-Busch Brewery. Visitors can also watch Oreo cookies and other

**St. Augustine Lighthouse near Jacksonville.**

confections move along the conveyor belt at the Peterbrooke Chocolatier production line on San Marco Boulevard. The World Golf Village is home to the World Golf Hall of Fame, a PGA Tour Academy, and an IMAX theater.

The Fort Caroline national memorial is the site of the first Protestant settlement in the United States. Established in 1564, the site overlooks the St. Johns River and includes a replica of the original fort. Located on Fort George Island, the 1792 Zephaniah Kingsley Plantation contains the remains of slave quarters. Nature walks are available at the Nature Trails at the University of North Florida, the only state university in the country located in a protected wildlife area. Self-guided and expert-guided walking tours of historical areas around the city are well worth the exploration.

Located 25 miles from the city, Fernandina Beach is a 300-year-old town that was once a haven for pirates and smugglers and today features many restored buildings and eighteenth-century homes. A half-hour south of Jacksonville by car is the nation's oldest city, St. Augustine. A walk along the recently restored St. George Street, with its authentic Spanish-Colonial homes and quaint shops, provides a view of more than 400 years of American history.

Camp Milton Historic Preserve is scheduled to be opened in September 2005. Named for Florida's Civil War governor, John Milton, the 124-acre park will feature an educational center, boardwalk, interpretive hiking trails, and a tree sanctuary.

## Arts and Culture

From musical theater to contemporary drama, the arts are alive and well in Jacksonville. This is partly due to the Cultural Council of Greater Jacksonville, which keeps the spotlight on the arts and encourages public and private partnerships to increase arts funding.

The Jacksonville Symphony Orchestra, one of the premier orchestras of the Southeast, offers classical performances with world-class guest artists in its more than 130 annual concerts at the Florida Theatre, the Times-Union Center for the Performing Arts, and in nearby communities. The Florida Community College at Jacksonville Artists Series brings top quality national and international entertainers to the Florida Theatre and to the Times-Union Center. The Alhambra Dinner Theatre, which has been producing professional Broadway style shows since 1967, features professional Equity actors.

Jacksonville's museums and galleries reflect the diverse historical and cultural interests of its residents. The Museum of Science and History features wonderful exhibits showing the history of the area, science and health demonstrations, and nature studies. An indoor playground at the museum and the adjacent Alexander Brest Planetarium bring fun to young and old alike. The Jacksonville Museum of Modern Art, on the city's south side, houses five galleries and features a collection of pre-Columbian artifacts as well as exhibits of painting, sculpture, and photography. Its adjacent outdoor sculpture garden is a famous place for picnicking. The Karpeles Manuscript Library Museum, located in the restored former First Church of Christ Scientist, is one of seven in the nation that exists to display the historical manuscript collection of David and Marsha Karpeles. Surrounded by two acres of beautiful English and Italian waterfront gardens in Riverside, the Cummer Museum of Art is the largest museum in northeast Florida. Its permanent collection of more than 4,000 objects includes works from prehistoric, medieval, Renaissance, Baroque, Rococo, 19th Century Impressionist, and modern art eras. The Ritz Theatre houses the LaVilla Museum, displaying a permanent collection of African American history. The Museum of Southern History features a collection of artifacts reflecting life in the southeastern United States, the Civil War, and genealogy of southern families. Other items of note are the Battle of Antietam replica, and more than 3,000 books, periodicals, military, and cultural items. Finally, the Jacksonville Maritime Museum is dedicated to artwork and large-scale models of maritime-related events and objects from the history of Jacksonville and the First Coast.

## Festivals and Holidays

The Jacksonville Jazz Festival is the city's best-known annual event. This three-day celebration takes place in the spring, and draws classic and contemporary jazz and blues celebrities and includes the Great American Jazz Piano Competition. The JaxParks Family Fest, held each March, features games, entertainment, and food for the whole family. Also in the spring are the Jacksonville Film Festival; the 15K River Run; the World of Nations Celebration, which provides an opportunity to experience the food, culture, and traditions of various countries around the globe; and the Kuumba Festival, devoted to African cultures.

The Fiesta Playera dia de San Juan Bautista is an annual summertime festival paying tribute to St. John the Baptist and celebrating the customs and culture of Puerto Rico. It has been voted among the top 20 festivals in the region by the Southeast Tourism Society. The Juneteenth Celebration celebrates the Emancipation Proclamation of 1863 with food, entertainment, and music. The Caribbean Carnival is held each autumn and features costumes, cuisine, and music. The Olustee Battle Festival re-enacts the 1864 Battle of Ocean Pond, a major Civil War battle, each winter.

Celebrations in Jacksonville are not limited to annual events. The First Wednesday Art Walk takes place on the first Wednesday of every month. On these days, Downtown

Jacksonville is transformed into a walkable art gallery. A variety of art is displayed in dozens of historic buildings, and is accompanied by live bands, sidewalk artists, and street vendors.

### Sports for the Spectator

More than 70,000 avid fans flock to watch the Jaguars of the National Football League, who play home games on Sundays from September to January at Alltel Stadium. This arena is also the site of two annual college event games: the Gator Bowl Classic and the University of Florida vs. University of Georgia contest. Jacksonville Veterans Memorial Arena, built on the site of the former Jacksonville Coliseum in 2003, is the venue for the Jacksonville Barracudas hockey games as well as other sporting and entertainment events. Memorial Arena also houses the Jacksonville Sports Hall of Fame. Jacksonville's newest professional sports team is the Jade, who compete in the W League, a nationally organized women's soccer league in the United States.

Athletic enthusiasts in Jacksonville also enjoy the tennis championships organized by the Association of Tennis Professionals as well as March's Players Championship, which attracts 150,000 spectators to Sawgrass Resort, the toughest course on the Professional Golfer's Association tour. Up to 10,000 fans fill the Baseball Grounds of Jacksonville, a stadium constructed in 2003, to watch the Class AA Jacksonville Suns minor league team. The Kingfish off-shore fishing tournament in July draws nearly 50,000 people. The 42-mile Mug Race Regatta in May attracts both local and Olympic sailors for the longest river sailboat race in the world. Jacksonville has a year-round greyhound racing season at St. Johns Greyhound Racing Park, the Jacksonville Kennel Club, and the Orange Park Kennel Club.

### Sports for the Participant

Jacksonville is home to the largest urban park system in the nation. Residents and visitors enjoy more than 82,000 acres of land that extends from the rivers to the beaches. Nearly 60 miles of free beaches avail themselves to boating, sailing, surfing, fishing, and swimming. Playgrounds, tennis courts, picnic areas, about 70 golf courses, and dozens of public pools offer more choices.

The Fort Clinch State Park, a restored Civil War fort built in 1847, has picnic grounds, beaches, and an ocean fishing pier. Adventure Landing features two miniature golf courses, batting cages, a go-cart track, an uphill water coaster, and Shipwreck Island water park. Hikers enjoy the trails at Timucuan Ecological Historic Preserve.

### Shopping and Dining

Jacksonville is a shopper's delight, offering interesting shops downtown and arty shops along the beaches. Jackson-ville Landing offers a festive marketplace atmosphere, with novelty and gift shops, name-brand apparel, antiques, toys, and locally made accessories along with entertainment venues. The Avenues Mall on the Southside and Regency Square in Arlington each offer more than 100 nationally known retailers. Avondale, one of the country's largest National Register of Historic Districts, is a charming place to stroll, shop, and dine. San Marco Square, in the style of St. Mark's Square in Venice, offers an open-air produce market, restaurants, and boutiques, together with a water fountain, bronze lions, and a gazebo.

Local fish camps and waterside restaurants with their fresh seafood fare add to the pleasure of dining in Jacksonville. Southern barbecue is also a tradition. A delectable selection of ethnic foods from Japanese to Greek to Indian or Tex Mex are offered by the city's many casual and upscale restaurants downtown or at suburban or beach locations.

*Visitor Information:* Jacksonville and the Beaches Convention and Visitors Bureau, 550 Water St., Ste. 1000, Jacksonville, FL 32202; telephone (904)798-9111; toll-free (800)733-2668

# Convention Facilities

The Prime F. Osborn III Convention Center, formerly the Jacksonville Railroad Terminal, is the largest convention facility in the region. It offers a 78,500 square foot exhibit hall in an architecturally interesting setting, with an additional 22 function rooms. The 1919 Neoclassical Revival railway terminal boasts a fully restored 10,000-square-foot ballroom (the Grand Lobby) and 22 meeting rooms. The convention center is connected to a nearby hotel by the Automated Skyway Express. The refurbished Times-Union Center for the Performing Arts includes 22,000 square feet of meeting space with a 3,200-seat concert theater, a 600-seat theater, and a new 1,800-seat symphony hall. The refurbished Jacksonville Veterans Memorial Coliseum multipurpose facility accommodates 10,000 people for meetings. Other meeting facilities are the restored Florida Theater, Conference Center at the Avenues, and the University Center at the University of North Florida, a 95,000 square foot, full-service conference and meeting facility.

*Convention Information:* Jacksonville and the Beaches Convention and Visitors Bureau, 550 Water St., Ste. 1000, Jacksonville, FL 32202; telephone (904)798-9111; toll-free (800)733-2668

# Transportation

### Approaching the City

Jacksonville International Airport (JIA), only minutes from the central business district, recently expanded its passenger terminal and expects to service more than 8 million passengers annually by the year 2009. Most major airlines provide more than 230 flights in and out of the city every day. In addition to JIA, Jacksonville has two general aviation facilities, Craig Airport and Herlong Airport, which facilitate travel by private or corporate aircraft. Amtrak offers rail service.

Drivers approach Jacksonville via three major interstates that lead to the city (I-10, I-95 and I-295); U.S. Highways 1, 17, 90 and 301 also traverse the city. Beltways built around the city and main arteries linked to key locations make all parts of Jacksonville easily accessible.

### Traveling in the City

The St. Johns River bisects the city and traveling across one or several bridges is commonplace. Seven bridges span the river within Duval County and the Intracoastal Waterway, and the area's many tributaries are crossed by dozens of small bridges. Local bus transportation is provided by the Jacksonville Transportation Authority (JTA). The Park-N-Ride service permits commuters to park in one of the JTA's outlying lots and ride the bus downtown. Community Transportation Services offers door-to-door transportation for the handicapped. The downtown area is also served by JTA's Automated Skyway Express, a monorail system.

# Communications

### Newspapers and Magazines

Jacksonville's major daily (morning) paper is the *Florida Times-Union. The Jacksonville Business Journal* and the *Jacksonville Daily Record* are the area's business newspapers. Other weekly newspapers are the *Florida Star Times,* serving the black community, and the *Florida Baptist Witness.* Newspapers published in Jacksonville Beach include the semiweekly *Beaches Leader* and the weekly *Sun-Times. Jacksonville Magazine* is a monthly publication devoted to the city's attractions, community resources, and recreational opportunities. *St. Augustine Catholic* is a religious magazine published in Jacksonville.

### Television and Radio

Jacksonville is served by seven television stations: six commercial and one PBS. There are 16 AM radio stations and 22 FM stations.

***Media Information:*** *Florida Times-Union,* 1 Riverside Ave., PO Box 1949, Jacksonville, FL 32231; telephone (904)359-4111

### Jacksonville Online

City of Jacksonville home page. Available www.coj.net

Downtown Jacksonville, Inc. Available www.downtown jacksonville.org

Duval County Public Schools. Available www.education central.org

Enterprise Florida. Available www.eflorida.com

*Florida Times-Union.* Available www.jacksonville.com

Jacksonville and the Beaches Convention & Visitors Bureau. Available www.jaxcvb.com

Jacksonville Historical Society. Available http://www .jaxhistory.com

Jacksonville Public Libraries. Available http://jpl.itd.ci.jax .fl.us

Jacksonville Regional Chamber of Commerce. Available www.myjaxchamber.com

Mayo Clinic Jacksonville. Available www.mayoclinic.org/ jacksonville

### Selected Bibliography

Buker, George E., *Jacksonville: Riverport-Seaport* (Columbia, South Carolina: University of South Carolina Press, 1992)

Crooks, Arsenault, and Mormino, *Jacksonville: The Consolidation Story, from Civil Rights to the Jaguars* (Gainesville, Florida: University Press of Florida, 2004)

Crooks, James B., *Jacksonville After the Fire, 1901-1919: A New South City* (Jacksonville: University of North Florida Press, 1991)

Jacksonville Historical Society, *Jacksonville in Vintage Postcards: Between the Great Fire and the Great War* (Mount Pleasant, South Carolina: Arcadia Publishing, 2001)

# Miami

## The City in Brief

**Founded:** 1836 (incorporated 1896)

**Head Official:** Mayor Manuel A. Diaz (I) (since 2001)

**City Population**
1980: 346,681
1990: 358,648
2000: 362,470
2003 estimate: 376,815
Percent change, 1990–2000: 1.0%
U.S. rank in 1980: 41st
U.S. rank in 1990: 46th (State rank: 2nd)
U.S. rank in 2000: 56th (State rank: 2nd)

**Metropolitan Area Population**
1980: 1,626,000
1990: 1,937,194
2000: 2,253,362

Percent change, 1990–2000: 16.3%
U.S. rank in 1980: 12th (CMSA)
U.S. rank in 1990: 11th (CMSA)
U.S. rank in 2000: 12th (PMSA)

**Area:** 36 square miles (2000)
**Elevation:** 12 feet above sea level
**Average Annual Temperature:** 76.7° F
**Average Annual Precipitation:** 58.53 inches

**Major Economic Sectors:** tourism, trade, banking, manufacturing
**Unemployment rate:** 5.4% (December 2004)
**Per Capita Income:** $15,128 (1999)

**2002 FBI Crime Index Total:** 33,952

**Major Colleges and Universities:** University of Miami, Miami-Dade Community College, Florida International University, Barry University, St. Thomas University

**Daily Newspapers:** *The Miami Herald; Diario Las Americas*

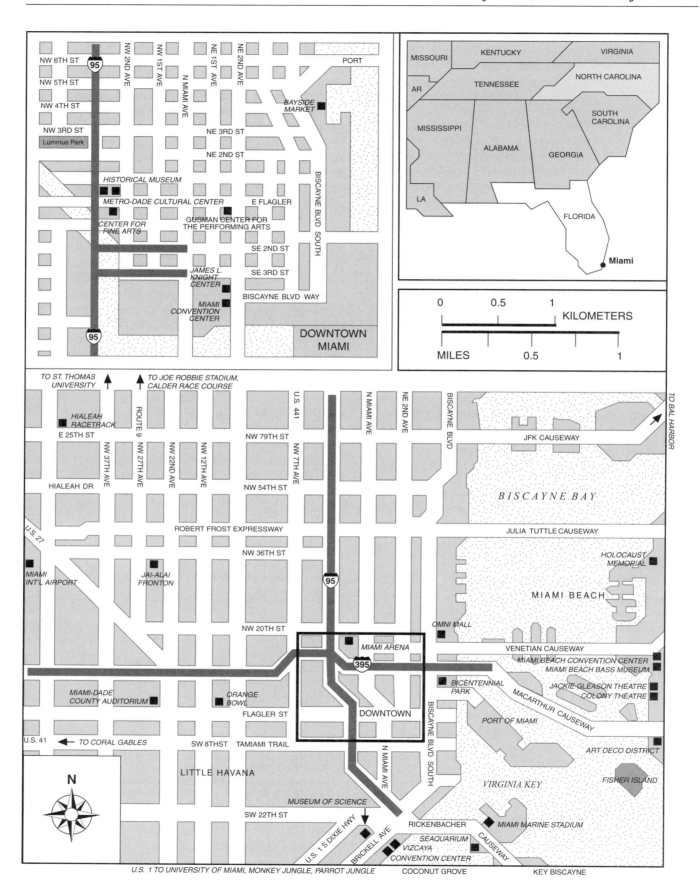

NW 6TH ST
NW 5TH ST
NW 4TH ST
NW 3RD ST
Lummus Park

NW 2ND AVE
NW 1ST AVE
N MIAMI AVE
NE 1ST AVE
NE 2ND AVE

PORT

BAYSIDE MARKET

NE 3RD ST
NE 2ND ST

HISTORICAL MUSEUM
METRO-DADE CULTURAL CENTER
CENTER FOR FINE ARTS
GUSMAN CENTER FOR THE PERFORMING ARTS
E FLAGLER
SE 2ND ST
JAMES L. KNIGHT CENTER
SE 3RD ST
MIAMI CONVENTION CENTER
BISCAYNE BLVD WAY

BISCAYNE BLVD SOUTH

DOWNTOWN MIAMI

MISSOURI  KENTUCKY  VIRGINIA
AR  TENNESSEE  NORTH CAROLINA
MISSISSIPPI  SOUTH CAROLINA
ALABAMA  GEORGIA
LA
FLORIDA
**Miami**

0    0.5    1    KILOMETERS
MILES    0.5    1

TO ST. THOMAS UNIVERSITY
TO JOE ROBBIE STADIUM, CALDER RACE COURSE
U.S. 441
N MIAMI AVE
NE 2ND AVE
BISCAYNE BLVD
TO BAL HARBOR
JFK CAUSEWAY
HIALEAH RACETRACK
E 25TH ST
ROUTE 9
NW 37TH AVE
NW 27TH AVE
NW 22ND AVE
NW 12TH AVE
NW 7TH AVE
NW 79TH ST
NW 54TH ST
BISCAYNE BAY
HIALEAH DR
JULIA TUTTLE CAUSEWAY
U.S. 27
ROBERT FROST EXPRESSWAY
HOLOCAUST MEMORIAL
NW 36TH ST
MIAMI INT'L AIRPORT
JAI-ALAI FRONTON
MIAMI BEACH
NW 20TH ST
OMNI MALL
MIAMI ARENA
VENETIAN CAUSEWAY
MIAMI BEACH CONVENTION CENTER
MIAMI BEACH BASS MUSEUM
MIAMI-DADE COUNTY AUDITORIUM
ORANGE BOWL
BICENTENNIAL PARK
JACKIE GLEASON THEATRE
COLONY THEATRE
FLAGLER ST
DOWNTOWN
PORT OF MIAMI
MACARTHUR CAUSEWAY
U.S. 41
TO CORAL GABLES
SW 8TH ST
TAMIAMI TRAIL
BISCAYNE BLVD SOUTH
ART DECO DISTRICT
LITTLE HAVANA
N MIAMI AVE
VIRGINIA KEY
FISHER ISLAND
N
MUSEUM OF SCIENCE
SW 22ND ST
U.S. 1 S DIXIE HWY
BRICKELL AVE
RICKENBACHER
MIAMI MARINE STADIUM
SEAQUARIUM
VIZCAYA
CONVENTION CENTER
CAUSEWAY

U.S. 1 TO UNIVERSITY OF MIAMI, MONKEY JUNGLE, PARROT JUNGLE       COCONUT GROVE       KEY BISCAYNE

# Introduction

Described as the "only great city of the world that started as a fantasy," Miami, with its subtropical climate, naturally protected harbor, and spectacular beaches, has traditionally been a haven for tourists and retirees. Since the late 1980s, however, the city has sustained unprecedented growth and, while transforming its image, has emerged as a center of international finance and commerce and as a regional center for Latin American and Haitian art.

An unincorporated village shortly before the turn of the twentieth century, Miami boasts a metropolitan area that includes a large unincorporated area and 30 incorporated areas or municipalities, all of which make up Miami-Dade County. Greater Miami offers a diversity of lifestyles and attractions to both residents and visitors in a variety of small towns and cities such as Coconut Grove, Miami Beach, South Beach, Coral Gables, Bal Harbor, and Hialeah. With easy access to other parts of the country, Miami has developed into one of America's major transportation hubs, and thriving job and housing markets have made it an ideal location for business expansion and new construction. At one time, Miami came to life only in the winter with the influx of tourists from the north. Today it is a year-round city that offers something for everyone.

# Geography and Climate

Located at the mouth of the Miami River on the lower east coast of Florida, Miami is bordered on the east by Biscayne Bay, an arm of the Atlantic Ocean. Further east, the islands of Key Biscayne and Miami Beach shelter the bay from the Atlantic Ocean, thus providing Miami with a naturally protected harbor. Once pine and palmetto flatlands, the Miami area boasts sandy beaches in its coastal areas and gives way to sparsely wooded outlying areas. A man-made canal connects the city to Lake Okeechobee, located 90 miles northwest of Miami.

Miami's year-round semi-tropical climate is free of extremes in temperature, with a long, warm summer and abundant rainfall followed by a mild, dry winter. Summer humidity levels—usually in the 86 to 89 percent range during the day—make Miami the second most humid city in the United States. Hurricanes occasionally affect the area in September and October; tornadoes are rare. Waterspouts are sometimes sighted from the beaches in the summer, but significant damage seldom occurs.

**Area:** 36 square miles (2000)

**Elevation:** 12 feet above sea level

**Average Temperatures:** January, 68.1° F; July, 83.7° F; annual average, 76.7° F

**Average Annual Precipitation:** 58.53 inches

# History

### Early Settlement Attempts Create Conflict

South Florida was settled more than four thousand years ago by primitive people who had established a thriving culture by the time Spanish explorers led by Ponce de Leon arrived in 1513. The principal native tribe in the region that is now Miami-Dade County was the Calusa (renamed Tequesta by de Leon), whose members built villages along the Miami River. The name Miami comes from the Calusa word "Mayami," meaning "Big Water." Tequesta—or Chequescha—their village on the north bank of the river, became the site of the future city of Miami.

Spanish conquistadors, attracted by the mild climate, abundant food sources, and fresh water supply—and by tales of gold and other riches—made repeated attempts to colonize the Miami region during the early sixteenth century but were met with hostility from the Calusas. Nevertheless, by the early 1700s, less than two hundred years after the arrival of the Spanish, most of the native population of south Florida had disappeared. European diseases like smallpox had severely reduced their numbers, as did inter-tribal wars. The few Calusas who remained were threatened by invading Creek and Seminole Indians, and in 1711 many fled to Havana, Cuba.

Spain, never really successful in settling the Miami region, supported France against the British during the French and Indian War, and as a result lost Florida to the victorious British in 1763. In 1783, after the American Revolution, Florida briefly reverted to Spanish possession, but in 1821 Spain ceded Florida to the United States for $5 million. Over the next two decades, settlers moving into the Biscayne Bay area encountered conflict with the Seminoles living there. In 1836, as part of an effort to quell the angry Seminoles, the U.S. Army took over Fort Dallas—originally a naval post at the mouth of the Miami River. In 1842, after numerous skirmishes, the remaining Seminoles were driven into the Everglades swamp, a region so unfit for human habitation that the government did not challenge their occupation of it. Seven years later a permanent structure was built at Fort Dallas from which the army could monitor the Seminoles.

While other outposts in Florida flourished after the final Seminole conflict, Miami and Dade County suffered. Farming had become impossible and settlers drifted to other locales. By 1860 the name Miami no longer appeared in public records. The Civil War barely touched the few people who lived in the isolated Miami River settlement; in fact, it was assumed by those in prosperous north Florida towns that the southern region was uninhabited. Although stragglers, deserters, and freed slaves passed through Miami after the war, few settled there.

### The City Becomes a Cosmopolitan Mecca

In the 1870s investors and developers from the midwest moved into the area, claiming old titles and buying land. Among them was Julia Tuttle, the wealthy widow of a Cleveland businessman, who enjoyed life in Miami and saw potential for a resort community there. She persuaded Henry Flagler to extend his Florida East Coast Railroad into the wilderness beyond Palm Beach. On April 15, 1896, Flagler brought his railroad into Miami and also began to develop the town, which was incorporated in 1896. Other entrepreneurs followed, and Miami grew from a village with a population of 343 people to a flourishing resort. Miami Beach was founded in 1915.

After World War I, improved highways gave greater access from the north and triggered an unprecedented building boom. In 1920 the city's population was 30,000 people; by 1925 real estate speculation swelled the population to 200,000 people. A year later the boom had collapsed, but it had laid the basis for future development in office buildings, hotels, housing, and a network of streets and roads. A hurricane in 1926 killed 243 people and caused damage estimated at $1.4 billion in 1990 dollars. Miami's phenomenal growth slowed.

World War II brought a second boom to Miami. Soldiers replaced tourists, and after the war servicemen who had trained in the city returned to make their homes there. This second boom has continued without significant interruption to the present. It was given impetus in the 1960s with the migration of more than 178,000 refugees from Communist Cuba. The Cuban migration transformed Miami into an international city, strengthening existing ties with the Caribbean and South America. Today the city is bilingual; Spanish-speaking employees work at most businesses, and downtown shops post signs in both English and Spanish. Still, racial tensions persisted. For example, an incident of alleged police brutality toward an African American caused major rioting in 1980. And African Americans staged a tourism boycott resulting from the snubbing by county commissioners of former South African President Nelson Mandela during his visit to Miami in 1990.

### End of Century Sees Political Turmoil, Reform Efforts

Capitalizing on its multinational character, Miami moved during the 1980s and 1990s into the forefront of world commerce and finance. Hundreds of thousands of European visitors discovered Miami Beach, popularizing the Art Deco hotels and adding to the city's cosmopolitan flair. But in the wake of racial and ethnic tensions, some highly publicized murders of foreign tourists, and Hurricane Andrew in 1992, at least 100,000 non-Hispanic whites fled the Greater Miami area between 1990 and 1996, leaving a city that was the only large U.S. city with a Hispanic majority.

The city struggled in the late twentieth century to balance the needs of its mostly poor citizens with the need for business development. In spite of its glamorous image, Miami was the nation's fourth poorest city. In 1997, faced with a $68 million budget shortfall, Miami became the first city in Florida to have an oversight board appointed by the state. City voters rejected a plan to dissolve Miami as separate entity and merge it with the county, though county voters approved to change the name of Dade County to Miami-Dade County. This name change did little to help Miami, whose problems had become more than financial. The 2000 incident involving Elian Gonzalez, a five-year-old Cuban boy who survived a shipwreck to arrive in the United States only to be returned to Cuba by the U.S. government, deepened ethnic tensions between Miami's Cuban and non-Cuban population. By the turn of the century, corruption in the city government and a number of controversial police shootings brought about scrutiny by the U.S. Department of Justice.

### A Radical with a Business Vision

Desperate for a positive change, disenchanted voters shook up Miami's government by electing Manuel A. Diaz as mayor in 2001. Diaz, a lawyer who had never held elected office, immediately and radically restructured the government. Modeling it on a private-sector organization, he eliminated some departments and consolidated others, and incorporated a vertical structure consisting of such positions as a Chief Executive Officer and Chief Financial Officer. Business processes were rewritten at each employee and government level, and a new emphasis was placed on accountability, training, and timely service to citizens. A number of programs were developed and implemented to boost the local economy and improve the quality of life for Miami's residents and visitors. By 2004, only three years after the city was nearly bankrupt and its bonds were junk grade, Wall Street gave its bonds an A+ rating, the highest in Miami's history. Diaz's remarkable results in such a short time earned him the Urban Innovator of the Year Award by the Manhattan Institute.

***Historical Information:*** Historical Museum of Southern Florida, 101 W. Flagler St., Miami, FL 33130; telephone (305)375-1492; email hasf@historical-museum.org

# Population Profile

**Metropolitan Area Residents**
*1980:* 1,626,000
*1990:* 1,973,194 (PMSA)
*2000:* 2,253,362 (PMSA)
*Percent change, 1990–2000:* 16.3%
*U.S. rank in 1980:* 12th (CMSA)
*U.S. rank in 1990:* 11th (CMSA)
*U.S. rank in 2000:* 12th (CMSA)

**City Residents**
*1980:* 346,681
*1990:* 358,648
*2000:* 362,470
*2003 estimate:* 376,815
*Percent change, 1990–2000:* 1.0%
*U.S. rank in 1980:* 41st
*U.S. rank in 1990:* 46th (State rank: 2nd)
*U.S. rank in 2000:* 56th (State rank: 2nd)

*Density:* 10,160.9 people per square mile (based on 2000 land area)

*Racial and ethnic characteristics* (2000)
White: 241,470
Black or African American: 80,858
American Indian and Alaska Native: 810
Asian: 2,376
Native Hawaiian and Pacific Islander: 130
Hispanic or Latino (may be of any race): 238,351
Other: 19,644

*Percent of residents born in state:* 26.6% (2000)

*Age characteristics* (2000)
Population under 5 years old: 21,222
Population 5 to 9 years old: 21,962
Population 10 to 14 years old: 22,182
Population 15 to 19 years old: 22,339
Population 20 to 24 years old: 23,023
Population 25 to 34 years old: 54,264
Population 35 to 44 years old: 55,682
Population 45 to 54 years old: 44,287
Population 55 to 59 years old: 17,983
Population 60 to 64 years old: 17,758
Population 65 to 74 years old: 32,233
Population 75 to 84 years old: 21,140
Population 85 years and older: 8,395
Median age: 37.7 years

*Births* (Miami-Dade County, 2003)
Total number: 32,551

*Deaths* (Miami-Dade County, 2003)
Total number: 18,369 (of which, 194 were infants under the age of 1 year)

*Money income* (1999)
Per capita income: $15,128
Median household income: $23,483
Total households: 134,344

*Number of households with income of . . .*
less than $10,000: 32,558
$10,000 to $14,999: 14,370
$15,000 to $24,999: 23,087
$25,000 to $34,999: 17,280
$35,000 to $49,999: 17,036
$50,000 to $74,999: 14,484
$75,000 to $99,999: 6,458
$100,000 to $149,999: 4,829
$150,000 to $199,999: 1,581
$200,000 or more: 2,661

*Percent of families below poverty level:* 23.5% (61% of which were female householder families with related children under 5 years)

*2002 FBI Crime Index Total:* 33,952

# Municipal Government

Miami's system of government is two-tiered: municipal and county. At the municipal level are a city mayor, five commissioners, and a city manager. The Miami-Dade County, or metropolitan government, consists of an executive mayor, a county manager, and 13 county commissioners, each of which represents a district and serves a four-year term. The county government administers issues that affect the greater metropolitan area, such as transportation and pollution control.

**Head Officials:** City Mayor Manuel A. Diaz (I) (since 2001, current term expires 2005); County Mayor Carlos Alvarez (since 2004)

**Total Number of City Employees:** 3,500 (2005)

*Government Information:* City Mayor's Office, 3500 Pan American Dr., Miami, FL 33133; telephone (305)250-5300; fax (305)854-4001; email mannydiaz@ci.miami.fl.us. County Mayor's Office, Stephen Clark Center, 111 NW 1st St., 29th Fl., Miami, FL 33128; telephone (305)375-5071; fax (305)375-3618; email mayor@miamidade.gov

# *Economy*

## Major Industries and Commercial Activity

For most of Miami's history, its economy has been based on tourism. In fact, it was not so long ago that the city came to life only during the winter months when tourists from cold northern regions flocked to its beaches, hotels, and resorts. That phenomenon is no longer the case, as tourists visit the region throughout the year. In 2003, 10.4 million overnight visitors came to Greater Miami, infusing the local economy with $9.9 billion in direct expenses, such as hotel rooms, restaurants, shopping, transportation, and attractions, and another $5.5 in indirect expenditures in such areas as real estate, medicine, and retail.

While tourism continues to be the principal industry in Miami, the city's economy has become more diversified. Trade is increasingly vital to the economy. Its close proximity to Latin America and the Caribbean make it the center of international trade with those areas. Nearly $50 billion in total merchandise trade came through the Miami Customs District in 2002. Because many companies choose to establish their Latin American headquarters in southern Florida, Miami-Dade County is known as the ''Gateway to the Americas.'' In 2003 approximately 1,200 multinational corporations were established in the region.

The city's international trade infrastructure is vast and varied. With an economic impact of $18.6 billion, Miami International Airport is the nation's top airport for international freight and third for international passengers. The Port of Miami, which contributes $8 billion to the local economy, ranks first among the state's containerized ports and ninth in the United States. The World Trade Center Miami is Florida's oldest international organization, and assists member companies to introduce and expand their international presence. It is also petitioning to establish Miami-Dade County as the site of the Permanent Secretariat of the 34-nation Free Trade Area of the Americas. Miami is home to more than 64 foreign consulates, 25 international trade offices, and 32 bi-national chambers of commerce. Two free trade zones exist in Greater Miami, the Homestead Free Zone and the Miami Free Zone, one of the world's largest privately owned and operated zones. The top imports into the Miami Customs District in 2002 were apparel and accessories; the leading exports were electrical machinery and photographic and medical equipment.

International banking is another growing segment of the economy. With total deposits of $74.3 billion in 2003, about 100 commercial banks, thrift institutions, foreign bank agencies, and Edge Act banks are located in downtown Miami, representing the largest concentration of domestic and inter-

national banks on the East Coast south of New York. Brazilian, British, Canadian, French, German, Israeli, Japanese, Spanish, and Venezuelan banks have offices in Miami-Dade County. Still, domestic banks dominate the market, led by Bank of America Corp., which has total deposits of over $7.8 billion in its 25 local offices.

*Items and goods produced:* apparel, textiles, books and magazines, pharmaceuticals, medical and diagnostic testing equipment, plastics, aluminum products, furniture, light manufactured goods, transportation equipment, cement, electronic components, agricultural products such as tomatoes, beans, avocadoes, and citrus fruits

## Incentive Programs—New and Existing Companies

*Local programs*—The Beacon Council is the agency responsible for recruiting new businesses to Miami-Dade County in an effort to create new jobs. The Council's many free services include site identification; labor recruitment and training; business data and economic research; packaging local, state, and federal business incentives; and import/export assistance. The Council promotes the many advantages of doing business in Miami-Dade County, including a number of business incentive programs and a favorable tax structure. Business location incentives at the local level include Empowerment Zone and Enterprise Zone opportunities, each of which offers tax or wage credits to businesses based on the number of new jobs created. The Miami-Dade County Targeted Jobs Incentive Fund is available to companies that are on the list of industries identified by the county as desirable additions to the local economy. The Grow Miami Fund grants qualified small businesses long-term, low-interest loans ranging from $50,000 to $2 million. In 2003 the city partnered with ACCION USA to make $4 million in micro loans available to the small business community.

*State programs*—Enterprise Florida is a partnership between Florida's government and business leaders and is the principal economic development organization for the state of Florida. Enterprise Florida's mission is to increase economic opportunities for all Floridians by supporting the creation of quality jobs, a well-trained workforce, and globally competitive businesses. It pursues this mission in cooperation with its statewide network of economic development partners.

Among the incentive programs managed at the state level is the Economic Development Transportation Fund, which provides up to $2 million to fund the cost of transportation projects, such as access roads and road widening, required for the establishment, expansion, or retention of businesses in Florida. The state's Qualified Target Industry Tax Refund is similar to the Miami-Dade program that rewards the creation of jobs in certain industries. Florida also offers various sales and use tax exemptions for machinery and equipment purchase, electric energy, research and development, and other aspects of doing business in the area.

*Job training programs*—The Workforce Development Board (WDB), commonly known as Jobs & Education Partnership, is a part of Enterprise Florida. WDB provides policy, planning, and oversight for job training programs funded under the federal Workforce Investment Act, along with vocational training, adult education, employment placement, and other workforce programs administered by a variety of state and local agencies. Regional Workforce Development Boards operate under charters approved by the Workforce Development Board. The 24 regional boards have primary responsibility for direct services through a state-wide network of One-Stop Career systems.

State and local workforce development efforts are concentrated on three broad initiatives. First Jobs/First Wages focuses on preparing workers for entry-level employment including the School-to-Work and WAGES (Work and Gain Self-Sufficiency) programs. High Skill/High Wages targets the higher skills needs of employers and training workers for advancement through such programs as Performance Based Incentive Funding, Occupational Forecasting Conference/ Targeted Occupations, Quick Response Training, and Incumbent Worker Training. One-Stop Career Centers are the central elements of the One-Stop system that provide integrated services to employers, workers, and job-seekers.

## Development Projects

Under the leadership of Mayor Manuel Diaz, the city of Miami experienced an unprecedented level of development and private investment. New projects valued at about $12.5 billion were planned or under construction in 2004. This influx of capital resulted in a tax base that grew 15 percent during the year, attributing to a $2.3 billion dollar increase in real estate values. Two of the largest projects under development are the Midtown Miami Project, which will result in the Shops at Midtown and the Midtown Miami residential center, and a $1.5 billion commitment by a group of private investors to develop several locations in the city; combined, these two projects will result in 3.5 million square feet of residential, commercial, office, and parking space in Miami. Another significant development is the Wagner Square project, slated to break ground in 2005, which will produce residential and commercial retail units from 2.95 acres of environmentally contaminated city land.

City leaders are determined to develop all areas of the Greater Miami region, not just the downtown area. The $1 billion Midtown Miami residential project will create more than 1,500 jobs in Wynwood, an area that lost 20,000 jobs during the 1990s. Approximately $175 million in private investment will help revitalize Overtown, the poorest neigh-

borhood in Miami. The University of Miami will bolster the region's foothold in biotechnology by constructing a 300,000 square foot Clinical Research Building along with two new wet lab facilities. The Miami International Airport launched a $4.6 billion program to renovate existing facilities and construct new ones.

In addition to attracting new business developments, Miami is focused on improving the existing environment. Mayor Diaz implemented the city's first Capital Improvement Plan, an initiative to rebuild the city's entire infrastructure by reconstructing, resurfacing, and repairing every road, sidewalk, and curb on a 12-year cycle. Operation Difference and a Quality of Life task force strive to make the city safer and cleaner by tackling garbage dumping and housing violations, along with such illegal activities as drug dealing, prostitution, and gambling. The *Miami Herald* reported that the city's crime rate dropped nine percent during 2004, the 11th consecutive year of decline.

The Clean Up Miami Campaign includes daytime street sweepers and litter and graffiti clean-up teams. The Adopt-a-Waterway program, the first of its kind in the nation, will improve water quality in the Miami River and its tributaries and will complement the city's $80 million dredging project that is expected to pull approximately 500,000 cubic yards of sediment from the river. Miami-Dade County's Adopt-a-Tree program distributes thousands of trees throughout the region. The Miami River Greenways Plan will develop a series of pedestrian and bicycle paths to link parks and neighborhoods on both sides of the river.

***Economic Development Information:*** Miami Department of Economic Development, 444 SW 2nd Ave., 3rd Fl., Miami, FL 33130; telephone (305)416-1435; fax (305)416-2156; email development@ci.miami.fl.us. The Beacon Council, 80 SW 8th St., Ste. 2400, Miami, FL 33130; telephone (305)579-1300; fax (305)375-0271; email info @beaconcouncil.com

## Commercial Shipping

Miami ranked 22nd among "America's 100 Most Logistics Friendly Metros" by *Expansion Management* magazine in 2004. The economic and logistical vitality of Miami comes in large measure from Miami International Airport (MIA). Served by more than 100 airlines, MIA is a hub of both domestic and international trade and is the primary commerce link between North and South America. In 2002 the airport transported nearly 1.8 million tons of cargo and more than 30 million passengers. MIA ranks first in the nation for international freight and third for both international cargo and international passengers. Its trade support infrastructure includes more than 300 freight forwarders and customs brokers, as well as a Cargo Clearance Center that provides 24-hour service by inspectors from the U.S. Customs Service, Department of Agriculture, Fish and Wildlife Service, and Food and Drug Administration.

The Port of Miami, in addition to being the world's largest cruise port, has achieved dominance in international commerce; it ranks first in Florida and ninth nationally in commercial tonnage. In 2002 the port handled 8.7 million tons of cargo and 3.6 million passengers, a 5.9 percent and 7.4 percent increase over the previous year, respectively. The Miami Free Zone's principal function is importing for domestic U.S. consumption. Fifteen minutes from the seaport and five minutes from the airport, the free zone is one of the largest duty-free zones in the United States. Two major railway systems, Amtrak and Tri-Rail, link the city locally and nationally. Interstates 95 and 195 run perpendicular through the Miami region. A network of 5,640 miles of roadway provides delivery and receiving routes for the nearly 100 motor freight lines operating in the area.

## Labor Force and Employment Outlook

The Miami-Dade County labor force is Florida's largest and most comprehensive, numbering over 1.1 million, of which college students and adult/vocational education students make up 100,000 each. The region's labor advantages include a large and diverse pool of Spanish-speaking and bilingual workers who contribute to Miami's expansion as a headquarters of international operations. The Beacon Council forecasts the largest employment growth sectors for the mid- to late-2000s will be professional and business services, education, health services, and construction.

The following is a summary of data regarding the Miami-Hialeah metropolitan area labor force, 2003 annual averages.

*Size of nonagricultural labor force:* 1,004,100

*Number of workers employed in . . .*
  *manufacturing:* 52,400
  *trade, transportation and utilities:* 252,800
  *information:* 28,400
  *financial activities:* 67,300
  *professional and business services:* 146,800
  *educational and health services:* 129,900
  *leisure and hospitality:* 92,100
  *other services:* 42,100
  *government:* 150,900

*Average hourly earnings of production workers employed in manufacturing:* $14.09 (2003 statewide average)

*Unemployment rate:* 5.4% (December 2004)

| Largest employers | Number of employees |
| --- | --- |
| Miami-Dade County Public Schools | 54,387 |
| Miami-Dade County | 32,265 |

| Largest employers | Number of employees |
| --- | --- |
| Federal Government | 20,100 |
| Florida State Government | 18,900 |
| Jackson Memorial Hospital/Health System | 11,700 |
| Baptist Health Systems of South Florida | 10,300 |
| University of Miami | 9,079 |
| American Airlines | 9,000 |
| Miami-Dade College | 7,500 |
| Florida International University | 5,000 |
| United Parcel Service Inc. | 5,000 |

## Cost of Living

The Beacon Council reports that Miami's 2003 cost of living, while above the national average, was lower than other major urban areas like New York, Boston, Los Angeles, and Washington DC.

The following is a summary of data regarding several key cost of living factors for the Miami area.

*2004 (3rd Quarter) ACCRA Average House Price:* $323,449

*2004 (3rd Quarter) ACCRA Cost of Living Index:* 111.5 (U.S. average = 100.0)

*State income tax rate:* None for personal income; 5.5 percent of net income for corporations

*State sales tax rate:* 6.0%

*Local income tax rate:* None

*Local sales tax rate:* 1.0%

*Property tax rate:* $26.23895 per $1,000 of assessed property value (2004)

**Economic Information:** The Beacon Council, 80 SW 8th Street, Suite 2400, Miami, FL 33130; telephone (305)579-1300; fax (305)375-0271; email info@beaconcouncil.com

# Education and Research

## Elementary and Secondary Schools

Like all public schools in the state of Florida, the public elementary and secondary schools of Miami are part of a county-wide district. The Miami-Dade County district, fourth largest in the United States, is administered by a partisan nine-member elected school board that appoints a superintendent.

The district operates the largest magnet school system in the nation, offering 77 specialized fields of study in such areas as mathematics, science, and technology; gifted; international education; Montessori; visual and performing arts; communications and humanities; and careers and professions. Additionally, 25 charter schools are under contract with the school district. In 2002–2003, more than 117,000 children were enrolled in the kindergarten through the twelfth grade at 286 schools and centers.

The following is a summary of data regarding Miami's public schools as of the 2002–2003 school year.

*Total enrollment:* 371,482

*Number of facilities*
*elementary schools:* 206
*junior high/middle schools:* 53
*senior high schools:* 36
*other:* 45

*Student/teacher ratio:* 19:1

*Teacher salaries*
*average:* $45,905

*Funding per pupil:* $5,858 (2001–2002 operating and special revenue funds)

Miami-Dade County has more than 400 private schools enrolling approximately 50,000 students.

***Public Schools Information:*** Miami-Dade County Public Schools, 1450 N.E. Second Avenue, Miami, FL 33132; telephone (305)995-1000

## Colleges and Universities

The Miami area has dozens of institutions of higher learning, including five vocational/technical schools. Florida International University, which enrolls more than 31,000 students, is the state's largest public university. The University of Miami is a private university noted for its business school. Miami-Dade Community College, with nearly 47,000 students, is recognized as one of the best in the nation. Barry University and St. Thomas University are both affiliated with the Roman Catholic Church; Florida Memorial College is affiliated with American Baptist Churches in the USA; and Trinity International University is affiliated with the Evangelical Free Church of America. International Fine Arts College offers Associate, Bachelor's, and Master's degrees.

## Libraries and Research Centers

In addition to its main branch in downtown Miami, the Miami-Dade Public Library System operates 34 branches and four regional libraries, with a regional library on Miami Beach and a branch in Sunny Isles Beach scheduled to open in 2005. Its collection numbers more than 3.8 million volumes; 1 million volumes can be found at the Main Library in the downtown Metro-Dade Cultural Center, where the largest collection of books and documents in the Southeast are housed. The library also holds numerous newspapers, magazines, films, records, tapes, sheet music, and photographs. The Main Library serves as a resource center for the system and provides information via eight subject departments: art, business, Florida, languages, music, science, urban affairs, and genealogy. Special collections are held in the Florida Room, the Foundations Center Regional Collection, and the U.S. and State Documents department; special interests include Florida and foreign languages, particularly Spanish. The library sponsors a wide array of educational and culturally enriching programs and exhibitions attended by more than 500,000 patrons annually. In 2002 the library system returned bookmobile service to outlying suburban neighborhoods.

Miami is home to more than 40 special libraries, including the University of Miami, which houses more than two million volumes. The library at the Wolfsonian Museum features a collection of about 36,000 books and other materials focusing on industrial arts, design, and architecture. The Wolfsonian's research and study center traces the interconnections of European culture with other cultures. Numerous other research centers are affiliated with academic institutions, conducting research activities in such fields as medicine, energy, marine science, economics, Latin America and the Caribbean, the environment, and aging.

***Public Library Information:*** Miami-Dade Public Library System, 101 W. Flagler St., Miami, FL 33130-1523; telephone (305)375-5026; email director@mdpls.org

# Health Care

Miami-Dade County, with 28 hospitals and more than 32,000 licensed healthcare professionals, has the state's largest concentration of medical facilities, which provide comprehensive human and social services through an array of programs. Hundreds of thousands of residents take part in a wide variety of county programs including emergency assistance, mental health care, substance abuse treatment and prevention, homeless shelter, veteran services, and other traditional social services.

Considered one of the best hospitals in the United States, Miami's Jackson Memorial Hospital (JMH) is also one of the nation's largest health care facilities. JMH, Miami-Dade County's only public hospital, is affiliated with the University of Miami School of Medicine and is known for research work in a number of fields, particularly eye and blood diseases, diabetes, and back pain. With the only Level 1 trauma center in South Florida, JMH treats more than 95 percent of the trauma victims in Miami-Dade County. The burn center, spinal cord injury center and organ transplant program are other JMH specialty areas unique to South Florida. Also at the Medical Center, the Bascom-Palmer Eye Institute/Anne Bates Leach Eye Hospital, Mailman Center for Child Development, Sylvester Comprehensive Cancer Center, National Parkinson Foundation, Diabetes Research Institute, and the Miami Project to Cure Paralysis, among many others, have earned Miami-Dade County high marks nationally and internationally as a center for groundbreaking research and treatment programs.

Baptist Hospital owns several facilities in the area and is highly regarded for the quality of its patient care. Miami Children's Hospital, a 268-bed facility, is South Florida's only licensed specialty hospital especially for the treatment of children. The not-for-profit hospital has a medical staff numbering over 650, is the largest freestanding pediatric teaching hospital in the Southeastern United States, and has a tele-education program reaching more than 40 sites in Latin America and the Caribbean. Other Miami-area hospitals are Mount Sinai Medical Center of Greater Miami, Cedars Medical Center, and Mercy Hospital.

*Health Care Information:* Jackson Memorial Hospital/Jackson Health System, 1611 NW 12th Ave., Miami, FL 33136-1094; telephone (305)585-1111; email info@um-jmh.org

# Recreation

## Sightseeing

Visitors to Miami will find a variety of activities, from an adventure-filled day at a nature park to a nostalgic stroll through a historic district. The city's principal attraction is Miami Seaquarium, south Florida's largest tropical aquarium and home of Flipper, television's star dolphin. At Seaquarium, Flipper, Lolita the Killer Whale, and Salty the Sea Lion appear in three shows daily. Seaquarium also features thousands of other sea creatures in display tanks, as well as tropical gardens and a wildlife sanctuary. Another popular family-oriented wildlife/nature park is Monkey Jungle, where hundreds of monkeys, gorillas, and trained chimpanzees swing freely through a natural rain forest. Chimpanzees perform daily. Similar to Monkey Jungle, Parrot Jungle Island presents more than 1,100 tropical birds that fly free. Featured are trained birds that perform daily in 40-minute shows, riding bicycles, playing poker, roller skating, and demonstrating arithmetic. Located between downtown

Miami and South Beach, Parrot Jungle occupies 18.6-acres with an Everglades exhibit, children's area with petting zoo, animal barn, playground and water play areas, baby bird and plant nurseries, picnic pavilions, food court, 500-seat theater, two amphitheaters, jungle trails, and aviaries.

Perhaps the ultimate wildlife experience can be found at Miami MetroZoo, rated the top attraction in Miami in 2004 by Zagat Survey. This cageless zoo is set on approximately 300 acres of natural habitats, where hundreds of species of the world's animals roam on islands separated from visitors by moats. Animal shows are presented daily, and elephant rides, monorail tours, walking tours, the children's petting zoo, PAWS, and an outdoor concert series are also available.

The Miami area maintains some of the nation's most beautiful tropical gardens. Fairchild Tropical Garden, in nearby Coral Gables, is the largest botanical garden in the continental United States. It features paths that wind through a rain forest, sunken gardens, a rare plant house, and 11 lakes displaying a wide variety of tropical vegetation. When the gardens sustained massive damage from Hurricane Andrew in 1992, scientists from around the globe gathered to begin to help restore this world-class botanical paradise. The Richard H. Simons Rainforest is a two-acre exhibit that features a 500-foot gurgling stream, waterfalls, paved paths, and rest areas.

Miami has preserved much of its rich past and embraced its social and ethnic diversity. A 30-block strip called Calle Ocho showcases Miami's Cuban culture in restaurants, nightclubs, sidewalk coffee shops, parks, cigar factories, and boutiques. The Art Deco District in Miami Beach contains more than 800 buildings designed in the Art Deco architecture and pastel colors of the 1930s. Another reminder of the past is Vizcaya Museum and Gardens, a 70-room Italian Renaissance-style palace with beautiful formal gardens overlooking Biscayne Bay. Vizcaya—which was built by James Deering, the founder of International Harvester—houses a collection of fifteenth- to early nineteenth-century European art.

## Arts and Culture

The primary venues for concerts and theatrical performances in Miami are the Gusman Center for the Performing Arts, the Jackie Gleason Theater of the Performing Arts (called TOPA), and the Miami-Dade County Auditorium. The Gusman Center, an ornate Baroque-style theater, has been transformed from a 1920s movie palace into an elegant stage for the performing arts. Its 40-week season includes classical music concerts by the Florida Philharmonic Orchestra and the New World Symphony (who are housed at the Lincoln Theatre in the Lincoln Road Shopping District). The Jackie Gleason Theater hosts the Miami Beach Symphony Orchestra and other entertainments. The Miami-Dade County Auditorium, featuring Art Deco revival decor, is a performance site for many local and international artists. At the historic Coconut Grove Playhouse, for more than 50 years south Florida's principal regional theater, Broadway and Off- Broadway shows are presented. The Florida Shakespeare Theater performs in a new space in the Historic Biltmore Hotel. The Miami Light Project, which performs artistic works such as musicals, stand-up comedy, and dance, performs in various locations. The Greater Miami Performing Arts Center is scheduled to open its doors in the 2005-2006 season, and will be one of the few facilities in the nation to feature three separate performance halls for ballet, opera, theater, and symphonic music. It will be home to the Concert Association of Florida, Florida Grand Opera, Miami City Ballet, and the New World Symphony.

The Metro-Dade Cultural Center, which consists of the Miami-Dade Public Library, the Historical Museum of Southern Florida, and the Miami Art Museum, is part of a reviving downtown Miami. The Historical Museum traces the 10,000-year history of humans in south Florida through permanent and traveling exhibits. The Miami Art Museum presents a variety of traveling exhibits.

Several Miami-area museums and galleries reflect the city's varied culture. For example, the Cuban Museum of Arts and Culture exhibits works by traditional and contemporary Hispanic artists; documents and memorabilia pertaining to the Cuban culture and history are presented, along with concerts, lectures, and films. Other historical museums include the 1891 Barnacle State Historic Site in Coconut Grove, Coral Gables' restored 1920s Merrick House, and the Holocaust Memorial.

The Bass Museum of Art in the heart of the Art Deco district in Miami Beach houses a permanent collection of Old Masters, sculptures, textiles and period furniture. Newer museums in the region include the Sanford L. Ziff Jewish Museum of Florida, the Museum of Contemporary Art, and the Wolfsonian. The Wolfsonian boasts a collection of more than 100,000 objects, including ceramics, glass, books, and furniture. Also instrumental in Miami's cultural life is the Art in Public Places program, one of the earliest of its kind, which has installed more than 450 works in the Metro-Dade area.

***Arts and Culture Information:*** Greater Miami Convention and Visitors Bureau, 701 Brickell Ave., Ste. 2700, Miami, FL 33131; telephone (305)539-3000; toll-free (800)933-8448

## Festivals and Holidays

Miami hosts countless festivals and fair throughout the year. Many reflect the city's rich cultural heritage. The Hispanic Heritage Festival runs throughout October with art, theater, dance, and Latin folklore, and cuisine. In March, the grounds of Vizcaya Palace are transformed into a sixteenth century marketplace of arts, crafts, and performance at the

Italian Renaissance Festival. The nation's largest Hispanic festival is Carnival Miami, also held in March, featuring salsa, brilliant costumes, and Cuban delicacies. It culminates in an all-day block party in the heart of Little Havana, the Calle Ocho Festival, which earned the title of the world's largest street party because it spans 23 city blocks. Cowbells, whistles, and washboard bands salute summer's Miami/Bahamas Goombay Festival, which celebrates Bahamian culture.

Art festivals abound. One of the largest and most prestigious is Art Basel Miami Beach. This fair, sister to the world famous Art Basel Switzerland, debuted in December 2002 and is now the most successful art fair in North America. January's annual Art Deco Weekend in South Miami Beach features tours of the historic Art Deco district, site of more than 800 buildings from the 1920s and 1930s, and includes an antique car show, a costume ball, films, and lectures. Other art events include the Coconut Grove Arts Festival, a three-day event held in February, as well as the Miami Beach Festival of the Arts, Art in the Tropics, and the South Miami Art Festival. Film festivals are just as common. The Miami International Film Festival showcases films from the United States, South America, Europe, the near East, and Australia that might not otherwise be seen in this country. Other festivals spotlight Jewish, gay and lesbian, Brazilian, African American, and Italian films.

The Orange Bowl Festival centers around the Orange Bowl football game on New Year's night. This festival, which has been held annually since 1933, includes the King Orange Jamboree and sports tournaments for children and adults. The season of Lent is kicked off with the Greater Miami Mardi Gras celebration. The Miami Wine & Food Festival, ranked as one of the nation's top ten wine events, is held each April. More than 100 rides and 50,000 exhibits are featured at the Miami-Dade County Fair & Exposition, an 18-day event held in the spring.

## Sports for the Spectator

Miami offers a variety of spectator sports at both the professional and collegiate level. The Miami Dolphins of the National Football League play their home games in Pro Player Stadium, which is also home to the Florida Marlins National League baseball team. The AmericanAirlines Arena houses the professional basketball team the Miami Heat, who play from November through April. The Florida Panthers of the National Hockey League play from October through April at the National Car Rental Center in neighboring Broward County. The excitement of Major League Soccer exists for the city in the form of the Miami Fusion, who play home games at Lockhart Stadium in Fort Lauderdale.

The city of Miami is the site of the Orange Bowl Classic and Festival, which features the annual New Year's Day football game between two top-ranked collegiate teams. The University of Miami Hurricanes play their home basketball games in the Orange Bowl, while the Florida International University Golden Panthers play at the Golden Panther Arena.

Other popular spectator sports in the Miami area are horse and auto racing. Hialeah Park holds thoroughbred races year-round; Calder Race Course in Miami also offers thoroughbred racing. One of Miami's major sporting events is the Grand Prix of Miami, an annual, week-long auto race in the European tradition. Held at the Metro-Dade Homestead-Miami Speedway, the event attracts more sports car entries than any other auto racing event in the United States and is televised throughout the world. It also features the season opener of the PPG Indy Car World Series. Jai-alai is played year-round at the Miami Jai-Alai fronton. Those interested in other sports can choose among golf tournaments, greyhound races, horse shows, regattas, soccer matches, and tennis tournaments. Golf enthusiasts enjoy the Royal Caribbean International Golf Classic and the Genuity Golf Championship, while tennis fans gather for the Florida Caribbean Tennis Championships, the NASDAQ-100 Open, and the Ericsson Open.

## Sports for the Participant

A complete range of outdoor activities is available year-round in Miami at numerous public and private facilities. Miami-Dade County offers more than 20 public golf courses. Nearly 500 tennis courts for day and evening play are located in many parks and recreation areas throughout Miami and the county; in addition, most hotels have their own tennis facilities.

The extensive public park system in the Miami area was called "one of the most innovative systems in the country" by the National Recreation and Parks Association. Of the more than 300 parks and nature centers, two are national parks: Everglades and Biscayne. Among the recreational activities that can be pursued in Miami's parks are picnicking, canoeing, boating, hiking, camping, fishing, swimming, basketball, softball, handball, racquetball, vita course trails, and 80 miles of Class I bike trails.

Water sports are pursued with great enthusiasm in Miami's ocean and bay. Most local dive shops offer lessons, certification courses, and dive trips for scuba and skin diving. Among the favorite diving spots are Haulover Park and Biscayne National Park. For surfing one can go to Haulover Beach in Sunny Isles and South Pointe in South Miami Beach. A popular place for windsurfing is Hobie Beach in Key Biscayne. Waterskiing schools, jumps, towing services, and ski boat rentals can be found along beaches and causeways throughout the Miami area. Many beach hotels also offer water sports equipment rental.

Fishing is another favorite pastime. A fresh water fishing license, obtainable at bait and tackle stores, is required for anyone between the ages of 15 and 65 years. The Florida Game and Fresh Water Commission publishes guides to fishing regions. In the Miami area the popular spots are Tamiami Canal, from west Miami along U.S. 41, which is noted for pan fish and bass; and Thompson Park fishing camp, a 29-acre campground near Hialeah, with three fishing lakes available only to campers. No license is required for salt water fishing, but minimum size and bag limits apply. Fishing piers are located at Haulover Park, Baker's Haulover Cut, and South Pointe. Full-service charter boats and party boats for deep sea fishing are available at area marinas. Annual events include the Mayor's Cup Billfish and Miami Billfish tournaments.

## Shopping and Dining

In keeping with its international image, Miami offers a cosmopolitan shopping experience. Every kind of shopping facility is available in the area, from indoor and outdoor malls to elegant specialty boutiques. Virtually all famous high-end retailers and designers, including Chanel, Versace, Saks Fifth Avenue, Cartier, and Bloomingdale's, have a presence in the area.

Aventura Mall, located in the northern portion of Miami-Dade County, is the largest super-regional mall in south Florida. It contains 250 upscale shops and restaurants, as well as a 24-screen movie theater. The Village at Merrick Park, which opened in 2002, features 115 stores and restaurants in a natural environment complete with landscaped fountains, tropical foliage, and serene gardens. At the Downtown Miami Shopping District are more than 1,000 retail businesses, including the country's second-largest jewelry district. In Little Havana ethnic shops offer a variety of exotic items, from Cuban coffee and rum-soaked pastries to mantillas and furniture. The Falls, located on the southern edge of the city and anchored by Bloomingdale's and Macy's, sets its more than 100 shops among covered walkways, footbridges, and waterfalls. In Coconut Grove, CocoWalk shopping district resembles a European village. Bal Harbor Shops are in Miami Beach in an area called the Rodeo Drive of the South because of their exclusive stores and designer boutiques. Lincoln Road Shopping District, located in the Art Deco District of Miami Beach, was the first pedestrian-only shopping street in the United States. In trendy South Miami, The Shops at Sunset Place, an entertainment-shopping complex, has waterfalls, fountains, a grand staircase, and 35-foot Banyan trees.

Dadeland Mall features more than 185 specialty stores. Biscayne Bay's open-air Bayside Marketplace, on 20 acres of waterfront property at the north end of Bayside Park, has more than 100 shops that offer merchandise not ordinarily found in regional shopping areas. Just west of Miami Beach is the Miami Design District, comprised of 18 blocks of interior design showrooms and home furnishings and furniture stores that are open to the public.

With its expanding role in international trade, cuisine from every culture as well as local specialties can be found in a wide variety of dining establishments in Miami. Enhancing the ethnic diversity of Miami's dining possibilities are the more than 30 restaurants, supper clubs, and cafeterias in Little Havana.

***Visitor Information:*** Greater Miami Convention and Visitors Bureau, 701 Brickell Ave., Ste. 2700, Miami, FL 33131; telephone (305)539-3000; toll-free (800)933-8448

# Convention Facilities

With several convention centers, including a new ultramodern downtown facility, Miami is an attractive gathering place for large or small groups. Generous hotel space and a warm climate, coupled with a diverse range of available leisure activities, make the city an ideal spot for business mixed with pleasure.

The Miami Convention Center is located on the Miami River in the heart of the business and financial district. One of the most advanced meeting, educational, sports, and entertainment complexes in the southeast, it offers 70,000 square feet of space for exhibits, shops, and restaurants, and its main convention floor can accommodate 5,000 people. The Hyatt Regency Miami is adjacent to the center, and also offers convention facilities. The 5,000-seat James L. Knight International Center can accommodate many types of events, and Riverfront Hall adds 28,000 square feet of space to the Convention Center. A scenic promenade leads from the center to Bayside Marketplace.

The Miami Beach Convention Center, which spans four city blocks and sits adjacent to the Jackie Gleason Theatre, offers 500,000 square feet of gross exhibition space and 70 meeting rooms. Promoted as the nation's only African American majority-owned convention hotel, the Royal Palm Crowne Plaza Resort features two 15-story oceanfront buildings within walking distance of the Miami Beach Convention Center. Ten minutes from downtown Miami, the unique Coconut Grove Exhibition Center, once a navy hangar, offers up to 150,000 square feet of contiguous space, which can subdivide into five halls ranging from 7,000 to 50,000 square feet apiece. Located on Biscayne Bay, it is within walking distance of the center of the village of Coconut Grove and Sailboat Bay and Kennedy Park. The

Radisson Mart Plaza Hotel & Convention Center is ranked as the largest hotel exhibit space in the region. It offers more than 24,000 square feet of meeting space, with another 115,500 square feet available in the adjoining Radisson Centre.

For groups ranging in size from 20 to 1,350 people, other downtown meeting sites can be found in numerous hotels. Some resort hotels located in Miami offer meeting facilities along with a variety of activities, including health clubs and water sports; similarly, some resort hotels located in nearby Coconut Grove, Key Biscayne, and Coral Gables also accommodate large and small meeting groups. Miami Beach, too, offers a number of hotels with meeting facilities, of which the best known are the Fontainebleau, the Eden Roc, and the Doral, popular for decades as tourist resorts.

***Convention Information:*** Greater Miami Convention and Visitors Bureau, 701 Brickell Ave., Ste. 2700, Miami, FL 33131; telephone (305)539-3000; toll-free (800)933-8448; email convservices@gmcvb.com

# Transportation

### Approaching the City

The visitor arriving in Miami by plane will stop at the Miami International Airport (MIA), an ultramodern facility only seven miles from downtown and served by more than 100 airlines. MIA is the one of the busiest in the world, and has the third highest international passenger traffic in the country. The Metropolitan Miami-Dade County Aviation Department, which is overseeing a $4.6 billion expansion of the airport, also maintains five general aviation facilities that handle corporate aircraft flights. The Port of Miami is the world's busiest cruise port, serving more than 3.6 million passengers annually. Amtrak provides passenger rail service into and out of the city. Tri-Rail links downtown Miami to three counties and to Miami International Airport via a 65-mile train system.

The major north-south expressways into Miami are Interstate 95, the Palmetto Expressway (also called State Road 826), and the Florida Turnpike. Main east-west routes are Interstate 195, the Dolphin Expressway (State Road 836), the Airport Expressway (State Road 112), the Tamiami Trail (U.S. 4, which is also Southwest Eighth Street), and the Miami Beach Causeways (MacArthur, Venetian, Julia Tuttle, and Seventy-ninth Street). Other east-west thoroughfares are the Bal Harbor (Broad Street), Sunny Isles (State Road 826) and William Lehman Causeways.

## Traveling in the City

Miami is laid out in a grid pattern organized around a downtown intersection of Miami Avenue (east-west) and Flagler Street (north-south), which divides the city into four quadrants. For ease in getting around, visitors have only to remember that "streets," "lanes," and "terraces" run east and west, while "avenues," "courts," and "places" run north and south.

Miami's Metrorail-Metrobus system is operated by the MetroDade Transportation Administration. A tourist attraction in its own right, Metrorail carries passengers in air conditioned, stainless steel trains on an elevated railway over a 21.5-mile route from south of the city to north Miami-Dade. It provides connections to all major areas of the city. With the completion of the downtown Metromover, Miami-Dade County became the first community in the world to have a people mover connected to a rail system. The Metromover is a free service that is made up of individual motorized cars running atop a 4.4-mile elevated track, looping around the downtown and connecting to the Metrorail. Interconnecting with the Metrorail and the Metromover is the fleet of buses known as Metrobus, which runs almost 24 hours a day.

Bus, boat, and even helicopter tours are a relaxing way to see Miami and its environs. Comprehensive tour service is provided by numerous tour companies that feature half- and full-day bus or trolley excursions in and around Miami. For those who would like to experience the full effect of the city's skyline, several cruise lines in Miami Beach offer luncheon and moonlight boat excursions.

# *Communications*

## Newspapers and Magazines

Miami's major daily newspaper, the morning *The Miami Herald* is supplemented by two Spanish-language dailies, *El Nuevo Patria* and *Diario Las Americas,* a Spanish-language weekly, *El Nuevo Herald*(Sunday), and the *Daily Business Review. The Miami Times* is an African American community newspaper. *Miami Today* is a weekly newspaper aimed at upper management. *New Times of Miami* is an alternative news and arts weekly. Among the more than 50 newspapers and magazines published in Miami are the Spanish-language version of *Harper's Bazaar, Hombre Internacional,* and *TV y Novelas,* which covers the lifestyles of Spanish-language soap opera stars.

## Television and Radio

Television stations broadcasting from Miami include seven network-affiliated stations, two public broadcasting stations, one independent, and one commercial station. Cable television service is also available throughout Miami-Dade County. Seventeen AM and FM radio stations broadcasting from Miami present programming ranging from popular, easy listening, country, rock and roll, jazz, and classical music to news, sports, religious and educational programs, and talk shows; several stations serve the special interests of African Americans and Spanish-language listeners.

*Media Information: The Miami Herald,* Knight-Ridder Inc., 1 Herald Plaza, Miami, FL 33132-1693; telephone (305)350-2111

## Miami Online

The Beacon Council. Available www.beaconcouncil.com

City of Miami home page. Available www.ci.miami.fl.us

*Diario las Americas.* Available www.diariolasamericas.com

*El Nuevo Herald.* Available www.miami.com/mld/elnuevo

Enterprise Florida. Available www.eflorida.com

Historical Museum of Southern Florida. Available www .historical-museum.org

Greater Miami Chamber of Commerce. Available www .greatermiami.com

Greater Miami Convention and Visitors Bureau. Available www.gmcvb.com

Jackson Memorial Hospital/Jackson Health System. Available www.um-jmh.org

*The Miami Herald.* Available www.miami.com/mld/ miamiherald

Miami-Dade County home page. Available http://miami dade.gov/wps/portal

Miami-Dade County Public Schools. Available www.dade schools.net

Miami-Dade Public Library System. Available www.mdpls .org

Miami Department of Economic Development. Available www.ci.miami.fl.us/economicdevelopment

## Selected Bibliography

Beebe, Morton, *Miami: The Sophisticated Tropics* (San Francisco: Chronicle Books, 1991)

Miller, Mark, *Miami and the Keys* (Washington, D.C.: National Geographic Society, 1999)

Muir, Helen, *Miami, U.S.A.* (Miami: Pickering Press, 1990)

Parks, Arva Moore, and Carolyn Klepser, *Miami Then & Now* (Berkeley, CA: Thunder Bay Press, 2003)

Portes, Alejandro, and Alex Stepick, *City on the Edge: The Transformation of Miami* (Berkeley: University of California Press, c1993)

# Orlando

## The City in Brief

**Founded:** 1857 (incorporated 1875)

**Head Official:** Mayor Buddy Dyer (I) (since 2003)

**City Population**
   **1980:** 128,291
   **1990:** 164,674
   **2000:** 185,951
   **2003 estimate:** 199,336
   **Percent change, 1990–2000:** 12.9%
   **U.S. rank in 1980:** 124th
   **U.S. rank in 1990:** 104th (State rank: 6th)
   **U.S. rank in 2000:** 122nd (State rank: 6th)

**Metropolitan Area Population**
   **1980:** 805,000
   **1990:** 1,224,844
   **2000:** 1,644,561
   **Percent change, 1990–2000:** 34.2%
   **U.S. rank in 1980:** 51st
   **U.S. rank in 1990:** 37th
   **U.S. rank in 2000:** 27th

**Area:** 94 square miles (2000)
**Elevation:** 127 feet above sea level (average)
**Average Annual Temperature:** 72.8° F
**Average Annual Precipitation:** 48.35 inches

**Major Economic Sectors:** tourism, software, film and television production, aviation and aerospace, biotechnology
**Unemployment rate:** 3.8% (December 2004)
**Per Capita Income:** $21,216 (1999)

**2002 FBI Crime Index Total:** 21,133

**Major Colleges and Universities:** University of Central Florida, Rollins College

**Daily Newspaper:** *Orlando Sentinel*

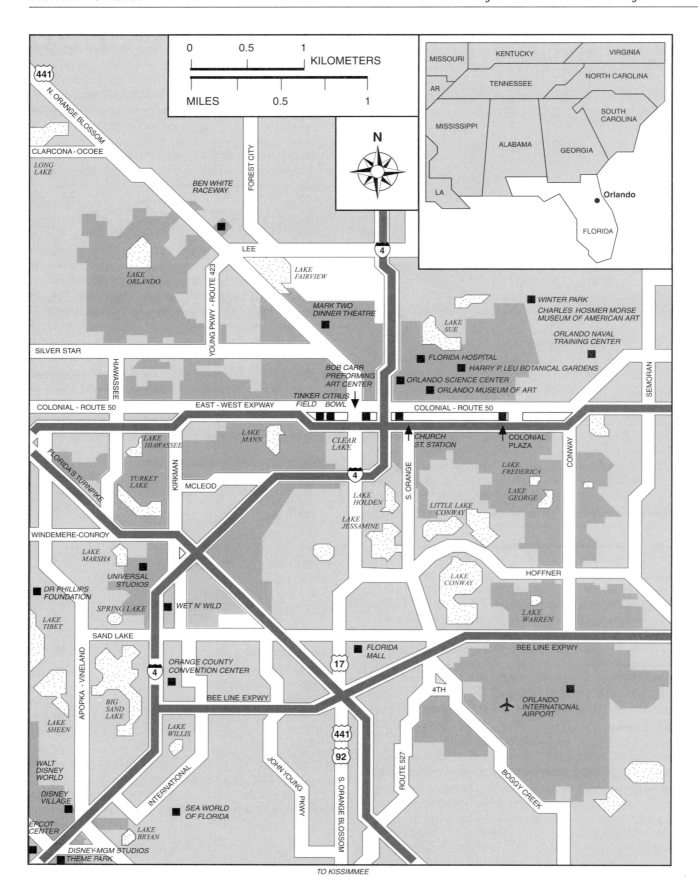

# Introduction

Orlando's pleasant weather, affordable housing, and location at the center of one of the country's fastest growing markets, have helped make the city a boom town. New residents are drawn by the city's attractive setting among the inland lakes and citrus groves and by the short drive from the coastal beaches. Growing numbers of manufacturers and distributors have relocated to the city to take advantage of its mushrooming work force, and major attractions like Walt Disney World, Sea World of Florida, and Universal Studios Florida bring millions of visitors annually. New industries such as film production, military simulation and training, and various technologies are adding to the booming local economy.

# Geography and Climate

Orlando is the seat of Orange County, though its metropolitan area also includes portions of Seminole, Lake, and Osceola counties. Located approximately 150 miles from the Florida/Georgia border, in an area surrounded by numerous citrus growers and 1,200 lakes, Orlando lies about 50 miles from the Atlantic to the east, 75 miles from the Gulf Coast to the west, and about 375 miles from the tip of the Florida Keys. Abundant sunshine and warm temperatures are the norm. Daily temperatures range from the low 70s to the mid 80s from October to May, and nighttime lows average from the low 50s to the mid 60s, with occasional freezes in between December and February. From May through September the daily average highs are in the upper 80s to mid 90s, and lows average from the upper 60s to mid 70s. Prevailing winds are southerly at nine miles per hour. The summers are humid and thundershowers occur frequently in the afternoon.

**Area:** 94 square miles (2000)

**Elevation:** Approximately 127 feet above sea level

**Average Temperatures:** January, 60.9° F; July, 82.4° F; annual average, 72.8° F

**Average Annual Precipitation:** 48.35 inches

# History

### City Built Around Fort

The last 170 years have been a time of phenomenal change for what was once referred to as "The Phenomenal City." Prior to the arrival of the first European settlers in 1837, the area that is now Orlando was occupied by the Seminole tribe of Native Americans. Historians believe that the Seminoles, whose named is said to mean "wild and separate," inhabited the Central Florida region for 6,000 to 12,000 years. The Second Seminole War, which spanned the period from 1835 to 1842, began when disagreements arose between the natives and the American settlers on such issues as land, cattle, and slaves. In the years following the war the natives moved away, leaving the pioneers who built their town around Fort Gatlin. Until 1845 Orange County, of which the city of Orlando is the county seat, was known as Mosquito County. Tradition holds that Orlando was named after Orlando Reeves, an American soldier on sentinel duty for a scouting party. While Reeves' companion slept, a native approached disguised as a rolling log. Reeves, seeing what was occurring, fired his gun, woke the other soldiers, and saved them from peril. However, Reeves himself succumbed to an arrow shot by the native. Prior to receiving the name Orlando in 1857, the town was known as Jernigan, after Aaron Jernigan, a settler from Georgia. The first post office was established in 1850.

### Citrus Industry Spurs Development

Prior to the 1880s, the two biggest industries in central Florida were cattle breeding and cotton growing. During the 1880s some of the pioneers started growing citrus trees. The growth of Orlando in size and prosperity was associated with the need for better transportation to citrus markets on the part of citrus growers. The city had its first rail lines by 1881, and during the 1880s and 1890s there was an influx of new fruit growers. In 1885 Rollins College was founded in Winter Park. By 1886 the city's streets were lined with office buildings, churches, hotels, and schools, and tourists from the north began to spend summers in the area.

Disaster struck in 1894 when a three-day freeze destroyed nearly all the citrus trees in Orange County. The freeze had a devastating effect on the community, which suffered losses of an estimated $100 million. Packing plants closed, banks closed, people lost their jobs, and it was 15 years before Orlando fully recovered.

### City Attains Major Status

Between 1910 and 1920 the population of Orlando doubled, and the city was transformed from a rural citrus growing area to a major city. During the 1920s a great building boom aided in Orlando's continuing prosperity, evidenced by the opening of the Orlando Public Library in 1923 and the Municipal Auditorium (now Bob Carr Auditorium) in 1926. During the Great Depression of the 1930s, the federal government's Works Progress Administration programs aided in the upgrading of the Municipal Airport, the building of a new football stadium at Tinker Field, and park development, and by 1944 many new jobs had been created.

Another building boom followed World War II, and new suburbs, new roadways, and new shopping centers were built. In 1956 the forerunner of the Lockheed Marietta company began operations, becoming the largest employer in Central Florida. Gradually many more companies and workers followed.

In 1968 Florida Technological University (now called the University of Central Florida) opened its doors. That same year marked the beginning of the Orlando Naval Training Center.

### City Becomes World-Class Tourist Site

The development of Walt Disney World in 1971 spurred a construction boom that included apartment buildings, hotels and motels, banks, commercial shopping areas, and tourist-related businesses. The city's Municipal Justice Building was erected in 1972 and Sea World of Florida followed in 1973. Tourism increased, thanks to tourist sites such as Epcot Center built in 1982, and the Disney-MGM Studios theme park, which opened in 1989. To the dismay of many local people, what had once been a sleepy backwater town was rapidly becoming a world class tourist mecca. The town of Orlando was recognized as one of the world's most popular vacation sites.

The economic climate during the 1990s and 2000s was marked by diversification. The tools and technologies that were once geared toward military services were applied to the business sector, and the region developed into a high technology corridor. Industries like software, simulation, digital media, and biotechnology began to boom, fueling further growth and development. Tourism is still the city's primary industry, but Orlando has also developed a reputation for high tech businesses and industries both related and unrelated to the entertainment industry.

**Historical Information:** Orange County Regional History Center, 65 E. Central Blvd., Orlando, FL 32801; telephone (407)836-8500; toll-free (800)965-2030

# Population Profile

### Metropolitan Area Residents
*1980:* 805,000
*1990:* 1,224,844
*2000:* 1,644,561
*Percent change, 1990–2000* 34.2%
*U.S. rank in 1980:* 51st
*U.S. rank in 1990:* 37th
*U.S. rank in 2000:* 27th

### City Residents
*1980:* 128,291
*1990:* 164,674
*2000:* 185,951
*2003 estimate:* 199,336
*Percent change, 1990–2000:* 12.9%
*U.S. rank in 1980:* 124th
*U.S. rank in 1990:* 104th (State rank: 6th)
*U.S. rank in 2000:* 122nd (State rank: 6th)

*Density:* 1,988.9 people per square mile (based on 2000 land area)

*Racial and ethnic characteristics* (2000)
White: 113,611
Black or African American: 49,933
American Indian and Alaska Native: 638
Asian: 4,982
Native Hawaiian and Pacific Islander: 150
Hispanic or Latino (may be of any race): 32,510
Other: 10,060

*Percent of residents born in state:* 34% (2000)

*Age characteristics* (2000)
Population under 5 years old: 12,287
Population 5 to 9 years old: 12,104
Population 10 to 14 years old: 10,623
Population 15 to 19 years old: 10,203
Population 20 to 24 years old: 15,639
Population 25 to 34 years old: 39,206
Population 35 to 44 years old: 30,163
Population 45 to 54 years old: 21,614
Population 55 to 59 years old: 7,208
Population 60 to 64 years old: 5,820
Population 65 to 74 years old: 10,577
Population 75 to 84 years old: 7,753
Population 85 years and older: 2,754
Median age: 32.9 years

*Births* (Orange County, 2003)
Total number: 14,917

*Deaths* (Orange County, 2003)
Total number: 6,556 (of which, 123 were infants under the age of 1 year)

*Money income* (1999)
Per capita income: $21,216
Median household income: $35,732
Total households: 80,996

*Number of households with income of . . .*
less than $10,000: 8,182
$10,000 to $14,999: 5,574
$15,000 to $24,999: 12,583
$25,000 to $34,999: 13,178

$35,000 to $49,999: 15,226
$50,000 to $74,999: 13,869
$75,000 to $99,999: 6,159
$100,000 to $149,999: 3,695
$150,000 to $199,999: 1,117
$200,000 or more: 1,413

*Percent of families below poverty level:* 13.3% (53.9% of which were female householder families with related children under 5 years)

*2002 FBI Crime Index Total:* 21,133

# Municipal Government

The city of Orlando has a mayor and six commissioners, each of whom are elected to four-year terms. The mayor is the full-time chief executive officer of the city and presides over all city council meetings. The city council must confirm all mayoral appointments of department heads. The six city commissioners are elected on a nonpartisan basis by district.

**Head Official:** Mayor Buddy Dyer (I) (since 2003; current term expires 2008)

**Total Number of City Employees:** 3,272 (2002)

*City Information:* City of Orlando, 400 S. Orange Ave., PO Box 4990, Orlando, FL 32802-4990; telephone (407)246-2121

# Economy

## Major Industries and Commercial Activity

Orlando is known around the world for its major entertainment attractions, especially Walt Disney World, Epcot, and the film studios. Representing a 4.7 percent increase from the previous year, nearly 45 million tourists and conventioneers visited Orlando in 2003, pumping about $24.9 billion into the region's economy.

Behind the scenes of the area's tourism and entertainment industry is a dynamic and diversified economy that has expanded enormously. Among its most important industry sectors are high technology, aviation and aerospace, film and television production, biotechnology, and manufacturing, warehousing, and distribution.

The aviation and aerospace industry has had a foothold in the Orlando area for decades. The flight training industry was drawn to the area's favorable year-round climate, and military air bases were established in World War II. Since then, with a number of international and regional airports and thriving high technology expertise, the area has given rise to companies providing aircraft and ground support services; Signature Air Services, one of the largest such companies in the world, is based in Orlando. Some of the world's most advanced flight training schools, such as Delta Connection Academy and FlightSafety International, are located in the area. Lockheed Martin Corp., a major defense contractor, has a strong presence in metro Orlando, and The Boeing Co. and Harris Corp. are among Florida's top contractors.

The influx of technology-related companies to the area has made Orlando one of the fastest growing high technology centers in the nation. The metro area has the country's largest concentration of modeling, simulation and training (MS&T) businesses, research centers, and educational facilities. The MS&T sector, which has its roots in military services, provides applications in such diverse fields as homeland security, emergency services, entertainment, information and medical technologies, optics and photonics, and transportation. It accounts for more than 100 area companies and $2.5 billion in gross regional product. Another strong segment of the high technology industry is software. This field, another off-shoot of military applications, focuses on financial services but includes other areas like utilities, billing, higher education, multimedia, animation, and military training. More than 1,000 software companies are based in Metro Orlando, generating nearly $1 billion in annual revenue.

Motion picture and television production is a major element in Orlando's economy. Metro Orlando was a $586 million market in 2003, up from $2.5 million only 15 years prior. Work ranges from major motion pictures and network series to studio activities. Digital media combines two of Orlando's top industries—MS&T and film/television production—into a $9 billion per year enterprise. Known as one of the nation's top 12 clusters for digital media, Orlando employs 30,000 workers in more than 1,000 digital media companies. The field's applications include website design, interactive video, video game development, military simulations, special effects, theme park ride and shows, and computer animation.

Also benefiting from the area's specialization in high technology is the field of advanced manufacturing. Companies involved in this field provide high tech parts for a broad range of products and applications, such as power generation systems, wireless communications, computers, medical imaging, instruments and control, and automotive systems. Among the largest advanced manufacturers in the area are Agere Systems Inc., Mitsubishi Power Systems Inc., and Westinghouse Power Corp.

In addition to advanced manufacturing, Orlando is a prime locale for other types of manufacturing, warehousing, and distribution. New manufacturers have been attracted in part by Orlando's efficient air service, low cost of doing business, growing work force, and high quality of life. Approximately 2,200 manufacturing companies are located there, including Hughes Supply Inc. and Constar International Inc. Plastics is a key sector, with Tupperware Corp. leading the field. Other important manufacturing segments include metal fabrication and parts, infrastructure materials, defense, power plant systems, microelectronics, and laser equipment. As for distribution, Metro Orlando is one of the world's few quadramodal transportation centers, with the ability to transport goods via land, air, sea, and space. The area's network of interstate highways, its international and regional airports, and its proximity to the Kennedy Space Center and the Port of Tampa, combine to give Orlando a distribution advantage over other areas. Major distributors in the area include DaimlerChrysler Corp., Kraft Foods Nabisco Division, Circuit City Stores Inc., and Whirlpool Corp. Moreover, Metro Orlando's warehousing capabilities include 67.9 million square feet of industrial space, in which such items as restaurant equipment, healthcare products, auto parts, and consumer electronics are stored.

Orlando's fertile farmlands, regional healthcare system, and expertise in photonics and MS&T have given rise to a strong biotechnology industry. More than 500 biotechnology and life sciences companies earn $3.6 billion each year in such areas as research, clinical trials, agricultural sciences, and medical training. This vibrant field has applications in industrial food ingredients, plant reproduction, bioterrorism defense, medical products, and modeling systems for laboratories.

*Items and goods produced:* aviation and aerospace equipment, computer software, power generation systems, wireless communications, processed foods, plastic products, agricultural products, data systems equipment, film and video productions, metal fabrication and parts, power plant systems, microelectronics, and laser equipment

### Incentive Programs—New and Existing Companies

*Local programs*—The Metro Orlando Economic Development Commission attracts new business investment by marketing the Orlando region worldwide as a top location for business. It also works with local companies to assist them with expansion plans and other business concerns. Its key services and support range from relocation and expansion expertise to export counsel to long-term planning with its community partners. Orange County commissioners aggressively provide inducements, such as tax credits and refunds for developing jobs and properties in targeted areas, to companies that will have a significant impact on the economy. The city of Orlando also offers incentives to new or expanding businesses, including tax credits, assistance with development fees, and discounts on film production costs.

*State programs*—Enterprise Florida is a partnership between Florida's government and business leaders and is the principal economic development organization for the state of Florida. Enterprise Florida's mission is to increase economic opportunities for all Floridians by supporting the creation of quality jobs, a well-trained workforce, and globally competitive businesses. It pursues this mission in cooperation with its statewide network of economic development partners.

Among the incentive programs managed at the state level is the Economic Development Transportation Fund, which provides up to $2 million to fund the cost of transportation projects, such as access roads and road widening, required for the establishment, expansion, or retention of businesses in Florida. The state's Qualified Target Industry Tax Refund rewards the creation of jobs in certain industries. Florida also offers various sales and use tax exemptions for machinery and equipment purchase, electric energy, research and development, and other aspects of doing business in the area.

*Job training programs*—Workforce Central Florida, representing Metro Orlando, is the regional arm of Workforce Florida Inc., an agency charged with administering the stat's workforce policy, programs, and services. Quick Response Training is a state-administered program that provides funding for customized training for new or expanding businesses, while Incumbent Worker Training serves existing businesses.

### Development Projects

In a developmental about-face, in recent years attention has shifted away from theme parks to downtown Orlando, where many of the most high-profile projects are taking place in the central city. High-rise offices and apartments are being built, and the city hopes that such projects will accelerate the downtown's evolution to a 24-hour hub of activity for the tens of thousands of newcomers who move to Orlando each year. In the city's northeast corner, the former Orlando Naval Training Center is slated to be redeveloped into a self-contained community where some 5,000 people could be living by 2010. In the city's southeast corner, new neighborhoods are taking shape near the ever-growing Orlando International Airport. The largely undeveloped area is expected to become home to more than 28,000 residents by 2020, with millions of square feet in retail, office, industrial, hotel, and government space also available. Millions of dollars have been spent to revitalize the city's historic, African-American Parramore neighborhood. By 2020 the Central Business District is expected to be a distinct family-oriented portion of downtown Orlando, complete with theaters, galleries, museums, and parks, as well as office and retail space.

The Sanctuary, a $60 million residential, office, and retail development, is slated for completion in 2005. The following year will see the completion of two other developments, The Vue at Lake Eola and the Premier Trade Plaza. Office, residential, and retail space will also be available at 55 West on the Esplanade, a $140 million project.

***Economic Development Information:*** Downtown Development Board/Community Redevelopment Agency, 400 S. Orange Ave., Orlando, FL 32801; telephone (407)246-2555; fax (407)246-3359. Metro Orlando Economic Development Commission, 301 E. Pine St., Ste. 900, Orlando, FL 32801; telephone (407)422-7159; fax (407)425-6428; email info @orlandoedc.com

## Commercial Shipping

With global shipping opportunities via air, land, sea, and space, Metro Orlando is one of the world's few quadramodal transportation centers. Orlando International Airport is the 15th largest in the U.S. and 23rd largest in the world. It offers non-stop service to 72 domestic cities, more than any other airport in Florida. The airport is also the site of Foreign Trade Zone #42, an area that permits foreign goods to be stored or processed without import duty. The Orlando/Sanford International Airport is the site of Foreign Trade Zone #250, the largest trade zone in Florida. The Orlando area has more than 30 trucking company terminals, and because Florida has deregulated the trucking industry within its borders, many shippers report rates of 10 percent or less than the national average. Interstates 4 and 95 provide access to many areas throughout the state and the Southeast, and 62 motor freight carriers have local terminals or warehouses. Amtrak provides commercial rail service, and CSX Transportation and Florida Central Railroad transport cargo. CSX Intermodal has a terminal located in Orlando. Orlando's nearest navigable waterways are at Sanford, 20 miles away, Port Canaveral, 40 miles away, and Port of Tampa, 84 miles away. The nearby Kennedy Space Center offers deep water ports as well as launch facilities.

## Labor Force and Employment Outlook

According to *National Real Estate Investor,* Metro Orlando added 19,300 jobs in 2003, an increase of 2.1 percent from the previous year. This momentum is expected to continue, as Orlando was projected by *Business 2.0* magazine in 2003 to have the nation's second-highest ten-year job growth rate, 31.9 percent, through 2013. Much of that increase will derive from the area's key growth sectors, including software, film and television production, aviation and aerospace, biotechnology, and modeling, simulation and training. The available labor pool in these industries is dependent on the availability of educational programs in those fields. In this respect, Orlando not only provides the demand for quality personnel, it creates the supply.

The University of Central Florida offers programs specifically designed to train students for many of these industries. Among them are the Institute for Simulation and Training, Center for Advanced Transportation Systems Simulation, School of Film and Digital Media, Florida Interactive Entertainment Academy, Center for Applied Human Factors in Aviation, Aerospace Engineering Program, Space Education and Research Center, and Biomolecular Science Center. Other regional schools, such as Valencia Community College and Seminole Community College, offer degrees in industry-related fields. The Florida Simulation Center, National Center for Simulation, and the Digital Animation and Visual Effects School offers similar programs. Flight training schools like Delta Connection Academy and FlightSafety International operate independently or in cooperation with such organizations as Lockheed Martin Corp. and Embry-Riddle Aeronautical University.

The following is a summary of data regarding the Orlando metropolitan area labor force, 2003 annual averages.

*Size of nonagricultural labor force:* 925,700

*Number of workers employed in . . .*
  *manufacturing:* 41,800
  *trade, transportation and utilities:* 174,000
  *information:* 24,900
  *financial activities:* 57,100
  *professional and business services:* 154,300
  *educational and health services:* 93,500
  *leisure and hospitality:* 169,900
  *other services:* 46,100
  *government:* 103,500

*Average hourly earnings of production workers employed in manufacturing:* $14.09 (2003 statewide average)

*Unemployment rate:* 3.8% (December 2004)

| *Largest employers* | *Number of employees* |
|---|---|
| Walt Disney World | 53,500 |
| Orange County Public Schools | 22,807 |
| State of Florida Government | 17,200 |
| Adventist Health System | 17,059 |
| Florida Hospital | 14,225 |
| Wal-Mart Stores Inc. | 13,139 |
| Orlando Regional Healthcare System | 12,754 |
| Universal Orlando | 12,000 |
| Federal Government | 10,800 |
| Publix Supermarkets, Inc. | 9,927 |

## Cost of Living

The cost of living in metro Orlando is lower than the national average. With the U.S. average at an index of 100,

Orlando's grocery index is 95.3 and its housing index is 87.8 in 2004 (ACCRA data).

The following is a summary of data regarding several key cost of living factors for the Orlando area.

*2004 (3rd Quarter) ACCRA Average House Price:*$223,128

*2004 (3rd Quarter) ACCRA Cost of Living Index:* 97.7 (U.S. average = 100.0)

*State income tax rate:* None for personal; 5.5% for corporations

*State sales tax rate:* 6.0%

*Local income tax rate:* None

*Local sales tax rate:* None for city; 0 to 1.0% for county

*Property tax rate:* $21.177 per $1,000 of assessed property value (2003)

***Economic Information:*** Metro Orlando Economic Development Commission, 301 E. Pine St., Ste. 900, Orlando, FL 32801; telephone (407)422-7159; fax (407)425-6428; email info@orlandoedc.com

# *Education and Research*

## Elementary and Secondary Schools

In the state of Florida, each county is its own school district. The Orange County public school system is the twelfth largest district in the nation and is the fifth largest in Florida. It is divided into five communities. The Orange County school board consists of seven members who represent individual districts but are elected countywide. Members must live in the districts they represent while serving staggered, four-year terms. The superintendent is appointed.

The Orange County school district offers pre-kindergarten classes in 85 of its elementary schools. All high schools offer some advanced placement and honors courses. Magnet programs are available in all high schools and some elementary schools in such areas aviation/aerospace, language, fine arts, science, economics, medicine, law, finance, animal science, and international studies. Tech Prep and Architects for Tomorrow are two public-school programs that prepare young students for life after graduation. Programs are available for students who are physically or emotionally handicapped, learning disabled, speech and language or hearing impaired, autistic, or visually impaired. Occupational and physical therapy programs are also available. Gifted educa-

tion programs are offered at elementary, middle, and high school level.

The following is a summary of data regarding Orlando's public schools as of the 2004–2005 school year.

*Total enrollment:* 174,060

*Number of facilities*
  *elementary schools:* 108
  *junior high/middle schools:* 27
  *senior high schools:* 16
  *other:* 4 alternative/exceptional schools

*Student/teacher ratio:* elementary, 16:1

*Teacher salaries*
  *average:* $38,139

*Funding per pupil:* $6,409

***Public Schools Information:*** Orange County Public Schools, 445 W. Amelia St., Orlando, FL 32801; telephone (407)317-3200

## Colleges and Universities

Within the Orlando area are two fully accredited four-year institutions of higher learning, Orlando's University of Central Florida (UCF) and Rollins College in Winter Park. UCF is a public state university based in Orlando and having three regional campuses. More than 42,000 students are offered undergraduate, graduate, and specialist programs in business, education, engineering, health sciences, nursing, as well as emerging fields of high technology, including aviation and aerospace, biotechnology, and modeling, simulation and training. Rollins College, a private institution, was founded in 1885. Primarily a coeducational liberal arts institution, Rollins College offers bachelor's degrees in 36 fields and graduate study in business administration, education, and psychology. With a total enrollment of 3,726, Rollins, which has produced Rhodes, Fulbright, Goldwater, and Truman scholars, is listed consistently by *U.S. News & World Report* magazine as one of "America's Best Colleges."

Valencia Community College, which serves more than 53,000 students, has six campuses and offers a science degree program in laser/electro-optics as well as a technical film training program. Seminole Community College, with an enrollment of 32,195, offers traditional academic and industry-oriented courses of study.

## Libraries and Research Centers

The Orange County Library System consists of the Orlando Public Library and 14 branches. The system houses approximately two million books, periodicals, DVDs, CDs, art reproductions, slides and maps. Its special collections include the Walt Disney World Collection, the Florida Collection, the Genealogy Collection, and state documents.

Located adjacent to the University of Central Florida (UCF) is the Central Florida Research Park, one of the top science parks in the world. The park is a joint venture between the university and Orange County to promote relations between industry and the university. Consisting of about 1,000 acres, it is occupied by more than 80 companies in the fields of simulation and training, lasers, optical filters, behavioral sciences, diagnostic test equipment, and oceanographic equipment. One of the park's major tenants is the Naval Air Warfare Center Training Systems Division, the world's leading simulation center for military training. Affiliated with UCF are a number of other research centers that focus on such diverse fields as electro-optics and lasers, tourism, sinkhole research, solar energy, and small business development.

*Public Library Information:* Orange County Library System, c/o Orlando Public Library, 101 E. Central Blvd., Orlando, FL 32801; telephone (407)835-7323.

# Health Care

Florida Hospital, based in Orlando, is a private, not-for-profit network of 17 hospitals and 12 Centra Care urgent care facilities. Treating more than one million patients each year, Florida Hospital is the second busiest in the United States. It is noted for its programs in cardiology, cancer, women's medicine, diabetes, orthopedics, and rehabilitation. In 2004 *U.S. News & World Report* ranked Florida Hospital 28th for the treatment of hormonal disorders, 29th in kidney disease, and 31st in neurology and neurosurgery. Another not-for-profit, Orlando Regional Healthcare System, has eight locations in central Florida, including the Arnold Palmer Hospital for Children & Women and the M. D. Anderson Cancer Center Orlando, as well as the only Level I trauma center in the area. With 1,640 beds, it treats 640,000 local patients and 4,500 international patients annually. Its specialties include pediatric emergency and cancer care, orthopedics, cardiology, brain injuries, burns, rehabilitation, women's services, infertility, mental health, sleep disturbances, and diabetes. *Modern Healthcare* magazine ranked Orlando Regional as one of the best cardiovascular hospitals in 2003.

The Nemours Children's Clinic–Orlando is a nationally recognized center for pediatric subspecialities. The clinic serves children from the greater Orlando area as well as around the United States and the world. In addition, four independent medical centers, several mental health care facilities, and two nationally recognized cancer centers (Walt Disney Memorial Cancer Institute at Florida Hospital, affiliated with Duke Comprehensive Cancer Center, and the M.D. Anderson Cancer Center Orlando) ensure residents the best medical care.

*Health Care Information:* Florida Hospital, 601 E. Rollins St., Orlando, FL 32803; telephone (407)303-5600; email fh.web@flhosp.org

# Recreation

### Sightseeing

Orlando's many attractions, particularly its theme parks, bring visitors to the area from all over the world. In order to draw tourists and keep them coming back, new projects are always under development. New rides and exhibits are unveiled every year at Walt Disney World's four parks: the Magic Kingdom, with its seven themed lands; Epcot, which provides "journeys" to Future World and to the World Showcase; Disney-MGM Studios, where spectators can experience actual movie and television production; and Animal Kingdom, Disney World's largest attraction at 500 acres. Universal Orlando's Islands of Adventure and Universal Studios, a high-technology movie-themed attraction with more than 40 rides, shows, shops, and restaurants, rank just below the Disney parks in annual attendance. Central Florida is served by Busch Gardens Tampa Bay, which is a combination amusement park and zoo with more than 2,700 animals. The area's newest family theme park is Cypress Gardens Adventure Park; once the first tourist attraction in central Florida, this park reopened in late 2004.

Gatorland offers the chance to observe thousands of alligators, birds, and animals; its alligator breeding marsh was seen in the movie *Indiana Jones and the Temple of Doom*. Shamu the Killer Whale is the focus at Sea World Orlando marine life park. River Country and Typhoon Lagoon near Walt Disney World are spectacular water parks with rapids, wave lagoons, slides and waterfalls. Wet 'n Wild, Blizzard Beach, and Water Mania offer family slide and tubing fun. Pleasure Island on the Disney site is an entire island of nighttime entertainment with music, shops, and movies.

A view of Florida's floral splendor is the attraction at Harry P. Leu Gardens, featuring the largest formal rose garden in Florida. Also on display are 50 acres of camellias, as well as palm, bamboo, herb, vegetable, and butterfly gardens.

### Arts and Culture

Once known primarily for sunshine and oranges, Orlando is developing its arts and cultural profile as the city continues to grow. Part of the Centroplex facility, the Bob Carr Performing Arts Centre stages performances by the Orlando

**Epcot Center, one of four popular Walt Disney parks in Orlando.**

Ballet, Orlando Opera, and Orlando Philharmonic Orchestra. It is also the venue for Broadway musicals as well the Festival of Orchestras, a permanent concert series featuring at least five internationally acclaimed orchestras each season. Among the region's other musical groups are the Florida Symphony Youth Orchestra, whose members range from the third grade through college sophomore, and the Bach Festival Society, located in Winter Park. The Central Florida Performing Arts Alliance takes a leadership role in the theater and cultural community in the region. Based in Orlando, the alliance seeks to unite the performing arts, including theater, dance and music, by providing information, developing awareness for the arts, and building relationships with the community.

Orlando Loch Haven Park, a 45-acre cultural oasis, is home to some of Florida's finest facilities for the arts, sciences, and humanities. Among them is the Orlando Museum of Art, considered one of the South's finest museums. It offers permanent collections of nineteenth- and twentieth-century American, pre-Columbian, and African art, as well as summer art camp and studio classes. Also in the park is 207,000-square-foot Orlando Science Center, the largest facility of its kind in the Southeast and home to the world's largest combined Iwerks dome and digital planetarium, and the Mennello Museum of American Folk Art, Florida's only museum devoted solely to displaying vernacular work. Loch Haven is also the site of the Central Florida Civic Theatre, the Orlando Garden Club, and ''The Mayor,'' one of Florida's oldest and largest oak trees.

The Charles Hosmer Morse Museum of American Art in Winter Park includes the world's most comprehensive collection of leaded and art glass by Louis Comfort Tiffany. An authentic 1926 firehouse complete with antique trucks, and Central Florida artifacts from pre-history, pioneer times, and the Victorian era are on view at the Orange County Regional History Center. Historic Bok Sanctuary, a national historic landmark located about 55 miles from Orlando in Lake Wales, offers tours of its historic bell tower, the visual centerpiece of a magnificent garden, which houses one of the world's great carillons.

The Albin Polasek Museum and Sculpture Gardens displays 200 of the sculptor's works; the museum was added to the National Register of Historic Places in 2002. The Cornell Fine Arts Museum at Rollins College houses more than 6,000 works of art. In nearby Eatonville, American's oldest African American municipality, the Zora Neale Hurston National Museum of Fine Arts rotates exhibits of works by artists of African descent.

### Festivals and Holidays

Fun and frolic abound at a variety of special events that attract residents and visitors alike in Greater Orlando. Kissimmee's Silver Spurs Rodeo in February attracts cowpokes from the U.S. and Canada to compete in an event billed as the largest rodeo east of the Mississippi. The Annual Bach Festival is also held in February, as are the GeorgeFest Washington's Birthday Festival, Valentine's Stroll at the Harry P. Leu Gardens, SeaWorld's Annual BBQ Fest, and the Festival of Rhythm & Blues in Kissimmee. The Central Florida Fair, which is approaching its centennial, is held in March. More than 110,000 Harley Davidson enthusiasts participate in Orlando Bike Week each March, and another 12,000 bikers arrive for Biketoberfest in October. Traditional and nontraditional Easter activities take place in Cocoa Beach at the Easter Surfing Festival, featuring an egg hunt and surfing competition, clinics, and demonstrations. April brings the Cabaret Festival, a two-week celebration of comedy and vocal performances, and the Fiesta Medina, Orlando's longest running Latin community festival. Orlando celebrates July Fourth with Fireworks Over the Fountain, a free fireworks display and laser show at Lake Eola. The two-week International Food & Wine Festival is held each autumn at Epcot. Halloween is celebrated at a number of local venues including Universal Studios Orlando, where the celebration lasts for 14 days. The lighting of Orlando's Great American Christmas Tree in early December ushers in the holiday season.

Several arts festivals are held in the region, including the Zora Neale Hurston Festival of Arts & Humanities in late January, and four spring festivals—the Leesburg Fine Art Festival, Winter Park's Sidewalk Art Festival, Maitland Spring Festival of the Arts, and Downtown Orlando Contemporary Arts Festival. The Orlando-UCF Shakespeare Festival presents Shakespearean works performed by professional actors at the Lake Eola Amphitheater in April. It is followed by the Florida Film Festival, one of the top film festivals in the nation, and the Orlando International Fringe Festival, featuring more than 300 performing artists and theatrical troupes.

### Sports for the Spectator

The wildly popular Orlando Magic National Basketball Association team plays its home games at the TD Waterhouse Centre from November through April. The Centre is also home to the Orlando Predators, who play arena football from April through August; the Orlando Miracles, a team in the Women's National Basketball Association; and the Orlando Seals, an Atlantic Coast Hockey League team founded in 2002. Tinker Field is the site of the minor league baseball contests of the Orlando Rays, the AA affiliate of the Chicago Cubs. Harness racing is the attraction at the Ben White Raceway and jai alai is the focus at Orlando-Seminole Jai Alai fronton.

Football fans kick off the new year with the Capital One Bowl, a college contest held on New Year's Day at the

Florida Citrus Bowl Stadium. This stadium is also home to University of Central Florida Knights football games, the Superbowl of Motorsports, and the AMA Supercross Series. The Champs Sports Bowl is an annual college event that takes place in December. Golf enthusiasts can enjoy the Bay Hill Invitational each in March and the Disney Oldsmobile Golf Classic in October.

### Sports for the Participant

Metro Orlando is a golf and tennis mecca with more than 80 golf courses and more than 800 tennis courts. Nearly 2,000 freshwater lakes offer a paradise for boating enthusiasts and swimmers. For lovers of the sea, Orlando has the Atlantic Ocean and the Gulf of Mexico within a one and one-half hour drive. More than 100 campgrounds and thousands of acres of national forest are available to hunters and campers. Orlando itself has about 3,000 acres of park land and more than 30 recreation facilities.

### Shopping and Dining

Orlando provides a delightful array of combination shopping/entertainment experiences. The Florida Mall, anchored by Saks, Gayfers, J.C. Penney, Dillard's, and Sears, is central Florida's largest shopping center. The Mall at Millenia, also located in Orlando, offers dozens of specialty retailers as well as Neiman Marcus, Bloomingdale's, and Macy's. Located across from the Orange County Convention Center, Pointe Orlando is an open-air complex that features more than 60 retailers, seven restaurants, and entertainment facilities. Unique settings are offered by the Mercado (A Festive World Marketplace), which features 75 specialty shops, themed restaurants, free nightly entertainment, and *Titanic—The Exhibition*. The Church Street Station has more than 40 shops and restaurants in a Victorian atmosphere. Discount shoppers may find treasures among the 110 shops at Orlando Premium Outlets and the more than 160 outlet stores in the Belz Factory Outlet World/Belz Designer Outlet Centre. Across the street from the Belz shopping centers is Festival Bay at International Drive, a retail and entertainment mall.

Orlando offers a wide array of dining experiences from fast-food and family restaurants, to lavish fine-dining establishments and novelty eateries. The region's 5,043 restaurants can satisfy any palate, from sushi to steak and pasta to grits. A unique specialty is gator tail or gator ''nuggets,'' true Florida-only fare. The pleasant weather permits many outdoor dining settings, as well as meals aboard a paddle wheel steamer. American, Indian, Italian, Chinese, Continental, Japanese, and Mediterranean cuisine—all are available in greater Orlando.

*Visitor Information:* Orlando/Orange County Convention and Visitors Bureau, Inc., 6700 Forum Dr., Ste. 100, Or-lando, FL; 32821-8017; telephone (407)354-5586; fax (407)370-5002

# Convention Facilities

As befits a city with a reputation as an exciting destination with plenty to do, Orlando is popular with meeting planners. Greater Orlando is capable of accommodating meetings and expositions both large and small. Orange County Convention Center, located just south of the city, ranks fifth among U.S. exhibition halls. It has more than two million square feet of exhibit space and 74 meeting rooms with an additional 62,000 square feet of space in the Valencia Room. Another major Orlando meeting space is the Centroplex, which is comprised of five separate facilities, three of which accommodate conventions, conferences, and exhibitions: the Expo Center, with 71,000 square feet of exhibit space and seven meeting rooms; the Bob Carr Performing Arts Center, which has 2,500 seats and can accommodate professional stage productions; and the TD Waterhouse Centre, which seats up to 17,740 for concert, sporting, and other events. The combined meeting space in Orlando area hotels adds up to more than one million square feet. Orlando offers nearly 111,000 hotel rooms with accommodations ranging from budget hotels to lavish themed resorts.

*Convention Information:* Orlando/Orange County Convention and Visitors Bureau, Inc., 6700 Forum Dr., Ste. 100, Orlando, FL; 32821-8017; telephone (407)354-5586; fax (407)370-5002

# Transportation

### Approaching the City

Many travelers to the city arrive at the Orlando International Airport, one of the fastest growing major airports in the nation. Its 72 non-stop domestic destinations are the most of any airport in Florida. More than 23 million passengers came through the airport in 2004, a 14.4 percent increase from the previous year. Even faster growing is the Orlando/Sanford International Airport, which served more than 1.7 million passengers in 2004, an annual growth of 51.1 percent. It is the third most active international airport in Florida. Other options for air passengers to Orlando are Orlando Executive Airport, Kissimmee Gateway Airport, Leesburg Municipal Airport, and Mid-Florida Airport.

For drivers to Orlando, two major limited-access highway systems bisect Central Florida, the crossroads of the state's highway network. Interstate Highway 4 runs east and west across Florida from Daytona Beach, and Interstate 95 runs from Tampa to the Atlantic coast. Florida's Turnpike runs south to Miami and north to join Interstate 95. Greyhound Lines offers interstate and intrastate bus service to Orlando, and there are four Amtrak stations in the Orlando area.

### Traveling in the City

State Road 408 (East-West Expressway) expedites traffic through Orlando. The Martin Andersen Bee Line Expressway (State Road 528) provides direct access to JFK Space Center, Port Canaveral, and the Atlantic Coast beaches. Other highways serving the city include U.S. 441, which runs east and west, U.S. 17, U.S. 92, and U.S. 27, which run north and south, as well as numerous state roadways. State Road 417 (Central Florida GreeneWay) was named one of the nation's top ten roads by the American Automobile Association.

LYNX, the Central Florida Regional Transportation Authority, operates 238 busses that serve Orange County and adjoining Seminole and Osceola counties. Free service in downtown Orlando is provided on the "FreeBee," and on a three-mile, dedicated-lane transit system called Lymmo.

# *Communications*

### Newspapers and Magazines

Orlando's daily (morning) newspaper is *The Orlando Sentinel. The Orlando Times* is a weekly newspaper focusing on the African American community, while the *Orlando Business Journal* speaks to the business community. *Orlando Weekly* is a weekly alternative newspaper covering news and entertainment in central Florida. A number of medical journals and religious magazines are also published in Orlando.

### Television and Radio

Seven television channels serve the Greater Orlando area, including five network affiliates, one public station, and a Christian station. Cable television offers 66 channels. The city's 15 FM and five AM stations offer a variety of entertainment from music, to talk radio to public interest programs.

***Media Information:*** *The Orlando Sentinel,* 633 North Orange Avenue, Orlando, FL 32801-1349; telephone (407)420-5000

### Orlando Online

City of Orlando's home page. Available www.ci.orlando.fl.us

Downtown Development Board/Community Redevelopment Agency. Available www.downtownorlando.com

Florida Hospital. Available www.floridahospital.org

Metro Orlando Economic Development Commission. Available www.business-orlando.org

Orange County Library System. Available www.ocls.info

Orange County Public Schools. Available www.ocps.k12.fl.us

Orange County Regional History Center. Available www.thehistorycenter.org

Orlando/Orange County Convention & Visitors Bureau. Available www.orlandoinfo.com

*Orlando Sentinel.* Available www.orlandosentinel.com

### Selected Bibliography

Hood, Bachmann, and Jones, *Orlando: The City Beautiful* (Memphis, TN: Towery Publishing, 1997)

McCain, Joan, *Orlando: The City Beautiful* (Orlando, FL: Tribune Publishers, 1991)

Snow, Michelle, *Walt Disney World & Orlando For Dummies*(New York, NY: Wiley Publishing Inc., 2004)

# St. Petersburg

## *The City in Brief*

**Founded:** 1887 (incorporated 1893)

**Head Official:** Mayor Rick Baker (since 2001)

**City Population**
   **1980:** 238,647
   **1990:** 240,318
   **2000:** 248,232
   **2003 estimate:** 247,610
   **Percent change, 1990–2000:** 3.2%
   **U.S. rank in 1980:** 58th
   **U.S. rank in 1990:** 65th (State rank: 4th)
   **U.S. rank in 2000:** 79th (State rank: 4th)

**Metropolitan Area Population**
   **1980:** 1,614,000
   **1990:** 2,067,959
   **2000:** 2,395,997
   **Percent change, 1990–2000:** 15.8%

   **U.S. rank in 1980:** 22nd
   **U.S. rank in 1990:** 21st
   **U.S. rank in 2000:** 20th

**Area:** 60 square miles (2000)
**Elevation:** Ranges from sea level to 60 feet above sea level
**Average Annual Temperature:** 73.1° F
**Average Annual Precipitation:** 44.77 inches

**Major Economic Sectors:** tourism, financial services, manufacturing, medical technology, information technology, marine sciences
**Unemployment rate:** 3.5% (December 2004)
**Per Capita Income:** $21,107 (1999)

**2002 FBI Crime Index Total:** 20,914

**Major Colleges and Universities:** University of South Florida, St. Petersburg College, Eckerd College, Stetson University College of Law

**Daily Newspapers:** *St. Petersburg Times; Tampa Tribune,* Pinellas Edition

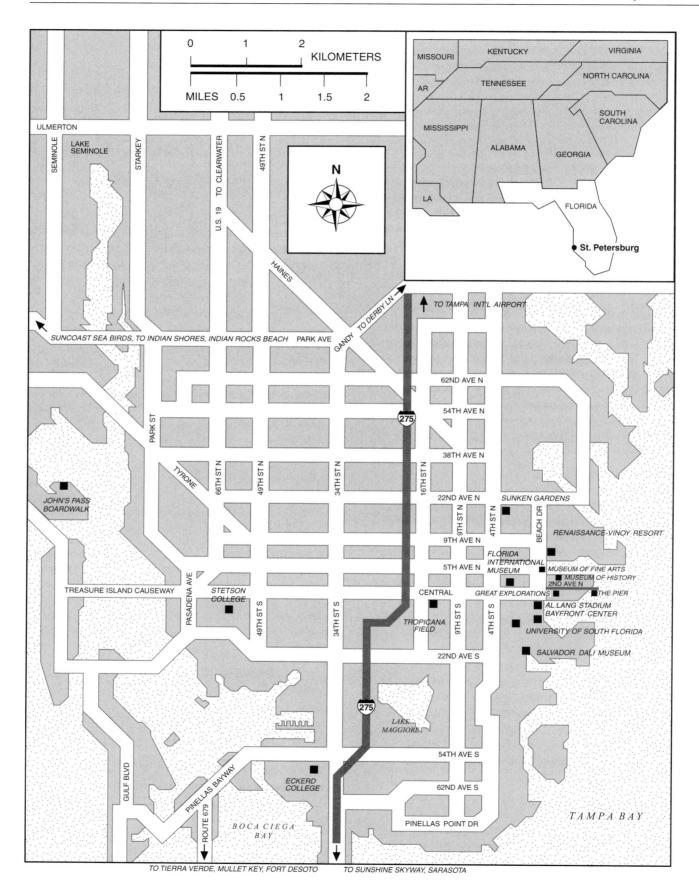

# Introduction

St. Petersburg is a city so confident of its good weather that one of the local papers had a long tradition of giving away that day's edition anytime the sun didn't shine. Surrounded by water and beaches on three sides, the city has drawn generations of winter sun seekers—many of whom return permanently. St. Petersburg has a booming local economy, especially in tourism, health care, manufacturing, and high technology. And "St. Pete," as it is frequently referred to, was the birthplace of spring training for several major league baseball teams in 1914; today Tropicana Field is home to the region's own team, the Tampa Bay Devil Rays. Part of the larger Tampa Bay area that also includes the major cities of Tampa and Clearwater, St. Petersburg is connected directly to a string of small Gulf of Mexico beach communities across the Intracoastal Waterway.

# Geography and Climate

St. Petersburg is situated on the Pinellas Peninsula in southernmost Pinellas County. It is surrounded by the Gulf of Mexico to the west and Tampa Bay to the east. To the north, the city borders Clearwater. The 345 miles of shoreline around the peninsula include the resort communities of Clearwater Beach, Dunedin, Indian Rocks Beach, Redington/Belleair Beach, Madeira Beach, St. Petersburg, St. Pete Beach, Safety Harbor, Tarpon Springs, and Treasure Island. The Sunshine Skyway bridge spans Tampa Bay to connect St. Petersburg with Manatee County to the south. More than 20 barrier islands buffer the Pinellas Peninsula from the Gulf of Mexico, resulting in a calm surf ideal for family water activities. The area's semitropical climate includes the summer thunderstorm season running from June through September, with frequent afternoon rains. St. Petersburg also claims the third highest relative humidity in the country at 70 percent, a figure it shares with neighboring Tampa. Nevertheless, the city boasts an average 361 days of sunshine per year.

**Area:** 60 square miles (2000)

**Elevation:** Sea level to 60 feet above sea level

**Average Temperatures:** January 61.3° F; August 82.7° F; annual average 73.1° F

**Average Annual Precipitation:** 44.77 inches

# History

**Railroad Line Leads to City's Founding**

Like much of Florida, the Tampa Bay area had been settled by Native Americans for generations before the first white explorer arrived. The region was visited in 1513 when Ponce de Leon of Spain anchored near Mullet Bay to clean barnacles from his ships. His party was greeted with a violent reception from Timucuan tribe and de Leon retreated. Eight years later, de Leon returned, suffered an arrow wound, and again fled, this time to Cuba, where he died of his injury. A statue of de Leon stands in the city's Waterfront Park today. Seven years after de Leon's disaster, another Spanish explorer, Panfile de Narvaez, landed in St. Petersburg on Good Friday of 1528. He, too, had notoriously bad relations with Native Americans, and following some preliminary explorations, Narvaez died in a storm while leaving the region.

The first modern settler to remain in the area was John Constantine Williams of Detroit, Michigan, where his father was the first mayor. Williams, like many who would come after him, moved to Florida for his health. An asthma sufferer, Williams bought thousands of acres in St. Petersburg, but lived in Tampa until an 1887 yellow fever epidemic there drove him across the bay.

Williams transferred part of his land to Russian exile Peter Demens and in return Demens extended his Orange Belt Railroad from Sanford, Florida, west to Tarpon Springs and then south along the Gulf coast to Williams's settlement. As part of the deal, Williams agreed to let the railway man name the settlement. Demens called it St. Petersburg after his Russian birthplace. When the railroad made its first run in 1888, the population of St. Petersburg numbered 30 people. Even with the new rail line, the population reached only 273 people two years later. Williams, who died in 1892, the same year St. Petersburg was incorporated, built the first big resort in the city at the corner of Central Avenue and Second Street. Called The Detroit, the hotel still stands today.

Tourism soon followed. By 1909, the first direct train arrived from New York City. The next year, Lew Brown, publisher of *The Independent* newspaper, began his tradition of giving away that day's papers anytime the sun didn't appear—a promise that was kept until the paper closed in the 1980s. Giveaways averaged just four a year, and according to the *Guinness Book of World Records,* the longest stretch of sunshine was 768 days in a row.

**Early Baseball Days**

Professional baseball's spring training had first come to Florida as early as 1888 in Jacksonville, but it was civic boosters in St. Petersburg who made "Grapefruit League" action an institution. The city's first game was played on February 27, 1914. The hosting St. Louis *Browns* lost to the Chicago *Cubs,* who were training in Tampa and made the trip by steamboat across Tampa Bay. Al Lang, a former Pittsburgh, Pennsylvania, launderer, moved to St. Petersburg in 1909 and soon became mayor. Lang, a baseball fan, enticed the Philadelphia *Phillies* to St. Petersburg in 1915. When Philadelphia got off to a rousing start back north for the regular season, St. Petersburg's good spring weather got much of the credit. City leaders later named their baseball stadium after Lang.

**Real Estate Boom Collapses**

Improved roads, increased automobile travel, and the search for warm weather helped make St. Petersburg one of the first Florida cities to live through the real estate boom of the 1920s. The city counted 14 residents in 1920 and 50,000 residents just five years later. The boom years left a legacy of landmarks built in the Mediterranean Revival style that today remain as a graceful reminder of the city's past.

But the first boom didn't last. By the Great Depression of the 1930s, all nine of the city's banks had collapsed, script was used instead of U.S. currency, and the population dropped back down to 40,000 people. Signs posted at the edge of the city warned newcomers against moving in.

On New Year's Day in 1914, commercial aviation was inaugurated in St. Petersburg, or, more precisely, in the waters just offshore. Pilot Tony Jannus flew a lone passenger (St. Petersburg's mayor), who had paid $400 for the honor, from the yacht basin in St. Petersburg to the foot of Lee Street in Tampa. The flight, on the wooden airboat "Benoist," took 23 minutes, and 3,000 spectators cheered its arrival. The St. Petersburg-Tampa Airboat Line survived for a year before interest flagged.

Foul weather has altered the area on several occasions. In 1843, four decades before the Detroiter Williams arrived, Antonio Maximo set up a fishing camp at the southernmost tip of the Pinellas peninsula. But five years later, a hurricane wiped out his holdings and Maximo disappeared. Much later, the hurricane of 1921 brought 106-mile-per-hour winds and more than 6 inches of rain in one 24-hour period, washing ships up to a half mile inland. The city's main pier was destroyed.

**Modern Development Extends to Gulf Beaches**

Despite these weather-related problems, development continued. Ten major hotels were built in the first half of the 1920s. More important, bridges were extended to the Gulf beaches, which are separated from St. Petersburg proper by the Intracoastal Waterway. Then, in late 1924, the Gandy Bridge, connecting St. Petersburg to Tampa, was opened,

eliminating dependence on unreliable ferry schedules or what could be a day-long train ride around Tampa Bay to the city of Tampa. When tourist-dependent St. Petersburg suffered because of gas rationing during World War II, the U.S. Air Corps filled the void by stationing many of its troops in the area's big hotels. The resorts returned to civilian use after the war. During the post-war years, a second bridge spanning Tampa Bay was added, and the Sunshine Skyway linking St. Petersburg to communities to the south was built.

In the 1960s the city moved to shift its image from a retirement haven to a prime spot for investment and business growth. Besides tourism, the fields of health care, manufacturing, high technology, marine sciences, and electronics were emerging to lead St. Petersburg into its future.

Following two nights of civil disturbances in October-November 1996, St. Petersburg united as a community and vowed to change the way it does business in the inner city by creating jobs, improving education, increasing property values, and reducing crime. In 2000 the National League of Cities awarded the city's efforts with its top award for promoting cultural diversity. Today's St. Petersburg thrives on its popularity with tourists and its flourishing economy.

***Historical Information:*** St. Petersburg Museum of History, 335 N. 2nd Ave., St. Petersburg, FL 33701; telephone (727)894-1052; email info@stpetemuseumofhistory.org

# *Population Profile*

**Metropolitan Area Residents**
  *1980:* 1,614,000
  *1990:* 2,067,959
  *2000:* 2,395,997
  *Percent change, 1990–2000:* 15.8%
  *U.S. rank in 1980:* 22nd
  *U.S. rank in 1990:* 21st
  *U.S. rank in 2000:* 20th

**City Residents**
  *1980:* 238,647
  *1990:* 240,318
  *2000:* 248,232
  *2003 estimate:* 247,610
  *Percent change, 1990–2000:* 3.2%
  *U.S. rank in 1980:* 58th
  *U.S. rank in 1990:* 65th (State rank: 4th)
  *U.S. rank in 2000:* 79th (State rank: 4th)

  *Density:* 4,163.1 people per square mile (based on 2000 land area)

*Racial and ethnic characteristics* (2000)
   White: 177,133
   Black or African American: 55,502
   American Indian and Alaska Native: 769
   Asian: 6,640
   Native Hawaiian and Pacific Islander: 130
   Hispanic or Latino (may be of any race): 10,502
   Other: 2,661

*Percent of residents born in state:* 36% (2000)

*Age characteristics* (2000)
   Population under 5 years old: 14,123
   Population 5 to 9 years old: 15,337
   Population 10 to 14 years old: 15,382
   Population 15 to 19 years old: 14,127
   Population 20 to 24 years old: 13,677
   Population 25 to 34 years old: 34,152
   Population 35 to 44 years old: 40,887
   Population 45 to 54 years old: 34,617
   Population 55 to 59 years old: 12,269
   Population 60 to 64 years old: 10,488
   Population 65 to 74 years old: 20,202
   Population 75 to 84 years old: 15,958
   Population 85 years and older: 7,013
   Median age: 39.3 years

*Births* (Pinellas County, 2003)
   Total number: 9,225

*Deaths* (Pinellas County, 2003)
   Total number: 12,049 (of which, 72 were infants under
      the age of 1 year)

*Money income* (1999)
   Per capita income: $21,107
   Median household income: $34,597
   Total households: 109,608

*Number of households with income of . . .*
   less than $10,000: 12,090
   $10,000 to $14,999: 8,536
   $15,000 to $24,999: 17,685
   $25,000 to $34,999: 17,032
   $35,000 to $49,999: 18,978
   $50,000 to $74,999: 18,489
   $75,000 to $99,999: 8,458
   $100,000 to $149,999: 5,183
   $150,000 to $199,999: 1,430
   $200,000 or more: 1,727

*Percent of families below poverty level:* 9.2% (39.7% of
   which were female householder families with related
   children under 5 years old)

*2002 FBI Crime Index Total:* 20,914

# Municipal Government

St. Petersburg has a strong mayor form of government, which combines a mayor with an eight-member elected council. The mayor and council members serve four-year terms. The mayor is responsible for the day-to-day affairs of the city, while the council looks after city policy, city budget, and mayoral appointments of other city officials.

**Head Official:** Mayor Rick Baker (since 2001; current term expires 2006)

**Total Number of City Employees:** 3,628 (2003)

*City Information:* City of St. Petersburg, 175 5th St. N., PO Box 2842, St. Petersburg, FL 33731; telephone (727)893-7171; email council@stpete.org

# Economy

### Major Industries and Commercial Activity

St. Petersburg's economy has traditionally been fueled by tourism. More than 4 million visitors flock to the greater Suncoast area annually, generating more than $2 billion in direct revenue. But the city's economy is actually more broad-based. Major growth industries in the metropolitan area include financial services, manufacturing, medical technologies, information technology, and marine sciences.

St. Petersburg's economy is rooted in financial services. Not only does the city and extending area serve as base for many financial companies, these companies in turn stimulate growth in other industries by providing the financial resources for development and expansion. Manufacturing companies are attracted to the region's transportation infrastructure. Pinellas County ranks second in the state for the number of manufacturing employees, and ranks first for the manufacture of such items as computer and office equipment and electronics components. The area's research hospitals make it a logical site for medical technology firms, with more than half of all such companies in Florida's High Tech Corridor based in Pinellas County. Similarly, information technology companies cluster in the region, and downtown St. Petersburg is home to numerous small- and medium-sized software and Web development enterprises. The city's proximity to Tampa Bay and the Gulf of Mexico make it a prime spot for marine science; in fact, it is the largest marine science community in the Southeast. This segment in the economy is augmented by local research facilities, including the Florida Institute for Oceanographic

Research and the University of South Florida's College of Marine Science.

*Items and goods produced:* computer and office equipment, electronics components, industrial and commercial machinery, plastic products, sensors, defense-related products, micro-electronics, lasers, medical devices, printed circuit boards, pharmaceuticals

### Incentive Programs—New and Existing Companies

*Local programs*—The city of St. Petersburg administers various programs to assist business start-up, expansion, and relocation. The Business Retention Program offers consulting services to already existing businesses with an emphasis on the Enterprise Zone adjacent to Tropicana Field. The Business Revolving Loan Fund assists businesses in acquiring or renovating real property, and for the purchase of capital machinery and equipment through loans with flexible terms at below market rates. The city offers tax credits or exemptions for businesses in the Enterprise Zone for material used in rehabilitation projects, business property used in the zone, creation of new jobs, hiring of zone residents, and credits for increased property taxes on improved properties. The city helps manufacturing or industrial plants, health care facilities and public works projects to obtain financing below the conventional borrowing rates through Industrial Revenue Bonds. An incentive program offers reduced taxes to employers who hire target groups of individuals for employment.

*State programs*—Enterprise Florida is a partnership between Florida's government and business leaders and is the principal economic development organization for the state of Florida. Enterprise Florida's mission is to increase economic opportunities for all Floridians by supporting the creation of quality jobs, a well-trained workforce, and globally competitive businesses. It pursues this mission in cooperation with its statewide network of economic development partners.

Among the incentive programs managed at the state level is the Economic Development Transportation Fund, which provides up to $2 million to fund the cost of transportation projects, such as access roads and road widening, required for the establishment, expansion, or retention of businesses in Florida. The state's Qualified Target Industry Tax Refund rewards the creation of jobs in certain industries. Florida also offers various sales and use tax exemptions for machinery and equipment purchase, electric energy, research and development, and other aspects of doing business in the area.

*Job training programs*—WorkNet Pinellas provides employment services to employers and job seekers throughout the county. Among its training services are the Quick Response Training Program, which provides customized employee training grants to new and expanding businesses, and Incum-

bent Worker Training, which offers customized training to existing companies in need of training for incumbent employees. The Industry Services Training Program provides basic employee training, consulting, and technical assistance through the Pinellas County School Board. The Success Training & Retention Services program extends intensive skills and development training to inexperienced, unemployed, or underemployed job seekers. The HB-1 Technical Skills Training Grant Program was designed to fill the gap in skills between U.S. technology employees and those entering the U.S. workforce via HB-1 visas. The Entrepreneurial Academy provides business training to new business owners or those who are planning to establish a business.

### Development Projects

St. Petersburg remains one of the fastest growing regions in Florida, and has been called the "megamarket of the South." Among the top growth areas is the Gateway Region, located in the northeast portion of the city, which was dubbed the "Hottest Business Address" by the St. Petersburg Area Chamber of Commerce. Over the past 20 years, it has grown from 4 companies with 26 employees to 350 companies with 30,000 employees. Recent development projects include a 14-acre expansion of the Home Shopping Network's campus, construction of Carillon Outpatient Center, which is a $37 million expansion by St. Anthony's Hospital, and a 9-story Hilton hotel, which will add more than 200 guest rooms and 15,000 square feet of meeting space. The new Brighton Bay development boasts 120 single-family homes, 150 townhomes, and 780 apartments.

Similar commercial, retail, and residential development occurs in other areas of St. Petersburg. All Children's Hospital announced the largest expansion plan in its history, a $270-million project to build a new 8-story hospital and add almost one million square feet of space. The St. Petersburg campus of the University of South Florida plans to create on-campus housing for nearly 750 students within the next 6 years. In 2004 the Poynter Institute for Media Studies nearly doubled its size by adding 26,000 square feet of space. That year also saw the completion of University Village, a 60,000-square-foot shopping center in downtown St. Petersburg.

The city is also dedicated to redeveloping brownfields, areas where environmental contamination exists in the soil, surface water, or ground water. Among the largest redevelopment projects are the Dome Industrial Park, a $1.5 million pilot project that is the first to be undertaken with grants from the U.S. Environmental Protection Agency and the State of Florida Brownfields program. Atherton Oil and Mercy Hospital are two other redevelopment projects, with a combined clean-up cost of nearly $600,000.

Other development projects are aimed at improving the quality of life for residents. In the early 2000s, the city allocated

$325,000 to 33 different neighborhood improvement projects. Pedestrians and bicyclists will benefit from CityTrails, a project that will add 150 miles of new pathways, 38 miles of new sidewalks, and better crosswalks at 81 intersections through 2008. A $2.5 million plan to clean up Lake Maggiore will result in the development of a waterfront park. St. Petersburg established a goal of providing a playground within a half mile of every child in the city. The city is also attempting to secure funds to link U.S. Highway 19 with Interstate 275 to create a north-south corridor through the county.

***Economic Development Information:*** City of St. Petersburg Economic Development Department, Municipal Services Center, One 4th St. N., 9th Fl., PO Box 2842, St. Petersburg, FL, 33731; telephone (727)893-7100; toll-free (800)874-9026; fax (727)892-5465; email business@stpete .org. St. Petersburg Area Chamber of Commerce, 100 2nd Ave. N., St. Petersburg, FL 33701; telephone (727)821-4069

## Commercial Shipping

Port Tampa and Port Manatee serve Pinellas County's shipping needs. Port Tampa, a crucial link between the United States and Central and South America, is the largest port in the Southeast and the nation's 10th largest by tonnage handled. Port Manatee, one of the state's busiest, is the closest of the area's deepwater ports to the Gulf of Mexico. Both ports provide custom house brokers, freight forwarding, and other services. St. Petersburg also has a port, though it is a "non-operating" port whose shipping activities are managed by the city.

Three airports—Tampa International, St. Petersburg/ Clearwater International, and Albert Whitted—serve the area, with Tampa International Airport being the largest. Through it, Florida's top exports are shipped, including industrial and commercial machinery, computers, optical instruments and lenses, medical and dental equipment, and photographic equipment. Freight is shipped by rail via CSX Corp.

## Labor Force and Employment Outlook

The Economic Development Department of the City of St. Petersburg reported in 2005 that the regional workforce numbered more than 1.2 million. This abundant labor pool will only rise, as the region is expected to experience a growth in its population by 15.3 percent over the next 10 years. In 2004, 16 percent of the St. Petersburg workforce was engaged in finance, insurance, and real estate, representing nearly double the figure for the state's workforce as a whole. The city also surpassed Florida in the percentage of workers engaged in manufacturing, with nine percent of the city's workforce so employed.

The following is a summary of data regarding the Tampa-St. Petersburg-Clearwater metropolitan area labor force, 2003 annual averages.

*Size of nonagricultural labor force:* 1,225,700

*Number of workers employed in . . .*
　*manufacturing:* 71,500
　*trade, transportation and utilities:* 216,400
　*information:* 34,700
　*financial activities:* 94,000
　*professional and business services:* 296,700
　*educational and health services:* 142,300
　*leisure and hospitality:* 108,100
　*other services:* 48,200
　*government:* 147,000

*Average hourly earnings of production workers employed in manufacturing:* $14.09 (2003 statewide average)

*Unemployment rate:* 3.5% (December 2004)

| Major private sector employers | Number of employees |
|---|---|
| Home Shopping Network | 2,500 |
| Raymond James & Associates, Inc. | 2,300 |
| Raytheon E-Systems | 2,300 |
| Times Publishing Co. | 2,255 |
| Bayfront Medical Center | 2,100 |
| All Children's Hospital | 2,100 |
| Bright House Networks | 2,000 |
| Jabil Circuit Inc. | 1,900 |
| Progress Energy, Inc. | 1,800 |
| Mortgage Investors Corp. | 1,200 |

## Cost of Living

Housing and food costs in St. Petersburg and the rest of the Tampa Bay area are slightly below national averages. Florida home owners do not have to pay taxes on the part of their property that is valued at less than $25,000 under the state's Homestead Exemption law.

The following is a summary of data regarding several key cost of living factors for the St. Petersburg area.

*2004 (3rd Quarter) ACCRA Average House Price:* $245,109

*2004 (3rd Quarter) ACCRA Cost of Living Index:* 95.7 (U.S. average = 100.0)

*State income tax rate:* None for personal; 5.5% for Type C corporations

*State sales tax rate:* 6.0% on most items

*Local income tax rate:* None

*Local sales tax rate:* 1.0%

*Property tax rate:* 24.3064 mills (2004)

***Economic Information:*** City of St. Petersburg Economic Development Department, Municipal Services Center, One

4th St. N., 9th Fl., PO Box 2842, St. Petersburg, FL, 33731; telephone (727)893-7100; toll-free (800)874-9026; fax (727)892-5465; email business@stpete.org

# Education and Research

## Elementary and Secondary Schools

Pinellas Public Schools is a county-wide system comprised of traditional public schools as well as several types of specialty schools. Seven fundamental elementary and middle schools emphasize parental involvement, daily homework assignments, and strict discipline. Magnet schools are special schools with programs geared toward academically and artistically talented students. Career academies offer high school instruction in academic subjects based on such industries or occupations as veterinary science, automobiles, architecture, and business technology. The district also has five charter schools, one in the city of St. Petersburg, that operate under a contractual agreement with the local school board.

The following is a summary of data regarding Pinellas County public schools as of the 2004–2005 school year.

*Total enrollment:* more than 113,000

*Number of facilities*
　　*elementary schools:* 88
　　*junior high/middle schools:* 28
　　*senior high schools:* 22
　　*other:* 6 exceptional schools; 6 adult schools

*Student/teacher ratio:* 29:1

*Teacher salaries*
　　*minimum:* $31,100
　　*maximum:* $55,900

*Funding per pupil:* $5,895

More than one hundred private and parochial schools serve the county.

*Public Schools Information:* Pinellas County Schools, 301 4th St. SW, Largo, FL 33770; telephone (727)586-1818

## Colleges and Universities

Eckerd College, Florida's only private national liberal arts college, offers work-study and overseas programs and bachelor's degrees. The highly regarded Stetson University College of Law, known as Florida's first law school, maintains its campus in St. Petersburg. The University of South Florida (USF), with a campus in St. Petersburg, is known for the Knight Oceanographic Research Center and its programs in marine science, accounting, management information sci-

ence, medicine, and psychology. The St. Petersburg College, formerly the state's oldest 2-year college, is now a 4-year college enrolling 28,000 students, and is one of the nation's leaders in number of associate degrees awarded. St. Petersburg is also home to the Poynter Institute for Media Studies, a journalism school that also owns the Times Publishing Company, publisher of the *St. Petersburg Times*.

## Libraries and Research Centers

The St. Petersburg Public Library System contains nearly a half million general subject titles, plus special collections of Florida history, genealogy, more than one thousand periodical subscriptions, and back issues of local newspapers. In addition to the Main Library, there are 5 branches throughout the city, and the resources of 14 municipalities participating in the Pinellas Public Library Cooperative are available to residents. Special libraries and collections include the St. Petersburg Museum of History archives and the Florida State Department of Natural Resources marine research library. The University of South Florida (USF) is home to the Knight Oceanographic Research Center, which is a collaborative effort of Florida public and private universities and conducts research in such fields as ocean currents, endangered species, beach erosion, water quality, tourism, and shipping. The U.S. Center for Coastal Geology and Regional Studies is located on the USF campus. The Tampa Bay Research Institute, which studies viruses and molecular genetics, is also located in the city.

*Public Library Information:* St. Petersburg Public Library System, 280 5th St. N., St. Petersburg, FL 33701; telephone (727)893-7736

# Health Care

The hospital industry is one of Pinellas County's largest employers. The city of St. Petersburg has seven major hospitals, including Bayfront Medical Center and St. Anthony's. St. Anthony's Hospital, located downtown, is one of only two facilities in the nation with a vascular rehabilitation program. Both Bayfront and All Children's hospitals are teaching centers affiliated with the University of South Florida (USF) in Tampa; together they operate a joint cardiac surgical program. USF and All Children's jointly operate a pediatric medical research facility, which seeks to solve the mysteries of illnesses in children. Palms of Pasadena Hospital, known for its Continent Ostomy Center, also specializes in treating infertility. Other major medical centers include Edward White Hospital, Northside Hospital and Heart Institute, St. Petersburg General, Vencor Hospital, and the Veterans Administration Medical Center at Bay Pines.

# Recreation

## Sightseeing

The center of St. Petersburg's tourist life is The Pier, five stories of shopping, restaurants, galleries, live musical entertainment, an aquarium, an art gallery, and a Children's Hands on Museum, right on the waterfront in downtown St. Petersburg. The observation platform at the end of The Pier, which juts 2,400 feet into Tampa Bay, provides a panoramic view of the city. During the winter months, a replica of the *H.M.S. Bounty* is docked. At the Sunken Gardens, a city-owned park, thousands of plants and flowers bloom on four acres that also contain a tropical forest, butterfly garden, trails, waterways, and flamingos. Weedon Island Preserve occupies 3,164 acres of historic parkland featuring a boardwalk, hiking trails, and a 45-foot high observation tower. Close to St. Petersburg, the Suncoast Seabird Sanctuary in Indian Shores has one of the world's few "hospitals" for injured pelicans, seagulls, and other shorebirds and seabirds.

Fort De Soto Park, with a beach ranked among the top ten in the country, stretches across five islands (or keys) at the south end of the peninsula. Open from sunrise to sunset, the park offers opportunities for bird watching, picnicking, swimming, biking, fishing, in-line skating, and camping on 900 acres on the Gulf of Mexico. The actual fort, on Mullet Key, was intended for coastal defense during the Spanish-American War, but construction was not completed until after hostilities ended. The guns at Fort De Soto, facing south, have never been fired in battle.

On the south side of the city, Boyd Hill Nature Park is a precious oasis—245 acres of unspoiled land—with over 3 miles of trails and boardwalks that lead visitors through hardwood hammocks, sand pine scrub, pine flatwoods, willow marsh, and lakeshore. On the other side of town, 400-acre Sawgrass Lake Park offers a one-mile elevated nature trail through marshland. Private operators offer boat tours on waterways around and through the city.

Docked in international waters just off the Port of St. Petersburg is the *Ocean Jewel,* a 450-foot-long gaming ship. The ship, which opened for business in October 2004, features eight decks of blackjack, poker, craps, roulette, sports book, and slot machines, as well as nightly entertainment and dining. Shuttles to and from the mainland are provided at no cost.

## Arts and Culture

St. Petersburg citizens—both retirees and younger residents—are active in community theater and musical groups. While the city has a full year-round arts calendar, many of the nationally known touring shows and acts visit in the winter at the height of the tourist season. More than 800 events are scheduled yearly for 9 million downtown visitors. The American Stage Company, a professional not-for-profit organization, presents a variety of productions in addition to its annual "American Stage in the Park" offerings. Other theater groups include the St. Petersburg Little Theatre, Florida's oldest continually-operated community theater, and the Palladium Theater, a restored movie house, that presents a varied venue of music and comedy events. The nationally known Florida Orchestra performs classics and pop favorites at the Mahaffey Theater, bringing in guest performers and conductors in addition to its own musicians. The Bayfront Center hosts traveling ice shows and dance troupes, and popular musical entertainers, circuses, and sporting events.

St. Petersburg boasts the world's largest collection of the works of the Spanish surrealist artist Salvador Dali. In a dramatic waterfront setting, Dali's sculptures, paintings, and other works, dating from 1914 forward, are discussed during regularly scheduled tours at the Salvador Dali Museum. The Florida International Museum, an affiliate of the Smithsonian Institute that spans one-half of a city block, welcomes traveling blockbuster cultural exhibitions. Recent exhibitions include the *The Cuban Missile Crisis, A Century of Jewels and Gems 1785–1885,* and *DIANA: A Celebration,* a tribute to the personal and public life of Diana Spencer, Princess of Wales, with apparel, paintings, letters, film footage, and funeral memorabilia on loan from the Althorp Estate in England, the Spencer family's ancestral home. The St. Petersburg Museum of Fine Arts, the only comprehensive art collection on the state's west coast, owns more than 4,000 pieces of European, American, Oriental, and pre-Columbian art, including works by Cezanne, Gauguin, and Renoir.

The St. Petersburg Museum of History features exhibits of Florida and St. Petersburg history and a Flight #1 wing housing a full-scale replica of the historic "Benoist" Airboat, which flew the world's first scheduled commercial airline trip in 1914. Great Expectations, situated adjacent to the Sunken Gardens, is a children's museum featuring a variety of hands-on exhibits. The Florida Holocaust Museum, located in the Tampa Bay area, honors the memory of the millions of innocent men, women, and children who suffered or died in the Holocaust. Exhibits include artifacts, memorabilia, letters by camp prisoners, and an original boxcar from Nazi-occupied Poland.

Nearby, the Clearwater Marine Aquarium is a working aquarium that serves to educate the public as well as rescue, treat, and release sick or injured whales, dolphins, otters, and sea turtles. Visitors can observe the treatment and care of these animals, view sharks and fish in their underwater environment, and touch stingrays, starfish, sea urchins, and

**St. Petersburg offers five public beaches for sun-seekers' enjoyment.**

sea turtle shells. The Science Center of Pinellas County, located in St. Petersburg, offers seven acres of exhibits, many hands-on, as well as a planetarium, observatory, 600-gallon marine touch tank, adoptable animal room, Laser Odyssey Theater, and exhibits relating to Native American and African American pioneers. The planetarium and observatory at St. Petersburg College presents star shows from September through April.

## Festivals and Holidays

St. Petersburg celebrates the birthday of Dr. Martin Luther King, Jr. each January in one of the nation's largest civic parades and festival of bands. The following months brings the Festival of Speed, featuring exotic cars, boats, and bikes from the past 100 years. The International Folk Fair Festival is the biggest event in March. This three-day event celebrates the many cultures in the area with entertainment, demonstrations, crafts, and cuisines from 40 different countries. Other events in March include the Cajun/Zydeco Crawfish Festival, with 10,000 pounds of crawfish and Cajun, Creole, and Louisiana cuisine; the Abilities Wine & Food Festival, offering premium wines, gourmet food, and hundreds of silent auction items; the Festival of the Sun, a beach fest with reggae music and food; and the Butterfly Festival & Plant Sale, held at the Sunken Gardens.

Spring also brings the Festival of States, a decades-long tradition of parades, fireworks, music, and bicycle races. An Easter Egg Hunt is held each year, as is the Mainsail Arts Festival, considered one of the best fine art shows in the nation. Earth Day and Arbor Day are celebrated with the Green Thumb Festival, which features tree and plant sales, a plant diagnostic clinic, flower shows, and a children's plant fair. Teens enjoy Pierfest, a two-day event of extreme alternative sports, skateboard and wakeboard competitions, and rock music held at The Pier.

Food is the theme of several June events, including Taste of Pinellas, an annual food and music festival with the fare of more than 60 restaurants, and Real Men Cook, a Father's Day celebration that began in Chicago in 1989 and is now celebrated in a dozen cities around the nation. The Tampa Bay Caribbean Carnival celebrates the islands' traditional food and Soca, Calypso, and Reggae music. American Stage Shakespeare in the Park presents the works of Shakespeare at Demen's Landing by the city's professional theater group. The Pier hosts an annual Fourth of July Celebration with concerts, activities, and, of course, fireworks.

SnowFest, held in November or December, features Nutcracker in the Park, the Santa parade, a Jingle Bell run, and a lighted boat parade. The annual Holiday Taste & Tour treats visitors to self-guided tours, music, and refreshments in area bed and breakfast inns. The First Night celebration, held on New Year's Eve, offers alcohol-free family activities in dozens of venues throughout downtown St. Petersburg.

## Sports for the Spectator

Major League Baseball's (MLB's) Tampa Bay Devil Rays are based in St. Petersburg and play at the city's Tropicana Field. Spring training brings three other MLB teams to the area, the Philadelphia Phillies to Clearwater, the Toronto Blue Jays to Dunedin, and the New York Yankees to Tampa. The MLB Players Alumni Association hosts the Legends of Baseball, the nation's largest old-timers game, in St. Petersburg each year.

World-class auto racing arrived in the city in 2003 with the first annual Grand Prix of St. Petersburg. The event takes place over three days in the spring on a waterfront circuit that incorporates part of a runway at Albert Whitted Municipal Airport. The Sunshine Speedway, located near the St. Petersburg/Clearwater Airport, hosts stock car racing every Saturday night. Greyhound racing is a big draw during the January-to-June season at Derby Lane; more than a million fans flock to the track to watch the races and dine in the Derby Club restaurant. The Tampa Bay Downs, located in Oldsmar, features thoroughbred horse racing from December to March. Each spring brings the Regata del Sol al Sol, an annual 456-mile yacht race from St. Petersburg to Isla Mujeres, Mexico. Powerboat racing is the attraction in the St. Petersburg Offshore Super Series held each June, featuring 35-40 powerboats competing on a 5-mile race course.

For sports fans who are willing to travel a short way, Tampa is the home of the National Football League's Tampa Bay Buccaneers, the National Hockey League's Tampa Bay Lightning, and the Tampa Bay Storm, a championship arena football team.

## Sports for the Participant

St. Petersburg's sunny climate means year-round outdoor activities for the sports-minded. The city boasts that it spends more per capita on its parks and recreation programs than any other city in the country. Anglers can harvest more than 300 species of fish in the Gulf of Mexico, Tampa Bay, and area lakes. Charters are available from boat captains along many piers, but shore-bound fishermen can still try their luck at Fort De Soto Park and The Pier in downtown St. Petersburg. Among the many annual fishing tournaments is the competitive Tarpon Roundup, held every summer from May through July.

The Pinellas Trail runs 45 miles from Tarpon Springs to St. Petersburg, linking parks, scenic coastal areas, and neighborhoods for bicyclists, pedestrians, and in-line skaters. St. Anthony's Triathlon, one of the nation's top triathlons in terms of prize money, attracts 2,000 athletes who compete each April in swimming, biking, and running events. The city provides 66 public tennis courts, 29 soccer/football fields, 42 baseball/softball fields, and 18 boat ramps. Golf enthusiasts can choose from three municipal courses, including Mangrove Bay Golf Course, which has been named one of the nation's best by *Golf for Women* magazine. St. Petersburg has 125 parks covering 2,400 acres. Sun bathers can enjoy 8 public pools and 5 public beaches stretching to Clearwater on 35 miles of gleaming white sand. The St. Petersburg Shuffleboard Club is the world's oldest and largest shuffleboard club, and is the site of the National Shuffleboard Hall of Fame.

### Shopping and Dining

St. Petersburg combines shopping opportunities at regional malls and charming downtown settings. University Village, a 60,000-square-foot shopping center located downtown, opened its doors in 2004. Plaza Tower offers 30,000 square feet of retail space, and Tyrone Square Mall, anchored by Burdines, Dillard's, JC Penney, and Sears, features 170 specialty stores. There are more than two dozen art galleries downtown. The city hosts three antique malls: the Antique Exchange Mall, Fourth Street Antique Alley Mall, and Gas Plant Antique Arcade, the largest antique mall in Florida. Stylish Beach Drive has recently been joined by the revived Central Avenue district to offer even more restaurant, shopping, art gallery, and entertainment choices. The Pier nearby offers tropical clothing, shell crafts, and other regional specialties. Nearby Dunedin's restored Main Street offers seafood restaurants, art galleries, and quaint shops.

Dining in St. Petersburg ranges from fresh seafood restaurants with scenic waterfront views to ethnic cuisines from Europe, Asia, Latin America, and the Caribbean. Favorite local dishes include paella Valenciana, a dish featuring shellfish, chicken, vegetables and rice; smoked local mullet; and locally caught grouper either blackened, baked, broiled, or fried. The greater Suncoast area provides a choice of more than 1,500 restaurants.

*Visitor Information:* St. Petersburg/Clearwater Area Convention & Visitors Bureau, 14450 46th St., Ste. 108, Clearwater, FL 33762; telephone (727)464-7200; toll-free 877-352-3224; fax (727)464-7222; email info@floridasbeach.com. St. Petersburg Area Chamber of Commerce, 100 2nd Ave. N., St. Petersburg, FL 33701; telephone (727)821-4069

## Convention Facilities

The St. Petersburg area offers 5 large halls totaling nearly 300,000 square feet of convention space. They are Tropi-

cana Field (St. Petersburg's largest venue), Bayfront Center and Mahaffey Theater, Harborview Center and Ruth Eckerd Hall (both in Clearwater), and The Coliseum (a historic 1924 setting). St. Petersburg's resort hotels, both large and small, can handle conventions, meetings, and other events, with five housing a large amount of meeting space; St. Petersburg Bayfront Hilton and the Renaissance Vinoy Resort have the largest single meeting rooms, measuring 7,221 and 6,724 square feet, respectively. Unusual settings for meetings and receptions include beaches, museums, and cruise ships.

*Convention Information:* St. Petersburg/Clearwater Area Convention & Visitors Bureau, 14450 46th St., Ste. 108, Clearwater, FL 33762; telephone (727)464-7200; toll-free 877-352-3224; fax (727)464-7222; email info@floridasbeach.com

## Transportation

### Approaching the City

The St. Petersburg/Clearwater International Airport, close to the beaches, carries approximately one million commercial passengers each year. The Albert Whitted Airport, situated on the waterfront in downtown St. Petersburg, serves corporate aircraft, private pilots, and helicopters. Most visitors arrive at the larger Tampa International Airport, a 30- to 45-minute drive away. CSX Corp. provides rail service to St. Petersburg, and the Port of Tampa accommodates international cruise ships.

Most drivers to St. Petersburg pass through Tampa and over Tampa Bay. Interstate 275, which runs through the city, connects to both interstates 4 and 75 in Tampa. U.S. 19 connects St. Petersburg to the rest of Pinellas County to the north. The Sunshine Skyway bridge, at the terminus of Interstate 275, spans the mouth of Tampa Bay to join St. Petersburg with Manatee County, including the cities of Sarasota and Bradenton to the south.

### Traveling in the City

St. Petersburg is laid out in an easy-to-navigate grid pattern with streets running north to south and avenues running east to west. Interstate 275 and U.S. 19 are the two major north-south arteries. Central Avenue cuts through downtown and runs out to the beaches on the Gulf coast. Public bus transportation is operated by Pinellas Suncoast Transit Authority. Sightseers may use Gray Line Sightseeing Tours and First Class Coach Company.

# *Communications*

## Newspapers and Magazines

The Pulitzer Prize-winning *St. Petersburg Times,* a morning paper, is frequently ranked as one of the top ten newspapers in the country. Pinellas County also has its own edition of the *Tampa Tribune. Florida Trend* magazine, a monthly publication circulated statewide, focuses on business and finance in the state.

## Television and Radio

Two television stations broadcast from St. Petersburg, an independent station and the CBS affiliate. Six other stations operate from Tampa and Clearwater, including network affiliates, two public stations, and the nationwide Home Shopping Network. Cable television is available to residential subscribers. Four FM and four AM radio stations are based in St. Petersburg, with other stations serving the area from Tampa, Clearwater, and Sarasota.

*Media Information: St. Petersburg Times,* 490 First Ave. S., St. Petersburg, FL 33701; telephone (727)893-8111. *Tampa Tribune,* (Pinellas Edition), PO Box 191, Tampa, FL 33601; telephone (813)259-7711

## St. Petersburg Online

City of St. Petersburg home page. Available www.ci.saint-petersburg.fl.us or www.stpete.org

Economic Development Department, City of St. Petersburg. Available http://stpeteshines.stpete.org

Pinellas County Schools. Available www.pinellas.k12.fl.us

St. Petersburg Area Chamber of Commerce. Available www.stpete.com

St. Petersburg/Clearwater Area Convention & Visitors Bureau. Available www.floridasbeach.com

St. Petersburg Museum of History. Available www.stpetemuseumofhistory.org

St. Petersburg Public Library System. Available http://st-petersburg-library.org

*St. Petersburg Times.* Available www.sptimes.com

*Tampa Tribune.* Available www.tampatrib.com

## Selected Bibliography

Arsenault, Raymond, *St. Petersburg and the Florida Dream, 1888–1950* (Norfolk: University Press of Florida, 1996)

Ayers, R. Wayne, *St. Petersburg: The Sunshine City* (Mount Pleasant, SC: Arcadia Publishing, 2001)

Rooks, Sandra W., *St. Petersburg Florida (Black America Series)* (Mount Pleasant, SC: Arcadia Publishing, 2003)

# Tallahassee

## *The City in Brief*

**Founded:** 1824 (incorporated 1825)

**Head Official:** Mayor John Marks (N-P) (since 2003)

**City Population**
  1980: 81,548
  1990: 124,773
  2000: 150,624
  2003 estimate: 153,938
  Percent change, 1990–2000: 20.1%
  U.S. rank in 1980: 221st
  U.S. rank in 1990: 146th (State rank: 8th)
  U.S. rank in 2000: 135th (State rank: 8th)

**Metropolitan Area Population**
  1980: 190,000
  1990: 233,598
  2000: 284,539

  2003 estimate: 273,489
  Percent change, 1990–2000: 21.8%
  U.S. rank in 1980: 203rd
  U.S. rank in 1990: 146th
  U.S. rank in 2000: 134th

**Area:** 96 square miles (2000)
**Elevation:** 150 feet above sea level
**Average Annual Temperature:** 68.0° F
**Average Annual Precipitation:** 63.21 inches

**Major Economic Sectors:** government, trade, services
**Unemployment rate:** 2.7% (December 2004)
**Per Capita Income:** $18,981 (1999)

**2002 FBI Crime Index Total:** 10,750

**Major Colleges and Universities:** Florida State University, Florida A & M University, Tallahassee Community College

**Daily Newspaper:** *Tallahassee Democrat*

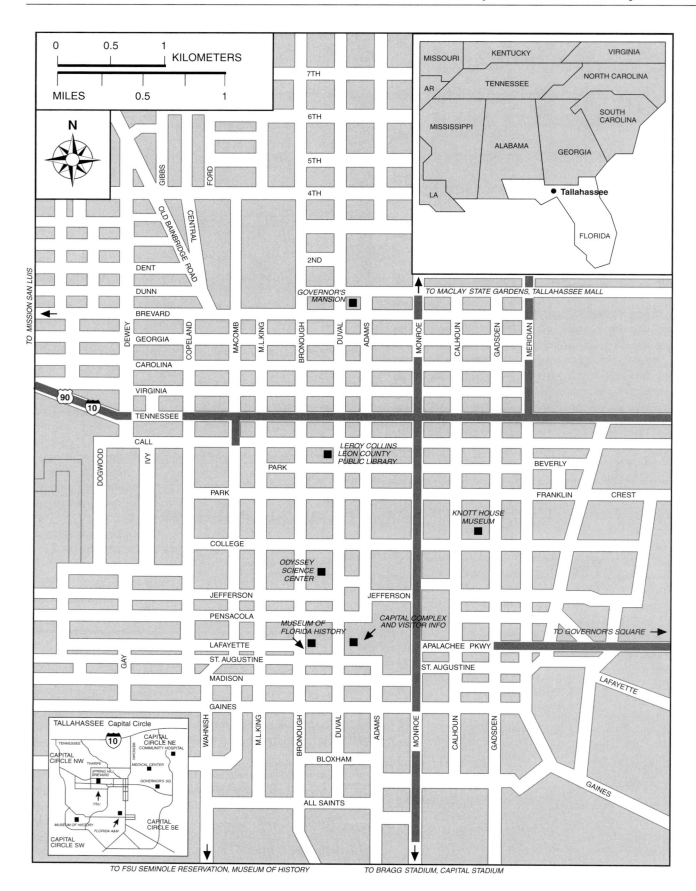

# Introduction

Tallahassee, which means "land of the old fields" in the Apalachee Indian language, still retains the feel of the Old South with its antebellum homes, historic churches, and Spanish moss-draped oaks. As the state capital, the city is a center of both government and education for the state of Florida. The number of young people in the city give Tallahassee a vitality that is somewhat different from other places in Florida with considerably older populations.

# Geography and Climate

Nestled among the rolling hills of northwest Florida, Tallahassee is located in a region of the Florida panhandle known as the Big Bend. The city is set 20 miles north of the Gulf of Mexico, 178 miles west of Jacksonville, and 200 miles east of Pensacola. Its hilly terrain abounds with lakes, forests, and gardens. Tallahassee has a mild, moist climate with four distinct seasons, including subtropical summers with frequent thunderstorms, and 90 days with above 90 degree temperatures annually. Winters are often rainy with less sunshine than in summer and occasional below freezing days. High winds occur most frequently in late winter and early spring, and, with the exception of 2004's unusual season, full-blown hurricanes directly hit about every 17 years.

**Area:** 96 square miles (2000)

**Elevation:** 150 feet above sea level

**Average Temperatures:** January, 51.8° F; July, 82.4° F

**Average Annual Precipitation:** 63.21 inches

# History

### Early Settlements of Tallahassee

As long ago as 10,000 B.C., Native Americans lived in the Red Hills of Tallahassee where they constructed temple mounds on the shores of what is now Lake Jackson (six of the mounds are preserved at Lake Jackson Mounds State Archaeological Site). Prior to the coming of the Europeans, Tallahassee had gained importance as a village of more than 30,000 people. The Apalachee tribes, who lived there from about 500 B.C. through the 1600s, were farmers. They developed impressive works of pottery, which were traded as far away as the Great Lakes. Remains of their communities can be observed at the city's Museum of Florida History.

Although the Spanish explorer Narvaez visited the region in 1628, the first important exploration by Europeans took place in 1539, when Hernando de Soto and hundreds of Spanish settlers and soldiers came and held the first Christmas celebration in the New World. By 1607, almost wiped out by diseases brought by the Europeans, many of the Apalachee left, earning the area the name Tallahassee, or "abandoned fields." The Apalachee who remained accepted the Christian faith, and nearly twenty missions were established in what later became Leon County. In 1704, after almost a century of peaceful co-existence, both the Spanish and the Apalachee were forced to flee from the area after an attack by Colonel James Moore of South Carolina and his Creek allies.

In 1739, encouraged by the Spaniards, who wanted to restore their foothold in the area, members of the Seminole tribe established towns and nearby farms. Following a brief period of British rule, the Spaniards again took charge of the area in 1783. General Andrew Jackson, soon to become governor of West Florida, banished the Seminoles in 1818, who by then were demonstrating resistance to growing American influence.

### Tallahassee Becomes Territorial, Then State Capital

The U.S. Territory of Florida was established in 1821, and the Territorial Legislature decided to found its new capital mid-way between St. Augustine and Pensacola, at the site of present-day Tallahassee. The area quickly gained a reputation as a rather lawless place where gunfire and knife duels were not uncommon. To bring law and order to the citizenry, the Tallahassee Police Department was established. Within a short time, a plantation economy developed around Tallahassee, which became part of the agricultural central region of Florida. Territorial Governor William P. DuVal laid out the city in 1824. By 1837, a rail line connected Tallahassee with its Gulf of Mexico port, St. Marks, and Tallahassee had become the commercial and social center for the region.

Early settlers faced difficult times with Indian attacks, a yellow fever epidemic, bank failures, hurricanes, and a terrible downtown fire. Despite these obstacles, by 1845 Tallahassee had become the capital of Florida, with government playing an ever more important role in the city's development.

### The City in the Civil War

In 1861, as part of the Confederacy, Florida seceded from the Union and Tallahassee was one of the sites where important battles were fought. Defended only by old men and young boys, the city was able to stave off a Union attack in 1865 at the Battle of Natural Bridge, the only Confederate capital east of the Mississippi to avoid capture.

Union leader Edward M. McCook took over governance of the city in 1865, and on May 20th read the Emancipation Proclamation freeing the slaves. While some African Americans moved to the city, most remained in rural areas working as tenant farmers.

Education began to attain prominence in Tallahassee around the mid-nineteenth century. In 1854, a school for boys was founded which later became Florida State University. The Florida Agricultural and Mechanical University was founded in 1884, the state's first institution for African Americans.

**Post Civil War, Twentieth-Century Developments**

Wealthy Northerners discovered the area in the 1870s and 1880s, and former cotton estates were bought up and turned into hunting retreats. Prompted by the concerns of plantation owners over the potential loss of the native quail population, Tall Timber Research Station was established in the 1920s, and soon became an international groundbreaker in the study of ecological issues. In 1929 Dale Mabry Air Field opened, and commercial aviation was first brought to the area. During the 1930s nearly 100 new buildings were constructed in Tallahassee and Leon County as a result of Franklin Roosevelt's New Deal programs.

By the twentieth century, government and education had replaced agriculture as the chief industries in Tallahassee. During the early part of the century, hotels and boarding houses developed to accommodate the growing number of legislators in the city. In an effort at beautification, hundreds of oaks and dogwood trees were planted. During the decade of the 1940s Tallahassee grew by nearly two-thirds, going from a population of nearly 32,000 people to a population of 52,000 people.

By the 1960s the dogwood had become the symbol of Tallahassee, and an annual parade and celebration called "Springtime Tallahassee" was initiated. The 1960s also saw the integration of the city's schools and the founding of Tallahassee Community College. A new Capital Complex was constructed and dedicated in 1978, and Tallahassee's new civic center opened in 1981.

Tallahassee's 1999 designation by the National Civic League as an All America City (AAC) was described by Mayor Scott Maddox as "clearly one of the most exciting things to ever happen to Tallahassee. . . . [It] verifies what we've known for so long—that we have one of the greatest cities in all of America." The Tallahassee Boys' Choir was one of the community projects that led to the AAC honor; the others were the Community Human Services Partnership, a joint human services funding program from the city, Leon County, and the United Way, and Kleman Plaza, a cornerstone of downtown development and revitalization.

Today's Tallahassee shares little of what brings many tourists to Florida, besides its weather. With no beaches, bays, oceanfront high-rises, cruise ship terminals, or theme parks, a slower pace seems to resound in Tallahassee, which is more a town of old-south charm than that of booming tourism.

***Historical Information:*** Black Archives Research Center and Museum, Historic Carnegie Library/FAMU Campus, off Martin Luther King Blvd. and Gamble St; telephone (850)599-3020

# *Population Profile*

**Metropolitan Area Residents**
   *1980:* 190,000
   *1990:* 233,598
   *2000:* 284,539
   *2003 estimate:* 273,489
   *Percent change, 1990–2000:* 21.8%
   *U.S. rank in 1980:* 203rd (MSA)
   *U.S. rank in 1990:* 146th
   *U.S. rank in 2000:* 134th

**City Population**
   *1980:* 81,458
   *1990:* 124,773
   *2000:* 150,624
   *2003 estimate:* 153,938
   *Percent change, 1990–2000:* 20.1%
   *U.S. rank in 1980:* 221st
   *U.S. rank in 1990:* 146th (State rank: 2nd)
   *U.S. rank in 2000:* 135th (State rank: 8th)

*Density:* 1,574 people per square mile (in 2000, based on 2000 land area)

*Racial and ethnic characteristics* (2000)
   White: 91,007
   Black or African American: 51,569
   American Indian and Alaska Native: 376
   Asian: 3,617
   Native Hawaiian and Pacific Islander: 82
   Hispanic or Latino (may be of any race): 6,309
   Other: 1,457

*Percent of residents born in state:* 51.6% (2000)

*Age characteristics* (2000)
   Population under 5 years old: 7,763
   Population 5 to 9 years old: 7,278
   Population 10 to 14 years old: 6,832
   Population 15 to 19 years old: 17,874
   Population 20 to 24 years old: 31,189

Population 25 to 34 years old: 24,008
Population 35 to 44 years old: 17,985
Population 45 to 54 years old: 16,397
Population 55 to 59 years old: 5,185
Population 60 to 64 years old: 3,694
Population 65 to 74 years old: 6,225
Population 75 to 84 years old: 4,598
Population 85 years and older: 1,596
Median age: 26.3 years

*Births* (2003)
Total number: 2,341

*Deaths* (2003)
Total number: 1,031 (Tallahassee), 1559 (Leon County, of which, 33 were infants under the age of 1 year)

*Money income* (1999)
Per capita income: $18,981
Median household income: $30,571
Total number of households: 63,165

*Number of households with income of . . .*
less than $10,000: 12,178
$10,000 to $14,999 5,016
$15,000 to $24,999: 9,721
$25,000 to $34,999: 8,086
$35,000 to $49,999: 8,795
$50,000 to $74,999: 9,414
$75,000 to $99,999: 4,911
$100,000 to $149,999: 3,248
$150,000 to $199,999: 807
$200,000 or more: 989

*Percent of families below poverty level:* 12.6% (47.1% of which were female householder families with related children under 5 years)

*2002 FBI Crime Index:* 10,750

# Municipal Government

Tallahassee has a council/manager form of government with a mayor and four council members elected at large who serve staggered four-year terms. The city commission appoints the city manager who oversees most city departments and administers the daily operation of the city.

**Head Official:** Mayor John Marks (since 2003; current term expires 2007)

**Total Number of City Employees:** about 2,200 (2005)

*City Information:* City of Tallahassee, 300 South Adams St., Tallahassee, FL 32301; telephone (850)891-8200

# Economy

## Major Industries and Commercial Activity

Government is the central focus of Tallahassee's economy, although education, printing and publishing, food processing, and the lumber industry play important roles as well. As Florida's state capital, Tallahassee enjoys a stable economy and a comparatively low unemployment rate. A recent survey of occupations and industries found a wide variety of employment sectors.

Tallahassee is a high technology center and is sometimes referred to as "Silicon Valley South." Institutions such as Innovation Park/Tallahassee, affiliated with Florida A&M University and Florida State University, and Smart Park, a privately owned 130-acre fiber-optic research center, place Tallahassee on the cutting edge of technology. The city boasts that it is the most wired community in the country.

*Items and goods produced:* pulpwood, pine extracts, insecticides, pre-stressed concrete, lumber, boats, feed

## Incentive Programs—New and Existing Companies

*Local programs*—Local city and county governments and the Tallahassee Area Chamber of Commerce have joined together to form the Economic Development Council, which works toward promoting a diversified economy that continues to grow and create more jobs and business opportunities for both new and existing industries. In 2004, the Chamber announced the creation of Action 2010, to promote Tallahassee as a center of art and culture, while expanding local business areas.

*State programs*—Enterprise Florida, Inc. is a partnership between Florida's government and business leaders and is the principal economic development organization for the state of Florida. Enterprise Florida's mission is to increase economic opportunities for all Floridians, by supporting the creation of quality jobs, a well-trained workforce, and globally competitive businesses. It pursues this mission in cooperation with its statewide network of economic development partners.

*Job training programs*—The Workforce Development Board (WDB), commonly known as Jobs & Education Partnership, is a part of Enterprise Florida, Inc. WDB provides policy, planning, and oversight for job training programs funded under the new federal Workforce Investment Act (WIA), formerly Job Training Partnership Act

(JTPA), along with vocational training, adult education, employment placement, and other workforce programs administered by a variety of state and local agencies. Regional Workforce Development Boards operate under charters approved by the Workforce Development Board. The 24 regional boards have primary responsibility for direct services through a statewide network of One-Stop Career systems. State and local workforce development efforts are concentrated on three broad initiatives: First Jobs/First Wages focuses on preparing workers for entry-level employment including the School-to-Work and WAGES (Work and Gain Self-Sufficiency) programs; High Skill/High Wages targets the higher skills needs of employers and training workers for advancement including Performance Based Incentive Funding (PBIF), Occupational Forecasting Conference/ Targeted Occupations, Quick Response Training (QRT), and Incumbent Worker Training (IWT); One-Stop Career Centers are the central elements of the One-Stop system for providing integrated services to employers, workers, and job-seekers.

### Development Projects

In 2005, planning began for a large community performing arts center. Several hotel and condo developments are also scheduled to begin, including the delayed Marriott Civic Center hotel, condo and convention center project.

*Economic Development Information:* The Economic Development Council of Tallahassee/Leon County, Inc., 100 N. Duval, PO Box 1639, Tallahassee, FL 32302; telephone (850)224-8116, fax (850)561-3860. Michael Parker, Director, City of Tallahassee Economic Development Department, 300 South Adams Street, Tallahassee, FL 32301; telephone (850)891-8625; email parkerm@talgov.com

### Commercial Shipping

Tallahassee is served by 13 motor freight carriers, as well as several package delivery services.

### Labor Force and Employment Outlook

Tallahassee businesses have access to a labor force in which more than 41 percent of working adults hold college degrees. *Inc.* magazine has ranked Tallahassee among the "Best Small Metro Areas to start and grow a business." In 2002, *Forbes* magazine listed Tallahassee as one of the Best Places for Business and Careers. The fastest growing business sectors are telecommunications, computer hardware vendors, software developers, and trade associations.

The following is a summary of data regarding the Talahassee metropolitan area labor force, 2003 annual averages.

*Size of nonagricultural labor force:* 158,600

*Number of workers employed in . . .*
*construction and mining:* 7,300
*manufacturing:* 3,600
*trade, transportation and utilities:* 22,200
*information:* 3,800
*financial activities:* 7,200
*professional and business services:* 17,600
*educational and health services:* 16,200
*leisure and hospitality:* 13,100
*other services:* 7,600
*government:* 60,100

*Average hourly earnings of production workers employed in manufacturing:* $14.09 (2003 statewide average)

*Unemployment rate:* 2.7% (December 2004)

| Largest employers | Number of employees |
|---|---|
| State of Florida | 25,204 |
| Florida State University | 8,784 |
| Leon County Schools | 4,403 |
| City of Tallahassee | 3,327 |
| Tallahassee Memorial Healthcare | 2,850 |
| Florida A & M University | 2,681 |
| Publix Super Markets | 2,000 |
| Leon County | 1,522 |
| Tallahassee Community College | 1,090 |
| Sprint | 740 |

### Cost of Living

The following is a summary of data regarding several key cost of living factors for the Tallahassee area.

*2004 (3rd Quarter) ACCRA Average House Price:* $261,680

*2004 (3rd Quarter) ACCRA Cost of Living Index:* 101.4 (U.S. average = 100.0)

*State income tax rate:* None

*State sales tax rate:* 6.0%

*Local income tax rate:* None

*Local sales tax rate:* 1.5

*Property tax rate:* 3.2 mills per $100 of assessed valuation

*Economic Information:* Tallahassee Area Chamber of Commerce, 100 N. Duval, PO Box 1639, Tallahassee, FL 32302; telephone (850)224-8116

# Education and Research

## Elementary and Secondary Schools

The Leon County School District offers programs in education for the gifted, physically and emotionally handicapped, and homebound, as well as programs in vocational education, special education, adult job preparation, and adult general education. Leon County students continue to score higher than students state-wide and nationally on the Scholastic Achievement Test.

The following is a summary of data regarding the Leon County School District as of the 2003–2004 school year.

*Total enrollment:* 31,857

*Number of facilities*
　　*elementary schools:* 24
　　*junior high/middle schools:* 7
　　*combination schools:* 3
　　*senior high schools:* 6
　　*other:* 2 charter and 9 other

*Student/teacher ratio:* 18.6

*Teacher salaries*
　　*average:* $39,117

*Funding per pupil:* $3,485

***Public Schools Information:*** Superintendent, Leon County School District, 2757 W. Pensacola St., Tallahassee, FL 32304; telephone (850)487-7100

## Colleges and Universities

Florida State University, with its more than 38,000 students, is known for its science program, performing arts curricula, and super computing; it recently added a new School of Computational Science and Information Technology. Florida A & M University, founded in 1888 as a primarily African American institution, has more than 9,000 students; it has received acclaim for its business, pharmacy, and engineering schools, as well as for being home of the high-stepping Marching 100 Band. Tallahassee Community College serves 10,000 students, most of whom are in the associates-in-arts transfer program.

Tallahassee is also the site of the Lively Technical Center, one of ten centers for electronic excellence in the state, offering entry-level training in disciplines such as electronics, drafting, aircraft maintenance, and computer service. Keiser College, a private college, provides associate and bachelor degree programs in such fields as criminal justice, business administration and culinary arts

## Libraries and Research Centers

LeRoy Collins Leon County Public Library maintains six branches housing nearly 319,000 volumes. The library offers a Tech/Media Section with a computer laboratory, books-on-tape, CD-ROMs, and a large video collection. Special features are its Youth Services section, Consumer Center, Map Resource Center, and Grants Information area. The library provides Tallahassee FreeNet, a free community internet provider that offers instruction and support.

The city of Tallahassee boasts more than 40 special and research libraries affiliated with educational institutions, state agencies, and private companies. Governmental libraries cover such subjects as environmental protection, agriculture, commerce, legal affairs, transportation, medical services, and public service.

Research centers affiliated with Florida State University (FSU) cover such topics as European politics, aquatic research, biomedical toxicology, environmental hazards, marine biology, neuroscience, communication science, computing, weather, insurance, management, real estate, population studies, and education. FSU's National High Magnetic Field Laboratory is one of the nation's newest high-tech laboratories for scientific research and engineering. Florida A & M University researches areas such as anti-inflammatory drugs, space life sciences, computers, transit, and child development.

Other research centers in the city include Tall Timbers Research Station, dedicated to protecting wildlands and preserving natural habitats; the Dyslexia Research Institute; and institutions that study conflict resolution, government, taxation, family services, and archeology.

***Public Library Information:*** LeRoy Collins Leon County Public Library, 200 West Park Avenue, Tallahassee, FL 32301-7720; telephone (850)487-2665

# Health Care

Tallahassee is served by two local hospitals plus walk-in clinics and a mental health center. The Tallahassee Memorial Healthcare, eighth largest hospital in Florida, is a 770-bed hospital that provides open-heart surgery and cardiac transplantation, renal dialysis, laser surgery, and lithotripsy. Other services are a community cancer treatment center, neurological intensive care services, a psychiatric center, and the area's only neonatal high-risk nursery. In 2004, Tallahassee Memorial Cancer Center became affiliated with H. Lee Moffitt Cancer Center in Tampa, FL.

Capital Regional Medical Center is a fully accredited, acute care hospital serving the residents of North Florida and

**The Florida State Capitol building.**

South Georgia. Established in 1979, Capital Regional Medical Center has 180 state-licensed beds and a 700-person hospital staff, including more than 300 physicians and approximately 250 professional nurses. Surgical specialties include a heart surgery program and orthopedic, urological, and neurosurgery centers. In 1998, the center completed a $1.1 million dollar renovation and expansion of their Emergency Department. More recent renovations and expansions (2004) include a new facility, with public areas and a facade designed by architect Michael Graves. The new hospital center includes all new equipment, private rooms, and a state-of-the-art Heart Center. Other services include a full range of outpatient services, specialized intensive care units, radiology, respiratory care, physical therapy, a Wound Care Center, Family Center, and a hyberbaric oxygen chamber.

Big Bend Hospice offers compassionate in-home care to people with terminal illnesses, with several satellite offices in Northern Florida. Hospice House, a homelike residence for patients who cannot remain at home through the end of their illness, offers short-term crisis care.

# Recreation

### Sightseeing

Tallahassee offers the visitor a handsome vista of rolling hills, abundant trees, and an interesting variety of Southern architectural styles. The downtown district was formed according to the plan of William DuVal, governor of the Florida Territory. The major symbols of the state of Florida's government are its Old and New Capitol Buildings. The old Greek Revival-style 1845 building was expanded in 1902, with the addition of grand porticoes and a majestic dome. The New Capitol, erected in 1978, is an example of the "new classicism" style. A fifth-floor observation deck allows visitors to watch the legislature in session.

Within the Park Avenue Historic District, visitors can stroll along streets lined with graceful ante-bellum and turn-of-the-century homes, explore the Old City Cemetery, and enjoy the newly renovated city parks. The district's historic Knott House Museum is known as the "house that rhymes," for the poems attached to its Victorian era furnishings. The Calhoun Street Historic District, once termed "gold dust street" because of its wealthy residents, is home to the 1856 Brokaw-McDougall House and Gardens.

Other historic houses worth noting are the Governor's Mansion, patterned after Andrew Jackson's The Hermitage, and the LeMoyne Art Foundation, listed on the National Register of Historic Places. Free tours are offered on the grounds of the Goodwood Plantation's house and gardens. Fine crystal, porcelain, and period furniture are among the collections of the Pebble Hill Plantation, which features gardens, a kennel, a fire house, a log cabin schoolhouse, and a cemetery. Nearby Alfred B. Maclay State Park displays flowers and shrubs in a setting of reflecting pools, bubbling fountains, and a natural lake.

Driving tours along the lush, moss-draped "Canopy Roads" of the region (so named for their arching trees overhead) include the Native Trail tour, which focuses on architectural history; the Cotton Trail, which traces the impact of the area's cotton trade; and the Quail Trail Tour, which highlights the ante-bellum hunting estates that dot the landscape.

The Museum of Florida History allows visitors to climb aboard a reconstructed steamboat, examine sunken treasures, and march to a Civil War musical beat. The Mission San Luis de Apalachee, site of the only reconstructed Spanish mission in Florida and a Native American village, offers ongoing excavations, exhibits, and living history demonstrations. Animals such as red wolves, Florida panthers, and alligators thrive on the 52 acres of the Tallahassee Museum of History and Natural Science, which offers a nature center, an 1880s farm, a child friendly Discovery Center, and special events throughout the year.

Fun and exploration in the world of science are the focus of the Mary Brogan Museum of Art and Science. The Challenger Learning Center features a planetarium, IMAX theater, and programs for students K–12, featuring mission control and space station simulators. The National High Magnetic Field Laboratory on the Florida State University campus offers tours of its state-of-the-art facility where such high-tech procedures as magnetic resonance imaging and tests with semiconductors and super-conductors are performed.

### Arts and Culture

Tallahassee's Civic Center and college auditoriums are the site for many musical and theatrical events throughout the year. The Tallahassee-Leon County Civic Center plays host to touring Broadway shows during its main September-through-March season. The renowned Florida State University (FSU) School of Theatre offers productions at its three facilities: the Mainstage, The Lab, and the Studio Theatre. The university's School of Music presents more than 400 concerts, recitals, and opera performances annually. FSU's Ruby Diamond Auditorium plays host to the Tallahassee Symphony Orchestra, whose season, which includes a Masterworks Series and a holiday concert, runs from October through April. The Tallahassee Ballet Company, also housed at FSU's Ruby Diamond Auditorium, presents three major performances annually, and provides ballet lessons for the community. Florida A & M University hosts a variety of concerts in the Foster-Tanner Fine Arts Center recital hall. The Tallahassee Little Theatre produces a September-through-May season of offerings as well as its avant-garde "Coffeehouse Productions."

## Festivals and Holidays

Tallahassee welcomes spring with March's Jazz and Blues Festival at the Tallahassee Museum of History and Natural Science, and the Springtime Tallahassee celebration, spanning dates in March and April. A parade kicks off the spring events, which include six stages of entertainment, and more than 250 food and craft vendors. The Flying High Circus, an actual circus found on the campus of Florida State University stages shows in Tallahassee during the first two weekends in April before moving to Callaway Gardens for the summer.

The spirit of the Renaissance inspires the Southern Shakespeare Festival, which culminates with a free performance of Shakespearean plays at Downtown Capitol Commons. July events include the area's largest fireworks display on July Fourth at Tom Brown Park, and the Swamp Stomp at the Museum of History and Natural Science, featuring guitar music in all its variety. Calypso rhythms and the smell of jerk chicken and salsa fill the air at the Caribbean Carnival, which takes place downtown during August.

The crafts and culture of the Seminole, Miccosukee, Creek, and Choctaw are the focus of the Native American Heritage Festival each September. The "World's Largest Free Fish Fry" lures visitors to the Florida Forest Festival in October. Autumn is also the time for the North Florida Fair with its livestock shows, performances, and carnival rides, and the Halloween Howl with its ghost stories and trick or treating on a circa-1800s farm. November brings Market Days at which 270 artists and craftspersons display their wares. The joys and lights of Christmas brighten up December's Winter Festival downtown, and at the Knott House Candlelight Tour. The early history of Tallahassee takes the spotlight at January's Hernando DeSoto Winter Encampment, which focuses on the Spanish and Apalachee cultures. In order to keep the Spanish speaking culture alive in Tallahassee, the North Florida Hispanic Association hosts a yearly Hispanic festival.

## Sports for the Spectator

Although Tallahassee does not field any professional teams, watching college sporting events is very popular—so popular, in fact, that the city sponsors Downtown Get Downs, high spirited, themed block-parties, on most Friday nights preceding college home football games. The free events feature food vendors, live entertainment, arts and crafts, and more. Football, baseball, and other intercollegiate sports are played by the Florida State Seminoles and Florida A & M Rattlers.The Nike Tallahassee Open takes place in April at the Golden Eagle Country Club.

The Tallahassee Sports Council is involved in hosting multisport and community partnership events, such as the hosting NCAA basketball and tennis championships and the Sunshine State Games. The Sports Council also serves as agent to such local sports entities as the Tallahassee Soccer Association, the Amateur Sports Association, and the Center Classic.

## Sports for the Participant

An undisturbed natural environment adds to the enjoyment of the many recreational resources in the area. In 2004, Tallahassee's Parks and Recreation Department won a Gold Medal Award from the National Recreation and Park Association, naming it the best in the country for cities with populations of 100,000 to 250,000 residents. The city has more than 2,700 acres of parkland. The popular St. Marks Trail, extending from Tallahassee south to the coast, is available to cyclists, skaters, hikers, and equestrians. The St. Marks National Wildlife Refuge is a popular eco-tourism attraction, with its undisturbed coastal marshes and a preserved lighthouse. A stretch of parks in the downtown area spans some five blocks. Several ocean beaches are less than seventy miles away, and Tallahassee has its own freshwater beaches. Lake Hall at Alfred B. Maclay State Park and Lake Bradford offer public beach access, swimming, boating, fishing and other water sports. Golfers can enjoy the city's several municipal and public courses as well as award-winning private courses. Three local parks provide lighted tennis courts.

## Shopping and Dining

Downtown Tallahassee offers a collection of specialty and gift shops at Downtown Market Place on Park, where fine arts, crafts, authors, writers/poets, live jazz, chefs, historic chats, children's storytelling and a farmer's market can be enjoyed on Saturdays from March to November. The Tallahassee Mall boasts more than 90 specialty stores. Governor's Square is home to over 100 stores and restaurants, anchored by four full-line department stores, and a 500-seat Food Court. Bradley's 1927 County Store is renowned for homemade sausage and Southern goods and is on the National Register of Historic Places.

Restaurant offerings in the city range from the international cuisines of France, Italy, and Thailand, to seafood in all its variety, classic American cooking, and steak and barbecues.

***Visitor Information:*** Tallahassee Area Visitor Information Center, 106 East Jefferson Street (across from City Hall); telephone (850)413-9200 or (800)628-2866; fax (850)487-4621; email vic@mail.co.leon.fl.us

# *Convention Facilities*

As the government center for the state of Florida, Tallahassee is the preferred headquarters location for most gatherings of Florida professionals. Tallahassee has more than 5,000 rooms in more than 50 hotels and motels. The Tallahassee-Leon County Civic Center is the main convention site in the city, with a 14,000-seat arena, and 52,000 square feet of meeting, dining, and exhibition space. The Dale Mabry Conference Center at Tallahassee Airport offers versatile amenities for meetings from small, closed-door sessions to large public receptions. The Augustus B. Turnbull III Conference Center at Florida State University can accommodate small conferences. Out of the ordinary meeting areas include the North Florida Fairgrounds, the Wakulla Springs Lodge and Conference Center, and The Capital Cultural Center, which also houses the Mary Brogan Museum of Art and Science. Historic Dorothy B. Oven Park, part of the Lafayette Land Grant awarded to General Marquis de Lafayette in 1824 by the United States Congress, has a Main House that is available to the public for rental use for seminars, meetings, and receptions.

*Convention Information:* Tallahassee Area Convention and Visitors Bureau, 106 East Jefferson Street Tallahassee, FL 32301; telephone (850)413-9200 or (800)628-2866; fax (850)487-4621

# Transportation

## Approaching the City

Florida law requires that drivers must turn on their headlights when rain is heavy enough to use windshield wipers. A number of interstate and state highways converge in Tallahassee including U.S. highways 27, 90, 319, as well as state highways 20 and 363. Amtrak offers east-west service on its Sunset Limited line, and Greyhound Bus Lines also serves the city. The Tallahassee Regional Airport, which is served by eight national airlines, is located five miles south of downtown. The airport reported serving a total of 1,155,072 travelers in 2004.

## Traveling in the City

Taltran, an extensive public transit system, offers 35 city routes and 9 routes to the city's college campuses, with a modern transfer facility, the C.K. Steele Plaza. Traveling downtown becomes a fun event on The Old Town Trolley, with its brass fittings and cable-car gong.

# Communications

## Newspapers and Magazines

The *Tallahassee Democrat* is the city's daily newspaper. The *Capital Outlook,* is an African-American weekly, while the *Elder Update,* published monthly, offers consumer information for senior citizens. The *Florida Bar News, the FSView* and other legal and college newspapers, are published in the city.

The North Florida Hispanic Association publishes a quarterly Spanish-language newsletter, *La Gaceta Hispana.* Journals on engineering, agriculture, and the funeral industry are also published in Tallahassee. *Tallahassee Magazine,* a bimonthly, is the region's only full-color lifestyle publication. It features award-winning writing on the people and business of the area, and carries a dining guide and calendar of events.

## Television and Radio

Tallahassee has three network television stations, one public station, four digital television stations, twelve FM radio stations and five AM stations.

*Media Information: Tallahassee Democrat,* 277 N. Magnolia Drive, Tallahassee, Florida, 32301; telephone (850)599-2100. *Tallahassee Magazine,* Rowland Publishing, Inc., 1932 Miccosukee Road, Tallahassee, Florida, 32308; phone (850)878-0554; fax (850)656-1871.

## Tallahassee Online

City of Tallahassee home page. Available www.state.fl.us./citytlh

Leon County home page. Available www.co.leon.fl.us

Leroy Collins Leon County Public Library. Available www.co.leon.fl.us/library

National High Magnetic Field Laboratory. Available www.nhmfl.gov

North Florida Hispanic Association. Available www.tnfha.org

Tallahassee Chamber of Commerce. Available www.talchamber.com

*Tallahassee Democrat.* Available www.tallahassee.com

Tallahassee Visitor's Guide. Available www.seetallahassee.com/Default.asp

## Selected Bibliography

Ellis, Mary Louise, *Tallahassee & Leon County* (Tallahassee: Historic Tallahassee Preservation Board, Florida Department of State, 1986)

Paisley, Clifton, *The Red Hills of Florida, 1528–1865* (Tuscaloosa: University of Alabama Press, 1989)

Rabby, Glenda Alice, *The Pain and the Promise: The Struggle for Civil Rights in Tallhassee, Florida* (Athens: University of Georgia Press, 1999)

# Tampa

## *The City in Brief*

**Founded:** 1824 (incorporated 1887)

**Head Official:** Mayor Pam Iorio (NP) (since April 2003)

**City Population**
    **1980:** 271,577
    **1990:** 280,015
    **2000:** 303,447
    **2003 estimate:** 317,647
    **Percent change, 1990–2000:** 8.1%
    **U.S. rank in 1990:** 55th (State rank: 3rd)
    **U.S. rank in 2000:** 57th (State rank: 3rd)

**Metropolitan Area Population**
    **1980:** 1,614,000
    **1990:** 2,067,959
    **2000:** 2,395,997

    **Percent change, 1990–2000:** 15.9%
    **U.S. rank in 1990:** 21st
    **U.S. rank in 2000:** 20th

**Area:** 112.1 square miles (2000)
**Elevation:** Ranges from sea level to about 48 feet above sea level
**Average Annual Temperature:** 73.1° F
**Average Annual Precipitation:** 44.8 inches

**Major Economic Sectors:** wholesale and retail trade, services, government
**Unemployment rate:** 3.5% (December 2004)
**Per Capita Income:** $29,728 (2002)

**2002 FBI Crime Index Total:** 35,380

**Major Colleges and Universities:** University of South Florida, University of Tampa, St. Petersburg College

**Daily Newspaper:** *Tampa Tribune; St. Petersburg Times*

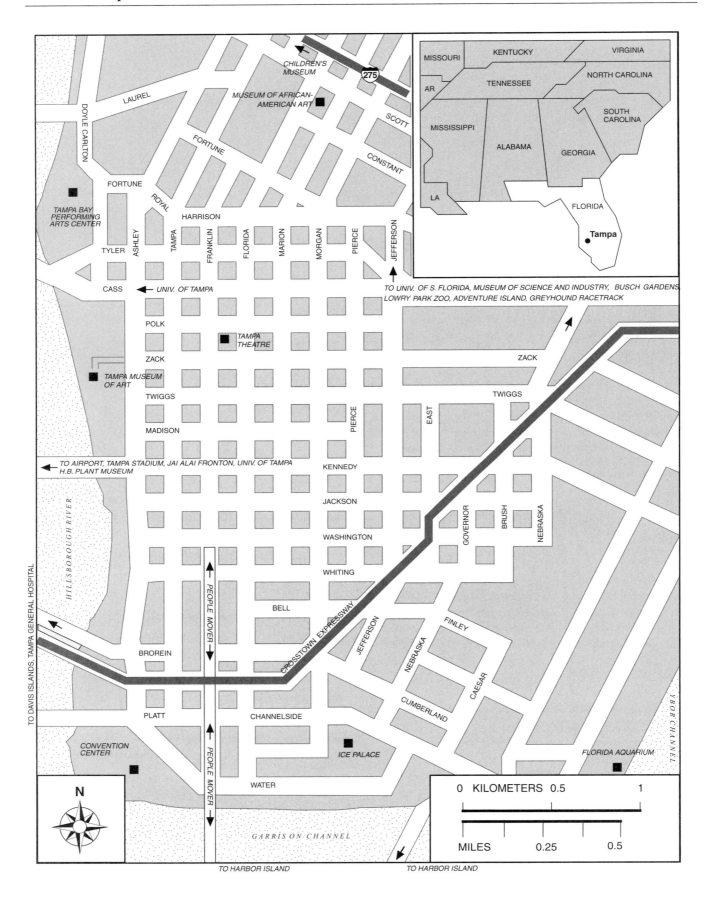

# Introduction

Tampa is Florida's third most populous city, and its chief treasure is its diversity. The city today combines elements of the Italian, Spanish, Indian, Cuban, and African American cultures that reflect its historical development and give Tampa a cosmopolitan flair. Its warm, sunny weather, Gulf Coast location, abundant labor supply, and spirit of cooperation between the public and private sectors have made it a very attractive choice for companies wishing to expand or relocate. The influx of new businesses and residents has in turn revitalized the city, sparking a multibillion-dollar construction and renovation boom that combines the best of old Tampa with dynamic new structures to better serve the growing community. Tampa is proud of its accomplishments and excited about the future.

# Geography and Climate

Located midway down Florida's west coast, about 25 miles east of the Gulf of Mexico, Tampa is bordered on the south and west by the Hillsborough and Old Tampa bays. Downtown is divided by the winding Hillsborough River, which originates northeast of the city and empties into Hillsborough Bay. The city's year-round semitropical climate is free from many of the extremes found elsewhere. Its most remarkable feature is the summer thunderstorm season. On an average of ninety days from June through September, late afternoon thundershowers sweep across the area, making Tampa one of the stormiest cities in the United States.

**Area:** 112.1 square miles (2000)

**Elevation:** Sea level to about 48 feet above sea level

**Average Temperatures:** January, 61.3° F; August, 82.7° F; annual average, 73.1° F

**Average Annual Precipitation:** 44.8 inches

# History

### First Established Settlement Called Fort Brooke

When Spanish explorers first arrived in the Tampa Bay region in 1528, they encountered a native civilization that had flourished there for at least 3,500 years. Several different tribes dominated the Gulf Coast, including the Tocobaga, the Timucua, the Apalachee, and the Caloosa (also spelled Calusa). It was a Caloosa village called *Tanpa* (a name meaning "stick of fire") that eventually became known to the Spanish as Tampa. Annihilated by an onslaught of European diseases against which they had no immunity, the various Tampa Bay tribes had all but vanished by 1700. Raiding parties comprised of English colonists from the north and members of other Indian tribes destroyed the few remaining settlements. Desolate and uninhabited, the Tampa Bay region was held briefly by the British in the late 1700s, then once again became a Spanish possession after the American Revolution. In 1821, Spain ceded the Florida territory to the United States for $5 million.

By this time, northern Florida had become a haven for displaced Seminole Indians and runaway black slaves from nearby southern states. Because white settlers were eager to move into the region and grow cotton, the federal government decided to relocate the Indians further south, around Tampa Bay. A fort was established on the eastern shore of the Hillsborough River to house the soldiers sent there to keep an eye on the angry Seminoles. Erected in 1824 and named Fort Brooke (after the army colonel in command), it was the first permanent, modern settlement on the site of present-day Tampa.

### Area's Economy Rollercoasters

The 1830s and 1840s were marked by repeated violent conflicts between the Seminoles and white soldiers and settlers. Although Tampa emerged from the so-called Second Seminole War (1835–1842) as a fledgling town rather than just a frontier outpost, it subsequently endured a variety of setbacks, including further skirmishes with the Seminoles, yellow fever epidemics, and, in 1848, a hurricane-generated tidal wave that leveled the village.

In the 1850s a rebuilt Tampa expanded, and by 1855 it had grown enough to incorporate as a city. After the Third Seminole War (1855–1858) saw most of the Indian population removed to Oklahoma, the town experienced a boom of sorts. An extremely lucrative beef trade with Cuba flourished, as did the related activities of shipping and shipbuilding. During and after the Civil War, however, Tampa, like much of the rest of the South, suffered economic ruin, compounded throughout the 1860s and 1870s by periodic outbreaks of yellow fever.

The 1880s ushered in a dramatic turnaround for the dying city—the discovery of rich phosphate deposits nearby and, more important, the coming of Henry Bradley Plant's Jacksonville, Tampa & Key West Railroad company. Potential new settlers streamed into the city in search of business opportunities. One of these was Cuban cigar manufacturer Vicente Martinez Ybor, who left Key West in 1885 to establish his operations in Tampa; within just a few years, cigars had become the city's trademark, as well as its chief industry.

The next fifty years were marked by continued economic growth for Tampa. At the turn of the century, subzero temperatures forced farmers in the northern part of the state to relocate farther south, Tampa became the new center for the expanding citrus industry. World War I led to a demand for ships that kept Tampa's docks humming with activity. During the early 1920s, land speculators and tourists from the North flocked to the state and gave rise to a building boom in Tampa and the surrounding area. Even after the rest of the Florida real estate market collapsed in 1926, Tampa managed to hold its own. But, like much of the rest of the country, Tampa suffered severe economic setbacks during the Depression of the 1930s. Its number-one industry, cigar manufacturing, went into a sharp decline as product demand decreased and more and more factories became automated; never again would cigar manufacturing figure as prominently in the city's economic makeup.

## Downtown Experiences Decline and Rebirth

The growing American involvement in World War II proved to be the stimulus Tampa's paralyzed economy needed. Thousands of troops were stationed in and around the city, and government contracts again revived the shipbuilding industry. But in the 1950s and 1960s Tampa lost residents and businesses to the suburbs, and the downtown area quickly deteriorated. During the early 1970s, government and business united to revive the ailing downtown area and change Tampa's image. After a rocky and unfocused start in the 1960s, Tampa's urban renewal program emerged in the 1970s and 1980s as a carefully and professionally planned alternative to the earlier chaotic approach. Downtown soon became the site of new office buildings, stores, stadiums, convention centers, and condominiums, and the local economy flourished. The city and the surrounding region saw a boom in business expansions and relocations in the 1990s that is only picking up speed today. Today, Tampa proclaims itself a city "where the good life gets better every day"—an urban area on the threshold of changes that will assure it of a vital role in the country's future.

*Historical Information:* Tampa Bay History Center, 225 South Franklin Street, Tampa FL 33602-5329; telephone (813)228-0097

# Population Profile

## Metropolitan Area Residents
*1980:* 1,614,000
*1990:* 2,067,959
*2000:* 2,395,997
*Percent change, 1990–2000:* 15.9%

*U.S. rank in 1990:* 21st
*U.S. rank in 2000:* 20th

## City Residents
*1980:* 271,577
*1990:* 280,015
*2000:* 303,447
*2003 estimate:* 317,647
*Percent change, 1990–2000:* 8.1%
*U.S. rank in 1990:* 55th (State rank: 3rd)
*U.S. rank in 2000:* 57th (State rank: 3rd)

*Density:* 2,707.8 people per square mile (in 2000)

*Racial and ethnic characteristics* (2000)
    White: 194,871
    Black or African American: 79,118
    American Indian and Alaska Native: 1,155
    Asian: 6,527
    Native Hawaiian and Pacific Islander: 281
    Hispanic or Latino (may be of any race): 58,522
    Other: 12,646

*Percent of residents born in state:* 44.8% (2000)

*Age characteristics* (2000)
    Population under 5 years old: 20,528
    Population 5 to 9 years old: 21,843
    Population 10 to 14 years old: 20,741
    Population 15 to 19 years old: 20,628
    Population 20 to 24 years old: 21,404
    Population 25 to 34 years old: 47,967
    Population 35 to 44 years old: 50,077
    Population 45 to 54 years old: 38,470
    Population 55 to 59 years old: 13,121
    Population 60 to 64 years old: 10,715
    Population 65 to 74 years old: 19,559
    Population 75 to 84 years old: 13,890
    Population 85 years and older: 4,504
    Median age: 34.7 years

*Births* (2003)
    Total number: 8,125

*Deaths* (2003)
    Total number: 8,725 (Hillsborough County) (of which, 137 were infants under the age of 1 year)

*Money income* (1999)
    Per capita income: $29,728 (2002)
    Median household income: $34,415
    Total households: 124,594

*Number of households with income of . . .*
    less than $10,000: 16,582
    $10,000 to $14,999: 9,866
    $15,000 to $24,999: 18,838

$25,000 to $34,999: 17,835
$35,000 to $49,999: 20,206
$50,000 to $74,999: 19,671
$75,000 to $99,999: 8,457
$100,000 to $149,999: 6,760
$150,000 to $199,999: 2,586
$200,000 or more: 3,793

*Percent of families below poverty level:* 14.0% (51.7% of which were female householder families with related children under 5 years)

*2002 FBI Crime Index Total:* 35,380

# Municipal Government

Tampa, the Hillsborough County seat, adopted a nonpartisan mayor-council form of government in 1945. Elections are held every four years, at which time city residents choose the mayor and seven council members.

**Head Official:** Mayor Pam Iorio (NP) (since April 2003; current term expires March 2007)

**Total Number of City Employees:** 4,631 (2004)

***City Information:*** City of Tampa, 306 E. Jackson St., Tampa, FL 33602; telephone (813)274-8211

# Economy

### Major Industries and Commercial Activity

Early in the twentieth century, Tampa was unquestionably a one-industry town. From the late 1880s through the 1930s, cigar manufacturing and related activities—primarily box construction and lithography—dominated the economy. Several hundred competing firms annually turned out well over 100 million hand-rolled examples of the city's best-known product.

The current story of Tampa, however, is quite different. Though still known for its cigars (now made with tobacco from sources other than Cuba), Tampa branched out to become the industrial, commercial, and financial hub of Florida's west coast; a third of the state's entire population, in fact, lives within a two-hour drive of the city.

Part of what has made Tampa's future so promising is its diversified economic base. The push to diversify first came after World War II, when the emphasis was on fostering the growth of heavy industry. But in the late 1970s, as the traditional stability and profitability of heavy industry seemed threatened, a movement began to make Tampa appealing to a wide variety of businesses, especially those that were more service-related and office-oriented. Since then, the city has been touted as an ideal location for companies in search of regional headquarters, for banking and other financial firms, and for various high-technology industries. The business world has responded with enthusiasm. Looking toward the future, city developers are aggressively seeking to expand into aerospace and medical technology and international trade and to attract additional electronics and financial firms. Today, Tampa is a center not only for cigars and tourism, but also for agriculture, food processing, electronics and other high-technology fields, health care and related industries, and finance.

To those who know Tampa only as a vacation spot, it may come as a surprise to learn that the city is a thriving agribusiness center. Hillsborough County markets an abundance of citrus fruit, beef cattle, dairy products, eggs, vegetables, ornamental plants and flowers, and tropical fish. As a result, many agriculture-related industries have been attracted to the area, including food processing firms; feed, fertilizer, and insecticide companies; and paper and metal container manufacturers. Two breweries, Anheuser-Busch and Pabst, also have facilities in Tampa.

Tampa has attained the status of a foreign trade zone, an area where goods can be unloaded for repacking, storage, or transshipment without being subject to import duties.

*Items and goods produced:* cigars, electronic equipment, medical equipment, beer, paint, cigars, fabricated steel, fertilizers, citrus products, livestock, processed shrimp, decorative plants, and flowers

### Incentive Programs—New and Existing Companies

In May 2000 the Greater Tampa Chamber of Commerce's Committee of One Hundred was named among *Site Selection* magazine's top ten development groups for the second year in a row. The editors wrote: "If there's anyplace where economic development customer service has been honed and polished to a brighter shine than in sunny Tampa and Hillsborough County, Fla., it would be hard to find." The Chamber's Committee of One Hundred has a number of resources available for people and businesses interested in relocating to the area.

*State programs*—Enterprise Florida, Inc. is a partnership between Florida's government and business leaders and is the principal economic development organization for the state of Florida. Enterprise Florida's mission is to increase economic opportunities for all Floridians, by supporting the creation of quality jobs, a well-trained workforce, and globally competitive businesses. It pursues this mission in cooperation with its statewide network of economic development partners.

*Job training programs*—The Workforce Development Board (WDB), commonly known as Jobs & Education Partnership, is a part of Enterprise Florida, Inc. WDB provides policy, planning, and oversight for job training programs funded under the federal Workforce Investment Act (WIA), along with vocational training, adult education, employment placement, and other workforce programs administered by a variety of state and local agencies. Regional Workforce Development Boards operate under charters approved by the Workforce Development Board. The 24 regional boards have primary responsibility for direct services through a statewide network of One-Stop Career systems. State and local workforce development efforts are concentrated on three broad initiatives: First Jobs/First Wages focuses on preparing workers for entry-level employment including the School-to-Work and WAGES (Work and Gain Self-Sufficiency) programs; High Skill/High Wages targets the higher skills needs of employers and training workers for advancement including Performance Based Incentive Funding (PBIF), Occupational Forecasting Conference/ Targeted Occupations, Quick Response Training (QRT), and Incumbent Worker Training (IWT); One-Stop Career Centers are the central elements of the One-Stop system for providing integrated services to employers, workers, and job-seekers.

## Development Projects

Business expansion and relocation of businesses to Tampa has been strong since 2000. An October 2004 article in the *Tampa Tribune* credits this to the comparatively low costs of buying or renting commercial real estate, as well as developers limiting the amount of speculative construction.

In 2002, Coca Cola opened a 33,000 square foot 210-employee service center, and a 58,000 square foot accounting center for the company's North American operations. In 2004, Depository Trust & Clearing Corp. opened a $34 million back-up operations center that will house 400 jobs.

A $120 million retail/entertainment/residential complex with theaters, restaurants, and retail shops is in the burgeoning Channelside district. At the center of the complex, called The Pinnacle, is an observation tower rising from a three-story podium building. At 624 feet in the air, the tower is taller than any of Tampa's downtown buildings. Serving as a gateway into the Channelside district is Heritage Park, which features a 4-acre park and amphitheater, and retail shops and cafes in three buildings. In 2004 work began on a $93 million Towers at Channelside project, a mixed-use development of 260 residential units spread across twin 30-story towers.

Segment D of the $80 million 40th Street Corridor Enhancement Project was underway in early 2005. In five phases, the 40th Street project was created to enhance a 4.2 mile stretch of 40th Street, from Hillsborough Avenue north to Fowler Avenue. The $1.9 million Segment D phase consists of a new bridge and is to be completed in July 2005. Design plans for all phases of the project include roadway lighting, bike lanes, a drainage system, and landscaped medians.

In early 2005, talks began on a new Riverwalk project as part of an effort by Mayor Pam Iorio to revitalize Tampa's downtown. The project hopes to create more than two miles of walkway along the Hillsborough River. Another announcement in early 2005 was the state allocation of $283 million to provide direct truck access from the Port of Tampa to Interstate 4. Pending Florida Legislature approval in July of the same year, the state money would be available in 2009. The total cost of the project is estimated to be $414 million; the mile-long, six-lane connector will also be a tollway.

Tampa's health care facilities are also undergoing expansion and renovation. In 2004, work began on a $65 million, four-story addition to Tampa General Hospital, adding a 280,000 square foot emergency department and Level 1 trauma center. The completion of a $10 million addition to the H. Lee Moffitt Cancer Center and Research Institute vivarium and laboratory research facility is expected in 2005.

***Economic Development Information:*** Greater Tampa Chamber of Commerce, PO Box 420, Tampa, FL 33601. Office Address: 401 E. Jackson Street, 21st Floor, Tampa, FL 33602. Information Center, telephone (813) 276-9418 (call this number for relocation information or email Info@tampachamber.com). Switchboard number (813)228-7777 or (800)298-2672.

## Commercial Shipping

Tampa's economy benefits greatly from its airport, where freight-hauling has been growing at a rate of 12 percent annually, the CSX railway system linking up with cities to the south and east, and nearby interstate and state highways providing convenient delivery and receiving routes for the eighteen motor freight lines operating in the city. Perhaps its greatest asset, however, is its port—the eleventh largest (by tonnage) in the country and the largest in the state of Florida—which handles more than 50 million tons of cargo annually.

The closest U.S. maritime center to the Panama Canal, the Port of Tampa serves as the gateway to Latin America. It is also home to one of the world's largest shrimp fleets and features modern shipbuilding and ship repair facilities. As the result of a federally-funded harbor-deepening project, super cargo ships have gained access to the port. International trade in Tampa got a boost from the year 2000 decision by the Tampa-Hillsborough International Affairs Commission to establish an office in the new Port of Tampa headquarters building. In 2005, a new cement terminal is scheduled to be completed, while the dredging of Big Bend Channel and the construction of a new general cargo warehouse will be started. The director is charged with establishing the Tampa metropolitan area as a center for international commerce and tourism for west central Florida.

## Labor Force and Employment Outlook

The Committee of One Hundred's recruitment efforts resulted in the creation of more than 54,543 direct new jobs and capital investment exceeding $2.6 billion between 1991 and 2002; announced jobs in 2003 numbered 1,101 and capital investment of $11.6 million. From October 2003–2004, 21,100 jobs were created in the area, making the Tampa area the second fastest growing region in Florida in terms of new jobs and businesses.

The following is a summary of data regarding the Tampa-St. Petersburg-Clearwater metropolitan area labor force, 2003 annual averages.

*Size of nonagricultural labor force:* 1,225,700

*Number of workers employed in . . .*
  *manufacturing:* 71,500
  *trade, transportation and utilities:* 216,400
  *information:* 34,700
  *financial activities:* 94,000
  *professional and business services:* 296,700
  *education and health services:* 142,800
  *leisure and hospitality:* 108,100
  *other services:* 48,200
  *government:* 147,000

*Average hourly earnings of production workers employed in manufacturing:* $14.09 (2003 statewide average)

*Unemployment rate:* 3.5% (December 2004)

| Largest employers | Number of employees |
|---|---|
| Hillsborough County School District | 21,426 |
| MacDill Air Force Base | 19,000 |
| Verizon Communications | 14,000 |
| University of South Florida | 12,477 |
| Hillsborough County Government | 10,886 |
| Tampa International Airport | 8,000 |
| James A. Haley Veterans Hospital | 5,900 |
| St. Joseph's Hospital | 5,242 |
| J.P. Morgan Chase | 5,237 |
| Publix Supermarkets | 4,630 |
| City of Tampa | 4,500 |
| U.S. Postal Service | 3,947 |

## Cost of Living

Compared to American cities of similar size and other Florida cities such as Miami, Fort Lauderdale, West Palm Beach, and Sarasota, Tampa enjoys a low cost of living.

The following is a summary of data regarding several key cost of living factors for the Tampa area.

*2004 (3rd Quarter) ACCRA Average House Price:* $241,125

*2004 (3rd Quarter) ACCRA Cost of Living Index:* 98.8 (U.S. average = 100.0)

*State income tax rate:* None (corporate income tax is 5.5%)

*State sales tax rate:* 6.0% on most items

*Local income tax rate:* None

*Local sales tax rate:* 7.0% (the county lodging tax is 5.0%)

*Property tax rate:* Ranges from $23.7362 to $29.1403 per $1,000

# Education and Research

## Elementary and Secondary Schools

Like all public schools in the state, the public elementary and secondary schools of Tampa are part of a county-wide district. The Hillsborough district, third largest in the state and tenth largest in the country, is administered by a nonpartisan, seven-member school board that appoints a superintendent.

The following is a summary of data regarding the Hillsborough County Public Schools as of the 2003–2004 school year.

*Total enrollment:* 175,454

*Number of facilities*
  *elementary schools:* 130
  *junior high/middle schools:* 42
  *senior high schools:* 26
  *other:* 20 charter schools

*Student/teacher ratio:* 16.7:1 average

*Teacher salaries*
  *average:* $38,762

*Funding per pupil:* $3,494

More than 120 private and parochial schools also operate in Hillsborough County. These range from institutions that stress achievement-oriented college preparatory courses to those that emphasize basic education combined with strict religious training.

**Public Schools Information:** Hillsborough County Public Schools, 901 E. Kennedy Blvd., PO Box 3408, Tampa, FL 33601-3408; telephone (813)272-4000

### Colleges and Universities

Hillsborough County has five fully accredited institutions of higher learning: the University of South Florida (with more than 34,000 students), the University of Tampa, Tampa College, Florida College, and Hillsborough Community College. Also in Tampa are Education America–Tampa Technical Institute Campus, a two-year program, and ITT Technical Institute, primarily a two-year institution that also awards bachelor's degrees in electronics engineering technology. A four-year program is offered at International Academy of Merchandising and Design.

### Libraries and Research Centers

In addition to its main branch in the downtown area (the John F. Germany Library), the Tampa-Hillsborough County Public Library system has 21 branches. Its collection numbers over four million books, plus numerous films, records, talking books, magazines, newspapers, maps, photographs, and art reproductions. Many of the systems libraries were undergoing refurbishment and expansion in the early 2000s; the new 15,000 square foot Upper Tampa Bay branch was dedicated in January 2005. Tampa also boasts more than 20 research centers, most of which are affiliated with the University of South Florida (USF) and are active in the fields of business, health care, and the development of high-technology equipment. USF's multimillion dollar public-private partnership with Lucent Technologies Inc. is part of a larger initiative through the 1-4 Technology Corridor, an initiative based on cooperative business and academic ventures from Pinellas to Brevard counties. Lucent agreed to donate millions of dollars in money and equipment to further local semiconductor research.

**Public Library Information:** John F. Germany Library, 900 N. Ashley, Tampa, FL 33602; telephone (813)273-3652; fax (813)272-5640

# Health Care

Well on its way to becoming one of the Southeast's premier centers for medical treatment of any kind, Tampa is home to more than a dozen major hospitals, a Children's Cancer Center, the University of South Florida's Medical Center (where teaching and research are combined with patient care), and the university's H. Lee Moffitt Cancer Center and Research Institute, a 162-bed hospital. The completion of a $10 million addition to the H. Lee Moffitt Cancer Center and Research Institute vivarium and laboratory research facility is expected in 2005. The city also has more than 2,000 physicians practicing in at least 50 different specialties.

The pride of the local medical establishment is Tampa General Hospital, which serves as the regional referral center in such fields as burn treatment, neonatal and pediatric care, and poison control. In 2004, work began on a $65 million, four-story addition to Tampa General Hospital, adding a 280,000 square foot emergency department and Level 1 trauma center. The primary teaching hospital for the University of South Florida's College of Medicine, Tampa General is operated by the Hillsborough County Hospital Authority.

The University Community Health system operates four hospitals throughout Tampa with a combined total of 1,019 beds. The system's new Pepin Heart Hospital and Research Institute is scheduled to begin operations in 2005.

# Recreation

### Sightseeing

Visitors to Tampa can pursue a wide variety of activities, from the thrills of a day at a popular theme park to the quiet beauty of a leisurely walk along a waterfront boulevard. The city's premier attraction—and the state's second busiest, after Walt Disney World in Orlando—is Busch Gardens, a 335-acre entertainment center, jungle garden, and open zoo in which several thousand animals roam free on a simulated African veldt. Open 365 days a year, the park has rides, live shows (some starring animals and birds), shops, and games, all linked by a nineteenth-century African theme—and all only a few minutes north of downtown. Next to Busch Gardens is Adventure Island, another family-oriented theme park centered around water-related activities, including flumes, a pool that produces five-foot waves, and several giant slides. More than 4,300 plants and animals, representing 550 native species, are on display at the Florida Aquarium. Explore-A-Shore is a 2.2 acre play and discovery zone just for kids.

City-run Lowry Park includes a zoo, shows, rides, and Fairyland Village, which features castles and characters from Mother Goose and other children's stories. In 2004, the first section of the new Safari Africa exhibit opened. Featuring many African animal species and amenities, it is expected to be completed in 2008.

Plant Hall, the administration building of the University of Florida, originally opened in 1891 as the opulent Tampa Bay Hotel. Entrepreneur Henry B. Plant's pet project, the 511-room palatial structure cost $3 million and defied categorization with its eclectic blend of Moorish, Near Eastern, and

The University of Tampa campus is situated on 100 acres of land in downtown Tampa.

Byzantine architectural styles. Never a commercial success, the hotel was deeded to the city in 1904, and for the next twenty-five years, it was the site of various social events. The University of Tampa, in need of room to expand, took over the Tampa Bay Hotel during the 1930s. Today, it is probably the city's most recognized landmark.

More than any other major Florida city, Tampa has retained much of its Latin flavor. Ybor City, Tampa's Latin Quarter, is a National Register Historic District and, as such, is one of the city's most architecturally intact neighborhoods. The area developed around two cigar factories built in the mid-1880s by Cubans forced from their homeland by Spanish oppression. It soon became a center for Cuban revolutionary activity, even serving for a time as a home to Jose Marti, a writer, poet, and patriot considered the George Washington of Cuba. Today, the former Ybor Cigar Factory goes by the name of Ybor Square; it houses shops, boutiques, and restaurants. Other historic buildings in the Ybor City area include the El Pasaje Hotel, formerly a private club for Ybor City notables who hosted visitors such as Teddy Roosevelt and Winston Churchill; the Ritz Theatre; and the Ferlita Bakery, now the home of the Ybor City State Museum.

Some of Tampa's most interesting sights are best explored on foot. From the 4.5-mile sidewalk along Bayshore Boulevard, one of the longest continuous walkways in the world, the casual stroller can marvel at the striking mansions on one side and a sweeping view of the bay and the city's skyline on the other. The residential neighborhoods of Hyde Park (adjacent to Bayshore Boulevard) and Davis Islands are also ideally suited for walking tours.

Bus tours and boat tours of Tampa are especially carefree ways to see the city and its surroundings. Though they originate in St. Petersburg, the Gray Line Bus Tours can be boarded in Tampa at the Greyhound and Trailways terminals.

## Arts and Culture

In 1967 the Florida State legislature created the Arts Council of Tampa to coordinate and promote the performing and visual arts in the Tampa region. Today, renamed the Arts Council of Hillsborough County, the council is actively involved in developing and administering school programs in dance, visual arts, music, poetry, creative writing, and theater; providing grants services to individual artists and arts organizations; scheduling events; and operating the Tampa Theatre, an ornate movie palace of the 1920s that has been restored to its former grandeur to serve film buffs, as well as fans of dance, music, and drama.

The Tampa Bay Performing Arts Center is a multipurpose facility located at the northern edge of downtown on a nine-acre riverfront site. It is a joint public-private venture designed to accommodate many different kinds of perfor-

mances. Its three halls and its rehearsal studio are used by local arts groups, touring drama companies, country music artists, and for the Center's own presentations.

Tampa is home to a variety of performing groups. American Stage, Stageworks, and the Alley Cat Players present seasons of drama, cabaret, classics and comedies. The University of South Florida and the University of Tampa both have theater training programs for actors, directors, and designers. Other local groups include the Carollwood Players community theater, and the Bits 'n Pieces Puppet Theater, which produces children's classics featuring giant puppets, as well as conventional actors. Ballet Folklorico of Ybor specializes in classic dances from Spain, Cuba, Italy, Mexico, and Latin America. The Kuumba Dancers and Drummers teach and perform traditional dances and rhythms of a variety of African cultures. At the University of South Florida, the dance department is housed in a state-of-the-art studio and theater, teaching and performing forms of dance from jazz to ballet to modern. Music is presented by the Florida Orchestra, which is based in the three west coast cities of Tampa, St. Petersburg and Clearwater. It performs 14 masterworks concerts with a pops and daytime series offered in each of the cities during its September-to-April season. Musical entertainment is also provided by the Master Chorale, Tampa Bay Chamber Orchestra, Tampa Oratorio, and myriad smaller community and college groups.

Several museums and galleries are based in Tampa. Among them are the Museum of Science and Industry, which offers hands-on displays and demonstrations of a scientific and technological nature pertaining specifically to Florida's weather, environment, agriculture, and industry. The Tampa Museum of Art features changing art exhibitions from across the country and houses the Southeast's largest and most significant permanent collection of Classical Art of Ancient Greece and Rome. The Henry B. Plant Museum features Victorian furniture and art objects in settings similar to those that would have greeted Tampa Bay Hotel guests in the late 1800s. The Ybor City State Museum provides an overview of the cigar industry and its history in Tampa, as well as information about the area's Latin community. Situated on the campus of the University of South Florida are two of the area's best contemporary art facilities. The Contemporary Art Museum, which has in its collection some of the finest of the world's modern artists, and organizes exhibitions of contemporary art to tour the United States and Europe. Graphicstudio, an experimental printmaking facility, has hosted such notables as Robert Rauschenberg, James Rosenquist, Jim Dine, and Miriam Shapiro. Kids City delights youngsters aged two to twelve with indoor, hands-on exhibits set in a realistic outdoor miniature village.

Other Tampa art facilities include the Florida Center for Contemporary Art, the state's only alternative artist's gallery, which highlights new work by emerging and established artists throughout Florida. The Lee Scarfone Gallery, the University of Tampa's fine arts college teaching gallery, exhibits works by students and faculty as well as artists of regional and national renown. Tampa has many fine galleries, and one of the highlights of the gallery season is a special event called Gallery HOP, an evening when all of the galleries are open and buses transport thousands of viewers on tours of the varied display sites around the city.

*Arts & Culture Information:* Arts Council of Hillsborough County, telephone (813)276-8250.

## Festivals and Holidays

The Gasparilla Pirate Fest, on the last Saturday in January and dating back to 1904, is a noisy and colorful Mardi Gras-like festival that takes place in the downtown waterfront area. Named in honor of Jose Gaspar, Tampa's legendary "patron pirate," the Gasparilla invasion calls for a group of more than 700 costumed pirates (usually some of the city's most prominent business and social leaders) to sail into Tampa harbor on a three-masted schooner (complete with cannons and flying a Jolly Roger flag), capture the city, and kidnap the mayor. They then parade along Bayshore Boulevard accompanied by lavish floral floats and marching bands. Other activities held during Gasparilla Week include world-class distance runs, a children's parade, and a bicycle race. The festival ends with Fiesta Day in Ybor City, a day-long party of dancing in the streets, free Spanish bean soup, sidewalk artists, and a torchlight parade during which the pirates make their final appearance of the year.

In February, the Florida State Fair opens its annual twelve-day run. The largest fair of its kind south of the Mason-Dixon Line, the Florida State Fair features traditional agricultural exhibits and demonstrations, items for display and for sale, food, rides, auto races, shows, and contests, all spread out on a 301-acre site beside seven lakes.

Other Tampa celebrations include the Gasparilla Festival of the Arts, the Winter Equestrian Festival, the statewide Florida Dance Festival, the outrageous Guavaween Halloween festival, The Greater Hillsborough County Fair, the Tampa-Hillsborough County Storytelling Festival, and a variety of ethnic festivals. First Night, a New Year's Eve festival to celebrate the arts, again rings in the start of the annual cycle of varied arts experiences. One of the city's newest events is the Hot Rod and Street Machine Nationals.

## Sports for the Spectator

The Tampa sporting scene has changed drastically in recent years with the addition of new stadiums and teams. The region's major league baseball team, the Tampa Bay Devil Rays, play at St. Petersburg's $206 million Tropicana Field.

The Bay Area has three other major professional sports teams, the Tampa Bay Buccaneers of the National Football League (NFL), the Tampa Bay Lightning of the National Hockey League (NHL), and the Tampa Bay Storm of the Arena Football League (AFL). The Buccaneers play at the $168 million, 66,321-seat Raymond James Stadium, the only NFL stadium with a theme-park element—a cannon-firing pirate ship located at one end of the playing field in Buccaneer Cove. The $153 million state-of-the-art St. Pete Times Forum is home to both the Lightning and the Storm.

The New York Yankees' major league team use Legends Field, modeled after the original Yankee Stadium in New York, for spring training. The Yankees' Minor League team plays each year from April through September at Legends Field. The Threshers, a Class A affiliate with the Philadelphia Phillies, play at brand-new Bright House Networks Field.

Horse racing and dog racing are popular spectator sports in the Tampa area. The renovated Tampa Bay Downs and Turf Club (located about fifteen miles west of the city) is the only thoroughbred track on Florida's west coast. It is open from mid-December through early May. The Tampa Greyhound Track, open since 1933, is one of the ten most popular in the United States. Located north of downtown, it is open from June through December. Top professional and amateur golfers compete each year in the Senior Professional Golfer's Association Tour's GTE Suncoast Classic which is played at the Tournament Players Club.

Collegiate athletic events of all kinds are regularly scheduled at the University of South Florida and the University of Tampa. Golf and tennis tournaments, wrestling and boxing matches, equestrian shows, and automobile and boat races are also held on a regular basis in and around the city.

## Sports for the Participant

With its warm climate, proximity to the water, and numerous public and private facilities, Tampa is ideal for those who enjoy golf, tennis, swimming, canoeing and boating, fishing, and other sports on a year-round basis. Golf is especially popular. Tampa has dozens of public courses, but several other local semiprivate clubs allow greens fee players. For tennis enthusiasts, the city has more than a thousand public and private tennis courts. The Tampa recreation department also maintains racquetball courts, basketball courts, shuffleboard courts, recreation centers, gym facilities, playgrounds and community centers, a softball complex, and more than a hundred other fields. For those who prefer less strenuous forms of relaxation, the city alone has 141 parks; numerous parks and wilderness areas are located nearby. Just to the northeast of the city is the Hillsborough River State Park, which is ideal for those who enjoy picnicking, camping, canoeing, fishing, and hiking.

Much of the sports activity in Tampa occurs in or on the water. The city maintains eleven swimming pools, including one handicapped facility and one supplied with water from a natural spring; and two beaches, Picnic Island and the Ben T. Davis Municipal Beach. Picnic Island, a park located near where Teddy Roosevelt and the Rough Riders camped during the Spanish-American War, offers swimming, boating, and fishing. Ben T. Davis Municipal Beach, only fifteen minutes from downtown on the Courtney Campbell Causeway, is popular with swimmers as well as with windsurfers and catamaran sailors.

Both saltwater and freshwater fishing are excellent in the Tampa Bay area. A license is required for saltwater fishing. Good spots are everywhere—off bridges and piers and even downtown off Davis Islands or Bayshore Boulevard. Deep-sea charters are also readily available for those who would rather venture out into the gulf. Tarpon, cobia, kingfish, sea trout, mackerel, blue-tailed redfish, and bass are among the many varieties in abundance.

**Shopping and Dining**

A wide variety of retail establishments flourish in and around Tampa, from six large regional malls featuring nationally known stores to small specialty shops promoting goods of a more local nature. Westfield Shoppingtown Citrus Park offers 120 upscale shops and a 20-screen movie theater. Ybor Square caters to those seeking a more unusual shopping experience. Capitalizing on its status as a historic landmark in an ethnic neighborhood, Ybor Square leans more toward antique stores and gift shops with a Latin American focus. Near downtown Tampa is Old Hyde Park Village, which offers more than 60 shops plus restaurants and movie theaters in a historic outdoor setting.

Ranging in type from typical fast food fare to specialties served in elegant or unique settings, Tampa's 1,300-plus restaurants offer diners many choices. Fresh seafood (from the Gulf of Mexico) and Cuban cuisine (including thick, crusty bread and black bean soup) are local favorites.

*Visitor Information:* Tampa Bay Convention and Visitors Bureau., 400 N. Tampa Street, #2800, Tampa, FL 33602; toll-free (800)826-8358; telephone (813)223-1111

# Convention Facilities

Tampa's $140-million Tampa Convention Center complex is located near Harbour Island. It contains approximately 200,000 square feet of exhibition space and 60,000 square feet of meeting rooms, a 36,000-square-foot ballroom, a 600-room hotel, and office and retail space. The Exposition Hall can accommodate up to 12,000 people for concerts.

The Sun Dome at the University of South Florida, a large multipurpose facility, can accommodate up to 11,500 people for concerts, lectures, trade shows, banquets, and large conventions.

For those seeking facilities for groups ranging in size from 10 to 2,500 people, Tampa has much to offer. Among the choices are the Egypt Temple Shrine, a well-equipped hall for banquets and more entertainment-oriented functions, and the National Study Center, a place for medical professionals to attend courses and lectures required for re-licensing or certification. The Florida State Fair and Expo Park also offers indoor and outdoor facilities. Spacious and convenient meeting areas for smaller groups are also available at nearly 50 hotels and resorts in Tampa, many of them recently renovated.

*Convention Information:* Tampa Bay Convention and Visitors Bureau, Inc., 400 N. Tampa St., 2800, Tampa, FL 33602; toll-free (800)826-8358; telephone (813)223-1111; fax (813)229-6616

# Transportation

**Approaching the City**

The Tampa International Airport (TIA), a modern facility 12 miles from downtown, was designed to be an optimally user-friendly origin-and-destination airport. It was the first airport in the country to use a people-mover system to transport passengers from remote buildings to terminals. It has been rated ''Best Airport in the U.S.'' by *Conde Nast Traveller* magazine. A second, smaller facility, the Peter O. Knight Airport, is located on Davis Islands. It serves Tampa's general aviation traffic and executive aircraft and even has a seaplane basin and ramp. Charters and flight instruction are also available.

Florida law requires that drivers must turn on their headlights when rain is heavy enough to use windshield wipers. Tampa's rush hours can be very congested. The major direct routes are Interstate 75 from the north or south (which becomes Interstate 275 as it passes through the city), Interstate 4 from the northeast (which merges with Interstate 275 downtown), State Road 60 from the southeast, and U.S. Highway 41 (a coastal road also known as the Tamiami Trail) from the south. U.S. Highways 41 and 301 roughly parallel Interstate 75 on the west and east, respectively.

Passenger rail service to Tampa is also available from Amtrak's Seaboard Coast Line trains.

## Traveling in the City

Allowing for constraints imposed by certain geographic features, Tampa is laid out in a basic grid pattern. Florida Avenue divides east from west, and John F. Kennedy Boulevard and Frank Adamo Drive (State Road 60) divide north from south.

Tampa's mass transit system is primarily bus-based and operated by the Hillsborough Area Regional Transit authority or, as it is more commonly known, HARTline. An express bus service links Hillsborough County with neighboring Pinellas County.

The TECO Line, an historic electric streetcar line, connects downtown Tampa with Ybor City, stopping at Tampa Convention Center, St. Pete Times Forum, the Channelside area, Port of Tampa cruise terminals and The Florida Aquarium.

# *Communications*

## Newspapers and Magazines

Tampa's major daily newspaper is *The Tampa Tribune,* a morning publication. Residents also read the *St. Petersburg Times.* Tampa's magazine that focuses on lifestyles, local events, shopping, dining, books, films, and entertainment is *Tampa Bay Magazine.*

## Television and Radio

Tampa has eight television stations, six commercial and two public. Other stations serve the area from the nearby towns of Largo and St. Petersburg. Additional stations are available via cable. Twelve AM and FM radio stations are based in Tampa, ten commercial and two public. Approximately forty other radio stations serve the metropolitan area from nearby locations.

***Media Information:*** *The Tampa Tribune,* 200 S. Parker St., Box 191, Tampa, FL 33601; telephone (813)259-7711; email readerservice@tampatrib.com

## Tampa Online

Central Florida Development Council. Available www.cfdc .org

City of Tampa home page. Available www.ci.tampa.fl.us

Greater Tampa Chamber of Commerce. Available www .tampachamber.com

Hillsborough County Public Schools. Available apps.sdhc .k12.fl.us

Tampa Bay Convention and Visitors Bureau. Available www.gotampa.com

Tampa Bay Library Consortium. Available snoopy.tblc.lib .fl.us

*Tampa Tribune.* Available www.tampatrib.com

Tampa-Hillsborough County Public Library System. Available www.thpl.org

## Selected Bibliography

Miller, Bill and Mary Fallon Miller, *Tampa Triangle Dead Zone* (St. Petersburg, Fla.: Ticket to Adventure, c1997)

# GEORGIA

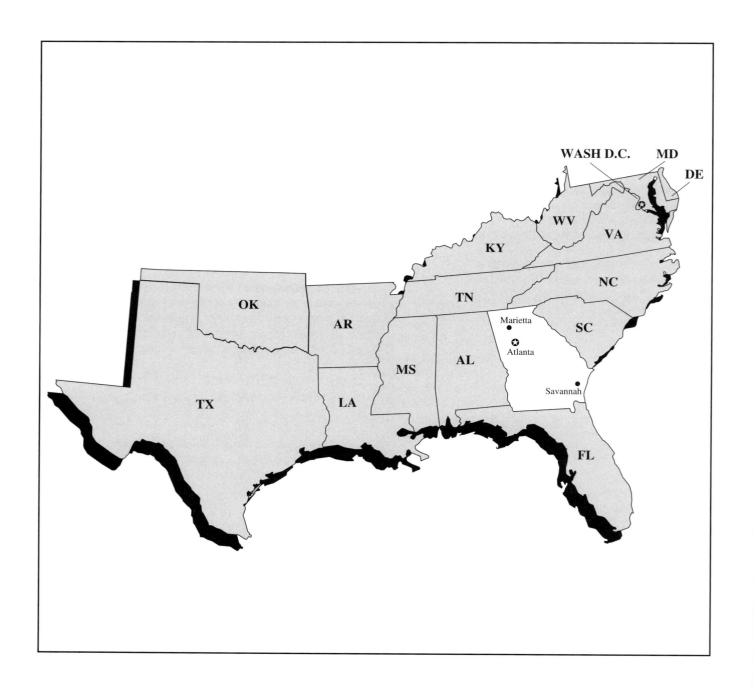

# The State in Brief

**Nickname:** Empire State of the South; Peach State
**Motto:** Wisdom, justice, and moderation

**Flower:** Cherokee rose
**Bird:** Brown thrasher

**Area:** 59,424 square miles (2000; U.S. rank: 24th)
**Elevation:** Ranges from sea level to 4,784 feet above sea level
**Climate:** Long, hot summers and short, mild winters

**Admitted to Union:** January 2, 1788
**Capital:** Atlanta
**Head Official:** Sonny Perdue (R) (until 2007)

**Population**
　1980: 5,463,000
　1990: 6,478,000
　2000: 8,186,453
　2004 estimate: 8,829,383
　Percent change, 1990–2000: 26.4%
　U.S. rank in 2004: 9th
　Percent of residents born in state: 57.8% (2000)
　Density: 141.4 people per square mile (2000)
　2002 FBI Crime Index Total: 385,830

**Racial and Ethnic Characteristics** (2000)
　White: 5,327,281
　Black or African American: 2,349,542
　American Indian and Alaska Native: 21,737
　Asian: 173,170
　Native Hawaiian and Pacific Islander: 4,246
　Hispanic or Latino (may be of any race): 435,227
　Other: 196,289

**Age Characteristics** (2000)
　Population under 5 years old: 595,150
　Population 5 to 19 years old: 2,414,770
　Percent of population 65 years and over: 9.6%
　Median age: 33.4 years

**Vital Statistics**
　Total number of births (2003): 135,831
　Total number of deaths (2003): 66,337 (infant deaths, 1,153)
　AIDS cases reported through 2003: 14,023

**Economy**
　Major industries: Paper and board, textiles, manufacturing, agriculture, forestry, chemicals
　Unemployment rate: 4.1% (December 2004)
　Per capita income: $29,259 (2003; U.S. rank: 28th)
　Median household income: $43,535 (3-year average, 2001-2003)
　Percentage of persons below poverty level: 12.0% (3-year average, 2001-2003)
　Income tax rate: Ranges from 1.0% to 6.0%
　Sales tax rate: 4.0% (food and prescription drugs are exempt)

# Atlanta

## The City in Brief

**Founded:** circa 1837 (incorporated as Marthasville, 1843; reincorporated 1847)

**Head Official:** Mayor Shirley Franklin (D) (since 2002)

**City Population**
1980: 425,022
1990: 393,929
2000: 416,474
2003 estimate: 423,019
Percent change, 1990–2000: 5.8%
U.S. rank in 1980: 29th
U.S. rank in 1990: 36th (State rank: 1st)
U.S. rank in 2000: 48th

**Metropolitan Area Population**
1980: 2,233,000
1990: 2,969,500
2000: 4,112,198
Percent change, 1990–2000: 38.9%

U.S. rank in 1980: 16th
U.S. rank in 1990: 12th
U.S. rank in 2000: 11th

**Area:** 132 square miles (2000)
**Elevation:** 1,010 feet above sea level
**Average Annual Temperature:** 64.2° F
**Average Annual Precipitation:** 50.77 inches

**Major Economic Sectors:** wholesale and retail trade, services, government
**Unemployment Rate:** 4.2% (December 2004)
**Per Capita Income:** $25,772 (1999)
**2004 (3rd Quarter) ACCRA Average House Price:** $247,229
**2004 (3rd Quarter) ACCRA Cost of Living Index:** 98.2 (U.S. average = 100.0)

**2002 FBI Crime Index Total:** 49,451

**Major Colleges and Universities:** Emory University, Georgia Institute of Technology, Atlanta University Center, Georgia State University

**Daily Newspaper:** *Atlanta Journal-Constitution*

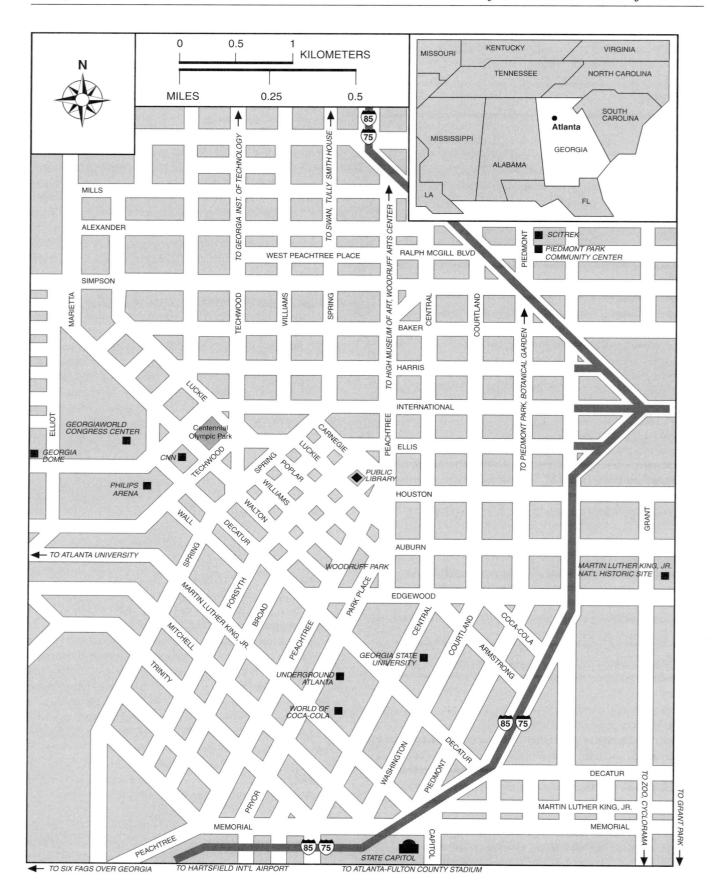

# Introduction

Georgia's capital and largest city, Atlanta is a major Southern financial and cultural force and the focus of a metropolitan statistical area that covers more than 6,000 square miles and includes more than 110 municipalities. People from all over the country, joined by immigrants from other lands, have flocked to Atlanta's mild climate, physical beauty, and job opportunities. Offering Old South graciousness blended with an ambitious zest for expansion and dominance, Atlanta has assumed an important position in national and international commerce. Ted Turner, one of the city's well-known citizens, has declared that Atlanta has ''absolutely everything going for it—climate, location, great transportation, easy air access, and a government that's both cooperative and supportive.'' This is a judgment widely shared by both residents and visitors.

# Geography and Climate

Located in the foothills of the southern Appalachians in the north-central part of the state, Atlanta has a mild climate that rotates through all four seasons. The city's elevation and relative closeness to the Gulf of Mexico and the Atlantic Ocean moderate the summer heat; mountains to the north retard the southward movement of polar air masses, thereby providing mild winters. Most precipitation falls in the form of rain, with the heaviest concentration in March. Snowfall is negligible, the yearly average being one-and-one-half inches, though a snowstorm of about four inches occurs about every five years. Tornado activity is also fairly frequent in the area.

**Area:** 132 square miles (2000)

**Elevation:** 1,010 feet above sea level

**Average Temperatures:** January, 40.5° F; July, 79.1° F; annual average, 64.2° F

**Average Annual Precipitation:** 50.77 inches

# History

### City Develops as Trade Center

Until the early nineteenth century, the site near the Chattahoochee River where Atlanta is located (originally named the Standing Peach Tree for a peach tree on a small hill about seven miles away) was virgin territory sparsely occupied by Creek and Cherokee Native American tribes. The first permanent white settlers arrived during the War of 1812, when Fort Gilmer was built at the Standing Peach Tree. After the war, the land around Fort Gilmer was slowly settled by farmers from northern Georgia, the Carolinas, and Virginia. Then, in the late 1830s, the Western & Atlantic Railroad was constructed, connecting the Chattahoochee River with the town of Chattanooga to the north. The area thus became an important trade center, and a village soon developed at the southern end of the railroad. Initially called Terminus (after the word for the engineer's final stake) the village was chartered as Marthasville in 1843, then renamed Atlanta in 1845 and reincorporated in 1847.

By the end of the 1850s, the population of Atlanta had grown to 10,000 people (up from approximately 2,500 people in 1847), and the city had undergone extensive industrial development to become a railway hub, a vital trade link between North and South. Retaining the rough-and-tumble spirit of a frontier town, Atlanta had also progressed as a center of civilization and culture. When the Civil War broke out, Atlanta ceased trade with the North and was established as a Confederate military post. Because of its railroads and factories the city was a prime target, and it was bombarded by Union forces in July 1864.

The Battle of Atlanta was fierce. For a time Southern troops were able to defend the city, but military and civilian casualties from enemy shells and typhoid fever were high. The battle lost, the mayor, James Calhoun, and a few citizens surrendered on September 2, 1864. The fall of Atlanta was catastrophic. All civilians were evacuated, and 90 percent of the structures in the city were destroyed by Union Army General William T. Sherman's troops as they marched toward Georgia's Atlantic coast. Reconstruction began almost immediately after Sherman's army departed. Slowed by smallpox epidemics in 1865 and 1866 that forced the building of a temporary hospital, efforts to rebuild the city were nevertheless successful, and in 1868 Atlanta became the state capital (officially confirmed in 1877).

### Atlanta Becomes a Major City

Expansion and growth continued through the nineteenth century and into the early decades of the twentieth, though the city was beset by periodic racial conflict. By 1920 the population of Atlanta had reached 200,000 people. The Great Depression brought more hard times, as it did throughout the country, but the city rose to meet the challenge of World War II. The transportation hub for the Southeast, Atlanta was one of the most important cities in the war effort.

After the war came renewed expansion in manufacturing, as well as a vital role in aviation. Having been a railroad center for most of its history, Atlanta was by the 1950s also the busiest and most important airline center in the South. In recent decades both the economy and cultural life have flourished, with Atlanta emerging as the major city of the "New South." While racial tension has troubled modern Atlanta, citizens have brought about a new spirit of cooperation and teamwork in the political process. Atlantans are optimistic about the future of their metropolis of more than four million inhabitants; a city that enjoys a nearly ideal climate and natural beauty, Atlanta has gained a momentum that promises continued growth and prosperity. Atlanta was the focus of world attention when it hosted the 1996 Centennial Summer Olympic Games. By most media accounts, the city has distinguished itself as world class and an economic leader. City leaders are buoyed by the trend back toward downtown living that has taken place in recent years. Business is thriving as many lucrative business projects are in development.

Atlanta's strength as a business community is reflected with its distinction as *Inc.* magazine's number one ranked city for doing business in America. Contributing to this is the dramatic growth of the metropolitan area's population between 1990–2000 of 38.9%, many of whom are employed at the wide variety of area corporations including two dozen on the *Fortune* 1000 list. The local economy is bolstered by the ldquo;the world's busiest passenger airport." of Hartsfield-Jackson Atlanta International Airport. Consumer goods find easy transport in the highly successful rail system.

Further, the area offers a vibrant arts scene along with beautiful parks and exciting activities. Many tourists are drawn to the historical significance of the area including its Civil War landmarks. This mix of history, tourism, job growth, and business opportunities all lends to the boundless prosperity that the area has enjoyed and its prospects for a bright future.

*Historical Information:* Atlanta History Center, 130 W. Paces Ferry Rd. NW, Atlanta, GA 30305-1366; telephone (404)814-4000

# Population Profile

## Metropolitan Area Residents
*1980:* 2,233,000
*1990:* 2,959,500
*2000:* 4,112,198
*Percent change, 1990–2000:* 38.9%
*U.S. rank in 1980:* 16th
*U.S. rank in 1990:* 12th
*U.S. rank in 2000:* 11th

## City Residents
*1980:* 425,022
*1990:* 393,929
*2000:* 416,474
*2003 estimate:* 423,019
*Percent change, 1990–2000:* 5.8%
*U.S. rank in 1980:* 29th
*U.S. rank in 1990:* 36th (State rank: 1st)
*U.S. rank in 2000:* 48th

*Density:* 3,161.2 people per square mile (2000)

*Racial and ethnic characteristics* (2000)
White: 138,352
Black or African American: 255,689
American Indian and Alaska Native: 765
Asian: 8,046
Native Hawaiian and Pacific Islander: 173
Hispanic or Latino (may be of any race): 18,720
Other: 8,272

*Percent of residents born in state:* 58.5% (2000)

*Age characteristics* (2000)
Population under 5 years old: 26,666
Population 5 to 9 years old: 27,386
Population 10 to 14 years old: 25,023
Population 15 to 19 years old: 30,048
Population 20 to 24 years old: 39,157
Population 25 to 34 years old: 82,083
Population 35 to 44 years old: 64,632
Population 45 to 54 years old: 50,178
Population 55 to 59 years old: 17,164
Population 60 to 64 years old: 13,602
Population 65 to 74 years old: 20,855
Population 75 to 84 years old: 13,649
Population 85 years and older: 6,031
Median age: 31.9 years

*Births* (2003, Fulton County)
Total number: 13,013

*Deaths* (2003, Fulton County)
Total number: 5,917 (of which, 106 were infants under the age of 1 year)

*Money income* (1999)
Per capita income: $25,772
Median household income: $34,770
Total households: 168,341

*Number of households with income of . . .*
less than $10,000: 28,669
$10,000 to $14,999: 12,267
$15,000 to $24,999: 23,191
$25,000 to $34,999: 20,403
$35,000 to $49,999: 21,704

$50,000 to $74,999: 23,819
$75,000 to $99,999: 12,859
$100,000 to $149,999: 12,398
$150,000 to $199,999: 4,475
$200,000 or more: 8,556

*Percent of families below poverty level:* 21.3% (56.8% of which were female householder families in poverty)

*2002 FBI Crime Index Total:* 49,451

# Municipal Government

Atlanta, the Fulton County seat, is governed by a mayor and a 16-member city council that is managed by the council president. The mayor is chief executive officer and oversees administration of city government.

**Head Official:** Mayor Shirley Franklin (D) (since 2002; current term expires 2006)

**Total Number of City Employees:** 7,500 (2005)

*City Information:* City of Atlanta, 55 Trinity Ave., Atlanta, GA 30303; telephone (404)330-6000; fax (404)658-7673

# Economy

## Major Industries and Commercial Activity

While the Coca-Cola Company wields considerable influence in Atlanta—much of it in areas outside its immediate manufacturing concerns—no single industry or firm truly dominates the local economy. Service industries employ the largest number of workers, but trade and manufacturing are also important elements. Having such diversity, Atlanta has been slower to suffer a downturn and quicker to recover from any temporary setback than many other major American cities. In fact, metropolitan Atlanta saw a decrease in unemployment and an increase in its labor force between 2002–2003 despite the country's economic recession during that time period.

In 2000, 24 *Fortune* 1000 corporations were headquartered in metropolitan Atlanta. Atlanta is home to BellSouth, Delta Airlines, Home Depot, UPS, and Georgia-Pacific, among other big names.

The Atlanta MSA added more than 1.1 million new residents between 1990–2000, which has attracted more and more new businesses. Metropolitan Atlanta has consistently led the nation in new housing permits every year since 1991,

leading the way in 2003 with 53,750 new permits, according to Bureau of Census figures. In 1991, according to the National Association of Home Builders, the number was nearly 25,000; in comparison, 2002 topped off at 66,550.

Efforts by Georgia Tech and local industry to make Atlanta a high-tech center are paying off; even though much of the technology field suffered losses, Atlanta held steady and was ranked third in 2003 among the top ten metropolitan areas in this field by the Milken Institute. Atlanta is also becoming a leading world center of business and trade. More than 1,300 foreign-based businesses have operations in metropolitan Atlanta, and they employ more than 81,000 residents.

*Items and goods produced:* metals, machinery, transportation, equipment, food and beverages, printing, publishing, textiles, apparel, furniture, telecommunications hardware, steel, chemicals

## Incentive Programs—New and Existing Companies

Georgia has the reputation for being a strong pro-business state. Many new companies have relocated to metro Atlanta and have either built new facilities or converted vacant office space. The various local and state business incentives offered have encouraged these company moves as well as expansions of local firms.

*Local programs*—Atlanta was an empowerment zone city named by the Clinton administration, but in 2002 it converted to a "Renewal Community" allowing the city to benefit from a nationwide pot of $17 billion in tax incentives. Businesses within the three "renewal clusters" that were created receive tax credits and deductions, capital gains exclusives, and bond financing.

*State programs*—Georgia has business-friendly tax laws; the state does not use the unitary tax method, but instead taxes businesses only on income apportioned to Georgia. In addition, at four percent the state sales tax rate has risen only one percentage point since 1951. Attractive inventory tax exemptions are available in all metropolitan Atlanta counties, and sales and property tax exemptions are available for certain pollution control equipment used in production. Georgia's Freeport zones, like Atlanta's, exempt for ad valorem taxation all or part of the value of certain tangible property held in certain inventories. Companies can apply for a permit from the Georgia Environmental Protection Division which can result in their obtaining their federal permit as well, via a single application.

*Job training programs*—The Georgia Department of Technical and Adult Education administers the Georgia Quick Start program, a three-way partnership between Quick Start, one of the state's technical institutions, and a company wishing to start up business in Georgia via 34 technical colleges and institutes, 4 associated university programs, and 18 satellite campuses. By developing and implementing high quality customized training programs and materials, Quick Start assists the company in obtaining a trained work force ready to begin as soon as the company opens for business. In addition, metro Atlanta's 43 colleges and universities provide a continuing supply of educated and ready-to-work graduates.

## Development Projects

The staging of the 1996 Centennial Olympic Games in Atlanta had a tremendous impact on development that extends today. More than $2 billion was spent on new construction, sporting arenas, entertainment venues, and beautification projects in preparation for the games. Another $100 million was spent on hotel renovations and expansions. The downtown area received the lion's share of the improvements as the city furthered its goal of becoming world class. Buildings were leveled and 21 acres were cleared to create the $57 million Centennial Olympic Park, which now serves as the centerpiece of downtown Atlanta. Following the Olympics, the city was left with several other multimillion-dollar sporting venues, including Turner Field, now home to the Atlanta Braves; the Georgia International Horse Park; and the Stone Mountain Tennis Center. While all of the Olympics-related construction was going on, downtown living was making a comeback with the construction of new housing units. In December 2004 Centennial Park West, which began building in 1999–2000, sold three of its million-dollar penthouse suites leaving it only four short of sellout. This property is part of Legacy Property Group, LLC who has also been involved in a 435,000 square foot, $100 million hotel and residential development that has brought the downtown area an Embassy Suites Hotel and several fine dining restaurants.

Meanwhile, in midtown Atlanta, the redevelopment of a 145-acre site (formerly a steel mill) as a community of homes, offices, shops, and hotels connected to surrounding areas by bicycle lanes, walking paths, and public transportation has been designated by the U.S. Environmental Protection Agency as a national model for innovative development that improves air quality. This designation allows developers to build a bridge across I-75/85, connecting midtown to areas west of the Downtown Connector.

Atlanta has long been the center of business activity and development in the Southeast. In October 2004 Cousins Properties Inc. announced leases with three companies to occupy the new building of a 31-story, 500,000 square foot office tower. Construction on a new headquarters building for the Centers for Disease Control and Prevention is to be completed in 2005 with an estimated cost of $81 million for the 12-story, 360,000 square foot facility. In February 2005 CSX Transportation opened its $8 million technology-

driven training center to future engineers, conductors, and other technicians.

***Economic Development Information:*** Metro Atlanta Chamber of Commerce, 235 Andrew Young International Blvd. NW, Atlanta, GA 30303; telephone (404)880-9000

## Commercial Shipping

An extensive array of air, rail, and truck connections makes Atlanta a city with a robust cargo industry. Hartsfield-Jackson Atlanta International Airport is the main focus of activity. A Foreign Trade Zone located near the airport at the Atlanta Tradeport provides companies with an opportunity to delay, reduce, or eliminate customs duty on imported items, while the U.S. Customs Service Model Inland Port is a highly computerized center designed to expedite quick clearance for international freight.

The railroad, for so long crucial to Atlanta's well-being, continues to serve the city through two major systems, CSX and Norfolk Southern, which operate more than 100 freight trains in and out of the city daily. In 2003 the Association of American Railroads named Atlanta as its first "Freight Rail Smart Zone" as two million railcars transport vast amounts of consumer goods throughout the region. Several hundred motor freight carriers also offer their services in Atlanta, as do many other carriers that transport only their own products.

## Labor Force and Employment Outlook

Atlanta enjoys an expanding labor pool derived from the surrounding counties and from people coming to the city from other parts of the country and the world. Skilled laborers are more than willing to relocate to Atlanta. Wages have been the fastest-growing in the country; that trend is predicted to continue for the next 20 to 30 years as Atlanta creates more high quality jobs.

According to figures released by the Bureau of Labor Statistics in 2000, between 1998-2025 metropolitan Atlanta is projected to gain 1.8 million net new jobs becoming the new hub for high-tech companies—some call it the "Silicon Valley of the South." Atlanta led the list of "Top 25 Cities for Doing Business in America" by *Inc.* magazine in March 2004; specifically mentioned was its diverse economic structure.

The following is a summary of data regarding the Atlanta metropolitan area labor force, 2003 annual averages.

*Size of nonagricultural labor force:* 2,158,600

*Number of workers employed in . . .*
*natural resources and mining:* 1,800
*construction:* 115,600
*manufacturing:* 170,300

*trade, transportation and utilities:* 492,000
*information:* 97,500
*financial activities:* 148,000
*professional and business services:* 337,900
*educational and health services:* 213,100
*leisure and hospitality:* 200,700
*other services:* 94,000
*government:* 287,800

*Average hourly earnings of production workers employed in manufacturing:* $13.29

*Unemployment rate:* 4.2% (December 2004)

| Largest employers | Number of employees |
|---|---|
| Delta Airlines | 26,237 |
| BellSouth Corp. | 22,000 |
| U.S. Postal Service | 16,099 |
| Wal-Mart | 15,600 |
| Emory University (including hospitals) | 13,619 |
| Cobb County School District | 12,372 |
| U.S. Army Garrison Headquarters | 10,485 |
| AT&T Corp. | 10,000 |
| Home Depot Inc. | 9,652 |
| IBM Corp. | 8,400 |

**Cost of Living**

Atlanta's cost of living figures, while high for the South, compare favorably with those of other major metropolitan areas in the United States.

The following is a summary of data regarding several key cost of living factors for the Atlanta area.

*2004 (3rd Quarter) ACCRA Average House Price:* $247,229

*2004 (3rd Quarter) ACCRA Cost of Living Index:* 98.2 (U.S. average = 100.0)

*State income tax rate:* Ranges from 1.0% to 6.0%

*State sales tax rate:* 4.0% (food and prescription drugs are exempt)

*Local income tax rate:* None

*Local sales tax rate:* Atlanta metropolitan counties levy taxes up to 3%

*Property tax rate:* $17.86 (within city) per $1,000 of fair market value) (2003)

***Economic Information:*** Metro Atlanta Chamber of Commerce, 235 Andrew Young International Blvd. NW, Atlanta, GA 30303; telephone (404)880-9000

# Education and Research

**Elementary and Secondary Schools**

The Atlanta system is located in the city of Atlanta, as well as in unincorporated portions of Fulton and DeKalb Counties. Policies are formed by the nine-member Atlanta Board of Education, all elected positions. The Atlanta schools work closely with parents and local businesses to ''stay the course and focus on student success,'' as Superintendent Beverly L. Hall, Ed.D. explained. Special programs within the Atlanta schools system include Early Childhood Development Centers, three planetariums, two teen parent programs, evening/community high schools and Alternate Schools, programs for exceptional children, exchange student programs, and the Atlanta Area Technical Schools.

Several schools have received state and national awards, including the 2003 National Blue Ribbon Award for Brandon Elementary, and Grove Park Elementary received a 2004 Georgia School of Excellence. In the state of Georgia, any student who graduates from high school with at least a B average is eligible for free college tuition and a $300 per academic book allowance at any of the state's colleges or universities. Those who choose a private college in Georgia get a $3,000 grant. The program is called HOPE (Helping Outstanding Pupils Educationally).

The following is a summary of data regarding Atlanta's public schools as of the 2004–2005 school year.

*Total enrollment:* 51,000

*Number of facilities*
*elementary schools:* 62
*middle schools:* 16
*senior high schools:* 10
*other:* 7 charter and 4 alternate schools

*Student/teacher ratio:* 14.2:1

*Teacher salaries*
*minimum:* $39,370
*maximum:* $78,602

*Funding per pupil:* $10,993 (2002-03)

More than 150 private schools also operate in the Atlanta area, ranging from residential preparatory institutions to church-affiliated programs. A number of private schools offer foreign language curriculums, including several Japanese schools, a German school and the Atlanta International School.

***Public Schools Information:*** Atlanta Public Schools, Administrative Office, 130 Trinity Ave. S.W., Atlanta, GA 30303; telephone (404)802-3500

## Colleges and Universities

Metropolitan Atlanta is home to 43 post-secondary institutions, including several of the most prestigious in the United States. They feature more than 300 programs of study and offer a variety of associate and undergraduate degrees, as well as graduate degrees in such fields as medicine, law, and theology. Among the city's principal schools are the 11,300-student body Emory University, nationally recognized for its business and medical research programs; Georgia Institute of Technology, with 16,000 students is famous for its research programs in dozens of different high-technology disciplines; and the Atlanta University Center, the largest assemblage of African American institutions in the world. The center is comprised of five colleges: Clark Atlanta University, Morehouse College, Morehouse School of Medicine, Spelman College, and the Inter-denominational Theological Seminary (it previously included a sixth member, Morris Brown College, which lost its accreditation in 2002). Other notable facilities in Atlanta include Georgia State University; Mercer University's Cecil B. Day Campus, its Stetson School of Business and Economics, and its Southern School of Pharmacy; Oglethorpe University; and Art Institute of Atlanta. The Atlanta Technical College offers more than 70 programs in a variety of fields including health and human services, information technology, and skilled trades. The metropolitan area also has large public two-year and four-year colleges to serve students, including Clayton College & State University and several schools that offer specialized vocational and religious instruction.

## Libraries and Research Centers

In addition to a modern central library located downtown, the Atlanta-Fulton Public Library operates 34 branches throughout the city and Fulton and DeKalb counties. The system's holdings include more than 2.1 million books, periodical subscriptions, films, and a large collection of compact discs, records, and audio- and videotapes. The Auburn Avenue Research Library, part of the public library system, is devoted to collecting materials on African American history and culture. Among Atlanta's several outstanding historical research libraries is the Jimmy Carter Library & Museum, dedicated to the former president. The University of Georgia Libraries hold more than 3.5 million books, and Emory University Libraries house more than 2.7 million books, 39,801 periodical subscriptions, 4.5 million microform units, and 15,653 film and video sources. The various campus libraries in Atlanta house special collections of material; many are open to the public for in-house reading and research.

Nearly 150 research centers are based in Atlanta, most of which are affiliated with either the Georgia Institute of Technology or Emory University. The topics under investigation are wide ranging; among them are health care, computers and software, bioengineering, economics, mining, biotechnology, business, women's studies, electronics, energy, pharmacology, cancer, and immunology.

Atlanta boasts four research centers of international renown. The U.S. Centers for Disease Control and Prevention studies some of the world's deadliest diseases in maximum security laboratories. The Yerkes Regional Primate Research Center is the oldest continuously operated center for research on the biological and behavioral characteristics of nonhuman primates. Georgia Tech Research Institute (GTRI), of the Georgia Institute of Technology, is one of the country's premier bioengineering programs producing advances in prosthetics and engineered assistance for the disabled. Tech's Medical Informatics Research Group, part of Georgia Institute of Technology, Graphics, Visualization and Usability Center, explores the ways in which computer science methods and techniques can help solve problems in medicine and biomedicine. Affiliated with Emory University and founded in 1982 by former President Jimmy Carter and his wife, Rosalynn, The Carter Center focuses on global environmental, agricultural, economic, and public health concerns; its Task Force for Child Survival and Development addresses issues of immunization, malnutrition, disease control, and child advocacy.

***Public Library Information:*** Atlanta-Fulton Central Library, 1 Margaret Mitchell Square, Atlanta, GA 30303; telephone (404)730-1700

# *Health Care*

A regional as well as a national leader in the field of health care, the Atlanta metropolitan area is home to more than 50 hospitals supporting 40,000 medical personnel and more than 10,000 beds. Twelve hospitals are located in the city proper. One of the major full-service institutions is Grady Health System, used as a teaching hospital by the medical schools of both Emory University and Morehouse College. Grady has operated a separate, state-of-the-art care facility for HIV and AIDS patients since 1994. In February 2005 it also received a grant to assist the CenterPregnancy program that focuses on prenatal care for immigrants and Spanish-speaking mothers. Emory University Hospital received high scores in 2004 from *Best Hospitals,* particularly their heart and heart surgery department and geriatrics. Other institutions in the city include Children's HealthCare of Atlanta, Georgia Baptist Healthcare System, Piedmont Hospital, and the 460-bed Atlanta Medical Center. Atlanta also serves as the home of the Centers for Disease Control and Prevention and the U.S. Public Health Service for the Southeast.

The Swan House was built in 1928 by Atlanta architect Philip Trammell.

# Recreation

## Sightseeing

The Atlanta area offers extraordinarily rich opportunities for leisure, pleasure, and culture. A popular site within the city is Grant Park, which includes scenic walking paths, the Zoo Atlanta featuring a Giant Panda exhibit until 2009, and some Civil War fortifications. The Civil War Museum on park grounds houses the famous Cyclorama, a huge three-dimensional panoramic painting of the Battle of Atlanta. Visitors sit on a revolving platform to view the work, the impact heightened by sound and light effects as well as a narration that explains the scene. Open since 1893, it is dubbed "The Longest Running Show in the Country." Various Civil War battle sites, parks, cemeteries, and memorials are also scattered throughout the city and are accessible to visitors. Scheduled to open in late 2005 is the $200 million Georgia Aquarium, featuring more than 55,000 animals in 5 million gallons of fresh and marine waters. The new Aquarium expects to serve more than 2 million visitors annually.

Also within the city is the Georgia State Capitol. Built in 1889 and patterned after the Capitol in Washington, D.C., it has a dome plated with gold mined in northern Georgia. Besides serving as the meeting place for the state's General Assembly, the Capitol is home to the Georgia Capitol Museum.

Underground Atlanta is an "adult playground" of bars, restaurants, and shops in the heart of the city's downtown. Every New Year's it plays host to the "Peach Drop" with music, fireworks, and an 800-pound peach resembling New York's Times Square ball. The Martin Luther King, Jr. National Historic District near Underground Atlanta honors the slain civil rights leader, a native of Atlanta. The entire area was renovated in time for the 1996 Olympic Games to give a sense of the neighborhood as it was during King's lifetime. The district encompasses King's childhood home, the Ebenezer Baptist Church (where he preached), and, adjacent to the church, his tomb. The district includes a visitors' center that tells the story of the civil rights movement and King's role in the movement. Nearby is the Martin Luther King, Jr., Center for Nonviolent Social Change that draws about 650,000 visitors annually.

Adjacent to Underground Atlanta in a three-story pavilion, The World of Coca-Cola, a collection of exhibits and more than 1,000 articles commemorating the history of Atlanta's most famous product, provides fun for the whole family. Another popular attraction is the CNN Center, the news and entertainment center of Turner Broadcasting's global headquarters, which offers tours, shops, and restaurants.

Outside Atlanta are several other notable attractions. The most popular is Stone Mountain, located about 20 miles east of downtown. The world's largest mass of exposed granite, the treeless dome stands more than 800 feet above the surrounding plain and measures approximately 5 miles in circumference. On the mountain's north face are carved colossal figures of Robert E. Lee, Jefferson Davis, and General Stonewall Jackson. Work began in 1923 but after several design changes it was not declared completed until 1972. A 3,200-acre park fans out from the base of the mountain, featuring a lake and recreational facilities for dozens of sports and other outdoor activities such as waterslides, golf, and tennis along with laser shows and a riverboat. Also within the park is Magnolia Hall, an authentic antebellum plantation house moved from another Georgia location and restored to its former elegance. Some 20 miles north of Atlanta is Kennesaw Mountain National Battlefield Park, which also combines history and recreation. The site of several major Civil War battles, the Kennesaw Mountain area now boasts a museum and some fortifications along with hiking trails and picnic grounds.

For those seeking pure entertainment, Six Flags parks bring three different venues to the area. Six Flags Over Georgia is located about 12 miles west of the city. The 331-acre family-oriented theme park features more than 100 rides, musical shows, and other attractions. During the summer months, thousands of visitors make it one of the busiest parks in the area. Six Flags White Water offers a variety of water-related activities such as giant slides, raft rides, and body flumes. Adjacent to it is Six Flags American Adventure, an outdoor park with roller coasters, bumper cars, and an array of rides for small children.

For nature-lovers, the Fernbank Science Center has trails, natural history exhibits, and one of the largest planetariums in the nation. The Fernbank Museum of Natural History offers 160,000 square feet of space providing dinosaur and wildlife exhibits and an IMAX theater. The Atlanta Botanical Garden, located in Piedmont Park, is also a favorite stop for those wishing to enjoy its vegetable, herb, rose, and oriental plantings on 15 acres. The Botanical Garden also includes a children's garden and a conservatory with rare and endangered plants from rainforests and deserts.

## Arts and Culture

Integral to Atlanta's cultural life is the Woodruff Arts Center, consisting of the Memorial Arts Building (itself a work of modern art) and the High Museum of Art. The cooperating units in the center include the Atlanta Symphony Orchestra, the Alliance Theatre, and the Atlanta College of Art. Another major center is the Callanwolde Fine Arts Center, located in a 1920s-era Gothic-Tudor-style mansion. The center accommodates 4,000 students annually with various arts classes, and offers a range of concerts, recitals, and exhibits.

Atlanta has a vital theater, dance, and music community that profits from the area's fine facilities and the generous patronage of its businesses and interested citizens. Performing at the Memorial Arts Building of the Woodruff Arts Center are the Alliance Theatre, which stages both standard and innovative works, and the Atlanta Symphony Orchestra. Entertainment is provided by numerous other professional and amateur groups based in Atlanta, including the Atlanta Ballet (the oldest regional ballet company in the United States, originating in 1929), the Atlanta Shakespeare Company, and the Georgia Ensemble Theatre. Since 1978, The Center of Puppetry Arts is said to be the only facility in the country devoted solely to puppetry and features three performance series, workshops, and a museum.

Local colleges and universities also sponsor a wide variety of performing arts programs in theater, dance, and music. Oglethorpe University's Georgia Shakespeare Festival presents a series of performances in the summer and fall.

Atlanta's museums and galleries cater to many different interests. State and local history are on view at the Atlanta History Center, whose main attractions are the Swan House, a former private residence that typifies the milieu of a wealthy Atlanta family during the 1930s; and Tullie Smith House, a restored 1835 farm house that illustrates how early Georgia farmers lived and worked; and several gardens.

Other museums in the city include the Wren's Nest, a Victorian mansion that was named a National Historic Landmark in 1962 and was home to Joel Chandler Harris, creator of the Uncle Remus stories, and now displays original furnishings, books, and memorabilia; the Margaret Mitchell house in midtown; the Governor's Mansion, a modern structure built in Greek Revival style and housing nineteenth-century furnishings; the Fernbank Museum of Natural History, whose exhibits include A Walk Through Time in Georgia; and the William Breman Jewish Heritage Museum, a 50,000-square-foot facility that opened in 1996 and has exhibits dating to 1733, when Jews first settled in Georgia, along with a Holocaust gallery.

With a few notable exceptions, private galleries showcase most of Atlanta's art. Public facilities include the High Museum of Art, which displays more than 11,000 works of primarily Western art from the early Renaissance to the present, and Chastain Gallery, which highlights the contemporary works of Georgia artists.

## Festivals and Holidays

Two of Atlanta's biggest celebrations are the Dogwood Festival, held every spring, and the Arts Festival, a staple on the fall calendar. The Dogwood Festival coincides with the blooming of dogwood trees in the area in April; events include a parade, tours, garden competitions, arts and crafts displays, canine competition, and musical performances. Held in downtown Atlanta, the Arts Festival is a week-long

affair that attracts nearly 2 million people to a multitude of different activities involving the visual and performing arts. Among Atlanta's other annual events are the Memorial Day weekend Jazz Festival and summer concert series, which features local and international talent; the Peachtree Road Race, a 10K run held annually since 1970 during the July 4th holiday; the National Black Arts Festival, held in late June and early July at the Woodruff Arts Center focusing on dance, music, and art; the Stone Mountain Highland Games and Scottish Festival, an October celebration since 1973 that brings international travelers to the region; and December's Chick-fil-A Peach Bowl football game and its related activities.

## Sports for the Spectator

Fans of sports of all kinds can usually find their favorite form of action somewhere in Atlanta, the sports capital of the South. The city is home to five professional franchises: the Falcons, a National Football League team; baseball's National League team, the Braves; the Hawks, a National Basketball Association team; the Thrashers, a National Hockey League team; and the Ruckus, of the American Professional Soccer League. The Falcons play at the Georgia Dome. The Braves play at Turner Field, formerly the Centennial Olympic Stadium downtown. The Hawks and Thrashers face their rivals at the $219 million Philips Arena, which opened in September 1999.

Since 1934 Atlanta has been home to the nation's largest recreational tennis league, Atlanta Lawn and Tennis Association (ALTA), with more than 81,000 members. Stone Mountain Tennis Center, which seats about 2,000 people around two center courts and has an 8,000-seat stadium, played host to the 1996 Centennial Olympic Tennis. The city also hosts many collegiate competitions in these same sports, among them the annual Peach Bowl football contest and the NCAA basketball championships, the Heritage Bowl, and others.

Auto racing buffs have two tracks to choose from just outside the metropolitan area. Atlanta Motor Speedway, about 25 miles south of the city, features NASCAR and other events. Forty-five miles north of the city is Road Atlanta, site of one of the world's largest sports car races, an event that draws top international drivers and thousands of spectators. The Grand Prix of Atlanta is held annually in April.

Atlanta also hosts numerous other sporting events throughout the year. Two of the most notable are the BellSouth Classic, a Professional Golfer's Association tournament held every spring at the Sugarloaf Country Club which raises money for Children's Healthcare of Atlanta, and the Atlanta Steeplechase, the area's major horse show. Tennis and polo are also growing in popularity as spectator sports in Atlanta.

### Sports for the Participant

Atlanta's physical setting and mild climate combine to make the city and its environs ideal for outdoor activities of all types. Running is an especially popular local sport; the Atlanta Track Club is one of the largest in the country, and it sponsors a number of annual events, including the Peachtree Road Race 10K and the Atlanta Women's 5K. Golfers may choose from 39 public courses and a host of new luxury golf communities growing up outside the city, while tennis players can visit any one of more than 200 courts.

Water sports enthusiasts can take advantage of the facilities along the Chattahoochee River to go canoeing, rafting, fishing, and camping. Within an hour's drive of the city are Lake Lanier and Lake Allatoona, both man-made lakes surrounded by recreation areas that encompass beaches, golf courses, horseback riding trails, and other amenities.

The Peachtree Center Athletic Club brings a number of activities to the downtown area such as aquatics, racquetball, pilates, squash, and group fitness.

### Shopping and Dining

Atlanta's modern shopping facilities draw consumers to the city from throughout the entire region. More than a dozen malls and outlet centers ring the metropolitan area. Lenox Square, in the Buckhead neighborhood, and nearby Phipps Plaza, offer exclusive shops such as Neiman Marcus, Macy's, and Rich's along with antique stores. Downtown, Peachtree Center offers shopping in the heart of the city while other shopping opportunities await at Underground Atlanta. Opened since 1999 just north of Atlanta is the Mall of Georgia, the southeast's largest shopping complex; it is anchored by Lord & Taylor, Penney's, Dillard's, Rich-Macy's, and Nordstrom, and its restaurants offer cuisines ranging from traditional Southern food to upscale and ethnic delicacies. The mall's decor incorporates the five regions of Georgia and their histories. Ten miles south of the city is the State Farmer's Market, a gigantic retail and wholesale center where visitors have the opportunity to buy fresh fruit, vegetables, eggs, meats, plants, shrubs, and flowers.

Atlanta diners have hundreds of restaurants to choose from, and traditional Southern cooking (catfish, hushpuppies, ham and redeye gravy, barbecue, fried chicken, and Brunswick stew) and soul food are widely available. Atlanta's growth as a center of international business has made haute cuisine and ethnic specialties extremely popular alternatives to traditional southern fare.

***Visitor Information:*** Atlanta Convention and Visitors Bureau, 233 Peachtree St., NE, Ste. 100, Atlanta, GA 30303; telephone (404)521-6600; fax (404)577-3293. The Convention Bureau publishes a city guide especially for African Americans called *Atlanta Heritage*. A visitor center is located at Underground Atlanta.

# Convention Facilities

Easy access to the city, a good public transportation system, an abundance of hotel rooms, and a mild climate have combined to make Atlanta one of the leading convention centers in the United States, by most accounts ranking just behind Chicago and Orlando. Atlanta's major convention facilities are the Georgia World Congress Center, which contains 3.9 million square feet of exhibit space and 76 meeting rooms and is among the 5 largest nationwide; the Georgia Dome, which seats 71,500 and has 102,000 square feet of exhibit space, and the Philips Arena, which offers an 18,000-seat and 17,000 square-foot facility for meetings, athletic events, and concerts. All three facilities are linked by the new Georgia International Plaza, a gathering place featuring fountains and outdoor sculpture. Three buildings that are connected by elevated walkways comprise AmericasMart, which provides 4.2 million square feet of exhibition space. The Boisfeuillet Jones Atlanta Civic Center provides a 5,800 square-foot ballroom and a 4,600-seat theater.

Atlanta also boasts dozens of smaller, more intimate meeting facilities, some of them in unusual settings. Among them are the Woodruff Arts Center, High Museum of Art, Fox Theatre (a renovated "movie palace" built in 1929), Academy of Medicine, Martin Luther King, Jr. Center for Non-Violent Social Change, Callanwolde (formerly a private residence), and Houston Mill House (a country estate). Other facilities are available at many of the city's hotels.

***Visitor Information:*** Atlanta Convention and Visitors Bureau, 233 Peachtree St., NE, Ste. 100, Atlanta, GA 30303; telephone (404)521-6600; fax (404)577-3293

# Transportation

### Approaching the City

Often referred to as Atlanta's number-one economic asset, Hartsfield-Jackson Atlanta International Airport has been distinguished as "the world's busiest passenger airport." The huge, ultramodern facility, only 10 miles from downtown on 4,700 acres of land, is served by 25 passenger airlines that fly non-stop or one-stop to more than 200 national and international destinations along with 19 cargo airlines. Terminals are connected by an automated underground train system. General aviation facilities in the Atlanta area number 19 (including Hartsfield-Jackson).

Three major interstates—I-75, I-20, and I-85—route traffic into and out of Atlanta, making it one of the leading interstate highways centers in the nation.

Amtrak provides passenger rail service to Atlanta; travelers can go west to New Orleans (via Birmingham, Alabama) or east to Washington, D.C. (via Charlotte, North Carolina). Greyhound has limited service into and out of the city at the Amtrak station.

## Traveling in the City

Atlanta can present a challenge to drivers for several reasons. For instance, the city is not laid out in a grid pattern, so there are few rectangular blocks or square intersections. Five main streets converge downtown in an area known as Five Points; these streets roughly divide the city into geographic quadrants (northeast, northwest, southeast, and southwest). Further complicating matters is the fact that more than 30 avenues, lanes, drives, and other thoroughfares in Atlanta contain the word ''Peachtree,'' but only Peachtree *Street* is truly a main road.

Public transportation in Atlanta is operated by the train- and bus-based Metropolitan Atlanta Rapid Transit Authority, or MARTA.

# Communications

## Newspapers and Magazines

One major daily newspaper serves Atlantans: the *Atlanta Journal-Constitution.* The major weeklies include *The Atlanta Bulletin, Atlanta Business Chronicle,* and *Mundo Hispanico* (a Hispanic-oriented paper published since 1979). Numerous African American-oriented newspapers and magazines are published in Atlanta, including the *Atlanta Daily World,* Atlanta's oldest continuously published (since 1928) African American newspaper, and *The Atlanta Inquirer.* About 16 other daily, weekly, and biweekly newspapers are circulated throughout the metropolitan area, most of them focusing on county and community news, consumer affairs, and business topics. *Atlanta Magazine* and *KNOW Atlanta Magazine* cover life in the city. Many other monthly magazines based in Atlanta are targeted at specific business, medical, educational, and hobbyist markets.

## Television and Radio

Seven television stations, including major network affiliates, one PBS, one commercial, and two independents, broadcast in the Atlanta area; cable service is also available. In the 1970s, Atlanta became a national media force when entrepreneur Ted Turner launched his independent ''super-station'' WTBS-TV Superstation and the Cable News Network (CNN), viewed by cable television subscribers across the United States. As for radio, 24 stations based in Atlanta offer news, public service programming, and a variety of musical formats to metropolitan listeners.

***Media Information:*** *The Atlanta Journal-Constitution,* 72 Marietta St., NW Atlanta, GA 30303; telephone (404) 522-4141; *Atlanta Magazine,* 260 Peachtree St., Ste. 300, Atlanta, GA 30303; telephone (404)527-5500; fax (404)527-5575

## Atlanta Online

AccessAtlanta (local news, entertainment listings, real estate information, and a section that covers the Atlanta-area technology scene). Available www.accessatlanta.com

Arts in Atlanta. Available www.artsinatlanta.org

Atlanta Convention & Visitors Bureau. Available www.atlanta.com or www.acvb.com

*Atlanta Daily World.* Available www.AtlantaDailyWorld.com

Atlanta Downtown. Available www.atlantadowntown.com

Atlanta-Fulton County Library System. Available www.af.public.lib.ga.us/library

Atlanta History Center. Available www.atlhist.org

*Atlanta Journal-Constitution. Available www.ajc.com*

*The Atlanta Nation* (daily internet newspaper). Available www.atlantanation.com

Atlanta Public Schools. Available www.atlanta.k12.ga.us

City of Atlanta home page. Available www.atlantaga.gov

Fulton County home page. Available www.co.fulton.ga.us

Metro Atlanta Chamber of Commerce home page. Available www.metroatlantachamber.com

## Selected Bibliography

Allen, Frederick, *Atlanta Rising: The Invention of an International City, 1946–1996* (Atlanta: Longstreet Press, 1996)

Craig, Robert M., and Richard Guy Wilson, *Atlanta Architecture: Art Deco to Modern Classic, 1929–1959* (Gretna: Pelican, 1995)

Mitchell, Margaret, *Gone with the Wind.* (New York: Macmillan, 1936)

Willard, Fred, *Down on Ponce: A Novel* (Atlanta, Ga.: Longstreet Press, 1997)

# Marietta

## *The City in Brief*

**Founded:** 1834 (incorporated 1852)

**Head Official:** Mayor Bill Dunaway (R) (since 2002)

**City Population**
  **1980:** 30,829
  **1990:** 44,129
  **2000:** 58,748
  **2003 estimate:** 61,282
  **Percent change, 1990–2000:** 33.1%
  **U.S. rank in 1990:** 582nd (State rank: 13th)
  **U.S. rank in 2000:** 557th (State rank: 13th)

**Metropolitan Area Population**
  **1980:** 2,233,000
  **1990:** 2,959,500
  **2000:** 4,112,198

**Percent change, 1990–2000:** 39.0%
**U.S. rank in 1980:** 16th
**U.S. rank in 1990:** 12th
**U.S. rank in 2000:** 11th

**Area:** 21.95 square miles (2000)
**Elevation:** 1,128 feet above sea level
**Average Annual Temperature:** 61.2° F
**Average Annual Precipitation:** 48.61 inches

**Major Economic Sectors:** wholesale and retail trade, services, government
**Unemployment rate:** 4.2% (December 2004)
**Per Capita Income:** $23,409 (1999)

**2002 FBI Crime Index Total:** not reported

**Major Colleges and Universities:** Kennesaw State University, Southern Polytechnic State University

**Daily Newspaper:** *Marietta Daily Journal*

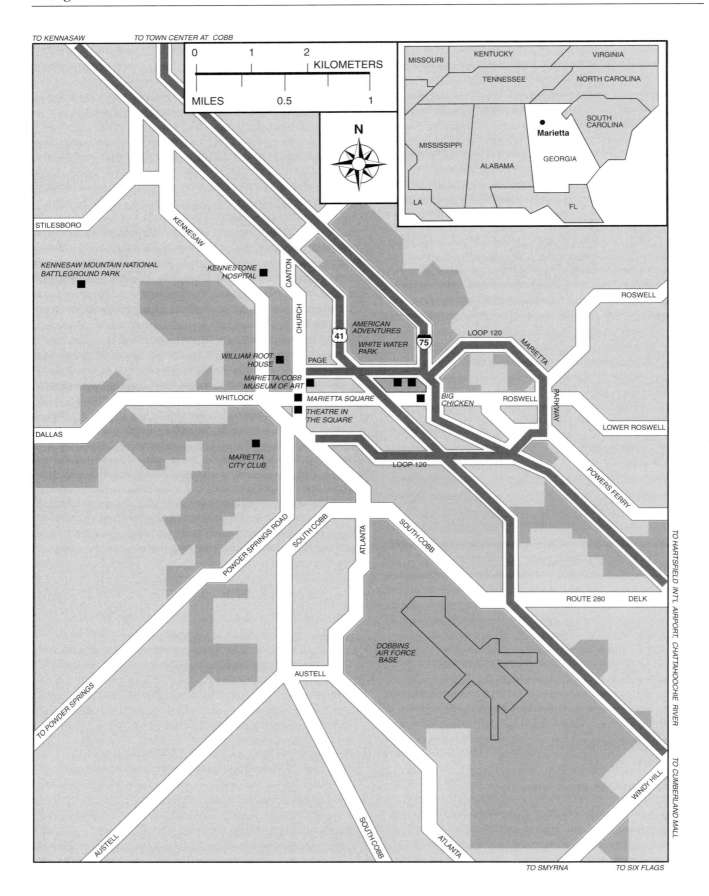

# Introduction

Marietta, located in Cobb County, approximately 20 miles from Atlanta, is one of the booming exurban job centers growing up around the country. Cobb County likes to market the area's recreational attractions by referring to itself as "the fun side of Atlanta," and Mariettans spend hundreds of thousands of dollars sowing seeds and planting trees and shrubs to promote beautification throughout the city. The town square, bleached-white gazebos, and the antebellum mansions give Marietta the misty feeling of the Old South. Yet the *Wall Street Journal* describes the city as "the intersection of great economic, social and geographic changes." The city and surrounding county were totally transformed with office buildings, warehouses, light manufacturing factories, and retail shops. Cobb County invested more in infrastructure, including water, sewer, road, and other utilities between 1970 and 1990 than any other county in Georgia, and during that period more houses were built in the county than anywhere else in the state. The influx of new residents has even resulted in the popular use of the new pronunciation of the city's name, MARRY-etta, rather than the traditional May-RETT-a. In 2002 an analysis produced by the Georgia Municipal Organization and a local magazine considered such things as fiscal management, public safety, infrastructure, citizen participation, cultural activities, and community partnerships, and concluded that Marietta was a "City of Excellence."

# Geography and Climate

Marietta is located north of Atlanta, along the Chattahoochee River. The city is bordered by Lake Allatoona to the northwest, while its southern boundary lies south of Interstate 20. Marietta is part of Cobb County, which is also made up of the cities of Acworth, Austell, Kennesaw, Powder Springs, and Smyrna. Seventy-eight percent of Cobb County's population lives in unincorporated areas. Citizens enjoy four seasons featuring a mild climate where winters seldom go below the thirties and summer highs are in the nineties.

**Area:** 21.95 square miles (2000)

**Elevation:** 1,128 feet above sea level

**Average Temperatures:** January, 41° F; July, 79° F; annual average, 61.2° F

**Average Annual Precipitation:** 48.61 inches

# History

### Europeans Take Over Indian Lands

For many years, Cobb County was the home of the Creek tribe, descendants of the Mississippian tribes that inhabited the northwest section of Georgia from approximately 800 A.D. The Creeks were driven south of the Chattahoochee River by the Cherokees in the early 1800s. Cobb County was still part of the Cherokee Indian Territory when Marietta's earliest European settlers came. They began to arrive in the early 1830s from other parts of Georgia, when they won land lotteries used to allocate the Indian lands. Other early migrants, most of English and Scotch-Irish descent, traveled south to Georgia through the mid-Atlantic states. The Cherokee land had been divided into 40-acre gold and 160-acre farm tracts with most of Cobb County originally settled by gold-seekers and people looking for good farmland. Despite several treaties to protect the rights of the Cherokees, in 1835 these Native Americans were forced to move west, and the whites moved in for good. Although some of the Native Americans left voluntarily, more than 17,000 were relocated by the federal government to Oklahoma by way of the infamous Trail of Tears. Traces of its Native American heritage remain in Cobb County in place names such as Sweetwater, Allatoona, and Kennesaw. Some of the Indian trails were widened to accommodate wagons, which in time brought in more settlers and launched trade in the county.

### Early History of Marietta

By 1833, nearly 100 people had settled in the area of Marietta, chosen as a town site in part because of the springs located near the present town square. The county was named in honor of Judge Thomas Willis Cobb, Georgia Congressman, U.S. Senator, and later a judge of the Ocmulgee Circuit of the Superior Court and the city for his wife. Marietta's first courthouse, a single room log cabin, was built in 1834. By the mid 1830s, several river ferries began operating to transport people, wagons, and livestock across the Chattahoochee.

In the mid-1840s, Marietta had more than 1,500 residents. By the next decade, it was a popular resort town for people from "the low country," who were attracted in part by the mild climate and the alleged therapeutic powers of local spring water. The state-owned Western & Atlantic Railroad began runs in 1845 and was completed in May 1850, providing access to a ready market for farmers and manufacturers and reducing the costs of conveying merchandise. Cities and towns sprang up along major rail lines running through Cobb County. In 1852 Marietta's formal incorporation took place. From 1850 to 1861, Marietta was considered a carefree town and was once described as "the fastest town in Georgia." During this period, businesses included tailor shops, warehouses, grocery stores, general stores, carriage and wagon shops, a tin and gunsmith shop, a bakery, professional services, and other small businesses.

## Civil War Brings Destruction

On April 11, 1862, the first disruptive effects of the Civil War were felt by the city's people when a group of 22 undercover Union agents arrived. After staying overnight at Kennesaw House, a former hotel, which still stands west of the town square, the agents boarded the W & A Railroad northbound train at the Marietta Station. At Big Shanty (now Kennesaw), the Union spies took control of the train. They were later caught by "Andrew's Raiders" after a now-famous locomotive chase with the backward pursuing "The Texas" overtaking "The General" near Ringgold, Georgia. The hard times of the War Between the States culminated with the Union occupation of the city on July 3, 1864, following battles around Kennesaw Mountain. During that time, the courthouse and all county records were destroyed when General Sherman's troops burned every public building on Marietta's town square.

## Prosperity Slowly Returns in Post-War Period

After the Civil War, recovery was slow for Marietta as for the rest of the South. Over time, however, the city began to prosper as new businesses moved in, and an 1860s account reveals that the city once again was beginning to attract visitors. In the 1870s, a new jail and courthouse were built, and summer tourists were honored at a reception in the city square. County finances gradually were improving, but the blackened ruin of the county courthouse remained as a reminder of the "War of Northern Aggression," as it was termed in the South, until the construction of a new building began in 1872. Industrialization came to the Marietta area in the late nineteenth century, gradually overtaking agriculture as the major factor in the county's economy over the next half century. The Marietta Bank (now called First National Bank of Cobb County) opened in 1888, and a paper mill, two chair and two marble companies, a textile mill, and a machine works sparked the economic recovery. By 1899, street lights illuminated the town, a local telephone company was operating, and there was a railroad depot in downtown Marietta. Still, the rural parts of Cobb County endured low cotton prices for years. In 1900 as many as 56 percent of the county's farmers paid rent as tenants with typical fees amounting to a fourth of their cotton crop along with a third of their corn. By 1905, an electric railway operated between Marietta and Atlanta, spawning residential development as Cobb County residents commuted to jobs in Atlanta.

Schools were established early in Marietta, and the city set up its independent school system in 1892. In 1919 the city organized the first Parent-Teacher Association (PTA) in the county. (In fact, The National PTA was founded in Wash-

ington, D.C. by Alice McLellan Birney (1858–1907), a former Marietta resident.)

Early construction of highways was concentrated in Marietta from 1917 to 1921, and the county began a federally-subsidized road program at that same time. Old Highway 41 was paved in 1926, allowing ready access between Marietta and Atlanta and encouraging trade.

## Aircraft Industry Aids Recovery

Cobb County's economy remained dependent on agriculture until 1940 when manufactured goods produced amounted to twice the value of agricultural products. Hard times took over during the Great Depression of the 1930s, and World War II played a part in the recovery. In 1941, Rickenbacker Field (now Dobbins Air Force Base) was built south of Marietta along with the adjoining 200-acre Bell Aircraft Plant. During World War II, B-29s were produced at the plant and employment reached 28,000 people. With the local population able to supply only a small part of the work force for the large plant, newcomers poured in, necessitating the construction of new housing projects. About that time a 45-acre complex was built and named Larry Bell Park, in honor of the President of Bell Aircraft Corporation. The plant closed in 1946, but reopened in 1951 as the Lockheed-Georgia Company. Some of the aircraft produced there include B-47s, C-130s, C-141s, C-5As, C-5Bs, and the Jetstar. Employment at the plant of the Bell Aircraft Corporation, Georgia's largest employer at that time, reached more than 31,000 people by the 1960s.

Businesses and the real estate industry burgeoned when thousands of people moved to Cobb County and the Greater Atlanta area. Construction of Interstate 75 through the county in the 1950s increased the impact of tourism, and brought outside investments for industry and housing. During the following years major developments included the opening of the first major office parks in the 1960s, the opening of Cumberland Mall in 1973, the opening of the first major hotels and shopping malls and the establishment of the Cobb Convention and Visitors Bureau in the 1980s, and the construction of the $47 million Galleria Convention Centre in 1992. With the area's economic growth showing no signs of slowing, by mid-2003 more than 27,000 businesses were licensed in Cobb County.

Cobb County, of which Marietta is the county seat, is Georgia's third largest county and growing. The city's and county's station as a commercial hub of north Georgia, blended with its "old South" charm and close proximity to Atlanta, combine to make it one of the fastest-growing counties in the country.

***Historical Information:*** Cobb County Public Library, 266 Roswell St., Marietta, GA 30060; telephone (770)528-2320

# Population Profile

### Metropolitan Area Residents

*1980:* 2,233,000
*1990:* 2,969,500
*2000:* 4,112,198
*Percent change, 1990–2000:* 39.0%
*U.S. rank in 1980:* 16th
*U.S. rank in 1990:* 12th
*U.S. rank in 2000:* 11th

### City Residents

*1980:* 30,829
*1990:* 44,129
*2000:* 58,748 (of which, 22,824 were male and 22,766 were female)
*2003 estimate:* 61,282
*Percent change, 1990–2000:* 33.1%
*U.S. rank in 1990:* 582nd (State rank: 13th)
*U.S. rank in 2000:* 557th (State rank: 13th)

*Density:* 2,684.1 people per square mile (in 2000, based on 2000 land area)

*Racial and ethnic characteristics* (2000)
　White: 33,185
　Black or African American: 17,330
　American Indian and Alaska Native: 188
　Asian: 1,744
　Native Hawaiian and Pacific Islander: 51
　Hispanic or Latino (may be of any race): 9,947
　Other: 4,694

*Percent of residents born in state:* 35.4% (2000)

*Age characteristics* (2000)
　Population under 5 years old: 4,655
　Population 5 to 9 years old: 3,776
　Population 10 to 14 years old: 3,023
　Population 15 to 19 years old: 3,391
　Population 20 to 24 years old: 6,615
　Population 25 to 34 years old: 14,134
　Population 35 to 44 years old: 9,031
　Population 45 to 54 years old: 6,021
　Population 55 to 59 years old: 1,932
　Population 60 to 64 years old: 1,276
　Population 65 to 74 years old: 2,174
　Population 75 to 84 years old: 1,929
　Population 85 years and older: 791
　Median age: 30.0 years

*Births* (2003, in Cobb County)
　Total number: 10,539

*Deaths* (2003, in Cobb County)
　Total number: 3,289 (of which, 51 were infants under the age of 1 year)

*Money income* (1999)
　Per capita income: $23,409
　Median household income: $40,645
　Total households: 23,945

*Number of households with income of . . .*
　less than $10,000: 2,068
　$10,000 to $14,999: 1,209
　$15,000 to $24,999: 3,165
　$25,000 to $34,999: 3,573
　$35,000 to $49,999: 4,579
　$50,000 to $74,999: 4,504
　$75,000 to $99,999: 2,081
　$100,000 to $149,999: 1,711
　$150,000 to $199,999: 493
　$200,000 or more: 562

*Percent of families below poverty level:* 11.5% (41.3% of which were female householder families with related children under 5 years)

*2002 FBI Crime Index Total:* Not reported

# Municipal Government

Marietta is governed by a mayor and seven-member city council who serve four-year terms, while the day-to-day administration is handled by the City Manager, who is appointed by the city council.

**Head Official:** Mayor Bill Dunaway (R) (since 2002; current term expires January 2006)

**Total Number of City Employees:** 750 (2004)

*City Information:* City of Marietta, 205 Lawrence St., Marietta, GA 30061; telephone (770)794-5530

# Economy

### Major Industries and Commercial Activity

Cobb County has a diverse business base that encompasses manufacturing and distribution, administrative headquarters operations, service industries, and retailers. The booming service economy and the large migration of Northern companies into the South have formed a new class of entrepreneurs. Marietta and Cobb County compete with cities such as Nashville, Birmingham, Charlotte, Dallas, and Fairfax, Virginia, for the attention of relocating businesses. Cobb County has the advantages of relatively low property taxes, as well as the diversity and availability of site and buildings. Marietta offers strong advantages in terms of low costs for building and leasing, as well as a moderate cost of living.

In the early 1990s when Lockheed, the area's largest employer, cut its work force, it didn't seem to faze the community, though in early 2005 more layoffs are predicted due to the proposed federal budget. The mix of new and diverse industries have made the area virtually recession-proof. Besides Lockheed Martin Aeronautical Systems, other large-scale employers in Cobb County include the Cobb County Public Schools, WellStar Health System, The Home Depot, Cobb County Government, and Publix.

Cobb County is the second most popular visitor destination in Georgia. More than 4 million visitors a year experience the area's attractions and stay in its hotels. Tourism was a $1.2 billion industry in 2001. While tourism increased 1.3 percent from the previous year, figures were still slightly impacted by the September 11, 2001 terrorist attacks. Tourism in the area is still experiencing major growth, and is responsible for nearly 40,000 direct and indirect jobs in the county.

*Items and goods produced:* computer software and hardware, aerospace equipment, aircraft parts, medical devices, printing, construction products, chemicals, plastics, paper products, foodstuffs, telecommunications equipment

## Incentive Programs—New and Existing Companies

*Local programs*—The Cobb Chamber of Commerce works to maintain a healthy economy by bringing business and industry to the area and helping established firms grow. Through six Area Councils in the Cumberland, East Cobb, Marietta, North Cobb, Smyrna, and South Cobb areas, the Cobb Chamber unifies and advocates for Cobb's business community. Each council is represented on the Cobb Chamber Board of Directors and promotes grassroots actions. The Cobb Chamber handles administration for the Development Authority of Cobb County and the Cumberland Community Improvement District, which supports the Cumberland Transportation Network.

*State programs*—Georgia has business-friendly tax laws; the state does not use the unitary tax method, but instead taxes businesses only on income apportioned to Georgia. In addition, the state sales tax rate has risen only one percentage point since 1951. Attractive inventory tax exemptions are available in most metropolitan Atlanta counties, and sales and property tax exemptions are available for certain pollution control equipment used in production. Companies can apply for a permit from the Georgia Environmental

Protection Division which can result in their obtaining their federal permit as well, via a single application.

*Job training programs*—The Georgia Department of Technical and Adult Education administers the Georgia Quick Start program, a three-way partnership of Quick Start, one of the state's technical institutions, and a company wishing to start up business in Georgia. By developing and implementing high quality, customized training programs and materials, Quick Start assists the company in obtaining a trained work force ready to begin as soon as the company opens for business.

## Development Projects

In late 2004, a new Chattahoochee Tunnel and R.L. Sutton Water Reclamation Facility was put into operation. Begun in 2000, the $113.6 million wastewater project included a 9.5 mile long tunnel and 40-million-gallon-a-day wastewater treatment facility. The new facility is expected to meet the needs of the county through the year 2050.

Also in late 2004, the county purchased the vacant Westpark Plaza shopping center on Whitlock Avenue for $2.8 million. Plans to begin renovation were underway, with an expected finish time of spring 2005; county offices will inhabit the new space. Groundbreaking took place in October 2004 on a new regional library in Marietta's historic Mableton area. As the third of five new library facilities in the county, the $3.7 million building is expected to be completed by early 2006.

*Economic Development Information:* Cobb Chamber of Commerce, PO Box 671868, Marietta, GA 30006-0032; telephone (770)980-2000

## Commercial Shipping

Norfolk Southern and CSX offer freight rail service at Marietta, and piggyback service at Atlanta, 18 miles away. For motor freight, Marietta and Cobb County are part of the Atlanta Commercial Zone, with 11 interstate and 51 inter/intrastate terminals, and 23 local terminals. General aviation aircraft are served by McCollum Field, which can handle operations of small jets and other craft weighing less than 33,000 pounds. The airport has a 4,600-foot bituminous runway and offers aircraft tiedown, airframe and power plant repair, a hangar, and lighted runway.

## Labor Force and Employment Outlook

Low unemployment levels and some of the lowest property tax levels in metro Atlanta continue to assist Marietta and Cobb County in their attractiveness to businesses and residents. Cobb County has metamorphosed from a sleepy bedroom community into the region's driving economic force. Good planning has built a solid infrastructure; Cobb Community Transit operates a bus system and major road improvements are underway. Cobb County is well positioned for further growth and economic expansion.

The following is a summary of data regarding Cobb County's labor force as of 2003.

*Size of labor force:* 355,501

*Number of workers employed in . . .*
   *agriculture and mining:* 357
   *construction:* 22,971
   *manufacturing:* 33,496
   *wholesale and retail trade:* 60,726
   *transportation and public utilities:* 23,442
   *information:* 16,380
   *finance, insurance, and real estate:* 27,472
   *services:* 60,123
   *education, health, and social services:* 54,720
   *arts, entertainment, leisure, and accommodation:* 21,128
   *government:* 14,316

*Average hourly earnings of production workers employed in manufacturing:* $14 (2003 statewide average)

*Unemployment rate:* 4.2% (December 2004)

| Largest employers | Number of employees |
| --- | --- |
| Cobb County Public Schools | 13,799 |
| WellStar Health System | 9,900 |
| Lockheed Martin Aeronautical | 7,800 |
| The Home Depot, Inc. | 6,686 |
| Cobb County Government | 5,001 |
| Six Flags Atlanta Properties | 2,765 |
| Publix Super Markets | 2,600 |
| Naval Air Station-Atlanta | 2,500 |
| IBM Corporation | 1,400 |
| WORLDSPAN | 1,310 |

## Cost of Living

The following is a summary of data regarding several key cost of living factors for the Marietta area.

*2004 (3rd Quarter) ACCRA Average House Price:* $209,258

*2004 (3rd Quarter) ACCRA Cost of Living Index:* 97.0 (U.S. average = 100.0)

*State income tax rate:* Ranges from 1.0% to 6.0%

*State sales tax rate:* 4.0% (food and prescription drugs are exempt)

*Local income tax rate:* None

*Local sales tax rate:* 1.0%

*Property tax rate:* $11.99 per $1000 of fair market value (2003)

***Economic Information:*** Cobb Chamber of Commerce, PO Box 671868, Marietta, GA 30006; telephone (770)980-2000; fax (770) 980-9510; email info@cobbchamber.org

# Education and Research

## Elementary and Secondary Schools

Marietta's city school system is governed by a seven-member elected Board of Education. Four of its 10 schools have been named Georgia Schools of Excellence along with one National School of Excellence, and in 2003 the system ranked in the top 15 percent of nationwide school systems. In 2004 the combined average of SAT scores exceeded the national average. Marietta offers a comprehensive program for exceptional and gifted children in elementary, middle, and high school. The system offers special education programs, reading recovery classes, and a program called Project Key aimed at pre-school handicapped children. In the fall of 2005 the Marietta Center for Advanced Academics, the city's first magnet school, is scheduled to open and will enroll 360 third to fifth grade students via application only.

In 2003, Cobb County taxpayers extended a "special purpose" sales tax of $637 million for new school construction and technology programs. Of that total, $76 million was allocated for technology and curriculum programs. The need for additional classrooms due to the expanding population is addressed as $205 million of the tax is directed to the building of nine new schools within the county (four elementary, three middle, and two high schools).

The following is a summary of data regarding Marietta's public schools as of the 2003–2004 school year.

*Total enrollment:* 7,558

*Number of facilities*
   *elementary schools:* 7
   *junior high/middle schools:* 2
   *senior high schools:* 1
   *other:* 1 alternative school

*Student/teacher ratio:* 12:1

*Teacher salaries*
   *minimum:* $33,455
   *maximum:* $70,568

*Funding per pupil:* $7,710

Several private schools, both church-affiliated and nonsectarian, are located in the area.

***Public Schools Information:*** Marietta City Schools, 250 Howard St., Marietta, GA 30060; telephone (770)422-3500; fax (770)425-4095

## Colleges and Universities

Marietta is the home of two senior colleges of the University System of Georgia. Kennesaw State University, with about 18,000 students, offers a broad selection of undergraduate majors as well as graduate programs in business administration and education. Southern Polytechnic State University, founded in 1948 and located within the city, offers its nearly 4,000 students associate degree transfer programs and 23 undergraduate majors in its bachelor degree programs including ten areas of engineering technology and related fields, as well as masters programs in Technology Management and Technical Communication.

The city has two post-secondary institutions. Chattahoochee Technical College offers its 5,000-plus students vocational-technical and supplementary education and industrial short-term training. The school offers four associate of applied technology degree programs and certificate programs in architectural drafting technology and dental assisting. Diploma programs are available in seventeen other fields. The North Metro Technical College offers the associate of applied science degree in business, electronics, and secretarial science. Diploma programs include accounting, information & office technology, electronics and telecommunications. Continuing education programs are also offered, as are customized industry-specific short term courses. Life University offers bachelor's degrees in business administration, nutrition for the chiropractic sciences, and pre-professional education for advanced careers in health care and business. Finally, the private Shorter College has six different schools focused on a liberal arts curriculum.

## Libraries and Research Centers

The Cobb County Public Library System, one of the largest in the state, is comprised of a 64,000-square-foot main library in Marietta and 16 branches with another expected to open in early 2006. The system has almost 680,000 volumes, 1,298 periodical subscriptions, almost 500 microfiches, nearly 8,000 audio and videotapes, 3,200 music CDs, a CD-ROM network, and Internet access. A number of databases are also available free of charge on the library's website. The library is also home to a special historical collection in its Georgia Room containing more than 12,000 items.

Special libraries in Marietta include the Genealogical Center Library, which lends books to the public by mail for a fee (write to them at PO Box 1343, Marietta GA 30007-1343); Lockheed's comprehensive Technical Information Center; and Southern Polytechnic State University's science and engineering library. Three research centers are located in Marietta, including the U.S. Army Corps of Engineers' South Atlantic Division Laboratory, which tests soil and water quality among other activities.

*Public Library Information:* Cobb County Public Library System, 266 Roswell St., Marietta, GA 30060-2004; telephone (770)528-2320; email cobbcat@cobbcat.org

# Health Care

The region supports four large hospitals; Marietta's largest is WellStar Kennestone Hospital with 493 beds. Kennestone has made treatment of minor illness and injuries more convenient to residents through its five satellite KenMed facilities throughout the community. Atherton Place, an independent and personal care living facility on the main campus, serves senior citizens, while Health Place, the system's 40,000-square-foot fitness center, is open to the public and specializes in cardiac rehabilitation. The system's emergency center in Marietta is the second busiest in Georgia. Kennestone Hospital is one of only four designated trauma centers in metro Atlanta. The city of Marietta operates its own emergency medical service. The Specialty Care of Marietta accommodates 138 patients in its postacute rehabilitation center.

# Recreation

### Sightseeing

The first stop to make on a visit to Marietta is at the Welcome Center to pick up tour maps; the Center is in the renovated train station right off Marietta Square. The revitalized square is an entertainment mecca with several popular nightspots, restaurants, and the renovated Theater in the Square. The focal point of the square is Glover Park, where winding brick paths lead to a majestic, three-tiered fountain, to an ornate Victorian gazebo, and to a scaled-down replica of "The General," a celebrated Civil War locomotive, where children can climb, slide, and pretend. The park is the location for frequent special events, festivals and concerts.

A walking tour of the downtown features at least 100 homes and buildings that span the period from antebellum to Victorian and evoke the sentiment and beauty of days gone by. The William Root House, the city's oldest residence, houses a museum depicting life in Cobb County during the 1840s and is open from Tuesdays to Saturdays. Other structures include classic Victorian, Queen Anne, Greek Revival, and Plantation Plain-style residences. The 1854 Greek classic style First Presbyterian Church, St. James Episcopal Church, and the 1866 Zion Baptist Church are part of the Historic District's walking tour. Other buildings of note include for-

**The Marietta Welcome Center is a renovated train station located off of Marietta Square.**

mer general stores, a ''Breakfast House'' hotel, and a former hardware store. The Episcopal Cemetery is the burial place of many early well-known local citizens.

Not far from the center of town, Kennesaw Mountain National Battlefield Park, a Civil War fortress, provides miles of wood trails, original earthworks and cannons that stand as silent witnesses to the decisive battle in which Confederate troops, vastly outnumbered, defended Kennesaw Mountain in a bloody effort to block Sherman's March to Atlanta. At the visitor's center a ten-minute slide presentation briefs visitors on the battle that took place and exhibits depict the harsh conditions the soldiers endured in the front ranks. At the park, visitors may walk on the grounds and view the family cemetery of the Kolb Farm, a significant battle site during the Civil War. Marietta is one of only two U.S. cities with both a Confederate and a Union Cemetery. The Confederate Cemetery is the final resting place for more than 3,000 Confederate soldiers. At the nearby 23-acre National Cemetery, more than 10,000 Union soldiers, 3,000 of whom are unknown, rest alongside veterans of five subsequent wars.

Well worth a visit is the Concord Covered Bridge, one of the few remaining covered bridges in operation, nestled on Nickajack Creek alongside historic Ruff's Mill. Both sites are national landmarks and part of a historic district that also features nineteenth century homes and the Concord Woolen Mills. Another interesting spot is home to the remains of the nineteenth-century Marietta Manufacturing Mill on the banks of the Sope Creek.

At the East Cobb Children's Museum, school-age children can participate in historical tours, and dress in authentic period costumes. The museum also offers live puppet shows and classroom excursions. The Aurora, a horse-drawn 1879 Silsby Steamer, is on display at the Marietta Fire Museum. It has been fully renovated and is said to be the best-restored engine of its kind in the world. The Kennesaw Civil War Museum, formerly know as The Big Shanty Museum, in Kennesaw provides a close-up look at ''The General,'' a steam locomotive that caused quite a stir in 1862 when Union soldiers known as Andrew's Raiders hijacked it and sped northwest to damage the line and seal off Chattanooga in the Civil War campaign. Classic cars and the largest selection of miniature die-cast cars in the Southeast are on display at the Auto Motif in Smyrna. Marietta also features a Gone With The Wind Museum: Scarlett on the Square opened in 2003 and maintains a wide variety of memorabilia from the 1939 classic. Located within the historic Kennesaw House is the Marietta Museum of History that displays such items as Civil War uniforms and a local photograpy collection.

Youngsters are enthusiastic participants at Six Flags White Water, a 35-acre park featuring more than two dozen specialty water rides including speed slides and body flumes.

Marietta's newest family draw is American Adventures, a ''turn of the century'' entertainment park with rides, games, and attractions that is also part of the Six Flags family. Another mammoth attraction, which is located in the southwestern corner of the county, is Six Flags Over Georgia amusement park, home of the Great American Scream Machine, The Free Fall, Z Force and other thrilling rides, musical revues and top name entertainers. Skull Island debuted there in 2004 and features three water-dumping towers, six water slides, and many other water-related activities. Sun Valley Beach, the South's largest swimming pool, with 2 million gallons, is located on one-and-a-half acres of land and provides sun and games at its Powder Springs location.

No visit to Marietta would be complete without paying respects to the ''Big Chicken,'' a local landmark. In 1963 a Marietta restaurateur wanted a focal point for his eatery and commissioned a Georgia Tech student to create a plucky, triangular-shaped fowl, complete with eyes that rolled, a beak that snapped open and shut, and a comb that dipped in the breeze. At one point, a hydraulic lift made the bird operational, but for the most part it stands as a silent object of wonder for foreign visitors who have declared it to be ''so American'' and an important element of Marietta folklore. The Big Chicken has inspired the ''Gran Poulet,'' an art festival featuring fowl-inspired works of every description.

**Arts and Culture**

The best in professional live theater, both contemporary and classical, is offered by the award-winning 225-seat Theatre In the Square opened in 1982 at its renovated home on Marietta Square. Classical music concerts are offered by the Cobb Symphony, established in 1951, and the Jubilee Concert Series at the Galleria Centre. The Georgia Ballet performs regularly at the Cobb County Civic Center.

The Marietta/Cobb Museum of Art is located just off the Square. The museum's permanent exhibit is complemented by workshops, lectures, poetry readings, special art showings and children's activities. Art lovers can also visit the Mable House Cultural Center in the southern portion of Cobb County. Smyrna's Lillie Glassblowers allows spectators to watch as liquid crystal is transformed into exquisite designs for artistic and scientific purposes.

**Festivals and Holidays**

Annual events in Marietta involve a wide variety of activities. The last weekend in April brings the Taste of Marietta food festival. In spring, Cobb Landmarks and Historical Society sponsors ''Through The Garden Gate,'' a spring tour of gardens in the city. In May and October, arts, crafts, and food concessions fill Glover Park at Historic Marietta Arts & Crafts Festival, and performances, exhibits, and an artists' market are presented at The Art Place-Mountain

View's Arts Fest and have been dubbed "May-Retta Daze" and "Harvest Square." Summer brings the Glover Park Concert Series, a variety of musical presentations that extend through June, July, and August. The Fourth of July celebration starts the day with a parade and is filled with food and completed by fireworks at dusk. Labor Day Weekend's Art in the Park at Marietta Square showcases local artists' paintings, photography and pottery in Glover Park. September ushers in the Historic Marietta Antique Street Festival that was established in 1992 and draws over 125 antiques dealers from across the state. Late September's North Georgia State Fair at Miller Park features carnival rides, top name entertainment, contests, and special attractions. Theatre In The Square Presents "the 1940's Radio Hour," a song and dance extravaganza performed at Marietta Square during November, December, and January. December brings The Marietta Pilgrimage: A Christmas Home Tour featuring six private historic homes decorated for the holidays. Audiences enjoy the holiday excitement of the Georgia Ballet's performances of "The Nutcracker" at Cobb County Civic Center. Each spring the city celebrates Founder's Day, when the City Square is decked out for a weekend festival, the highlight of which is an antique show.

### Sports for the Spectator

Al Bishop Softball Complex is the site of numerous national/regional softball tournaments on its five lighted playing fields. Marietta's professional sports fans have an exciting series of events to choose from by making the fifteen-mile trip to nearby Atlanta, home to five professional franchises. Atlanta also hosts many collegiate competitions.

### Sports for the Participant

The Cobb County Parks, Recreation, & Cultural Affairs Department, one of the largest in the Southeast, consists of 35 parks covering more than 2,000 acres. Tennis, swimming, softball, gymnastics, and soccer are offered, as are arts and crafts classes and informational programs. Marietta has an impressive network of municipal parks, most fully equipped with playground facilities, athletic fields and tennis courts. Wildwood Park, a beautiful 28-acre site, is equipped with a unique "Adventure Challenge Course," one of the largest in the state, plus a one-third mile self-guided Sensory Trail for the Blind. At the site of the former Marietta County Club, the Marietta City Club opened as Cobb County's first public Professional Golfer's Association standard golf course on 126 acres and a professional shop. Visitors to Kennesaw Mountain National Battlefield Park enjoy five marked hiking trails, the longest of which extends for sixteen miles. Laurel Park has a jogging trail, basketball court, picnic facilities, thirteen tennis courts, and two volleyball courts on 25 acres. The Chattahoochee River National Recreation Area consists of more than 1,700 acres in four parks along the waterway. Concessionaires rent canoes, rafts, or kayaks at various points along the river so that water buffs can experience the river's whitewater thrills firsthand. The Lake Allatoona Reservoir, which boasts a 330-acre lake and 124 land-acres, is ideal for fishing, boating, swimming, camping, hiking, and picnicking. At the town of Acworth, Acworth Beach and Lake Acworth offer swimming, fishing, picnicking, and sunbathing.

### Shopping and Dining

Cobb County offers shoppers a variety of options from the corner store to huge regional shopping malls like Cumberland Mall and Town Center at Cobb, each with more than one million square feet. Opened in 1973 as the area's first enclosed mall, Cumberland Mall has a projected $65 million in improvements scheduled to conclude in 2006. Marietta is the home of Providence Square, which is anchored by Home Depot, Upton's, and Parkaire Landing. Quaint shops surrounding Marietta Square offer antiques, art, fine china, jewelry, clothing, and novelty items. Other shopping areas include Marietta Trade Center, Town and Country Shopping Center, Merchants Walk, Cobb Place, Belmont Hills Shopping Center, and Akers Mill Shopping Center. The Church Street Market provides foods native to the area along with quaint home and garden products.

Southern cuisine, featuring such treats as baked squash casserole or turnip greens, or palate-tempting fare served in classic plantation style, makes for memorable dining experiences. A variety of ethnic cuisines, including Japanese, Mexican, Italian, Chinese, and standard American and continental fare are available at the more than 200 dining rooms, outdoor cafes, and casual eateries which proliferate throughout the area.

***Visitor Information:*** Cobb County Convention & Visitors Bureau, One Galleria Pkwy., Atlanta, GA 30339; telephone (800)451-3480; fax (678)303-2625; email cobbcvb @cobbcvb.com. Marietta Welcome Center, 4 Depot St. NE, Marietta, GA 30060; telephone (770)429-1115

# Convention Facilities

Cobb County's Galleria Centre provides 320,000 square feet of meeting and exhibit space. The $40 million facility offers a 144,000-square-foot exhibit/arena space; a 25,000-square-foot ballroom; nearly 24,000 square feet of registration/prefunction space, and 20 meeting rooms ranging from 528 to 1,750 square feet. Connected to the center is the Renaissance Waverly Hotel with 27 meeting room and 60,000 square feet of meeting space and 521 deluxe hotel suites. The county offers more than 70 hotels/motels with more than 12,000 sleeping rooms in a variety of price ranges. Unique off-site meeting spots include a Victorian-styled park, an 1830's historic home/museum, a Victorian country inn, an amusement park, and the Cobb County Civic Center.

Within the city itself is the Marietta Conference Center & Resort, which has 20,000 square feet of meeting space and features 17 meeting rooms that can accommodate up to as many as 500 people.

*Convention Information:* Cobb County Convention & Visitors Bureau, One Galleria Pkwy., Atlanta, GA 30339; telephone (800)451-3480; fax (678)303-2625; email cobbcvb @cobbcvb.com

# Transportation

## Approaching the City

Atlanta's Hartsfield-Jackson Atlanta International Airport serves the greater metro area, including Marietta. Airlines serving Hartsfield-Jackson include domestic and international carriers, as well as commuter and freight lines. Cobb County is bisected by Interstate 75 and Highway 41/Cobb Parkway. It is bordered on the east by Atlanta's perimeter highway Interstate 285 and the Chattahoochee River, and on the south by Interstate 20. In 2004 the state of Georgia announced that approximately $1.2 billion in transportation renovation monies would be available to Cobb County with a focus on developing high-occupancy vehicle lanes on I-575 and bus lanes on I-285 and I-75.

## Traveling in the City

Cumberland Transportation Network and Cobb Community Transit offer alternative ways to get around and connect Cobb County with Atlanta and the MARTA rapid transit system.

# Communications

## Newspapers and Magazines

Marietta's daily newspapers are the *Marietta Daily Journal* and *The Atlanta Journal-Constitution,* both published in Atlanta. *East Cobber* and *Cobb Extra* are published weekly. Several magazines are published in Marietta, including *The Game & Fish Magazine, Georgia Sportsman,* and *North American Whitetail Magazine.*

## Television and Radio

Cobb County has access to eight television stations, all but one from Atlanta. There are two local radio stations.

*Media Information:* *Marietta Daily Journal,* 580 Fairground St. SE, Marietta, GA 30060; telephone (770) 428-9411. *The Atlanta Journal-Constitution,* 72 Marietta St. NW, Atlanta, GA 30303

## Marietta Online

City of Marietta home page. Available www.city.marietta .ga.us

Cobb Chamber of Commerce. Available www.cobbchamber .org

Cobb County Board of Education. Available www.cobb.k12 .ga.us

Cobb County Convention and Visitors Bureau. Available www.cobbcvb.com

Cobb County Public Library. Available www.cobbcat.org

Marietta City Schools. Available www.marietta-city.org

*Marietta Daily Journal.* Available www.mdjonline.com

Marietta Square (downtown visitor information). Available www.mariettasquare.com

## Selected Bibliography

Lassiter, Patrice Shelton, *Generations of Black Life in Kennesaw & Marietta, Georgia* (Charleston, S.C.: Arcadia Pub., c1999)

# Savannah

## *The City in Brief*

**Founded:** 1733 (chartered 1789)

**Head Official:** Otis S. Johnson (D) (since 2003)

**City Population**
  1980: 141,654
  1990: 137,560
  2000: 131,510
  2003 estimate: 127,573
  Percent change, 1990–2000: − 4.4%
  U.S. rank in 1980: 158th
  U.S. rank in 1990: 129th
  U.S. rank in 2000: 182nd (State rank: 6th)

**Metropolitan Area Population**
  1980: 231,000
  1990: 257,899
  2000: 293,000

Percent change, 1990–2000: 13.5%
U.S. rank in 1990: 137th
U.S. rank in 2000: 133rd

**Area:** 75 square miles (2000)
**Elevation:** approximately 46 feet above sea level
**Average Annual Temperature:** 66.4° F
**Average Annual Precipitation:** 49 inches

**Major Economic Sectors:** services, wholesale and retail trade, government, manufacturing, tourism, military, healthcare and port operations
**Unemployment rate:** 3.4% (December 2004)
**Per Capita Income:** $16,921 (1999)

**2002 FBI Crime Index Total:** 11,595

**Major Colleges and Universities:** Savannah State University, Armstrong Atlantic State University, Savannah Technical Institute, Savannah College of Art and Design

**Daily Newspaper:** *Savannah Morning News*

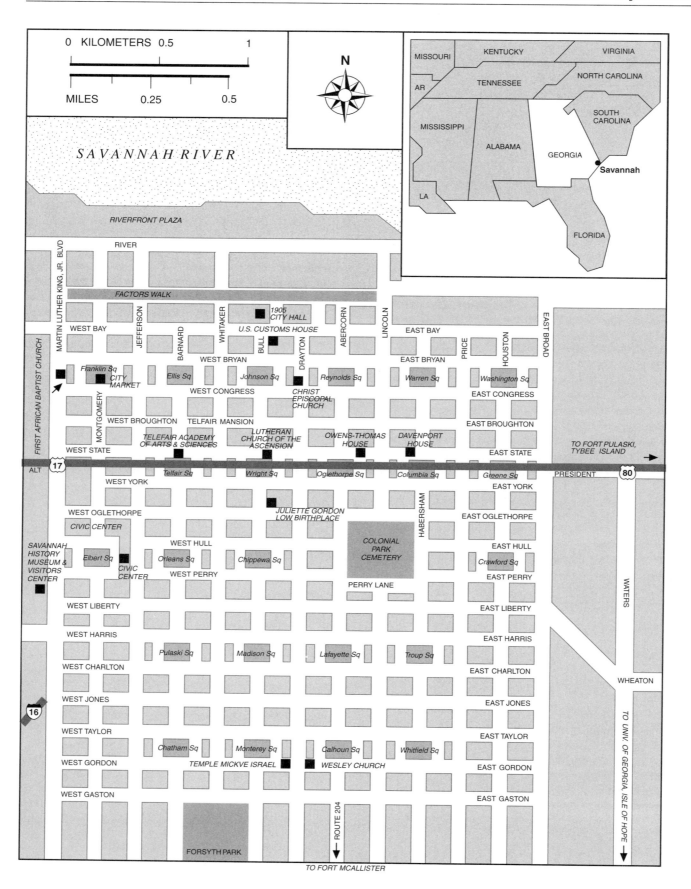

# Introduction

"The most beautiful city in North America," is the way Paris's famed *Le Monde* newspaper describes Savannah. Visitors in growing numbers flock to experience the city's mild climate, old world charm and atmosphere, moderately priced accommodations, and unique historic downtown district. Savannah is attracting retirees, too, who are looking for alternatives to an increasingly crowded Florida. Savannah consistently appears on "Top 10" lists for assets such as its attractiveness as a tourist destination and its walkability. The Toronto *Sunday Sun* says of this alluring city: "Savannah wears her past like a fine old cape, draped in Southern graciousness, pockets filled with treasures of a rich, proud history."

# Geography and Climate

Savannah is located on the Georgia-South Carolina border where the Savannah River and the Atlantic Ocean are the natural boundaries of both the city and the state. In its semi-tropical location, Savannah usually has warm, and frequently hot, humid weather throughout the year. The city is set on the coastal plain and is surrounded by flat and low marshland to the north and east, and higher land, rising as high as 51 feet above sea level to the south and west. About half of the land to the west and south is clear of trees; the other half is woods, much of which lie in swamp. The intercoastal waterway runs down the Savannah coast, as do numerous rivers and inlets. There are seven months in which the average temperature is 70 degrees or higher. Summer temperatures are moderated by frequent afternoon showers. Average snowfall is less than one-half inch per month in winter.

**Area:** 75 square miles (2000)

**Elevation:** approximately 46 feet above sea level

**Average Temperatures:** January, 49.2° F; July, 81.2° F; annual average, 66.4° F

**Average Annual Precipitation:** 49 inches

# History

### City Designed by British Colonist

On February 12, 1733, James E. Oglethorpe and 114 colonists from Gravesend, England, arrived at Yamacraw Bluff on the Savannah River to found America's thirteenth colony, Georgia. Many of the new settlers were poor. Their purpose was to increase imperial trade and navigation along the coastal waterway and to establish a protective buffer between Spanish Florida and the northern English colonies during the Spanish War. It is said that Oglethorpe had four rules for his new community: no slaves, no Roman Catholics, no strong drink, and no lawyers. The name Savannah is said to have derived either from the Sawana people who inhabited the region or from a Shawnee word for the Savannah River.

Oglethorpe designed the basic layout of Savannah into blocks of five symmetrical 60-by-90-foot lots. Included in his plan were 24 public squares (21 of which are still in existence). They were intended to serve both as public meetings places and as areas where citizens could camp out and fortify themselves against attack from natives, Spaniards (who ruled Florida), and even marauding pirates. Thus Savannah became "America's first planned city." This system of public squares was intended as central areas of fortification, as well as social areas for the colonists.

Immigrants from around the world were attracted to Oglethorpe's city. By the time the American Revolution started, the population of Savannah exceeded 3,000, making it the twentieth largest town in the American colonies.

### Savannah During the Revolution

During the Revolutionary War, Savannah was taken by colonial insurgents. The following year, in 1778, the British recaptured the city. In 1779 the American army was unsuccessful in its attempts to retake the city. Finally, in 1782, the British left the city to return to England. Savannah was the chief city and capital of the Georgia colony until after the war ended in 1783.

### Cotton Dominates Economy

From the outset, Savannah was an important seaport. In 1755 James Habersham and Francis Harris organized the first import-export businesses of the colony with the selling of cattle products. Before the American Revolution, the products of agriculture and trade with the Indians were sent back to England. At one time, diked rice paddies almost surrounded the city. Savannah prospered, and many of its historic homes were built. When the scourge of yellow fever swept through the city in 1820, the rice culture was abandoned and cotton became the dominant crop. For nearly a century, trading in the Cotton Exchange on Savannah's waterfront set world cotton prices. Cotton farming was greatly expanded following Eli Whitney's invention of the cotton gin, an event that took place near Savannah in 1793. Shortly thereafter, cotton shipments from the area soared to more than two million bales annually.

## Marine History Events

Transportation history was made in 1819 when the SS *Savannah* became the first steamship to cross an ocean, traveling from Savannah to Liverpool, England. Later, in 1834, the shift from sail to steam was furthered when the country's first all-iron vessel, the *John Randolph,* was built, owned, and operated in Savannah.

## The City During the Civil War and Beyond

Savannah, which had a large free African American population before the Civil War, suffered from the Union navy's coastal blockade during the war. The city was captured by General William T. Sherman in 1864 after the citizens surrendered rather than risk total destruction of Savannah (as had already happened in Atlanta). As a result, Sherman sent a famous message to President Abraham Lincoln in which he said: "I beg to present to you as a Christmas gift, the city of Savannah with 140 heavy guns and plenty of ammunition and also about 25,000 bales of cotton."

The capture of Savannah brought on rampant vandalism. Throughout the reconstruction period (1865–1877) and beyond, the city went through hard times. Nevertheless, the first art museum in the Southeast, Telfair Academy of Arts And Sciences, was opened in 1886. Still, it is said that the city's civic pride did not revive until the early 1900s, when the National Park Services restored nearby Fort Pulaski. This revival inspired a group of Savannah citizens to begin restoration efforts. In March 1912, Savannah citizen Juliette Gordon Low formed the first Girl Scout troop in the nation, and later her birthplace was made into the national Girl Scout museum and national program center. World War I and its aftermath put restoration efforts on hold. The years following the war were harsh ones for Savannah. The boll weevil wiped out cotton crops and the city fell into a decline. Many of its beautiful structures fell into disrepair.

Some say it was the proposal to demolish the 1815 Davenport House that galvanized the city. In 1955 city residents created the Historic Savannah Foundation with the purpose of restoring old buildings in the city's original town center. Many sites in and around Savannah received the National Historic Landmark designation in 1966, and the city has been heralded as a masterpiece in urban planning. A multimillion-dollar riverfront revitalization in 1977 peaked the restoration efforts. Today, the historic district encompasses more than 2,300 architecturally and historically significant buildings in its 2.5-square-mile area. Restoration of these buildings continues to the present day. Restoration efforts have also included the existing City Market, including adaptive re-use of historic warehouses. Construction of the $83 million waterfront complex of the Savannah International Trade and Convention Center was completed in May 2000 on Hutchinson Island. The island also boasts a new

409-room Westin Savannah Harbor Golf Resort, featuring a Greenbrier spa and a world-class, 18-hole Troon golf course. These developments are part of the conversion of the island into an upscale community which is to include high-rise condominiums, town houses and single family homes.

*Historical Information:* Georgia Historical Society—Library and Archives, 501 Whitaker Street, Savannah, GA 31401; telephone (912)651-2125; Library (912)651-2128; Fax (912)651-2831; email ghslib@georgiahistory.com

# *Population Profile*

## Metropolitan Area Residents
*1980:* 231,000
*1990:* 258,060
*2000:* 293,000
*Percent change, 1990–2000:* 13.5%
*U.S. rank in 1990:* 137th
*U.S. rank in 2000:* 133rd

## City Residents
*1980:* 141,654
*1990:* 137,560
*2000:* 131,510
*2003 estimate:* 127,573
*Percent change, 1990–2000:* −4.4%
*U.S. rank in 1980:* 158th
*U.S. rank in 1990:* 129th (State rank: 3rd)
*U.S. rank in 2000:* 182nd

*Density:* 1,759.5 people per square mile (2000)

*Racial and ethnic characteristics* (2000)
  White: 51,108
  Black or African American: 75,072
  American Indian and Alaska Native: 303
  Asian: 1,997
  Native Hawaiian and other Pacific Islander: 92
  Hispanic or Latino (may be of any race): 2,938
  Other: 1,224

*Percent of residents born in state:* 66.5% (2000)

*Age characteristics* (2000)
  Population under 5 years old: 9,186
  Population 5 to 9 years old: 5,163
  Population 10 to 14 years old: 9,423
  Population 15 to 19 years old: 10,139
  Population 20 to 24 years old: 12,653
  Population 25 to 34 years old: 19,419
  Population 35 to 44 years old: 18,027
  Population 45 to 54 years old: 15,260

Population 55 to 59 years old: 5,656
Population 60 to 64 years old: 4,717
Population 65 to 74 years old: 8,503
Population 75 to 84 years old: 6,582
Population 85 years and older: 2,382
Median age: 32.3 years

*Births* (2003)
Total number: 4,222

*Deaths* (2003)
Total number: 4,205 (of which, 77 were infants under the age of 1 year)

*Money income* (1999)
Per capita income: $16,921
Median household income: $29,038
Total households: 51,378

*Number of households with income of . . .*
less than $10,000: 8,842
$10,000 to $14,999: 4,794
$15,000 to $24,999: 8,815
$25,000 to $34,999: 6,956
$35,000 to $49,999: 8,359
$50,000 to $74,999: 7,241
$75,000 to $99,999: 3,399
$100,000 to $149,999: 1,678
$150,000 to $199,999: 448
$200,000 or more: 846

*Percent of families below poverty level:* 17.7% (54.6% of which were female householder families with related children under 5 years)

*2002 FBI Crime Index Total:* 11,595

# Municipal Government

Savannah has an elected mayor, eight alders, and an appointed city manager. Elections are held every four years. Savannah is in Chatham County.

**Head Official:** Otis S. Johnson (D) (since 2003; current term expires 2006)

**Total Number of City Employees:** 2,212 in more than 350 positions (2004)

*City Information:* City of Savannah, Public Information Office, telephone (912)651-6410

# Economy

## Major Industries and Commercial Activity

Savannah has a five-tiered economy consisting of manufacturing, the port and transportation, tourism, the military, and miscellaneous businesses such as health care. Retail and service businesses are also important factors. Manufacturing is the largest part of the economy, with 251 manufacturing facilities in Chatham County in 2002 with annual payrolls exceeding $713 million. The largest plants include Gulfstream Aerospace, an executive jet aircraft manufacturer; International Paper, the largest producer of paper for paper bags in the United States; Georgia Pacific Savannah River Site, which makes paper products; Great Dane Trailers, which makes large truck trailers; and Derst Baking Company, which makes bread, rolls and cakes. The transportation industry, centered on the Port of Savannah, is a vital element of the economic mix. It is the fifth largest container port in the country, handling more than 1.5 million container units in 2004 and shipping to more than 150 countries around the world.

Tourism is an active and rapidly growing segment of the economy. The city's attractiveness as a visitor destination is enhanced by its charming historic district, accommodations, and accessibility. In 2003 Savannah's nearly six million visitors spent $1.542 billion, supporting nearly 16,000 jobs locally.

The military plays an important role in the economic health of the city as well. The U.S. Army's Third Infantry Division (Mechanized) is housed at Fort Stewart, 40 miles from Savannah. Hunter Army Airfield, part of the army complex, is located in Savannah. The Stewart/Hunter complex has more than 22,000 soldiers and approximately 3,500 civilians making it coastal Georgia's largest employer. Combined payrolls totaled $934.48 million in 2003.

Retail and services today generate most new jobs. Savannah, with two enclosed malls and 41 large shopping centers, is the retail center for a six-county area. Retail sales totaled $4.5 billion in 2004.

*Items and goods produced:* transportation equipment, chemicals, cotton, food products, stone, clay, glass, fabricated metals, printing and publishing, computer equipment and machinery, paper, paper products, aircraft, petroleum products, wood products, tea, sugar, construction materials

## Incentive Programs—New and Existing Companies

The Savannah Economic Development Authority (SEDA) is the business solicitation organization in the City of Savannah and Chatham County. It assists companies interested in relocating to, or expanding in, the Savannah area at no cost to the client. SEDA was recently named one of the top ten development groups in the country for the second time.

*Local programs*—Savannah offers incentives and inducements to companies considering investments that will impact the labor market in a positive way. Programs include a variety of job tax credits, including a special job tax credit for new corporate headquarters facilities, a one to three percent tax credit for an investment of $50,000 or more, a research and development tax credit, and up to $500 tax credit per program per employee for retraining. There are tax abatements and exemption programs, including material handling equipment sales tax exemptions, pollution equipment sales tax exemptions, manufacturing machinery sales tax exemption, and tax-exempt industrial revenue bonds for manufacturing facilities. Parts of Savannah fall under the blanket of the Foreign Trade Zone program. Other programs include a childcare credit, electricity rate discounts, county inventory tax exceptions, rapidly expanding business tax credit for Georgia companies growing faster than 20 percent per year, and eligibility for the HOPE Scholarship and HOPE Grant (tuition and fees at Georgia public and state technical colleges). In addition, the Savannah Area Chamber of Commerce has established a one-stop resource program for small and minority businesses.

*State programs*—Georgia has business-friendly tax laws; the state does not use the unitary tax method, but instead taxes businesses only on income apportioned to Georgia. In addition, the state four percent sales tax rate has risen only one percentage point since 1951. Georgia's Freeport zones, like Savannah's, exempt for ad valorem taxation on all or part of the value of certain tangible property held in certain inventories. Companies can apply for a permit from the Georgia Environmental Protection Division, which can result in their obtaining a federal permit as well, via a single application. Georgia also exempts sales and use tax on certain computer equipment.

*Job training programs*—Several workforce development and training programs provide students educational and technical skills through apprenticeships, internships and professional development programs. Among them are Project Workforce, administered by the Savannah Area Chamber of Commerce; Coastal Empire Tech Prep Consortium; Junior Achievement; youth apprenticeship through First District Regional Educational Service Agency; Coastal Workforce Services; and the Intellectual Capital Partnership Program (ICAPP) through the University System of Georgia. The Quick Start Pre-employment Training program is a three-way partnership of Quick Start, the Georgia Department of Labor, and a Georgia company wishing to obtain a qualified workforce. The program is a coordinated applicant

screening and on-going training process for groups of 25 or more workers.

## Development Projects

Savannah is unique in having a large tract of waterfront land open for development and located close to the central business and historic districts. Recently completed projects on the tract include the Savannah International Trade & Convention Center and Westin Savannah Harbor Resort, a 403-room luxury facility.

Icon Health & Fitness, a manufacturer of fitness equipment headquartered in Logan, Utah, announced plans in 2004 to build a 600,000 square foot distribution facility in Crossroads Industrial Park in Savannah. The facility will bring 300 new jobs to Savannah when it opens in 2005.

***Economic Development Information:*** Savannah Economic Development Authority, 8001 Chatham Center Drive, Suite 300, Savannah, GA 31405; telephone (912)447-8450 or (800)673-7388; fax (912)447-8455; email moreinformation @seda.org

## Commercial Shipping

Savannah is one of the southeast's leading seaports and cargo hubs. Shipping activity is focused on the Port of Savannah, which is supported by two railroads and two interstate highways as well as Savannah International Airport. Improvements at the port focus on handling more containerized cargo. The port moves 300,000 containers annually through more than 9 million square feet of warehousing. Because of its location on the coast, the port serves as a major distribution point to and from a 26-state region, which services 75 percent of the country. The port has been designated as a Foreign Trade Zone to encourage international commerce.

## Labor Force and Employment Outlook

Georgia is a right-to-work state. Labor costs in Georgia are low and union activity is minimal. The area population is growing and the number of jobs is increasing, especially in the service sector. Though job growth in Georgia was slowing, in 2005 jobs in the Savannah area were expected to grow at a rate of 3.1 percent, the largest percentage gain for any metro area in the state.

Hospitality, port activities, tourism, convention business, and information technology (IT) were expected to be major sources of job growth in 2005 and beyond.

The following is a summary of data regarding the Savannah metropolitan area labor force, 2003 annual averages.

*Size of nonagricultural labor force:* 149,022

*Number of workers employed in . . .*
  *construction and mining:* 8,500
  *manufacturing:* 13,500
  *trade, transportation and utilities:* 30,300
  *information:* 1,900
  *financial activities:* 6,100
  *professional and business services:* 14,400
  *educational and health services:* 19,400
  *leisure and hospitality:* 17,600
  *other services:* 7,100
  *government:* 21,000

*Average hourly earnings of production workers employed in manufacturing:* $16.30

*Unemployment rate:* 3.2% (November 2004)

| *Largest employers* | *Number of employees* |
|---|---|
| Memorial Health | 4,583 |
| Savannah-Chatham County Board of Education | 4,309 |
| Gulfstream Aerospace | 4,300 |
| St. Joseph's/Candler Hospital | 3,800 |
| Fort Stewart Hunter Army Airfield | 3,485 |
| City of Savannah | 2,408 |
| International Paper | 1,800 |
| Wal-Mart | 1,675 |
| Chatham County | 1,600 |
| Georgia-Pacific Savannah River Mill | 1,461 |
| Kroger | 1,300 |
| Savannah College of Art & Design | 1,200 |

**Cost of Living**

Savannah is a relatively inexpensive town in which to live and do business. *Outlook Magazine* ranked Savannah as "one of the top 25 places to live and work."

*2004 (3rd Quarter) ACCRA Average House Price:* $254,612

*2004 (3rd Quarter) ACCRA Cost of Living Index:* 97.6

*State income tax rate:* Ranges from 1.0% to 6.0%

*State sales tax rate:* 4.0% (food and prescription drugs are exempt)

*Local income tax rate:* None

*Local sales tax rate:* 2.0%

*Property tax rate:* Set and reviewed twice yearly and applied to the assessed value, which is 40 percent of the fair market value. The city's millage rate has seen a gradual reduction since 1996 and was 13.30 mills in 2002.

***Economic Information:*** Savannah Area Chamber of Commerce, 101 E Bay Street, Savannah, GA 31402; telephone (912)644-6400; fax (912)644-6497

# Education and Research

## Elementary and Secondary Schools

The Savannah-Chatham County Public Schools system consists of 49 schools and 9 educational centers educating 36,000 students, and featuring outstanding curricula as well as a number of special programs for students from K-12. The Savannah-Chatham County Public Schools Academy Programs (formerly the Magnet program) offer students the opportunity to pursue specialized courses of study. The system also offers Select Schools, a group of four schools with one or more special features, as well as majority-to-minority transfers. Other special programs include the Business, Legal, and Financial Academy at Savannah High, which provides practical working experience; the Performing Arts Academy at Savannah High, which requires auditions for acceptance; and special elementary school programs that focus on the cultures of the world, interdisciplinary instruction through modern technology, computer expertise, and music. A Savannah-Chatham County Public Schools' construction program, with projects totaling $221 million, resulted in the opening of 13 new schools between 1996 and 2003.

In the state of Georgia, any student who graduates from high school with at least a B average is eligible for free college tuition and a book allowance at any of the state's public colleges, universities or technical colleges. Those who choose a private college in Georgia get a $3,000 grant. The scholarship and grant program is called HOPE (Helping Outstanding Pupils Educationally).

The following is a summary of data regarding Savannah-Chatham County public schools as of the 2003-2004 school year.

*Total enrollment:* 34,554

*Number of facilities*
  *elementary schools:* 31
  *junior high/middle schools:* 11
  *senior high schools:* 7
  *other:* 9 educational centers

*Student/teacher ratio:* 14:1

*Teacher salaries*
  *average:* $43,000

*Funding per pupil:* $7,272

Private schools in Savannah include Benedictine Military School, Bible Baptist Day School, Blessed Sacrament School, Calvary Baptist Day School, Hancock Day School, Memorial Day School, Notre Dame Academy, Providence Christian

School, Ramah Junior Academy, Rambam Day School, St. Andrew's School, St. James Catholic School, St. Michael's Catholic School, St. Peter the Apostle, St. Vincent's Academy, Savannah Christian Preparatory School, Savannah Country Day School, and Urban Christian Academy.

*Public Schools Information:* Marketing Services Department, Savannah-Chatham County Public School System, 208 Bull Street, Room 204, Savannah, GA 31401; telephone (912)651-5685

### Colleges and Universities

Savannah State University, part of the University System of Georgia, enrolls more than 2,700 students and offers bachelor's degrees through its schools of humanities and social sciences, business, and sciences and technology. Master's degrees can be earned in business administration, public administration, and social work. Armstrong Atlantic State University enrolls more than 6,000 students and offers 75 undergraduate and graduate degrees in arts and sciences, health professions, and education. A new 84,000-square-foot building houses the university's Criminal Justice Training Center.

One of the largest art and design schools in the country, Savannah College of Art and Design offers bachelor and master of fine arts programs and graduate courses in architecture. Founded in 1993, the School of Visual Arts/Savannah, part of the School of Visual Arts/New York, awards bachelor's degrees in arts, computer graphics, sculpture, and other arts-related disciplines. South University, whose main campus is on Mall Blvd. in the heart of the Southside offers bachelor's, masters's and doctoral degrees. Savannah Technical College offers job training and skills in more than 50 certificate, professional, diploma, and associate degree programs. The Coastal Georgia Center for Continuing Education provides adult continuing education. Georgia Southern University in Statesboro, 50 miles from Savannah, enrolls 15,075 students.

Brewton-Parker College offers bachelor's degrees as well as evening courses for students employed full-time. The Embry-Riddle Aeronautical University is located on the Hunter Army Airfield and offers courses in aviation-related fields. Online as well as campus-based courses are offered at Saint Leo University's Savannah center.

### Libraries and Research Centers

Savannah's Live Oak Public Libraries serve Chatham, Effingham, and Liberty counties. It has 19 branches and one bookmobile. The library has more than 500,000 volumes and makes available thousands of periodicals, records, cassettes, compact discs and videocassettes, CD-ROM resources, and special collections on local history. The library also offers access to state-of-the-art computerized indexes,

on-line information services, and the Internet. Other libraries in the area include college-related and medical libraries, a municipal research library, the Georgia Historical Society Library and other historical libraries, Skidaway Institute of Oceanography Library, and a U.S. Army Corps of Engineers technical library.

Marine research is conducted at the University of Georgia and at Skidaway Institute of Oceanography. At Herty Foundation Research and Development Center, fibrous materials are studied. Armstrong Research Institute assists industry with problems in engineering, chemistry, mechanics, and other technical areas. The Department of Energy's Savannah River National Laboratory and Savannah River Ecology Laboratory are science and technology centers.

*Public Library Information:* Chatham-Effingham-Liberty Regional Library, 2002 Bull Street, Savannah, GA 31401; telephone (912)652-3600

# Health Care

With its two major hospital systems and more than 600 private physicians in the city alone, Savannah is the healthcare hub of a 40-county area encompassing coastal Georgia and parts of South Carolina. St. Joseph's/Candler Health System is responsible for innovative programs that focus on early detection and prevention. St. Joseph's Hospital, with 305 beds, is a general acute care facility considered one of the best in the country. Its LifeCare Center and its Center for Heart Disease Prevention are national models. Memorial Health University Medical Center, with 530 beds, provides tertiary care to 35 counties and is a regional referral center for cancer care, trauma, rehabilitation, high-risk obstetrics, neonatology, pediatrics, and cardiac care. Georgia Regional Hospital at Savannah is an inpatient psychiatric facility. Coastal Harbor Treatment Center provides residential psychiatric treatment for children and adolescents. Willingway Hospital is a recognized leader in the treatment of alcoholism and drug dependency.

# Recreation

### Sightseeing

Visitors are attracted to Savannah for many reasons, the primary one being the opportunity to tour the city's beautiful Historic District, the country's largest historic urban landmark district. The Savannah Visitors Center, located at the

**The Gaston House.**

former Central of Georgia Railroad Station, itself a national historic landmark, offers helpful brochures, maps, and publications. Walking, driving, and carriage tours of the city are also available. The nearby Roundhouse Complex contains the oldest and most complete railroad repair shop in the U.S.

Tours of the Historic Landmark District include six different neighborhoods and views of garden-like public squares and hundreds of restored eighteenth- and nineteenth-century buildings with ornate ironwork, gingerbread trim, and picturesque fountains (about seven houses are open as museums). Highlights of the district include the Owens-Thomas House, circa 1816–1819, which was designed by John Jay and considered to be the finest example of Regency architecture in America; the Davenport House Museum, built between 1815–1820, a fine example of Federal architecture and period decorative arts; and Juliette Gordon Low Birthplace of the founder of the Girl Scouts, which is restored and furnished to depict the 1870s.

Interesting churches in the district are the First African Baptist Church (1861), the oldest African American congregation in the United States; the 1890 Wesley Monumental United Methodist Church; Temple Mickve Israel, the third oldest synagogue in the United States; Lutheran Church of the Ascension (1878-89), which has an exquisite Ascension window; Christ Episcopal Church (1838), which was the first church established in the colony; and the Cathedral of St. John the Baptist, the oldest Roman Catholic congregation in the state.

The Cotton and Naval Stores Exchange (1886) was the center of commerce when Savannah was the world's foremost cotton port. Other interesting civic sites include the U.S. Customs House (1852); the 1905 City Hall; Colonial Park Cemetery, the second oldest burial ground (1750–1853) for colonists; and Bonaventure Cemetery, resting place of many local residents, made famous by the publication of *Midnight in the Garden of Good and Evil*. The recently restored City Market features City Market Art Center, shops, restaurants, and taverns. Particularly scenic streets include Factor's Walk, known for iron bridges and cobblestones; Riverfront Plaza/River Street, with restaurants, pubs, and shops housed in old cotton warehouses; Gaston Street, distinguished by its stately old homes; and Oglethorpe Avenue, a fashionable residential street. Beauty abounds at Emmett Park, with its Harbor Light and fountain, and at Forsyth Park, with its beautiful azalea blooms, Confederate monument, and recently restored fountain. The district's museums are detailed in the Arts and Culture section.

The city of Savannah has many other interesting attractions outside the Historic District. The Bethesda Home for Boys on Isle of Hope is the oldest continuously operated home for boys in America. Its Cunningham Museum houses items connected with Bethesda's history dating back to the 1700s.

The Massie Heritage Interpretation Center is the only remaining original building of Georgia's oldest chartered school system. The University of Georgia Marine Education Center & Aquarium, ten miles southeast of the city on Skidaway Island, features an aquarium exhibit of marine life found in Georgia's waters. Old Fort Jackson, the oldest remaining brickwork fort in Georgia, and the Savannah History Museum at the Visitors Center offers artifacts and exhibits from the eighteenth and nineteenth centuries. Fort Pulaski National Monument, fifteen miles east of Savannah, Fort McAllister State Historic Park, 22 miles south, and the Tybee Island Museum provide exhibits concerning the Civil War period. Also on Tybee Island, the Tybee Island Lighthouse, guardian of the Savannah River since 1736, offers tours, a museum, and gift shop. The Ships of the Sea Museum presents a large collection of models and maritime memorabilia representing man's 2,000-year quest to conquer the seas. Hands-on exhibits in natural history, astronomy, the sciences, prehistoric animals of the Georgia Coast, and a discovery room dealing with natural and physical sciences are offered at the Savannah Science Museum. Trustees Garden Village was the site of the first public agricultural experimental garden in America. It is now a residential area and home of the famous Pirates' House (1759) frequented by seamen and pirates alike. The Roundhouse Railroad Museum offers a glimpse of the oldest and most complete pre-Civil War railroad repair facility in the country.

The city's newest museums are the Mighty Eighth Air Force Heritage Museum in Pooler and the Ralph Mark Gilbert Civil Rights Museum. The Mighty Eighth honors the sacrifices made during and after World War II by the largest air strike force in history, which was formed in Savannah in 1942. The Civil Rights Museum tells the story of Savannah's role in the movement.

**Arts and Culture**

With its splendid squares and parks, elegant architecture, and lush vegetation, Savannah creates a studio and stage artscape for its performing and visual arts. The City Lights Theater Company, permanently housed in the newly renovated Avon Theater, moves to historic Telfair Square each spring to produce "Shakespeare on the Square." The Savannah Theatre, the oldest continuously operating theater site in the country, is home to the Savannah Theatre Company which performs a season of live drama plus a summer musical. The Savannah Concert Association offers a five-concert season at the Lucas Theatre for the Arts. Various entertainments are offered at the Savannah Civic Center throughout the year.

Opened in 1885 as the first public art museum in the southeast, the Telfair Museum of Art in the historic district is Savannah's premier art museum. The handsome William

Jay-designed mansion features American painting and art of the eighteenth and nineteenth centuries, as well as the 1818 Octagon Room, dining room, and the restored 1886 rotunda gallery. The Jepson Center for the Arts, the Museum's third building in downtown Savannah, is scheduled to open in fall 2005. It features gallery spaces, expanded educational resources, sculpture gardens, auditorium, storage facilities, cafe and museum store. The King-Tisdell Cottage museum in the historic district is dedicated to preserving aspects of African American culture and heritage and displays documents, furniture, and art objects of the 1890s. The Negro Heritage Trail Tours embark from the site. The Spirit of the South Museum offers a special retrospective exhibit of the song writing career of Savannahian Johnny Mercer.

*Arts and Culture Information:* telephone (912)233-ARTS

## Festivals and Holidays

Savannah is host to more than 200 festivals and events annually. During the first two weeks in February, the Georgia Heritage Celebration's Colonial Faire and Muster, sponsored by the Historic Savannah Foundation, celebrates the state's colonial history. The Black Heritage Festival, held the second week in February, is a series of events featuring the cultural and artistic contributions of African Americans. The Savannah Irish Festival is held in February at the Civic Center Area in the Historic District. Sheep to Shawl Festival at Oatland Island in early March provides the opportunity to watch the annual shearing of the sheep and the processing and handweaving of the wool. The St. Patrick's Day Parade is Savannah's biggest event, and the second largest St. Pat's celebration in the country. More than one-quarter of a million people participate in this event, which began in the early 1800s. Savannah Music Festival is a 15-day fest featuring concerts in downtown venues and includes international talent in blues, jazz, and classical music. The Savannah Tour of Homes and Gardens offers self-guided walking tours of private homes in six historic neighborhoods over four days in late March. An ecumenical Easter Sunrise service is a Tybee Island tradition. April is the month for four Savannah festivals including the International Festival, Sidewalk Art Festival, Blues and BBQ Festival and the Spring Fling Art and Music Festival.

The Savannah Seafood Festival, Savannah Shakespeare Festival, Scottish Games Festival, Tybee Island Beach Bum Parade, and the SCAD Sands Art Festival round out the list of activities in May. The Tybee Island Summer Concert Series during the summer months hosts concerts for beach music lovers. Picnics, music, arts, food, and fireworks at sites around the city help residents and visitors hail the Fourth of July holiday.

City Market and Forsyth Park are the sites for the week-long Savannah Jazz Festival in September. National, regional, and local jazz stars assist in the workshops, jazz seminars, and other events. Oktoberfest is held early in the month of October and features German food, imported beer, arts, and entertainment. Greek music and food aromas fill the air three days in mid-October at the Savannah Greek Festival. The Savannah Film Festival features films and videos from around the world. The Savannah Harbor Boat Parade of Lights in November with its fireworks extravaganza and tree lighting kicks off the Savannah Harbor Holiday Series. Christmas in Savannah offers a Christmas parade, tours of historic homes, Civil War reenactments and other events.

## Sports for the Spectator

Historic Grayson Stadium is the site of the home games of the Class A South Atlantic League Savannah Sand Gnats, a farm team of baseball's Washington Nationals. Armstrong Atlantic State University, Savannah State University, and Savannah College of Art and Design field teams in such sports as football, basketball, baseball, softball, and volleyball.

## Sports for the Participant

Savannah's warm weather allows participation in outdoor activities year round. Savannah offers excellent facilities for jogging, tennis, golf, swimming, boating, and other water sports. The city has more than 100 public recreational neighborhood parks, 13 swimming pools, more than 70 athletic fields (including 4 fully equipped complexes,) more than 75 basketball courts, 50 tennis courts, and 2 public golf courses. For boating, fishing and swimming enthusiasts, Savannah offers marinas throughout the 420 miles of navigable waters and 87,000 acres of tidal marshland, as well as the intercoastal waterway.

## Shopping and Dining

Savannah offers numerous choices for enthusiastic shoppers, including two traditional enclosed malls, 41 large shopping centers, boutiques, antique shops, flea markets, and restored warehouse complexes. Oglethorpe Mall in midtown offers 5 major department shops and more than 100 other stores. Savannah Mall on the south side has four major department stores and an indoor carousel. Savannah Festival Factory Outlet Center offers brand name merchandise at substantial savings. Magnolia Bluff Factory Outlet is located about 45 minutes away in Darien. River Street's nineteenth-century warehouses have been converted into shops, restaurants, and nightclubs. "First Saturday" festivals (every month but January) present a grand display of arts and crafts in Rousakis Plaza.

Savannah is a city renowned for its hospitality. While the city offers a wide choice of dining establishments, visitors are particularly delighted by the "down-home southern cookin' " for which the area is famous. The diverse land and water of the region produces catfish and chicken for frying, hush puppies, grits, sweet potatoes for pie, collards and turnip greens, okra, scallions, dried peas, ham and turkey for smoking, meat for barbecuing, peanuts for boiling, white butter beans, white and yellow turnips, cornmeal for bread, tomatoes, oysters, crab for crabcakes, and shrimp. In addition to this sort of delectable fare, the city's many restaurants offer the cuisines of China, Japan, Italy, and Greece, as well as continental dishes.

***Visitor Information:*** The Savannah Area Convention & Visitors Bureau, 101 East Bay Street, Savannah, GA 31402; telephone (877)-SAVANNAH; email info@savannah-visit.com Visitors may wish to request a copy of the "Savannah Travel Planner," "Tybee Island Brochure," or the "Calendar of Events."

# Convention Facilities

The $83 million Savannah International Trade & Convention Center is the centerpiece of a remarkable renaissance blending the best of the Old and New South into a unique meetings destination. The state-of-the-art, 365,000-square-foot complex features 100,000 square feet of customizable exhibit space with impressive vistas of Savannah's bustling waterfront. An additional 50,000 square feet of prime meeting space accommodates large general sessions to small private retreats. Highly flexible, these first-class facilities include the 25,000-square-foot Grand Ballroom, a variety of 13 meeting rooms, and four executive class boardrooms. The Oglethorpe Auditorium offers exceptional comfort and convenience both for audiences and presenters, including state-of-the art audio-visual and telecommunications technology.

***Convention Information:*** The Savannah Area Convention & Visitors Bureau, 101 East Bay Street, Savannah, GA 31402; telephone (877)-SAVANNAH; email info@savannah-visit .com. Savannah International Trade & Convention Center, One International Drive, PO Box 248, Savannah, GA 31402-0248; telephone (888)644-6822; fax (912)447-4722; email vgainor@savtcc.com

# Transportation

## Approaching the City

Savannah/Hilton Head International Airport, which is located 12 miles west of the city, is served by AirTran,

Continental Express, Delta, Delta Express, Independence Air, Northwest Airlink, United Express and U.S. Airways. Forty-five daily departures and eleven destinations are offered by the airport. Non-stop service is provided to Atlanta, Charlotte, Chicago, Cincinnati, Detroit, Houston, Newark, New York (LaGuardia and JFK), Orlando, and Washington D.C. Savannah Aviation, a charter service, is also located at the facility.

Savannah is reached by automobile on Interstate Highway 95 north-south (which links Savannah with other cities along the East Coast), and I-16 east-west (via I-75 from Atlanta.) Amtrak provides rail service to and from the city; Greyhound-Trailways provides intercity bus transportation and charter service.

## Traveling in the City

Just west of the city, Interstate Highway 95 runs north and south. I-16 comes from the west and stops at the city's center. The city's historic district is ten miles east of the intersection of I-95 and I-16. U.S. 80 from Tybee Island and the Atlantic Ocean, 17 miles away, crosses the city going east and west, and U.S. 17 bisects the northwest quadrant of the city, coming from the north. Chatham Area Transit (CAT) provides local bus service and wheelchair-accessible shuttle service from downtown hotels, inns, and the visitors center to the historic district and other attractions.

# Communications

## Newspapers and Magazines

Savannah's major daily newspaper is the *Savannah Morning News*. Local weeklies include *The Herald, Connect Savannah, Creative Loafing, Savannah Business Report and Journal,* and *Savannah PennySaver. The Savannah Jewish News* is published monthly. Magazines published in Savannah are *SCUBA Diving, Savannah Magazine,* and *Cash Magazine.*

## Television and Radio

Represented in the Savannah area are all four major television networks. Savannah's 18 (12 AM and 6 FM) radio stations cover a wide variety of formats including talk and public radio, classical, jazz, rock, religious, and adult contemporary.

***Media Information:*** *Savannah Morning News* PO Box 1088, Savannah, GA 31402; telephone (912)236-9511

## Savannah Online

Chatham County home page. Available www.chatham county.org

City of Savannah government home page. Available www .ci.savannah.ga.us/cityweb/webdatabase.nsf

Georgia Historical Society. Available www.georgiahistory .com

Live Oak Public Libraries. Available www.liveoakpl.org

Savannah Area Convention and Visitors Bureau. Available www.savannah-visit.com

Savannah Chamber of Commerce. Available www .savannahchamber.com

Savannah-Chatham County Public Schools. Available www .savannah.chatham.k12.ga.us

Savannah City Guide. Available www.ourcoast.com/ cityguides

Savannah Economic Development Authority. Available www.seda.org

Savannah International Trade and Convention Center. Available www.savtcc.com

*Savannah Morning News.* Available www.savannahnow .com

Savannah Online. Available www.savannahonline.com

## Selected Bibliography

Beney, Peter, *The Majesty of Savannah* (New York: Pelican, 1992)

Berendt, John, *Midnight in the Garden of Good and Evil* (New York: Vintage Books, 1999)

Harris, William Charles Jr., *Delirium of the Brave: A Novel of Savannah* (St. Martin's, 1999)

Jakes, John *Savannah or A Gift for Mr. Lincoln* (Dutton Books, 2004)

# KENTUCKY

# The State in Brief

**Nickname:** Bluegrass State
**Motto:** United we stand, divided we fall

**Flower:** Goldenrod
**Bird:** Cardinal

**Area:** 39,728 square miles (2000, U.S. rank: 37th)
**Elevation:** Ranges from 257 feet to 4,145 feet above sea level
**Climate:** Temperate, with plentiful rainfall; occasional winter temperature extremes in the mountains

**Admitted to Union:** June 1, 1792
**Capital:** Frankfort
**Head Official:** Governor Ernie Fletcher (R) (until 2007)

### Population
**1980:** 3,661,000
**1990:** 3,685,296
**2000:** 4,041,769
**2004 estimate:** 4,145,922
**Percent change, 1990–2000:** 9.7%
**U.S. rank in 2004:** 26th
**Percent of residents born in state:** 73.7% (2000)
**Density:** 101.7 people per square mile (2000)
**2002 FBI Crime Index Total:** 118,799

### Racial and Ethnic Characteristics (2000)
**White:** 3,640,889
**Black or African American:** 295,994
**American Indian and Alaska Native:** 8,616
**Asian:** 29,744
**Native Hawaiian and Pacific Islander:** 1,460
**Hispanic or Latino (may be of any race):** 59,939
**Other:** 22,623

### Age Characteristics (2000)
**Population under 5 years old:** 265,901
**Population 5 to 19 years old:** 847,743
**Percent of population 65 years and over:** 12.5%
**Median age:** 35.9 years

### Vital Statistics
**Total number of births (2003):** 54,954
**Total number of deaths (2003):** 39,927 (infant deaths, 341)
**AIDS cases reported through 2003:** 2,359

### Economy
**Major industries:** Food products, agriculture, coal mining, construction, manufacturing
**Unemployment rate:** 4.2% (December 2004)
**Per capita income:** $26,252 (2003; U.S. rank: 41st)
**Median household income:** $38,161 (3-year average, 2001-2003)
**Percentage of persons below poverty level:** 13.7% (3-year average, 2001-2003)
**Income tax rate:** ranges from 2.0% to 6.0%
**Sales tax rate:** 6.0% (food, utilities, and prescription drugs are exempt)

# Frankfort

## *The City in Brief*

**Founded:** 1786 (chartered 1786)

**Head Official:** Mayor William I. May, Jr. (D) (since 1995)

**City Population**
   **1980:** 25,973
   **1990:** 25,968
   **2000:** 27,741
   **2003 estimate:** 27,408
   **Percent change, 1990–2000:** 6.8%

**Franklin County Population**
   **1980:** 41,830
   **1990:** 44,143
   **2000:** 47,687
   **2003 estimate:** 48,051

**Percent change, 1990–2000:** 8.9%
**U.S. rank in 2000:** 957th

**Area:** 15 square miles (2000)
**Elevation:** 510 feet above sea level
**Average Annual Temperature:** 54.9° F
**Average Annual Precipitation:** 44.55 inches

**Major Economic Sectors:** Government, services, trade, manufacturing
**Unemployment rate:** 2.8% (November 2004)
**Per Capita Income:** $21,229 (2000)
**2004 ACCRA Average House Price:** Not reported
**2004 ACCRA Cost of Living Index:** Not reported

**2002 FBI Crime Index Total:** Not reported

**Major Colleges and Universities:** Kentucky State University

**Daily Newspaper:** Frankfort *State Journal*

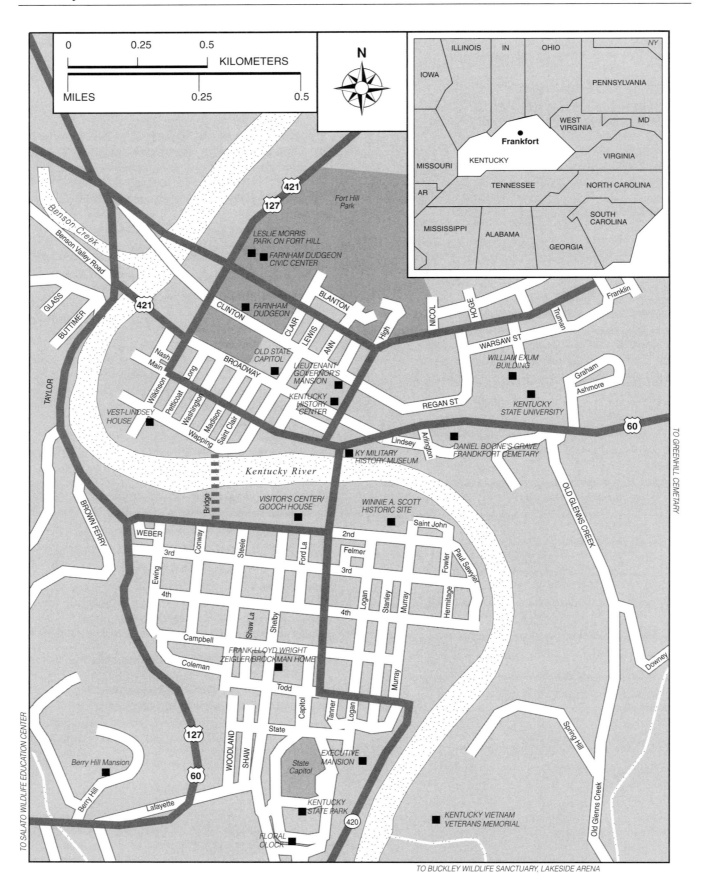

# Introduction

Frankfort, capital city of Kentucky, is one of the country's oldest and smallest state capitals. It is a quaint little town cut through by the Kentucky River. Bluegrass country residents boast of Frankfort's quality of life, the natural beauty of the Kentucky River and its palisades, the graciousness of the local people, and the area's wealth of cultural offerings. Often rated highly in polls measuring top small metropolitan cities in which to live, Frankfort offers the charm of small-town living with both big-city amenities and rolling country-side only a stone's throw away.

# Geography and Climate

Frankfort, county seat of Franklin county, is located in a beautiful valley in the Bluegrass region of Kentucky. The city lies within an hour's drive of the major metropolitan areas of Louisville (to the west) and Lexington (to the east). Cincinnati is less than two hours drive to the north. The city sits on an alluvial plain between the Kentucky River and 150-foot-high steep bluffs, on an S-loop in the river 60 miles above its mouth. The river divides the city into north and south sides, which are connected by bridges. The Bluegrass terrain is rocky and gently rolling, and the land is well suited to agriculture. Disastrous flooding of the Kentucky River at Frankfort occurred in 1937, 1974, and 1997.

**Area:** 15 square miles (2000)

**Elevation:** 510 feet above sea level

**Average Temperatures:** January, 30° F; July, 75° F; annual average, 54.90° F

**Average Annual Precipitation:** 44.55 inches

# History

### Easterners Hear of Garden of Eden in Kentucky

Before Europeans first began to explore the area where Frankfort now stands, the land was heavily forested and teeming with wild game. Shawnee, Delaware, and Cherokee hunting parties followed migrating herds of buffalo, deer, and elk across the Kentucky River near present-day Frankfort. The tribes frequently fought among themselves to control the hunting grounds of Kentucky. In the mid-eighteenth century, backwoodsmen in Pennsylvania, Virginia, and the Carolinas began to feel overcrowded; they complained of land shortages, falling supplies of wild game, and depleted soil, and they cast their eyes on the lush land of Kentucky. In 1751, North Carolina backwoodsman Christopher Gist may have been the first white man to set eyes on the beautiful valley in which Frankfort now lies, but he was forced to leave after learning that Frenchmen and their Indian allies occupied the area (then claimed by France). Frontiersman John Finlay built a log cabin in the area in about 1752, but his hunting and trading—and any further white settlement—were interrupted by the outbreak of the French and Indian War in 1754. The British won that war, but King George's Proclamation of 1763 then prohibited white settlement of the area. It was not until 1769 that Finley was able to return; he brought with him legendary frontiersman Daniel Boone and four other men intent on hunting and exploration.

Boone, Finley, and other so-called Long Hunters (named for the long periods of time they spent hunting) inflamed the public back East with their stories about the rich land of Kentucky and the opportunities it offered to get rich quick. In 1773, Governor John Murray of Virginia, better known as Lord Dunmore, sent survey parties to Kentucky (then a Virginia county), including one led by Robert McAfee. McAfee and his group surveyed and laid claim to 600 acres of land in and around Frankfort. More settlers poured westward, the Natives reacted with hostility, and in 1774 Lord Dunmore's War erupted. The war ended with the defeat of the Indians and the signing of a peace treaty in the spring of 1775, at about the same time the battle of Lexington and Concord ushered in the American Revolution.

### Town Rises, Prospers on Banks of Kentucky River

Land speculators took advantage of the distractions of wartime and laid claim to vast areas of Kentucky. Meanwhile, McAfee's doubtful claim to the area around Frankfort lapsed, lawsuits were filed, and in 1786, General James Wilkinson, a fellow soldier and friend of George Washington, found himself in possession, at a very cheap price, of most of what is now the downtown district of Frankfort (north of the Kentucky River). Wilkinson set to work organizing a town. He chose the name Frankfort to honor the memory of a man named Stephen Frank, a Jewish pioneer who had been shot by Indians, possibly near a river crossing known as "Frank's Ford." Streets were laid out and named in honor of Wilkinson, his wife (Ann), his friends from the Revolutionary War, and even for some Spanish friends (Wilkinson was said to be a secret agent of the Spanish government, and it was rumored that he planned to make Kentucky a Spanish colony). Wilkinson built the second house in Frankfort, a log cabin, but his wife refused to live in the crude structure. The house became a tavern that over the years hosted such celebrities as Aaron Burr, the Marquis de Lafayette, and Henry Clay.

Land speculators and pioneers flocked to Frankfort; they cleared land for farms and built houses. By the late 1780s, a church and schoolhouse had been built, and large quantities of tobacco were growing on farms around Frankfort. While the town did not grow as quickly as Wilkinson had envisioned and he decided not to live there himself, he saw that there was money to be made, and in 1791 he built a tobacco warehouse on his Frankfort land. In 1792 Frankfort was named the capitol of the recently admitted state of Kentucky. Up until the last raid took place in 1794, Frankfort settlers were kept busy fending off hostile Indians; thereafter, the tobacco business thrived and salt pork, animal skins, and hemp joined the economic mix, followed by livestock and lumbering. By 1800, Frankfort was the second largest town in Kentucky after Lexington, with a population of 628. A library opened in 1814; several beautiful and elegant homes and churches were built, some of which are still standing; and the central business district began to expand.

The Lexington and Ohio railroad came to town in 1835 and soon Frankfort began to prosper as a manufacturing center. The population grew from 4,755 people in 1860 to 5,396 people in 1874; by 1900, the population was 9,487 people. Residents processed wood from the huge timberlands of Kentucky and produced cotton goods, carriages, paper, lumber, and distilled liquors, including the "corn liquor" for which the state became famous.

## Politics, War, and the Modern City

Lexington and Louisville had vied to be Kentucky's capital, and when Frankfort's capitol building burned twice, in 1815 and 1824, the two cities challenged the rebuilding in Frankfort. Each time, the structure was rebuilt. The presence of government has flavored the social life and affected the economy of the town. National political figures such as Henry Clay, U.S. Senators John J. Crittenden and John G. Carlisle, and Supreme Court Justice John M. Harlan trained in Frankfort. Nineteenth-century visitors to Frankfort, expecting to encounter backwoodsmen in the legislature, reported astonishment at the eloquence of Kentucky orators.

Kentucky was officially a part of the Union during America's Civil War but many of its citizens were slave owners and Southern sympathizers. The peace of Frankfort was disturbed in 1862 when General Bragg's Confederate Forces seized the city and set up a Confederate State Government. Before the first session met, Yankee guns began firing on the town and the Southerners withdrew. The years following the Civil War saw the development of a modern city on the Kentucky. A school system developed, and by 1900, a movement began urging legislators to fund and construct a modern Capitol. In June 1910 citizens throughout Kentucky gathered to witness the formal dedication of architect Frank Mills Andrews's masterpiece, the Beaux Arts design Kentucky State Capitol.

The early twentieth century brought more disturbances to the peace of Frankfort, punctuated by some periods of prosperity. The city dealt with the assassination of Governor William Goebel during a hotly contested election in 1900, as well as outbreaks of racial violence, a legacy of Civil War days, when more than a third of the town's residents were slaves. The Prohibition era brought a decline in the distilling industry and thus in agricultural production. The Great Depression and a severe drought in the 1930s led to hardship and a decline in population. Further misery came when the Ohio River flooded in 1937, engulfing basements and lifting small homes and businesses off their foundations. Estimated damage was $5 million. But beginning in 1935, the New Deal stimulated a growth in government employment and the beginning of a housing boom. By the time World War II ended, the city, which had changed little since the turn of the century, stood poised to enter its greatest era of growth.

Frankfort experienced a population explosion between 1940 and 1970, from 11,492 residents to 21,356 residents. Demand for housing skyrocketed and farmland rapidly disappeared to make way for subdivisions. Frankfort tripled in size as suburbs were annexed by the city. Realizing the need for a more formal style of government to suit its larger size, in 1956 Frankfort voters approved the manager-commission form of government. Frankfort's infrastructure was modernized and roads were improved, resulting in the move of manufacturing industries to the suburbs, leaving a concentration of government workers downtown. Gradually, the small and compact city, with its charming blend of architectural styles developed over more than a century, expanded into a sprawling city characterized by a more uniform, less ornamental style of construction. Commercial strips grew up where homes once stood; shopping centers sprang up on the outskirts of town, further reducing the importance of downtown Frankfort as a retail center.

The 1960s and 1970s saw considerable downtown building activity, with modern high rises replacing slums but also displacing many African American residents. Capital Plaza, a convention center (which became the home of Kentucky State University Thoroughbreds basketball), and the Federal Building created a new skyline for Frankfort. The city experienced a severe tornado in 1974 that caused millions of dollars in damage. Four years later, in December 1978, the Kentucky River rose to 48.5 feet, breaking the 1937 record by almost a foot. This time the damage exceeded $14.5 million and brought home the need for flood control, a challenge that Frankfort leaders were still grappling with when another disastrous flood occurred in 1997.

Today, Frankfort residents and visitors enjoy the history and quaint charm of small-town living with modern conveniences and larger cities nearby. Frankfort's business climate is cost-effective and has attracted new manufacturing and technology companies. The historic downtown is enjoying revitalization as new businesses move in and become successful.

**Historical Information:** Kentucky Historical Society at the Kentucky History Center, 100 West Broadway, Frankfort, KY 40601; telephone (502)564-1792

# Population Profile

## Franklin County Residents
*1980:* 41,830
*1990:* 44,143
*2000:* 47,687
*2003 estimate:* 48,051
*Percent change, 1990–2000:* 8.9%
*U.S. rank in 2000:* 957th

## City Residents
*1980:* 25,973
*1990:* 25,968
*2000:* 27,741
*2003 estimate:* 27,408
*Percent change, 1990–2000:* 6.8%

*Density:* 1,883.2 people per square mile (2000)

*Racial and ethnic characteristics* (2000)
    White: 23,078
    Black or African American: 4,351
    American Indian and Alaska Native: 149
    Asian: 348
    Native Hawaiian and Pacific Islander: 22
    Hispanic or Latino (may be of any race): 411
    Other: 279

*Percent of residents born in state:* 77.6% (2000)

*Age characteristics* (2000)
    Population under 5 years old: 1,719
    Population 5 to 9 years old: 1,688
    Population 10 to 14 years old: 1,636
    Population 15 to 19 years old: 1,884
    Population 20 to 24 years old: 2,321
    Population 25 to 34 years old: 4,235
    Population 35 to 44 years old: 4,164
    Population 45 to 54 years old: 3,776
    Population 55 to 59 years old: 1,362
    Population 60 to 64 years old: 1,086
    Population 65 to 74 years old: 1,950
    Population 75 to 84 years old: 1,412
    Population 85 years and over: 508
    Median age: 35.9 years

*Births* (2003)
    Total number: 511

*Deaths* (2003)
    Total number: 397

*Money income* (1999)
    Per capita income: $20,512
    Median household income: $34,980
    Total households: 12,250

*Number of households with income of . . .*
    less than $10,000: 1,613
    $10,000 to $14,999: 1,025
    $15,000 to $24,999: 1,784
    $25,000 to $34,999: 1,706
    $35,000 to $49,999: 2,112
    $50,000 to $74,999: 2,060
    $75,000 to $99,999: 1,163
    $100,000 to $149,999: 568
    $150,000 to $199,999: 109
    $200,000 or more: 110

*Percent of families below poverty level:* 9.5% (54.0% of which were female householder families with related children under 5 years)

*2002 FBI Crime Index Total:* Not reported

# Municipal Government

Frankfort is governed through the commission-manager form of government. The members of the city commission are elected to two-year terms and the mayor is elected to a four-year term. The city manager is responsible for the day-to-day operations of the city, while the mayor and commissioners make policy decisions and enact ordinances.

**Head Official:** Mayor William I. May, Jr. (D) (since 1995; current term expires 2007)

**Total Number of City Employees:** 300 (2004)

**City Information:** Mayor's Office, City of Frankfort, PO Box 697, Frankfort, KY 40602; telephone (502)875-8500, fax (502)875-8502

# Economy

## Major Industries and Commercial Activity

As the home of Kentucky's state government, Frankfort has long been a regional employment center. State government employment and private professional service firms doing business with the state have had a stabilizing effect on the area's economy. Nearly half of the local citizens are employed by state or local government.

Major local manufacturers produce automotive wheels and stamped automotive parts, automotive wire products, as well as air brake components, pipes, and oil valves for the heating industry. Other local industries make tool and die products, pallets and wood furniture, and fabrics. World-famous Kentucky whiskey is also produced locally.

Frankfort serves as a trading center for mid-Kentucky. The Capital Community Economic/Industrial Authority (CCE/IDA) assists existing companies in expanding their local operations and helps recruit new manufacturers to Frankfort. The result has been 1,774 new jobs, $120 million in new investment, and more than $32 million in new payroll in recent years. Through the creation of two industrial parks and several business/office parks, the CCE/IDA claims to be a "one stop shop" for businesses seeking a base of operations; the group has provided such infrastructure as double-loop-fed electricity, high-speed bandwidth telecommunications cable, water, and county maintained roads. They also provide financial assistance through low-rate loans for capital investment.

A comprehensive industrial survey conducted by the Frankfort Area Chamber of Commerce showed that industrial employers had a very positive perspective on doing business in the Frankfort area. Ninety-four percent indicated that the Frankfort area was "a very good" or "good" place to do business. This indicator of the business climate was better than that for the state as a whole.

*Items and goods produced:* corn, bourbon whiskey, candy, tobacco, furniture, electronic parts, automotive parts and stampings, plastics, construction products, machinery, textiles, thoroughbred horses.

## Incentive Programs—New and Existing Companies

Several programs help city areas in their efforts to revitalize and attract new businesses to their downtown.

*Local programs*—Downtown Frankfort's Facade Grant Program offers a 50-50 owner match reimbursement for revitalization of downtown buildings. Renaissance Kentucky is formed by an alliance of four state agencies and three private entities, and works with communities to plan and locate resources for restoration and revitalization projects. The Main Street Program is based on a four-point approach and addresses organization, promotion, design, and economic restructuring. The program's goal is "to encourage downtown revitalization within the context of historic preservation." The Capital Community Economic/Industrial

Development Authority offers assistance to new and existing businesses with site and investment matters. Downtown Frankfort, Inc. offers assistance with retail and office location information in the city's historic downtown.

*State programs*—The state of Kentucky offers an extensive array of incentives for business start-up and expansion. The Kentucky Cabinet for Economic Development oversees a wide array of programs and services available to businesses including existing businesses, newly locating companies, start-ups, small and minority businesses, and many others. Kentucky has the lowest overall cost of doing business east of the Mississippi River and ranks fourth nationally as the most favorable state for the cost of doing business. Kentucky's variety of incentives include corporate tax credits, loan financing, training grants, and opportunities for foreign trade zone operations. Local Kentucky sales taxes are taboo, and property taxes are among the lowest in the nation. Kentucky prides itself as an industry-friendly state; only property tax on manufacturing equipment is figured at $1.50 per $1,000. Local jurisdictions may offer inventory tax reduction or exemption options.

## Development Projects

Frankfort's Grand Theater on St. Clair Street was purchased in January 2005 by a nonprofit group with plans to raise $3.7 million for renovations. Currently used for arts programming, once renovated the theater will be an arts center for the city.

***Economic Development Information:*** Downtown Frankfort, Inc., 100 Capital Ave., Frankfort, KY 40601; telephone (502)227-2261, fax (502)227-2604; email downtown@dcr .net

## Labor Force and Employment Outlook

Low unemployment rates relative to state and national averages attest to the industriousness and desirability of Franklin County workers, contributing to an overall Kentucky workforce that measures over 5 percent more productive than the national average and 13th among the 50 states in Gross State Product per wage. Additionally, one in every five adults residing in Franklin County has a college degree.

The following is a summary of data regarding the Franklin County labor force, 2003 annual averages.

*Size of nonagricultural labor force:* 18,457

*Number of workers employed in . . .*
   *construction and mining:* 811
   *manufacturing:* 3,886
   *trade, transportation, and utilities:* 5,098
   *information:* 291
   *financial activities:* 1,032

*professional and business services:* 5,643
*educational and health services:* 649
*leisure and hospitality:* 399
*other services:* 466
*government:* 1,642

*Average hourly earnings of production workers employed in manufacturing:* $15.44

*Unemployment rate:* 4.2% (December 2004, statewide)

| Largest manufacturing employers | Number of employees |
|---|---|
| Topy Corp. | 531 |
| Fruit of the Loom | 426 |
| Allied/Bendix Corp. | 336 |
| Ohi-America | 318 |
| Jim Beam Brands Co. | 309 |
| American Wire Products, Inc. | 227 |
| Frankfort Habilitation | 181 |

## Cost of Living

Within an easy drive of big city amenities in Louisville and Lexington, Frankfort retains a small-town feel with small-town living expenses. Housing in Frankfort is more affordable than in most other parts of the country. The median home price in 2002 was 98,000.

The following is a summary of data regarding several key cost of living factors for the area.

*2004 ACCRA Average House Price:* Not reported

*2004 ACCRA Cost of Living Index:* Not reported

*State income tax rate:* 2% to 6% (2004)

*State sales tax rate:* 6% (2005)

*Local income tax rate:* 1.75% occupational tax

*Local sales tax rate:* None

*Property tax rate:* .201/$100 assessed value of real estate (2005)

**Economic Information:** Frankfort Area Chamber of Commerce, 100 Capitol Ave., Frankfort, KY 40601; telephone (502)223-8261, fax (502)223-5942

# *Education and Research*

## Elementary and Secondary Schools

Frankfort Independent Schools operates its elementary (Second Street School), high school (Frankfort High School), and alternative schools (Wilkingson Street School for troubled middle and high schoolers; EXCEL for skills enrichment; and the Panther Enrichment Program for additional learning opportunities) as a joint venture with the greater Franklin County Public School system. Frankfort schools open in early August, continue for nine weeks, then break for a three-week intersession. The combination continues through the year until summertime, when the students take a six- to seven-week break.

The following is a summary of data regarding the Frankfort public school system as of the 2004–2005 school year.

*Total enrollment:* 939

*Number of facilities*
    *elementary schools:* 1
    *junior high/middle schools:* 1
    *senior high schools:* 1

*Student/teacher ratio:* 13.3: 1 (2005)

*Teacher salaries (2003–2004 school year)*
    *minimum:* $27,500
    *maximum:* $48,000

*Funding per pupil:* $7,665 (2005)

Frankfort and Franklin County are also home to a number of private and religious primary and middle schools, including Capital Day School (K-8), which focuses on accelerated learning with a traditional approach, along with Good Shepherd School (K-8) and the Montessori School of Frankfort (K-5). Millville Baptist Academy is a small school that covers grades 1-12.

**Public Schools Information:** Franklin County Public Schools, 315 Steele St., Frankfort, KY, 40601; telephone (502)875-8661; fax (502)875-8663.

## Colleges and Universities

Kentucky State University, smallest of the state's public institutions, is a 2,300-student school consisting of the College of Arts and Sciences, the College of Applied Sciences, the School of Business, the School of Public Affairs, and the Whitney M. Young, Jr. College of Leadership Studies. It also offers community college degrees. From the 1980s through 2004 more than 30 new structures or major building expansions have enhanced the University's 511-acre campus, which includes a 203 acre agricultural research farm. The school's close proximity to the Kentucky state government affords students a unique opportunity to participate in government administration internships and earn from 3 to 12 credit hours per semester. Pre-law students can also earn credits as interns in the State Office of the Attorney General.

Once strictly an African American institution, the student body of about 2,500 is now racially blended.

**Libraries and Research Centers**

With one building and one bookmobile, the Paul Sawyier Public Library serves both Frankfort and Franklin County. The library's book collection numbers more than 98,000 and its audio-visual collection is more than 10,000. The library has a strong program for children from one year to adolescence.

The Thomas D. Clark Research Library of the Kentucky Historical Society offers rare books, maps, and manuscripts on the state's past. It houses more than 90,000 books, more than 6,000 oral history interviews, and 12,000 reels of microfilm, including some of nineteenth-century newspapers, as well as more than 10,000 historic photographs. The Kentucky Department of Library & Archives provides state research facilities and governmental records. The Kentucky Military Records and Research Branch houses archives of the Kentucky Department of Military Affairs going back to 1791. The Archives of CESKAA at Kentucky State University include images, manuscript collections, and oral histories of African American Kentuckians, as well as the Fletcher collection on African American theater. The Aquaculture Program at Kentucky State University seeks to meet future world food demands through research on more than 15 varieties of farmed fish.

***Public Library Information:*** Sawyier Paul Public Library, 305 Wrapping St., Frankfort, KY 40601; telephone (502)223-1658, fax (502)227-2250

# Health Care

Frankfort Regional Medical Center, a 173-bed acute care facility, features a team approach and offers emergency care, maternity services, diagnostic imaging, and intensive care. The medical center provides outpatient service and treatment programs for substance abuse, as well as psychiatric care. The Medical Center's Center for Women's Health provides medical care for all phases of a woman's life, and the Breast Center provides diagnostic and biopsy services for early detection of cancers and other breast diseases. Medical facilities within 20 miles of Frankfort include Bluegrass Community Hospital in Versailles, KY; New Horizons Health Systems in Owenton, KY; and the Georgetown Community Hospital in Georgetown, KY.

***Health Care Information:*** Frankfort Regional Medical Center, 299 King's Daughters Dr., Frankfort, KY 40601; telephone (502)875-5240, fax (502)226-7936.

# Recreation

**Sightseeing**

The Frankfort/Franklin County Tourist and Convention Commission's Visitors Center, located five blocks from the Kentucky statehouse, offers maps and information about local sites. Two good places to get a feeling for the personalities that formed Frankfort's history are the Corner of Celebrities, which is actually one square block behind Wilkinson Street in the north part of town, and the Frankfort Cemetery, located on a high cliff overlooking the city. Dozens of famous Kentuckians have lived on and near the Corner. Historic residences there that are open to the public include Orlando Brown House, a Greek Revival home designed by architect Gideon Shryock; and the adjacent Liberty Hall, built in 1796 in the Federalist style for John Brown, Orlando Brown's brother and Kentucky's first U.S. Senator. The Frankfort Cemetery is dominated by the marble marker over the graves of Daniel and Rebecca Boone; it is carved with scenes from the lives of the pioneer couple. In addition to the graves of at least 16 Kentucky governors, the cemetery features the Kentucky Vietnam Veterans Memorial, a 65-foot-tall monument that acts as a giant sundial.

The 1910 Kentucky State Capitol's Beaux Arts design features 70 Ionic columns, decorative murals, and sculptures of Kentucky dignitaries, as well as the First Lady Doll Collection. Tourists throw coins for good luck at the floral clock that is located on the West Lawn of the Capitol Grounds. Next to the Capitol and overlooking the Kentucky River, the Executive Mansion, built of native limestone, was modeled after France's Petit Trianon, Marie Antoinette's Summer villa. The Greek Revival Old State Capitol, which served as the seat of state government from 1830–1910, features a self-supporting staircase held together by precision and pressure. These state buildings are open for touring. Another outstanding local site is the 1910 Prairie-style Ziegler-Brockman House, designed by Frank Lloyd Wright.

Nature lovers will find native flora and fauna at the Kentucky Department of Fish & Wildlife Game Farm and Salato Wildlife Education Center in Frankfort. Bird watchers will be particularly interested in the Clyde F. Buckley Wildlife Sanctuary-Trust; a 374-acre haven with hiking trails, a bird blind, and a nature center operated by the National Audubon Society.

Kentucky is famous for its whiskey, and visitors may tour the Woodford Reserve Distillery, which dates back to 1812, to see how it is produced. Guides lead tourists to see the bulb-shaped stills, huge fermenting vats, and a warehouse where the charred white oak barrels are stored. Bottling into the distillery's unique-shaped bottles still is accomplished by

**Built by John Brown from 1796–1801, Liberty Hall was one of the first brick buildings constructed in the town of Frankfort.**

hand. The Buffalo Trace Distillery, first to ever ship bourbon down the Mississippi River and a worldwide winner of more than 40 awards for it's whiskey, offers tours each weekday.

## Arts and Culture

The site of many major cultural, musical, and sporting events is the Farnham Dudgeon Civic Center, which seats 5,365 people. The RiverPark Center in nearby Owensboro is another multi-purpose cultural and events facility that hosts touring productions as well as community theater, recitals, children's theater, and ensemble concerts. The Bluegrass Theatre Guild offers musicals, workshops, and touring productions of its shows. The Capital Art Guild promotes public knowledge of the visual arts by educational activities by way of art exhibits, technique demonstrations, art classes, and community art projects.

The new Kentucky History Center displays the survey notes penned by Daniel Boone as he helped to map the new frontier. Also on display are early civil rights documents. Visitors may take a journey along Kentucky's time line, from the rustic life of early pioneer times through modern life. The Center, which houses a gift shop as well as the state museum and research library, presents educational programs and special events. It features the Hall of Governors of Kentucky, and a permanent exhibit gallery showcasing "A Kentucky Journey," which tells the state's story, and a changing exhibit gallery spotlighting the artifacts of the Kentucky Historical Society.

Displays of weapons, uniforms, flags, and other memorabilia at the Kentucky Military History Museum honor the service of the state militia, state guard, and other volunteer military organizations. The museum is located in the 1850 Old State Arsenal, a brick Gothic Revival "castle" on a cliff overlooking the Kentucky River.

## Festivals and Holidays

The festival season begins with May's Governor's Derby Breakfast, featuring guided tours of the Capitol building and gardens. The first full weekend in June brings the Capital Expo Arts & Crafts Festival, three days of arts and crafts, live entertainment, an antique car show, hot air balloon rides, and fireworks; June also brings Boone Day, the Kentucky Historical Society's annual symposium to commemorate Daniel Boone's first observance of Kentucky. The Kentucky Herb Festival takes place on the second Saturday in June; it offers lectures on gardening, music, and an outdoor herbal luncheon. July's Franklin County Fair & Horse Show features antiques, a flower and doll show, a demolition derby, a gospel sing, a beauty contest, and childrens' events. Also in July, Frankfort teams with other central Kentucky cities to host the week-long Central Kentucky Civil War Heritage Trail.

In September, the state's diverse job, ethnic, and family traditions are celebrated at the Kentucky Folklife Festival downtown. The Great Pumpkin Festival features the Black Cat 5K run, a haunted house, hayrides, and a costume parade down Main Street. The Candlelight Tour of the downtown takes place in November. An evening of food, music, and shopping kicks off the holiday season. Also in November, the Kentucky Book Fair at the KSU draws more than 100 authors of national and worldwide renown. The city rings in December with a parade, tree lighting ceremony, caroling and viewing the wares of more than 100 craft exhibitors.

The Center of Excellence for Study of Kentucky African Americans at Kentucky State University sponsors a number of exhibits and displays throughout the year. They include an annual "Many Cultures, One Art" quilt exhibit, a Civil War symposium, a forum on the Great Black Jockeys, and other special events. Dates vary from year to year.

## Sports for the Spectator

Kentucky State University is a member of the National Collegiate Athletic Association (NCAA). At present, all sports are classified in Division II. KSU is affiliated with the Southern Intercollegiate Athletic Conference (SIAC) and competes for conference championships in all sports. Men's Thorobreds teams include basketball, football, baseball, cross country & track, golf, and tennis. Football games are played at the university's Alumni Stadium. Many of the indoor sports, including basketball, are played at the William Exum Center on campus. The Thorobrettes women's teams include basketball, softball, cross country and track, volleyball, and tennis.

## Sports for the Participant

When urban planners first noticed, back in the 1950s, that Frankfort was one of the few cities in the country with no public parks or recreational areas, city officials went to work to create a parks system. Beginning with the creation of Juniper Hills Park, the system expanded into six large public parks offering picnic areas, courts for basketball, tennis, and volleyball, plus baseball, softball, and soccer fields. Riverview Park offers trails along the Kentucky River. Headquartered in Peaks Mill, 8 miles north of Frankfort, Canoe Kentucky offers canoeing, kayaking, innertubing, and guided or self-guided canoe and kayak trips over whitewater Class 1 and 2 waters.

## Shopping and Dining

On downtown Frankfort's tree-lined streets, shops offer such items as art pieces, gifts, clothing, books, antiques, and model trains. Shaded under flowering trees, the St. Clair Mall features an old-fashioned general store as well as boutiques. Visitors flock to Rebecca-Ruth Candy shop on the East Side of town to buy bourbon-flavored sweets made on the same curved marble bar top where the secret recipe was developed more than 60 years ago. The city's major mall is Franklin Square, which features a department store, music, clothing, and gift shops, as well as cinemas and restaurants.

Dining choices in Frankfort run the gamut from homestyle and barbecue, to ethnic varieties including Thai, Chinese, Mexican, Irish, and Italian, to seafood and steak. Gabriel's Chop House in the Holiday Inn Capital Plaza has Kentucky Bourbon ribs and steak. Visit Tink's on St. Clair Street for barbecue in an outdoor setting. Cajun cooking is the draw at Rick's White Light Diner, while Jim's Seafood specializes in catfish, trout, and fried banana peppers. At Daniel's Restaurant patrons may enjoy a bourbon-tasting experience.

*Visitor Information:* Frankfort/Franklin County Tourist & Convention Commission, 100 Capitol Ave., Frankfort, KY 40601; telephone (502)875-8687; toll-free (800)866-7925; fax (502)227-2604

# Convention Facilities

Nestled along the Kentucky River within short walking distance of downtown's shops and restaurants, The Farnham Dudgeon Civic Center Complex adjoining Capital Plaza seats 5,365 people in arena seating, 5,047 people for concerts, and 800 people for banquets. The adjacent Holiday Inn Capital Plaza is equipped with an additional 8,000 square feet of meeting/convention space offered in 10 flexible meeting rooms. In addition to extensive audio-visual equipment, the hotel offers expert catering services and award-winning banquet menus.

*Convention Information:* Frankfort Convention Center, 405 Mero St., Frankfort, KY 40601; telephone (502)564-5335; fax (502)564-3310.

# Transportation

## Approaching the City

Air travelers to Frankfort usually arrive at Lexington's Blue Grass Airport, 25 miles east of downtown Frankfort (a trip of about 35 minutes), then take a taxi to the city (fare about $42). Greyhound offers bus service into Frankfort.

## Traveling in the City

Frankfort is laid out in grid patterns in sections north and south of the Kentucky River. The north side includes the older residential section, the Old Capitol, and the downtown business section; its major north-south thoroughfare is Wilkinson Boulevard, named for the city's founder. The Kentucky State Capitol is located in the mostly residential south section. Mass transport is offered by the Frankfort Transit System, which runs three fixed routes covering all major shopping centers, hospital, senior centers, and most state office buildings. Fares are $.50 each way ($.25 for seniors) with free transfers.

# Communications

## Newspapers and Magazines

*The State Journal* is Frankfort's daily newspaper. Magazines published in Frankfort include *Kentucky Bench & Bar Magazine,* and *Kentucky Afield.*

## Television and Radio

Frankfort's four radio stations feature news, nostalgia, country, oldies, and contemporary music. NBC, CBS, ABC, and Fox affiliates broadcast from Lexington and Louisville. Cable television service is provided by the Frankfort Plant Board.

*Media Information: The State Journal,* 321 West Main St., PO Box 368, Frankfort, KY 40203; telephone (502)227-4556; fax (502)227-2831

## Frankfort Online

City of Frankfort home page. Available www.cityof frankfortky.com

Frankfort Area Chamber of Commerce. Available www .frankfortky.org

Frankfort Convention Center. Available www.frankfort conventioncenter.com

Frankfort/Franklin County Tourist and Convention Commission. Available www.franklin.k12.ky.us

Frankfort Regional Medical Center. Available www .frankfortregional.com

Franklin County Public Schools. Available www.frankfort .k12.ky.us

Kentucky Cabinet for Economic Development. Available history.ky.gov

Kentucky Historical Society. Available history.ky.gov

Kentucky State Government and Tourism Information. Available www.state.ky.us

Kentucky State University. Available www.kysu.edu

Paul Sawyier Public Library. Available www.pspl.org

## Selected Bibliography

Kramer, Carl E., *Capital on the Kentucky: A Two Hundred Year History of Frankfort & Franklin County* (Frankfort: Historic Frankfort, Inc., 1986)

Wallace, James C. and Gene Burch, *Frankfort: Capital of Kentucky.* (Louisville, KY: Merrick Printing Co., 1994)

# Lexington

## The City in Brief

**Founded:** 1775 (incorporated 1781)

**Head Official:** Mayor Teresa Isaac (D) (since 2002)

**City Population**
1980: 204,165
1990: 225,366
2000: 260,512
2003 estimate: 266,798
Percent change, 1990–2000: 7.6%
U.S. rank in 1980: 68th
U.S. rank in 1990: 70th (State rank: 2nd)
U.S. rank in 2000: 70th (State rank: 1st)

**Metropolitan Area Population**
1980: 371,000
1990: 405,936

2000: 479,198
Percent change, 1990–2000: 15.2%
U.S. rank in 1980: 103rd
U.S. rank in 1990: 106th
U.S. rank in 2000: 85th

**Area:** 284 square miles (Lexington-Fayette) (2000)
**Elevation:** Approximately 966 feet above sea level
**Average Annual Temperature:** 54.9° F
**Average Annual Precipitation:** 44.6 inches

**Major Economic Sectors:** horses, tobacco, services, whole-sale and retail trade, government
**Unemployment rate:** 2.8% (December 2004)
**Per Capita Income:** $26,912 (2004)

**2002 FBI Crime Index Total:** 12,521

**Major Colleges and Universities:** University of Kentucky, Transylvania University

**Daily Newspaper:** *Lexington Herald-Leader*

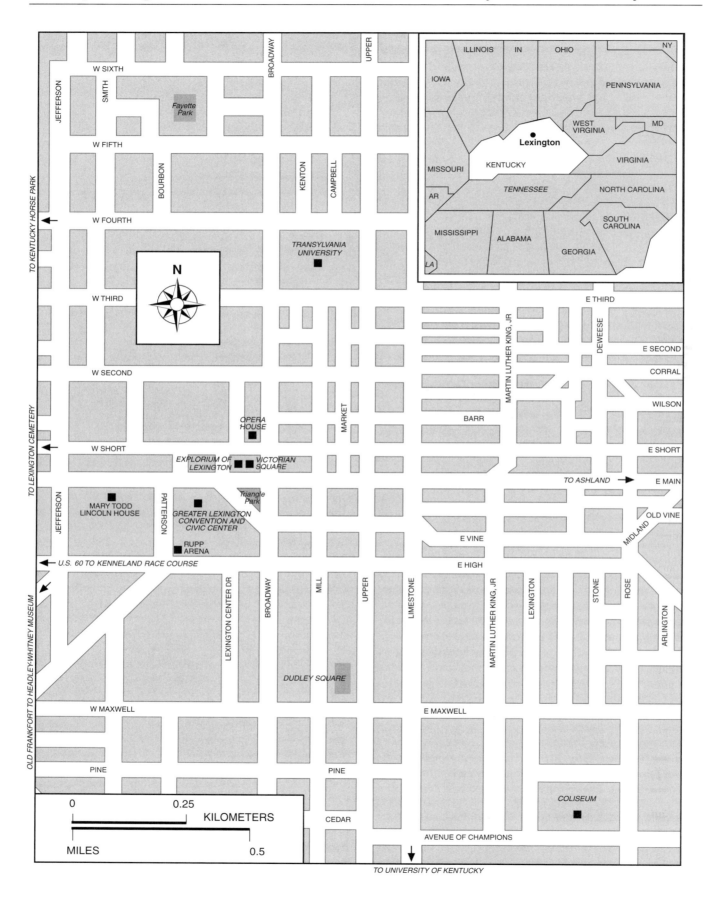

# Introduction

In the heart of the nation's Bluegrass Country, Lexington, Kentucky, is a city that has artfully blended history, horses, culture, and industry to create a uniquely desirable quality of life. With its graciously restored downtown buildings complementing its modern office and convention facilities, Lexington exemplifies the benefits of a successful public-private partnership. In 1974 the city merged its government with Fayette County to streamline services. The efficient consolidation became known as Lexington-Fayette County Urban County Government. A spirit of cooperation propels the community toward its goals of excellence in education as well as economic growth. Lexington was once known as the ''Athens of the West'' because many early artists, poets, and architects settled in the region; each left a sense of his or her own style.

# Geography and Climate

Located on the lush, grassy plateaus of Kentucky's central Bluegrass Country at the edge of the Cumberland Gap, Lexington is the county seat of Fayette County. The fertile 283-square-mile region is dotted with numerous small creeks that run to the nearby Kentucky River. The largest bodies of water in the area are the reservoirs of the Lexington Water Company.

Lexington has four distinct seasons, and while the region endures few extremes of weather, it is subject to unexpected changes in temperature of relatively short duration. Precipitation is fairly constant year round, with an average of three to four inches per month. September and October in Lexington are considered the most agreeable months of the year.

**Area:** 284 square miles (Lexington-Fayette—Lexington proper is approximately 60 square miles) (2000)

**Elevation:** Approximately 966 feet above sea level

**Average Temperatures:** January, 33.1° F; July, 76.7° F; annual average, 54.9° F

**Average Annual Precipitation:** 44.6 inches

# History

### Permanent Community Established in 1779

Pioneer Daniel Boone was one of the first white men to explore the territory known today as the Bluegrass Country. The births of the United States and the city of Lexington occurred at nearly the same moment in history. In June 1775, a small band of pioneers who were camped in the bluegrass amid buffalo and Native American trails received word of the battle of Lexington, Massachusetts, that marked the beginning of the American Revolution. In a spirit of adventure and independence, the pioneers named their campsite for the historic conflict. Development of a permanent settlement was postponed for four years when several members of the patriotic group departed to enlist in the Continental Army. Hostile natives also discouraged pioneer incursion into this wilderness. Neighboring pioneer villages were plagued by the often violent resistance of the natives and many believed this opposition was incited and encouraged by the British.

The present-day state of Kentucky was, at that time, part of the far-flung properties of Virginia, visited only by hunters, surveyors, and explorers. In 1779 a party of settlers journeyed to Lexington from nearby Harrodsburg and erected several cabins and a stockade in an effort at establishing a permanent community. In 1780 the Virginia Assembly divided its sprawling Kentucky District into three counties—Lincoln, Jefferson, and Fayette (named for the Revolutionary War hero, French General Mortier de Lafayette). The following year Lexington incorporated, became county seat of Fayette County, and was granted township status.

### City Develops as Trading Center

The popular and fertile Bluegrass Country quickly attracted settlers from Virginia, North Carolina, Maryland, and Pennsylvania. Within two decades, Lexington, with eighteen hundred citizens, was the largest town in ''western America.'' A thriving community of stores, taverns, hotels, and industries grew steadily in the protective curve of the Kentucky River, and Lexington became known as a major supply center linking east to west. Stores kept their shelves stocked with goods carted overland from Philadelphia and Baltimore and paid eastern merchants with hides, skins, furs, home-made linens, beef, ham, lard, and lumber. The development of farming added whiskey, tobacco, and hemp to the list of products exported to eager merchants to the east, west, and south.

### Local Horse Industry Gets Its Start

Local fascination with the breeding, rearing, training, and racing of thoroughbred horses has always been an important element of life in the Bluegrass Country. The limestone soil, rich bluegrass, and mild climate combined to make the area prime horse country. The town's first race course was established shortly after 1788, when civic leaders banned the sport on downtown streets. Thoroughbreds, trotters, and saddle horses brought from Virginia and the Carolinas joined breeding stallions from England and Arabia during the early 1800s, and another industry was launched.

In 1787, the flourishing Lexington community expanded its communication and education services. John Bradford's printing press produced the state's first newspaper, the *Kentucky Gazette.* Log cabin schools gave way to a succession of private and semi-public schools, and a group of persuasive Lexington businessmen convinced the trustees of Transylvania College to relocate from Danville. The college established law and medical departments, attracted students from throughout the South, and added immeasurably to the prestige of the frontier town.

## City Falters Economically Then Rallies

The Commonwealth of Kentucky split from Virginia in 1792 and was admitted as the fifteenth state in the Union. Lexington was its temporary capital and enjoyed considerable status as a seat of higher learning and an industrial center until shortly after the turn of the century, when the success of the steamboat gave the rival city of Louisville, located on the Ohio River, a distinct advantage. Development faltered in Lexington with the rise of the river cities, and by the time railroads established a much-needed link to the Ohio River, the economic damage was already evident in the unemployment rate, the number of declared bankruptcies, and the declining population.

Lexington's civic and business leaders then began to steer the town away from its fading industrial economy and encourage an emphasis on culture and education instead. Tax dollars were diverted toward promotion and support of the arts and the growth of Transylvania University. Gradually the frontier town gained a reputation as the "Athens of the West," and Transylvania was referred to by many as the "Harvard of the West." A measure of Lexington's success can be seen in rival Louisville's unsuccessful attempt, during the 1830s, to lure Transylvania's medical school to that town.

Although the state officially declared itself neutral, the Civil War pitted neighbor against neighbor within Kentucky. While their traditions were southern, many political and industrial influences were of the North. During the war years the horse racing industry was suspended, but progress was made in other areas. The University of Kentucky was established at Lexington in 1865 and thrives today, attracting students, researchers, and athletes. Horse racing experienced a resurgence after the war, and as the popularity of cigarettes grew among soldiers during the Civil and World Wars, tobacco farming became a major industry in the Lexington area.

## Present-Day City in Growth Spurt

Modern Lexington's economy is still firmly based in horses, cattle, burley tobacco, and of course, the academic community of the University of Kentucky. During recent times, downtown Lexington has been revitalized by a surge of growth and new development, especially in the corporate service sectors of the economy; yet, through the work of such organizations as the Lexington Downtown Development Authority, the city has been diligent in preserving its roots through renovation and preservation of many of its historic buildings and neighborhoods. Called "the city in the park" because of its location in the middle of hundreds of beautiful, park-like horse farms, Lexington offers a charming blend of big-city amenities and small-town friendliness. In fact, Lexington was the first city in the country to create an urban service boundary to protect the surrounding countryside. Before, after and between meeting sessions at the modern Lexington Center convention complex, visitors will find plenty to see and do. History, art, and culture are all within easy and safe walking distance and include: beautiful historic office buildings, churches, and homes; many of Lexington's finest restaurants, specialty shops and galleries; and major performance and sports arenas. The city takes pride in the fact that crimes reported in 2004 were the lowest in more than 30 years. Lexington is part of a metropolitan statistical area comprised of Bourbon, Clark, Fayette, Jessamine, Madison, Scott, and Woodford counties.

***Historical Information:*** Lexington Historic Preservation Office, 200 East Main St., Lexington, KY 40507; telephone (606)258-3265

# *Population Profile*

## Metropolitan Area Residents
*1980:* 371,000
*1990:* 405,936
*2000:* 479,198
*Percent change, 1990–2000:* 15.2%
*U.S. rank in 1980:* 103rd MSA
*U.S. rank in 1990:* 106th MSA
*U.S. rank in 2000:* 85th MSA

## City Residents
*1980:* 204,165
*1990:* 225,366
*2000:* 260,512
*2003 estimate:* 266,798
*Percent change, 1990–2000:* 7.6%
*U.S. rank in 1980:* 68th
*U.S. rank in 1990:* 70th (State rank: 2nd)
*U.S. rank in 2000:* 70th (State rank: 1st)

*Density:* 914.1 people per square mile (2000; Lexington-Fayette County)

*Racial and ethnic characteristics* (2000)
   White: 211,120

Black or African American: 35,116
American Indian and Alaska Native: 507
Asian: 6,407
Native Hawaiian and Other Pacific Islander: 83
Hispanic or Latino (may be of any race): 8,561
Other: 4,390

*Percent of residents born in state:* 94.1 (2000)

*Age characteristics* (2000)
Population under 5 years old: 16,146
Population 5 to 9 years old: 15,711
Population 10 to 14 years old: 14,947
Population 15 to 19 years old: 18,422
Population 20 to 24 years old: 28,355
Population 25 to 34 years old: 44,542
Population 35 to 44 years old: 41,824
Population 45 to 54 years old: 34,491
Population 55 to 59 years old: 11,275
Population 60 to 64 years old: 8,625
Population 65 to 74 years old: 13,890
Population 75 to 84 years old: 9,149
Population 85 years and older: 3,135
Median age: 33.0 years

*Births* (2002)
Total number: 3,614

*Deaths* (2002)
Total number: 2,049 (of which, 22 were infants under the age of 1 year)

*Money income* (1999)
Per capita income: $23,109
Median household income: $39,813
Total households: 108,411

*Number of households with income of . . .*
less than $10,000: 11,076
$10,000 to $14,999: 7,669
$15,000 to $24,999: 15,426
$25,000 to $34,999: 13,862
$35,000 to $49,999: 17,501
$50,000 to $74,999: 20,068
$75,000 to $99,999: 10,334
$100,000 to $149,999: 7,527
$150,000 to $199,999: 2,227
$200,000 or more: 2,721

*Percent of families below poverty level:* 8.2% (of which 45.3% were female householder families with related children under 5 years)

*2002 FBI Crime Index Total:* 12,521

# Municipal Government

On January 1, 1974, Lexington and Fayette County made Kentucky history by merging their governments into a single system. Called the Lexington-Fayette County Urban County Government, the consolidation was the result of nearly four years of study and eliminated many duplicate services as well as the need for two separate property taxes. The government is administered by the mayor and a fifteen-member legislative body.

**Head Official:** Mayor Teresa Isaac (D) (since 2002; current term expires 2006)

**Total Number of City Employees:** 3,090 (Lexington-Fayette; 2005)

***City Information:*** City of Lexington, Government Center, 200 E. Main St., Lexington, KY 40507; telephone (859)258-3000

# Economy

## Major Industries and Commercial Activity

Horses are a billion-dollar industry in the Bluegrass Country. Home to more than 450 horse farms, Lexington is surrounded by the greatest concentration of thoroughbred horse farms in the world. Rich limestone soil, lush grasses, and a moderate climate combine to create an ideal spot for the raising, breeding, and training of horses. The Bluegrass Country is the birthplace of the state's native breed—the American Saddlebred—and a center for the breeding of the Standardbred.

While horse breeding is the area's big business, horse racing is probably its claim to fame. The local economy greatly benefits from tourists who come from around the world in large numbers. Keeneland Race Course and the Red Mile attract horse-lovers, experts, and gamblers from around the world. Kentucky Horse Park, a 1,032-acre park built on a former thoroughbred stud farm, is a major attraction.

Agriculture also benefits from the mineral-rich land. Kentucky is the leading producer of burley tobacco in the United States, with Lexington-Fayette County producing the largest crop. Corn, soybeans, alfalfa hay, wheat, and barley are also produced in the area, and Lexington is a major market for beef cattle as well. The Lexington metropolitan area exports more than $2.5 billion worth of goods and services annually; in addition to agricultural products, major exports include cars and printers.

The University of Kentucky, located in Lexington, is a center for educational conferences and sports attractions and is one of the Lexington area's major employers. The University provides local businesses and corporations with a ready supply of educated manpower and its considerable resources for problem solving and research. The school was established in 1865 as a flagship for agricultural research and development, and it owns 2,400 acres of land throughout the Bluegrass Country that is still used for that purpose.

But while the city and state of Kentucky fervently protect and promote the region's strong agricultural and horse-country identity, they also are making attempts to keep pace with economic trends. In the decade covering 1995 through 2005, Lexington has emerged as one of a handful of leading American cities in economic growth. *Entrepreneur* magazine recently named the city one of the top five in the southeast for small-business start-ups. *Forbes* magazine recognized Lexington as the 14th best place for business and careers in 2003; in 2004 the magazine named Lexington as the 9th best place in America for business. This reflects a concerted effort to diversify the area's economy toward more manufacturing and high-technology ventures. More than 100 major companies have located headquarters or facilities in Lexington. Toyota's multimillion-dollar assembly plant just north of Lexington employs close to 7,500 workers. Lexmark International, a *Fortune* 500 company, is the city's largest employer (6,784 people).

More than two dozen national organizations—medical, research, scholarly and business—make Lexington their home base. Industry analysts forecast continued progress for Lexington, targeting the area for both population growth and economic development into the 21st century. They predict particular strides in the areas of finance, insurance, and real estate, while community leaders continue to encourage the growth of high technology industries and planning marketing strategies to capitalize on tourism.

*Items and goods produced:* Paper products, air conditioning heating equipment, electric typewriters and computer printers, metal products, bourbon whiskey, industrial valves, peanut butter, furniture, feed, tobacco products, equine-related products, automobiles, construction equipment

## Incentive Programs—New and Existing Companies:

*Local programs*—State laws exempt a broad group of commercial entities from local property taxation and limit local government taxation to a few classes of property. Commerce Lexington, the local Chamber of Commerce, provides an array of assistance to businesses thinking of starting up or relocating in greater Lexington, particularly minority-owned business through its Minority Business Development Program.

*State programs*—The state of Kentucky offers an extensive array of incentives for business start-up and expansion. Cities or counties may issue Industrial Revenue Bonds to finance land, buildings and machinery, and equipment and pollution control equipment. Low-interest state loans for fixed assets, Small Business Administration guaranteed loans, venture capital loans, bond financing of manufacturing plants, and state community development block grants are available under various circumstances. Both state and local property tax rates on real estate and tangible personal property remain low. Businesses are eligible for credits on annual debt service costs, start-up and annual rental costs, and recycling equipment. Credits are allowed for the hiring of persons who have been unemployed for more than 60 days. Credits are allowed for using Kentucky coal for industrial heating or processing. Major exemptions on state sales tax are available for resale items, machinery for new and expanded industry, raw material that becomes part of a manufactured product, certain supplies and industrial tools, and many other items. By way of Lexington's Foreign Trade Zone, companies may be exempt from customs duties if they meet specified criteria.

*Job training programs*—The Mayor's Career Resource and Training Center in Lexington offers corporate participants customized testing and assessment, pre-employment skills training, on-the-job training, entry-level skills training, skills upgrade training, and reimbursement of up to 50 percent of gross wages for the hiring of older workers. The state's employment service provides recruiting, testing, and job placement of industrial workers at no cost to employers. The Kentucky Bluegrass State Skills Corporation offers custom training of industrial worked to skill levels specified by industrial employers.

## Development Projects

College basketball is a certifiable passion in Kentucky in general and Lexington in particular. Rupp Arena is home to the Kentucky Wildcats, one of the most storied basketball teams in college athletics. The arena and attached Lexington Convention Center underwent $50 million in renovations in 1999 and 2000; it also hosts major concerts, exhibitions, and other events.

Valvoline recently opened a new product development lab; the 25,000-square-foot, two-story facility cost $4.5 million.

The Lexington Downtown Development Authority announced plans in 2004 for construction of a 54-unit loft/residential development on Martin Luther King Boulevard near College Town. The non-profit group (in a joint venture with the city-county government, the University of Kentucky, and major downtown employers) also seeks to attract more people to live in downtown Lexington through a unique ''Live Where You Work'' program, which provides up to $15,000 in forgivable loans to individuals who build or renovate homes in the downtown area. Additionally, planning has begun on some major road work in downtown Lexington. The Newtown Pike Extension will alleviate traffic problems and create a modern thoroughfare carrying up to 25,000 automobiles daily and affecting more than 1,400 residents and businesses in the downtown area. Construction was scheduled to begin around 2010. The newly renovated Lexington Center provides 66,000 square feet of convention space and an additional 40,000 square feet of meetings and ballrooms.

In 2004 the city announced that the Belcan Engineering Group would open a new Engineering Design Center for the Sikorsky Aircraft Corporation. The project could bring up to 300 high-tech jobs downtown by the end of 2005. The city's largest employer, the University of Kentucky, also announced plans for a significant expansion of its medical complex.

Completed major development projects included Hamburg Pavilion, a 950,000-square-foot shopping center anchored by a Target and a 20-screen movie theater, and Lexmark International's investment of $70 million for research and development, and a new building which added 700 jobs. The downtown area is experiencing a resurgence attributed to the location of new businesses, two new business parks, and a courthouse.

***Economic Development Information:*** Greater Lexington Chamber of Commerce, 330 E. Main St., P.O. Box 1968, Lexington, KY 40588-1968; telephone (606)226-1600; fax (859)233- 3304

## Commercial Shipping

Lexington's central location within Kentucky and the United States is attractive to manufacturers, distributors, and business interests. Easy access to two major interstate systems makes motor carrier service readily available. The city is within a day's drive of 75 percent of the nation's business activity. Since Toyota Motor Manufacturing chose to locate its multi award winning Camry/Avalon/Sienna manufacturing plant just 14 miles north of Lexington, the I-75/I-64 corridors have come to be known as "America's Auto Axis," reflecting the profusion of automotive suppliers which have located near enough to meet just-in-time inventory requirements for the Toyota, Saturn, Nissan, Honda, Ford and Corvette plants located within the immediate area. Two railroads provide freight service to Lexington. Lexington Bluegrass Airport (LEX) is a major international hub; numerous air freight companies maintain facilities there as well. There are also full-service international airports in nearby Louisville and Cincinnati.

## Labor Force and Employment Outlook

Analysts rate Lexington high on the scale of available, quality labor. The University of Kentucky and eleven other nearby accredited colleges produce an ample supply of management-level workers, a particular concern of corporate and high technology businesses seeking to locate in the Bluegrass Country. Analysts also describe the area as having an abundance of clerical, skilled, semi-skilled, and unskilled workers. According to executives at Toyota Manufacturing U.S.A., the "bottom line [for opening its $800 million American factory near Lexington] was the Central Kentucky work force and its ethic." The Fayette County School system is consistently rated as one of the nation's best, and of the 75 largest cities in the United States, Lexington ranks 6th in percentage of population having completed 16 years of school. The city's Partnership for Workforce Development coordinates efforts of employers, workers, educational and training facilities; offers access to testing and assessment services; and maintains a data base of area employers' needs and workers' capabilities. In 2000 *Employment Review* placed Lexington at number 15 on its list of the 20 best places to live and work in America; deciding factors included cost of living and job opportunities among others.

The following is a summary of data regarding the Lexington-Fayette metropolitan area labor force, 2003 annual averages.

*Size of nonagricultural labor force:* 275,700

*Number of workers employed in . . .*
　*construction and mining:* 13,700
　*manufacturing:* 40,700
　*trade, transportation, and utilities:* 49,100
　*information:* 5,900
　*financial activities:* 11,000
　*professional and business services:* 27,300
　*educational and health services:* 34,800
　*leisure and hospitality:* 27,300
　*other services:* 10,500
　*government:* 55,500

*Average hourly earnings of production workers employed in manufacturing:* $21.07

*Unemployment rate:* 2.8% (December 2004)

| *Largest employers (Lexington MSA, 2004* | *Number of employees* |
|---|---|
| University of Kentucky | 10,668 |
| Toyota | 7,990 |
| Fayette County Schools | 4,906 |
| Lexmark (laser printers) | 4,000 |
| University of Kentucky Hospital | 3,458 |
| Lexington Fayette Urban County Government | 3,090 |
| Central Baptist Hospital | 2,400 |
| St. Joseph Hospital | 2,000 |
| Eastern Kentucky University | 1,750 |
| Johnson Controls | 1,500 |

## Cost of Living

The following is a summary of data regarding several key cost of living factors for the Lexington area.

*2004 (3rd Quarter) ACCRA Average House Price:* $237,188

*2004 (3rd Quarter) ACCRA Cost of Living Index:* 96.6 (U.S. average = 100.0)

*State income tax rate:* ranges from 2.0% to 6.0%

*State sales tax rate:* 6.0% (food, utilities, and prescription drugs are exempt)

*Local income tax rate:* 2.25% on wages plus 0.5% school tax

*Local sales tax rate:* None

*Property tax rate:* ranges from $.7690 to $.845 per $100 of assessed value (2004)

*Economic Information:* Greater Lexington Chamber of Commerce, 330 E. Main St., P.O. Box 1968, Lexington, KY 40588-1968; telephone (606)226-1600; Commonwealth of Kentucky, Cabinet for Workforce Development, Dept. for Employment Services, Frankfort KY 40621-0001

# Education and Research

## Elementary and Secondary Schools

Historically known as an educational center in the South, Lexington has maintained its concern with providing excellence in education. The Fayette County Public School System was established when the Lexington and Fayette County Boards of Education merged in 1967. The district is managed by a five-member elected board and an appointed superintendent. In 2005 the district was comprised of 53 schools, including two schools for applied technology and one alternative school. SRI (Scholastic Reading Inventory), STAR Math, and Commonwealth Accountability Testing (CATS) are district-administered assessment tests given to all Fayette County Public School enrollees. All elementary and select high schools in the district have English as a Second Language programs available. The Extended School Services program, a component of the Kentucky Education Reform Act of 1990, provides programs for students who need additional assistance with academic coursework; and the Kentucky Educational Technology System (KETS) was established to provide funding, standards, and procedures for connecting all classrooms in Kentucky to the Internet and to improve student achievement through the instructional use of technology.

The following is a summary of data regarding the Lexington-Fayette County public schools as of the 2004–2005 school year.

*Total enrollment:* 32,980

*Number of facilities*
  *elementary schools:* 34
  *middle schools:* 11
  *senior high schools:* 5
  *other:* 3 (2 technical schools and 1 alternative school)

*Student/teacher ratio:* 12.82

*Teacher salaries*
  *average:* $42,748

*Funding per pupil:* $7,627

In addition to the public school system, Lexington has more than 12 private schools, including religious and nondenominational institutions.

*Public Schools Information:* Fayette County Public Schools, 701 E. Main St., Lexington, KY 40502-1699; telephone (859)381-4100

## Colleges and Universities

Lexington is the home of the University of Kentucky (UK), which enrolls more than 24,000 students and was established in 1865. UK is home to 16 major colleges including schools of medicine, law, engineering, arts and sciences, and business. Lexington Community College is located on the campus of the University of Kentucky. Transylvania University is a small four-year institution affiliated with the Christian Church; it was established in 1780. Within a 40-mile radius are Eastern Kentucky University and seven other colleges: Asbury, Berea, Centre, Georgetown, Kentucky State, Midway, and Southeastern Christian Junior. Together they award undergraduate and advanced degrees in a full range of fields, including medicine, law, engineering, economics, architecture, and library science. The city is also home to two theological seminaries and several vocational and business schools.

## Libraries and Research Centers

The Lexington Public Library's collection includes more than 650,000 book volumes plus magazines, films, audio and video tapes, filmstrips, microfiche and microfilm, and art reproductions. The library system includes the Central Branch on East Main St., plus five branch libraries, a full-service outreach program, and an innovative new English/Spanish Information Kiosk that allows access to library databases from a nearby Wal-Mart store. The library also houses a collection of early Kentucky newspapers and books and the Lexington Urban County Documents Collection. The Uni-

**Memorial Hall at University of Kentucky was built in 1929 as a memorial to those who died in World War I.**

versity of Kentucky Libraries hold more than 2.5 million book volumes and numerous special collections, including Appalachiana and government documents. Other Lexington-area libraries include those associated with academic institutions, hospitals, museums, religious organizations, and corporations. The unique Keeneland Library is devoted to thoroughbred horse racing and contains 10,000 volumes, 1,500 videocassettes, 225,000 photo negatives and nearly every edition of the Daily Racing Form dating back to 1896.

Nearly 42 of the 66 research centers in Lexington are affiliated with the University of Kentucky. They conduct research activities in such fields as life sciences, social and cultural studies, private and public policy and affairs, physical sciences, engineering, tobacco production, and multidisciplinary programs. The Kentucky Rural Health Works Program, an offshoot of the school's Agricultural College, seeks to help rural Kentucky communities make informed decisions in the development of their health facilities. The University of Kentucky Coldstream Research Campus is dedicated to the development of knowledge-based firms. Once a prominent bluegrass horse farm, Coldstream provides a synergetic research camp environment for science and technology-focused businesses, and University of Kentucky faculty, staff, and students. The Massachusetts Institute of Technology conducts research at Lexington centers in astronomy and other areas. Other subjects of research facilities include horses, asphalt, energy (particularly coal), and tobacco. The Kentucky Center for Public Issues focuses on matters of concern to the general public.

***Public Library Information:*** Lexington Public Library, 140 E. Main St., Lexington, KY 40507-1376; telephone (859)231-5504; fax (859)231-5598

# Health Care

Lexington offers a wide choice of quality medical treatment facilities to its residents. There are nine hospitals located in the city. Area facilities include several cardiac rehabilitation centers and medical research centers. The largest hospital in Lexington is the 446-bed St. Joseph Hospital, which recently added another 174 beds at its St. Joseph East campus (former facility of the Jewish Hospital). Other facilities include Charter Ridge Behavioral Health System, University of Kentucky Hospital, Samaritan Hospital, Shriners Hospital for Children, and the Veterans Administration Medical Center. Both St. Joseph and the University hospital have full-service cancer centers. The University of Kentucky Hospital is also a teaching hospital, with colleges of Dentistry, Health Sciences, Medicine, Public Health, Nursing, and Pharmacy.

***Health Care Information:*** St. Joseph Hospital, (859)313-1000

# Recreation

### Sightseeing

Lexington-area residents enjoy an abundance of cultural and recreational activities and attractions. A rejuvenated downtown features Triangle Park, a 1.5-million-acre oasis of pear trees and cascading waterways; Gratz Park historic area; Victorian Square, an entire city block of restored turn-of-the-century buildings transformed into fine shops; and Dudley Square, a renovated 1800s schoolhouse with a craft center and restaurant. For strolling and browsing, the ArtsPlace is a multi-purpose arts center which houses a gallery showcasing the works of Central Kentucky artists, and is also the site of free music and dance performances.

One of Lexington's best-known attractions is Kentucky Horse Park, a 1,200-acre tribute to the animal that makes the area famous. The park features a larger-than-life-size statue of the champion racehorse Man O'War; more than 50 breeds of horses, from racing thoroughbreds to miniature ponies; twin theaters, and the International Museum of the Horse, which traces the history of horses. Special events include horse shows, rodeos, polo matches, and national competitions involving horses and their riders or trainers. In 2005 the museum will present an exhibit dedicated to the life and work of Henry Clay, famous Kentucky horseman and one of the most influential senators in U.S. history.

The Spendthrift Training Center is an operating horse farm and training facility for more than 4,000 thoroughbreds, including two Triple Crown winners. Visitors learn how horses are trained, view a multimedia film, and tour the farm itself. The Kentucky Horse Center provides tours of thoroughbred training facilities, including barns and training tracks.

Many sights in the Lexington area are points of historic interest. The Lexington History Museum (free admission), Lexington's newest attraction, is housed in the beautiful old Fayette County Courthouse (circa 1900). Inaugural exhibits include a timeline of the area's history, a photographic study of Lexington's African American community and a special display of the IBM Selectric Typewriter, once produced locally. Perryville Battlefield in nearby Perryville, Kentucky is the site of Kentucky's bloodiest, and most important, Civil War battle. The battle marked a fatal loss of the initiative for the South. Each October, the battle is re-enacted; throughout the year, living history activities with costumed interpreters are available.

Henry Clay's twenty-room mansion, Ashland, is furnished with Clay family heirlooms and set on 20 acres of woodland and formal gardens. Hopemont, the Hunt-Morgan House, is a Federal-style home built in 1814 for Kentucky's first millionaire, John Wesley Hunt; it was also the boyhood home of Lexington's first mayor, Charlton Hunt, Confederate General John Hunt Morgan, and geneticist and Nobel Prize winner Thomas Hunt Morgan. The restored house features a collection of Civil War memorabilia, early nineteenth-century paintings, a garden, and a courtyard. Built in 1802, the Mary Todd Lincoln House is the former first lady's childhood home. The Georgian-style building contains displays of personal articles that once belonged to the Todd-Lincoln families, including part of Mary's Meissen china collection. The downtown Lexington Cemetery was chartered in 1848 and features landscaped grounds, two lakes, and monuments to such Kentucky greats as statesman Henry Clay, Confederate General John Hunt Morgan, the Mary Todd Lincoln family, and author James Lane Allen. An elegant Greek Revival mansion built in 1847 is the center of the 10-acre Waveland State Shrine, named for the acres of wind-blown bluegrass that once surrounded this historical complex. The home is furnished in nineteenth-century style and is surrounded by servant's quarters, a country store, gardens, an orchard, and a craft shop. Transylvania University, founded in 1780, was the first college west of the Alleghenies and features the Old Morrison Hall, built in 1833; Patterson Cabin, built by Lexington's pioneer founder Robert Patterson and perhaps the first building constructed in Lexington; and the Mitchell Fine Arts Center, housing the Morlan Gallery and a rare collection of scientific apparatus.

Nature can be enjoyed at Lexington-area attractions such as the University of Kentucky Landscape Garden Center, a collection of plants, flowers, and herbs managed by the Horticulture and Landscape Architecture Department in the College of Agriculture. Raven Run Nature Sanctuary, a 274-acre park dedicated to the preservation of the Kentucky River Palisades, features more than 400 species of wildflowers and a 7-mile network of hiking trails. The Lexington Cemetery is nationally recognized as one of America's most beautiful arboretums and is listed in the National Register of Historic Places for landscape design.

**Arts and Culture**

Lexington was an acknowledged center for art and culture as early as the mid-1800s, earning the nickname ''Athens of the West.'' The commitment to culture continues today. The Lexington Arts and Cultural Council (LACC) was formed in 1989 through a merger of two former arts organizations. The LACC operates two facilities in downtown Lexington, ArtsPlace and the Downtown Arts Center, providing high quality performance space, galleries, rehearsal space and office space for nonprofit arts organizations. At these loca-

tions, the LACC organizes visual art exhibitions and performances showcasing the region's creative talent. The Council is located downtown in a renovated 1904 Beaux-Arts Classical building called ArtsPlace that originally housed the Lexington YMCA. ArtsPlace is a working center for individual and group activities in the visual and performing arts and features the juried work of Kentucky artists in its gallery, as well as free performances that range from classical music to jazz and from ballet to modern dance. The four-story building contains studios, a rehearsal and performance hall, and offices for numerous cultural groups; it is adjacent to the Lexington Opera House, where many of its organizations stage their presentations. The seasons of Lexington's performing arts groups generally run September through May; in summer, Shakespeare in the Park presents free outdoor performances.

Some of the groups housed at ArtsPlace are the Lexington Philharmonic, performing popular and classical concerts; Lexington Children's Theater, offering a full schedule of plays and dramatic workshops aimed at the younger set; the Lexington Ballet, which sponsors classic ballet performances and a dance school; and the Central Kentucky Youth Orchestra Society, Inc., which sponsors two orchestras for young musicians, as well as the Actors' Guild of Lexington. The Living Arts and Science Center, which is housed in the restored Kinkead House mansion, encourages artistic expression and learning. Cinema buffs view new and classic films at the newly renovated Italian Renaissance style Kentucky Theater.

Musical groups in Lexington include the Guitar Society of Lexington—Central Kentucky, a nonprofit arts organization that promotes and fosters awareness of the guitar as an instrument of classical music and sponsors several concerts annually; the University Artist Series, which annually sponsors a season of musical performances; and the Lexington Singers, a choral group of more than 120 singers who perform several holiday, pops, and classical concerts annually.

Lexington-area museums display a wide variety of art and artifacts. The Headley-Whitney Museum contains the unique artifacts and reflects the interests of Lexington artist George Headley. The museum consists of three buildings and features a shell grotto, a jewel room filled with miniatures fashioned from precious gems and metals, an Oriental gallery, an art library, and other changing exhibits. The Lexington Children's Museum provides interactive exhibits for children from one to twelve years old. Special galleries focus on the environment, human growth, local history, play, foreign travel, and science. At the University of Kentucky Art Museum, a collection of fourteenth- through twentieth-century European, American, African, and Pre-Columbian art is on display. Tracing the culture and development of Kentucky man from the Paleoindians to the

Shawnee, the William S. Webb Museum of Anthropology at the University of Kentucky features textiles, kinship art, and religion. The American Saddle Horse Museum at the Kentucky Horse Park offers a multimedia theater presentation and a touch-screen interactive video photo file of world champion horses. The Aviation Museum of Kentucky features restored historic aircraft.

Notable buildings in Lexington include Loundon House, a unique castellated Gothic Villa that serves as the headquarters of the Lexington Art League, and the restored Senator John Pope House, one of the last remaining examples of the work of architect Benjamin Henry Latrobe, who designed the U.S. Capitol.

## Festivals and Holidays

Seasonal events in Lexington include the LexArts weekend in February; a St. Patrick's Day parade in March; a Festival of the Bluegrass in June; a week-long July Fourth celebration; a Woodland Arts Fair in August; a Roots and Heritage Festival in September; and the Southern Lights Holiday Festival in November and December, which includes a downtown Christmas Parade. Downtown Lexington hosts an annual Mayfest that features more than 100 artists, traditional Maypole dances, strolling entertainment, and tours of historic Gratz Park, where the event takes place. There are dozens of horse shows around town and at the Kentucky Horse Park throughout the year, including the Kentucky Three-Day Event in April that is the only four-star event of its kind. Touchdown Downtown takes place before and after home UK football games, providing fans transportation to and from the stadium and encouraging shopping and dining downtown. Equestrian events abound in the Lexington area, highlighted by the Blue Grass Stakes Race in April; July's Junior League Horse Show, the nation's largest outdoor saddlebred show; and Summer Yearling Sales at Keeneland, also in July. Lexington's arts calendar includes such summertime events as Festival of the Blue Grass, Shakespeare Festival, and the Woodland Arts Fair.

## Sports for the Spectator

In 2001, minor-league baseball returned to Lexington for the first time in 50 years when the Lexington Legends began play at state-of-the-art Applebee's Park. The $13.5 million ballpark seats 6,000 and features more than 20 luxury suites as well as two lawn areas where fans can picnic as they watch the game. The Lexington Horsemen play at UK's Rupp Arena and were 2004 champions of the United Indoor Football league. Of course, the University of Kentucky (UK) competes in a wide variety of Division I collegiate sports. The Wildcats basketball team plays at Rupp Arena and has won more NCAA championships than any program in history and is arguably, next to horse racing, the overriding sports passion in the Bluegrass State. The UK football team

also plays in the top-tier Southeastern Conference; games are played at Commonwealth Stadium. Memorial Coliseum is the site of the University of Kentucky Lady Cats games and the Transylvania Pioneers play at McAlister Auditorium.

The real sports attraction in Lexington, however, involves its famous four-legged athletes. Thoroughbreds are the champions of the Bluegrass Country, and Lexington is considered the world's horse capital. Lexington's full calendar of equestrian events includes horse shows, dressage events, racing, polo, steeplechases, fox hunting, and horse sales.

The Keeneland Race Course is the scene of fine thoroughbred racing during April and October. The highlight of the spring meet is the Blue Grass Stakes, the last major race before the Kentucky Derby (held in Louisville but simulcast and celebrated wholeheartedly in Lexington). Horse sales are scheduled four times annually in a world-famous pavilion; facilities include a private clubhouse, a grandstand that accommodates 5,000 people, and stables for 1,200 horses. Transcontinental aircraft from Greece, the United Arab Emirates, and England berth at Bluegrass Field each year while their passengers participate in the Keeneland Summer Select Sales. The beautifully landscaped course was established in 1936 on Keene family property, which was part of a 1783 land grant from patriot Patrick Henry, a cousin of the family. Steeped in the gentile tradition of the Old South, the track even provides ladies with parasols when the sun is reflecting off the copper roof.

The Red Mile Harness Track, built in 1875, is the nation's oldest active harness course. It has the reputation of being the fastest track in the world because more world records have been set at this one-mile, red clay track than at any other. Racing meets are held here in the spring, summer, and fall, with the Kentucky Futurity, the final jewel in trotting's Triple Crown, held in October. The Junior League Horse Show, the nation's largest outdoor Saddlebred show, is held at the Red Mile in July of each year. The Lexington Polo Club holds matches from June through October at the Kentucky Horse Park, and the U.S. Open Polo Championship occurs in September.

## Sports for the Participant

The Lexington Area Sports Authority was established in 2002 to promote amateur sports in the area by bringing in, and supporting, quality amateur athletic events, including youth tournaments in a variety of sports and the unique Bluegrass State Games every summer.

Lexington sees its beautiful countryside as both an attraction and an enhancement to its way of life, and the city has long sought to protect and preserve green space. More than 100 parks comprising four thousand acres serve citizens and visitors with a variety of services, facilities, and programs, including ballfields, summer playground programs, cultural activities, fitness trails, golf courses, swimming pools, and city-wide special events and contests. Special parks include McConnell Springs, a 26-acre natural pocket within an industrial area; Shillito Park, which contains softball, baseball, soccer, and football fields, tennis courts, a fitness trail with 18 exercise stations, and picnic shelters; Jacobson Park, which features a lake stocked with fish for anglers, a marina with pedalboats, a nature center, and an amphitheater; Masterson Station Park, the site of unique, comprehensive equestrian programs including clinics, lectures, and horseback riding lessons; and Raven Run Nature Sanctuary, which contains rare wildflowers, hiking trails, and picnicking facilities in a beautiful, informal setting.

Lexington's moderate climate offers plenty of incentive and opportunities for outdoor recreation, and when the temperatures dip low enough, residents can be found cross-country skiing, sledding, or ice skating in the parks and surrounding countryside. Lexington Ice Center and Sports Complex is open year-round for day and night sessions of skating lessons and hockey games. Lexington's milder climate and natural beauty makes golf an option throughout all but the coldest months. Fifteen public and semi-private courses are available to golfers, including such Pete Dye-designed layouts as Kearney Hill and Peninsula, as well as Picadome, Connemara, and High Point.

**Shopping and Dining**

Lexington has more than a dozen major shopping centers, including modern indoor malls that feature both large department stores and smaller specialty shops. Turfland Mall has department stores and retail shops, and Fayette Mall is the second-largest mall in Kentucky with more than 120 stores. The Shops at Lexington Center is convenient to downtown and the convention center. The city also offers plenty of boutique and specialty shopping areas. Clay Avenue Shops are a collection of stores in a former turn-of-the-century residential neighborhood. Victorian Square and Dudley Square are historic, renovated areas in the downtown with restaurants, fashions and Kentucky/Appalachian handicrafts. Chevy Chase Village is a thriving and eclectic mix of shops near the University. The Kentucky Store on Victorian Square has Kentucky souvenirs. Festival Market is a specialty food, retail, and entertainment center adjacent to Victorian Square. Also downtown are the Civic Center Shops, featuring Berea College crafts. Lexington's Farmers' Market is held every Saturday on West Vine Street and each Tuesday and Thursday at Maxwell and South Broadway, featuring fruits and vegetables, herbs, flowers, jams and jellies, honey, Kentucky specialties and more. The J. Peterman Company, based in Lexington, operates a store in the city. Lexington is legendary for antique hunters; as a writer

for *The New York Times* put it, antiquing in the Bluegrass is "a chance to unearth some great buys in American antiques and, in the bargain, enjoy some of the most beautiful rural countryside anywhere." There are three antique malls within the city limits, and more than 200 shops in the surrounding area.

Cuisines from around the world can be had in Lexington in myriad restaurants that range from casual to fine dining. Mid-south regional food specialties found in Lexington include the Kentucky Hot Brown sandwich, Derby Pie, catfish, country ham, southern fried chicken, spoonbread, hushpuppies, and chess pie. Some of the more popular restaurants serving up Bluegrass Fare include Café Jennifer on Woodland Ave., any of the several Ramsey's Diner restaurants around town, deShea's in Victorian Square, or Horse & Barrel right next door. For fine dining patrons visit Jonathan at Gratz Park, Metropol on West Short Street, or Le Deauville in the Historic District, among others. Lygnah's Irish Pub near the University of Kentucky campus was commended for its burgers in *Southern Living* magazine. Alfalfa's in the bottom floor of the new Downtown Arts Center has vegetarian fare.

***Visitor Information:*** Lexington Convention and Visitor's Bureau, 301 East Vine Street, Lexington, KY 40507-1513; telephone (859)233-7299 or (800)845-3959

# Convention Facilities

Lexington Center, an 11-acre downtown complex, is the city's largest convention facility. The center includes Rupp Arena, which can be configured to accommodate seating requirements ranging from 3,500 to 23,000 people. The adjacent Heritage Hall makes available 66,000 square feet of space for exhibits, meetings, performances, or assemblies; as of early 2005, an additional 20,000 square feet of meeting space was temporarily unavailable due to renovations. The Lexington Opera House is also part of the complex and is available for meeting and convention trade in addition to its full schedule of performing arts events. The Radisson Plaza and Hyatt Regency hotels are connected to the center by skywalks. They offer more than 700 guest rooms, and an additional 46,000 square feet of exhibit space adjacent to meeting rooms. Meeting space is available in several unusual and historic settings near downtown, including ArtsPlace, Bell House, and the Bodley-Bullock House. Also connected to the convention center is Triangle Park, with cascading fountains and acres of flowering pear trees. Shopping and a specialty food court are available at the Shops at Lexington Center collection.

Lexington contains more than 6,000 rooms in its 52 hotels and motels. Most of the major chains are represented and offer ballrooms, conference rooms, or meeting rooms. The city prides itself on being able to handle conventions of nearly every size and type.

*Convention Information:* Lexington Convention and Visitor's Bureau, 301 East Vine Street, Lexington, KY 40507-1513; telephone (800)848-1224 or (859)233-1221

# Transportation

## Approaching the City

Lexington's modern airport, Blue Grass Airport, is 5 miles west of the city and 10 minutes from the heart of downtown. It is served by 11 regional and national carriers, who together make about 120 direct flights daily. In 2004 the airport set a new record with 1.17 million passengers served. For those arriving by car, Lexington is conveniently located along the juncture of two interstate highways: Interstate-75 approaches from the north and south, while I-64 approaches from the east and west. Blue Grass Parkway, a four-lane toll road, provides access to western Kentucky via U.S. 60, and Mountain Parkway can be reached via I-64. Kentucky Route 4, New Circle Road—a four-lane beltway—completely encircles the city.

## Traveling in the City

Lexington Transit Authority provides several transportation options to visitors and area residents, including the LexTran bus system and LexDART's dial-a-ride transit service to rural Fayette County; LexVan facilitates vanpool ridesharing for commuters. Recent improvements to LexTran made the buses wheelchair accessible and added bicycle racks. A free trolley service in the downtown area completes a circular route in twenty minutes. The city's Transit Authority created a Transit Center, which provides more than 700 handicapped-accessible parking spaces for the downtown.

# Communications

## Newspapers and Magazines

The *Lexington Herald-Leader* is Lexington's major daily newspaper. Several other specialty publications are based in Lexington, including *Annals of the Association of American Geographers, The Blood-Horse, Horseman and Fair World, Kentucky Kernel,* and *State Government News. Around the Town* is Lexington's entertainment and restaurant guide.

### Television and Radio

ABC, NBC, CBS, and Fox all have Lexington affiliate stations, as does PBS. In addition, the region's viewers can tune in stations originating in nearby cities. The local cable television provider is Insight Communications. Thirteen public and commercial radio stations are based in Lexington and offer music, sports, and news.

*Media Information: Lexington Herald-Leader,* 100 Midland Avenue, Lexington, KY 40508-1999; telephone (606)231-3257

### Lexington Online

City of Lexington home page. Available www.lfucg.com

The Downtown Lexington Corporation. Available www.downtownlex.com

Fayette County Public Schools. Available www.fayette.k12.ky.us

Greater Lexington Chamber of Commerce. Available www.lexchamber.com

Lexington Downtown Development Authority. Available www.lexingtondda.com

*Lexington Herald-Leader.* Available www.kentuckyconnect.com/heraldleader/index.htm

Lexington, Kentucky Convention and Visitors Bureau. Available www.visitlex.com

Lexington Public Library. Available www.lexpublib.org

### Selected Bibliography

Strode, William, *Keeneland: A Half-Century of Racing* (Louisville: Harmony House Publishing/Louisville, 1986)

Walter, Jeff and Susan Miller *Insider's Guide to Lexington and Kentucky Bluegrass, 4th edition* (Globe Pequot Publishing)

Wright, John D., Jr., *Heart of the Bluegrass* (Lexington, KY: Lexington-Fayette, 1982)

# Louisville

## *The City in Brief*

**Founded:** 1778 (incorporated 1828)

**Head Official:** Mayor Jerry E. Abramson (since 2003)

**City Population**
  1980: 298,694
  1990: 269,555
  2000: 256,231
  **2003 estimate:** 248,762
  **Percent change, 1990–2000:** −5.0%
  **U.S. rank in 1980:** 49th
  **U.S. rank in 1990:** 58th
  **U.S. rank in 2000:** 69th (State rank: 1st)

**Metropolitan Area Population**
  1980: 954,000
  1990: 949,012

  2000: 1,025,598
  **Percent change, 1990–2000:** 8.1%
  **U.S. rank in 1980:** 38th
  **U.S. rank in 1990:** 43rd
  **U.S. rank in 2000:** 49th

**Area:** 66.65 square miles (2000)
**Elevation:** 488 feet above sea level
**Average Annual Temperature:** 56.1° F
**Average Annual Precipitation:** 44.4 inches

**Major Economic Sectors:** services, wholesale and retail trade, manufacturing
**Unemployment rate:** 4.2% (December 2004)
**Per Capita Income:** $18,193 (1999)

**2002 FBI Crime Index Total:** 15,439

**Major Colleges and Universities:** University of Louisville, Bellarmine College, Spalding University

**Daily Newspaper:** *Courier-Journal*

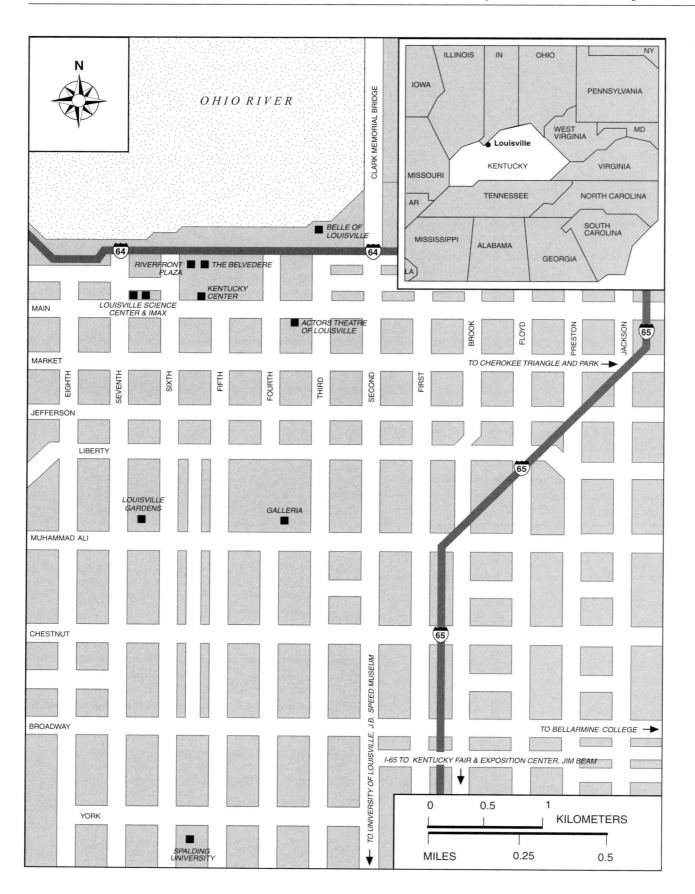

# Introduction

Noted for the Kentucky Derby, mint juleps, and southern charm, Louisville preserves the best of the past while looking forward to the future. The city's economy is in transition, combining a reliance on traditional industries with redevelopment to attract new business enterprises. The face of the city has been changed by a downtown renaissance fueled by $2 billion in public and private investment. The metropolitan area spans seven counties in Kentucky and Indiana and boasts the advantages of both urban and rural living. Today, the city boasts a thriving art community, an affordable cost of living, eclectic neighborhoods, safe streets and a diverse population. The 2000 edition of *Places Rated Almanac* ranked Louisville the 14th-best place to live in North America. The city where for more than one hundred years the best thoroughbreds in the world have run for the roses has moved full-stride into the twenty-first century.

# Geography and Climate

Louisville is located on the south bank of the Ohio River, about 377 miles above its confluence with the Mississippi River. Beargrass Creek and its south fork divide the city into two sectors with different types of topography. Louisville's eastern portion, with an elevation of 565 feet, is hilly, while the western part, lying in the flood plain of the Ohio River, is flat, with an average elevation of 465 feet. The climate is variable because of the city's position in mid-altitudes and in the interior of the continent; in both winter and summer there are hot and cold spells of brief duration. On the average, winters are moderately cold and summers are very warm.

**Area:** 66.65 square miles (2000)

**Elevation:** 488 feet above sea level

**Average Temperatures:** January, 31.7° F; August, 75.8° F; annual average, 56.1° F

**Average Annual Precipitation:** 44.4 inches

# History

### Canal Completion Spurs City's Development

One historian has noted that chances of a settlement being established where Louisville now stands—adjacent to the Falls of the Ohio on a plain along the Ohio River—for a long time appeared unlikely because of treacherous rapids that had forced many prospective Native American, French, and Spanish settlers to turn back. In 1773, Thomas Bullitt was sent with a small surveying party to the site to plan a town, but they remained for less than a year. Then, in 1778, Colonel George Rogers Clark, accompanied by 120 soldiers and twenty families, established the first permanent settlement on nearby Corn Island, a land mass in the Ohio River that has since been worn away by water. The following year Clark and his party moved to a fort on the mainland that served as a base for supplying Clark's expeditions into the Northwest Territory. This settlement, on the site of what is now 12th Street, was officially designated a town by the Virginia legislature in 1780 and named in honor of France's King Louis XVI for French service against the British during the American Revolution. A year later, Clark again moved his group and built Fort Nelson at the foot of present-day 7th Street.

Louisville, incorporated as a city in 1828, became an important river port because of its location on the Ohio River, a main artery for westward expansion. The economy profited greatly from the portaging of goods around the falls, but the advent of steamboats from New Orleans made it apparent that the falls were a barrier to development. In 1830 the Louisville & Portland Canal was completed, thus providing a water by-pass around the falls and opening the way for increased river traffic from Pittsburgh to New Orleans.

### Cultural and Economic Growth Continues

By the mid-nineteenth century Louisville was a prosperous industrial center and had begun to thrive culturally, its citizens surprising European visitors with their sophistication and cultivated tastes. As part of the New Orleans commercial empire, Louisville attracted two new groups of people who were to make permanent contributions to the life of the city—the French from New Orleans and the Germans from Pittsburgh.

During the Civil War the city served as an important Union supply depot, but the conflicting loyalties among its residents reflected the often bitter division between pro-Union and pro-Confederate sentiments that existed throughout the state of Kentucky. After the war Louisville was forced to adjust to the collapse of the southern plantation economy; new merchandising methods were initiated and railroad links were established with other major cities in the South.

The city continued to grow, and by 1900 the population had surpassed 200,000 people. During the 1920s a building boom brought skyscrapers to Louisville's silhouette, and in 1925 an electrical power plant was constructed at the Falls of the Ohio. The city was relatively untouched by the depression, as the tobacco trade and manufacturing maintained their normal levels; federal job programs during the 1930s helped to alleviate unemployment. In the winter of 1937, the Ohio River flooded and devastated the city, but by the summer of that same year Louisville was able to resume its usual way of life through rehabilitation loans and Red Cross assistance.

The city has recently undergone extensive redevelopment and revitalization with completion of many projects including Riverfront Plaza and Belvedere, an urban plaza overlooking the Ohio River, 4th Street Live!, Glassworks, Louisville Extreme Park and the Kentucky Center for African American Heritage. A direct link to the past has been retained with the restoration of old buildings that are being used as museums, theaters, shops, and restaurants. A challenge for the twenty-first century is to make downtown Louisville a place where people want to live and work.

*Historical Information:* Louisville Free Public Library, 301 W. York Street, Louisville, KY 40203; telephone (502)574-1611

# Population Profile

## Metropolitan Area Residents
*1980:* 954,000
*1990:* 949,012
*2000:* 1,025,598
*Percent change, 1990–2000:* 8.1%
*U.S. rank in 1980:* 38th
*U.S. rank in 1990:* 43rd
*U.S. rank in 2000:* 49th

## City Residents
*1980:* 298,694
*1990:* 269,555
*2000:* 256,231
*2003 estimate:* 248,762
*Percent change, 1990–2000:* −5.0%
*U.S. rank in 1980:* 49th
*U.S. rank in 1990:* 58th
*U.S. rank in 2000:* 69th (State rank: 1st)

*Density:* 4,124.9 people per square mile (2000)

*Racial and ethnic characteristics* (2000)
White: 161,261
Black or African American: 84,586
American Indian and Alaska Native: 578
Asian: 3,705
Native Hawaiian and other Pacific Islander: 111
Hispanic or Latino (may be of any race): 4,755
Other: 1,709

*Percent of residents born in state:* 75.6% (2000)

*Age characteristics* (2000)
Population under 5 years old: 16,926
Population 5 to 9 years old: 17,359
Population 10 to 14 years old: 16,627
Population 15 to 19 years old: 17,362
Population 20 to 24 years old: 18,923
Population 25 to 34 years old: 37,541
Population 35 to 44 years old: 40,354
Population 45 to 54 years old: 33,755
Population 55 to 59 years old: 10,716
Population 60 to 64 years old: 9,211
Population 65 to 74 years old: 18,577
Population 85 years and older: 5,075
Median age: 35.8 years

*Births* (Jefferson County, 2000)
Total number: 9,565

*Deaths* (Jefferson County, 2000)
Total number: 7,158 (of which, 113 were infants under the age of 1 year)

*Money income* (1999)
Per capita income: $18,193
Median household income: $28,843
Total households: 111,414

*Number of households with income of . . .*
less than $10,000: 19,542
$10,000 to $14,999: 10,471
$15,000 to $24,999: 18,883
$25,000 to $34,999: 16,258
$35,000 to $49,999: 17,695
$50,000 to $74,999: 15,227
$75,000 to $99,999: 6,654
$100,000 to $149,999: 3,990
$150,000 to $199,999: 1,193
$200,000 or more: 1,471

*Percent of families below poverty level:* 21.6% (61.7% of which were female householder families with related children under 5 years)

*2002 FBI Crime Index Total:* 15,439

# Municipal Government

In January 2003, Louisville became the first major metropolitan city in three decades to merge its city and county governments. The Louisville-Jefferson County Metro Government, dubbed ''Louisville Metro,'' is led by Mayor Jerry

E. Abramson and a 26-member Metro Council. Abramson is the former mayor of Louisville, in office from 1985 to 1998. Louisville Metro serves a community of approximately 700,000 people. The new government is focused on working on economic development, transportation, increasing research efforts to bring high-tech jobs to the area, land-use and workforce training.

**Head Official:** Mayor Jerry E. Abramson (since 2003, current term expires 2007)

**Total Number of City Employees:** 6,243 (2005)

*City Information:* Louisville Metro Hall, 527 W. Jefferson, Louisville, KY 40202-2814; telephone (502)574-2003; email mayor@louky.org

# Economy

## Major Industries and Commercial Activity

The geography of Louisville, specifically its river accessibility, central location, and mild climate have contributed to its importance as a center for industry and commerce. Kentucky has historically been a mining and agricultural state, but Louisville has greatly diversified its economic base in recent years. The city has traditionally been a manufacturing center for durable goods including appliances, cars and trucks. More recently, the area's economy has diversified, bringing with it more skilled and high-tech employment opportunities.

Like the rest of Kentucky, Louisville is undergoing a new era of economic development, with the public and private sectors working together to attract new industries while retaining existing businesses. In 2003, *Entrepeneur* magazine ranked Louisville #1 for ''Best City for Small Business Growth.'' The same magazine also ranked the city #15 nationally and 2nd in the Midwest in a list of the ''Top 25 Best Cities for Entrepreneurs.''

The Louisville area is headquarters to some of the nation's top companies, including *Fortune* 500 companies Yum! Brands Inc., which includes KFC (formerly Kentucky Fried Chicken), Kindred Healthcare and Humana Inc. One of the better-known industries based in Louisville is Hillerich & Bradsby, makers of the famous ''Louisville Slugger'' baseball bat. The headquarters for Presbyterian Church (USA) and the American Printing House for the Blind, the official source of texts for the visually impaired, are also in the city. Ford Motor Co. has two plants in the area that produce the Explorer, Sport Trac, Mountaineer, commercial light trucks, and F-series pick-ups. Manufacturing plants for GE Con-

sumer Products and Swift & Co. are also located in Louisville. Companies new to the area since 2000 are Charter Communications (cable TV), Gordon Foods, Linens n Things, and Reynolds/Alcoa.

The services sector is the leading economic sector in the region. In Greater Louisville, nearly 14,000 facilities employed 234,000 workers in 2001. Tourism leads the region's service industries; approximately 26,000 of these jobs are generated by the tourism industry in Jefferson County. Travelers spend nearly $1.2 billion a year in the county, and more than 880,000 convention delegates visited Louisville in 2000-2001. Greater Louisville is also an important center for local, state, and federal government agencies, which employ more than 71,000 area residents. The Kentucky Air National Guard and Army National Guard are headquartered at the Louisville International Airport's Standiford field; the U.S. Defense Department operates the Defense Mapping Agency and a veteran's hospital in the area; and the U.S. Corp of Engineers maintains the McAlpine Locks and Dam.

*Items and goods produced:* chemicals, automobiles, machinery, electrical appliances, processed foods, published materials, farm tools, aluminum, industrial machinery, lumber, timber products, baked goods, office products

## Incentive Programs—New and Existing Companies

*Local programs*—Greater Louisville Inc. is the agency responsible for working with new and existing businesses to create new jobs and capital investment in Louisville. It was formed by the merger of the Greater Louisville Economic Development Partnership and the Louisville Chamber of Commerce. A $3 million grant from the U.S. Department of Labor, Employment and Training Administration in 2002 is providing support to Greater Louisville Inc. for the recruitment and training of healthcare workers. The award became known as the Kentuckiana Healthcare Workforce Initiative. In addition to low taxes and low costs of doing business, Louisville offers a variety of financial incentives. Among them are the Louisville Metro Manufacturing Tax Moratorium which offers new or expanding manufacturing operations a five-year moratorium on all assessed property and real estate taxes. The Louisville Metro Brownfields Loan Program provides financing for economic development in older industrial areas of the city. Greater Louisville's Foreign Trade Zone is located within Clark Maritime Center, Eastpoint Business Center, Jefferson Riverport International and the Greater Louisville Technological Park.

*State programs*—The following incentives are available: Kentucky Jobs Development Act, Kentucky Industrial Development Act, low interest loans, industrial revenue bonds, community development block grants, enterprise zone, foreign trade zone, Bluegrass State Skills Corporation, job recruitment and placement, and Indiana incentives.

*Job training programs*—The unique partnership of the University of Louisville, Jefferson Community College, Jefferson Technical College and UPS established the Metropolitan College. The College addresses workforce needs by providing special curricula and work-friendly class schedules that cater to the needs of college students who work at night, enabling them to study for technical certifications, two-year, or four-year degrees. The Bluegrass State Skills Corporation (BSSC) provides training grants and investment credits for job training projects.

## Development Projects

In 2001 a $121 million, two-phase plan was unveiled for major construction and renovations at one of the area's biggest attractions, Churchill Downs. With Phase One construction finished by 2003, part of the changes included more seating, new viewing suites, a new club and meeting space, renovation of the first floor grandstand, and new elevators. Phase Two of the construction, underway in early 2005, includes modernization of the clubhouse, installation of lights around the track, new restaurant and entertainment areas, and a year-round satellite wagering facility with seating. Phase Two is expected to be completed by the 2005 Kentucky Derby, held on the first Saturday in May.

Construction and revitalization activity in Louisville was brisk in the mid-2000s. Recent development in the city includes the Southeastern Christian Church with its $31 million, 294,100-square-foot Worship Center, a seven-story, nearly circular-shaped structure featuring white precast concrete exterior wall panels and a copper-colored roof. The Louisville Extreme Park is a public skatepark owned and operated by Metro Louisville. Opened to the public in 2002, the park features a 24-foot full pipe, 40,000 square feet of outdoor concrete skating surface and a wooden vertical ramp for skateboarders, inline skaters, and bikers. Glassworks, an eight-story historic building in downtown Louisville, has been converted into 41 loft apartments, office and commercial space, an artglass studio and restaurant. The new 4th Street Live! is a $75 million redevelopment of the former antiquated Louisville Galleria in the heart of downtown. Opened in 2004, the refurbished entertainment and retail district offers restaurants, bars, nightclubs, a comedy club, and live music, as well as a food court and a half dozen retail shops.

Louisville also has several development projects on the drawing board or in the first stages of completion. The Kentucky Center for African American Heritage project encompasses the renovation of four historic trolley barns as a center for the telling of the story of African Americans in Kentucky. The Center, scheduled for completion in March 2005 in the historic Russell district of Louisville, houses a museum, research center, artists' studio, sculpture garden and shops. Also scheduled to open in spring 2005 is the

Muhammed Ali Center, a museum dedicated to the ideals of Muhammed Ali. Exhibits showcase his biography and other Center features include educational classrooms, theater, auditorium, exhibits gallery, library, shops, and a cafe. The Louisville Medical Center Development Corporation, created to capitalize on the economic development opportunities in the Medical Center, has plans to add to its three research park facilities which currently house life science, medical device, and health care technology companies. The planned expansion includes 700,000 square feet of wet lab and office space. Two new office/warehouse facilities will be built at Freeport Center at Riverport, about 10 miles outside Louisville's central business district in a thriving part of town. Park DuValle is a new $180 million revitalization project scheduled for completion in 2008. This development will restore a 125-acre urban neighborhood and feature 450 homes, 600 apartments, schools, parks, a health center, shops, and churches.

***Economic Development Information:*** Greater Louisville Inc., 614 West Main Street, Louisville, KY 40202; telephone (502)625-0000. Kentucky Cabinet For Economic Development, 500 Mero Street, Capital Plaza Tower, Frankfort KY 40601; telephone (502)564-7140; (800)626-2930. Louisville Metro Development Authority, 444 South Fifth Street, Suite 600, Louisville, KY 40202; telephone (502)574-4140; fax (502)574-4143.

## Commercial Shipping

Louisville's economy is served by 40 motor carriers and Louisville is home to CSX and Norfolk Southern Railroad systems that connect the city with major markets in the United States, Canada, and Mexico. Louisville is the international air-freight hub for United Parcel Service; UPS Worldport handles the twelfth-largest amount of cargo tonnage in the world and offers next-day air service to 200 markets, including China, the Far East, Europe and Russia. The Louisville International Airport handles 3.6 billion tons of cargo annually. Another important component in the local economy is the Port of Louisville, which handles an average of seven million tons of cargo yearly.

## Labor Force and Employment Outlook

Louisville boasts a steadily growing number of workers. Between 1990 and 2000, Greater Louisville added more than 160,000 net jobs, the greatest growth in the area's history, according to *The Louisville Labor Force 2003* report by the University of Louisville. The employment rate grew 13 percent during this period, compared to an 11 percent growth nationally. A key element in this job picture is the growth in female employment. While the male employment rate in the area has seen little change since 1980, the female employment rate has risen 12 percent. Also contributing to the increasingly attractive employment outlook is the growth in the area's population. Despite a twenty-year trend of low birth rates and high mortality rates, the Louisville metropolitan area population began to reverse its declines through migration to the area in the 1990s. By the new millenium, its population grew almost as fast as the nation as a whole.

Louisville's workforce continues to suffer from a lack of educational attainment, especially compared to competitive markets. Its low rate of college attainment translates into relatively low earnings for workers. But Louisville has seen an improvement in the higher education of its young adult population in recent years. In the decade 1990 to 2000, young people aged 25 to 34 completing college increased from 20 percent to 27 percent.

The following is a summary of data regarding the Louisville metropolitan area labor force, 2003 annual averages.

*Size of nonagricultural labor force:* 561,400

*Number of workers employed in . . .*
  *mining and construction:* 29,300
  *manufacturing:* 72,100
  *transportation, communication, and utilities:* 123,500
  *information:* 11,100
  *financial activities:* 37,400
  *professional and business services:* 62,900
  *educational and health services:* 70,700
  *leisure and hospitality:* 107,100
  *other services:* 30,300
  *government:* 70,800

*Average hourly earnings of production workers employed in manufacturing:* $19.66

*Unemployment rate:* 4.2% (December 2004)

| *Largest private-sector employers (2004)* | *Number of employees* |
|---|---|
| United Parcel Service | 17,206 |
| Ford Motor Company | 9,903 |
| Norton Healthcare | 7,850 |
| Jewish Hospital Healthcare Services | 5,450 |
| GE Consumer Products | 5,200 |
| The Kroger Company | 4,960 |
| Humana Inc. | 4,889 |
| Catholic Archdiocese of Louisville | 2,468 |
| Baptist Hospital East | 2,308 |
| Caritas Health Services | 2,147 |

## Cost of Living

Costs are lower than might be expected in a metropolitan area of Louisville's size, due in part to the fact that the population is spread out over seven largely rural counties in Kentucky and Indiana.

The following is a summary of data regarding several key cost of living factors for the Louisville area.

*2004 (3rd Quarter) ACCRA Average House Price:* $203,091

*2004 (3rd Quarter) ACCRA Cost of Living Index:* 92.9 (U.S. average = 100.0)

*State income tax rate:* Ranges from 2.0% to 6.0%

*State sales tax rate:* 6.0% (groceries, medicines, and utility bills are exempt)

*Local income tax rate:* Averages 1.75%

*Local sales tax rate:* None

*Property tax rate:* Taxable property is assessed at 100% of the fair cash value of the property held on January 1. Rates per $100 of assessed valuation in 2003: State, $0.133; Jefferson County, $0.128; City of Louisville, $.3764; Jefferson County Schools, $0.5760.

**Economic Information:** Greater Louisville Inc., 614 West Main Street, Louisville, KY 40202; telephone (502)625-0000. Commonwealth of Kentucky, Department of Workforce Investment, Capital Plaza Tower, 500 Metro St., Frankfort, KY 40621-0001; telephone (502)564-6606.

# *Education and Research*

### Elementary and Secondary Schools

The public elementary and secondary schools in Louisville are part of a county-wide district operated by the Jefferson County Board of Education. The school system offers students a variety of optional programs including advanced programs for gifted students; career/technological programs for middle school students; magnet programs; strict, traditional school curriculums; trade schools; Learning Choice schools offering specialized instructional areas; and special programs for handicapped students. The Jefferson County Public School System has been recognized for its outstanding availability of technology for students. The county is home to the Gheens Professional Development Academy, a national model for teacher training. The SAT scores of county students are consistently higher than the national average. Eighty-one percent of county teachers have attained at least a master's degree. Student attendance rate was 93.8 in the 2003-2004 school year.

The following is a summary of data regarding Jefferson County's public schools as of the 2003–2004 school year.

*Total enrollment:* 97,000

*Number of facilities*
  *elementary schools:* 87
  *junior high/middle schools:* 23
  *senior high schools:* 20
  *other:* 23 learning centers

*Student/teacher ratio:* 17:1

*Teacher salaries*
  *average:* $41,000

*Funding per pupil:* $5,463

Also operating in the area are Catholic and Christian schools, Academy for Individual Excellence, Louisville Collegiate School, Kentucky Country Day School, Summit Academy of Greater Louisville, The DePaul School, Walden School, and Waldorf School of Louisville.

***Public Schools Information:*** Jefferson County Public Schools Administrative Offices, VanHoose Education Center, 3332 Newburg Rd., PO Box 34020, Louisville, KY 40232; telephone (502)485-3357

### Colleges and Universities

Louisville has three major institutions of higher learning: the University of Louisville, Bellarmine College, and Spalding University. The University of Louisville offers Ph.D.'s in 23 areas, including engineering (its Speed School of Engineering is nationally known), medicine, dentistry, law, and education. Bellarmine College offers master of arts degrees in social and business administration, education, and nursing, in addition to 44 undergraduate degrees. Spalding University offers extensive programs for the part-time student. In the Greater Louisville region are located 20 institutions of higher learning.

### Libraries and Research Centers

The main branch of the Louisville Free Public Library is located downtown, with 16 other branches and two bookmobiles throughout the metropolitan area. The library, which was founded in 1816, houses periodicals, films, records, art reproductions, government documents, and a Kentucky History and Kentucky Author Collection. It is a Federal Depository library for government documents. An even larger number of volumes is stored at the University of Louisville Libraries, home to more than 1.9 million books and special collections on Astronomy, Mathematics, and Irish Literature.

More than 30 research centers are located in Louisville; some are affiliated with local colleges and hospitals, and others concentrate on such fields as genealogy, health, engineering, law, crime prevention, and alcoholic beverage production. The Donald E. Baxter, M.D. Biomedical Research

Building is part of the University of Louisville School of Medicine and one of the cornerstones for attracting new research scientists to its Health Sciences Center. Construction of a companion to the Baxter Research Building is now underway. The University's transplantation research program received international acclaim when it performed the second successful hand transplant in the world.

***Public Library Information:*** Louisville Free Public Library, 301 York St., Louisville, KY 40203-2257; telephone (502)574-1611

# Health Care

Greater Louisville offers world-class medical facilities; the health care industry employs more than 45,000 people, many of whom work in downtown Louisville's medical center, hospitals, and related facilities close to the University of Louisville School of Medicine. Health care costs remain below the national average, and the city was one of the first in the nation to guarantee health care for the indigent. Major area medical facilities are Baptist Hospital East, affiliated with Duke Comprehensive Cancer Center; Caritas Medical Center, offering advanced treatment in cancer, pain management diabetes, and cardiopulmonary services; Floyd Memorial Hospital and Health Services in New Albany, Indiana, which has the area's only full-service urologic center; Jewish Hospital, internationally known as a high-technology specialty center; Norton Health Care, with five locations in Louisville offering a Women's Pavilion and centers for spine, neuroscience, and cancer treatment and advanced orthopedics as well as Kosair Children's Hospital; Tri-County Baptist Hospital; University of Louisville Hospital, featuring the area's only Level I trauma center and bone-marrow transplant unit; Vencor Hospital, which treats medically complex, chronically ill patients; and Veterans Affairs Medical Center.

***Health Care Information:*** Jefferson County Medical Society, 101 South Chestnut St., Louisville, Ky 40202; telephone and fax (502)589-2001.

# Recreation

### Sightseeing

Louisville offers a variety of recreational activities, from a leisurely steamboat excursion on the Ohio River to a fun-filled day at a theme park. The city's most famous attraction is Churchill Downs, the site of the Kentucky Derby, held annually on the first Saturday in May. With a grandstand featuring trademark twin Edwardian spires, the track was established in 1874, and the first Derby was run the following year. Another of the area's most popular attractions is Six Flags Kentucky Kingdom, a family adventure theme park featuring Chang, the tallest, longest, fastest stand-up roller coaster in the world.

The city retains a flavor of the past with its historic Main Street, a restored district that features the second-largest collection of cast-iron buildings in the United States (only New York City has more). Many homes have also been restored; regular tours are offered to visitors who wish to experience a taste of life as it was in the eighteenth and nineteenth centuries. Among the most popular residences are Locust Grove, the last home of Louisville founder George Rogers Clark; Farnsley-Moreman Landing, a nineteenth-century Kentucky ''I'' house with a two-story Greek Revival portico; the Farmington Historic Site, which features octagonal rooms; the Brennan House, the last remaining private home in downtown Louisville; the Culbertson mansion, an example of Second Empire architecture; and the Whitehall House and Gardens, a classic Revival antebellum mansion on ten acres. The Thomas Edison Butchertown House/Museum, a shotgun cottage, contains a collection of Edison inventions. Tours are available at the 1871 Spalding University Mansion and at Conrad-Caldwell House, a completely renovated 1895 home in ''Old Louisville,'' a neighborhood of elegant nineteenth-century mansions. The Filson Historic Society is headquartered in a 1900s home and features artifacts, manuscripts, portraiture, special collections, and a library for historical and genealogical research. The Kentucky Center for African-American Heritage tells the story of African-Americans in Kentucky. The Zachary Taylor National Cemetery and Monument honors the dead of many wars, and the Cave Hill Cemetery and Arboretum is a historic 297-acre cemetery and botanical garden.

Nature lovers can visit the Louisville Zoo, which displays more than 1,300 animals in a 73-acre park-like setting. Twelve western lowland gorillas are on display at the zoo's popular Gorilla Forest habitat. The Louisville Nature Center is an urban oasis where visitors can enjoy more than 150 species of birds, wild animals and flower-decked trails. Buffalo Crossing is a working buffalo ranch in Shelbyville, complete with pony rides, a petting zoo, playground and restaurant.

Several local industries provide tours of their facilities. Among them are Jim Beam American Outpost, located about 25 miles south of the city; Hillerich & Bradsby, makers of the Louisville Slugger baseball bat; Philip Morris, one of the largest cigarette companies under one roof; and Louisville Stoneware Company, where visitors can paint their own pottery. American Printing House for the Blind and Callahan Museum, which creates products and services for the blind and visually impaired, offers plant and museum tours. Gray Line specializes in bus tours of the city. Horse-drawn carriages ride past historical sites, and public excursions on the Ohio River aboard the *Belle of Louisville, Spirit of Jefferson,* and *Star of Louisville* can also be arranged.

Caesar's Glory of Rome riverboat casino in Elizabeth, Indiana, provides gambling entertainment just across the Ohio River from Louisville. The complex includes a 503-room hotel, a 200,000-square-foot pavilion with a sports and entertainment coliseum seating 1,500 people, three restaurants, a retail shopping area, and an 18-hole golf course called Chariot Run designed by architect Arthur Hills.

**Arts and Culture**

The performing and visual arts flourish in Louisville, the first city to create a community fund for the arts. The Kentucky Center has four theaters that stage a variety of performances ranging from symphony, opera, and ballet to children's theater, a Broadway series, and country music.

Louisville's historic Water Tower is the home of Louisville Visual Art Association, a nonprofit, artist-oriented organization dedicated to the creation and appreciation of visual art in all media. The center offers free art classes for talented elementary and high school students; it also hosts year-round exhibitions and special events such as jazz concerts and the Boat Race Party during Derby Week. The new Glassworks galleries feature artists from around the world, as well as glass blowing workshops and classes.

Louisville is also home to theater groups, a symphony orchestra, an opera and a ballet company. Housed in a historic landmark built in 1837, the Tony-Award-winning Actor's Theatre of Louisville is internationally known for the annual Humana Festival of New American Plays, one of the world's most important showcases for aspiring playwrights; other theater groups include Kentucky Shakespeare Festival, Bunbury Theatre, Music Theatre Louisville which performs at Iroquois Amphitheater, the Kentucky Contemporary Theatre at Spalding University, and the Derby Dinner Playhouse in Clarksville, Indiana. Stage One: The Louisville Children's Theatre offers professional productions throughout the year at The Kentucky Center. The Louisville Orchestra offers five concert series. The Louisville Ballet offers a full subscription season of classical and contemporary dance, including performances of *The Nutcracker*. The Kentucky Opera has produced operas in Louisville since 1952.

The museums and galleries of Louisville highlight much that is unique to the city and the region. For example, the Kentucky Derby Museum is the world's largest equine museum, offering hands-on computerized simulated racing, a 360-degree audio-visual presentation about the Kentucky Derby, and a live thoroughbred exhibit. The Howard Steam-

**Churchill Downs is one of two horse racing tracks in the city.**

boat Museum—the only museum of its kind in the United States—displays models of famous steamboats, tools, pilot wheels, and pictures. Located on the University of Louisville campus, J. B. Speed Art Museum is Kentucky's oldest; it houses collections of traditional and contemporary art and sculpture. The Louisville Slugger Museum showcases the famous bat and the history of the family that created it. Other local museums include the Eisenburg Museum; the Filson Club, which houses one of the nation's finest historical libraries; The Frazier Historical Arms Museum; and the Col. Harland Sanders Museum located at the KFC headquarters.

Among the museums dedicated to science and technology are Louisville Science Center, formerly the Museum of History and Science, which features hands-on exhibits and an aerospace collection as well as an IMAX theater. The Portland Museum features a light and sound show that carries viewers back to nineteenth-century Louisville. Located on the University's Belknap campus, Gheens Science Hall and the Rauch Memorial Planetarium offer multimedia astronomy presentations.

## Festivals and Holidays

Louisville's major annual events calendar is full, beginning in February with the National Farm Machinery Show and Tractor Pull Championships, the nation's most popular and best-attended function of its kind. In April and May the city hosts the Kentucky Derby Festival offering 70 events. Held in conjunction with the running of the Kentucky Derby, it is one of the country's largest civic celebrations. The Great Steamboat Race and the Great Balloon Race are two of the more popular Derby events. The Cherokee Art Fair also occurs in April. May is the month for the Kentucky Reggae Festival.

The Greek Festival, Waterside Festival and Street Ball Showdown kick off the summer festivals and events in June. Taking place during the summer months is one of the oldest Shakespeare festivals in the nation, Shakespeare in Central Park. July brings the Operation/Coca-Cola Volleyball Classic, the Kentucky Music Weekend and the Waterfront Independence Festival celebration of the Fourth of July. The National Street Rod Association attracts more than 11,000 cars to the world's largest automotive participation event. The Kentucky State Fair runs for 10 days beginning in mid-August. The Strassenfest celebrating Louisville's German heritage and the World Championship Horse Show round out the summer activities.

September opens with the Bluegrass Festival of the United States, the country's largest free bluegrass music event featuring top-name bands. In mid-September is the Corn Island Storytelling Festival, the largest event of its kind in the United States. The Rock the Water Tower, Irish Family Festival and the Captain's Quarters Regatta are also held this month. October is the month for the St. James Court Art Show, the Bluegrass Fan Festival and the Lewis and Clark Ohio River Festival. The year ends with Christmas in the City, a Victorian Christmas celebration involving street vendors, carolers, and house tours. The Mayor's Midnight Special on New Year's eve is an outdoor family party.

## Sports for the Spectator

Louisville's best-known sporting event is the Kentucky Derby. For racing fans, Louisville offers two horse-racing tracks, Churchill Downs (for thoroughbred racing) and Louisville Downs (for harness racing). Churchill Downs' spring racing dates are April through June; fall racing takes place in October and November. Louisville Downs features nighttime races in early spring, summer, and fall. Auto races are held at the Louisville Motor Speedway.

Louisville's $26 million, 13,000-seat Louisville Slugger Field is home to the RiverBats (formerly the Redbirds), a Triple-A affiliate of the Cincinnati Reds. Slugger Field was named the 2004 Professional Baseball Field of the Year by the Sports Turf Managers Association for the second time in three years. The Louisville Fire is the city's Arena Football League team. The University of Louisville fields highly regarded football and basketball teams; the Cardinals play football at Papa John's Cardinal Stadium.

## Sports for the Participant

The Louisville park system maintains 11 urban parks, including four designed by Frederick Law Olmsted. These public parks contain more than 200 tennis courts, four 18-hole golf courses, five nine-hole golf courses, and 15 swimming pools. Twenty lakes in nine parks in the metropolitan area are stocked for fishing. Five parks located along the Ohio River provide access to river fishing. Water sports are also a favorite pastime on the river during the summer. The new Louisville Extreme Park offers skateboarding, in-line skating and biking on 40,000 square feet of concrete surface. Bicycling is a popular sport in Kentucky, and each fall the Louisville Wheelmen sponsor My Old Kentucky Home Bicycle Tour, a two-day event that draws more than 400 cyclists. Ice skating is another favorite sport; enthusiasts skate at the Alpine Ice Arena and the outdoor rink on the Belvedere downtown.

## Shopping and Dining

Louisville offers a wide variety of retail establishments in more than 100 shopping centers, including enclosed malls and several neighborhood shopping areas. Starks Court atrium includes more than 30 distinctive retail shops and restaurants in the heart of downtown. The Forum Center is home to some of Louisville's most exclusive shops and Oxmoor Center features 110 specialty stores and three department stores. Jefferson Mall is a regional shopping center located near the airport. The Summit on the East End is one of Louisville's newest open air shopping centers. For outlet shoppers, Factory Stores of America is located in nearby Georgetown. In addition to the malls, many neighborhoods and individual streets have become meccas for shoppers. Main and Market Streets between 5th and 9th is the primary downtown shopping area. Antique shops, galleries and unique boutiques are plentiful in the Bardstown Road, Frankfort Avenue areas, and Chenoweth Lane in St. Matthews.

Dining in one of the city's restaurants can range from a casual meal at a fast-food establishment or a family treat at an ethnic cafe to an elegant event at a gourmet restaurant. Foods that have made Louisville famous are burgoo, originally a game stew made with squirrel, venison, or opossum—but now more likely to contain a blend of pork, beef, mutton, and chicken—in a spicy tomato sauce with a mixture of vegetables that might include cabbage, peppers, and potatoes; the Hot Brown, a layered sandwich of country ham, turkey, bacon, tomatoes, and cheese served bubbling hot; and the Benedictine, a delicate sandwich incorporating cream cheese and chopped cucumber.

*Visitor Information:* Greater Louisville Convention and Visitors Bureau, 401 W. Main St., Suite 2300, Louisville, KY 40202; telephone (502)584-2121, (800)626-5646

# Convention Facilities

Louisville's largest meeting facility is the Kentucky International Convention Center, expanded and renovated at a cost of $72 million. The expansion part of the project increased the facility's exhibit space to 200,000 square feet and added a 360-seat theater and a 30,000-square-foot ballroom. The center is located in the heart of downtown and connected by skywalks to the Hyatt Regency Hotel and two parking garages. This exposition center hosts conventions, trade, civic, and entertainment events. Another downtown facility is the all-purpose Louisville Gardens, located in the shopping district. The Gardens can accommodate groups ranging from 100 to 7,000 people.

The Convention Center's sister facility, the Kentucky Fair and Exposition Center, is located just two minutes from Louisville International Airport. It is one of the world's largest multipurpose buildings on one floor. Offering 30 acres and 1 million square feet of space, together with paved parking for 1,200 cars, it is within easy driving distance of hotels and motels. Its indoor arena, Freedom Hall, seats 19,000 people. The six-building complex hosts more than 500 events and four million people each year. Its multipurpose building, Broadbent Arena, is the site of tractor pulls,

basketball tournaments, and graduation ceremonies. The Hilton Garden hotel recently opened there.

Unique meeting space is available on the recently renovated *Belle of Louisville,* a 1914 paddlewheel steamboat; the *Belle* hosts receptions for up to 800 people or seated dinners for up to 308 people from April through October. *Spirit of Jefferson,* a sternwheeler excursion boat, also hosts chartered cruises and features two indoor climate-controlled decks. The Speed Art Museum accommodates groups of up to 1,000 people for receptions and 300 people for banquets after six p.m. except Mondays and Thursdays.

Hotel space in Louisville is plentiful—approximately 17,000 rooms are available in the metropolitan area. More than 3,000 hotel rooms are located downtown, with most within walking distance of the Kentucky International Convention Center. The Marriott Louisville Downtown, which opened in March 2005 adjacent to the Convention Center, boasts 616 rooms and 50,000 square feet of meeting space. It is connected to the Convention Center via an enclosed pedestrian walkway. Other downtown properties include the 1,300-room Galt House Hotel, the 388-room Hyatt Regency Louisville, the 321-room Seelbach Hilton, the 298-room Camberley Brown Hotel, the 287-room Holiday Inn Louisville Downtown, the 182-room Doubletree Club Louisville-Downtown, and the 160-room Courtyard by Marriott Louisville Downtown. The dual appeal of a vital urban climate steeped in history makes Louisville an ideal place for large and small meetings.

*Convention Information:* Greater Louisville Convention and Visitors Bureau, 401 W. Main St., Suite 2300, Louisville, KY 40202; telephone (502)584-2121, (800)626-5646

# Transportation

### Approaching the City

Louisville International Airport is located fifteen minutes from downtown and enjoys easy access to interstate highways. It is served by 10 passenger airlines and a commuter line and offers nearly 100 flights daily. The airport terminal recently underwent a $41 million upgrade to its facility, including new restroom facilities, security enhancements, smoking lounge, and business center, plus additional gates and improved signage. A new Wyndham Airport hotel connected to the terminal is slated for completion in 2006. A second, smaller airport at Bowman Field provides a variety of local and state aviation services.

Louisville is at the center of three major interstates: Interstate 65 from the north or south, Interstate 64 from the east or west and Interstate 71 from the northeast. U.S. Highway 60 (Broadway) intersects the city east and west.

## Traveling in the City

Louisville is laid out on a grid pattern slightly tilted on the east-west axis. Broadway (U.S. 60) divides the city north from south, and Second Street divides east from west.

The Transit Authority of River City (TARC) provides the city's bus-based mass transit system. The service area covers the Louisville metropolitan area as well as Jefferson, Oldham and Bullitt Counties; it also includes Floyd and Clark Counties in Southern Indiana, with the state of Indiana contributing to TARC's funding.

# Communications

## Newspapers and Magazines

Louisville's major daily newspaper is the *Courier-Journal* (morning). *The Voice Tribune* is a weekly business newspaper. *Louisville Business First* and a number of special-interest magazines are also based in Louisville, including the weekly *Leo,The Louisville Defender,Snitch,*the annual *Kentucky Travel Guide,* and the monthly lifestyle publication *Louisville Magazine.* Other publications serve readers involved in the building trades, agriculture, computers, and religion.

## Television and Radio

Louisville is served by eight television stations. Fourteen radio stations (eight AM and six FM) broadcast a variety of musical formats plus news and talk.

*Media Information: Louisville Courier-Journal,* telephone (502)582-4011

## Louisville Online

City of Louisville Home Page. Available www.louky.org/main.htm

Greater Louisville Convention and Visitors Bureau. Available www.louisville-visitors.com

Greater Louisville Inc. Available www.greaterlouisville.com

Jefferson County Public Schools. Available www.jefferson.k12.ky.us

Louisville Free Public Library. Available www.lfpl.org

Metro Chamber of Commerce. Available www.greaterlouisville.com

## Selected Bibliography

Bolus, Jim, *Derby Dreams* (Gretna, La.: Pelican Pub Co., 1996)

Wright, George C., *Life Behind a Veil: Blacks in Louisville, Kentucky 1865–1930* (Baton Rouge: Louisiana State University Press, 1985)

# LOUISIANA

# The State in Brief

**Nickname:** Pelican State
**Motto:** Union, justice, and confidence

**Flower:** Magnolia
**Bird:** Eastern brown pelican

**Area:** 51,839.7 square miles (2000; U.S. rank: 31st)
**Elevation:** Ranges from eight feet below sea level to 535 feet above sea level
**Climate:** Subtropical and humid, with long, hot summers and short, mild winters

**Admitted to Union:** April 30, 1812
**Capital:** Baton Rouge
**Head Official:** Governor Kathleen Blanco (D) (until 2008)

**Population**
  **1980:** 4,206,000
  **1990:** 4,220,164
  **2000:** 4,468,976
  **2004 estimate:** 4,515,770
  **Percent change, 1990–2000:** 5.9%
  **U.S. rank in 2004:** 24th
  **Percent of residents born in state:** 79.4% (2000)
  **Density:** 102.6 people per square mile (2000)
  **2002 FBI Crime Index Total:** 228,528

**Racial and Ethnic Characteristics** (2000)
  **White:** 2,856,161

**Black or African American:** 1,451,944
**American Indian and Alaska Native:** 25,477
**Asian:** 54,758
**Native Hawaiian and Pacific Islander:** 1,240
**Hispanic or Latino (may be of any race):** 107,738
**Other:** 31,131

**Age Characteristics** (2000)
  **Population under 5 years old:** 317,392
  **Population 5 to 19 years old:** 1,050,637
  **Percent of population 65 years and over:** 11.6%
  **Median age:** 34 years (2000)

**Vital statistics**
  **Total number of births (2003):** 65,020
  **Total number of deaths (2003):** 42,676 (infant deaths, 596)
  **AIDS cases reported through 2003:** 7,592

**Economy**
  **Major industries:** Chemicals, construction, mining, transportation equipment, trade, government, manufacturing
  **Unemployment rate:** 5.5% (December 2004)
  **Per capita income:** $26,048 (2003; U.S. rank: 44th)
  **Median household income:** $34,307 (3-year average, 2001-2003)
  **Percentage of persons below poverty level:** 16.9% (3-year average, 2001-2003)
  **Income tax rate:** Ranges from 2.0% to 6.0%
  **Sales tax rate:** 4.0% (food sales exempt)

# Baton Rouge

## *The City in Brief*

**Founded:** 1719 (incorporated 1817)

**Head Official:** Mayor Melvin "Kip" Holden (since 2005)

**City Population**
    **1980:** 220,394
    **1990:** 219,531
    **2000:** 227,818
    **2003 estimate:** 225,090
    **Percent change, 1990–2000:** 3.77%
    **U.S. rank in 1980:** 62nd
    **U.S. rank in 1990:** 73rd (State rank: 2nd)
    **U.S. rank in 2000:** 85th (State rank: 2nd)

**Metropolitan Area Population**
    **1980:** 494,000
    **1990:** 528,261
    **2000:** 602,894

    **Percent change, 1990–2000:** 12.37%
    **U.S. rank in 1980:** 68th
    **U.S. rank in 1990:** 90th
    **U.S. rank in 2000:** 69th

**Area:** 76.84 square miles (2000)
**Elevation:** 83 feet above sea level
**Average Annual Temperature:** 67.5° F
**Average Annual Precipitation:** 55.55 inches of rain; 0.1 inch of snow

**Major Economic Sectors:** services, government, retail trade, construction
**Unemployment rate:** 5.4% (December 2004)
**Per Capita Income:** $18,512 (1999)

**2002 FBI Crime Index Total:** 18,949

**Major Colleges and Universities:** Louisiana State University, Southern University, Baton Rouge Community College

**Daily Newspaper:** *The Advocate*

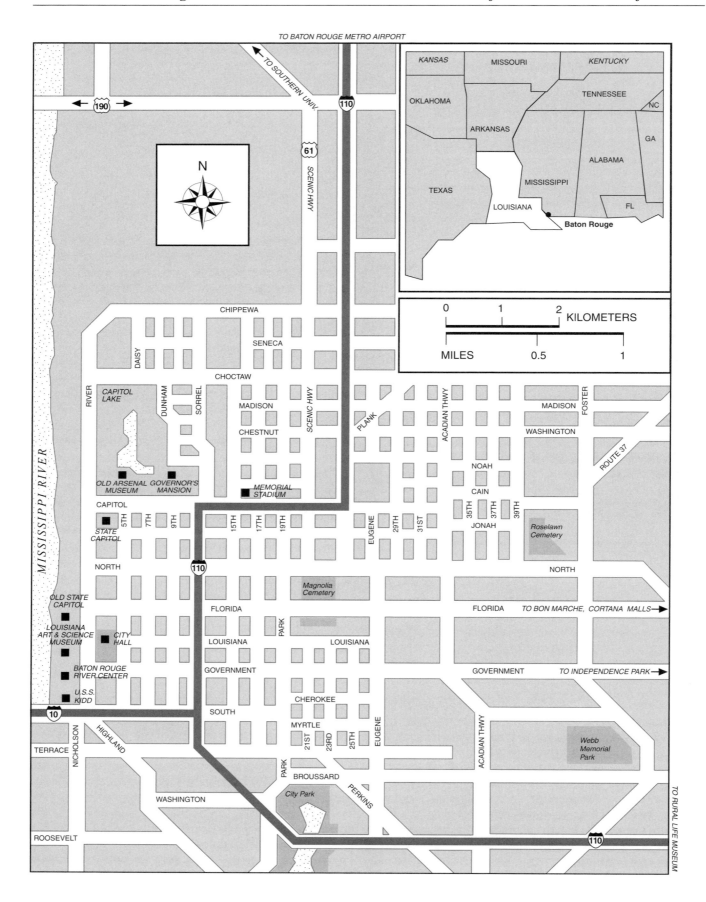

# Introduction

Baton Rouge, the state capital of Louisiana and the county seat of Baton Rouge Parish, has been described as ''a happy blend of Cajun *joie de vivre* and progressive American know-how.'' Situated on the Mississippi River in the heart of the state, the city is an important center in the Sun Belt market. Moderate year-round temperatures and a relaxed environment make Baton Rouge a desirable place to live. Significant construction projects taking place in the twenty-first century are bringing city planners' dreams of a pedestrian-centered downtown community a step closer to realization.

# Geography and Climate

Located on the east side of the Mississippi River and situated on the first series of bluffs north of the river delta's coastal plain, Baton Rouge is about 60 miles inland from the Gulf of Mexico in southeastern Louisiana. The city's subtropical climate is free of extremes in temperature, except for occasional brief winter cold spells. Precipitation is ample, placing Baton Rouge fifth among the ten wettest cities in the United States.

**Area:** 76.84 square miles (2000)

**Elevation:** 83 feet above sea level

**Average Temperatures:** January, 51.21° F; August, 80.54° F; annual average, 67.5° F

**Average Annual Precipitation:** 55.55 inches of rain; 0.1 inch of snow

# History

### French Settlers Found City

The second largest city in Louisiana, Baton Rouge was established as a military post by the French in 1719. The present name of the city, however, dates back to 1699, when French explorers noted a red cypress tree stripped of its bark that marked the boundary between Houma and Bayou Goula tribal hunting grounds. They called the tree ''le baton rouge,'' or red stick. The native name for the site had been Istrouma. From evidence found along the Mississippi, Comite, and Amite rivers, and in three native mounds re- maining in the city, archaeologists have been able to date habitation of the Baton Rouge area to 8000 B.C.

### Capital City Grows Steadily

Since European settlement, Baton Rouge has functioned under seven governing bodies: France, England, Spain, Louisiana, the Florida Republic, the Confederate States, and the United States. In the mid-1700s when French-speaking settlers of Acadia, Canada's maritime regions, were driven into exile by British forces, many took up residence in rural Louisiana. Popularly known as Cajuns, descendants of the Acadians maintained a separate culture that immeasurably enriched the Baton Rouge area. Incorporated in 1817, Baton Rouge became Louisiana's state capital in 1849. During the first half of the nineteenth century the city grew steadily as the result of steamboat trade and transportation; at the outbreak of the Civil War the population was 5,500 people. The war halted economic progress but did not actually touch the town until it was occupied by Union forces in 1862.

In August of that year, the Third Battle of Baton Rouge was fought at Port Hudson, less than 25 miles north of the city. Six thousand Confederate troops were ultimately defeated by 18,000 Union soldiers in one of the longest sieges in American military history.

### Petrochemical Industry Develops

During the war, the state capital had been moved to Shreveport, but it was returned to Baton Rouge in 1880. By the beginning of the twentieth century, the town had undergone significant industrial development as a result of its strategic location for the production of petroleum, natural gas, and salt. In 1909 the Standard Oil Company built a facility that proved to be a lure for other petrochemical firms. Throughout World War II, these plants increased production for the war effort and contributed to the growth of the city.

In the 1950s and 1960s, Baton Rouge experienced a boom in the petrochemical industry, causing the city to expand away from the river and threatening to strand the historic downtown area. In recent years, however, government and business have begun a move back to the central district. A building boom that began in the 1990s continues today, with multi million dollar projects for quality of life improvements and new construction happening all over the city. With a renewed interest and focus in the downtown area, it appears that the twenty-first century will mark a new phase in the life of the city.

***Historical Information:*** Foundation for Historical Louisiana, 900 North Blvd., Baton Rouge, LA, 70802; telephone (225)387-2464. Baton Rouge Genealogical & Historical Society, PO Box 80565, Southeast Station, Baton Rouge, LA 70898-0565. Louisiana Genealogical & Historical Society,

PO Box 82060, Baton Rouge, LA 70884-2060. Louisiana State Archives, Secretary of States Building, 3851 Essen Lane, Baton Rouge, LA; telephone (225)922-1209

# Population Profile

## Metropolitan Area Residents
*1980:* 494,000
*1990:* 528,261
*2000:* 602,894
*Percent change, 1990–2000:* 12.37%
*U.S. rank in 1980:* 68th
*U.S. rank in 1990:* 90th
*U.S. rank in 2000:* 69th

## City Residents
*1980:* 220,394
*1990:* 219,531
*2000:* 227,818
*2003 estimate:* 225,090
*Percent change, 1990–2000:* 3.77%
*U.S. rank in 1980:* 62nd
*U.S. rank in 1990:* 73rd (State rank: 2nd)
*U.S. rank in 2000:* 85th (State rank: 2nd)

*Density:* 2,964.7 people per square mile (2000)

*Racial and ethnic characteristics* (2000)
White: 105,691
Black or African American: 114,860
American Indian and Native Alaskan: 1,035
Asian: 6,547
Native Hawaiian and Pacific Islander: 176
Hispanic or Latino (may be of any race): 3,918
Other: 1,888

*Percent of residents born in state:* 76.7% (2000)

*Age characteristics* (2000)
Population Under 5 years: 15,502
Population 5 to 9 years: 15,609
Population 10 to 14 years: 15,248
Population 15 to 19 years: 21,954
Population 20 to 24 years: 27,230
Population 25 to 34 years: 31,719
Population 35 to 44 years: 30,343
Population 45 to 54 years: 27,166
Population 55 to 59 years: 9,495
Population 60 to 64 years: 7,490
Population 65 to 74 years: 13,312
Population 75 to 84 years: 9,611
Population 85 years and over: 3,139
Median age: 30.4 years

*Births* (2002)
Total number: 4,878

*Deaths* (2002)
Total number: 2,604 (of which, 55 were infants under the age of 1 year)

*Money income* (1999)
Per capita income: $18,512
Median household income: $30,368
Total households: 88,913

*Number of households with income of . . .*
Less than $10,000: 15,805
$10,000 to $14,999: 7,903
$15,000 to $24,999: 14,039
$25,000 to $34,999: 11,366
$35,000 to $49,999: 12,451
$50,000 to $74,999: 12,538
$75,000 to $99,999: 6,544
$100,000 to $149,999: 4,813
$150,000 to $199,999: 1,526
$200,000 or more: 1,928

*Percent of families below poverty level:* 20.3% (72.7% of which were female householder families with related children under 5 years)

*2002 FBI Crime Index Total:* 18,949

# Municipal Government

Baton Rouge operates under a city-parish form of government, administered by a mayor/president and a twelve-member council.

**Head Official:** Mayor Melvin "Kip" Holden (since 2005; current term expires 2009)

**Total Number of City Employees:** 2,530 (2004)

*City Information:* Baton Rouge Municipal Government, PO Box 1471, Baton Rouge, LA; telephone (225)389-3000

# Economy

## Major Industries and Commercial Activity

Baton Rouge has one of the nation's largest deep-water ports, equipped to handle both ocean-going vessels and river barges. A 45-foot channel on the lower Mississippi River has established the region as one of the nation's most attractive locations for large-scale industrial development. The region served by the port thrives on the large industrial and chemical complexes, as well as agricultural interests, along the 85 miles of the Mississippi River in the port's jurisdiction. Forest and agricultural products, steel and pipe, ores, coal, and petroleum products top the list of cargoes shipped through the port. In the Greater Baton Rouge area a natural resources basin exists, giving industries inexpensive access to the natural resources of gas, oil, water, timberland, sulphur, salt, and other raw materials. In 2004, the Port of Greater Baton Rouge handled more than 6.1 million tons, an increase of 11.5 percent over the previous year.

The travel industry continues to figure prominently in the Baton Rouge economy. Future growth in the Baton Rouge area appears to be in this industry, as well as in finance and insurance, and health care.

*Items and goods produced:* petrochemicals, rubber, plastic, wood, paper products, food, concrete, scientific instruments

## Incentive Programs—New and Existing Companies

*Local programs*—Companies wishing to expand or establish roots in Baton Rouge are eligible for a variety of investment incentives. The industrial tax exemption provides that new industrial buildings, machinery, and equipment are exempt from property taxes for five years with provision for a five-year renewal. A five-year property tax abatement on improvements to a structure is available when renovation has not yet begun, with a five-year option for renewal. Existing structures in downtown, historic or economic development districts are eligible, including Spanish Town and Beauregard Town. Urban Enterprise Zones offer a one-time tax credit of $2,500 for newly created jobs, for up to a five-year period. For each new net job created, employers attain job tax credits ranging from $100 up to $225. Foreign trade zones allow foreign goods to enter the zone duty-free and quota-free. The Freeport Law permits most manufacturers to avoid paying taxes on raw materials brought to the state until they enter the manufacturing process. Financing assistance is offered through industrial revenue bonds, general obligation bonds, agriculture revenue bonds, plant loans, and other programs.

*State programs*—Louisiana has pledged itself to broaden its business base through liberal development incentives and loan programs. The Louisiana Quality Jobs Act offers a tax rebate of up to 5 percent of payroll paid each year for 10 years to new or expanding labor-intensive companies that create $1 million in gross annual payroll, conduct 75 percent of their business out of the state, and provide at least 50 percent of premium coverage for basic health insurance. The Louisiana Capital Investment Tax Credit incentive program is aimed at capital-intensive industries and will give a fran-

chise tax credit of 5 percent per year over 20 years on invested capital in new or expanded facilities.

*Job training programs*—The Louisiana State Board of Elementary and Secondary Education offers the Quick Start Program whereby participating businesses can obtain workers who are trained with skills to match the needs of the company. Training is offered either at a neutral site or at the company facility. The Job Training Partnership Act assists industries in choosing applicants, provides customized training for specific occupational skills and reimburses industry up to 50 percent for wages paid. Other opportunities are available through the Louisiana Department of Labor.

## Development Projects

In what community leaders called the first significant expression of confidence by a private investor in Baton Rouge's long-term plan for downtown renewal, Argosy Gaming Company constructed a 300-room convention center hotel, the first hotel to be built downtown in 50 years. The Argosy Casino Baton Rouge is a three-deck riverboat casino featuring over 29,000 square feet of gaming area. Argosy has invested an $80 million in downtown's Catfish Town on a gambling boat, dock, garage, and 100,000 square feet of retail space.

Plan Baton Rouge, the city's downtown revitalization program, was developed by Andres Duany, a pioneer of the New Urbanism movement. Part of Plan Baton Rouge calls for a $30 million expansion and renovation of The Baton Rouge River Center, the city's entertainment, government, and convention center. Projects in the plan continued into 2005 and included improvements and developments throughout the entire city.

While several new parking garages were built in the early 2000s, the issue of parking and getting around the downtown area was still a challenge. In 2003 and in hopes of alleviating vehicle congestion, freestanding trolleys began running, moving passengers to and from a variety of downtown destinations.

Opened in early 2005, the $55 million, 125,500 square foot Shaw Center for the Arts houses the Louisiana State University (LSU) Museum of Art, a 350-seat performing arts theater, rehearsal halls, LSU School of Art galleries and classrooms, and retail space. In early 2005, ground broke on the massive, 36-story RiverPlace project, a $45 million development that will consist of 99 residential units, retail space, a spa, meeting space, and a fitness center. The first high-rise condominium development in Baton Rouge's downtown, the center is expected to be completed in 2007.

Other projects in the planning or construction phase in early 2005 include a $30 million expansion of the Riverside Centroplex; a $34 million expansion of the City Plaza; a new $2.7 million State Visitors Center; a new $30 million

Education-Bienville Building; a bike and pedestrian path costing $2 million; a new Capitol House Hilton at $50 million; and many others.

**Economic Development Information:** Greater Baton Rouge Chamber of Commerce, 564 Laurel Street, PO Box 3217, Baton Rouge, LA 70801-1808; telephone (225)381-7125

## Commercial Shipping

The Port of South Louisiana (LaPlace) led the nation in cargo tonnage, and the ports of New Orleans, Baton Rouge and Plaquemines were in the Top 10. The Port of Greater Baton Rouge, the sixth largest deep water port in the United States, links the city to markets throughout the world. The port has a bulk coke handling facility handling more than 1 million tons of green and calcine coke annually. The port also houses one of the largest molasses terminals in the world, with a liquid storage capacity of 16.3 million gallons. The terminal also handles chemicals such as acids and glycol-based products. Forest products are Baton Rouge's leading commodity, including such products as woodpulp, linerboard, flitches, logs, plywood, lumber, milk carton stock, newsprint, and other paper products.

Two major railroads furnish daily service, connecting Baton Rouge with key points throughout the country. A system of interstate highways permits access to and from Baton Rouge for more than 40 common motor carriers that ship a broad range of materials through the area. More than 50 barge and steamship companies offer services to the interior of the United States.

## Labor Force and Employment Outlook

The efforts of the Baton Rouge Joint Labor-Management Committee, in conjunction with the passage of the right-to-work law, have created a positive labor-management situation in Baton Rouge. The employment base is diverse, with most jobs occurring in the retail, government, and services sectors.

The following is a summary of data regarding the Baton Rouge metropolitan area labor force, 2003 annual averages.

*Size of nonagricultural labor force:* 305,700

*Number of workers employed in . . .*
  *construction and mining:* 33,000
  *manufacturing:* 21,400
  *trade, transportation and utilities:* 58,400
  *information:* 5,300
  *financial activities:* 16,700
  *professional and business services:* 35,900
  *educational and health services:* 33,800
  *leisure and hospitality:* 28,400
  *other services:* 11,500
  *government:* 61,200

*Average hourly earnings of production workers employed in manufacturing:* $17.57

*Unemployment rate:* 5.4% (December 2004)

| *Largest area employers* | *Number of employees* |
|---|---|
| Louisiana Department of State Civil Service | 24,985 |
| The Shaw Group Inc. | 12,500 |
| East Baton Rouge Paris | 11,312 |
| Turner Industries Holding Co. LLC | 11,092 |
| Louisiana State University | 6,809 |
| ExxonMobil | 5,261 |
| City of Baton Rouge/Parish of East Baton Rouge | 4,389 |
| Jacobs | 4,000 |
| Our Lady of the Lake Regional Medical Center | 3,500 |

## Cost of Living

With an exceptionally low property tax, plus a generous state homestead exemption, Baton Rouge is a desirable place to own a home.

The following is a summary of data regarding several key cost of living factors for the Baton Rouge area.

*2004 (3rd quarter) ACCRA Average House Price:* not reported

*2004 (3rd quarter) ACCRA Cost of Living Index:* not reported

*State income tax rate:* Ranges from 2.0% to 6.0%

*State sales tax rate:* 4.0% (food sales exempt)

*Local income tax rate:* None

*Local sales tax rate:* 5.0%

*Property tax rate:* average 91.3 mills per $1,000 of assessed valuation (2004) (residential property is assessed at 10% of fair market value with a $7,500 homestead exemption)

**Economic Information:** The Chamber of Greater Baton Rouge, 564 Laurel Street, PO Box 3217, Baton Rouge, LA 70801-1808; telephone (225)381-7125

# Education and Research

## Elementary and Secondary Schools

Public elementary and secondary schools in Baton Rouge are part of the East Baton Rouge Parish (county) system, administered by a school board that appoints a superintendent. The system offers specialized programs for gifted students as well as arts, English as a second language, magnet, Montessori, college preparatory, and vocational programming. Adult education is provided to more than 5,000 students each year. A 1998 vote approved the five-year collection of a one-cent sales tax to be used for educational improvements; the tax generated nearly $300 million, which funded the construction of four new schools, and additions, improvements and repairs to all of the others. In 2003 voters renewed the tax-collecting program for another five years. District plans include seven new schools, and more renovations and repairs to existing schools.

The following is a summary of data regarding East Baton Rouge Parish's public schools as of the 2002–2003 school year.

*Total enrollment:* 52,434

*Number of facilities*
   *elementary schools:* 52
   *junior high/middle schools:* 13
   *senior high schools:* 11
   *other:* 12

*Student/teacher ratio:* 14.8:1

*Teacher salaries*
   *minimum:* $36,604
   *maximum:* $53,001

*Funding per pupil:* $7,478

About 50 parochial and private schools also operate in the Baton Rouge area, enrolling more than 60,000 students.

***Public Schools Information:*** East Baton Rouge Parish School System, 1050 S. Foster Drive, Baton Rouge, LA 70806; telephone (225)922-5400

### Colleges and Universities

Baton Rouge is home to two major universities, Louisiana State University (LSU) and Southern University (SU). LSU, with more than 31,000 students, offers undergraduate programs in more than 100 fields and advanced degrees in many fields, including law and medicine and is one of only 25 universities nationwide holding both land-grant and sea-grant status. SU, with more than 10,000 students, is the largest African American university system in the nation. SU offers degrees through 13 different colleges and includes programs in arts and science and engineering. Baton Rouge Community College enrolls about 4,000 students and is expanding its campus to include a Science and Technology Building and a Learning Resources Center, which will feature a library, a theater, and an academic learning center. Industrial training programs are available at 14 vocational-technical schools in greater Baton Rouge, including the Baton Rouge Technical Institute.

### Libraries and Research Centers

In addition to its main library in Baton Rouge, the East Baton Rouge Parish Library operates 12 branches. Its collection includes nearly one million volumes, plus magazines, newspapers, films, cassette tapes, compact discs, videos, talking books, and art reproductions. The library's popular Information Services answers more than 600,000 questions annually, many of them telephone inquiries. Baton Rouge residents also have access to libraries at Louisiana State University and Southern University and to several governmental libraries.

About 70 research centers are located in the Baton Rouge area; many of them are affiliated with LSU and conduct research in such fields as agriculture, mining, and environmental studies. Key LSU research institutes include the $125 million Pennington Biomedical Research Center and the $25 million Center for Advanced Microstructures and Devices. Private-sector research facilities include Exxon's R&D Laboratories and the Allied Signal High Density Polyethylene Laboratory.

***Public Library Information:*** East Baton Rouge Parish Library, 7711 Goodwood Blvd., Baton Rouge, LA 70806-7699; telephone (225)389-3360

# Health Care

The Baton Rouge region includes seven general hospitals providing more than 2,100 beds plus 28 nursing homes providing nearly 3,000 beds. Woman's Hospital specializes in care for mothers and newborns but offers services to women of all ages. Earl K. Long Medical Center is the teaching arm of LSU Medical School, as well as part of the state's charity hospital system. Patients throughout the region and the state seek treatment at Baton Rouge General Medical Center's burn center and at Our Lady of the Lake Regional Medical Center's eye bank. Additionally, Our Lady of the Lake Heart Center specializes in heart disease with a staff which works only in cardiac care.

# Recreation

### Sightseeing

Baton Rouge offers a variety of recreational activities. A visitor can experience the city's past by touring the elegant plantations in the area. Among the most beautifully restored are Magnolia Mound, Oak Alley and Myrtles. History has

**The Old State Capitol is the site for the FestForAll festival.**

also been preserved in the Old State Capitol, built in 1849, featuring ornate architecture and gardens. Other points of interest are the New State Capitol, at 34 stories the tallest capitol building in the nation; the Old Governor's Mansion; and the New Governor's Mansion.

Baton Rouge features one of the country's finest zoos, the initial funding for which came from children collecting pennies. Its natural habitat exhibits contain more than 1,800 animals and birds. The newest exhibit is the Otter Pond which offers above- and below-water views of a naturalistic otter habitat. Plans are being developed for a new Endangered Tiger Survival Center.

Bus and boat tours are available through various charter companies that offer services ranging from brief excursions in the city to overnight trips through Cajun country. Baton Rouge is about a 1.5-hour drive from the French Quarter in New Orleans.

### Arts and Culture

With 18 major arts groups, 25 smaller groups, and a network of artists in the community and at local universities, Baton Rouge is a culturally vital city. A renewed interest in the arts beginning in the late 1980s resulted in large part from the construction of performing arts facilities in the 12,000-seat Riverside Centroplex and the designation of the Arts and Humanities Council of Greater Baton Rouge as the official arts agency.

Theater, dance, and music are available to Baton Rouge's audiences of all tastes. Housed in The Baton Rouge River Center, the Baton Rouge Symphony offers a full season of orchestral programming. The Baton Rouge Opera and the Baton Rouge Ballet Theatre also reside and perform in The Baton Rouge River Center; the ballet performs classical and modern works. The Baton Rouge Little Theater is the area's most successful community theater. Among other groups integral to the cultural life of Baton Rouge are the music and drama departments at Louisiana State University (LSU) and Southern University.

Museums and galleries in Baton Rouge also offer variety. At the Louisiana Arts and Science Center Riverside Museum, a renovated railroad station features restored cars dating from 1883 to 1940, the Discovery Depot for young children, and the Lindy Boggs Space Station and Mission Control (reservations required). Historical Baton Rouge firefighting equipment and memorabilia are featured at the Old Bogan Fire Station. A complex of more than twenty buildings reproducing life on a nineteenth-century Louisiana plantation awaits visitors to the LSU Rural Life Museum. The LSU campus also offers and art museum and an art gallery, a natural science museum, historic Indian Mounds, and other interesting attractions.

The Old Arsenal Museum offers a tour of an old powder magazine. The Enchanted Mansion exhibits rare and unusual dolls. Baton Rouge's USS Kidd WWII destroyer and the Louisiana Naval War Memorial is a "Southern Travel Treasure" (a designation given by AAA's magazine *Southern Traveler*). Old State Capitol is home to a new interactive audio-visual museum, the Louisiana Center for Political and Governmental History. Baton Rouge's riverfront can be toured on a riverboat, and the Atchafalaya Swamp can be toured by boat.

### Festivals and Holidays

February (or March) brings Baton Rouge's best known special event, Mardi Gras, with its Krewe of Mystique Parade and other events. Also in February, the LSU Livestock and Rodeo show takes place at the Parker Agricultural Center on the LSU campus. Other Baton Rouge celebrations are the Jambalaya Jamboree (April), FestForAll (May), Bastille Day and 4th of July Freedom Fest (July), and the Baton Rouge Blues Fest and State Fair (both in October).

### Sports for the Spectator

Baton Rouge is also home to the Louisiana State University Tigers and the Lady Tigers, and the Southern University Jaguars. The LSU sports complex, site of National College Athletic Association football, basketball, and track competition, is rated among the best in the country. Southern's refurbished A. W. Mumford Stadium hosts Southwestern Athletic Conference football games.

### Sports for the Participant

BREC, the Recreation and Park Commission for the Parish of East Baton Rouge, maintains and operates 184 neighborhood parks with a broad array of facilities and programming. Facilities in the parks include a theatre and cultural center at Independence Park; Cohn Arboretum on Foster Road; the Highland Observatory on Highland Road; four fitness centers; and facilities for golf, BMX, archery, rugby, mountain biking, swimming, tennis, and other athletic pursuits. In 2004, plans were underway for expansions at 12 parks that would enhance each park's level of family programming.

Among the private sports facilities in Baton Rouge is the Country Club of Louisiana, which features an 18-hole Jack Nicklaus golf course, 10 outdoor and 3 indoor tennis courts, and a swimming pool. Riverboat and casino gambling are also popular diversions.

### Shopping and Dining

According to the Baton Rouge Convention and Visitors Bureau, the visitor who has only one free afternoon to spend in Baton Rouge should spend it at the Historic Merchants District on Perkins Road, which has been compared to New

Orleans' Magazine Street shopping area. The visitor will find a dozen charming shops and galleries and four restaurants featuring local cuisine, hamburgers and crawfish pies, and possibly the best Italian food in town. Downtown Baton Rouge offers shopping opportunities for those interested in fine art, gifts, designer furnishings, stained glass, and other novelties. The new Mall of Louisiana offers quality stores on two levels. Baton Rouge offers unique shopping at several locations, including The Royal Standard on Perkins Road, where more than two dozen merchants offer international wares.

Baton Rouge's numerous restaurants satisfy any dining taste, from fast food to gourmet continental, served in casual or elegant settings. Specialties include Cajun and Creole cooking and fresh seafood from the Gulf of Mexico.

*Visitor Information:* Baton Rouge Area Convention and Visitors Bureau, 730 North Blvd., Baton Rouge, LA 70802; telephone (225)383-1825; (800)LA-ROUGE; fax (225)346-1253

# Convention Facilities

Louisiana's hotel room demand is fourth in the nation, with 63.6% of rooms sold. The principal convention facility in Baton Rouge is The Baton Rouge River Center, which is located downtown on the banks of the Mississippi River. Connected to the Louisiana Arts and Science Center and the Old State Capitol, The Baton Rouge River Center is within walking distance of hotels, restaurants, shops, and major attractions. Municipally owned, The Baton Rouge River Center is maintained by a private management company called SMG. Since SMG assumed management of the facility events have grown to more than 500 per calendar year and attendance at these events continues to increase. The Baton Rouge River Center is comprised of three main facilities: the Arena, the Exhibition Hall and the Theater for Performing Arts. The River Center Arena is a 10,000-seat arena, with over 30,000 square feet of exhibition space and more than 7,000 square feet of meeting space. The new 70,000 square-foot Convention Center can be combined with the arena to create more than 100,000 square-feet of contiguous exhibit space. The River Center hosts events such as concerts, conventions, sporting events, trade shows and theater productions. As the downtown area continues to grow, The Baton Rouge River Center has responded with the current expansion of the new Convention Center. This new venue will include 100,000 square feet of continuous, state-of-the-art exhibition space and will prove to be a cornerstone development in Baton Rouge.

Among other meeting facilities in Baton Rouge are the LSU Assembly Center and LSU Union, located on the campus of Louisiana State University, and F. G. Clark Activity Center and Smith-Brown Memorial Union, both on the Southern University campus.

There are more than 7,000 hotel rooms in Baton Rouge, most in the College Drive area; many offer convention and meeting facilities.

*Convention Information:* Baton Rouge Area Convention and Visitors Bureau, 730 North Blvd., Baton Rouge, LA 70802; telephone (225)383-1825; (800)LA-ROUGE; fax (225)346-1253

# Transportation

**Approaching the City**

Located off Interstate 110 approximately 5 miles north of downtown Baton Rouge, the Baton Rouge Metropolitan Airport is served by 4 major airlines. The recently renovated facility provides direct service to 24 cities, with connecting service also available through major southern cities.

The major routes into Baton Rouge by car or bus are Interstates 10, 12, and 55. Interstate 10, which runs across the continent from Jacksonville, Fla., to Los Angeles, gives the motorist a fine view of Baton Rouge. Interstate 55 connects the city with points as far north as Chicago.

**Traveling in the City**

Baton Rouge is laid out on a grid pattern, with streets in the northern half of the city intersecting at right angles; in the southern half, however, streets run diagonally. Florida Boulevard divides north from south; east is divided from west by the Acadian Throughway. Public bus service in the city is provided by Capitol Area Transit System (CATS), which offers 17 different routes. Charter bus services are also available.

# Communications

**Newspapers and Magazines**

Baton Rouge's major daily newspaper is *The Advocate,* a morning paper. News is also available in *The Baton Rouge Post,* an online only news daily. *Gambit,* a weekly, covers local politics, dining, and entertainment. Scholarly/literary magazines published in Baton Rouge include the *Henry*

*James Review* and *The Southern Review*. In addition, magazines on engineering, agriculture, the oil industry, library science, business, and pharmacy are published in the city.

### Television and Radio

Baton Rouge has four television stations: three network and one public. Five television stations are located in surrounding communities, and cable is available. In addition, eleven radio stations broadcast from Baton Rouge: six AM and five FM.

*Media Information:* *The Advocate,* 525 Lafayette Street, Baton Rouge, LA 70802; telephone (225)767-1400

### Baton Rouge Online

The Advocate. Available www.2theadvocate.com

Baton Rouge city guide. Available www.baton-rouge.com/BatonRouge

Baton Rouge Convention & Visitors Bureau. Available www.visitbatonrouge.com

The Baton Rouge Post. Available www.batonrougepost.com

The Chamber of Greater Baton Rouge. Available www.brchamber.org

City of Baton Rouge home page. Available brgov.com

The State Library of Louisiana. Available www.state.lib.la.us

### Selected Bibliography

Bannon, Lois Elmer, Martha Carr, et. al., *Magnolia Mound: A Louisiana River Plantation* (Gretna, La.: Firebird Press, 1984)

Carleton, Mark T. *River Capital: An Illustrated History of Baton Rouge.* Pictorial research by M. Stone Miller, Jr. (Sierra Madre, CA: Windsor Publications, 1981).

Dedicated Friends of Magnolia Mound Plantation. *The Magnolia Mound Plantation Kitchen Book: Being a Compendium of Foodways and Customs of Early Louisiana, 1795–1841, Interspersed with Anecdotes, Incidents and Observations.* (Baton Rouge, LA: Magnolia Mound Plantation House, 1986)

East, Charles. *Baton Rouge, A Civil War Album.* (Baton Rouge, LA: East, 1977)

Meyers, Rose. *A History of Baton Rouge, 1862.* (Baton Rouge, LA: Louisiana State University Press for the Baton Rouge Bicentennial Corporation, 1976)

# New Orleans

## *The City in Brief*

*Note: This profile of the city of New Orleans was updated prior to August 2005, when Hurricane Katrina caused severe damage to the Gulf Coast region of the United States. The long-term impact of Katrina on New Orleans is unknown at the time of publication.*

**Founded:** 1718 (incorporated 1805)

**Head Official:** Mayor C. Ray Nagin (since 2002)

**City Population**
1990: 496,938
2000: 484,674
2003 estimate: 469,032
Percent change, 1990–2000: −2.46%
U.S. rank in 1990: 24th (State rank: 1st)
U.S. rank in 2000: 38th (State rank: 1st)

**Metropolitan Area Residents**
1990: 1,285,262
2000: 1,337,726

Percent change, 1990–2000: 4.08%
U.S. rank in 1990: 32nd
U.S. rank in 2000: 34th

**Area:** 181 square miles (2000)
**Elevation:** Ranges from 5 feet below sea level to 15 feet above sea level
**Average Annual Temperature:** 68.1° F
**Average Annual Precipitation:** 61.88 inches

**Major Economic Sectors:** entertainment, tourism and hotels, construction, financial services, oil and gas, maritime/transportation, shipbuilding and aerospace
**Unemployment rate:** 5.0% (December 2004)
**Per Capita Income:** $17,258 (2000)

**2002 FBI Crime Index Total:** 31,206

**Major Colleges and Universities:** University of New Orleans, Tulane University, Louisiana State University School of Medicine, Southeastern Louisiana University, Loyola University, Xavier University, Dillard University

**Daily Newspaper:** *The Times-Picayune*

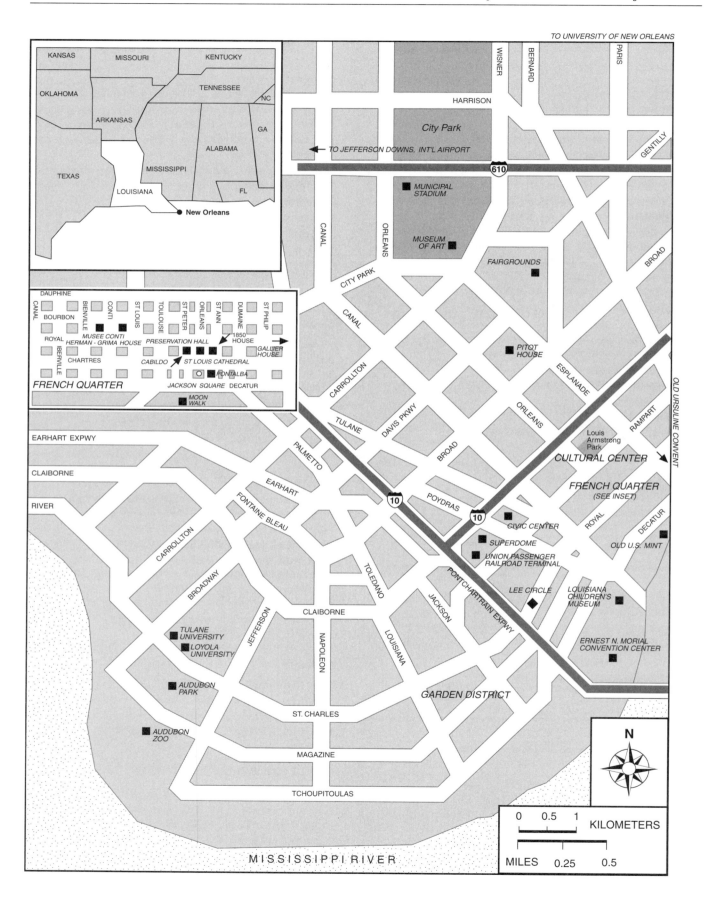

# Introduction

An international seaport with direct water connections to half the United States, New Orleans would not exist without the Mississippi River. Its roots are deep in the saturated soils of the delta; its history is a pageant of canoes, rafts, paddlewheels, and barges from mid-America converging with sails and steamships from around the world. Under four flags New Orleans has grown from a tiny swamp outpost populated by French convicts to a major economic center, a sports-minded city of rare elegance, culture, and high spirits. The city consistently appears on "Top Ten" lists as a vacation destination, cited particularly for its many attractions and for its fine cuisine.

# Geography and Climate

With miles of waterfront in three directions, New Orleans is partly peninsular. The heart of the city spreads around a curve of the Mississippi River—source of the nickname "Crescent City"—while edging Lake Pontchartrain on the north. Lake Pontchartrain connects to Lake Borgne, a broad opening to the Gulf of Mexico. Lakes, marshlands, and bayous extend from the city in all directions. Louisiana is divided into parishes rather than counties; New Orleans itself occupies the entirety of Orleans Parish, while metropolitan New Orleans extends west into St. Charles, St. John, and St. James; south into Jefferson, Plaquemines, and St. Bernard Parishes, and north into St. Tammany Parish, and into other parishes as well.

A humid, semi-tropical climate in New Orleans is kept from extremes by surrounding waters. While snowfall is negligible, rain occurs throughout the year. Waterspouts caused by small tornadoes are frequently seen on nearby lakes.

**Area:** 181 square miles (2000)

**Elevation:** Ranges from 5 feet below sea level to 15 feet above; mean elevation, 5 feet above sea level

**Average Temperatures:** January, 51.3° F; July 81.9° F; annual average, 68.1° F

**Average Annual Precipitation:** 61.88 inches

# History

**French Settlers Leave Their Mark**

The first Europeans known to travel past the site of New Orleans were followers of Hernando Cortez, a Spanish soldier of fortune who died on the banks of the Mississippi River in 1543. One hundred forty years later French explorer Robert Cavelier de La Salle, led an expedition from Canada that traced the Mississippi, called "Father of Waters," as far as the Gulf of Mexico, and boldly claimed all land between the Alleghenies and Rockies for his sovereign, France's Louis XIV. La Salle was assassinated before he could direct the building of a settlement in the land he called "Louisiane." In 1718 Jean Baptiste Le Moyne, Sieur de Bienville, a founder of outposts in what are now Biloxi, Mississippi, and Mobile, Alabama, placed a cross at a point where the Mississippi curved near Lake Pontchartrain to mark the site for a new settlement. The proposed town was named for the Duc d'Orleans, who was governing France during Louis XV's childhood.

To establish a population in the new settlement, France sent prisoners, slaves, and bonded servants. An unscrupulous speculator, John Law, beguiled the Duc d'Orleans into giving him a 25-year charter to exploit the new territory and managed to lure a few Europeans across the seas with tales of nearby gold. The men who arrived found only a village of cyprus huts and criminals surrounded by swamp, disease, and hostile Native American tribes. Under threat of a revolt, France then sent "wives" for the colonists: about ninety women from Paris jails, a wild group chaperoned by Ursuline nuns until they were married. Later, poor girls of good reputation were also recruited to bring the settlement a core of respectability, but by then the ribald side of New Orleans's lifestyle had been established. Swamp conditions were hard on its inhabitants, yet the settlement grew into a French crown colony and soon served as territorial capital.

**Origins of Creoles and Cajuns**

In 1762 New Orleans citizens suddenly found themselves subjects of Charles III of Spain; France's Louis XV had paid a debt to his Spanish cousin by giving away Louisiana. The thoroughly French colony drove out the Spanish commissioner sent to govern them. In the summer of 1763, 22 Spanish warships and 3,000 troops arrived to restore order and install another governor, this time without provoking open opposition. Descendants of these early French-Spanish colonial times are known as Creoles. French-speaking families also began emigrating from Canada's maritime region, Acadia—now Nova Scotia and New Brunswick—to flee British occupation. Referred to as Acadians, and eventually Cajuns, they found sanctuary in

New Orleans and in the bayous of the wide Mississippi Delta not far from the city.

In 1788 and 1794 devastating fires destroyed most of the buildings in New Orleans's French Quarter, or Vieux Carre (Old Square); these were replaced by structures of a decidedly Spanish nature. About the same time a process for making granulated sugar made sugar cane an important cash crop in a market soon dominated by cotton. When Spain transferred Louisiana back to France in 1803, U.S. President Thomas Jefferson adroitly bought the territory for $15 million. New Orleans was incorporated two years later. The city was unsuccessfully attacked by British forces during the War of 1812; that same year the first steamboat arrived from Natchez, and Louisiana became a state. The years following the Louisiana Purchase saw rapid development and swift growth in the city's slave and free population. United States and foreign interests invested in the expanding port and immigration increased.

### City Boasts Multicultural Neighborhoods

Americans settling in nearby Faubourg Ste. Marie, the present business district, developed a suburb very different in nature from the old French Quarter. Other individualistic neighborhoods developed, including the Irish Channel, a rowdy waterfront area; Bucktown, a one-street fishing village on the shore of Lake Pontchartrain in Jefferson Parish; and the wealthy residential Garden District.

The city's prosperity depended heavily on slave labor, however, and economic threats to this trade made New Orleans intensely pro-Confederate in the Civil War. After the war, reconstruction in New Orleans was hampered by rivalry between ethnic and economic factions, yet eventually, the city emerged as a railroad and shipping center. New Orleans survived a yellow fever and cholera outbreak in 1853 in which nearly 11,000 people died; a malaria outbreak in 1871; a yellow fever outbreak in 1878 in which more than 4,000 people died; a severe hurricane in 1915; and an influenza epidemic in 1918 in which 35,000 people died statewide.

Jazz, considered the unique American music idiom, developed in New Orleans at the beginning of the twentieth century while the city continued to celebrate its cultural origins with the phenomenally successful Mardi Gras and world-renowned cuisine. Tourists began to flock to the city to experience its heralded celebrations and unique neighborhoods. While crime troubled the city in later years of the twentieth century—a blight the city has continued to fight against—New Orleans fiercely protects its legendary heritage. Eighteenth- and nineteenth-century buildings nestle in the shadow of sleek modern towers, convention centers, and shopping facilities, part of the mix of business, history, and good times that characterizes the city's charm.

At the beginning of the twenty-first century, a downtown rebirth was on the minds of city planners. "The Downtown Revival!," a multi-million dollar project that includes a long list of improvements to New Orleans' entire downtown area, is aimed at restoring the downtown and Canal Street for the millions of tourists that flock to the city each year. Today's New Orleans is a successful blend of southern historical charm and modern tourist mecca.

**Historical Information:** Musee Conti, 917 Conti Street, New Orleans, LA 70112; telephone (504)525-2605; (800)233-5405

# Population Profile

### Metropolitan Area Residents
*1980:* 1,303,800
*1990:* 1,285,262
*2000:* 1,337,726
*Percent change, 1990–2000:* 4.08%
*U.S. rank in 1980:* 27th
*U.S. rank in 1990:* 32nd
*U.S. rank in 2000:* 34th

### City Residents
*1980:* 557,515
*1990:* 496,938
*2000:* 484,674
*2003 estimate:* 469,032
*Percent change, 1990–2000:* −2.46%
*U.S. rank in 1980:* 21st
*U.S. rank in 1990:* 24th (State rank: 1st)
*U.S. rank in 2000:* 38th (State rank: 1st)

*Density:* 2,684.3 people per square mile (2000)

*Racial and ethnic characteristics* (2000)
   White: 135,956
   Black or African American: 325,947
   American Indian and Alaska Native: 991
   Asian: 10,972
   Native Hawaiian and Pacific Islander: 109
   Hispanic or Latino (may be of any race): 14,826
   Other: 7,240

*Percent of residents born in state:* 77.4% (2000)

*Age characteristics* (2000)
   Population Under 5 years: 33,496
   Population 5 to 9 years: 37,133
   Population 10 to 14 years: 36,769
   Population 15 to 19 years: 38,312
   Population 20 to 24 years: 38,932

Population 25 to 34 years: 70,466
Population 35 to 44 years: 71,497
Population 45 to 54 years: 63,690
Population 55 to 59 years: 21,068
Population 60 to 64 years: 16,658
Population 65 to 74 years: 28,949
Population 75 to 84 years: 20,296
Population 85 years and over: 7,408
Median age: 33.1 years

*Births* (Orleans Parish, 2002)
Total number: 7,068

*Deaths* (Orleans Parish, 2002)
Total number: 5,656 (of which, 92 were infants under the age of 1 year)

*Money income* (1999)
Per capita income: $17,258
Median household income: $27,133
Total Number of households: 188,365 (2000)

*Number of households with income of . . .*
Less than $10,000: 39,617
$10,000 to $14,999: 17,991
$15,000 to $24,999: 29,760
$25,000 to $34,999: 25,460
$35,000 to $49,999: 26,399
$50,000 to $74,999: 23,724
$75,000 to $99,999: 10,802
$100,000 to $149,999: 7,920
$150,000 to $199,999: 2,620
$200,000 or more: 4,072

*Percent of families below poverty level:* 23.7% (of which, 61.4% were female householder families with related children under 5 years)

*2002 FBI Crime Index Total:* 31,206

# Municipal Government

New Orleans operates under a mayor-council form of government; the mayor is elected for a four-year term, as is the seven-member city council.

**Head Official:** Mayor C. Ray Nagin (since May 2002; current term expires 2006)

**Total Number of City Employees:** 6,370 (2004)

*City Information:* Mayor's Office, 1300 Perdido Street, New Orleans, LA 70112; telephone (504)565-6400

# Economy

## Major Industries and Commercial Activity

The New Orleans economy is dominated by four major sectors: oil/gas and related activities, tourism, the port and ship/boat building, and aerospace manufacturing. The presence of universities, hospitals, legal/accounting and other professional services, together with key installations of the U.S. Navy and other military operations in the region adds further to its diversified economic base.

Tourism continues to be the driving force of New Orleans' economy. Boasting attractions such as its magnetic French Quarter, America's largest Mardis Gras festival, and riverboat gambling, New Orleans has a history of solid tourist trade. In a city with more than 10 million visitors annually, the hospitality business supplies more than 66,000 jobs in the service sector such as accommodations and restaurants. In 2004, tourists spent $4.9 billion in New Orleans.

At the beginning of the twenty-first century, New Orleans was heralded by several magazines as a top place for small businesses and entrepreneurs. One magazine noted that statistics from the Small Business Administration showed that small businesses in the area create more than 75 percent of new jobs.

Some of New Orleans's largest private employers are shipbuilding firms, where workers build and repair vessels for the U.S. Navy, merchant fleets and cruise ship lines. Martin Marietta, manufacturers of aerospace components for NASA space projects, uses a large work force at its New Orleans operations. In recent years the economy has diversified into such varied fields as health services, aerospace, and research and technology.

The New Orleans region is also a major transportation hub and a leader in production of crude oil and natural gas processing facilities.

*Items and goods produced:* ships, petrochemical products, food processing, stone, clay and glass products, printing and publishing

## Incentive Programs—New and Existing Companies

*Local programs*—An exemption from ad valorem property taxes levied by local parishes and municipalities is offered to new and expanding manufacturing industries. In addition, the Louisiana Urban Enterprise Zone program offers tax credits and other incentives to businesses locating in specially designated areas. Manufacturers, distributors, and retailers are eligible to have ad valorem property taxes on inventories levied by municipal government credited against the state corporate and personal income taxes and the corporation franchise tax.

Greater New Orleans, Inc.'s International Business and Trade Development Department was created to position the region as a prominent player in global marketplace. The strategy includes developing the New Orleans Region as a hub for north-south trade with the Americas, thus generating new business opportunities and accelerating job growth. Among these efforts are matchmaking meetings between local companies and international trade delegations and partnerships such as the Louisiana/Honduras Alliance, which is a broad-reaching effort with five major universities in Southeast Louisiana to rebuild Honduras in the wake of Hurricane Mitch. In partnership with other international trade organizations and public-sector officials in the region, Greater New Orleans, Inc. is helping to anchor the New Orleans Region as the Gateway to Latin America.

*State programs*—Louisiana has pledged itself to broaden its business base through liberal development incentives and loan programs. To that end the governor signed three tort reform bills intended to signal the state's new commitment to improving the state's business climate. In addition, the state legislature overwhelmingly passed two new incentives to attract new business. The Louisiana Quality Jobs Act offers a tax rebate of up to five percent of payroll paid each year for 10 years to new or expanding labor-intensive companies that create $1 million in gross annual payroll, conduct 75 percent of their business out of the state, and provide at least 50 percent of premium coverage for basic health insurance. The Louisiana Capital Investment Tax Credit incentive program is aimed at capital-intensive industries and will give a franchise tax credit of five percent per year over 20 years on invested capital in new or expanded facilities.

New Orleans, site of the world's first trade center, has been designated a Foreign Trade Zone. A freeport exemption law allows property tax exemptions on goods imported into the United States and held for export outside of the state or the country, as well as goods in interstate commerce that are stored while in transit through the state. The region of New Orleans has diverse business incentives sponsored by the state as well as special financing programs for companies of all sizes.

*Job training programs*—Greater New Orleans, Inc., whose mission is to attract new businesses to the New Orleans region, is responsible for the School-to-Career Initiative, which has organized local businesses into industry consortia in the fields of Architecture, Design, Engineering and Construction (ADEC); Culinary Arts; Financial Services; Hospitality, Travel and Tourism; Law-Related Careers; and Petrochemical. An Information Technologies Consortium and a Healthcare Consortium were recently developed. A Consortium on Out-of-School Youth (COSY) has also been established. The industry consortia provide teacher and student shadowing opportunities and internships, assisting with curriculum development and providing guidance and financial support. Speaking through the consortia, the local business community is able to voice its workforce needs and expectations of its entry-level employees. Having heard their needs, the School-to-Career Initiative focuses on creating systems that deliver the quality employees that will ensure profit and success for not only these businesses, but ultimately for the region as a whole.

**Development Projects**

''The Downtown Revival!,'' a multi-million dollar project that includes a long list of improvements to New Orleans' entire downtown area, is aimed at restoring the downtown and Canal Street for the millions of tourists that flock to the city each year. By 2005 $2 million had been spent on downtown-wide improvements that included new signs to help visitors find their way, extensive street landscaping, and street pole banners. Beginning in spring of the same year, developers expect to begin a $15 million project that involves major renovations and improvements to Canal Street for businesses and visitors. As part of the project, the About Face Façade Improvement Fund consists of a $156 million program to enhance the city's public transportation by way of a new Canal Street Streetcar Line program and new transit shelters.

***Economic Development Information:*** Greater New Orleans, Inc., 601 Poydras Street, Suite 1700, New Orleans, LA 70130; telephone (504)527-6900; fax (504)527-6950

**Commercial Shipping**

The Port of South Louisiana (LaPlace) led the nation in cargo tonnage, and the ports of New Orleans, Baton Rouge and Plaquemines were in the Top 10. The Port of New Orleans, the largest inland port in the United States, is a hub of national and international transportation. It is connected to a network of 19,000 miles of inland waterways consisting of the Mississippi River, its tributaries, and other systems. More than 4,000 ship calls are made at the region's deepwater ports every year. French explorers were the first to identify the Mississippi rivermouth region as an important port location that was connected by waterways to a vast section of interior territory. American traders and farmers floated their goods downstream to New Orleans and, after 1812, steamboats transported upriver commodities that ocean-going vessels landed at New Orleans. The modern history of the Port of New Orleans, however, began in 1896 when the Louisiana state legislature created a state agency to serve as port authority. In 1925 the Inner Harbor Navigational Canal was built to connect the Mississippi River and Lake Pontchartrain. Also known as the Industrial Canal, it serves as the mouth of the Mississippi

River-Gulf Outlet, built in the 1960s as a route to the Gulf of Mexico that is more than forty miles shorter than the Mississippi River route.

Seventy percent of the nation's waterways drain through the Port of New Orleans, which operates a Foreign Trade Zone, where foreign and domestic goods can be stored and processed without being subject to U.S. customs and regulations. Commercial vessels and ship tonnage entering and leaving the area make the Port of New Orleans one of the world's busiest harbors, with imports and exports serving the iron and steel, manufacturing, agricultural, and petrochemical industries. Port-related activities involve shipbuilding and repair, grain elevators, coal terminals, warehouses, and distribution facilities, as well as steamship agencies, importers and exporters, international banks, transportation services, and foreign consular or trade offices. The port is also a departure point for a variety of pleasure cruises to Caribbean destinations and for upriver riverboat and paddlewheel cruises.

## Labor Force and Employment Outlook

In a bold and sweeping move, regional business leaders have closed the books on their 140 year old regional chamber and its economic development arm MetroVison, to take on a new five-year plan to generate 30,000 new jobs and $1 billion in new payroll. Recognizing that the most relevant issue for the region is a stalled economy, leaders have created Greater New Orleans, Inc. to be the new, streamlined organization to implement best-practice strategies to achieve these measurable objectives. Louisiana ranked 19th in the country in high-tech job growth for 2001, with a growth rate of 3 percent.

The following is a summary of data regarding the New Orleans metropolitan area labor force, 2003 annual averages.

*Size of nonagricultural labor force:* 615,500

*Number of workers employed in . . .*
   *construction and mining:* 40,700
   *manufacturing:* 31,500
   *trade, transportation and utilities:* 122,400
   *information:* 9,800
   *financial activities:* 35,900
   *professional and business services:* 71,900
   *educational and health services:* 83,700
   *leisure and hospitality:* 82,200
   *other services:* 23,200
   *government:* 104,200

*Average hourly earnings of production workers employed in manufacturing:* $16.91

*Unemployment rate:* 5.0% (December 2004)

| *Largest private employers* | *Number of employees* |
|---|---|
| Schwegmann Bros. Giant Supermarket | 4,600 |

| *Largest private employers* | *Number of employees* |
|---|---|
| Hibernia Corp. (banking) | 3,100 |
| First Commerce Corp. of Louisiana | 3,026 |
| South Central Bell | 3,000 |
| Shell Oil Company | 2,700 |
| Martin Marietta Manned Space System | 2,400 |
| Exxon Corporation | 1,750 |
| Union Carbide Corp. | 1,150 |
| Whitney National Bank | 1,305 |
| Hilton Hotels | 1,300 |
| Ruth's Chris Steak House | 1,100 |

## Cost of Living

The following is a summary of data regarding several key cost of living factors for the New Orleans area.

*2004 (3rd Quarter) ACCRA Average House Price:* $226,244 (Slidell–St. Tammany Parish reporting)

*2004 (3rd Quarter) ACCRA Cost of Living Index:* 96.1 (U.S. average = 100.0)

*State income tax rate:* Ranges from 2.0% to 6.0%

*State sales tax rate:* 8.75% (food sales exempt)

*Local income tax rate:* None

*Local sales tax rate:* Varies by parish ranging from 5.0% in Orleans Parish (City) to 4.75% in Jefferson Parish

*Property tax rate:* 1.70% (residential property is assessed at 10% of fair market value with a $7,500 homestead exemption)

**Economic Information:** Greater New Orleans, Inc., 601 Poydras Street, Suite 1700, New Orleans, LA 70130; telephone (504)527-6900; fax (504)527-6950

# Education and Research

## Elementary and Secondary Schools

Public schools in the New Orleans area are noted for their dedication to excellence. For instance, the Ben Franklin public high school produces a high number of National Merit scholars among its college-bound graduates, while the public New Orleans Center for Creative Arts is designed to provide special instruction to artistically gifted students.

The following is a summary of data regarding New Orleans public schools as of the 2002–2003 school year.

*Total enrollment:* 70,246

*Number of facilities*
 *elementary schools:* 78
 *junior high/middle schools:* 35
 *senior high schools:* 26
 *other:* 12

*Student/teacher ratio:* Average 16.6:1 (2002–2003)

*Teacher salaries*
 *minimum:* $25,439
 *maximum:* $41,478

*Funding per pupil:* $6,501

New Orleans area public elementary and secondary schools are supplemented by 67 private schools. Catholic schools comprise the majority of the area's private schools, which also include other church-affiliated, non-denominational schools and special schools, including the nationally acclaimed Isidore Newman School.

***Public Schools Information:*** New Orleans Public Schools, 4300 Almonaster Ave., New Orleans, LA 70126; telephone (504)942-3531

### Colleges and Universities

The New Orleans region supports eight four-year colleges and universities and two 2-year community colleges. Those in New Orleans include the University of New Orleans; Tulane University, a private nonprofit institution that includes Sophie Newcomb College for Women; Louisiana State University Medical Center, offering medical and dental education; Dillard University, one of the oldest predominantly African American institutions in the country; Loyola University; Our Lady of Holy Cross College; New Orleans Baptist Theological Seminary; Xavier University of Louisiana; and a branch of Southern Louisiana University, as well as several two-year colleges and vocational-technical schools.

### Libraries and Research Centers

The New Orleans Public Library, consisting of the Main Library and 12 branches, numbers nearly one million books in its collection, in addition to recordings, tapes, and films. It maintains the New Orleans City Archives as well as The Louisiana Division located on the third floor of the Main Library. The Division collects, through purchase and gift, all types of printed, manuscript, graphic, and oral resources relating to the study of Louisiana and its citizens. Other areas of interest include the Mississippi River, the Gulf of Mexico, and the South. Included are books by or about Louisianians; city, regional, and state documents; manuscripts, maps, newspapers, periodicals, microfilms, photographs, slides, motion pictures, sound recordings, video tapes, postcards, and ephemera of every sort. The Genealogy

Collection contains books, periodicals, microfilms, and CD-ROMs with emphasis on the Southeast United States, Nova Scotia, France, and Spain. The library also hosts a literacy program and a new African American Resource Center.

New Orleans also boasts several special libraries and collections. For instance, the W. R. Hogan Archive of New Orleans Jazz is housed by Tulane University's library. The Louisiana State Museum Historical Center library maintains a collection of French and Spanish colonial documents, eighteenth- and nineteenth-century maps, and nineteenth-century personal manuscripts. A 20,000-volume library at the World Trade Center of New Orleans collects works on import and export trade, travel, international relations, economics, and transportation.

Louisiana State University Medical Center conducts research on a variety of medical topics, such as oncology, cystic fibrosis, human development, hearing, eye diseases, and arteriosclerosis. The Louisiana Business and Technology Center at LSU is the "Best Of The Class," and is in the Top 10 Technology Incubators in the United States. It placed first in terms of average revenue growth in its client companies. Nearly 20 research centers at Tulane University conduct research on such topics as AIDS, politics, Mesoamerican ecology, and Latin America. Tulane University received a National Institutes of Health grant to build an $18 million biosafety lab specializing in the development of treatments and vaccines for emerging infectious diseases. The state-of-the-art facility is expected to have a global impact. The Amistad Research Center at Tulane University pursues research and maintains a library and archives in such subject areas as African American history and culture, ethnic minorities of the United States, civil rights, abolitionism, and Protestant denominations.

The Audubon Nature Institute's Center for Research of Endangered Species conducts research programs on reproductive physiology, endocrinology, genetics, embryo transfer, and others in hopes of ensuring survival of endangered species.

***Public Library Information:*** New Orleans Public Library, 219 Loyola Avenue, New Orleans, LA 70112; telephone (504)529-READ; fax (504)596-2609

## *Health Care*

Internationally known as a center for medical care and research, New Orleans is home to 25 acute care hospitals, with approximately 5,200 staffed beds and 1,800 medical and surgical specialists, serving the health care needs of a multistate area as well as Latin America and other foreign countries. One of the largest medical complexes in the United States is located in the city's central business district and consists of the U.S. Veterans Administration Hospital, the state-operated Charity Hospital, and the medical schools of both Louisiana State University and Tulane University. The Tulane Center for Abdominal Transplant specializes in the treatment of all diseases involving the liver, pancreas, and kidneys. Other New Orleans area hospitals include DePaul Hospital and Mental Health Center, United Medical Center, Eye and Ear Institute of Louisiana, Baptist Hospital, St. Charles General Hospital, and East Jefferson General Hospital. Terminally ill patients and their families are also served by the Hospice of Greater New Orleans.

# Recreation

### Sightseeing

Visitors can tour New Orleans by bus, boat, seaplane, street-car, or horse-drawn carriage, whether seeking a general-interest excursion or a specialized trip. Points of interest include Cajun country; picturesque homes, plantations, and gardens; and historic sites. Self-guided driving and walking tours are also available in the city.

Part of Jean Lafitte National Historic Park, New Orleans' French Quarter is one of America's most famous neighborhoods. Park rangers offer free walking tours that begin at the park information center. A living slice of history, the French Quarter's Vieux Carre is home to people from all walks of life. Its intriguing architecture is mainly Spanish, dating from the late 1700s after two fires destroyed nearly all of the city's French buildings. Visits to the French Quarter usually begin in Jackson Square, originally a municipal drill field and parade ground known as the ''Place d'Armes.'' Painters and musicians hone their arts in the square while pigeons flock around the famed equestrian statue of General Andrew Jackson. The square is dominated by St. Louis Cathedral, built in 1794 and remodeled in 1850. Next door, the Cabildo, the one-time Spanish government building where Jefferson's Louisiana Purchase agreement was signed, houses French Emperor Napoleon Bonaparte's death mask and a collection of folk art.

A section of the Mississippi River levee adjacent to Jackson Square serves as a promenade. Renamed the Moon Walk when renovated, it offers a scenic view of the river. The Woldenburg Riverfront Park, stretching from Canal Street to the Moonwalk, gives direct access to the Mississippi River. Elsewhere in the French Quarter landmarks such as the Old Ursuline Convent—the oldest recorded building in the Mississippi Valley and now restored as Archbishop

Antoine Blanc Memorial—and Preservation Hall—the city's most famous jazz club where pioneers of the idiom still perform nightly—join with antique shops, confectioneries, Bourbon Street jazz clubs, world-famous restaurants, historic homes, art galleries, sidewalk cafes, and outdoor markets to make the French Quarter New Orleans's top tourism drawing card.

The Audubon Nature Institute comprises several attractions throughout New Orleans. Its Audubon Zoo displays more than 2,000 animals in natural habitats, and the spectacular Aquarium of the Americas displays exhibits of 530 species of fish, birds and reptiles. Adjacent to the Aquarium is the Entergy IMAX Theater. The Louisiana Nature Center is an 86-acre forest and wetland, featuring trails, interpretive galleries, exhibits, and a planetarium. The Audubon Insectarium is scheduled to open in fall 2005. The ''largest free-standing museum in the country devoted to 900,000+ known species of insects and their relatives,'' the museum will encompass 23,000 square feet of exhibit space at the U.S. Customs House in New Orleans.

New Orleans's varied neighborhoods, central business district, and surrounding areas provide a wide range of other attractions as well. City Park, one of the largest municipal parks in the country, showcases an 18-foot sundial, a carousel, a children's story land, and a miniature train, as well as points of historic interest. Six Flags New Orleans theme park provides roller coasters and New Orleans-themed entertainment for families. Construction began on the fortifications at Fort Pike Commemorative Area in 1818 and the buildings were used in various capacities until after the Civil War; now a 125-acre park surrounds the fort. Six Flags New Orleans theme park provides roller coasters and New Orleans-themed entertainment for families.

In the business district, sights include the K & B Plaza at Lee Circle, featuring a 5-acre sculpture garden; the International Trade Mart, which offers spectacular views of the New Orleans area from its 31st and 33rd floors; and the Civic Center, which anchors a complex of state and city buildings around an attractive plaza. Creole cottages and shotgun houses dominate the scene in many New Orleans neighborhoods. Both have a murky ancestry. The Creole cottage, two rooms wide and two or more rooms deep under a generous pitched roof with a front overhang or gallery, is thought to have evolved from various European and Caribbean forms. The shotgun house is one room wide and two, three or four rooms deep under a continuous gable roof. As legend has it, the name was suggested by the fact that because the rooms and doors line up, one can fire a shotgun through the house without hitting anything.

Among the area's picturesque and historic sights is the Longue Vue House and Gardens, a Greek Revival mansion

**The famous New Orleans French Quarter.**

with eight acres of meticulously tended grounds showcasing a spectacular Spanish Court. Conveying residents and visitors past antebellum homes, the St. Charles Avenue Streetcar Line is listed on the National Register of Historic Places and represents the nation's only surviving historic streetcar system. All 35 electric cars were manufactured by the Brill & Perley Thomas Company between 1922 and 1924 and are still in use. The Riverfront Line connects the cultural and commercial developments along the riverfront. In the Garden District, a New Orleans neighborhood registered with the Historic Landmarks Commission, stately nineteenth-century homes line wide streets.

Because the high water table restricts burials in New Orleans to above-ground edifices, the city's old cemeteries (called "cities of the dead") are often sought out for their unusual beauty. There are 42 cemeteries in the metropolitan New Orleans area. Metairie Cemetery is thought by many to be the most beautiful as well as the most unique cemetery, not only in New Orleans, but anywhere in the world, featuring architecture styles from around the world.

Crossing 24 miles of open water between Jefferson and St. Tammany parishes, the Lake Pontchartrain Causeway is the world's longest overwater highway bridge; other drives along area waterfronts and bayou country afford scenic views as well. The Louisiana Nature Center, the Michoud NASA facility, Fairgrounds and Jefferson Downs racetracks, the Pitot House Museum, and the Chalmette National Historical Park are among the many other points of interest in and around New Orleans.

## Arts and Culture

New Orleans enjoys an extensive cultural life. The New Orleans Cultural Center with its Municipal Auditorium and Theater of Performing Arts hosts ballets, operas, and concerts. Broadway productions are staged at the Saenger Performing Arts Center, while Le Petit Theatre du Vieux Carre offers community theater on two stages housed in historic architecture. University theaters, dinner theaters, the Contemporary Arts Center, and other area stages also mount various performing arts productions. With a repertoire that ranges from classical to popular music, the New Orleans Philharmonic performs in the Orpheum Theater. The New Orleans Opera Association, a resident company, features renowned guest soloists in its full productions, while concerts by chamber groups spotlight music for smaller groups. Various university and church organizations also offer musical performances in the New Orleans area, while at nightspots around the city listeners can find rhythm and blues, rock and roll, reggae, Cajun, and country music performed by national and local talent.

But music in New Orleans means just one thing to many residents and visitors: jazz. In the late nineteenth and early twentieth centuries African American musicians evolved a style of music that fused African American rhythms and improvisatory methods with European musical styles and the syncopated St. Louis-based piano music known as ragtime. This blend formed the basis for a musical idiom heard in Storyville—New Orleans's brothel district—as well as in parades and at parties, picnics, and funerals. Gradually the new style of musical expression, called jazz, began to take hold outside the city's African American community; the first jazz recording was made in 1917 by a white New Orleans group called the Original Dixieland Jazz Band. Many consider jazz to have come of age with the trumpet genius of Louis Armstrong, a New Orleans native whose music is familiar worldwide and whose statue graces New Orleans's Armstrong Park. Traditional straight-ahead jazz such as Armstrong played is the predominant style heard in present-day New Orleans nightclubs, on Bourbon Street in the French Quarter, and elsewhere across the birthplace of jazz.

The importance of jazz to New Orleans can be seen in the jazz exhibit at the Louisiana State Museum system's Old U.S. Mint facility, which also features a Mardi Gras Carnival exhibit. The state museum system, which maintains several facilities, also presents folk art and traveling exhibitions. The Confederate Museum, the oldest museum in New Orleans, preserves Civil War flags, uniforms, weapons, currency, and other mementos. Jackson Barracks houses a large number of military artifacts, Kenner Historical Museum features various Jefferson Parish items of interest, and Historic New Orleans Collection exhibits imaginative displays in the eighteenth-century home of the collection's founder.

At the Voodoo Museum in the French Quarter, occult displays and a Witchcraft Shop merge a part of old and modern New Orleans. Marie Laveau's grave in St. Louis Cemetery #1 is visited and meticulously maintained by legions of followers, who still place offerings there, including food or various symbols of Voodoo. One ritual that still lives on is the marking of her tomb with chalk in the shape of a cross or an X. The New Orleans Pharmacy Museum preserves antique remedies and apothecary equipment in an 1823 pharmacy building. The Louisiana Children's Museum presents hands-on exhibits, puppet workshops, and storytelling, and includes one of the few interactive math exhibits in a children's museum.

*ARTnews* magazine has noted that citizens of New Orleans are enthusiastic supporters of the arts. The prestigious New Orleans Museum of Art exhibits works ranging from Renaissance to avant-garde. The Contemporary Arts Center has three galleries and two theaters. It features art exhibits, as well as music, drama, and videotapes in its facility. The new Sydney and Walda Besthoff Sculpture Garden adjacent to the New Orleans Museum of Art in City Park features 42 extraordinary sculptures installed among 100-year-old oaks, mature pines, magnolias and camellias. The sculptures, valued in excess of $25 million, include works by world-renowned twentieth-century artists as Henry Moore, George Rickey, Jacques Lipchitz, and George Segal. The Besthoff Sculpture Garden is open to the public without charge. There are about 150 other art galleries in the city where local, national, and international artists show their work throughout the year.

Scenes of New Orleans history are on display at the Musee Conti Wax Museum. The Cabildo, site of the signing of the Louisiana Purchase, exhibits steamboat artifacts and paintings and Louisiana historical items, as well as Napoleon's death mask. House museums, such as the Gallier House in the French Quarter, carefully restored to its mid-nineteenth-century elegance, and the Pitot House in Bayou St. John, containing Federal period antiques, are available for touring.

### Festivals and Holidays

The Nokia Sugar Bowl on New Years' Day is the oldest annual sporting event in New Orleans; besides football, festivities include tennis, yachting, and other events. In spring the New Orleans Jazz and Heritage Festival is an extravaganza attracting thousands of musicians, craftsmen, and chefs to New Orleans for ten days of concerts, displays, and revelry featuring blues, gospel, ragtime, Cajun, swing, folk, and jazz performances. During the seven-day Spring Fiesta, plantations, courtyards, and private homes throughout New Orleans can be viewed on special tours. In July, the city hosts Carnaval Latino, the Gulf South's most elaborate Hispanic Festival. From April to October various food festivals in the New Orleans area highlight crawfish, catfish, crab, andouille sausage, strawberries, gumbo, and other delicacies. New Orleans Christmas is a series of special events spanning the month of December.

The most famous of all celebrations in New Orleans—and perhaps in the nation—is Mardi Gras. Rooted in the Roman Catholic liturgical calendar, Mardi Gras season begins on January 6, or Twelfth Night. Parades, private balls, and parties continue through Mardi Gras Day, the day before Ash Wednesday, which signifies the beginning of the six-week period of Lent that precedes Easter. Carnival celebrations culminate in rollicking street revelry, formal masked balls, and ritualistic torchlight parades featuring elaborate floats, dancing, lavish costumes, and merriment that infects visitors and residents alike.

### Sports for the Spectator

The Louisiana Superdome is home to the National Football League's New Orleans Saints football team; the annual Sugar Bowl football classic and Tulane University's football contests are also played there. The Zephyrs, a farm team of the Houston Astros, play minor-league baseball at Zephyr Field. The New Orleans Arena is home to the Arena Football League's New Orleans VooDoo and the National Basketball Association's New Orleans Hornets.

Consecutive racing schedules at Jefferson Downs and the Fairgrounds racetracks fill the equestrian calendar. Sports spectators can also see tennis tournaments and the Compaq Golf Classic of New Orleans, as well as the annual 10K (6.2 mile) Crescent City Classic road race. In nearby Slidell, the Bayou Liberty Pirogue Races test the skill of boaters skippering dugout canoes known as pirogues. The Ted Gormely Stadium in City Park, refurbished as a state-of-the-art sports facility, hosted the 1992 Olympic Track & Field Triad. The Grand Prix du Mardi Gras is a major league road race held in June in downtown's historic riverfront area. Riverboat gambling is available on the paddleboat vessels "America" and "Queen of New Orleans."

### Sports for the Participant

New Orleans's 1,500-acre City Park offers four golf courses, a two-tiered driving range, 48 tennis courts, rental canoes and paddleboats, and riding stables. Six other public parks also maintain public golf, tennis, and similar facilities.

Popular water sports such as wind surfing, sailing, and boating are possible year-round on New Orleans-area lakes and through the region's lush bayous and marshlands. The delta has always been a prime area for deep-water and freshwater fishing, crawfishing, crabbing, and shrimping, in addition to seasonal duck and deer hunting.

### Shopping and Dining

Canal Street has historically been a center in New Orleans for department stores and specialty shops, and the locale continues its tradition with such retail and office developments as One Canal Place and the nearby Riverwalk, which features not only shops but restaurants, cafes, bars, and magnificent views of the Mississippi River. At once-famous Jackson Brewery, now a marketplace, shops, entertainment, and Louisiana food specialties lure visitors. In the French Quarter, handicraft, antique, and candy stores draw buyers from around the country. Accessible via the St. Charles Street streetcar, Magazine Street's clusters of small shops begin in the Garden District and extend for more than three miles of antique shops and art galleries.

For more than 160 years the long, narrow French Market across from Jackson Square in the French Quarter has furnished area cooks with exotic spices, fresh produce, and cheeses at stalls encompassing coffee houses and craft shops as well. Shops retailing health food, books, brassware, perfume, and other specialty items are also popular among visiting and resident consumers.

New Orleans, dubbed the nation's culinary capital, considers cooking and dining to be art forms. Local chefs excel in variety while specializing in unique Cajun and Creole cuisines. Creole cooking, originally the region's urban gastronomic style, combines several elements: the French provincial talent for incorporating a wide variety of ingredients into its repertoire, the Spanish taste for zest, the Choctaw affinity for herbs and spices, the African understanding of slow cooking, the American Southern tradition, and subsequent ethnic infusions. Creole cuisine is perhaps best exemplified by its complex sauces with Mediterranean and Caribbean inflections. Cajun cuisine, on the other hand, originally the region's rural cooking style, is more robust and savory and is typified by such dishes as boudin, a smoky pork sausage; crawfish etouffe, a tomato-based stew of small lobster-like crustaceans served over rice; boiled crawfish liberally seasoned with cayenne pepper; or blackened redfish, a highly seasoned fillet of fish charred in a hot skillet.

Cajun and Creole elements are combined in the cuisine of present-day New Orleans, where diners at the more than 3,000 restaurants find numerous local specialties: jambalaya, a spicy blend of shrimp, ham, tomatoes, vegetables, and rice; andouille, a salty sausage; gumbo, from an African word meaning okra, now signifying a thick soup; red beans and rice, traditionally a washday recipe featuring kidney beans; dirty rice, pan-fried leftover rice cooked with giblets, spices, and onions; mirliton, a vegetable pear cooked like squash; plantains, large starchy bananas served as a side dish; seafood, from oysters Rockefeller and shrimp Creole to boiled crab and broiled pompano; and the po' boy, a fried sandwich on crusty French bread typically featuring oysters but possibly instead featuring roast beef, crab, or shrimp. Diners in New Orleans are likely to encounter eggplant, avocados, yams, and mangoes in the regional cuisine as well. Sweet offerings typical of the Crescent City include pecan pralines, bread or rice pudding with caramel or whiskey sauce, and beignets—square, fried doughnuts sprinkled with powdered sugar. Coffee in New Orleans is brewed strong and sometimes blended with roasted chicory root or chocolate, and it can be served as cafe au lait—half hot milk—or cafe brulot—mixed with spices, orange peel, and liqueurs and set aflame. Residents and visitors alike find dining in New Orleans to be an event in itself.

*Visitor Information:* The New Orleans Metropolitan Convention and Visitors Bureau, 2020 St. Charles Avenue, New Orleans, LA 70130; telephone (504)566-5011 or (800)672-6124

# Convention Facilities

A central location, spacious facilities, and famous off-hour activities make New Orleans an extremely popular choice for trade show and professional conferences. More than 21,000 hotel guest rooms are available downtown, and more than 37,000 are found in the metropolitan area. New Orleans is home to one of America's most popular meeting venues, the Morial Convention Center, located on the Mississippi River in the heart of the business district and within easy walking distance of the French Quarter, which offers 1.1 million square feet of contiguous exhibit space in 12 separate/combinable exhibit halls

The enormous Louisiana Superdome seats 77,000 people at one event, and offers 166,000 square feet of unobstructed convention floor space plus smaller meeting rooms. Situated in the northwest corner of the business district, the Superdome is close to government offices and hotels.

Located near the river amid major hotels and only steps from the French Quarter, the Rivergate is another name for the Port of New Orleans Exhibition Center, where 580,000 square feet of space and numerous conference rooms are available. On the north side of the French Quarter, the Municipal Auditorium is the city's fourth largest convention center, with 52,000 square feet of show space.

Additional exhibit space and meeting rooms for large gatherings can be found at the Pontchartrain Center, which recently added the Belle Grove Plantation Ballroom, and at the Fairmont, Hyatt Regency, and Hilton Riverside hotels. Smaller groups of 200 to 300 people, however, often seek out New Orleans's unique atmosphere for gatherings in such unusual settings as the Storyville Jazz Hall and the New Orleans Paddlewheels Creole Queen—at the International Cruise Terminal—or in Terrell House, a guest home lavishly furnished in Victorian antiques.

*Convention Information:* The New Orleans Metropolitan Convention and Visitors Bureau, 2020 St. Charles Avenue, New Orleans, LA 70130; telephone (504)566-5011 or (800)672-6124

# Transportation

## Approaching the City

The Louis Armstrong New Orleans International Airport, which is located west of the city in Kenner, provides full service on 20 carriers to every part of the United States with flights to and from South and Central America and Toronto and Mexico City. Private planes and corporate and charter flights often prefer to use Lakefront Airport, on the Lake Pontchartrain coast near the central business district. Interstate Highways I-59, I-55, and U.S. 61 approach New Orleans from the north, while I-10 and US 90 carry east-west drivers into the city. Auto ferries cross the Mississippi at various locations. Overnight Amtrak trains from and to Chicago, Washington, D.C., and western locales arrive at and depart from the Union Passenger Railroad Terminal. The Port of New Orleans facilitates the inclusion of New Orleans as a port of call for commercial pleasure cruises in the Gulf of Mexico.

### Traveling in the City

The New Orleans Transit Authority in New Orleans operates an extensive bus system connecting all areas of the city. In the downtown business district, a shuttle traverses a route that connects the city's three largest convention facilities with major hotels and with the French Quarter. Visitors often include a ride on the historic electric streetcar along the St. Charles Streetcar Line as a part of their New Orleans experience, while the Riverfront Streetcar Line transports visitors to cultural and shopping destinations in that district.

# Communications

### Newspapers and Magazines

*The Times-Picayune* is the city's leading newspaper. Other periodicals originating from New Orleans are the *Clarion Herald, Gambit* (covering local politics, dining and entertainment), *Offbeat,* a free monthly music magazine, *Naval Reservist News,* and *Louisiana Weekly* and *New Orleans Data News Weekly* (both covering the African American community). Trade and university papers, scholarly journals, and quarterly publications are also published in the ''Crescent City.''

### Television and Radio

Five television stations broadcast in New Orleans. Four are affiliated with the national networks, and one is a public television station. Talk shows, gospel music, news, religion, and contemporary music head the programming of the 19 AM and FM stations in the New Orleans area.

***Media Information:*** *New Orleans Time-Picayune,* 3800 Howard Ave., New Orleans, LA 70140; telephone (504)826-3300

### New Orleans Online

City of New Orleans Home Page. Available www.cityofno .com

The Greater New Orleans, Inc. Available www.norcc.org

Individual public school report cards. Available www.doe .state.la.us/DOE/asps/home.asp?I = REPORTC

Louisiana Bureau of Tourism and Travel. Available crt .g2digital.com

New Orleans Metropolitan Convention and Visitors Bureau. Available www.neworleanscvb.com

New Orleans Public Library. Available www.gnofn.org/ ~nopl

### Selected Bibliography

Kennedy, Richard S., ed., *Literary New Orleans: Essays & Meditations* (Baton Rouge, LA: Louisiana State University Press, 1992)

Rice, Anne, *The Feast of All Saints* (New York: Ballantine Books, 1992)

Sexton, Richard, *New Orleans: Elegance and Decadence* (San Francisco: Chronicle Books, 1993)

Young, Andrew, *An Easy Burden: The Civil Rights Movement and the Transformation of America* (New York: HarperCollins, 1996)

*Note: This profile of the city of New Orleans was updated prior to August 2005, when Hurricane Katrina caused severe damage to the Gulf Coast region of the United States. The long-term impact of Katrina on New Orleans is unknown at the time of publication.*

# MARYLAND

# The State in Brief

**Nickname:** Old Line State, Free State
**Motto:** *Fatti maschii, parole femine* (Manly deeds, womanly words)

**Flower:** Black-eyed susan
**Bird:** Baltimore oriole

**Area:** 12,407 square miles (2000; U.S. rank: 42nd)
**Elevation:** Ranges from sea level to 3,360 feet above sea level
**Climate:** Temperate, with mild winters and hot summers; cooler in mountains

**Admitted to Union:** April 28, 1788
**Capital:** Annapolis
**Head Official:** Governor Robert L. Ehrlich (R) (until 2007)

**Population**
    **1980:** 4,217,000
    **1990:** 4,781,468
    **2000:** 5,296,486
    **2004 estimate:** 5,558,058
    **Percent change, 1990–2000:** 10.8%
    **U.S. rank in 2004:** 19th
    **Percent of residents born in state:** 49.3% (2000)
    **Density:** 541.9 people per square mile (2000)
    **2002 FBI Crime Index Total:** 259,120

**Racial and Ethnic Characteristics** (2000)
    **White:** 3,391,308
    **Black or African American:** 1,477,411
    **American Indian and Alaska Native:** 15,423
    **Asian:** 210,929
    **Native Hawaiian and Pacific Islander:** 2,303
    **Hispanic or Latino (may be of any race):** 227,916
    **Other:** 95,525

**Age Characteristics** (2000)
    **Population under 5 years old:** 353,393
    **Population 5 to 19 years old:** 1,139,572
    **Percent of population 65 years and over:** 11.3%
    **Median age:** 36 years (2000)

**Vital Statistics**
    **Total number of births (2003):** 75,487
    **Total number of deaths (2003):** 44,629 (infant deaths, 645)
    **AIDS cases reported through 2003:** 12,911

**Economy**
    **Major industries:** Electrical equipment, food products, transportation equipment, metals, tourism
    **Unemployment rate:** 3.7% (December 2004)
    **Per capita income:** $37,424 (2003; U.S. rank: 5th)
    **Median household income:** $55,213 (3-year average, 2001-2003)
    **Percentage of persons below poverty level:** 7.7% (3-year average, 2001-2003)
    **Income tax rate:** Ranges from 2.0% to 4.75%
    **Sales tax rate:** 5.0% (food and prescription drugs are exempt)

# Annapolis

## *The City in Brief*

**Founded:** 1649 (chartered 1708)

**Head Official:** Mayor Ellen O. Moyer (D) (since 2001)

**City Population**
   **1980:** 31,740
   **1990:** 33,195
   **2000:** 35,876
   **2003 estimate:** 36,178
   **Percent change, 1990–2000:** 10.2%
   **U.S. rank in 2000:** 878th (State rank: 15th, in 2002)

**Metropolitan Area Population (CMSA)**
   **1990:** 6,727,050
   **2000:** 7,608,070
   **Percent change, 1990–2000:** 13.1%
   **U.S. rank in 1980:** 4th

**U.S. rank in 1990:** 4th
**U.S. rank in 2000:** 4th

**Area:** 7.2 square miles (2004)
**Elevation:** 92 feet above sea level
**Average Temperatures:** January, 35.5° F; July, 85.2° F
**Average Annual Precipitation:** 39.03 inches of rain; 14.4 inches of snow

**Major Economic Sectors:** Services, trade, government, technology
**Unemployment rate:** 3.7% (State of Maryland, December, 2004)
**Per Capita Income:** $27,180 (1999)

**2002 FBI Crime Index Total:** 2,330

**Major Colleges and Universities:** U.S. Naval Academy, Saint John's College, Anne Arundel Community College

**Daily Newspaper:** *The Capital*

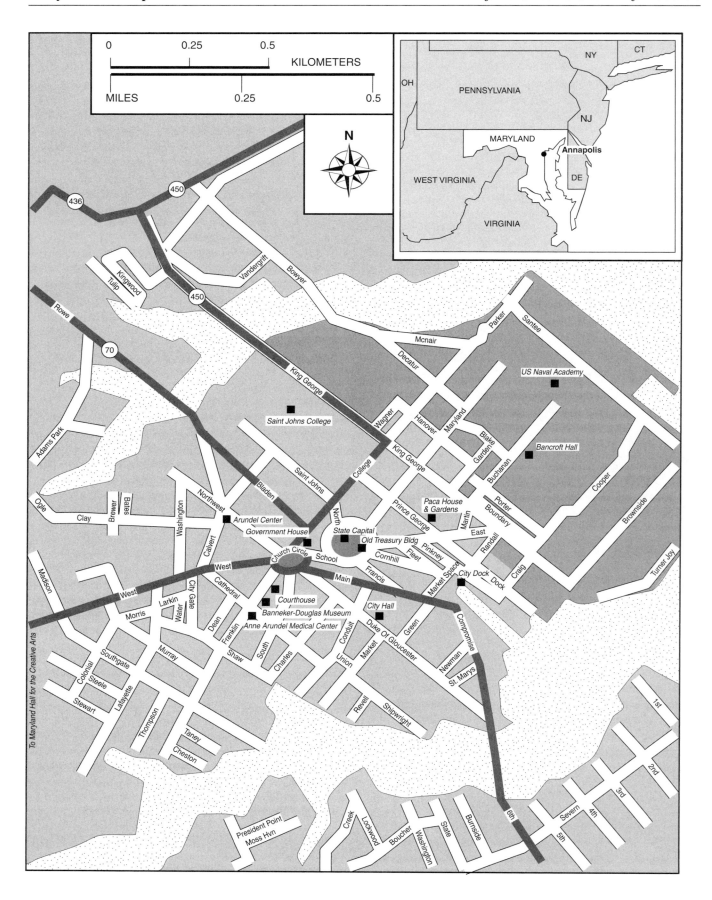

# Introduction

Annapolis is a cosmopolitan American city with a small-town atmosphere. For more than 350 years it has played an integral part in national affairs. The city has long been the site of the U.S. Naval Academy, and marine activities remain a vital part of community life. Despite being home to high-tech industries and modern businesses, the city has managed to maintain its seventeenth-century charm. Visitors can enjoy the more than three centuries of American architecture on display there.

# Geography and Climate

Annapolis is located in central Maryland on the south bank of the Severn River, near the mouth of the Chesapeake Bay. It is 27 miles south-southeast of Baltimore and 27 miles east of Washington, D.C. The lowest land in Annapolis is near sea level at the City Dock, and the level climbs to 92 feet between Bay Ridge Avenue and Forest Drive. Excluding the U.S. Naval Academy, the city has 17 miles of waterfront.

Annapolis has a temperate mid-latitude climate with warm, humid summers and mild winters. The weather during spring and autumn is generally pleasant. There are no pronounced wet and dry seasons, but summer often bring sudden heavy showers, damaging winds, and lightning. Breezes from the Chesapeake Bay and nearby creeks moderate the city's temperature. Regional rainfall averages slightly more than 39 inches annually, while snowfall averages below 15 inches per year.

**Area:** 7.2 square miles (2004))

**Elevation:** 92 feet above sea level

**Average Temperatures:** January, 35.5° F; July, 85.2° F

**Average Annual Precipitation:** 39.03 inches of rain; 14.4 inches of snow

# History

### Early settlement

Before white settlers arrived in Maryland, the Algonquin and other Native American tribes occupied the region. By the time Annapolis was settled in 1649, the Algonquins were gone from the area, forced out by raiding parties of the Susquehannock tribe.

The original white settlement of the area near Annapolis was at Greenbury Point, although the land is now mostly covered by the Severn River. In the middle of the seventeenth century, Puritans living in Virginia were threatened with severe punishments by the Anglican Royal Governor if they did not conform to the worship of the Anglican church. Then Cecil Calvert, the second Lord Baltimore, offered the Pilgrims generous land grants, freedom of worship, and trading privileges if they agreed to move to Maryland, which he wanted to have settled. In 1649 they started a community on a site at the mouth of the Severn River on the western shore of Chesapeake Bay.

The Puritans named their new settlement Providence. In 1650, Lord Baltimore, the overseer of the colony, granted a charter to the county that surrounded Providence. He named it Anne Arundel County after his beloved wife, Anne Arundel, who had died shortly before at the age of thirty-four. But the Puritans refused to sign an oath of allegiance to Lord Baltimore, in part because he was a Roman Catholic. In 1655 he sent the St. Mary's militia, headed by Governor William Stone, to force the Puritans into submission. A battle between the two groups took place on March 25, 1655. The Puritans won the conflict, which was the first battle between Englishmen on the North American continent. Eventually, Maryland became a royal colony. The capital was moved further north in 1694 to the site of present-day Annapolis. By that time, for reasons unknown, the Puritan settlement of Providence had all but disappeared.

### Development of Annapolis

Over time a small community began to develop on the peninsula that is the site of present-day Annapolis. It was known as Anne Arundel Town, taking its name from the county. The settlement grew and by the late 1600s the population of the province had reached nearly 25,000 residents. People started to object that the then-capital, St. Mary's, was too far away from where the majority of the people lived.

Royal Governor Francis Nicholson decided a more centrally located capital was needed and chose the site of what is now Annapolis. He named the new capital Annapolis in honor of Princess Anne, who became queen of England in 1702. It was Nicholson who determined that the city be built on a grand baroque street plan much like the great capitals of Europe. Streets were designed to radiate from a circle that was to contain the capitol. In a second circle was built an Anglican church. Residential areas were built for the prosperous families, for artisans, and for working men and their families. In 1696, Nicholson granted a charter to King William's School, which was built in Annapolis's center.

During the second half of the seventeenth century, the people of colonial Anne Arundel County had violent encounters with the Algonquins and other tribes along the shores of the Magothy River. The Indians staged raids there to try to protect their tribe and their lands from colonists, who often used devious methods to take advantage of them. Eventually the colonists won out.

## Annapolis Prospers

In time Annapolis became the political, social, cultural, and economic hub of Maryland. The city gained its charter in 1708. Annapolis and Anne Arundel County continued to grow into a major shipping port. By the last third of the 1700s, the only town in Maryland to rival Annapolis as a shipping center was Baltimore.

Those were prosperous times for some. With the help of the fertile soil and a slave economy, plantation owners and wealthier citizens were able to furnish their houses with luxury items from Europe. Young ladies and gentlemen wore elegant clothing and attended fancy balls at various large homes.

During the years shortly before the start of the Revolutionary War, and even during wartime, citizens of Annapolis enjoyed racing, dancing, and gambling. Luckily for Annapolitans, the Revolutionary War and the wars of the nineteenth century bypassed the area. During the war's later years, French volunteer Marquis de Lafayette helped enliven the city's social scene.

## Site of Annapolis Convention

From 1783 to August 1784, Annapolis served as the United State's first peacetime national capital. There in 1783 General George Washington resigned from the Continental Army. The next year, the Treaty of Paris ending the American Revolution was ratified there. In 1786 the city served as the seat of the Annapolis Convention, at which delegates from five states met to discuss proposed changes to the Articles of Confederation by which the country was then run.

During this period slavery played a large role in the economy. Alex Haley, the late author of the world-famous account of his family entitled *Roots*, was able to trace back the arrival of his ancestors, who had been kidnapped from Africa, to the Annapolis City Dock. Although Maryland was formally a slave state, many of its citizens opposed the institution. Archaeologists have found that there was a large, free African American population in the area before the Civil War.

## From Post-Revolution to Civil War Times

After the Revolutionary War, Baltimore forged ahead of Annapolis as a center of commerce. However, in 1808, Fort Severn was built on Windmill Point to prevent the British from attacking Annapolis during the War of 1812. (Soldiers

inhabited the fort until 1845. Then the post was transferred to the U.S. Navy, becoming the U.S. Naval Academy in 1850.)

As early as 1800 Annapolis had developed into a city of stately residences and public buildings patterned on those in London, England. Members of local high society enjoyed such diversions as fox hunts and racing meets. During the Civil War years most Annapolitans sympathized with the South but did not engage in acts of violence. At that time, facilities at the Naval Academy and St. John's College were used to house injured soldiers.

## Agriculture and Tourism

Until well into the nineteenth century, Anne Arundel County remained agrarian, with tobacco the main crop. Other important crops were wheat, corn, and fruit. Seafoods such as oysters and crab were also a mainstay of the local diet. The addition of steamboats to the local scene after the Civil War brought many visitors to the area, as vacationers fled to the shore to leave behind the heat of the larger cities. This prompted the growth of resorts, beaches, yacht clubs, and summer communities.

In the 1880s the railroad brought a period of development in the area. By 1890 the population of the city had reached 7,604 people. Crops were shipped to markets in Washington, D.C., Philadelphia, and beyond.

## The City in the Twentieth Century

During the twentieth century, the area continued to develop, due to such factors as the growth of the state government, the presence of U.S. Navy and Coast Guard facilities, the completion of a bridge to the Delmarva peninsula, and the development of Baltimore-Washington International Airport. The population grew from 7,657 people in 1900 to 10,047 people by 1950.

Today, Annapolis remains a thriving naval and government center. It has enjoyed the benefits of having its own developing local high-tech firms, while also serving as a commuter community for nearby Washington, D.C. and Baltimore.

***Historical Information:*** Maryland Historical Society, PO Box 385, 7101 Aviation Boulevard, Linthicum, MD 21090-0385; telephone (410)685-3750. Anne Arundel County Historical Society, telephone (410)768-9518; email director @MaHS.org

# *Population Profile*

**Metropolitan Area Population (CMSA)**
*1990:* 6,727,050

*2000:* 7,608,070
*Percent change, 1990–2000:* 13.1%
*U.S. rank in 1980:* 4th (CMSA)
*U.S. rank in 1990:* 4th (CMSA)
*U.S. rank in 2000:* 4th (CMSA)

**City Residents**
*1980:* 31,740
*1990:* 33,195
*2000:* 35,876
*2003 estimate:* 36,178
*Percent change, 1990–2000:* 10.2%
*U.S. rank in 2000:* 878th (State rank: 15th, in 2002)

*Density:* 5,326 people per square mile (in 2000)

*Racial and ethnic characteristics* (2000)
  White: 22,457
  Black or African American: 11,267
  American Indian and Alaska Native: 60
  Asian: 650
  Native Hawaiian and Pacific Islander: 11
  Hispanic or Latino (may be of any race): 2301
  Other: 796

*Percent of residents born in state:* 50.6% (2000)

*Age characteristics* (2000)
  Population under 5 years old: 2,385
  Population 5 to 9 years old: 2,160
  Population 10 to 14 years old: 2,005
  Population 15 to 19 years old: 2,102
  Population 20 to 24 years old: 2,455
  Population 25 to 34 years old: 6,352
  Population 35 to 44 years old: 5,620
  Population 45 to 54 years old: 5,137
  Population 55 to 59 years old: 1,907
  Population 60 to 64 years old: 1,439
  Population 65 to 74 years old: 2,241
  Population 75 to 84 years old: 1,564
  Population 85 years and over: 471
  Median age: 35.7 years

*Births* (Anne Arundel County, 2003)
  Total number: 6,913

*Deaths* (Anne Arundel County, 2003)
  Total number: 3,567 (of which, 56 were infants under the age of 1 year)

*Money income* (1999)
  Per capita income: $27,180
  Median household income: $49,243
  Total households: 15,231

*Number of households with income of . . .*
  less than $10,000: 1,405

$10,000 to $14,999: 652
$15,000 to $24,999: 1,716
$25,000 to $34,999: 1,636
$35,000 to $49,999: 2,330
$50,000 to $74,999: 3,051
$75,000 to $99,999: 1,937
$100,000 to $149,999: 1,508
$150,000 to 199,999: 518
$200,000 or more: 478

*Percent of families below poverty level:* 9.59% (41.6% of which were female householder families with related children under 5 years)

*2002 FBI Crime Index Total:* 2,330

# Municipal Government

Annapolis is the capital of Maryland and the seat of Anne Arundel County. The Annapolis city council includes eight aldermen, who serve four-year terms and the mayor, who presides at meetings. Each alderman represents one of eight wards, or geographical areas, of the city. The mayor serves full-time as the chief executive officer of the city and may serve two consecutive four-year terms. City services are provided by 10 departments staffed by some 550 full-time employees.

**Head Official:** Mayor Ellen O. Moyer (D) (since 2001; current term expires December 2005)

**Total Number of City Employees:** 550 (2005)

*City Information:* Mayor's Office, City of Annapolis, Annapolis City Hall, 160 Duke of Gloucester Street, Room 105, Annapolis, MD 21401; telephone (410)263-7997; email mayor@annapolis.gov

# Economy

## Major Industries and Commercial Activity

Annapolis has long had its economic base in federal, state, and local government, aided by its quick access to Washington, D.C. But in more recent years Annapolis is rapidly becoming a center for high-tech industrial development as well. The city's location in the high-tech corridor between Baltimore and Washington, D.C. helps attract and retain technology companies and services. New companies concentrate primarily in the areas of fiber optics, telecommunications, computer-related technologies, Internet-based services, regional data centers, medical equipment and supplies distribution, and environmental concerns.

The main industries in the city are the production of radar electronic equipment and underwater military devices, as well as research and development, and communications. Annapolis is a port of entry and a farm produce shipping center for nearby agricultural areas.

Anne Arundel County's largest employer, the National Security Agency, is a high-technology organization responsible for the collection and processing of foreign signals intelligence and for the communications and computer security of the U.S. government. The county's second largest employer, Fort George G. Meade, has been evolving from a troop training facility into a federal business park for military and civilian tenants.

Tourism is a thriving industry in Annapolis, with many tourists drawn by the city's authentic colonial character and the U.S. Naval Academy. Tourism brings more than $1.4 billion annually into Anne Arundel County, with more than 12,000 people employed in the industry.

*Items and goods produced:* radar and electronics equipment, undersea warfare equipment, seafood processing, small boats, concrete products, plastic, beverages

## Incentive Programs—New and Existing Companies

*Local programs*—The Anne Arundel Economic Development Corporation (AAEDC) provides loans of up to $300,000 to county-based or new companies seeking a county presence. Loans are made through the Arundel Business Loan Fund in the form of direct loans and Small Business Administration guaranteed loans.

*State programs*—The Maryland Industrial Development Financing Authority (MIDFA) provides financing assistance for capital assets and working capital to small and mid-sized businesses that demonstrate a significant economic impact. This assistance includes programs that insure loans made by financial institutions up to 80% and not exceeding $2.5 million; taxable bond financing; tax-exempt bond financing for 501(c)(3) non-profit organizations and manufacturing facilities; linked deposits that provide loans below market rates to qualified small businesses in rural areas with high unemployment rates; and trade financing for industrial or commercial businesses that are engaged in the export and import of goods through Maryland ports and airport facilities. Other programs are the Maryland Industrial Land Act, the Community Development Block Grant for Economic Development, and the Economic Development Opportunities Program Fund. The Maryland Small Business Development Financing Authority (MSBDFA) provides financing

for small businesses through a variety of programs, including a contract financing program, an equity participation investment program, a long-term guaranty program, and a surety bonding program.

Major incentive programs include Job Creation Tax Credits amounting to the lesser of $1,000 or 2.5 percent of annual wages for each qualifying permanent job, Employment Opportunity Tax Credit, Neighborhood Partnership Program Tax Credit, Research and Development Tax Credit, and Employer Commuter Tax Credit. Some areas of the state are also eligible for Enterprise Zone Tax Credits. The Clean Energy Incentive Act of 2000 also provides a number of tax incentives and exemptions for businesses that purchase products that use less energy and generate less pollution, including solar energy systems, hybrid electric vehicles, and biomass energy fuel sources.

*Job training programs*—The Office of Business and Industry Training at Anne Arundel Community College offers business training programs in computers, management and leadership, communication, and customer service. The University of Maryland provides training specialists to review, analyze, and recommend safety training programs.

The Maryland Industrial Training Program helps with training for new employees, and Partnership for Workforce Quality targets training grants to firms to improve business competitiveness and worker productivity. The Partnership for Workforce Quality (PWQ) offers skill training grants and support services designed to improve the competitive ability of small and mid-sized manufacturing and technology companies throughout the state. The Maryland Community Colleges' Business Training Network (MCCBTN) serves as a clearinghouse for workforce training at the 16 community colleges serving the state of Maryland. Other programs help employers who wish to establish apprenticeship programs and provide customized technology training.

## Development Projects

Major projects in Anne Arundel County underway in early 2005 include Annapolis Towne Centre at Parole, a 33-acre site featuring 650,000 feet of retail space, 90,000 square feet of office space, 900 residential units, and a full-service hotel; the 500,000 square foot Arundel Mills Corporate Park; the 1,622-acre Odenton Town Center; Park Place, an 11-acre development designed to offer 250,000 square feet of office space in two five-story office buildings, plus retail stores, a four-star hotel, a performing arts center, and a concierge condominium complex; and the 100,000 square foot National Business Office Park.

*Economic Development Information:* Annapolis Economic Development & Public Information Office, 160 Duke of Gloucester St., Annapolis, MD, 21401; telephone (410)263-

7940; email econdev@annapolis.gov. Anne Arundel Economic Development Corporation, 2660 Riva Road, Suite 200, Annapolis, MD 21401; telephone (410)222-7415; email info@aaedc.org

## Commercial Shipping

Freight carriage is provided by the Chessie System and the Consolidated Rail Corporation (CONRAIL). More than 100 motor freight common carriers serve Anne Arundel County. The international Port of Baltimore is nearby, providing a 42-foot shipping channel. To take advantage of the channel by bringing its products to the port, Anne Arundel County has invested in the local transportation infrastructure by upgrading and expanding its highway, commuter, and light rail system.

## Labor Force and Employment Outlook

Maryland's is among the best educated and highly skilled work forces in the nation. It is projected to grow 14 percent by 2008. More than 82 percent of the Annapolis work force has a high school diploma and 38.7 percent hold a college degree. Anne Arundel County has 223 businesses that employ 100 or more workers.

The following is a summary of annual data regarding the Annapolis/Baltimore metropolitan area labor force as of 2003.

*Size of nonagricultural labor force:* 1,246,400

*Number of workers employed in . . .*
  *construction and mining:* 73,700
  *manufacturing:* 80,200
  *trade, transportation, and utilities:* 237,000
  *information:* 20,600
  *financial activities:* 81,800
  *professional and business services:* 172,000
  *educational and health services:* 199,500
  *leisure and hospitality:* 107,100
  *other services:* 55,700
  *government:* 218,900

*Average hourly earnings of production workers employed in manufacturing:* $15.75 (state of Maryland, 2003 average)

*Unemployment rate:* 3.7% (December 2004, state of Maryland)

| *Largest employers*<br>*(Anne Arundel County)* | *Number of employees* |
|---|---|
| National Security Agency | 16,000 |
| Ft. Meade | 14,150 |
| A.A. County Public Schools | 10,500 |
| State of Maryland | 9,396 |
| Northrup Grumman ES3/Oceanic | 7,500 |

| *Largest employers*<br>*(Anne Arundel County)* | *Number of employees* |
|---|---|
| Anne Arundel County | 3,800 |
| Anne Arundel Health System, Inc. | 2,432 |
| Southwest Airlines | 2,425 |
| U.S. Naval Academy | 2,052 |
| Computer Sciences Corporation | 1,829 |

## Cost of Living

In 2004 the average cost of a home in Annapolis was $335,746. The following is a summary of data regarding several key cost of living factors for the Annapolis area.

*2004 (3rd Quarter) ACCRA Average House Price:* Not reported

*2004 (3rd Quarter) ACCRA Cost of Living Index:* Not reported

*State income tax rate:* 2–4.75% (corporate business tax rate, 7%)

*State sales tax rate:* 5%

*Local income tax rate:* None

*Local sales tax rate:* None

*Property tax rate:* $6.93 per $100 of assessed value (2005)

***Economic Information:*** Annapolis and Anne Arundel County Chamber of Commerce, 49 Old Solomon's Island Road, Suite 204, Annapolis, MD 21401; telephone (410)266-3960; fax (410)266-8270; email info@aaaccc.org

# Education and Research

## Elementary and Secondary Schools

Annapolis students attend the Anne Arundel County Public Schools, ranked in 2005 as the 41st largest school system in the United States and the 5th largest school system in Maryland. In addition to basic academic subjects, the school system offers classes in computer education, music, art, health, physical education, foreign languages, library media, and technology. It also boasts a special gifted and talented program.

The following is a summary of data regarding the Annapolis public school system as of the 2004–2005 school year.

*Total enrollment:* 75,000

*Number of facilities*
  *elementary schools:* 77
  *middle schools/combined:* 19

*senior high schools:* 12
*other:* 12

*Student/teacher ratio:* 16.6:1

*Teacher salaries*
   *minimum:* $34,691
   *maximum:* $73,525

*Funding per pupil:* $7,793 (2002-03)

The city is also served by two private schools and one parochial school.

***Public Schools Information:*** Anne Arundel County Public Schools, 2644 Riva Rd., Annapolis, MD 21401; telephone (410)222-5000

## Colleges and Universities

Annapolis is home to St. John's College, the third oldest college in the nation. The co-educational, four-year liberal arts institution, with a 1:8 faculty-student ratio, has an enrollment of about 1,000, and offers bachelor and master of arts degrees. It has a second campus in Santa Fe, New Mexico. Rather than employing typical college classes and lectures, St. John's instructors teach primarily by way of seminars, tutorials, and laboratories. St. John's students follow a curriculum that is based on in-depth reading of the major works of European thought.

Annapolis is also served by the University of Maryland's University College, which provides undergraduate and graduate courses at its Annapolis Center. In addition, Anne Arundel Community College, a public two-year college, enrolls more than 14,400 students at its two campuses near Annapolis.

The United States Naval Academy in downtown Annapolis, founded in 1845, provides undergraduate education for the members of the U.S. Navy. On its more than 338-acre campus, the institution enrolls more than 4,000 students from every state and several foreign countries. The academy offers a core curriculum of required courses as well as a choice of 18 major fields of study. The Brigade of Midshipmen, as the student body is known, undergoes a rigorous academic program and intense physical training to prepare them for being commissioned as ensigns in the Navy or second lieutenants in the Marine Corps.

## Libraries and Research Centers

The Anne Arundel County Public Library, founded in 1921, has its headquarters in Annapolis. Its 15 countywide library branches contain more than one million items, and the staff responds to more than 300,000 inquiries annually. In addition to popular materials and information services, the library provides storytime programs, special business and health collections, a bookmobile, and services for disabled persons and adult new readers. Public Internet access is available at all branches.

The U.S. Naval Academy's Nimitz Library houses more than 413,000 books in its general collections and some 27,000 books in special collections that focus on naval history, naval and military science, and science and technology. The U.S. Navy Library, with 12,000 volumes, focuses on energy research and materials and environmental control.

Other libraries in the city include the Maryland State Archives Library, the Maryland State Law Library, the Maryland Department of Legislative Services Library, St. John's College Library, the Anne Arundel Medical Center Library, the Environmental Protection Agency Office of Analytical Services Library, and *The Capital* Newspaper Library.

A number of research institutes make their home in Annapolis. The Historic Annapolis Foundation Research Center has special subject interests in architecture, city planning, urban design, and local and state history. The ITT Research Institute Technical Information Services concentrates on communications and electronics equipment areas. The Center for Public Justice offers public policy research from a Christian perspective, while the Environmental Research Foundation examines toxic, hazardous, and solid waste problems.

***Public Library Information:*** Anne Arundel County Public Library, 5 Harry S Truman Pkwy., Annapolis, MD 21401; telephone (410)222-7371

# Health Care

Annapolis is served by the city's Anne Arundel Medical Center, which treats patients at its location at the Carl A. Brunetto Medical Park. The Medical Center, which provides 303 beds, served more than 22,100 patients in the year ending June 30, 2004. The Clatanoff Pavilion offers a variety of women's health care services, including obstetrics and gynecology services, maternity suites, and a critical care nursery; more than 4,600 babies are delivered there each year. The Donner Pavilion houses the DeCesaris Cancer Institute, a state-of-the-art cancer treatment center. Patients needing same-day surgery are treated at the Edwards Surgical Pavilion, where more than 600 surgeries are performed every month. The Sajak Pavilion includes the hospital's Breast Center, focusing on the needs of breast cancer patients, as well as other medical and administrative offices such as Anne Arundel Diagnostics, the Diabetes Center, and the AAMC Foundation. The Medical Park also makes available critical care treatment, outpatient surgery, and health education.

**The U.S. Naval Academy, established in 1845, is an undergraduate college that prepares men and women for careers as officers in the U.S. Navy and Marine Corps.**

*Health Care Information:* Anne Arundel Medical Center, 2001 Medical Parkway, Annapolis, MD 21404; telephone (443)481-4700; email aamcpr@aahs.org

# Recreation

## Sightseeing

Charming Annapolis boasts more surviving colonial buildings than any city in the country, and the entire downtown is a registered National Historic Landmark. More than 60 eighteenth-century structures survive in the Annapolis downtown area. Annapolis is a great city to tour on foot with its unusual street layout in the center city—there are two major circles with streets spoking around them. Sightseers can observe an attractive mix of Colonial, Federal, and Victorian architecture, especially in the National Historic Landmark District. Visitors can also observe the comings and going of yachts at the waterfront.

The focal point of sightseeing in Annapolis is the Maryland State House with its unique narrow dome, which is topped by an unusual tower and observation deck. Built in 1779, it is the oldest capital building in the United States that has been in continuous use. The old Senate Chamber was the site of the meetings of the Continental Congress during 1783–84 and also functioned as the U.S. capitol. It was here that George Washington resigned his position as commander-in-chief of the Continental Army in 1784. Just a few weeks later, the building was the site of the signing of the Treaty of Paris that ended the Revolutionary War. Tours of the building are offered daily.

From the State House visitors can see the colorful streets featuring houses and shops from different periods and in various styles as they wander down to the riverfront and Market Square, a popular tourist spot. City Dock is the only remaining pre- Revolutionary seaport in the country.

Annapolis provides tours of a number of interesting private residences. The Banneker-Douglass Museum, set in the first African Methodist Episcopal Church of Annapolis, dates from 1803. It houses the Douglass Museum of African American Life and History. The Charles Carroll House, with its terraced gardens, is also open for visitors. It was the home of the only Roman Catholic to sign the Declaration of Independence.

Tours of the Chase-Lloyd House, with its large and magnificent facade, allow visitors to view its prized interior woodwork, furniture from three centuries, and a dramatic arched triple window. The brick Hammond-Harwood House, the Georgian masterpiece work of famed architect William

Buckland, contains unique wood- carved trim and an authentic period garden. The William Paca House and Garden was the home of a three-term Maryland Governor and signer of the Declaration of Independence. The Georgian mansion, built in the 1760s, has a carved entrance and formal rooms and stands as another fine example of William Buckland's design skills. Another residence, called The Barracks, is a typical dwelling of a colonial tradesman and is furnished to depict the life of a Revolutionary War soldier.

Tours are available of the magnificent grounds of the U.S. Naval Academy, often referred to as "the Yard," where highlights of the history of the American Navy are represented by statues, artifacts, paintings, and ships. Memorial Hall honors Academy graduates who were killed in action. The Lejeune Physical Education Center contains the Athletic Hall of Fame. Among other highlights of a visit to the academy grounds are the U.S. Naval Academy Museum, the crypt of naval hero John Paul Jones, and the 600-year-old Liberty Tree, the site where in 1652 the early settlers made peace with the local Susquehannock Indians.

## Arts and Culture

Annapolis is home to excellent museums and performing arts groups. The Maryland Federation of Art Gallery on the Circle provides juried exhibitions by regional artists. The Mitchell Art Gallery at St. John's College features art shows, gallery talks, and tours.

Local residents and visitors enjoy performances by the Annapolis Chorale, a 150-member chorus; the Annapolis Opera, which presents one full opera each year plus special events such as vocal competitions and children's operas; the Annapolis Symphony Orchestra, which features a family series, a classic series, and a pops series, plus an annual gala event, the Black and White Ball; and the Annapolis Brass Quintet. The Ballet Theatre of Maryland, the state's largest professional ballet company, offers a mix of classical and modern ballet. Patrons can take a variety of classes from pottery to puppetry at the Maryland Hall for Creative Arts. Other local arts groups include the Annapolis Summer Garden Theatre, featuring Broadway and Shakespearean productions; the Chesapeake Music Hall, a dinner theater; the Colonial Players of Annapolis theater group; the Talent Machine Company, a children's theater group; and Them Eastport Oyster Boys, who provide a comical musical history of the area.

## Festivals and Holidays

September brings The Anne Arundel County Fair and the Maryland Seafood Festival, both of which provide many opportunities for food and fun. October's highlights are the U.S. Sailboat Show and Powerboat Show and the Scottish Highland Games, which feature piping, fiddling, and physical fitness competitions. Candlelight tours through historic homes and public buildings and the Lights on the Bay holiday displays herald the arrival of the holiday season. December features include the Lights Parade of decorated sailboats and First Night Annapolis, a New Year's Eve celebration of jugglers, dancers, and choirs. January is enlivened by the Annapolis Heritage Antique Show. The City Dock is the site of April's Spring Boat Show, while May offers the Waterfront Arts Festival and the Children's Fair.

Summer activities include June's Annapolis JazzFest and the Star-Spangled Celebration and Fourth of July fireworks. August's Kunta Kinte Heritage Festival at St. John's College commemorates the landing of the ancestors of Alex Haley, the author of *Roots,* the book and television series that tell the story of Haley's family who were slaves in America. Also in August, the Annapolis Rotary Club Crab Feast is the world's largest event of its kind. The Maryland Renaissance Festival takes place in an English village setting with ten stages and a jousting arena and continues through October.

### Sports for the Spectator

Annapolis calls itself the Sailing Capital of the World. Sailboat racing is a popular sport and enthusiastic fans can watch water events such as regattas, boat festivals, and races. The Chesapeake Bay Yacht Racing Association provides information on the racing scene. March brings the Marlborough Hunt Races in which horses race around a three-mile track. Sports fans also enjoy athletic events at the U.S. Naval Academy including football, basketball, and lacrosse contests as well as women's basketball.

### Sports for the Participant

Annapolis provides endless opportunities for yachting and water sports. The Annapolis Department of Recreation and Parks maintains more than 15 neighborhood parks on 96 acres, including street-end or "pocket" parks; they have basketball courts, ball fields, tennis courts, playgrounds, and boating facilities. The department offers a variety of programs including athletic tournaments, arts and crafts, and fun runs. Truxton park offers outdoor activities on 70 acres, including 12 tennis courts, 5 basketball courts, 3 outdoor playing fields, and 1 multi-purpose facility. The public may also use recreational facilities at public schools in Anne Arundel County for sports and leisure activities. The Arundel Olympic Swim Center has a 50-meter pool, wading pool, poolside spa, and diving boards. Residents can also enjoy the county's parks, sports leagues, fitness and self-defense classes, and other activities.

### Shopping and Dining

The city is served by Annapolis Mall, also known as Westfield Shoppingtown, which features more than 175 specialty stores and restaurants, including Nordstrom, JC Penney, Lord and Taylor, and Hecht's. Other malls include the Annapolis Harbour Shopping Center, boasting more than 290,000 square feet of retail space, and Harbor Square Mall. The city's downtown has a variety of exclusive gift and specialty shops, galleries, antique shops, and jewelry stores. The city is also served by the Colonial Parole, Eastport, and Forest Plaza shopping areas.

Annapolis has a fine array of restaurants. Although many of them specialize in seafood, there are also Mexican, French, Mediterranean, Chinese, Italian, Irish, and Japanese dining spots to enjoy. The Treaty of Paris Restaurant offers fine dining in a lovely eighteenth-century dining room. The 49 West Cafe is a European-style café providing light gourmet fare in a relaxed atmosphere filled with art, music, books, and newspapers.

***Visitor Information:*** Annapolis & Anne Arundel County Conference & Visitors Bureau, 26 West St., Annapolis, MD 21401; telephone (410)280-0445; email info@visit-annapolis.org

# Convention Facilities

The Historic Inns of Annapolis's Governor Calvert Center provides meeting rooms for groups from 10 to 250 people. Governor's Hall can handle a banquet for 210 people or a reception for 300 people, as well as offering theater-style seating for 250 people. The Loews Annapolis Hotel offers more than 17,000 square feet of flexible meeting space and can accommodate groups of up to 450 people. The Annapolis Marriott Waterfront Hotel offers eight meeting rooms. The Chesapeake Ballroom has 3,850 square feet of space and can accommodate 600 people for a reception and 400 people theater-style. The Wyndham Garden Hotel has eleven meeting rooms with a total of 12,108 square feet of meeting space. It can accommodate receptions for up to 800 people, and banquets of up to 400 people.

***Convention Information:*** Annapolis & Anne Arundel County Conference & Visitors Bureau, 26 West St., Annapolis, MD 21401; telephone (410)280-0445; email info @visit-annapolis.org

# Transportation

### Approaching the City

Major highways to Annapolis include U.S. 50/301 (I-595) and Maryland Route 2/170/450. U.S. 50/301 passes on the city's west side and continues eastward over the Bay Bridge. Coming from the north, I-97 exits onto Route 50/301 just west of the city. Coming from the South, Maryland Route 2 enters the city in the Parole area, and U.S. Route 301 comes northward and joins U.S. Route 50 west of the city.

The closest major airport to Annapolis is Baltimore-Washington International, about 20 miles northwest of downtown, which has 18 scheduled carriers. Air travelers can proceed from the airport to Annapolis via Light Rail, passenger trains, limo, van, or taxi service.

The Maryland Mass Transit Administration (MTA) operates several bus routes and light rail to Washington and nearby suburbs. Carolina Trailways operates limited bus service through nearby Baltimore and Glen Burnie, and Greyhound also provides bus service. Amtrak offers rail service to Baltimore's Penn Station, and Union Station in Washington, D.C.

### Traveling in the City

Annapolis's main east-west thoroughfare is West Street, also known as Route 50. Radiating northwest and southeast from downtown's Church Circle is Duke of Gloucester Street. College Avenue runs northeast from the circle.

Annapolis Transit has five bus routes that serve more than 180 stops throughout the city and the Eastern Shore area, including stops at Annapolis Mall, Anne Arundel Medical Center, and many area hotels. There are also commuter shuttles from downtown to nearby Kent Island and to the Navy-Marine Corps Memorial Stadium. Gasoline-powered trolleys run within the central business district. Several taxi and limousine companies also serve the city. Local waterways are served by the Jiffy Water Taxi, which can be picked up at the waterfront. Bicycles are a welcomed form of transportation in Annapolis. The city offers several designated bike routes that use a combination of grade-separated trails and city streets. Most city buses have bike racks. Helmet use is encouraged for bicycle riders in the city, and visitors to the U.S. Naval Academy are required to wear helmets there.

# *Communications*

### Newspapers and Magazines

*The Capital* is Annapolis's daily paper. *Publick Enterprise* is the local twice-monthly community newspaper, and the

*Maryland Farmer* is an area agricultural newspaper. The city's local magazine is called *Inside Annapolis*.

Other locally published magazines include *Chesapeake Bay Magazine,* a boating publication; *Chesapeake Family,* a consumer parenting magazine; the *Maryland Register,* which focuses on public administration and law; *Municipal Maryland,* a publication of the Maryland Municipal League aimed at elected and appointed Maryland city officials; the Naval Institute's *Proceedings,* a magazine on naval and maritime news; and alumni magazines of the local colleges.

### Television and Radio

The city is served by seven commercial television stations and one public station from metropolitan Washington, D.C. and Baltimore. Annapolis area radio stations include FM stations WHFS, an alternative/modern rock station and WFSI, a religious station, and AM stations WNAV, an adult contemporary station and WBIS, a business news station. The U.S. Naval Academy broadcasts on station WRNV, while Anne Arundel Community College is served by station WACC.

***Media Information:*** *Capital Gazette Newspapers*, 2000 Capital Drive, Annapolis, MD 21401; telephone (410)268-5000

### Annapolis Online

Annapolis and Anne Arundel County Chamber of Commerce. Available www.annapolischamber.com

Annapolis and Anne Arundel County Conference & Visitors Bureau. Available www.visitannapolis.org

Anne Arundel County Public Library. Available www.aacpl.lib.md.us

Anne Arundel Economic Development Corporation. Available www.aaedc.org

Anne Arundel Medical Center. Available www.aa-healthsystem.org

*The Capital* newspaper. Available www.capitalonline.com

City of Annapolis. Available www.ci.annapolis.md.us

### Selected Bibliography

Martin, William, *Annapolis* (New York, NY: Warner Books, 1997)

Risjord, Norman K., *Builders of Annapolis: Character and Enterprise in a Colonial Capital* (Baltimore: Maryland Historical Society, 1997)

# Baltimore

## *The City in Brief*

**Founded:** 1696 (incorporated 1797)

**Head Official:** Mayor Martin O'Malley (D) (since 1999)

**City Population**
1980: 786,741
1990: 736,014
2000: 651,154
2003 estimate: 628,670
Percent change, 1990–2000: −11.5%
U.S. rank in 1980: 10th (MSA)
U.S. rank in 1990: 12th (MSA)
U.S. rank in 2000: 23rd (State rank: 1st)

**Metropolitan Area Population (CMSA)**
1990: 6,727,050
2000: 7,608,070
Percent change, 1990–2000: 13.1%

U.S. rank in 1980: 15th
U.S. rank in 1990: 18th
U.S. rank in 2000: 4th

**Area:** 80.8 square miles (2000)
**Elevation:** 148 feet above sea level
**Average Annual Temperature:** 55.1° F
**Average Annual Precipitation:** 41.94 inches (22.7 inches of snow)

**Major Economic Sectors:** services, government, wholesale and retail trade
**Unemployment rate:** 4.2% (December 2004)
**Per Capita Income:** $16,978 (1999)

**2002 FBI Crime Index Total:** 55,820

**Major Colleges and Universities:** Johns Hopkins University, Towson State University, University of Baltimore, University of Maryland, Baltimore County Morgan State University Loyola College

**Daily Newspaper:** *The Baltimore Sun*

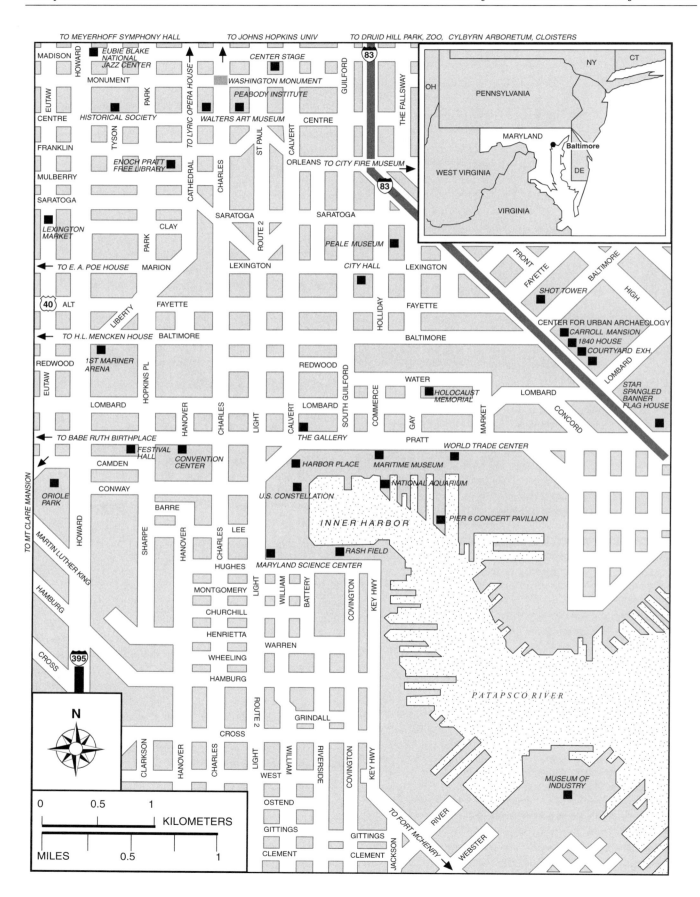

# Introduction

Baltimore's fortuitous location on the northern Chesapeake Bay has been at the heart of its social and economic development. Farther inland than other eastern seaport, the city is convenient to landlocked areas. Water-related industry quickly developed around Baltimore harbor, and when tracks for the nation's first railroad were laid there in 1829, the thriving port city increased both its accessibility to other cities and its attractiveness to immigrants and investors.

Through careful city planning and cooperation between public and private investors, Baltimore has entered the ranks of America's "comeback cities" in recent years. Its downtown business district has been transformed into a mecca of sparkling new hotels, retail centers, and office buildings. But Baltimore has not wholly exchanged its traditional working-class image for high-technology polish. Many of its urban renewal programs focus on the preservation or renovation of historical buildings and neighborhoods amidst new construction. For example, its wildly popular Oriole Park at Camden Yards offers state-of-the-art amenities in a turn-of-the-century style baseball stadium. Nicknamed the "charmed city," Baltimore has become a top tourist destination.

# Geography and Climate

Located on the Mid-Atlantic coast, Baltimore was built at the mouth of the Patapsco River, which empties directly into the Chesapeake Bay. The city is protected from harsh weather variations year-round by the Chesapeake Bay and Atlantic Ocean to the east and the Appalachian Mountains due west. Freezing temperatures generally do not occur after mid-April or before the end of October, allowing the area approximately 194 frost-free days. Precipitation, averaging 41 inches annually, tends to be equally distributed throughout the year, but the greatest amounts accrue during summer and early fall—the thunderstorm and hurricane seasons, respectively. Since snow is often mixed with rain and sleet due to Baltimore's relatively mild winter temperatures, freezing rain is considered a greater hazard to motorists and pedestrians than the infrequent snowfall that remains on the ground more than several days.

**Area:** 80.8 square miles (2000)

**Elevation:** 148 feet above sea level

**Average Temperatures:** January, 31.8° F; July, 77° F; annual average, 55.1° F

**Average Annual Precipitation:** 41.94 inches (22.7 inches of snow)

# History

### City Founded on Tobacco-Centered Economy

The geology at the mouth of the Patapsco River determined the location of Baltimore. The area lies on a fall line where hard rocks of the piedmont meet the coastal plains of the tidewater region. A large, natural harbor had formed, and streams coursing from the north and west toward the Patapsco fall line had tremendous velocity. This made them ideal sites for water-driven mills. Additionally attractive to early settlers were the plentiful forests, fertile countryside, and moderate climate that was ideal for agriculture.

In 1632, England's King Charles I gave George Calvert (Lord Baltimore) a vast area in colonial America that became Baltimore County in 1659. During the 1660s the Maryland General Assembly appointed commissioners who granted land patents and development privileges to enterprising colonists. Although the Piscataway and Susquehannock tribes originally lived in neighboring regions, tribal competition and the onslaught of colonial diseases dissipated all but a few hundred of the Native Americans in Maryland by 1700.

The sandy plains bordering the Chesapeake Bay were ideal for growing tobacco, and a tobacco-based economy quickly developed in pre-Revolutionary Maryland. An area of 550 acres, formerly known as "Cole's Harbor," was sold to Baltimore landowners Daniel and Charles Carroll in 1696; they sold a parcel of this land in one-acre lots for development. These lots became Baltimore Town, which grew quickly in both size and trade. By 1742 regular tobacco shipments were leaving Baltimore harbor for Europe.

### Radical Politics Gain Popularity

Productive mills had also sprung up along the northwestern tributaries of the Patapsco; the market for locally-milled flour and grain was primarily directed toward the British slave and sugar colonies in the West Indies. This trade was cut off at the outset of the American Revolution, a loss that cost Baltimore. The loss was partly mitigated when Congress authorized private citizens to arm and equip their own vessels for war in 1776; privateering became a growth industry in Baltimore, since the city had become an important center for shipbuilding. Anti-British activities in the city during this era earned Baltimore a reputation for radical politicking that lasted through the nineteenth century. Baltimore was the meeting place of the Continental Congress after the British occupied Philadelphia in 1777.

## City Prospers During Reconstruction

After the Revolutionary War, Baltimore, incorporated in 1797, resumed its commercial success by exporting grain, particularly to South America. A slump in maritime trade prompted the building of America's first public railroad in Baltimore in 1828, thus linking the city to other parts of the country and expanding commercial possibilities. During the Civil War, Maryland remained Unionist but Baltimore was split. Trade was cut off with the South and badly hurt with the North, but Baltimore managed to profit as a military depot. The city recovered rapidly from the physical and economic damages of the war, embarking during the reconstruction era on the period of its greatest prosperity.

## Renewal Follows Destruction

In 1904 Baltimore was struck by a fire that had started in a cotton warehouse and soon spread to destroy more than 2,000 buildings. This calamity initiated improvements in the streets and the harbor and the construction of a sewer system that was considered one of the most modern of its time. The city again prospered during World War I, its economy remained relatively untouched by the 1930s Depression, and Baltimore continued to flourish as a military supply center during World War II.

Baltimore's urban renewal began in 1947, when inner city decay was so extensive that more than 45,000 homes were considered substandard. A rigorous construction and rehabilitation program reduced this number to 25,000 by 1954. In 1955 public and private cooperation resulted in the formation of the Greater Baltimore Committee, a group of influential businessmen who worked with municipal agencies to develop civic programs. Extensive neighborhood revitalization and development were undertaken in the 1970s and 1980s. Projects included the construction of shops and restaurants in Harbor Place, the Maryland Science Center, the National Aquarium, the American Visionary Art Museum and the construction of a rapid transit line to the suburbs. Waterfront development carried in the 1990s and into the new millennium, with many old neighborhoods experiencing a growth in popularity. Development continues along with historical preservation and the careful blending of the past and the present. More than $1 billion in new development is in the works, including hotels, retail space, increased arts offerings and technology improvements to Baltimore's harbor.

The 1990s were also a time of sharp population declines. Like many of the older, urban areas of the northeast, Baltimore faced an exodus to the suburbs and lost 11.5 percent of its population. Today, Baltimore is beginning to buck the trend. From 2000 to 2003, it lost only 3.2 percent.

In 1999, white city councilman Martin O'Malley won the Baltimore Democratic mayoral primary, defeating 16 candidates, 8 of whom were African American, in this predominantly African American city. Mr. O'Malley went on to win the mayoral election after a campaign in which he promised to clean the streets of open-air drug markets and have zero tolerance for crime. By 2004, Baltimore led the nation's 25 largest cities in a five-year reduction in violent crime, with the city experiencing a drop of 40 percent in violent crimes from 1999 to 2004.

*Historical Information:* City Life Museums, 33 South Front Street, Baltimore, MD 21202; telephone (410)545-3000 or (410)396-3279; (open to the public with permission and payment of a fee). Maryland Historical Society, 201 W. Monument Street, Baltimore, MD 21201-4674; telephone (410)685-3750. Jewish Historical Society of Maryland, 15 Lloyd Street, telephone (410)732-6400

# Population Profile

## Metropolitan Area Residents (CMSA)
*1990:* 6,727,050
*2000:* 7,608,070
*Percent change, 1990–2000:* 13.1%
*U.S. rank in 1980:* 4th
*U.S. rank in 1990:* 4th
*U.S. rank in 2000:* 4th

## City Residents
*1980:* 786,741
*1990:* 736,014
*2000:* 651,154
*2003 estimate:* 628,670
*Percent change, 1990–2000:* −11.5%
*U.S. rank in 1980:* 10th (MSA)
*U.S. rank in 1990:* 12th
*U.S. rank in 2000:* 23rd (State rank: 1st)

*Density:* 7,986 people per square mile (2000)

*Racial and ethnic characteristics* (2000)
    White: 205,982
    Black or African American: 418,951
    American Indian and Alaska Native: 2,097
    Asian: 9,985
    Native Hawaiian and other Pacific Islander: 222
    Hispanic or Latino (of any race): 11,061
    Other: 4,363

*Percent of residents born in state:* 71.2% (2000)

*Age characteristics* (2000)

Population under 5 years old: 41,694
Population 5 to 9 years old: 46,968
Population 10 to 14 years old: 46,835
Population 15 to 19 years old: 47,710
Population 20 to 24 years old: 49,287
Population 25 to 34 years old: 93,248
Population 35 to 44 years old: 101,544
Population 45 to 54 years old: 83,408
Population 55 to 59 years old: 29,499
Population 60 to 64 years old: 35,040
Population 65 to 74 years old: 44,716
Population 85 years and older: 9,956
Median age: 35 years

*Births in Baltimore County* (2001)
Total number: 9,056

*Deaths in Baltimore County* (2001)
Total number: 7,663

*Money income* (1999)
Per capita income: $21,240
Median household income: $32,400
Total households: 257,788

*Number of households with income of . . .*
less than $10,000: 48,249
$10,000 to $14,999: 21,649
$15,000 to $24,999: 40,516
$25,000 to $34,999: 35,520
$35,000 to $49,999: 39,873
$50,000 to $74,999: 38,724
$75,000 to $99,999: 16,903
$100,000 to $149,999: 10,053
$150,000 to $199,999: 2,689
$200,000 or more: 3,612

*Percent of families below poverty level:* 18.8% (of which, 48.5% were female householder families with related children under 5 years)

*2002 FBI Crime Index Total:* 55,820

# Municipal Government

Baltimore is the only city in the state of Maryland not located within a county. It is governed by a mayor and a sixteen-member city council who are elected to four-year terms.

**Head Official:** Mayor Martin O'Malley (D) (since 1999, current term expires 2007)

**Total Number of City Employees:** 15,099 (2005)

*City Information:* City Hall, 100 N. Holliday St., Baltimore, MD 21202; telephone (410)396-4941; City Hall tourist information, telephone (410)837-5424

# Economy

## Major Industries and Commercial Activity

Baltimore's heritage as a strategically-located East Coast port is drawn upon by its developers today. The city's revived downtown and central location among major East Coast cities has made it increasingly attractive to new or expanding businesses. The blue-collar tradition exemplified by Bethlehem Steel's ranking as top employer in the 1980s is being replaced by jobs in the service sector in fields such as law, finance, medicine, hospitality, entertainment, maritime commerce and health. Growth in the high-technology market in areas such as electronics, information technology, telecommunications and aerospace research has also created new jobs.

Baltimore is an established center of medicine and biosciences. It is a national headquarters for advanced medical treatment and research with two pioneering teaching hospitals, Johns Hopkins Hospital and University Hospital at the University of Maryland. The Baltimore area is the research center for the mapping of the human genome and its resulting commercial applications.

Year after year, Greater Baltimore ranks among the nation's top twenty markets in key retail categories. Tourism, spurred on by the opening or expansion of downtown attractions, has boosted construction and the success of the Inner Harbor renovation has lured city residents back downtown. Tourism in Baltimore brought increased revenues from 2003 to 2004, with increased hotel occupancy rates, convention–related spending, overall air travel to the city, increased tax revenues and growth in the number of leisure and hospitality jobs.

Among the city's major exports are coal, grain, iron, steel, and copper products. Baltimore also remains a center for shipbuilding.

The Baltimore metropolitan area is home to three companies on the *Fortune* 500 list of the largest companies in the country: food distributor U.S. Foodservice Inc., power tool giant Black & Decker Corp., and Constellation Energy, the utility holding company that owns Baltimore Gas & Electric Co.

*Items and goods produced:* steel pipe; plate, sheet, and tin mill products; ships and ship-related products; aerospace equipment; sugar and processed foods; copper and oil refining; chemicals; clothing

### Incentive Programs—New and Existing Companies

*Local programs*—The Economic Alliance of Greater Baltimore helps businesses to access the broad range of competitive incentives offered by the State of Maryland and local jurisdictions, as well as Baltimore Gas and Electric. Municipalities and the State of Maryland offer attractive financing programs including industrial revenue bonds, small business and high technology loans, and community development block grants. Many of these loans offer interest rates that are below market. Payment-in-lieu-of Taxes (PILOT) agreements with the City of Baltimore exempt businesses from property taxes on certain real estate within the city for a specified length of time and substitute a negotiated payment.

*State programs*—The One Maryland Tax Credit Program for development in a "qualified distressed county" allows up to $5 million in project tax credits and an additional $500,000 in start-up tax credits. In addition to the One Maryland program, four other business finance programs are offered through the state, consisting of loans and grants. Enterprise zone property and income tax credits are available. Foreign Trade Zone #74 houses port-related activities and includes facilities for assembly, distribution, packaging, manufacturing and warehousing.The zone, which saw a reorganization and major expansion of more than 1,000 acres in 2001, now encompasses 1,464 acres.

*Job training and recruitment programs*— The Economic Alliance also partners with area colleges and universities to provide customized training to ensure a quality workforce. The Maryland Industrial Training Program (MITP), as well as some local programs, provides reimbursement grants for the development and training of new employees in firms that are locating or expanding their workforce in Maryland. The level of funding provided is negotiated between the company and the State of Maryland, with specific cost sharing items spelled out in a training grant agreement. The Partnership for Workforce Quality (PWQ) provides matching skill training grants. The Business Training Network (BTN) is a network of regional community colleges providing training and recruitment programs. Maryland Apprenticeship and Training Program (MATP) offers free technical assistance to companies who want to set up apprenticeship programs. Additional workforce resources include the Greater Baltimore Regional Transitional Assistance Program (TAP) Initiative, providing employers the opportunity for recruitment directly from the regional and national military population. Career Net is a workforce database linking employers and job seekers.

### Development Projects

Baltimore is continuing its redevelopment program for its Inner Harbor and downtown areas. The $71 million Calvert Mercier Lombard Grant Street redevelopment project is designed to include 300 apartments, retail space and a 542-car parking garage in the heart of the central business district. Improved water taxi/commuter service at Inner Harbor provides tourists and commuters with easy access to the city's cultural, business, entertainment, historic and recreational venues. The city also plans to redevelop Oldtown Mall, a once thriving pedestrian mall in East Baltimore. The west side of the city is also seeing revitalization in the Westside Initiative which incorporates the redevelopment of 100 square blocks and links the finance district to the University of Maryland's graduate and medical schools.

Ten of Baltimore's neighborhood commercial districts received a financial boost over three years under a national Main Street program. The revitalization initiative followed the National Trust for Historic Preservation model, using more than $1.5 million in city, state, and private funds. The program has been successful in creating 210 new businesses, more than 700 new full– and part–time jobs, and 291 facáde improvement projects.

***Economic Development Information:*** Economic Alliance of Greater Baltimore, 111 South Calvert Street, Suite 2220, Baltimore, MD 21202-6180; telephone (888)298-4322. Baltimore Development Corporation, 36 South Charles Street, Baltimore, MD 21201-3015; telephone (410) 837-9305; fax 410-837-6363

### Commercial Shipping

Baltimore-Washington International Airport is a major cargo carrier for the mid-Atlantic region. CSX and Norfolk Southern railroad systems service industry throughout the Baltimore area. Several major interstate highways run through Baltimore; I-95 links Baltimore with major cities from New England to Florida, and I-70 connects it with the Midwest. More than 100 trucking lines also accommodate the Baltimore area.

The most significant mover of goods in the area is the port of Baltimore, the fifth largest and one of the busiest deep-water ports in the nation. One hundred fifty miles closer to key midwestern markets than any other Atlantic Coast port, the port of Baltimore has lower transportation costs between its marine terminals and inland points of cargo origin or destination. Baltimore also benefits by having two access routes to its port: from the north through the Chesapeake & Delaware Canal, and from the south up the Chesapeake Bay. Since 1980, more than one-half billion dollars has been invested in maritime-related improvements to the Port.

### Labor Force and Employment Outlook

Sixty-eight percent of population over 25 in the City of Baltimore has a high school diploma and 19.1 percent has a bachelor's degree or more. Baltimore's job growth rate was up in 2004 and ranked in the top quarter of the nation's metro areas. Education and health services, financial activities, and leisure and hospitality were the major industries facing job gains. The largest job losses were in the information and manufacturing sectors.

The following is a summary of data regarding the Baltimore Metropolitan area (PMSA) labor force, 2003 annual averages.

*Size of civilian labor force:* 1,344,649

*Number of workers employed in . . .*
  *construction and mining:* 73,700
  *manufacturing:* 80,200
  *trade, transportation and utilities:* 237,000
  *information:* 20,600
  *financial activities:* 81,800
  *professional and business services:* 172,000
  *educational and health services:* 199,500
  *leisure and hospitality:* 107,100
  *other services:* 55,700
  *government:* 218,900

*Average hourly earnings of production workers employed in manufacturing:* $15.36 (MSA)

*Unemployment rate:* 4.2% (December 2004)

| *Largest Baltimore employers* | *Number of employees* |
|---|---|
| Northrop Grumman Corp. (Electronic Sensors & Systems incl. Oceanic Sys. Div.) | 9,500 |
| Johns Hopkins Medicine | 7,000 |
| University of Maryland Cancer Center | 5,000 |
| University of Maryland Medical System | 5,000 |
| U.S. Department of Health and Human Services | 4,282 |

**Cost of Living**

When it comes to buying groceries, paying a mortgage or hopping on a subway, Baltimore is one of the most affordable of all East Coast cities. The following is a summary of data regarding several key cost of living factors for the Baltimore area.

*2004 (3rd Quarter) Average House Price:* $301,143

*2004 (3rd Quarter) Cost of Living Index:* 108.7 (U.S. average = 100.0)

*State income tax rate:* Ranges from 2.0% to 4.75%

*State sales tax rate:* 5.0% (food and prescription drugs are exempt)

*Local income tax rate:* 3.05% (City of Baltimore)

*Local sales tax rate:* None

*Property tax rate:* $2.328 per $100.00 assessed value (2005 Fiscal year)

***Economic Information:*** Economic Alliance of Greater Baltimore, 111 South Calvert Street, Suite 2220, Baltimore, MD 21202-6180; toll-free (888)298-4322; telephone (410) 468-0100

# Education and Research

**Elementary and Secondary Schools**

The Baltimore City Public School System (BCPSS) serves the largest number of low income and special needs students in the state of Maryland. It is struggling to create an effective educational environment for its children despite disastrous financial problems. The system's Master Plan is part of a city-state partnership aimed at reforming the troubled system by focusing on student assessment, program evaluation, institutional research, and shared planning and accountability. Master Plan II directs reform efforts through the 2007-2008 school year. These efforts are paying off with improvements in math and reading scores and reductions in class size.

The following is a summary of data regarding Baltimore's public schools as of fall 2003.

*Total enrollment:* 91,738

*Number of facilities*
  *elementary schools:* 80
  *middle/combined schools:* 57
  *high schools:* 16
  *other:* 6 alternative schools; 8 special centers; 3 pre-K schools; 2 non-technical schools

*Student/teacher ratio:* 14.6:1 (all grades, 2003)

*Teacher salaries*
  *average:* $48,205

*Funding per pupil:* $8,315

About 124 private and parochial schools operate in the Baltimore area.

***Public Schools Information:*** Baltimore City Public School System, 200 East North Avenue, Room 319, Baltimore, MD 21202; telephone (410)396-8577

**Colleges and Universities**

Of the approximately 30 colleges and universities located in the Baltimore metropolitan area, nearly half lie within the city limits. Towson State University, the oldest four-year college in Maryland and the largest in the Baltimore area, offers bachelor's degrees in 57 fields and master's degrees in 29. Considered one of Baltimore's outstanding assets, Johns Hopkins University boasts a world-renowned medical school and an affiliation with a prestigious music conservatory, the Peabody Institute. Loyola College offers a joint program in medical technology with Baltimore's Mercy Medical Center. The University of Baltimore, a state-supported institution, awards upper-division, graduate, and law degrees. One of five campus units of the University of Maryland, the University of Maryland at Baltimore offers professional programs in health and medical fields, social work, and law, as well as undergraduate degrees in a variety of fields. At Morgan State University students can earn advanced degrees in architecture, city and regional planning, and urban education. Coppin State University benefits from a cooperative program with local industries and offers both bachelor's and master's degree programs.

The Baltimore area's other large academic institutions include University of Maryland, Baltimore County, the U.S. Naval Academy, the Maryland Center for Career and Technology Education Studies, the Ner Israel Rabbinical College, College of Notre Dame of Maryland, the Maryland Institute College of Art, Anne Arundel Community College in Arnold, Harford Community College in Bel Air, Western Maryland College in Westminster, Howard Community College, and Carroll Community College.

### Libraries and Research Centers

Baltimore's public library system, The Enoch Pratt Free Library, has 24 branches, a bookmobile, and a Central Library that also serves as the state Library Resource Center. Holdings consist of more than two million books, 4,000 current magazines, thousands of films and federal government documents, and more than 600,000 magazines, newspapers, and monographs on microform, videotapes, filmstrips, and other media. Special collections include African-American materials, the works of Baltimore authors H. L. Mencken and Edgar Allan Poe, the Howard Beck Memorial Philatelic Collection, and the Maryland Department, which holds extensive books, periodicals, and other documents on all aspects of life in the state of Maryland and its cities.

Research activities at centers affiliated with Johns Hopkins University focus on such subject areas as biophysics, Alzheimer's Disease, STDs, inherited diseases and other maladies, alternatives to animal testing, communications, and mass spectrometry. The University of Maryland at Baltimore also supports medical research work through its Center of Marine Biology. The Space Telescope Science Institute, the principal scientific element of the NASA Hubble Space Telescope Project, is based in Baltimore.

*Public information:* Enoch Pratt Free Library, 400 Cathedral St., Baltimore, MD 21201-4484; telephone (410)396-5430; fax (410)396-1441; email GenInfo@mail.pratt.lib.md.us

# Health Care

Thirty accredited hospitals offering a wide range of general and specialized services are located within the Baltimore city limits. Cardiac rehabilitation units, hospice programs, extensive psychiatric and drug rehabilitation programs, and neonatal intensive care are among the special services available in various Baltimore hospitals. In addition to the many fine teaching hospitals throughout the city, Baltimore's institutions include two world-class medical schools: the Johns Hopkins University School of Medicine and the University of Maryland School of Medicine.

Johns Hopkins Hospital, affiliated with the university, is one of the largest, most advanced, most prestigious hospitals in the South; its oncology center and eye clinic are world famous. The Johns Hopkins $125 million Comprehensive Cancer Center, opened in 2000, provides the most advanced cancer care in the country. The Johns Hopkins Bayview Medical Center and the Baltimore Regional Burn Center are recognized programs for the treatment of burn injuries. Another of Baltimore's teaching hospitals, the University of Maryland Medical System, boasts a shock trauma center that was one of the first of its kind. Sinai Hospital of Baltimore is one of the city's largest and most completely equipped hospitals. Another teaching facility, Union Memorial Hospital, is known for its work in sports medicine; Maryland General Hospital is also a teaching hospital. Other Baltimore hospitals are Bon Secours Hospital serving West Baltimore, Mercy Medical Center, and Children's Hospital.

# Recreation

### Sightseeing

With its extensively developed waterfront, overhead skywalks, and numerous plazas and promenades, downtown Baltimore is ideally geared to the pedestrian tourist. Many visitors begin their tour of the city at Baltimore's Inner Harbor, easily the city's most picturesque area. A one-half-mile brick promenade along the water enables visitors to walk to the many attractions at water's edge.

The Maryland Science Center, set directly on the water, is especially popular with children. Three block-length floors of science exhibits, hands-on displays, and live science

**The Baltimore Washington Monument, designed by Robert Mills, was the first major memorial built in honor of George Washington.**

demonstrations are featured. The Davis Planetarium boasts 350 projectors and presents multimedia and topical shows. Nearby is the world's tallest five-sided building, the thirty-story World Trade Center, designed by I. M. Pei. The "Top of the World" observation deck on the building's 27th floor offers a panoramic view of the harbor.

One of the most spectacular sights at the Inner Harbor is the seven-level National Aquarium, whose unique glass pyramid roofs create dramatic reflections in the water. It is the city's top attraction and was rated one of the country's best family attractions in 2004, according to *USA Today*. More than 10,500 aquatic specimens and 560 species of animals are housed in the exhibits and the Aquarium is crowned by a 64-foot-high model of an Amazon rain forest that looks out over the harbor.

Port Discovery is Baltimore's children's museum and offers interactive exhibits and features a three-story urban tree house. *Child* magazine ranked it among the country's five top children's museums in 2002.

Visitors to Baltimore's Inner Harbor may take advantage of the Water Taxi, which from mid-April to mid-October shuttles between major points of interest around the harbor. For longer excursions, public and charter cruises, as well as brunch and dinner cruises, are available through Harbor Cruises.

Among Baltimore's many historical landmarks is the National Park at Fort McHenry, the unusual star-shaped fort that was the site of Baltimore's victory over the British bombardment during the War of 1812, and the inspiration for the U.S. national anthem. The fort's battlements have been carefully preserved. The Star-Spangled Banner Flag House, built in 1793, preserves the site where Mary Pickersgill sewed the 30-inch by 42-inch flag that flew at Fort McHenry during the War of 1812. A collection of early American art, Federal period furniture, and a unique map of the United States composed of stones from each state are presented.

Homes of several famous Baltimore residents are open to the public. The Babe Ruth Birthplace and Museum offers exhibits commemorating baseball legend Babe Ruth and Maryland baseball history, with numerous photos and memorabilia of Baltimore's major-league teams, the Orioles. The childhood home of Babe Ruth is preserved as it was at the time of his birth in 1895. Continuing the baseball theme, the Baseball Center located in the Camden Station Passenger Terminal building at Oriole Park at Camden Yards. About four times the size of Babe Ruth's birthplace, the facility houses archives, classrooms, a baseball theater, a baseball-themed restaurant, and a main corridor that resembles a 1920s railroad car. The Benjamin Banneker Historical Park and Museum on Banneker's 142-acre homesite commemorates this son of a freed slave and grandson of an African prince.

Edgar Allan Poe lived and wrote in Baltimore from 1832 to 1835. His home on North Amity Street is open to the public. Writer and journalist H. L. Mencken, locally known as the "Sage of Baltimore," lived in Baltimore for more than 68 years until his death in 1956. His nineteenth-century rowhouse overlooking scenic Union Square has been carefully restored with its original furniture and much of Mencken's personal memorabilia. The H. L. Mencken House is part of a seven-museum and park complex collectively known as Baltimore City Life Museums. Other historical buildings around Baltimore include the Baltimore City Hall, Shot Tower, The Washington Monument, and the George Peabody Library of Johns Hopkins University.

Baltimore has many public gardens and parks. The largest is Druid Hill Park, at 674 acres one of the country's largest natural city parks. One hundred fifty acres are devoted to the popular Baltimore Zoo, which features the largest captive colony of African black-footed penguins. Also in Druid Hill Park is the Conservatory, a remarkable glass pavilion similar in construction to the Victorian-era "Crystal Palace" built in 1888. Known as "The Palm House," the building contains an extensive collection of tropical and desert plants. Other gardens include Cylbyrn Arboretum, on the grounds of Cylbyrn Mansion, and Sherwood Gardens, located in the beautifully-landscaped neighborhood of Guildford.

## Arts and Culture

Those seeking fine music, theater, and dance performances will not be disappointed in Baltimore, which has seen a recent renewal of interest in the arts, including new construction or major renovation of existing performing centers. The acoustically impressive Joseph Meyerhoff Symphony Hall is home to the Baltimore Symphony Orchestra. In addition to its classical programs, which include a number of celebrity performers each year, the orchestra presents a Pops series. The Baltimore Opera Company performs full-scale grand opera at the restored Lyric Opera House, a replica of Germany's Leipzig Music Hall. Summer concert series are held at the Pier Six Concert Pavilion, a unique fabric-covered structure where jazz, country, and classical music, and musical comedy programs are presented by top-name performers. The Eubie Blake National Museum and Cultural Center, dedicated to the famous Baltimore-born pianist, fosters the development and sponsors performances of community artists. Classes are held at the center in music, dance, and drama. The Creative Alliance at the Patterson showcases a variety of entertainment in a 1930s movie theatre.

Baltimore theater-goers will find dramatic productions to suit every taste. The Morris A. Mechanic Theatre offers a wide range of pre- and post-Broadway productions. Center Stage is among the nation's top ten regional theaters and produces six classic and modern plays each year. Cockpit in

Court Summer Theatre offers musicals, comedies, dramas and a children's each summer on the CCBC Essex campus. The Arena Players is one of the foremost black theater companies on the East Coast and the Theatre Project is known internationally for its experimental music, drama, and dance.

Baltimore's museums and galleries offer a variety of art and artifacts for viewing. The lifetime collections of Baltimore residents William and Henry Walters are gathered at the Walters Art Museum. Its treasures include more than 30,000 objects from 5,500 years of history—from pre-Dynastic Egypt to twentieth century Art Nouveau. Particularly resplendent collections are held in ivories, jewelry, enamels, bronzes, illuminated manuscripts and rare books. Baltimore's other major art museum is the Baltimore Museum of Art, designed by John Russell Pope, architect of Washington's National Gallery. The museum's prize holding is the "Cone Collection," a large and valuable collection of paintings and sculpture by such European Post-Impressionist masters as Matisse, Cezanne, Picasso, and Van Gogh. The museum also has important collections of eighteenth- and nineteenth-century American paintings, sculpture, and furniture, art from Africa and Oceania, and the works of Andy Warhol. One of Baltimore's newest museums, the American Visionary Art Museum, combines two historic buildings with modern museum architecture. Said to be the only such institution in the country, the museum was officially designated by the U.S. Congress as "the national museum, education and repository center, the best in self-taught, outsider or visionary artistry." The Contemporary Museum is part of an emerging "arts row" on Centre Street.

In the historical former residence of nineteenth-century Baltimore philanthropist Enoch Pratt is the Maryland Historical Society. The Society's Museum and Library of Maryland History are of particular interest to researchers; of general interest are collections of portraits by famous American artists, valuable nineteenth-century silver, furniture from 1720 to 1950, and Francis Scott Key's original manuscript of "The Star-Spangled Banner." Near the heart of industrial South Baltimore, the Baltimore Museum of Industry, housed in the former Platt Oyster Cannery, features recreations of turn-of-the-century machinery, printing, and metalworking workshops, as well as a garment loft.

The B & O Railroad Museum is designed around Mount Clare Station, which was built in 1830 for the Baltimore & Ohio Railroad as the nation's first passenger and freight station. The original 1884 roundhouse, tracks, and turntable have been preserved. Among the more than 130 railroad cars on display here, both originals and replicas, is "Tom Thumb," the first steam locomotive. The Museum has renovated the roundhouse, added exhibits, train rides, visitor facilities and a museum store and had scheduled a grand reopening for spring 2005. The Baltimore Public Works Museum preserves the history of the city's public works with a collection of more than 2,000 items including early wooden water pipes, water meters, numerous photographs, and an early twentieth-century water-pumping truck. The museum itself was once a sewage pumping station, built in 1912. Much of the art collection of Baltimore's artistic Peale family can be seen at the Peale Museum, which has three floors of exhibits, including a floor dedicated to a history of the Baltimore rowhouse.

The National Great Blacks in Wax Museum is the first of its kind and represents black history and heritage through more than 100 historical wax figures as well as paintings, sculpture, and carvings. The Reginald F. Lewis Museum of Maryland African American History and Culture, located at Inner Harbor, was scheduled to open June 2005. Its focus is on the lives, history and culture of African Americans in Maryland. It has partnered with the State Board of Education which has adopted a curriculum linked to the museum's programs. The Frederick Douglass-Isaac Myers Maritime Park on the Fells Point Riverfront is also scheduled to open in the summer 2005. The $12 million park is sponsored by the Living Classrooms Foundation and features exhibits and monuments dedicated to the two entrepreneurs, a shipbuilding workshop, a working marine railway, outdoor amphitheater, dockage for historic ships, and other multicultural displays.

**Festivals and Holidays**

Most of Baltimore's festivals begin in late spring and continue on weekends throughout the fall. The colorful Maryland Kite Festival, held on the last Saturday in April, is a competition with homemade kites, judged for their beauty, flight performance, and design. Also in April is the highly acclaimed Baltimore International Film Festival, held for one month and presenting numerous entries in such categories as documentaries, movies by women or children, and animation. The Blues Fest is usually held in June. The African American Heritage Festival is held for three days in June at Oriole Park in Camden Yards.

Artscape is a lively outdoor festival held in July showcasing local artistic and musical talent. Baltimore's famous and very popular Showcase of Nations—a series of weekly ethnic festivals held from June through September—celebrates the heritage of many cultures through music, dance, crafts, and international cuisine.

September is the month of the Maryland State Fair, held at the Fairgrounds in nearby Timonium. The week-long state fair features livestock, produce, and equestrian competition from Maryland 4-H groups, as well as an amusement midway and horse racing. September also brings the Baltimore Book Festival, a celebration of the literary arts.

In October the Fells Point Fun Festival celebrates the historical waterfront neighborhood with two days of arts and crafts, entertainment, maritime exhibits, neighborhood tours, and music ranging from jazz and blues to Polish polkas. December's parade of lighted boats adds to the festive season and New Year's Eve Extravaganza offerings include parties at the convention center, ice skating demonstrations, live music and fireworks at the harbor (on January 1st).

### Sports for the Spectator

Baltimore's American Conference East Division indoor soccer team, the Baltimore Blast, plays at Baltimore Arena; the team's season runs from October to March, with post-season play in April.

Professional football returned to the city with great fanfare after a 12-year absence when the newly christened Baltimore Ravens (formerly the Cleveland Browns and renamed in honor of the Edgar Allan Poe poem) played their first official National Football League game in 1996. The team now plays in the state-of-the-art M & T Bank Stadium. College football and basketball are represented by the University of Maryland Terrapins, Towson State Tigers, Johns Hopkins Blue Jays, and the Naval Academy Midshipmen at nearby stadiums.

Baseball fans come out to watch the American League Baltimore Orioles at Oriole Park at Camden Yards. Architects have praised its distinctive turn-of-the-century style, which is in keeping with its old urban neighborhood. The 48,000-seat stadium incorporates a landmark B & O Railroad warehouse that has been converted to office space for the ball club and the Maryland Stadium Authority. Another popular warm-weather sport is lacrosse, played by the champion Johns Hopkins University Blue Jays at Homewood Field; the Lacrosse Museum and National Hall of Fame is located adjacent to Homewood Field.

Thoroughbred racing, always popular with Maryland horse breeders and followers, can be seen at Pimlico Racecourse, Maryland's oldest racetrack. The famous Preakness Stakes, second jewel in the Triple Crown, is run here in May. In October on Maryland Million Day, thoroughbreds race at Pimlico Racecourse and purses total more than $1 million. Maryland's most famous steeplechase is the annual Maryland Hunt Cup, held in Baltimore County.

### Sports for the Participant

Baltimore's proximity to the Chesapeake Bay makes all sorts of water-related activities are favorite pastimes of many area residents. Sail- and powerboat regattas are held at the Inner Harbor, nearby Annapolis, and Havre de Grace throughout the summer months. Numerous marinas and yacht clubs dot the bay and river inlets near Baltimore, and local pleasure boats can be seen all along the Chesapeake on a clear day. Fishing, crabbing, and clamdigging are also very popular, even within city limits.

Numerous public and private golf clubs dot the Baltimore area. Art Links Baltimore is a miniature course designed by regional artists and architects. Art Links' 18 holes celebrate the culture of the Baltimore region, incorporating tracks of the B & O Railroad or depicting a crab feast, for example. Tennis courts are available in many of the city's parks, as are bike paths and swimming pools.

### Shopping and Dining

Most of the malls in the Baltimore area are located in Baltimore and Anne Arundel counties, close to the city, but many specialized shopping centers can be found within city limits, at Lexington Mall and along Antique Row, for instance. The twin pavilions of Harborplace and The Gallery offer shops and restaurants at the water's edge. Lexington Market, which underwent a revitalization in 2002, features more than 140 merchants selling fresh seafood, produce, and international delights. Lexington Market is part of Market Center, a bustling and colorful collection of more than 400 diverse shops. One of the oldest and most luxurious shopping districts in Baltimore is the Charles Street Corridor, where shoppers can find numerous art galleries, jewelers, stationers, furriers, and specialty boutiques; new stores are interspersed with enduring older ones.

As with many other aspects of Baltimore living, restaurant dining is greatly influenced by the city's proximity to the Chesapeake Bay. A wide range of Baltimore restaurants specialize in preparation of crabs, oysters, clams, mussels, and fish from the Bay. Many Baltimore restaurants also reflect the port city's rich ethnic heritage, and diverse international cuisines can be enjoyed throughout the downtown area.

*Visitor Information:* Baltimore Area Visitors Center, Constellation Pier, 301 East Pratt Street, Baltimore, MD; telephone (410)837-4636 or (800)282-6632. For information on group visits, Baltimore Area Convention and Visitors Association, 100 Light Street, 12th Floor, Baltimore, MD 21202; telephone (410)659-7300 or (800)343-3468; fax (410)727-2308

# Convention Facilities

With its mid-Atlantic coast location and easy access by air, rail, or automobile, Baltimore has long been a strategic choice for convention-holders. The recent redevelopment of the city's downtown Inner Harbor area has made Baltimore even more attractive to conventioneers, who enjoy the many fine restaurants, retail centers, and cultural attractions on or near the water.

Baltimore's largest meeting facility is the Baltimore Convention Center located at the Inner Harbor. An expansion of the facility completed in 1996 tripled its size to more than 1.2 million square feet. A 36,672-square-foot ballroom, 50 meeting rooms, and 300,000 square feet of exhibition space on one level make for an extremely flexible facility.

The Baltimore Arena is used primarily for sporting events and travelling circuses, but it also has 25 meeting rooms for 20 to 300 people. The facility has an auditorium with a capacity for 13,000 people, and parking accommodations for 5,000 cars. Oriole Park at Camden Yards is available for trade shows. Many of Baltimore's downtown hotels also provide meeting facilities. There are more than 8,000 hotel rooms within a mile radius of the Baltimore Convention Center. The Baltimore Marriott-Waterfront, which opened in 2000, is a 31-story hotel with 750 guestrooms, 80,000 square feet of total meeting space, exhibition space and 38 meeting rooms.

***Convention Information:*** Baltimore Area Convention and Visitors Association, 100 Light Street, 12th Floor, Baltimore, MD 21202; telephone (410)659-7300 or (800)343-3468; fax (410)727-2308

# Transportation

## Approaching the City

The recently expanded Baltimore-Washington International (BWI) Airport, located just 10 miles from downtown Baltimore, is one of the fastest-growing major airports in the country. BWI has 18 carriers that provide more than 600 daily flights, including nonstop flights to 72 cities in the United States, Canada, Europe and the Caribbean.

Major highway links between Baltimore and other cities are Interstate-95, which runs all along the East Coast, and I-70, which crosses through western Maryland to the Midwest. Interstate 395 runs south from Baltimore to Washington and Virginia; I-83 runs north through the city toward central Pennsylvania. All these interstates intersect with I-695, the Baltimore Beltway, which circles the city. Those approaching the central city by car should be aware that most of the streets are one way.

Just north of downtown is the historical, restored Pennsylvania Station, where Amtrak trains pull in and out. For commuters, the Maryland Rail Commuter Service (MARC) provides weekday service on the most extensive track commuter rail system in the Greater Baltimore region, including 43 stations over three lines (Brunswick, Camden and Penn) covering a total of 187 miles. Twenty trains run from the Maryland/Delaware border, south to Montgomery County, MD. MARC also provides convenient access to both downtown Baltimore and Washington, D.C.

## Traveling in the City

Baltimore's highly regarded mass transit system consists of 850 buses, the Metro (subway), light rail, and the Maryland Area Rail Commuter system (MARC). The Metro's 15.5 mile system extends from the Owings Mills corporate and shopping complex in Baltimore County, through the heart of the downtown business, shopping and sightseeing districts to Johns Hopkins Hospital.

# Communications

## Newspapers and Magazines

Baltimore is served by one major daily newspaper, *The Baltimore Sun*. The *Daily Record* provides daily business and legal news, and *The Baltimore Business Journal* and *The Jeffersonian* (Baltimore County) are business weeklies. Weekly newspapers published in Baltimore include *The Baltimore Times,* (part of the BlackPressUSA Network) *Baltimore City Paper; Baltimore Guide;* and *Baltimore Messenger. The Baltimore Chronicle & Sentinel* is published monthly.

More than 200 newspapers, periodicals, and directories are published in Baltimore, including numerous medical journals such as *The Lancet (North American Edition)*. Quarterly publications include *Maryland Historical Magazine.*

## Television and Radio

Seven television stations broadcast from Baltimore: affiliates of ABC, CBS, NBC, Fox, public television, and the Home Shopping Network. Stations originating in nearby communities are also accessible to Baltimore-area residents, as is cable service.

The 17 Baltimore and nine area AM and FM radio stations broadcast programming that ranges from news, religious material, and public broadcasting to music that includes classical, jazz, country, gospel, easy listening, top-40, and contemporary styles.

***Media Information:*** *The Sun,* 501 N. Calvert St., Baltimore, MD 21278; telephone (410) 332-6300

## Baltimore Online

Baltimore Area Convention & Visitor's Bureau. Available www.baltimore.org

Baltimore City Public School System. Available www.bcps .k12.md.us

Baltimore County Public Library. Available www.bcpl online.org/libpg/aboutyourlibrary.html

Baltimore Development Corporation. Available www .baltimoredevelopment.com

Baltimore Washington Corridor Chamber of Commerce. Available www.baltwashchamber.org/home.cfm

*Baltimore Sun.* Available www.sunspot.net

City of Baltimore home page. Available www.ci.baltimore .md.us

Economic Alliance of Greater Baltimore. Available www .greaterbaltimore.org

Enoch Pratt Free Library. Available www.pratt.lib.md.us

Maryland Department of Business & Economic Development. Available www.mdbusiness.state.md.us

## Selected Bibliography

Bready, James, H., *Baseball in Baltimore: The First 100 Years* (Baltimore: Johns Hopkins University Press, 1998)

Fein, Isaac M. *The Making of an American Jewish Community: The History of Baltimore Jewry from 1773 to 1920* (Philadelphia: Jewish Publication Society of America, 1971)

Stockett, Letitia, *Baltimore: A Not Too Serious History* (Baltimore: Johns Hopkins University Press, 1997)

# MISSISSIPPI

# The State in Brief

**Nickname:** Magnolia State
**Motto:** *Virtute et armis* (By valor and arms)

**Flower:** Magnolia
**Bird:** Mockingbird

**Area:** 48,430 square miles (2000; U.S. rank: 32nd)
**Elevation:** Ranges from sea level to 806 feet above sea level
**Climate:** Temperate in north and subtropical in south, with long, hot summers and mild winters

**Admitted to Union:** December 10, 1817
**Capital:** Jackson
**Head Official:** Governor Haley Barbour (R) (until 2008)

**Population**
**1980:** 2,521,000
**1990:** 2,573,216
**2000:** 2,844,658
**2004 estimate:** 2,902,966
**Percent change, 1990–2000:** 10.5%
**U.S. rank in 2004:** 31st
**Percent of residents born in state:** 74.3% (2000)
**Density:** 60.6 people per square mile (2000)
**2002 FBI Crime Index Total:** 119,442

**Racial and Ethnic Characteristics** (2000)
**White:** 1,746,099
**Black or African American:** 1,033,809
**American Indian and Alaska Native:** 11,652
**Asian:** 18,626
**Native Hawaiian and Pacific Islander:** 667
**Hispanic or Latino (may be of any race):** 39,569
**Other:** 13,784

**Age Characteristics** (2000)
**Population under 5 years old:** 204,364
**Population 5 to 19 years old:** 668,850
**Percent of population 65 years and over:** 12.9%
**Median age:** 33.8 years (2000)

**Vital Statistics**
**Total number of births (2003):** 42,150
**Total number of deaths (2003):** 28,882 (infant deaths, 425)
**AIDS cases reported through 2003:** 2,875

**Economy**
**Major industries:** Transportation equipment, food products, government, trade, agriculture, manufacturing
**Unemployment rate:** 6.4% (December 2004)
**Per capita income:** $15,853 (2003; U.S. rank: 51st)
**Median household income:** $31,887 (3-year average, 2001-2003)
**Percentage of persons below poverty level:** 17.9% (3-year average, 2001-2003)
**Income tax rate:** Ranges from 3.0% to 5.0%
**Sales tax rate:** 7.0%

# Biloxi

## The City in Brief

*Note: This profile of the city of Biloxi was updated prior to August 2005, when Hurricane Katrina caused severe damage to the Gulf Coast region of the United States. The long-term impact of Katrina on Biloxi is unknown at the time of publication.*

**Founded:** 1719, incorporated 1981

**Head Official:** Mayor A. J. Holloway, Jr. (R) (since 1993)

**City Population**
**1990:** 46,319
**2000:** 50,644
**2003 estimate:** 48,972
**Percent change, 1990–2000:** 9.3%
**U.S. rank in 1990:** 535th (State rank: 2nd)
**U.S. rank in 2000:** 707th (State rank: 3rd)

**Metropolitan Area Population**
**1990:** 312,368
**2000:** 363,988
**Percent change, 1990–2000:** 16.5%
**U.S. rank in 1990:** 157th
**U.S. rank in 2000:** 113th

**Area:** 46.53 square miles (2000)
**Elevation:** 20 feet above sea level
**Average Annual Temperature:** 68° F
**Average Annual Precipitation:** 61 inches

**Major Economic Sectors:** services, casinos, government, and trade
**Unemployment rate:** 4.0% (December 2004)
**Per Capita Income:** $17,809 (1999)

**2002 FBI Crime Index Total:** 3,852

**Major Colleges and Universities:** Mississippi Gulf Coast Community College, The University of Southern Mississippi-Gulf Coast

**Daily Newspaper:** *Sun Herald*

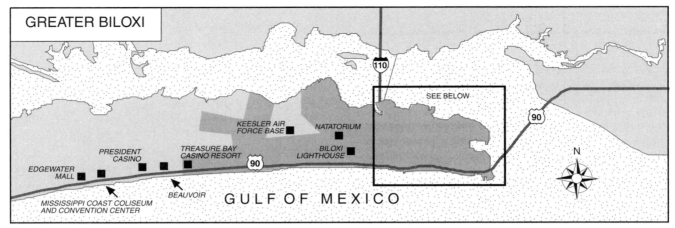

GREATER BILOXI

KEESLER AIR FORCE BASE

NATATORIUM

PRESIDENT CASINO

TREASURE BAY CASINO RESORT

BILOXI LIGHTHOUSE

EDGEWATER MALL

SEE BELOW

BEAUVOIR

MISSISSIPPI COAST COLISEUM AND CONVENTION CENTER

GULF OF MEXICO

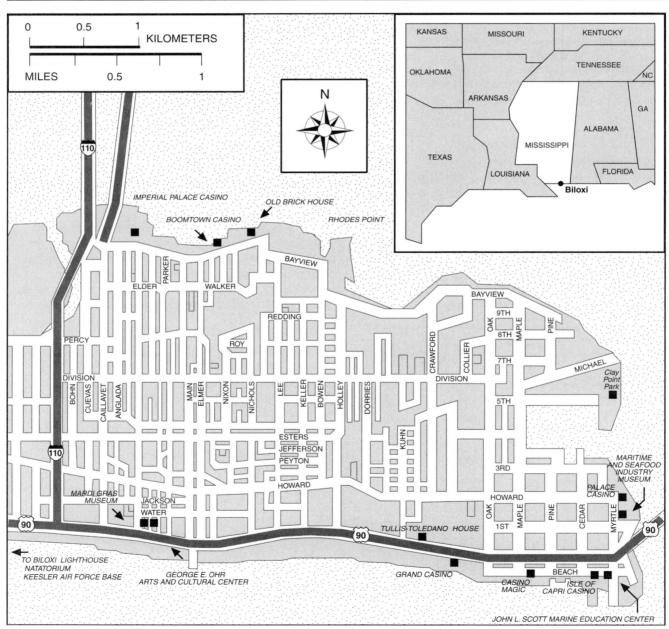

KILOMETERS

MILES

KANSAS
MISSOURI
KENTUCKY
OKLAHOMA
TENNESSEE
NC
ARKANSAS
GA
TEXAS
ALABAMA
MISSISSIPPI
LOUISIANA
FLORIDA
**Biloxi**

IMPERIAL PALACE CASINO

OLD BRICK HOUSE

BOOMTOWN CASINO

RHODES POINT

BAYVIEW

PARKER

ELDER

WALKER

REDDING

BAYVIEW

9TH

OAK

MAPLE

PINE

8TH

ROY

7TH

PERCY

CRAWFORD

COLLIER

MICHAEL

Clay Point Park

DIVISION

BOHN

CUEVAS

CAILLAVET

ANGLADA

MAIN

ELMER

NIXON

NICHOLS

LEE

KELLER

BOWEN

HOLLEY

DORRIES

DIVISION

5TH

ESTERS

JEFFERSON

PEYTON

KUHN

3RD

HOWARD

MARITIME AND SEAFOOD INDUSTRY MUSEUM

MARDI GRAS MUSEUM

JACKSON

WATER

HOWARD

OAK

MAPLE

PINE

CEDAR

MYRTLE

PALACE CASINO

1ST

TULLIS-TOLEDANO HOUSE

TO BILOXI LIGHTHOUSE NATATORIUM KEESLER AIR FORCE BASE

GEORGE E. OHR ARTS AND CULTURAL CENTER

GRAND CASINO

BEACH

CASINO MAGIC

ISLE OF CAPRI CASINO

JOHN L. SCOTT MARINE EDUCATION CENTER

# Introduction

Biloxi, with its 25 miles of white Gulf Coast beaches, is one of the oldest cities in the United States. Historically a sleepy resort town, originally serving vacationers from Mobile and New Orleans, it is noted for its oyster and shrimp fisheries. The introduction of legalized gambling at offshore casinos has led to the city's renaissance and a booming economy. Biloxi's rich history and cultural attractions have also contributed to its becoming one of the new "hot spots" for Southern tourism.

# Geography and Climate

Biloxi is located on a little peninsula between Biloxi Bay and the Mississippi Sound on the Gulf of Mexico. It is 70 miles northeast of New Orleans, 70 miles southwest of Mobile, and 150 miles west of Jacksonville. The city has a moist semitropical climate, and sunny days with frequent cool breezes predominate. From May through September the hot, humid weather can be uncomfortable at times, and afternoon thundershowers are not uncommon. Winter brings primarily warm, clear weather and occasional cold spells lasting no longer than three or four days. Cyclones occur most often during June through November.

**Area:** 46.53 square miles (2000)

**Elevation:** 20 feet above sea level

**Average Temperatures:** January 50.8° F, July, 81.7° F, average 68° F

**Average Annual Precipitation:** 61 inches

# History

### Many Flags Have Flown over Biloxi

An area across Biloxi Bay from the city, called Old Biloxi, was first visited by French explorer Pierre LeMoyne d'Iberville in 1699. The explorer, who was looking for the mouth of the Mississippi River, was instructed by the King of France to claim the coastal region. D'Iberville sailed into Biloxi Bay with a small group of men and established Fort Maurepas and a similar colony on the east shore, now the site of Ocean Springs. The word Biloxi means "First People" and was the name of a local Native American tribe met by d'Iberville and his men when they explored the land.

Since its discovery, eight flags have flown over the city including the French, English, Spanish, West Florida Republic, Mississippi Magnolia, Confederate State, Mississippi State, and that of the United States.

In 1719 Fort Louis was founded on the site of the present-day city, which served as the capital of French colonial Louisiana from 1720 to 1722. In 1783 Biloxi was taken over by the Spanish, who merely collected tariffs, while the area retained its strong French influence. The Spanish maintained their rule until 1810, when a rebellion occurred and the area was seized by American insurgents. At that time, Biloxi became part of the Republic of West Florida. Although petitions for statehood were denied, the Biloxi region became part of the Territory of Orleans (which had been part of the Louisiana Purchase). Two years later, in 1812, Biloxi became part of the Mississippi Territory. In 1814 a British attempt to capture New Orleans failed, but the British remained on nearby Ship Island until 1815. Finally, on December 10, 1817, Mississippi became the twentieth state of the United States.

### Biloxi Established as a Resort

During the 1820s Biloxi became a popular summer resort for New Orleanians wishing to escape their city's heat and yellow fever epidemics. Biloxi was incorporated officially in 1838. The city grew as families and their servants flocked to the area, which by 1847 had become the most important of the Gulf Coast's resort towns. By the middle of the nineteenth century even more people came for the ostensible healing powers of the waters, and for the balls, outings, and hunting events that enlivened the social scene.

At the time of the Civil War, Union troops took over nearby Ship Island and carried out a blockade of the gulf. Citizens protected the city from invasion by the Yankees through the threatening appearance of fake cannons, which were really only logs planted in the sand. Mullet fish, called "Biloxi bacon," saved the local populace from starvation in the war years. The first fish cannery opened in 1881, and the city's seafood industry quickly developed. By 1900 Biloxi was termed the "seafood capital of the world." Polish, Austrian, and Acadian French soon came to the city to work in the industry, adding their own cultural influences. Tourism flourished and more hotels were built to accommodate the visitors, many of them from the Midwest, who came to escape the harsh northern winters.

During the early twentieth century, the city grew and new developments included electricity, a street railway system, and telephone service. During the 1920s a paved highway was built along the beach, and more hotels were constructed as tourism increased. In 1928 the world's longest seawall, which spanned 25 miles of Biloxi's coastline, was dedicated. The 1930s saw the decline of the area's seafood industry, but a new boom took place during World War II when Biloxi was chosen to be the site of a new air force base.

## Legalized Gambling Revitalizes City

Mid-century saw the construction of a four-lane superhighway and the production of a sand beach, thanks to the use of hydraulic dredges. The development of Edgewater Plaza Shopping Center took place in the early 1960s, and the mall has served to draw people from all over the region ever since. In 1969 Biloxi suffered considerable damage when Hurricane Camille ravaged the entire Gulf Coast area, but the citizens soon rallied and rebuilt their town. A new era began in the city in 1992 with the opening of the first Las Vegas-style gambling casino. The resort casinos with their 24-hour entertainment availability spurred a tremendous growth in both local and tourist populations, and restaurants and other businesses grew accordingly.

Biloxi suffered some damage from Hurricane Georges in 1998 but rallied a year later to celebrate its tricentennial with music fests, sporting events, exhibits, and tours. The city's ninth casino, the Beau Rivage, opened in 1999, further stimulating Biloxi's economy through tourism and gaming revenues.

*Historical Information:* Harrison County Library System, 1300 21st Ave., Gulfport, MS 39501; telephone (228)868-1383; fax (228)863-7433

# Population Profile

## Metropolitan Area Residents

*1980:* 300,000
*1990:* 312,368
*2000:* 363,988
*Percent change, 1990–2000:* 16.5%
*U.S. rank in 1980:* 174th
*U.S. rank in 1990:* 157th
*U.S. rank in 2000:* 113th

## City Residents

*1980:* 49,311
*1990:* 46,319
*2000:* 50,644
*2003 estimate:* 48,972
*Percent change, 1990–2000:* 9.3%
*U.S. rank in 1980:* 428th
*U.S. rank in 1990:* 535th (State rank: 2nd)
*U.S. rank in 2000:* 707th (State rank: 3rd)

*Density:* 1,331.8 people per square mile (2000)

*Racial and ethnic characteristics* (2000)
White: 36,177
Black or African American: 9,643
American Indian and Alaska Native: 248
Asian: 2,590
Native Hawaiian and Pacific Islander: 58
Hispanic or Latino (may be of any race): 1,848
Other: 725

*Percent of residents born in state:* 46.2% (2000)

*Age characteristics* (2000)
Population under 5 years old: 3,721
Population 5 to 9 years old: 3,634
Population 10 to 14 years old: 3,078
Population 15 to 19 years old: 4,290
Population 20 to 24 years old: 4,779
Population 25 to 34 years old: 7,645
Population 35 to 44 years old: 7,695
Population 45 to 54 years old: 5,822
Population 55 to 59 years old: 2,044
Population 60 to 64 years old: 1,861
Population 65 to 74 years old: 3,390
Population 75 to 84 years old: 2,076
Population 85 years and older: 609
Median age: 32.5 years

*Births* (2002)
Total number: 864

*Deaths* (2002)
Total number: 478 (of which, 6 were infants under the age of 1 year)

*Money income* (1999)
Per capita income: $17,809
Median household income: $34,106
Total number of households: 19,606

*Number of households with income of . . .*
less than $10,000: 2,348
$10,000 to $14,999: 1,368
$15,000 to $24,999: 3,137
$25,000 to $34,999: 3,196
$35,000 to $49,999: 3,616
$50,000 to $74,999: 3,321
$75,000 to $99,999: 1,473
$100,000 to $149,999: 730
$150,000 to $199,999: 177
$200,000 or more: 240

*Percent of families below poverty level:* 11.2% (50.7% of which were female householder families with related children under 5 years)

*2002 FBI Crime Index Total:* 3,852

# Municipal Government

Biloxi has a strong Mayor-Council form of government, with council members elected by each of seven local districts. The mayor and council members serve four-year terms.

**Head Official:** Mayor A.J. Holloway, Jr. (R) (since 1993; current term expires 2005)

**Total Number of City Employees:** 674 (2005)

*City Information:* City of Biloxi, PO Box 429, Biloxi, MS 39533; telephone (228)435-6254; fax (228)435-6129; email mayor@biloxi.ms.us

# Economy

## Major Industries and Commercial Activity

Gaming and tourism is Biloxi's most important industry. By the end of the twentieth century, there were 12 Las Vegas-style casinos in the region, nine of which were in the city of Biloxi. The casinos feature restaurants, floor shows, and round-the-clock gambling. According to a formula devised when gambling was legalized, 8 percent of gross gaming revenue goes to the state and 3.2 percent of gross gaming revenue is distributed among city institutions, including the general fund, the city public safety department, the city school system, the county school system, and the county public safety department. The revenue of Biloxi's casinos exceeded $879 million in 2003, representing the city's greatest single source of revenue. This economic impact is only expected to increase with the opening of the Hard Rock Hotel & Casino Biloxi in the summer of 2005. The lure of gaming has also bolstered the region's tourism industry in general, as many gamblers also visit other area attractions outside of the casinos. In fact, most visitors are no longer merely overnight guests; now the average tourist stays 2.5 days.

The seafood industry contributes $450 million dollars to the Mississippi Gulf Coast economy, supporting an estimated 1,600 shrimp workers and 1,200 employees in seafood processing. Shrimp accounts for about half of the seafood market, contributing $250 million to the economy, followed by oysters, menhaden, and crabs. Thirty-eight seafood processing plants are situated along the Gulf Coast, with 11 in Biloxi. Building boats and producing boat paraphernalia are also big businesses in the area. Ingalls Shipbuilding, based 20 miles east of Biloxi in Pascagoula, employs approximately 10,000 workers, more than any other private employer in Mississippi.

Military and federal government installations are another key sector of the area's economy. The presence in the city of Keesler Air Force Base is responsible for a great part of the employment in the government sector of the economy, which represents nearly a quarter of all employment in the city. Keesler's economic impact on the Mississippi Coast equaled $1.4 billion dollars in 2002. In addition to the 12,600 active-duty personnel, Keesler employs 3,600 civilians and pays $179 million to military retirees. Local contracts initiated through Keesler in 2002 include $120 million in construction and $46.7 million in other local services and supply contracts. The John C. Stennis Space Center, located 45 miles west of Biloxi, impacts the local economy by employing approximately 30,000 military and personnel in more than 20 federal and state agencies. Other federal installations in the region are the Naval Construction Battalion Center, Naval Station Pascagoula, the National Guard facilities in Gulfport, and the Office of Supervisor of Shipbuilding, Conversion & Repair, located about 30 miles east of Biloxi.

*Items and goods produced:* seafood products, canning, boat building and repair, fishing nets

## Incentive Programs—New and Existing Companies

*Local programs*—The Harrison County Development Commission works with companies interested in developing or expanding their business in the county. Its services include the coordination of financial incentives, including tax abatements, as well as assisting in industrial park and Foreign Trade Zone activities. The Biloxi Department of Economic & Community Development offers a renovated building tax exemption to businesses that renovate existing structures in the city's central business district.

*State programs*—A tax credit program is offered through the Mississippi Department of Archives & History for the restoration of buildings listed on the National Register of Historic Places or designated as Mississippi Landmarks. The Mississippi Development Authority (MDA), through the Financial Resources Division, administers a variety of incentive programs to assist businesses in development and expansion. For large projects, a primary financial incentive is the Major Economic Impact Authority, which allows the state to issue general obligation bonds to secure up to $300 million for development. Other financial incentive programs administered by the MDA are the Rural Economic Development Assistance Program, Industrial Development Revenue Bond Program, Agribusiness Enterprise Loan, Business Investment Act Program, Energy Investment Program, Guaranty Loan Program, Minority Business Enterprise Loan, Minority Surety Bond Guaranty Program, Small Business Assistance Program, and Small Enterprise Development Finance Program. Additionally, in an effort to attract national and regional headquarters to Mississippi, the state offers income tax credits for each new job created and sales tax exemptions on construction materials and equipment used to build the new facility.

*Job training programs*—The state of Mississippi provides custom-designed pre-employment training, post-employment training, and upgrade/retraining services for new, expanding, or existing industries. The Employment Training Division of the Mississippi Development Authority administers the Workforce Investment Network (WIN). This network, the state's response to the federal Workforce Investment Act, combines federal, state, and community workforce resources to provide employment and training services to Mississippi employers and job seekers. WIN Job Centers, located throughout the state, provide access to employment, education, training, and economic development services. Other WIN services for employers include a database of qualified job candidates, assistance in writing job descriptions, proficiency testing, labor market data, and information on work opportunity tax credits. The Mississippi Contract Procurement Center, located in Biloxi, provides information about bid opportunities from federal, state, and local government agencies; it also offers training, marketing assistance, technical support, and counseling. The Gulf Coast Business Services Training Program assists local business with employee training.

### Development Projects

Construction in Biloxi nearly doubled between 2000 and 2003, rising from an estimated value of $70.7 million to $120.1 million. By early 2005, more than $800 million in construction was in varying stages of development on the Gulf Coast. It is, perhaps, no surprise that some of the largest projects are casinos. The Isle of Capri Casino Resort's $170 million expansion of its Biloxi facility will be completed in the spring of 2005. The Hard Rock Hotel & Casino Biloxi broke ground on a $235 million facility that is expected to open in the summer of 2005. Scheduled to open later in 2005 is the Silver Slipper, an $80 million project that will feature the only riverboat casino on the Gulf Coast.

A number of large-scale construction projects outside the realm of the gaming industry were underway in Biloxi in the mid-2000s. Voters in 2004 approved a $68 million expansion of the Mississippi Coast Coliseum & Convention Center that will be completed in 2007. The Gulfport-Biloxi International Airport was undergoing a series of expansion projects to increase its physical size, thereby increasing the number of airlines and passengers it can handle. Among projects in the amusement industry were a new $29 million Ohr-O'Keefe Museum of Art, expected to open in phases until its completion in 2007; the Gulf Islands Water Park, which will open in Gulfport in spring 2005; and a $35 million NASA space attraction that is scheduled to open in 2007.

*Economic Development Information:* Mississippi Development Authority, 501 N. West St., PO Box 849, Jackson, MS 39205; telephone (601)359-3449; fax (601)359-2832. Mississippi Gulf Coast Convention & Visitors Bureau, PO Box 6128, Gulfport, MS 39506-6128, telephone (228)896-6699; toll-free (800)237-9493; email tourism @gulfcoast.org.

### Commercial Shipping

Biloxi is located within one day's drive of more than half of the country's population and is within an hour from the major cities of New Orleans, Louisiana, and Mobile, Alabama. The Gulfport-Biloxi International Airport is the site of Foreign Trade Zone #92, a 1,000-acre area where foreign goods bound for international destinations can be temporarily stored without incurring an import duty. Cargo railroads serving Biloxi include CSX Corp. and Kansas City Southern Rail Line. The Mississippi State Port, located at nearby Gulfport, is the second largest handler of tropical fruit in North America and the nation's top exporter of frozen poultry to Russia and other former Soviet countries. In 2002 this port handled more than 2.1 million tons of cargo, including bananas and other fresh fruits, ores and other bulk cargo, frozen cargo, lumber and wood products, and containerized general cargo. Nine industrial parks on the Gulf Coast offer prime waterfront industrial sites on navigable water. Worldwide overnight and local shipping capability is provided by express, courier, and parcel companies that serve the coast region.

### Labor Force and Employment Outlook

The success of gaming in Biloxi is responsible for the creation of many new jobs in the area. Some, like those in the hospitality and tourism industries, are directly linked to gaming; others, like those in the construction, medical services, and general retail industries are indirect offshoots of an economy driven by casinos. In 2003 the Biloxi-Gulfport-Pascagoula metropolitan area ranked 127th among the "Best Places for Business and Careers" by *Forbes* magazine.

The following is a summary of data regarding the Biloxi metropolitan area labor force, 2004 annual averages.

*Size of nonagricultural labor force:* 113,500

*Number of workers employed in . . .*
   *construction and mining:* 5,200
   *manufacturing:* 6,000
   *trade, transportation and utilities:* 20,400
   *leisure and hospitality:* 29,600
   *government:* 24,000

*Average hourly wage of production workers employed in manufacturing:* $12.88 (2003 statewide annual average)

*Unemployment rate:* 4.0% (December 2004)

| Largest employers | Number of employees |
|---|---|
| Keesler Air Force Base | 15,674 |
| Grand Casino/Park Place Entertainment | 5,460 |
| Beau Rivage | 4,150 |
| President Casino | 1,991 |
| VA Gulf Coast Veterans Health Care System | 1,500 |
| Imperial Palace | 1,500 |
| Casino Magic Corp. | 1,360 |
| Treasure Bay Casino | 1,200 |
| Isle of Capri Casino | 1,077 |
| Boomtown Casino | 1,000 |

## Cost of Living

According to the City of Biloxi, the Gulf Coast's cost of living was 5.6 percent below the national average in 2003.

The following is a summary of data regarding several key cost of living factors for the Biloxi area.

*2004 (3rd Quarter) ACCRA Average House Price:* $188,335

*2004 (3rd Quarter) ACCRA Cost of Living Index:* 96.2 (U.S. average = 100.0)

*State income tax rate:* Ranges from 3.0% to 5.0%

*State sales tax rate:* 7.0%

*Local income tax rate:* None

*Local sales tax rate:* None

*Property tax rate:* 30 mills (2002)

*Economic Information:* Mississippi Development Authority, 501 N. West St., PO Box 849, Jackson, MS 39205; telephone (601)359-3449; fax (601) 359-2832

# Education and Research

## Elementary and Secondary Schools

The Biloxi Public School District reorganized its schools in 2002. Upon completion of the new Biloxi High School, the three junior high schools were consolidated. As a result, all seventh grade students attend Michel 7th Grade School and all students in grades eight and nine attend Biloxi Junior High School. The district offers a curriculum ranging from remedial education to college level advanced placement courses, as well as specialized programs in technology or vocational studies. There are four private schools in Biloxi: one high school and three elementary/junior high schools.

The following is a summary of data regarding Biloxi's public schools as of the 2002–2003 school year.

*Total enrollment:* 6,200

*Number of facilities*
*elementary schools:* 7
*junior high/middle schools:* 2
*senior high schools:* 1

*Student/teacher ratio:* 15:1

*Teacher salaries (2004–2005)*
*minimum:* $33,650
*maximum:* $62,965

*Funding per pupil:* $6,415

*Public Schools Information:* Biloxi Public School District; 160 St. Peters Ave., PO Box 168, Biloxi, MS 39533; telephone (228)374-1810; fax (228)436-5171

## Colleges and Universities

Mississippi Gulf Coast Community College has two campuses in Gulfport, and also offers classes in Biloxi through the Keesler Center of the Keesler Air Force Base. Also operating out of Keesler Air Force Base is the University of Southern Mississippi-Gulf Coast, which offers a variety of classes for civilians and military personnel. University College, one of 11 colleges of New Orleans-based Tulane University, has a campus in Biloxi that offers associate's and bachelor's degrees. Located in nearby Gulfport are William Carey College and Madison University, both within comfortable commuting range of students from Biloxi.

## Libraries and Research Centers

The Biloxi Public Library, part of the Harrison County Library System, consists of a main building and three branches. Its collection exceeded 300,000 items in 2003, an increase of approximately 5,000 items over the prior year. Special collections include genealogy, local history, and Mississippiana. The Gulf Coast Research Laboratory, located in Ocean Springs, is a state-funded institution administered by the University of Southern Mississippi. It offers a broad marine science curriculum and collaborates with the local commercial seafood industry to devise efficient methods of harvesting the waters and to develop future ventures, such as aquaculture.

*Public Library Information:* Harrison County Library System, 1300 21st Ave., Gulfport, MS 39501; telephone (228)868-1383; fax (228)863-7433

# Health Care

Biloxi has two hospitals, while the entire Gulf Coast region has seven general hospitals with more than 2,450 beds. Services at the Biloxi Regional Medical Center, which has 153 beds, include a cardiac intensive care unit, an emergency department, an outpatient care center, HIV services, a medical surgical intensive care unit, a neonatal intensive care unit, oncology services, pediatric intensive care, physical rehabilitation, psychiatric care, and a radiation department. The Gulf Coast Medical Center, with 144 beds, offers a variety of services including outpatient care, geriatric services, a medical-surgical intensive care unit, outpatient surgery, and psychiatric care. The Veterans Affairs Gulf Coast Veterans Health Care System consists of two hospital divisions—one of which is located in Biloxi—and three outpatient clinics to serve veterans in seven counties in Mississippi, four counties in Alabama, and seven counties in Florida. Keesler Medical Center, the second largest medical treatment facility in the Air Force, treats more than 52,000 active duty and retirees in the area and houses the only genetics laboratory in the U.S. Department of Defense. Cedar Lake Medical Park is privately owned by physicians and offers a variety of medical services.

# Recreation

### Sightseeing

Biloxi's bygone eras are captured in a number of historical structures. Visitors to Beauvoir, the last home of Jefferson Davis, only president of the Confederacy, can see where he lived, worked, and entertained the notables of his day. The house is set on a 52-acre estate containing museums with Confederate artifacts, two pavilions, and a cemetery with the Tomb of the Unknown Soldier. French and American architectural styles of the nineteenth century are exhibited in the Old Brick House, overlooking Back Bay. The restored Tullis-Toledano Manor, built in 1856, is one of the area's finest examples of the antebellum style. The Pleasant Reed House was named for its builder, who was born into slavery in 1854 and moved to Biloxi after the Civil War. The Redding House is a Colonial Revival home that is listed on the National Register of Historic Places. The Biloxi Lighthouse, erected in 1848, has been welcoming sailors since the days of the sailing schooners, and provides a wonderful view of the Gulf Coast area. The Spanish Captains Quarters and the Old French House, reflecting two distinct architectural styles and cultures that were once powerful in the area, date to the early 1700s; the Old French House is now a restaurant. Visitors to the Old

Biloxi Cemetery can read the gravestones of the first French settlers. Fort Massachusetts, on the western tip of Ship Island, was inhabited by the Confederate Army and later recaptured by Union Troops who used it for a prison. On the grounds are a library, a summer cottage, and a Confederate cemetery; tours are offered during the spring, summer, and fall.

Nine casinos are located in Biloxi, with three others elsewhere along the Mississippi Gulf. They are open 24 hours a day, seven days a week, and offer Las Vegas-style gaming, entertainment, hotel rooms, and retail shops, as well as other amenities. The Biloxi casinos are Beau Rivage Resort & Casino, Boomtown Casino, Casino Magic–Biloxi, Grand Casino–Biloxi, Imperial Palace Hotel & Casino, Isle of Capri Casino Resort, Palace Casino Resort, President Casino Broadwater Resort, and Treasure Bay Casino Resort. Casino Magic–Bay St. Louis is located in Bay St. Louis, and Copa Casino and Grand Casino–Gulfport are both situated in Gulfport.

Biloxi also provides family entertainment. The J.L. Scott Marine Education Center and Aquarium features 47 aquariums, a 44,000-gallon Gulf of Mexico tank, hands-on exhibits, and a touch tank. Time In Family Fun Center is the largest indoor playground on the Mississippi Gulf, and features putt putt, a two-story soft playground, video games, and food. Public swimming pools and miniature golf courses are also present in the city.

### Arts and Culture

Biloxi is home to a diverse collection of museums. The Maritime and Seafood Industry Museum traces Biloxi's 300-year history as the seafood capital of the world. The George E. Ohr Arts and Cultural Center exhibits work by ''the Mad Potter of Biloxi,'' whose pottery was so unique that it is housed in the Smithsonian. The Mardi Gras Museum showcases the splendor of that celebration at the restored antebellum Magnolia Hotel, the oldest hotel structure on the Gulf Coast. Moran's Art Studio displays original works of Joe Moran, George E. Ohr, and Mary and Tommy Moran.

The Saenger Theatre for the Performing Arts is home to the Gulf Coast Opera Theatre, Gulf Coast Symphony Orchestra, Gulf Coast Symphony Youth Orchestra, and KNS Theatre, a non-profit community theater. Biloxi Little Theatre, an all-volunteer community theatre, presents four major productions each year, and Center Stage presents a variety of regular performances, children's theater, and workshops.

### Festivals and Holidays

The Gulf Coast's variety of festivals, many of them centering on water events, delight both hometown crowds and visitors. Country Cajun Crawfish Festival in April draws thousands who want to share in the delicious Southern fare. May brings

**Visitors may enjoy a shrimp boat or a sail along the city's beachfront.**

the Great Biloxi Schooner Races & Blessing of the Fleet, a celebration of the onset of shrimping season that features a street festival, coronation of the Shrimp King and Queen, and a parade of boats. The Mississippi Arts Fair for the Handicapped is held in June, as is the 11-day Mississippi Coast Coliseum Summer Fair & Music Festival. A variety of Independence Day celebrations enliven the area in July. September is the time for the Biloxi Seafood Festival and the Scottish Games & Celtic Festival, held in Gulfport. The Arts are celebrated at the G. E. Ohr Fall Festival, and spectators line the beaches in autumn to enjoy the Mayor's Regatta. Christmas on the Gulf Coast features Biloxi's Christmas on the Water boat parade, the Lighting of the Fish Net Christmas Tree and parade, and Tullis Manor's Ethnic Christmas Trees.

Vietnamese New Year and the Black Heritage Festival salute local ethnic groups in January, and the area's French heritage is celebrated at Coast History Week with its French Encampment. Queen Ixolib (Biloxi spelled backwards) presides over the festivities at Mardi Gras, which has been celebrated longer in Biloxi than in New Orleans. March brings the St. Patrick's Day Parade, the Irish Heritage Festival, and the Oyster Festival.

### Sports for the Spectator

Biloxi has one professional sports team, the Mississippi Sea Wolves, one of 28 teams in the East Coast Hockey League. Up to 9,150 fans can watch their home games at the Mississippi Coast Coliseum & Convention Center, located in Biloxi. The coliseum is also the arena for the Professional Cowboys Championship Finals, held over four days each January.

### Sports for the Participant

The city of Biloxi maintains 26 parks encompassing 170 acres, as well as five community centers, 13 baseball and softball fields, four soccer fields, and 13 tennis courts. The Natatorium offers an Olympic-sized indoor-outdoor pool with a retractable top. Biloxi boasts three of the area's 23 public golf courses that attract golfers from all over the country.

The Mississippi Deep Sea Fishing Rodeo is the world's largest event of its kind. Held on the Fourth of July weekend, the event features a fishing competition open to all ages, as well as carnival rides, live entertainment, and fireworks. The Kingmaster 100 finishing tournament is held each May at the Isle of Capri Crowne Plaza Resort in Biloxi. The Great Biloxi Schooner Races are held in May, and the Race for the Case sailing regatta is held in July. In addition to organized events, boating and fishing enthusiasts can participate in the sports whenever they please. The Mississippi Gulf Coast houses more than 200 varieties of saltwater fish. Fishing and boating trips are available by charter, and the Biloxi Schooners take groups on a sail along the beachfront on two-masted replicas of nineteenth-century oyster schooners.

### Shopping and Dining

Edgewater Mall is the largest enclosed mall on the Gulf Coast. Totaling more than one million square feet, the mall is anchored by four major retailers, including Dillard's and J.C. Penney, and is occupied by more than 100 specialty stores. Edgewater Village Shopping Center features more than 40 stores occupying 200,000 square feet of retail space. Nearby, more than 60 retailers offer discounted wares at the Prime Outlets of Gulfport. In all, more than 1,300 retail establishments were operating in Biloxi in 2002, generating $924 million in revenue.

Biloxi's cuisine is an enticing blend of Spanish, French, Cajun, and traditional Southern cuisine. Gumbo, a succulent blend of seafood, okra, celery, scallions, and chopped bell peppers, is the featured item on the menu of Mary Mahoney's Old French House Restaurant. The restaurant, which was built in 1737, was once the site of the headquarters of the Louisiana Territory.

*Visitor Information:* Biloxi Chamber of Commerce, 1048 Beach Blvd., Biloxi, MS 39530; telephone (228)374-2717; fax (228)374-2764. Mississippi Gulf Coast Convention & Visitors Bureau, PO Box 6128, Gulfport, MS 39506-6128; telephone (228)896-6699; toll-free (800)237-9493; email tourism@gulfcoast.org

# Convention Facilities

The Mississippi Gulf Coast offers total convention space in excess of 500,000 square feet and more than 18,000 hotel rooms. The largest beachfront meeting and convention center in the South is the Mississippi Coast Coliseum & Convention Center, which has 180,000 square feet of convention space, up to 32 meeting rooms, and a 15,000-seat arena. The majority of Biloxi's nine casinos also provide meeting space, the largest of which is the 54,000 square feet of the Imperial Palace Hotel & Casino.

*Convention Information:* Mississippi Gulf Coast Convention & Visitors Bureau, PO Box 6128, Gulfport, MS 39506-6128; telephone (228)896-6699; toll-free 800-237-9493; email tourism@gulfcoast.org

# Transportation

### Approaching the City

More than 816,000 passengers moved through Gulfport-Biloxi International Airport in 2002. By 2006, upon completion of a $25.4 million expansion that will allow more airlines to operate at it, the airport is expected to serve 2.2 million passengers. The airlines serving the facility are AirTran Airways, ASA/Delta, Continental/Continental Express, and Northwest. For those who choose to approach the city by rail, Amtrak's Sunset Limited line provides service to Biloxi and Gulfport, among other cities along the Gulf Coast. Biloxi also has private and public marinas for those who choose to arrive by boat.

### Traveling in the City

Seven interstate highways provide access to the Alabama-Mississippi-Louisiana region via Interstate 10, which runs east and west across the northern part of Biloxi. U.S. Highway 90 also runs east and west, but along the beaches of the Gulf. Interstate 110 extends north and south through the city, and Highways 67 and 15 run north toward central Mississippi. Local bus service is provided by the Coast Transit Authority.

# Communications

### Newspapers and Magazines

The *Sun Herald,* Biloxi's daily paper, is published every morning. Weeklies include the *Biloxi-D'Iberville Press, Gulf Pines Catholic,* and the *Keesler News,* which is produced at Keesler Air Force Base.

### Television and Radio

Biloxi has one network affiliate, one cable station, and one public television station. Two FM stations—one commercial and one religious—and three AM stations broadcast from the city.

*Media Information:* The *Sun Herald,* Gulf Publishing Company, Inc., PO Box 4567, Biloxi, MS 39535-4567; telephone (800)222-9502.

### Biloxi Online

Biloxi Chamber of Commerce. Available www.biloxi.org

Biloxi Public School District. Available www.biloxischools .net

City of Biloxi Home Page. Available www.biloxi.ms.us

Harrison County Development Commission. Available www.mscoast.org

Harrison County Library System. Available www.harrison .lib.ms.us

Mississippi Development Authority. Available www .mississippi.org

Mississippi Gulf Coast Convention & Visitors Bureau. Available www.gulfcoast.org

*Sun Herald.* Available www.sunherald.com

### Selected Bibliography

*The Buildings of Biloxi: An Architectural Survey.* (City of Biloxi, 1975)

Husley, Val, *Maritime Biloxi* (Mount Pleasant, South Carolina: Arcadia Publishing, 2000)

Sullivan, Charles, *Mississippi Gulf Coast: Portrait of a People* (Northridge, CA: Windsor Publications, 1985)

*Note: This profile of the city of Biloxi was updated prior to August 2005, when Hurricane Katrina caused severe damage to the Gulf Coast region of the United States. The long-term impact of Katrina on Biloxi is unknown at the time of publication.*

# Jackson

## The City in Brief

**Founded:** 1821 (incorporated 1833)

**Head Official:** Mayor Harvey Johnson, Jr. (since 1997)

**City Population**
   **1980:** 202,895
   **1990:** 202,062
   **2000:** 184,256
   **2003 estimate:** 179,599
   **Percent change, 1990–2000:** −8.8%
   **U.S. rank in 1980:** 71st
   **U.S. rank in 1990:** 78th (State rank: 1st)
   **U.S. rank in 2000:** 127th (State rank: 1st)

**Metropolitan Area Population**
   **1980:** 362,000
   **1990:** 395,396
   **2000:** 440,801

**Percent change, 1990–2000:** 11.5%
**U.S. rank in 1980:** 92nd
**U.S. rank in 1990:** 92nd
**U.S. rank in 2000:** 95th

**Area:** 106.82 square miles (2000)
**Elevation:** 291 feet above sea level
**Average Annual Temperature:** 64.1° F
**Average Annual Precipitation:** 55.95 inches

**Major Economic Sectors:** services, government, manufacturing
**Unemployment rate:** 4.2% (December 2004)
**Per Capita Income:** $17,116 (1999)

**2002 FBI Crime Index Total:** 17,648

**Major Colleges and Universities:** Jackson State University, Belhaven College, Millsaps College, University of Mississippi Medical Center

**Daily Newspaper:** *The Clarion Ledger*

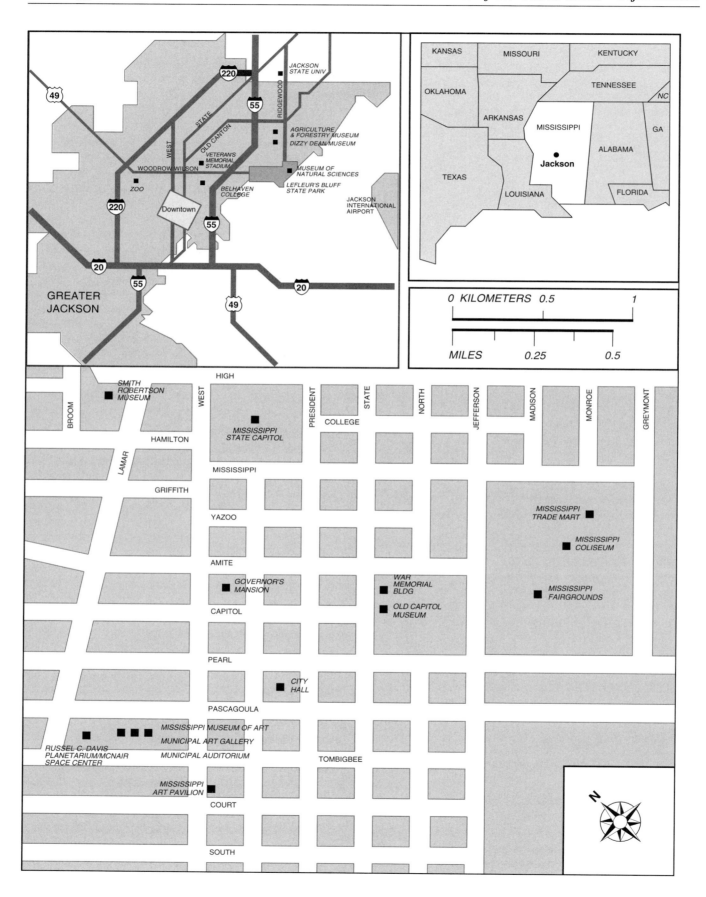

# Introduction

Jackson, Mississippi's capital and largest city, is still essentially a proud Southern city where the living is gracious and activities move at a relaxed pace. But Jackson is also a financial center and a rapidly growing major distribution center, with interstate highways and railroads affording access to all parts of the Sun Belt. Jackson is a forward-looking community with many cultural attractions.

# Geography and Climate

Standing on the west bank of the Pearl River about 150 miles north of the Gulf of Mexico, Jackson is about 45 miles east of the Mississippi River. The city is the seat of Hinds County, though parts of Jackson are also located in Rankin and Madison counties. The terrain surrounding Jackson is gently rolling; alluvial plains up to 3 miles wide extend along the river near Jackson, where some levees have been built on both sides of the river. Jackson receives approximately 55 inches of rainfall per year, but only trace amounts of snow, making it rather wet and significantly humid most of the year. The vicinity enjoys a fairly long warm season with light winds late in the day during summer.

**Area:** 106.82 square miles (2000)

**Elevation:** 291 feet above sea level

**Average Temperatures:** January, 45.0° F; August, 80.9° F; annual average, 64.1° F

**Average Annual Precipitation:** 55.95 inches

# History

## City Named for "Old Hickory"

The earliest inhabitants of the Jackson area were of the Choctaw and Chickasaw Native American tribes. During the late eighteenth century, a French-Canadian named Louis LeFleur began operating a trading post on a high bluff along the west bank of the Pearl River. The subsequent settlement became known as LeFleur's Bluff. In October 1821 when the Choctaws ceded their land to the federal government as part of the Treaty of Doak's Stand, LeFleur's Bluff was recommended as the most suitable location for a seat of government. A November 1821 act of the U.S. Congress established Mississippi's state government at this site, re-

named Jackson in honor of General Andrew "Old Hickory" Jackson. The city's development cannot be separated from its role as Mississippi's capital.

In little more than a year, a two-story brick statehouse was ready for the historic opening session of the Mississippi state legislature in December 1822. A second capitol, now known as the "Old Capitol," opened in 1840; that edifice, now a historical museum, was in turn replaced. Based on the design of the nation's capitol in Washington, Jackson's architecturally splendid New Capitol has, since its dedication in 1903, been the focus of Mississippi's government activities.

## Jackson Rebuilds After Fires

The cotton industry had made Jackson the capital of a wealthy state, but during the Civil War, when Union forces occupied Jackson under the command of General George Sherman, the city suffered three major fires. Because brick chimneys were the most visible structures left standing, Jackson earned the nickname "Chimneyville." The City Hall was spared from burning, probably because it was used as a hospital. Jackson residents had to begin slowly rebuilding after 1865. Railroads radiating out from the city contributed to the growth of transportation and trade in Jackson.

While Jackson's population was less than 8,000 people at the close of the century, by 1905 it had nearly doubled. Natural gas fields near the city were opened in the 1930s, providing inexpensive fuel for factories. Abundant energy coupled with existing transportation systems began to attract industries to the Jackson area. Since the 1960s an active program for economic development has stimulated building of many kinds, spurred industrial expansion, and attracted new residents to Jackson.

Jackson's lingering reputation as a racially divided city changed in 1997, when Harvey Johnson was elected the city's first African American mayor. He won 70 percent of the vote with a campaign that transcended race. Continuing to reinvent itself as a diverse and progressive city, Jackson made a major foray into the automobile industry by enticing Nissan Motor Co. to construct a $930 million automotive plant in 2003.

***Historical Information:*** Mississippi Department of Archives and History, 200 North St., PO Box 571, Jackson, MS 39205-0571; telephone (601)576-6850; email pubinfo @mdah.state.ms.us

# Population Profile

**Metropolitan Area Residents**
*1980:* 362,000

*1990:* 395,396
*2000:* 440,801
*Percent change, 1990–2000:* 11.5%
*U.S. rank in 1980:* 92nd
*U.S. rank in 1990:* 92nd
*U.S. rank in 2000:* 95th

**City Residents**
*1980:* 202,895
*1990:* 202,062
*2000:* 184,256
*2003 estimate:* 179,599
*Percent change, 1990–2000:* −8.8%
*U.S. rank in 1980:* 71st
*U.S. rank in 1990:* 78th (State rank: 1st)
*U.S. rank in 2000* 127th (State rank: 1st)

*Density:* 1,756.4 people per square mile (2000)

*Racial and ethnic characteristics* (2000)
White: 51,208
Black or African American: 130,151
American Indian and Alaska Native: 236
Asian: 1,056
Native Hawaiian and Pacific Islander: 24
Hispanic or Latino (may be of any race): 1,451
Other: 344

*Percent of residents born in state:* 82.9% (2000)

*Age characteristics* (2000)
Population under 5 years old: 14,438
Population 5 to 9 years old: 15,053
Population 10 to 14 years old: 14,388
Population 15 to 19 years old: 15,418
Population 20 to 24 years old: 16,015
Population 25 to 34 years old: 26,751
Population 35 to 44 years old: 26,944
Population 45 to 54 years old: 22,215
Population 55 to 59 years old: 7,086
Population 60 to 64 years old: 5,887
Population 65 to 74 years old: 10,105
Population 75 to 84 years old: 7,161
Population 85 years and older: 2,795
Median age: 31 years

*Births* (2002)
Total number: 2,929

*Deaths* (2002)
Total number: 1,615 (of which, 36 were infants under the age of 1 year)

*Money income* (1999)
Per capita income: $17,116
Median household income: $30,414
Total households: 67,782

*Number of households with income of . . .*
less than $10,000: 11,415
$10,000 to $14,999: 5,901
$15,000 to $24,999: 10,934
$25,000 to $34,999: 9,617
$35,000 to $49,999: 10,756
$50,000 to $74,999: 10,081
$75,000 to $99,999: 4,158
$100,000 to $149,999: 2,561
$150,000 to $199,999: 808
$200,000 or more: 1,551

*Percent of families below poverty level:* 16.6% (of which, 53.5% were female householder families with related children under 5 years)

*2002 FBI Crime Index Total:* 17,648

# Municipal Government

Jackson has operated through a mayor-council form of government since 1985. Its seven councilmen are elected by districts while the mayor is elected at-large for a four-year term.

**Head Official:** Mayor Harvey Johnson, Jr. (since 1997; current term expires 2005)

**Total Number of City Employees:** 2,400 (2002)

*City Information:* City of Jackson, PO Box 17, Jackson, MS 39205; telephone (601)960-1084; fax (601)960-2193

# Economy

**Major Industries and Commercial Activity**

Known as the ''Best of the New South,'' Jackson is a major business force in Mississippi. Its diversity of business and industry and its position as the state capital help insulate the metropolitan area from the economic downturns experienced by other cities. Jackson's success in drawing high-paying industrial operations is attributed to the city's combination of an attractive labor pool and a good quality of life.

The Jackson metropolitan area is home to 16 banks, 4 of which are headquartered in the city of Jackson: Consumer National Bank, First American Bank, First Commercial Bank, and Trustmark National Bank. Agriculture commodities represent a $180 million business in the tri-county area. Cattle is the primary commodity in Hinds County, though other commodities important to the region are cotton, grains, poultry, and timber. Government jobs, ranging from municipal to federal, employ approximately 40,000 residents of metropolitan Jackson. Manufacturing remains an important economic sector, with nearly 500 manufacturers present in the area. Construction, distribution and trade, health care, retail, telecommunications, and travel and tourism are also vital to the local economy.

One of the most promising sectors for Jackson is the automobile industry. For years, city officials had worked to lure automotive manufacturers to the area by highlighting its assets, namely the availability of large parcels of land, a well-developed energy and utility infrastructure, and low industrial expenses. Nissan Motor Co. responded to their efforts, and in 2003 produced the first truck in Jackson's new, $930 million automobile plant. This investment by Nissan helped offset the downturn the Jackson area had incurred with the bankruptcy of WorldCom Inc., whose headquarters were in nearby Clinton, Mississippi, as well as the losses it faced in 2004 when Tyson Foods Inc. announced the closing of its Jackson processing plant, which cut about 900 jobs.

*Items and goods produced:* automobiles and related automotive components, fabricated metals, electrical and electronic equipment, food products, apparel, wood products, furniture, transportation equipment, rubber and plastic products, portable electric tools, welded steel tubing, aircraft parts

## Incentive Programs—New and Existing Companies

*Local programs*—MetroJackson Economic Development Alliance (MEDA), an alliance consisting of the City of Jackson, Entergy Mississippi Inc., Jackson Municipal Airport Authority, MetroJackson Chamber of Commerce, and Hinds and Rankin county economic development organizations, markets and promotes the metropolitan Jackson area and encourages economic development through the expansions of existing businesses and industries and locations. Incentives for new businesses locating in the metropolitan Jackson area include low taxes, high quality labor, training programs, and tax credits for companies who create new jobs and provide basic skills for training and/or childcare. The City of Jackson Storefront Improvement Program offers grants for exterior structural improvements to businesses located in designated areas of the city.

*State programs*—The Advantage Mississippi Program was created by lawmakers in 2000 to attract businesses by improving the state's infrastructure and upgrading incentive packages. The Mississippi Development Authority (MDA), through the Financial Resources Division, administers a variety of incentive programs to assist businesses in development and expansion. For large projects, a primary finan-

cial incentive is the Major Economic Impact Authority, which allows the state to issue general obligation bonds to secure up to $300 million for development. Other financial incentive programs administered by the MDA are the Rural Economic Development Assistance Program, Industrial Development Revenue Bond Program, Agribusiness Enterprise Loan, Business Investment Act Program, Energy Investment Program, Guaranty Loan Program, Minority Business Enterprise Loan, Minority Surety Bond Guaranty Program, Small Business Assistance Program, and Small Enterprise Development Finance Program. Additionally, in an effort to attract national and regional headquarters to Mississippi, the state offers income tax credits for each new job created and sales tax exemptions on construction materials and equipment used to build the new facility. A tax credit program is offered through the Mississippi Department of Archives & History for the restoration of buildings listed on the National Register of Historic Places or designated as Mississippi Landmarks.

*Job training programs*—The state of Mississippi provides custom-designed pre-employment training, post-employment training, and upgrade/retraining services for new, expanding, or existing industries. The Employment Training Division of the Mississippi Development Authority administers the Workforce Investment Network (WIN). This network, the state's response to the federal Workforce Investment Act, combines federal, state, and community workforce resources to provide employment and training services to Mississippi employers and job seekers. WIN Job Centers, located throughout the state, provide access to employment, education, training, and economic development services. Other WIN services for employers include a database of qualified job candidates, assistance in writing job descriptions, proficiency testing, labor market data, and information on work opportunity tax credits. The Mississippi Contract Procurement Center provides information about bid opportunities from federal, state, and local government agencies; it also offers training, marketing assistance, technical support, and counseling. The Workforce Development Center of Hinds Community College provides industry-specific training, as well as additional educational courses and career exploration services.

## Development Projects

By far, the largest development project of the early 2000s was the new Nissan Motor Co. truck plant. The $930 million facility created 3,300 new jobs and has the capacity of producing 250,000 vehicles each year, the first of which rolled off the line in the spring of 2003. This factory, in turn, attracted suppliers and other support services to the area. In 2003 just over 100 new facilities were announced in the metropolitan Jackson area, with a total capital investment of $435.6 million and the creation of 2,065 jobs. The city is actively pursuing the restoration of Farish Street, a formerly vibrant business district, into an entertainment center. The historic King Edward Hotel, vacant since 1967, has been entertaining bids from potential redevelopers who are considering turning it into apartments and office space.

The new TelCom Center and the Capital City Convention Center were under construction and in the final planning stages, respectively, in early 2005. The Capital City Convention Center will sit adjacent to, and connect with, the new Mississippi TelCom Center, a 74,000 square foot conference center that is scheduled to open in 2005. Together, the two centers will act as a complex offering a variety of options for meetings and events. The Capital City Convention Center, with more than 240,000 square feet, is expected to be completed by 2009 at an estimated total cost of $61 million.

***Economic Development Information:*** Hinds County Economic Development District, 909 N. President St., PO Box 248, Jackson, MS 39205; telephone (601)353-6056; email exedir@hcedd.com. MetroJackson Economic Development Alliance, PO Box 3318, Jackson, MS 39207-3318; toll-free 800-566-5267; fax (601)352-5539; email info@metro jacksoneda.com.

## Commercial Shipping

Equidistant from Memphis to the North, New Orleans to the south, Atlanta to the east, and Dallas to the west, Jackson is advantageously positioned to serve the South's distribution needs. A transportation network of major carriers, regional airlines, major trucking lines, and rail lines operated by the Canadian National Railway and the Kansas City Southern Railway Co. assures Jackson's position as a vital provider of the nation's freight service. The Jackson Municipal Airport Authority operates Jackson-Evers International Airport (JIA) and Hawkins Field, both of which handle considerable freight activity. JIA is the site of Foreign Trade Zone #158, where foreign goods bound for international destinations can be temporarily stored without incurring an import duty, as well as the Mississippi Air Cargo Logistics Center. The nearest full-service port is the Port of Vicksburg, located on the Mississippi River 45 miles west of Jackson.

## Labor Force and Employment Outlook

Industrial leaders credit the metropolitan Jackson work force with a demonstrated willingness to adapt to rapidly changing technologies. High profit margins result from hourly manufacturing wages that are lower than the national average. Office space is inexpensive and abundant, and business operating expenses in Jackson are among the lowest in the nation.

The following is a summary of data regarding the Jackson metropolitan area labor force, 2003 annual averages.

*Size of nonagricultural labor force:* 232.6

*Number of workers employed in . . .*
  *natural resources and mining:* 700
  *construction:* 11,400
  *manufacturing:* 17,900
  *trade, transportation and utilities:* 48,500
  *information:* 5,700
  *financial activities:* 15,900
  *professional and business services:* 25,800
  *educational and health services:* 28,300
  *leisure and hospitality:* 19,600
  *other services:* 8,600
  *government:* 50,300

*Average hourly earnings of production workers employed in manufacturing:* $14.07

*Unemployment rate:* 4.2% (December 2004)

| *Largest employers* | *Number of employees* |
|---|---|
| State of Mississippi | 31,556 |
| University of Mississippi Medical Center | 7,200 |
| United States Government | 5,500 |
| Jackson Public School District | 4,500 |
| Nissan North America Inc. | 4,000 |
| Baptist Health Systems | 2,700 |
| St. Dominic Health Services | 2,600 |
| Mississippi State Hospital | 2,500 |
| City of Jackson | 2,400 |
| Rankin County School District | 2,000 |

## Cost of Living

According to the December 2003 issue of *SmartMoney* magazine, Jackson was the nation's most underpriced housing market, with an undervalue of approximately 10 percent.

The following is a summary of data regarding several key cost of living factors for the Jackson area.

*2004 (3rd Quarter) ACCRA Average House Price:* $215,368

*2004 (3rd Quarter) ACCRA Cost of Living Index:* 92.8 (U.S. average = 100.0)

*State income tax rate:* Ranges from 3.0% to 5.0%

*State sales tax rate:* 7.0%

*Local income tax rate:* None

*Local sales tax rate:* 1% on hotels and restaurants

*Property tax rate:* 169.14 mills

***Economic Information:*** MetroJackson Chamber of Commerce, PO Box 22548, Jackson, MS 39225-2548; telephone (601)948-7575; fax (601)352-5539; email contact @metrochamber.com

# Education and Research

## Elementary and Secondary Schools

Public education in Jackson is provided by Jackson Public Schools, the largest school district in Mississippi. Jackson is notable for being the city where Parents for Public Schools was founded in 1989. The group began a national movement to make public schools truly integrated.

The following is a summary of data regarding Jackson public schools as of the 2003–2004 school year.

*Total enrollment:* 31,580

*Number of facilities*
  *elementary schools:* 38
  *junior high/middle schools:* 10
  *senior high schools:* 8
  *other:* 1 alternative learning center, 1 career development center, 1 academic advancement center, 1 academy of academics and performing arts

*Student/teacher ratio:* 15:1

*Teacher salaries*
  *average:* $36,030

*Funding per pupil:* $7,429.73

Public facilities are supplemented by several private and parochial schools that serve the area.

***Public Schools Information:*** Jackson Public Schools, PO Box 2338, Jackson, MS 39225-2338; telephone (601)960-8700

## Colleges and Universities

Jackson State University is a public institution that has a total of 7,785 students enrolled in undergraduate and graduate programs. The University of Mississippi Medical Center has schools of medicine, dentistry, nursing, and health-related professions, and a graduate school of medical sciences. Hinds Community College, a two-year public institution enrolling 9,798 students, has a campus in Jackson. Belhaven College, affiliated with the Presbyterian Church, awards bachelor's, master's, and associate's degrees. Millsaps College, a private college affiliated with the United Methodist Church, awards bachelor's and master's degrees. Antonelli College is a private, two-year college based in Ohio with a campus in Jackson. Other Jackson-area colleges include Tougaloo College and the Mississippi College School of Law.

## Libraries and Research Centers

The Jackson-Hinds Library System supports 15 branches, 8 of which are located in the city of Jackson. Its collection numbers more than 535,000 books, videos, audio cassettes, compact discs, and multimedia kits, in addition to periodicals, microfiche, magazine and newspapers on microfilm, and CD-ROMs. The main library, the Eudora Welty Library, houses a special collection on Mississippi writers and serves as the Hinds County Bar Association's public law library.

Jackson State University maintains a large library holding 400,000 book titles, government documents, and a special Black Studies collection. The University's Center for Business Development and Economic Research conducts small business research. The Institute for Technology Development, a public/private interdisciplinary research corporation located at the Stennis Space Center, also contributes to the development of the area's business economy. The University of Mississippi Medical Center is a leader in innovative medical research.

***Public Library Information:*** Jackson-Hinds Library System, c/o Eudora Welty Library, 300 N. State St., Jackson, MS 39201; telephone (601)968-5811; fax (601)968-5817; email cmccallum@jhlibrary.com

# Health Care

With 11 hospitals and nearly 3,200 beds available for patient care, Jackson is a fully equipped regional health care center. Two of the largest facilities are the Mississippi Baptist Health System and the Central Mississippi Medical Center, with 642 and 429 beds, respectively. A major asset is the University of Mississippi Medical Center. Besides providing instruction in medicine, dentistry, nursing, and health-related professions, the University Medical Center operates the renowned University Hospitals and Clinics, which serve as Jackson's major teaching institutions. The Montgomery Veterans Affairs Medical Center, also a teaching facility, has 443 beds for long-term care. Other health care institutions in Jackson include Brentwood Behavioral HealthCare of Mississippi, Jackson State College Health Center, Methodist Rehabilitation Center, Mississippi Hospital for Restorative Care, River Oaks Hospital, St. Dominic-Jackson Memorial Hospital, and Woman's Hospital at River Oaks.

# Recreation

## Sightseeing

As the capital of the Magnolia State, Jackson offers visitors several buildings of historical interest. The New Capitol, built in 1903 in the Beaux Arts style of architecture and patterned

**Construction on the Mississippi State Capitol building was completed in 1903.**

after the nation's capitol in Washington, is the working seat of Mississippi's government. The restored Old Capitol, which was built in 1833 and served as the government seat for 70 years, is the home of the State Historical Museum. The Governor's Mansion was headquarters for Union Generals Grant and Sherman during the Civil War and has been home to 35 governors since 1842; it is one of only two executive residences designated a National Historic Landmark. City Hall is one of the few buildings left standing after Union troops set fire to the city. At the Gothic Revival Manship House, the 1857 home of Jackson's Civil War-era mayor, the daily life of a nineteenth-century Mississippi family is recreated.

On 100 acres in the heart of the city, the Jackson Zoological Park houses more than 300 birds, reptiles, and mammals representing 130 species from all over the world, as well as a children's petting zoo. At Mynelle Gardens, also known as Jackson's Botanical Gardens, more than a thousand varieties of plants are tended among several distinct gardens situated on seven acres. Battlefield Park is a memorial to Civil War battles fought there, with areas available for tennis and baseball. About 10 miles north of Jackson is the historic Natchez Trace Parkway, where a series of Indian paths became a post road. Mississippi Crafts Center, a showcase for folk arts, and pleasant picnic areas are located along the historic drive.

## Arts and Culture

With pride in their southern hospitality and culture, Jacksonians have created facilities and assured an atmosphere where the arts flourish. Mississippi Arts Center includes Thalia Mara Hall, home of the Mississippi Symphony Orchestra and the Mississippi Museum of Art, with its vast permanent collections, regular monthly exhibits, and visiting shows. Next door, the Russell C. Davis Planetarium offers a variety of public shows and educational programs, including Sky Shows and Laser Light Concerts, designed to give students of all ages a better understanding of the universe and space exploration. In one of the largest theaters in the country, Cinema-360 completely surrounds the viewer.

The performing arts offer variety to Jackson residents and visitors. New Stage Theatre and the Community Children's Theatre stage live dramatic performances, as do local colleges and national touring companies. Ballet is hugely popular in Jackson. It is presented locally by Ballet Mississippi, which is affiliated with the Ballet Mississippi Youth Ballet and the Ballet Mississippi School. Every four years Jackson is proud to host the two-week USA International Ballet Competition. The Mississippi Opera, Mississippi Symphony Orchestra, Mississippi Academy of Ancient Music, Jackson Choral Society, and Metropolitan Chamber Orchestra Society offer a full calendar of live music to the region's audiences. Jackson-area nightspots feature music for every taste, including reggae, blues, Dixieland, country, jazz, and rock.

The region's museums provide a wide range of arts and artifacts for viewing. The Mississippi Museum of Art is the oldest and largest professional arts organization in the state, and holds a collection of more than 3,000 works. Old Capitol Museum, formerly the seat of state government, now exhibits Mississippi's state historical collections. Wildlife specimens, aquariums, and ecological exhibits are on display at the Mississippi Museum of Natural Science. The Municipal Art Gallery displays month-long exhibitions of works that are available for sale.

The Mississippi Agriculture and Forestry Museum, spanning 40 acres, depicts the stories of men and women who made their living as farmers and woodsmen. African American culture and African American Mississippi history are featured in the Smith Robertson Museum and Cultural Center. The International Museum of Muslim Cultures is devoted to contributions Muslims have made to the city of Jackson, the state, the nation, and the world. Other Jackson museums of note are the Oaks House Museum, which is the oldest house in the city; the Manship House Museum, a rare example of Gothic Revival architecture in Mississippi; and the Mississippi Sports Hall of Fame and Museum, which features interactive exhibits and more than 500 televised interviews with famous Mississippi athletes.

## Festivals and Holidays

Jackson hosts the nation's second largest parade in honor of Dr. Martin Luther King, Jr. This two-week celebration in January also features gospel music, a talent show, and live entertainment. Right on its heels is the Dixie National Livestock Show, Parade, and Rodeo; held over three weeks at the Mississippi Fairgrounds, the event also includes a three-day Western Festival, a rodeo dance, and two trade shows. March brings Mal's St. Paddy's Parade & Festival, featuring the local favorite and world-famous Sweet Potato Queens. Spring ushers in the Crossroads Film Festival, McB's Crawfish Festival, the Returning Powwow & Frontier Rodeo, and the Mississippi Cultural Festival, which celebrates the diversity of cultures in the state.

Jubilee! JAM, held in downtown Jackson each June, is a celebration of music, arts and crafts, and food. Several events celebrate our nation's independence each July, such as the Old Fashioned 4th of July Celebration at the Mississippi Agriculture & Forestry Museum. September is the month for several cultural festivals, including Celtic Fest, the Farish Street Heritage Festival, and Festival Latino. Each October brings the huge Mississippi State Fair, a 12-day event that attracts nearly 550,000 visitors. Trustmark's Red Beans & Rice Celebration, featuring Southern-style food, music, and activities, is also held in the autumn, as are the Halloween Carnival and the Harvest Festival. Numerous musical and theatrical performances, a parade, and tours of architecturally significant buildings contribute to festive Christmas and Kwanzaa seasons.

### Sports for the Spectator

Mississippi's only professional baseball team is the Jackson Senators, who play at Smith-Wills Stadium from May through August. College football is a local favorite; thousands of spectators turn out for the annual Capital City Classic between the Jackson State University Tigers and the Alcorn State University Braves, along with other contests, pageants, and events at Memorial Stadium. The National Cutting Horse Association event is held each March at the Mississippi State Fairgrounds, with competition from amateur and professional riders. The Tour LeFleur Bike Race, a regional cycling event with multiple races throughout downtown Jackson, takes place the following month. The Southern Farm Bureau Golf Classic, Mississippi's only regular PGA tour event, is held over a week in late September.

### Sports for the Participant

Taking advantage of its warm climate, many of Jackson's sports facilities emphasize outdoor life. With 54 lovely parks in the city park system, residents and visitors can enjoy facilities ranging from playground to primitive camping. Public and private golf courses, tennis and basketball courts, baseball and soccer fields, jogging and biking routes, nature trails, swimming pools, bowling and roller skating facilities, a go-cart track, and a model airplane field are all available in the area. Sports leagues suited to children include T-ball, baseball, football, and soccer.

An outdoor asset to Jackson, only 10 miles northeast of the city center, is the 33,000-acre Ross Barnett Reservoir, where water sports—boating, sailing, water skiing, swimming, and fishing—abound, with additional areas designated for camping and picnicking. LeFleur's Bluff State Park offers camping, fishing, picnic spots, hiking trails, and a 9-hole golf course situated on 305 acres.

### Shopping and Dining

The central business district offers a variety of stores for shopping pleasure. Three major shopping malls are located in the city of Jackson. One of the largest is MetroCenter Mall, which houses more than 120 specialty stores in addition to its anchors of Dillard's, McRae's, and Sears. Numerous specialty shopping centers located outside of the major malls offer unique merchandise. Among these are the Chimneyville Crafts Gallery, specializing in crafts made by local artists, and two local outlets featuring the work of members of the Craftsmen's Guild of Mississippi. More than 40 antique dealers operate in the Jackson area.

Dining opportunities in Jackson's 400 restaurants can suit every taste, from fast food or southern style cuisine, such as southern fried chicken, biscuits, and pecan pie, to fresh Gulf Coast seafood, including shrimp, oysters, and crab. International establishments in the Jackson area feature French, Continental, Greek, Oriental, and Mexican menus.

***Visitor Information:*** Jackson Convention & Visitors Bureau, 921 N. President St., Jackson, MS 39202; telephone (601)960-1891; toll-free 800-354-7695; fax (601)960-1827; email info@visitjackson.com

# Convention Facilities

In November 2004, voters decided that Jackson would no longer be one of the only capital cities without a convention center. The Capital City Convention Center will have a $40 million economic impact on the city by creating 700 new jobs and attracting convention delegates, thereby boosting tourism and hospitality revenue. This center will sit adjacent to, and connect with, the new Mississippi TelCom Center, a 74,000 square foot conference center that is scheduled to open in 2005. Existing facilities include the Mississippi Fair Grounds Complex, which is comprised of the Mississippi Coliseum, an all-season arena with 6,500 permanent seats and up to 3,500 additional temporary seats, and the Mississippi Trade Mart, which offers 66,000 square feet of exhibit space and is ideal for professional conventions and exhibits of automobiles and other types of equipment. Thalia Mara Hall, adjacent to the Mississippi Arts Center downtown, offers 8,000 square feet of exhibit space and seating space for 2,500 people. Mississippi Veterans Memorial Stadium has 60,000 seats, while Smith-Wills Stadium, near the Agriculture and Forestry Museum, can seat 5,200 people. A number of area hotels offer meeting facilities, including the Hilton Jackson & Convention Center with seating up to 1,200 and meeting space of 8,100 square feet, and the Marriott of Jackson with 19 meeting rooms totaling 35,000 square feet.

***Convention Information:*** Jackson Convention & Visitors Bureau, 921 N. President St., Jackson, MS 39202; telephone (601)960-1891; toll-free 800-354-7695; fax (601)960-1827; email info@visitjackson.com

# Transportation

### Approaching the City

Most air passengers arrive in Jackson through Jackson-Evers International Airport. American Eagle, Continental Express, Delta/ASA/Comair/SkyWest, Northwest/Airlink,

Southwest, and US Airways Express serve the airport, transporting a total of nearly 1.2 million passengers in 2004. Hawkins Field, located in northwest Jackson and serving Hawkins Industrial Park, accommodates private and company planes. Motor traffic is handled by two primary interstate highways, I-55 running north and south, and I-20 going east and west; a third interstate, I-220, connects I-20 with I-55. Additional approaches to the city are U.S. highways 49, 51, and 80, and state highways 18, 25, and 468. Amtrak and Greyhound-Trailways Bus Lines accommodate rail and bus passengers traveling to Jackson.

### Traveling in the City

Jackson's urban mass transit is furnished by 45 city buses operated by JATRAN. The system's fixed route service carried 782,610 passengers for more than one million miles in 2003. More than 37,000 passengers with disabilities utilized the system's handlift service transportation that year.

# Communications

### Newspapers and Magazines

*The Clarion-Ledger* publishes an evening paper seven days a week. Weekly newspapers include the *Jackson Advocate,* Mississippi's oldest African American newspaper; *Mississippi Business Journal,* Mississippi's only statewide business publication; and *Northside Sun,* serving 9,500 paid subscribers. *The New Southern View* is a quarterly magazine featuring articles, local information, and a community calendar for residents of the Greater Jackson metropolitan area. Several other publications available in Jackson feature regional, religious, professional, and educational material.

### Television and Radio

Jackson has 13 television stations, with additional coverage available through cable television service and stations based in surrounding communities. Eleven AM and 18 FM radio stations broadcast from Jackson.

***Media Information:*** *The Clarion-Ledger,* 201 S. Congress St., Jackson, MS 39201; telephone (601)961-7000

### Jackson Online

City of Jackson Home Page. Available www.city.jackson.ms.us

*The Clarion-Ledger.* Available www.clarionledger.com

Hinds County Economic Development District. Available www.hcedd.com

Jackson Convention & Visitors Bureau. Available www.visitjackson.com

Jackson-Hinds Library System. Available www.jhlibrary.com

Jackson Public Schools. Available www.jackson.k12.ms.us

MetroJackson Chamber of Commerce. Available www.metrochamber.com

MetroJackson Economic Development Alliance. Available www.metroeda.com

Mississippi Department of Archives and History. Available www.mdah.state.ms.us

### Selected Bibliography

Brown, Jennie, *Medgar Evers* (Los Angeles: Holloway House, 1994)

Brown, Rosellen, *Civil Wars* (New York: Knopf, 1984)

Kimbrough, Julie L., *Jackson, MS: Images of America Series* (Mount Pleasant, South Carolina: Arcadia Publishing, 1998)

Patterson, James, ed., and Judy H. Tucker, *Wyatt Waters: Another Coat of Paint: An Artist's View of Jackson, Mississippi* (Brandon, Miss.: Quail Ridge Press, 1997)

# NORTH CAROLINA

# The State in Brief

**Nickname:** Tar Heel State; Old North State
**Motto:** *Esse quam videri* (To be rather than to seem)

**Flower:** Dogwood
**Bird:** Cardinal

**Area:** 53,818 square miles (2000, U.S. rank: 28th)
**Elevation:** Ranges from sea level to 6,684 feet above sea level
**Climate:** Warm and mild with abundant rainfall; subtropical in southeast, cooler in the mountains

**Admitted to Union:** November 21, 1789
**Capital:** Raleigh
**Head Official:** Governor Mike F. Easley (D) (until 2009)

**Population**
  **1980:** 5,882,000
  **1990:** 6,628,637
  **2000:** 8,049,313
  **2004 estimate:** 8,541,221
  **Percent change, 1990–2000:** 21.4%
  **U.S. rank in 2004:** 11th
  **Percent of residents born in state:** 63.0% (2000)
  **Density:** 165.2 people per square mile (2000)
  **2002 FBI Crime Index Total:** 392,826

**Racial and Ethnic Characteristics** (2000)
  **White:** 5,804,656
  **Black or African American:** 1,737,545
  **American Indian and Alaska Native:** 99,551
  **Asian:** 113,689
  **Native Hawaiian and Pacific Islander:** 3,983
  **Hispanic or Latino (may be of any race):** 378,963
  **Other:** 186,629

**Age Characteristics** (2000)
  **Population under 5 years old:** 539,509
  **Population 5 to 19 years old:** 1,653,851
  **Percent 65 years and older:** 12.0%
  **Median age:** 35.3 years (2000)

**Vital Statistics**
  **Total number of births (2003):** 117,981
  **Total number of deaths (2003):** 73,443 (infant deaths, 931)
  **AIDS cases reported through 2003:** 6,545

**Economy**
  **Major industries:** Textiles, agriculture, tobacco, furniture, bricks, metalworking, chemicals, paper, tourism, manufacturing
  **Unemployment rate:** 5.2% (December 2004)
  **Per capita income:** $28,301 (2003; U.S. rank: 37th)
  **Median household income:** $38,096 (3-year average, 2001-2003)
  **Percentage of persons below poverty level:** 14.2% (3-year average, 2001-2003)
  **Income tax rate:** Ranges from 6.0% to 8.25%
  **Sales tax rate:** 4.5% (food and prescription drugs are exempt; food sales are subject to local sales taxes)

# Charlotte

## *The City in Brief*

**Founded:** circa 1750 (incorporated 1768)

**Head Official:** Mayor Patrick McCrory (R) (since 1995)

**City Population**
   **1980:** 315,474
   **1990:** 419,558
   **2000:** 540,828
   **2003 estimate:** 584,658
   **Percent change, 1990–2000:** 28.9%
   **U.S. rank in 1980:** 47th
   **U.S. rank in 1990:** 35th (State rank: 1st)
   **U.S. rank in 2000:** 33rd (State rank: 1st)

**Metropolitan Area Population**
   **1980:** 971,000
   **1990:** 1,162,000
   **2000:** 1,499,293

**Percent change, 1990–2000:** 29.0%
**U.S. rank in 1980:** 36th
**U.S. rank in 1990:** 34th
**U.S. rank in 2000:** 34th

**Area:** 242.87 square miles (2000)
**Elevation:** Ranges from 730 to 765 feet above sea level
**Average Annual Temperature:** 60.1° F
**Average Annual Precipitation:** 43.1 inches

**Major Economic Sectors:** wholesale and retail trade, services, manufacturing
**Unemployment rate:** 5.2% (December 2004)
**Per Capita Income:** $26,823 (1999)

**2002 FBI Crime Index Total:** 49,052

**Major Colleges and Universities:** University of North Carolina at Charlotte, Queens University of Charlotte, Johnson C. Smith University, Davidson College

**Daily Newspaper:** *The Charlotte Observer*

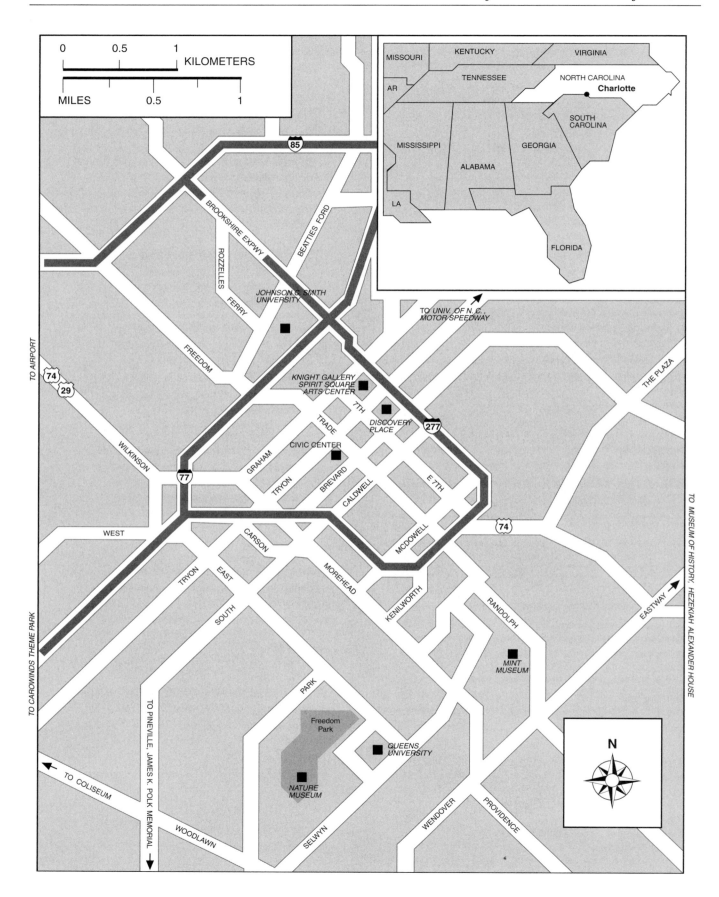

# Introduction

Charlotte, known as the "Queen City," offers a fascinating mix of southern culture and growing business mecca. A major economic center with growing finance and defense industries, the city's economic base continues to develop at a rate more than twice that of the rest of the country. An excellent interstate highway system, good railroad access, and an inland port facility are other factors that have made Charlotte the major distribution center of the Southeast and one growing in both national and international importance.

Even as Charlotte has emerged as a major city of the new South—and of the nation—its people continue to keep a clear vision of what makes a good life. Neighborhood streets are filled with majestic 90-foot water and willow oaks. Uptown's major thoroughfare is lined with trees. Each spring, the entire county is filled with delirious color as dogwoods and azaleas bloom. Just two hours east of the Appalachian Mountains and three hours west of the Atlantic Ocean, life in this comfortable, mid-sized city provides the best of all worlds.

# Geography and Climate

Charlotte is located in southwestern North Carolina's Piedmont region of rolling hills. The city is about 85 miles south and east of the Appalachian Mountains, and about 180 miles northwest of the Atlantic Ocean. Situated near the South Carolina state line, Charlotte is the Mecklenburg county seat.

Charlotte's moderate climate enjoys a sheltering effect from the mountains; its cool winters seldom bring extreme cold temperatures or heavy snowfall, while the city's long, quite warm summer days are mitigated by considerably cooler nights. Summer precipitation falls principally in the form of thundershowers, followed by comparatively drier fall weather.

**Area:** 242.87 square miles (2000)

**Elevation:** 730 to 765 feet above sea level

**Average temperatures:** January, 39.3° F; July, 79.3° F; average annual temperature, 60.1° F

**Average Annual Precipitation:** 43.1 inches

# History

### Colonists Curry King's Favor

The first colonial settlers—German, Scotch-Irish, English, and French Huguenot—in the region that is now Charlotte encountered a friendly, peaceful native tribe, the Catawba. The area's fertile soil brought more settlers, and by 1761 the Catawba were restricted to assigned territory in South Carolina. The colonists were aggressive in seeking political advantages. In the mid-1750s, for example, to curry favor with England's King George III, the first settlers to the area named their town Charlotte, after the king's wife, Charlotte Sophia of Mecklenburg-Strelitz (Germany). The town was incorporated in 1768. Their next step was to convince the royal government that they deserved to be a separate county. They diplomatically named their new county Mecklenburg, in honor of the queen.

But their ambitions did not stop there. Thomas Polk, one of the town's first settlers, and his neighbors wanted Charlotte as the county seat. Although there really was not much in Charlotte to justify such a designation, that did not stop these enterprising individuals. They built a log cabin where two Indian trails converged and called it a courthouse, and the existence of that courthouse led to the royal government's appointing Charlotte as the county seat in 1774.

### Gold Fever Spurs Boom

Charlotteans' "can-do" attitude also included a strong streak of stubbornness and independence. It was in Charlotte that the Mecklenburg Declaration of Independence was signed on May 20, 1775, predating the colonies' joint declaration by more than a year. During the Revolutionary War, British General Lord Cornwallis referred to Charlotte as "a damned hornet's nest of rebellion."

From 1781 to 1800 Charlotte added a flour mill and a saw mill to its growing settlement. In 1799, a young boy came upon a 17-pound gold nugget at the Reed Gold Mine, 30 miles east of the city. Soon, mines dotted the area and business in Charlotte boomed. Gold fever lasted until starry-eyed prospectors were lured west by the California Gold Rush of 1849.

### City Becomes A Financial and Textile Center

As the importance of the mines diminished, cotton took hold as the town's money producer. The invention of the cotton gin helped to establish Charlotte as a ginning and exchange center, and the town evolved into a textile power. The beginning of the city's development as a major distribution center began in the mid-1880s with the convergence of several railroad lines in Charlotte. After the Civil War, hydroelectric power was developed on the Catawba River near Charlotte. The city began to serve as a textile center in the late nineteenth century, and by 1903, more than half of the nation's textile production was located within a 100-mile radius of Charlotte. The evolution of North Carolina's interstate highway system in the 1900s further paved the way for Charlotte to become the major distribution center that it is today. Charlotte enjoyed great expansion after World War I. The location of a branch of the Federal Reserve Bank in the 1920s also had a major impact, and Charlotte subsequently evolved into a top banking center. In the 1940s Charlotte contributed to military efforts and in the 1950s underwent another period of growth. Charlotte became a banking and distribution center that grew more than 30 percent in the 1970s, profiting from a historic desegregation ruling and a dedication to metropolitan renewal and development.

In the 1990s, large-scale business expansions and relocations created many new jobs and an economy that continued to thrive despite the recession in the early 2000s. In 2005 the *Charlotte Business Journal* reported on a study that indicated Charlotte was the second-most popular destination for relocating families. Several factors contribute to the success of the area, including a cost of living below the national average and a graceful blend of historical homes alongside new development. The city's population is projected to grow nearly four percent annually, resulting in an expanding job market accompanied by a diverse business community that allows for prosperity even during difficult economic times.

**Historical Information:** Public Library of Charlotte & Mecklenburg County, 310 N. Tryon St., Charlotte, NC 28202-2176; telephone (704)336-2725. Hezekiah Alexander Foundation, 3500 Shamrock Dr., Charlotte, NC 28215; telephone (704)568-1774

# Population Profile

## Metropolitan Area Residents
*1980:* 971,000
*1990:* 1,162,140
*2000:* 1,499,293
*Percent change, 1990–2000:* 29.0%
*U.S. rank in 1980:* 36th
*U.S. rank in 1990:* 34th
*U.S. rank in 2000:* 34th

## City Residents
*1980:* 315,474
*1990:* 419,558
*2000:* 540,828
*2003 estimate:* 584,658

*Percent change, 1990–2000:* 28.9%
*U.S. rank in 1980:* 47th
*U.S. rank in 1990:* 35th
*U.S. rank in 2000:* 33rd (State rank: 1st)

*Density:* 2,232.4 people per square mile (2000)

*Racial and ethnic characteristics* (2000)
   White: 315,061
   Black or African American: 176,964
   American Indian and Alaska Native: 1,863
   Asian: 18,418
   Native Hawaiian and Pacific Islander: 283
   Hispanic or Latino (may be of any race): 39,800
   Other: 23,743

*Percent of residents born in state:* 46.3% (2000)

*Age characteristics* (2000)
   Population under 5 years old: 38,529
   Population 5 to 9 years old: 38,895
   Population 10 to 14 years old: 36,269
   Population 15 to 19 years old: 34,442
   Population 20 to 24 years old: 41,513
   Population 25 to 34 years old: 103,103
   Population 35 to 44 years old: 92,561
   Population 45 to 54 years old: 69,537
   Population 55 to 59 years old: 22,470
   Population 60 to 64 years old: 15,844
   Population 65 to 74 years old: 25,616
   Population 75 to 84 years old: 16,650
   Population 85 years and older: 5,399
   Median age: 32.7 years

*Births* (2003)
   Total number: 10,566

*Deaths* (2003)
   Total number: 3,903 (of which, 78 were infants under the age of 1 year)

*Money income* (1999)
   Per capita income: $26,823
   Median household income: $46,975
   Total households: 215,803

*Number of households with income of . . .*
   less than $10,000: 15,422
   $10,000 to $14,999: 9,254
   $15,000 to $24,999: 24,030
   $25,000 to $34,999: 28,791
   $35,000 to $49,999: 36,318
   $50,000 to $74,999: 44,158
   $75,000 to $99,999: 23,612
   $100,000 to $149,999: 18,999
   $150,000 to $199,999: 6,404
   $200,000 or more: 8,815

*Percent of families below poverty level:* 7.8% (35.6% of which were female householder families with related children under 5 years)

*2002 FBI Crime Index Total:* 49,052

# Municipal Government

Charlotte-Mecklenburg County is governed by two elective entities: an 11-member city council with an elected mayor, all of whom serve two-year terms; and a professional city manager, a position appointed by the city council.

**Head Official:** Mayor Pat McCrory (R) (since 1995; current term expires 2005)

**Total Number of City Employees:** 5,838 (2005)

*City Information:* Charlotte Mecklenburg Government Center, 600 E. Fourth St., Charlotte, NC 28202-2840; telephone (704)336-7600

# Economy

## Major Industries and Commercial Activity

Distribution and banking are the two major forces responsible for the emergence of Charlotte as a major urban center where economic growth and business development are flourishing.

Located in one of the nation's largest urban regions, Charlotte has more than six million people living within a 100-mile radius. In fact, more than half the population of the United States can be reached from Charlotte within one hour's flight time or one day by vehicle. Its proximity to a wide variety of markets has led to Charlotte's maturation as a financial, distribution, and transportation center for the entire urban region. The city has developed into a major wholesale center with the highest per capita sales in the United States, ranking sixth nationally in total wholesale sales.

Charlotte is also becoming recognized as a national and international financial center. The city is already the major banking center of the Southeast and only New York City has more banking resources. With more than $1 trillion in bank holding company assets and two major banking institutions (Wachovia and Bank of America), Charlotte is in a position to provide businesses with a wide array of sophisticated corporate banking services, as well as resources for financing and investing.

Several factors attract foreign businesses to Charlotte from such countries as Germany, Great Britain, Japan, France, Switzerland, Italy, and Canada. These include an inland port facility, a foreign trade zone, and the area's customs and immigration offices. More than 600 foreign-owned companies have facilities in the Charlotte region, representing one-third of all foreign companies in North Carolina and South Carolina combined.

In October 2000, *Entrepreneur* magazine listed metropolitan Charlotte as fifth on their ranking of the "Top 20 Large Cities" to own a business. As the subsidiary headquarters for a variety of major national companies, its urban region continues to attract sophisticated industries such as microelectronics, metal working, and vehicle assembly, as well as research and development, high-technology and service-oriented international and domestic firms. Charlotte boasted 286 *Fortune* 500 firms in 2004 within its city limits along with 1,200 manufacturing companies.

In recent years, Charlotte has emerged as a magnet for defense-related industries, with four of the nation's top ten defense contractors locating facilities in the area. In 2003, 149 defense-related firms were awarded contracts totaling more than $47 million; more than $160 million in defense related contracts have been awarded to Charlotte companies in the past three years.

Charlotte's business future is expected to remain diverse. More corporate headquarters, transportation- and distribution-related industries will lead growth, with knowledge-based industries following. In 2005, 48 biotech firms are located in Charlotte and 18 optoelectronic facilities exist within the region.

*Items and goods produced:* textiles, food products, printing and publishing, machinery, primary and fabricated metals, aircraft parts, computers, paper products

## Incentive Programs—New and Existing Companies

A variety of incentives, grants, bonds, and other programs are offered by the City of Charlotte and Mecklenburg County to help local businesses. Among them, two brownfield programs offer reimbursement for site development or tax breaks; a Façade Improvement Grant Program offers reimbursements up to $10,000 for façade renovations, landscaping, or signage improvements; a Business Investment Grant Program offers funds for eligible companies.

*State programs*—North Carolina, a right-to-work state with a low unionization rate, offers a revenue bond pool program through various banks. Several venture capital funds operate in the state and inquiries can be made through North Carolina's Council for Entrepreneurial Development (CED). Industrial Revenue Bonds issued by the state provide new and expanding businesses the opportunity to provide good employment and wage opportunities for their workers. North Carolina offers State Technology Based Equity Funds providing financing for new technology based enterprises, as well as TDA incubators for firms transferring new technologies into commercial applications. The state offers an income tax allocation formula that permits the double weighting of sales in calculating corporate income tax. The North Carolina Department of Transportation administers a program which provides for the construction of access roads to industrial sites and road improvements in areas surrounding major corporate installations. The William S. Lee Act makes available to new and expanding companies a 4 percent tax credit on machinery and equipment investments over $2 million, a jobs tax credit, worker training tax credit, research and development tax credits, and business property tax credits. The State Development Zones program offers tax credits for investments in machinery or equipment, creation of new jobs, worker training, credit on training expenditures, and research and development.

*Job training programs*—The state of North Carolina's Division of Employment and Training offers a unique system of job training programs that are available to any new or expanding manufacturing employer creating a minimum of 12 new production jobs in the state, and to any new or prospective employee referred for training by a participating company. The industrial training service provides great versatility in terms of types and length of training, and classes can be held in a company's plant or on the campus of one of the state's community colleges. The state of North Carolina furnishes instructors and, at the company's request, may test and screen job candidates. Employees may go through training before or after employment by the company. The industrial training service is financed solely by the state of North Carolina.

**Development Projects**

In the 10 years between 1994 and 2003, Charlotte gained 8,888 firms, announced more than $9.1 billion in new business, and created 79,646 new jobs on 99 million square feet of floor space. During that 10-year period, significant announcements were made by a variety of firms, including the Charlotte Bobcats, Carolina Panthers, Carrier Corporation, Carolina Place Mall, GM Onstar, Hearst Corporation, Transamerica, Solectron, SeaLand, T.J. Maxx Distribution Center, and B.F. Goodrich. The Charlotte-Mecklenburg Development Corporation (CMDC) began selling parcels of land in 2003 on the site of the Wilkinson Park Business Center. One investor was the real estate firm Beacon Partners, who in August 2004 planned the $5 million development of 5 free-standing buildings ranging from 12,500 to 22,080 square feet. Johnson & Wales University opened its new campus to about 1,000 students that will also provide

exceptional student housing featuring expansive floor plans, a fitness center, and game room.

Today's retail building in Charlotte is being shaped by a court ruling made in 2000. The retail building boom the area witnessed during the 1990s might have gone on indefinitely, but in a far-reaching development neighborhood opponents of a shopping center project took Charlotte and the developer to court and won. In a decision handed down by a Superior Court judge in May 2000, it was ruled that the city must change how it makes about 80 percent of its zoning decisions. The judge said that Charlotte's fast-track zoning process, under which approvals were made without a hearing, was illegal as it violated state laws. The decision impacted at least 50 projects that ranged from multimillion-dollar shopping center expansions to apartment buildings. The SouthPark Mall, at the center of the controversy, was set to grow by 50% and bring in tenants such as Saks Fifth Avenue and Nordstrom, but the ruling resulted in a limitation on square footage that prevented or delayed those retailers from setting up shop.

Prominent among Charlotte's success is the New Charlotte Arena that will serve as home to the NBA expansion Bobcat team along with the WNBA's Charlotte Sting beginning in the fall of 2005. Occupying about 780,000 square feet at a cost of $200 million, it will host college basketball, concerts, and other shows.

***Economic Development Information:*** Charlotte Chamber of Commerce, 330 S. Tryon St., PO Box 32785, Charlotte, NC 28232; telephone (704)378-1300

**Commercial Shipping**

Providing exceptional air service in and out of the city, Charlotte/Douglas International Airport ranked 33rd nationally in annual air cargo volume in 2004 with nearly 96,000 tons deplaned. Both domestic and international air freight moves quickly and economically to its destination. Charlotte also serves as a major hub for small package express. Ten air couriers have Charlotte operations in addition to commercial passenger carriers and large freight forwarders.

Charlotte is at the center of the largest consolidated rail system in the United States. Two major rail systems, Norfolk Southern and CSX Transportation, link 27,000 miles of rail systems between the region and 23 states in the eastern half of the country. About 300 trains pass through the city each week. The railroads, in fact, have enabled Charlotte to become a "port city," although the city is located about 175 miles from the coast. The Charlotte Intermodal Terminal (CIT), operated by the North Carolina Ports Authority, is a facility that links Charlotte with the port of Wilmington, Delaware, through a Seaboard Railroad System piggyback ramp operation. CIT is the first fully operational inland container staging and storage facility in the United States operated by a port authority.

More than 200 trucking companies move products and materials through the area. Forty percent of the nation's 100 largest trucking firms have Charlotte operations.

**Labor Force and Employment Outlook**

The work force in both Mecklenburg County and surrounding areas is plentiful. Studies have found North Carolina workers are more productive than other workers in the same industries nationally. Several area educational institutions provide education and training for employees, including classes in technical skills and management development, as well as graduate degree programs. In 2003 alone, new Charlotte firms created 16,171 new jobs.

The following is a summary of data regarding the Charlotte-Gastonia-Rock Hill labor force, 2003 annual averages.

*Size of nonagricultural labor force:* 823,400

*Number of workers employed in . . .*
   *manufacturing:* 106,200
   *trade, transportation, and utilities:* 176,500
   *information:* 24,300
   *financial activities:* 69,000
   *professional and business services:* 118,700
   *educational and health services:* 68,200
   *leisure and hospitality:* 71,000
   *other services:* 36,600
   *government:* 104,700

*Average hourly earnings of production workers employed in manufacturing:* $14.54

*Unemployment rate:* 5.2% (December 2004)

| Largest employers | Number of employees |
|---|---|
| Wachovia Corporation | 18,967 |
| Carolinas HealthCare System | 15,257 |
| Charlotte-Mecklenburg Schools | 15,134 |
| Bank of America | 13,000 |
| City of Charlotte | 5,838 |
| US Airways | 5,749 |
| Duke Energy Corp. | 5,400 |
| Mecklenburg County | 5,373 |
| Presbyterian Healthcare/Novant Health | 5,166 |
| Excel Staffing Services of Charlotte, Inc. | 4,500 |

**Cost of Living**

A slightly lower than national average cost of living and broad economic base converge to make Charlotte attractive to new residents.

The following is a summary of data regarding several key cost of living factors for the Charlotte area.

*2004 (3rd Quarter) ACCRA Average House Price:* $218,000

*2004 (3rd Quarter) ACCRA Cost of Living Index:* 92.9 (U.S. average = 100.0)

*State income tax rate:* Ranges from 6.0% to 8.25%

*State sales tax rate:* 4.5% (food and prescription drugs are exempt; food sales are subject to local sales taxes)

*Local income tax rate:* None

*Local sales tax rate:* 3.0% (county-wide) (restaurant food sales are subject to local sales tax of 7.5%; 2.0% in grocery stores for food)

*Property tax rate:* City, $.42 plus County, $.7567 per $100 assessed value; assessed value based on 100% of established market value (2005)

**Economic Information:** Charlotte Chamber of Commerce, 330 S. Tryon St., PO Box 32785, Charlotte, NC 28232; telephone (704)378-1300

# Education and Research

**Elementary and Secondary Schools**

Charlotte is at the forefront of innovation in education today. The public school system, which implemented court-ordered busing to achieve desegregation in 1970, is now considered a model for the entire country in terms of race relations. In 2002 the Council of Great City Schools issued a report profiling the school district as one of four nationwide having "reduced racial disparities in academic achievement." A key component to their success comes from the Equity Plus program that operates in specific schools and features reduced student-teacher ratios, added teacher incentives, and additional supplies and equipment.

As one of four finalists in the Broad Foundation's 2004 annual competition, Charlotte-Mecklenburg schools received $125,000 in scholarship monies for graduating seniors in recognition of bridging the inequities in achievement among ethnic groups as well as between high and low income students. A study by *Forbes* in February 2004 ranked the district seventh on its "The Best Education in the Biggest Cities" list that focused on various factors such as housing values and high school graduation rates. In the 2004–2005 school year, the district is testing a "Pay for Performance" program that links specific student academic performance directly to teacher bonuses.

The following is a summary of data regarding Charlotte's public schools as of the 2004–2005 school year.

*Total enrollment:* 121,640

*Number of facilities*
  *elementary schools:* 91
  *junior high/middle schools:* 32
  *senior high schools:* 17
  *other:* 11

*Student/teacher ratio:* kindergarten-grade 3, 19:1; grades 4-8, 22:1; 9-12, 29:1

*Teacher salaries*
  *minimum:* $28,724
  *maximum:* $65,566

*Funding per pupil:* $7,311

Education in grades kindergarten through twelve is also provided at more than 60 private schools in the area.

***Public Schools Information:*** Charlotte-Mecklenburg Schools, 701 E. Second St., Charlotte, NC 28202; telephone (980) 343-7450; fax (980)343-5164; email cms@cms.k12.nc.us

### Colleges and Universities

The University of North Carolina at Charlotte, the fastest growing campus in the University of North Carolina system, offers dozens of undergraduate options in 7 colleges to its nearly 20,000 students, including approximately 4,000 graduate students. Three local institutions are affiliated with the Presbyterian Church: Davidson College, Queens University of Charlotte, and Johnson C. Smith University. With 1,600 students, Davidson College in northern Mecklenburg County was founded in 1837 and is considered one of the most competitive liberal arts and sciences colleges in the nation. Queens University of Charlotte, formerly (in 2002) Queens College, offers bachelor's degree programs in arts, science, nursing, and music. Originally chartered as the Biddle Memorial Institute in 1867, Johnson C. Smith University is one of the oldest historically African American colleges in the country with more than half of its 1,500 students coming from out-of-state. Winthrop College, located in Rock Hill, South Carolina, is highly regarded for its executive master's in business administration program, as well as its training of future teachers and home economists. In fall 2004 Johnson & Wales University, opened the doors to its career-focused institution that operates in five other states nationwide.

### Libraries and Research Centers

The Public Library of Charlotte & Mecklenburg County is North Carolina's largest system, with a 187,000-square-foot main library, six regional libraries, and 16 branch locations. The library system lends books, CDs, tapes, videos, and soft-ware along with providing many searchable online resources. The main library downtown contains a large local history and genealogy library, a depository for U.S. Government publications, an International Business Library, and the Virtual Library—a computer learning laboratory. Other libraries in the area include those affiliated with academic institutions (such as the one million volume collection at the University of North Carolina's J. Murrey Atkins Library), commercial concerns, and medical and legal organizations. Research centers affiliated with the University of North Carolina at Charlotte conduct activities in such fields as microelectronics, bimolecular engineering, social science and urban studies. The University Research Park, located on a 3,200-acre campus near the University of North Carolina at Charlotte, has attracted a combination of regional and national businesses engaged in research, manufacturing, and services.

***Public Library Information:*** Public Library of Charlotte & Mecklenburg County, 310 N. Tryon St., Charlotte, NC 28202-2176; telephone (704)336-2725

# Health Care

The importance of the availability of quality, cost-efficient health care has long been recognized by Charlotte's citizens. Early recognition in the community of future cost problems and cooperative efforts to keep cost increases under control have resulted in reasonable costs, thoughtful use of services by physicians, and efficient hospital management. Four major hospitals in the area fall under the Carolinas HealthCare System and include Carolinas Medical Center (861 beds), Carolinas Medical Center–Mercy Hospital (305 beds), Carolinas Medical Center–Pineville (109 beds), and Carolinas Medical Center–University (130 beds). Another major hospital system is Presbyterian Healthcare, comprised of three area hospitals in Charlotte, Matthews, and Huntersville.

# Recreation

### Sightseeing

Sightseers in Charlotte enjoy the Mecklenburg County park system, which includes 175 parks with more than 14,000 acres, plus an extensive growing greenway system. Latta Plantation Nature Preserve—1,290 acres off Mountain Island Lake in northern Mecklenburg County—is a prime example, and the park is becoming a major recreational center in the Southeast. Special features include the Equestrian Center, with riding trails and a major show facility; the

Carolina Raptor Center, a unique facility for caring for and exhibiting birds of prey, and an environmental center that includes a museum and permanent research and rehabilitation facilities; and Historic Latta Plantation, a restored plantation home dating from the early 1800s that includes a small operating farm that is also listed on the National Register of Historic Places. Nature trails and picnic areas are available.

History buffs can take in the Hezekiah Alexander Home, built in 1774 and considered the oldest building in Mecklenburg County. Listed on the National Register of Historic Places, the home is furnished with authentic articles from the eighteenth century, and the adjacent Charlotte Museum of History presents a variety of changing exhibits. Located at Pineville is the James K. Polk Memorial, a state historic site devoted to the country's eleventh president with log buildings and their furnishings that serve as period pieces dating from the early 1800s and a visitor's center featuring a film on Polk's life. At Reed Gold Mine, where gold was discovered in 1799, visitors today can still pan for gold.

Within the city, Ray's Splash Planet Waterpark has 117,000 gallons of water in its indoor waterpark and also features a fitness center, concessions, and a summer camp.

Fun beckons just outside of Charlotte, too. To the south, but within Mecklenburg County, is Paramount's Carowinds, a 105-acre amusement park featuring rides, a 13-acre WaterWorks park with a 25,000-square-foot wave pool named Big Wave Bay, and in 2005 *Nickelodeon Live* presents favorite characters from their cable television shows. The North Carolina Transportation Museum in Spencer provides train rides, antique autos, and transportation displays on its 53-acre site.

**Arts and Culture**

Culturally minded residents and visitors in Charlotte can view a wide array of collections at the Mint Museum of Art, founded in 1936, that houses more than 27,000 items including American art, pre-Columbian art, and American and European ceramics by such artists as Winslow Homer, Andrew Wyeth, and Frederic Remington. As the oldest art museum and emerging as a major southern landmark in North Carolina, the museum's building formerly served as the first branch of the U.S. Mint from 1837–61. Other collections include a 6,000-piece costume collection, antique maps, and contemporary American prints. In 1999 its sister museum, the Mint Museum of Arts & Crafts, opened to present ceramics, glass, jewelry, wood, and metalworks from historical to contemporary times.

The crown jewel of Charlotte's arts scene is the North Carolina Blumenthal Performing Arts Center, home to the Charlotte Symphony, which offers 115 performances each season with frequent guest artists; and Opera Carolina, which stages four major operas annually. Also anchored

there are the Charlotte Choral Society, the Carolinas Concert Association, the Oratorio Singers of Charlotte, the Charlotte Repertory Theatre Company, and the North Carolina Dance Theatre. The city's other musical groups include the Charlotte Boys & Girls Choir, Carolina Pro Musica, Chamber Music of Charlotte, and the Charlotte Music Club. The Charlotte Pops Orchestra brings a summer series of 16 free open air concerts to Symphony Park at SouthPark.

The state-of-the-art Verizon Wireless Pavilion (formerly Blockbuster Pavilion), which showcases world-class concerts, Broadway shows, opera, and ballet, is an outdoor amphitheater that can accommodate 19,000 people. For theater buffs, Charlotte Repertory Theatre, the city's first and only resident Equity theater company, presents three productions each summer. Theatre Charlotte, the state's oldest community theater, presents over 2,600 performances productions fueled by more than 500 local volunteers each year. Central Piedmont Community College's (CPCC) Summer Theatre has chased away the summer doldrums with its mostly-musicals schedule for over three decades. Since 1954, the Children's Theatre of Charlotte produces plays for and by children, presents special events, and holds classes.

The Charlotte City Ballet, a local company founded in 1985, offers classical and non-traditional performance throughout the year as does the Charlotte Youth Ballet. Cultural events, lectures, and entertainment are presented at the Afro-American Cultural Center.

Offerings in theater—as well as the other arts—are enriched in Charlotte because of its many colleges and universities. The University of North Carolina at Charlotte, Davidson College, Queens University of Charlotte, and Johnson C. Smith University all offer a variety of cultural programs for the general public. UNCC is the site of WFAE-FM, Charlotte's National Public Radio affiliate.

Spirit Square is located in the historic First Baptist Church, built in 1909. The arts center is the result of private and corporate support, as well as a $2.5 million bond issue. More than 500,000 people visit the facility each year to enjoy its four galleries, take classes in such areas as theater, fiber, clay, and dance, and view performances in its intimate 750-seat theater. Watch performing artists, in all their variety and from all over the world at Spirit Square's 180-seat, black-box Duke Power Theatre, which is home to the Actor's Theater of Charlotte. Spirit Square is also home for area arts groups and has helped to spur the revitalization of Charlotte's uptown. It is considered the keystone of Charlotte's cultural center on North Tryon Street, which includes restaurants, several art galleries, the public library, and Discovery Place.

Located adjacent to Freedom Park, the Nature Museum is geared to younger visitors and features nature trails, live animals, classes, a planetarium, and a puppet theater.

Collectible treasures from around the world are on display at the Farvan International Gallery.

There are 14 galleries located in "NoDa" as Charlotte's historic northern district is called. The ArtHouse Center for Creative Expression has fine art, photography, textile art, and sculptures. The Center of the Earth Gallery (CTE) is award-winning and displays an eclectic collection of contemporary works from both regional and national artists.

Visitors can explore the wonders of science at Discovery Place, ranked among the 10 most outstanding hands-on science and technology museums in the country, which includes an IMAX Dome Theatre.

### Festivals and Holidays

Charlotteans like to celebrate, and festivals abound almost year-round. The biggest is the three-day Spring Fest, which draws more than 300,000 people uptown to celebrate the rites of spring each April. Among the offerings are food, entertainment by local and nationally known performers, games, art exhibits, and an art competition. Also, during May, the city celebrates the 600 Festival, an auto-racing event tied to the Coca-Cola 600 that includes a parade, fireworks, and unusual competitive events such as a bathtub derby and culminates with a charity ball.

Numerous neighborhoods have festivals and celebrations throughout the summer. In the fall, Festival in the Park, held in Freedom Park, says farewell to summer in a fun-filled 4 days featuring 175 artists and nearly 1,000 entertainers. The free event has art awards totaling about $4,000. The annual Greek Yiasou Festival celebrates Charlotte's largest ethnic community, and November's Southern Christmas Show, the largest indoor event in the Carolinas and Virginia, is a holiday crafts show that extends over 10 days at Charlotte's Merchandise Mart. Each year the Christmas season is launched in Charlotte with the Carolinas' Carousel Parade on Thanksgiving Day.

### Sports for the Spectator

The Carolina Panthers, a National Football League expansion team, began play in Charlotte in the 1996 season in Bank of America Stadium (originally Ericsson Stadium), a $187 million state-of-the-art black and silver 73,258-seat stadium that was custom built for them. Local basketball fans were disappointed when the Charlotte Hornets decided to move their professional National Basketball Association team to New Orleans. However, in 2004 the expansion Bobcats picked up play at the Charlotte Coliseum while they await a brand new $264 million arena located in the city. Since 1997 the Charlotte Sting has played for the Women's National Basketball League (WNBA). Professional golf comes to town during May for the Wachovia Championship at Quail Hollow Club, founded in 2003. To date, the event has sold out all of its 35,000 daily tickets.

The annual Continental Tire Bowl has been extremely popular since its inception in 2002. The University of North Carolina at Charlotte 49ers plays basketball at the Halton Arena. The Shrine Bowl Game at Memorial Stadium pits the top high-school stars from North and South Carolina. Proceeds from the event, which began in 1937, go to the Shriners Hospital for Crippled Children in Greenville, South Carolina.

Until 2005 the *Charlotte Observer* Marathon Run for Peace had some of the top name runners in the country. However, it suffered a setback when the former director pled guilty to embezzlement; the group is planning to revive the run in January 2006. A local running store has inserted itself into the picture by announcing a Run for Your Life marathon to occur in December 2005. Spring signals the opening of the 167,000-seat Lowe's Motor Speedway, which attracts fans to its NASCAR events, including the Coca-Cola 600 during Memorial Day weekend, among other races. Summer ushers in a full season of baseball played by the Charlotte Knights, the city's Triple A minor league team in the Chicago White Sox farm system.

### Sports for the Participant

For active pursuits, Charlotte-Mecklenburg County boasts 14,000 acres of parks and over 20 recreation centers. The city's more than 175 parks include recreation centers, a petting zoo, playgrounds, more than 1,000 swimming pools, volleyball, basketball, 100 tennis courts, soccer and softball fields, 10 golf courses, and a motocross track. A BMX bike track (which has hosted national tournaments) is located at the Hornets Nest Park, which sits on 102 acres and also has facilities for baseball, softball, basketball, and volleyball; 10 playgrounds; and a lake with a fishing pier. One of the park system's oldest recreation centers, the Enderly Recreation Center, underwent a major renovation and in May 2005 opened with 21,000 square feet that includes a gymnasium, three multipurpose rooms, senior and youth activity rooms, a computer lab, and an adult fitness center. Skateboarders can enjoy expansive new courses, a multi bowl, and a variety of terrains at Grayson Skatepark, opening in spring 2005.

For those who prefer water activities, Lake Wylie and Lake Norman are about a 20-minute drive from uptown. Boating, swimming, water skiing, and fishing can be enjoyed in an unspoiled wooded environment. The mountains of North Carolina—the highest east of the Mississippi—are just two hours away by car, and they offer the delights of skiing, backpacking, hiking, and mountain climbing. Two hundred miles of Atlantic Ocean beach, with beckoning surf and offerings of swimming, sunning, boating, and fishing, are a three-hour drive away.

### Shopping and Dining

A variety of shopping experiences are available to Charlotteans. The Eastland Mall offers more than 100 stores including Sears and Burlington Coat Factory, an ice rink called "Ice House" that offers lessons and party packages, and cinemas. Midtown Square is a discount mall with a central food court that is in the midst of redevelopment that will, by 2007, include high-profile stores such as Target and Home Depot EXPO Design Center. Meanwhile SouthPark Mall, Charlotte's most upscale facility, offers 1.2 million square feet of shopping space in one of America's top selling retail centers, with plans to add a Nordstrom and Neiman Marcus by the holiday season of 2006. Adjacent to Carowinds amusement park is the Outlet Marketplace Mall, which features more than 50 outlet and off-price stores, a farmer's market, a flower market, and a food court. Charlotte Regional Farmers Market features locally grown produce, baked goods, flowers, and crafts from March through December. The North Davidson district is Charlotte's version of New York's SoHo and has been dubbed "NoDa" by locals; the district counts antique and boutique shops among its eclectic mix.

From an elegant dinner by candlelight to a rollicking night of food with Dixieland jazz, a variety of dining options is offered in the city. Visitors may chose from Chinese, Japanese, Indian, Egyptian, Arabian, Greek, French, Indian or Mexican cuisines, as well as "good old down-home" Southern cooking. Among the mid-South regional food specialties diners may seek in Charlotte are southern fried chicken, barbecue, country ham, and Brunswick stew—a mixture of chicken, pork, corn, tomatoes, beans, and hot peppers, as well as biscuits and hushpuppies, and pecan pie and banana pudding.

***Visitor Information:*** Visit Charlotte, The Convention & Visitors Bureau, 500 S. College St., #300, Charlotte, NC 28202; telephone (704)334-2282; toll-free (800)722-1994; fax (704)342-3972; email info@visitcharlotte.com

# *Convention Facilities*

Boasting more than 23,000 hotel rooms, Charlotte has become the major business travel center in the Carolinas and a prime meeting and convention center in the Southeast. The Charlotte Convention Center offers 850,000 square feet and hosts trade shows, conventions, conferences, and expositions. The exhibit space consists of 280,000 square feet and is divisible into one to four halls. There are 46 meeting rooms with 90,000 square feet of flexible meeting space, a deluxe hotel-quality ballroom measuring 35,000 square feet, and wide, light-filled concourses that converge at the heart of the center, the Grand Hall. The Charlotte Coliseum seats 24,041 people in comfort, providing superior sight lines, television monitors, state of the art video monitors, and

ample concession service. A two-story scoreboard features instant replay, and monitors on four sides; banquet rooms allow for 400 sit-down guests and 700 reception-style. The 275-room Renaissance Charlotte Suites Hotel is adjacent to the Charlotte Coliseum and features 19,000 square feet of meeting space, 18 meeting rooms, and an 11,400 square foot ballroom. The Ovens Auditorium is a 2,457-seat facility where arts-related events and business meetings are held. Featuring a 9,100 square-foot ballroom along with more than 20,000 square feet of meeting space, the Marriott Charlotte Center City offers a unique atrium for events.

***Convention Information:*** Visit Charlotte, The Convention & Visitors Bureau, 500 S. College St., #300, Charlotte, NC 28202; telephone (704)334-2282; toll-free (800)722-1994; fax (704)342-3972; email info@visitcharlotte.com

# *Transportation*

## Approaching the City

Charlotte/Douglas International Airport, a U.S. Airways hub, is about twenty minutes from uptown and is ranked among the nation's busiest airports (thirteenth in operations and seventeenth in passengers in 2003) averaging more than 500 daily departures serving about 25 million passengers every year. For motor travel to the region, Interstates 77 and 85 intersect in Charlotte, and I-40 is a half-hour away.

## Traveling in the City

The Charlotte Department of Transportation's (CDOT) 400 employees work to maintain the local commuter system. The Charlotte Area Transit System (CATS) operates more than 40 routes for about 12 million passengers annually; the system also offers two vanpool programs, special transportation services for the disabled, and shuttle services. In 2002 CATS proposed a "Transit Corridor System Plan" meant to provide rapid public transportation via six main corridors within the city.

# *Communications*

## Newspapers and Magazines

*The Charlotte Observer* is Charlotte's major daily newspaper (morning). Also published in Charlotte is *SportsBusiness Journal,* a national tabloid-size glossy weekly that reports on the glitzy and the mundane of sports business. Other publications originating in the area include the weekly *The*

*Charlotte Post,* serving the African American community; the twice-weekly *The Mecklenburg Times,* featuring financial, legal, and realty news; *Charlotte Business Journal;* community weeklies such as *The Leader;* and several periodicals serving such industries as iron, chemistry, hosiery, and botany.

## Television and Radio

Seven television stations broadcasting from Charlotte include three network affiliates (ABC, CBS, and NBC), a PBS affiliate, and three independent stations (Fox, UPN, and WB). Programming from independent and educational stations originating in neighboring cities is also available to Charlotte-area television viewers. Sixteen AM and FM radio stations in Charlotte broadcast a variety of offerings that include religious and sports programming as well as contemporary, rock and roll, gospel, and country music.

***Media Information:*** *Charlotte Observer,* Knight-Ridder Inc., 600 S. Tryon St., Charlotte, NC 28202; telephone (704)358-5000

## Charlotte Online

Charlotte Center City Home Page. Available www.charlotte centercity.org

Charlotte Chamber of Commerce. Available www.charlotte chamber.org

Charlotte-Mecklenburg Schools. Available www.cms.k12 .nc.us

*Charlotte Observer.* Available www.charlotte.com/mld/ observer

Charlotte Regional Partnership Home Page. Available www .charlotteusa.com/crp

City of Charlotte Home Page. Available www.charmeck.nc .us/living/home.htm

Historic Charlotte Home Page. Available www.historic charlotte.com

Public Library of Charlotte & Mecklenburg County. Available www.plcmc.org

Visit Charlotte (Charlotte Convention & Visitors Bureau). Available www.visitcharlotte.com or www.charlottecvb.org

## Selected Bibliography

Claiborne, Jack, *The Charlotte Observer: Its Time and Place, 1869–1986* (Chapel Hill, NC: University of North Carolina Press, 1986)

Mayes, Doug, and Nancy Stanfield, *Charlotte—Nothing Could Be Finer* (Memphis, TN: Towery Publishing, 1996)

# Greensboro

## *The City in Brief*

**Founded:** 1808 (incorporated 1829)

**Head Official:** Mayor Keith A. Holliday (since 1999)

**City Population**
    **1980:** 155,642
    **1990:** 185,125
    **2000:** 223,891
    **2003 estimate:** 229,110
    **Percent change, 1990–2000:** 20.9%
    **U.S. rank in 1980:** 100th
    **U.S. rank in 1990:** 88th
    **U.S. rank in 2000:** 88th (State rank: 3rd)

**Metropolitan Area Population**
    **1980:** 951,000
    **1990:** 1,050,304
    **2000:** 1,251,509

    **Percent change, 1990–2000:** 19.2%
    **U.S. rank in 1980:** 44th
    **U.S. rank in 1990:** 45th
    **U.S. rank in 2000:** 36th

**Area:** 109.25 square miles (2000)
**Elevation:** 897 feet above sea level
**Average Annual Temperature:** 57.8° F
**Average Annual Precipitation:** 50.24 inches (3.8 inches of snow)

**Major Economic Sectors:** manufacturing, wholesale and retail trade, services
**Unemployment rate:** 4.7% (December 2004)
**Per Capita Income:** $22,986 (1999)

**2002 FBI Crime Index Total:** 15,128

**Major Colleges and Universities:** University of North Carolina at Greensboro, North Carolina Agricultural and Technical State University

**Daily Newspaper:** *News & Record*

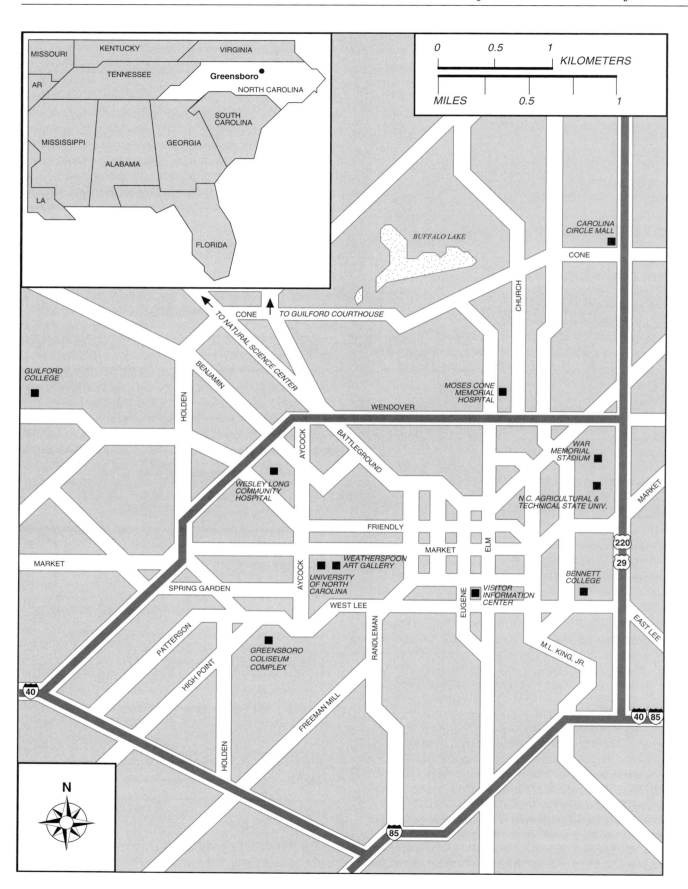

# Introduction

"It is perhaps the most pleasing, the most bewitching country which the continent affords." So wrote J. Hector St. John de Crevecoeur in the 1770s when he bestowed the eighteenth-century equivalent of a "quality-of-life" award on a Quaker community called New Garden, located in Piedmont, North Carolina, between the mountains and the sea.

Much has changed since then. New Garden grew to be part of a community called Greensboro, founded in 1808; and Greensboro grew to be part of a thriving metropolitan area called the Triad, which encompasses three major cities (Greensboro, High Point, and Winston-Salem) and more than a million people. Greensboro evolved from a small center of government to an early 1900s textile and transportation hub, and today is emerging as one of the South's up-and-coming centers for relocating businesses. Two centuries later Greensboro is still collecting accolades for its beauty and livability. In 2004 the Department of Energy (DOE) awarded Greensboro with entry into the Clean Cities Hall of Fame.

# Geography and Climate

Located in the northern Piedmont section of North Carolina, near the headwaters of the Haw and Deep rivers, Greensboro enjoys a relatively mild climate, partly due to the moderating influence of the mountains to the north and west of the city. Freezing temperatures occur on more than half the winter days; zero degree days are virtually unknown. Snowfall can range from trace amounts to as much as 15 or 20 inches in a single season, but usually there are only two storms each winter that bring an inch or more. Summer temperatures vary depending on cloud cover and thundershower activity, which itself varies greatly from year to year.

**Area:** 109.25 square miles (2000)

**Elevation:** 897 feet above sea level

**Average Temperatures:** January, 38.1° F; July, 77.9° F; annual average, 57.8° F

**Average Annual Precipitation:** 50.24 inches (3.8 inches of snow)

# History

## City Named for Revolutionary Hero

Greensboro is the county seat of Guilford County, which was founded in 1771 and named after England's first Earl of Guilford, Lord Francis North. Perhaps the first thing that newcomers notice about Greensboro is how green the city is. They are often surprised to learn that Greensboro is named for a man—not its lush landscape.

They soon hear the story of Nathanael Greene, a Revolutionary War general, who in 1781 played a major role in the colonists' fight for independence at a battlefield called Guilford Courthouse just north of present-day Greensboro. Greene lost the battle to Britain's Lord Charles Cornwallis, but historians credit him with so weakening Cornwallis's army that surrender soon followed.

More than 25 years later, the settlers of Guilford County decided to replace their county seat of Martinville with a more central city. They measured out the exact center of the county, and in 1808, a new 42-acre city was created. It was named Greensborough (meaning town of Greene) to honor Nathanael Greene. By 1895 Greensborough had become Greensboro.

## City Rises to the Confederate Call

The city grew slowly at first, but by the mid-1800s the seeds for its future as a textile, insurance, and transportation center had been planted. In 1828 the first textile mill opened, and in 1850, the first insurance company. In 1851 men began laying railroad tracks. The progressiveness of the county's educational community was showing, too. A log college for men had been operated there since 1767, and in 1837 the first coeducational institution in North Carolina opened. Called the New Garden Boarding School, it continues today as Guilford College.

The founders of the school were Quakers, many of English and Welsh descent, who were among Guilford County's first permanent settlers. Other early arrivals were a group of Germans who settled in the eastern portion of the county, and a number of Pennsylvanians of Scots-Irish descent who traveled south in search of land and opportunity.

The peace-loving nature of the Quakers influenced the area and its development. Quakers established the first Underground Railroad in Greensboro in the 1830s. When the Civil War was at hand, Guilford County citizens voted 2,771 to 113 against a state convention to consider secession from the union, writes local author Gayle Hicks Fripp in her history, *Greensboro: A Chosen Center*. North Carolina eventually became the last state to secede on May 20, 1861, and Guilford

County citizens accepted the decision. They turned churches into hospitals and melted church bells for ammunition. For a few days in April 1865, Greensboro even was the seat of the Confederate government as President Jefferson Davis contemplated surrender in a meeting with his military leaders.

## Transportation and Textiles Spur Growth

The turn of the nineteenth century brought tremendous growth to Greensboro. Much of the prosperity then and now can be traced to one man and the moving of a line. The man was John Motley Morehead, state governor from 1841–1845. He used his influence to curve an east-west line of railroad tracks miles north so it would pass through his hometown of Greensboro. The city soon became known as the Gate City for its busy train station (60 running daily), and ever since, transportation has remained a key to the city's development.

In 1892 two Maryland salesmen, the Cone brothers, chose Greensboro as the site for the first textile-finishing plant in the South. Thus began an enterprise called Cone Mills, which would become one of the largest makers of denim and corduroy in the world. By 1920 Blue Bell was making bib overalls there, and Burlington Mills, which later became Burlington Industries, had moved to Greensboro by 1935. Both companies added to the textile industry's influence on the economy.

## Modern Era Sees Racial Problems; Skyline Changes

The influence of the insurance industry showed on Greensboro's skyline in 1923, when the city became the site of the tallest building between Atlanta and Washington, D.C. The 17-story Jefferson Standard Building still stands beside the 20-story Jefferson-Pilot Tower, today the tallest building in Greensboro; it was built in 1990.

The 1940s brought people from all over the country to Greensboro. During World War II, the military located an Overseas Replacement Depot in the city in 1944, and more than 300,000 men and women were processed or trained for service there.

The 1960s to the mid 1990s brought immense change to the city socially, cosmetically, and economically. In 1960 Greensboro was the site of the first Civil Rights-era sit-in when four African American students refused to accept a lunch-counter color bar; their actions led to the collapse of segregation in the American South. A new face—a blend of old character and new maturity—was put on downtown. Modern office buildings and a government center were built; The Carolina Theatre, founded in 1927, was saved and restored; arts events downtown breathed new life into the inner city; and a campaign was launched to save a turn-of-the-century area called Old Greensborough.

## Economic Diversification Spurs Growth

The civil rights movement brought economic change to Greensboro. Tradition and innovation mixed, as high-technology electronics manufacturers and international firms, like the CIBA-GEIGY Corporation (later CIBA Corp. and now Novartis), moved in alongside the city's textile and tobacco plants. The U.S. Postal Service opened one of the nation's 21 bulk-mail centers, a huge facility spanning 7 acres. Kmart and Polo-Ralph Lauren chose the Greensboro area for their major distribution centers. In 2002 Powell Co., a home furniture importer/distributor, moved into the 300,000-square-foot location formerly occupied by Sears' distribution center. The opening of the Piedmont Triad International Airport (PTIA) terminal in 1996 to serve Greensboro and its Triad neighbors set off a spurt of industrial growth there and united the cities more closely than ever. This will be enhanced when FedEx completes the building of its cargo hub for $500 million on 1,000 acres of the eastern side of the airport. The spring of 2005 brought a brand-new $20 million stadium for the Class A Grasshoppers (formerly Bats). City financial officials projected in 2005 steady to moderate gains in revenue that would parlay into a solid economic forecast. The continued influx of new businesses (75 in 2004) and the expansion of existing businesses (759 in 2004) in a variety of fields translates to an overall general prosperity for the area's workforce and the city as a whole.

***Historical Information:*** Greensboro Historical Museum, 130 Summit Ave., Greensboro, NC 27401; telephone (336)373-2043; fax (336)373-2204

# *Population Profile*

## Metropolitan Area Residents
*1980:* 951,000
*1990:* 1,050,304
*2000:* 1,251,509
*Percent change, 1990–2000:* 19.2%
*U.S. rank in 1980:* 44th
*U.S. rank in 1990:* 45th
*U.S. rank in 2000:* 36th

## City Residents
*1980:* 155,642
*1990:* 185,125
*2000:* 223,891
*2003 estimate:* 229,110
*Percent change, 1990–2000:* 20.9%
*U.S. rank in 1980:* 100th
*U.S. rank in 1990:* 88th
*U.S. rank in 2000:* 88th (State rank: 3rd)

*Density:* 2,138.3 people per square mile (in 2000, based on 2000 land area)

*Racial and ethnic characteristics* (2000)
White: 124,243
Black or African American: 83,728
American Indian and Alaska Native: 989
Asian: 6,357
Native American and Other Pacific Islander: 89
Hispanic or Latino (may be of any race): 9,742
Other: 4,647

*Percent of residents born in state:* 57.8% (2000)

*Age characteristics* (2000)
Population under 5 years old: 14,214
Population 5 to 9 years old: 14,606
Population 10 to 14 years old: 13,620
Population 15 to 19 years old: 16,773
Population 20 to 24 years old: 22,183
Population 25 to 44 years old: 37,483
Population 45 to 54 years old: 33,296
Population 55 to 59 years old: 28,068
Population 60 to 64 years old: 9,621
Population 65 to 74 years old: 13,607
Population 75 to 84 years old: 9,400
Population 85 years and older: 3,572
Median age: 33.0 years

*Births* (2003)
Total number: 3,394

*Deaths* (2003)
Total number: 1,916 (of which, 33 were infants under the age of 1 year)

*Money income* (1999)
Per capita income: $22,986
Median household income: $39,661
Total households: 92,084

*Number of households with income of . . .*
less than $10,000: 8,481
$10,000 to $14,999: 5,512
$15,000 to $24,999: 13,154
$25,000 to $34,999: 13,635
$35,000 to $49,999: 16,054
$50,000 to $74,999: 17,254
$75,000 to $99,999: 7,674
$100,000 to $149,999: 5,967
$150,000 to $199,999: 2,035
$200,000 or more: 2,318

*Percent of families below poverty level:* 8.6% (38.8% of which were female householder families with related children under 5 years)

*2002 FBI Crime Index Total:* 15,128

# Municipal Government

Greensboro adopted a city council-manager form of government in 1921. The council consists of the mayor and eight members, all of whom are elected on a nonpartisan ballot for two-year terms. The council in turn appoints a city manager to administer government policy.

**Head Official:** Mayor Keith A. Holliday (D) (since 1999; current term expires 2006)

**Total Number of City Employees:** 2,935 (2004)

*City Information:* Greensboro City Hall, PO Box 3136, Greensboro, NC 27402-3136; telephone (336)373-2065

# Economy

### Major Industries and Commercial Activity

For decades, the products of Greensboro's approximately 500 factories, such as Kent cigarettes and No Nonsense pantyhose, were known better than the city itself. However, an increasing number of companies have since discovered its award-winning quality of life, a low crime rate, and its thriving business climate including low lease rates and facility costs, below-average wages, and moderate overall costs appealing and have moved in or expanded their existing business.

The traditional industries—textiles, furniture, and tobacco—remain a dominant influence on the local economy, as does manufacturing in general. But unlike many other areas of the country with a heavy dependence on manufacturing, Greensboro has prospered—not suffered—as jobs have been lost to automation and foreign imports. Diversification has been the key. For example, the city has been an insurance center for decades. Jefferson-Pilot Corporation is headquartered in Greensboro, as is mortgage insurance provider United Guaranty Corp. Printing and publishing are growing industries. Gilbarco, a maker of service station equipment, is headquartered in Greensboro. Electronics firms such as Analog Devices, A M P Inc., and RF Micro Devices also have plants in the city. In December 2004 RF Micro Devices announced a $75 million expansion plan with a projected 75-position job growth. Vicks VapoRub, invented in Greensboro more than 75 years ago, is still produced there, as are other familiar products, such as Nyquil nighttime cold medicine, Vicks Formula 44 cough mixture, Vicks cough syrup, and Vicks cough drops (although the company has been taken over by Procter & Gamble).

International flavor has been added, courtesy of Twinings Tea of England and Fuji Foods of Japan, which located their U.S. manufacturing plants in Greensboro. Switzerland's Novartis located its dyestuffs and agricultural divisions in Greensboro, Sweden's Volvo Truck Corp. chose Greensboro for the headquarters of its Volvo-GM Heavy Truck Corporation, and Japan's Konica Manufacturing USA, Inc. located its plant for the manufacture of photographic paper in the city.

The opening of the Piedmont Triad International Airport terminal just west of the city in 1982 set off a building boom along nearby Interstate 40 and the feeder roads to the airport that has not yet shown signs of abating. The corridor is being called the ''downtown of the Triad,'' and the chambers of commerce from the three Triad cities have joined forces to attract businesses to the area.

*Items and goods produced:* furniture, textiles, apparel, tobacco products, chemicals, electronic equipment

## Incentive Programs—New and Existing Industries

*Local programs*—Both the city of Greensboro and Guilford County have incentive policies available to assist new and expanding businesses. One example is the Targeted Loan Pool Program that began making funds available in November 2003 to small businesses from a $1 million pool if they currently operate or plan to open in one of Greenboro's State Development Zones.

*State programs*—North Carolina, a right-to-work state with a low unionization rate, offers a revenue bond pool program through various banks. Several venture capital funds operate in the state and inquiries can be made through North Carolina's Council for Entrepreneurial Development (CED) that was founded in 1984. About 8,000 entrepreneurs also utilize CED's programs and services statewide. North Carolina offers State Technology Based Equity Funds providing financing for new technology-based enterprises, as well as TDA incubators for firms transferring new technologies into commercial applications. The state issues Industrial Revenue Bonds for new and expanding businesses empowering them to provide good employment and wage opportunities for their workers. The state offers an income tax allocation formula that permits the double weighting of sales in calculating corporate income tax. The North Carolina Department of Transportation administers a program that provides for the construction of access roads to industrial sites and road improvements in areas surrounding major corporate installations. A 4 percent tax credit is available to new and expanding companies via the William S. Lee Act for machinery and equipment investments over $2 million, along with a jobs tax credit, worker training tax credit, research and development tax credits, and business property tax credits.

*Job training programs*—The state of North Carolina's Division of Employment and Training offers a unique system of job training programs available to any new or expanding manufacturing employer creating a minimum of 12 new production jobs in the state, and to any new or prospective employee referred for training by a participating company. The industrial training service provides great versatility in terms of types and length of training, and classes can be held in a company's plant or on the campus of one of the state's community colleges. The state of North Carolina furnishes instructors and, at the company's request, may test and screen job candidates. Employees may be trained before or after employment by the company. The industrial training service is financed solely by the state of North Carolina.

## Development Projects

Greensboro's Economic Development Office manages and supports development projects throughout the community. One critical project was the $20 million First Horizon Park that opened in the spring of 2005 with more than 5,000 seats and a wide variety of amenities for the Class A baseball team, the Greensboro Grasshoppers (name changed from the Bats, concurrent with the move). At a cost of $500 million, a FedEx hub, to be only the fifth in the nation, is targeted for completion in 2009 and is expected to create 1,500 jobs at the Piedmont Triad International Airport. In February 2005 computer giant Dell began building in nearby Winston-Salem, a deal that Greenboro's officials were prominent in procuring as it will bring the region about 1,500 jobs. A 29-acre development was in progress in spring 2005 along Eastchester Drive that is to include a rebuilt version of Kepley's Barn (a reception hall destroyed by a 2001 fire) plus retail stores and a hotel.

*Economic Development Information:* Greensboro Chamber of Commerce, 342 N. Elm St., Greensboro, NC 27401; telephone (336)275-8675; fax (336)275-9299

## Commercial Shipping

Greensboro is a hub for moving freight nationwide by rail or truck. More than 50 motor freight trucking firms have offices in Greensboro, and Norfolk Southern Railway Corporation operates one of the most active intermodal facilities in its 20-state system in Greensboro. Dedicated piggybacks hauling trailers travel out of Greensboro. Norfolk Southern provides second-morning service for freight going to Chicago from Greensboro and third-day service to the West Coast.

## Labor Force and Employment Outlook

In addition to its role as a government center, Greensboro serves as a business, financial, and retail hub for the county and for a semicircle of more rural counties to the north, south, and east. The city's major industry is manufacturing, from textiles to electronics, but retail and wholesale trade, finance, insurance, real estate, and the service sector also are major parts of the economy. Factors that are attracting companies to Greensboro include a large and growing Triad population base of nearly 1.4 million people (projected in 2005) from which to draw employees; a motivated and trainable work force; a physical site available at a reasonable price; sophisticated telecommunications capabilities; a location near a major airport and highway network; and a respected community college system that provides employee training assistance at no charge through a state program. With the expansion of existing business (759 in 2004, generating nearly $145 million) and the creation of new business (75 in 2004 and nearly $225 million) the job market will continue to be an active one.

The following is a summary of data regarding the Greensboro metropolitan area labor force, 2004 annual averages.

*Size of nonagricultural labor force:* 354,900

*Number of workers employed in . . .*
  *construction and mining:* 18,800
  *manufacturing:* 66,100
  *trade, transportation, and utilities:* 72,100
  *information:* 6,700
  *financial activities:* 19,700
  *professional and business services:* 43,100
  *educational and health services:* 42,200
  *leisure and hospitality:* 29,500
  *other services:* 15,500
  *government:* 41,300

*Average hourly earnings of production workers employed in manufacturing:* $13.49

*Unemployment rate:* 4.7% (December 2004)

| *Largest employers*<br>*(Greensboro MSA)* | *Number of employees* |
|---|---|
| Guilford County Public Schools | 7,900 |
| Moses H. Cone Health System &<br>  Affiliates | 7,000 |
| U.S. Postal Service | 3,367 |
| American Express | 3,200 |
| Guilford County | 3,000 |
| City of Greensboro | 2,935 |
| Volvo Trucks North America | 2,200 |
| United Parcel Service | 2,100 |
| Bank of America, N.A. | 2,000 |
| Lorillard Tobacco | 1,950 |

### Cost of Living

The cost of housing in Greensboro is slightly below the national average, as are costs for food, utilities, and other necessities.

The following is a summary of data regarding several key cost of living factors for the Greensboro area.

*2004 (3rd Quarter) ACCRA Average House Price:* $216,660 (Winston-Salem)

*2004 (3rd Quarter ACCRA Cost of Living Index:* 89.3 (U.S. average = 100.0) (Winston-Salem)

*State income tax rate:* Ranges from 6.0% to 8.25%

*State sales tax rate:* 4.5% (food and prescription drugs are exempt; food sales are subject to local sales taxes)

*Local income tax rate:* None

*Local sales tax rate:* 2.5% (county-wide) (restaurant food sales are subject to local sales tax of 7.5%; 2.0% in grocery stores for food)

*Property tax rate:* $.5675 per $100 of assessed valuation (assessed valuation = 100% of market value)

**Economic Information:** Greensboro Area Chamber of Commerce, 324 N. Elm St., Greensboro, NC 27401; telephone (336)275-8675; fax (336)275-9299

# Education and Research

### Elementary and Secondary Schools

The Guilford County Schools (GCS) system was created on July 1, 1993, when the former Greensboro, High Point, and Guilford County school systems merged to form the third largest school district in North Carolina. The system continues to grow each year by approximately 1,200 new students. The academic achievement of GCS students has risen each year since the merger, as well. GCS offers its high school students two directions to help them prepare for future careers: College Tech Prep and College Prep. The system has earned a state and national reputation for its technological innovations that help its own students and students in other districts statewide.

Sixteen Magnet Schools focus on specialized topics such as communications, cultural arts, and foreign language. Other local high schools include International Baccalaureate programs while Middle College High Schools operate on area college campuses. The Early College at Guilford provides high school students the opportunity to earn college credits, and the Saturn Academy has flexible schedules. High school students may also take advantage of performing arts courses, television production classes, and courses in photography and commercial food service. Students with autism, cerebral palsy, orthopedic impairments, and severe and profound handicaps can attend GSC's Gateway Education Center, a facility that is world-renowned for its exceptional programs. McIver Education Center serves about 100 mentally challenged students from age 3 to 22.

The following is a summary of data regarding the Guilford County Schools as of the 2003–2004 school year.

*Total enrollment:* 65,828

*Number of facilities*
*elementary schools:* 64
*junior high/middle schools:* 19
*senior high schools:* 22
*other:* 2

*Student/teacher ratio:* 20:1 (kindergarten-grade 5); 23:1 (grades 6-8); 20:1 (grades 9-12)

*Teacher salaries*
*minimum:* $28,890
*maximum:* $64,320

*Funding per pupil:* $6,587 (2001–2002)

The city also is served by 48 private schools, including church-related (37) and nonreligious (11) institutions.

**Public Schools Information:** Guilford County Schools, 712 N. Eugene St., Greensboro, NC 27401; telephone (336)370-8100

### Colleges and Universities

The 200-acre University of North Carolina at Greensboro (UNCG), with more than 14,300 students and 800 full-time faculty members, is the largest of the colleges and universities in Greensboro. Founded in 1891 as a women's school, it became coeducational in the fall of 1964. Undergraduate degrees are offered in more than 100 fields, and graduate and professional degrees are granted in more than a dozen areas of study.

The city's other state university, North Carolina Agricultural and Technical State University (A & T), was founded in 1891 as a land-grant institution offering agricultural and mechanical training to African Americans. In 2004 more than 10,000 students were enrolled at the university. Known for its nationally accredited engineering department, the university offers undergraduate and master's degrees in a half dozen engineering specialties.

The oldest college in Greensboro, Guilford College, is also one of the city's most respected institutions. Founded in 1837 by the Religious Society of Friends, or Quakers, Guilford is the third oldest coeducational institution in the United States. Majors are offered in more than three dozen areas, ranging from accounting to criminal justice to women's studies.

One year after Guilford College was founded, Greensboro College opened its doors, becoming the third college char-

tered for women in the United States. It became coeducational in 1954. Located in the historic College Hill area, Greensboro College today is a Methodist-affiliated institution with 1,300 students that emphasizes individual attention (student-teacher ratio is 14:1) within a traditional liberal arts framework.

Rounding out the private liberal arts colleges in Greensboro is Bennett College, which opened in 1873 as a school for the children of former slaves, and became a women's college in 1926. Bennett is still for women only and is affiliated with the United Methodist Church. Among the most popular areas of study for its approximately 600 students are interdisciplinary studies, biology, and business administration.

A wide variety of opportunities, from career exploration to high-technology business training, are offered through Guilford Technical Community College (GTCC), which has a main campus in nearby Jamestown and satellite campuses in downtown Greensboro. Established in 1958, GTCC is the third largest public two-year college in the state and has a student body in excess of 11,000 along with nearly 21,000 in continuing education programs. The college provides important training to the local work force.

The Greater Greensboro Consortium (GGC) provides the unique opportunity to degree-seeking students of the eight participating institutions in the metropolitan area (Bennett College, Elon College, Greensboro College, Guilford Technical Community College, High Point University, North Carolina Agricultural and Technical State University (A & T), and the University of North Carolina at Greensboro) to take classes at any of the schools that meet specific criteria.

### Libraries and Research Centers

The Greensboro Public Library, opened in 1902, consists of a central facility (founded in 1998) and six branches, has some 541,000 books and more than 17,000 serial volumes in its collection, as well as audio tapes and video tapes, CD ROMs, DVDs, slides, maps, and art prints. All locations have computers with Internet access (about 200 in total) and some provide classes. Special collections are maintained in the areas of business and management, local history, and genealogy; resources are available for the use of nonprofit agencies.

The University of North Carolina at Greensboro is the home of the 220,000-square-foot Walter Clinton Jackson Library. It maintains more than 3.4 million items featuring 700,000 federal and state documents and 5,100 serial subscriptions.

Several research centers are based in Greensboro; most are affiliated with either the University of North Carolina at Greensboro or North Carolina Agricultural and Technical State University. The topics under investigation include business and economics, transportation, nutrition, semiconductors, and the effects of social, economic, and cultural deprivation. The city also boasts a Center for Creative Leadership that has a variety of programs geared toward the development of leaders in the business world.

*Public Library Information:* Greensboro Public Library, 219 N. Church St., Greensboro, NC 27401; telephone (336)373-2471

# Health Care

From lifesaving open-heart surgery to the newest diagnostic technologies, Greensboro is a city where advanced medical technology is available. The city and surrounding area has specialized and general physicians, representing virtually every specialty and most subspecialties. Four acute-care hospitals and a psychiatric hospital offer a combined total of more than 1,100 beds.

The Moses Cone Health System provides most of the health care in the Greensboro area. It offers a complete range of medical and surgical services. There are five hospitals in the system with more than 7,000 employees. The largest hospital is the 535-bed Moses H. Cone Memorial Hospital, founded in 1953, which has a national reputation for cardiovascular research. The Wesley Long Community Hospital is a modern 204-bed hospital that features a regional cancer center. The 134-bed Women's Hospital of Greensboro is the only free-standing hospital dedicated to women's services in the area. The 110-bed Annie Penn Hospital provides specialty services such as a cancer center and sleep center and is located 20 miles north of the city. The Behavioral Health Center supplies 80 beds—50 for adults and 30 for children—to assist those with mental health issues. A 124-bed acute care facility, Kindred Hospital Greensboro, focuses on patients requiring more extensive treatment for pulmonary problems and those who are ventilator-dependent while partnering with regional hospitals.

# Recreation

## Sightseeing

A tour of Greensboro might begin with Blandwood Mansion, a 19th-century Italian villa in downtown Greensboro, which is a National Historic Landmark and former home of Governor John Motley Morehead. Not far from Blandwood is the William Fields House, a Gothic Revival-style structure that is listed on the National Register of Historic Places. Since 1973 Carolina Model Railroaders has displayed scale

trains and equipment that, after relocating in 2003, were rebuilt into a different configuration. Guilford Courthouse National Military Park, located in North Greensboro, provides a fascinating look at a battle that helped win America's independence. The 220-acre park, which was the first Revolutionary War battleground to be preserved as a national military park, includes a museum and interpretive automobile, bicycle, and foot trails for retracing the battle. The adjacent eight-acre Tannenbaum Historic Park/Colonial Heritage Center served as a staging area for British troops under Cornwallis's command during the Revolutionary War Battle of Guilford Courthouse. Today, the park features a visitor's center, gift shop, and exhibits depicting colonial life. Not far from the two parks is the Natural Science Center, a hands-on museum, zoo, and planetarium.

The Greensboro Children's Museum is an exciting, colorful place with interactive exhibits and activities designed for kids up to age 12 as well as summer camp, programs, and workshops. Fun for the whole family can be had at Celebration Station, featuring miniature golf, water bumper boats, arcade games, batting cages, and more. Wet 'n Wild Emerald Pointe is the largest water park in the state with a giant wave pool and other water activities. More than 60,000 tropical plants and 1,100 exotic animals are the main attraction at North Carolina Zoological Park, 25 miles southeast of Greensboro, that includes an impressive 37-acre African Plains exhibit.

## Arts and Culture

The energy behind Greensboro's vibrant arts scene is the United Arts Council, located in the Greensboro Cultural Center at Festival Park, downtown's performing arts showplace and home base for 25 visual and performing art organizations as well as art galleries, a sculpture garden, and an outdoor amphitheater. The council serves as the fund-raising umbrella for the city's many arts groups. The council funds 14 organizations and provides support to other groups. It also operates an artists' center, where serious, talented writers, painters, potters, and others may rent inexpensive studio space.

The Greensboro Symphony Orchestra, founded in the 1920s, performs masterworks and pops concerts from September to May at the War Memorial Auditorium in the Greensboro Coliseum Complex. Since 1980 the Greensboro Opera Company has presented performances by local talent year-round and an annual production featuring international talent in operatic works performed in the original language, also at the War Memorial Auditorium. The Greensboro Ballet, also the home of the home of the School of Greensboro Ballet, offers three performances each season and delights holiday audiences each December with a presentation of *The Nutcracker*. The North Carolina Dance project holds an annual concert in Greensboro and features two dance troupes that travel throughout the state.

**Tannenbaum Park/Colonial Heritage Center contains exhibits depicting colonial life and is host to Revolutionary War reenactments.**

Jazz is very popular in Greensboro with nationally known musicians performing in the 1927 vintage Carolina Theatre and in local clubs. The Carolina Theatre is the principal venue for performing arts productions sponsored by City Arts Drama of the Greensboro Parks and Recreation Department. City Arts oversees the Livestock Players Musical Theatre, which presents Broadway musicals in November, April, and July; Children's Theatre, which performs during the school year; Razz-Ma-Tazz Musical Revue Company; the Music Center; Greensboro Concert Band; Philharmonia of Greensboro; Choral Society of Greensboro; Youth Chorus; and We Are One Youth Choir.

Theatrical entertainment also abounds in Greensboro. At the Barn Dinner Theatre audiences have enjoyed dinner and a Broadway-style play year-round since 1962. Professional theater in an intimate setting is the specialty of the Broach Theatre in the Old Greensborough Historic District, which produces seven adult plays from February to December. Community Theatre of Greensboro presents five Broadway plays and musicals.

Greensboro's universities and colleges sponsor arts events throughout the year that are open to the public. The artists series at Guilford College, for example, brought the Prague Chamber Orchestra to Greensboro, and the UNCG Concert and Lecture Series has sponsored such notables as violinist Isaac Stern and actor Hal Holbrook. In 2005 a Nigerian art and literature series kicks off a biennial cultural program.

Museum lovers enjoy the Greensboro Historical Museum, which traces the development of Guilford County from Native American times through the present. Special collections include memorabilia of author William Sydney Porter, better known as O. Henry, who grew up in Greensboro, as well as a variety of items and information related to Edward R. Murrow and First Lady Dolley Madison, who lived in Guilford County. The museum also has two restored log homes open for touring on its downtown site and has recreated a 1880s village of Greensboro, showing the city as it might have been when O. Henry left in 1882. The Richard Petty Museum, located south of Greensboro, contains memorabilia relating to the race car driver.

North Carolina Agricultural and Technical State University (A & T) is the site of a nationally recognized facility, the Mattye Reed African Heritage Center in the Dudley Building, a repository for more than 3,500 artifacts from more than 30 African and Caribbean countries. The Old Mill of Guilford provides a view of the past through its working water-powered mill.

Greensboro is not lacking in art galleries. The Greensboro Artists' League gallery, founded in 1956, promotes the visual arts of the Piedmont Triad with changing exhibitions by local artists and a sales gallery. The Weatherspoon Art Museum, on the campus of the University of North Carolina at Greensboro is widely recognized for having one of the most outstanding collections of post-World War II American art in the Southeast. The African American Atelier in the Cultural Center features works by local artists and presents six to eight exhibitions per year. North Carolina artists are the focus at Green Hill Center for North Carolina Art. The Guilford Native American Art Gallery was the first of its kind in the Southeast.

***Arts and Culture Information:*** United Arts Council of Greensboro, 200 N. Davie St., Greensboro, NC 27402; telephone (336)373-7523; fax (336)373-7553

## Festivals and Holidays

Many of Greensboro's biggest celebrations focus on music. The nationally acclaimed Eastern Music Festival began in 1962 and brings the world's most promising music students to Greensboro each year for six weeks of intense study with the world's most accomplished musicians. The performers, who spend the summer on the Guilford College campus, present more than 40 concerts from June through August.

St. Patrick's Day brings the Green Party to the downtown area in the form of several bands performing at various venues. Fun Fourth Festival in the downtown National Register Historic District is a street festival that thousands flock to in the inner city to celebrate the Fourth of July. Arts and crafts from all over the country take center stage at two events sponsored by the Gilmore Shows' Carolina Craftsmen: the annual Spring Show in April and the Christmas Classic in late November. African American arts and culture take the spotlight during the two-month African American Arts Festival (since 1988) that begins in mid-January and extends to mid-March. Also in March is the African American Heritage Extravaganza with dance, music, art exhibits, and "soul food" sampling.

## Sports for the Spectator

When it comes to recreation, Greensboro is a city for all seasons and all sports. From May through August, the United Soccer League's Carolina Dynamo play at the 3,000-seat Macpherson Stadium that opened in 2002 and is part of the extensive Bryan Park. Summer used to mean "batter up" at War Memorial Stadium with the Greensboro Bats, a Class A farm team of the Florida Marlins. The team's former stadium was built in 1926 and in 2004 was the fourth oldest active minor league park in the country. However, in the spring of 2005 the brand-new $20 million First Horizon Park opened with more than 5,000 seats and featuring suites, party decks, and a children's play area; the team also changed its name to the Grasshoppers. The Greensboro Generals, an East Coast Hockey League Team affiliate of the Carolina Hurricanes take to the ice from October through March at the Greensboro Coliseum Arena.

The Chrysler Classic of Greensboro golf tournament, sponsored by the Greensboro Jaycees, attracts top names in golf to Greensboro in the fall (previously held in the spring until 2003).

The sports fan can also find plenty of collegiate sports in the area. Fall's kicks come when the successful Spartan soccer team takes to the field at the University of North Carolina at Greensboro (UNCG), and winter often brings Carolinians' favorite rivalry, the Atlantic Coast Conference (ACC) basketball tournament at the Greensboro Coliseum. The North Carolina Agricultural and Technical State University (A & T) basketball team often lands a berth in the NCAA tournament, but the football team also draws crowds to the 22,000-seat Aggie Stadium. Women's sports include basketball and track. UNCG women's soccer, basketball and tennis teams have been prominent nationally.

### Sports for the Participant

Greensboro is a launching site for just about any interest. The state's beaches are just four hours away, and the cool Blue Ridge Mountains are a three-hour drive. One of the highlights of Greensboro itself is the extensive parks and recreation system, which includes 170 parks on more than 3,500 acres. Bicycling routes, fitness and hiking trails, swimming pools, and a network of community parks and 11 recreation centers are spread throughout the city. Tennis is an especially popular sport in Greensboro, both for players and spectators. The city has tennis courts in 16 locations, three of which are fully equipped tennis centers. The United States Tennis Association's (USTA) Greensboro January Indoor Junior Championships is played annually at the Simkins Indoor Pavilion in Barber Park in Greensboro. Jaycee Park, site of the Love Tennis Center, is home to the North Carolina Tennis Hall of Fame along with the Junior USTA-Sanctioned Tennis Tournaments and Junior Novice Tennis Tournaments.

The area's many golf aficionados find challenging golf in the 600-acre Bryan Park, as well as at the area's many private golf courses. The park includes two 18-hole championship golf courses, two putting greens, a driving range, and a golf school. Facilities at Bryan Park also include a tennis center, a nature trail, and a wildlife sanctuary.

The Greensboro Sportsplex has many amenities on its 106,000 square feet of space including 8 basketball and volleyball courts and 3 state-of-the-art indoor soccer fields along with a hockey program and summer camps.

Another well-used city park is Country Park, a 126-acre facility in northern Greensboro listed as a National Historical Landmark property that includes two stocked fishing lakes; hiking, bicycling, and jogging trails; pedal-boat rentals; and plenty of places for a quiet picnic. It also is the site of the annual Carolina Cup Bicycle Road Race in September sponsored by U.S. Cycling.

### Shopping and Dining

North of downtown Greensboro, visitors can stroll through a relaxed neighborhood of 37 unique shops, restaurants, and boutiques housed in elegantly refurbished 1920s vintage buildings at State Street Station. On the city's southwest side, the Four Seasons Town Centre features three levels with more than 200 shops and restaurants in 1.3 million square feet. With 95 stores on 75 acres of open-air shopping, the Friendly Center has three department stores and many national retailers. In the section of downtown called Old Downtown Greensborough, browsers will find more than a dozen antique stores housed in turn-of-the-century storefronts. The city and neighboring communities are also home to dozens of outlet stores. Products manufactured locally, such as clothing and furniture, are especially popular with shoppers.

As for dining, barbecue, hushpuppies, and coleslaw are North Carolina staples, and restaurants serving these local favorites are plentiful in the metropolitan Greensboro area's 500 eateries. Hungry visitors will also find upscale eateries and a variety of ethnic cuisines.

The locals enjoy going down to the Greensboro Farmers Curb Market year-round for an abundance of fresh produce, baked goods, flowers, and crafts.

***Visitor Information:*** Greensboro Area Convention and Visitors Bureau, 317 S. Greene St., Greensboro, NC 27401-2615; telephone (336)274-2282; toll-free (800)344-2282; fax (336)230-1183; email gso@greensboronc.org

# Convention Facilities

The city-owned Greensboro Coliseum Complex, the largest facility of its kind in the state, seats 23,500 people in its Coliseum Arena; the War Memorial Auditorium has 2,376 seats. The special events center has 120,000 square feet for trade and consumer shows featuring three wings, a pavilion, and 12 meeting rooms while seating 4,300 for concerts and sporting events. The smaller Town Hall theater has 298 seats.

Greensboro is home to the largest privately owned, self-contained hotel-convention complex between Washington, D.C. and Atlanta, and boasts more than 8,600 total hotel rooms. In addition, there are a number of private and public meeting areas.

The largest hotel-convention complex is the more than 1,000-room Sheraton, which includes about 250,000 square feet of meeting space and 100,000 square feet of exhibition space with 75 meeting rooms, located adjacent to the three-level Four Seasons Town Centre mall with more than 200 shops and restaurants and a multi-theater cinema. The hotel's largest meeting area, the 40,000-square-foot Guilford Ballroom, can accommodate in excess of 4,000 people for a banquet or 6,000 people for a meeting with full trade-show capabilities.

The Greensboro-High Point Marriott Airport hotel, adjacent to Piedmont Triad International Airport, provides a convenient meeting place for groups arriving by air. With 296 guest rooms and 14 meeting rooms, the Marriott can accommodate large groups in its 9,850 square feet of meeting space.

Grandover Resort and Conference Center features 45,000 square feet of meeting space, including a 13,500-square-foot ballroom. Hotel amenities include 274 guest rooms and two championship, 18-hole golf courses designed by David Graham and Gary Panks.

Also in the heart of downtown is the Biltmore Greensboro Hotel, a charming meeting location for small groups. The inn, which dates to 1895 and originally housed corporate offices for Cone Mills, today is a 23-room hotel furnished with eighteenth-century reproductions. A maximum of 80 people can be accommodated for meetings.

Meeting space is available at many other local facilities, including the Embassy Suites Hotel Greensboro Airport; the Carolina Theatre; in the 1840s Blandwood Mansion and Carriage House. Kepley's Barn had featured a rustic country atmosphere for events and was located near the airport; it burned down in 2001 and in 2005 discussions continued by the city's planning department regarding a new 29-acre area that would include the rebuilding of the barn. The Conference Center at Bryan Park can handle business or social events in its 22,000-square-foot facility overlooking the championships golfing greens.

*Convention Information:* Greensboro Area Convention and Visitors Bureau, 317 S. Greene St., Greensboro, NC 27401-2615; telephone (336)274-2282; toll-free (800)344-2282; fax (336)230-1183; email gso@greensboronc.org

# Transportation

## Approaching the City

Greensboro is proud of its convenient and efficient transportation network. The city is located at the juncture of two major arteries, the east-west Interstate 40 and north-south Interstate 85, and major U.S. and state highways lead in all directions. In addition to cities served directly by I-40 and I-85, those highways provide connections to other major arteries throughout the region and the nation, such as Interstates 77, 75, 81 and 95, leading virtually anywhere along the eastern seaboard.

The Piedmont Triad International Airport (PTIA) terminal, located only minutes from downtown, is served by seven major airlines and had more than 1.3 enplaned passengers in 2004. Travelers can also catch the train in Greensboro; Amtrak trains going north and south stop daily at the Greensboro station.

## Traveling in the City

The smooth traffic flow in Greensboro, which often amazes newcomers, gives Greensboro the feel of a smaller city. It is an impression that has been carefully created through years of planning that began when the city developed its transportation plan in the 1950s. As development has taken place over the years since then, planners have kept pace to meet city needs. One key to Greensboro's smooth-flowing traffic is Wendover Avenue, an expressway that takes motorists from I-40 on the west through Greensboro to U.S. 29 on the east in a matter of minutes. Many of the city's other major thoroughfares are four-lane. The Greensboro Urban Loop is a prominent project in progress that literally links several highways on the perimeter of the city limits. One portion, the Southern Urban Loop, opened in February 2004 while the Western Urban Loop is slated for completion in 2007. Part of the Eastern Urban Loop was operational in May 2002; however, most of the work is expected to wrap up by 2010.

Good public transportation is provided by the 27 buses of Greensboro Transit Authority. Special bus service for elderly and handicapped persons is provided through Specialized Community Area Transportation (SCAT).

# Communications

## Newspapers and Magazines

Greensboro's major daily (morning) newspaper is the *News & Record.* Several weekly or biweekly newspapers are published in Greensboro, including *Carolina Peacemaker,* for the African American community, and *The North Carolina Christian Advocate.* Several magazines and journals are published in Greensboro, including *Elegant Bride, Carolina Gardener,* two in-flight magazines, and other literary, collegiate, and children's publications.

**Television and Radio**

Four commercial television stations broadcast from Greensboro. Several other stations are based in nearby towns and serve viewers in the entire metropolitan region. Additional stations are available via cable. As for radio, 11 stations offering entertainment that ranges from eclectic, top 40 and classical music to news and talk shows broadcast to area listeners.

*Media Information:* News & Record, Landmark Communications, PO Box 20848, Greensboro, NC 27420-0848; telephone (336)274-5476; toll-free (800)553-6880

**Greensboro Online**

City of Greensboro home page. Available www.ci.greensboro.nc.us

County of Guilford home page. Avaiilable www.co.guilford.nc.us

The Depot (Piedmont Triad, NC). Available www.thedepot.com

Downtown Greensboro. Available www.downtowngreensboro.net

Greensboro Area Convention & Visitors Bureau. Available www.greensboronc.org

Greensboro Chamber of Commerce. Available www.greensboro.org

Greensboro Historical Museum. Available www.greensborohistory.org

Guilford County Public Schools. Available www.guilford.k12.nc.us

News and Record. Available www.news-record.com

**Selected Bibliography**

Redding, Sarah and Sherry Roberts, eds., *Greensboro: A Portrait of Progress* (Montgomery, Ala.: Community Communications, 1998)

Thompson, Deanna, L., and Sherry Roberts, *Greensboro: A New American Metropolis: A Contemporary Portrait of Greensboro, North Carolina* (Greensboro: Community Communications, 1991)

Wolff, Miles, *Lunch at the 5 & 10* (Chicago: Ivan R. Dee, 1990)

# Raleigh

## The City in Brief

**Founded:** 1792 (incorporated 1795)

**Head Official:** City Manager J. Russell Allen (since April 2001)

**City Population**
  **1980:** 150,255
  **1990:** 218,859
  **2000:** 276,093
  **2003 estimate:** 285,639
  **Percent change, 1990–2000:** 26%
  **U.S. rank in 1980:** 106th
  **U.S. rank in 1990:** 75th
  **U.S. rank in 2000:** 73rd (State rank: 2nd)

**Metropolitan Area Population**
  **1980:** 665,000
  **1990:** 858,000
  **2000:** 1,187,941
  **Percent change, 1980–1990:** 29.1%
  **U.S. rank in 1980:** 61st
  **U.S. rank in 1990:** 54th
  **U.S. rank in 2000:** 40th

**Area:** 117.3 square miles (2000)
**Elevation:** 434 feet above sea level
**Average Annual Temperature:** 59.3° F
**Average Annual Precipitation:** 52.6 inches

**Major Economic Sectors:** services, government, wholesale and retail trade
**Unemployment rate:** 3.3% (December 2004)
**Per Capita Income:** $25,113 (1999)

**2002 FBI Crime Index Total:** 17,833

**Major Colleges and Universities:** North Carolina State University, Shaw University, Meredith College, St. Augustine's

**Daily Newspaper:** *The News and Observer*

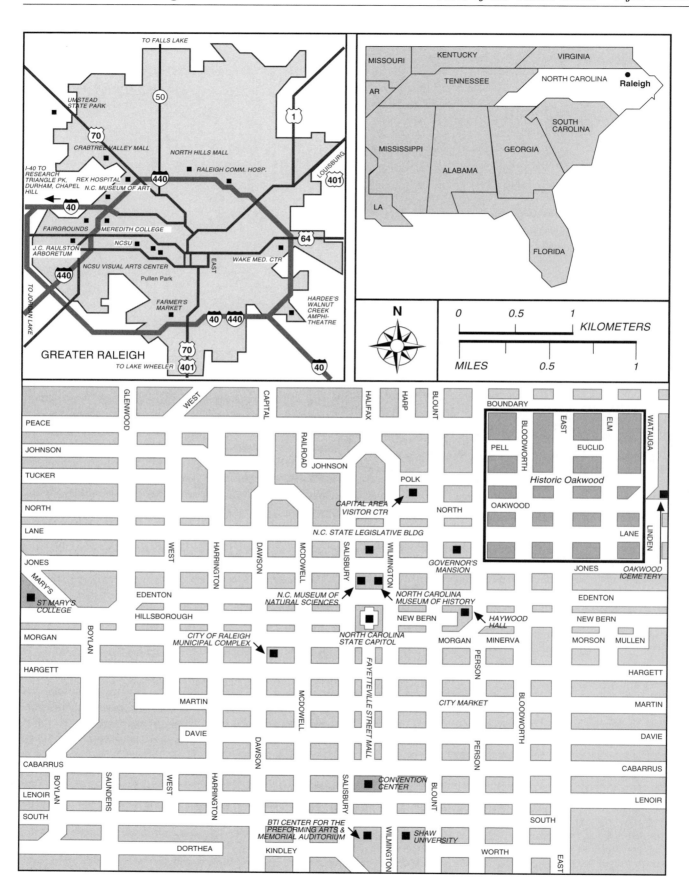

# Introduction

Blessed with beautiful residential areas, expansive parks, and historic buildings, the city of Raleigh exudes southern charm. Along with Durham and Chapel Hill, it is the largest city of an area in central North Carolina known as the Research Triangle. Raleigh's North Carolina State University joins two other stellar research institutions—the University of North Carolina at Chapel Hill and Duke University in Durham—to form the intellectual nucleus of the Research Triangle.

Over the past decade and a half, Raleigh prospered as an education, government, and research and development center. The city has a superior system of local parks and lakes, easy access to the ocean and the mountains, and a moderate climate, all of which encourage year-round outdoor activities. High-caliber health care services are offered by the many physicians who trained at the state's several top-rated medical colleges, fell in love with the area, and decided to settle in Raleigh. Cultural activity abounds in the city, which offers a major symphony orchestra, an art museum with an outstanding collection of European and American paintings, and the world's premier modern dance festival. Residents and visitors enjoy an ever-widening culinary scene.

As the new century gets underway, downtown Raleigh is one area of focus for city and county planners. Ground will be broken in 2005 for a 500,000-square-foot convention center, as well as a four-star convention headquarters hotel. Both are scheduled to open in early 2008. The city is also currently planning a redevelopment for a regional commuter rail system linking downtown Raleigh with downtown Durham.

# Geography and Climate

Raleigh is located in the gently rolling pine woods of the central Piedmont section of North Carolina, midway between the Great Smoky Mountains to the west and the Atlantic Ocean to the east, each about a three-hour drive. Temperatures average around 38.9 degrees in mid-winter, 59.3 degrees in mid-spring, 78.1 degrees in mid-summer and 59.7 degrees in mid-autumn. Snowfall averages 7.9 inches per year.

**Area:** 117.3 square miles (2000)

**Elevation:** 434 feet above sea level

**Average Temperatures:** January, 38.9° F; July, 78.1° F; annual average, 59.3° F reported

**Average Annual Precipitation:** 52.6 inches

# History

## City Named Capital of State

In 1771 a new North Carolina county was created by the state assembly. They named the county Wake, in honor of Margaret Wake, wife of Governor William Tryon. In 1792 the General Assembly purchased 1,000 acres of Wake County and established the city of Raleigh, which was named in honor of Sir Walter Raleigh, to serve as the first permanent state capital. The word "Raleigh" comes from two Anglo-Saxon words meaning "meadow of the deer," which captures the essence of the city's peaceful setting.

## Early Citizens Seen as "Roughnecks"

William Christmas of Franklin County, North Carolina, was hired to create a plan for the new city. Christmas designed a layout with one square mile of perpendicular streets and one-acre lots. Union Square, future home of the State House, lay at the center. Equidistant from it the planner designated four squares to serve as green space. Even now, the original city boundaries can be recognized by their original names, North, South, East, and West.

Enthusiastic about Christmas's plans, legislators authorized the building of a new courthouse in Raleigh, making it the county seat as well as the capital. During its early days, Raleigh had a questionable reputation because of the bachelors and saloons that dominated the scene. Its citizens were not granted the right to vote until the beginning of the nineteenth century.

## Raleigh in the Nineteenth Century

Raleigh grew larger at a slow but steady pace during this time when most of its residents were in the business of agriculture. Eventually towns developed along railroad lines and market centers. In time, small textile and furniture factories grew up. In 1831 the original State House burned down. The legislature agreed that the new State House should be a more durable structure. For this purpose solid granite was quarried in the east side of the county and brought to Raleigh via a specially built rail line. The permanent Executive Mansion was designed by architects Samuel Sloan and Gustavus Bauer, and constructed entirely of North Carolina materials, from the slate roof to the pine balustrade and brick facade. Construction was performed by prison inmates whose names and initials can still be seen in the brick sidewalks surrounding the mansion.

During the Civil War, Raleigh did not experience the tremendous suffering at the hands of Union forces as did many other southern towns and cities. Destruction was narrowly averted when some torch-carrying troops from the 60,000 troops quartered in the city approached the downtown upon hearing of the assassination of President Abraham Lincoln. Their commander, General John A. Logan, turned them back at gunpoint.

### City Takes Off After WWII

Raleigh's major growth occurred after World War II ended in 1945. The seeds of the city's modern renaissance were sewn in the 1950s when the state of North Carolina created the world-famous Research Triangle Park west of the city. The concept of Dr. Howard Odom, a University of North Carolina sociologist, the original purpose of the development was to use the talents of the highly trained graduates of North Carolina's colleges and universities who were leaving for more promising careers elsewhere. The area boomed following the establishment of IBM's facilities there in 1965.

Raleigh is now recognized around the world for the basic and applied research and development conducted by the occupants of Research Triangle Park. The downtown area is currently undergoing a revitalization with the groundbreaking in 2005 for a new 500,000-square-foot convention center, scheduled for completion in early 2008. With a population of more than 330,000, Raleigh enjoys a combination of the two most sought after and envied economic characteristics: low unemployment and rising incomes. Major companies are regularly launching new operations or expansions in the Raleigh area, keeping the local economy healthy. Furthermore, the city's housing stock is robust, increasing at a healthy pace to welcome newcomers to the area.

***Historical Information:*** North Carolina (State) Department of Cultural Resources, Division of Archives and History, 109 East Jones Street, Raleigh, NC 27601-2807; telephone (919)733-3952

# *Population Profile*

### Metropolitan Area Residents
*1980:* 665,000
*1990:* 858,485
*2000:* 1,187,941
*Percent change, 1990–2000:* 38.2%
*U.S. rank in 1980:* 61st
*U.S. rank in 1990:* 54th
*U.S. rank in 2000:* 40th

### City Residents
*1980:* 150,255
*1990:* 218,859
*2000:* 276,093
*2003 estimate:* 285,639

*Percent change, 1990–2000:* 26%
*U.S. rank in 1980:* 106th
*U.S. rank in 1990:* 75th
*U.S. rank in 2000:* 61st (State rank: 2nd)

*Density:* 2,409.2 people per square mile (2000)

*Racial and ethnic characteristics* (2000)
White: 174,786
Black or African American: 76,756
American Indian and Alaska Native: 981
Asian: 9,327
Native Hawaiian and Other Pacific Islander: 118
Hispanic (may be of any race): 19,308
Other: 5,179

*Percent of residents born in state:* 56.1% (2000)

*Age characteristics* (2000)
Population under 5 years old: 17,461
Population 5 to 9 years old: 16,444
Population 10 to 14 years old: 15,254
Population 15 to 19 years old: 19,864
Population 20 to 24 years old: 32,458
Population 25 to 34 years old: 57,105
Population 35 to 44 years old: 43,826
Population 45 to 54 years old: 32,984
Population 55 to 59 years old: 10,308
Population 60 to 64 years old: 7,394
Population 65 to 74 years old: 12,025
Population 75 to 84 years old: 8,143
Population 85 years and older: 2,827
Median age: 30.9 years

*Births* (2000)
Total number: 5,187

*Deaths* (2000)
Total number: 1,725 (of which, 32 were infants under the age of 1 year)

*Money income* (1999)
Per capita income: $25,113
Median household income: $46,612
Total households: 112,727

*Number of households with income of . . .*
less than $10,000: 8,113
$10,000 to $14,999: 5,154
$15,000 to $24,999: 12,758
$25,000 to $34,999: 14,896
$35,000 to $49,999: 19,062
$50,000 to $74,999: 23,007
$75,000 to $99,999: 13,262
$100,000 to $149,999: 10,843
$150,000 to $199,999: 3,081
$200,000 or more: 2,551

*Percent of families below poverty level:* 7.1% (60.6% of which were female householder families in poverty)

*2002 FBI Crime Index Total:* 17,833

# Municipal Government

Raleigh has a council/manager form of government with a mayor and seven council members, two elected at large and five from districts.

**Head Official:** City Manager J. Russell Allen (since April 2001)

**Total Number of City Employees:** 3,000 (2004)

*City Information:* City of Raleigh, PO Box 590, Raleigh, NC 27602; telephone (919)890-3000

# Economy

## Major Industries and Commercial Activity

Raleigh and the Research Triangle Park area consistently rank among the nation's best economies year after year. Unemployment remains low and per capita income remains high. Wake County's biggest industries—government, education, and healthcare—are virtually recession proof. Although the region has felt some of the pinch of the nation's economic slowdown, many factors point to Raleigh's continued fiscal health.

Numerous high-technology and medical corporations have been attracted to the Raleigh-Durham area because of the outstanding educational and research facilities at area universities, such as North Carolina State University, which is home to the nation's tenth largest school of engineering, Duke University, and the University of North Carolina-Chapel Hill.

Nearby Research Triangle Park is one of the leading centers for high-technology research and development in the country. Roughly 140 corporate, academic, and government agencies in the Park employ more than 38,500 (plus 5,000 additional contract employees) workers and provide an annual payroll in excess of $2 billion.

Business is booming in Raleigh, both as companies move into the area from other parts of the country and through the growth of home-grown enterprises. In early 2002, Red Hat, the market leader for the Linux marketing system, moved its

630 employees from nearby Durham to downtown Raleigh. Asea Brown Boveri, a $31-billion company that provides large-scale equipment, systems, and services for electric power transmission, continues to expand its presence in Raleigh. The city has witnessed the growth of lower-technology, sophisticated, and highly specialized new manufacturing companies that produce intricate machinery and electronic parts. The Raleigh workforce is fueled by the annual graduation of thousands of students from the area's universities and colleges, and the influx of new residents looking for opportunities.

With excellent road, rail, and air transportation systems, and easier access to the deepwater port at Wilmington as a result of the completion of I-40, Raleigh is a growing distribution center.

*Items and goods produced:* pharmaceuticals, electronic equipment, electrical machinery, processed foods, metal products

### Incentive Programs—New and Existing Companies

*Local programs*—The Greater Raleigh Chamber of Commerce believes that public funds "should not be used to subsidize a private company's bottom line." The city does not provide free land, free buildings, interest-free loans, direct grants, or preferential tax treatment. However, infrastructure improvements, human capital development, and public financing programs have been put in place to encourage new business development. The chamber's Site Selection Services offers companies considering moving to the city tours, an inventory of facilities, research portfolios, and newcomer assistance. For major corporate relocations, chamber members may provide services to new firms at reduced rates. The chamber, together with MCI Communications Corp and the North Carolina Small Business and Technology Development, has established the MCI Small Business Resource Center, which offers free international trade aid to North Carolina entrepreneurs. Wake County offers Industrial Revenue Bonds and assistance with water and sewer utility expansions. The Capital Economic Development Corporation administers Small Business Administration (SBA) loan guarantee and other financing programs for small business as well as the SBA 503 program for long-term capital asset acquisition.

*State programs*—North Carolina is one of 22 states with a "right-to-work" law. Several venture capital funds operate in the state and inquiries can be made thorough the North Carolina Council for Entrepreneurial Development. North Carolina offers State Technology Based Equity Funds providing financing for new technology based enterprises, as well as TDA incubators for firms transferring new technologies into commercial applications. The state offers an income tax allocation formula that permits the double weighting of sales in calculating corporate income tax. The North Carolina

Department of Transportation administers a program which provides for the construction of access roads to industrial sites and road improvements in areas surrounding major corporate installations. The William S. Lee Quality Jobs and Expansion Act makes available to new and expanding companies tax credits on investment, a jobs tax credit, worker training tax credit, research and development tax credits, and business property tax credits. Additional tax credits are also available for portions of Raleigh and Wake County designated as "development zones."

*Job training programs*—Screening, testing, and placement services are provided free of cost by the North Carolina Job Service. Extensive, cost-free customized training is provided by Wake Technical Community College for any new or expanding industry that created new jobs. The Capital Area Private Industry Council offers funding for various U.S. Department of Labor on-the-job training programs and youth summer employment programs.

## Development Projects

From 1990 to 2002, there were 273 new industries in Wake County, bringing 16,507 new jobs, and 400 expanded industries in Wake County, bringing 31,810 new jobs. In 2003, the Chamber of Commerce assisted 33 new or expanding companies, yielding 677 jobs and $50.9 million in investment. Among companies announcing expansion are Ascom Wireless Solutions, Iams Company, Time Warner Cable, and Relativity. The area continues to be an encouraging place for high-tech entrepreneurial companies, as evidenced by the amount of venture capital that is available. Investors continue to provide funds to companies with a focus on profits. Programs offered by groups such as the Council for Entrepreneurial Development routinely help turn innovative ideas and technological developments into capital-rich companies.

The downtown Raleigh Renaissance, a revitalization process designed to create a stronger and more vibrant downtown, includes three major projects totaling almost $250 million that will move the city toward becoming a more viable meetings destination. A new 500,000-square-foot convention center, a 400-room Marriott headquarters hotel, and the reopening of Fayetteville Street to vehicular traffic are scheduled for completion in early 2008. Progress Energy, one of the country's largest energy providers and the only Fortune 500 company headquartered in Raleigh, plans to build a mixed-use development on approximately 2 acres located east of its current location. The 19-story structure will include three elements: one level of street retail, six levels of parking, and 12 levels of office space.

*Economic Development Information:* Wake County Economic Development, PO Box 2978, 800 South Salisbury Street, Raleigh, NC 27602-2978; telephone (919)644-7040; fax (919)664-7099. Greater Raleigh Chamber of Commerce,

800 S. Salisbury St., Raleigh, NC 27601; telephone (919)664-7000

## Commercial Shipping

Raleigh is an integral part of Norfolk Southern's rail service linking the east coast to Midwest markets and is in the center of CSX's 27,000-mile network serving 22 states and Canada. More than 300 motor freight carriers operate in the area, which has more than 40 motor freight terminals. The city is located within 500 miles of half the population of the United States. The state's 78,000-mile highway network makes the area a highway hub for the Northeast, Mid-Atlantic, and Southeast states, while providing rapid access to Midwest markets.

## Labor Force and Employment Outlook

Raleigh-Durham boasts a skilled, educated, enthusiastic, and growing workforce. The economy is thriving and the unemployment rate consistently registers below the national average. The technical and medical industries are in particular need of qualified personnel. Education, services, and wholesale/retail sectors also offer abundant job opportunities. From 1990 to 2002, there were 273 new industries in Wake County, bringing 16,507 new jobs, and 400 expanded industries in Wake County, bringing 31,810 new jobs. Raleigh was voted the number one city with the happiest workers by the Hudson Employment Index in 2004, and the number one "hottest job market" in *Business 2.0* magazine in 2005.

The following is a summary of data regarding the Raleigh metropolitan area labor force, 2003 annual averages.

*Size of nonagricultural labor force:* 680,700

*Number of workers employed in . . .*
  *manufacturing:* 69,100
  *trade, transportation, and utilities:* 112,900
  *information:* 22,000
  *financial activities:* 32,200
  *professional and business services:* 101,700
  *education and health services:* 82,100
  *leisure and hospitality:* 1,100
  *government:* 33,200

*Average hourly earnings of production workers employed in manufacturing:* $14.45

*Unemployment rate:* 3.3% (December 2004)

| *Largest employers* | *Number of employees* |
|---|---|
| State of North Carolina | 23,539 |
| IBM Corporation | 13,000 |
| Wake County Public School System | 12,997 |
| North Carolina State University | 7,787 |
| WakeMed | 5,000 |

## Cost of Living

The following is a summary of data regarding several key cost of living factors for the Raleigh area.

*2004 (3rd Quarter) ACCRA Average House Price:*$236,450

*2004 (3rd Quarter) ACCRA Cost of Living Index:* 97.7 (U.S. average = 100.0)

*State income tax rate:* Ranges from 6.0% to 7.75%

*State sales tax rate:* 4.5% (food and prescription drugs are exempt; food sales are subject to local sales taxes)

*Local income tax rate:* None

*Local sales tax rate:* 2.0%

*Property tax rate:* $.95 (combined city and county) per $100 of assessed value (2004)

***Economic Information:*** Greater Raleigh Chamber of Commerce, 800 S. Salisbury St., Raleigh, NC 27601; telephone (919)664-7000. Employment Security Commission of North Carolina, Labor Market Information Division, PO Box 25903, Raleigh, NC 27611-5903

# *Education and Research*

## Elementary and Secondary Schools

The Wake County Public School System is a comprehensive system with 134 schools serving the entire county. The system is the 2nd largest in the state and the 27th largest in the nation. Since 1981 students have had the option of either attending their neighborhood school or a network of 50 magnet schools, including year-round schools, schools with gifted and talented programs, and schools with other programs, including Montessori, creative arts, extended day, and accelerated studies. Special programs are available for physically and mentally handicapped children. Project Enlightenment targets preschool youngsters who may need some extra assistance. In 2003, voters approved a bond referendum for $450 million to fund the building of 13 new schools, one pre-K center, renovations at 16 schools, and minor repairs at 61 schools.

The following is a summary of data regarding Raleigh's public schools as of the 2003–2004 school year.

*Total enrollment:* 114,092 (2004–2005)

*Number of facilities*
    *elementary schools:* 84

*junior high/middle schools:* 28
*senior high schools:* 17
*other:* 5 special/optional schools

*Student/teacher ratio:* 23:1

*Teacher salaries*
    *minimum:* $28,725
    *maximum:* $65,566

*Funding per pupil:* $5,634

Private school education in Raleigh thrives under many forms, with more than 60 schools in the metropolitan area including church-related schools, preschools, college preparatory schools, a school whose entire curriculum is taught in French, and special institutions for the learning disabled. Nearby Durham is home to the North Carolina School of Science and Mathematics, a statewide, public, residential high school for juniors and seniors with special interest and talent in the sciences and mathematics. North Carolina is also a leader in home schooling.

***Public Schools Information:*** Wake County Public School System, 3600 Wake Forest Road, PO Box 28041, Raleigh, NC 27611; telephone (919)850-1600

## Colleges and Universities

Higher education plays an important role throughout the Raleigh area, which boasts 12 colleges and universities. North Carolina State University (NCSU), with nearly 30,000 students, is the state's largest university. The most popular programs are engineering and humanities/social sciences. Faculty at North Carolina State set a new record in 2003 and 2004 by earning $208 million in external support for research and sponsored programs. In addition, faculty took the initiative to develop and submit proposals for an additional $96.5 million in funding. Meredith College is a Baptist-affiliated women's liberal arts college that offers its more than 2,000 students more than 40 undergraduate programs and four master's programs. The oldest historically African American university in the South, Shaw University enrolls more than 2,500 students. Peace College, a women's college affiliated with the Presbyterian Church, offers its 630 students more than 30 two-year associate degree programs as well as 5 B.S. degree programs. St. Augustine's College was founded by the Episcopal Church after the Civil War to educate freed slaves. Today, the school offers four-year curricula to the 1,600 students in its predominantly African American student body. Wake Technical Community College provides vocational programs and two-year associate degree programs in such areas as business computer programming, automatic robotics technology, criminal justice, hotel and restaurant management, and early childhood education to its nearly 50,000 curriculum and continuing education students.

## Libraries and Research Centers

The Wake County Public Library operates 18 branches within Wake County. The library has 1.4 million volumes, 52,430 audio materials, 39,248 video materials, and 1,850 serial subscriptions. Special Collections include the Mollie Houston Lee Collection on African American subjects and the North Carolina History Collection. The library system at North Carolina State University's 5 facilities numbers 2.2 million books and more than 18,000 periodicals.

Research Triangle Park near Raleigh-Durham is one of the country's leading centers for high technology research. Its 7,000-acre campus is the largest planned research facility in the world. North Carolina State University is world-renowned for its research in biotechnology, chemical engineering, polymer science, electrical engineering, genetics, and microelectronics. There are many other college-related and independent research facilities throughout the area.

***Public Library Information:*** Wake County Department of the Public Library, 4020 Carya Drive, Raleigh, NC 27610-2900; telephone (919)250-1200.

# Health Care

The Raleigh area offers world-class care and state-of-the-art technology in the health field, in part because of the proximity of nearby pharmaceutical, nursing, and medical schools at the University of North Carolina and Duke University at Durham. Raleigh itself is served by 518.4 physicians per 100,000 people. Wake Medical Center, a major medical and referral facility for the state, offers a top-rate heart program, a trauma center, a neuroscience unit, and neonatal intensive care. Wake is the flagship for a five-hospital private, nonprofit system totaling 752 beds, which includes four community facilities and a 45-bed rehabilitation hospital. Rex Hospital, a not-for-profit facility, has specialized centers for cancer, obstetrics, and same-day surgery. Its 388-bed facility encompasses a home healthcare division and a convalescent center, as well as the Rex Wellness Center. Part of the Duke University Health System, Duke Health Raleigh Hospital is a 186-bed acute care facility. Mental health and addiction treatment programs are the focus of Dorothea Dix Hospital, Holly Hill, and Charter Hospital. Located within 30 miles of the city are a Veteran's Administration Hospital and Lenox Baker Children's Hospital, as well as North Carolina Memorial Hospital in Chapel Hill.

# Recreation

### Sightseeing

Visitors to Raleigh should start their explorations with a trip to the Capital Area Visitor Center, which provides free brochures, maps, and a film about the city's offerings. Tours are available of the North Carolina Executive Mansion, a masterpiece of Queen Ann Victorian architecture completed in 1891. Historic Oakwood, a neighborhood of restored Victorian homes built between 1870 and 1900, occupies a 20-block area adjacent to the 1876 Oakwood Cemetery. The birthplace of President Andrew Johnson can be viewed at Mordecai Historic Park, which is the site of the Mordecai House, a 200-year-old furnished plantation house. Haywood Hall, a Federal-style house built in 1799, is the oldest residence in the city still on its original site. A life-sized bronze statue of civil rights leader Martin Luther King Jr. is on view at the MLK Memorial Gardens, which are surrounded by trees, shrubs, and flowering plants. The State Capitol, built between 1833 and 1840, is an excellent preserved example of the Greek Revival style. Tours are also available through the North Carolina State Legislative Building, home of the General Assembly. Built in the 1760s, the Wakefield/Joel Lane House, decorated with furnishings and gardens of the period, is Raleigh's oldest dwelling.

Dubbed "the Smithsonian of the South," Raleigh is home to a number of museums, including three free state museums. The North Carolina Museum of History displays more than 100,000 artifacts reflecting the history of the state. Holdings include furniture, fashions, crafts, military artifacts, dolls, toys, and period exhibits. Free lectures, films, and demonstrations are presented in its "Month of Sundays" series. The North Carolina Museum of Natural Sciences has four floors of exhibits, live animals, and the only Acrocanthosaurus dinosaur fossil in existence. The North Carolina Museum of Art houses paintings and sculpture representing more than 5,000 years of artistic heritage. It also features the Museum Park outdoor amphitheater. Exploris, the nation's first children's museum devoted to global learning and awareness, is a 70,000-square-foot interactive learning center. The IMAX theater is also located there.

Eight acres with 6,000 varied plants from almost 50 countries are the highlights of the North Carolina State University's Arboretum, which also features a Victorian gazebo, Japanese garden, and special areas such as water and reading gardens. Playspace is a creative play area for children of all ages, which encompasses a large sandbox, water play area, climbing structure, and a child-sized bank, grocery store, and hospitals with costumes, a video, and a television area. Tours are available of the 5 acres of landscaped garden surrounding the WRAL-TV studio, which features more than 2,000 azaleas, trees, and plants.

The North Carolina State Capitol building.

## Arts and Culture

Raleigh's downtown arts district is a collection of galleries clustered in a three-block area around the historic City Market and Moore Square. The district comprises a variety of galleries, including Artspace, Inc., a downtown renovation project, offering 26,000 square feet of studio and gallery space to working visual and performing artists. Visitors can tour the gallery and studios while the artists are working.

The Visual Arts Center on the campus of North Carolina State University features changing exhibits of ceramics, furniture, photography, textiles, drawings, and graphic design. Also on campus is the Crafts Center, the largest campus-based crafts facility of its kind in the Southeast, which features changing exhibitions of local, regional, and national craftspersons. At the Wake Visual Arts Association and Gallery, classes, workshops, and exhibits are offered to members and the public. Ninety-day exhibitions of works produced or collected by Raleigh residents are on view at the City of Raleigh Arts Commission.

Raleigh's premier music venue is the ALLTEL Pavilion at Walnut Creek. In its natural setting on 212 acres, the amphitheatre presents big-name rock and pop performers in its 7,000-seat open air pavilion and to an additional 13,000 people seated on a sloping lawn. The North Carolina Symphony Orchestra, the first state-supported orchestra in the nation, performs 55 times annually in the city, with an additional 200 performances and 70 educational concerts statewide. Programming includes solo performances by world-class performers as well as classical, pops, and children's series, outdoor summer programs, and special holiday performances. The National Opera Company, based in Raleigh, performs operatic classics in English, and the Friends of the College Series at North Carolina State University presents world-renowned singers and dancers. NCSU also presents dance, opera, orchestra, and other cultural events at its student center and at Reynolds Coliseum. The city is also the site of the Raleigh Chamber Music Guild series, which brings in international guest performers, and the Raleigh Oratorio Society. Musical performances are also available throughout the Triangle region by such groups and events as Durham's Ciompi Quartet; the North Carolina International Jazz Festival, a two-week festival held annually in Durham; the Piedmont Council for Traditional Music's many concerts of blues, gospel, bluegrass, and other folk music; and the Durham Civic Choral Society, as well as numerous civic symphonies, youth symphonies, concert bands, community choruses, boys' choirs, and barbershop groups.

The performing arts are flourishing in the city with performances by both local groups and touring troupes and Carolina Ballet, Raleigh's professional ballet company, which often collaborates with the North Carolina Symphony. The Raleigh Ensemble Players feature contemporary dramas, including original works by North Carolina playwrights. The North Carolina Theatre brings touring musicals to its home at the Raleigh Memorial Auditorium. The city's community theater groups include the Raleigh Little Theatre, which has been performing for more than 50 years, and Burning Coal Theatre Company. Pullen Park's Theatre In the Park community group presents dramas, musicals, and occasional children's programs. Stewart Theatre at NCSU presents a professional series of theater, music, film, and lectures. Theatrical productions are also offered by Thompson Theatre at NCSU, Peace College, Meredith College Theatre, and Shaw University Theatre.

The completion of the BTI Center for the Performing Arts in 2001 offered Raleigh three new theaters to offer an additional 2,470 seats daily for arts lovers. The Fletcher Opera Theater is designed for opera, dance, and theatrical productions, offering performances from such groups as Carolina Ballet, National Opera Company, and A. J. Fletcher Opera Institute. Meymandi Concert Hal is the home of the North Carolina Symphony. The Kennedy Theater is an experimental theater that provides performance space for innovative groups as Burning Coal Theatre.

## Festivals and Holidays

Raleigh welcomes spring in May with the Artsplosure Jazz and Arts Festivals, which combines exhibitions, food, and open air performances. July Fourth activities include the Capital's Celebration with a parade and free live entertainment; exhibits, rides, and fireworks at the State Fairgrounds; and the North Carolina Symphony's annual extravaganza with a concert and fireworks at Regency Park. In August, attendees can meet, greet, and perhaps eat some of the coolest critters around at Bugfest! Autumn brings the Pops in the Park in September with the North Carolina Symphony performing pop music in a picnic setting.

The North Carolina State Fair in mid-October offers craft demonstrations, livestock exhibits and competitions, top-notch concerts, games, rides, side shows, food, and other family-friendly entertainment. The Greater Raleigh Antique Show at the State Fairgrounds takes place in November, as does the six-day handicrafts and entertainment of the Carolina Christmas Show. November's Raleigh Christmas Parade kicks off the holiday season, which includes December's Holiday Festival at the North Carolina Museum of Art; the Christmas Celebration on the Mall in downtown Raleigh which features the lighting of the state Christmas tree; annual performances of *A Christmas Carol* and *The Nutcracker*; and candlelight tours through a variety of historic homes decked out for the holiday season. First Night Raleigh on December 31 welcomes the new year with performances, visual arts, food, and a midnight countdown downtown. The Home and Garden Show in February offers 100,000 square feet of springtime gardens, flowers, designer rooms, seminars, and hundreds of home product displays at the Raleigh Convention and Conference Center.

### Sports for the Spectator

*Sports Travel* magazine has rated Raleigh as one of the "hottest sports cities" in the country. Raleigh's state-of-the-art Entertainment and Sports Arena hosts the city's first major league professional franchise, the National Hockey League's Carolina Hurricanes. With seating for more than 20,000 people, the arena is one of the premier event venues in the southeast. The Arena Football League's Carolina Cobras also play at the Entertainment and Sports Arena.

Celebrated college sports teams in Raleigh and the Research Triangle area include the North Carolina State University Wolfpack, who play their basketball games at the Entertainment and Sports Arena and their football games at Carter-Finley Stadium; the University of North Carolina Tarheels; and the Duke University Blue Devils. Two professional baseball teams are located within a 30-mile radius. A farm team of the Tampa Bay Devil Rays, the Durham Bulls play from April through August at Durham Bulls Athletic Park. The Carolina Mudcats, a Double A professional baseball affiliate of the Colorado Rockies, play home games at Five County Stadium in Zebulon. Sports fans also enjoy the athletic events at Raleigh's Shaw University and St. Augustine's College.

### Sports for the Participant

Raleigh citizens take pride in their extensive recreational assets. The city's Parks and Recreation Department has more than 7,300 acres of park land and green spaces and more than 1,300 acres of water. Forty-one miles of greenway with 24 different trails can be found throughout the city. Park facilities include 19 community centers and 8 different organized sports teams for adults and youths, as well as 21 public golf courses, 112 lighted tennis courts, and 8 public swimming pools.

Major recreational sites include Pullen Park, a 65-acre inner city children's play facility with an aquatic center, complete with a 50-meter indoor pool; Umstead State Park, which offers picnicking, camping and hiking; Lake Wheeler, 650 acres of lake and park land offering boating, skiing, fishing, and picnicking; Shelley Lake, which can accommodate boating as well as bird watching, fishing, nature walks, jogging, and concerts; Falls Lake, a 12,000-acre facility with beaches, boat ramps, fishing, and picnic areas; Jordan Lake, a lakeside recreation area and marina that is the largest summertime home of the bald eagle in the eastern U.S.; and Lake Johnson, a 137-acre creek-fed lake with forests and a boathouse.

### Shopping and Dining

Six shopping malls, featuring major department stores and popular clothing chains, and more than 100 shopping centers serve the Raleigh area. The shopping scene is made more interesting by the variety of local shops featuring original art, crafts, jewelry, children's boutiques, native gem jewelers, and garden shops, as well as burgeoning outlet stores. Antique shops are located all over the city, and settings range from flea markets to upscale import-export emporiums. Among the city's favorite shopping sites are Crabtree Valley Mall, North Hills, Tower Shopping Complex, Cameron Village, and Triangle Towne Center, which is currently undergoing redevelopment. The old mission-style City Market Building and adjacent Moore Square have been transformed into a festive retail district. The State Farmer's Market is also a fun place to shop for fresh produce, crafts items, and plants.

Greater Raleigh offers a wide variety of dining experiences, from steak houses, chain restaurants, and ethnic eateries (featuring French, Middle Eastern, Indian, Mexican, Chinese, Italian, and Japanese food) to down-home cooking. Ambience ranges from casual cafes to big screen sports bars to elegant dining rooms.

*Visitor Information:* Greater Raleigh Convention and Visitor's Bureau, 421 Fayetteville Street Mall, Suite 1505, PO Box 1879, Raleigh, NC 27602-1879; telephone (919)834-5900; toll-free (800)849-8499

# Convention Facilities

The City of Raleigh and Wake County have approved plans to build a new 500,000-square-foot downtown convention center. The existing convention center, which is just east of the new convention center site, will be demolished. The new facility will have a total of 212,000 square feet of rentable space, including 150,000 square feet designated for exhibits and 30,000 square feet for meetings, as well as a 32,000-square-foot ballroom. Memorial Auditorium, which will continue to serve as the performing arts wing of the complex, has seats for 2,277 people, a stage with proscenium arch, and a lobby that can handle receptions for up to 1,000 people.

Other unique meeting sites in Raleigh include Artspace, which can handle receptions for 600 people; the Capital City Club, which can accommodate up to 600 people; and the Angus Barn Wine Cellar, an intimate dining room offering an extensive wine list and seating for groups of 12 to 28 people.

*Convention Information:* Greater Raleigh Convention and Visitor's Bureau, 421 Fayetteville Street Mall, Suite 1505, PO Box 1879, Raleigh, NC 27602-1879; telephone (919)834-5900; toll-free (800)849-8499

# Transportation

### Approaching the City

Raleigh-Durham International Airport (RDU), located 15 miles from downtown Raleigh, is served by 14 major airlines and 10 regional airlines that offers more than 200 daily departures to 41 nonstop destinations. Recent improvements include renovations, expansions, roadway widening, and a new 6,000-space parking garage. By 2015, when RDU's annual total is projected to be 20 million passengers arriving and departing, some 16,000 garage spaces will be located between the terminals with an additional 10,000 available in surface lots outside the terminal area. Raleigh can be reached by an extensive network of state highways and roads. With one of the largest state-maintained highway systems in the nation, the Triangle area lies at the intersection of three interstate highways: Interstate 40, 85, and 95. Other major highways serving the area include U.S. Highways 1, 64, 70, and 401. Interstate 540 connects I-40 and U.S. 70 and provides easy access to RDU. The Raleigh Beltline, or I-440, is approximately 21 miles long and circles the city. Carolina Trailways and Greyhound Bus Lines provide service to points in the eastern United States, and Amtrak offers rail service from its recently renovated downtown station.

### Traveling in the City

Raleigh is a comfortable city to get around in. The main thoroughfares give easy access to the heart of the city from any direction. Local bus service is provided by Capital Area Transit and the Raleigh Trolley.

# Communications

### Newspapers and Magazines

Raleigh's daily (morning) newspaper is *The News and Observer.* About nine weekly and semimonthly newspapers are published there, including *Triangle Business Journal, The Independent,* and *The Carolinian,* an African American community newspaper. Nearly 30 magazines are published in Raleigh, including *Carolina Country*; *Balanced Life Center*; *North Carolina Historical Review; Social Science Computer Review,* published by Duke University Press; and a host of others focusing on agriculture, religion, Southern women, toy collectors, and assorted professions.

### Television and Radio

Eighteen television stations broadcast in Raleigh, five of which are affiliated with the major networks. Thirty-three radio stations broadcast from the area, offering programming such as Top Forty, country, classical, religious, Hispanic, and jazz.

***Media Information:*** *The News and Observer,* 215 South McDowell Street, PO Box 191, Raleigh, NC 27602; telephone (919)829-4500

### Raleigh Online

City of Raleigh home page. Available www.raleigh-nc.org

Greater Raleigh Convention & Visitors Bureau. Available www.raleighcvb.org

*The News and Observer.* Available www.news-observer .com

Raleigh Chamber of Commerce. Available www .raleighchamber.org

Wake County Public Libraries. Available www.co.wake.nc .us/library

Wake County Public Schools. Available www.wcpss.net

### Selected Bibliography

Gaddy, Charlie, *Celebrating a Triangle Millenium* (Memphis, Tenn.: Towery Publishing, 1999)

# OKLAHOMA

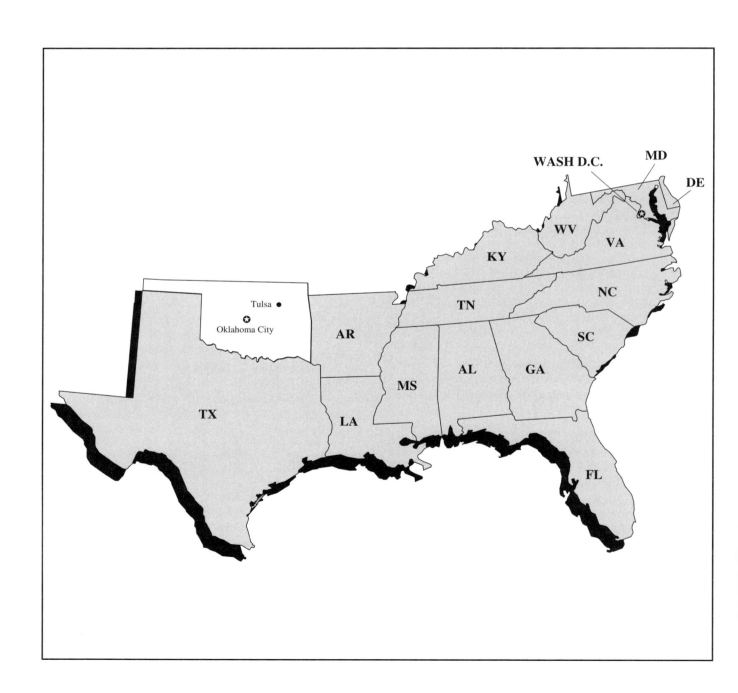

# The State in Brief

**Nickname:** Sooner State
**Motto:** *Labor omnia vincit* (Labor conquers all things)

**Flower:** Mistletoe
**Bird:** Scissor-tailed flycatcher

**Area:** 69,898 square miles (2000; U.S. rank: 20th)
**Elevation:** Ranges from 289 feet to 4,973 feet above sea level
**Climate:** Temperate and continental, with seasonal extremes

**Admitted to Union:** November 16, 1907
**Capital:** Oklahoma City
**Head Official:** Governor Brad Henry (D) (until 2007)

**Population**
    **1980:** 3,025,000
    **1990:** 3,145,585
    **2000:** 3,450,654
    **2004 estimate:** 3,523,553
    **Percent change, 1990–2000:** 9.7%
    **U.S. rank in 2004:** 28th
    **Percent of residents born in state:** 62.6% (2000)
    **Density:** 50.3 people per square mile (2000)
    **2002 FBI Crime Index Total:** 165,715

**Racial and Ethnic Characteristics** (2000)
    **White:** 2,628,434

**Black or African American:** 260,968
**American Indian and Alaska Native:** 273,230
**Asian:** 46,767
**Native Hawaiian and Pacific Islander:** 2,372
**Hispanic or Latino (may be of any race):** 179,304
**Other:** 82,898

**Age Characteristics** (2000)
    **Population under 5 years old:** 236,353
    **Population 5 to 19 years old:** 765,927
    **Percent of population 65 years and over:** 13.2%
    **Median age:** 35.5 years (2000)

**Vital Statistics**
    **Total number of births (2003):** 51,040
    **Total number of deaths (2003):** 35,325 (infant deaths, 378)
    **AIDS cases reported through 2003:** 2,085

**Economy**
    **Major industries:** Machinery, oil, gas, agriculture, food processing, manufacturing
    **Unemployment rate:** 4.2% (December 2004)
    **Per capita income:** $26,567 (2003; U.S. rank: 40th)
    **Median household income:** $36,733 (3-year average, 2001-2003)
    **Percentage of persons below poverty level:** 14.0% (3-year average, 2001-2003)
    **Income tax rate:** Ranges from 0.5% to 6.75%
    **Sales tax rate:** 4.5%

# Oklahoma City

## *The City in Brief*

**Founded:** 1889 (incorporated 1890)

**Head Official:** Mayor Mick Cornett (since 2004)

**City Population**
1980: 404,014
1990: 444,724
2000: 506,132
2003 estimate: 523,303
Percent change, 1990–2000: 13.8%
U.S. rank in 1980: 31st
U.S. rank in 1990: 29th (State rank: 1st)
U.S. rank in 2000: 36th

**Metropolitan Area Population**
1980: 861,000
1990: 959,000
2000: 1,083,346
Percent change, 1990–2000: 12.9%

U.S. rank in 1980: 43rd
U.S. rank in 1990: 42nd
U.S. rank in 2000: 48th

**Area:** 606.99 square miles (2000)
**Elevation:** 1,291 feet above sea level
**Average Annual Temperature:** 60.1° F
**Average Annual Precipitation:** 32.03 inches of rain, 9.0 inches of snow

**Major Economic Sectors:** energy, aviation, services, trade, government, manufacturing
**Unemployment rate:** 3.7 % (December 2004)
**Per Capita Income:** $19,098 (1999)

**2002 FBI Crime Index Total:** 49,929

**Major Colleges and Universities:** University of Oklahoma, University of Oklahoma Health Sciences Center, University of Central Oklahoma, Oklahoma State University-Oklahoma City

**Daily Newspaper:** *Oklahoman*

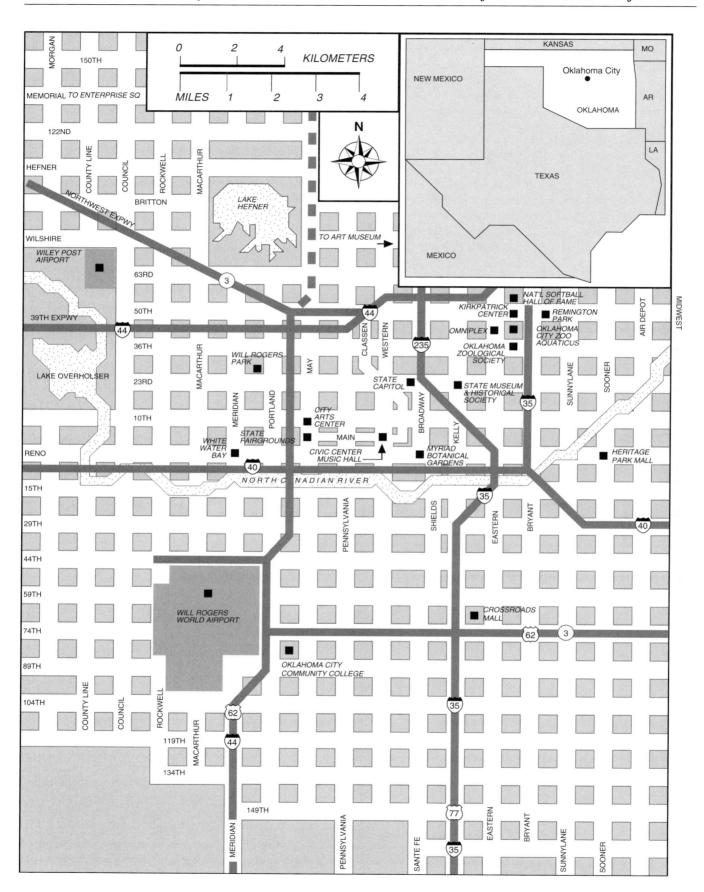

# Introduction

From its birth at high noon on April 22, 1889, Oklahoma City, the state capital of Oklahoma, has grown to become one of the nation's largest cities in terms of area. A low unemployment rate, continuing steady economic expansion, and a prime Sun Belt location are attractive to new businesses. Its sunny climate, educational and job opportunities, numerous cultural assets, and recreational attractions entice new residents. After experiencing economic difficulties with the 1980s oil slump and enduring one of the nation's worst terrorist attacks with the 1995 Murrah Federal Building bombing, Oklahoma City continues a vigorous rebound with a growing population and increasingly diversified economy.

# Geography and Climate

Surrounded by gently rolling prairie and plains along the North Canadian River, Oklahoma City is at the geographic center of the state. With a climate influenced by the Great Plains region, Oklahoma City is one of the sunniest, windiest cities in the country. Summers are long and hot; winters, short and mild. Tornadoes are not uncommon; in May 1999 central Oklahoma was hit by the most devastating tornadoes in its history, a series of twisters that flattened entire neighborhoods in the city and caused $40 million in damage in central Oklahoma.

**Area:** 606.99 square miles (2000)

**Elevation:** 1,291 feet above sea level

**Average Temperatures:** January, 45.9° F; July, 80.7° F; annual average, 60.1° F.

**Average Annual Precipitation:** 32.03 inches of rain; 9.0 inches of snow

# History

### Land Run Leads to City's Founding

Inhabited by Plains tribes and sold to the United States by France as a part of the 1803 Louisiana Purchase, much of what is now Oklahoma was subsequently designated as Indian Territory. As such, it was intended to provide a new home for tribes forced by the federal government to abandon their ancestral lands in the southeastern United States. Many of those forced to relocate in the 1830s were from what were called the Five Civilized Tribes—Cherokee, Choctaw,

Chickasaw, Creek, and Seminole—who soon set up independent nations in the new territory. After the Civil War, however, the pressure of westward expansion brought railroads into the Indian Territory, where the U.S. government began to declare some land available for white settlement. Prairie land surrounding a Santa Fe railroad single-track boxcar station was designated as a townsite when presidential proclamation opened the central portion of Indian Territory to claims stakers on noon of April 22, 1889. Thousands crossed the borders of the "unassigned lands" at high noon when a cannon was fired. By sunset of that day the land run had produced a tent city of 10,000 people on the townsite, which eventually became Oklahoma City.

The settlement attained official status in 1890, just a few weeks after the western half of Indian Territory was redesignated Oklahoma Territory, named for a Choctaw phrase meaning "red man." Incorporated as Oklahoma City on May 23, 1890, Oklahoma City swiftly became one of the new territory's largest cities. More railroad connections to the city helped make it a center for trade, milling, and meat packing. The Oklahoma and Indian territories merged and were admitted to the union as the state of Oklahoma in 1907. Oklahoma City became the state capital in 1910.

### Oil Brings Prosperity

The capital city was flourishing as a financial and manufacturing center when in 1928 an oil field beneath the city proved to be what was then the largest oil strike ever made. Oklahoma City joined neighboring regions in the petroleum industry with vast economic benefits. A gigantic deposit at the Mary Sudik well in Oklahoma City gushed wildly for 11 days in 1930, spewing 10,000 barrels of oil each day in a great geyser and spreading an oily cloud that deposited petroleum as far away as 15 miles. By the time it was closed down, the Mary Sudik well had produced a total of one million barrels of oil.

### Future Points Toward Diversity

The end of the oil boom dealt the city a severe blow. During its height in the early 1980s, developers added 5.2 million square feet of office space downtown. When the boom went bust, so did the real estate market. By the 1990s, downtown Oklahoma City was in a decline, with few shopping areas and too much empty office space. While the petroleum industry continues to be a solid part of Oklahoma City's economy in the early 21st century, the region has also been involved in the development of the state's other natural resources, such as coal and metals. In addition, the city supports such industries as livestock, agriculture, energy, aviation, and manufacturing.

Oklahoma City made international headlines on April 19, 1995, when a Ryder truck fitted with a homemade oil-and-fertilizer bomb exploded in the Alfred P. Murrah Federal Building, killing 168 men, women, and children, and injuring more than 400 others. In December 1996, the *Wall Street Journal* reported: "Twenty months after the bombing that vaulted it on to front pages around the world, this gutsy city is hoping a rapidly growing economy and a $300 million public-works program will revive one of the nation's sickest downtowns." Feelings of optimism were running high that a dramatic comeback for the city was in the works.

In April 2000 Oklahoma City unveiled its monument to the victims of the bombing. The main component of the memorial is 168 bronze-and-glass chairs, one for each victim, positioned in rows that correspond to the floors of the building where the victims were when the bomb exploded. It is a potent symbol in a city that still continues to grieve a tragedy even as it rebuilds and tries to modernize its image.

As the 21st century dawns, many of the city's efforts at revitalization and moving forward appear to be paying off. With up to $1 billion in new downtown investment, Oklahoma City was named one of the "Best Places to Live in North America" by *Places Rated Almanac*. The city continues an economic revitalization that has seen it move prominently into the areas of medicine, aviation, high technology, and diversified energy resources.

**Historical Information:** Oklahoma Historical Society, Historical Building, 2100 North Lincoln Boulevard, Oklahoma City, OK 73118; telephone (405)522-5209

# *Population Profile*

## Metropolitan Area Residents
*1980:* 861,000
*1990:* 958,839
*2000:* 1,083,346
*Percent change, 1990–2000:* 12.9%
*U.S. rank in 1980:* 43rd
*U.S. rank in 1990:* 42nd
*U.S. rank in 2000:* 48th

## City Residents
*1980:* 404,014
*1990:* 444,724
*2000:* 506,132
*2003 estimate:* 523,303
*Percent change, 1980–2000:* 13.8%%
*U.S. rank in 1980:* 31st
*U.S. rank in 1990:* 29th (State rank: 1st)
*U.S. rank in 2000:* 36th

*Density:* 833.8 people per square mile (2000)

*Racial and ethnic characteristics* (2000)
   White: 346,226
   Black or African American: 77,810
   American Indian and Alaska Native: 17,743
   Asian: 17,595
   Native Hawaiian and Other Pacific Islander: 360
   Hispanic or Latino (may be of any race): 51,368
   Other: 31,382

*Percent of residents born in state:* 60.6% (2000)

*Age characteristics* (2000)
   Population under 5 years old: 37,194
   Population 5 to 9 years old: 35,486
   Population 10 to 14 years old: 34,759
   Population 15 to 19 years old: 36,501
   Population 20 to 24 years old: 39,703
   Population 25 to 34 years old: 76,444
   Population 35 to 44 years old: 79,344
   Population 45 to 54 years old: 66,659
   Population 55 to 59 years old: 23,420
   Population 60 to 64 years old: 18,524
   Population 65 to 74 years old: 30,874
   Population 75 to 84 years old: 20,292
   Population 85 years and older: 6,932
   Median age: 34.0 years

*Births* (2002; Oklahoma County)
   Total number: 11,464

*Deaths* (2002; Oklahoma County)
   Total number: 6,421

*Money income* (1999)
   Per capita income: $19,098
   Median household income: $34,947
   Number of households: 204,493

*Number of households with income of . . .*
   less than $10,000: 23,882
   $10,000 to $14,999: 15,699
   $15,000 to $24,999: 32,485
   $25,000 to $34,999: 30,306
   $35,000 to $49,999: 34,729
   $50,000 to $74,999: 35,424
   $75,000 to $99,999: 15,965
   $100,000 to $149,999: 10,614
   $150,000 to $199,999: 2,341
   $200,000 or more: 3,048

*Percent of families below poverty level:* 12.4% (54.4% of which were female householder families with related children under 5 years)

*2002 FBI Crime Index Total:* 49,929

# Municipal Government

Oklahoma City has a city manager-council form of government. Its mayor and eight councilmen are elected to staggered four-year terms.

**Head Official:** Mayor Mick Cornett (since 2004; current term expires 2008)

**Total Number of City Employees:** 4,320 (2005)

*City Information:* Oklahoma City Hall, 200 N. Walker Ave., Oklahoma City, OK 73102; telephone (405)297-2345

# Economy

## Major Industries and Commercial Activity

Although in its early days oil dominated the economy, Oklahoma City today hosts a wide range of businesses and employers. Agriculture, energy, aviation, government, health care, manufacturing, and industry all play major roles in the city's economic well-being. Oklahoma City is the seat of government for the state of Oklahoma as well as Oklahoma County. There are also many regional federal agency offices located in the City. The government sector accounts for about 20 percent of the Oklahoma City metropolitan area non-agricultural employment. The health care industry is a major economic driver in the city. Mike Monroney Aeronautical Center, which is the largest trainer of Air Traffic Controllers in the world, and Tinker Air Force Base are major drivers as well. As the largest industrial operation in Oklahoma, Tinker serves the U.S. Air Force as a repair depot and provides logistic services for the U.S. Air Force throughout the world. Tinker employs 26,000 military and civilian personnel with a combined annual payroll of more than $775 million. There is also a growing high technology sector in the Oklahoma City economy, with more than 400 companies employing 30,000 in the fields of high technology, information technology, and software development.

As one of the nation's largest processing centers for a variety of farm products, the city is home to the world's largest stocker and feeder cattle market. Horses are also big business in Oklahoma City, stretching back to the region's days as a key cattle center and gateway to westward expansion. The city is known as the Horse Show Capital of the World for the nine major national and international horse shows held annually. Many large oil and energy-related companies have headquarters or major branches in the city. Other present and projected future growth industries include fabri-cated metal, computers, clothing, oil-field equipment, crude oil, back office, distribution and food processing.

*Items and goods produced:* motor vehicles, food products, steel, electronic devices, computers, oil-well supplies, paper products, rubber tires

### Incentive Programs—New and Existing Companies

*Local programs*—The Greater Oklahoma City Chamber of Commerce Economic Development Division provides full-service expansion and/or new business services. The Oklahoma City's Development Center offers one-stop shopping for permits, inspections, and building guidelines. The mission of the Oklahoma Small Business Development Center is to provide high quality one-to-one business counseling, economic development assistance, and training to small businesses and prospective small businesses. Many zones and neighborhoods of Oklahoma City have been designated as Federal Empowerment Zones that offer incentives to businesses looking to start-up or relocate. Incentives include tax credits of up to $3,000 for each employee newly hired or already on the payroll who lives and works in the zone; tax-exempt facility bonds to finance property, equipment and site development; and increased expense deductions of up to $35,000 for depreciable assets acquired during the first year.

*State programs*—The innovative Oklahoma Quality Jobs Program is a method to allow businesses that are creating large numbers of new quality jobs to receive a special incentive to locate or expand in Oklahoma. It is an easy-access program that provides direct payment incentives (based on new wages paid) to companies for up to ten years. The Investment/New Jobs Tax Credit Package provides growing manufacturers a significant tax credit based on either an investment in depreciable property or on the addition of full-time-equivalent employees engaged in manufacturing, processing, or aircraft maintenance. Other key Oklahoma incentives include a five-year ad valorem tax exemption, sales tax exemptions, freeport exemption, foreign trade zones, financing programs, export assistance, government contracting assistance, and limited industrial access road assistance. With reference to industrial financing programs, Oklahoma has simplified the laws governing businesses incorporated in the state. Oklahoma's new company legislation, based on the Delaware model, simplifies the procedures for incorporating businesses in the state and gives boards of directors more authority and flexibility in determining capital structures of companies.

*Job training programs*—The city's Office of Workforce Development administers the federal Workforce Investment Act program. Services include skills assessment, basic skills and GED instruction, career planning and counseling, tuition assistance, and job search assistance. Workforce Oklahoma, also created under the federal Workforce Investment Act, is a new training and education development system that partners business leaders, educators, and employment professionals to achieve job growth, employee productivity, and employer satisfaction. This system includes a network of 52 statewide offices called Workforce Oklahoma Centers, where employment, education, and training providers integrate a wide range of services that benefit both employers and employees. Customized industrial training programs, at no cost to the employer, are provided by the Oklahoma State Department of Vocational and Technical Education.

Known nationwide for its excellence, Oklahoma's Career and Technology Education system provides customized employer training and gives Oklahomans of all ages the opportunity to learn advanced technical skills they can put to use in the workforce. The centerpiece of the effort is the Training for Industry Program or TIP, which is offered free to new and expanding companies. Career Tech works closely with the business to develop a program that meets the company's needs and prepares their new workforce for success. To date, TIP has served over 1,700 companies including Boeing, MCI WorldCom, American Airlines, Goodyear, General Motors, Whirlpool, America Online, Southwest Airlines, Lucent Technologies, Mutual of Omaha, Bama Foods, Best Buy, Armstrong and Xerox.

## Development Projects

Several cultural, educational, tourist, and sports-related Metropolitan Area Projects (MAPS), from investments totaling more than a quarter billion dollars, were approved and built in Oklahoma City in the late 1990s and early in the new century. New projects included the 20,000-seat Ford Center arena, the aforementioned ballpark and riverwalk in Bricktown, and a vintage-style trolley system that makes getting around the downtown area much easier. MAPS also included extensive renovations to the Myriad Convention Center, State Fair Park, and the Civic Center. The $30 million Oklahoma City National Memorial and Memorial Museum, a 30,000 square foot memorial park, museum, and anti-terrorism institute, was dedicated on April 19, 2000, five years to the day after a terrorist bombing claimed the lives of 168 people at the Alfred P. Murrah Federal Building downtown.

Development has been brisk in Oklahoma City in the beginning of the 21st century. The Oklahoma City Metropolitan Area Public Schools Trust was approved by voters in 2002 to earmark $470 million for a massive, 100 project, 10-year effort to make Oklahoma City schools a national model for urban education reform. In 2004 the city rezoned property at the northern tip of Lake Stanley Draper for a proposed commercial and recreational development project that would include a 36-hole golf course, retail stores, and RV and camping grounds. The Civic Center Music Hall was recently renovated into a modern performance center for the Downtown Arts District; nearby stands the new Oklahoma

City Museum of Art, featuring Dale Chihuly's 55-foot glass sculpture, as well as the new Ronald J. Norick Downtown Library. The Bricktown riverwalk area features shops and restaurants in turn-of-the-century industrial buildings; a new Bass Pro Shop and 16-screen theater add to the district's entertainment scene. Towering over Bricktown is the SBC Bricktown Ballpark, home of the Oklahoma RedHawks Triple A baseball team. Work continues on a Bricktown East canal, where 45 larger-than-life statues will depict those settlers who made the April 22, 1889 Oklahoma Land Run.

*Economic Development Information:* Greater Oklahoma City Chamber of Commerce, 123 Park Avenue, Oklahoma City, OK 73102; telephone (405)297-8900; fax (405)297-8916. Oklahoma Department of Commerce, Office of Business Location Division, PO Box 26980, Oklahoma City, OK 73126-0980; telephone (405)815-6552

## Commercial Shipping

Freight such as grain, minerals, and steel products are shipped at low cost via the McClellan Kerr River Navigation System, which offers access to the Mississippi River. The Port of Catoosa is only 140 miles from Oklahoma City. Many area motor freight carriers, two major railroads offering Class I and Class III service by 20 rail operators, and five nearby airports serve the region's shipping needs. Trucking is made convenient by the city's central location at Interstate Highways I-35, I-40, and I-44.

## Labor Force and Employment Outlook

Oklahoma City boasts a productive labor force with a strong work ethic. Absenteeism, work stoppages, and turnover levels are below average. Present and future growth areas include, among others, such diverse fields as aircraft, fabricated metal, computers, clothing, oil-field equipment and crude oil, back office, distribution, and food processing. A growing high-technology sector now employs more than 30,000 in Oklahoma City; key high-tech firms include Lucent Technologies with more than 4,800 employees and Dell Inc., which broke ground in late 2004 on a 120,000 square-foot facility that will employ more than 700 people in a new customer contact center.

The following is a summary of data regarding the Oklahoma City metropolitan area labor force, 2003 annual averages.

*Size of nonagricultural labor force:* 531,700

*Number of workers employed in . . .*
  *natural resources and mining:* 6,900
  *construction:* 22,200
  *manufacturing:* 38,000
  *trade, transportation and utilities:* 96,500
  *information:* 13,400
  *financial activities:* 34,400

*professional and business services:* 65,900

*educational and health services:* 66,600

*leisure and hospitality:* 52,200

*other services:* 27,800

*government:* 107,800

*Average hourly earnings of production workers employed in manufacturing:* $14.24

*Unemployment rate:* 3.7% (December 2004)

| Largest employers | Number of employees |
|---|---|
| State of Oklahoma | 38,100 |
| Tinker Air Force Base | 26,000 |
| U.S. Postal Service | 8,706 |
| University of Oklahoma | 7,902 |
| Oklahoma City Public Schools | 5,900 |
| US FAA Mike Monroney Aeronautical Center | 5,600 |
| City of Oklahoma City | 5,320 |
| INTEGRIS Baptist Medical Center | 4,102 |
| General Motors Corp. | 3,400 |

## Cost of Living

The following is a summary of data regarding several key cost of living factors for the Oklahoma City area.

*2004 (3rd Quarter) ACCRA Average House Price:* $209,232

*2004 (3rd Quarter) ACCRA Cost of Living Index:* 91.8 (U.S. average = 100.0)

*State income tax rate:* Ranges from 0.5% to 6.75%

*State sales tax rate:* 4.5%

*Local income tax rate:* None

*Local sales tax rate:* 3.875%

*Property tax rate:* Varies due to city limits that extend into different counties and school districts; for example, the rate in school district #89 is $57.84 (2004)

*Economic Information:* Greater Oklahoma City Chamber of Commerce, 123 Park Avenue, Oklahoma City, OK 73102; telephone (405)297-8900; fax (405)297-8916

# Education and Research

## Elementary and Secondary Schools

Oklahoma City Public Schools is the second largest public school district in the state. The district offers specialty programs at all grade levels, including Spanish language immersion programs, international studies, performing arts, media/communications and even a Montessori-based education program. A 2001 MAPS for Kids program, in conjunction with the citizens of Oklahoma City and the public school system, was created to help revitalize the school system. This program called for building seven new schools and revitalization work in 65 others, at a cost of more than $500 million. The metropolitan area includes more than 20 other school districts.

The following is a summary of data regarding the Oklahoma City public schools as of the 2003–2004 school year.

*Total enrollment:* 40,703

*Number of facilities*
  *elementary schools:* 59
  *middle schools:* 8
  *senior high schools:* 9
  *other:* 9 charter and 6 alternative schools

*Student/teacher ratio:* 16.2:1

*Teacher salaries*
  *average:* $29,810

*Funding per pupil:* $6,541

Many private and parochial elementary schools and two parochial high schools also serve students in the Oklahoma City area, including the Oklahoma School of Science and Mathematics for gifted high school students.

*Public Schools Information:* Oklahoma City Public Schools, 900 North Klein, PO Box 25428, Oklahoma City, OK 73125-0428; telephone (405)297-6522

## Colleges and Universities

Sixteen college and university campuses and two community colleges, with a combined enrollment of more than 100,000 students, are located in the greater Oklahoma City area. The largest institution is the University of Oklahoma, which enrolls about 24,800 students in the main school, the Oklahoma University Health Sciences Center, and the College of Law. The University ranked among the nation's top 10 percent in the *Fiske Guide to Colleges* and is the nation's number one school for national merit scholars, as well as the top 5 for graduation of Rhodes scholars. Other institutions of higher education include Oklahoma State University-Oklahoma City, University of Central Oklahoma, Rose State College, Oklahoma City Community College, University of Science and Arts of Oklahoma, Oklahoma City University, and Oklahoma Christian University of Science and Arts.

## Libraries and Research Centers

The Metropolitan Library System in Oklahoma County has 17 area libraries that serve the community needs of more than 600,000 people living in Oklahoma City or Oklahoma County. Its more than 1,000,000 volumes include books, newspapers, magazines, microfilms, video collections, and books on tape. In 2003 the city opened a new central library, the 108,000 square foot Downtown Library and Learning Center, which is a state-of-the-art facility built with more than $24 million in MAPS taxes and library building funds. In addition to traditional library services, the Downtown Library also has a high-tech theater, classrooms, learning center, Oklahoma Literacy Council Services, on-site business assistance from the Small Business Development Center, and college classes through the Downtown College Consortium. Special collections include local history and local black history. A large collection of books on Native Americans, genealogy, and the history of Oklahoma is housed at the Oklahoma Historical Society Archives and Manuscripts Division. Libraries at city colleges and universities and at state offices also offer reference materials on a wide range of topics.

Much of the state's cutting-edge research is conducted at the nearby University of Oklahoma. The Sarkeys Energy Center is a 4-square-block, 7-acre, 340,000 square-foot teaching and energy research complex where faculty, students, and energy industry researchers can explore interdisciplinary energy issues, train future energy researchers and leaders, and enhance national energy security. The Oklahoma Medical Research Foundation is developing into a research institute of national importance, especially in the field of immunology. Research centers affiliated with academic institutions in Oklahoma City study state constitutional law and conduct business research and consulting.

*Public Library Information:* Metropolitan Library System in Oklahoma County, 131 Dean A. McGee Avenue, Oklahoma City, OK 73102-6499; telephone (405)231-8650

# Health Care

With 20 general medical and surgical hospitals, four specialized hospitals, and two federal medical installations with a combined total of more than 5,000 beds in the area, Oklahoma City has become a leading health referral center in the Southwest. The state-owned OU Medical Center and The Children's Hospital of OU Medical Center merged with Oklahoma City-based, for-profit Presbyterian Hospital in a private-public partnership called University Health Partners in 1998 to form the largest medical care and research center in Oklahoma. In 2003 the hospital's governing board announced plans for a $180 million expansion and renovation project that will update all current facilities while providing the Children's Hospital with its own separate entrance and facilities to make navigation easier on pediatric patients and their families. Other facilities include the INTEGRIS Baptist Medical Center and INTEGRIS Southwest Medical Center, Deaconess Hospital, the Bone and Joint Hospital, Mercy Health Center, and St. Anthony Hospital.

*Health Care Information:* Oklahoma State Department of Health—Information and Referral Healthline, 1100 N.E. 10th Street, Box 53551, Oklahoma City, OK 73152; telephone (405)271-5600

# Recreation

## Sightseeing

Oklahoma City offers the visitor a full range of sights and activities. Frontier City Theme Park offers more than 50 acres of rides and western shows. The Oklahoma City Zoo, one of the top zoos in the nation, features more than 2,100 exotic species on 110 lushly-planted acres, including a children's zoo, and state-of-the-art primate and lion exhibits. The Oklahoma City Stockyards represents one of the largest cattle markets in the world. The State Capitol Building stands out as the only capitol with producing oil wells on the grounds, while Enterprise Square, U.S.A., explains America's free enterprise system and features a spacecraft landing. The Martin Park Nature Center offers self-guided trails, and its Garden Exhibition Building and Horticulture Gardens bloom with azaleas, roses, and orchids, and showcase collections of cacti and succulents. The Myriad Gardens features a unique 224-foot Crystal Bridge and a 17-acre outdoor park with a 1.5-acre sunken lake. Crystal Bridge, a seven-story enclosed botanical garden, displays an interesting array of more than 1,000 horticultural specimens from all over the world. The tropical atmosphere is enhanced by the roar of water cascading down a 35-foot waterfall. Kirkpatrick Planetarium at the Omniplex provides views of the heavens, and Celebration Station, a family amusement center, provides family fun.

Guided tours are offered at several attractions, including the Oklahoma Governor's Mansion, the Oklahoma State Capitol, and the Overholser Mansion, which was the first mansion in Oklahoma City.

For those who enjoy exploring on foot, Oklahoma City's Metro Concourse offers a unique way to see downtown. The concourse, an underground tunnel system connecting most of the downtown buildings, is lined with offices, restaurants, and shops. The renovated Bricktown historic site features shops, restaurants, and entertainment spots.

The *End of the Trail* sculpture at the National Cowboy Hall of Fame and Western Heritage Center.

## Arts and Culture

Oklahoma City provides year-around enjoyment for the visitor interested in arts and culture. In 2002, with the success of a $40 million Legacy Campaign that included a $14.5 million grant from the Donald W. Reynolds Foundation, the Oklahoma City Museum of Art in the Donald W. Reynolds Visual Arts Center opened. This 3-story, 110,000 square foot facility features 15 galleries, 3 education rooms, a library/resource center, a store, a cafe, and the 252-seat Noble Theatre. Since relocating to its new facility, the Museum hosts approximately 100,000 visitors annually and has tripled its membership and increased its staff from 8 people in 1994 to over 60 at present. The Museum has been accredited by the American Association of Museums for 28 years and houses an extensive permanent collection of European, Asian, and American art, featuring such artists as Pierre Auguste Renoir, Gustave Courbet, Maurice de Vlaminck, Mary Cassatt, Thomas Moran, Robert Henri, Ellsworth Kelly, Alexander Calder, Henry Moore, and Frank Stella. The Museum also owns the largest, most comprehensive collection of Chihuly glass in the world, including a 55 foot tall tower, commissioned for the atrium of the new facility in memory of Eleanor Blake Kirkpatrick.

Civic Center Music Hall is home to the Oklahoma City Philharmonic Orchestra, which performs classical and pop music; a professional ballet company, Ballet Oklahoma, with an October through April season; and the Canterbury Choral Society, a 140-voice chorus that performs the major choral masterworks with full orchestral accompaniment during its 3-concert series. The Prairie Dance Theatre performs three times annually (in February, May, and November) and tours throughout the remainder of the year in nine states. Musical theater is performed by the Lyric Theatre of Oklahoma, the Oklahoma Opera and Music Theatre, and the Oklahoma Opry.

A variety of works from contemporary playwrights is presented by the Carpenter Square Theatre, and African American productions are offered by the Black Liberated Arts Center. Oklahoma City's oldest community theater, the Jewel Box Theatre, offers performances from August through May.

Many other Oklahoma City area's museums and galleries display a wide variety of art and artifacts. The 1889 Harn Museum and William Fremont Harn Gardens commemorate the land run of 1889 with a restored homestead. Objects and equipment unique to Oklahoma's citizen soldiers from past to present are exhibited at the Forty-Fifth Infantry Division Museum. The history of Oklahoma from prehistoric times to the present is preserved at the State Museum of History.

The Omniplex, a cultural, educational, and recreational center with craft and zoological exhibits, maintains three art galleries featuring African, Native American, and Japanese art. The center also houses the Air Space Museum, which documents Oklahoma's contributions to aviation; the International Photography Hall of Fame and Museum, which displays photographic prints from around the world; and the Kirkpatric Science Museum, a blend of science exhibits, shows, and displays.

Art and cultural materials representing several Native American tribes are highlighted at the Red Earth Indian Center. The National Cowboy Hall of Fame and Western Heritage Center showcases a collection of fine western art by Frederick Remington, Charles Russell, and others, and portraits of western television and movie stars; each June the museum hosts its annual Prix de West Invitational Art Exhibition to showcase the work of the country's finest contemporary western artists. Approximately 300 works of art, by more than 100 artists, are featured in the exhibition. The history of softball is the focus of the National Softball Hall of Fame, which also includes a softball library and research center. Turn-of-the-century fire engines are displayed at the Oklahoma Firefighters Museum.

## Festivals and Holidays

A variety of annual events are held in Oklahoma City, and horses are a prime attraction. Each January the International Finals Rodeo brings the top 15 cowboys and cowgirls in for the Professional Rodeo Association's season finale. The March Oklahoma Youth Expo has more than 5,000 animals for competition and auction. In April the OKC Centennial Horse Show at State Fair Park features Morgans, Arabians, National Show Horses, American Saddlebreds, and a Hackney/Harness division. Designated as one of the top outdoor festivals in the United States, the Oklahoma City Spring Festival of the Arts at Myriad Gardens and Festival Plaza displays works of art from across the nation in downtown Oklahoma City. In June, Red Earth at the Myriad Convention Center attracts thousands of Native Americans, who display their heritage and culture through artwork, crafts, and traditional and modern dancing. Aerospace America, held each June at Will Rogers Airport, features a mix of aerobatic acts, military aircraft, and displays. Held during mid-September, the State Fair of Oklahoma is one of the largest in the country. Festivities vary from celebrity shows and carnival activities to livestock, arts and crafts, and home economics exhibits. Also in September, Septemberfest at the Governor's Mansion is a celebration of Oklahoma's heritage. The November World Championship Quarter Horse Show is the largest out-of-state visitor attraction held in Oklahoma City, with more than $1 million in prizes handed out over 15 days of competition. Opening Night in downtown Oklahoma City is an annual family New Year's Eve celebration with live country and rock music, magic shows, theater, and fireworks at midnight.

## Sports for the Spectator

Oklahoma City is home to four professional sports teams. The Oklahoma RedHawks are a Triple A baseball farm team for the Texas Rangers who play their games at the Southwestern Bell Bricktown Ballpark. Hockey action is the forte of the Oklahoma City Blazers, a Central Hockey League team, who play 35 home games per season before an average of 9,300 fans per game at the new Ford Center arena. The Oklahoma City Yard Dawgs, a professional arena football team, also play before packed crowds at the Ford Center. The University of Oklahoma Sooners is a member team of the Big Twelve football conference and compete in a wide variety of sports on campus in nearby Norman, Oklahoma. The Sooners' football program is legendary and consistently ranks near the top of the NCAA's Division One.

Spectators enjoy auto racing at the Fairgrounds Speedway and parimutuel betting at Remington Park's $97 million racetrack. Oklahoma City is home to the Amateur Softball Association and the International Softball Federation, which govern the sport, maintain the National Softball Hall of Fame on 50th Street, and hold events such as the Women's College World Series at the ASA Hall of Fame Stadium. Several national and international horse shows and competitions are held each year at State Fair Park, Lazy E Arena, and Heritage Place. The World Championship Quarter Horse Show is held in November at the State Fair Arena and the International Finals Rodeo takes place in January.

**Sports for the Participant**

Public recreation opportunities abound in and around Oklahoma City with its many municipal parks, swimming pools, picnic facilities, public and private golf courses, softball diamonds, soccer and baseball fields, tennis and basketball courts, fitness trails, and recreation centers. The area's lakes offer boating, fishing, sailing, and water skiing. White Water, a 20-acre water park, provides a wave pool, rapids, and water slides. Lake Hefner is an excellent place for sailing and sailboat racing, and Bird watchers treasure its 17-mile shoreline for bird migrations that make this one of the best locations in Oklahoma. The Oklahoma City Community College Aquatics Center has hosted the U.S. Olympic Festival and is open to the public for classes, state and community competitions, and major national competitions.

**Shopping and Dining**

Just a block east of the Myriad Convention Center in downtown Oklahoma City is Bricktown, Oklahoma City's newest entertainment, shopping, and dining district. Oklahoma City has four major enclosed shopping malls, each anchored by major department stores. They are Crossroads Mall, Northpark Mall, Penn Square Mall, and Quail Springs Mall. Upscale shopping is the attraction at 50 Penn Place and the Nichols Hills Plaza on Western Avenue. Sportsmen throughout the region come to the massive new Bass Pro Shops Outdoor World near the I-35 and I-40 Interchange. Choctaw Indian Trading Post features silver and turquoise

jewelry, Indian paintings, Kachina dolls, rugs, and blankets. Shepler's Western Wear on W. Meridian is the world's largest western store and catalog, carrying a vast assortment of boots, jeans, shirts, and hats for the entire family, plus accessories and home decor. Fancy western wear can be found at Tener's Western Outfitters. The Spanish-style Paseo Artist District is the showcase for the works of Oklahoma artists and also features restaurants and shops. Shoppers can immerse themselves in western culture at Stockyards City, a National Register Historic District near downtown that features western shops, restaurants, art galleries, and crafters producing boots, spurs, hats, belt buckles the size of hubcaps, and other western gear.

Oklahoma City restaurants offer menus ranging from the city specialty—Oklahoma-raised beef—to French and Vietnamese cuisine. The specialty of the house at the city's oldest restaurant, Cattlemen's Café, is calves brains and eggs. Steaks and barbecue lead the way at Cimarron Steak House, Earl's Rib Palace, Murphy's Chop House, and Nikz high atop the United Founders Tower. Diners will also discover authentic Mexican food at Abuelo's, sushi at Sushi Neko, fine dining at the award-winning Mantel Wine Bar & Bistro, and Japanese fare Musashi's.

***Visitor Information:*** Oklahoma City Convention & Visitors Bureau, 189 W. Sheridan, Oklahoma City, OK 73102; telephone (405)297-8912; toll-free (800)225-5652; email okccvb@okccvb.org

# Convention Facilities

A sunny climate, abundant hotel space—more than 14,000 rooms in Oklahoma City and the metropolitan area—and a wide range of leisure, cultural, and recreational opportunities make Oklahoma City attractive to large and small groups of convention-goers.

The Cox Business Services Center, located in the city's business district, offers facilities for sports, banquets, concerts, exhibitions, trade shows, and stage performances. A recent $50 million renovation added 105,000 square feet of exhibit space, nearly doubling the old square footage. High ceilings and wide expanses of glass overlooking the downtown landscape evoke the open feel of the Oklahoma prairie. Meeting, exhibit, and entertainment areas totaling 1 million square feet include the Exhibit Hall, the Great Hall for banquets and ballroom dancing, and the Arena, which can seat up to 16,000 people. The arena houses an ice rink, basketball floor, and a portable indoor track. The Renaissance, a $32 million, 15-story, 311-room luxury hotel is connected to the center via skywalk, and a climate-controlled walkway also connects to the nearby Westin Hotel. Four blocks from the Cox Center is the Civic Center Music Hall (which underwent a $52 million renovation in 2001) with facilities for concerts, lectures, meetings, conventions, and stage shows. It can seat up to 3,200 people.

Funded by a one percent sales tax increase, the sleek new Ford Center arena opened in 2002 with seating for 20,000 and facilities to accommodate professional sporting events and national touring concerts. A premier project of MAPS, Oklahoma City's unique capital improvement program to upgrade the city's convention and municipal facilities, the Ford Center has 49 private suites and is home to professional hockey and arena football franchises.

The Oklahoma City Fairgrounds, with over a million square feet, also offers a 12,500-seat arena, a racetrack, and a baseball stadium. Among the city's other convention facilities are Frontier City, with its themed indoor banquet facilities that seat 5 to 1,000 people, and the popular Wagon Wheel Picnic Ranch, which can seat 25 to 5,000 people. Groups of up to 1,000 people can be accommodated at Metro Tech's Business Conference Center. Smaller and medium-sized groups can find meeting and event space at the Clarion Meridian Hotel and Convention Center or the Will Rogers Theater.

***Convention Information:*** Oklahoma City Convention & Visitors Bureau, 189 W. Sheridan, Oklahoma City, OK 73102; telephone (405)297-8912; toll-free (800)225-5652; email okccvb@okccvb.org

# *Transportation*

## Approaching the City

Oklahoma City's Will Rogers World Airport, just 10 miles northwest of the city, is served by 12 commercial carriers that carry more than 3.2 million passengers a year. As of 2005 construction was underway on a five-year expansion project totaling more than $100 million and expected to add 9 new gates, bigger ticketing and lobby areas, and better traffic flow to handle capacity requirements into 2012 and beyond. Located near the center of the United States, Oklahoma City is connected to the east and west coasts and north and south borders of the nation by interstate highways I-40, I-35, I-44, and I-240. Numerous state highways and a turnpike system provide easy access to any location in the metropolitan area. Amtrak provides train service, and Greyhound/Trailways Bus Lines schedules buses into and out of the city.

## Traveling in the City

Streets in downtown Oklahoma City are generally laid out in an east-west, north-south grid pattern, with numbered streets running east-west. Taxis and buses are available for transportation to all parts of the city. The extensive bus system was upgraded in 2004 with the addition of the new $6.2 million METRO Transit Downtown Transit Center, an air-conditioned transfer center. As part of the city's downtown revitalization efforts, the Oklahoma Spirit trolley system now takes visitors around Bricktown and downtown for just a quarter. In warm weather, Pedicabs and horse-drawn carriages ferry customers all over Bricktown. A mile-long pedestrian canal through Bricktown turns south at the new ballpark, then heads under the highway to a waterfall-and-forested park area. Water taxis carry visitors to canal-side restaurants.

# *Communications*

## Newspapers and Magazines

Oklahoma City has one morning daily newspaper, the *Oklahoman,* and one business newspaper, *The Journal Record.* More than a dozen weekly, semiweekly, and bimonthly newspapers are published there, including *The Black Chronicle* and *Capital Hill Beacon,* and *The Sooner Catholic.* Among the more than two dozen magazines and journals published in Oklahoma City are the lifestyle magazine *Oklahoma Living Magazine*; *Oklahoma Today Magazine,* focusing on travel, nature, recreation, and American Indian and New West issues; and others focusing on livestock, pharmacy, retailing, and trades.

## Television and Radio

Oklahoma City has ten television stations: one commercial station broadcasting religious programming, two independents, three PBS stations, and four stations affiliated with the major networks. Stations also broadcast from nearby towns and cable television is available throughout the metropolitan area. In addition, Oklahoma City radio provides listeners with a choice of 13 AM and 20 FM stations.

***Media Information:*** *Oklahoman,* PO Box 25125, Oklahoma City, OK 73114; telephone (405)475-3311

## Oklahoma City Online

City of Oklahoma City Home Page. Available www.okc.gov

Metropolitan Library System. Available www.mls.lib.ok.us

Oklahoma City Chamber of Commerce. Available www .okcchamber.com

Oklahoma City Convention and Visitors Bureau. Available www.okccvb.org

Oklahoma City Public Schools. Available www.okcps.k12 .ok.us

Oklahoma Community Links. Available www.state.ok.us/ osfdocs/county.html

Oklahoma Department of Commerce. Available www .kcommerce.com

*Oklahoman.* Available www.oklahoman.com

Tinker Air Force Base (unofficial site). Available wwwext .tinker.af.mil/default.asp

**Selected Bibliography**

Knight, Marsha (compiler), *Forever Changed: Remembering Oklahoma City, April 19, 1995* (Amherst, N.Y.: Prometheus Books, 1998)

# Tulsa

## The City in Brief

**Founded:** 1836 (incorporated 1898)

**Head Official:** Mayor Bill LaFortune (since 2002)

**City Population**
   **1980:** 360,919
   **1990:** 367,302
   **2000:** 393,049
   **2003 estimate:** 387,807
   **Percent change, 1990–2000:** 7.03%
   **U.S. rank in 1980:** 38th
   **U.S. rank in 1990:** 43rd (State rank: 2nd)
   **U.S. rank in 2000:** 52nd (State rank: 2nd)

**Metropolitan Area Population**
   **1980:** 657,000
   **1990:** 709,000
   **2000:** 803,235

**Percent change, 1990–2000:** 13.3%
**U.S. rank in 1980:** 52nd
**U.S. rank in 1990:** 56th
**U.S. rank in 2000:** 58th

**Area:** 186.84 square miles (2000)
**Elevation:** 700 feet above sea level
**Average Annual Temperature:** 63.0° F
**Average Annual Precipitation:** 38.77 inches

**Major Economic Sectors:** aerospace and air transportation, petroleum and natural gas, healthcare, telecommunications, business and financial services, wholesale and retail trade, manufacturing
**Unemployment rate:** 4.2% (December 2004)
**Per Capita Income:** $21,534 (1999)

**2002 FBI Crime Index Total:** 30,119

**Major Colleges and Universities:** University of Tulsa, Oral Roberts University

**Daily Newspaper:** *Tulsa World*

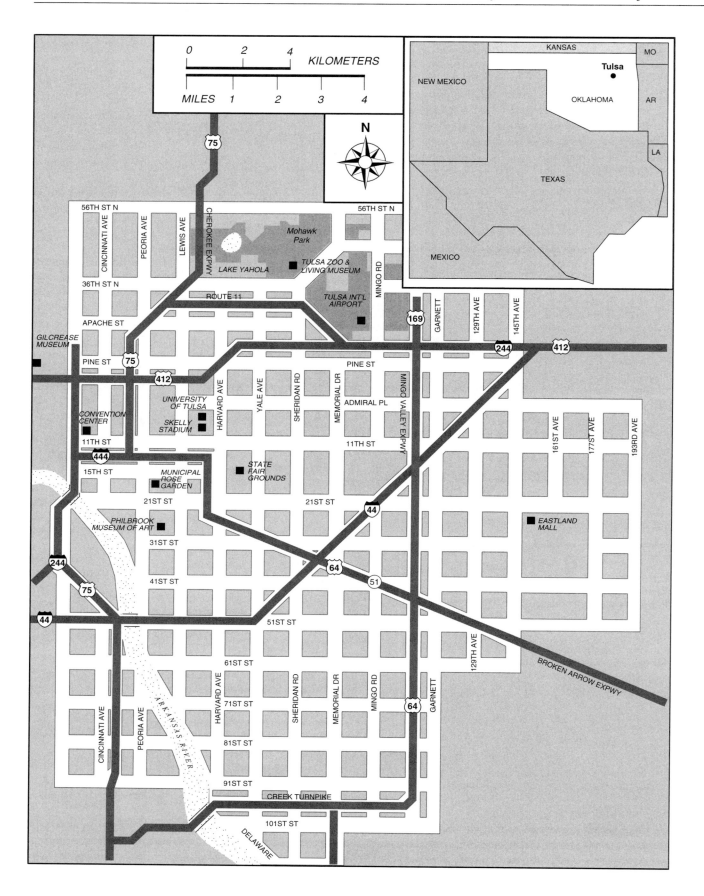

# Introduction

Tulsa is the second largest city in Oklahoma. From its earliest ranching and oil boom days to the present, Tulsa has recognized the need for economic diversity and has continually taken appropriate steps. With a history of steady expansion, a unique geographic location as an important shipping port, and wide range of employment opportunities, Tulsa has made itself attractive to new businesses. It is equally enticing to new residents, with its moderate Sun Belt climate, abundant recreational areas, continuing cultivation of the arts, and educational opportunities. Thus prepared for, and anticipating, steady economic growth, Tulsa enters the twenty-first century with confidence.

# Geography and Climate

Located 90 miles northeast of Oklahoma City and surrounded by gentle hills stretching toward the Ozark foothills, Tulsa lies along the Arkansas River at a latitude providing a moderate climate. Winters are generally mild with light snowfall, and the high temperatures of mid- to late-summer are often moderated by low relative humidity and southerly breezes. Tornadoes and windstorms characterize spring and early summer, but sunny days and cool nights prevail throughout the fall. Rainfall is heaviest in the spring.

**Area:** 186.84 square miles (2000)

**Elevation:** 700 feet above sea level

**Average Temperatures:** January, 36.7° F; August, 82.0° F; annual average, 63.0° F

**Average Annual Precipitation:** 38.77 inches

# History

### City's Native American Roots

French traders and plains-culture Osage tribes occupied the region now surrounding Tulsa when the United States bought the land from France as part of the Louisiana Purchase in 1803. Soon the federal government sought to remove communities of the Five Civilized Tribes—Cherokee, Choctaw, Chickasaw, Creek, and Seminole—from their traditional lands in the southeastern United States to Indian Territory in what is now Oklahoma. After violent protest, in 1826 the Osages ceded their land in the Tulsa area to the U.S. government, which in turn gave it to exiled Creeks and Cherokees. Many of the Native Americans who were forced to resettle in Oklahoma brought black slaves with them. In 1836 Archie Yahola, a full-blood Creek, presided over the region's first council meeting, held under an oak tree that came to be known as the Council Oak. The tree still stands in Tulsa's Creek Nation Council Oak Park.

The settlement convened at the Council Oak was first named Tallassee-Lochapoka, for the Alabama regions the Creeks had left behind; eventually it became known as Tulsey—or Tulsee—Town. The name Tulsa became official for the settlement in 1879 with the establishment of the post office, which also marked the beginning of Tulsa as an economic force in the area. When a railroad connection reached Tulsa in 1882, the town began to supply beef and other staples to the East, South, and Midwest. Ranching and farming—mostly by Creeks or Cherokees—flourished. Tulsa grew steadily and became incorporated as a municipality on January 18, 1898.

### Oil Spurs White Settlement; Racial Uneasiness Surfaces

In 1901 oil reserves were discovered in Red Fork, across the Arkansas River from Tulsa. Enterprising Tulsans built a toll bridge to connect their city with the oil country, and oil men crossed the river to make Tulsa their home. Despite Indian Territory laws that discouraged white settlement, the region became increasingly open to whites, and Tulsa grew into a business and residential center. Oil gushed again in 1905, this time from the Glenn Pool well. Oil companies built headquarters in Tulsa, bringing families of corporate executives, urban tastes, and money. In 1906 the U.S. Congress passed the Enabling Act, which merged Indian Territory and Oklahoma Territory, achieving statehood for Oklahoma and bringing down the last barriers to settlement of the region. The decade of the 1920s was a tumultuous period for Oklahoma as a whole, with oil wells gushing, whites and Native Americans becoming fabulously wealthy, and the Ku Klux Klan boasting close to 100,000 members statewide. A race riot erupted in Tulsa in 1921 that has been described as one of this country's worst incidents of racial violence. Some 300 people died and 35 city blocks of Tulsa's Greenwood section, known as ''the Black Wall Street,'' were destroyed after a black man was arrested for allegedly assaulting a white woman. In 1997 the Oklahoma state legislature named an 11-member Tulsa Race Riot Commission to unearth the facts behind the incident. In early 2000 the commission recommended direct payments to survivors and victims' descendants, scholarships, a tax checkoff program to fund economic development in the mostly black Greenwood district, and a memorial to the dead.

## Modern Economy Diversified

Between 1907 and 1930, Tulsa's population grew by 1,900 percent. By the 1920s Tulsa was being called the Oil Capital of the World. But not content to be an oil capital only, Tulsa continued its expansion into other commercial and industrial areas as well. In fact, several of Tulsa's firms had a part in the U.S. moon-thrust endeavor, Project Apollo. Today, oil retains importance but Tulsa primarily relies on aerospace, telecommunications, energy, and environmental engineering/ manufacturing for its industrial base. In 1996 *Nation's Cities Weekly* described Tulsa as "a unique social, cultural and corporate melting pot that somehow maintains a 'downhome' feeling."

Due in large part to planning and intelligent growth, as well as a general demographic shift that has seen continued growth in the southern and southwestern states, Tulsa joins a number of other mid-sized cities enjoying revitalization in the early 21st century. In 2004, based on Tulsa's strides in preparing itself for the new global economy and its opportunities for tourism, business investment, relocation, education, retirement, and better quality of life, the city was selected as one of America's Most Livable Communities by the Partners for Livable Communities in Washington, D.C.

***Historical Information:*** Tulsa Historical Society, 2445 South Peoria, Tulsa, OK 74114; telephone (918)712-9484

# *Population Profile*

## Metropolitan Area Residents
*1980:* 657,000
*1990:* 708,954
*2000:* 803,235
*Percent change, 1990–2000:* 13.3%
*U.S. rank in 1980:* 52nd
*U.S. rank in 1990:* 56th
*U.S. rank in 2000:* 58th

## City Residents
*1980:* 360,919
*1990:* 367,302
*2000:* 393,049
*2003 estimate:* 387,807
*Percent change, 1990–2000:* 7.03%
*U.S. rank in 1980:* 38th
*U.S. rank in 1990:* 43rd (State rank: 2nd)
*U.S. rank in 2000:* 52nd (State rank: 2nd)

*Density:* 2,103.4 people per square mile (2000)

*Racial and ethnic characteristics* (2000)
White: 275,488
Black or African American: 60,794
American Indian and Alaska Native: 18,551
Asian: 7,150
Native Hawaiian and Pacific Islander: 202
Hispanic or Latino (may be of any race): 28,111
Other: 13,564

*Percent of residents born in state:* 56.2% (2000)

*Age characteristics* (2000)
Population under 5 years old: 28,318
Population 5 to 9 years old: 27,606
Population 10 to 14 years old: 25,980
Population 15 to 19 years old: 27,180
Population 20 to 24 years old: 31,286
Population 25 to 34 years old: 58,659
Population 35 to 44 years old: 58,916
Population 45 to 54 years old: 52,383
Population 55 to 59 years old: 18,179
Population 60 to 64 years old: 14,034
Population 65 to 74 years old: 25,982
Population 75 to 84 years old: 18,256
Population 85 years and older: 6,270
Median age: 34.5 years

*Births* (2002, Tulsa County)
Total number: 9,288

*Deaths* (2002, Tulsa County)
Total number: 5,225

*Money income* (2000)
Per capita income: $21,534
Median household income: $35,401
Total households: 165,881

*Number of households with income of . . .*
less than $10,000: 17,625
$10,000 to $14,999: 13,268
$15,000 to $24,999: 26,886
$25,000 to $34,999: 24,407
$35,000 to $49,999: 28,203
$50,000 to $74,999: 26,638
$75,000 to $99,999: 12,766
$100,000 to $149,999: 9,249
$150,000 to $199,999: 2,977
$200,000 or more: 3,862

*Percent of families below poverty level:* 10.9% (51.9% of which were female householder families with related children under 5 years)

*2002 FBI Crime Index Total:* 30,199

## Municipal Government

Incorporated as a municipality on January 18, 1898, Tulsa operates under a mayor-council form of city government. Nine council members are elected to two-year terms.

**Head Official:** Mayor Bill LaFortune (since 2002; current term expires 2006)

**Total Number of City Employees:** 3,862 (2005)

***City Information:*** City of Tulsa, 200 Civic Center, Tulsa, OK 74103; telephone (918)596-7777

## Economy

### Major Industries and Commercial Activity

Tulsa's central location in the United States makes it a desirable place to locate nearly any type of business, from manufacturing to retail, telecommunications, and service-oriented industries. Operating costs generally run well below the national average. According to a 2004 study published by *Forbes* magazine, the Tulsa metropolitan area ranks as the third lowest metro area in terms of cost-of-living in the United States.

Tulsa was literally the "Oil Capital of the World" from the early 1920s until World War II. By the time the companies moved operations closer to offshore production, Tulsa had begun to develop the aircraft and aerospace industry, which is now the region's largest industry. Today Tulsa has more than 300 aviation-related companies, contributing to more than 32,000 Tulsa jobs and 140,000 statewide jobs in aviation. The industry generates $960 million in annual payroll and contributes an additional $3.3 billion annually to the region. In addition, two insurance companies are major employers, as are major manufacturers such as Ford Glass and Whirlpool. Three car rental company headquarters and a major car rental reservation center are located in Tulsa. Telecommunications is also a major industry, employing about 15,000 people annually.

In early 1971, Tulsa opened the Tulsa Port of Catoosa on the Verdigris River, thereby becoming a major inland port along the 445-mile McClellan-Kerr Navigation System. The port provides low-cost shipping for such products as oil, coal, fertilizer, and grain to the Mississippi River, and from there on to the Great Lakes or the Gulf of Mexico and around the world.

In 2004 the Tulsa Metropolitan Statistical Area (MSA) had a gross product of $27.1 billion, about one-third of the Okla-

homa economy. Healthcare has become big business in Tulsa, employing over 30,000 people and contributing $1.4 billion in payroll income to the Tulsa economy. Employment figures reveal Tulsa industries as major employers on the national scene. The Tulsa MSA ranks nationally in the areas of aircraft engines and aircraft, ranked 6th and 17th respectively; oil and gas products and services, ranked 7th; fabricated platework, ranked 2nd; metal pumps, ranked 4th; and hoists and cranes, fabricated metal pipe, and laundry and cleaning appliances all ranked 3rd.

*Items and goods produced:* airplane parts, appliances, metal pipes and pumps, fiber optics, meat, feed, boilers, burners, fishing rods, natural gas

### Incentive Programs—New and Existing Companies

*Local programs—* The Tulsa Port of Catoosa has been designated an Enterprise Zone and can offer businesses tax credits for job creators, tax exemptions of up to 6 years for qualifying businesses, and low-interest loans. Most incentive programs are at the state level.

*State programs—*In 2002 Oklahoma became the nation's 22nd state to adopt the Right-to-Work law, creating a business friendly environment that has directly benefited state workers. State officials credit the law with creating 94 percent more jobs due to start-ups and expansions, as well as raising average hourly wages for workers in manufacturing and bringing the state to the lead in household income growth. In 2004 Pollina Real Estate Corporation ranked Oklahoma third in the nation in its list of Top Ten Pro-Business States. The Oklahoma Tax and Incentives Guide, published by the Oklahoma Department of Commerce, summarizes state tax advantages and business incentives. For instance, Oklahoma's Quality Jobs Program pays cash payments up to five percent of payroll to companies that create new jobs in the state. It is targeted toward manufacturers and certain service companies that have a new payroll investment of $2.5 million or more. A lower payroll threshold is available for certain food processing and research and development projects or as a result of location in targeted areas. Investment/Jobs Income Tax Credit and Construction Sales Tax Refunds Package is geared primarily toward manufacturing. It allows a five-year tax credit on the greater of one percent per year of investment in qualified new depreciable property or a credit of $500 per year per qualified new job. The Sales Tax Refunds are available on construction materials for certain manufacturers and aircraft maintenance repair facilities; on purchases of computers, data processing equipment for certain aircraft facilities; and for purchases of computer services and data processing for qualified computer services or research and development companies. Additional incentives include five-year ad valorem tax exemption for manufacturing, research and development, certain computer/data services, and certain distribution services; customized employee training; key sales tax exemptions; Freeport Law; Industrial Access Road Assistance; Foreign Trade Zones; and financing through various programs and agencies.

*Job training programs*—Customized industrial training programs, at no cost to the employer, are provided by the Oklahoma State Department of Vocational and Technical Education. Management training is also available through vocational-technical schools at 48 sites statewide.

## Development Projects

Tulsa voters approved a one-cent sales tax increase in 2003 to fund several Tulsa 2025 initiatives; the fund would create tax incentives that would benefit two key area employers—Boeing and American Airlines, among others. Of the $885 million, nearly 40 percent was earmarked as incentives for Boeing Corp. to land the final assembly plant for Boeing's new 7E7 jetliner. Another $22.3 million in incentives was slotted to retain and expand American Airlines' Tulsa maintenance center. The proposal also designates 40 percent of the penny tax, or $350.3 million, for economic development, education, and updates to the highly valuable Tulsa County EXPO Square facility and a new and modernized convention and events center to sustain and grow Tulsa's meeting and events industry. The remaining 17.5 percent, or $157.4 million, would go toward community enrichment projects ranging from two low water dams, to new soccer fields, parks, museums, swimming pools, and community centers. The low water dams stand to enrich the development of Tulsa's Arkansas River, which runs next to the downtown region and connects Tulsa's suburban communities.

*Economic Development Information:* Metropolitan Tulsa Chamber of Commerce, 616 S. Boston, Suite 100, Tulsa, OK 74119; telephone (918)585-1201. Oklahoma Department of Commerce, Office of Business Location Division, PO Box 26980, Oklahoma City, OK 73126-0980; telephone (405)815-6552

## Commercial Shipping

The Tulsa Port of Catoosa is an inland port and foreign trade zone along the Arkansas River, with more than 2,000 acres of adjacent industrial parks. Barge tonnage through the port was more than 2.3 million tons in 2004. Five railroad systems network throughout the region.

## Labor Force and Employment Outlook

A 2002 Labor Market Survey commissioned by the Tulsa Metro Chamber revealed that the Tulsa region is a somewhat undiscovered area for employers seeking office, high-technology, distribution, and manufacturing labor. The local population is generally well-educated and growing, with the number of workers in the key 12-15 years of education range exceeding the national average. Tulsa workers were found to be above state and national averages in terms of computer and technology skills, experience, and diversity of skills. Professional and managerial talent can be recruited to the area with relative ease. Contributing to this favorable recruiting climate is a large number of students enrolled in and graduating from the region's post-secondary institutions. Tulsa has 6 technology centers and 4 two-year institutions that graduate 2,800 students annually, 8 four-year schools that graduate 4,800 annually, and one medical college. The overall payoff for employers is excellent, with labor costs at only about 75 percent of the national average. Present and future economic growth areas are primarily in the service and trade sectors, specifically reservations, data and credit card processing, telecommunications, aviation and aerospace, transportation, communications, and utilities.

The following is a summary of data regarding the Tulsa metropolitan area labor force, 2003 annual averages.

*Size of nonagricultural labor force:* 381,400

*Number of workers employed in . . .*
  *natural resources and mining:* 4,200
  *construction:* 19,300
  *manufacturing:* 45,900
  *trade, transportation and utilities:* 81,000
  *information:* 12,100
  *financial activities:* 24,100
  *professional and business services:* 47,600
  *educational and health services:* 51,100
  *leisure and hospitality:* 32,400
  *other services:* 19,800
  *government:* 44,000

*Average hourly earnings of production workers employed in manufacturing:* $16.65

*Unemployment rate:* 4.2% (December 2004)

| *Largest employers* | *Number of employees* |
|---|---|
| American Airlines | 9,100 |
| Tulsa Public Schools | 7,000 |
| City of Tulsa | 4,220 |
| St. Francis Hospital | 4,100 |
| St. John Medical Center | 4,050 |
| Bank of Oklahoma | 2,520 |
| Hillcrest Medical Center | 2,350 |
| Tulsa Community College | 2,200 |

## Cost of Living

In 2005 the Tulsa Chamber of Commerce reported that Tulsa's cost of living was 8% below the national average while per capita income was 11% above the national average. Tulsa remained below the national average in unemployment with gains in net new job growth.

The following is a summary of data regarding several key cost of living factors for the Tulsa area.

*2004 (3rd Quarter) Average House Price:* $201,365

*2004 (3rd Quarter) ACCRA Cost of Living Index:* 93.6 (U.S. average = 100.0)

*State income tax rate:* Ranges from 0.5% to 6.75%

*State sales tax rate:* 4.5%

*Local income tax rate:* none

*Local sales tax rate:* 3.0% (county sales tax rate: 1.417%)

*Property tax rate:* the average effective tax rate for locally assessed property is about 1.0% of the value of the property (2005)

***Economic Information:*** Metropolitan Tulsa Chamber of Commerce, 616 S. Boston, Suite 100, Tulsa, OK 74119; telephone (918)585-1201

# Education and Research

## Elementary and Secondary Schools

The largest public school system in the state of Oklahoma, the Tulsa Public Schools (TPS) system has received national acclaim for its voluntary desegregation plan, which includes magnet schools and open-transfer. Tulsa Public Schools offers a wide range of curriculum to students living in a 172.78 square mile radius, spread throughout Tulsa, Wagoner, Osage and Creek counties. More than 80 percent of students reside inside Tulsa city limits. Approximately 39 percent of TPS teachers have advanced degrees and 47 percent have more than 10 years of experience. Overall the state of Oklahoma teachers rank in the top 10 in certification and top 5 in No Child Left Behind requirements; the state ranks 4th in classroom internet connectivity. TPS owns its own fiber optic network. In addition to the district's 81 schools, a number of special and alternative programs are also in operation, such as the Street School, Project 12, Margaret Hudson and Franklin Youth Academy. Tulsa County Area Vocational-Technical Schools, recognized as one of the leading model programs in the nation, offers more than 200 subject areas for approximately 3,000 high school students and more than 15,000 adults.

The following is a summary of data regarding the Tulsa Public Schools as of the 2004–2005 school year.

*Total enrollment:* 43,029

*Number of facilities*
   *elementary schools:* 57

*junior high/middle schools:* 15
*senior high schools:* 9

*Student/teacher ratio:* 16:1

*Teacher salaries*
   *average:* $43,810

*Funding per pupil:* $7,322 (2003)

There are more than 20 private religious schools or secular secondary and elementary schools in greater Tulsa.

***Public Schools Information:*** Tulsa Public Schools, PO Box 470208, Tulsa, OK 74147; telephone (918)746-6298

## Colleges and Universities

Metropolitan Tulsa has five major state and several private institutions of higher learning. Public institutions include Oklahoma State University at Tulsa (enrollment 2,600), the University of Oklahoma at Tulsa, Oklahoma City University at Tulsa, Rogers State University (enrollment 3,600), and Tulsa Community College (enrollment 22,866).

Tulsa's three private universities are the University of Tulsa (enrollment 4,072), Oral Roberts University (enrollment 5,700), and Oklahoma Wesleyan University (enrollment 799). The University of Tulsa, the state's oldest private university, was founded as a school for Indian girls. Today it offers programs through the doctoral level to its more than 4,200 students. The most popular recent majors are liberal arts/general studies, elementary education, and nursing. Oral Roberts University is a Christian-centered liberal arts college, education students from 50 states and more than 50 countries in 138 areas of study, including business administration/commerce/management, telecommunications, and elementary education. Southern Nazarene is another private institution that offers undergraduate and graduate programs for business people who can only attend classes in the evening.

The renowned Spartan School of Aeronautics, one of the oldest continually operating aviation schools in the world, has graduated more than 80,000 in its 75 years of education in the fields of aviation maintenance technology, avionics technology, communications technology, quality control, and aviation. Other kinds of specialized education and training are available at the Tulsa Technology Center, which trains high school juniors and seniors as well as adults. Students in Tulsa also attend several business and trade schools.

## Libraries and Research Centers

The Tulsa City-County Library has a Central Library, four regional libraries, and 19 branches. Approximately 308,000 cardholders check out more than 3.7 million volumes annually. In addition to its permanent collection of 1.7 million volumes and 2,600 periodical subscriptions, the library houses government documents, maps, art reproductions, and audio/videotapes, plus talking and large-print books. Special collections include the Land Office Survey Map Collection and the Shakespeare Collection. The Library's American Indian Resource Center provides cultural, educational, and informational resources, and activities and services honoring American Indian heritage, arts, and achievements. The center provides access to more than 7,000 books and media for adults and children by and about American Indians, including historical and rare materials, new releases, videos and music compact discs. Subjects include American Indian languages, art, culture, fiction, genealogy, history, and religion. In 2005 the Center held its American Indian Festival of Words. Among the special collections at the Thomas Gilgrease Institute of American History and Art Library are Hispanic documents from the period 1500–1800 and the papers of Cherokee Chief John Ross and Choctaw Chief Peter Pitchlynn. Tulsa has 27 other libraries offering reference materials on a wide range of topics, many having to do with petroleum. Research centers affiliated with the University of Tulsa conduct projects in such fields as women's literature and petroleum engineering, while a center affiliated with Oral Roberts University researches the Holy Spirit, among other topics.

***Public Library Information:*** Tulsa City-County Library, 400 Civic Center, Tulsa, OK 74103; telephone (918)596-7977

# Health Care

Metropolitan Tulsa has 25 hospitals providing a full range of medical treatment including Tulsa Life Flight, 24-hour emergency helicopter service to and from the region's hospitals. Six general hospitals serve Tulsa: Doctors' Medical Center, Hillcrest Medical Center, St. Francis Hospital, St. John Medical Center, Children's Medical Center, and Tulsa Regional Medical Center and Cancer Treatment Center. Most have medical school affiliation and serve as approved learning centers for medical interns and residents. Treatment and consultation are offered in virtually all fields of medicine, including such specialties as burn care, open-heart surgery, cardiac rehabilitation, genetic counseling, and neonatal intensive care. Hospice and long-term-care facilities are also available.

# Recreation

## Sightseeing

Tulsa boasts one of the nation's largest city-owned parks, 2,800-acre Mohawk Park. Along with picnic and recreation areas, the park contains the Tulsa Zoological Park with its Nocturnal Animal Building, Chimpanzee Colony, Children's Zoo, and North American Living Museum showcasing Native American artifacts and replicas of dinosaurs. The Tulsa Zoo has emerged as one of the most impressive zoos in the region and was named "America's Favorite Zoo" by the Microsoft Corporation. The Tulsa Garden Center features beautiful dogwood and azalea plantings. Nearby is the award-winning Tulsa Rose Garden. Tulsa's oldest landmark is a tree, the Council Oak, which still stands in the Creek Nation Council Oak Park as a memorial to the Lachapokas and Tallassee Creek tribes, the first settlers of what later became Tulsa.

Industrial tours of Tulsa are offered by several facilities, including the Frankhoma Pottery Factory, which uses Oklahoma clay for its creations; the Sun Petroleum Products Company; and the American Airlines Maintenance Engineering Base, which overhauls and repairs aircraft. Sightseers may also tour the campus of Oral Roberts University with its unique Prayer Tower.

## Arts and Culture

Long known as a cultural center and leading the state in the number and quality of cultural events, Tulsa offers the visitor year-round entertainment. A blooming arts scene is happening in the new Greenwood Cultural Center in the historic Greenwood District. Stage performances, art galleries, and the annual Juneteenth Jazz Festival are part of this area's resurgence. In 2004 the county announced the purchase of the district's Tulsa Union Depot, an historic train station, as the new home of the Oklahoma Jazz Hall of Fame. The Hall was created to educate the public about the significant contributions of Oklahoma's jazz musicians. During Greenwood's heyday, such notable jazz and blues performers as Nat "King" Cole, Louis Armstrong, Duke Ellington, Cab Calloway, Dizzy Gillespie, and Lionel Hampton, all visited Tulsa to play at white clubs and then jam afterwards with local musicians on Greenwood Avenue. For performances of theater, dance, and music, the six-level Performing Arts Center (or PAC), located in the Williams Center in downtown Tulsa, seats 2,400 people in its music hall and 450 people in the performing theater. Among groups and programs in residence are the Tulsa Philharmonic Orchestra, Tulsa Ballet, Tulsa Opera, Tulsa Philharmonic, Tulsa Town Hall, and the Broadway series. Ten miles from Tulsa is the Discoveryland! Outdoor Theater, which presents the popular musical classic "Oklahoma!" during the summer.

Among the many museums and galleries in the Tulsa area is the Thomas Gilcrease Museum, which features more than 10,000 works by American artists from colonial times to the present. The centerpiece is the country's most impressive collection of works by famous western artists such as Frederic

**River Parks Amphitheater provides a view of the Tulsa skyline.**

Remington, Charles Russell, and George Catlin, plus maps, manuscripts, rare books, and prehistoric and modern Indian artifacts. The Tulsa County Historical Society Museum displays photographs, rare books, furniture, and tools representative of Tulsa's early days. Objects of Jewish art, history, ceremony, and everyday life are presented at the Gershon and Rebecca Fenster Museum of Jewish Art. The Philbrook Museum of Art exhibits Chinese jades, paintings of the Italian Renaissance and of nineteenth-century England and America, plus Native American basketry, paintings, and pottery. The center is surrounded by several acres of formal gardens. The Alexandre Hogue Gallery of Art at Tulsa University showcases traveling art collections as well as works by local artists, including students and instructors. The Tulsa Air and Space Center museum promotes Tulsa's rich aviation history; the center planned to move into a brand new facility near the Tulsa Zoo and Mohawk Park in late 2005.

*Arts and Culture Information:* Arts & Humanities Council of Tulsa, 2210 S. Main, Tulsa, OK 74114; telephone (918)584-3333; email tulsaarts@mail.webtek.com

## Festivals and Holidays

Mayfest, a celebration of spring held in late May, is Tulsa's most prominent downtown event. The festivities include arts, crafts, music, and food. In late May, the Gilcrease Rendezvous Fair at the Gilcrease Museum is patterned after long-ago fur-trading events. The Tulsa Powwow, one of the largest Native American powwows in the world, takes place in early June. Highlights include authentic arts and crafts plus ceremonial dances and fancy-dress competitions. Every June, the Oklahoma Jazz Hall of Fame inducts new members into its ranks during the Juneteenth Heritage Festival on Greenwood Avenue. The yearly festival draws more than 50,000 people. The end of September brings the Tulsa State Fair; with more than 1 million fairgoers, it is one of the largest in the country. Other celebrations include the Tulsa Indian Arts Festival (February), the Boom River Celebration (4th of July), the Bok/Williams Jazz Festival (August), the Chili Cookoff/Bluegrass Festival (September), Oktoberfest, and the Christmas Parade of Lights.

## Sports for the Spectator

Fans of professional sports will find the Double A Tulsa Drillers, a farm team of the Texas Rangers, rounding the bases from April through August at renovated Drillers Stadium, where a capacity of 10,997 makes it the largest Double A ballpark in the country. The Tulsa Talons have been playing professional arena football since 2000, and the Tulsa Oilers of the Central Hockey League take to the ice, both at the Tulsa Convention Center from November through March. In collegiate sports, the University of Tulsa fields Golden Hurricane football and basketball teams. The football season lasts from September through November and

games are played at Skelly Stadium. Both the Golden Hurricane and the Oral Roberts University Golden Eagles play basketball from November through March. The Oral Roberts University Lady Titans play baseball at the Mabee Center from mid-February to mid-May.

Tulsa's numerous equestrian events include the Longhorn Championship Rodeo, in which the top money-winners on the rodeo circuit compete. Tulsa also plays host to several prestigious golf tours and championships at its challenging Southern Hills Country Club, including the 2007 PGA championship. Other spectator sports include tennis and horse racing as well as stock-car races.

## Sports for the Participant

Public recreation opportunities abound on and around the seven large lakes surrounding Tulsa. The area has become known locally as "Green Country," encompassing thousands of miles of shoreline on Grand Lake, Lake Eufala, Keystone Lake, Lake Tenkiller, and others. In the River Parks system along the Arkansas River in the heart of Tulsa, visitors can enjoy more than 50 miles of hiking/biking trails as well as picnic and playground areas. Mohawk Park offers bridle trails and a polo field. Other facilities include several golf courses, more than 100 tennis courts, several municipal swimming pools, Bell's Amusement Park, and Big Splash Water Park.

## Shopping and Dining

From nationally known stores to specialty shops, Tulsa provides shoppers with a wide range of choices. Three large malls serve the metro area, including the largest, Woodland Hills, as well as Eastland Mall and Tulsa Promenade. Utica Square is a tree-lined avenue of posh stores and diverse retailers. Just northwest of Utica Square, trendy boutiques and restaurants cater to more Bohemian tastes, while the Brookside area, a little south of the Square, offers still more individualized shopping, with some of Tulsa's best dining. The Cherry Street historic district has been restored and many small shops have opened there. Jenks, America is the city's antiques center near the downtown Jenks neighborhood. Smaller shops featuring Native American crafts and Oklahoma memorabilia abound. Saturday's Flea Market at Expo Square is also a favorite shopping destination.

Dozens of restaurants offer menus ranging from traditional American cuisine to those with an international flavor. Regional specialties include chicken-fried steak, Santa Fe-style Mexican food, and authentic western barbecues.

*Visitor Information:* Tulsa Convention & Visitors Bureau, 616 S. Boston Ave. #100, Tulsa, OK 74119-1298; telephone (918)585-1201; toll-free (800)558-3311; fax (918)592-6244; email TulsaCVB@tulsachamber.com

# Convention Facilities

A moderate climate, abundant hotel space—approximately 9,000 rooms in Tulsa and the metropolitan area—and a wide range of leisure, cultural, and recreational opportunities make Tulsa attractive to large and small groups of convention-goers.

In 2005 ground was broken on the city's most exciting development project in many years, the 18,000 seat Regional Convention and Events Center, featuring a stunning, futuristic design by world-renowned architect Cesar Pelli. The Tulsa Convention Center, in the heart of the business district and only six blocks from the Performing Arts Center (which is also available for meetings), offers facilities for sports, banquets, concerts, exhibitions, trade shows, and stage performances. The facility provides 102,000 square feet of exhibit space, a banquet area seating up to 5,100 people, an arena seating 8,992 people plus additional arena floor space, and 25 conference rooms for break-out sessions seating 45 to 275 people. The Tulsa Exposition Center contains four meeting centers providing an exhibit area with a total of 548,798 square feet, a banquet area seating 1,700 to 20,000 + people, 7,523 arena seats, and a race track with 8,900 covered seats.

Among the city's other convention facilities are the Downtown Doubletree Hotel, the Doubletree Hotel at Warren Place, Adam's Mark Tulsa, Tulsa Marriott Southern Hills, Tulsa Sheraton, and Grandview.

*Convention Information:* Tulsa Convention & Visitors Bureau, 616 S. Boston Ave. #100, Tulsa, OK 74119-1298; telephone (918)585-1201; toll-free (800)558-3311; fax (918)592-6244; email TulsaCVB@tulsachamber.com

# Transportation

## Approaching the City

Visitors arriving by air will touch down at Tulsa International Airport, just nine miles northeast of downtown—approximately 15 minutes by taxi. Employing more than 17,000 people, the modern 22-gate facility is served by 10 passenger air carriers and supports about 170 daily arrivals and departures. South of the city is the Richard Lloyd Jones, Jr., Airport, a smaller facility serving general aviation traffic. For those traveling to Tulsa by car, the major direct routes are Interstate Highways 44 from the east and south—which merges with U.S. Highway 75-Alternate and State Highway 33 a few miles southwest of the city—and 244

from the east—which intersects with I-44 a few miles east of Tulsa and leads directly into the city, then merges with U.S. 75 southwest of the city; U.S. Highway 75 from the north and south, 64 from the southeast—which merges with State 51 southeast and northwest of the city—and 169 from the northeast; and by State highways 412—an east-west highway south of the city—and 51 from the east and west. Four toll expressways radiate from the city, the Red Fork and Crosstown (both are Interstate 244), Cherokee (U.S. 75), and Broken Arrow (U.S. 64/State 51).

## Traveling in the City

Downtown Tulsa is bounded on the north by Interstate 244/U.S. 64/State 51, on the east by U.S. 75, on the south by U.S. 64/State 51, and on the west by Interstate 244/U.S. 75.

Tulsa's bus-based mass transit system, Tulsa Transit, has routes to most business, shopping, and recreation areas and is operated by the Metropolitan Tulsa Transit Authority. Unique to the system are trackless trolleys. To make commuting easier, the city also offers Rideshare, a free computerized service matching individuals who drive similar routes daily.

# Communications

## Newspapers and Magazines

Tulsa's morning and Sunday newspaper is the *Tulsa World*. In addition, an African American community newspaper, *The Oklahoma Eagle,* two business newspapers, and several suburban and metro area weeklies serve the city. Tulsa also publishes a wide variety of periodicals, including *Geophysics: The Leading Edge of Exploration, James Joyce Quarterly,* and others covering such topics as science, petroleum, dentistry, and medicine.

## Television and Radio

Seven television stations broadcast from Tulsa—affiliates of NBC, PBS, CBS, ABC, and Fox, plus two independents. Other stations operate in the area from nearby towns. In addition, Tulsa radio provides listeners with a choice of 23 AM and FM stations broadcasting religious programs, country music, oldies and contemporary hits, talk, and sports.

*Media Information:* *Tulsa World,* 315 S. Boulder Avenue, PO Box 1770, Tulsa, OK 74102; telephone (918)582-0921; toll-free (800)444-6552

## Tulsa Online

City of Tulsa. Available www.cityoftulsa.org

Metropolitan Tulsa Chamber of Commerce. Available www .tulsachamber.com

Oklahoma Community Links. Available www.state.ok.us/ osfdocs/county.html

Oklahoma Department of Commerce. Available www.odoc .state.ok.us

Tulsa City-County Library. Available www.tulsalibrary.org

Tulsa Oklahoma Convention & Visitors Bureau. Available www.tulsachamber.com/cvb.htm

Tulsa Public Schools. Available www.tulsaschools.org

*Tulsa World.* Available www.tulsaworld.com

## Selected Bibliography

Bernhardt, William, *Dark Justice* (New York: Ballantine Books, 1999)

Johnson, Hannibal B. *Black Wall Street: From Riot to Renaissance in Tulsa's Historic Greenwood District*(Marion Koogler Mc-Nay Art Museum, 1998)

# SOUTH CAROLINA

# The State in Brief

**Nickname:** Palmetto State
**Motto:** *Animism opibusque parati* (Prepared in mind and resources); *Dum spiro spero* (While I breathe, I hope)

**Flower:** Carolina jessamine
**Bird:** Carolina wren

**Area:** 32,020 square miles (2000; U.S. rank: 40th)
**Elevation:** Ranges from sea level to 3,560 feet above sea level
**Climate:** Humid and subtropical, with long, hot summers, short, mild winters, and abundant rainfall

**Admitted to Union:** May 23, 1788
**Capital:** Columbia
**Head Official:** Governor Mark Sanford (R) (until 2007)

**Population**
**1980:** 3,122,000
**1990:** 3,486,703
**2000:** 4,012,012
**2004 estimate:** 4,198,068
**Percent change, 1990–2000:** 15.1%
**U.S. rank in 2004:** 25th
**Percent of residents born in state:** 64.0% (2000)
**Density:** 133.2 people per square mile (2000)
**2002 FBI Crime Index Total:** 217,569

**Racial and Ethnic Characteristics** (2000)
**White:** 2,695,560
**Black or African American:** 1,185,216
**American Indian and Alaska Native:** 13,718
**Asian:** 36,014
**Native Hawaiian and Pacific Islander:** 1,628
**Hispanic or Latino (may be of any race):** 95,076
**Other:** 39,926

**Age Characteristics** (2000)
**Population under 5 years old:** 264,679
**Population 5 to 19 years old:** 871,099
**Percent of population 65 years and over:** 12.1%
**Median age:** 35.4 years (2000)

**Vital Statistics**
**Total number of births (2003):** 55,869
**Total number of deaths (2003):** 38,060 (infant deaths, 451)
**AIDS cases reported through 2003:** 6,379

**Economy**
**Major industries:** Textiles, tourism, chemicals, agriculture, lumber, machinery, automobiles, manufacturing
**Unemployment rate:** 6.7% (December 2004)
**Per capita income:** $26,139 (2003; U.S. rank: 43rd)
**Median household income:** $38,791 (3-year average, 2001-2003)
**Percentage of persons below poverty level:** 14.0% (3-year average, 2001-2003)
**Income tax rate:** Ranges from 2.5% to 7.0%
**Sales tax rate:** 5.0%

# Charleston

## *The City in Brief*

**Founded:** 1670 (incorporated 1783)

**Head Official:** Mayor Joseph P. Riley, Jr. (D) (since 1975)

**City Population**
   **1980:** 69,779
   **1990:** 88,256
   **2000:** 96,650
   **2003 estimate:** 101,024
   **Percent change, 1990–2000:** 6.7%
   **U.S. rank in 1980:** 286th
   **U.S. rank in 1990:** 266th
   **U.S. rank in 2000:** 272nd (State rank: 2nd)

**Metropolitan Area Population**
   **1980:** 430,346
   **1990:** 506,875
   **2000:** 549,033
   **Percent change, 1990–2000:** 8.3%
   **U.S. rank in 1980:** 77th
   **U.S. rank in 1990:** 73rd
   **U.S. rank in 2000:** 76th

**Area:** 97 square miles (2000)
**Elevation:** Ranges from sea level to 20 feet above sea level
**Average Annual Temperature:** 65.6° F
**Average Annual Precipitation:** 51.53 inches

**Major Economic Sectors:** services, trade, government
**Unemployment rate:** 4.6% (December 2004)
**Per Capita Income:** $22,414 (1999)

**2002 FBI Crime Index Total:** 6,997

**Major Colleges and Universities:** Medical University of South Carolina, College of Charleston and University of Charleston, The Citadel, Trident Technical College

**Daily Newspaper:** *The Post & Courier*

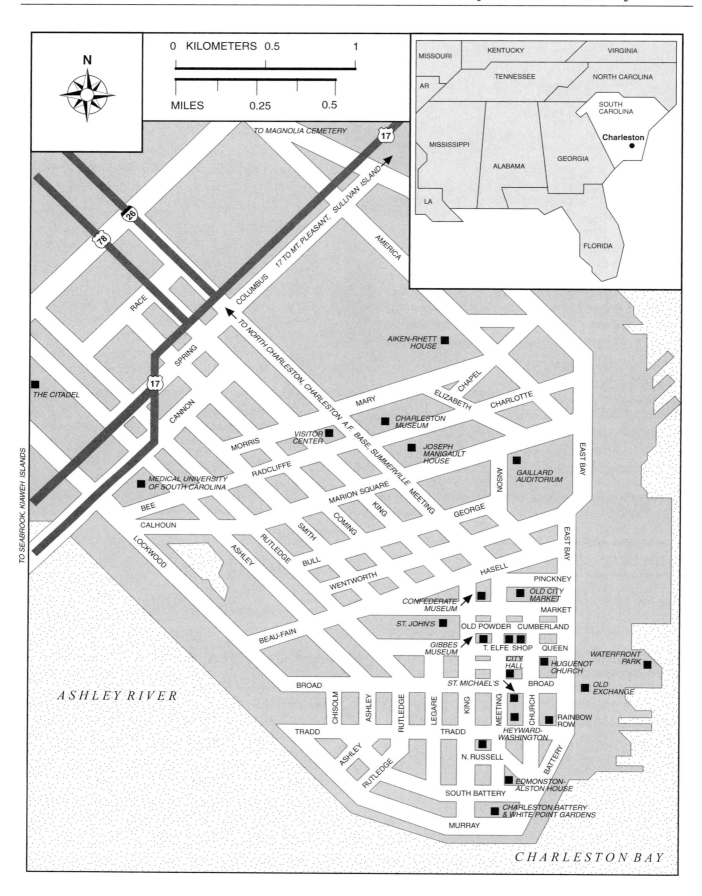

# Introduction

Charleston is the flagship city of three South Carolina counties: Charleston, Dorchester, and Berkeley. They share social, economic, and political ties, and cover 2,600 square miles of what is called the low country. Charleston owes much to its warm, sunny climate and proximity to the sea. Although the Charleston Naval Base closed in 1996, Charleston still has a large military presence. The Port of Charleston ranks as one of the fastest-growing in the nation. Visitors flock to the luxury resorts on the Atlantic coast barrier islands to play golf, stroll secluded beaches, observe wildlife, and enjoy deep water fishing off Charleston's mainland. In recent years *Conde Nast Traveler* has consistently ranked Charleston among its top 10 U.S. destinations and top 20 world destinations.

Charleston also owes much to those who worked to preserve its historic buildings. Cobblestone streets, quaint gardens, historic homes and buildings, mingled with flower stalls and specialty shops draw tourists to Charleston for a glimpse at a gracious and genteel lifestyle long gone. Waterfront and downtown renovation and new construction planned to blend with historic structures have rejuvenated not only the body, but the spirit of the city as well, as it looks to the future.

# Geography and Climate

Prior to 1960, Charleston proper was limited to the South Carolina peninsula bounded on the west and south by the Ashley River, on the east by the Cooper River, and on the southeast by an excellent harbor almost completely landlocked from the Atlantic Ocean. The city has expanded to include other areas, but most residents still think of Charleston as the peninsula. In fact, the physical size of Charleston has increased from approximately 17 square miles in 1975 to 97 square miles today. A chain of barrier islands between Charleston's mainland and the Atlantic Ocean adds sandy beaches and marshland to the region's geography.

Charleston's proximity to the Atlantic Ocean provides a temperate climate. During the winter months temperatures on the peninsula can be as much as 15 degrees warmer than inland because of the ocean's influence. In summer, sea breezes cool the city to a temperature about three degrees below higher country. The summer is Charleston's rainiest season with 41 percent of the annual rainfall occurring in the form of thundershowers and occasional tropical storms. Hurricanes threaten in late summer and early fall. It is estimated that Charleston is affected by hurricanes every

4.62 years. In September 1989 Hurricane Hugo inflicted more than $5 billion in property damage to the region. In September 1999 Hurricane Floyd forced hundreds of thousands of people to evacuate Charleston. More recent hurricanes were Charley and Gaston, both in 2004.

**Area:** 97 square miles (2000)

**Elevation:** Sea level to 20 feet above sea level

**Average Temperatures:** January, 47.8° F; August, 80.6° F; annual average, 65.6° F

**Average Annual Precipitation:** 51.53 inches

# History

### Settlement Named for British King

In April 1670, the first English colonists sailed into Charleston harbor. This band of some 150 men and women soon established themselves on what they called Albemarle Point on the Ashley River. Ten years later, the colony was moved to Oyster Point, a peninsula of land between the Ashley and Cooper Rivers, the present site of Charleston. The settlement was named Charles Towne in honor of King Charles II of England, who had granted the land for colonization. The colony began to grow as people arrived first from England and the Caribbean islands. They were followed by Huguenots and Quakers who, along with Scottish, Irish, and Belgian colonists settled the area. The thriving port became known as one of the most religiously tolerant of the colonies. About 5,000 people inhabited the town by 1700, and friendly relations with the area's tribal natives had been established.

### City Incorporated Following Revolution

By this time, the town was protected by a formidable wall; situated along the river bluff, it stood five feet thick and was made of brick on a base of palmetto logs and wood planks; on the land side, the wall was made of earth and bordered by a moat. The mere sight of it turned back a frontal attack on the settlement from a combined French-Spanish fleet in 1706. Ships sailed out of the harbor carrying corn, pork, lumber, deerskins, and rice, conveying goods to England and the West Indies. But shipping was threatened when, following a devastating 1713 hurricane and renewed tribal hostility, pirates became bold enough to attack the sea trade. Notable among the pirates was Edward Teach, known as Blackbeard. He seized several ships carrying Charles Towne residents and demanded, and received, ransom. Teach was eventually captured and executed, but residents of Charles Towne had become dissatisfied with the administration of the colony, especially in regard to the protection of the populace. England's Privy

Council took over responsibility for the government of South Carolina and appointed the first royal governor in 1720. With the threat of hostile native and pirate attacks effectively quelled by the new administration, Charles Towne residents took down most of the city walls, opened and extended the streets, and built spacious homes with well-tended grounds. The shoreline was developed, and shipping activity was brisk. Left standing was the Battery, a large retaining wall that today overlooks the harbor and Fort Sumter.

Beginning with the Stamp Act of 1765, Charles Towne was seriously torn over conflicts between loyalty to England and resistance to England's imposition of unjust taxes on the colonies. Residents protested the tea tax at a mass meeting held in 1773 and set up the formal governmental structure of South Carolina in July 1774. In September 1775, the last royal governor left the colony and took refuge aboard a British ship in the harbor. Then on June 28, 1776, a British fleet attempted to sail into the harbor at Charles Towne and was repulsed by revolutionary patriots. This victory persuaded the South Carolina delegates to the Continental Congress to sign the Declaration of Independence. Following the Revolution, Charles Towne remained politically troubled. Violence was directed against suspected British sympathizers, and various factions of the town faced each other with open animosity. Finally, in an attempt to restore order, the city was incorporated under the name of Charleston in 1783. Three years later, the South Carolina General Assembly voted to move the state capital from Charleston to the new city of Columbia.

**The Citadel Founded to Quell Uprisings**

Several innovations improved Charleston's economy in the 1790s. The invention of the cotton gin made the cotton business profitable. A method of using tidal force to irrigate rice plantings expanded the possibilities for rice cultivation. New and more efficient rice mills were built. Meanwhile, the shipping industry, no longer forced to comply with British mercantile laws, found new markets for American goods; wagon trade expanded, rolling cotton and other produce into Charleston's King Street for sale. When other regions began to draw trade away from Charleston, the city began construction of the South Carolina Railroad. By 1833, rail service began out of Charleston, but while the railroad did improve the economy, Charleston never again regained its dynamic growth pattern.

In 1822, just as Charleston was beginning to feel economic woes, it also experienced an attempted slave rebellion led by a former slave from the West Indies, Denmark Vesey, a dynamic, well-educated leader. Vesey had laid plans for obtaining weapons and had determined which buildings would be attacked when he was betrayed by two house servants and arrested. After a trial during which he engaged counsel and

expertly examined witnesses himself, he was condemned to be hanged along with 36 of his co-conspirators. Others involved in the rebellion were deported. Following this attempted uprising, the Old Citadel was built as an arsenal and staffed by federal troops, and stricter laws governing slaves and their activities were adopted. The Citadel was later staffed by state troops, and in 1843 by a 20-man force that became the first Corps of Cadets of The Citadel.

**"Cradle of Secession" Surrenders to Yankees**

Unresolved economic and philosophical conflicts between northern and southern states reached a crisis on December 20, 1860, when the South Carolina Secession Convention unanimously voted to adopt the Ordinance of Secession, leading other southern states in an attempt to leave the Union and form their own Confederacy. On April 12, 1861, Confederate batteries fired on Union forces occupying Fort Sumter, an installation off Charleston's coast. The Union forces on the island surrendered, Confederate forces occupied the fort, and one week later President Abraham Lincoln ordered all southern ports blockaded. While preparing for Union attack, Charleston was ravaged by a fire that destroyed 540 acres. Blockade runners were able to slip some supplies past the Union's blockade of Charleston harbor, but as the war continued it brought shortages of all vital supplies, including meat, sugar, and salt. Charleston, the "Cradle of Secession," withstood Union attacks until February 17, 1865, when, with the Confederacy crumbling, hundreds of fires swept through the city. After four years of siege, Charleston succumbed to Union forces, and two months later the Confederacy surrendered.

**Navy Yard Helps Stabilize Economy**

Following the Civil War, Charleston was powerless. The city lay in ruins, railroads were destroyed, banking capital was depleted, and private capital was scarce. An industry eventually developed around phosphate deposits mined from local rivers and land sites and by 1880 was the most profitable industry in the state. Other commercial concerns recovered or developed, such as lumber mills, locomotive engine manufacturing, cotton presses and mills, breweries, and grist and flour mills. Port trade thrived, and the cotton business revived. Charleston recovered from an 1885 hurricane and an 1886 earthquake only to battle political trade obstacles, industrial competition from other regions, and insect destruction of the cotton industry. By the turn of the century, the city had to look to new industries and new developments for new hope.

In a move that proved to be the single most important gesture affecting the city's economy in the twentieth century, the United States Navy Yard was located at Charleston in 1901. Although other industries established themselves in the area, the military facility fueled the city's economy through two world wars and provided the stability that enabled Charleston to solidify its identity. In the 1920s and 1930s, although the rest of the country was mired in the Great Depression, efforts to preserve and capitalize on Charleston's historic buildings began. Leading the way were wealthy people with well-known names like Doubleday, du Pont, and Whitney, who used Charleston's abandoned rice fields as quail- and duck-hunting preserves, and also began the task of restoring the city's beautiful old mansions. In 1989 Hurricane Hugo, one of the most destructive hurricanes to ever have struck the U.S. mainland, inflicted more than $5 billion in property damage on the region. Citizens quickly repaired the damage, restoring the city to the pristine freshness that still beguiles its four and a half million annual visitors. Although the U.S. Naval Base in Charleston closed in 1996, a significant U.S. Naval and Air Force presence remains.

Today's Charleston is considered a "living museum" with a rich, 300 year history. Its blend of history with a diverse economic mix, favorable climate, and true southern charm not only attracts visitors and new residents but businesses as well. Charleston's future, fueled in part by a multi-billion dollar tourism business, is bright.

**Historical Information:** South Carolina Historical Society Library, Fireproof Building, 100 Meeting Street, Charleston, SC; telephone (803)723-3225. College of Charleston, Avery Research Center for African American History and Culture–Library, 125 Bull Street, Charleston, SC 29424; telephone (803)727-2009

# Population Profile

## Metropolitan Area Residents
*1980:* 430,000
*1990:* 506,877
*2000:* 549,033
*Percent change, 1990–2000:* 8.3%
*U.S. rank in 1980:* 77th
*U.S. rank in 1990:* 73rd
*U.S. rank in 2000:* 76th

## City Residents
*1980:* 69,779
*1990:* 88,256
*2000:* 96,650
*Percent change, 1990–2000:* 6.7%
*U.S. rank in 1980:* 286th
*U.S. rank in 1990:* 266th
*U.S. rank in 2000:* 272nd (State rank: 2nd)

*Density:* 996.5 people per square mile (2000)

*Racial and ethnic characteristics* (2000)
   White: 60,964
   Black or African American: 32,864
   American Indian and Alaska Native: 145
   Asian: 1,197
   Native Hawaiian and other Pacific Islander: 55
   Hispanic or Latino (may be of any race): 1,462
   Other: 518

*Percent of residents born in state:* 58.2% (2000)

*Age characteristics* (2000)
   Population under 5 years old: 5,252
   Population 5 to 9 years old: 5,263
   Population 10 to 14 years old: 5,572
   Population 15 to 19 years old: 8,555
   Population 20 to 24 years old: 11,274
   Population 25 to 34 years old: 14,725
   Population 35 to 44 years old: 13,142
   Population 45 to 54 years old: 11,969
   Population 55 to 59 years old: 4,397
   Population 60 to 64 years old: 3,469
   Population 65 to 74 years old: 6,471
   Population 75 to 84 years old: 5,005
   Population 85 years and older: 1,556
   Median age: years 33.2

*Births* (Charleston County, 2003)
   Total number: 4,655

*Deaths* (Charleston County, 2003)
   Total number: 2,724 (of which, 37 were infants under the age of 1 year)

*Money income* (1999)
   Per capita income: $22,414
   Median household income: $35,295
   Total households: 40,791 (2000)

*Number of households with income of . . .*
   less than $10,000: 6,401
   $10,000 to $14,999: 2,869
   $15,000 to $24,999: 5,586
   $25,000 to $34,999: 5,279
   $35,000 to $49,999: 5,902
   $50,000 to $74,999: 6,724
   $75,000 to $99,999: 3,187
   $100,000 to $149,999: 2,647
   $150,000 to $199,999: 852
   $200,000 or more: 1,103

*Percent of families below poverty level:* 13.3% (59.8% of which were female householder families with related children under 5 years)

*2002 FBI Crime Index Total:* 6,997

# Municipal Government

Charleston is governed by a mayor and a twelve-member city council. Council members are elected on a single-member district basis for four-year terms. Every two years, six members are elected.

**Head Official:** Mayor Joseph P. Riley, Jr. (D) (since 1975; current term expires January 2008)

**Total Number of City Employees:** 1,278 (2004)

*City Information:* City of Charleston, Executive Office, 80 Broad St., Charleston, SC 29401; telephone (843)577-6970

# Economy

### Major Industries and Commercial Activity

The economy in the Charleston region rests upon several sturdy bases. The military has traditionally been the major industry in the area since 1901 when the Charleston Naval Shipyard was founded. Even after the Naval Base and Shipyard closed in 1996, the military has remained the largest single employer in the Charleston region. The Department of Defense has remained at installations such as the Charleston Naval Weapons Station, Naval Hospital and the SPAWAR Systems Center Charleston. The Department of the Navy employed more than 12,500 active duty and civilian personnel in the region in 2003. At the same time, Charleston Air Force Base employs more than 5,000 personnel as the home for the U.S. Air Force's 437th Airlift Wing, adding substantially to the region's economic foundation.

Oil, electronics, computers, mining, and health care are also major industries in the Charleston area. Three of the region's largest employers are in the health care industry. They are Medical University of South Carolina, Roper St. Francis Healthcare and Trident Health System, and HCA division headquarters.

Tourism is another significant factor in the area's economy. The Charleston Metro Chamber of Commerce, the nation's oldest chamber of commerce, has long been interested in promoting Charleston as a place to visit, and despite wars, fires, hurricanes, and earthquakes, Charleston has preserved and restored hundreds of historic buildings that draw some four and a half million tourists per year. Visitors enjoy shopping and dining, as well as touring historic plantations, landmarks, and churches. According to research from the Chamber's Center for Business Research, Charleston visitors surveyed say that the area's greatest assets are its historic charm, historic sites and attractions, restaurants and climate. While most visitors to Charleston come from the nearby states of North Carolina, Georgia, Ohio and Tennessee, as well as their home state of South Carolina, about four percent of visitors are from outside the U.S. Charleston's world-famous barrier islands feature outstanding resort facilities in a semi-tropical climate, serving as powerful elements in the area's allure for tourists. The number of visitors to the Charleston region has grown steadily since 1997 when 2.5 million people visited to 4.6 million visitors in 2003. The number of accommodations in the area has also increased to keep pace with the growing demand. Tourism contributes $5.1 billion to the local economy annually.

*Items and goods produced:* marine products, fertilizer, rubber products, textiles, aircraft parts, paper, textiles, food products, lumber, metal components, heavy machinery, transportation equipment, furniture, instruments and chemicals

### Incentive Programs—New and Existing Companies

Both the State of South Carolina and the Charleston community offer a number of business incentives designed to provide measurable economic advantages and reduce the cost of start-up operations.

*Local programs*—The Berkeley-Charleston-Dorchester Council of Governments operates a revolving loan fund offering financing for projects meeting certain criteria. Charleston County may negotiate a fee in lieu of property taxes with prospects or existing industries that commit to large new capital investment in the state. Five-year property tax abatements for new manufacturing facilities locating in the tri-county area and an exemption from the county portion of ordinary property taxes for five years on all additions to existing facilities are available under certain circumstances. The Charleston Citywide Local Development Corporation (LDC) offers financial assistance through six different loan programs for small businesses.

*State programs*—The following incentives and financing sources may be available to qualifying companies: Job Tax Credit for corporate income tax for job creation; displaced worker jobs tax credit; corporate headquarters tax credit; credit for hiring Family Independence Recipients; employer child care credit; job development credit; income tax credits for infrastructure construction; tax credit for the construction of water resources; income tax credit for investments in the Palmetto Seed Capital Corporation; property tax abatements; and sales tax exemptions for certain business expenditures. South Carolina's Jobs-Economic Development Authority provides funding assistance through Community Development Block Grants and through Carolina capital investment loans. South Carolina also offers Enterprise Zone incentives. There is no local tax on corporate income as well as no tax on worldwide profits.

*Job training programs*—The Center for Acccelerated Technology Training (CATT), a division of the State Board of Technical and Comprehensive Education, provides new and expanding companies with fully trained and productive employees. The program may include trainee recruitment and testing, instructor recruitment and training, provision of training sites, development of instructional materials, and complete program management. South Carolina administers the Job Training Partnership Program, which provides both training for new and expanding businesses, as well as customized skill training for specific employer needs. Finally, funds for retraining employees in existing industries are available from the Coordinating Council for Economic Development.

## Development Projects

Major corridors in the city are getting a boost from the City's Streetscape program. Scheduled for completion by 2007, improvements include reconstruction of sidewalks, curbing, lighting, handicap ramps, the addition of street trees, brick crosswalks, and burial of overhead wires to the King Street commercial area and other downtown areas of the city. The South Carolina legislature has mandated additional expansion to the Port of Charleston, and by 2004 the South Carolina State Ports Authority had begun the permitting process for a sixth container terminal located at the former Charleston Naval Complex. This terminal will accommodate the expanding international container trade and the increasingly larger container ships that arrive in the port. In 2004, the Ports Authority also completed a $24 million project to deepen the Charleston channel and widen the harbor to improve navigation and accommodate larger vessels. The 2005 planned completion of a $635 million new bridge across the Port of Charleston's shipping channel will feature eight traffic lanes and improved clearance over the channel. The Arthur Ravenel Jr. Bridge over the Cooper River and Town Creek replaces two aging truss bridges. The city has initiated work on the renovation of the Camden Tower Sheds, an historic railway property, into a cultural Arts District and Children's Museum. The Children's Museum of the Lowcountry opened to the public in 2003.

***Economic Development Information:*** Charleston Regional Development Alliance, 5300 International Blvd., Suite 103A, North Charleston, SC 29418; telephone (843)767-9300; fax (834)760-4535

## Commercial Shipping

International trade is a growing sector of the regional economy and the Port of Charleston is making strides to accommodate that growth. Known as one of the most efficient ports in the world, it handles one quarter of all containers from Norfolk to Miami. The port is also ranked sixth in the country by value of cargo moved through its terminals. Containerized shipments such as textiles, chemicals, and rubber are the main commodities handled by the port. The Port of Charleston contributes greatly to the economic impact of the city in areas of employment, personal income, and tax revenues. Adding to the efficiency of shipping into and out of Charleston is the Charleston International Airport. Its air cargo facilities include a 21,000 square yard facility and a separate cargo/freight area on the airport's east side. In addition, about 100 motor freight carriers, three railroad systems, and an expansive system of interstates and U.S. highways move cargo through the region.

## Labor Force and Employment Outlook

Charleston boasts a plentiful supply of skilled labor; its civilian labor force has grown 4.3 percent from 1998 to 2003. Most Charleston residents are employed in the trade, transportation and utilities sector and government sector. High school graduates account for 81.1 percent of the city's labor force and 16 percent are college graduates. Most employment opportunities can be found in the tourism industry, transportation services, health care, military installations, and manufacturing.

The following is a summary of data regarding the Charleston metropolitan area labor force, annual averages 2003.

*Size of nonagricultural labor force:* 260,300

*Number of workers employed in . . .*
   *construction and mining:* 19,900
   *manufacturing:* 20,900
   *trade, transportation and utilities:* 53,600
   *information:* 3,700
   *financial activities:* 10,800
   *professional and business services:* 33,600
   *educational and health services:* 27,400
   *leisure and hospitality:* 32,100
   *other services:* 7,600
   *government:* 50,800

*Average hourly earnings of production workers employed in manufacturing:* Not reported

*Unemployment rate:* 4.6% (December 2004)

| *Largest employers* | *Number of employees* |
|---|---|
| U.S. Navy | 12,543 |
| Medical University of South Carolina | 8,200 |
| Charleston Air Force Base | 5,000 |
| Charleston County School District | 5,000 |
| Roper St. Francis Health Care | 4,000 |
| Berkeley County School District | 3,457 |
| Piggly Wiggly Carolina Co. Inc. | 2,447 |
| Charleston County | 2,243 |
| HCA Carolinas division headquarters & medical centers | 2,082 |

| Largest employers | Number of employees |
|---|---|
| Robert Bosch Corp. (fuel injection & braking systems) | 2,062 |
| MeadWestvaco | 1,755 |

## Cost of Living

The following is a summary of data regarding several key cost of living factors for the Charleston area.

*2004 (3rd Quarter) ACCRA Average House Price:* $229,315

*2004 (3rd Quarter) ACCRA Cost of Living Index:* 97.3 (U.S. average = 100.0)

*State income tax rate:* Ranges from 2.5% to 7.0%

*State sales tax rate:* 5.0%

*Local income tax rate:* None

*Local sales tax rate:* 1.5% (Charleston County)

*Property tax rate:* Millage rates set annually by local government tax authorities and applied to 4.0% of fair market value. In 2003 the city's combined millage rate was 337 (tax credit factor was .000365).

***Economic Information:*** Charleston Metro Chamber of Commerce, 81 Mary Street, PO Box 975; Charleston, SC 29402-0975; telephone (843)577-2510; fax (843)723-4853

# Education and Research

## Elementary and Secondary Schools

There are four school districts serving about 87,500 students in the Charleston Metropolitan Area. Berkeley County, Charleston County, Dorchester II, and Dorchester IV collectively operate 134 schools serving grades K-12. Charleston County has the largest enrollment of the four. Charleston County's average SAT score in 2004 for college-bound seniors was 964, compared to a U.S. average of 1,026. The 2004 South Carolina Annual Report Card for the Charleston County schools assigned an Absolute Rating of ''good'' based on student test scores and an Improvement Rating of '' average'' which compares student test scores from one year to the next.

The following is a summary of data regarding the Charleston County School District for the 2003–2004 school year.

*Total enrollment:* 42,226

*Number of facilities*
  *elementary schools:* 42
  *middle schools:* 13

*senior high schools:* 8
*other:* 4 charter schools, 12 magnet schools, and 8 alternative programs

*Student/teacher ratio:* 21:1

*Teacher salaries*
  *average:* $40,092

*Funding per pupil:* $7,661

In addition, about 11,200 students are educated at nearly 75 private and parochial schools in the region, including the exclusive Charleston Day School, where children from Charleston's oldest families matriculate.

***Public Schools Information:*** Center for Business Research, Charleston Metro Chamber of Commerce, 81 Mary Street, PO Box 975, Charleston, SC 29402-0975; telephone (843)805-3042; fax (843)723-4853

## Colleges and Universities

Students can choose from among 17 institutions of higher learning in the Charleston region. The Medical University of South Carolina, the South's oldest medical school, has five health-related colleges. The College of Charleston offers 34 undergraduate degree programs; in conjunction with the college, the University of Charleston offers 15 graduate degree programs. The Charleston Air Force Base is home to four academic institutions. Webster University, a St. Louis-based facility granting master's degrees, offers courses in business and management, liberal arts and sciences, and fine arts. City Colleges of Chicago, Southern Illinois University and Embry-Riddle Aeronautical University also have campuses on the base. Johnson and Wales University at Charleston offers bachelor and associate degrees in the culinary arts and hospitality management. Trident Technical College is a two-year institution that emphasizes training in job skills and offers 150 programs of study. Charleston Southern University enrolls about 2,990 students in its College of Arts and Science, ROTC program, and schools of business, education, and nursing. Southern Wesleyan University offers accelerated learning programs for working adults. Limestone College offers bachelor's and associate's degrees in several disciplines, including art, biology, and computer science. Miller-Motte Technical College offers both certificate and college degree programs in art direction, accounting, design and photography, among others. Springfield College offers undergraduate and graduate degrees in 50 majors and programs. In addition, The Citadel, The Military College of South Carolina, a four-year liberal arts school with a strict military structure, is also located in Charleston. Voorhees College is a private, historically African American, coeducational, liberal arts school affiliated with the Episcopal Church. The Charleston School of Law is the city's newest addition to its academic institutions. Opened in August 2004, the law school enrolled 200 students in its first class.

### Libraries and Research Centers

The city of Charleston is served by the Charleston County Library, the first public library in the country, with 16 branch libraries and a traveling bookmobile. The library system houses about 2.2 million catalogued items including books, magazine subscriptions, compact discs, records, videotapes, films and film strips, cassettes, as well as an excellent collection of Charleston and South Carolina historical and genealogical materials. It maintains a complete business reference library, as well as legal resources pertaining to federal, state, and local law. Research centers affiliated with area academic institutions conduct activities in such fields as pharmacology and toxicology, marine biomedicine, public affairs and policy studies, and medicine.

*Public Library Information:* Charleston County Library, 68 Calhoun Street, Charleston, SC 29401; (843)805-6801

# Health Care

Medical University of South Carolina, a leading teaching and research center, has 775 beds and 8,200 employees. The hospital has announced plans for the construction of a new four-story diagnostic and treatment center, state-of-the-art cardiology center, and a seven-story patient tower. Roper St. Francis Health Care is the next largest health system in the metro Charleston area. Its two hospitals are Bon Secours St. Francis Hospital, specializing in acute care, and Roper Hospital, a tertiary care facility. Other medical facilities serving the region's health care needs include the U.S. Naval Hospital, which serves military personnel; Charleston Memorial Hospital (172 beds); Charter Behavior Health System, a psychiatric and rehabilitation hospital with 102 beds; East Cooper Regional Medical Center (100 beds); R.H. Johnson Veterans Administration Medical center (117 beds); and Trident Health System (Columbia/HCA), with two hospitals, 400 beds, and 2082 employees.

# Recreation

### Sightseeing

Visitors to Charleston are greeted with a delightful array of sights and activities all year around. The colonial port city is famous for its horse-drawn carriage tours that take visitors over cobblestone streets through quaint colonial neighbor-

hoods. The historic district consists of more than 2,000 preserved and restored buildings, 73 of which are pre-Revolutionary, 136 date from the 1700s, and 600 from the early 1800s.

Using guide services, boat and motorized trolley tours, or walking or bicycling with directions on audio cassettes, visitors can view Charleston's historic and stately buildings and churches. Opened in 1736, the Dock Street Theatre was one of the nation's first theaters. Later, the Planters Hotel, built around the ruins of the theater, was a gathering spot where "Planters Punch" is said to have originated; the hotel was remodeled into the Dock Street Theatre in the mid-1930s. Performances are currently given in the theater and its foyer. Completed in 1772 by Daniel Heyward, the Heyward-Washington House was the property of Thomas Heyward, delegate to the Continental Congress and signer of the Declaration of Independence; the house is furnished with period furnishings, and visitors may tour the only restored eighteenth-century kitchen open to the public in Charleston. The Aiken-Rhett House, built in 1817, contains some of the finest rooms of the Greek Revival and rococo styles in the city. Built between 1767 and 1771, the Old Exchange was the site of the election of South Carolina's delegates to the first Continental Congress in 1774. Although its Provost Dungeon was used by the British to confine prisoners during the Revolution, the U.S. Constitution was ratified at the Old Exchange in 1787; the building was later used as a customs house and post office and is now open to the public. The Avery Research Center for African-American History and Culture in the beautifully restored former Avery School preserves and makes public the historical and cultural heritage of South Carolina low country African Americans. The Cabbage Row section of Church St. was the inspirational setting for Gershwin's "Porgy and Bess" opera.

The oldest church in the city is St. Michael's Episcopal Church, which was completed in 1761. The edifice was designed after St. Martin's-in-the-Field in London; richly ornamented, the church includes a clock and bells operating since 1764. The mother church of the province, St. Philip's Episcopal Church originally stood on the site where St. Michael's Episcopal Church stands today; the present edifice was constructed between 1835 and 1838. St. Philip's churchyard contains the graves of John C. Calhoun, Secretary of War and Vice President of the United States; Edward Rutledge, signer of the Declaration of Independence; Charles Pinckney, signer of the U.S. Constitution; and DuBose Heyward, author of the novel *Porgy*. Construction for the Unitarian Church was begun in 1772, but work was stopped during the Revolution and not completed until 1787; remodeled in 1852, the church is noted for its fan-tracery ceiling and striking stained-glass windows. The Circular Congregational Church was designed by Robert Mills, built in 1806, and destroyed by fire in 1861; 30 years later the

**Magnolia Plantation and Gardens.**

original brick was used to erect the present building on the site. The First Baptist Church, also designed by Robert Mills, was completed in 1821; its original congregation founded the Anabaptist Church in 1682 in Kittery, Maine, and, fleeing persecution from the Puritans, settled in colonial Charles Towne. Congregation Beth Elohim, an imposing Greek Revival building dating from 1841, is the oldest synagogue in the United States in continuous use; this synagogue introduced a liberalized ritual using instrumental music during the service for the first time and is recognized as the birthplace of Reform Judaism in the nation.

Built before 1760, the perfectly scaled miniature of a Charleston "single house" known as the Thomas Elfe Workshop features cypress woodwork, collections of cabinetmaking tools, and excavated artifacts in a privately restored setting. The first Adam-style house in Charleston, the Joseph Manigault House, was designed by Charleston architect Gabriel Manigault; completed in 1803, the house is a parallelogram with half-moon bows at either end and features French, English, and Charleston-made furniture, as well as a restored garden. The Nathaniel Russell House, built in 1808, is noted for its astonishing flying staircase spirals, oval drawing rooms, and extensive interior detailing, as well as for its fine china, silver, and furniture. St. John's Lutheran Church, the mother church of the South Carolina Synod of the Lutheran Church in America, is noted for its wrought iron gates and fence; the first church on the site was built in 1759, and the present building dates from 1817. The French Huguenot Church was built in the 1840s; each spring a French liturgy service is held to commemorate the French Huguenots who fled religious persecution and settled in Charleston.

Visitors to Charleston will also enjoy the numerous gardens, parks, and plantations. Rainbow Row, north of the Battery along East Bay Street, is one of Charleston's most famous sections. Throughout the district are walled gardens, noted for their lavish floral displays and lacy ironwork. Charles Towne Landing is the original site of South Carolina's first permanent English settlement; this extensive park features the original colony's history at an interpretive center and reconstructed earthworks and palisade, as well as a replica of a seventeenth-century trading vessel moored in Old Towne Creek. Animals indigenous to South Carolina in 1670 roam in the Animal Forest behind concealed barriers, while the Settlers' Life Area invites visitors to participate in activities typical of early colonists' lives. Fort Sumter, where the Civil War's armed conflict began, is on a man-made island; visitors reach the island, now a National Monument, by boat from the Municipal Marina and Patriots Point. Snee Farm is a remnant of the plantation home of Charles Pinckney, a principal architect and signer of the U.S. Constitution. Boone Hall Plantation, McLeod Plantation on James Island, Drayton Hall, Magnolia Plantation and Middleton Place rice plantation are other area plantations not to be missed.

Caw Caw Interpretive Center is a 643-acre park highlighting Charleston's historical, natural and cultural heritage, especially the practice of rice cultivation brought to the country by Africans. Its eight miles of trails and boardwalks meander through marshland, swamp and oak forest. A famous landmark in Charleston is the Angel Oak; estimated to be about 1,400 years old, this giant tree has a circumference of 23 feet and a limb spread of 151 feet. James Island County Park allows crabbing and fishing from floating docks along tidal creeks and lagoons, and offers bike paths, pedal boats, kayaks, picnicking, and 50-foot climbing wall. Its Splash Zone waterpark is open seasonally. North Charleston Wannamaker County Park in North Charleston features family fun and a Whirlin' Waters waterpark. Other Charleston-area parks include Cypress Gardens and the Audubon Swamp Garden.

Among the tours offered to Charleston visitors is a "Ghosts of Charleston" guided walking tour of haunted sites. Other tours feature a history of the pirates of the area and the story of Charleston. Drayton Hall conducts daily walking tours of Charleston's preservation movement, architecture, and history departing from Marion Square. Carriage tours, van tours and water and harbor tours are also popular.

**Arts and Culture**

In 1735 Charleston's Dock Street Theatre opened as the first building in the American colonies to be used for theatrical productions. In that same year Charleston audiences saw the first opera performed in the New World, and by the 1790s the city supported a symphony orchestra. Jenny Lind, Sarah Bernhardt, Adelina Patti and other internationally known performers brought their talents to Charleston theaters in the nineteenth century. Local playwright and novelist DuBose Heyward collaborated with composer George Gershwin in the 1930s to produce the musical drama "Porgy and Bess," based on Heyward's novel *Porgy*.

Today the vitality of the arts in Charleston can be deduced from the tremendous success of the Spoleto Festival U.S.A., recognized as the world's most comprehensive arts festival. A version of an annual festival held in Spoleto, Italy, Charleston's Spoleto was brought to the city by Maestro Gian Carlo Menotti in 1977. For three weeks in late spring, Charleston, draped in banners and showered with fireworks, becomes a showplace for music, dance, opera, theater, and the visual arts. Internationally known performers entertain audiences in Charleston's historic churches, theaters, and plantations. Established works and performers are showcased; however, Spoleto is also an exciting opportunity for new artists and new works, and the festival generates a wide variety of activity. An imaginative spinoff to the Spoleto Festival is Piccolo Spoleto (piccolo is Italian for "small"), a festival that runs concurrently with Spoleto and features a full spectrum of artistic events, many of which are free to the public. Children and adults alike enjoy face-painting, jazz concerts, street musicians, organ and chamber music recitals, and street fairs.

Charleston is also home to two ballet companies. The Charleston Ballet Theatre presents numerous public performances each season plus matinees for school children, and the Robert Ivey Ballet is the company-in-residence at the College of Charleston. The Charleston Symphony Orchestra performs a September-through-May season and also performs masterworks, pops and children's concerts. The Charleston Symphony Orchestra, as a nonprofit organization, receives funding from the South Carolina Arts Commission, the National Endowment for the Arts, and the city of Charleston. World-famous musicians are brought to Charleston each year by the Charleston Concert Association. Broadway shows, Shakespeare, and eighteenth-century classics are all part of the repertoire of the Footlight Players, who offer six or more plays a season at the Footlight Players Theatre. The Charleston Stage Company is the company-in-residence at the Dock Street Theatre.

Museums and galleries in the region display a wide range of art and artifacts. The Charleston Museum, founded in 1773, is the country's oldest municipal museum; it focuses on South Carolina and the Southeast with displays on history, the arts, archaeology, and natural history, and houses a full-scale replica of the Confederate submarine *Hunley*. The Citadel Memorial Museum, located at the entrance to The Citadel, displays items pertaining to the history of the college and its graduates, including two of the largest flags from the Civil War; each Friday at 3:45 p.m. the Citadel Corps of Cadets conducts a dress parade. The American Military Museum displays uniforms and artifacts of soldiers from all the American wars. The Confederate Museum, housed in Market Hall, contains flags, uniforms, swords, and other Confederate memorabilia. Patriots Point Naval and Maritime Museum, two miles east of Charleston, is one of the world's largest naval and maritime museums; featured is the USS *Yorktown*, a retired aircraft carrier that saw service in World War II, Korea, and Vietnam, as well as the nuclear merchant ship *Savannah*, the World War II submarine *Clamagore*, and the destroyer *Laffey*, and displays of missiles, guns, mines, and aircraft. Built in 1713, the Old Powder Magazine, Charleston's oldest public building, was used during the Revolutionary War as a powder storehouse; it now serves as a historical museum. The Karpeles Manuscript Museum showcases the world's largest private collection of historically significant manuscripts. One of four sites that comprise the African-American National Heritage Museum, the Slave Mart Museum showcases the contributions of African Americans from 1670 to the civil rights movement. The Children's Museum of the Lowcountry has hands-on exhibits appealing to children through 12 years of age.

The South Carolina Aquarium on Charleston Harbor is Charleston's most visited attraction. Opened in May 2000,

its more than 60 exhibits showcase aquatic animals from river otters and sharks to loggerhead turtles. Special traveling exhibits are changed annually. Next door to the aquarium on Aquarium Wharf is the Charleston IMAX Theatre. Also for kids of all ages is the Edisto Island Serpentarium, a reptile park open in the summer months.

Featuring a fine collection of American paintings, Japanese woodblock prints, and sculpture, the Gibbes Museum of Art also offers an excellent collection of miniature portraits. The portrait gallery in the Council Chamber of the City Hall contains portraits of important leaders, including John Trumbull's portrait of George Washington and Samuel F. B. Morse's portrait of James Monroe. The City Gallery at the Dock Street Theatre exhibits the work of Charleston area artists, especially experimental and contemporary work.

**Festivals and Holidays**

In addition to the celebrated Spoleto Festival U.S.A., held in Charleston for three weeks in May and June (described above in Arts and Culture), the city hosts many other events throughout the year. Begun in 1984, the Moja Arts Festival is held for two weeks each October; Moja, the Swahili word meaning "the first" or "one," aptly describes this festival, which features the rich heritage of the African continent presented through dance, theater, films, lectures, and music. Charleston's International Film Festival runs each year for 10 days at the end of October and the beginning of November; at this world-class film festival, international film makers exhibit their work in restored eighteenth-century theaters and other historic buildings. For one week each mid-February Charleston hosts the Southeastern Wildlife Exposition; the largest show of its kind, the exposition brings more than 500 wildlife artists and artisans to a show of crafts, wildlife arts, and collectibles in Charleston's historic buildings. Also in February is the Bonterra Lowcountry Blues Bash, a 10-day festival featuring authentic blues music in selected clubs, hotels and restaurants.

The city's architectural heritage is showcased at various times throughout the year. Each March and April the Historic Charleston Foundation sponsors the Festival of Houses and Gardens, a series of walking tours of private homes and gardens in Charleston's historic district; in October the Preservation Society of Charleston sponsors the Fall Candlelight Tour of Homes and Gardens, 16 different walking tours featuring private houses and gardens in the historic district. Tickets for these tours, which are considered the best way to get an intimate view of the city, are highly sought after.

Other Charleston-area festivals include the Lowcountry Oyster Festival in early February; September's Scottish Games and Highland Gathering; and the Christmas in Charleston Festival, with its parade of boats, held every mid-November through mid-January. In April visitors can enjoy a little taste of Louisiana at the Charleston Lowcountry Cajun Festival at James Island County Park, featuring live Zydeco and Cajun music, authentic food, crafts, and activities for children. Also in April is the World Grits Festival in St. George. The Charleston Maritime Festival in May features tours of tall ships, shipyard tours, model ships, and family boatbuilding. Holiday Magic is a month-long celebration of the holidays downtown including special shopping days, a Christmas parade, entertainment, a parade of boats and a Taste of Charleston, celebrating the city's culinary delights. First Night Charleston features activities and entertainment throughout the city including music, dance, children's act ivities, and a parade, all on New Year's Eve.

## Sports for the Spectator

Baseball fans can watch the Charleston RiverDogs, the San Diego Padres' minor league team, face opponents at Joe Riley Stadium. Fans of professional ice hockey enjoy the South Carolina Stingrays, while professional soccer action is the forte of the Charleston Battery at Blackbaud Stadium on Daniel Island. Collegiate action is provided by teams fielded by the College of Charleston, The Citadel, and Charleston Southern University. Plantation Polo matches are held each Saturday in April, October, and November at Boone Hall Plantation in Mt. Pleasant.

## Sports for the Participant

Almost any sport that can be enjoyed under the sun is found in the Charleston area with its warm sun and sea breezes. Golf, tennis, horseback riding, swimming, sailing, water skiing, snorkeling, clamming, crabbing, fishing, hunting, bird watching—all are available within minutes of the city. Many visitors to the area are attracted by the challenge of its world-famous golf courses, some of which have been designed by celebrated course designers such as Tom Fazio, Gary Player, Jack Nicklaus, and Robert Trent Jones. The area's breathtaking coastal terrain and lowcountry woodlands offer great golfing. Many of the area's courses are on Isle of Palms, Kiawah and Seabrook Islands. Charleston's Department of Recreation operates the Tennis Center, which offers lessons, drills, clinics, and league play, as well as sanctioned tournaments. Most of the numerous public and private tennis courts in and around Charleston employ resident professionals. Young people may participate in soccer, football, volleyball, basketball, indoor soccer, and tennis. Softball and soccer leagues are also popular for adults, as is running. The challenging 10K Cooper River Bridge Run is held each year in April and attracts nearly 17,000 runners. For those who prefer the less strenuous activity of walking, several lovely parks invite strolling. Many of the parks have biking trails, and bicycles may be rented at several locations.

Charleston affords ample opportunity to pursue sports near, in, or on the water. The Charleston County Parks and Recreation Department operates Beachwalker Park at the south end of Kiawah Island, Palmetto Island County Park, Folly Beach County Park, and James Island County Park, for the enjoyment of swimming, as well as bicycling and other sports. The six barrier island beaches have been called the finest in the world. The Santee-Cooper Lake beaches near Moncks Corner and St. Stephen, and the network of inlets, coves, and tidal creeks provide water skiers with seemingly endless waterways. The public has access to 20 boat landings in the area. Sailing is the most popular summer sport in Charleston. Regattas are held throughout the season, drawing sailors from the entire southeast coast. Charleston Race Week in the Charleston Harbor in April draws 100 sailboats and crews of 500 sailors to the city each year. Private marinas along the coast provide facilities for both large and small boats. Surf and pier fishing are popular pastimes, and boats heading for deep water are a common sight in Charleston Harbor. Freshwater fishing for the famous land-locked striped bass in the freshwater lakes of the Santee-Cooper is a challenge few anglers can resist, and in season crabbing and shrimping attract even novices.

The opportunity to bag quail, duck, and deer lures hunters to local hunting clubs. For those who hunt with binoculars and cameras, Bulls Island, part of the Cape Romain National Wildlife Refuge, is a wintering ground for many species of migratory birds and a nesting area for sea turtles. Drum Island shelters the largest wading bird rookery in the eastern United States.

## Shopping and Dining

Two of the focal points for shopping in Charleston are the Old City Market area and King Street area, home to a number of antique shops. Antiques shoppers in Charleston can choose from more than a dozen shops with items ranging from crystal, china, and English mahogany furniture to oriental rugs. Charleston Place offers 50,000 square feet of elegant shops. Specialty shops abound, stocked with imported sportswear, resort wear, perfume, fine jewelry, lingerie, housewares, candies, and other items. The Charleston Farmers Market in Marion Square, open Saturdays from March through December, brims with fresh vegetables, fruit, and flowers. Juried arts and crafts are also available as are a variety of activities and amusements for children. The major malls are Citadel Mall, which contains three major anchors and more than 90 specialty shops, and Northwoods Mall, with more than 130 stores. Fountain Walk, Charleston's newest waterfront destination located at Aquarium Wharf, also has many shops and restaurants.

Eating well has long been a Southern tradition; in Charleston, however, that tradition was honored in homes, not in restaurants. The growth of tourism in the area has spurred development of new, first-rate eating establishments, and now visitors and locals alike reap the benefits: American, Southern, Chinese, Italian, French, Indian, Japanese, German, Greek, and Mexican cuisine are available. In historic Charleston the atmosphere lends a special touch to dining. Along Shem Creek in Mt. Pleasant, several seafood restaurants afford patrons a view of the shrimp boats moving over the water, while another establishment south of the city is actually built on piers above the ocean. Almost all restaurants, regardless of ambience, feature seafood, a South Carolina staple. The nearby waters provide millions of pounds of seafood in a harvest that includes shrimp, crabs, oysters, mussels, clams, whiting, spot, mullet, red snapper, grouper, king mackerel, flounder, and catfish. Visitors to Charleston can sample the famous she-crab soup and other low country specialties such as soft shell crab, shrimp and grits, and red rice.

***Visitor Information:*** Charleston Convention and Visitors Bureau, PO Box 975, Charleston, SC 29402; telephone (843)853-8000

# *Convention Facilities*

The largest meeting facility in Charleston is the Charleston Convention Center Complex. The center boasts a 76,960 square foot exhibition hall, a 25,000 square foot ballroom, 20 meeting rooms, and the attached 2,300-seat Performing Arts Theater. The 14,000-seat North Charleston Coliseum offers an additional 30,000 square feet of exhibition space and is connected by covered walkway to the convention center. Completing the complex is an adjacent 255-room Embassy Suites hotel which services the ballroom and meeting rooms at the Convention Center.

Lodgings in the Charleston area range from small and medium hotels to gleaming full-range hostelries and provide more than 11,300 hotel/motel rooms. That figure was expected to grow by seven percent by the year 2006. Charleston Place hotel boasts a ballroom with a capacity of 1,700 people and 18 other rooms of varying capacities. In the heart of this historic district and adjacent to the Old City Market and King Street shops, Charleston Place also contains a fitness center and a parking garage in addition to its 320 guest rooms. The Riviera at Charleston Place is the hotel's conference center located across the street, featuring 9,000 square feet of space, with an amphitheater, ballroom, and rooftop terrace.

Visitors who value history, luxury, and personal service will not be disappointed in Charleston, where numerous historic buildings have been restored and furnished with reproductions of Charleston antique furniture. These highly individualized accommodations couple old world, international charm with modern, expert, personal attention. For those who prefer to stay in a home when away from home, some 60 rooms are available on a bed-and-breakfast basis. Next to its historic district, Charleston is best known for its nearby pristine barrier islands: Isle of Palms, Sullivan's Island, Folly Beach, Kiawah Island, and Seabrook Island, featuring top-rated resort amenities. Along with beachfront meeting facilities and conference rooms, seaside facilities offer opportunities for world-class golf, tennis, sailing, and fishing, plus secluded beach walks, nature safaris, and fine dining.

***Convention Information:*** Charleston Convention and Visitors Bureau, PO Box 975, Charleston, SC 29402; telephone (843)853-8000. Charleston Area Convention Center Complex, 5001 Coliseum Drive, Charleston, SC 29418; Ed Riggs, Director of Sales, telephone (843)529-5011; fax (843)529-5040.

# *Transportation*

## Approaching the City

Visitors arriving at the Charleston International Airport will appreciate that the air exits, baggage claim area, and ground transportation facilities are all on one level for speedy accommodation to and from the terminal complex. The airport is located in North Charleston adjacent to the Charleston Air Force Base and uses the airport facilities and runways jointly with the USAF. Six commercial airlines (Continental Airlines, Delta, Northwest Airlines, Independence Air, U.S. Airways and United Express) offer national and international flights daily. Six private airports in the region can accommodate corporate and private aircraft.

For those motoring to Charleston, the major approaches from the north and south are U.S. Highway 17, a favorite coastal route, and I-95. Interstate 26, which terminates at Charleston, approaches from the west and links with Interstate 95 running north-south. U.S. Highway 52, paralleling Interstate 26 west of Charleston, and U.S. Highway 701 both approach Charleston from the north. Interstate 526, the Mark Clark Expressway, is a 19-mile freeway that forms a semicircle across the region from St. John's Island in the west to east of the Cooper River.

## Traveling in the City

The peninsular city of Charleston is laid out in a grid pattern; however, city blocks are not uniform in size or shape. The downtown/historic district is bisected by King Street and Meeting Street. In the north, East Bay Street branches off Meeting Street and becomes East Battery Street and Murray Boulevard around the edge of the Battery. Ashley and

Rutledge connect with the west end of Murray Boulevard. Major east-west streets are Calhoun, Broad, and Tradd.

Public bus service in Charleston is provided by the Charleston Area Regional Transportation Authority (CARTA). The Downtown Area Shuttle (DASH) trolley provides affordable and convenient transportation from the Visitors Center to various points throughout the Historic District. The Mount Pleasant Shuttle provides service from the airport to area hotels. Charleston is easily explored on foot.

# Communications

## Newspapers and Magazines

One major daily (morning) newspaper serves the area: *The Post & Courier*. Publications for the African American community are the *Charleston Black Times, The Charleston Chronicle* and *Charleston Trident Black Pages. The Charleston City Paper* and the *Charleston Jewish News* are other local papers. Magazines published in Charleston include *Commerce Magazine, Good Dog!, South Carolina History Magazine,* and *Charleston Magazine.*

## Television and Radio

The four television stations broadcasting from Charleston are network affiliates; additional television viewing is available through cable service. The city's seven radio stations broadcast educational, sports, religious, public, and special interest programming in addition to music ranging from popular and country-western to jazz and classical.

***Media Information:*** *The Post & Courier,* Evening Post Publishing Company, 134 Columbus Street, Charleston, SC 29403; telephone (843)577-7111

## Charleston Online

Charleston: A National Register of Historic Places Travel Itinerary. Available www.cr.nps.gov/nr/travel/charleston

Charleston Area Convention Center Complex. Available www.charlestonconvention.com

Charleston Area Regional Transportation Authority. Available www.ridecarta.com

Charleston Convention and Visitors Bureau. Available www.charlestoncvb.com

Charleston County Library. Available www.ccpl.org

Charleston Metro Chamber of Commerce. Available www.charlestonchamber.net

Charleston Regional Development Alliance. Available www.charleston-for-business.com

City of Charleston home page. Available www.ci.charleston.sc.us

*The Post & Courier.* Available www.charleston.net

## Selected Bibliography

Beardsley, John, ed., Roberta Kefalos et al., *Art and Landscape in Charleston and the Low Country: A Project of Spoleto Festival USA* (Washington, D.C.: James G. Trulove, 1998)

Jakes, John, *Charleston: A Novel* (New York: Signet Books, 2003)

Straight, Susan, *I Been in Sorrow's Kitchen and Licked Out All the Pots* (New York: Hyperion, 1992)

Vlach, John Michael, *Charleston Blacksmith: The Work of Philip Simmons* (Columbia, S.C.: University of South Carolina Press, 1992)

# Columbia

## *The City in Brief*

**Founded:** 1786 (chartered 1805)

**Head Official:** Mayor Bob Coble (D) (since 1990)

**City Population**
  **1980:** 101,229
  **1990:** 110,734
  **2000:** 116,278
  **2003 estimate:** 117,357
  **Percent change, 1990–2000:** 1.6%
  **U.S. rank in 1990:** 203rd
  **U.S. rank in 2000:** 198th (State rank: 1st)

**Metropolitan Area Population**
  **1980:** 410,000
  **1990:** 454,000
  **2000:** 536,691

  **Percent change, 1990–2000:** 18.4%
  **U.S. rank in 1980:** 82nd
  **U.S. rank in 1990:** 79th
  **U.S. rank in 2000:** 79th

**Area:** 125 square miles (2000)
**Elevation:** Ranges from 200 to 350 feet above sea level
**Average Annual Temperature:** 65° F
**Average Annual Precipitation:** 50.14 inches

**Major Economic Sectors:** government, wholesale and retail trade, services
**Unemployment rate:** 4.9% (December 2004)
**Per Capita Income:** $18,853 (1999)

**2002 FBI Crime Index Total:** 10,307

**Major Colleges and Universities:** University of South Carolina, Benedict College, Columbia College

**Daily Newspaper:** *The State*

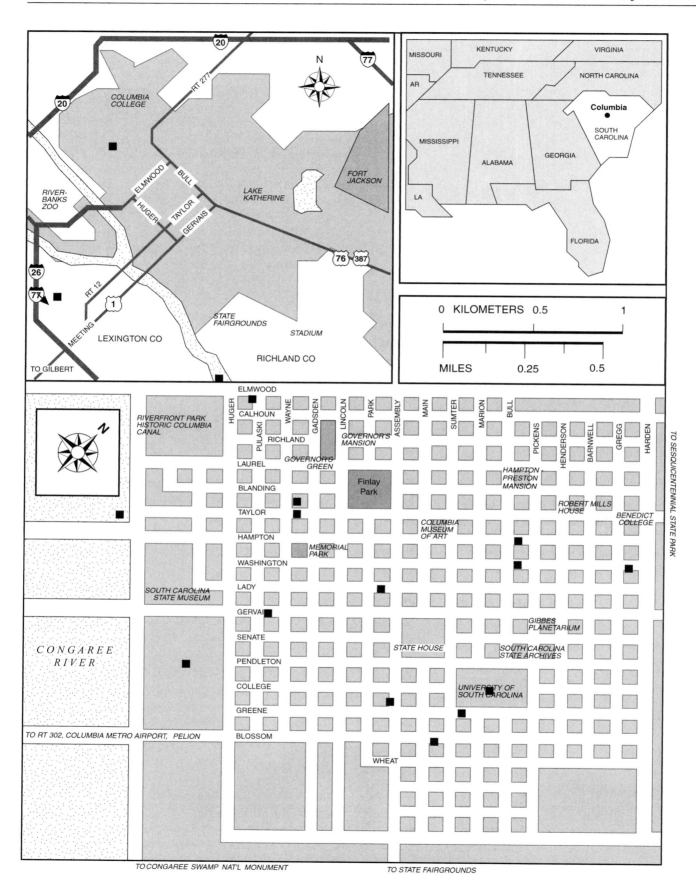

# Introduction

The capital city of South Carolina is a major industrial, cultural, and educational center located in the heart of a fertile farm region. The romance of the nineteenth century is writ large in the buildings and historical markers that grace its broad, tree-lined streets. Chosen as a compromise site for the interests of wealthy low country planters and fiercely independent small farmers and merchants from the hill country, this city located directly in the center of the state was specifically designed to serve as its seat of government. From the beautifully preserved antebellum architecture to the riverbanks and swamps to the State House with its battle-scarred walls and rich interiors, Columbia is an enchanting city. Columbia was ranked 2nd of "America's Most Livable Mid-Sized Communities" in 2005 by the national non-profit organization Partners for Livable Communities.

# Geography and Climate

Columbia is situated near the geographic center of South Carolina, midway between New York City and Miami. Set near the "fall line" dividing the South Carolina Piedmont and Coast Plains, the rolling hills surrounding the city slope from approximately 350 feet above sea level in the city's northernmost part to 200 feet above sea level in the southeast. The Appalachian and Blue Ridge Mountains northwest of the city often delay the approach of cold weather, and the winters are mild with the lowest temperatures extending from November to mid-March. Below-freezing temperatures are experienced during only one-third of the winter days. Nearly every year brings one day with a one-inch snowfall. Temperatures in spring range from March's occasional cold snap to warm, pleasant days in much of May. Long summers are the norm, and short-lived late afternoon thundershowers a common occurrence. Typically, there are about 6 days of over-100 degree weather in summer, but the heat is eased by frequent summer showers. Sunny days and lack of rain characterize Columbia's typically beautiful fall weather.

**Area:** 125 square miles (2000)

**Elevation:** ranges from 200 to 350 above sea level

**Average Temperatures:** January, 44.7° F; July, 81.0° F; annual average, 65° F

**Average Annual Precipitation:** 50.14 inches

# History

Located at the middle of South Carolina, the city of Columbia was carved out of the countryside by order of the state legislature, which wanted to establish a new capital more centrally situated than Charleston. By that time, the area had been important in the state's development for more than a century. Early settlers were mostly Scots-Irish, German, and English farmers who moved to the hills of northwestern South Carolina, having little in common with the wealthy planters of Charleston. "The Congarees," a frontier fort on the river's west bank, was the head of navigation on the Santee River system. In 1754 a ferry service was initiated to connect the fort with the settlement that was developing on the east bank's higher ground.

The new capital, named Columbia in honor of Christopher Columbus, was set on Taylor's Hill where the Broad and Saluda rivers merge to form the Congaree River. The General Assembly moved to Columbia in 1791. History tells of a visit by George Washington during that year as part of his tour of South Carolina.

### Development of America's First "Planned City"

One of the first planned cities in America, Columbia was laid out in a two-mile square surrounding the site of the State House. The city's streets, designed in a grid, were named for heroes of the Revolution and for the state's agricultural products, such as rice, wheat, blossom, and indigo.

By the early 1880s the town had become an agricultural center, and soon the state had become the leading cotton producer in the nation. The first textile mill was introduced in 1832, and saw mills, cotton gins, tanneries, carriage manufacturers, and iron foundries were soon to follow. With the establishment of steamship connections to the Congaree and Santee rivers, many of the city's cotton merchants handled shipments that earlier had moved overland to the port at Charleston. South Carolina College (now the University of South Carolina) was founded in 1801, and the ensuing close relationship between the college, the city, and the legislature endures to the present day.

By mid-century, the local economy was strengthened by growing accessibility to the eastern United States via the railroad. A distinctive style of architecture, known as Columbia Cottage, had emerged. To help assuage the often unpleasant summer heat, builders designed a structure to maximize the effect of natural breezes. The building featured a raised cottage with an enclosed basement above the ground, halls from front to back, windows that reached the floor, and ceilings often 15 feet high.

## Civil War Brings Destruction

Columbia, with a population of 8,000, was the site of the First Secession Convention and was instrumental in establishing the Confederacy and keeping it supplied with uniforms, swords, cannonballs, and other supplies over the course of the Civil War. The city was destroyed by the fiery rampage of General William T. Sherman in 1865, which left almost everything in ruins except the university. Reconstruction was a time of great hardship, but by the 1890s the city finally reemerged as a center of agricultural commerce.

## Major Fort Important to City

By 1900 large cotton mills had been built and nearly 9,000 people worked in the city's mill district. The period prior to World War I and until the Great Depression of the 1930s was one of prosperity. Trade was growing, banks and hospitals multiplied, and the city became the state's business center. East of the city the U.S. Army built Fort Jackson, presently one of the country's largest infantry training bases. Thanks to a diversified economy, the city survived the Great Depression without as much pain as some other areas of the country. Between 1940 and 1950 the population grew by more than one-third, in part due to Fort Jackson's role in the training of soldiers for World War II.

## Economic and Social Progress Made Since Mid-Century

By the post-War 1950s, small and medium-sized factories were developing, and new industries such as electronics, military equipment, textiles, cameras, and structural steel further diversified the economy. During the period of the civil rights struggle in the 1960s, Mayor Lester Bates and a biracial committee of 60 citizens worked together to quietly and systematically encourage the desegregation of the city. By 1963 the university was integrated, and in 1964, 24 African American students entered previously all-white public schools.

The 1970s saw the creation of downtown's Main Street Mall and the completion of Riverbanks Zoological Park. In subsequent years Riverfront Park was developed, the Koger Center for Performing Arts opened, and new interstate highways made the city even more accessible regionally and nationally. Today, more people are moving to Columbia and its crime rate has fallen 25 percent. The city is making strides to revitalize old neighborhoods, improve its city center streetscapes and make the area's river system more accessible and enjoyable for its residents. Foreign investors are realizing the benefits of locating their manufacturing and production businesses to the area and Columbia is becoming a leading research and technology center of the region.

***Historical Information:*** South Carolina (State) Department of Archives and History, Archives and History Center, 8301

Parklane Rd., Columbia, SC 29223; telephone (803) 896-6100. South Carolina Confederate Relic Room and Museum Library, Columbia Mills Building, 301 Gervais Street, Columbia, SC 29214-0001; telephone (803)737-8095

# *Population Profile*

## Metropolitan Area Residents
*1980:* 410,000
*1990:* 453,932
*2000:* 536,691
*Percent change, 1990–2000:* 18.4%
*U.S. rank in 1980:* 82nd
*U.S. rank in 1990:* 79th
*U.S. rank in 2000:* 79th

## City Residents
*1980:* 101,229
*1990:* 110,734
*2000:* 116,278
*2003 estimate:* 117,357
*Percent change, 1990–2000:* 1.6%
*U.S. rank in 1990:* 203rd
*U.S. rank in 2000:* 198th (State rank: 1st)

*Density:* 928.6 people per square mile (2000)

*Racial and ethnic characteristics* (2000)
 White: 57,236
 Black or African American: 53,465
 American Indian and Alaska Native: 296
 Asian: 2,008
 Native Hawaiian and other Pacific Islander: 104
 Hispanic or Latino (may be of any race): 3,520
 Other: 1,582

*Percent of residents born in state:* 59.2% (2000)

*Age characteristics* (2000)
 Population under 5 years old: 6,478
 Population 5 to 9 years old: 6,495
 Population 10 to 14 years old: 6,195
 Population 15 to 19 years old: 13,248
 Population 20 to 24 years old: 17,556
 Population 25 to 34 years old: 19,541
 Population 35 to 44 years old: 15,466
 Population 45 to 54 years old: 12,381
 Population 55 to 59 years old: 3,948
 Population 60 to 64 years old: 2,988
 Population 65 to 74 years old: 5,846
 Population 75 to 84 years old: 4,595
 Population 85 years and older: 1,541
 Median age: 28.6 years (2000)

*Births* (Richland County, 2002)
Total number: 4,375

*Deaths* (Richland County, 2002)
Total number: 2,582 (of which, 29 were infants under the age of 1 year)

*Money income* (1999)
Per capita income: $18,853
Median household income: $31,141
Total households: 41,960

*Number of households with income of . . .*
less than $10,000: 7,012
$10,000 to $14,999: 3,535
$15,000 to $24,999: 6,666
$25,000 to $34,999: 5,976
$35,000 to $49,999: 6,409
$50,000 to $74,999: 5,721
$75,000 to $99,999: 2,647
$100,000 to $149,999: 2,128
$150,000 to $199,999: 760
$200,000 or more: 1,116

*Percent of families below poverty level:* 17.0% (38.1% of which were female householder families in poverty)

*2002 FBI Crime Index Total:* 10,307

# Municipal Government

The city of Columbia has a mayor-council form of government. The mayor is elected at large and there are six council members, four elected from districts and two elected at large; all are elected to staggered four-year terms.

**Head Official:** Mayor Bob Coble (D) (since 1990; current term expires 2006)

**Total Number of City Employees:** 1,700 (2005)

*City Information:* Columbia City Hall, 1737 Main Street, PO Box 147, Columbia, SC 29217; telephone (803)545-3000

# Economy

## Major Industries and Commercial Activity

Columbia prides itself on a diverse and stable economy based on jobs in local and state government, manufacturing, and services and on being the site of the Fort Jackson military base. In recent years, distribution, manufacturing, and research and development have increased that diversity. The city is relying on its technology infrastructure, active entrepreneurial community, major research university, and diverse quality of life to attract and keep new business. Columbia's diverse economic base includes 31 *Fortune* 500 companies, and the city serves as a service center for the insurance, telecommunications, computer, and real estate industries. Dozens of international companies from Australia, France, Italy, Germany, Great Britain, Denmark, Japan, South Korea, Belgium, Luxembourg, Taiwan and Canada have operations in the region.

The University of South Carolina bolsters the economy through the expenditures of its more than 32,000 students as well as 7,900 faculty, staff, and support personnel. Fort Jackson, which is located within the city's boundaries, employs more than 4,400 civilians and spends nearly $716.9 million annually for salaries, utilities, contracts and other services, much of it in Columbia. It hires local firms for construction work and buys its supplies from local businesses.

Ample rainfall and the temperate climate promote the area's success as an agricultural center. The wholesale trade industry, which began its growth in the years prior to World War I, benefits from the fact that approximately 70 percent of the nation's population and 70 percent of its industrial/commercial power are within 24-hour ground access.

*Items and goods produced:* electronics, military equipment, marine products, chemicals, processed foods

### Incentive Programs—New and Existing Companies

*Local programs*—The City of Columbia Economic Development Office stands ready to provide a wide range of services to companies interested in the Columbia region; incentives range from new business tax incentives to site planning. The Central Carolina Alliance is a public/private partnership engaged in the recruitment of capital investment and jobs to the Columbia region.

*State programs*—South Carolina is a "right-to-work" state and has the lowest unionization rate in the country at only 3.7 percent. The State provides a variety of business incentives. South Carolina emphasizes helping companies expand by offering low tax structures. The following incentives and financing sources may be available to qualifying companies: 20 percent state tax credit for development or lease of qualified office facilities; elimination of inventory, intangibles, unitary and value added taxes; job creation tax credits for five years up to $1,500 per employee; the Childcare Program Credit; Sales Tax Exemptions on a variety of production goods; fee-in-lieu of taxes option for investment and job creation; Enterprise Zones incentive; and property tax incentives.

*Job training programs*—The Columbia Work Initiative Program is a work training program developed by the City of Columbia and the Sumter-Columbia Empowerment Zone. It provides opportunities for empowerment zone residents to develop marketable skills in carpentry and masonry to supply area industry with a pool of trained workers. South Carolina's Special Schools program, a division of the State Board of Technical and Comprehensive Education, assumes the entire training responsibility and designs programs to suit a company's needs. The program may include trainee recruitment and testing, instructor recruitment and training, provision of training sites, development of instructional materials, and complete program management. South Carolina's Center for Accelerated Technology Training (CATT) pre-employment training program provides new and expanding companies with a fully trained and productive work force on the first day of operation. In Columbia, the Midlands Education and Business Alliance is one of the 16 School-to-Work consortiums, which offer pre-employment, internships and worker training programs to ensure that high school graduates are prepared to enter the workforce. South Carolina administers the Job Training Partnership Program.

## Development Projects

Attracting area residents to live and work in Columbia is a main objective of the city's Economic Development Office. Its City Center Residential Initiative aims to increase the number of people living in the heart of the city. A 40,000 square foot Confederate Printing Plant has been redeveloped into a Publix grocery store, which opened in 2004 to accommodate the needs of urban residents. This redevelopment is part of an effort to revitalize the Huger Street corridor, which once housed a steel business. Other developments in the corridor include two office buildings and two multi-million dollar residential projects. Six other properties in the corridor have potential for redevelopment.

The Three Rivers Greenway is a multi-year ongoing project which has brought together a partnership of city and county governments and other area institutions to develop a 12-mile linear park system for the 90-mile interconnecting Saluda, Congaree and Broad Rivers. Conceived in 1995, the River Alliance has constructed parks, river walks, an amphitheater, bike lane, running trail, housing communities, and water sport activities along the rivers. In 2005, plans for student housing apartments and an upscale condominium project near the river were underway. Work on the Columbia side of the river is scheduled in phases.

The Charles R. Drew Wellness Center, scheduled for completion in late 2005, is one of the city's newest municipal projects. The 40,000 square foot complex features an indoor swimming pool and gymnasium, cardio/weight room, jogging track, and meeting and activity rooms. The Five Points District, Downtown Columbia's shopping and nightlife destination, is the beneficiary of a $28 million revitalization. Scheduled for completion in mid-2006, the two year project is designed to renovate and rejuvenate not only the streets, sidewalks, streetlights and signage, but to also repair some major underground sewer lines and other utility lines. Columbia's Main Street is also undergoing a renovation with new landscaping, paving, lighting and the installation of a fiber duct bank. Lady Street, Harden Street, and North Main Street are other city roads which have recently benefited from streetscape improvements. Other economic development projects on the city's drawing board include a plan to develop a technology-focused industrial park and plans to attract research projects to the University of South Carolina and the community.

***Economic Development Information:*** Economic Development Division, Greater Columbia Chamber of Commerce, 930 Richland Street, P.O. Box 1360, Columbia, SC 29202-9896; telephone (803)733-1110. City of Columbia Economic Development Office; telephone (803)734-2700; email development@columbiasc.net.

## Commercial Shipping

With the benefit of its location where three major interstate highways cross within its regional boundaries and two rail systems operate, Columbus is positively positioned for businesses that require major transportation access. The Columbia Metropolitan Airport handles more than 10,400 tons of cargo annually plus an additional 93 tons of airmail. The airport's Foreign Trade Zone #27 is a 108-acre tract with a 40,000 square foot warehouse and office building and an additional 52,000 square feet of multi-tenant space. The U.S. Customs Services offices, Port of Columbia, are also located in this zone along with several Custom House brokers. Columbia is served by more than 60 motor freight carriers and is the site of United Parcel Service's southeastern regional air cargo hub, ensuring low costs and timely delivery for local industry. Charleston, the second busiest seaport on the east coast, is just 110 miles away.

## Labor Force and Employment Outlook

Columbia boasts a large and growing workforce, especially in the 20-to-40 age group. Many retirees from Fort Jackson choose to stay in the area, adding skill and maturity to the available workforce. Workers are described as efficient and productive, and work stoppages are rare. *Forbes* magazine ranked Columbia 17th of the best cities for business climate in 2003. South Carolina is a right-to-work state and is one of the country's least unionized states. The Columbia area workforce is also an educated one, ranking 23rd in the nation for doctoral degrees and 32nd for college degrees, according to the Columbia Office of Economic Development.

While Columbia has been successful in creating jobs, it has not achieved the same success in raising its residents' standard of living. Growth in wages in the state from 1994-2004 fell below the national average. Per capita income was 80 percent of the national average. The Columbia region, historically insulated because of State government, the University of South Carolina, and Fort Jackson, lost more than 10,000 jobs between 2002 and 2004. The city's challenge is to create more high-paying jobs, according to Mayor Bob Coble in his 2004 State of the City address. To that end, the city has plans to increasingly focus on attracting technology companies to the area and especially to the University of South Carolina Research Campus.

The following is a summary of data regarding the Columbia metropolitan area labor force, 2003 annual averages.

*Size of nonagricultural labor force:* 303,800

*Number of workers employed in . . .*
　　*construction and mining:* 17,400
　　*manufacturing:* 23,800
　　*trade, transportation and utilities:* 55,800
　　*information:* 5,600
　　*financial activities:* 25,200
　　*professional and business services:* 33,800
　　*educational and health services:* 32,800
　　*leisure and hospitality:* 26,200
　　*other services:* 9,300
　　*government:* 73,800

*Average hourly earnings of production workers employed in manufacturing:* not reported

*Unemployment rate:* 4.9% (December 2004)

| *Largest private sector employers (Greater Columbia)* | *Number of employees* |
|---|---|
| Palmetto Health | 7,500 |
| Blue Cross & Blue Shield of SC | 5,100 |
| Richland School District One | 5,000 |
| SCE&G | 4,000 |
| United Parcel Service | 3,528 |
| Wachovia Bank of South Carolina | 3,422 |
| Richland School District Two | 2,500 |
| Branch Banking and Trust Company | 2,093 |
| School District Five of Lexington and Richland Counties | 2,000 |
| Santee Cooper | 1,650 |

### Cost of Living

The following is a summary of data regarding several key cost of living factors for the Columbia area.

*2004 (3rd Quarter) ACCRA Average House Price:* $246,380

*2004 (3rd Quarter) ACCRA Cost of Living Index:* 96.2 (U.S. average = 100.0)

*State income tax rate:* Ranges from 2.5% to 7.0%

*State sales tax rate:* 5.0%

*Local income tax rate:* none

*Local sales tax rate:* none

*Property tax rate:* Millage rates set annually by local government tax authorities and applied to 4.0% of fair market value.

***Economic Information:*** Greater Columbia Chamber of Commerce, 930 Richland, Columbia, SC 29202; telephone (803)733-1110

# Education and Research

### Elementary and Secondary Schools

Richland County has three school districts: Richland School District One and Two and School District Five of Lexington and Richland Counties. Richland School District Two is a suburban school district serving the rapidly growing northeast section of Richland County. Thirteen of its eighteen schools have been named national Blue Ribbon Schools by the U.S. Department of Education's Excellence in Education Program. Three elementary schools and two middle schools have been named ''Palmetto's Finest schools.''

The following is a summary of data regarding Richland County School District Two as of the 2003–2004 school year.

*Total enrollment:* 18,969

*Number of facilities*
　　*elementary schools:* 13
　　*middle schools:* 5
　　*high schools:* 4
　　*other:* 1 child development center with 5 satellites districtwide; 2 magnet schools; 1 secondary alternative school for non-violent, chronically disruptive students

*Student/teacher ratio:* 20.7:1

*Teacher salaries*
　　*average:* $41,321

*Funding per pupil:* $7,547

Greater Columbia is home to 72 private and parochial schools.

***Public Schools Information:*** Richland School District Two, 6831 Brookfield Road, Columbia, SC 29206; telephone (803)787-1910

### Colleges and Universities

Columbia is the home of ten institutions of higher learning, including the University of South Carolina (USC), which has gained regional recognition for its programs in law, marketing, geography, medicine, marine science, nursing, engineering, business administration, and social work. The Columbia campus of South University offers programs in accounting, business administration, computer information systems, medical assisting and paralegal/legal studies and a paralegal certificate program. Baptist-affiliated Benedict College, a traditionally African American college, offers four-year degrees in more than 30 majors. Columbia College, a Methodist-related women's liberal arts school, offers bachelor's of arts and science and master's of arts degrees in such areas as public affairs and human relations, business administration, and communications, as well as a coeducational Evening College and Graduate School. Allen University, an African Methodist Episcopal four-year college, offers liberal arts and teacher education. Midlands Technical College, a two-year multi-campus college, offers technical and academic training. Other local colleges are Newberry College, a Lutheran liberal arts college; Columbia International University and Lutheran Theological Southern Seminary, both specializing in religious studies; and Columbia Junior College, offering associate degrees in eleven professional programs.

### Libraries and Research Centers

In addition to its main library, the Richland County Public Library has nine branches and a bookmobile. The library has more than 1.13 million volumes and subscribes to 2,840 periodical titles. It also has more than 45,554 audio materials and 30,630 visual materials. They include microforms, audio cassettes/tapes, compact discs, CD-ROM titles, maps, and art reproductions. Its special collections include a local history collection, large print books, and rare and out-of-print books. The library offers many programs for children and adults, including frequent lectures by authors. The library enjoys many programming partnerships with the University of South Carolina (USC), the Historic Columbia Foundation, and the Cultural Council of Richland and Lexington counties. Since 1987 it has co-sponsored the annual A(ugusta) Baker's Dozen—a Celebration of Stories with the College of Library and Information Science Department at USC. The celebration honors Augusta Baker and features well-known, award-winning authors and illustrators of children's books and outstanding storytellers each year.

Also located in Columbia is the South Carolina State Library, which houses nearly 250,000 volumes, more than 26,000 periodicals, plus microfilm, government publications, and audio visual materials. Its special collections include ERIC, Foundation Center Cooperating Collection,

South Carolina collection, and state documents. A special feature of the library's web site home page is the South Carolina Reference Room, a guide to a broad range of information on state topics. The University of South Carolina campus library system has more than 2 million volumes and almost 17,000 periodical subscriptions.

Many of Columbia's research centers are affiliated within the University of South Carolina (USC). More than 80 institutes and centers comprise the University's research effort. In 2004, USC received $149 million in federal, state and private funding for its research, outreach and training programs. Notable among the funding recipients is the University's NanoCenter which is engaged in researching the applications of the world's smallest electronic circuits.

***Public Library Information:*** Richland County Public Library, 1431 Assembly Street, Columbia, SC 29201; telephone (803)799-9084; fax (803)929-3448. South Carolina State Library, PO Box 11469, Columbia, SC 29211; telephone (803)734-8666.

# Health Care

The city of Columbia prides itself on being a regional leader in providing quality health care services. The University of South Carolina's School of Medicine adds invaluable research and training resources. The university is one of the few in the country offering a graduate program in genetic counseling. Palmetto Health is the State's largest and most comprehensive health care systems; its institutions in Columbia include Palmetto Richland Memorial Hospital, a 649-bed regional community teaching hospital serving all of South Carolina, and Palmetto Baptist Medical Center with 489 beds. The Dorn Veterans Affairs Medical Center complex includes a 216-bed hospital and 5 community outpatient clinics located in Anderson, Florence, Greenville, Orangeburg, Rock Hill, and Sumter. Other Columbia hospitals are the William S. Hall Psychiatric Institute providing psychiatric and chemical addiction inpatient care for children and adolescents; G. Werber Bryan Psychiatric Hospital for adults; and the 64-bed Moncrief Army Community Hospital in Fort Jackson, among others. Also serving the health care needs of Columbia metropolitan area residents are Fairfield Memorial Hospital, a 50-bed hospital located in Winnsboro; Providence Hospital and Providence Heart Institute, a nationally recognized referral center for the diagnosis, prevention, and treatment of cardiovascular disease; and Lexington Medical Center, offering specialized care for breast cancer and prostate problems, plus advanced cardiac, vascular and pulmonary rehabilitation, outpatient surgery, a state-of-the-art emergency department, outpatient surgery and diagnostics, radiation oncology, radiology, surgery, and physical therapy.

# *Recreation*

### Sightseeing

Columbia has an interesting array of historical, cultural, and recreational sites to delight both visitors and residents. Consistently rated as one of the top travel attractions in the Southeast, the Riverbanks Zoo and Botanical Garden is home to more than 2,000 mammals, reptiles, fish, and invertebrates. Animals roam freely in the zoo's unique recreated environment. Visitors can watch the daily feeding of penguins and sea lions. Across the Saluda River from the zoo, the Riverbanks Botanical Garden features 70 acres of woodlands, gardens, historic ruins, and plant collections. Gibbes Planetarium, located within the Columbia Museum of Art on the campus of the University of South Carolina, provides spectacular views of the skies through its permanent and changing programs.

Columbia's newest family attraction is the EdVenture Children's Museum. Opened to the public in November 2003, the $19.4 million facility is located next to the South Carolina State Museum and features 74,000 square feet of hands-on exhibit space in 8 indoor and outdoor galleries, as well as laboratories and other visitor amenities. Special exhibit areas are designed to appeal to very young children.

The Historic Columbia Foundation conducts bus and walking tours of the city and heritage education programs (such as the Black Heritage Trail). An especially popular sight is Governor's Green, a nine-acre complex made up of the 1830 Caldwell-Boylston House, the 1854 Lace House, and Governor's Mansion, home to the state's first family since 1868. Other historic houses are the Hampton-Preston Mansion, an elegant, restored antebellum society home, and the fully restored and furnished boyhood home of Woodrow Wilson. The State Archives has contemporary exhibits and houses the state and county official records. The South Carolina Criminal Justice Hall of Fame traces the history of law enforcement, including the gun collection of Melvin Purvis, the FBI agent who captured John Dillinger. The Robert Mills Historic House and Park, designed by the state's most famous architect, has been refurbished with period pieces and has park gardens covering an entire block.

### Arts and Culture

Columbia boasts an active arts environment. The showcase of Columbia's cultural sites is the Koger Center for the Performing Arts, an acoustically excellent facility with three-tier seat-

ing for 2,300 patrons. The center is home to the South Carolina Philharmonic, which presents Saturday Symphonies, Friday Classics, and Philharmonic Pops. The Bolshoi Ballet, the Polish National Radio Symphony Orchestra, and many others perform at the Township Auditorium.

Theater in its many forms is available from the city's 10 professional theater groups. The Longstreet Theatre, an 1855 Greek Revival structure, is the site for many University of South Carolina-sponsored productions at its theater-in-the-round. Trustus Theatre presents quality alternative productions with a different show each month. The Town Theatre, the oldest continuously operating community theater in the nation, stages Broadway comedies and musicals. The Workshop Theatre offers modern and classical productions by its amateur group. The Chapin Community Theatre performs plays for children as well as musicals and dramatic productions. The South Carolina Shakespeare Company performs for a week in October at Finlay Park. Columbia Marionette Theatre is one of only 20 such theaters in the country.

The Columbia Museum of Art, the city's premier museum, maintains more than 5,000 objects, including pieces from the Baroque and Renaissance periods. The museum also offers a hands-on children's gallery and traveling exhibits, as well as European and American works of the eighteenth and nineteenth centuries, decorative arts, and contemporary crafts. The South Carolina State Museum, located in a renovated textile mill, contains a comprehensive array of exhibits on art, natural history, and science and technology. The Mann-Simons Cottage, a fine example of the Columbia Cottage style of architecture, is the site of the Museum of African-American Culture, which contains the history of the lives of an African American family in the antebellum period. The Confederate Relic Room and Museum contains relics from the Colonial period to the Space Age, with special emphasis on Civil War objects.

The original 1801 campus of the University of South Carolina is today known as the Historic Horseshoe. It has been restored and is open for tours. There visitors will find the McKissick Museum, which features changing exhibitions of art, science, and regional history and folk art; as well as the Baruch Silver Collection, the Mineral Library, and Fluorescent Minerals and Gemstones. The history of the American soldier is the focus of the Fort Jackson Museum, which displays photos, weapons, uniforms, and military items from the Revolution onward. Memorial Park is the site of the South Carolina Vietnam Monument, the largest monument of its type outside Washington, D.C.

### Festivals and Holidays

The wearin' of the green is a common sight at the parade, children's areas, and arts and music events that highlight Columbia's St. Patrick's Day Celebration in Five Points.

The South Carolina State Capitol building.

The Earth Day festival in Finlay Park brings together environmental booths and traditional festival favorites. Also held in spring is the Riverfest Celebration featuring a 5K run, music, arts and crafts and food specialties. River activities, rides, and food are the focus of the Cayce Congaree Carnival and A Taste of Columbia in September at the Convention Center. Dance, arts and crafts, music, and a road race combine to celebrate spring's Mayfest. The spectacle of decorated boats, a parade, and fireworks light up the July Fourth celebration at Lake Murray. Peanuts galore—roasted, boiled and raw—are the stars of August's Pelion Peanut Party. Autumnfest in uptown Columbia in October brings street dances, music, arts and crafts, and catfish races to the grounds of the historic Hampton Mansion and Robert Mills House. Columbia's music festivals include the Three Rivers Music Festival, three days of national and regional musical acts, and Main Street Jazz which attracts world-renown jazz musicians. One of the biggest events in Columbia is the ten-day South Carolina State Fair in October, which draws more than one-half million visitors. The fair features agricultural and handicraft displays, rides, and entertainment. Jubilee: Festival of Heritage celebrates African American heritage with crafts, storytelling, music and dance. Vista Lights festival combines walking tours of area homes and musical entertainment with carriage rides through the antique district. The Christmas season is ushered in by December's Christmas Candlelight Tour of Historic Houses and Lights Before Christmas at the Riverbanks Zoo.

## Sports for the Spectator

Sporting News' "Best Sports Cities 2002" ranked Columbia 54th among 300 U.S. and Canadian cities for its sports climate. The Columbia Inferno tear up the ice at the Carolina Coliseum. The Inferno are a professional hockey team in the East Coast Hockey League. The University of South Carolina's Fighting Gamecocks play football at the Williams-Brice Stadium. The university's basketball team plays at the Frank McGuire Arena in the Carolina Coliseum, and its soccer team is on view at "The Graveyard." Male and female intercollegiate sports teams from other local colleges offer sporting opportunities for spectators. Major League baseball, NFL and NBA teams all play within easy driving distance in nearby Charlotte and Atlanta.

## Sports for the Participant

Columbia's mild climate encourages outdoor recreation year-round. Water skiers, campers, windsurfers, fishermen, boating enthusiasts, bikers, and runners enjoy the myriad regional and municipal parks in and around Columbia. Lake Murray boasts 540 miles of scenic shoreline perfect for boaters of all types. Dreher Island State Park on its shores offers RV and primitive camping, fishing, boating and swimming. Columbia's Saluda River, a navigable whitewater river with thrilling rides down the rapids, also offers gentler waters for canoeists and rafters. The 1,445-acre Sesquicentennial State Park offers nature trails, camping and picnic sites, swimming, fishing, and miniature golf. The Congaree National Park and Monument, located 20 miles southeast of the city, is a national monument offering nature walks and self-guided canoe trails affording views of old-growth bottomland hardwood forest.

The City of Columbia maintains nearly 50 parks and green spaces. Finlay Park in the downtown area is host to many festivals and celebrations. Granby Park is the gateway to the rivers in Columbia. Memorial Park is a tribute to those South Carolinians who served their country. Soccer enthusiasts enjoy the nine fields located at Owens Park. Winding along the Congaree River is the Riverfront Park and Historic Columbia Canal. Planned around the city's original 1906 waterworks plant, the park features an old pump house and jogging and bicycle paths. City and county parks offer organized baseball, youth and adult basketball, youth football, soccer, softball, volleyball, racquetball, and roller skating, as well as a variety of other activities. City residents enjoy five public and eight semi-private golf courses, plus public tennis courts and swimming pools. Private tennis and golf clubs extend the recreational choices. Several local private golf clubs offer special golf packages to visitors. Rock climbers can master their skills at the Earth Treks Climbing Center, which features two large indoor climbing walls. The new Charles R. Drew Wellness Center offers indoor swimming, jogging, and weight training.

## Shopping and Dining

Shopping is a many-dimensional affair in a city that offers spacious malls, fashionable boutiques, specialty stores, antique shops, and antique malls. Richland Mall features Belk's, Parisian, and The Bombay Co. among other stores. The most popular shopping center is Columbiana Centre, with more than 100 specialty shops. Columbia Place is the region's largest, offering more than 100 specialty stores. Old Mill Antique Mall and City Market Antique Mall offer out-of-the-ordinary shopping experiences. The Dutch Square Center's major shops include Belk's, Burlington Coat Factory, and Office Depot. The State Farmers Market, open daily across from the USC Football Stadium, is one of the largest produce markets in the southeast.

Dining out in Columbia presents myriad possibilities, from the fresh seafood provided by its proximity to the state's Atlantic Coast, to a variety of ethnic cuisines such as Greek, Chinese, Cajun, or Japanese, as well as traditional Southern. Southern cooking favorites may include tasty barbecue, vegetable casseroles, sweet potato pie, biscuits and gravy, red beans and rice, country fried steak, pecan pie, and the ever popular fried chicken. From simple lunchtime fare to haute cuisine, the area boasts quality restaurant fare. Five Points and the Congaree Vista neighborhoods draw visitors to their nightlife.

*Visitor Information:* Columbia Metropolitan Convention and Visitors Bureau, P.O. Box 15, Columbia, SC 29202; telephone (803)545-0000; toll-free (800)264-4884

# Convention Facilities

The newest jewel in the city's crown is the Columbia Metropolitan Convention Center which opened in summer 2004 in the historic downtown Vista area. It features 120,000 square feet of space including a 25,000 square-foot exhibit hall, 18,000 square-foot ballroom, divisible meeting rooms, and a full banquet kitchen. Construction on the 222-bed Columbia Hilton convention center hotel was expected to begin in spring 2005. Columbia's Carolina Coliseum offers 60,000 square feet of exhibit space. The South Carolina State Fair Grounds accommodates up to 3,000 delegates in 100,000 square feet of space. The Township Auditorium has a stage and seats 3,224 people. Special services such as teleconferencing are available. The Columbiana Hotel & Conference Center offers 12 meeting rooms and an 11,000 square foot ballroom which accommodates up to 1,800 people for receptions or 1,200 people for banquets. Other area meeting facilities include Williams Brice Stadium, Koger Center for the Arts, and Jamil Temple. Saluda Shoals Park offers a secluded 5,200 square-foot state-of-the-art facility on the shores of the Saluda River, located minutes from downtown. Columbia provides choice accommodations with 7,000 rooms in a variety of hotels and motels.

*Convention Information:* Columbia Metropolitan Convention and Visitors Bureau, PO Box 15, Columbia, SC 29202; telephone (803) 545-0000; toll-free (800)264-4884

# Transportation

## Approaching the City

Columbia is centrally located and easily accessible from cities throughout the state and the nation. Six airlines serve Columbia Metropolitan Airport, which is located eight miles from downtown. The airport recently underwent a $3.1 million road improvement project and the construction of a multilevel parking garage for 1,837 cars plus an additional 1,668 uncovered spaces. Airlines include Continental Airlines, Delta Airlines and Delta Connection, Northwest Airlines,

Independence Air, United Express, and U.S. Airways Express. Amtrak offers daily rail departures and arrivals from the Eastern seaboard from New York City to Miami. Three interstate highways (I-20, I-26, I-77) crisscross the city of Columbia, with two other major interstates (I-85 and I-95) within an hour's drive. The area also has eight U.S. highways. Columbia is directly linked to Atlanta, GA; Richmond, VA; Jacksonville, FL; and Charlotte, NC, via these roadways. Greyhound/Trailways supplies inter-city bus service.

## Traveling in the City

Columbia is an easily navigable city. While rush hour traffic is heavy on I-26 and other major thoroughfares, it most often moves steadily. The Central Midlands Regional Transit Authority (CMRTA) serves the heart of the Midlands, including Columbia, Cayce, West Columbia, Forest Acres, Arcadia Lakes, Springdale and the St. Andrews area. Its services include the trolleys in Downtown Columbia and the DART service (Dial-a-Ride Transit). Five taxi companies provide a fleet of more than 175 cabs.

# Communications

## Newspapers and Magazines

Columbia's daily (morning) newspaper, *The State,* is also South Carolina's major paper. In addition, the city publishes three weekly newspapers including the *Columbia Star,* which covers human interest and legal news, *Free Times,* Columbia's free paper, and *Columbia Black News.* About 20 magazines and journals are published in Columbia, including the *Business and Economic Review,* published by the University of South Carolina's Moore School of Business, *Columbia Metropolitan Magazine,* and *South Carolina Game and Fish,* and three magazines directed at farmers.

## Television and Radio

Five television stations broadcast in Columbia, affiliates of ABC, NBC, CBS and FOX, as well as South Carolina Educational Television. Three cable stations also serve the area; a government information station is available on a local cable network. Six AM and 14 FM radio stations offer music, information, news, call-in talk programs, and religious programming.

*Media Information: The State,* Knight-Ridder, Inc., P.O. Box 1333, Columbia, SC 29202; telephone (800)888-5353

## Columbia Online

Central South Carolina Alliance. Available www.centralsc .org

City of Columbia Home Page. Available www.columbiasc
.net

Columbia Metropolitan Convention Center. Available www
.columbiacvb.com

Columbia Today. Available www.columbiatoday.com

Greater Columbia Chamber of Commerce. Available www
.columbiachamber.com/new/index.htm

Richland County Public Library. Available www.richland
.lib.sc.us

Richland School District One. Available www.richlandone
.org

Richland School District Two. Available my.richland2.org/
portal/server.pt#

South Carolina State Library. Available www.state.sc.us/
scsl

*The State.* Available www.thestate.com

## Selected Bibliography

Edgar, Walter B. and Deborah K. Wolley, *Columbia: Portrait of a City,* 1976.

Maxey, Russell, *South Carolina's Historic Columbia: Yesterday and Today in Photographs,* 1980.

Moore, John Hammond, *Columbia and Richland County: A South Carolina Community, 1740–1990,* 1993.

Rawl, Miriam Freeman, *From the Ashes of Ruin* (Columbia, S.C.: Summerhouse Press, 1999)

# TENNESSEE

# The State in Brief

**Nickname:** Volunteer State
**Motto:** Agriculture and commerce

**Flower:** Iris
**Bird:** Mockingbird

**Area:** 42,143 square miles (2000; U.S. rank: 36th)
**Elevation:** Ranges from 178 feet to 6,643 feet above sea level
**Climate:** Continental; mild weather with abundant rainfall in the east; hot humid summers in the western region; severe winters in mountains

**Admitted to Union:** June 1, 1796
**Capital:** Nashville
**Head Official:** Governor Phil Bredesen (D) (until 2007)

**Population**
　**1980:** 4,591,000
　**1990:** 4,877,185
　**2000:** 5,689,262
　**2004 estimate:** 5,900,962
　**Percent change, 1990–2000:** 3.7%
　**U.S. rank in 2004:** 16th
　**Percent of residents born in state:** 64.7% (2000)
　**Density:** 138 people per square mile (2000)
　**2002 FBI Crime Index Total:** 290,961

**Racial and Ethnic Characteristics** (2000)
　**White:** 4,563,310

**Black or African American:** 932,809
**American Indian and Alaska Native:** 15,152
**Asian:** 56,662
**Native Hawaiian and Pacific Islander:** 2,205
**Hispanic or Latino (may be of any race):** 123,838
**Other:** 56,036

**Age Characteristics (2000)**
　**Population under 5 years old:** 374,880
　**Population 5 to 19 years old:** 1,186,152
　**Percent of population 65 years and over:** 12.4%
　**Median age:** 35.9 years (2000)

**Vital Statistics**
　**Total number of births (2003):** 78,811
　**Total number of deaths (2003):** 56,909 (infant deaths, 717)
　**AIDS cases reported through 2003:** 5,817

**Economy**
　**Major industries:** Construction, chemicals, textiles, apparel, electrical machinery, furniture, leather goods, food processing, tobacco, leather, agriculture, automobiles, aluminum, tourism
　**Unemployment rate:** 5.2% (December 2004)
　**Per capita income:** $28,565 (2003; U.S. rank: 34th)
　**Median household income:** $37,529 (3-year average, 2001-2003)
　**Percentage of persons below poverty level:** 14.3% (3-year average, 2001-2003)
　**Income tax rate:** Limited to dividends and interest income
　**Sales tax rate:** 7.0%

# Chattanooga

## The City in Brief

**Founded:** 1838 (chartered 1839)

**Head Official:** Mayor Bob Corker (R) (since 2001)

**City Population**
- **1980:** 169,514
- **1990:** 152,393
- **2000:** 155,554
- **2003 estimate:** 154,887
- **Percent change, 1990–2000:** 2.1%
- **U.S. rank in 1980:** 87th
- **U.S. rank in 1990:** 113th (State rank: 4th)
- **U.S. rank in 2000:** 148th (State rank: 4th)

**Metropolitan Area Population**
- **1980:** 418,000
- **1990:** 424,000
- **2000:** 465,161

**Percent change, 1990–2000:** 9.7%
**U.S. rank in 1980:** 78th (MSA)
**U.S. rank in 1990:** 82nd (MSA)
**U.S. rank in 2000:** 89th (MSA)

**Area:** 135.2 square miles (2000)
**Elevation:** Ranges from 675 feet above sea level in city to 2,391 feet at Lookout Mountain
**Average Annual Temperature:** 60.5° F
**Average Annual Precipitation:** 54.5 inches

**Major Economic Sectors:** wholesale and retail trade, services, manufacturing
**Unemployment rate:** 3.6% (December 2004)
**Per Capita Income:** $19,689 (1999)

**2002 FBI Crime Index Total:** 15,867

**Major Colleges and Universities:** University of Tennessee at Chattanooga

**Daily Newspaper:** *The Chattanooga Times Free Press*

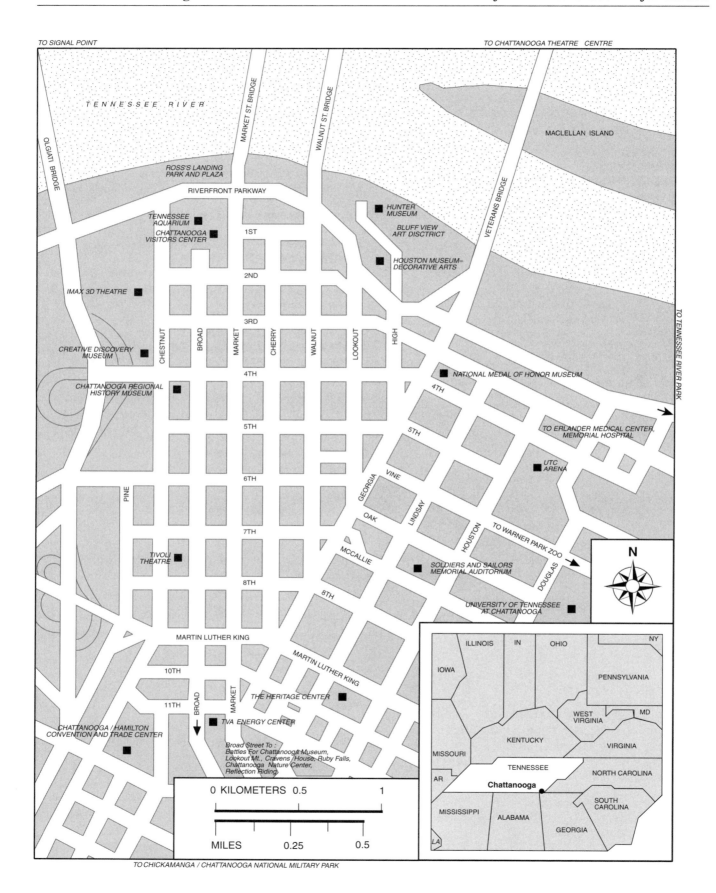

TO SIGNAL POINT

TO CHATTANOOGA THEATRE CENTRE

*TENNESSEE RIVER*

MACLELLAN ISLAND

OLGIATI BRIDGE

MARKET ST. BRIDGE

WALNUT ST. BRIDGE

VETERANS BRIDGE

ROSS'S LANDING PARK AND PLAZA

RIVERFRONT PARKWAY

TENNESSEE AQUARIUM

CHATTANOOGA VISITORS CENTER

1ST

HUNTER MUSEUM

BLUFF VIEW ART DISCTRICT

2ND

HOUSTON MUSEUM– DECORATIVE ARTS

IMAX 3D THEATRE

3RD

TO TENNESSEE RIVER PARK

CHESTNUT

BROAD

MARKET

CHERRY

WALNUT

LOOKOUT

HIGH

CREATIVE DISCOVERY MUSEUM

4TH

NATIONAL MEDAL OF HONOR MUSEUM

CHATTANOOGA REGIONAL HISTORY MUSEUM

4TH

5TH

TO ERLANDER MEDICAL CENTER, MEMORIAL HOSPITAL

5TH

VINE

UTC ARENA

PINE

6TH

GEORGIA

OAK

LINDSAY

HOUSTON

TO WARNER PARK ZOO

7TH

MCCALLIE

SOLDIERS AND SAILORS MEMORIAL AUDITORIUM

DOUGLAS

N

TIVOLI THEATRE

8TH

8TH

UNIVERSITY OF TENNESSEE AT CHATTANOOGA

MARTIN LUTHER KING

MARTIN LUTHER KING

10TH

BROAD

MARKET

THE HERITAGE CENTER

ILLINOIS

IN

OHIO

NY

IOWA

PENNSYLVANIA

11TH

TVA ENERGY CENTER

WEST VIRGINIA

MD

CHATTANOOGA / HAMILTON CONVENTION AND TRADE CENTER

MISSOURI

KENTUCKY

VIRGINIA

Broad Street To :
Battles For Chattanooga Museum,
Lookout Mt., Cravens House, Ruby Falls,
Chattanooga Nature Center,
Reflection Riding

AR

TENNESSEE

NORTH CAROLINA

Chattanooga

SOUTH CAROLINA

0 KILOMETERS 0.5 1

MISSISSIPPI

ALABAMA

GEORGIA

LA

MILES 0.25 0.5

TO CHICKAMANGA / CHATTANOOGA NATIONAL MILITARY PARK

# Introduction

Located in the heart of the beautiful Tennessee Valley, Chattanooga is a small industrial city rich in history. It is becoming well known today for its commitment to sustainable economic growth and quality of life. Perhaps nowhere in the country has a city undergone as dramatic an improvement as that experienced by Chattanooga, a city named America's most polluted by the U.S. Department of Health, Education, and Welfare in 1980. The privately-funded Vision 2000 program was initiated in 1982 to revitalize the city's riverfront and downtown by the year 2000 and change its grimy image. And change it did; by the twenty-first century Chattanooga is now one of the cleanest U.S. cities, known especially for its breathtaking beauty and natural attractions. Pride in this change is evident in more recent downtown revitalization projects, including the citywide 21st Century Waterfront Plan. Today's Chattanooga boasts a vital and diverse economy, rich cultural history, and gleaming new downtown attractions loved by residents and visitors alike.

# Geography and Climate

Chattanooga is located at the juncture of Tennessee, Alabama, and Georgia, in a valley in southeastern Tennessee between the Appalachian and the Cumberland mountain ranges. The city lies on both banks of the Tennessee River at Moccasin Bend and is bordered by Signal Mountain on the north and Lookout Mountain to the south, with Missionary Ridge running through the eastern section of the city. The mountains shelter the city from major weather systems.

The city has a moderate climate, with cool winters and hot summers, and springs and falls characterized by plentiful sunshine and rainfall, mild temperatures, and lush foliage. Extreme cold is rare, and the annual average snowfall is only 2.8 inches.

**Area:** 135.2 square miles (2000)

**Elevation:** Ranges from 675 feet above sea level in city to 2,391 feet at Lookout Mountain

**Average Temperatures:** January, 39.4° F; July, 79.6° F; annual average, 60.5° F

**Average Annual Precipitation:** 54.5 inches

# History

### Native Americans Displaced by Early Settlers

In 1663 the British established the colony of Carolina, which included all of the Tennessee country. The French from the Mississippi Valley also claimed the land at that same time. About 1769, a crude structure known as the "Old French Store" was established, most likely on Williams Island, marking the first white settlement in the area. England gained undisputed title to the territory in 1763 at the end of the French and Indian War.

The Chickamaugas, a splinter group of the Cherokee tribe, moved to the South Chickamauga Creek villages in 1777. They resisted white settlement and cooperated with the British during the American Revolution. Frontiersmen destroyed the Chickamauga villages in 1779. Three years later, on the slope of Lookout Mountain, the Native Americans engaged the frontiersmen who had destroyed their villages. This confrontation has become known as the "last battle of the American Revolution." In 1785, the United States government took control of Native American affairs.

Tennessee became the sixteenth state in 1796. At that time Native American lands made up about three-fourths of the region, including the Chattanooga area. Ross's Landing was established in 1816 as a trading post on the banks of the Tennessee River by Chief John Ross, leader of the Cherokee nation. Chattanooga became a center of education and culture for the Native Americans when the Brainerd Mission was created in 1817. Hamilton County was established in 1819 on land north of the Tennessee River. With the Cherokee removal in 1838, the county expanded south of the river to encompass Ross's Landing.

Cherokee removal was part of the 1837–1838 episode known as the "Trail of Tears," one of the most shameful events in American history. As the result of a treaty from a disputed land sale, the Cherokee were driven from their homes in several southeastern states and were assembled at various camps, including Ross's Landing, for expulsion to Oklahoma. Forced on a harsh journey through wilderness and bad weather, more than one-half of the 16,000 Native Americans died along the way or upon arrival, largely because of the strenuous trip.

### Railroads Key To Chattanooga's History

The name of Ross's Landing was changed to Chattanooga by the U.S. Post Office in 1838. Although the origin of the city's name is uncertain, some say the name was a Native American expression meaning the "rock that comes to a point," describing Lookout Mountain. Legislation establishing Chattanooga and its boundaries was passed in 1839.

Rail transportation began in Chattanooga in the 1850s. Connections to other cities were constructed by the Western & Atlantic, Nashville & Chattanooga, Memphis & Charleston, and East Tennessee & Georgia Railroads. The city's population stood at approximately 2,500 people at the beginning of the Civil War. Although Chattanoogans supported secession, Hamilton County as a whole voted to remain in the Union. The county became one of the key battlegrounds of the war, as both the Confederate and Union armies attempted to keep possession of this important railway hub.

## City Experiences Major Civil War Battles

Union soldiers, under the command of General William Rosecrans, marched into Chattanooga in September of 1863, intent on holding the key railroad center. The Battle of Chickamauga took place on September 19 and 20, 1863, followed by the Battle of Lookout Mountain (which was commanded by General Ulysses S. Grant) on November 24, and the Battle of Missionary Ridge on November 25. Confederate defenses were broken during the last battle and the southerners began their retreat into Georgia. According to Confederate General D. H. Hill, "Chattanooga sealed the fate of the Confederacy."

In November 1863, the nation's first National Cemetery was established in Chattanooga. Of the 12,000 Union soldiers buried at the cemetery, 5,000 are unknown. The cemetery is the site of 31,000 graves of soldiers from every American war and conflict. Most Confederate soldiers were buried at the city's Citizens Cemetery.

## Gradual Recovery Follows War

Following the war, the city began to experience economic progress. Disaster struck in March 1867, when the largest flood on record—56.8 feet—washed away the city's only bridge spanning the Tennessee River. Chattanooga remained without a bridge until 1891 when the Walnut Street Bridge was built.

Major events occurring in the nineteenth century include the publishing of the first issue of *The Chattanooga Times* in 1869; creation of the public school system in 1872; a Yellow Fever epidemic in 1878 that claimed 366 lives; the advent of telephone service in 1880; and the introduction of the first electric lights in 1882.

During the late nineteenth century, as the city's rail access increased, so did the push to develop mineral and timber resources. Two industries that still thrive in the community today, manufacturing and tourism, began during that period. In 1899, Chattanooga became the site of the first franchised Coca-Cola bottling plant.

Early in the twentieth century there occurred a boom in downtown construction, and "skyscrapers" of the time, such as the James Building, were erected. The Hamilton

County Courthouse, struck by lightning in 1910, was rebuilt, Market Street Bridge was dedicated in 1917, and airport facilities opened at Lovell Field in 1930.

Chattanooga entered the annals of musical history in 1923 when Bessie Smith, who began her career singing for coins on Chattanooga's streets, gained prominence with the release of her recording "Downhearted Blues" by Columbia Records. The city received special notoriety with the popularity of the Glenn Miller Orchestra's big band hit, "Chattanooga Choo-Choo," in 1941.

## TVA Crucial to City's Development

The Great Depression struck Chattanooga hard, as it did the rest of the country, and in 1933 the U.S. Congress created the Tennessee Valley Authority (TVA) which proved to be the most successful of all Franklin Roosevelt's New Deal programs. Construction of TVA's most dramatic plan, the Chickamauga Dam, began in 1936. TVA's extensive system of power-producing and flood-control dams created a number of lakes, which are widely used for commercial transportation and recreation. In 1941 the city became the center for all TVA power operations.

## Suburbs Grow, Bridges Built

Over time, communities began to develop around the city in areas such as Cameron Hill, Riverview, Lookout Mountain, and Signal Mountain. Although these were primarily enclaves for the wealthy, middle-class communities developed in Brainerd, East Ridge, and Red Bank.

Beginning in the 1950s, the growth of the city necessitated the building of additional bridges to span the Tennessee River. The Wilkes T. Thrasher Bridge across Chickamauga Dam opened in 1955; the Olgiati Bridge was dedicated in 1959; the C. B. Robinson Bridge opened in 1981; and the Veterans Bridge opened in 1984.

## Moves to Insure Racial Equality

The history of local race relations began a new era in 1962 when the Chattanooga and Hamilton County school systems were desegregated. More recently, in 1990 a new city council form of government was mandated by the federal court for the purpose of insuring fair racial representation.

## A New City Emerges

From the late 1960s to the early 1980s, Chattanooga was known as America's dirtiest city. By 1982, city residents and leaders were tired of the bad reputation of the city, and an $850 million plan was devised to revitalize the city's downtown and riverfront by the year 2000.

In 1986 the River City Company was formed to promote, encourage, and assist local economic development along 22 miles of river frontage and in the central business district. It was succeeded by a new agency formed in 1993 when River City Company merged with Partners for Economic Progress, forming a public-private economic development agency called RiverValley Partners. Also in 1986, the Chattanooga Neighborhood Enterprise Housing Program was founded to make housing affordable for local residents and to eliminate substandard housing.

In the 1990s, Chattanooga Venture, a community think tank, was begun to introduce new programs for local residents. In 1991 the Target '96 Plan, an environmental initiative—the first of its kind in the country—was established to deal with education, business development, and community action in a comprehensive, coordinated manner. At the end of the century, Chattanooga's focus on sustainable development centers and creating an environment that would attract and retain companies that provide good jobs in businesses that would continue to grow in the twenty-first century. Today, Chattanooga is realizing those goals with a new focus enhancing its allure for conventioneers, tourists, and Chattanoogans alike through the completion of several major renovation projects throughout the city.

*Historical Information:* Chattanooga-Hamilton County Bicentennial Library, Local History and Genealogical Collections, 1001 Broad Street, Chattanooga, TN 37402; telephone (423)757-5317

# Population Profile

## Metropolitan Area Residents
*1980:* 418,000
*1990:* 424,347
*2000:* 465,161
*Percent change, 1990–2000:* 9.7%
*U.S. rank in 1980:* 78th (MSA)
*U.S. rank in 1990:* 82nd(MSA)
*U.S. rank in 2000:* 89th (MSA)

## City Residents
*1980:* 169,514
*1990:* 152,393
*2000:* 155,554
*2003 estimate:* 154,887
*Percent change, 1990–2000:* 2.1%
*U.S. rank in 1980:* 87th
*U.S. rank in 1990:* 113th (State rank: 4th)
*U.S. rank in 2000:* 148th (State rank: 5th)

*Density:* 1,150.5 people per square mile (2000)

*Racial and ethnic characteristics* (2000)
White: 92,874
Black or African American: 56,086
American Indian and Alaska Native: 446
Asian: 2,396
Native Hawaiian and Pacific Islander: 164
Hispanic or Latino (may be of any race): 3,281
Other: 3,588

*Percent of residents born in state:* 63.5% (2000)

*Age characteristics* (2000)
Population under 5 years old: 9,449
Population 5 to 9 years old: 10,009
Population 10 to 14 years old: 9,811
Population 15 to 19 years old: 10,236
Population 20 to 24 years old: 12,114
Population 25 to 34 years old: 22,176
Population 35 to 44 years old: 22,610
Population 45 to 54 years old: 21,227
Population 55 to 59 years old: 7,673
Population 60 to 64 years old: 6,554
Population 65 to 74 years old: 12,203
Population 75 to 84 years old: 8,285
Population 85 years and older: 3,207
Median age: 36.8 years

*Births* (2003; Hamilton County)
Total number: 3,943

*Deaths* (2003; Hamilton County)
Total number: 3,166 (of which, 46 were infants under the age of 1 year)

*Money income* (1999)
Per capita income: $19,689
Median household income: $32,006
Total households: 65,513

*Number of households with income of . . .*
less than $10,000: 10,010
$10,000 to $14,999: 5,124
$15,000 to $24,999: 10,913
$25,000 to $34,999: 8,977
$35,000 to $49,999: 10,569
$50,000 to $74,999: 10,615
$75,000 to $99,999: 4,348
$100,000 to $149,999: 2,881
$150,000 to $199,999: 929
$200,000 or more: 1,147

*Percent of families below poverty level:* 14.0% (25.5% of which were female householder families with related children under 5 years)

*2002 FBI Crime Index Total:* 15,867

# Municipal Government

The city of Chattanooga government consists of a full-time mayor elected at-large and a nine-member city council elected by districts. The mayor and council serve four-year terms.

**Head Official:** Mayor Bob Corker (R) (since 2001; current term expires 2005)

**Total Number of City Employees:** 2,363 (2000)

*City Information:* Chattanooga City Hall, Chattanooga, TN 37402; telephone (423)757-5152

# Economy

## Major Industries and Commercial Activity

Chattanooga, the hub of a thriving economic region, is located at the crossroads of three states: Alabama, Georgia, and Tennessee. Among the city's economic advantages are abundant natural resources (chiefly iron and steel), a strong tourism industry, a trained labor force, and a centralized location. An extensive system of highway, air, water, and rail transportation helps make the city a major transportation and distribution center. In addition, the city has a designated Foreign Trade Zone.

One of the nation's oldest manufacturing cities, Chattanooga's employment in that sector has decreased slightly in recent years (mirroring national trends) to 16.5 percent. Again mirroring national trends, increases have occurred in information, financial activities, and professional and business services. In addition, Chattanooga has experienced a modest growth trend in transportation, trade, and utilities. As a whole, the city is a diversified and profitable business location with no single dominant industry.

Locally based UNUM Provident Corp. is a *Fortune* 500 service company. Other large companies with headquarters in the city include Blue Cross/Blue Shield of Tennessee, Brach & Brock Confections, Chattem Inc., Dixie Yarns, The Krystal Company, McKee Banking Company, North American Royalties, and Olan Mills, Inc.

The city is the headquarters for the Division of Power of the Tennessee Valley Authority (TVA), the largest utility in the United States. TVA is a federal corporation that works to develop the natural resources of the Tennessee Valley. Chattanooga is in an enviable position: both electricity and natural gas are readily available at very reasonable rates. Water supplies are also plentiful and sewage treatment has considerable excess capacity to support industrial expansion. In addition, TVA and its power distributors offer a growth credit program that provides significant savings to new commercial and industrial customers requiring a large capacity.

*Items and goods produced:* processed foods, iron and steel products, textiles, apparel, cosmetics, pharmaceuticals, clay products, furniture, machinery, paper, petroleum products

## Incentive Programs—New and Existing Companies

*Local programs*—The city of Chattanooga, Hamilton County, and the state of Tennessee have joined with the private sector to form RiverValley Partners, a non-profit public-private organization that has responsibility for economic development in Chattanooga and Hamilton County. The organization provides assistance to new and expanding businesses and industry in securing business financing. Services include networking with community financial resources, assistance in obtaining state aid, and business counseling for start-up operations experiencing difficulties. The city of Chattanooga Community Development Block Grant Program makes loans to locating or expanding businesses for terms of up to five years. The Enterprise Fund of Greater Chattanooga provides capital on a loan or equity basis to new and existing businesses in Chattanooga, Hamilton County, and surrounding areas for purposes of creating jobs and strengthening the tax base. The Local Development Corporation Revolving Loan Fund can provide limited fixed asset financing when necessary to leverage other loan funds or bridge a financing gap. The Tennessee Valley Authority provides loans to business and industry in Hamilton County and other regional counties. Valley Capital Corporation provides long-term debt and equity capital to small businesses which are at least 51 percent owned by economically or socially disadvantaged entrepreneurs.

*State programs*—Tennessee, a right-to-work state, provides a low cost of doing business. It boasts the lowest utility costs in the nation and offers numerous tax incentives. State-administered financial programs for businesses include: the Small and Minority-Owned Business Assistance Program, currently being developed by the state Treasury Department and expected to provide assistance to small and minority-owned businesses through loans, technical assistance, and program services; the Small Business Energy Loan Program, which helps qualified Tennessee-based businesses upgrade their level of energy efficiency in their buildings and manufacturing processes; the FastTrack Infrastructure Program, which assists in the funding of infrastructure improvements for businesses locating or expanding in Tennessee; and the FastTrack Training Services Program, which helps companies provide training for their staff.

*Job training programs*—Tennessee's FastTrack Training Services Program is the state's primary source of financial support for new and expanding business and industry training. FastTrack staff work with businesses to plan, develop, and implement customized training programs. Training may be done in a classroom setting, or on the job. The Southeast Tennessee Private Industry Council also assists businesses in meeting labor force training needs. The Council strives to provide businesses with a more competent workforce, higher employee productivity, a reduction in employee turnover, lower employee retraining costs, and highly motivated employees. The council works with Chattanooga State Technical Community College on vocational training, and helps new companies combine resources to meet their training needs. Several four-year institutions and two-year colleges serve the area with a wide range of programs designed to train personnel for new and expanding industry. The Tennessee Industrial Training Service provides specialized services at low or no cost to manufacturing, warehouse/distribution, and service industry employers, including task and job analysis, training program design and material development, coordination of programs with employee recruitment activities, provision of facilities and equipment for developing specific job skills, and provision of funding.

### Development Projects

Perhaps the most visible sign of Chattanooga's renewal is its continuing revitalization to its riverfront area. The 21st Century Waterfront Project, a $120 million enhancement to 129 acres along both shores of the Tennessee River, is scheduled for completion in May of 2005. The project encompasses a $30 million expansion to the Tennessee Aquarium, a $19.5 million expansion to the Hunter Museum of Art, a $3 million renovation and enhancement to the Children's Creative Discovery Museum, a new pedestrian bridge with a lit glass deck, a new pier, waterfront parks and dining, unique retail, and a poignant pedestrian passageway, linking the downtown and river, that marks the beginning of the Trail of Tears and celebrates Native American culture.

*Economic Development Information:* Chattanooga Area Chamber of Commerce, 811 Broad Street, Chattanooga, TN 37402; telephone (423)756-2121; fax (423)267-7242; email info@chattanooga-chamber.com

### Commercial Shipping

Chattanooga is located at the crossroads of several major U.S. highways, including Interstates 75, 24, and 59. The city is within one day's drive of nearly one-third of the major U.S. markets and population, and within 140 miles of Nashville, Atlanta, Knoxville, Huntsville, and Birmingham. Chattanooga is the distribution center for the region that includes southeast Tennessee, northwest Georgia, southwest North Carolina, northeast Alabama, and parts of several neighboring states. More than 70 motor freight lines are certified to transport shipments in the area. Two ports—the

Port of Chattanooga and Centre South Riverport—are within city limits. Chattanooga remains an important port as a result of the Tennessee Valley Authority's system of locks and dams, and the Tombigbee waterway, which saves days, miles, and dollars on shipments to and from ports along the Ohio and Mississippi Rivers and the Gulf of Mexico. Freight rail transportation is provided by divisions of the CSX Transportation system and the Norfolk Southern Railway. Air cargo service carriers operate out of Chattanooga Metropolitan Airport/Lovell Field.

### Labor Force and Employment Outlook

Chattanooga's work force is said to be distinguished by its pride in individual workmanship. Workers are prepared for specialized professions by the state's excellent industrial training programs. Tennessee is a right-to-work state, and the city's cost of labor remains lower than in many other areas of the United States. Between July of 2003 and July of 2004, Chattanooga netted 1,900 new jobs (the fastest job growth rate the city has seen in 4 years) and average wages rose 4.2 percent, compared with the national average of 2.7 percent.

The following is a summary of data regarding the Chattanooga metropolitan area labor force, 2003 annual averages.

*Size of nonagricultural labor force:* 233,500

*Number of workers employed in . . .*
　*manufacturing:* 35,400
　*trade, transportation and utilities:* 55,100
　*information:* 2,800
　*financial activities:* 17,800
　*professional and business services:* 25,400
　*educational and health services:* 23,100
　*leisure and hospitality:* 19,200
　*other services:* 10,600
　*government:* 35,100

*Average hourly earnings of production workers employed in manufacturing:* $13.24

*Unemployment rate:* 3.6% (December 2004)

| Largest employers | Number of employees |
|---|---|
| Hamilton County Dept. of Education | 4,723 |
| BlueCross BlueShield | 3,683 |
| McKee Foods Corporation | 3,300 |
| UnumProvident Corporation | 3,147 |
| Memorial Health Care System | 2,583 |

### Cost of Living

At the end of 2004, Chattanooga's cost of living, based on average cost of housing, utilities, gasoline, doctor visits, and taxes, was nearly eight percent below the national average.

The following is a summary of data regarding several key cost of living factors for the Chattanooga area.

*2004 (3rd Quarter) ACCRA Average House Price:*$238,224

*2004 (3rd Quarter) ACCRA Cost of Living Index:* 92.8 (U.S. average = 100.0)

*State income tax rate:* Limited to dividends and interest income

*State sales tax rate:* 7.0%

*Local income tax rate:* None

*Local sales tax rate:* 2.25%

*Property tax rate:* $2.52 per $100 of assessed valuation (2005)

*Economic Information:* Chattanooga Area Chamber of Commerce, 811 Broad Street, Chattanooga, TN 37402; telephone (423)756-2121; fax (423)267-7242; email info @chattanooga-chamber.com

# Education and Research

## Elementary and Secondary Schools

The Hamilton County Department of Education (HCDE) is the largest employer in Chattanooga. HCDE was formed in 1997 upon the merger of Chattanooga Public Schools and Hamilton County Schools. The resulting Hamilton County School system has built upon the strengths of Chattanooga's Paideia active learning curriculum, the county's site-based management approach, and other recognized programs. Hamilton County's 15 magnet schools, focusing on such areas of study as math, science, and technology, fine arts, liberal arts, and classical studies, add to the diversity of the school system.

The following is a summary of data regarding Hamilton County public schools as of 2002-2003.

*Total enrollment:* 44,217

*Number of facilities*
  *elementary schools:* 47
  *junior high/middle schools:* 15
  *senior high schools:* 14
  *other:* 15 magnet schools

*Student/teacher ratio:* 15.2:1

*Teacher salaries*
  *average:* $34,494

*Funding per pupil:* $7,229

Chattanooga has a strong tradition of private and parochial elementary and secondary education, including the nationally recognized Girls' Preparatory School, the McCallie School for Boys, and the coeducational Baylor School. More than 15,000 students attend 33 private and parochial schools.

*Public Schools Information:* Hamilton County Schools, 6703 Bonny Oaks Drive, Chattanooga, TN 37421; telephone (423)209-8400

## Colleges and Universities

There are 17 junior colleges, colleges, and universities located in the Chattanooga region. The University of Tennessee at Chattanooga (UTC), a primary campus of the University of Tennessee system, is comprised of a College of Arts and Sciences, College of Business Administration, College of Engineering and Computer Science, and College of Health, Education, and Professional Studies, schools of Nursing and Engineering, and a graduate school offering master's degrees in 22 subjects.

Chattanooga State Technical Community College, with more than 8,000 students, is a two-year college offering the following areas of study: arts and sciences; engineering, business, and information technologies; industrial technology; and nursing and allied health.

Three private colleges operate in the Chattanooga area: Tennessee Temple University, with more than 500 students; Southern Adventist University, in nearby Collegedale, TN, with nearly 2,300 students; and Covenant College, in Lookout Mountain, GA, with more than 1,200 students. Vocational education and training programs are also offered through continuing vocational education of the public school systems.

## Libraries and Research Centers

The Chattanooga-Hamilton County Bicentennial Library consists of a main downtown library and four branches. The library has holdings of nearly 500,000 volumes, 1,382 periodical subscriptions, and 19,416 audio and video materials. Special collections include interviews on Chattanooga and Hamilton County history, Genealogy, and Tennesseana. The library also offers special events, concerts, and programs, including preschool story hours and film festivals.

The University of Tennessee at Chattanooga (UT) makes the following research and testing resources available to business and industry: The Center for Excellence in Computer Applications, which provides resources associated with high technology; and The Center for Economic Education and its associated Probasco Chair of Free Enterprise, which designs and implements research projects and education programs about basic economic principles. At UT's SimCenter, established in fall of 2002, research professionals, UT faculty, and students serve government and industry through research in computational engineering. The Bass Research Foundation studies ways to increase the quantity of America's bass fishery resources. The Tennessee Valley Authority has several research centers in Chattanooga.

***Public Library Information:*** Chattanooga-Hamilton County Bicentennial Library, 1001 Broad Street, Chattanooga, TN 37402-2652; telephone (423)757-5310; email library@lib.chattanooga.gov

# Health Care

Among the health services available to Chattanooga residents are public and private mental health facilities, drug and alcohol abuse recovery facilities, rehabilitation centers, a sports medicine center, speech and hearing services, facilities for the handicapped, free standing emergency medical centers, and community hospitals. Erlanger Medical Center, the region's largest and oldest public hospital with 818 acute-care beds and 50 long-term beds, offers Miller Eye Center, T. C. Thompson Children's Hospital, Erlanger North Hospital, Regional Trauma Center, Regional Heart and Vascular Center, Regional Cancer Center, Regional Women's Center, Regional Burn Center, Kidney Transplant Center, the Southside/Dodson Avenue Community Health Centers, and Tennessee Craniofacial Center, and is the only medical center in the region offering LifeForce Air Ambulance. Memorial Hospital, a 365-bed affiliate of the Kentucky-based Sisters of Charity of Nazareth Health System, offers an ambulatory intensive care unit. North Park Hospital, an 83-bed acute-care facility, offers a 24-hour emergency room. The 109-bed Siskin Hospital for Physical Rehabilitation offers treatment programs in brain injury, amputation, stroke, spinal cord injury, orthopedics, and major multiple trauma. It is one of only two rehabilitation hospitals in the country specializing in treatment of lymphedema. Parkridge Medical Center, with 517 beds, is known for its strong open-heart and cardiac services program and bypass surgeries. Parkridge East Hospital (formerly East Ridge Hospital), provides specialty services including a women's center, a sleep disorder center, bariatric surgery services, neonatal intensive care, and a spine and orthopedic center. Parkridge Valley hospital specializes in behavioral health. Other Chattanooga health care facilities include HealthSouth Chattanooga Rehabilitation Hospital, which offers comprehensive physical rehabilitation services; Greenleaf Health Systems Psychiatric and Chemical Dependency Center; and Women's East Pavilion (a component of Erlanger Medical Center), the only area hospital exclusively for women.

# Recreation

### Sightseeing

More than four million people visit Chattanooga annually to explore the city's past, take part in activities, and enjoy the region's unique sights and diversions. The $45 million Tennessee Aquarium, the world's largest freshwater aquarium, takes spectators everywhere a river goes— from small mountain streams, to raging currents, to deep reservoirs, to the sea. Displays of thousands of living plants, fish, birds, and other river animals show how water supports life. A $30 million, 60,000 square foot addition, scheduled to open in April 2005, will hold 650,000 gallons of water, with ten-foot sharks, stingrays, and barracuda swimming among coral formations. This expansion is only part of a $120 million Waterfront Plan scheduled for completion by May 2005, which includes a $19.5 million expansion to the Hunter Museum of American Art, and a $3 million renovation and enhancement to the Children's Creative Discovery Museum, as well as other riverside revitalization projects. The story of Chattanooga's rich cultural, historical, and geographical significance is related through chronologically progressive exhibits at Ross's Landing Park and Plaza, which is adjacent to the Aquarium. The Chattanooga Regional History Museum was established in 1978 to collect, preserve, and exhibit the written, spoken, pictorial, and artifactual record of Chattanooga and the surrounding region.

The Chattanooga Zoo at Warner Park presents a variety of exotic animals and birds, including primates, jaguars, nocturnal animals, and a petting zoo, as well as classes about animal life. Its newest exhibit, "Himalayan Passage" features red pandas. The Tennessee Valley Railroad Museum offers an impressive collection of classic railroad memorabilia, including a 1911 steam locomotive, a 1917 office car with three bedrooms, a 1926 dining car, a Pullman sleeping car, and a 1929 wooden caboose. Visitors can ride the train on its 40-acre site with its four railroad bridges and a historic tunnel through Missionary Ridge; four-hour roundtrip train rides to historic Chickamauga, Georgia, are also available. The National Knife Collector Association and Museum, which promotes the hobby of knife collecting, has many interesting knives on display.

The Chattanooga Choo-Choo is a 30-acre complex offering accommodations in restored Victorian railroad cars, dining options including dinner in an elegant dining car, browsing in unique shops, and touring the entertainment complex via old-fashioned trolley. At Ross's Landing, the sternwheeler *Southern Belle,* which can carry 500 people, conducts excursions up the Tennessee River on its dining and entertainment cruises. The river's newest excursion boat, the *Chattanooga*

*Star,* is an authentic side paddle wheeler that can accommodate up to 145 passengers.

The Lookout Mountain Incline Railway ascends and descends the mountain every half hour with trolley-style railcars, offering panoramic views of the city. One of the steepest railways in the world, its gradient reaches 72.7 percent. The self-guided tour of famous Rock City on Lookout Mountain reveals giant prehistoric rock formations, breathtaking views, and visits to Fairyland Caverns and Mother Goose Village, where fairy tales are celebrated. Ruby Falls-Lookout Mountain Caverns is a cave providing a view of a 145-foot waterfall that is 1,120 feet underground. The Tennessee Wildlife Center is an environmental educational facility featuring exhibits such as a wildlife diorama, interactive computer games, and a crawl-in beaver lodge, as well as a 1,200-foot Wetland Boardwalk, and a Wildlife Rehabilitation laboratory. Adjoining Lookout Mountain is Reflection Riding, a 300-acre nature preserve that permits visitors to drive through a grand variety of trees, shrubs, and wildflowers similar to those in an English landscape.

Straddling the Tennessee-Georgia border, the 9,000-acre Chickamauga and Chattanooga National Military Park is the nation's oldest and largest preserved area of Civil War sites. Chickamauga Battlefield unit offers ''living history'' programs, the Fuller gun collection, a self-guided tour, and a multimedia presentation on the battle. Lookout Mountain unit offers free programs, the Craven's House Museum, and magnificent views from Point Park. The National Medal of Honor Museum displays memorabilia, artifacts, equipment, and history about the Medal of Honor. An exciting three-dimensional presentation of Chattanooga's Civil War history is presented at the Battles for Chattanooga Museum, which features 5,000 miniature figures, 650 lights, sound effects, and details of major battles. Signal Point, atop Signal Mountain, is the site where messages were relayed to clear the way for supplies coming down the Tennessee River for Union soldiers during the Civil War.

A number of interesting historical houses and buildings are located around the city. The Brabson House, built in 1857 and later used as a hospital during the 1878 yellow fever epidemic, was destroyed by fire in 1881 and rebuilt in the early 1990s. The John Ross House, a memorial to the man who was the greatest chief of the Cherokee Nation, was built in 1779 by Ross's grandfather. Craven's House, built circa 1854, was the center of action in the Battle of Lookout Mountain, and the 1840s Gordon Lee Mansion served as headquarters to General William Rosecrans in 1863 as well as serving as a soldiers' hospital. After the Confederate evacuation of Chattanooga in 1863, General Braxton Bragg established his headquarters at the Lee & Gordon's Mill.

Other area attractions include water fun at the Alpine Slide, views of the underground lake of Lost Sea at Sweet-water, tours of the Jack Daniels Distillery at Lynchburg, and the games and rides at Lake Winnepesaukah Amusement Park.

## Arts and Culture

Chattanooga has a very active performing arts community. The Symphony and Opera Association presents symphony concerts, operas, chamber music, pops programs, young people's concerts and operas, and youth orchestras, with guest artists of international renown at the Tivoli Theatre. The restored Tivoli is a fine example of 1920s baroque elegance. With its ample stage depth and first-rate backstage and rehearsal facilities, the theater is the site of some of the city's major entertainment and cultural events, including touring Broadway productions. The Soldiers and Sailors Memorial Auditorium was built in 1924 and rededicated in 1991 after being refashioned into a theatrical venue with a sloped concert hall with permanent seating. The auditorium is an ideal venue for concerts, theatrical performances, meetings, andconventions.

Founded in 1923 as the Little Theatre of Chattanooga, the Chattanooga Theatre Centre is a 40,000 square-foot facility with a main stage seating 380 and a smaller Circle stage seating 200. The Theatre Center offers a variety of locally produced programs featuring professionally directed local and regional talent in its eight main stage shows, four smaller and more adventurous Circle Series shows, and four youth theater productions each year. The Backstage Dinner Playhouse, the Mountain Opry, and other area and regional theaters offer a variety of locally produced performances year-round.

Chattanooga has a number of dance companies including Ballet Tennessee, Chattanooga Ballet, Contemporary Performing Arts of Chattanooga, and Dance Theatre Workshop. These companies present a variety of programs from the holiday classic *The Nutcracker* to avant garde drama. The Chattanooga Boys Choir, which includes approximately 200 boys in the program each year, and Girls Choir, composed of nearly 150 girls, travel throughout the United States and abroad. Rock and popular concerts are held at Memorial Auditorium.

The Heritage Center features the 264-seat Bessie Smith Performance Hall, a legacy of the city's ''Empress of the Blues.'' Adjacent to the Bessie Smith Hall is the Chattanooga African-American History Museum, which contains a library and a collection of artifacts including African art, original sculptures, paintings, musical recordings, and local African American newspapers. The Houston Museum of Decorative Arts is famous for its outstanding collection of American decorative arts assembled by Anna S. Houston, a local antiques dealer. The museum features beautiful pieces of porcelain, glass, furniture, and ceramics. With one of the largest and finest collections of American art in the Southeast, the Hunter Museum of American Art is situated high on a bluff overlooking the Tennessee River. The museum houses masterworks from Thomas Hart Benton, Winslow Homer, and Andrew Wyeth. As of March 2005, the museum is undergoing a $19.5 million expansion and renovation; its new addition will be home to temporary exhibits and galleries.

The University of Tennessee at Chattanooga (UTC) provides the community with numerous offerings in the cultural and fine arts. The University Theatre presents several stage productions annually while faculty, student, and guest musicians participate in the Cadek Department of Music and Conservatory offerings. The University's Cress Gallery of Art, part of the UTC Fine Arts Center, houses visiting exhibitions as well as local and student art work. Patten Performances, formerly The Dorothy Patten Fine Arts Series, hosts top quality theatrical, concert, and dance presentations.

## Festivals and Holidays

Held in May, the two-day 4 Bridges Arts Festival celebrates the visual arts. The annual River Roast, also in May, draws thousands to the riverfront and features a barbeque, volleyball tournament, and Mayor's Regatta. The Bessie Smith Traditional Jazz Festival, another May event, is a three-day jazz extravaganza held at the Chattanooga Choo Choo's Station House. One of the recreational highlights in Chattanooga is June's nine-day Riverbend Festival, a musical celebration on the riverfront at Ross's Landing, which draws more than 540,000 people each year to see top-name entertainers. Musical performances on its six stages range from jazz, blues, rock, folk, country, bluegrass, classic and more. At the Southern Brewers Festival in Auguest, microbrewers from across the country offer more than 30 ales and lagers; the event also features music and food. October brings visitors from across the country to attend the two-week Fall Color Cruise and Folk Festival, which includes boat trips down the Tennessee River, food events, music, and crafts. The holiday season is highlighted by Christmas on the River, a parade of festively decorated lighted boats on the Tennessee River.

## Sports for the Spectator

Chattanooga boasts professional sports teams in baseball (Chattanooga Lookouts, Class AA Southern League) and football (Chattanooga Locomotion, National Women's Football Association Southern Division), and major collegiate sports entertainment at the University of Tennessee at Chattanooga (UTC). The Lookouts play in the 6,500-seat BellSouth Park, which opened for the 2000 season, while as of April 2005 the Locomotion will play home games at Howard Stadium, at Howard School of Academics and Technology. UTC's NCAA Division I basketball Mocs play at the McKenzie Arena, formerly called the UTC Arena

(capacity 11,218), while the Division I-AA Mocs football team plays its Southern Conference schedule at the 20,668-seat Max Finley Stadium, the site for the annual NCAA Division I-AA National Football Championship Games. UTC also fields NCAA Division I teams in cross country, golf, softball, tennis, indoor/outdoor track and field, volleyball, and wrestling.

## Sports for the Participant

Surrounded by parks, mountains, and nearly 50,000 acres of rivers and lakes, the Chattanooga area offers recreation opportunities of all kinds. The mountains circling the city feature camping, rock climbing, rappelling, and spelunking. The mountain rivers offer exciting white water rafting, kayaking, and canoeing. Fishing on the Tennessee River is always an attraction, and nearby Lake Chickamauga provides more than 35,000 acres of water for sailing, water skiing, and rowing. Another site for water enthusiasts is the 192 miles of shoreline on Nickajack Lake.

More than 200 tennis courts, as well as hundreds of basketball courts, softball and baseball fields, dot city neighborhoods. Golfers are beckoned by 25 area golf courses. Chattanooga has dozens of recreation centers and supervised playgrounds to occupy the young set. Around the city, organized team sports include softball, baseball, wrestling, polo, boxing, soccer, rugby, gymnastics, and swimming, while sporting clubs center on hunting, fishing, running, biking, and skiing.

The Tennessee Riverwalk, a scenic pedestrian pathway connecting a string of parks and playgrounds along the riverfront, was largely the reason for that designation. The Passage, slated to open in May of 2005, is a new pedestrian link between the river and the downtown area. One of the jewels in the Tennessee Riverpark system is Coolidge Park, located on Chattanooga's north shore waterfront. The 6-acre park is named in honor of Charles Coolidge, a World War II Medal of Honor recipient. The park boasts a restored Denzel carousel originally built in 1895 for Atlanta's Grant Park; it features 52 intricately painted, hand-carved animals created by students of artisan Bud Ellis at Horsin' Around, a year-round carousel animal carving school in Chattanooga.

## Shopping and Dining

Chattanooga is a shopping mecca for a region covering a 50-mile radius in Tennessee, Alabama, and Georgia. Residents are served by more than 40 shopping centers, including several enclosed major malls. Hamilton Place, with more than 200 stores, is the state's largest shopping mall; it is located in southeast Hamilton County. Rehabilitation efforts in the city's downtown have restored its vitality as a popular shopping and dining site. There, Warehouse Row, a $30 million upscale outlet complex, features designer shops located in 8 cavernous former turn-of-the-century railroad warehouses. Chattanooga's riverfront area has numerous shops alongside piers, boatslips, and waterfront parks. The East Ridge Flea Market, open on weekends and holidays, is a huge indoor/outdoor market featuring more than 200 vendors selling new and used items, and three restaurants.

Dining experiences in Chattanooga can be as varied as having dinner while walking or cruising along the Tennessee River or while watching a stage production or eating in a former railway dining car. Fine dining and more moderately priced traditional American fare are offered in many areas of the city. Casual eateries include burger joints, delis, buffets and cafeterias, and novelty settings. Ethnic cuisine runs the gamut from Chinese, Italian, and Tex-Mex to Jamaican.

*Visitor Information:* Chattanooga Area Convention & Visitors' Bureau, 2 Broad Street, Chattanooga, TN 37402; telephone (423)756-0001; toll-free (800)962-5213

# Convention Facilities

Chattanooga offers several facilities designed to hold such diverse events as trade shows, conventions, meetings, banquets, or any other special event. The Chattanooga/Hamilton Convention Center and Trade Center underwent a $56 million renovation completed in the summer of 2002. Located in the heart of downtown, the 298,000 square-foot trade center offers 180,000 square feet of exhibit space and has a seating capacity of 8,500. The Tivoli Theatre, which is listed on the National Register of Historic places and was once known as ''The Jewel Box of the South,'' can host meetings and conventions for more than 1,700 people. Soldiers & Sailors Memorial Auditorium features two theaters, the larger of which seats 3,866, and an exhibit hall providing 9,600 square feet of display space, suitable for small trade shows. For larger groups, McKenzie Arena at the University of Tennessee seats 12,000 people, and can provide 27,000 square feet of exhibit space.

*Convention Information:* Chattanooga Area Convention & Visitors' Bureau, 2 Broad Street, Chattanooga, TN 37402; telephone (423)756-8687; toll-free (800)964-8600

# Transportation

## Approaching the City

Three interstate highways, I-75, I-24, and I-59 converge near the city. I-75 runs southwest toward the city from Knoxville, and north-northwest from Atlanta; I-59 runs

north, then east from Birmingham; and I-24 runs south, then east from Nashville. The city is a convenient stop en route to cities such as New Orleans, Orlando, and many other deep south destinations. Chattanooga Metropolitan Airport/Lovell Field, just 15 minutes from downtown, offers 52 flights daily, including direct flights to New York City, Washington D.C., Chicago, Memphis, Cincinnati, and Charlotte. Greyhound/Trailways Bus Lines provides interstate service.

## Traveling in the City

The three Interstate Highways, I-75, I-24 and I-59, are particularly busy during the rush hour to and from work. Major thoroughfares include Hixson Pike, which runs north-south, and Brainerd Road, which runs east-west then turns north into Lee Highway. Ringgold Road is another important east-west route. Riverside Drive curves around many major downtown sites. The Chattanooga Area Regional Transportation Authority (CARTA) provides regularly scheduled public bus transportation for the area. CARTA also offers free downtown electric shuttle service for visitors, residents, and downtown workers.

# Communications

## Newspapers and Magazines

The *Chattanooga Times Free Press* is the city's daily morning paper. The Chattanoogan.com is a daily internet-only news source available at www.chattanoogan.com. There are several general and special weekly newspapers, among them the *Chattanooga Courier,* which serves the area's African American community, and *The Pulse,* which provides alternative news. Magazines covering Chattanooga include *Commerce* and *Tennessee Business Journal,* both published monthly; and *Chattanooga CityScope* and *Chattanooga Magazine,* published quarterly.

## Television and Radio

Seven television stations and 15 radio stations serve the Chattanooga area.

*Media Information:* The *Chattanooga Times/Chattanooga Free Press,* 400 E. 11th St., PO Box 1447, Chattanooga, TN 37403; telephone (423)756-6900

## Chattanooga Online

Chattanooga Area Chamber of Commerce. Available www.chattanooga-chamber.com

Chattanooga Area Convention & Visitors Bureau. Available www.chattanoogafun.com

Chatanooga-Hamilton County Bicentennial Library. Available www.lib.chattanooga.gov

Chattanooga Regional History Museum. Available www.chattanoogahistory.com

City of Chattanooga Home Page. Available www.chattanooga.gov

*Free Press and Times*. Available www.timesfreepress.com

Hamilton County School System. Available www.hcde.org

Virtual Chattanooga. Available www.chattanooga.net

## Selected Bibliography

Burton, Linda L., *Chattanooga Great Places* (Chattanooga, TN: Phase II Publications, 1995).

Rodgers, June Scobee, Jack Makuch, and Chattanooga Area Chamber of Commerce, *Chattanooga: River City Renaissance* (Memphis, Tenn.: Towery Publishers, 1998)

Wann, Libby, *Chattanooga: Delivering the Dream* (Nashville, TN: Towery Publishing Co., 1991).

# Knoxville

## *The City in Brief*

**Founded:** 1786 (incorporated 1791)

**Head Official:** Mayor Bill Haslam (R) (since 2003)

**City Population**
  **1980:** 175,045
  **1990:** 169,761
  **2000:** 173,890
  **2003 estimate:** 173,278
  **Percent change, 1990–2000:** 2.4%
  **U.S. rank in 1980:** 77th
  **U.S. rank in 1990:** 101st (State rank: 3rd)
  **U.S. rank in 2000:** 135th (State rank: 3rd)

**Metropolitan Area Population**
  **1980:** 546,488
  **1990:** 585,960 (MSA)
  **2000:** 687,249 (MSA)

**Percent change, 1990–2000:** 17.3%
**U.S. rank in 1980:** 60th (MSA)
**U.S. rank in 1990:** 65th (MSA)
**U.S. rank in 2000:** 62nd (MSA)

**Area:** 92.7 square miles (2000)
**Elevation:** Approximately 936 feet above sea level
**Average Annual Temperature:** 60.0° F
**Average Annual Precipitation:** 48.2 inches

**Major Economic Sectors:** wholesale and retail trade, services, government
**Unemployment rate:** 3.3% (December 2004)
**Per Capita Income:** $18,171 (1999)

**2002 FBI Crime Index Total:** 11,983

**Major Colleges and Universities:** University of Tennessee at Knoxville, Knoxville College, Pellissippi State Technical Community College

**Daily Newspaper:** *The Knoxville News-Sentinel*

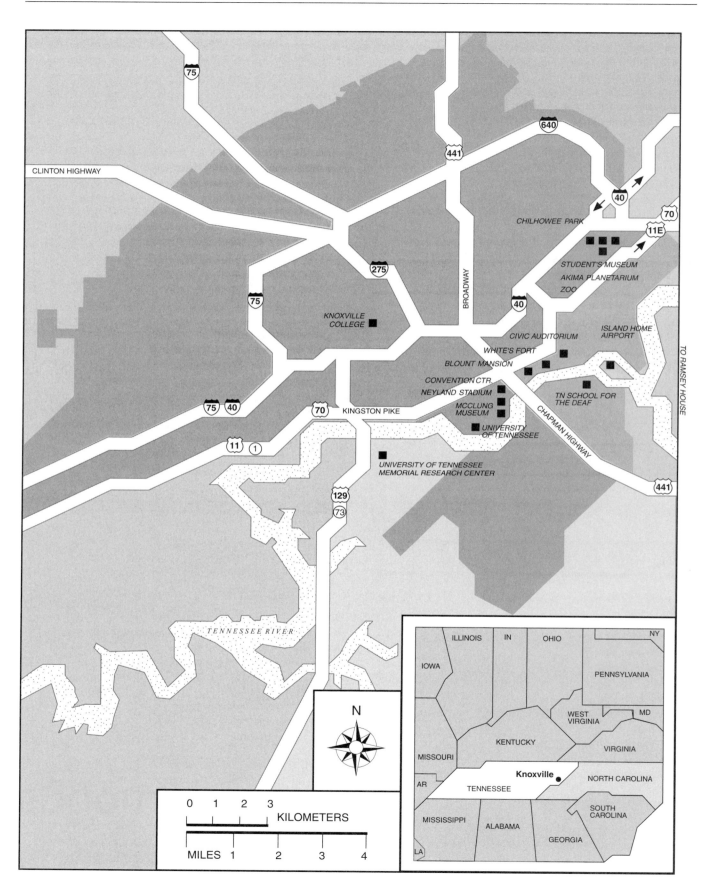

# Introduction

Just 30 miles north of the country's most visited national park, Knoxville, Tennessee, has long been known as the "Gateway to the Smokies." The greater Knoxville area has won accolades for its "livability"—a combination of qualities that encompasses such factors as economic outlook, climate, cost of living, education, transportation, and the arts. The corporate hub of east Tennessee and home to the Tennessee Valley Authority (TVA) and the University of Tennessee at Knoxville's main campus, the city is not yet among the South's urban giants. In the last several decades Knoxville has experienced impressive gains, particularly in high-technology industries and related firms. Because of the influence of TVA, the University of Tennessee at Knoxville and world-famous Oak Ridge, 30 miles away, Knoxville has become known as one of the foremost energy centers in the world. Knoxvillians are determined to enjoy the fruits of development without sacrificing those qualities that have made their city stand out among the country's smaller urban areas.

# Geography and Climate

Knoxville is located at the headwaters of the Tennessee River in a broad valley between the Cumberland Mountains to the northwest and the Great Smoky Mountains to the southeast. Both mountain ranges modify the type of weather that plains areas at the same latitude experience by slowing and weakening cold winter air from the north and tempering hot summer winds from the west and south. Precipitation is usually in the form of rain, and falls primarily during the winter and in late spring, though sudden thunderstorms are also quite common in summertime and provide relief on extremely warm days in the valley. Snowfall averages approximately 12 inches annually, most often in amounts of less than four inches at one time; it rarely stays on the ground for more than a week.

**Area:** 92.7 square miles (2000)

**Elevation:** Approximately 936 feet above sea level

**Average Temperatures:** January, 37.6° F; July, 77.7° F; annual average, 60.0° F

**Average Annual Precipitation:** 48.2 inches

# History

## Settlement Becomes Supply Center

Archaeological evidence suggests that the first humans to live in what is now Knoxville were of the Woodland tribe, a group of hunters and trappers driven south from the Great Lakes region by climatic changes, probably about 1000 B.C. Their simple culture eventually gave way to that of the more sophisticated mound builders, whose influence was felt throughout most of the South. By 1761, the year the first white men were known to have explored Knoxville, the mound builders had been displaced by yet another group of Native Americans, the Cherokee.

Early contacts between the white settlers and the Cherokee were fairly cordial, which encouraged colonial expansion into the land west of the Great Smoky Mountains. In 1783 North Carolina's James White and several friends crossed the mountains in search of a place to stake a claim. White later returned to the area with his family, and in 1786 he became Knoxville's first permanent settler when he built a log cabin on a hill overlooking a stream that fed into the Tennessee River. A peace treaty with the Cherokee sparked additional migration into the region, and soon White's cabin was joined by several others. After the pioneers connected their cabins with a stake fence, the settlement took on the name White's Fort. Because of its strategic location, it quickly began serving as a repair and supply center for westbound wagon trains.

In 1790 William Blount, newly appointed governor of the territory south of the Ohio River and superintendent of Indian affairs for the same region, arrived at White's Fort and established his headquarters there. One of his first tasks was to meet with the Cherokee and establish territorial boundaries; this he accomplished almost immediately, purchasing from the Cherokees much of the East Tennessee Valley and opening the area to even more settlers. In 1791, at Blount's suggestion, streets were laid out around White's Fort and a town was incorporated that the governor named Knoxville in honor of the Secretary of War, Major General Henry Knox. By 1792, Knoxville had become the county seat, and it continued to grow steadily as a trading post. When Tennessee was admitted to the Union in 1796, Knoxville even served as the state's first capital, a designation it retained until 1812. Despite its political and economic status, Knoxville at the turn of the century was little more than a rowdy village of taverns and smithies that catered to teamsters, flatboatmen, soldiers, and homesteaders on their way west.

## City Grows Slowly

Knoxville's first industries were related to its function on the frontier; among the most common were grist mills, sawmills, tanyards, cotton-spinning factories, and wool-carding mills. Because of the transportation difficulties posed by the mountains and unnavigable parts of the Tennessee River, no attempt was made to mine nearby coal, iron, and marble for shipping out of the region. As a result, Knoxville grew rather slowly in comparison with the rest of the state, posting a population of barely more than 2,000 people in 1850. The arrival of the railroad in the 1850s promised change, but the advent of the Civil War put a halt to further development.

A majority of east Tennessee citizens were loyal to the Union before and even during the Civil War, and their opposition to secession made Tennessee the last state to join the Confederate States of America. Alarmed at the thought of so many Union sympathizers in a critical border state, the Confederate Army occupied the city from early 1861 until August 1863, shortly before Union troops arrived and established headquarters there. In November of that same year, Confederate troops tried to recapture Knoxville. After a two-week-long siege, they were eventually repulsed, but victory for the Union forces came at a great cost to Knoxville—railroad shops, factories, virtually all public buildings, and some private homes were either burned to the ground or badly damaged.

The Reconstruction period was a boon to the city as hundreds of former Union soldiers chose to return to Knoxville to settle permanently, bringing with them the business and labor skills so desperately needed to rebuild what had been destroyed during the war. The population swelled to almost 10,000 people in 1870, up from less than 3,000 people in 1860. The rest of the century brought still more development; iron plants, cloth mills, furniture factories, marble quarries, and foundry and machine companies were established, and Knoxville began to emerge as a major southern commercial center.

### Economic Problems Abound

Throughout much of the twentieth century, however, Knoxville saw its postwar progress eroded by racial tension, periodic economic downturns, the Great Depression of the 1930s, loss of population to the suburbs, and a series of ineffective city governments. The 1920s provided a brief respite from economic woes as the city benefited from the national boom, but social and political conditions continued to deteriorate when conservative leaders clashed with progressive elements over the best way to tackle Knoxville's problems. Like so many other cities, Knoxville was hit hard by the Great Depression; factories closed, major banks failed, and the optimism of the previous decade faded, leaving in its place a cautiousness that influenced decision-makers for years to come.

### Wartime Brings Prosperity

World War II brought prosperity to the area, especially at Alcoa Aluminum, Oak Ridge National Laboratory, the Ten-

nessee Valley Authority, and Rohm & Haas, manufacturers of plexiglass for airplanes. The influx of federal money and jobs led to increased activity in other areas, including construction, service industries, and retail and wholesale trade. But Knoxville failed to capitalize on the wartime gains and instead entered another period of stagnation during the 1950s.

### City Celebrates Progressive Spirit

Since the mid-1960s, however, Knoxville has been busy reversing the trends of previous years. A new generation of progressive business and political leaders has worked to make the city more attractive to developers, initiating facelifts for downtown buildings, arranging financing for new projects, cleaning up the riverfront, and demolishing or upgrading substandard housing. The 1982 World's Fair and its theme of "Energy Turns the World" focused even more attention on the city's attempts to stage a comeback. New industries, especially high-technology ones, have established facilities in the area, and old industries have expanded. This in turn has led to gains in construction, services, and retail trade as thousands of young, well-educated, and affluent workers have followed the high-technology firms to Knoxville. In 2005, *Expansion Management* magazine ranked Knoxville 14th on its list of "America's 50 Hottest Cities" for businesses looking to expand or relocate. Knoxville intends to build on the progress of the past to make the twenty-first century the best years yet for the "Gateway to the Smokies."

*Historical Information:* East Tennessee Historical Society, McClung Historical Collection, 314 W. Clinch Ave., Knoxville, TN 37902; telephone (865)544-5744

## Population Profile

### Metropolitan Area Residents

*1980:* 546,488
*1990:* 585,960
*2000:* 687,249
*Percent change, 1990–2000:* 17.3%
*U.S. rank in 1980:* 60th (MSA)
*U.S. rank in 1990:* 65th (MSA)
*U.S. rank in 2000:* 62nd (MSA)

### City Residents

*1980:* 175,045
*1990:* 169,761
*2000 estimate:* 173,890
*2003 estimate:* 173,278
*Percent change, 1990–2000:* 2.4%

*U.S. rank in 1980:* 77th

*U.S. rank in 1990:* 101st (State rank: 2nd)

*U.S. rank in 2000:* 135th (State rank: 2nd)

*Density:* 1,876.7 people per square mile (2000)

*Racial and ethnic characteristics* (2000)
White: 138,611
Black or African American: 28,171
American Indian and Alaska Native: 541
Asian: 2,525
Native Hawaiian and Pacific Islander: 60
Hispanic or Latino (may be of any race): 2,751
Other: 3,982

*Percent of residents born in state:* 67.6% (2000)

*Age characteristics* (2000)
Population under 5 years old: 10,296
Population 5 to 9 years old: 9,610
Population 10 to 14 years old: 9,033
Population 15 to 19 years old: 13,652
Population 20 to 24 years old: 20,800
Population 25 to 34 years old: 27,311
Population 35 to 44 years old: 24,062
Population 45 to 54 years old: 20,702
Population 55 to 59 years old: 7,361
Population 60 to 64 years old: 6,069
Population 65 to 74 years old: 11,977
Population 75 to 84 years old: 9,393
Population 85 years and older: 3,624
Median age: 33.4 years

*Births* (2003; Knox County)
Total number: 5,058

*Deaths* (2003; Knox County)
Total number: 3,661 (of which, 39 were infants under the age of 1 year)

*Money income* (1999)
Per capita income: $18,171
Median household income: $27,492
Total households: 76,550

*Number of households with income of . . .*
less than $10,000: 14,282
$10,000 to $14,999: 7,255
$15,000 to $24,999: 13,643
$25,000 to $34,999: 10,878
$35,000 to $49,999: 11,958
$50,000 to $74,999: 10,089
$75,000 to $99,999: 4,085
$100,000 to $149,999: 2,690
$150,000 to $199,999: 705
$200,000 or more: 965

*Percent of families below poverty level (2000):* 14.4% (29.8% of which were female householder families with related children under 5 years)

*2002 FBI Crime Index Total:* 11,983

# Municipal Government

Knoxville operates via a mayor-council form of government. The mayor and nine council members are elected to four-year terms.

**Head Official:** Mayor Bill Haslam (R) (since 2003; current term expires 2006)

**Total Number of City Employees:** 2,858 (2004)

*City Information:* City of Knoxville, PO Box 1631, 400 Main St., Knoxville, TN 37902; telephone (865)215-2000

# Economy

**Major Industries and Commercial Activity**

The stable economy of the Greater Knoxville Area is one of the region's major assets. It is highly diversified with no one employment sector accounting for more than 22 percent of the area's total employment. Recent years have seen substantial growth in the areas of trade, transportation, utilities, and financial activities.

Knoxville's economy is bolstered by the presence of the Tennessee Valley Authority headquarters and the University of Tennessee at Knoxville. Added benefits accrue with the location of ORNL, a major U.S. Department of Energy facility, in nearby Oak Ridge. Scientists and engineers at ORNL labs do research and development work to bring scientific knowledge and technological solutions that strengthen U.S. leadership in the area of science; increase the availability of clean energy; restore and protect the environment; and contribute to national security. These institutions provide unlimited education and training opportunities for area businesses and are active in a cooperative technology transfer program that has successfully spawned many spin-off companies. The Spallation Neutron Source (SNS) project, based in Oak Ridge, is scheduled for completion in mid 2006. SNS development is carried out by collaboration of six national laboratories, and is based at an 80-acre site at ORNL. The $1.4 billion project will produce the most powerful pulsed neutron sources in the world for scientific research and industrial development, making the region a world leader in technology. The project is expected to have applications in the areas of chemistry, physics, biology, genetics, semiconductors and aerospace engineering.

As another nurturing aspect of the local business climate, the area features an unusually high number of incubator facilities, particularly in Oak Ridge—a city whose roots can be traced to the Manhattan Project of the late 1930s and early 1940s.

Through the assistance of the ORNL and University of Tennessee (UT), spin-off companies have been formed. UT, Lockheed Martin Energy Systems, and TVA, have been successful in recruiting national high-technology consortiums. The city itself is very technology-forward, with fiber-optic lines threaded throughout its downtown core. Knoxville Telecommunication infrastructure is a critical factor in the site selection process of relocating companies, and Knoxville's state-of-the-art telecommunications structure has helped the city attract several telemarketing divisions of large corporations.

Another key element in the Greater Knoxville area's economic prosperity is location. Knoxville is at the center of the eastern half of the United States and within one day's drive of three-fourths of the U.S. population. Location is one important reason why many manufacturing businesses have relocated or expanded in the area. In 2004, new or expanding industrial businesses in the Knoxville Metropolitan MSA invested $283,345,000; those investments were made by 4 new businesses and 16 existing companies. Location is also a factor in the area's booming tourism industry, particularly in nearby Sevier County, where approximately 10 million people annually visit the Great Smoky Mountains National Park—the most visited national park in the United States—and the many other attractions in Gatlinburg, Pigeon Forge and Sevierville.

Knoxville remains an urban center for mining in the Cumberland range. Zinc and coal mining are carried on in the region. Burley tobacco and a variety of food crops are harvested on farms just outside the city, and livestock and dairy products are also important to the local economy. Knox County ranks fifth in the state of Tennessee for visitor expenditures; in 2001 tourism brought the county $549 million.

*Items and goods produced:* motor vehicles supplies, manufactured housing, aluminum products, clothing, computer peripherals, electrical equipment, plastics, pleasure boats, processed foods

## Incentive Programs—New and Existing Companies

*Local programs*—Knoxville has a Foreign Trade Zone, is an inland Port of Entry, and has a U.S. Customs Office. The city and county offer sales tax exemptions on new equip-

ment and special revenue bond financing programs. Knoxville's Jobs Now! campaign, launched in 2003, aims to attract new businesses to the Knoxville area and encourage expansion of local businesses, primarily through marketing, via advertising, trade show exhibitions, distribution of brochures, and calling on prospects. The city of Knoxville and Knox County have been the campaign's biggest backers, with annual contributions of $400,000 each; approximately 200 other backers bring the annual figure to $2 million.

*State programs*—Tennessee is a right-to-work state and its overall state and local tax burden is among the lowest of all 50 states. Tennessee has no personal income tax on wages or salaries. Finished goods inventories are exempt from personal property tax and industrial machinery is totally exempt from state and local sales taxes. Manufacturers receive other tax exemptions and reduced property assessments under specified circumstances. State-administered financial programs for businesses include: the Small and Minority-Owned Business Assistance Program, currently being developed by the state Treasury Department and expected to provide assistance to small and minority-owned businesses through loans, technical assistance, and program services; the Small Business Energy Loan Program, which helps qualified Tennessee-based businesses upgrade their level of energy efficiency in their buildings and manufacturing processes; the FastTrack Infrastructure Program, which assists in the funding of infrastructure improvements for businesses locating or expanding in Tennessee; and the FastTrack Training Services Program, which helps companies provide training for their staff.

*Job training programs*—Tennessee's FastTrack Training Services Program is Tennessee's primary source of financial support for new and expanding business and industry training. FastTrack staff work with businesses to plan, develop, and implement customized training programs. Training may be done in a classroom setting, or on the job. The Southeast Tennessee Industrial Training Service provides specialized services at low or no cost to employers, including task and job analysis, training program design and material development, coordination of programs with employee recruitment activities, provision of facilities and equipment for developing specific job skills; and provision of funding. Pellissippi State Technical Community College offers technical programs, and the Knoxville State Area Vocational Technical School offers career-oriented programs.

## Development Projects

Knoxville's healthy economy is exemplified by the many renovation and expansion projects underway or recently completed around the city. The newly-expanded Knoxville Convention Center, opened in July of 2002, is a sparkling, technologically-advanced facility boasting a 119,922 square-foot exhibit hall, a 27,300 square-foot divisible ball-room, 14 functional meeting rooms seating attendees in theater style, a lecture hall with seating for 461, and three luxury conference rooms. The East Tennessee Historical Center's Museum of East Tennessee History, McClung Historical Collection, and Knox County Archives will double in size upon the completion of a $20 million expansion in 2005. This will bring more exhibit and collection space to the museum; more space for growing number of books, manuscripts, and microfilm of the McClung Historical Collection; and more room for the Knox County Archives' permanent records of historic Knox County. An extensive $23.5 million restoration of the magnificent Tennessee Theatre was completed in January of 2005, returning the 1928 theatre to its former glory. Several new exhibits have opened at the Knoxville Zoological Park in recent years, including an elephant preserve and African grasslands exhibit, both opened in 2002, and a meerkat exhibit opened in 2003; the zoo's Kid's Cove, a fun environment designed for children, is scheduled to open in April of 2005.

***Economic Development Information:*** Knoxville Area Chamber Partnership, 601 West Summit Hill Drive, Suite 300, Knoxville, TN 37902; telephone (865)637-4550

## Commercial Shipping

All major air shipments in Knoxville originate out of Mc-Ghee Tyson Airport. A new cargo facility was constructed in the early 1990s, more than doubling the airport's cargo capacity. In the fall of 2000, McGhee Tyson Airport completed a $70 million renovation and expansion project of its main terminal and concourses. Rail is another option for those needing to transport freight to and from the Greater Knoxville area. Main rail service is provided by the Norfolk/Southern and the CSX rail systems. Fifty-seven regular-route, common-carrier truck lines have terminals in Knox County. Many irregular routes and special-contract carriers also supply the area with efficient ground freight services.

Because of navigation improvements made by the Tennessee Valley Authority on the Tennessee River system, Knoxville enjoys barge commerce with 21 other states on the Tennessee, Ohio, and Mississippi Rivers. This interconnected inland water system runs from the Gulf of Mexico to the Great Lakes, allowing shipments on water to such distant points as Houston, Tampa, Pittsburgh, Minneapolis, and Little Rock.

## Labor Force and Employment Outlook

The Knoxville area labor force is drawn from a nine-county region in eastern Tennessee. The presence of a variety of instructional centers, combined with the city's proximity to key U.S. markets and the state's commitment to nurturing research and development firms, has made Knoxville a considerable force in the world of high-technology industry.

The labor force has one of the lowest turnover and absenteeism rates in the country.

The following is a summary of data regarding the Knoxville metropolitan area labor force, 2003 annual averages.

*Size of nonagricultural labor force:* 355,400

*Number of workers employed in . . .*
   *manufacturing:* 42,100
   *trade, transportation and utilities:* 74,700
   *information:* 6,300
   *financial activities:* 18,000
   *professional and business services:* 40,400
   *educational and health services:* 37,600
   *leisure and hospitality:* 45,800
   *other services:* 14,800
   *government:* 58,700

*Average hourly earnings of production workers employed in manufacturing:* $14.10

*Unemployment rate:* 3.3% (December 2004)

| *Largest employers* | *Number of employees* |
| --- | --- |
| Covenant Health | 8,000 |
| The University of Tennessee at Knoxville | 7,934 |
| Knox County Public School System | 7,848 |
| Wal-Mart Stores, Inc. | 4,600 |
| St. Mary's Health System | 3,461 |
| Baptist Health System of East Tennessee | 3,000 |
| City of Knoxville | 2,858 |
| University of Tennessee Medical Center | 2,764 |

## Cost of Living

Knoxville's overall cost of living, assisted by low taxes and low utility charges, is among the most reasonable in the country. Home buyers everywhere in the Greater Knoxville Area benefit from housing prices that are lower than the national average, as well as low taxes and low utility bills. Electric power rates here are among the lowest in the nation. The Tennessee Valley Authority, a publicly owned utility, is headquartered in Knoxville and generates much of the electrical power used in homes.

The following is a summary of data regarding key cost of living factors for the Knoxville area.

*2004 (3rd Quarter) ACCRA Average House Price:* $192,000

*2004 (3rd Quarter) ACCRA Cost of Living Index:* 87.8 (U.S. average = 100.0)

*State income tax rate:* Limited to dividends and interest income

*State sales tax rate:* 7.0%

*Local income tax rate:* None

*Local sales tax rate:* 2.25%

*Property tax rate:* $2.96 per $100 assessed value in Knox County, $3.05 per $100 assessed value in city of Knoxville (2004)

**Economic Information:** Knoxville Area Chamber Partnership, 601 West Summit Hill Drive, Suite 300, Knoxville, TN 37902; telephone (865)637-4550

# Education and Research

## Elementary and Secondary Schools

Knoxville public schools are considered models of quality. They recently received an A+ rating from the Tennessee State Department of Education. The system offers diverse options, including advanced programs for gifted students, and comprehensive services for students with learning disabilities or physical challenges. Knox county's five magnet schools offer enhanced arts and science curriculums.

The following is a summary of data regarding Knox County public schools as of spring 2004.

*Total enrollment:* 62,000

*Number of facilities*
  *elementary schools:* 51
  *junior high/middle schools:* 14
  *senior high schools:* 12
  *other:* 12 (2 vocational schools and 10 special education centers)

*Student/teacher ratio:* 16:1

*Teacher salaries (2004-2005)*
  *minimum:* $30,530
  *maximum:* $51,770

*Funding per pupil:* $5,701 (2000-2001)

In addition to the public schools, students in metropolitan Knoxville may attend one of the area's 31 private or parochial schools. Hearing-impaired children from across the state attend the Knoxville-based Tennessee School for the Deaf.

**Public Schools Information:** Knox County Public School System, PO Box 2188, Andrew Johnson Building, 912 S. Gay St., Knoxville, TN 37901; telephone (865)594-1800

## Colleges and Universities

Knoxville is home to one public and three private institutions of higher learning. The largest and most influential by far is the main campus of the University of Tennessee at Knoxville (UT), located near downtown. The centerpiece of a statewide university system, it has 21 different schools and colleges (among them a College of Veterinary Medicine). UT offers bachelor's, master's, doctoral, and professional degrees in a total of 809 fields of study ranging from engineering and business to history and music. Several of the university's programs are highly ranked nationally, including its Physician Executive MBA program (ranked 1st), graduate program in printmaking (ranked 3rd), pharmacy (ranked 7th), and nuclear engineering (ranked 11th). The university works closely with area industries and research centers, including the Tennessee Valley Authority and nearby Oak Ridge National Laboratory, to provide leadership and expertise in a variety of high-technology fields.

The city's other major facilities are Knoxville College and Johnson Bible College, both of which provide four-year degrees in liberal arts and sciences, and Bristol University which offers bachelor of science degrees in business and computer science. Located nearby are Carson-Newman College and Maryville College. Pellissippi State Technical College offers two-year college transfer and technical programs, and State Area Vocational Technical School at Knoxville offers career-oriented programs.

## Libraries and Research Centers

The Knox County Public Library System (KCPLS) consists of the Central Library downtown (the East Tennessee Historical Center and Lawson McGhee) and 17 branches located throughout Knox County. Its annual circulation is over two million. The system's holdings encompass approximately one million volumes as well as numerous films, videos, compact discs, and other materials. Special interest fields include the history and genealogy of Tennessee, and the city of Knoxville and Knox County archives. The KCPLS offers free Internet access to patrons. The University of Tennessee (UT) at Knoxville and Knoxville College also maintain their own large libraries. Additionally, several Knoxville-area hospitals and city, county, and federal offices maintain libraries.

In addition to the Tennessee Valley Authority and Oak Ridge National Laboratory, the region's two largest research and development facilities, Knoxville is home to several other research centers, most of which are affiliated with the University of Tennessee at Knoxville. In 2000, UT created nine Research Centers of Excellence in the following areas: information technology research, food safety, neurobiology of brain diseases, diseases of connective tissue, environmental biotechnology, structural biology, vascular biology, genomics and bioinformatics, and advanced materials.

**Public Library Information:** Knox County Public Library System, Lawson McGhee Library, 500 West Church Avenue, Knoxville, TN 37902-2505; telephone (865)544-5750; email kplref@aztec.lib

# Health Care

Quality, affordable health care is available through the Knoxville region's five general-use hospitals, offering about 2,590 beds and providing practically every imaginable specialty, including many that are generally not found in communities of this size. In addition, Knoxville's East Tennessee Children's Hospital devotes itself exclusively to prenatal and intensive care, pediatrics, and children's surgery.

The largest hospital in the area is the University of Tennessee Medical Center at Knoxville (UT). UT is nationally renowned for its research programs in heart disease, cancer, and genetics. Pediatrics, intensive care for newborns, and organ transplants are among its expanding services. Another of Knoxville's outstanding hospitals is Fort Sanders Regional Medical Center. Fort Sanders features the Patricia Neal Rehabilitation Center, an $8 million facility specializing in treatment for disabled accident or stroke victims and a Kidney Stone Treatment Center with lithotripsy, the latest in kidney stone treatment. The hospital houses the Thompson Cancer Survival Center, a $20 million regional cancer unit closely affiliated with the prestigious Duke University Cancer Center. East Tennessee Baptist Hospital, offering a full range of services, is particularly known for its heart clinic.

St. Mary's Health System features a substance abuse center, a diabetes management center, and an Alzheimer treatment and research program. The hospital excels in laser eye care treatment as well as programs related to adolescent emotional behavior problems and home health care. Baptist Hospital of East Tennessee is known for its leading edge techniques in carotid artery treatment, and has the only Gamma Knife treatment center in the region, offering an alternative for brain tumor patients facing traditional surgery. Parkwest Medical Center's specialties include bariatric surgery, and treatment of breast cancer and heart disease.

# Recreation

### Sightseeing

A good place to begin a tour of Knoxville is at Volunteer Landing on the riverfront, the site of the Women's Basketball Hall of Fame, which recounts the first 100 years of women's basketball, and the new Gateway Regional Visitor Center, 500,000 square feet of total space showcasing information about the scenic beauty surrounding Knoxville. In the four-county Knoxville area are hundreds of thousands of acres of parks and recreational space, including 800 miles of forests, 800 square miles of trout streams, and seven major Tennessee Valley Authority lakes that provide more than 11,000 miles of shoreline and 1,000 square miles of water surface. Knoxville itself boasts the east-side Chilhowee Park and Tyson Park in the University of Tennessee at Knoxville area, and the Ijams Nature Center, a non-profit regional environmental education center located minutes from downtown Knoxville. A raptor center and snapping turtle exhibit were added in 2004.

Much of Knoxville's outdoor and tourism activity centers around the Great Smoky Mountains National Park, America's most visited national preserve, with more than nine million visitors annually. The Smokies—located 45 minutes from downtown Knoxville and skirted by Gatlinburg, Pigeon Forge, Sevierville and Townsend—provide both active and passive recreation. The park boasts 800 square miles, 95 percent of which is forested, including 20 percent old-growth forest; 700 miles of trout streams; and more than 800 miles of trails.

Many more miles of trails and trout streams are found in Cherokee National Forest, an hour's drive south of Knoxville. Five whitewater rivers flow through Cherokee National Forest's 640,000 acres. Commercial outfitters will rent equipment or provide guided trips on some of the rivers. There are five state parks located nearby: Big Ridge State Park, Cove Lake State Park, Frozen Head State Park and Natural Area, Norris Dam State Park, and Panther Creek State Park.

The area's lakes, known as the Great Lakes of the South, are a major source of pleasure to residents and visitors. They include Norris Lake to the north, recognized nationwide for its striper fishing, and Melton Hill Lake in Oak Ridge, known for its world-class rowing conditions. The climate stays warm from May through September, and water skiing, sailing, and swimming are popular pastimes.

The site of the 1982 World's Fair has developed into a permanent recreation area in the heart of the city. The 266 foot-tall Sunsphere is still within the park, and is Knoxville's unofficial symbol. Visitors can take in a 365-degree view of Knoxville from 26 stories up on the observation deck of the Sunsphere.

Historical homes are also popular with sightseers. Among the best known in Knoxville are the Armstrong-Lockett House (often called Crescent Bend because of its location in a bend of the Tennessee River), a stately mansion built in 1834 as the centerpiece of a 600-acre farm; Blount Mansion, the oldest frame house west of the Allegheny Mountains (it was built in 1792 by Governor William Blount); the Craighead-Jackson House, a brick home built in 1812 adjacent to Blount Mansion; and Ramsey House, a two-story stone structure built in 1797. James White's Fort, Knoxville's most visited historic site, is still standing on a bluff high above the Tennessee River near downtown; seven log cabins now house pioneer artifacts and furnishings, giving a glimpse into regional life of the past.

Built in 1858, Mabry-Hazen House retains its original furniture. The site is on eight acres atop the highest hill north of the Holston River. It was once a fort—first for Confederate soldiers and then for Union troops. Mark Twain memorialized the home's builder, Joseph A. Mabry, Jr., in *Life on the Mississippi.* The second generation to live in the house was fictionalized in the best seller *Christy,* and the third and last generation at Mabry-Hazen House was featured in *Life Magazine.*

With more than 800 exotic animals, many in their natural habitats, including gorillas, red pandas, and rhinos, the Knoxville Zoological Park is full of family fun, adventure, and learning. The zoo is nationally known for its work with red pandas (it has the highest birth rate of red pandas in the Western Hemisphere), white rhinoceroses, and reptiles. Popular exhibits include Gorilla Valley, Penguin Rock, North American River Otters, and the Birds of Central America Aviary. Special attractions include the Bird Show, featuring free-flying birds of prey, and camel rides, elephant encounters, and a children's petting zoo. The zoo's Kid's Cove, a fun environment designed for children, is scheduled to open in April of 2005; an elephant preserve and African grasslands exhibit opened in 2002, and a meerkat exhibit opened in 2003.

The historic Candy Factory Building was built circa 1917. There visitors can see chocolatiers at work at the South's Finest Chocolate Factory, which features more than 100 candies made and sold on the site. Nearby, visitors will encounter a row of beautifully restored Victorian houses. These quaint, brightly hued dwellings were built in the 1920s and are now home to antique and curiosity shops as well as studios and art galleries.

## Arts and Culture

Organizations like the Arts Council of Greater Knoxville support an active arts community. The Tennessee Amphitheater, located in World's Fair Park, is a popular venue and is used for numerous free concerts and productions sponsored by the city of Knoxville and private groups. The Oak Ridge Art Center is also a boon for the cultural climate of the region. It has a studio and a gift shop and displays both local and traveling artists' and photographers' exhibits. Classes are offered in such artistic endeavors as pottery, oil painting, watercolor, drawing, and sculpture.

Knoxville boasts two symphony orchestras: the world-class Knoxville Symphony Orchestra (KSO) and the Knoxville Chamber Orchestra. KSO, established in 1935, plays several concerts a year to sold-out houses at the magnificent Tennessee Theatre, which reopened in January of 2005 following an extensive $23.5 million restoration, and at the Civic Auditorium/Coliseum. The orchestra's core group also makes up the Knoxville Chamber Orchestra, which was founded in 1981 and performs a five-concert series in the historic Bijou Theatre.

The Knoxville Opera Company, which has achieved a position of prominence among American opera companies, produces several major operas annually. The Civic Music Association brings internationally known musicians to Oak Ridge; their performances alternate with concerts by the Oak Ridge Symphony and Chorus, composed of local musicians and with full-time professional directors.

A variety of dance forms are presented to Knoxville audiences by the Appalachian Ballet Company, Circle Modern Dance Company, the City Ballet, and the internationally acclaimed Tennessee Children's Dance Ensemble.

The University of Tennessee at Knoxville and Maryville College also serve as cultural centers for the region. UT's Department of Theatre is committed to providing drama education and exposure to outstanding theatrical productions—both to university students seeking a career in theater and to East Tennessee audiences desiring quality dramatic fare. The Ula Love Doughty Carousel Theatre, the Music Hall, and the Clarence Brown Theatre present musical, comedies, dramas and dance performances. Maryville College supports a Playhouse and College-Community Orchestra series.

The Knoxville Civic Auditorium/Coliseum brings to the area the best in professional traveling companies presenting Broadway hits. Local residents can not only view fine theater but also are encouraged to participate at the Oak Ridge Community Playhouse. The playhouse has a full-time professional director and offers a full season of plays and musicals.

Highlighting the history of the Knoxville region are many excellent museums and historic sites. The history of the entire area is the focus at the Museum of East Tennessee History, housed at the East Tennessee Historical Center along with the public library's McClung Historical Collection and the Knox County Archives. The Museum, Historical Collection, and Archives will double in size upon the completion of a $20 million expansion in 2005. African American history and culture reaching as far back as the 1840s is chronicled at the Beck Cultural Exchange Center in downtown Knoxville. Confederate Memorial Hall, an antebellum mansion that once served as General Longstreet's headquarters during the siege of Knoxville, is now a museum that houses artifacts, documents, and furniture of the Civil War era. The University of

Tennessee at Knoxville's McClung Museum highlights collections of history, anthropology, archaeology, natural history, science, fine arts, and furnishings.

The Knoxville Museum of Art is a dynamic institution providing exciting exhibitions from the surrounding region, the country, and the world. This state-of-the-art facility, located in downtown Knoxville's World's Fair Park, presents an average of 20 traveling exhibitions annually in its five galleries; its permanent collection is drawn from American art of the twentieth century and later. The Arts Council of Greater Knoxville sponsors exhibits and varied galleries at the Candy Factory at World's Fair Park, at the Ewing Gallery of Art and Architecture, and at the Joseph B. Wolffe Sculpture Gallery. The University of Tennessee Gallery Concourse focuses on the work of local, regional, and national artists.

To the north of Knoxville, Oak Ridge lures visitors with its American Museum of Science and Energy. One of the world's largest energy exhibitions, it features interactive displays, live demonstrations, computer games, and films for all ages.

In nearby Norris, the Museum of Appalachia offers the most authentic and complete documentation of the Appalachian way of life in the world. The museum houses one of the nation's largest collections of pioneer, country, mountain, and contemporary artifacts such as baskets, coverlets, quilts, early animal traps, thousands of tools, and early musical instruments. Enhancing the main display are 35 other authentic log structures—houses, cabins, a school, a church, and barns—all fully furnished with period relics.

**Festivals and Holidays**

Knoxville presents a variety of popular seasonal activities for residents and visitors. The 17-day Dogwood Arts Festival in April offers more than 350 events. The Dogwood Arts Festival is the largest civic celebration in North America, with more than 8,000 volunteers helping with its staging. This nationally renowned festival includes craft shows, concerts and sporting events, and features 500 miles of marked motor trails in Knoxville to showcase the abundant spring blossoms on the dogwood trees. The Bearden Festival of Art is the newest Festival event. Visitors can enjoy the galleries, shops, and restaurants of Bearden Village.

The Tennessee Valley Fair runs for 10 days every September, followed by the Foothills Fall Festival in October, featuring music from local and famous entertainers, arts and crafts, and a Children's Adventure Land. Tennessee Fall Homecoming, also in October, celebrates Appalachian crafts and mountain music. December's Christmas in the City is sponsored jointly by the city of Knoxville and downtown businesses. This two-month long center-city event is a combination of more than 100 activities featuring music, lights, a parade, trees on the rooftops, whimsical window scenes, and memories of Christmases past.

**Sports for the Spectator**

The Tennessee Smokies provide professional baseball for the area; they play at Smokies Baseball Park, located in Sevierville, Tennessee, just 15 miles from downtown Knoxville. The Knoxville Ice Bears, part of the Atlantic Coast Hockey League, play at the Knoxville Civic Coliseum. Area residents also enthusiastically attend the sporting events of the University of Tennessee at Knoxville. The 104,079-seat Neyland Stadium on the UT campus is the largest collegiate stadium in the South, and the second largest in the country. The Thompson-Boling Assembly Center and Arena, a 25,000-seat basketball arena, is home to the University of Tennessee Volunteers and the Lady Volunteers basketball teams. It also hosts a variety of other community events.

**Sports for the Participant**

Knoxville city and county parks contain more than 5,700 acres of parks and recreational space. Facilities include 144 playgrounds; 103 tennis courts, including some of the finest facilities in the South at Tyson Park, located just minutes from downtown Knoxville; 20 public golf courses; 27 recreation centers; numerous ball fields; and a variety of country clubs and indoor commercial recreation establishments. At Volunteer Landing Marina, watercraft including houseboats, pontoons, paddleboats, and aqua-cycles can be rented. In March 2005 Knoxville will host its first Knoxville Marathon, a 26.2-mile run beginning at World's Fair Park and ending at UT's Neyland Stadium.

**Shopping and Dining**

Knoxville boasts three large shopping malls, Knoxville Center, Simpson Enterprises, and West Town Mall, and more than two dozen other shopping centers. In the downtown area, there are several areas of retail activity, including Market Square Mall. Knoxville's historic downtown warehouse district, called The Old City, is a bustling area of dining, shopping, and entertainment nestled in restored nineteenth-century brick warehouses. Near the University of Tennessee at Knoxville campus, Cumberland Avenue is noted for its shops.

Visitors and residents alike can sample a broad array of foods at Knoxville-area dining establishments. Barbecue and country-style cooking are especially popular, but other choices abound, among them continental cuisine and ethnic specialties such as Greek, Italian, Mexican, and Asian.

***Visitor Information:*** Knoxville Convention and Visitors Bureau, 301 S. Gay Street, Knoxville, TN 37920, telephone (865)523-7263 or (800)727-8045

# Convention Facilities

Knoxville played host to the world in 1982 when the city staged a highly successful World's Fair. Situated within World's Fair Park is the Knoxville Convention Center, a sparkling, technologically-advanced facility boasting a 119,922 square-foot exhibit hall, a 27,300 square-foot divisible ballroom, 14 functional meeting rooms seating attendees in theater style, a lecture hall with seating for 461, and three luxury conference rooms. Opened in July of 2002, the Convention Center is within walking distance of excellent dining, charming shops, and major hotels.

While the Knoxville Convention Center is the area's newest and largest meeting facility, the Knoxville Civic Auditorium and Coliseum has served the community well for many years. It has been the site of political rallies, rock concerts, major theatrical presentations, international circuses, glitzy ice shows, and grueling sports events. Conveniently situated in the downtown area, the Coliseum Convention Hall provides 34,000 square feet of uninterrupted exhibition space, with an additional 11,000 square feet available for storage. Seating capacity in the Convention Hall is 2,200 people. Smaller shows can be accommodated in the 11,130-square-foot Exhibition Hall. The ballroom is a multifunctional area of the Civic Coliseum used for banquets, exhibits, dancing and meetings. It has a seating capacity for meetings of 500 people. The Civic Auditorium, which seats up to 2,407 people, features two balconies, upholstered seating arranged in tiers, excellent acoustics, and a fully equipped stage.

Unusual meeting spaces include the Lamar House—Bijou Theatre and the Tennessee Theater. Knoxville's fine hotels and motor lodges not only furnish more than 7,500 rooms throughout the county (with approximately 1,200 in the downtown/convention area), but also provide additional private meeting rooms.

*Convention Information:* Knoxville Convention and Visitors Bureau, 301 S. Gay Street, Knoxville, TN 37902; telephone (865)523-7263

# Transportation

### Approaching the City

Knoxville's McGhee Tyson Airport, located 12 miles south of downtown, is served by three national carriers and six regional carriers. The city's other major facility is downtown's Island Home Airport, which is a base for smaller general aviation traffic and privately-owned planes.

Access to the city via car, truck, or bus is made easy by the fact that three of the nation's busiest interstate highways—I-40, I-75, and I-81—intersect in Knoxville. Completion of an extension of the Pellissippi Parkway, designed to relieve congestion on Alcoa Highway, is expected in June of 2005.

### Traveling in the City

Public transportation is provided in Knoxville by Knoxville Area Transit (KAT) buses; lift service for the disabled and handicapped is available. KAT routes reach within a quarter-of-a-mile of 90 percent of Knoxville's population, with discount rates offered to students and senior citizens. Colorful trolleys reminiscent of those of the turn of the century provide free service in the downtown area.

# Communications

### Newspapers and Magazines

Knoxville has one daily (morning) newspaper, *The Knoxville News-Sentinel.* Numerous other weekly, bi-weekly, and monthly publications are published in Knoxville, as well as quarterly academic journals on such topics as mental health nursing, education for the gifted, nematology, economics, and journalism.

### Television and Radio

Five television stations—four network affiliates, and one public education channel—operate in Knoxville. In addition, 17 AM and FM stations broadcast to listeners in metropolitan Knoxville, offering programs to suit every taste.

*Media Information:* Knoxville News-Sentinel Co., 208 W. Church Avenue, P.O. Box 59038, Knoxville, TN 37950; telephone (423)523-3131

### Knoxville Online

City of Knoxville Home Page. Available www.ci.knoxville .tn.us

Knox County Public Library System. Available www .knoxcounty.org/library

Knox County Schools. Available www.kcs.k12tn.net

Knoxville Area Chamber Partnership. Available www .knoxvillechamber.com

Knoxville News-Sentinel. Available www.knoxnews.com

## Selected Bibliography

Agee, James, *A Death In The Family,* (New York: McDowell Oblensky, 1957)

Manning, Russ, and Sondra Jamieson, *Historic Knoxville and Knox County* (Norris, Tenn.: Mountain Laurel Place, 1991)

# Memphis

## *The City in Brief*

**Founded:** 1818 (incorporated 1826)

**Head Official:** Mayor Willie W. Herenton (D) (since 1992)

**City Population**
   **1980:** 646,174
   **1990:** 618,652
   **2000:** 650,100
   **2003 estimate:** 645,978
   **Percent change, 1990–2000:** 5.1%
   **U.S. rank in 1980:** 14th
   **U.S. rank in 1990:** 18th (State rank: 1st)
   **U.S. rank in 2000:** 24th (State rank: 1st)

**Metropolitan Area Population**
   **1980:** 939,000
   **1990:** 1,007,000
   **2000:** 1,135,614

**Percent change, 1990–2000:** 12.8%
**U.S. rank in 1980:** 40th (MSA)
**U.S. rank in 1990:** 41st (MSA)
**U.S. rank in 2000:** 43rd (MSA)

**Area:** 279.3 square miles (2000)
**Elevation:** 331 feet above sea level
**Average Annual Temperature:** 62.0° F
**Average Annual Precipitation:** 48.9 inches

**Major Economic Sectors:** services, wholesale and retail trade, government
**Unemployment rate:** 6.1% (December 2004)
**Per Capita Income:** $17,838 (1999)

**2002 FBI Crime Index Total:** 51,034

**Major Colleges and Universities:** The University of Memphis, Rhodes College, University of Tennessee Center for Health Sciences, Christian Brothers University

**Daily Newspaper:** *The Commercial Appeal*

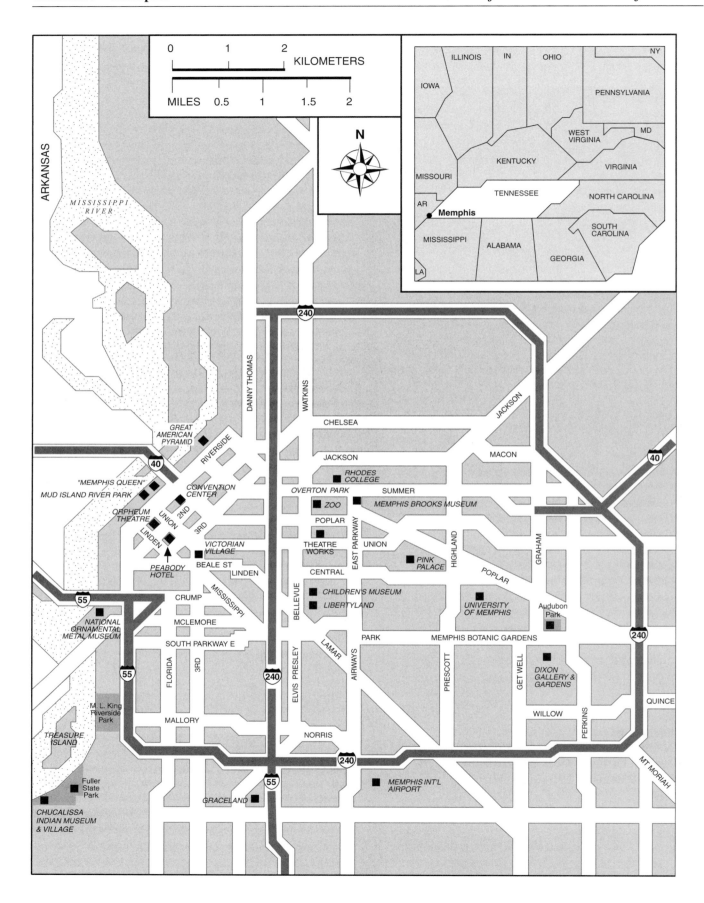

# Introduction

Situated on bluffs overlooking the Mississippi River, Memphis, Tennessee, has historically served as a commercial and social center for western Tennessee, northern Mississippi, and eastern Arkansas, and is considered by many to be the true capital of the Mississippi River delta. The city's rich history includes eighteenth-century French and Spanish forts, colorful riverboat traffic, and a driving economic force—cotton. The city numbers barbecue cooking among its contributions to the national culture and calls itself ''Home of the Blues'' and ''Birthplace of Rock 'n Roll.'' A five-time winner of the ''Nation's Cleanest City'' award, Memphis boasts a high quality of life enhanced by a pleasant climate, top-notch schools, and abundant recreational opportunities. Already a distribution hub and headquarters for leaders in services such as hotels and package express, Memphis proceeded through the end of the twentieth century with a technological focus on agribusiness and health care. Today, its Memphis Medical Center and St. Jude Children's Hospital are leaders in research and medical care, and the city continues to be an important commercial center; despite its development, Memphis retains an unhurried approach to life and remains close to its musical roots.

# Geography and Climate

Located in southwestern Tennessee on the east bank of the Mississippi River, Memphis is surrounded by slightly rolling countryside. The area, while subject to frequent changes in weather, experiences few temperature extremes. Precipitation is fairly evenly distributed throughout the year. May and October are considered to be particularly pleasant months in Memphis.

**Area:** 279.3 square miles (2000)

**Elevation:** 331 feet above sea level

**Average Temperatures:** January, 41.2° F; July, 81.2° F; average annual temperature, 62.0° F

**Average Annual Precipitation:** 48.9 inches

# History

### Jackson Helps Found City

Lush wilderness covered the Mississippi River bluffs (now known as the Memphis metropolitan area) when Spanish explorer Hernando De Soto encountered the area's Chickasaw inhabitants in 1541. In 1673, French explorers Louis Joliet and Jacques Marquette explored the region, called the Fourth Chickasaw Bluffs, which in 1682 was claimed for France by Robert Cavelier de La Salle as part of the vast Louisiana Territory. The French established Fort Assumption at the Fourth Chickasaw Bluffs in 1739. As ownership of the region was disputed by various nations, Fort Assumption was followed by the Spanish Fort San Fernando, built on the site in 1795, and the American Fort Adams, erected in 1797. The Chickasaw ceded West Tennessee to the United States in 1818, and the following year John Overton, James Winchester, and Andrew Jackson founded a settlement on the Mississippi River bluffs that they named Memphis, after an ancient Egyptian city on the Nile River.

### ''King Cotton'' Spurs City's Growth

Irish, Scots-Irish, Scottish Highlanders, and German immigrants joined westward-advancing pioneers from the eastern United States in settling the new town, which was incorporated in 1826. They served as gunsmiths and blacksmiths and operated saw mills, cotton mills, and cotton warehouses. The economy of the region was based primarily on the cotton industry, which utilized slave labor, and Memphis became the largest slave market in the mid-South. The necessity of transporting cotton to the marketplace made Memphis the focus of transportation improvements. The Memphis-to-New Orleans steamship line was established on the Mississippi River in 1834; six miles of railroad had been constructed around Memphis by 1842; and four major roads were carved out in the 1850s. In 1857 the Memphis-to-Charleston railroad line linked the Mississippi River to the Atlantic Coast. From 1850 to 1860 Memphis's population more than quintupled, swelling to 33,000 people.

When the economic and social differences between northern and southern states that led Tennessee to secede from the United States and join the Confederacy erupted in war, Memphis served temporarily as Tennessee's state capital. But in 1862 a Confederate fleet near Memphis was defeated by Union forces, which then captured Memphis. At the conflict's conclusion, Tennessee was the first state to rejoin the Union and the following year, in 1867, Memphis was made Shelby County seat. A series of yellow fever epidemics in the 1870s ravaged the city, leaving it deserted and bankrupt; in 1879 its charter was revoked.

Subsequent improvements to the city's sewage and drinking water systems helped reduce the threat of epidemic, trade resumed in Memphis, and its population mounted to almost 65,000 by 1890. The first railroad bridge across the Mississippi south of St. Louis opened in Memphis in 1892, increasing the city's trade opportunities. The following year Memphis regained its city charter, and by the turn of the century the city was once again established as a booming trading center for cotton and lumber.

### King Assassinated in City

In the first half of the twentieth century adversities in Memphis—such as the 1937 Mississippi River flood that brought 60,000 refugees into the city—were offset by advances—such as the formation of the Memphis Park Commission, the establishment of colleges, airports, military installations, and municipal utilities, and construction of port improvements. In the 1960s Memphis annexed neighboring areas and was the subject of federal court decisions ordering desegregation of the city's schools, parks, and recreational facilities. The city's sanitation workers, protesting discriminatory labor practices in a 1968 strike, attracted civil-rights leader Martin Luther King Jr., to their cause. On April 4, 1968, King, an advocate of nonviolent protest, was slain by a sniper at a Memphis motel. A steel structure entitled "The Mountaintop" honors King in Memphis's Civic Center Plaza. By 1973 court-ordered busing for school desegregation in Memphis was adopted without major incident, and the 1980 Memphis Jobs Conference, a broad-based economic planning initiative, was praised for its thorough integration of various Memphis sectors.

### Economic Growth

Present-day Memphis boasts renovated historic districts and city landmarks, striking new developments, and a diversified community of residents and workers. Traditional economic mainstays (such as cotton, lumber, and distribution) mix with services (including overnight package express, insurance, and hoteliery) and with newer enterprises (especially agricultural technology and biomedical technology) to make Memphis a strong economic community. Its strength supports academic institutions, health care facilities, and recreational assets and draws on a rich cultural and historical heritage, attracting both tourists and new residents to the river city on the bluffs.

*Historical Information:* Western Tennessee Historical Society Library, University of Memphis, McWherter Library Special Collections, Memphis, TN 38152; telephone (901)678-2210. Center for Southern Folklore Archives, 119 South Main Street, Memphis, TN 38103; telephone (901)525-3655. Memphis Pink Palace Museum Library, 3050 Central Avenue, Memphis, TN 38111; telephone (901)320-6368

# *Population Profile*

### Metropolitan Area Residents

*1980:* 939,000

*1990:* 1,007,306
*2000:* 1,135,614
*Percent change, 1990–2000:* 12.8%
*U.S. rank in 1980:* 40th (MSA)
*U.S. rank in 1990:* 41st (MSA)
*U.S. rank in 2000:* 43rd (MSA)

### City Residents

*1980:* 646,174
*1990:* 618,652
*2000:* 650,100
*2003 estimate:* 645,978
*Percent change, 1990–2000:* 5.1%
*U.S. rank in 1980:* 14th
*U.S. rank in 1990:* 18th (State rank: 1st)
*U.S. rank in 2000:* 24th (State rank: 1st)

*Density:* 2,327.4 people per square mile (2000)

*Racial and ethnic characteristics* (2000)
   White: 223,728
   Black or African American: 399,208
   American Indian and Alaska Native: 1,217
   Asian: 9,482
   Native Hawaiian and Pacific Islander: 239
   Hispanic or Latino (may be of any race): 19,317
   Other: 16,226

*Percent of residents born in state:* 64.4% (2000)

*Age characteristics* (2000)
   Population under 5 years old: 50,396
   Population 5 to 9 years old: 53,115
   Population 10 to 14 years old: 49,652
   Population 15 to 19 years old: 47,761
   Population 20 to 24 years old: 50,832
   Population 25 to 34 years old: 102,417
   Population 35 to 44 years old: 97,060
   Population 45 to 54 years old: 80,832
   Population 55 to 59 years old: 26,061
   Population 60 to 64 years old: 20,948
   Population 65 to 74 years old: 36,730
   Population 75 to 84 years old: 25,476
   Population 85 years and older: 8,820
   Median age: 31.9 years

*Births* (2003; Shelby County)
   Total number: 14,155

*Deaths* (2003; Shelby County)
   Total number: 7,768 (of which, 211 were infants under the age of 1 year)

*Money income* (1999)
   Per capita income: $17,838
   Median household income: $32,285
   Total households: 250,907

*Number of households with income of . . .*
    less than $10,000: 37,061
    $10,000 to $14,999: 19,816
    $15,000 to $24,999: 39,227
    $25,000 to $34,999: 37,471
    $35,000 to $49,999: 41,547
    $50,000 to $74,999: 40,510
    $75,000 to $99,999: 16,841
    $100,000 to $149,999: 10,811
    $150,000 to $199,999: 3,194
    $200,000 or more: 4,429

*Percent of families below poverty level:* 17.2% (33.9% of which were female householder families with related children under 5 years)

*2002 FBI Crime Index Total:* 51,034

# Municipal Government

Since 1966 Memphis has operated via a mayor-council form of government. The thirteen council members serve four-year terms; six are elected at-large, and seven are elected by district.

**Head Official:** Mayor Willie W. Herenton (D) (since 1992; current term expires 2008)

**Total Number of City Employees:** 6,680 (2005)

*City Information:* Memphis City Hall, 125 North Main Street, Memphis, TN 38103-2017; telephone (901)576-6766

# Economy

## Major Industries and Commercial Activity

At the center of a major distribution network, Memphis works from a broad economic base as it continues to diversify its employment opportunities. Historically a trading center for cotton and hardwood, Memphis is the headquarters for major manufacturing, services, and other business concerns.

The city is home to three *Fortune* 500 company headquarters: FedEx, AutoZone, and International Paper. FedEx began its operations in 1973, with 14 small aircraft delivering packages from Memphis International Airport. Today, FedEx averages more than 6 million shipments per day, and serves more than 220 countries and territories. AutoZone opened its first Auto Shack in Forrest City, Arkansas, in 1979; the company is now a leading auto parts retailer, with more than 3,400 stores nationwide. International Paper, organized in 1878, is the largest paper and forest products company in the world, with operations in more than 40 countries.

Memphis's economy is diverse. Services centered in Memphis include banking and finance (First Tennessee, National Commerce Bancorp, Union Planters); real estate (Belz Enterprises, Boyle Investment Co., and Weston Co.); nonprofits including the world's largest waterfowl and wetlands conservation organization (Ducks Unlimited); and a restaurant chain (Backyard Burgers). Science and technology business is very well represented in Memphis; Brother Industries USA, Buckman Laboratories, Medtronic Sofamor Danek, Morgan-Keegan, Sharp Manufacturing of America, Smith & Nephew, and Wright Medical Technologies all have headquarters there. Memphis is considered a mid-South retail center and an attractive tourist destination. Its early and continued role as a major cotton market makes agribusiness an economic mainstay in Memphis. Forty percent of the nation's cotton crop is traded in Memphis, home of three of the world's largest cotton dealers: Dunavant Enterprises, Hohenburg Brothers (now Cargill Cotton), and the Allenberg Company. Memphis is important in other areas of agribusiness. The city has long been established as a prime marketing center for hardwood, as well as wood and paper products. Memphis concerns are also major processors of soybeans, meats, and other foods. Enhancing Memphis's position at the center of agribusiness is Agricenter International, an $8 million, 140,000 square foot exhibition center for agricultural exhibitions, experimentation, and information exchange. It brings together the most technologically advanced methods of farming and farm equipment available in one location. The exhibition hall, where independent farm-related companies (chemical concerns, irrigation businesses, farm management companies, etc.) lease space, is totally computerized, allowing farmers and consumers to ask specific information of the computer and receive specific answers. The facility also includes about 1,000 acres of farmland, 120 acres of field displays, and a 600-seat amphitheater. Agricenter, a nonprofit entity that operates on a management contract with the Shelby County Agricenter Commission, was built amid 2,000 acres of old Shelby County penal farm land, in the eastern section of the county about 30 minutes from downtown Memphis.

Memphis business activities are facilitated by the city's Uniport Association, which coordinates a Foreign Trade Zone, and river, air, rail, and road transportation services into a top-ranked distribution network.

In the late 1990s Memphis made a name for itself as a center for movie making. Movies filmed there since then include *Mystery Train, Great Balls of Fire, The Firm, The Client, The People Vs. Larry Flynt, A Family Thing, The Rainmaker, Cast Away, 21 Grams, Forty Shades of Blue,* and *Walk the Line.*

*Items and goods produced:* chemicals, machinery, clothing, foodstuffs, electronic equipment, pharmaceuticals, cosmetics, ceiling fans, smokeless tobacco, gift wrap, bubble gum

## Incentive Programs—New & Existing Industries

*Local programs*—Think Memphis: Partnership for Prosperity is a public-private initiative whose goal is to make Memphis and Shelby County more globally competitive and attractive to businesses looking to relocate and expand. The program is in part a continuation of Memphis 2005, an economic development program begun in 1996 that aimed to diversify the economy, raise the per capita income, generate 12,000 net new jobs annually, increase minority and woman-owned business development, and lower the crime rate. Memphis 2005 has been credited with Memphis' average nonresidential capital investment of more than $1 billion a year, 10,000 net new jobs annually, and increased per capita income above the national average. Further, Think Memphis aims to enhance the economic vitality of the Memphis area through collaboration with its chambers of commerce, local and state governments, and other organizations; and aims to attract 10,000 newcomers to the region, and encourage Memphis residents to remain here, through a ten-year, multi-million dollar marketing effort.

*State programs*—Tennessee is a right-to-work state and its overall state and local tax burden is among the lowest of all 50 states. Tennessee has no personal income tax on wages or salaries. Finished goods inventories are exempt from personal property tax, and industrial machinery is totally exempt from state and local sales taxes. Manufacturers receive other tax exemptions under specified circumstances and reduced property assessments. State-administered financial programs for businesses include: the Small and Minority-Owned Business Assistance Program, currently being developed by the state Treasury Department and expected to provide assistance to small and minority-owned businesses through loans, technical assistance, and program services; the Small Business Energy Loan Program, which helps qualified Tennessee-based businesses upgrade their level of energy efficiency in their buildings and manufacturing processes; the FastTrack Infrastructure Program, which assists in the funding of infrastructure improvements for businesses locating or expanding in Tennessee; and the FastTrack Training Services Program, which helps companies provide training for their staff.

*Job training programs*—The state of Tennessee provides funds for eligible projects that can offset costs that are incurred during the training process. Each project is considered separately based on its economic impact to the state. This program does not include wage payments to persons involved in the training program. Vocational training in

Memphis is available through the Tennessee Technology Center, State Technical Institute of Memphis, Mid-South Quality Productivity Center, Southeast College of Technology, and through the public schools.

## Development Projects

In January of 2003, Cannon Center, a world-class performing arts center at the north end of Main Street, opened its doors. On the South end, Peabody Place Entertainment and Retail Center, a multifaceted entertainment center, opened in fall of 2001. This city within a city attracts more than 8 million visitors annually; it encompasses three blocks of Beale Street, and includes the Peabody Hotel, the Orpheum Center, Fed Ex Forum (home of the NBA Memphis Grizzlies) and Autozone Park (home of the AAA Memphis Redbirds), plus 80 restaurants. A $30 million Westin Hotel is being built next to the Fed Ex Forum, replacing a parking lot. Autozone park is a world-class baseball stadium that has been credited with stimulating nearby developments ranging from restaurants, night clubs, retail developments, and commercial and residential projects. The major one is Echelon at the Ballpark, a residential/business facility whose amenities include nine-foot ceilings, pass-through fireplaces, balconies with a ballpark view, a fitness center, and business facilities. In 2005 projects include the renovation of the Kress Building (listed in the National Historic Register) into an annex of the adjacent Marriot hotel, and renovation of the Lawrence Building into a luxury condominium with unique ''live/work'' areas on the first floor for professionals who work at home.

*Economic Development Information:* Memphis Chamber of Commerce, 2969 Elmore Park Road, Memphis, 38134, telephone (901) 372-9457. Tennessee Department of Economic & Community Development, 312 Eighth Avenue North, Nashville, TN 37243; telephone (615)741-1888

## Commercial Shipping

Memphis's Uniport combines a Foreign Trade Zone with river, air, rail, and road facilities to make Memphis one of the nation's most important distribution centers. The Memphis River Port, which connects the city to 25,000 miles of interconnected inland waterways, is the second largest inland port on the Mississippi River, and the fourth largest port in the nation. There are three still-water harbors, which include public terminals, loading facilities, grain elevators, and intermodal connections.

Memphis International Airport is less than 15 minutes from most business centers in the area and serves major airlines and commuter lines. One of the nation's fastest-growing airports, it is often the site of expansion projects, including improvements to cargo facilities. It is the world's busiest cargo airport because of FedEx, UPS, and other air freight companies that move approximately 2.4 million tons of cargo annually.

*Transport Topics,* a national newspaper for the trucking industry, has called Memphis ''an intermodal transportation hub like no other.'' The area is served by over 300 common carriers, including all major truck lines. Over 100 terminals offer direct services to all 48 contiguous states, as well as to Canada and Mexico. The presence of five Class I rail systems makes Memphis a center for world distribution in the new economy; Memphis is one of only three U.S. cities served by five or more such systems. Eight federal highways, three interstate highways, and seven state highways connect the Memphis trucking industry with both the rest of the nation and with other vital forms of transportation.

## Labor Force and Employment Outlook

Memphis boasts a diverse work force, prepared by nationally recognized schools and training programs. Memphis ranks high among business analysts for low taxes, competitive wages, and cost of living.

Memphis has seen substantial job growth in recent years; its Memphis 2005 program is credited with adding an average of 10,000 new jobs annually during the years 1996 to 2004. Currently, the high-tech bio and agri-research and health-related industries are thought to have particularly impressive growth potential, and the city's chamber of commerce seeks to attract technically skilled and creative workers to contribute leadership and manpower to those and other areas.

The following is a summary of data regarding the Memphis metropolitan area labor force, 2003–2004 annual averages.

*Size of nonagricultural labor force:* 616,400

*Number of workers employed in . . .*
  *construction and mining:* 26,400
  *manufacturing:* 53,000
  *trade, transportation and utilities:* 169,300
  *information:* 8,800
  *financial activities:* 33,000
  *professional and business services:* 72,200
  *educational and health services:* 71,700
  *leisure and hospitality:* 67,700
  *other services:* 24,400
  *government:* 90,100

*Average hourly earnings of production workers employed in manufacturing:* $14.96

*Unemployment rate:* 6.1% (December 2004)

| *Largest employers* | *Number of employees* |
|---|---|
| Federal Express Corp. | 30,000 |
| Memphis City Schools | 16,000 |

| *Largest employers* | *Number of employees* |
|---|---|
| United States Government | 14,800 |
| Methodist Healthcare | 10,000 |
| Baptist Memorial Healthcare | 8,000 |
| Shelby County Government | 7,183 |
| Memphis City Government | 6,680 |
| Wal-Mart Stores, Inc. | 6,500 |

## Cost of Living

The city of Memphis has a relatively low cost of living in comparison to other major cities in the country. The following is a summary of data regarding key cost of living factors for the Memphis area.

*2004 (3rd Quarter) ACCRA Average House Price:* $194,150

*2004 (3rd Quarter) ACCRA Cost of Living Index:* 90.7 (U.S. average = 100.0)

*State income tax rate:* Limited to dividends and interest income

*State sales tax rate:* 7.0%

*Local income tax rate:* None

*Local sales tax rate:* None; Shelby County sales tax is 2.25%

*Property tax rate:* In October 2003, the tax rate was $3.23 per $100 of property assessment. Property assessment is 25% of the property appraisal for residential real estate property.

***Economic Information:*** Memphis Chamber of Commerce, 2969 Elmore Park Road, Memphis, 38134; telephone (901)372-9457.

# *Education and Research*

## Elementary and Secondary Schools

The Memphis City Schools is the largest school system in the state of Tennessee and the 21st largest metropolitan school system in the nation. All Memphis City Schools are accredited; in comparison, 60 percent of elementary and 62 percent of secondary schools statewide are accredited. Shelby County schools have the largest PTA membership in Tennessee. Through Memphis' Adopt-A-School program, recognized by the U.S. Department of Labor as the best program of its kind in the nation, local businesses ''adopt'' a school to provide special support. All Memphis public schools are partnered with area businesses, and the program is so successful that many schools have numerous adopting sponsors.

Memphis City Schools offers gifted and talented programs, alternative schools for students who have problems in a regular school environment, and optional school programs that focus on such areas as college preparation, creative and performing arts, aviation, travel, tourism, health sciences, banking and finance, international studies and a variety of approaches to education.

The following is a summary of data regarding Memphis's public schools as of the 2004–2005 school year.

*Total enrollment:* 120,162

*Number of facilities*
  *elementary schools:* 112
  *junior high/middle schools:* 25 middle, 4 junior high
  *senior high schools:* 31
  *other:* 6 vocational, 6 charter schools, 7 alternative/specialty schools

*Student/teacher ratio:* 15:1

*Teacher salaries*
  *average:* $38,000

*Funding per pupil:* $6,326

Residents of Memphis and Shelby County also support a network of 70 private elementary and secondary schools. Premier among the list are St. Mary's Episcopal School, a school for girls in grades junior kindergarten through graduation, and Memphis University School, an all-boys preparatory school. Both are located within scenic surroundings in the eastern section of Memphis. Others often considered stepping stones to National Merit Scholarships are the Briarcrest Christian School System, Presbyterian Day School, and Harding Academy.

*Public Schools Information:* Memphis City School System, 2597 Avery Avenue, Memphis, TN 38112; telephone (901)416-5300

**Colleges and Universities**

The University of Memphis (U of M) is the largest college campus in Shelby County, both in size and student enrollment (more than 20,000). The U of M offers 15 bachelor's degrees in more than 50 majors, master's degrees in more than 45 subjects, and doctoral degrees in more than 20 disciplines. Set on 1,160 acres, its sprawling campus includes a College of Arts and Sciences, Fogelman College of Business and Economics, College of Communication and Fine Arts, College of Education, Herff College of Engineering, University College, Loewenberg School of Nursing, Humphreys School of Law, and Graduate School.

Rhodes College, recognized by *Time* magazine as ''one of the nine colleges challenging the nation's elite schools for

prominence'' is the oldest four-year liberal-arts school in the city. Founded before the Civil War (in 1848) in Clarksville, Tennessee, the college was moved to Memphis in 1925 and quartered in ivy-covered Gothic buildings, 13 of which are now listed on the National Register of Historic Places.

LeMoyne-Owen College, a four-year liberal-arts college, was founded in 1862 as LeMoyne to educate emancipated slaves; it later merged with Owen College and offers majors in 21 areas of study leading to three degrees: bachelor of arts, bachelor of science, and bachelor of business administration. The Memphis College of Art is an independent professional college of artistic study that offers bachelor's and master's of fine arts degrees in a number of visual arts disciplines.

Future doctors, pharmacists, dentists, research academicians, and others interested in the medical field flock to Memphis to attend and graduate from the University of Tennessee (UT) Memphis. Among the colleges of the system are those of Allied Health Sciences, Dentistry, Health Science Engineering, Medicine, Nursing, and Pharmacy, in addition to the UT Graduate School. UT is ranked among the largest and most progressive health science centers in the country.

Christian Brothers University is one of only a few private colleges in the nation to offer degrees in mechanical, electrical, civil, and chemical engineering. Chrichton College awards bachelor's degrees through its schools of arts and sciences; bible and theology; education and behavioral studies; and business.

Vocational schools such as State Technical Institute at Memphis provide a further dimension to educational opportunities available in Memphis and Shelby County.

**Libraries and Research Centers**

The Memphis/Shelby County Public Library and Information Center has an annual circulation of more than 3.3 million books. Its special collections focus on Memphis history, art and architecture, and business and management. The system maintains 23 branches and a bookmobile. Its Central Library, designed by Memphis architect Frank Ricks, opened in 2001; it is more than twice the size of the previous Main Library. The University of Memphis Libraries hold more than 1.1 million books, more than 10,000 periodical subscriptions, and many special collections, such as Confederate history, Lower Mississippi Valley history, and blues and jazz oral histories.

There are more than 40 research centers in Memphis. Research activities at the University of Memphis focus on such areas as business and economics, substance addiction, earthquakes, child development, neuropsychology, women, anthropology, ecology, oral history, educational policy, communication disorders, and genomics. Research conducted at centers affiliated with the University of Tennessee Center for the Health Sciences in Memphis focuses on fields such as neuroscience, vascular biology, genomics, and a variety of diseases and disorders. Christian Brothers University supports the M. K. Gandhi Institute for Nonviolence. St. Jude Children's Research Hospital studies pediatric diseases and abnormalities and is the only independent pediatric research center supported by a National Cancer Institute support grant.

*Public Library Information:* Memphis-Shelby County Public Library, 3030 Poplar Avenue, Memphis, TN 38111; telephone (901)415-2700

# Health Care

The Memphis and Shelby County region supports numerous hospitals, including Methodist and Baptist Memorial health systems, two of the largest private hospitals in the nation. Methodist Healthcare system operates seven hospitals as well as several rural clinics; it is the largest healthcare provider in the Mid-South. *Modern Healthcare* magazine recently ranked Methodist Healthcare among the top 100 integrated healthcare networks in the nation. Baptist Memorial Healthcare operates 15 hospitals, three of which are within the city of Memphis, including Baptist Memorial Hospital for Women, one of only a few freestanding women's hospitals in the nation. For nine consecutive years (1996-2004) Mid-Southerners have named Baptist Memorial Hospital–Memphis their ''preferred hospital choice for quality'' according to *Health Care Market Guide*'s annual studies. Memphians point with pride to St. Jude's Children's Research Hospital, a premier research/treatment facility for children with catastrophic diseases, particularly pediatric cancers. The institution was conceived and built by the late entertainer Danny Thomas in 1962 as a tribute to St. Jude Thaddeus, patron saint of impossible, hopeless, and difficult causes. Recent research at St. Jude's has focused on gene therapy, bone marrow transplant, chemotherapy, the biochemistry of normal and cancerous cells, radiation treatment, blood diseases, resistance to therapy, viruses, hereditary diseases, influenza, pediatric AIDS, and the psychological effects of catastrophic diseases. A billion-dollar expansion to double the size of St. Jude's and bolster its research facilities is well underway and parts of it will be completed and functional in early 2005: the new GMP building, an on-site facility for research/production of highly specialized medicines and vaccines; the Integrated Research Center, with a Children's Infection Defense Center; and an enlarged Immunology Department. Further expansion will include a new Integrated Patient Care and Research Build-

ing. Shelby County has more than 100 specialty clinics, including the nationally known Campbell orthopaedic center, Semmes-Murphey Neurologic and Spine Institute, and Shea Ear Clinic. Memphis has two mobile intensive care units providing prehospital emergency care.

# Recreation

## Sightseeing

Sightseeing in Memphis encompasses historical and modern attractions. At Chucalissa Archaeological Museum and Village in south Shelby County it is easy to step back in time—via slide shows, case exhibits, and village reconstruction—and learn about the Indian farmers, craftsmen and artists who lived in the area from 1000 to 1500 A.D. Operated by the University of Memphis, the archaeological site features tours and craft demonstrations by members of the Choctaw tribe.

The city's oldest private museums are located in an area known as Victorian Village, just a few miles east of downtown Memphis. Where once horse-drawn carriages kicked up dust as settlers arrived for afternoons of ''calling'' on their friends, Victorian Village today is a busy hubbub of tourist buses, cars, and bicycles as thousands come to see what life was like before electricity—when tea was poured from silver pots and ladies wore long, billowing frocks. The two most notable museum houses are the Woodruff-Fontaine House and the Mallory-Neely House (which, in 2005 is temporarily closed and awaiting funding). Woodruff-Fontaine, built in 1870, is French Victorian in style; Mallory-Neely was built in 1852. Several blocks away is the Magevney House; also temporarily closed, it is the oldest and by far the quaintest of the homes-turned-museums. The small white-frame building was built circa 1836. The home is furnished as it would have been in the 1850s.

Memphis's cultural heritage is strongly rooted in the mystical, magical sounds of jazz, blues, and rock and roll. W. C. Handy, the father of the blues, lived in Memphis when he heard bluesy music on Beale Street and then wrote such memorable songs as ''The Memphis Blues'' and ''The Beale Street Blues.'' Beale Street has been restored and redeveloped, serving as both a center for African American culture and entertainment and as a tourist attraction since 1983. A restaurant and nightclub district, historic Beale Street also contains the renovated Old Daisy Theatre; just across the street is the new Daisy Theater, a blues and jazz venue for all ages. The Center for Southern Folklore documents Southern traditions through live entertainment, folk art, and photography exhibits.

Sightseers in Memphis also visit the Peabody, the classic hotel in downtown that was originally built in the 1920s and renovated in 1981. Of interest are the hotel's Art Deco elevator doors, its stained glass work above the lobby bar, its reconstructed 1930s nightclub, and its resident ducks. By a tradition that started as a practical joke, a group of ducks occupies the hotel lobby's baroque fountain from eleven in the morning until five in the evening. During their arrival and departure, to the strains of John Phillip Sousa's "King Cotton March," they march over a red carpet unrolled between the fountain and the elevator that rises to the ducks' rooftop quarters. The Peabody's Plantation Roof attracts crowds of several hundred for Thursday evening Sunset Serenades. It is the very same spot where Paul Whiteman's and Tommy Dorsey's bands were once heard after their familiar radio introduction, "from high atop the Hotel Peabody, overlooking Ole Man River, in beautiful, downtown Memphis, Tennessee." In 2005, the Peabody will undergo a multimillion dollar renovation and refurbishment.

Fun can be found in many colors and hues at Libertyland, an educational and recreational theme park in Memphis. Built in 1976, the nonprofit park incorporates the themes of adventure, patriotism, and freedom under one giant, outdoor umbrella. The Memphis Zoo features 2,000 mammals, reptiles, birds, and fish in facilities that include an aquarium and a petting zoo. In March of 2005, a motion simulator ride opened at the zoo to take visitors on a thrilling trip to "Dino Island."

More than 700,000 people annually visit Memphis's Graceland, home of the late world-famous musician Elvis Presley; the entertainer moved to Memphis at age twelve, attended school there, and recorded his first songs at a studio in the city. He made Graceland, built in 1939, his home in 1957. Set on nearly 14 acres of lush grounds, Graceland is open to the public for tours that include glimpses of Presley's exotic Jungle Room, his gold-leafed piano, numerous television sets, and mirrored walls. Graceland's Trophy Building contains the singer's gold and platinum records, his costumes, and other memorabilia; the carport houses Presley's vehicles, including his legendary pink Cadillac. Graceland's Meditation Garden, the Presley family burial site, is also on view, as is the singer's private jet.

Another prime Memphis attraction is the mid-river Mud Island. What began as a sandbar in the Mississippi River grew into what is now called Mud Island, which was officially declared to be above the flood stage in 1965. Development of the island eventually resulted in the entertainment complex opened in 1982. It features a monorail, marina, amphitheater, playgrounds, River Museum, and a spectacular four-block-long River Walk that is an exact working replica of the Mississippi River; office workers and children alike are encouraged to wade in the River Walk's flowing waters. Mud

Island affords visitors a magnificent view of the Memphis skyline. Another Memphis-style experience is a sightseeing cruise along the Mississippi River aboard riverboat replicas.

## Arts and Culture

Touring Broadway productions are presented at the Orpheum Theatre, a lavish turn-of-the-century theater in downtown Memphis. Memphians and mid-South residents enthusiastically support other area theaters, including Theatre Memphis, Germantown Community Theatre, Jewish Community Center, Old Daisy Theatre (located on renovated Beale Street), Playhouse on the Square, and Circuit Playhouse. In addition, the University of Memphis and Rhodes College theater groups mount stage productions. Dance companies performing in Memphis include Ballet Memphis and the Memphis Youth Concert Ballet. Opera Memphis also performs in the city.

Besides the Memphis Symphony Orchestra, musical groups performing in the Memphis area include Roscoe's Surprise Orchestra, devoted to presenting audiences with the top new compositions in modern serious music. The University of Memphis and Rhodes College also support musical performances in the city. Live popular music is plentiful in Memphis, where audiences can hear the unique blend of blues, soul, and rock and roll that has been identified as the "Memphis Sound." Jazz, bluegrass, and country music are also found at Memphis nightspots, which thrive on historic Beale Street and at Overton Square. Next door to Beale Street, the new Gibson Guitar Plant is an active manufacturing facility that offers tours plus the Smithsonian Institute's "Rock 'n Soul: Social Crossroads," a permanent exhibit of the social and cultural history of music in the Mississippi Delta and Memphis.

Memphis-area museums and galleries display a range of art and artifacts. The Memphis Brooks Museum of Art exhibits Renaissance pieces, English portraits and landscapes, regional works, and traveling shows. The Art Museum of the University of Memphis features Egyptian and African collections, as well as regional, faculty, and student work. Exhibits are also mounted at the Memphis College of Arts (formerly the Memphis Academy of Arts.) The Dixon Gallery and Gardens showcases French and American impressionist art and 17 acres of landscaped formal gardens. At the Memphis Botanic Garden, 96 acres form the setting for roses, irises, wildflowers, magnolias, lemon trees, banana trees, orchids, and a Japanese garden. Also located in Memphis is the National Ornamental Metal Museum, which displays weapons, model trains, sculpture, furniture, fencing, tools, and utensils. The Memphis Pink Palace Museum and Planetarium, named for the pink marble used in its construction in the 1920s, houses archaeological gems, prehistoric fossils, a Civil War display, regional exhibits, and a highly ranked planetarium; the museum is one of the largest of its kind in the Southeast.

## Festivals and Holidays

The Memphis in May International Festival is a month-long series of festive activities offering celebrations to suit every taste. Events include foot races, canoe and kayak races, a triathlon competition, fireworks, and seminars. A main feature of the festival is the International Fair held at Tom Lee Park, each year honoring a different foreign country with exhibitions and demonstrations of arts, crafts, foods, and culture. The festival also hosts the World Championship Barbecue Cooking Contest, which rewards showmanship as well as culinary talent; the Desti-Nations International Family Festival; the Beale Street Music Festival with top-name jazz and blues artists; and the Sunset Symphony, a beloved Memphis in May tradition with orchestral selections including "Ole Man River," and the "1812 Overture," a bombastic symphonic standard by nineteenth-century Russian composer Petr Ilich Tchaikovsky; the concert is played as the sun sets over the Mississippi River.

In late May and early June the Great River Carnival is celebrated with a river pageant, exhibits, parades, and a MusicFest. The Elvis Tribute Week held in mid-August honors the late entertainer Elvis Presley, who made his home in Memphis and inspired intense fan loyalty. During Labor Day weekend in Memphis, historic Beale Street is the center of the Memphis Music and Heritage Festival, which underlines Memphis's claim as the birthplace of blues, soul, and rock music. September is also the month for the Mid-South Fair, featuring one of the largest rodeos east of the Mississippi, and agricultural, commercial, and industrial exhibits and events. October events in Memphis include the Oktoberfest and the week-long Pink Palace Crafts Fair.

## Sports for the Spectator

Memphis provides sports enthusiasts with a variety of spectator action. The NBA Memphis Grizzlies play professional basketball at the Pyramid Arena, a spectacular structure which, at 32 stories high, is the third largest pyramid in the world; it provides seating for 21,000. It is also home to the University of Memphis's basketball team, the Tigers. Baseball fans can cheer for the Memphis Redbirds, AAA affiliate of the St. Louis Cardinals, who play at the 12,000-seat AutoZone Stadium downtown. The Memphis Riverkings of the Central Hockey League provide hockey action. Early each spring, tennis buffs can enjoy the Kroger/St. Jude International Indoor TPA Tennis Tournament. During mid-summer, golfing devotees can enjoy the FedEx/St. Jude Classic PGA Golf Tournament, a professional golfing championship held each year at Colonial Country Club. Motorsports are increasingly popular in Memphis, and more than 200 events take place at Motorsport Park, which has a three-quarter-mile paved track and quarter-mile drag strip. Dog racing is also popular in the Memphis area; fans place wagers on favorites at Southland Greyhound Park in nearby West Memphis, Arkansas.

## Sports for the Participant

Memphis has 187 parks, totaling 5,387 acres; the oldest and most notable is Overton Park, where 342 acres offer picnic areas, sports fields, natural woods hiking, and bicycle trails, combined with a nine-hole golf course, the zoo, and the Memphis Brooks Museum of Art. Other large parks are M. L. King-Riverside, with facilities for golf and tennis; and Audubon, offering water skiing, boating, swimming, and sailing. Memphis offers a total of 11 public golf courses and more than 100 public tennis courts. The T. O. Fuller State Park, at the southern city limits, is the only State Park within Memphis. Its 1,138 acres, primarily of forest land, feature a swimming pool, picnic area, nature trails, and 18-hole golf course. In the north end of Shelby County is 13,467-acre Meeman-Shelby Forest State Park. Located parallel to the Mississippi River 15 miles north of the heart of Memphis, Meeman-Shelby offers horseback riding, swimming, fishing, and miles of camping and hiking trails.

Boating, sailing, and water skiing are popular leisure-hour pursuits at dozens of lakes in the Memphis/Shelby County area. The Memphis Yacht Club, located next to Mud Island, accommodates a vast array of member craft, ranging from small houseboats to ocean-going vessels. Visiting craft are also accommodated at the club's dock.

Hunting dogs from all over the United States compete each year in the National Bird Dog Championship just outside Memphis. Climate allows year-round fishing for bass, crappie, trout, bream, and catfish. Lichterman Nature Center, an urban nature center in the heart of metropolitan Memphis, encompasses 65 acres of sanctuary and nature trails and an exhibit center.

## Shopping and Dining

Notable among the city's shopping centers and malls is the Main Street Mall, a downtown array of department stores, boutiques, and eating establishments that together form one of the world's largest pedestrian shopping malls. The city's largest enclosed malls include Southland, Hickory Ridge, and Oak Court malls; the region's largest shopping mall is Wolfchase Galleria, with more than 130 stores, in eastern Shelby County. The city's historic Beale Street district contains unusual shops, including A. Schwab Dry Goods Store, a landmark on Beale Street since 1876, where general merchandise is enhanced by the Beale Street Museum housed in the establishment's basement. Overton Square in the city's midtown features antique shops and art galleries along with cafes and restaurants.

For those who like to combine dining with entertainment, Memphis offers Peabody Place Retail & Entertainment Center, a mixed-use development and historic preservation project. Opened in 2001, Peabody Place offers sports restaurants and bars, video games, dancing, bowling, billiards, and restaurants. A veritable city within the city, Peabody Place encompasses three blocks of Beale Street, and includes the Peabody Hotel, the Orpheum Center, Fed Ex Forum, Autozone Stadium, plus 80 restaurants; it attracts more than 8 million visitors annually. Overton Square and Beale Street boast a concentration of sidewalk cafes, restaurants, and nightclubs that contribute to the range of culinary experiences awaiting diners in Memphis. Besides European, Asian, and Mexican cuisines, Memphis-area restaurants offer traditional American choices such as steaks and seafood, as well as a number of typically Southern dishes. Regional specialties include main dishes such as fried chicken, catfish, ham hocks, chitlins, and seafood gumbo; side dishes such as turnip greens, sweet potato souffle, black-eyed peas, collard greens, yams, and cornbread; and desserts such as banana pudding, fruit cobblers, pecan pie, strawberry shortcake, and fried pie—a type of portable filled pastry. But Memphis is mainly known for its pork and barbecue masterpieces, ranging from dry ribs—prepared without sauce—to barbecue sandwiches.

***Visitor Information:*** Memphis/Shelby County Visitors Center, 12036 Arlington Trail, Arlington, TN 38002; telephone (901)543-5333. Memphis Convention and Visitors Bureau, 47 Union Avenue, Memphis, TN 38103; telephone (901)543-5300; fax (901)543-5350

## Convention Facilities

The advantages of Memphis's meeting sites include accessibility, adequate space, elegant places for overnight visits, leisure sites to visit, and fine dining. Located at the north end of Main Street Mall, the recently expanded, 350,000 square-foot Memphis Cook Convention Center offers 190,000 square feet of exhibition space. The convention center has 31 meeting rooms; an Executive Conference Center; a 125,000 square foot, column-free exhibit hall; a second, 35,000 square foot hall; a 28,000 square-foot ballroom; and the 2,100-seat Cannon Center for the Performing Arts.

There are more than 3,000 hotel rooms in downtown Memphis. Many hotels and motels throughout the city provide elegantly decorated spots for meetings. Among them are The Peabody, the renovated ''grand old lady'' famed the world over for its lobby fountain and daily parade of ducks across a red carpet from the hotel's elevators to the fountain; the Holiday Inn Select Downtown, a hotel directly across from The Peabody; Radisson Hotel adjacent to the Peabody; and the Holiday Inn Select Airport. At the Holiday Inn Select, a sprawling, contemporary-styled hotel within min-

utes of Memphis International Airport, accommodations provide 33,000 square feet of meeting space.

***Convention Information:*** Memphis Convention and Visitors Bureau, 47 Union Avenue, Memphis, TN 38103; telephone (901)543-5300

## Transportation

### Approaching the City

Located minutes from downtown, Memphis International Airport is served by international, regional, and commuter airlines. Expansion efforts in the late 1990s valued at $100 million included improvements to the concourse, taxiways, control tower, waiting areas, ticketing operations, parking facilities, and servicing systems, as well as land acquisition for further development. More enhancements at a cost of approximately $25 million are currently underway with completion expected in summer of 2005, including a concourse renovation, jet bridge improvements, and concessionaire upgrades. Other airports in the Memphis area include General DeWitt Spain Airport, Charles W. Baker Airport, Arlington Municipal Airport, Olive Branch Airport, and West Memphis Municipal Airport. Interstate highway I-40 approaches Memphis from North Carolina to the east and California to the west, while interstate highway I-55 approaches the city from Chicago, Illinois, to the north and New Orleans, Louisiana, to the south. Interstate loop I-240 rings the city. Motor traffic also enters Memphis via U.S. highways 51, 61, 64, 70, 72, 78, and 79. Amtrak offers passenger train service through Memphis's historic, recently renovated Central Station.

### Traveling in the City

A fleet of more than 200 buses and vans operated by Memphis Area Transit Authority (MATA) meets public mass transportation needs. Ten specially designed double-decker Showboat buses connect major activity centers in midtown Memphis with downtown Memphis. The Main Street Trolley, utilizing vintage trolley cars, operates between Auction and Calhoun streets.

## Communications

### Newspapers and Magazines

Memphis is served by *The Commercial Appeal,* a morning-circulated daily newspaper. Business and local news is reported weekday mornings in *The Daily News,* while the *Memphis Business Journal* and *Tri-State Defender* are published weekly. *Memphis Magazine* is the area's monthly general-interest magazine. *The Memphis Flyer* is a weekly tabloid that discusses the arts, entertainment, and lifestyles, while the *Mid-South Hunting & Fishing News* is a bi-weekly tabloid covering outdoor recreation. Special-interest publications originating in Memphis focus on such subjects as environmental legislation, poetry, and hunting, and such industries as glass and metal, trucking, rice and cotton growing, and other agricultural concerns.

## Television and Radio

Memphis-area television viewers are served by seven stations: affiliates of ABC, CBS, NBC, UPN, Fox, PBS, and one independent. 33 AM and FM radio stations present Memphis audiences with a range of programming from classical, jazz, blues, folk, bluegrass, reggae, easy listening, contemporary, and country music to religious, news, public radio, talk-show, agricultural, and educational broadcasts.

***Media Information:*** *The Commercial Appeal,* E. W. Scripps Co., 495 Union Avenue, Memphis, TN 38103; telephone (901)529-2211. *The Daily News,* 193 Jefferson Avenue, Memphis, TN 38103; telephone (901)523-1561; fax (901)526-5813

## Memphis Online

City of Memphis Home Page. Available www.ci.memphis.tn.us

*Commercial Appeal.* Available www.commercialappeal.com

*Daily News.* Available www.memphisdailynews.com

Memphis Chamber of Commerce. Available www.memphischamber.com

Memphis City Schools. Available www.memphis-schools.k12.tn.us

Memphis Convention and Visitors Bureau. Available www.memphistravel.com

Memphis Shelby County Public Library. Available www.memphislibrary.lib.tn.us

Tennessee Department of Tourist Development. Available www.tourism.state.tn.us/index.html

## Selected Bibliography

Faulkner, William, *The Reivers* (New York: Random House, 1962)

Grisham, J, *The Firm* (New York: Doubleday, 1991)

Guralnick, Peter, *Last Train to Memphis: The Rise of Elvis Presley* (Boston: Little, Brown, and Company, 1994)

# Nashville

## *The City in Brief*

**Founded:** 1779 (incorporated 1784)

**Head Official:** Mayor Bill Purcell (D) (since 1999)

**City Population**
1980: 455,651
1990: 488,366
2000: 545,524
2003 estimate: 544,765
Percent change, 1990–2000: 11.7%
U.S. rank in 1980: 25th
U.S. rank in 1990: 25th (State rank: 2nd)
U.S. rank in 2000: 32nd (State rank: 2nd)

**Metropolitan Area Population**
1980: 851,000
1990: 985,000
2000: 1,231,331

Percent change, 1990–2000: 25.0%
U.S. rank in 1980: 40th (MSA)
U.S. rank in 1990: 40th (MSA)
U.S. rank in 2000: 38th (MSA)

**Area:** 473 square miles (Nashville-Davidson) (2000)
**Elevation:** 550 feet
**Average Annual Temperature:** 59.5° F
**Average Annual Precipitation:** 48.0 inches

**Major Economic Sectors:** services, wholesale and retail trade, manufacturing
**Unemployment rate:** 3.5% (December 2004)
**Per Capita Income:** $22,018 (1999)

**2002 FBI Crime Index Total:** 46,018

**Major Colleges and Universities:** Vanderbilt University, Fisk University, Tennessee State University, Belmont University, David Lipscomb University

**Daily Newspaper:** *The Tennessean*

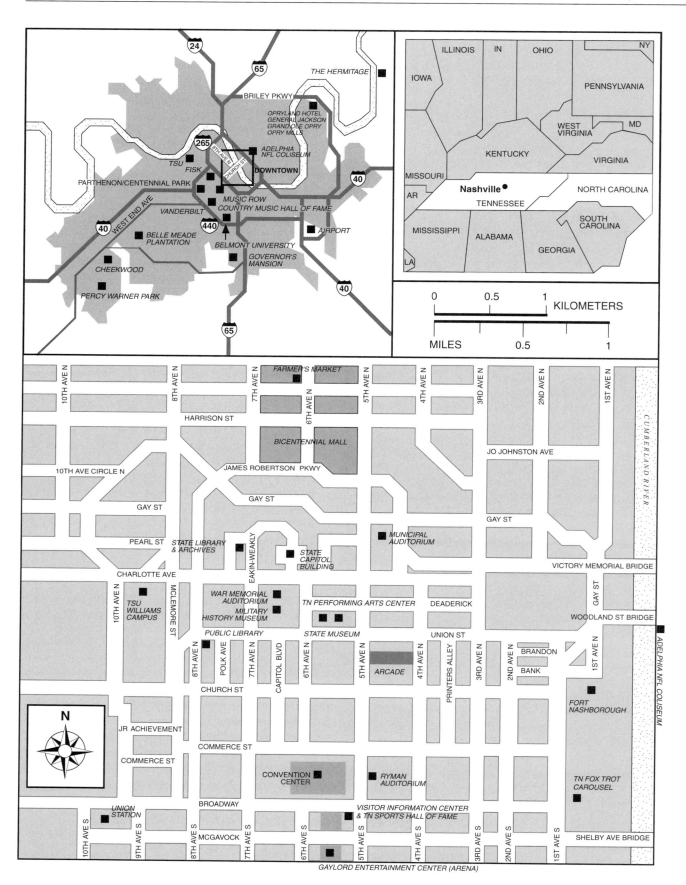

# Introduction

Nestled in rolling hills in the part of the state known as Middle Tennessee, Nashville is often called the "garden spot of the world." The lush natural vegetation, changing seasons, and mild climate of the area make a pretty picture that is the setting for miles of green neighborhoods, shaded shopping districts, thick forests, and wide-open pastures, all inside the city limits. It is a city large enough to be headquarters for scores of international corporations, yet small enough for the neighborhood banker to call his customers by name. Local people can hear the Nashville Symphony perform *Pagliacci* one night and see The Grand Ole Opry in all its glory the next. They can live in steel and glass high-rise condominiums near the center of the city or in secluded frame farmhouses on rural routes.

Nashville is not only a choice city, but it also is a city of choices. The traditional values of the rural people who settled the area have blended with influences brought in by international business, film crews, gourmet restaurants, university scholars, couture clothiers, and conventioneers to create an unusual blend of lifestyles. The combination of country charm and city savvy makes Nashville attractive to residents and visitors alike.

# Geography and Climate

Situated in the center of middle Tennessee on the Cumberland River, Nashville is rimmed on three sides by an escarpment rising three to four hundred feet. The city ranks with Houston, Texas, and Los Angeles, California, as one of the nation's largest cities in terms of area. Nashville's climate is moderate, with seasonal variation rarely lapsing into temperature extremes. Its humidity is also considered moderate for the Southeast. Precipitation is heaviest in winter and early spring, though when it falls in the form of snow it is seldom disruptive. Thunderstorms in Nashville are moderately frequent from March through September. Tornados occur occasionally, such as one in 1933 and more recently in 1998; the 1998 tornado caused property damages in excess of $100 million.

**Area:** 473 square miles (Nashville-Davidson) (2000)

**Elevation:** 550 feet above sea level

**Average Temperatures:** January, 38.7° F; July, 79.4° F; average annual temperature, 59.5° F

**Average Annual Precipitation:** 48.0 inches

# History

**First Settlers Face Perils**

The first settlers in the area that now forms Nashville were attracted by the fertile soil, huge trees, plentiful water, and an abundance of animal life. Native Americans such as the Cherokee, Chickasaw, and Shawnee hunted throughout Middle Tennessee in the 1700s, but ongoing fighting over hunting rights kept them from establishing any permanent settlements. The first Europeans to reach the area were French fur traders, who built trading posts in the dense woods. As more and more hunters brought glowing reports back to settlements in the East of the abundant, unoccupied land in the "west," 400 people in North Carolina eventually decided to band together and move to the area.

On Christmas Eve 1779, they reached the future site of Nashville. The men, women, and children of the James Robertson party (named for the man who would eventually become an early community leader) first survived in primitive camps at the base of what is now the state Capitol Hill. As spring arrived, they spread out to build cabins, the largest group settling on the banks of the Cumberland River in a "fort" of log blockhouses. They christened the community "Nashborough" for North Carolina's General Francis Nash, a hero of the American Revolution. Months later the pioneers found themselves swept up in war as the settlement became a western front for the American Revolution. Incited by the British, the Native Americans in the area turned on the white settlers, which caused most of them to move to safer ground in nearby Kentucky. The 70 people who remained gathered in the fort and managed to hold off their attackers until frontier conditions became less hostile.

In 1784 the community incorporated and changed its name to Nashville, dropping the English "borough" as a result of anti-British sentiment. The years following the war were a time of growth and prosperity. James Robertson helped to establish Davidson Academy, which would later become the University of Nashville. Churches were erected, public buildings developed, doctors' offices opened, and stores began doing business. In 1796, Tennessee became the sixteenth state of the Union.

**"The Age of Jackson"**

The period in Nashville history between 1820 to 1845 is quite simply known as "The Age of Jackson." Andrew Jackson, a brash, young local lawyer and public prosecutor, was a formidable figure in the new frontier. He first came to national attention as a hero of the Creek (Native American) War. When he trounced the British army in New Orleans at the end of the War of 1812, he was wildly embraced as a national hero. Jackson served in the U.S. House of Representatives and the Senate, and he was eventually elected the seventh president of the United States in 1829. Jackson's popularity gave Nashville considerable prestige, power, and clout in the nation's eye, and the city was made the permanent capital of Tennessee in 1843. State leaders soon commissioned construction of a new state capitol building, an impressive neo-classic structure erected over the next 14 years on the summit of the city's highest hill. Designed by noted nineteenth-century architect William Strickland, the Capitol ushered in an era of unprecedented building and design in Nashville of which Strickland was the uncontested leader. His distinct, clean, classic structures shaped the frontier town into a city, and left a lasting imprint on the community. Many buildings, such as the Capitol and St. Mary's Roman Catholic Church, are still in use today.

The mid-1800s was also an era of unprecedented development for the city. Traffic on the Cumberland River made Nashville a shipping and distribution center. Wealthy businessmen built lavish estates. A medical school was founded. The Adelphi Theater opened with a series of plays by Shakespeare. The first passenger train pulled into the depot. A board of education was established. P. T. Barnum even brought Jenny Lind, the world-renowned singer, to town. By 1860, all the qualities that had made Nashville such a boom town in times of peace also made it a city of strategic importance in times of war. At first a giant supply arsenal for the Confederates, Nashville was soon taken during the Civil War by Union troops who seized control of the railroad and river. They occupied the city for three years. In a last attempt to turn the war around, Southern troops tried to retake the town in December of 1864. The Battle of Nashville was one of the bloodiest confrontations between the North and South, and the last major conflict of the Civil War.

## Post-War Rebuilding

It took nearly ten years to pick up the pieces, but Nashville recovered to experience new growth in business and industry. The city became a printing center, an educational center (both Vanderbilt University and Fisk University were established in 1873), and an important distributing and wholesale center. An elegant new hotel, the Maxwell House, opened its doors and began serving a special blend of coffee that President Teddy Roosevelt said was "good to the last drop." One hundred years after Tennessee was admitted to the Union, the city celebrated with a giant Centennial Exposition that attracted visitors from throughout the United States. A wood and stucco replica of the Parthenon built for the fair was such a popular attraction that the city constructed a permanent version that now stands in Centennial Park. The railroad built a magnificent terminal building, Union Station, making Nashville a major railway center and greatly spurring population growth.

## Development During Twentieth Century and into Twenty-First Century

The twentieth century brought business and skyscrapers. The National Life and Accident Company was formed along with Life & Casualty Insurance Company. In the area, local financial institutions blossomed, manufacturing reached all-time highs, and the city's neighborhoods swelled with workers as a result of World War I and World War II. After the wars, Nashville was part of the country's new wave of technology with a new airport, factory automation, and even a local television station. In time, the recording industry became a mainstay of the local economy, and tourism and convention business became big business. By the 1960s, Nashville was infused with a spirit of urban renewal. Surrounding Davidson County had become a fragmented collection of local governments that lacked unified direction. On April 1, 1963, the city voted to consolidate the city and the county to form the first metropolitan form of government in the United States.

The system of metropolitan government has streamlined the city's organization and become an effective agent of progress. The city has undergone major municipal rehabilitation projects, and has renovated the historical district near the old Ft. Nashborough site. Second Avenue, once a row of dilapidated turn-of-the-century warehouses, has become a bustling center of shopping, offices, restaurants, clubs, and apartments. In recent years, many historic buildings have been saved from the wrecking ball. The Hermitage Hotel, built in 1910 as a showplace of Tennessee marble floors and staircases, was totally renovated in the 1990s and is once again packed with guests. Renovation has also come to Union Station, the massive railroad house that now towers over Broadway as one of Nashville's premiere hotels. Unprecedented investment in Nashville in the mid-1990s placed the city on the verge of explosive growth as a sports and entertainment venue. Its Gaylord Entertainment Center, home of the National Hockey League team the Nashville Predators, has become a major catalyst for urban development, which continues into the twenty-first century. In addition to Nashville's mainstay industries of banking, insurance, printing, education, health, and medicine, the city is becoming recognized for its growth as a hotspot for biotechnology and plastics companies, and growing real estate market. Nashville enters the twenty-first century as a thriving metropolis with extensive kudos for its quality of life, business climate, diversified economy, and top tourist destinations.

***Historical Information:*** Nashville Public Library, The Nashville Room, 615 Church Street, Nashville, TN 37219; telephone (615)862-5782. Tennessee State Museum Library, Fifth and Deaderick Streets, Nashville, TN 37243; telephone (615)741-2692. Tennessee Western History Association Library, PO Box 111864, Nashville, TN 37222; telephone (615)834-5069

# Population Profile

## Metropolitan Area Residents
*1980:* 851,000
*1990:* 985,026
*2000:* 1,231,331
*Percent change, 1990–2000:* 25.0%
*U.S. rank in 1980:* 40th (MSA)
*U.S. rank in 1990:* 40th (MSA)
*U.S. rank in 2000:* 38th (MSA)

## City Residents
*1980:* 455,651
*1990:* 488,366
*2000:* 545,524
*2003 estimate:* 544,765
*Percent change, 1990–2000:* 11.7%
*U.S. rank in 1980:* 25th
*U.S. rank in 1990:* 25th (State rank: 2nd)
*U.S. rank in 2000:* 32nd (State rank: 2nd)

*Density:* 1,152.6 people per square mile (2000)

*Racial and ethnic characteristics* (2000)
   White: 359,581
   Black or African American: 146,235
   American Indian and Alaska Native: 1,639
   Asian: 12,992
   Native Hawaiian and Pacific Islander: 400
   Hispanic or Latino (may be of any race): 25,774
   Other: 24,677

*Percent of residents born in state:* 57.7% (2000)

*Age characteristics* (2000)
   Population under 5 years old: 36,335
   Population 5 to 9 years old: 34,022
   Population 10 to 14 years old: 31,536
   Population 15 to 19 years old: 36,972
   Population 20 to 24 years old: 46,482
   Population 25 to 34 years old: 97,370
   Population 35 to 44 years old: 89,589
   Population 45 to 54 years old: 70,963
   Population 55 to 59 years old: 23,445
   Population 60 to 64 years old: 18,931
   Population 65 to 74 years old: 31,468
   Population 75 to 84 years old: 20,762
   Population 85 years and older: 7,649
   Median age: 33.9 years

*Births* (2003; Davidson County)
   Total number: 8,900

*Deaths* (2003; Davidson County)
   Total number: 5,187 (of which, 69 were infants under
      the age of 1 year)

*Money income* (1999)
   Per capita income: $22,018
   Median household income: $39,232
   Total households: 227,559

*Number of households with income of . . .*
   less than $10,000: 23,404
   $10,000 to $14,999: 13,316
   $15,000 to $24,999: 30,873
   $25,000 to $34,999: 33,863
   $35,000 to $49,999: 40,219
   $50,000 to $74,999: 43,207
   $75,000 to $99,999: 20,355
   $100,000 to $149,999: 14,075
   $150,000 to $199,999: 3,696
   $200,000 or more: 4,551
   Percent of families below poverty level (2000): 10.2%
      (31.7% of which were female householder families
      with related children under 5 years)

*2002 FBI Crime Index Total:* 46,457

# Municipal Government

Since 1963, when Nashville merged with surrounding Davidson County, Nashville has operated via a consolidated metropolitan mayor-council government. Voters elect 40 council members, 35 of which serve separate districts.

**Head Official:** Mayor Bill Purcell (D) (since 1999; current term expires 2007)

**Total Number of City Employees:** approximately 12,000 (2005)

*City Information:* City of Nashville, 107 Metro Courthouse, Nashville, TN 37201; telephone; (615)862-5000

# Economy

## Major Industries and Commercial Activity

Nashville's strength as a community truly rests on one solid foundation—its economic diversity. The city is a great ''neighborhood'' of private and public business and industry, where people are as likely to go to work each morning in banks, hospitals, or government offices as to drive trucks, punch cash registers, or work on assembly lines. The area has benefited from low unemployment, consistent job growth, heavy outside investment and expansion, and a broadening of the labor force. Although the city's economy is not reliant on any one area of production, Nashville is a leader in finance and insurance, health care, music and entertainment, publishing, transportation technology, higher education, biotechnology, plastics, and tourism and conventions. In June 2003, Moody's Investors Service placed Nashville 8th in a ranking of the top 10 most diversified local economies. Also in 2003, Nashville ranked 25th in *Forbes* magazine's May issue listing top places for business and careers.

Health care is one of Nashville's top industries; according to the Nashville Health Council, the city is known as the nation's health care center. Twenty-one healthcare companies are based within the city; in total 350 health care companies have operations here. Many service firms specializing in the industry (including accounting, legal, and others) are based in Nashville, including 12 investment and venture capital companies dealing primarily with health care. Health care services companies based in Nashville control more than 2,400 operations outside the city, as well. In 2002, almost 90,000 people in the Nashville metro area worked in the health care industry, earning more than a $4 billion payroll.

Nashville is the largest publishing center in the Southeast and one of the top ten largest in the country. Some of the nation's leading printers operate alongside scores of small, family-owned shops. The city is home to Thomas Nelson, the world's foremost publisher of Bibles, and two of the country's largest religious publishing houses. Nashville is also becoming a major distribution center for books and other print media.

Of all of the products manufactured in the city, music is what makes Nashville most famous. The local recording industry and its offshoots have not only brought worldwide recognition to what was once a sedate southern city, but they have also pumped billions of dollars into the local economy, created a thriving entertainment business scene ranked behind only New York and Los Angeles, and given the city a distinctly cosmopolitan flavor. Nashville music—country, pop, gospel, and rock—generates well over a billion dollars in record sales each year. As a result, spinoff industries have flourished: booking agencies, music publishing companies, promotional firms, recording studios, trade publications, and performance rights associations such as BMI, the Broadcast Music Inc. There are approximately 200 recording studios in Nashville, and most major record labels have offices on Nashville's Music Row, Sony, RCA, Mercury Nashville, MCA, Warner Brothers, Capitol, and Columbia. As Nashville remains a center for the music industry, it continues to draw support businesses and industry to the area. Local music-related advertising firms (especially jingle houses) bring in vast revenues, music video production in the city is at an all-time high, while a burgeoning radio, television, and film industry has enticed some of the country's top producers, directors, and production houses to set up shop in Nashville. The music industry in Nashville is responsible for a good chunk of the city's tourism activity.

An influx of new industry in recent years has resulted in hundreds of jobs and on-site training opportunities for local actors, editors, artists, technicians, and other production people. Nashville's entertainment scene brings in more than revenue, however. It draws millions of people to the city each year as well. Tourism is one of Tennessee's biggest businesses with annual revenues of $2.2 billion, and Nashville is known as the hottest spot in the state.

New technology is a burgeoning factor in the Nashville economy. Dell Computers operates a manufacturing and technical support center near the airport, which opened in 1999 and employs about 3,000 people. The plastics industry is growing here, as is the biotechnology (including pharmaceuticals and life sciences) industries.

Partnership 2010 (formerly Partnership 2000) was created as a regional, public-private economic development initiative for the region. The four cornerstones of the program strategy are business recruiting of corporate headquarters and administrative offices, retention of existing businesses, entrepreneurship through fostering growth and supporting start-up businesses, and community improvement. By 2005 the initiative has resulted in more than 350 companies relocating their corporate headquarters to Nashville. Expectations for the initiative include a $10 billion impact on the region's economy as well as the creation of 50,000 new jobs. Partly as a result of the initiative, Nashville ranked among Expansion Management's 2005 "America's 50 Hottest Cities."

*Items and goods produced:* printing and publishing, automotive products, trucks, automotive parts, clothing, shoes, lawnmowers, bicycles, telecommunications equipment, aerospace products, thermos bottles, kerosene lamps, computers

## Incentive Programs—New and Existing Companies

*Local programs*—The One Stop Business Assistance Program helps new and expanding businesses avoid delays by expediting their dealings with local, state, and federal government offices regarding regulatory permits, and by assisting with any problems they may have in the process. The Payment in Lieu of Tax (PILOT) program offers qualifying businesses a property tax freeze or reduction on projects involving a large capital investment or creating large numbers of new jobs. Requests for PILOT assistance are considered on a case-by-case basis by the city and county. Industrial Revenue Bonds are available to eligible companies for land, building, or equipment purchases.

*State programs*—The Jobs Tax Credit incentive provides qualified new or expanding businesses with a $2,000 tax credit when the business creates at least 25 new full-time jobs and makes a capital investment of $500,000. The Corporate Excise Tax Credit allows companies a one percent tax credit on industrial machinery for new or expanding businesses. Sales tax exemptions or reductions are available to qualified companies purchasing industrial machinery, or products used in the manufacturing of resale items. The program also offers credits of 5.5 percent towards building materials, equipment, and machinery for company headquarters with a construction price tag over $20 million. The Economic Development Loan Fund assists new and expanding industrial companies with loans for up to $2 million.

*Job training programs*—The State of Tennessee FastTrack Job Assistance program offers training assistance for new or existing businesses that are investing in facilities, equipment, or new jobs. FastTrack utilizes educational facilities and FastTrack staff to develop and implement customized training programs. The Tennessee Job Skills program is a work force incentive grant program for new and existing businesses that focuses on elevating employees skill levels.

## Development Projects

Nashville's aggressive Partnership 2010 program was responsible for a flurry of business activity in the early part of the new century, including company relocations, expansions, and new corporations. According to the Partnership 2010 annual report for 2003-2004, Asurion relocated its corporate headquarters to Nashville in 2003, creating 800 jobs by late 2004. In that year, 90 companies announced expansions or relocations to the Nashville region.

A major private investment in Nashville marks Dell's first U.S. expansion outside of Central Texas. In fall of 2000, Dell opened new manufacturing and office facilities in Nashville, and has since increased its Tennessee workforce from approximately 200 to nearly 3,000. Nashville has been building upon its considerable cultural cache in recent years, with the opening of the First Center for the Performing Arts, and a new main public library four times the size of the former library. Nashville expects to reap significant benefits when the state completes I-840, a limited-access highway that will form another outer ring of roadway around the city. The new highway, partially complete at the end of 2004, had already influenced business location decisions in Middle Tennessee.

*Economic Development Information:* Nashville Area Chamber of Commerce, 211 Commerce Street, Nashville, TN 37201; telephone (615)743-3000

## Commercial Shipping

Nashville's central location has made it one of the busiest transportation centers in the Mid-South. Today more than 80 miles of interstate highways weave in and out of the city, making Nashville a vital link to every corner of the region.

The bulk of local transportation services are designed to move freight. For high priority or overnight deliveries Nashvillians often turn to the rapidly expanding air freight industry. However, Nashville's strength as a distribution center for the Southeast still lies in the traditional and highly competitive industries of trucking, rail freight, and river barge.

Millions of tons of goods are moved through the city each year via truck by a multitude of motor freight lines serving the area. Nashville has become a regional headquarters for the trucking industry primarily because of its tight, efficient network of accessible interstate highways, its conveniently centralized location, and the fact that approximately 150 local terminals provide easy break-bulk distribution and specialized services for products such as produce (refrigeration), gasoline, and hazardous waste.

Since the turn of the century, Nashville has historically been considered the hub of railway activity for the Southeast. The local division of CSX provides service over 2,700 route miles to 23 states, the District of Columbia, and two Canadian provinces. An average of 90 trains pass through Nashville each day. The CSX Intermodal provides Nashville with a piggyback loading/unloading system that is one of the most modern in the nation, handling about 8,300 containers or trailers each month. Rail service is also provided by the Nashville Eastern and the Nashville Western short line railroads.

The Cumberland River, an artery of the Ohio River that weaves in and out of the Nashville Metropolitan area, links the city to points on the Mississippi River and the Gulf of Mexico coast. More than 30 commercial operators operate barges on the river. The distance to Gulf ports was cut by 563 miles in the mid-1980s when the United States Army Corps of Engineers opened its $1.8 billion Tennessee-Tombigbee Waterway, connecting the Tennessee River in northern Alabama with the Tombigbee River of southern Alabama 234 miles away. This ambitious man-made water route connected Nashville to the port of Mobile, resulting in an estimated savings of millions in shipping costs.

The Nashville Air Cargo Link is designated as foreign trade zone and is an all-cargo complex serving the Nashville International Airport. In 2003, more than 65 thousand tons of cargo was shipped through Nashville.

## Labor Force and Employment Outlook

Nashville has experienced significant economic expansion in recent years, to the extent that employers in certain sectors, such as skilled production and the hospitality industry, are experiencing labor shortages. Population growth continues, however, especially in suburban Nashville, which offers a long-term solution to the labor supply problem. With the influx of expansions and new businesses, and in concert with Nashville's diverse and stable economy and growing population, continued economic expansion is predicted.

The following is a summary of data regarding the Nashville metropolitan area labor force, 2003 annual averages.

*Size of nonagricultural labor force:* 680,800

*Number of workers employed in . . .*
  *manufacturing:* 78,400
  *trade, transportation and utilities:* 139,000
  *information:* 19,600
  *financial activities:* 44,300
  *professional and business services:* 82,600
  *educational and health services:* 93,100
  *leisure and hospitality:* 71,000
  *other services:* 30,200
  *government:* 89,400

*Average hourly earnings of production workers employed in manufacturing:* $14.44

*Unemployment rate:* 3.5% (December 2004)

| *Largest employers* (excludes government agencies) | *Number of employees* |
|---|---|
| Vanderbilt University & Medical Center | 13,601 |
| HCA, The Healthcare Company | 10,525 |
| Saturn Corporation | 7,609 |
| Nissan Motor Manufacturing USA | 6,500 |
| Gaylord Entertainment | 4,950 |
| Shoney's Incorporated | 3,670 |
| The Kroger Company | 3,350 |
| CBRL Group Inc. | 3,275 |
| Dell Computer Corporation | 3,000 |
| BellSouth | 3,000 |

## Cost of Living

The following is a summary of data regarding key cost of living factors for the Nashville area.

*2004 (3rd Quarter) ACCRA Average House Price:* $194,533

*2004 (3rd Quarter) ACCRA Cost of Living Index:* 94.5 (U.S. average = 100.0)

*State income tax rate:* Limited to dividends and interest income

*State sales tax rate:* 7.0%

*Local income tax rate:* None

*Local sales tax rate:* 2.25%

*Property tax rate:* For 2005 the tax rate was $2.52 per $100 of assessed value; residential property is assessed at 25 percent

***Economic Information:*** Nashville Area Chamber of Commerce, 211 Commerce Street, Nashville, TN 37201; telephone (615)743-3000

# Education and Research

## Elementary and Secondary Schools

In 1855 Nashville became the first southern city to establish a public school system. A program started in Nashville in 1963 became the prototype for Head Start. That same year the Metropolitan Nashville Public Schools, the 42nd largest urban school district in the country as of fall 2004, was formed when the city and Davidson County governments were consolidated. The schools offer diverse educational opportunities recognized statewide for their innovation. There are programs in Nashville for the gifted, the handicapped, and the foreign student who wants to catch up. Sixty-four percent of the city's high-school students continue their education after graduation. A nine-member elected board and its appointed director of schools are responsible for the running of the public schools.

The following is a summary of data regarding the Metro Nashville-Davidson County public schools as of the 2002-2003 school year.

*Total enrollment:* 67,954

*Number of facilities*
  *elementary schools:* 72
  *junior high/middle schools:* 38
  *senior high schools:* 23

*Student/teacher ratio:* 14.7:1

*Teacher salaries*
  *average:* $40,440

*Funding per pupil:* $6,648 (2001)

Numerous school-age children in Davidson County attend private schools. There are 66 preparatory academies, church-affiliated, and alternative schools operating in the area, focusing on specific academic and religious needs. A number of widely renowned preparatory schools are found on this list.

***Public Schools Information:*** Nashville Metropolitan Schools, 2601 Bransford Avenue, Nashville, TN 37204; telephone (615)259-8400

## Colleges and Universities

Perhaps the most famous school in Nashville is Vanderbilt University, alma mater of Vice President Al Gore and recording artist Amy Grant. The private, independent institution is highly competitive, maintains impeccable standards, and prides itself on what it calls a "quality liberal arts" undergraduate program. In addition, the school is widely known for its advanced academic offerings in medicine, law, business, nursing, divinity, and education. *U.S. News and*

*World Report,* in a recent study of U.S. universities, named Vanderbilt's Peabody College 4th (among graduate schools of education); ranked Vanderbilt's law school 17th; and ranked Vanderbilt 18th overall.

The first predominantly African American institution in the country to be awarded university status—Fisk University—is also located in Nashville. Fisk, alma mater of social critic and NAACP co-founder W. E. B. DuBois, is a four-year, private school designed to meet the special needs of minority students. Fisk offers three bachelors degrees along with a master of arts. Nashville's Meharry Medical College, established to train African American physicians, provides specialized instruction in medical science, public health, and dental surgery.

Nashville's largest state-operated university, Tennessee State University (TSU), maintains two campuses in the city. TSU offers undergraduate and graduate programs in arts and sciences, agriculture, health professions, business, education, engineering and technology, nursing, and public administration.

Belmont University, a private, four-year Baptist school located near downtown's Music Row, offers 50 undergraduate degree programs as well as graduate programs in accountancy, business administration, education, English, music, nursing, occupational therapy, physical therapy, and sport administration. Belmont's notable Mike Curb College offers majors in Audio Engineering Technology and Music Business, and a specialization in Entertainment and Music Business is offered within the University's M.B.A. program. Students from all over the country who want a career in the record industry have enrolled in specialized courses ranging from record promotion to studio engineering.

### Libraries and Research Centers

The Public Library of Nashville and Davidson County boasts more than 1.4 million volumes and more than 3,100 periodical subscriptions in a system that includes 20 branches and a bookmobile. Annual circulation is approximately four million. The main library also holds recordings, audio- and videotapes, compact discs, and maps. Its special collections include government documents, business, ornithology, genealogy, and oral and regional history. A new Main Library of approximately 300,000 square feet, quadruple the size of the library it replaced, was completed in 2001; it faces the Tennessee State Capitol building.

Special libraries in the Nashville area include two at Cheekwood Botanical Garden and Museum of Art. The Botanical Gardens Library specializes in works on environmental studies, garden design, horticulture, landscape architecture, plant science, wildflowers, arranging, and botanical illustration. The art museum library collects works on art, art history, decorative arts, contemporary U.S. artists, and photography.

Many research facilities in the city are linked to the academic community. Fisk University supports research on computing and molecular spectroscopy. Meharry Medical College's research activities focus on health sciences and the college has a research center devoted to the study and treatment of sickle cell disease. Research centers affiliated with Tennessee State University conduct studies in such areas as agriculture and the environment, information systems, business and economics, health, and education. Vanderbilt University is quite active in the research sector, promoting research through more than 120 centers and institutes devoted to a wide variety of subjects in such fields as sociology and culture, medicine, and science.

***Public Library Information:*** Nashville Public Library, 615 Church Street, Nashville, TN 37219; telephone (615)862-5800

# Health Care

Nashville boasts more than 350 health care companies operating in the city, 21 of which are headquartered in the city. More than 2,700 doctors work in Nashville's 30 hospitals, medical centers, and specialty centers. Nashville is home to HCA Inc., which manages 191 hospitals and 82 outpatient surgery centers throughout the U.S.—including Nashville's Centennial, Skyline, and Southern Hills medical centers—as well as in England and Switzerland. Centennial Medical Center is recognized for its work in cardiology, stroke, orthopaedics, and breast cancer management. Its campus includes The Women's Hospital at Centennial, and the Parthenon Pavilion, a full-service mental health center. Skyline Medical Center, a 59-acre campus overlooking downtown Nashville, opened in September 2000. It is notable for its treatment of stroke, back and neck surgery, and spinal fusion. Southern Hills Medical Center is a smaller, community hospital with a full range of heart, oncology, orthopaedic, and neurology services. Baptist Hospital is the Nashville region's largest not-for-profit medical center, with 685 beds. It offers a number of specialty units, including the Mandrell Heart Center, Institute for Aesthetic and Reconstructive Surgery, and Sports Medicine Center. St. Thomas Hospital, with 515 staffed beds, was founded by the Daughters of Charity and is nationally recognized for its heart and cancer units, while Meharry Medical College, one of the country's most prestigious predominantly African American colleges, has been a leading producer of African American physicians and dentists since its founding in 1876. Two Veterans Administration medical centers exist within the city.

The Vanderbilt University Medical Center, which adjoins the university's campus near downtown Nashville, is one of the most noted research, training, and health care facilities in the country. The main hospital boasts 658 beds, ultramodern surgical units, a labor and delivery area designed around the birthing room concept, a comprehensive burn center, and a coronary care wing. Vanderbilt Children's Hospital, formerly housed within the University Medical Center, moved to a new eight-floor facility in 2004. Patients and their families were involved in planning the new hospital, which took five years to build at a cost of $172 million. The hospital offers comprehensive pediatric care, boasting 19 specialty services. For adults and children who need immediate medical attention because of accident or sudden illness, Vanderbilt University also operates a helicopter ambulance service called "Life Flight," which quickly moves patients within a 130-mile radius of the city to the hospital.

# Recreation

## Sightseeing

A roster full of sports, the unspoiled countryside, and an endless choice of attractions have made Nashville one of the most popular vacation spots in the nation. Foremost among the city's historical attractions is The Hermitage, home of the seventh president of the United States, Andrew Jackson. The beautiful 1821 plantation house sits nestled in rolling farmland on the eastern edge of the city. The mansion has been a national shrine since the years shortly following Jackson's death there in 1845. Its vintage rooms display original pieces such as the Jackson family's furniture, china, paintings, clothes, letters, books, and wallpaper. Also on the grounds are the president's official carriage, his wife's flower garden, and both of their tombs.

Beautiful Belle Meade Plantation on the west side of the city is also open to the public. The restored antebellum farm has been called "Queen of the Tennessee Plantations." The mansion itself, built in 1853, displays period furniture and decor, while the mammoth stables on the grounds provide a glimpse of one of the most famous thoroughbred horse farms of that time.

Perched on a hill in the center of the downtown area is the Tennessee State Capitol Building, a renowned architectural monument constructed in 1859. Also open for tours is Belmont Mansion, an 1850s Italianate villa on the Belmont University campus, recognized as one of the most elaborate and unusual houses in the South. Cheekwood Botanical Garden and Museum of Art is a horticulturalist's delight. The sprawling complex, nestled in Nashville's prime residential area, showcases 55 acres of lush gardens, including a color garden, water garden, seasons garden, and the wood-land sculpture trail. The huge Georgian mansion houses a permanent display of 20th-century American art and American and English decorative arts.

More than 10,000 acres of land in 99 parks and greenways are operated by the Metro Board of Parks and Recreation, including Centennial Park, famous for its full-size replica of the ancient Greek temple to the goddess Athena, the Parthenon. Sitting in the midst of the busy central city near Vanderbilt University, the Parthenon was originally built as part of Tennessee's Centennial Exposition of 1897, but it has remained one of the most popular places in town for a century. The city maintains impressive gardens around the structure, which houses rotating art exhibits in a permanent gallery. Just down the street in the heart of the historical district is Riverfront Park, home to historic Fort Nashborough. Here the public can stroll along the banks of the Cumberland River or listen to concerts under the stars. The Tennessee Fox Trot Carousel by artist Red Grooms is housed in Riverfront Park. The 36 "horses" are actually characters depicting the state's history and culture.

The Nashville Zoo features exotic animals from around the world, including a 300-pound anaconda, in a themed setting plus educational programs. Cumberland Science Museum underwent a $2.7 million renovation and emerged as Adventure Science Center in 2002. The center offers unique health and science programs, hands-on exhibitions, live animal shows, and the Sudekum Planetarium. The Nashville Toy Museum presents a priceless display of more than 1,000 antique toys, including an entire room of rare toy trains from the U.S. and Europe.

The Grand Ole Opry, America's oldest and most cherished live country music show, is one of the most popular attractions in the city. Fans from all over the world pack the 4,400-seat Opry House each weekend to see top stars of traditional and country music. Begun in 1925 as the WSM Barn Dance, the Opry is still broadcast over WSM Radio to points all along the Eastern seaboard, providing audiences with a rare behind-the-scenes look at a tradition that literally launched popular country music. The Opry House, built in 1974 at a cost of $22 million, is said to be one of the most acoustically perfect auditoriums in the country; another is the famed Ryman Auditorium, home of the Opry from 1943-1974, recently renovated and now used as a performance venue for concerts and plays. The Opryland complex also includes the impressive Gaylord Opryland hotel, Opry Mills shopping and entertainment complex.

## Arts and Culture

Taking center stage in the area of performing arts, the Nashville Symphony Orchestra has a reputation as one of the leading city orchestras in the Southeast. Since 1980, the symphony has regularly performed on the stage of the Tennessee

**Belle Meade Mansion.**

Performing Arts Center (TPAC), the first state-funded facility of its kind in the nation, which also is home to the Nashville Ballet, the Nashville Opera, and the Tennessee Repertory Theatre. Built in a cantilevered style that allows large auditoriums to be column-free, TPAC houses state offices, the State Museum, and three acoustically advanced theaters with expansion capabilities for nearly any kind or size of production imaginable. One of the oldest companies in town is the Nashville Children's Theater, a group that has been entertaining the area's children and young adults for six decades. Started by the Junior League as a strictly volunteer organization, the Children's Theater is now partially funded by the metropolitan government and stages its shows in facilities especially built for the group by the city of Nashville. Nashville is also home to the American Negro Playwright Theatre, Darkhorse Theatre, and Tennessee Dance Theatre, which presents dance with a Southern theme.

In the area of visual arts, Nashville is a city-wide gallery of creativity. Cheekwood is the area's foremost cultural arts center and its most physically impressive gallery as well. Part of a 55-acre complex that once formed the estate of prominent Nashville businessman Leslie Cheek, the fine arts center is housed in a magnificent 60-room Georgian mansion that sits high atop a hill overlooking most of West Nashville. The Van Vechten Gallery at Fisk University houses more than 100 pieces from the collection of Alfred Stieglitz. Donated to Fisk in 1949 by Stieglitz's widow, noted artist Georgia O'Keeffe, the collection includes works by Cezanne, Picasso, Renoir, Toulouse-Lautrec, and O'Keeffe. The seat of Tennessee's government overlooks a plaza of government office buildings that house parts of the State Museum, a collection of more than 2,000 historical objects from the city's past. The museum includes 15,000 square feet of artifacts from the period in Tennessee history between 1840 and 1865. As it did in mid-nineteenth-century life, the Civil War dominates the collection: battle flags, pistols, and portraits of the war's most colorful personalities are displayed alongside period silver, sewing handiwork, furniture, and photographs. A vast collection of permanent and traveling exhibits is on display at the Frist Center for the Visual Arts downtown, which opened in 2000 with an exhibit on loan from Ontario, featuring works by Rubens, Renoir, Monet, Van Gogh, Picasso, Sargent, and others.

In downtown Nashville, the heart of the country music business beats on a single square mile of city streets known to the world as Music Row. A hodgepodge of contemporary office buildings and renovated houses, Music Row houses complexes belonging to all the major record labels and many individual recording artists. The top attraction on Music Row is the Country Music Hall of Fame and Museum, a quaint building resembling a chapel, which anchors the neighborhood to the surrounding business community. This is the most visited museum in the South, and it houses one of the country's finest collections of country music artifacts and memorabilia. The Hall of Fame moved from its home on Music Row to a new state-of-the-art downtown facility in 2001. Admission includes a visit to RCA Studio B, the oldest surviving recording studio in Nashville, where Elvis Presley, Dollie Parton, Charlie Pride and other music greats recorded their hits.

***Visitor Information:*** Nashville Convention and Visitors Bureau, 211 Commerce Street, Nashville, TN 37201; telephone (615)259-4700

**Festivals and Holidays**

Nashville's musical heritage is the focus of many of the city's festivals, including Tin Pan South and Gospel Week, both in April; Nashville River Stages in May; and Fan Fair, held in June. Dancing is added to the mix during Dancin' in the District, a huge street party held on Thursdays throughout the summer. The three-day Fest de Ville Nashville premiered in September 2000; this three-day outdoor festival on the streets of downtown Nashville features 60 hours of the best of the commercial and non-commercial music and entertainment made and performed in Nashville.

The winter holidays are celebrated in a series of events taking place throughout November and December. Highlights are A Country Christmas at the Opryland Hotel, and Victorian Celebrations at Belle Meade Plantation. Other events include decorated antebellum homes and the Christmas Sampler Craft, Folk Art and Antique Fair, which features 200 craftspersons and artisans from 28 states.

**Sports for the Spectator**

The Tennessee Titans play football at The Coliseum, a 67,000-seat, open-air, natural-grass venue. The Gaylord Entertainment Center is home to the National Hockey League Predators, the Nashville Kats arena football team, and the new Tennessee Sports Hall of Fame.

Each spring and summer, crowds turn out in record numbers at Herschel Greer Stadium to cheer on the Nashville Sounds, the local Triple A minor league baseball club that is the farm team for the Pittsburgh Pirates. In college action, fall brings Southeastern Conference football with the Commodores of Vanderbilt University. The university also boasts outstanding basketball and tennis teams. Across town, Tennessee State University's Tigers have consistently been a powerhouse in football. The school is also famous for its internationally recognized track team, the Tiger Belles, which has produced Olympic runners like Wilma Rudolph.

On weekends, NASCAR stock-car racing takes off at the Nashville Speedway, where top drivers compete in the weekly Winston Racing series. Special events are also held throughout the year at the speedway. Each May, Percy

Warner Park is the site for what Nashville sports writers call the city's "Rite of Spring," the Iroquois Memorial Steeplechase, 2- to 3-mile amateur races that pit the area's top riders and ponies in a benefit run for Vanderbilt Children's Hospital. And the Electrolux Ladies Professional Golfer's Association Golf Tournament in May at Hermitage Golf Course is just one of the special events that bring top U.S. golfers to Nashville.

**Sports for the Participant**

Two major lakes flank the city of Nashville, Old Hickory to the north and Percy Priest to the east. They offer miles of peaceful, accessible shoreline to the entire Middle Tennessee region. Just a short drive from downtown, these man-made wonders are favorite weekend spots for local outdoor enthusiasts. A series of public docks houses nearly every kind of freshwater craft and campgrounds are plentiful. The 385-acre Nashville Shores, with more than 2,500 feet of white sandy beach and three miles of lakefront, is Nashville's largest water playground. Here families can enjoy waterslides, a waterfall, pools, a pond, a young children's play area, parasailing, jet skiing, and banana boat rides.

Nashville is an angler's dream and fishing enthusiasts seek out the crystal-clear reservoirs that lie beneath Nashville area dams. Although most popular in the spring and summer, fishing is excellent year-round. The Harpeth River, which meanders through the western part of Davidson County, provides a peaceful look at the quiet countryside for canoers, while a little further west the Buffalo River, one of the few designated "wild" rivers in the nation, provides the challenge of white water.

Nashville has more than 10,000 acres of city, state, and federal parks in or near its borders, providing a full range of activities for people of all ages. The Metro Board of Parks and Recreation operates 99 parks and greenways that include 85 ball fields, 16 indoor and outdoor swimming pools, 7 golf courses, and 26 community centers. Percy and Edwin Warner Parks provide 2,665 acres of woods and meadows that dominate the southwestern side of Nashville.

**Shopping and Dining**

Shopping opportunities in Nashville include unique choices that reflect the local attractions. For instance, shoppers seeking musical recordings might visit the Ernest Tubb Record Shop, where radio's "Midnight Jamboree" is broadcast live on Saturday nights. Cowboy boots and western clothing are featured in several Nashville-area establishments, such as Robert's Western World, by day a shop and by night a musical free-for-all. On the banks of the Cumberland River, The District is a trendy shopping scene housed in Victorian-era buildings. Shoppers interested in collectibles frequent the city's many antiques malls, or attend the Tennessee State Fairgrounds Flea Market, a monthly gathering of hundreds of traders considered among the top 10 flea markets in the country. CoolSprings Galleria, one of the city's largest shopping centers, also houses a variety of eating establishments; other area malls include Hickory Hollow, Rivergate, and Bellevue Center, home to the Tennessee Museum Store. Exclusive shops are found at the Mall of Green Hills. More than 28 stores can be found at Factory Stores of America, across from the Opryland Hotel. Alongside the Opry House is the 1.2-million-square-foot Opry Mills. This shopping/dining/entertainment complex features top designers and manufacturers, theme restaurants such as Rainforest Café and Jillian's, and entertainment venues including an IMAX theater and the Gibson Bluegrass Showcase.

Nashville restaurants offer diners a wide range of cuisines, including continental, oriental, Mexican, French, Italian, and German menus, as well as traditional choices of steaks and seafood. Regional specialties (and often music) are showcased at several Nashville-area establishments that feature entrees such as fried chicken, catfish, barbecue, and country ham; side dishes such as okra, turnip greens, black-eyed peas, yams, cornbread, beans and rice, and biscuits; and desserts such as chess pie, fudge pie, and fruit cobblers.

*Visitor Information:* Nashville Convention and Visitors Bureau, 211 Commerce Street, Nashville, TN 37201; telephone (615)259-4700. The Visitor's Center, main entrance of the Gaylord Entertainment Center, corner of Fifth and Broadway; telephone (615)259-4747.

# Convention Facilities

Convention business and tourism form one of the Nashville area's most important industries, launched primarily by the growth of country music and entertainment. One of the most versatile convention-oriented hotels in Nashville is the Gaylord Opryland Resort and Convention Center, offering more than 600,000 square feet of meeting and exhibit space. Its Ryman Exhibit Hall is the largest in-hotel exhibit facility in the world, at 289,000 square feet. The elegant, white-columned facility is located on 30 acres of rolling Tennessee countryside just 8 miles east of downtown Nashville. It is approximately five minutes from the airport and close to shopping, restaurants, and attractions, with the Grand Ole Opry House next door.

The Nashville Convention Center offers 118,675 square feet of meeting space, ballrooms, and 25 meeting rooms. The city's Municipal Auditorium seats more than 9,600 people. For conventions and trade shows, the exhibit floor contains 63,000 square feet of space. Gaylord Entertainment Center offers 49,000 square feet of exhibition and meeting space. The Adelphia Coliseum offers a total of 200,000 square feet of space on the club levels for special events and functions; one side of the coliseum offers sweeping vistas of downtown Nashville. Parts of the Tennessee Performing Arts Center and the Tennessee State Fairgrounds are also available for sizable events.

Two miles west of the center city, the Loew's Vanderbilt Hotel rises next to Vanderbilt University in the middle of one of Nashville's busiest areas of commercial office development. Promoting itself as an "executive-class" hotel, the Vanderbilt has more than 24,000 square feet of flexible meeting space.

*Convention Information:* Nashville Convention and Visitors Bureau, 211 Commerce Street, Nashville, TN 37201; telephone (615)259-4730

# Transportation

### Approaching the City

East of the city, the Nashville International Airport, located just eight miles from the central business district, is approximately a 12-minute ride away. Passengers landing in Nashville may choose from any number of commercial vehicles to take them to their destinations. There is an airport limousine service available along with metered taxicabs, Metro Transit Authority buses, shuttle service to downtown hotels, and car rental agencies with representatives in the lobby of the terminal building.

Six major highways intersect in the heart of Nashville: Interstate-65 N leads to the industrialized cities of Chicago, Indianapolis, and Pittsburgh; I-40 takes travelers to the cities of Richmond, Washington, D.C., and Philadelphia, plus the Carolina ports; I-24 E extends to Atlanta and Florida; I-65 S reaches Birmingham, New Orleans, and the Gulf; I-40 W leads to Dallas, Oklahoma, and the West Coast; and I-24 W extends to St. Louis and Kansas City, the midwestern heartland.

The inner-city loop, I-265, encircles the downtown area to facilitate a smooth flow of interstate traffic, while an extensive outer loop, I-440, rings the city. The southern half of Interstate-840, a project that will circle the city at a 30-mile radius, is nearly complete at the end of 2004, while development of the northern half is on hold.

### Traveling in the City

Within Nashville, visitors usually travel by cab, rental or private car, or public bus. The Metropolitan Transit Author-

ity provides a large network of bus service both in the downtown area and outlying suburbs. Serving approximately 35,000 passengers daily, MTA buses cover 39 routes, including many neighborhood park-and-ride lots designed especially for commuters. Trolleys running around downtown and the Music Valley area are a fun way to see the city.

# Communications

### Newspapers and Magazines

*The Tennessean,* the daily paper, is published every morning and prints the Opry lineup in its Friday edition. *Nashville Scene,* a weekly alternative newspaper, offers the most in-depth coverage of local events. *Urban Journal* is a weekly alternative newspaper representing Nashville's African American community; *Nashville Pride,* a weekly, is read by a large portion of the African American community. Professional periodicals published in Nashville serve the furniture, insurance, banking, logging, agriculture, and paper industries, and the music and education fields. Numerous directories and newsletters are published in Nashville.

### Television and Radio

Nashville-area television viewers are served by seven stations affiliated with PBS, ABC, NBC, CBS, UPN, and Fox plus two independents. 30 AM and FM radio stations in Nashville offer educational, cultural, religious, and foreign language programming as well as rock and roll, gospel, blues, jazz, and country music.

*Media Information:* *The Tennessean,* 1100 Broadway St., Nashville, TN 37203; telephone (615)259-8000

### Nashville Online

Metropolitan Government of Nashville and Davidson County. Available www.nashville.gov

Metropolitan Nashville-Davidson County Schools. Available www.nashville-schools.davidson.k12.tn.us

Nashville Area Chamber of Commerce (including JobsLink). Available www.nashvillechamber.com

Nashville Convention and Visitors Bureau. Available www.nashvillecvb.com

Nashville/Davidson County Public Library. Available www.nashv.lib.tn.us

*The Nashville Digest.* Available www.nashvilledigest.com

*Tennessean.* Available www.tennessean.com

## Selected Bibliography

Feiler, Bruce S., *Dreaming Out Loud: Garth Brooks, Wynonna Judd, Wade Hayes, and the Changing Face of Nashville* (New York: Spike, 1999)

Goodstein, Anita S., *Nashville, 1789–1860: From Frontier to City.* (Gainesville, FL: University Press of Florida, 1989)

Squire, James D. *The Secrets of the Hopewell Box: Stolen Elections, Southern Politics, and a City's Coming of Age.* (New York: Times Books/Random House, 1996)

# TEXAS

# The State in Brief

**Nickname:** Lone Star State
**Motto:** Friendship

**Flower:** Bluebonnet
**Bird:** Mockingbird

**Area:** 268,580 square miles (2000; U.S. rank: 2nd)
**Elevation:** Ranges from sea level to 8,749 feet above sea level
**Climate:** Semi-arid in western region and central plains; subtropical on coastal plains; continental in the panhandle

**Admitted to Union:** December 29, 1845
**Capital:** Austin
**Head Official:** Governor Rick Perry (R) (until 2007)

**Population**
1980: 14,229,000
1990: 16,986,510
2000: 20,851,820
**2004 estimate:** 22,490,022
**Percent change, 1990–2000:** 22.8%
**U.S. rank in 2004:** 2nd
**Percent of residents born in state:** 62.2% (2000)
**Density:** 79.6 people per square mile (2000)
**2002 FBI Crime Index Total:** 1,130,292

**Racial and Ethnic Characteristics** (2000)
**White:** 14,799,505
**Black or African American:** 2,404,566
**American Indian and Alaska Native:** 118,362
**Asian:** 562,319
**Native Hawaiian and Pacific Islander:** 14,434
**Hispanic or Latino (may be of any race):** 6,669,666
**Other:** 2,438,001

**Age Characteristics** (2000)
**Population under 5 years old:** 1,624,628
**Population 5 to 19 years old:** 4,921,608
**Percent of population 65 years and over:** 9.9%
**Median age:** 32.3 years (2000)

**Vital Statistics**
**Total number of births (2003):** 377,414
**Total number of deaths (2003):** 153,944 (infant deaths, 2,400)
**AIDS cases reported through 2003:** 30,043

**Economy**
**Major industries:** Machinery, agriculture, chemicals, food processing, oil, transportation equipment
**Unemployment rate:** 5.8% (December 2004)
**Per capita income:** $29,076 (2003; U.S. rank: 30th)
**Median household income:** $40,934 (3-year average, 2001-2003)
**Percentage of persons below poverty level:** 15.8% (3-year average, 2001-2003)
**Income tax rate:** None
**Sales tax rate:** 6.25% (food and prescription drugs are exempt)

# Austin

## The City in Brief

**Founded:** 1835 (incorporated 1839)

**Head Official:** Mayor Will Wynn (since 2003)

**City Population**
    **1980:** 345,890
    **1990:** 472,020
    **2000:** 656,562
    **2003 estimate:** 672,011
    **Percent change, 1990–2000:** 39.0%
    **U.S. rank in 1980:** 42nd
    **U.S. rank in 1990:** 27th (State rank: 5th)
    **U.S. rank in 2000:** 22nd (State rank: 4th)

**Metropolitan Area Population**
    **1980:** 585,000
    **1990:** 846,227
    **2000:** 1,249,763

    **Percent change, 1990–2000:** 47.7%
    **U.S. rank in 1980:** 63rd
    **U.S. rank in 1990:** 52nd
    **U.S. rank in 2000:** 37th

**Area:** 258.43 square miles (2000)
**Elevation:** Ranges from 425 feet to 1,000 feet above sea level
**Average Annual Temperature:** 68.6° F
**Average Annual Precipitation:** 31.35 inches

**Major Economic Sectors:** services, government, wholesale and retail trade
**Unemployment rate:** 4.0% (December 2004)
**Per Capita Income:** $24,163 (1999)

**2002 FBI Crime Index Total:** 42,979

**Major Colleges and Universities:** University of Texas at Austin, St. Edward's University, Houston-Tillotson College

**Daily Newspaper:** *Austin American-Statesman*

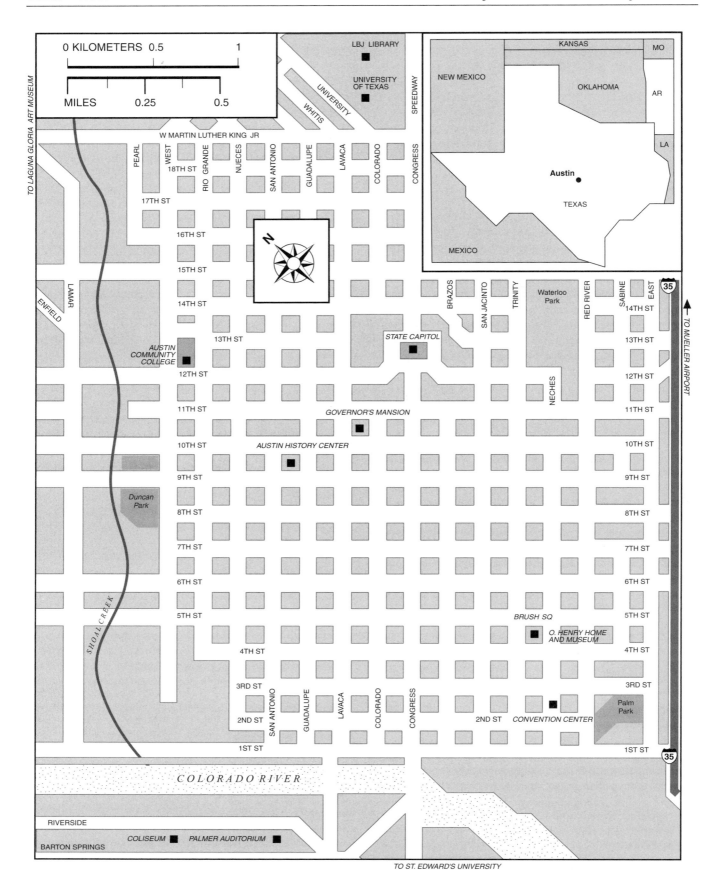

# Introduction

Nestled in the Texas Hill Country, Austin strikes a balance between nature, education, the arts, and commerce. Austin, the Texas state capital and the Travis County seat, is fueled by an entrepreneurial attitude that has resulted in the city's placement at the top of numerous business and cultural lists. Austin is known for its quality of life, which enables companies to attract and retain the very best talent from around the world. Its good jobs, easy living, excellent health care facilities, and low crime rate are a few of the reasons that *Men's Journal* ranked Austin the fifth best place to live in America in June 2004.

# Geography and Climate

Austin is located in south central Texas, where the Colorado River crosses the Balcones Escarpment, separating the Texas Hill Country from the black-land prairies to the east. The Colorado River flows through the heart of the city, creating a series of sparkling lakes that stretch for more than 100 miles. Austin's climate is subtropical with prevailing southerly winds and an average of 300 days of sunshine each year. Summers are hot; winters are mild, with only occasional brief cold spells. Most precipitation falls in the form of rain in late spring and early fall. Snow is rare; Austin may experience several winters in succession with no measurable amount.

**Area:** 258.43 square miles (2000)

**Elevation:** Ranges from 425 feet at lakeside to 1,000 feet in the northwest city hills

**Average temperatures:** January, 50.1° F; July, 84.3° F; annual average, 68.6° F.

**Average Annual Precipitation:** 31.35 inches

# History

## City Named State Capital

Lured to the area by tales of seven magnificent cities of gold, Spanish explorers first passed through what is now Austin during the 1530s. But instead of gold, they encountered several hostile Native American tribes; for many years, reports of the natives' viciousness (which included charges of cannibalism) discouraged further expeditions and restricted colonization. Spain nevertheless retained control of the region for nearly 300 years, withdrawing after Mexico gained its independence in 1821.

All of eastern Texas then experienced a boom as hundreds of settlers sought permission to establish colonies in the "new" territory. One of these early settlements was the village of Waterloo, founded in 1835 on the north bank of the Colorado River. In 1839 Mirabeau B. Lamar, vice-president of the Republic of Texas, recommended that Waterloo be chosen as the capital, noting among its assets its central location, elevation, mild climate, and freedom from the fevers that plagued residents of the republic's coastal areas. Despite stiff competition from those whose preference was Houston, Lamar's proposal was eventually accepted, and Waterloo was incorporated as Austin in 1839 and renamed in honor of Stephen F. Austin, "Father of Texas." Austin remained the capital when Texas was annexed by the United States in 1845.

During the 1850s the country's regional conflicts mounted, and Texans were fractured into three distinct camps: those who advocated supporting northern policies, those who wished to ally themselves with secessionist southern states, and those who urged the reestablishment of the independent Republic of Texas. Although Travis County citizens voted strongly against secession, Texas as a whole sided with the South when the Civil War erupted. Austin's contributions to the war effort included the manufacture of arms and ammunition and the mustering of the Austin City Light Infantry and a cavalry regiment known as Terry's Texas Rangers after its leader, B. F. Terry.

Despite some political strife following the Civil War, Reconstruction brought prosperity to Austin. The coming of the Houston & Texas Central Railroad in 1871 and the International-Great Northern five years later provided stimulus to the city's growth and commerce.

### Modern Development Linked to University

Austin's development received further impetus when, in 1883, the University of Texas at Austin held its first classes. In its early decades, the school was rich in real estate but poor in cash. The discovery of oil on university land in 1924 led to enormous wealth which, along with private donations and federal assistance, has made the University of Texas at Austin one of the best-endowed schools in the country.

Much of Austin's growth and development in the twentieth century was linked to the University of Texas at Austin. Its presence lent a cosmopolitan air to the city; visitors who expected to see cowboy boots and hats in abundance were usually disappointed because Austin was the least "Texan" of all the cities in the state. Besides making Austin a bastion of liberalism and tolerance, the university attracted much high-technology industry and fostered the city's image as the arts capital of Texas.

The recession of the early 2000s hit technology companies especially hard. As a result of its over-reliance on the high technology industry, Austin suffered an economic slump, losing jobs along with public and private revenues. The economy's road toward recovery coincided with the implementation of Opportunity Austin, an initiative launched in 2003 to rejuvenate the industries of existing companies and to diversify into such segments as automotive, biomedicine and pharmaceuticals, and corporate and regional headquarters.

Meanwhile, the resident of the Governor's Mansion moved from Austin into the White House. After a protracted recount effort centered on Florida ballots, George W. Bush resigned as Texas governor in December 2000 to accept his new post as the 43rd President of the United States. He was succeeded as governor by Rick Perry, Bush's lieutenant governor.

***Historical Information:*** Austin History Center, 9th and Guadelupe, PO Box 2287, Austin, TX 78768-2287; telephone (512)974-7480

# *Population Profile*

## Metropolitan Area Residents
*1980:* 585,000
*1990:* 846,227
*2000:* 1,249,763
*Percent change, 1990–2000:* 47.7%
*U.S. rank in 1980:* 63rd
*U.S. rank in 1990:* 52nd
*U.S. rank in 2000:* 37th

## City Residents
*1980:* 345,890
*1990:* 472,020
*2000:* 656,562
*2003 estimate:* 672,011
*Percent change, 1990–2000:* 39.0%
*U.S. rank in 1980:* 42nd
*U.S. rank in 1990:* 27th (State rank: 5th)
*U.S. rank in 2000:* 22nd (State rank: 4th)

*Density:* 2,610.4 people per square mile (2000)

*Racial and ethnic characteristics (2000)*
   White: 429,100
   Black or African American: 65,956
   American Indian and Alaska Native: 3,889
   Asian: 30,960
   Native Hawaiian and Pacific Islander: 469
   Hispanic or Latino (may be of any race): 200,579
   Other: 106,538

*Percent of residents born in state:* 54.9% (2000)

*Age characteristics* (2000)
   Population under 5 years old: 46,715
   Population 5 to 9 years old: 41,227
   Population 10 to 14 years old: 37,108
   Population 15 to 19 years old: 48,809
   Population 20 to 24 years old: 82,945
   Population 25 to 34 years old: 138,643
   Population 35 to 44 years old: 104,874
   Population 45 to 54 years old: 75,844
   Population 55 to 59 years old: 21,440
   Population 60 to 64 years old: 15,052
   Population 65 to 74 years old: 23,008
   Population 75 to 84 years old: 15,074
   Population 85 years and older: 5,823
   Median age: 29.6 years

*Births* (2002)
   Total number: 12,387

*Deaths* (2002)
   Total number: 3,370 (of which, 59 were infants under the age of 1 year)

*Money income* (1999)
   Per capita income: $24,163
   Median household income: $42,689
   Total households: 265,594

*Number of households with income of . . .*
   less than $10,000: 24,799
   $10,000 to $14,999: 14,492
   $15,000 to $24,999: 32,628
   $25,000 to $34,999: 35,546
   $35,000 to $49,999: 43,524
   $50,000 to $74,999: 51,029
   $75,000 to $99,999: 27,568
   $100,000 to $149,999: 21,889
   $150,000 to $199,999: 6,742
   $200,000 or more: 7,377

*Percent of families below poverty level:* 9.1% (39.3% of which were female householder families with related children under 5 years)

*2002 FBI Crime Index Total:* 42,979

# *Municipal Government*

Austin operates via a council-manager form of government. The mayor and six council members appoint the city manager, who is the chief administrator for the city. Each member serves staggered three-year terms. Term limits allow the mayor and council members to serve in their respective seat for a maximum of six years, or two consecutive terms.

**Head Official:** Mayor Will Wynn (since 2003; current term expires June 2006)

**Total number of city employees:** 10,692 (2004)

*City Information:* City of Austin, PO Box 1088, Austin, TX 78767; telephone (512)974-2000

# Economy

## Major Industries and Commercial Activity

Austin's role as a center for high technology made it particularly vulnerable to the recession that struck the nation's economy in the early 2000s. For three consecutive years, Austin suffered layoffs and job reductions; even the city government slashed 1,000 jobs. In an effort to reverse the tide, the city launched Opportunity Austin in September 2003. This plan aimed to bolster existing industries, such as computer software, digital media, wireless technology, semiconductors, and tourism, as well as attract new companies from diverse segments, like automotive, medical products, transportation and logistics, and national and regional headquarters. The 5-year goal of Opportunity Austin is to add 72,000 new jobs and a $2.9 billion increase in payroll.

An off-shoot of Austin's leadership in the semiconductor and software industries is the wireless segment. With a developed infrastructure of telecommunication, transportation, electric, and water capacities, Austin is a leading site for wireless technologies. Named one of the hottest wireless cities by *Newsweek* magazine in June 2004, Austin offers more free wireless spots—including its city parks—per capita than any other city in the nation. Moreover, the University of Texas at Austin is the nation's most unwired university in the country. Qualcomm Corp. constructed a computer chip design center in Austin in 2004, the same year that Verizon Wireless selected Austin as the first city for the launch of its BroadbandAccess 3G Network, a high-speed wireless Internet access service. Other wireless companies with a presence in Austin include AT&T Wireless Corp., Dell Inc., Intel Corp., and T-Mobile.

Drawing on the same expertise in high technology and innovation, the city is venturing into the biomedical and pharmaceuticals industry. The University of Texas at Austin is a primary asset in this arena. It has world-class programs in bioengineering, nanotechnology, bioinformatics, and pharmaceutical research, and is a leader in the number of science and engineering doctoral degrees it awards. Austin ranks high in patent activity—a measure of innovation. The 2,789 patents that were granted to Austin inventors in 2003 translates to 200 patents per 100,000 residents, more than 5 times the national rate of 36 patents per 100,000 residents. The city is home to approximately 85 biotech/pharmaceutical companies, including Apogent Technologies Inc., Luminex Corp., and TOPAZ Technologies Inc.

Austin has a history of success in striving to attract regional office and national headquarters. Dell Inc. is not only based in Austin, it is one of the area's largest employers. A diverse array of companies also elected to make Austin their headquarters: Hoover's Inc. (business/market intelligence), National Instruments Corp. (industrial automation), Schlotzsky's Inc. (sandwich chain), and Whole Foods Market Inc. (natural foods chain). In 2004 alone, a number of companies established or expanded their Austin headquarters, including 360Commerce Inc. (software), Britestream Networks Inc. (semiconductors), HealthTronics Inc. (surgical services/medical devices), Opus Healthcare Solutions (medical software), SigmaTel Inc. (semiconductors), Silicon Laboratories Inc. (integrated circuits), TriCoast Funding (mortgages), and the wireless industry association Wi-Fi Alliance. The city also serves as divisional or regional headquarters for such companies as 3M Co. (conglomerate well-known for adhesives), Progressive Corp. (insurance), and Waste Management Inc. (garbage collection).

*Items and goods produced:* computers, computer peripherals, software, electronic instruments, semiconductors, biotechnology, pharmaceuticals, business equipment, video games

## Incentive Programs—New and Existing Companies

*Local programs*—The city of Austin offers tax abatements, enterprise zone exemptions, public utility incentives, and financing programs for qualified new and existing companies. The Economic Development staff of the Greater Austin Chamber of Commerce can provide ongoing assistance to relocating companies, from initial inquiry to full employment. Chamber staff can act as area-wide resources for community presentations, initial interface with company employees, spousal employment assistance, residential real estate brokers/tours, special mortgage and banking programs, child care/elder care, and cultural acclimation.

*State programs*—The state of Texas offers a number of incentive programs to attract new and expanding businesses to the state. The Texas Economic Development Act of 2001 encourages large-scale manufacturing, research and development, and renewable energy by offering an eight-year reduction in property taxes. Other property tax incentives are offered to companies owning certain abated property and those that are located in specified areas known as reinvestment zones. The Texas Enterprise Zone Program offers sales and use tax refunds to companies that create jobs in certain economically distresses areas of the state. Other sales and use tax refunds are extended toward manufacturing machinery and equipment, with agricultural products and semi-conductor components targeted in particular. Research and development expenditures may be qualified for franchise tax credits, as can businesses creating jobs or injecting capital into "strategic investment areas."

*Job training programs*—The Texas Workforce Commission (TWC) provides workforce development assistance to employers and jobseekers across the state through a network of 28 workforce boards. Programs for employers include recruitment, retention, training and retraining, and outplacement services for employees. TWC also administers the Skills Development Fund, a program that assists public community and technical colleges create customized job training for local businesses. In the 2000-2001 school year alone, the Center for Career and Business Development, operated by Austin Community College, trained more than 5,800 employees of local high technology companies. This college also developed the Robotics and Automated Manufacturing program to produce skilled technicians for such highly automated industries as automotive manufacturing, an industry targeted by the city for growth. The Greater Austin Chamber of Commerce and the city of Austin founded the Capital Area Training Foundation (CATF) as an industry-led, non-profit organization dedicated to establishing long-term education and workforce development solutions. CATF courses provide college credit, internships, industry tours, and guest speakers who help students make the connection between high school and the world of work.

## Development Projects

Defined by the Opportunity Austin initiative, the city's focus for the mid-2000s was to strengthen its core high technology industry while attracting new diverse businesses and national, regional, or divisional headquarters. The first company recruited under this program was TASUS Corp., which announced plans in January 2004 to relocate from Indiana to Austin in a move that will create 100 new jobs in the area. Harris Publishing Co. announced a 150-job expansion the following month. In a large coup for the city, The Home Depot Inc. started construction in July 2004 on a new technology center that will create 500 new jobs and have an economic impact of $30 million each year. U.S. Aquaculture broke ground in February 2005 on a $5 million, 60,000 square foot facility that will produce organically raised fish.

In the culture and recreation arena, Austin continued to develop projects that would improve the quality of life for residents and visitors. Construction began in 2005 on the Lozano Long Center for the Performing Arts as well as the Lance Armstrong Crosstown Bikeway, named for the seven-time winner of the Tour de France, which will provide a six-mile bike route through downtown Austin. The Jack S. Blanton Museum of Art is scheduled to open at the University

of Texas at Austin in February 2006. In the planning stage are the Austin Museum of Art and the Mexican-American Cultural Center, a 126,000 square foot facility that will be dedicated to Mexican-American cultural arts and heritage.

*Economic Development Information:* Greater Austin Chamber of Commerce, 210 Barton Springs Rd., Ste. 400, Austin, TX 78704; telephone (512)478-9383; fax (512)478-6389

## Commercial Shipping

*Expansion Management* magazine ranked the Austin-San Marcos area one of the top metropolitan areas for logistics, taking into account its transportation/distribution climate, road infrastructure and traffic, railroads, water ports, and air service. Austin-Bergstrom International Airport has a 338,000-square-foot cargo port, and handled more than 254 million pounds of freight in 2004. Of this figure, international cargo totaled more than 12 million pounds, a 45 percent increase over the previous year. The airport's freight carriers are Federal Express, Airborne Express, and Menlo Worldwide Forwarding. Austin's busy Port of Entry is served by three brokers: LE Coppersmith Inc., Robert F. Barnes, and UPS Supply Chain Solutions Inc. Freight also travels to and from the city via Burlington Northern, Santa Fe Railway, Union Pacific Railroad, Georgetown Railroad, and Austin Area Terminal Railroad.

## Labor Force and Employment Outlook

Austin boasts a high quality labor force, based in large part on its highly trained, youthful population. In 2003 the percentage of college graduates in the Austin metropolitan area was 36.7 percent, compared to 26.5 percent nationally. The region's seven colleges and universities, particularly the University of Texas at Austin, produce highly skilled, innovative graduates seeking entry into the workforce. At the same time, 47 percent of the area's population was between the ages of 18 and 44 years, while the national average was 39 percent. As a result of these and other factors, *Business 2.0* magazine ranked Austin number four on its ranking of "Boom Towns" in March 2004.

The following is a summary of data regarding the Austin metropolitan area labor force, 2003 annual averages.

*Size of nonagricultural labor force:* 652,300

*Number of workers employed in . . .*
  *natural resources and mining:* 1,500
  *construction:* 35,700
  *manufacturing:* 57,700
  *trade, transportation and utilities:* 112,000
  *information:* 20,900
  *financial activities:* 39,400
  *professional and business services:* 85,500

*educational and health services:* 65,700
*leisure and hospitality:* 63,500
*other services:* 24,500
*government:* 145,800

*Average hourly wage of production workers employed in manufacturing:* $13.94 (2003 statewide annual average)

*Unemployment rate:* 4.0% (December 2004)

| *Largest employers* | *Number of employees* |
|---|---|
| Austin Independent School District | (each employs |
| City of Austin | 5,000 people |
| Dell Inc. | or more) |
| Federal Government | |
| Freescale Semiconductor Inc. | |
| IBM Corp. | |
| St. David's Healthcare Partnership | |
| Seton Healthcare Network | |
| State of Texas | |
| Texas State University-San Marcos | |
| University of Texas at Austin | |

## Cost of Living

Austin was ranked one of the nation's top 40 real estate markets by *Expansion Management* magazine in 2003. With a rate of 114.2 percent, the area also ranked first in fastest growing household income between 1990 and 2003, according to *Cities Ranked & Rated,* published by Wiley Publishing in 2004.

The following is a summary of data regarding several key cost of living factors for the Austin area.

*2004 (3rd Quarter) ACCRA Average House Price:* $216,000

*2004 (3rd Quarter) ACCRA Cost of Living Index:* 94.1 (U.S. average = 100.0)

*State income tax rate:* none

*State sales tax rate:* 6.25% (food and prescription drugs are exempt)

*Local income tax rate:* none

*Local sales tax rate:* 2.0% (of which, 1.0% goes to Metropolitan Transit Authority)

*Property tax rate:* 2.6431%

***Economic Information:*** Greater Austin Chamber of Commerce, 210 Barton Springs Rd., Ste. 400, Austin, TX 78704; telephone (512)478-9383; fax (512)478-6389. Texas Workforce Commission, 101 E. 15th St., Rm. 651, Austin, TX 78778-0001; telephone (512)463-2236; email customers @twc.state.tx.us

# *Education and Research*

## Elementary and Secondary Schools

The Austin Independent School District (AISD), the largest public school system in the metro Austin area, was ranked one of the nation's top eight public education systems by *Forbes* magazine in March 2004. Magnet schools such as the Science Academy and the Liberal Arts Academy serve outstanding students from throughout the school district. Through the Austin Partners in Education program, every school in Austin is in partnership with one or more businesses and organizations that donate millions of dollars in cash and in-kind resources such as school supplies, lab and technology equipment, and landscape materials to support AISD schools and programs. In an effort to enhance its fundraising capacities, Austin Partners in Education reorganized as a non-profit organization in 2004.

The following is a summary of data regarding Austin Independent School District as of the 2004–2005 school year.

*Total enrollment:* 79,788

*Number of facilities*
  *elementary schools:* 74
  *junior high/middle schools:* 17
  *senior high schools:* 12
  *special campuses:* 4

*Student/teacher ratio:* 22:1 (kindergarten through grade 4); 25-26:1 (grades 5-6); 28:1 (grades 7-12)

*Teacher salaries*
  *minimum:* $35,080
  *maximum:* $56,800

*Funding per pupil:* $6,644

A number of private and parochial schools also offer diverse educational opportunities to city students.

***Public Schools Information:*** Austin Independent School District, 1111 W. Sixth Street, Austin, TX 78703; telephone (512)414-1700

## Colleges and Universities

When it comes to higher education, Austin has a proud tradition. The city had barely been established when the Congress of the Republic of Texas mandated establishment of a "university of the first class." Today, the University of Texas at Austin is joined by six other institutions of higher education in the metropolitan area. The city's 2000 census paints a picture of a learned populous: 83.4 percent of adults have a high school diploma, while 25.7 percent have earned a bachelor's degree, and 14.7 percent have obtained a graduate degree. Austin's educational bent is a major attraction for businesses. The University of Texas at Austin is the nation's third largest university (Fall 2004 enrollment) and has a well-deserved reputation as one of the top research institutions in the country. Its network of research and resources creates a stimulating environment for businesses, and companies benefit from a highly trained workforce.

The area's other institutions of higher education include Austin Community College, St. Edward's University, Concordia University at Austin, Huston-Tillotson College, Southwestern University at Georgetown, Texas State University at San Marcos, and Episcopal and Presbyterian seminaries.

### Libraries and Research Centers

Best-selling author and Austin resident James Michener once commented, ''The libraries in Austin—you can't imagine how good they are.'' The large central public library and its 20 branches maintain a collection of more than 1.5 million volumes and about 2,500 periodical titles; special collections are maintained at the Austin History Center near the main library. Each of the colleges and universities has its own library whose collection reflects that institution's research interests and curriculum. Austin is also home to numerous special libraries that preserve the records of businesses, research firms, associations, and governmental agencies; the Lyndon Baines Johnson Library and Museum houses the 36th president's papers and other memorabilia. At least 80 research centers affiliated with the University of Texas at Austin sponsor investigations into everything from classical archaeology to artificial intelligence. Other of the city's notable research centers are Sematech, a consortium of U.S. semiconductor producers and the U.S. government; and the National Wildflower Research Center, brainchild of former first lady Lady Bird Johnson, whose facilities are open for tours.

***Public Library Information:*** Austin Public Library (Faulk Central Library), 800 Guadalupe, Austin, TX 78701; telephone (512)974-7400

# Health Care

Austin offers the best that modern medicine can supply and serves as a base for innovative technologies such as remote telecommunications uplinks and telephonic monitoring systems that carry health services into outlying areas or extend it to the home. With a total of 2,500 beds, the area has 12 major hospitals, including the Austin Women's Hospital that opened in 2004. These facilities provide an array of

specialized services such as major trauma care, coronary care, organ transplants, cancer treatments, and kidney dialysis. Other facilities specialize in mental health services, including chemical dependency treatment and counseling, and several also offer health classes and fitness centers for both individual and corporate clients. Families who are experiencing traumatic injury or illness also find a supportive environment. The community's Ronald McDonald House, located near Children's Hospital of Austin, and Seton League House, located near Seton Medical Center, each provide families with comfortable, affordable accommodations, regardless of which hospital cares for the patient. Hospice Austin and its affiliate in Williamson County provide comprehensive in-home services for those with terminal illnesses.

# Recreation

### Sightseeing

Austin beckons the tourist with its carefully maintained natural beauty, historic buildings, art museums and galleries, and vibrant night life. On a walking tour of the downtown area, highlights include the Texas State Capitol, a pink granite structure with a magnificent rotunda, and the antebellum Greek Revival Governor's Mansion. Early Texas history is reflected in the French Legation, a French provincial cottage built in 1841 for the French Charge d'Affaires to the Republic of Texas. Visitors may take guided tours of all three attractions. The State Cemetery, considered the Arlington of Texas, is the final resting place of many notable historical figures. The Umlauf Sculpture Gardens display 130 sculptures by Charles Umlauf. Both the curious and the lover of wildlife may appreciate seeing the largest colony of urban bats in North America. More than one million Mexican free-tailed bats—the namesake of the Austin Ice Bats hockey team—live under the Congress Avenue Bridge between April and September.

Other facets of Austin's past and present are reflected in the landmarks on the University of Texas at Austin campus. In addition to several museums, notable sights include the Center for American History, containing the most extensive collection of Texas history ever assembled; 1893 Littlefield House; and one of only five Gutenberg Bibles in the United States.

Zilker Park, the city's largest, is a popular destination for Austinites wanting to go for a swim, take a canoe ride, play soccer with friends, or just stroll through the gardens. Just a few minutes from downtown, it features Barton Springs, fed by natural spring water, as well as a nature center, a fanciful

**The State Capitol Building as viewed from the *'Dillo Express*.**

playground, several specialized gardens, a miniature train, large picnic and play areas, and a theater. Wild Basin Wilderness Preserve's 227 acres offer hiking and educational opportunities. Also within the city limits is the 744-acre McKinney Falls State Park.

## Arts and Culture

Austin is hailed as the "Live Music Capital of the World," and has more than 120 live music venues (including the Austin-Bergstrom International Airport). The PBS television program "Austin City Limits" has brought the city nationwide attention as a major center for progressive country music, popularized by such entertainers as Willie Nelson, a native Austinite. This is only part of a cultural scene that includes private theaters, two ballet companies, a symphony orchestra, an opera company, dozens of film theaters, and numerous art galleries and museums. The University of Texas Cultural Entertainment Committee hosts a constant stream of visiting entertainers, many of whom perform at the lavish University of Texas at Austin Performing Arts Center, comprised of Bass Concert Hall, Hogg Auditorium, Bates Recital Hall, B. Iden Payne Theatre, McCullough Theatre, and Oscar G. Brockett Theatre. Construction began in 2005 on the Joe R. and Teresa Lozano Long Center for the Performing Arts, which will serve 250 performing groups including the Austin Symphony, Ballet Austin, and the Austin Lyric Opera. Other classical groups in the city include the Austin Vocal Arts Ensemble and the Austin Civic Orchestra.

Aficionados of the stage may choose from traditional or more avant-garde fare presented by Austin's 35 independent theater companies. The Paramount Theatre, a restored 1915 vaudeville house, hosts traveling and children's productions. Repertory venues include Live Oak Theater, Capitol City Playhouse, and Zachary Scott Theatre. The city supports Shakespearean productions and a children's troupe. Musical theater is the forte of the Gilbert and Sullivan Society, which stages an annual "grand production" and free monthly musicales. Satirical performances are staged by Esther's Follies.

Austin claims to be home to the highest number of artists per capita of any city in Texas, and offers a wide variety of art galleries. Among Austin's 35 galleries and museums is the Elisabet Ney Museum, which displays the work of the state's first important sculptress in her former home. One of the world's largest collections of Latin American art is on display at the two locations of the Huntington Art Gallery on the University of Texas at Austin campus, while the Jack S. Blanton Museum of Art at the university has a large collection of Old Master paintings and drawings.

Austin's other museums celebrate Texas history and some of its notable citizens. For instance, the General Land Office Building, where William Sydney Porter, better known as O. Henry, once worked, was used as the setting for one of his stories and is open for tours. The O. Henry Home and Museum exhibits the writer's personal effects, and on the first Sunday of May, is the site of the O. Henry Pun-Off. The collections of the Daughters of the Republic of Texas are on view at the Republic of Texas Museum. The George Washington Carver Museum and Cultural Art Center is Texas' first African American history museum. The Lyndon B. Johnson Presidential Library and Museum maintains a collection of the late president's documents and displays memorabilia and a re-creation of his White House Oval Office. The state's natural history is the focus of the Texas Memorial Museum. Old and young alike enjoy Discovery Hall, a hands-on science museum, and the Austin Children's Museum.

## Festivals and Holidays

Austin hosts several major events throughout the year, the largest of which are centered on the arts. The South by Southwest (SXSW) music, film, and media festival is an internationally acclaimed, 10-day extravaganza held each March. Spring brings the Old Settler's Music Festival, the Austin International Poetry Festival, and the Austin Fine Arts Festival. The Austin City Limits Music Festival, an extension of the popular "Austin City Limits" television show, has been held each September since its 2002 debut. The following month is the Austin Film Festival, a showcase of commercial and independent films. Festivals with an ethnic flavor include the Carnival Brasiliero, a celebration of Brazilian culture and music held each February, and Cinco de Mayo (May 5th) and Diez y Seis (September 16th), which honor Mexican Independence. The Star of Texas Fair & Rodeo takes place over two weeks in March at the Travis County Exposition Center, which is also the site of the Republic of Texas Biker Rally in June. Numerous holiday celebrations, including Chuy's Christmas Parade, enliven the winter.

## Sports for the Spectator

Austin's first professional sports team was the Ice Bats of the Western Professional Hockey League. Named for the world-famous bats that live under the Congress Avenue Bridge, the team plays at the Travis County Exposition and Heritage Center. The Round Rock Express, a AA baseball affiliate of the Houston Astros, began play in the nearby city of Round Rock after relocating there from Mississippi in 2000. Four years later the city added another professional team, the Austin Wranglers, the nineteenth franchise of the Arena Football League. Spectators can watch the Dallas Cowboys at their pre-season football training camp at St. Edward's University in July and August. Professional basketball fans can view the National Basketball Association's San Antonio Spurs train at the University of Texas at Austin Rec Center.

In college action, the city is gripped with football fever each fall as the University of Texas at Austin Longhorns take on the Big 12 Conference at Memorial Stadium. University athletes engage in a full range of other sports as well, including volleyball, baseball, basketball, cross country, golf, track, tennis, swimming, rowing, diving, and women's soccer.

### Sports for the Participant

Amateur athletes delight in Austin's extensive sports facilities. The city's 208 parks and playgrounds total about 16,800 acres, and the city boasts numerous municipal golf courses and more than 28 miles of hiking and biking trails. The 150-mile chain that makes up Highland Lakes offers opportunities for swimming, canoeing, fishing, and boating. Austin has earned a reputation as one of the best tennis and golf environments in the nation.

Annual sporting events invite residents and visitors to put their best foot forward. The Freescale Marathon, a 26.2 mile race from Northwest Austin to Auditorium Shores, draws more than 7,000 participants each February. Texas' largest footrace, the Capitol 10,000, takes place in April and attracts approximately 10,000 runners on a 10K course between Congress Avenue and Auditorium Shores.

### Shopping and Dining

The infusion of wealthy high tech, film, and music professionals into Austin has turned it into a retail boom town. Austin offers residents and visitors a variety of shopping experiences. Downtown, for example, the streets around the capitol and other government buildings feature a wide array of upscale shops. One of the city's liveliest areas for both shopping and other forms of entertainment is Old Pecan Street, also known as Sixth Street, a seven-block strip of renovated Victorian and native stone buildings. Sporting more than 70 shops, restaurants, and clubs, Old Pecan Street displays a Bourbon Street flair in the evening. Adjacent to the University of Texas at Austin campus—especially along a street known as ''The Drag''—are dozens of small clothing boutiques and bookstores; on weekends, sidewalk vendors sell handcrafted items. More traditional mall shopping is common in the fast-growing northern part of the city.

Austin has more fine restaurants and clubs per capita than any other city in the nation. The city's restaurants feature everything from down-home Texas barbecue to the most elegant continental cuisine. Mexican restaurants are particularly abundant, and Asian restaurants have been proliferating.

*Visitor Information:* Austin Convention & Visitors Bureau, 301 Congress Ave., Ste. 200, Austin, TX 78701; telephone (512)474-5171; toll-free 800-926-2282; email visitorcenter @austintexas.org

## Convention Facilities

With its mild climate, many restaurants and live entertainment, and proximity to other Texas cities, Austin offers convention planners an attractive package. Its facilities, which include more than 12,000 hotel rooms, are well suited to the needs of large gatherings. The Austin Convention Center boasts 246,000 square feet of exhibit space, and its 54 meeting rooms total 61,440 square feet of space. At 43,300 square feet of space, its Grand Ballroom is the largest ballroom in Texas. In 2005 construction began to transform the Lester E. Palmer Auditorium into the Joe R. and Teresa Lozano Long Center for the Performing Arts. This $77 million project will produce a grand performance hall with seating for 2,400, as well as a smaller theater to accommodate conventions and receptions. The Texas Exposition and Heritage Center lies east of the downtown area. The Performing Arts Center and the Erwin Center on the University of Texas at Austin campus offer a variety of large meeting and performance spaces, while a number of hotels can provide banquet and meeting rooms for smaller gatherings.

*Convention Information:* Austin Convention & Visitors Bureau, 301 Congress Ave., Ste. 200, Austin, TX 78701; telephone (512)474-5171; toll-free 800-926-2282; email visitorcenter@austintexas.org

## Transportation

### Approaching the City

Located eight miles from downtown, the Austin-Bergstrom International Airport offers nonstop flights to 32 destinations, including New York, Chicago, Washington DC, Atlanta, Phoenix, Los Angeles, and Detroit. Total passenger traffic exceeded 7.2 million in 2004, up eight percent from the previous year. The airport is served by seven airlines: Southwest, American, Continental, Delta, Northwest, America West, and Frontier.

Drivers approach Austin via Interstate Highway 35, which runs north-south through the city and links it with Dallas and San Antonio, and Interstate Highway 10, running east-west along the southern edge of the city. Austin is also accessed via U.S. highways 79, 90, 183, and 290. Rail riders can board

Amtrak's Texas Eagle line (from Chicago to San Antonio) or its Sunset Limited line (Orlando to Los Angeles).

## Traveling in the City

Austin is bisected by interstate highways 10 and 35, and is also served by federal highways 79,90,183, and 290. Two other main roads, Loop 360 and Route 1, run north-south. The city is easy to explore by car and parking is plentiful. Visitors should note that only vehicles with special permits are allowed to drive through or park on the University of Texas at Austin campus.

Capital Metropolitan Transportation Authority provides the city's bus service. Each day, an average of 130,000 one-way passengers ride the system, which stops at more than 3,000 points throughout central Texas. The downtown area is served by the Armadillo Express trolleys known as 'Dillos, which offer free service to such places as the State Capitol and the University of Texas at Austin. Students and visitors to the University of Texas campus enjoy their own shuttle bus system.

# *Communications*

## Newspapers and Magazines

Austin's major daily newspaper is the *Austin American-Statesman,* a morning paper. Readers also have available the *Austin Daily Herald. The Daily Texan* is the student newspaper of the University of Texas at Austin. Weekly publications include the *Austin Chronicle,* a free tabloid that publishes entertainment listings, and the *Austin Business Journal,* which reports on local commerce. *Texas Monthly* chronicles state politics and culture. Also among the more than 80 newspapers and periodicals published in Austin are *Southwestern Historical Quarterly,* published by the Texas State Historical Association; *Capitol Times; El Mundo; Buddhist-Christian Studies; El Norte; Borderlands: Texas Poetry Review;* and *The Southwestern Musician.*

## Television and Radio

Seven television stations broadcast in Austin: one independent and affiliates of ABC, CBS, Fox, NBC, PBS, and WB. Access to dozens of cable channels is also available. The number and variety of the radio stations reflect Austinites' passion for music. Thirty-two AM and FM stations offer everything from contemporary and Christian music to talk radio.

*Media Information: Austin American-Statesman,* 305 S. Congress Ave., PO Box 670, Austin, TX 78767; telephone(512)445-4040; toll-free (800)445-9898; email circulation@statesman.com

## Austin Online

*Austin American-Statesman.* Available www.statesman.com

Austin Convention & Visitors Bureau. Available www.austintexas.org

Austin Independent School District. Available www.austinisd.org

Austin Public Library. Available www.ci.austin.tx.us/library

City of Austin Home Page. Available www.ci.austin.tx.us and www.cityofaustin.org

Greater Austin Chamber of Commerce. Available www.austinchamber.org

Texas Workforce Commission. Available www.twc.state.tx.us

## Selected Bibliography

Cantrell, Gregg, *Stephen F. Austin: Empresario of Texas* (New Haven: Yale University Press, 1999)

Douglass, Curan, *Austin Natural and Historic* (Austin, TX: Eakin Press, 2001)

Endres, Clifford, *Austin City Limits* (Austin: University of Texas Press, 1987)

Rather, Dan, and the Greater Austin Chamber of Commerce, *Austin: Celebrating the Lone Star Millennium* (Memphis, TN: Towery Publishing, 1999)

# Dallas

## The City in Brief

**Founded:** 1841 (incorporated 1871)
**Head Officials:** Mayor Laura Miller (since 2002)

**City Population**
  **1980:** 904,599
  **1990:** 1,007,618
  **2000:** 1,188,580
  **2003 estimate:** 1,206,667
  **Percent change, 1990–2000:** 17.95%
  **U.S. rank in 1980:** 7th
  **U.S. rank in 1990:** 8th (State rank: 2nd)
  **U.S. rank in 2000:** 12th (State rank: 2nd)

**Metropolitan Area Residents**
  **1980:** 2,055,000 (PMSA)
  **1990:** 4,037,282 (CMSA)
  **2000:** 5,221,801 (CMSA)

  **Percent change, 1990–2000:** 29.3 % (CMSA)
  **U.S. rank in 1980:** 10th (CMSA)
  **U.S. rank in 1990:** 9th (CMSA)
  **U.S. rank in 2000:** 9th (CMSA)

**Area:** 342.54 square miles (2000)
**Elevation:** Ranges from 500 to 800 feet above sea level
**Average Annual Temperature:** 66.42° F
**Average Annual Precipitation:** 35.77 inches

**Major Economic Sectors:** professional, scientific and technical services, finance and insurance, trade, utilities
**Unemployment rate:** 5.5% (December 2004)
**Per Capita Income:** $22,183 (1999)

**2002 FBI Crime Index Total:** 112,040

**Major Colleges and Universities:** Southern Methodist University, University of Dallas, University of Texas at Dallas, Dallas Baptist University

**Daily Newspaper:** *Dallas Morning News*

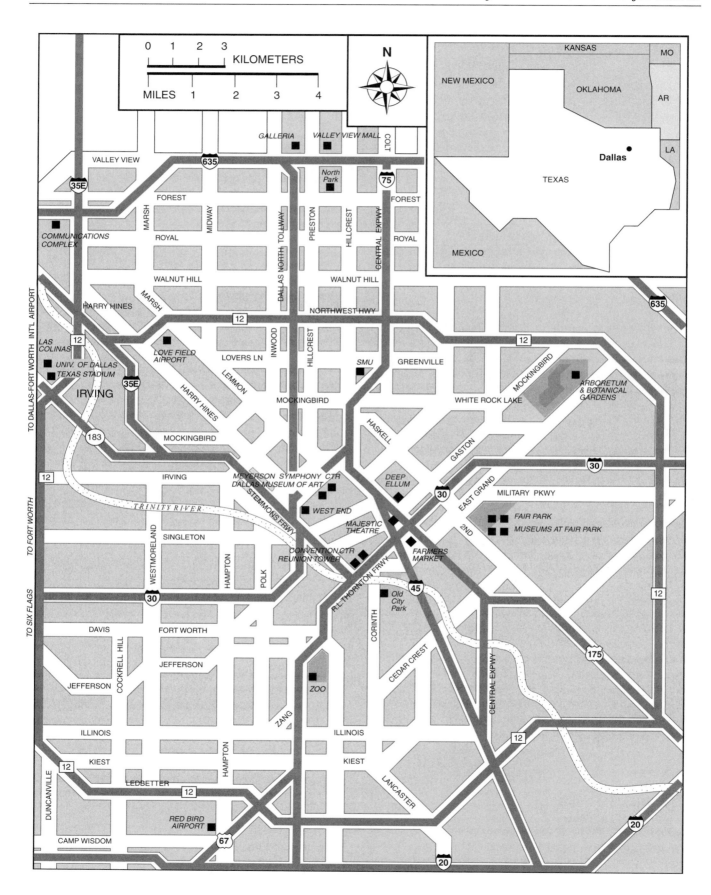

# Introduction

Nestled in the rolling prairies of north-central Texas, Dallas is a sophisticated, bustling metropolis that has earned its reputation in the marketplace of the world. Dallas is separated from its Fort Worth neighbor by less than 30 miles, leading many to link the two cities and their surrounding suburbs in the term "Metroplex," but each retains a distinctive identity. Basking in the glow of the nation's Sun Belt, Dallas has attracted people and businesses from colder regions for a number of years. The steady influx has caused Dallas to grow in size and importance, resulting in its status as a leader in culture, industry, fashion, transportation, finance, and commerce. The Dallas/Fort Worth area is the country's ninth most populated metropolitan area; with its continuous population growth, by 2010 it is expected to rank fourth.

# Geography and Climate

Dallas is located in north-central Texas, 70 miles south of the Oklahoma border, 174 miles west of Louisiana, and approximately 250 miles north of the Gulf of Mexico. The city is situated on the rolling plains near the headwaters of the Trinity River in an area known as the black-land prairies, midway between the Piney Woods of east Texas and the Great Plains. The general area has an unusual concentration of man-made lakes. Its climate is humid and subtropical, characterized by hot summers and mild winters, with snowfall rare. Within a 100-mile radius of the city, there are more than 60 lakes and over 50,000 acres of public parkland. The rainy season occurs in April and May; July and August are the driest summer months.

**Area:** 342.54 square miles (2000)

**Elevation:** Ranges from 500 to 800 feet above sea level

**Average Temperatures:** January, 45.44° F; August, 85.72° F; annual average, 66.42° F

**Average Annual Precipitation:** 35.77 inches

# History

### Bryan Designs Town

Since its pioneer days, Dallas has grown from a fledgling frontier trading post to a bustling city of more than one million people. Dallas was founded in 1841 when a bachelor lawyer from Tennessee, John Neely Bryan, settled on a small bluff above the Trinity River to open a trading post and lay claim to free land. The area, where three forks of the river merge, was part of a large government land grant, Peters Colony. Bryan decided the location was ideal for a town. He quickly sketched a plan, designating a courthouse square and 20 streets around it. He planned for his settlement to become the northernmost port on the river, which stretched to the Gulf of Mexico, but the unpredictable, too-shallow Trinity thwarted efforts at navigation.

Without a navigable river, an ocean harbor or plentiful natural resources, Dallas had little reason to thrive. Fortunately, Bryan's town was close to a shallow spot in the river often used by Native Americans and early traders as a natural crossing, and the Republic of Texas was already surveying two "national highways," both of which were to pass nearby. As a result, farmers, tradesmen, and artisans were attracted to the small community.

In 1849 Dallas County was created and named after George Mifflin Dallas, supporter of the annexation of Texas and vice president of the United States under James Knox Polk. The city of Dallas is thought to be named after either the vice president or his brother, Alexander James Dallas, a commander of the U.S. Navy's Gulf of Mexico squadron.

### Railroad spurs Growth

Although the Civil War never actually reached Dallas, its effect on the town was significant. Dallas became a food-producing and Texas recruitment center for the Confederacy. In 1872, when the railroad line from Houston reached Dallas, the town claimed 3,000 inhabitants, and in 1873, the east-west line of the Texas & Pacific Railroad was completed through Dallas, making it the first railroad crossing town in the state. The railroads made Dallas a major distribution center and the home of merchants, bankers, insurance companies, and developers. By 1890, Dallas was the largest city in Texas, with a population of more than 38,000 people.

### Economy Forms Around Oil

In 1920, the Trinity River, a source of some early central city flooding, was re-channeled westward as part of an ambitious construction project of the U.S. Army Corps of Engineers. Farming gained importance in the early twentieth century and Dallas was the largest cotton trading center in the nation. The city's position as a regional financial center was enhanced when a branch of the Federal Reserve Bank opened in 1914. Dallas attracted oil company headquarters, partly because Dallas banks were willing to finance exploration and production. Manufacturing arrived as companies were formed to produce supplies for the petroleum industry and, later, for the defense effort in World War II.

## City Experiences Tragedies

No city is without its share of fires (Dallas' worst destroyed most of its business district in 1860), floods, other tragedies, and infamous citizens. The notorious thieves Bonnie Parker and Clyde Barrow were Depression-era Dallas residents who captured the imagination and property of a large segment of the American public before their deaths in 1934. But Dallas' greatest trauma came on November 22, 1963, when President John F. Kennedy was assassinated in a cavalcade through the Dallas streets. Harsh world attention was focused on the city and its leaders. As a result, Goals for Dallas, a private planning program that helped promote a climate of involvement, openness, and sensitivity, was formed.

## Recent Economic Patterns

While much of the nation suffered an economic recession during the late 1970s and early 1980s, Dallas enjoyed unprecedented growth. As northern factories were idled, a rush to the "Sun Belt" created new businesses, industry, and jobs in Dallas. The downtown skyline changed rapidly as construction boomed. In 1984 Dallas was the site of the Republican National Convention, and many saw the occasion as a chance for the city to erase some lingering negative memories in the minds of the American public. In the 1980s Dallas witnessed a real estate bust that drove prices so low that in time many thriving businesses began to move in and take advantage of the bargain real estate. By 1990 Dallas ranked first in the country for the number of its new or expanded corporate facilities.

In the mid-1990s Dallas ranked as Texas' second largest city, next to Houston, and the eighth largest in the United States. Closing in on the twenty-first century, the city continued to thrive with a healthy and diversified economy and ranked high in the nation in convention activity, as an insurance and oil industry center, in concentration of corporate headquarters, in manufacturing, and in electronics and other high-technology industries.

After national economic downturns in the early part of the new century, Texas is primed for growth. Abundant job growth in many business sectors, coupled with a rapidly-growing population and a healthy economy, mean Dallas is poised for a bright future.

***Historical Information:*** Dallas Historical Society, G.B. Dealey Library, Hall of State, Fair Park, PO Box 150038, Dallas, TX 75315; telephone (214)421-4500

# *Population Profile*

## Metropolitan Area Residents

*1980:* 2,055,000

*1990:* 4,037,282 (CMSA)
*2000:* 5,221,801 (CMSA)
*Percent change, 1990–2000:* 29.3 % (CMSA)
*U.S. rank in 1980:* 10th (CMSA)
*U.S. rank in 1990:* 9th (CMSA)
*U.S. rank in 2000:* 9th (CMSA)

## City Residents

*1980:* 904,599
*1990:* 1,007,618
*2000:* 1,188,580
*2003 estimate:* 1,206,667
*Percent change, 1990–2000:* 17.95%
*U.S. rank in 1980:* 7th
*U.S. rank in 1990:* 8th (State rank: 2nd)
*U.S. rank in 2000:* 12th (State rank: 2nd)

*Density:* 3,469.9 people per square mile (2000)

*Racial and ethnic characteristics* (2000)
  White: 630,419
  Black or African American: 314,678
  American Indian and Alaska Native: 11,334
  Asian: 36,665
  Native Hawaiian and Pacific Islander: 1,461
  Hispanic or Latino (may be of any race): 422,587
  Other: 227,850

*Percent of residents born in state:* 53.8% (2000)

*Age characteristics* (2000)
  Population Under 5 years: 98,785
  Population 5 to 9 years: 89,942
  Population 10 to 14 years: 79,546
  Population 15 to 19 years: 81,733
  Population 20 to 24 years: 106,190
  Population 25 to 34 years: 235,824
  Population 35 to 44 years: 184,218
  Population 45 to 54 years: 132,491
  Population 55 to 59 years: 44,247
  Population 60 to 64 years: 33,303
  Population 65 to 74 years: 53,554
  Population 75 to 84 years: 35,808
  Population 85 years and over: 12,939
  Median age: 30.5 years

*Births* (2002)
  Total number: 42,863

*Deaths* (2002)
  Total number: 14,103 (of which, 285 were infants under the age of 1 year)

*Money income* (1999)
  Per capita income: $22,183
  Median household income: $37,628
  Total households: 452,009

*Number of households with income of . . .*
  Less than $10,000: 47,522
  $10,000 to $14,999: 27,270
  $15,000 to $24,999: 65,666
  $25,000 to $34,999: 68,020
  $35,000 to $49,999: 77,132
  $50,000 to $74,999: 74,160
  $75,000 to $99,999: 36,030
  $100,000 to $149,999: 29,478
  $150,000 to $199,999: 10,896
  $200,000 or more: 15,835

*Percent of families below poverty level:* 14.9% (42.3% of which were female householder families with related children under 5 years)

*2002 FBI Crime Index Total:* 112,040

# Municipal Government

Dallas is the third largest city in the country with the council-manager form of government. Citizens adopted this form of municipal government in 1931. The system divides responsibility between a policy-making council and the administration of a city manager. The Dallas City Council is comprised of 15 members elected by voters in non-partisan elections. Fourteen are elected from single-member districts, while the mayor is elected at-large.

**Head Official:** Mayor Laura Miller (since 2002; current term expires 2006)

**Total Number of City Employees:** 17,640 (2004)

*City Information:* Dallas City Hall, 1500 Marilla, Dallas, TX 75201; telephone (214)670-3302

# Economy

## Major Industries and Commercial Activity

Dallas boasts a broadly diverse business climate, with technological industries in the lead. Major industries include defense, financial services, information technology and data, life sciences, semiconductors, telecommunications, transportation, and processing. According to the Greater Dallas Chamber of Commerce, the Dallas-Fort Worth Metroplex holds about 43 percent of the state's high-tech workers. Further, 13 privately-held companies with at least $1 billion in annual revenues are headquartered in the area. Among the 19 *Fortune* 500 companies headquartered in the area are Advance PCS, Dean Foods, ExxonMobil, Kimberly-Clark, Neiman Marcus, Southwest Airlines, and Texas Instruments.

Dubbed the "Silicon Prairie," Dallas is among the country's largest employment centers for high technology. In addition, Dallas is known as a center for telecommunications manufacturing employment in the United States. The Telecom Corridor is an area in Richardson, Texas, north of Dallas. Its nickname is in recognition of the proliferation of telecommunications companies in a small section of the community. The area is a strip about three miles long on Highway 75, north of Interstate 635; Nortel, Ericsson, Alcatel, Southwestern Bell and other telecom companies call the area home.

Real estate and tourism are other major industry sectors in Dallas.

*Items and goods produced:* chemicals and allied products, electronic components, parts for defense and airline industries, machinery, transportation equipment, and food products

## Incentive Programs—New and Existing Companies

*Local programs*—Tax Increment Finance Districts (TIFs) are designated areas targeted for development, redevelopment, and improvements. Increases in tax revenues from new development and higher real estate values are paid into TIF funds to finance improvements. Public Improvement Districts (PIDs) are created at the request of property owners in the district, who pay a supplemental tax which is used for services beyond existing city services, such as marketing, security, landscaping, and other improvements. There are seven TIFs and five areas designated as PIDs in Dallas.

*State programs*—State-designated Enterprise Zone Projects may be eligible for state sales or use tax refunds of taxes paid for building materials, machinery and equipment for use in the enterprise zone. Other state sales tax refunds and franchise tax refunds or reductions are available to qualified businesses in state-designated enterprise zones. Classification by the Public Utilities Commission as a qualified business in a state designated enterprise zone may qualify the business for up to a 5 percent reduction on electric utility rate upon negotiation with local electric utility service provider.

*Job training programs*—The Greater Dallas Chamber promotes economic opportunities for all women through a series of seminars and training sessions. The College for Texans statewide campaign launched in the fall of 2002 by the Texas Higher Education Coordinating Board (THECB) works to send more Texans to college, training them for the workforce beyond. Through this program, GO Centers, a grassroots network of community-managed college recruiting centers, serve as primary points of coordination between the campaign efforts and local communities. Leadership Dallas is a program that trains business leaders in community responsibility through discussion of issues, consideration of options, and first-hand exploration of the needs and concerns of the Greater Dallas Region.

### Development Projects

The Dallas-Fort Worth (DFW) Airport has invested $2.7 billion in its five-year Capital Development Program (CPD), which includes a two million square foot international terminal with an integrated Grand Hyatt Hotel and a high-speed train. Airfield, roadway, and airport infrastructure support projects make up the rest of the program. The development program is expected to generate an estimated $34 billion impact on the North Texas economy and create 77,000 new jobs during the next 15 years. Currently, DFW has more than 2.6 million square feet of cargo facilities.

Among the city's seven Tax Increment Finance Districts (TIFs) is the City Center TIF at the historic center of downtown Dallas. With a budget of nearly $62 million, City Center TIF projects focus on streetscaping, lighting, acquisition and restoration of historic buildings, façade improvements, and others. Due in part to the TIF program, the City Center TIF area has brought about more than 1,300 already-built or in-planning residential units; more than 2,300 planned or completed hotel rooms; and more than 300,000 square feet of retail space. Another Tax Increment Finance District, the Sports Arena TIF contains about 65 acres of land surrounding the American Airlines Center. Funds to the tune of nearly $26 million will be used mainly for roadway improvements and future development of entertainment and retail space, residential units, and office space.

***Economic Development Information:*** Greater Dallas Chamber, Economic Development, 700 North Pearl Street, Suite 1200, Dallas, TX 75201; telephone (214)746-6600

### Commercial Shipping

A major mid-continent gateway to the world, the Dallas-Fort Worth International Airport's international cargo shipments have more than tripled in the last 10 years, reaching 244,515 metric tons in 2004, a nearly 28 percent increase over 2003. In addition to its excellent airport services, interstate highways, and railroad connections, Dallas maintains its edge as a leading distribution center of the Southwest with a healthy trucking industry whose carriers offer direct service to major points in the United States.

### Labor Force and Employment Outlook

Dallas' job market is primed to grow slightly faster than the nation in 2005. The expansion of the professional and business sector and the leisure and hospitality services sector is aiding the state's improving economy, along with solid growth in health and educational services. Additionally, the construction and transportation sectors are reporting accelerating year-over-year job growth, while the economic drag from the ailing manufacturing and information sectors is diminishing. Professionals are moving back to the urban center to take advantage of the educational and health care opportunities as well as professional business services that Dallas provides. Many of these new residents were enticed to relocate by the expanding leisure and hospitality industry, which has finally seen a revival since the September 11, 2001 terrorist attacks. This influx of new residents provides the metro area with an abundant labor supply and increased prospects for local lenders. The Dallas area enters the twenty-first century experiencing some of the highest economic expansion in the nation. Dallas' entrepreneurial spirit and pro-business atmosphere paved the way for the city to be named "the best city in North America for business" twice by *Fortune* magazine. The Sprint Business Survey called Dallas the most productive area in the U.S., based on its vibrant economic climate and its fast-growing industries in technology, communications, professional services, banking and financial services.

The following is a summary of data regarding the Dallas metropolitan area labor force, 2003 annual averages.

*Size of nonagricultural labor force:* 1,901,600

*Number of workers employed in . . .*
   *construction and mining:* 104,900
   *manufacturing:* 200,000
   *trade, transportation and utilities:* 410,500
   *information:* 80,600
   *financial activities:* 168,100
   *professional and business services:* 269,000
   *educational and health services:* 188,400
   *leisure and hospitality:* 170,300
   *other services:* 73,400
   *government:* 236,400

*Average hourly earnings of production workers employed in manufacturing:* $13.50

*Unemployment rate:* 5.5% (December 2004)

| Largest employers | Number of employees |
|---|---|
| AMR (American Airlines) | 26,700 |
| Wal-Mart Stores, Inc. | 19,200 |
| Lockheed Martin Aeronautics Co. | 15,500 |
| SBC Communications, Inc. | 14,100 |
| Verizon Communications, Inc. | 13,000 |
| Baylor Health Care System | 12,600 |
| Brinker International Inc. | 12,000 |
| Citigroup, Inc. | 9,400 |
| Electronic Data Systems Corp. | 9,000 |
| Raytheon | 8,000 |

| Largest employers | Number of employees |
|---|---|
| Bank of America Corp. | 7,700 |
| Parkland Health and Hospital System | 7,350 |
| TXU Corporation | 7,000 |
| Southwest Airlines Co. | 6,200 |
| Bell Helicopter Textron Inc. | 5,950 |
| United Parcel Service, Inc. | 5,550 |
| Delta Airlines | 5,000 |
| FedEx Corp. | 4,050 |

## Cost of Living

The following is a summary of several key cost of living factors for the Dallas area.

*2004 (3rd Quarter) ACCRA Average House Price:* $189,137

*2004 (3rd Quarter) ACCRA Cost of Living Index:* 93.9 (U.S. average = 100.0)

*State income tax rate:* none

*State sales tax rate:* 6.25% (food and prescription drugs are exempt)

*Local income tax rate:* none

*Local sales tax rate:* 8.25%, of which 1.0% is a transit system tax

*Property tax rate:* $2.93 per $100 of assessed valuation; ratio of assessment = 100% of market value (2003)

***Economic Information:*** The Greater Dallas Chamber of Commerce, 700 North Pearl Street, Suite 1200, Dallas, TX 75201; telephone (214)746-6600

# Education and Research

## Elementary and Secondary Schools

The Dallas Independent School District is the 12th largest school district in the nation, covering 351 square miles and 11 municipalities. Its commitment to student success and a progressive learning environment is reflected in a challenging core curriculum and special programs, such as career education, character education, advanced placement, talented and gifted, science and engineering, fine arts, and multilingual and multicultural enrichment.

The following is a summary of data regarding the Dallas Public Schools as of the 2003–2004 school year.

*Total enrollment:* 161,000

*Number of facilities*
   *elementary schools:* 157 (including charter, magnet, and special programs)

*junior high/middle schools:* 27 (grades 7-8)
*senior high schools:* 21
*other:* 14 (7 magnet high schools and 7 alternative programs)

*Student/teacher ratio:* 23:1

*Teacher salaries*
   *minimum:* $38,500
   *maximum:* $63,828

*Funding per pupil:* $7,178

More than 140 accredited private schools, both secular and parochial, are located in the Dallas area.

***Public Schools Information:*** Dallas Independent School District, 3700 Ross Avenue, Dallas, TX 75204; telephone (972)925-3700

## Colleges and Universities

The Dallas County Community College District educates almost 80,000 credit and non-credit students and operates seven campuses in Dallas County, each offering two-year programs in a variety of fields. Southern Methodist University in Dallas is a private school with undergraduate and graduate degree programs and an enrollment of 10,000. Other Dallas colleges include the University of Texas Southwestern Medical Center educating 3,520 students annually; Dallas Christian College, offering biblical and theological study; Louise Herrington School of Nursing of Baylor University; Baylor College of Dentistry; Other institutions offering biblical or religious studies or programs from a religious perspective include The Criswell College, Dallas Theological Seminary, Dallas Baptist University, Paul Quinn College, and the University of Dallas.

The University of Texas at Dallas is located in Richardson and consists of seven schools, which educate 14,000 students annually. In 2004 the university broke ground on an $85 million Natural Science and Engineering Research Building. The new building is part of the university's 25-year master plan, which proposes a host of new buildings on its growing campus. In downtown Dallas a unique consortium of educational institutions exists in a former department store building on Main Street. The Universities Center at Dallas is operated by the Federation of North Texas Area Universities and offers undergraduate and graduate courses by seven partner institutions including Midwestern State University, Texas A&M University–Commerce, Texas Woman's University, University of North Texas, University of Texas at Arlington, University of Texas at Dallas, and Dallas County Community College District.

## Libraries and Research Centers

The Dallas Public Library system consists of a central library and 22 branch libraries. The system has nearly 2.6

million volumes and serials and a large collection of government documents. The library also maintains a historical section that contains an extensive collection of books, letters, and historical documents of Texas, Dallas, and Dallas black history. The Dallas Public Library in Downtown Dallas has one of the original copies of the Declaration of Independence, printed on July 4, 1776 and William Shakespeare's First Folio of Comedies, Histories' Tragedies on permanent display at the library. The library's Children's Center is one of the largest in the country. Southern Methodist University's library has more than 2.5 million volumes, with special collections on Western Americana and Texana. Most of the other area universities and colleges also operate their own libraries.

Dallas has nearly 60 research centers, many affiliated with local colleges, universities, and hospitals. For example, at Baylor University, research is carried out on hair and treatment, bone marrow transplantation, biomedicine, and sports science. The University of Texas Southwestern Medical Center at Dallas conducts more than 2,000 research projects each year at a cost of more than $330 million. Eight of the nine Texas medical members of the National Academy of Sciences, three recent Nobel Laureates, and thirteen of the most-cited scientists in the world, are on faculty at the University of Texas Southwestern Medical Center. The Institute of Biomedical Sciences and Technology conducts interdisciplinary projects with a focus on cures for disease and enhancing health and quality of life.

*Public Library Information:* Dallas Public Library, 1515 Young Street, Dallas, TX 75201; telephone (214)670-1400; fax (214)670-1752

# Health Care

The Dallas area has an extensive network of public and private hospitals, including six major hospital systems with more than 13,000 beds.

Parkland Memorial Hospital, a public hospital operated by the Dallas County Hospital District, is the major trauma center for North Texas and the principal teaching hospital for the University of Texas Southwestern Medical Center. Parkland, considered among the top 25 hospitals in the country, offers specialized care in its pediatric trauma and burn centers.

Baylor Health Care System's University Medical Center at Dallas—consistently ranked by *U.S. News & World Report* as among the best hospitals in the United States—offers many areas of specialty. The Kimberly H. Courtwright and Joseph W. Summers Institute of Metabolic Disease at the

center provides comprehensive diagnostic and treatment services to children and adults suffering from metabolic diseases. Baylor Dallas has several specialty centers that focus on diabetes: The Ruth Collins Diabetes Center, The Professional Diabetes Educator Program, and the Louise Gartner Center for Hyperbaric Medicine.

The Dallas Craniofacial Center at Medical City Children's Hospital is one of the world's leading medical centers for treatment of children with craniofacial birth defects and facial trauma. A member of the National Association of Epilepsy Centers, The Center for Epilepsy at Medical City treats adult and pediatric patients with complex neurological disorders. Methodist Dallas Transplant Institute is one of the largest and most active transplant centers in the southwestern United States.

Other major medical facilities in Dallas include Presbyterian Hospital of Dallas, Veterans Affairs Medical Center, St. Paul Medical Center, and other facilities that specialize in psychiatric, orthopedic, or mental health.

# Recreation

### Sightseeing

Dallas is rich in entertainment opportunities. Whether one's preference runs to culture, sports, nightlife, or family fare, the Metroplex—including Fort Worth, Arlington, Irving, Grand Prairie, the "Mid-Cities," and many suburbs—has plenty to offer. Beginning in downtown Dallas, visitors can see Dallas founder John Neely Bryan's log cabin at Founder's Plaza, wander through the city's historic districts, enjoy a shopping excursion among the shops and stores located in the underground network of downtown office buildings, or seek out merchandise at Neiman-Marcus department store, which maintains a unique fifth-floor museum. Other downtown Dallas attractions include the beautifully restored Majestic Theatre, the chimes in the bell tower, Thanks-Giving Square, the marvelous bronze steers of Pioneer Plaza, the bargains at Farmers Market, the observation deck on top of the 50-story tall Reunion Tower, and the ice rinks at Plaza of the Americas complex and at downtown's West End (open December through March).

Fair Park is a 277-acre entertainment, cultural, and recreational complex located on the site of the Texas Centennial Exposition of 1936 and home each year to the State Fair of Texas, the country's largest. Fair Park includes the Cotton Bowl Stadium, a 3,400-seat Music Hall, a 7,200-seat coliseum, a 4,000-seat open-air Band Shell, Starplex Amphitheatre, six major exhibit buildings, livestock facilities, a permanent Midway amusement park, the technologically

**Fair Park, designated a National Historic Landmark in 1986, is home to nine museums and six peformance facilities.**

advanced TI Founders IMAX Theater, and nine museums including the Museum of Natural History, African American Museum, Texas Hall of State, Dallas Horticulture Center, Dallas Aquarium, The Science Place I and II, and Age of Steam Railroad Museum. Fair Park has the largest collection of art-deco structures in the world. More than seven million people visit Fair Park events each year, with 3.5 million visiting during the State Fair of Texas each fall.

Six Flags over Texas in nearby Arlington is a 205-acre theme park that includes more than 100 rides, shows, concerts, games, and restaurants. Six Flags, themed for the six nations that have governed Texas, is open for special events during the holidays. Fossil Rim Wildlife Center in Glen Rose, southwest of Dallas, is dedicated to conservation of endangered species. Programs here focus on conservation, management of natural resources, and public education. Most of the animals here are free to roam the 1,500 acres of savannahs and woodlands, offering visitors a rare chance to see and learn about how species live in the wild.

The Dallas Zoo features more than 2,000 animals, including many rare and endangered species. The 25-acre Wilds of Africa exhibit features a mile-long monorail, nature trail, African plaza, gorilla conservation center, and lots of animals in their natural habitats. "Lemur Lookout" features several examples of the endangered, primitive primate in a 4,000-square-foot naturalistic exhibit. The Zoo's Monorail Safari takes visitors on a one-mile tour through the six habitats. The Dallas Nature Center has 4.5 miles of hiking trails and picnic areas amid a variety of native wildflowers. Dallas Arboretum and Botanical Garden has 66 acres of gardens plus the historic DeGolyer Mansion and features the largest public selection of azaleas in the United States.

Old City Park is a living history museum portraying life in North Texas from 1840-1910. The museum features 38 historic structures, including a working Civil War era farm, a traditional Jewish household, Victorian homes, a school, a church, and commercial buildings. Deep Ellum, a former industrial neighborhood and center of the Dallas jazz scene is home to avant-garde culture in the form of a variety of restaurants, nightclubs, galleries, and shops.

## Arts and Culture

The performing arts enjoy a healthy patronage in Dallas. The Dallas Symphony Orchestra (DSO), acclaimed as one of the world's premier orchestras, presents numerous subscription concerts, pops concerts, youth concerts, and free park concerts. The DSO performs at the magnificent Morton H. Meyerson Symphony Center (designed by renowned architect I.M. Pei) in the 60-acre downtown Arts District, the largest urban arts district in the country. Classical music is also provided by the Dallas Chamber Orchestra, the Dallas Classic Guitar Society, and the Greater Dallas Youth Orchestra.

The Kalita Humphreys Theatre, home to the Dallas Theater Center, is the only public theater designed by Frank Lloyd Wright. It houses the city's professional theater company, which offers live drama and conducts a children's theater. The Theater Center has a second performance facility in the downtown Arts District. Dallas Children's Theater offers special fare for youngsters. Others on the Dallas theater scene include Water Tower Theatre, Deep Ellum Opera Theatre, Pocket Sandwich Theatre, Pegasus, Theatre Three, Actors' Theatre of Dallas, Dallas Summer Musicals, the Junior Black Academy of Arts and Letters, and Undermain Theatre. Teatro Dallas features plays about Hispanic culture, and the Callier Theatre for the Deaf offers performances throughout the year.

The Dallas Opera, an international company founded in 1957, presents numerous performances each winter and spring in the Music Hall at Fair Park and the Morton H. Meyerson Symphony Center. Three operettas in English are performed each year by the Lyric Opera. The Music Hall at Fair Park is home of the Dallas Summer Musicals and hosts annual shows during the State Fair each October. The Grapevine Opry and Mesquite Opry are sites for country music performances. One of Dallas' oldest dance troupes, Anita N. Martinez Ballet Folklorico, is particularly active during Dance for the Planet festivals. Dallas Black Dance Theatre is a contemporary modern dance company that performs a modern, jazz, ethnic, and spiritual works by nationally and internationally known choreographers.

Dallas-area museums and galleries offer a wide range of exhibits and displays. The Dallas Museum of Art has 370,000 square feet of space on an 8.9-acre site in the Arts District. Its collections include works by renowned American and European artists; the Crow Collection of Asian Art features more than 600 paintings, objects, and architectural pieces from China, Japan, India, and Southeast Asia.

The Dallas Aquarium at Fair Park features electric eels, moon jellyfish, and endangered green sea turtles among the 5,000 aquatic animals from around the world. Also at Fair Park, the Dallas Museum of Natural History contains native-habitat displays of animals—including a hall housing tremendous dinosaur fossils—and minerals, birds, and plants, a photographic gallery, and changing exhibits. Other Fair Park museums include: Hall of State, built in 1936 and home to the Dallas Historical Society; The Science Place, featuring science exhibits, a planetarium, and IMAX theater; The Age of Steam Railroad Museum, a collection of railroad locomotives; the African American Museum; Texas Discovery Gardens; and The Women's Museum.

Old City Park in downtown Dallas is an architectural and cultural museum whose authentic restorations trace Texas history from 1840 to 1910. Buildings include a depot, railroad section house, hotel, physician's office, bank, church, school, and various homes. The Biblical Arts Center features early Christian architecture, Biblical and secular art, a 30-minute light-and-sound presentation of the "Miracle at Pentecost" mural, and an atrium gallery that displays a replica of the garden tomb of Christ. The cultures and lifestyles of South American Indians are depicted at the International Museum of Cultures, where exhibits include pottery, habitat displays, and scenes of everyday life. The Sixth Floor Museum at the former Texas School Book Depository chronicles the life and legacy of President John F. Kennedy. The 30-foot-high JFK Memorial downtown commemorates the late president.

The Nasher Sculpture Center is a 54,000-square-foot building and outdoor sculpture garden featuring the art collection of philanthropist and collector Ray Nasher and his late wife, Patsy. Considered by many as one of the foremost private or public collections of twentieth-century sculpture in the world, consists of more than 300 pieces by artists such as Matisse, Picasso, Rodin and others.

The Dallas Firefighters Museum permits visitors to walk through Dallas' oldest in-service fire station, which houses "Old Tige," a turn-of-the-century steam pumper, and a variety of antique fire-fighting equipment. The Dallas Memorial Center for Holocaust Studies includes a museum, library, and educational institute. The Dollhouse Museum of the Southwest features displays of international dolls and toys.

## Festivals and Holidays

Dallas starts off its year with New Year's celebrations and continues strong throughout the year with numerous festivals featuring art, music, food, fun, and more. The Wildflower! Arts & Music Festival is held every May and features national, regional, and local entertainment. The Shakespeare Festival is held each summer and features Camp Shakespeare and Festival Workshops for kids. ArtFest is held each year in Fair Park, a celebration of art, food and drink, and good times. Dallas Farmers Market is the scene of seasonal festivals, and the great State Fair of Texas is held each year at Fair Park from late September through mid-October. Additionally, One of the largest wine festivals in the Southwest is Grapefest, held in Grapevine, Texas, a suburb of Dallas.

## Sports for the Spectator

Dallas sports fans can follow their local favorites at the professional or college level. Since 1972 the Dallas Cowboys professional football team has made its home at Texas Stadium in Irving. The American Airlines Center is home to National Basketball Association's expansion franchise team Dallas Mavericks, as well as the Dallas Desperados of the Arena Football League (AFL). Also at the American Airlines Center, the Dallas Stars face-off against other National Hockey League teams from September through April. The Texas Rangers play Major League Baseball from April thru October at Ameriquest Field in Arlington. Major League Soccer's FC Dallas (formerly the Dallas Burn) play at the Frisco Soccer & Entertainment Center, opened in 2005. The new 115-acre facility features a 20,000-plus-seat soccer stadium.

Real championship cowboys compete at the Mesquite Championship Rodeo at Resistol Arena from April to September in Mesquite, Texas. In May, the TPC at Four Seasons Resort in Irving, Texas hosts the annual Byron Nelson Golf Classic, one of the major events on the professional golf tour.

College and university sports fans follow the Southern Methodist University Mustang teams and the Texas Christian University Horned Frogs. The Cotton Bowl Football Classic each year pits two of the nation's best college teams.

## Sports for the Participant

The city of Dallas has more than 21,000 acres of parks and 17 lakes, with nearly 62 miles of jogging and biking paths. Residents and visitors can find almost every kind of recreation in one or more of the municipal facilities. The system's 406 neighborhood, community, and regional parks offer 263 tennis courts, 146 soccer fields, 226 pools, 45 recreation centers, 6 golf courses, and a variety of other fields, shelters, play areas, and recreational facilities.

Sixty lakes and reservoirs lie within a 100-mile radius of Dallas. The largest within the city is Lake Ray Hubbard, with more than 20,000 acres and a public marina. The Dallas Nature Center features 360 acres of preserved wilderness and mesquite prairie, including six miles of hiking trails.

In 2002 and after six years in development, Lake Tawakoni State Park opened 50 miles east of Dallas. The park covers 376 rolling, wooded acres on the shore of a large reservoir and provides a variety of recreational activities, including catfish and bass fishing.

## Shopping and Dining

Dallas offers visitors a unique blend of Southwestern warmth, cosmopolitan flair, Old West charm and modern sophistication. One of the wholesale and retail centers of the nation, Dallas has more shopping centers per capita than any major American city. Valley View Center is one of the city's largest shopping centers with more than 175 merchants occupying 1.5 million square feet of space. NorthPark Mall is home to more than 160 stores. The Galleria Dallas features more than 200 stores, including high-end retailers like Tiffany & Co., Gianni Versace, Gucci, Louis Vuitton, Nordstrom and others; the mall also features an ice skating rink inspired by the Galleria Vittorio Emanuele in Milan, Italy. The West End Marketplace downtown has over 30 specialty shops featuring Texas/Dallas memorabilia and unique gifts; shoppers also have their choice from a variety of restaurants and night clubs in the renovated historic district. More than three million antique and bargain hunters visit Traders Village in Grand Prairie, Texas each year. Spread over 120 acres, more than 2,500 dealers set up shop each weekend in the open-air bargain hunters' paradise.

Dallas, with four times more restaurants per person than New York City, can serve up Texas beef or French cuisine, fiery Texas chili, or a variety of ethnic specialties. According to the Texas Restaurant Association, Dallas has more than 7,000 restaurants to enjoy. TexMex fare is supplemented by the ethnic dishes of Greece, Mexico, Germany, Japan, China, Vietnam, India, and Italy at fine restaurants and eateries. Although some restaurants specialize in traditional southern cooking, this fare is mostly served at home in Dallas. Dallas boasts the invention of the frozen margarita, a popular cocktail made of tequila, lime juice, sugar, and salt.

*Visitor Information:* Dallas Convention and Visitors Bureau, 325 North St. Paul Street, Suite 700, Dallas, TX 75201; telephone (214)571-1000; fax (214)571-1008

# Convention Facilities

Dallas ranks among the top cities in the nation in convention and meeting attendees, with more than 3.8 million people attending more than 3,600 conventions and spending more than $4.2 billion annually. With more than 65,000 hotel rooms available in a variety of hotels throughout the city, the Dallas metro area is the top visitor destination in the state. The city's convenient location in the central United States makes Dallas no more than a three-hour flight from either coast. And Dallas' outstanding airport facilities make coming and going even easier. Major hotels with meeting facilities include the Adam's Mark, Wyndham Anatole, the Adolphus, the Doubletree Hotel, the Hyatt Regency, the Dallas Hilton, and the Fairmont Hotel.

Visitors to Dallas have available to them other fine convention facilities. The Dallas Convention Center, one of the country's largest, offers more than one million square feet of exhibit space, with 203,000 square feet in its column-free exhibit hall, which is the largest in the U.S.; a 9,816 seat arena, a 1770-seat theater, 105 meeting rooms, and 2 ballrooms. The center underwent its most recent expansion in 2002.

*Convention Information:* Dallas Convention & Visitors Bureau, 325 North St. Paul Street, Suite 700, Dallas, TX 75201; telephone (214)571-1000; toll-free 800-C-DALLAS (232-5527); fax (214)571-1008. Dallas Convention Center,

650 South Griffin Street Dallas, TX 75202; telephone (214)939-2700; fax (214)939-2795

# Transportation

## Approaching the City

Most visitors to Dallas arrive via the Dallas/Fort Worth International (DFW) Airport, located approximately 17 miles from the downtown areas of both cities and is served by 22 airlines. DFW is four hours or less by air from nearly every major North American market, with direct service to more than 165 nonstop destinations worldwide. Current construction at the airport includes a new international terminal and high-speed train scheduled to open in summer 2005. Future development is planned to keep up with national expectations of air travel increases by 2010.

Prior to construction of DFW Airport, Dallas' principal airfield was the city-owned Love Field. Today it is both a general aviation and commercial air facility with Southwest Airlines serving other Texas cities and adjacent states. Love Field is conveniently close to Dallas' central business district. Redbird Airport and many smaller municipal airports serve the Metroplex.

The Dallas area is served by four major highways: Interstate 20 (east-west); I-35 E (north-south); I-30 (northeast-west); and I-45 (south). All Dallas highways are connected by a twelve-lane loop—LBJ Freeway (I-635)—that encircles the city. Loop 12 is situated primarily within the city limits of Dallas. A third loop circles the Dallas central business district. Amtrak operates an intercity passenger line.

## Traveling in the City

Dallas Area Rapid Transit (DART) moves more than 200,000 passengers per day across a 700-square-mile service area of 13 cities with rail, bus, paratransit, light rail system, HOV lane and rideshare services. DART serves DFW International Airport and Fort Worth via the Trinity Railway Express' (TRE) commuter rail system links downtown Fort Worth, downtown Dallas, and DFW Airport.

# Communications

## Newspapers and Magazines

Dallas is served by one daily newspaper, the *Dallas Morning News,* and by the weeklies *Dallas Observer* and *Dallas*

*Business Journal.* Residents are able to subscribe to a variety of suburban and neighborhood papers, and numerous magazines, such as *D Magazine.*

## Television and Radio

Dallas-area residents are entertained and informed by 9 commercial and public television stations. Other stations are available through cable subscription. Dallas PBS station, KERA, is the most watched public television station in the nation. The 19 radio stations serving Dallas broadcast a variety of program formats, including all-news and country, rock, and classical music.

The Dallas Communications Complex, a multimillion-dollar film production center developed by Dallas real estate magnate Trammell Crow, includes a 15,000-square-foot soundstage and has been the site for the filming of several major motion pictures and television specials. The Dallas-Fort Worth Teleport is a full-service satellite communications facility specializing in broadcast quality video transmission.

*Media Information: The Dallas Morning News,* PO Box 655237, Dallas, TX 75265; telephone (800)925-1500

## Dallas Online

City of Dallas Home Page. Available www.dallascityhall.com

Dallas Convention & Visitors Bureau. Available www.dallascvb.com

Dallas Independent School District. Available www.dallasisd.org

*Dallas Morning News.* Available www.dallasnews.com

*Dallas Observer.* Available www.dallasobserver.com

Dallas Public Library. Available dallaslibrary.org

The Greater Dallas Chamber. Available www.gdc.org

## Selected Bibliography

Beckett, Haznel W., *Growing Up in Dallas* (Washington, D.C.: Beacham, 1985)

Warren, Leslie, *Dallas Public and Private: Aspects of an American City* (Dallas, Tx.: Southern Methodist University Press, 1998)

# El Paso

## *The City in Brief*

**Founded: 1598** (incorporated 1873)

**Head Official:** Mayor Joe Wardy (since 2003)

**City Population**
    **1980:** 425,259
    **1990:** 515,342
    **2000:** 563,662
    **2003 estimate:** 584,113
    **Percent change, 1990–2000:** 9.4%
    **U.S. rank in 2000:** 22 (State rank: 5th)

**Metropolitan Area Population**
    **1980:** 479,899
    **1990:** 591,610
    **2000:** 679,622

**Percent change, 1990–2000:** 14.9%
**U.S. rank in 2000:** 64th

**Area:** 249 square miles (2000)
**Elevation:** Average 3,762 feet above sea level
**Average Annual Temperature:** 63.3° F
**Average Annual Precipitation:** 8.81 inches

**Major Economic Sectors:** agriculture, clothing, oil, retail, military
**Unemployment rate:** 7.7% (December 2004)
**Per Capita Income:** $14,388 (1999)

**2002 FBI Crime Index Total:** 26,998

**Major Colleges and Universities:** University of Texas at El Paso, El Paso Community College, New Mexico State University, and Texas Tech University Health Sciences Center.

**Daily Newspaper:** *El Paso Times*

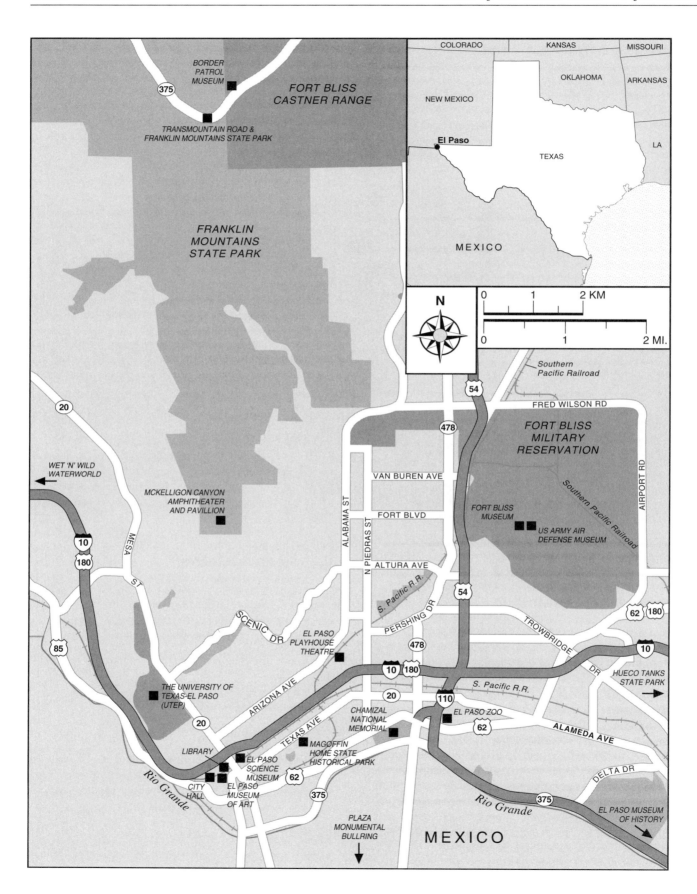

# Introduction

The county seat of El Paso County, El Paso is located on the far western edge of Texas on the north bank of the Rio Grande. At Mexico's border, El Paso and its Mexican sister city, Ciudad Juárez (in Chihuahua, Mexico), have downtowns that are within walking distance from one another. The fertile valley and surrounding mountains of El Paso del Norte (the Pass of the North), christened by Don Juan de Oñate in 1598, was the first all-weather pass through the Rockies. El Paso is a major transportation hub and is known for its cutting-edge medical facilities, top educational institutions, year-round recreation, vibrant cultural and entertainment life, and favorable cost of living. El Paso boasts a diverse population, with a majority of its residents speaking both English and Spanish. El Paso attracts new residents with its favorable weather, tax rates, comparably low cost of living, and multiple educational opportunities. United States Army Air Defense Center, Fort Bliss, has made El Paso its home for nearly 150 years. The fourth (in 2005) largest city in Texas, El Paso is the 22nd largest city in the U.S. and the country's third fastest-growing metropolitan area.

# Geography and Climate

Located in the westernmost corner of Texas, El Paso resides in the Chihuahuan Desert at the confluence of Texas, New Mexico, and Mexico, nestled between the Franklin Mountains and the Rio Grande. With only about 8 inches of precipitation per year, a summer high of 95 degrees and mild winter temperatures, El Paso residents enjoy sun about 300 days of the year.

**Area:** 249 square miles (2000)

**Elevation:** Average 3,762 feet above sea level

**Average Temperatures:** January, 42.8° F; July, 82.3° F; annual average, 63.3° F

**Average Annual Precipitation:** 8.81 inches

# History

### Spanish Lay Claim Over a Vast Land

Inhabited for centuries by various Indian groups, El Paso saw its first Europeans when Spaniards passed through in the mid-1500s. During 1540 to 1542, an expedition under Francisco Vázquez de Coronado explored the area now known as the American Southwest. These earliest Spanish explorers saw on their approach from the Rio Grande two mountain ranges rising from the desert, with a deep chasm between. They named the site ''El Paso del Norte, '' or ''the Pass of the North.'' The Rodríguez-Sánchez expedition in 1581 was the first party of Spaniards to explore the Pass of the North, bringing about the beginning of El Paso's modern history. Further expeditions followed, culminating in an April 30, 1598 ceremony near the site of present-day San Elizario in which expedition leader Juan de Oñate took formal possession of the territory drained by the Rio del Norte (now the Rio Grande). Called ''La Toma,'' (the claiming) this act brought Spanish civilization to the Pass of the North, laying the foundation for more than two centuries of Spanish rule.

Population of the area grew when the Pueblo Indian Revolt of 1680 sent Spanish colonists and Tigua Indians of New Mexico southward in search of safety. By 1682, five settlements were thriving on the south bank of the Rio Grande. By the middle of the eighteenth century, approximately 5,000 people populated the El Paso area; among them were Spaniards, *mestizos,* and Indians. The region became known for its vineyards, with residents producing wine and brandy. In 1789, the presidio of San Elizario was founded to defend the El Paso settlements against encroaching Apaches.

### Spanish Rule Ends, Tensions Begin

With Mexico's independence from Spain in 1821, the entire El Paso area became part of Mexico. Agriculture and commerce flourished, but the unpredictable levels of the Rio Grande made for difficulties with crops, fields, and structures frequently damaged by the rising water levels. In the 1830s, the river flooded much of the lower Rio Grande valley, creating a new channel and displacing several towns.

May 1846 saw more difficulties as hostilities erupted between the United States and Mexico. During the Mexican War, Col. Alexander Doniphan and a force of American volunteers defeated Mexican fighters at the battle of Brazito, entering El Paso del Norte. The Treaty of Guadalupe Hidalgo on February 2, 1848, ended the dispute and again changed the boundary between the two nations, bringing El Paso territory under the blanket of the United States.

El Paso's settlements grew in 1849 as easterners rushed west in search of gold. Lines between Mexico and the United States were revised yet again; this time the three Mexican towns of Ysleta, Socorro, and San Elizario ended up on the United States side of the line. The military post of Fort Bliss was established in 1858; one year later pioneer Anson Mills completed his plat of the town of El Paso. The name ''El Paso'' brought about confusion with the Mexican town across the Rio Grande, El Paso del Norte, so the Mexican town's name was changed to Ciudad Juárez in 1888.

During the Civil War, El Paso's alliance was to the South, though the Union presided and local Southern sympathizers eventually received pardons. In 1877, Texans and Mexicans became embroiled in a bitter civil war, the Salt War of San Elizario, which lasted six months.

## A Modern City Emerges

A rail system was established through the area in 1881–82, which transformed the village into a lively frontier community with a growing population. El Paso's early years are tinted by a colorful reputation from its many saloons, brothels, and high crime. By 1890 citizens were demanding reform, and by 1905 El Paso ordinances banned gambling and prostitution. At the turn of the century El Paso's frontier image was fading and its fresh start as a modern city began. The population grew from 15,906 in 1900 to 77,560 in just 25 years. Refugees of the Mexican Revolution contributed to the city's growth, as did burgeoning commercial, industrial, agricultural, and transportation business, along with El Paso's strategic location as a gateway to Mexico. Prohibition boosted the city's tourism as neighboring residents flocked to El Paso to cross the border for drinking and gambling in Juárez.

In 1930 census reports showed 102,421 residents in El Paso, though the city's growth began to slow soon after with the census reporting only 96,810 residents in 1940. After the war, development brought new residents and the 1950 census once again showed growth, with 130,003 people living in El Paso. Fort Bliss grew as well in the 1940s and 1950s. The 1960 census saw a doubling of residents; steady growth continued and by 1970 the population was 339,615. El Paso's population grew again when the city absorbed the Mexican town of Isleta, stretching the reaches of the metropolitan area even further. By the mid-1980s, Fort Bliss' military personnel and family members made up nearly a quarter of the city's population. Petroleum, textiles, tourism, metals, cement, and food processing became major industries by the 1980s.

Since 1990 El Paso's economy has suffered from competition with low labor rates from abroad and the closure of its main copper smelter. As well, El Paso has the unpleasant distinction of being one of the main entry points for drug smuggling into the United States, an attribute that has plagued the area for decades. The North American Free Trade Agreement (NAFTA) passage helped local service and transportation firms to expand their businesses, but hurt the city's industrial industry. Since El Paso is sensitive to changes in Mexico's economy, the devaluation of the Mexican peso in the 1990s and the border traffic controls instituted after the September 11, 2001 terrorist attacks both

affected El Paso's economy. Still, the area is recovering from these incidences, and the El Paso of today consists of a rich mix of culture with a strong military presence and the excitement of a border town. The El Paso-Juárez international metropolitan area is the largest bi-national community on an international border in the world.

**Historical Information:** Texas State Historical Association, 1 University Station D0901, Austin, TX 78712-0332; telephone (512)471-1525; fax (512)471-1551

# Population Profile

## Metropolitan Area Population
*1980:* 479,899
*1990:* 591,610
*2000:* 679,622
*Percent change, 1990–2000:* 14.9%
*U.S. rank in 2000:* 64th

## City Residents
*1980:* 425,259
*1990:* 515,342
*2000:* 563,662
*2003 estimate:* 584,113
*Percent change, 1990–2000:* 9.4%
*U.S. rank in 2000:* 22 (State rank: 5th)

*Density:* 2,263 people per square mile (2000)

*Racial and ethnic characteristics* (2000)
  White: 413,061
  Black or African American: 17,586
  American Indian and Alaska Native: 4,601
  Asian: 6,321
  Native Hawaiian and Pacific Islander: 583
  Hispanic or Latino (may be of any race): 431,875
  Other: 102,320

*Percent of residents born in state:* 54.3% (2000)

*Age characteristics* (2000)
  Population under 5 years old: 47,646
  Population 5 to 9 years old: 50,170
  Population 10 to 14 years old: 47,996
  Population 15 to 19 years old: 46,858
  Population 20 to 24 years old: 38,564
  Population 25 to 34 years old: 80,568
  Population 35 to 44 years old: 83,703
  Population 45 to 54 years old: 65,808
  Population 55 to 59 years old: 22,636
  Population 60 to 64 years old: 19,592
  Population 65 to 74 years old: 35,041

Population 75 to 84 years old: 19,279
Population 85 years and older: 5,801
Median age: 31.1 years

*Births* (2001, El Paso County)
Total number: 14,189

*Deaths* (2001, El Paso County)
Total number: 4,035 (of which, 66 were infants under the age of 1 year)

*Money income* (1999)
Per capita income: $14,388
Median household income: $32,124
Total households: 182,237

*Number of households with income of . . .*
less than $10,000: 25,341
$10,000 to $14,999: 15,622
$15,000 to $24,999: 30,009
$25,000 to $34,999: 26,661
$35,000 to $49,999: 30,185
$50,000 to $74,999: 29,283
$75,000 to $99,999: 12,585
$100,000 to $149,999: 8,127
$150,000 to $199,999: 1,946
$200,000 or more: 2,478

*Percent of families below poverty level:* 19.0% (51.2% of which were female householder families with related children under 5 years)

*2002 FBI Crime Index Total:* 26,998

# Municipal Government

El Paso operates under a mayor-council form of government. The mayor is elected every four years; the eight council members are also elected and serve staggered two- or four-year terms. The city manager oversees operations. Residents, who are appointed by the council or the mayor, serve as volunteers on a variety of boards and commissions that help to steer the direction of municipal issues.

**Head Official:** Mayor Joe Wardy (since 2003; current term expires May 2007)

**Total Number of City Employees:** 6,500 (2005)

*City Information:* City of El Paso, 2 Civic Center Plaza, El Paso, TX, 79901; telephone (915)541-4000

# Economy

## Major Industries and Commercial Activity

More than 70 *Fortune* 500 companies call El Paso their home, including Hoover, Eureka, Boeing, and Delphi.

El Paso is an important entry point to the U.S. from Mexico. Once a major copper refining area, chief manufacturing industries in El Paso now include food production, clothing, construction materials, electronic and medical equipment, and plastics. Cotton, fruit, vegetables, livestock, and pecans are produced in the area. With El Paso's attractive climate and natural beauty, tourism has become a booming industry as well as trade with neighboring Ciudad Juárez.

Education is also a driving force in El Paso's economy. El Paso's three large school districts are among the largest employers in the area, employing more than 19,000 people between them. The University of Texas at El Paso (UTEP) has an annual budget of nearly $250 million and employs nearly 3,600 people. A 2002 study by the university's Institute for Policy and Economic Development stated that the University's impact on local businesses has resulted in $349 million.

The military installation of Fort Bliss is a major contributor to El Paso's economy. Fort Bliss began as a Calvary post in 1848. Today, Fort Bliss is the site of the United States Army's Air Defense Center and produces approximately $80 million in products and services annually, with about $60 million of those products and services purchased locally. Fort Bliss' total economic impact on the area has been estimated at more than $1 billion, with 12,000 soldiers currently stationed at the Fort. A February 2005 article in the *El Paso Times* stated that as many as 20,000 troops could be arriving at Fort Bliss pending the Defense Department's removal of thousands of troops from overseas assignments. This would be in addition to 3,800 soldiers who would arrive as part of a new brigade combat team stationed at the Fort. The growth is expected to create a strong economic ripple throughout the El Paso area.

In addition to the military, the federal government has a strong presence in El Paso to manage its status and unique issues as a border region. The Immigration and Naturalization Service (INS), the Drug Enforcement Agency (DEA), and the U.S. Customs Service all have agency operations in El Paso to regulate traffic and goods through ports of entry from Mexico. Including these agencies, government job growth in the area is expected to rise to 64,390 jobs by 2007.

Call center operations make up 7 of the top 10 business employers in El Paso. With no signs of growth slowing in this industry, in 2005 the 14 largest call centers in El Paso employed more than 10,000 people. The largest of these in terms of employees are EchoStar, MCI/GC Services, and West Telemarketing.

Analysts in the area say that job growth in 2005 will be in the form of health care, business and trade services, international trade, and telecommunications.

*Items and goods produced:* petroleum, metals, medical devices, plastics, machinery, automotive parts, food, defense-related goods, tourism, boots

## Incentive Programs—New and Existing Companies

El Paso's economy is impacted significantly by the Mexican government's Maquiladora Program. Established in 1965, the program was created to help alleviate unemployment on the U.S.–Mexico border by allowing non-Mexican companies to establish manufacturing operations in Mexico to produce goods for exportation. El Paso's sister city Ciudad Juárez has more than 300 such plants employing approximately 195,000 workers, many of them El Paso residents. More than 70 of the maquiladora plants established in Ciudad Juárez are owned by *Fortune* 500 companies operating in telecommunications, manufacturing of medical supplies, consumer appliances, electronics, and automotive parts.

The Texas Workforce Commission (TWC) provides assistance to new companies in screening and pre-qualifying applicants for employment to the client's specifications. TWC is also the agency for the Federal Targeted Job Tax Credits Program. The state of Texas targets many of its incentive programs toward smaller and rural communities.

*Local programs*—The City of El Paso gives consideration for tax abatements for projects within specified Strategic Redevelopment Zones. The Tax Abatement Policy is organized to stimulate capital investment needed for residential, retail, commercial, and industrial redevelopment within the zones.

*State programs*—Texas is a right-to-work state. The Texas Enterprise Zone Programs offer tax abatement at the local level, and refunds of state sales and use taxes under certain circumstances to businesses operating in enterprise zone areas. Parts of El Paso benefit from the state's designation as Foreign Trade Zone #68. The state of Texas targets many of its incentive programs toward smaller and rural communities.

El Paso is a designated United States Department of Housing and Urban Development Empowerment Zone, which provides special tax incentives and bond provisions to encourage private investment in housing development. El Paso was the only city in Texas to receive this type of designation. The Enterprise Business program and the Micro-Loan program both assist new businesses with start-up funding.

*Job training programs*—The Greater El Paso Chamber Foundation and a coalition of El Paso workforce development agencies partnered to develop The Center for Workforce Preparedness. The Center houses several agencies and projects, and helps custom-train workers for local businesses. The Upper Rio Grande @ Work organization provides help with recruitment, job fairs, locating tax incentive programs, researching labor and employment laws, labor market details, and other services.

On-the-Job Training allows participants to work for an employer, receive payment, and develop the skills necessary to continue working. The program provides reimbursement to the employer for up to half of the wages paid for a maximum of three months.

The Texas Workforce Commission administers the Skills Development Fund, which helps Texas community and technical colleges finance customized job-training programs for local businesses. Qualifying companies are allowed up to $1,000 per trainee.

The Advanced Technology Center at El Paso Community College provides workforce training for local industry. The College also administers programs through the Workforce Development Center, the Career Training Center, and other centers throughout its four campuses.

## Development Projects

The city of El Paso has been involved in extensive improvement projects since 2000, when a plan for specific ''Quality of Life Capital Improvements'' was approved to span a 10-year period. New zoo facilities were completed, and still underway are plans for a new $6.65 million History Museum building (construction began in 2004), and improvements to city parks and libraries. As part of that initiative, the city's 5-year plan for capital improvements begins in 2005 and includes specific projects such as new fire stations, additional library branches, new animal care facilities, new parks and recreation facilities, further renovations and improvements to the zoo, street improvements, airport improvements, and public transportation improvements. At the end of 2009, projected spending for the 5-year improvement plan is a massive $440,924,631.

Developments completed in 2004 included a new $27.4 million, 110,000 square foot wing at Thomason Hospital. The wing generated an additional 100 high-paying jobs and expanded the number of critical care beds at the hospital from 18 to 30. The new unit includes an ambulatory surgery unit, an emergency department observation unit, a critical care unit, and a new labor and delivery unit. After $9 million in renovations, the 60-year-old El Paso County Coliseum is bringing in record revenues; additional seats and new air conditioning were part of the renovations.

Underway in 2005 were plans for a new golf course, federal courthouse, and restoration of a historic theatre. Slated for finish in 2006, the tentatively-named The Dunes at Butterfield Trail golf course will be a high-end course, designed by renowned golf course designer Tom Fazio. To be built near the airport, the course and its 8,800 square foot clubhouse will cost $11 million. Construction is expected to start in 2005 on the new downtown courthouse, with a budget of $63.4 million. The 8-story, 235,000 square foot courthouse will be built on two city blocks. Plans to restore the city's historic Plaza Theatre, at a cost of $25 million, began in 2005. An adjacent building will become the theatre's annex and will be converted into a restaurant on the first floor and a performing arts center, seating about 195 people, on the second floor.

Construction projects to the tune of $50 million were underway in 2005 at University of Texas at El Paso, including a new academic services building, biosciences building, a softball complex, an expansion of the engineering building, and a new research and business development complex. Projects in the planning stages in early 2005 include a new 5-level garage.

***Economic Development Information:*** City of El Paso Department of Economic Development, 2 Civic Center Plaza, El Paso, TX 79901; telephone (915)533-4284; fax (915)541-1316

## Commercial Shipping

According to the U.S. Department of Transportation, El Paso is the nation's "fifth busiest land border gateway by value for imports and exports transported across the border by highways, railroads, and pipelines." In 2003, $39 billion in merchandise trade passed through El Paso. Trucks carry most of the freight passing through the city, followed by rail. The Union Pacific Railway provides intermodal and other services to Los Angeles, Chicago, and Dallas. The Burlington Northern Santa Fe Railroad also travels to Los Angeles and Chicago. El Paso's position as an international gateway means it is a major thoroughfare for imports and exports.

## Labor Force and Employment Outlook

In 1994, half of El Paso's 50,000 manufacturing jobs were in the apparel and textile industry. Due to the devaluation of the Mexican peso in 1994, several large apparel manufacturers relocated over the border to Mexico, taking jobs with them. Growth in other areas have made up for this decline, however, as El Paso's job growth continues to rise after a rocky beginning to the 21st century. Still, El Paso's unemployment rate remains higher than the national average.

El Paso's labor force has shown a steady growth over the past decade. International trade in the region, stimulated by the North American Free Trade Act (NAFTA) and the Mexican Maquiladora Program, has helped to ensure El

Paso's success in the global economy. Jobs in globalization and information technology are helping to revitalize the area economy after its past dependency on ever-reducing manufacturing jobs. A 2002 study estimated that local employment for the El Paso MSA was expected to grow to 278,056 by 2006, or a compound annual growth rate of 1.52 percent over that 5-year period.

The following is a summary of data regarding the El Paso metropolitan area labor force, 2003 annual averages.

*Size of nonagricultural labor force:* 254,900

*Number of workers employed in . . .*
   *construction and mining:* 11,900
   *manufacturing:* 26,500
   *trade, transportation and utilities:* 55,000
   *information:* 5,400
   *financial activities:* 12,000
   *professional and business services:* 25,000
   *educational and health services:* 28,600
   *leisure and hospitality:* 23,500
   *other services:* 7,500
   *government:* 59,500

*Average hourly earnings of production workers employed in manufacturing:* $13.98 (statewide)

*Unemployment rate:* 7.7% (December 2004)

| Largest county employers | Number of employees |
|---|---|
| El Paso Independent School District | 8,663 |
| Fort Bliss (civilian employees) | 6,803 |
| Ysleta Independent School District | 6,500 |
| City of El Paso | 6,264 |
| University of Texas at El Paso | 4,871 |
| Socorro Independent School District | 3,995 |
| Sierra Providence Health Network | 3,761 |
| El Paso Community College | 3,728 |
| Wal-Mart | 3,706 |
| County of El Paso | 2,700 |
| Las Palmas and Del Sol Regional Health Care System | 2,244 |
| Echostar Satellite Corp. | 2,012 |

## Cost of Living

El Paso's cost of living, as well as its housing prices, are slightly below the national average.

The following is a summary of data regarding several key cost of living factors for the El Paso area.

*2004 (3rd Quarter) ACCRA Average House Price:* $205,450

*2004 (3rd Quarter) ACCRA Cost of Living Index:* 90.6%

*State income tax rate:* none

*State sales tax rate:* 6.25%

*Local income tax rate:* none

*Local sales tax rate:* 1.0% (city) and .5% (county)

*Property tax rate:* $.719833 per $100 assessed value (2002) (City of El Paso only)

**Economic Information:** Office of Economic Development, City of El Paso, 2 Civic Center Plaza, 1st Floor, El Paso, TX 79901; telephone (915)533-4284; fax (915)541-1316

# Education and Research

## Elementary and Secondary Schools

El Paso County is served by nine school districts. Of those nine, El Paso city public schools are divided into three districts: the El Paso Independent School District, Ysleta Independent School District, and Socorro Independent School District. The El Paso Independent School District (EPISD) is the largest, educating 62,000 students in 88 buildings. The EPISD offers three magnet programs: the new Capt. John L. Chapin High School, an engineering and science magnet school, is the only public high school built on military land in the U.S.; Silva Health Magnet's curriculum focuses on health and sciences; the new (2003) Academy for International Business and Public Affairs at Bowie High School in South El Paso focuses on international business and public affairs education.

The Ysleta Independent School District (YISD) is the second largest in the area, educating 50,000 students in 58 buildings. In the mid-1980's, YISD operated at state minimum levels. With effort and determination by administration, teachers, and families, the district accomplished a major turnaround which culminated in 1998 when the district was named a ''Recognized District'' for state testing performance. Since then, nine of the district's schools have been named National Blue Ribbon Schools; eight others are National Title One Distinguished Campuses.

Though large in its own right, the Socorro Independent School District is the smallest district of the three and educates more than 30,000 students in southeastern El Paso County. In 2004 more than 82 percent of the district's high school graduates were bound for college.

The following is a summary of data regarding the El Paso Independent School District public schools as of the 2004–2005 school year.

*Total enrollment:* 62,000

*Number of facilities*
*elementary schools:* 57
*junior high/middle schools:* 15
*senior high schools:* 11

*other:* 7 (3 magnet schools, 1 alternative school, 1 at-risk recovery program, 1 adult education school, 1 occupational center

*Student/teacher ratio:* 16.1:1 (2005)

*Teacher salaries (2004-05)*
*minimum:* $34,000
*maximum:* $55,705

*Funding per pupil:* $6,627

More than 25 parochial and 50 private schools educate El Paso students. Many of El Paso's private schools have received national awards: Loretto Academy for girls and St. Clement's Episcopal Parish School are both recipients of the Blue Ribbon award, a prestigious standing for high-performing schools. Other private schools offer technical programs, specialized programs, or mechanical education.

## Colleges and Universities

Four major institutions of higher learning are located in the El Paso region. They offer undergraduate and graduate degrees in engineering, business, science, education, health sciences, and liberal arts; and associate degrees and certificate programs in technology.

The University of Texas at El Paso (UTEP) prides itself on its status as the only major research university in the country with the majority of its students being predominately Mexican American. UTEP celebrated its 90th birthday in 2004. From its humble beginnings in 1914 as a small mining school, UTEP is now a recognized institution with an enrollment of more than 18,900 students and a $50 million building and expansion budget. UTEP ranks second in the nation of schools awarding undergraduate degrees to Hispanics.

Established in 1969, El Paso Community College (EPCC) has 5 campuses throughout El Paso and educates approximately 28,000 credit and continuing education students each semester. With 130 academic programs, 350 enrichment and continuing education courses, and a commitment to innovation in educational programs, EPCC is the fastest growing community college in the state.

In nearby Las Cruces, New Mexico, New Mexico State University educates 16,000 students, many of which are El Paso residents. Both the University of Phoenix and Webster University operate campuses in El Paso. Another regional educational institution is Howard Payne University extension campus. Texas Tech University's Health Sciences Center at El Paso confers degrees in medicine, nursing, pharmacy, and in biomedical and allied health sciences.

## Libraries and Research Centers

The El Paso Public Library operates a main library, 11 branches, a bookmobile, and a literacy center. In December

2004 the main library closed for expansion and renovation with an expected completion date of late 2005. The expansion will add 45,000 square feet, bringing the library's total square footage to 110,000. The newly-renovated facility will also have a new 250-seat auditorium, a 50-station computer lab and classroom, an expanded children's area, and a new area for teenagers called "Teen Town." As part of the city's Quality of Life Improvement Program, many of the system's branch libraries are undergoing renovations and expansions between 2000 and 2009.

The University of Texas at El Paso (UTEP) Library houses over 1.2 million volumes, including 200,000 government documents, in its 6-floor, 275,000 square foot facility. The library sits atop a hill and is built in the Bhutanese style of architecture, like of many of the university's structures.

Other libraries include the Texas Tech University Health Sciences Library at El Paso, the El Paso Community College library system, and the El Paso Scottish Rite Historical Library and Museum.

The University of Texas at El Paso's research facilities sponsored projects with expenditures of $52 million in 2003. The National Institutes of Health recently awarded UTEP and the University of Texas Houston Health Science Center more than $4 million to establish the Hispanic Health Disparities Research Center at the UTEP campus. Other research centers at UTEP include the Border Biomedical Research Center, the Center for Environmental Resource Management, the Center for Transportation Infrastructure Sytems, the Institute for Manufacturing and Materials Management, the Materials Research and Technology Institute, and the W.M. Keck Border Biomedical Manufacturing and Engineering Laboratory. New research centers on tap for development in 2005 include the Paso del Norte Research and Business Development Complex, which will house four new research facilities focusing on policy and economic development, economic forecasting, science, and entrepreneur development.

*Public Library Information:* El Paso Public Library, 501 N. Oregon, El Paso, TX; telephone (915)543-5401

# Health Care

El Paso's 9 hospitals, with approximately 2,200 beds total, serve the general public and the military in El Paso and bordering areas of Mexico. The Las Palmas Regional Healthcare System's facilities include the Las Palmas Medical Center and Heart Institute hospital, the Rehabilitation Hospital, the Life Care Center, the Regional Oncology and Wound Management Center, the Diabetes Treatment Center, and the Del Sol Medical Center. Specialties include

women's and children's services, oncology, heart health, and surgical services. In late 2004 Las Palmas broke ground on a new building that will house an expanded emergency room and intensive care unit. Opened in 2004, the system's new Rehabilitation Hospital is a 40-bed center specializing in treatment of strokes, spinal cord injuries, and other orthopedic or neurological diagnosis.

The Sierra Providence Health Network operates three hospitals consisting of two acute care hospitals (Sierra Medical Center and Providence Memorial Hospital) and a physical rehabilitation hospital (Rio Vista Physical Rehabilitation Hospital), with a total of 927 beds. Other centers include the Border Children's Health Center and the Sierra Teen Health Resource Center.

Thomason Hospital serves El Paso and neighboring Ciudad residents with its location directly on the U.S.-Mexico border. Part of the Texas Tech University's School of Medicine, the hospital is a teaching facility with 335 beds. The William Beaumont Army Medical Center specializes in trauma care and is one of the largest U.S. Army general hospitals in the country.

# Recreation

### Sightseeing

The El Paso area's attractions celebrate the region's rich history and culture, as well as its natural resources of the Franklin Mountains and the Rio Grande.

More than 313,000 people visited the El Paso Zoo in 2004, the same year the zoo opened a new sea lion exhibit. On 18 acres, the El Paso Zoo houses more than 600 animals from over 250 species. The zoo's Asia exhibit highlights endangered Indochinese tigers, Sumatran orangutans, Malaysian tapirs, and the critically endangered Amur leopard. Animals in the Americas exhibit include Mexican wolves, the California sea lion, and the Galapagos tortoise. A new exhibit featuring the animals of Africa is expected to open in 2006.

Magoffin Home State Historic Site is a 1.5 acre park and homage to pioneer Joseph Magoffin. The centerpiece of the park is the Magoffin Home, built in 1875 by Magoffin. The 19-room adobe home, built in the Territorial style of architecture, showcases period style with mid-Victorian wood trim and original appointments. Guided tours offer a glimpse into the life of the Magoffin family, who occupied the home until its sale to the city of El Paso in 1976.

The Chamizal National Memorial is part of the National Parks system. Established to commemorate diplomatic rela-

**Hueco Tanks State Park.**

tions between Mexico and the United States in 1963, Chamizal honors the peaceful settlement of a century-long boundary dispute between neighboring counties. Visitors can learn about this historic event at the Chamizal Museum or through interpretive performances at the indoor theatre. The Los Paisanos Gallery features the work of local and international artists in a variety of media; the gallery also hosts traveling museum exhibits.

Downtown El Paso's "Museum Row" includes the Museum of Art, El Paso Museum of History, and Insights Science Museum. The El Paso Museum of Art is a celebrated fine arts museum housing a permanent collection of more than 5,000 works of art, including the Samuel H. Kress Collection of European art from the 13th through 18th centuries, American art from the 19th and 20th centuries, Mexican colonial art, and contemporary art from the southwestern United States and Mexico. Temporary exhibitions, educational programs, lectures, and concerts are part of the museum's yearly event schedule. The Museum of History showcases the colorful people who shaped El Paso's history. Insights Science Museum features 60 hands-on exhibits that teach visitors about all aspects of science. Temporary exhibits, classes, and a "Museum on Wheels" round out Insight's offerings to the community.

The Museum of Archaeology at Wilderness Park showcases prehistoric artifacts from the Southwest, including pottery, stone objects, basketry, weavings, and figurines. Exhibits tell the story of El Paso and the region's first inhabitants. The museum's 15 acres feature walking trails and gardens that highlight more than 250 native plants.

The Fort Bliss Museum resides at a reconstructed site of the original Fort. Adobe walls shelter from the heat of the summer as well as create warmth in the winter. Displays include photographs, maps, and personal items. One block south of the museum is the new Air Defense/Artillery Museum, showcasing the history of air defense equipment.

The Natural History Museum features more than 300 exhibits in 30,000 square feet. The Border Patrol Museum highlights the work of those who tirelessly patrol the U.S./Mexico border in El Paso. The El Paso Holocaust Museum and Study Center chronicles events of the holocaust and memorializes those who suffered.

The Mission Trail offers visitors a glimpse into the El Paso of the past. One of the oldest roads in the country, the Mission Trail dates back more than 400 years. Along the route are three missions, one of which is the oldest building in Texas.

## Arts and Culture

The city's Arts & Culture Department (ACD) has been working to bring art and cultural events to residents since

1978. The ACD supports local art organizations through funding, grants programs, and educational programs. In 2003, the ACD was responsible for 1,058 art and cultural events throughout the city, with an overall attendance of 391,165. Some of the ACDs programs include the Young at Art Series, which presents children's theatrical performances; the Discovery Series, which offers dance performances by such renowned troops as Alvin Ailey; Alfresco Fridays, presenting free summer outdoor concerts at various city locations; Music Under the Stars World Festival offers free outdoor music from around the world on summer evenings at Chamizal National Memorial; and the Galleries program, which sponsors art exhibits at City Hall and the El Paso Regional Airport.

The Abraham Chavez Theatre in the El Paso Convention & Performing Arts Center hosts both the El Paso Opera and the El Paso Symphony performances. The El Paso Opera brings full-scale, professional opera to the area in addition to several educational outreach programs. Established in the 1930s, the El Paso Symphony is the longest continuously-running symphony orchestra in Texas, offering a full classical and special events season.

The Aardvark Theatre on N. Mesa presents a full season from September through June; the El Paso Playhouse presents a year-round season of plays and a monthly Dinner Theatre performance. The Adair Margo Gallery on E. Yandell exhibits the work of regional, U.S. and foreign fine artists.

## Festivals and Holidays

The events calendar begins with January's El Paso Chamber Music Festival, featuring performances over two weekends at University of Texas at El Paso's Fox Fine Arts Recital Hall. The Southwest International Livestock Show and Rodeo (in its 76th year in 2005) happens at the El Paso County Coliseum and fairgrounds in January or February. Over two weekends in late February and early March, the Siglo de Oro Drama Festival is held in the Chamizal National Memorial Theatre. This annual celebration honors Spain's Golden Age with professional and collegiate performing groups from Spain, Mexico, the United States, and South America. Presentations are often performed in Spanish.

Spring events include the city's semi-annual arts and crafts fair called Art in the Park, held over a weekend in late May at Memorial Park; the KLAQ Balloon Festival in May features hot air balloon rides and concerts at Wet & Wild Waterworld in nearby Anthony, Texas.

Summer events include the annual Independence Day Parades, one each on the city's west and east sides. The Downtown Street Festival follows in downtown El Paso, with four stages featuring live performances and more than 100 booths featuring arts, crafts, food, and drink. The July

2005 Ruisidoso Art Festival is the festival's 33rd; this weekend in late July offers goods from more than 100 juried artists at the Ruidoso Convention Center on Hwy. 48. The KLAQ "Taste of El Paso" happens mid-August at Western Playland. In addition to sampling the wares of local restaurants, visitors can enjoy rides and live entertainment. The St. Nicholas Greek Festival celebrates Greek food, music, and culture in late August at the Greek Orthodox Church.

On Labor Day weekend the Fiesta de las Flores (in its 52nd year in 2005) is held at the El Paso County Coliseum and includes games, food, arts and crafts, a car show, a children's area, and a variety of entertainment options. Mexican Independence Day is celebrated mid-September at Chamizal National Memorial, and honors Mexico's independence through song and dance.

In October, the annual Chamizal Festival celebrates the many cultural influences in the El Paso region through traditional arts and music with workshops, performances, demonstrations, and displays. Throughout October, the month-long "Celebration of Our Mountains" features events such as hikes, field trips, driving tours, nature walks, bike rides, and other activities that celebrate the Franklin Mountains. Thanksgiving Day events in El Paso include the Las Palmas Del Sol Sun Bowl Parade in downtown El Paso, and the Thanksgiving Day 5K run and 3K walk benefiting youth and teen programs at the YMCA. Ballet Folklórico Paso del Norte depicts the art and history of Mexico through dance and music at Chamizal National Memorial Theatre in late November.

For a month during late November through December, sports fans enjoy a variety of festivities related to the Vitalis Sun Bowl football game on December 31. Events include a parade, a new year's eve party, a 5K run, sports skills camps, and more. Visitors and residents enjoy the El Paso/Juárez Trolley Company's Christmas Light Tour, which circuits through the area's best-known seasonal sights at San Jacinto Plaza, the University of Texas at El Paso campus, Rim Road, Scenic Drive, and Eastwood. Holiday Lights at the Zoo features more than 200,000 lights creating a "winter wonderland" scene in the zoo throughout 10 days in December.

## Sports for the Spectator

The El Paso region abounds with opportunities for sports fans to watch their favorite activities. The El Paso Diablos, a double A team affiliated with the Arizona Diamondbacks, have been playing since 1974; 15 of those years have been at Cohen Stadium in northeast El Paso. In a 2004 announcement, however, the Diablos will be sold and will move to Springfield, Missouri at the end of the 2004-05 season. The El Paso Patriots play indoor soccer as a Premier Development League (PDL) team. The El Paso Scorpions professional rugby team has been playing since 1979. Their home

is the 5,000 seat Dudley field, the original home of the El Paso Diablos. The University of Texas at El Paso's athletics include the Miners football, soccer, track, tennis, and men's and women's basketball. The Southwestern International Livestock Show & Rodeo comes to the El Paso County Coliseum in January or February; polo is a popular spectator sport in nearby La Union, New Mexico.

## Sports for the Participant

El Paso's Parks & Recreation Department maintains 175 park sites with 2,372 acres throughout the city. These parks provide 12 recreation centers, 14 city pools (8 indoor and 6 outdoor), sports and fitness programming, and senior centers. In El Paso County, Ascarate Park is the largest public-use recreational park at 448 total acres. Ascarate Park is home to a golf course, an aquatic center, and an amusement park.

Franklin Mountains State Park is the largest urban park in the nation, with 24,247 acres spanning approximately 37 miles within the city limits of El Paso. By fall 2005 the trail network will encompass 118 miles of hiking trail, with 51 miles slated for use for both hikers and mountain bikers, and 22 miles open for hiking, mountain biking, and horseback riding. The park's natural rock formations invite rock climbers to the area. After a recent $1.7 million renovation, the park's 44 picnic sites offer new shelters, picnic tables, and grills. Recently opened, the Wyler Aerial Tramway offers riders an exhilarating 4 minute gondola ride offering unmatched views of the Franklin Mountains.

The Hueco Tanks State Historic Site, 32 miles northeast of the city in El Paso County, offers some of the best rock climbing opportunities in the area. Named for its natural rock formations, the park's rock basins, or *huecos*, have furnished a supply of trapped rain water to travelers to the region for thousands of years. The park also features rock paintings from hunters and foragers from thousands of years ago, as well as from tribes of the not-so-distant past, including Apaches, Kiowas, and earlier groups. The pictographs include more than 200 paintings of faces left behind by the prehistoric Jornada Mogollon Culture. The park is the site of the last Indian battle in the county.

Wet n' Wild Waterworld in nearby Anthony, Texas and Western Playland Amusement Park in El Paso offer family fun and adventure.

## Shopping and Dining

El Paso's three main shopping malls are Bassett Center, Sunland Park Mall, and Cielo Vista Mall. Sunland Park, the newer of the three, is located on the west side of the city and offers four anchors and a variety of popular shops and restaurants. Bassett Center has three department stores and more than 80 specialty shops. On the east side of the city,

Cielo Vista Mall features 5 department stores and more than 140 specialty shops. The Mission Trail Harvest Market is a program administered by the city in partnership with the Ysleta del Sur Pueblo Indian Tribe and the Texas Cooperative Extension. Open from June through October, the Market brings farm-fresh goods and handmade crafts for sale to the community. The Market operates at Zaragosa and Socorro Road, across from the Ysleta Mission.

While El Paso may have been known in the past as a place for steaks and traditional and often simple Mexican fare such as enchiladas, today's El Paso restaurants serve a variety of ethnic cuisines that reflect an even bigger variety of cultural influences. Dining in El Paso is a cultural blend drawing from Native Americans, Spanish Colonists, Mexican neighbors and residents, as well as Easterners drawn south for warmer climes. Ethnic and international restaurants include Chinese, Korean, German, Italian, and Middle Eastern, but the majority of El Paso's restaurants are steak houses, barbecue places, and Mexican restaurants. Highly popular in El Paso fare is the chile pepper, which is used in everything from eggs and *chorizo* (spicy sausage), to steaks, salsas, and sauces, and even on its own stuffed with cheese or meat and baked as *chile rellenos.*

*Visitor Information:* El Paso Convention and Visitors Bureau, One Civic Center Plaza, El Paso, TX 79901; telephone (800)351-6024; email info@elpasocvb.com

# Convention Facilities

The El Paso Convention & Performing Arts Center's Judson F. Williams Convention Center was remodeled and expanded in May 2002. The new center features three halls, 80,000 square feet of exhibit space, and 14,900 square feet of meeting space in 17 meeting rooms. Its Mt. Franklin Lobby offers 23,300 square feet of additional exhibit space. The Abraham Chavez Theatre in the Center features an 800 square foot meeting room and theatre seating for 2,500 people.

Across the street from the Convention Center, the Camino Real El Paso has 19 meeting rooms and 36,000 square feet of meeting space that can accommodate groups of up to 1,300. Listed in the National Historic Register, the Camino Real El Paso was established in 1912 and boasts crystal chandeliers, a Tiffany cut-glass dome, and ''the most photographed grand staircase in the Southwest.'' Other El Paso hotels offer 7,000 rooms total throughout the city.

*Convention Information:* El Paso Convention and Visitors Bureau, One Civic Center Plaza, El Paso, TX 79901; telephone (800)351-6024; email info@elpasocvb.com

# Transportation

## Approaching the City

The El Paso International Airport offers passenger services and air cargo services and is the gateway to West Texas, southern New Mexico, and northern Mexico. El Paso International Airport is served by American Airlines, AeroLitoral, Frontier, America West, Continental, Delta, Southwest, and United, and provides an average of 136 daily arrivals and departures. In 2003 the airport served 2,910,663 customers and transported 81,922 tons of cargo. The airport was recently expanded, adding two 144,000 square foot air cargo buildings, more than 34 acres of aircraft parking, and an additional 6.4 miles of roadways. Once a thriving Air Force Base, Biggs Army Airfield lies adjacent to the El Paso International Airport and boasts more miles of runway than any Army airfield in the world. Now part of Fort Bliss, the airfield is used for Army exercises and refueling.

Two major highways transport drivers in, out, and through El Paso: I-10 runs east and west, and Highway 54 runs north and south; Highway 375 loops around the outskirts of the city, through Fort Bliss, and close to downtown. Several bus lines offer service to and from El Paso, and Amtrak provides passenger rail service west to California and east as far as Florida.

## Traveling in the City

The Franklin Mountains literally split the city of El Paso down the middle, creating what El Pasoans call the city's east and the west sides. The Rio Grande flows along the city's southern edge. The city is laid out around these two natural features. Sun Metro provides bus and trolley service throughout the city, with 51 weekday routes, 41 Saturday routes, and 38 Sunday routes.

# Communications

## Newspapers and Magazines

El Paso's major daily newspaper is the *El Paso Times. The Prospector* is a weekly newspaper published by the University of Texas at El Paso. *Twin Plant News,* a magazine covering manufacturing and business in Mexico, is published in El Paso, as well as *NOVA Quarterly,* a quarterly magazine published by the University of Texas at El Paso.

## Television and Radio

El Paso is served by eight television stations, of which four are affiliated with the major commercial networks, two with public broadcasting, and one with Spanish-language Univision. The city's five AM and eight FM radio stations broadcast a variety of programs, including sports, talk, religious, country, rock, and Hispanic programming.

***Media Information:*** *El Paso Times,* PO Box 20, El Paso, TX 79999; telephone (800)351-1677

## El Paso Online

City of El Paso. Available www.ci.el-paso.tx.us

County of El Paso. Available www.co.el-paso.tx.us

El Paso: A Guestlife Destination Guide. Available www .guestlife.com/elpaso

El Paso Convention and Visitors Bureau. Available www .elpasocvb.com

El Paso Independent School District. Available www.episd .org

El Paso International Airport. Available www.elpasointer nationalairport.com/index.htm

El Paso Public Library. Available www.elpasotexas.gov/ library

El Paso Scene. Available wwwcene.com

El Paso Times. Available www.elpasotimes.com

Fort Bliss. Available www.bliss.army.mil

Texas State Historical Association. Available www.tsha .utexas.edu

University of Texas at El Paso. Available www.utep.edu

## Selected Bibliography

Metz, Leon C., *City at the Pass: An Illustrated History of El Paso* (Woodland Hills, California: Windsor, 1980)

Sonnichsen, C.L., *Pass of the North: Four Centuries on the Rio Grande* (2 vols., El Paso: Texas Western Press, 1968, 1980)

Timmons, W.H. ed., *Four Centuries at the Pass* ( El Paso: Guynes Printing, 1980)

# Fort Worth

## *The City in Brief*

**Founded:** 1849 (incorporated 1873)

**Head Official:** Mayor Michael J. Moncrief (NP) (since 2003)

**City Population**
  1980: 385,164
  1990: 447,619
  2000: 534,694
  2003 estimate: 585,122
  Percent change, 1990–2000: 19.3%
  U.S. rank in 1980: 33rd
  U.S. rank in 1990: 28th (State rank: 6th)
  U.S. rank in 2000: 27th (State rank: 6th)

**Metropolitan Area Population (CMSA)**
  1990: 4,037,282
  2000: 5,221,801
  Percent change, 1990–2000: 29.3%
  U.S. rank in 1990: 9th
  U.S. rank in 2000: 9th

**Area:** 292.5 square miles (2000)
**Elevation:** Ranges from 500 to 800 feet above sea level
**Average Annual Temperature:** 65.5° F
**Average Annual Precipitation:** 34.73 inches

**Major Economic Sectors:** services, wholesale and retail trade, manufacturing
**Unemployment rate:** 5.0% (December 2004)
**Per Capita Income:** $18,800 (2000)

**2002 FBI Crime Index Total:** 41,280

**Major Colleges and Universities:** University of Texas at Arlington, Texas Christian University, Texas Wesleyan College

**Daily Newspaper:** *Fort Worth Star-Telegram*

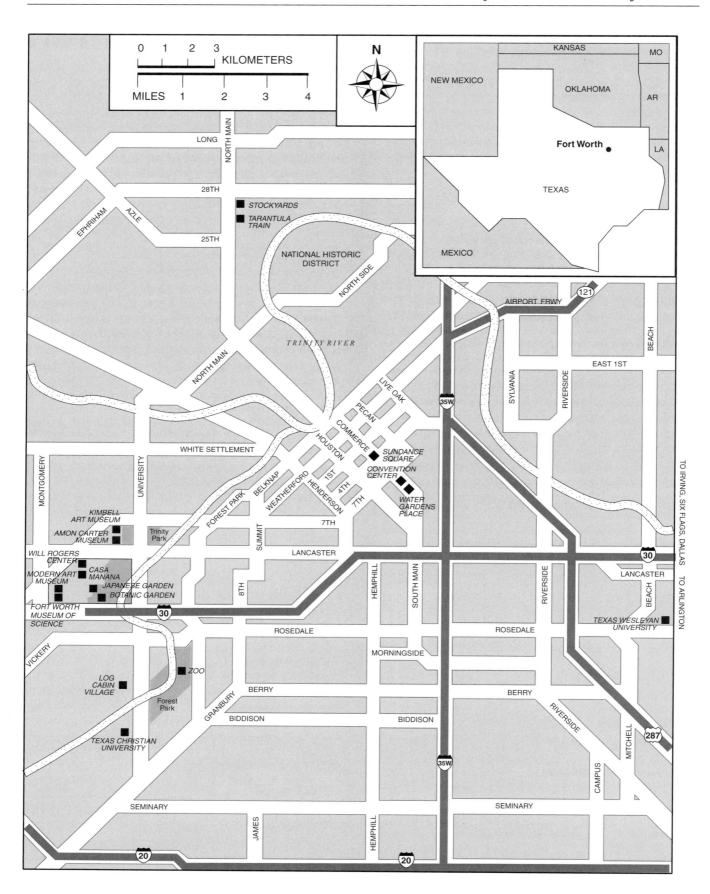

# Introduction

Fort Worth, western anchor city of the Dallas/Fort Worth Metroplex, identifies itself as "Where the West Begins." Proud of its colorful western heritage and rowdy past, the city carefully preserves its history even as it plans for the future. Within its downtown, cowboys, cattle auctions, and horse-drawn carriages coexist with cultural centers and modern office towers. Glass and steel skyscrapers housing headquarters of aviation, aerospace, and high-technology companies share sidewalks with renovated historic districts such as the Fort Worth Stockyards National Historic District and downtown's Sundance Square. With a population growth of 29.3 percent between 1990 and 2000, Fort Worth/Dallas is among the fastest growing metropolitan areas in the country.

# Geography and Climate

Fort Worth is located in the rolling hills of the Great Plains region of north-central Texas. It is the seat of Tarrant County and the major city in the western half of the Fort Worth/Dallas Metroplex. Fort Worth is 30 miles from Dallas and separated from it by the Dallas/Fort Worth International Airport and several smaller central cities, such as Irving, Arlington, and Grand Prairie. The Clear and West forks of the Trinity River join near the center of Fort Worth and Lake Worth, Eagle Mountain Lake, Benbrook, and Arlington Lakes form parts of its northwest and southern borders.

Fort Worth's climate is continental and humid subtropical, characterized by wide variations in annual weather conditions, long, hot summers, and short, mild winters. For more than 150 years Fort Worth was the only major city in the United States that had never had a fatal tornado. The city's luck ran out in March 2000 when a spectacular tornado tore through residential neighborhoods and the downtown area. Five people died in the storms, which caused an estimated $450 million in damage.

**Area:** 292.5 square miles (2000)

**Elevation:** Ranges from 500 to 800 feet above sea level; mean elevation is 670 feet

**Average Temperatures:** January, 44.1° F; August, 84.4° F; annual average, 65.5° F

**Average Annual Precipitation:** 34.73 inches

# History

## "Cowtown" Served As Trading Center

Fort Worth's wild and wooly past began in 1849 when Major Ripley Arnold led a small detachment of U.S. Dragoons to the banks of the Trinity River and established an outpost to protect early settlers from Native American attack. The garrison was named for General William Worth, a Mexican War hero. It was more of an encampment than a fort, but after several years the natives ceased their opposition to the settlement. When the soldiers left, the settlers stayed, and in 1860 Fort Worth was chosen to serve as Tarrant County seat.

Its location on the Old Chisholm Trail, the route along which ranchers drove their herds, helped establish Fort Worth as a trading and cattle center and earned it the nickname "Cowtown." Cowboys took full advantage of their last brush with civilization before the long drive north from Fort Worth. They stocked up on provisions from local merchants, visited the town's colorful saloons for a bit of gambling and carousing, then galloped northward with their cattle.

## Problems Accompanied Prosperity

Post-Civil War reconstruction brought many disillusioned Confederates to Texas in search of jobs and new beginnings. Commerce grew along with the population. Yankees wanted meat, and Texas had a ready supply. During this time rumors grew of a panther that stalked and slept on the city streets at night. A Dallas newspaper ran a story claiming that Fort Worth was so drowsy, a panther was found sleeping on Main Street. Fort Worth citizens good-naturedly dubbed their hometown "Panther City," and many local merchants and sports teams adopted the animal in their logos.

The Texas & Pacific Railroad arrived in Fort Worth in 1876, causing a boom in the cattle industry and in wholesale trade. The city was the westernmost railhead and became a transit point for cattle shipment. With the boom times came some problems. Crime was rampant and certain sections of town, such as Hell's Half Acre, were off-limits for proper citizens. Cowboys were joined by a motley assortment of buffalo hunters, gunmen, adventurers, and crooks. Butch Cassidy and the Sundance Kid were said to roam the streets of Fort Worth between robberies.

## Boom Town Is Tamed

During the 1880s and 1890s, an influx of home-seekers helped quiet the rowdy streets and create a more stable community. More railroads led to more industry. Meat packing companies, a brewing company, more newspapers, and a stronger banking system arrived. Community leaders modernized the fire department, started a municipal water system, built sanitary sewers, and paved streets. Free public schools were legalized in Texas and colleges were founded. By then most major religious denominations were represented with congregations in the city. Fort Worth women organized teas, dances, dinners, and cakewalks to raise funds for a public library. In 1907, the Texas Legislature helped tame the town by outlawing gambling.

During the early days of the twentieth century, Fort Worth became the meat packing center of the Southwest. Nearly all West Texas cattle stopped there for sale or reshipment. Merchants were delighted to discover that when ranchers brought their cattle to market, they also brought their wives to shop in Fort Worth's stores.

### Oil/Aviation Spur Economy

In 1917, oil was discovered in West Texas on McCleskey Farm about 90 miles west of Fort Worth. The gusher meant another boom for the city and helped meet the fuel demand created by World War I. Five refineries were built by 1920 and the city became a center for oil operators. Oil-rich ranchers and farmers moved to Fort Worth and built luxurious homes and towering office buildings.

During World War I three flying fields were established near Fort Worth, all eventually taken over by the U.S. government. In 1927, an airport opened and the aviation industry began. During World War II, B-24 bombers were manufactured at the Convair Plant in Fort Worth, while bomber pilots trained at the nearby Tarrant Field (renamed Carswell Air Force Base in 1948). The opening of Dallas/Fort Worth International Airport in 1974 ushered in a new era of aviation history. At the time it was built, the airport was the largest in the world. The aviation/aerospace industry remains an important factor in Fort Worth's economy today.

Partners for Livable Communities voted Fort Worth as one of America's Most Livable Large Cities in 2004. With a vibrant cultural life, continuing development, and expanding economy in high tech industries, Fort Worth forecasts a vibrant future.

***Historical Information:*** Fort Worth Public Library, Genealogy and Local History Department, 500 W. 3rd Street, Fort Worth, TX 76102; telephone (817)871-7740

# Population Profile

## Metropolitan Area Residents (CMSA)
*1990:* 4,037,282
*2000:* 5,221,801
*Percent change, 1990–2000:* 29.3%

*U.S. rank in 1990:* 9th
*U.S. rank in 2000:* 9th

## City Residents
*1980:* 385,164
*1990:* 447,619
*2000:* 534,694
*2003 estimate:* 585,122
*Percent change, 1990–2000* 19.3%
*U.S. rank in 1980:* 33rd
*U.S. rank in 1990:* 28th (State rank: 6th)
*U.S. rank in 2000:* 27th (State rank: 6th)

*Density:* 1,827.8 people per square mile (2000)

*Racial and ethnic characteristics* (2000)
  White: 319,159
  Black or African American: 108,310
  American Indian and Alaskan Native: 3,144
  Asian: 14,105
  Native Hawaiian and other Pacific Islander: 341
  Hispanic (may be of any race): 159,368
  Other: 75,100

*Percent of residents born in state:* 60.8% (2000)

*Age characteristics* (2000)
  Population under 5 years old: 45,452
  Population 5 to 9 years old: 42,413
  Population 10 to 14 years old: 39,943
  Population 15 to 19 years old: 39,984
  Population 20 to 24 years old: 43,562
  Population 25 to 34 years old: 91,042
  Population 35 to 44 years old: 83,691
  Population 45 to 54 years old: 61,472
  Population 55 to 59 years old: 20,240
  Population 60 to 64 years old: 15,433
  Population 65 to 74 years old: 26,614
  Population 75 to 84 years old: 18,496
  Population 85 years and older: 6,352
  Median age: 30.9 years

*Births* (2002)
  Total number: 11,466

*Deaths* (2002)
  Total number: 4,520 (of which, 86 were infants under the age of 1 year)

*Money income* (1999)
  Per capita income: $18,800
  Median household income: $37,074
  Total households: 195,309

*Number of households with income of . . .*
  less than $10,000: 20,658
  $10,000 to $14,999: 13,486

$15,000 to $24,999: 27,887
$25,000 to $34,999: 28,592
$35,000 to $49,999: 34,179
$50,000 to $74,999: 35,369
$75,000 to $99,999: 16,814
$100,000 to $149,999: 11,123
$150,000 to $199,999: 2,822
$200,000 or more: 3,379

*Percent of families below poverty level:* 12.7% (46.8% of which were female householder families with related children under 5 years)

*2002 FBI Crime Index Total:* 41,280

# Municipal Government

Fort Worth has a council-manager form of government with a mayor elected for a two-year term, an eight-member council, and an appointed city manager. The city is the seat of Tarrant County.

**Head Official:** Michael J. Moncrief (NP) (since 2003; current term expires 2005)

**Total Number of City Employees:** 5,708 (2005)

*City Information:* City of Fort Worth, 1000 Throckmorton Street, Fort Worth, TX 76102; (817)871-6000

# Economy

## Major Industries and Commercial Activity

Fort Worth has traditionally been a diverse center of manufacturing, and the city had demonstrated strong economic growth since the 1980s. However, an economic slowdown in the sector accounted for job losses for the first time in many years between 2001 and 2003. Forecasts call for an increase of manufacturing jobs, supplying 32,048 new manufacturing jobs between 2004 and 2025 for an annual growth rate of 1.2 percent. Government sector jobs are expected to show continued growth, and the transportation, communication, and utilities sector is forecasted to show growth as well. Mining business in Texas is driven by oil and gas production and has shown losses as oil prices dip.

Major employers in the area are American Airlines, Lockheed Martin Tactical Aircraft Systems, Bell Helicopter Textron, Radio Shack Corporation, SABRE, Pier 1 Imports, and Burlington Northern Santa Fe. Emerging economic

sectors in the new century include semiconductor manufacturing, communications equipment manufacturing, corporate offices, and distribution.

Between 1990 and 1996 defense downsizing resulted in the loss of 44,000 jobs in the Fort Worth area. That development set Fort Worth's economic diversification effort into motion. A plan was adopted called "Strategy 2000, Diversifying Fort Worth's Future," which had as its goal the creation of a healthy, diverse, less defense-dependent economy supported by business development, emerging technologies, international trade, and a world class workforce. Tech Fort Worth, an off-shoot of "Strategy 2000," is a business incubator that works with the Fort Worth Business Assistance Center to foster new start-up companies. Tech Fort Worth opened a new facility in 2004 with over 160,000 feet of office space, laboratories and conference rooms.

Tourism is an important contributor to the local economy. According to the Fort Worth Convention and Visitors Bureau, in 2004 there were 8.7 million visitors to Fort Worth, who spent $1.2 billion in the city and even more in the surrounding areas.

*Items and goods produced:* aircraft, communication equipment, electronic equipment, machinery, refrigeration equipment, containers, clothing, food products, pharmaceuticals, computers, clothing, grain, leather

## Incentive Programs—New and Existing Companies

*Local programs*—Fort Worth offers many incentive programs to develop and redevelop the city. As of 2005 Fort Worth had nine active Tax Increment Finance (TIF) districts. There are two Enterprise Zones in Fort Worth, with fee wavers, tax refunds, and other assistance provided by both the city and state. Under a policy adopted in February 2000, the City of Fort Worth, on a case-by-case basis, gives consideration to the granting of property tax incentives to eligible residential, commercial, and industrial development projects. It is the objective of the city of Fort Worth to encourage applications from projects that (a) are located in enterprise zones or other designated target areas; or (b) result in a development with little or no additional cost to the City; or (c) result in 1,000 or more new jobs, with a commitment to hire Fort Worth and inner city residents. Fort Worth has two state-designated Urban Enterprise Zones.

*State programs*—Texas is a right-to-work state. The Texas Enterprise Zone Programs offer tax abatement at the local level, and refunds of state sales and use taxes under certain circumstances to businesses operating in enterprise zone areas. The state of Texas primarily targets its incentive programs toward smaller and rural communities.

*Job training programs*—The state of Texas provides training funds through its Smart Jobs program, which offers up to

$2,000 in matching funds for training employees who will work for new and expanding Texas companies that pay at or above the state average wage. Job training funds are made available through the federal Workforce Investment Act (WIA). Employers using WIA participants can be reimbursed for up to 50 percent of the cost of training new employees. Fort Worth Works is a program run by the city to help both employers and job seekers by coordinating job fairs and placement agencies, and eliminating barriers to low-income workers. The Texas Department of Commerce has a work force incentive program for industrial start-up training and funding. Local state-supported educational institutions provide the training. The program provides up to $1,000 per trainee.

### Development Projects

The National League of Cities awarded Fort Worth the James C. Howland Award for Urban Enrichment for innovative redevelopment in 1995, and the building boom continues. In 2004, Pier 1 Imports moved into its new $90 million 440,000 square foot headquarters, employing more than 350 people. In 2005, work began on the city's new 37,000 square foot recreation center which will be completed by the end of the year. A $65 million renovation of the 37-story landmark Bank One Tower is being redeveloped into 294 luxury residential condominiums and 60,000 square feet of space for shops, restaurants, and boutique office space. Omni Hotels will build a $90 million, 600-room hotel next to the Fort Worth Convention Center, to be completed in 2007. Also in 2005, the Montgomery Ward building and warehouse, a 1928 Mission Revival-style structure, becomes an urban retail center after a $50 million redevelopment.

Other plans underway in 2005 were for construction of a 5-story, 221,000 square foot expansion of the JPS Hospital, including a new emergency department, surgery department, and sky bridge connector to the existing hospital, to begin mid-2005. So7, a residential and retail development near Trinity Park, will add an additional 150,000 square feet of retail space as well as additional condominiums and apartments.

***Economic Development Information:*** Fort Worth Chamber of Commerce, 777 Taylor Street, Suite 900, Fort Worth, TX 76102-4997; telephone (817)336-2491. Fort Worth Economic Development Office, Office of the City Manager, Third Floor City Hall, 1000 Throckmorton, Fort Worth, TX 76102; telephone (817)871-6103

### Commercial Shipping

A central location combined with superior air and ground transportation resources makes Fort Worth an ideal location for distribution. The Dallas/Fort Worth International Airport has a huge economic impact. Its Foreign Trade Zone, U.S. Customs Office, and U.S. Port of Entry status afford business and industry easy access to many important services. Nearby

Alliance Airport is used solely by distribution and manufacturing firms to reach national and international markets, and is home every October to its International Air Show. Several local and long distance carriers provide commercial motor freight service. For firms with their own trucks, support services are abundant. A full complement of rail services is available in the city where Burlington Northern Santa Fe, the largest railroad in the nation, is headquartered.

### Labor Force and Employment Outlook

The Dallas/Fort Worth area is a major trade center and distribution hub as well as the state's telecommunications center. It is the sixth-ranked metropolitan area in the nation for *Fortune* 500 companies, of which 17 have headquarters in the area.

The following is a summary of data regarding the Fort Worth metropolitan area labor force, 2003 annual averages.

*Size of nonagricultural labor force:* 776,900

*Number of workers employed in . . .*
   *mining:* 3,900
   *construction:* 43,700
   *manufacturing:* 96,700
   *trade, transportation and utilities:* 187,300
   *information:* 71,800
   *financial activities:* 45,800
   *business and professional services:* 81,500
   *educational and health services:* 84,500
   *leisure and hospitality:* 76,300
   *other services:* 31,700
   *government:* 107,800

*Average hourly earnings of production workers employed in manufacturing:* $17.18

*Unemployment rate:* 5.0% (December 2004)

| *Largest employers (2003)* | *Number of employees* |
| --- | --- |
| American Airlines | 28,500 |
| GameStop | 20,000 |
| Lockheed Martin Aeronautics | 16,800 |
| Fort Worth Independent School District | 10,300 |
| Bell Helicopter-Textron | 6,000 |
| City of Fort Worth | 5,700 |
| Radio Shack | 4,300 |
| Tarrant County Government | 4,200 |
| Harris Methodist Fort Worth Hospital | 3,800 |
| Cook Children's Medical Center | 3,800 |

### Cost of Living

The cost of living in Fort Worth is low compared to other major cities in the United States.

The following is a summary of data regarding several key cost of living factors for the Fort Worth area.

*2004 (3rd Quarter) ACCRA Average House Price:* $189,855

*2004 (3rd Quarter) ACCRA Cost of Living Index:* 92.4 (U.S. average = 100.0)

*State income tax rate:* none

*State sales tax rate:* 6.25% (food and prescription drugs are exempt)

*Local income tax rate:* none

*Local sales tax rate:* 2.0%

*Property tax rate:* $.8650 per $100 of assessed valuation (assessed valuation = 100% of market value)

*Economic Information:* Fort Worth Chamber of Commerce, 777 Taylor Street, Suite 900, Fort Worth, TX 76102-4997; telephone (817)336-2491.

# Education and Research

## Elementary and Secondary Schools

The Fort Worth Independent School District (FWISD) is the largest of the 20 school districts in Tarrant County. With a dedicated administration, in less than a decade the district saw a massive 833 percent increase in high-performing schools, from only 6 in 1994 to 59 in 2002. As part of a bond program, improvements and renovations have been ongoing since 2000 to many of the district's schools.

The FWISD continues to show leadership in innovative teaching techniques, including applied learning; new standards; elementary, reading, and math initiatives; and instructional support teams to enhance teaching. The FWISD's Vital Link program, which places 12-year-old students in workplace situations to show them the link between classroom learning and workplace needs, is nationally recognized. The FWISD's Teaching Chairs program to recognize teaching excellence in a variety of disciplines, is based on the university-level teaching chair concept and is unique in the nation at the public school level. Another feature of the system is a high school for medical professionals. Middle and elementary schools offer preparatory, Montessori, and baccalaureate education. The FWISD is one of only a few schools in the nation to hold the Kennedy Center Imagination Celebration, the national children's arts festival program. In Fort Worth the Imagination Celebration continues on a year-round basis.

The following is a summary of data regarding Fort Worth's public schools as of the 2004–2005 school year.

*Total enrollment:* 80,223

*Number of facilities*
 *elementary schools:* 80
 *middle schools:* 24
 *senior high schools:* 13
 *other:* 28

*Student/teacher ratio:* 16.7:1

*Teacher salaries (2004)*
 *minimum:* $38,500
 *maximum:* $64,176

*Funding per pupil:* $6,252 (2004-2005)

Around 75 private and parochial schools serve Fort Worth, including special schools for the learning disabled.

*Public Schools Information:* Fort Worth Independent School District, 100 North University Dr., Fort Worth, TX 76107-1360; telephone (817)871-2455; fax (817)871-2460

## Colleges and Universities

Fort Worth boasts seven colleges and universities. The University of Texas at Arlington (UTA) is the area's largest university, with more than 25,000 students enrolled in its schools of business, engineering, liberal arts, science, architecture, nursing, social work, and education. UTA is known for programs in high technology applied research.

Texas Christian University (TCU) educates more than 8,500 students. It specializes in a liberal arts education and offers research-oriented PhD programs in chemistry, divinity, English, history, physics, and psychology. Texas Wesleyan University has more than 2,800 students in its schools of business, education, fine arts, sciences, and humanities. The city's other colleges are Tarrant County Junior College (on several campuses), Southwestern Baptist Theological Seminary, and Arlington Baptist College. There are some 30 other colleges and universities within a 50-mile radius, including technical, business, and nursing schools.

## Libraries and Research Centers

The Fort Worth Public Library system operates a central library, a Southwest Regional location, an East Regional location, two satellite libraries in public housing communities, and nine branches. Its holdings number 2.3 million items, including more than 2,000 periodical subscriptions. Special collections include bookplates, early children's books, books in Spanish and Vietnamese, genealogy, earth science, popular sheet music, government documents, and oral history. Nearly 30 special libraries are located in Fort

Worth, affiliated with local businesses, art museums, hospitals and colleges, and U.S. government agencies. Among them are the Lockheed Martin Fort Worth Company Research Library and the National Archives Southwest Region collection of inactive records of U.S. government agencies in the Southwest.

The University of Texas at Arlington executes advanced research in a number of areas, notably at its Automation and Robotics Research Institute, and its Nanotechnology Research & Teaching Facility. The University of North Texas Health Science Center supports several research centers dealing with such topics as substance abuse and wound healing. Texas Christian University operates an Institute of Behavioral Research and the Center for Texas Studies.

*Public Library Information:* Fort Worth Public Library, 500 W. 3rd Street, Fort Worth, TX 76102-7305; telephone (817)871-7701

# Health Care

The Southside Medical District, located south of Fort Worth's Central Business District, encompasses approximately 1,400 acres and includes the area's major hospitals, medical institutions, and support services. It has more than 30,000 employees, representing the second largest employment center in the City of Fort Worth.

Fort Worth is home to 20 hospitals, including general care facilities, a children's medical center, urgent care center, emergency clinics, a cardiac center, and an osteopathic hospital. Harris Methodist Fort Worth Hospital, with more than 600 beds, is the largest hospital in the city and features emergency service, a CareFlite helicopter, open-heart surgery facilities, kidney transplant procedures and a rehabilitation program for head and spinal cord injuries.

JPS Health Network/John Peter Smith Hospital announced plans to build a $75 million patient tower to increase beds, host new operating suites, and add a new emergency department, scheduled to be completed in 2007. The Plaza Medical Center of Fort Worth is undergoing a $57 million renovation that will include a new critical cardiac care center and expanded emergency room. Among the services of All Saints Episcopal Hospital are wellness and fitness programs, a cardiac rehabilitation unit, and the largest freestanding center for radiation cancer therapy in the Southwest. Other health care facilities in Fort Worth are Rehabilitation Hospital, which offers programs for the brain-injured and those with other physical disabilities, and Cook-Fort Worth Children's Medical Center, which specializes in pediatrics.

# Recreation

### Sightseeing

Fort Worth and the Metroplex rank high on the list of U.S. tourist destinations. Many attractions are located in the city or within the mid-cities region of the Dallas/Fort Worth area, including Arlington, Grand Prairie, and Irving. Tourists have a wide range of diversions from which to choose.

The Stockyards National Historic District is a multiblock historic district featuring specialty shops, rodeos, saloons, and livestock auctions. Twice daily in the Stockyards, authentic cowhands drive the Fort Worth Herd, a group of Texas longhorn steer, down Exchange Avenue. Billy Bob's Texas in the Stockyards, is the world's largest honky tonk bar/entertainment center and can accommodate a crowd of 6,000 people to hear top western entertainers, play pool and video games, and shop. Sundance Square is another historic district of red-bricked streets, shops, and restaurants. Visitors to Fort Worth can walk through historic Van Zandt Cottage, Thistle Hill mansion, or the Eddleman McFarland House, an elegant Victorian residence. Tourists can also tour downtown Fort Worth and Sundance Square in a carriage. Fort Worth Water Garden Park is an impressive four blocks of concrete-terraced waterfalls, fountains, pools, and gardens. Trinity Trail consists 32 miles of paved trails for walking, biking, or rollerblading, winding from Northside Drive to Foster Park. The Tarantula Steam excursion train takes passengers between Grapevine and the Stockyards. Stockyards Station also includes retail and dining facilities, plus a children's carnival.

The Fort Worth Zoo is home to 5,000 exotic animals. Exhibits include a 2.5-acre World of Primates, African Savannah, Asian Falls, Parrot Paradise, and Texas Wild!, an exhibit that opened in 2001 which focuses on showcasing animals that are native to Texas. Nearby Log Cabin Village features 1850s-era restored cabins, a working grist mill, and pioneer craft demonstrations. Noble Planetarium in the Museum of Science and History features a Texas sky show that changes monthly. Fort Worth Nature Center and Refuge in Lake Worth is a 3,400-acre habitat and National Natural Landmark. The Fort Worth Botanic Garden, including the Japanese Garden, contains acres of plants, and a pagoda, teahouse, and meditation garden. The Forest Park Miniature Railroad takes visitors on a 40-minute trip from Forest Park to Trinity Park and back. Hurricane Harbor in Arlington is a family-oriented water park. Six Flags over Texas is a large amusement park complex in Arlington. Visitors can tour American Airlines Flight Academy, Mrs. Baird's Bakery, or the Bandera Hat Company.

**The Stockyards National Historic District features specialty shops, rodeos, saloons, and livestock auctions.**

## Arts and Culture

Cowboys and culture mix in Fort Worth. Community and commercial groups are generous and cooperative in their support of the arts. The city offers cultural experiences ranging from fine opera and ballet to knee-slapping country hoedowns. Its museums house the art and artifacts of European masters and Texas cattlemen.

The beautiful Nancy Lee and Perry R. Bass Performance Hall, a $67 million facility that opened in 1998, is the first-ever home of the Fort Worth Symphony, Texas Ballet Theater, and the Fort Worth Opera, as well as the Van Cliburn International Piano Competition. The 2,054-seat performance hall is located in Sundance Square; it makes a grand impression with its pair of 48-foot angels gracing the entrance.

Casa Manana, a theater-in-the-round under a geodesic dome, seats 1,800 people and features Broadway touring productions, a children's playhouse series, and produces its own shows featuring local talent. The Rose Marine Theater is home to the Latin Arts Association of Fort Worth, the only Hispanic theater company in the city, and presents theater, film, and live music series. Other thriving Fort Worth-area theaters include StageWest, Circle Theater, Jubilee, and the avant-garde group Hip Pocket. A number of area community orchestra and professional ensembles present classical music concerts throughout the year. Electrifying film performances are presented at the Omni Theater's 80-foot dome screen in the Fort Worth Museum of Science and History. The Scott Theatre hosts the Fort Worth Theatre, special film productions, and cultural activities. Hyena's Comedy Club features national acts; ''Four Day Weekends'' improvisational comedy show is Fort Worth's longest running show.

Fort Worth's museums and galleries also offer variety. The Kimbell Art Museum was designed by Louis Kahn and houses collections of classical and prehistoric art, and western European and early twentieth century paintings. The Amon Carter Museum, named for the late Fort Worth newspaper magnate whose foundation supports it, contains a collection of nineteenth- and early twentieth-century Western and American paintings and American photographs. Twentieth-century multimedia art including sculpture, photography, and painting are displayed at the Modern Art Museum of Fort Worth. The Sid Richardson Collection of Western Art in Sundance Square displays 60 paintings by artists of the American West such as Frederic Remington and Charles Russell.

The Fort Worth Museum of Science and History houses the Omni Theater and Museum School, the Noble Planetarium, and 35,000 square feet of exhibits, including the Hall of Medical Science, Man and His Possessions, Antique Calculators and Computer Technology, Geology, and Texas History. The American Airlines C.R. Smith Museum is devoted to the history of commercial aviation, having over 1,000 items in its collection, including a restored DC-3 airplane. The history of the ranching industry in Texas is traced through film, photographs, and memorabilia at the Cattle Raiser's Museum. The Texas Cowboy Hall of Fame and National Cowboys of Color Museum and Hall of Fame pay tribute to the people who built Texas. The National Cowgirl Museum and Hall of Fame, the only one of its kind in the world, opened a new home in the city's Cultural District in 2002. Fire Station No. 1 is the city's earliest fire house and contains an exhibit entitled ''150 Years of Fort Worth.''

Tours are available at the Bureau of Engraving and Printing's Visitor Center, allowing the public to watch the printing of paper currency. The Pate Museum of Transportation, located on a ranch near Cresson, maintains a collection of varying modes of transportation including antique, classic, and special interest cars, airplanes, railroad cars, and space exhibits. On the campus of Southwestern Baptist Theological Seminary, the Tandy Archaeological Museum houses a collection of biblical artifacts. The Texas Civil War Museum is scheduled to open in mid-2005 with a large collection of uniforms, weapons, and flags from both North and the South.

## Festivals and Holidays

In January/February the Fort Worth Stock Show and Rodeo is held over two weeks at the Will Rogers Memorial Coliseum and includes an indoor rodeo, exhibits, arts and crafts, rides, and a carnival midway. Cowtown Goes Green is Fort Worth's unique, western-style St. Patrick's Day celebration. The festival is held in the National Historic Stockyards District and features a parade, cattle drive, pub crawl, arts and crafts sales, and Irish music. For four days in April, Fort Worth's Main Street becomes a marketplace of food, arts and crafts, and live entertainment during the Main St. Fort Worth Arts Festival.

The arrival of spring is observed with Mayfest activities, games, sports, and arts and crafts in Trinity Park. The Van Cliburn International Piano Competition is held at the Bell Performance Center every four years. At the Texas Frontier Forts Muster and Quanah Parker Comanche Pow Wow & Honor Dance, Fort Worth's frontier past is highlighted with re-enactors showing off the skills and equipment needed in the days of the old West, along with Comanche dancers performing traditional dances. Shakespeare in the Park is also held in June at the Trinity Park Playhouse with nightly shows, music, and dance. In June and the beginning of July is the American Paint Horse Association World Championship Show & Sale at the Will Rogers Center. Pioneer Days in September commemorates the early days of the cattle industry with a fiddler's contest, fajita cook-off, parade, and footrace. Also in September, the Forth Worth International Air Show at Alliance Airport is a family-oriented event conceived as a tribute to Fort Worth's aviation industry. Oktoberfest features music, dance, and food events to raise money for symphonic activities. The Red Steagall Cowboy Gathering & Western Swing Festival fills the Stockyard District with music, rodeo and cowboy poetry in October. November and December are filled with holiday observances including the Zoobilee of Lights and the Christmas Parade of Lights.

### Sports for the Spectator

Fort Worth professional sports fans follow the American League's Texas Rangers baseball, NFL Dallas Cowboys football, NBA Dallas Mavericks basketball, and the Dallas Stars NHL teams. None of these is based in Fort Worth, but all are close enough to claim fans. Fort Worth's own Brahmas are in the Western Professional Hockey League; they play at Will Rogers Coliseum. College fans in Fort Worth pay close attention to the Texas Christian University Horned Frogs and the Texas Wesleyan University Rams, both of which compete in major collegiate sports. The Colonial National Invitational Golf Tournament and the GTE Byron Nelson Classic are held in May.

The Texas Motor Speedway, a 1.5-mile NASCAR oval track with a seating capacity of 155,000 (plus 53,000 more in the infield), is the second largest sports facility in the country; it schedules three major racing weekends a year.

### Sports for the Participant

Six large lakes within 25 miles of downtown provide Fort Worth residents with ample opportunities for water sports and recreation. Burger's Lake is a 20-acre recreational park with a swimming pool and picnic grounds. Greenhills Environmental Center is a 1,000-acre nature preserve and recreational area with hiking trails. Heritage Park Boat & Recreation Center bills itself as "a one-hour vacation in the heart of Fort Worth."

Fort Worth maintains 231 developed city parks with more than 10,000 acres, 98 public tennis courts, 3 bicycle trails, 6 public golf courses, and 20 municipal pools.

### Shopping and Dining

Fort Worth boasts one of the most beautiful and vibrant downtown areas in Texas. The centerpiece of the revitalized downtown is the Sundance Square entertainment and shopping district, a 20-block area filled with historic buildings, movie theaters, live theaters, nightclubs, coffee houses, art galleries and, of course, shopping in a 40-store mall with an indoor skating rink. Other popular shopping areas are Hulen Mall, the Fort Worth Outlet Square, University Park Village, Stockyards Station, the Camp Bowie Boulevard shops, Exchange Avenue Shops, and Ridgmar Mall in west Forth Worth.

Restaurants are plentiful in Fort Worth, offering everything from Continental, Texas Ranch, New American, and ethnic cuisines. The historic districts in particular, such as The Stockyards and Sundance Square, abound in restaurants and saloons. Texas beef, chili, and Tex-Mex are specialties. At Ellington's Southern Table in Sundance Square, diners' plates are piled high with Southern specialties like pot roast, chicken-fried steak, fried catfish, and liver and onions.

*Visitor Information:* Fort Worth Convention and Visitors Bureau, 415 Throckmorton, Fort Worth, Texas 76102; telephone (817)336-8791 or (800)433-5747

## Convention Facilities

The Fort Worth Convention Center in downtown Fort Worth is the city's major facility. The center has 253,226 square feet of exhibit space, 41 meeting rooms, a 28,160 square foot ballroom, a 3,000-seat theater, and a 14,000-seat arena. The Fort Worth Water Gardens are directly across the street and Sundance Square is only 5 blocks away.

Will Rogers Memorial Center is located in the museum district within walking distance of museums such as the Kimbell, Amon Carter, Modern Art, and the Science and History museums. The Botanic and Japanese Gardens are also nearby. The center contains 100,000 square feet of exhibit space, a 6,000-seat coliseum, a 3,000-seat auditorium, an equestrian center with 2,000-seat arena, and meeting/banquet facilities. The Bass Performance Hall can host events for as many as 500 people in the lobby to well over 2,000 people in the auditorium.

The Renaissance Worthington Hotel, the Radisson Plaza, and the Ramada Plaza Hotel are other downtown facilities equipped with meeting rooms and exhibit space. The city has more than 130 hotels/motels with more than 11,000 rooms, and the Metroplex area, including the Dallas/Fort Worth Airport, boasts even more convention facilities.

*Convention Information:* Fort Worth Convention and Visitors Bureau, 415 Throckmorton, Fort Worth, TX 76102; telephone (817)336-8791 or (800)433-5747

## Transportation

### Approaching the City

The Dallas/Fort Worth International Airport (DFW) is located approximately 17 miles from the downtown areas of both cities. With a U.S. Customs District, a Fish and Wildlife Port of Entry, its own Foreign Trade Zone, and official

U.S. Gateway status, DFW is a major U.S. transportation facility. In 2005 the airport will open a new International Terminal, and Skylink, a high-speed terminal-linking train, begins operation. Alliance Airport, the first major industrial airport in the U.S., is located 20 miles north of the city. Meachum Airport is Fort Worth's leading aviation airport.

Four interstate highways serve Dallas/Fort Worth: I-20 (east-west), I-35 (north-south), I-30 (northeast-west), and I-45 (south).

Intercity passenger service to Fort Worth is available on Amtrak train lines. The Trinity Railway Express, a commuter rail line, connects downtown Dallas, downtown Fort Worth, DFW airport, and the Fort Worth Intermodal Transportation Center, which houses the largest hub for the T and Amtrak trains. In 2004 it carried 2.16 million passengers.

### Traveling in the City

The Fort Worth mass transportation system is called "The T," and includes more than 130 vehicles that travel more than 50 routes. The city recently introduced a trolley service that transports visitors from the downtown area to the Stockyards National Historic District, the Fort Worth Cultural District, and the Fort Worth Zoo.

# Communications

### Newspapers and Magazines

Fort Worth's daily newspaper is the morning *Fort Worth Star-Telegram,*. Other newspapers and magazines focus on horses or cattle, including *Christian Ranchman,* which covers Cowboys for Christ events; several others deal with nurseries, gardening, and religious topics. Two airline inflight magazines are published in Fort Worth.

### Television and Radio

Due to their proximity, Fort Worth and Dallas share a number of television and radio stations with other Metroplex cities. Four television stations broadcast from Fort Worth: NBC, CBS and UPN affiliates and an independent. Five AM and six FM radio stations broadcast from the city, including two Hispanic stations and one owned by Texas Christian University.

*Media Information: Fort Worth Star-Telegram,* Capital Cities/ABC, Inc., 400 W. 7th St., Fort Worth, TX 76102; telephone (817)390-7400

### Fort Worth Online

City of Fort Worth Home Page. Available ci.fort-worth.tx.us

Fort Worth Chamber of Commerce. Available www .fortworthcoc.org

Fort Worth Convention and Visitors Bureau. Available www.fortworth.com

Fort Worth Independent School District. Available www .fortworthisd.org

Fort Worth Public Library. Available www.fortworthlibrary .org

*Fort Worth Star-Telegram.* Available www.star-telegram .com

### Selected Bibliography

Patterson, R. Michael, *Fort Worth: New Frontiers in Excellence* (Chatsworth, CA: Windsor Publications, Inc., 1990)

Roark, Carol and Byrd Williams, *Fort Worth's Legendary Landmarks* (Fort Worth: Texas Christian University Press, 1997)

# Houston

## *The City in Brief*

**Founded:** 1836 (incorporated 1837)

**Head Official:** Mayor Bill White (since 2004)

**City Population**
   1980: 1,595,138
   1990: 1,654,348
   2000: 1,953,631
   2003 estimate: 2,009,690
   Percent change, 1990–2000: 18.0%
   U.S. rank in 1980: 5th
   U.S. rank in 1990: 4th (State rank: 1st)
   U.S. rank in 2000: 6th (State rank: 1st)

**Metropolitan Area Population**
   1980: 2,753,000
   1990: 3,321,926
   2000: 4,177,646
   Percent change, 1990–2000: 25.8%
   U.S. rank in 1980: 9th (CMSA)
   U.S. rank in 1990: 10th (CMSA)
   U.S. rank in 2000: 10th (CMSA)

**Area:** 601.69 square miles (2000)
**Elevation:** Ranges from sea level to about 50 feet above sea level
**Average Annual Temperature:** 68.8° F
**Average Annual Precipitation:** 47.84 inches

**Major Economic Sectors:** services, finance/insurance/real estate, trade, government
**Unemployment rate:** 5.5% (December 2004)
**Per Capita Income:** $20,101 (1999)

**2002 FBI Crime Index Total:** 149,247

**Major Colleges and Universities:** Rice University, University of Houston, Texas Southern University

**Daily Newspaper:** *Houston Chronicle*

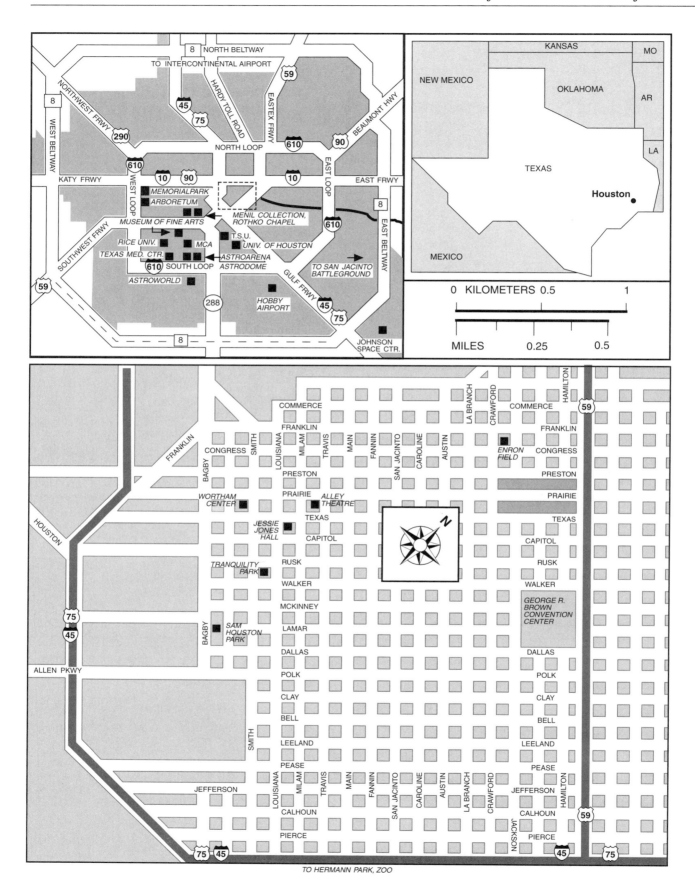

# Introduction

During the late 1970s Houston epitomized opulence, glitter, and opportunity. The city's major industry, petrochemicals, rode the crest of a boom "in the oilpatch," as Houstonians say. Get-rich-quick growth became a predominant feature across the sprawling landscape of the city. By 1982, however, a national recession, coupled with a wildly fluctuating oil market and devaluation of the Mexican peso, changed Houston's outlook from boom to bust. Unemployment and the local economy reached depression levels by 1985, prompting a painful retrenchment. Houston's recovery and subsequent expansion are the result of the growth of energy independent industry and diversification. Optimism is back in Houston as the city looks to new opportunities in high-technology and service industries. As a result of the boom, and despite the bust, Houston's consolidated metropolitan area now exceeds 8,700 square miles and the population has more than doubled from the 1960 level. Now the nation's fourth largest metropolitan area, with nearly 4.2 million people, Houston is looking up again and approaching the future with confidence.

# Geography and Climate

Houston lies near the Gulf of Mexico and sprawls westward from the shores of Galveston Bay on the coastal prairie of eastern Texas. Major waterways include the San Jacinto River, part of which is encompassed by the man-made Houston Ship Channel, and an intricate network of meandering creeks and bayous, the largest of which are Buffalo Bayou and Bray's Bayou. The climate is humid and semitropical in the summertime, with an average annual temperature of about 69 degrees. Houston's winters are mild, although freezing sometimes occurs, and its summers are potent. The threat of severe weather, especially hurricanes that form when northern cold fronts collide with moisture-laden Gulf coast weather systems, is taken seriously by the local population. Houston has been directly hit by two hurricanes in the last forty years, Carla in 1960 and Alicia in 1983, and has been threatened by many others. With Alicia, Houston became the nation's largest city to have endured the passage of a hurricane's eye directly over its downtown area.

**Area:** 601.69 square miles (2000)

**Elevation:** Sea level to about 50 feet above sea level

**Average Temperatures:** January, 51.8° F; July, 83.6° F; annual average, 68.8° F

**Average Annual Precipitation:** 47.84 inches

# History

### Early Days Full of Perils

Inhabited by cannibals, visited by Spanish explorers and missionaries, a base for pirates, former capital of a fledgling nation, and site of a battle that ultimately added millions of acres to the United States—all of this can be said for the rich and varied history of the Houston area.

Amerinds, descended from the early races of mankind that crossed into North America via the Bering land bridge, are known to have occupied the southwestern United States many thousands of years before Christ. As these tribal groups fanned out across North and South America over thousands of years, a primitive culture evolved along what is now the upper Texas coast. The first recorded meetings between Europeans and the native populations of eastern Texas are found in fifteenth- and sixteenth-century accounts of Spanish explorers. These accounts are not particularly pleasant, for the natives of the Gulf Coast region that one day became Houston were notorious cannibals of the small Atakapan and Karankawa tribes. These were ferocious tribal groups, described by the Spaniards as bloodthirsty and barbaric.

The Europeans chose to move on, and despite Galveston Bay's relative attraction as a safe harbor, the upper Gulf Coast of Texas remained largely unsettled by the Spanish, who came to control virtually all of the American Southwest by the early eighteenth century. The area now known as Houston remained a malarial coastal prairie, dotted by marshes and bayous, and home to a few remaining Karankawa.

In the aftermath of the War of 1812, various Caribbean buccaneers, notably Jean Lafitte, established short-lived settlements on Galveston Island, just south of present-day Houston. Local legends persisting to this day in Houston's southeastern suburbs along Galveston Bay, tell of buried pirate treasure, placed there by the crafty Lafitte.

### War Breaks Out with Santa Ana

By the 1820s settlers from the United States were moving into Texas, then owned by the newly independent nation of Mexico. It was in Mexico's interest at the time to allow these settlements. Later, as the American emigrant population grew, so did Mexico's troubles in Texas. By the 1830s the former Americans, calling themselves Texicans, were eager to form their own government and felt abused by dictates from Mexico City. Disputes emerged as a full-blown war with the Mexican government of General Antonio López de Santa Anna in 1836.

That year the area now encompassed by Houston came foursquare onto the national stage. In April, following the massacres of Texas troops at San Antonio's Alamo, General

Sam Houston, leading the main body of the Texas resistance, intercepted a courier and learned of military dispositions planned by Santa Anna, the "Napoleon of the West." Houston, stalling for time, veered away from the superior Mexican force until, at the San Jacinto River near present-day Houston, he used the intercepted information to deploy his small army in an advantageous position. The two armies fought a light skirmish on April 20. Santa Anna, accused by historians of having become contemptuous of Houston, bided his time before pressing home the attack. On the afternoon of April 21, while the Mexican troops prepared for what they expected would be a major engagement the next morning, Houston attacked. By the end of the day, the future of Texas was sealed as Santa Anna lost and Houston won.

## Houston Incorporated

In August a settlement named for the hero of San Jacinto began to take shape along the Buffalo Bayou. By the end of the year, even as the town was still being laid out, Sam Houston, by then the first president of the Republic of Texas, moved his capital from Columbia to the town named in his honor. Houston was incorporated in 1837. The capital remained there until 1839, when the town of Austin became Texas's permanent seat of government.

## Oil, Port, and Space Center Spur Development

As a settlement, Houston grew slowly but steadily in the mid-nineteenth century. By 1870, with 9,000 citizens, it was the third largest city in Texas behind San Antonio and Galveston. Located 50 miles inland, Houston lagged behind the two larger cities as a transportation center, although even then it was a major steamboat and rail terminus. Houston was mainly a distribution center, and manufacturing of paper products made use of the abundant lumber in the nearby pine forests of east Texas.

Three events, spread out over the first 60 years of the twentieth century, transformed the quiet community into the Southwest's largest metropolis. The first was the discovery of oil at Spindletop, near Houston, in 1901. Vast fortunes were made in the oil business, and Houston quickly began to accumulate the financial power it had once seen displayed by its neighbor to the south—Galveston—known in the nineteenth century as the "Wall Street of the South." The second major development came in 1914, when a colossal project began to reshape the Buffalo Bayou into a ship channel, navigable by more than shallow draft riverboats.

The combination of the new port with Houston's position as a major petrochemical center enabled the city to surpass San Antonio's population in the 1930s, becoming the largest city in what was then the nation's largest state. After World War II the petrochemical industry and Houston grew even more rapidly, but Houston remained a large city with a small-town flavor.

A third major development changed that small-town flavor in 1961, when the National Aeronautics and Space Administration chose Houston as the site of its new Manned Spacecraft Center. Suddenly, the quiet little city was home to oil tycoons and glamorous astronauts, world-famous surgeons, and a professional baseball team called the Astros. Eight years later the electric phrase, "Houston, Tranquility Base here, the Eagle has landed," made the city's name the first human word spoken from the surface of a heavenly body other than Earth.

## Oil-Dependency Hurts Economy

When the Arab Oil Embargo of 1973 precipitated a world energy crisis, oil prices rose and earnings doubled and tripled, and so did stock in Houston. New towers of commerce, many designed by world-class architects such as Philip Johnson and I. M. Pei, rose up to forever change the face of Houston's central business district. Companies expanded, venture capital looked for ways to spend new-found wealth, and Houston's population shot up as northern industrial workers, eager for a share of the opportunity, flocked to the city.

Houston became in many ways a one-industry town, with both oil and chemical production feeding one another through the petroleum distillation process. By the mid-1980s Houston was the headquarters for 8 of the 10 largest energy companies, and some 5,000 businesses related to energy were located either in Houston or within 100 miles of the city. The chemical industry in Houston accounted for almost 50 percent of the total U.S. production capacity by 1987, with more than 200 refining and processing plants in the Houston area. But by then the oil market had slumped.

Since the heady days of the oil boom, Houston's importance on the national scene has been largely economic. Reacting to the oil slump, civic and industrial leaders, intent on decreasing the city's reliance on the ups and downs of oil, were determined to build on Houston's strengths. Out of mutual interest, closer ties between the leaders of Houston's three major industries—oil, medicine, and aerospace—were forged in concert with city government and an aggressive chamber of commerce. Houston's story became one of diversity and new growth. The goal of diversification has proven successful, and Houston can count technology, finance, insurance, real estate, and manufacturing among the industries in which it plays a leadership role.

***Historical Information:*** The Heritage Society Research Library, 1100 Bagby, Houston, TX 77002; telephone (713)655-1912; fax: (713)655-7527; email info@heritage society.org. Houston Public Library, Texas and Local History Department, 500 McKinney St., Houston, TX 77002; telephone (832)393-1313

# Population Profile

## Metropolitan Area Residents
*1980:* 2,753,000
*1990:* 3,321,926
*2000:* 4,177,646
*Percent change, 1990–2000:* 25.8%
*U.S. rank in 1980:* 9th (CMSA)
*U.S. rank in 1990:* 10th (CMSA)
*U.S. rank in 2000:* 10th (CMSA)

## City Residents
*1980:* 1,595,138
*1990:* 1,654,348
*2000:* 1,953,631
*2003 estimate:* 2,009,690
*Percent change, 1990–2000:* 18.0%
*U.S. rank in 1980:* 5th
*U.S. rank in 1990:* 4th (State rank: 1st)
*U.S. rank in 2000:* 6th (State rank: 1st)

*Density:* 3,371.7 people per square mile (2000)

*Racial and ethnic characteristics* (2000)
   White: 962,610
   Black or African American: 494,496
   American Indian and Alaska Native: 8,568
   Asian: 103,694
   Native Hawaiian and Pacific Islander: 1,182
   Hispanic or Latino (may be of any race): 730,865
   Other: 321,603

*Percent of residents born in state:* 53.4% (2000)

*Age characteristics* (2000)
   Population under 5 years old: 160,797
   Population 5 to 9 years old: 154,638
   Population 10 to 14 years old: 139,691
   Population 15 to 19 years old: 138,762
   Population 20 to 24 years old: 161,754
   Population 25 to 34 years old: 354,444
   Population 35 to 44 years old: 305,738
   Population 45 to 54 years old: 235,249
   Population 55 to 59 years old: 79,055
   Population 60 to 64 years old: 59,438
   Population 65 to 74 years old: 93,086
   Population 75 to 84 years old: 53,439
   Population 85 years and older: 17,540
   Median age: 30.9 years

*Births* (2002)
   Total number: 44,869

*Deaths* (2002)
   Total number: 14,532 (of which, 318 were infants
      under the age of 1 year)

*Money income* (1999)
   Per capita income: $20,101
   Median household income: $36,616
   Total households: 718,897

*Number of households with income of . . .*
   less than $10,000: 83,410
   $10,000 to $14,999: 49,047
   $15,000 to $24,999: 105,887
   $25,000 to $34,999: 104,792
   $35,000 to $49,999: 117,451
   $50,000 to $74,999: 116,362
   $75,000 to $99,999: 57,368
   $100,000 to $149,999: 49,446
   $150,000 to $199,999: 16,419
   $200,000 or more: 18,715

*Percent of families below poverty level:* 16.0% (44.8% of
   which were female householder families with related
   children under 5 years)

*2002 FBI Crime Index Total:* 149,247

# Municipal Government

Houston, the Harris County seat, has a mayor-council form
of government. The mayor, 14-member city council, and
city controller are elected concurrently to two-year terms.
The mayor serves as the chief executive, the council as the
legislature, and the controller as the financial manager.

**Head Official:** Mayor Bill White (since 2004; current term
   expires 2006)

**Total Number of City Employees:** 21,621 (2004)

*City Information:* City of Houston, 900 Bagby, PO Box
1562, Houston, TX 77251-1562; telephone (713)837-0311

# Economy

## Major Industries and Commercial Activity

Energy has been the primary factor in the Houston economy
since oil was first discovered in the region in 1901. Even
during the oil and gas bust era of the 1980s and the recession
of the early 2000s, the expertise, technology, and resources

remained in the area, providing the crucial base required to meet current national and international market demands while laying the groundwork for future growth. Houston is home to major U.S. energy firms in every segment, including exploration, production, oil field service and supply, and development. About 3,600 energy-related companies lie within the Houston area, including 600 exploration and production firms and 170 pipeline companies. Given the existence of these firms, and the technically trained and experienced work force, Houston no doubt will remain the center of the energy industry in the United States.

During the last decades of the twentieth century, Houston's dependence on the upstream energy industry—which comprises oil and gas exploration and production, oilfield equipment manufacturing and wholesaling, and pipeline transportation—made it particularly vulnerable to economic downturns determined by energy prices, the national economy, and the value of the dollar against foreign currencies. In order to insulate itself from further economic distress, the city began diversifying into downstream energy (refining and chemicals manufacturing) as well as industries unrelated to the energy sector. In 1981 upstream energy represented 68.7 percent of the job market, while downstream energy represented 15.6 percent and diversified sectors represented 15.7 percent. By 2004 upstream energy's percentage was reduced to 31.4 percent while downstream energy increased to 17 percent and diversified industries nearly quadrupled to 51.6 percent.

Houston is also a world leader in the chemical industry, with nearly 40 percent of the nation's capacity for producing the basic chemicals that are used by downstream chemical operations. The Houston-Baytown-Huntsville area is home to 405 chemical plants employing roughly 36,000 people. With an extensive infrastructure that includes the world's most elaborate pipeline network, Houston is a key production center for derivatives and specialty chemicals. Nearly every major chemical company operates a plant near Houston, including BASF AG, Bayer Corp., Chevron Phillips Chemical Co., E. I. du Pont de Nemours Co., ExxonMobil Chemical Co., and Shell Chemical LP.

Through more than a quarter century of manned space flight, Houston has played an important role in space exploration. The Johnson Space Center of the National Aeronautics & Space Administration (NASA) is the focal point of the U.S. manned space flight program. It has primary responsibility for the research, design, development, and testing of the space shuttle, and also selects and trains astronauts and controls manned space flights. Opened in 1962, the 1,620-acre Johnson complex is an international powerhouse of technological development, employing approximately 17,000 engineers, scientists, and administrative personnel.

Financial services are a key component to Houston's economy. The finance/insurance/real estate sector represented 15.4 percent of the Houston region's gross area product in 2003. A number of major financial corporations are headquartered in the city, including American National Insurance Co., real estate firm Century Development, and AIG Retirement Services. Situated near the center of a twenty-county coastal prairie agricultural region, Houston is a major international agribusiness center emphasizing the marketing, processing, packaging, and distribution of agricultural commodities. The city also has a strong presence in computer software, electronics, engineering, and nanotechnology.

*Items and goods produced:* computer software, containers, processed foods, petrochemicals, steel, industrial gases, oil and gas field equipment, synthetic rubber, cement

## Incentive Programs—New and Existing Companies

*Local programs*—The City of Houston offers four types of tax abatements to attract new businesses. Economic development tax abatements are offered to certain types of businesses to encourage investment and job creation. Redevelopment abatements are extended to new development within Tax Abatement Districts or Enterprise Zones, while residential abatements are restricted to Enterprise Zones. Brownfield abatements encourage the redevelopment of brownfields, areas where environmental contamination exists in the soil, surface water, or ground water.

The city also attracts investments in Tax Increment Reinvestment Zones. These zones usually cover portions of the inner city, raw land in suburban fringe areas, or major activity center under decline. Several types of incentives are offered to businesses investing capital and creating new jobs in these areas, and can include capital costs, financing costs, real property assembly, relocation costs, professional services, and administrative costs.

*State programs*— The state of Texas offers a number of incentive programs to attract new and expanding businesses to the state. The Texas Economic Development Act of 2001 encourages large-scale manufacturing, research and development, and renewable energy by offering an eight-year reduction in property taxes. Other property tax incentives are offered to companies owning certain abated property and those that are located in specified areas known as reinvestment zones. The Texas Enterprise Zone Program offers sales and use tax refunds to companies that create jobs in certain economically distressed areas of the state. Other sales and use tax refunds are extended toward manufacturing machinery and equipment, with agricultural products and semiconductor components targeted in particular. Research and development expenditures may be qualified for franchise tax credits, as can businesses creating jobs or injecting capital into ''strategic investment areas.''

*Job training programs*—The Texas Workforce Commission (TWC) provides workforce development assistance to employers and jobseekers across the state through a network of 28 workforce boards. Programs for employers include recruitment, retention, training and retraining, and outplacement services for employees. TWC also administers the Skills Development Fund, a program that assists public community and technical colleges create customized job training for local businesses.

The Houston Community College System (HCC) is the city's leading vehicle for ongoing training and business development. With five regional colleges, HCC has quality, cost-effective training programs conveniently located throughout the Houston area. HCC staff members also can customize training programs to meet a company's specific needs and conduct those classes on site. The HCC Workforce Development Division oversees 67 degree and certificate programs, including accounting, biotechnology, computer science technology, international business, and real estate.

### Development Projects

Two of Houston's biggest initiatives in the early 2000s were to improve the general quality of life and address the traffic situation. These goals were encompassed by Project Houston Hope, under which the city will begin to reverse the downward spiral of distressed neighborhoods by eliminating abandoned property, building affordable housing, attacking the problem of crime, collecting unpaid property taxes, and improving water, sewer, road, and educational services. Improvements to the timing of most of Houston's traffic lights eased traffic congestion and shortened commute times by 10 to 20 percent in 2004.

Houston also took steps to increase its trade infrastructure. Union Pacific Corp. committed $1.5 billion to railway improvements in the Houston-Gulf Coast region. The U.S. government and the State of Texas agreed to the construction of Interstate 69, which will connect Houston with the northeastern U.S. and Canada. An investment of $1.7 billion in George Bush Intercontinental Airport, William P. Hobby Airport, and Ellington Field will improve air connections for passengers and cargo by 2006. Several projects, including construction of new facilities and a channel deepening and widening, are underway at the Port of Houston.

***Economic Development Information:*** Greater Houston Partnership, 1200 Smith, Ste. 700, Houston, TX 77002; telephone (713)844-3600; fax (713)844-0200; email ghp @houston.org

### Commercial Shipping

The Port of Houston is the world's sixth largest port. It ranked first in the nation in total foreign tonnage handled in 2003, and second in total tonnage. More than 6,300 ships called on the port that year, moving 190 million short tons of cargo. This 25-mile long complex is served by the port authority and more than 150 private industrial companies. The port is also the site of Foreign Trade Zone #84, at which foreign goods can be temporarily stored or processed without an import duty. Two major railroads and 150 trucking lines connect the port to the rest of the continental United States, Canada, and Mexico. Major commodities traded at the port include chemicals, petroleum and petroleum products, machinery, motor vehicles, and iron and steel. The Port of Houston Authority is undertaking a number of projects, all scheduled for completion by the end of 2005, to increase and improve the capacity of the port. Among these projects are a deepening and widening of the Houston Ship Channel and a $1.2 billion expansion of its container facilities.

Houston is the international air gateway to the Southwest. George Bush Intercontinental Airport, the 11th largest international air cargo gateway in the nation, shipped 355,000 metric tons in 2004. The William P. Hobby Airport is primarily a domestic passenger airport, though 5,725 cargo tons passed through it in 2003.

Houston is one of the nation's busiest rail centers, with more than 700,000 rail cars passing through the system each year. In addition to links with the three airports, the Port of Houston, and local highways, the rail system is linked with the local trucking industry by six intermodal terminals. The Houston area is served by more than 1,100 trucking firms.

### Labor Force and Employment Outlook

Houston lags just behind the national rate for high school graduates. According to the 2000 census, 76.3 percent of Houston adults completed high school, compared to 80.4 percent for the United States. However, its concentration of college graduates exceeds the national average, with Houston at 26.6 percent and the U.S. average at 24.4 percent.

The Texas Workforce Commission reports that between 1990 and 2005, the service industry accounted for 87 percent of all job growth across the Gulf Coast. Among the fastest growing sectors were computer systems design; architectural and engineering; arts, entertainment, and recreation; employment services; education; and health care and social assistance. The commission projects that the service industry will also be one of the fastest growing sectors throughout the first decade of the twenty-first century, second only to professional occupations. Between 2000 and 2010, professional and related occupations will experience a job growth of 28.9 percent, and service occupations will grow by 24.3 percent. These will be followed by management, business, and financial occupations (19 percent) and construction and extraction occupations (16.3 percent). The slowest growing sector will be farming, fishing, and forestry occupations, with a growth of only 9.8 percent. Overall, the labor force is expected to grow by 22.4 percent.

The following is a summary of data regarding the Houston metropolitan area labor force, 2003 annual averages.

*Size of nonagricultural labor force:* 2,095,800

*Number of workers employed in . . .*
  *natural resources and mining:* 63,400
  *construction:* 158,300
  *manufacturing:* 188,900
  *trade, transportation and utilities:* 440,900
  *information:* 37,300
  *financial activities:* 124,500
  *professional and business services:* 293,000
  *educational and health services:* 233,600
  *leisure and hospitality:* 178,000
  *other services:* 86,300
  *government:* 291,700

*Average hourly earnings of production workers employed in manufacturing:* $17.16

*Unemployment rate:* 5.5% (December 2004)

| Largest downtown employers | Number of employees |
|---|---|
| Shell Oil Co. | 5,744 |
| Harris County | 4,750 |
| Exxon Mobil Corp. | 4,420 |
| City of Houston | 4,000 |
| JPMorgan Chase | 3,000 |
| Continental Airlines Inc. | 2,824 |
| Foley's | 2,500 |
| U.S. Post Office | 2,314 |
| CenterPoint Energy Inc. | 2,199 |
| U.S. Government | 2,100 |

### Cost of Living

Historically, the cost of living has ranked lower in Houston than in most major U.S. cities because residents pay no state or local income tax. Housing in general is extremely attractive in Houston; low housing costs are the main reason Houston's overall living costs in 2004 were about 24 percent below the nationwide average for places of all sizes and run 45 percent below the average for metropolitan areas with a population of more than two million.

The following is a summary of data regarding several key cost of living factors for the Houston area.

*2004 (3rd Quarter) ACCRA Average House Price:* $186,722

*2004 (3rd Quarter) ACCRA Cost of Living Index:* 90.3 (U.S. average = 100.0)

*State income tax rate:* none for personal; $2.50 per $1,000 taxable capital for corporations

*State sales tax rate:* 6.25% (food and prescription drugs are exempt)

*City income tax rate:* none

*City sales tax rate:* 2.0% (of which 1.0% goes to transit authority)

*Property tax rate:* $0.655 per $100 assessed valuation

**Economic Information:** Greater Houston Partnership, 1200 Smith, Ste. 700, Houston, TX 77002; telephone (713)844-3600; fax (713)844-0200; email ghp@houston.org. Texas Workforce Commission, 101 E. 15th St., Rm. 651, Austin, TX 78778-0001; telephone (512)463-2236; email customers @twc.state.tx.us

# Education and Research

### Elementary and Secondary Schools

The Houston Independent School District (HISD) is the largest in Texas and the seventh largest in the United States. In 2002 HISD was named the nation's top-performing urban school district by the California-based Broad Foundation, due in part to its success in narrowing the achievement gap between economic and ethnic groups.

The following is a summary of data regarding Houston's public schools as of the 2003–2004 school year.

*Total enrollment:* 211,157

*Number of facilities*
  *elementary schools:* 183
  *middle schools:* 34
  *senior high schools:* 32
  *other:* 28 charter schools, 114 magnet programs, and 18 combined-level schools

*Student/teacher ratio:* 17:1

*Teacher salaries (2004–2005)*
  *minimum:* $34,068
  *maximum:* $62,774

*Funding per pupil:* $7,589 (2001–2002)

More than 52,000 students are enrolled in the area's 211 private and parochial schools.

**Public Schools Information:** Houston Independent School District, Hattie Mae White Administration Bldg., 3830 Richmond Ave., Houston, TX 77027-5802; telephone (713)892-6391

## Colleges and Universities

Houston's 289,000 college students make it one of the nation's leading academic centers. Forty-one public colleges, universities, and institutes dot the Houston landscape. The oldest is Rice University, while the largest is the University of Houston, with three campuses in the immediate Houston area. Other major educational centers include Texas Southern University, University of St. Thomas, and Houston Baptist University. The city also has three law schools and abundant medical training, including the Baylor College of Medicine and the University of Texas-Houston Health Science Center. The Houston Community College System is one of the city's largest, enrolling 33,821 students in 2002.

## Libraries and Research Centers

Houston has two major public library systems: the Houston Public Library system and the Harris County Public Library system. In addition to the central Houston Public Library downtown, a 333,000-square-foot facility with a capacity of 2 million volumes, the Houston Public Library system encompasses 38 branches along with the Clayton Library for Genealogical Research and the Parent Resource Library in the Children's Museum of Houston. Its collections include the Greenberg Collection, Texas and Local History Collection, U.S. Government Documents, and the Video Library. The system also includes the Houston Metropolitan Research Center, a cooperative project formed in 1976 with Rice University, Texas Southern University, and the University of Houston. Housed in the Julia Ideson Building, this collection makes available the documentary, oral, and visual evidence of Houston's past, including African American, Mexican American, architectural, photographic, jazz music, and oral history components.

The Harris County Public Library maintains 26 branches and 2.3 million items in its collection. Specialized libraries and research centers in Houston range from numerous medical and legal facilities to a library run by the American Brahman Breeders Association.

NASA's Johnson Space Center coordinates a great deal of development and design work for the U.S. Space Station. The University of Houston's 24 research entities include the Texas Learning & Computation Center, the Institute for Space Systems Operations, the Environmental Institute of Houston, Center for Materials Chemistry, Center for Public Policy, and Center for Immigration Research. Rice University conducts more than $40 million in grant research annually in such fields as computing, nanotechnology, laser technology, robotics, groundwater management, toxic chemical clean-up, global warming, material science, astronomy, space physics, and biomedical engineering. The Houston Advanced Research Center combines the facilities of nine major universities in translating scientific advances into practical

applications. Between 2000 and 2004, the Texas Medical Center committed $3.5 billion to research in such areas as cardiovascular, cancer, cell biology, and genetics. Baylor College houses a major center for AIDS research.

***Public Library Information:*** Harris County Public Library, 8080 El Rio, Houston, TX 77054; telephone (713)749-9000. Houston Public Library, 500 McKinney St., Houston, TX 77002; telephone (832)393-1313

# Health Care

With more than 85 hospitals within the metropolitan area, Houston is a world leader in medicine and boasts the world's largest medical complex. Approximately 5.2 million patients—more than 10,000 of them foreign—are treated each year in the Texas Medical Center alone, a centralized facility begun in 1943. The facility's 42 nonprofit and government institutions include 13 hospitals and two specialized patient facilities. It comprises Texas Children's Hospital, Methodist Hospital, and St. Luke's Episcopal Hospital, as well as the M.D. Anderson Cancer Center, which was ranked as the best hospital for cancer treatment by *U.S. News & World Report* in 2004, along with top 10 rankings in the fields of gynecology, urology, and ear, nose, and throat. Houston's medical community is known for its major contributions in the areas of cardiac care, cancer research and therapy, trauma care, and innovative medical treatment. Some of Houston's other major hospitals include the Menninger Clinic and TIRR: The Institute for Rehabilitation & Research.

# Recreation

### Sightseeing

As the nation's fourth largest city, Houston offers a wide selection of recreational opportunities, ranging from professional football, basketball, and baseball to permanent companies in opera, ballet, theater, and symphony. Houston's retail offerings are world class, with several major shopping malls and urban entertainment centers. With mild annual temperatures, abundant lakes, rivers, and wildlife areas, and more than 400 parks, Houston is also very much an outdoor city.

A principal point of interest is the Johnson Space Center, which offers self-guided public tours every day except Christmas. A unit of the National Aeronautics & Space Administration (NASA), the center features a museum,

The San Jacinto Monument.

tours of the Mission Control Center, and viewing of samples returned from the Moon. Space Center Houston allows visitors to "experience" manned space flight, explore shuttle and skylab facilities, and operate the simulator.

The historically minded may be interested in the San Jacinto Battleground State Historical Park, the world's tallest masonry structure. It houses documents, art, and memorabilia, and is a permanent berth for the battleship USS *Texas,* a veteran of both world wars and the only surviving dreadnought of its class.

Hermann Park includes the Houston Zoological Gardens, Miller Outdoor Theatre, the Houston Museum of Natural Science, and the first desegregated public golf course in the nation. Among other parks offering sightseeing opportunities are Memorial Park, featuring an arboretum, herb gardens, and a botanical hall; Sam Houston Park, with seven historical buildings located downtown; and Tranquility Park, in the Houston Civic Center. In the Harris County Park system attractions include Armand Bayou Park and Nature Center, with its wilderness preserve, nature trails, working turn-of-the-century farm, and scenic Armand Bayou boat tours; Mercer Arboretum, featuring gardens, a wilderness preserve, and nature trails; and Bay Area Park, featuring a marsh walkway. Moody Gardens on Galveston Island features a tropical setting with white sand beaches, penguins, and a discovery pyramid.

## Arts and Culture

Houston ranks second only to New York City by number of theater seats in a concentrated downtown area. Moreover, it is one of only a handful of cities in the country to feature permanent dance, theater, symphony, and opera companies. The Wortham Theater Center, a $75 million complex housing the Houston Grand Opera and the Houston Ballet, is the centerpiece of Houston's vital cultural community. That community is supported by a one percent hotel tax dedicated to the city's arts, which have become nationally prominent. The city also features Jesse H. Jones Hall for the Performing Arts, home of the Houston Symphony and Society for the Performing Arts; the Hobby Center for the Performing Arts, the home of Theatre Under the Stars and the SFX Broadway Series; and the Alley Theatre, one of the oldest resident professional theater companies in the nation.

Other famed theater groups include Stages Repertory, Main Street Theater, A.D. Players, De Camera of Houston, Theatre LaB Houston, Opera in the Heights, and the Ensemble Theatre, one of the nation's most respected African American theaters.

The Houston Symphony was formed in 1913 and performs more than 200 concerts each year in Jesse H. Jones Hall for the Performing Arts, plus summer concerts in Miller Theatre. Among other musical groups are the acclaimed Houston

Grand Opera; the Houston Opera Studio, an international apprenticeship center; the Houston Youth Symphony; and the orchestras of four local universities. The Houston Ballet, a professional company, performs at home and abroad. Other dance companies include the Delia Stewart Dance Company, the Discovery Dance Group, Allegro Dance Group, Chrysalis Dance Company, City Ballet of Houston, Cookie Joe and the Jazz Company, and Several Dancers Core.

With 15 world-class museums, Houston is the fourth largest museum district in the nation. The Houston Museum of Natural Science, located near Hermann Park, features the Burke Baker Planetarium, the Wortham IMAX Theatre, and the Cockrell Butterfly Center, as well as exhibits in space science, geography, oceanography, medical science, and Texas wildlife. The Museum of Fine Arts-Houston is the sixth largest museum in the United States and houses more than 27,000 works from antiquities to the present. It also features the Bayou Bend Collection of American decorative arts, housed in the historic home of local philanthropist Ima Hogg and surrounded by 14 acres of gardens. Houston also boasts the world-famous Menil Collection, 15,000 pieces representing twentieth-century, medieval, and Byzantine art, antiquities, and tribal art. The Contemporary Arts Museum exhibits modern works and is free to the public.

Other facilities include Children's Museum of Houston, Holocaust Museum Houston, Art Car Museum, National Museum of Funeral History, Buffalo Soldiers National Museum, American Cowboy Museum, the Moody Mansion & Museum, Museum of Health & Medical Science, Museum of Printing History, and the Byzantine Fresco Chapel Museum, repository for the only intact Byzantine frescoes in the Western Hemisphere. Among the area's galleries are Farish Gallery and Sewall Art Gallery, both on the Rice University campus, and the Sarah Campbell Blaffer Gallery, on the University of Houston campus.

*Arts and Culture Information:* Greater Houston Convention & Visitors Bureau, 901 Bagby, Ste. 100, Houston, TX 77002; telephone (713)227-3100; toll-free: 800-4-HOUSTON

## Festivals and Holidays

Houston celebrates with countless festivals throughout the year. A Grande Parade is held downtown each January in honor of Martin Luther King, Jr. The late-winter Houston Livestock Show & Rodeo commands Reliant Stadium and draws a crowd in excess of 1.8 million over three weeks. Spring is welcomed by the Budweiser Original Zydeco Jamm Festival, an outdoor celebration featuring zydeco music and Cajun-Creole cuisine. April brings the Houston International Festival, a multicultural event spanning 20 city blocks and attracting more than one million visitors across 10 days of performances, art expositions, and open-air markets. The Texas Renaissance Festival is held for eight themed weekends in October and November, while later in November Houston gathers for Washington Mutual's Thanksgiving Day Parade. In December Moody Gardens presents a Festival of Lights, the Heritage Society holds a Christmas Candlelight Tour, and lighted boats are displayed in the Christmas Boat Parade on Clear Lake.

Ethnic celebrations are held throughout the year. They include the Greek Festival, Bayou City Cajun Festival, Japan Festival, Asian Pacific Heritage Festival, Cinco de Mayo Celebration, Scottish Highland Games & Celtic Festival, Fiestas Patrias, Houston Turkish Festival, Festa Italiana, and the Texas Championship Pow Wow. Texans' love of a variety of cuisines is apparent from Houston's numerous food celebrations, such as the Clear Lake Crawfish Festival, Houston Pod Chili Cook-Off, Bayou Boil, and the Pasadena Strawberry Festival, held 20 minutes southeast of Houston. Celebrations of arts are nearly as frequent. Spring brings the Dance Salad Festival, which presents dancers from the Americas, Europe, Asia, and Africa, followed by the Houston International Film Festival. ArtHouston, Houston International Jazz Festival, Houston Shakespeare Festival, Bluegrass Festival, and Caribbean Luau are held in succession between mid-summer and early autumn.

Some events celebrate the unusual, and others are held just for fun. The Houston Comedy Festival features 20 performances across 8 days in April. Galveston Island hosts the FeatherFest, a birding celebration coinciding with the annual spring migration of nearly 300 species. Each May corporate and community teams race 40-foot dragon boats in the Dragon Boat Festival. Ballunar Festival Liftoff, presented by the Johnson Space Center each August, features a weekend of hot-air ballooning, sky-diving exhibitions, and food and entertainment. The U.S. Air Force Thunderbirds and the Navy's Blue Angels thrill spectators with aerial acrobatics each October in the Wings Over Houston Airshow.

## Sports for the Spectator

After losing the Oilers to Tennessee in 1996, Houston regained a National Football League (NFL) franchise when the Houston Texans took the field in 2002. Their home is the 69,500-seat Reliant Stadium, featuring the world's first retractable roof in the NFL. Reliant also hosted Super Bowl XXXVII in February 2004, at which the New England Patriots beat the Carolina Panthers. The Houston Astros, a franchise of the National League of Major League Baseball, play home games at Minute Maid Park. This park was christened Enron Field upon its completion in 2000, then renamed Astros Field when Enron Corp. went bankrupt in 2002, and later that year took its current name in a $170 million, 28-year naming deal with Minute Maid Co., which has been headquartered in Houston since 1967. The Toyota Center opened in September 2003, and is home to the Houston Rockets, of the National Basketball Association; the Houston Comets of the Women's

National Basketball Association; and the Houston Aeros of the American Hockey League. Houston Energy, a franchise of the Women's Professional Football League, play their home games at Rice Stadium.

Collegiate teams participate in most major sports by Houston-area academic institutions. Football is particularly notable, with Rice University in the Western Athletic Conference, the University of Houston in Conference USA, Texas Southern University in the Southwest Athletic Conference, and Houston Baptist University in the Trans America Athletic Conference. Horse racing can be enjoyed at Sam Houston Race Park, while dogs race at Gulf Greyhound Park. More than 150 of the world's best golfers vie for a $5 million purse in the Shell Houston Open Golf Tournament each April.

## Sports for the Participant

Harris County and the City of Houston's 429 parks embrace 43,700 land acres and 12,200 water-covered acres. They offer such attractions for the recreation-minded as seven 18-hole golf courses (plus dozens of non-municipal public and private courses), 43 swimming pools, 236 tennis courts, 174 baseball/softball fields, 124 football/soccer/rugby fields, 164 basketball courts, 80 hiking and cycling trails, 55 community recreation centers, and Lake Houston. Cullen Park, one of the largest municipal parks in the nation, boasts a velodrome equipped for Olympic cycling events. A driving range is available at Memorial Park, fishing is enjoyed at Eisenhower Park, and a three-story man-made mountain graces Herman Brown Park. Harris County parks include Clear Lake Park, with boating and fishing; Alexander Deussen Park, with boating, fishing, and camping on Lake Houston; Bear Creek Park, with an aviary on Addicks Reservoir lands; Bay Area Park, with canoeing; and Tom Bass Regional Park, offering fishing. Houston lies within an hour of 70 miles of Gulf Coast beaches; deep-sea fishing on the Gulf is available through charter companies.

Annual events invite participants of all athletic levels. In March the Tour de Houston attracts competitors in a 20- or 40-mile bike race. For many, the Tour de Houston is a warm-up for the BP MS 150 Bike Tour. Held each April, it is the largest non-profit sporting event in Texas, drawing 12,000 riders and raising more than $47 million in the last two decades to combat multiple sclerosis. Also held in April is the Running of the Bulls, a 5K run attracting 2,500 participants. The Hoopla Streetball Tournament, a weekend of three-on-three basketball games as well as other family attractions, is also held in the spring. The Buffalo Bayou Regatta, Texas' largest canoe and kayak race, is held each October.

## Shopping and Dining

The 375 stores and restaurants of The Galleria, the fifth largest shopping center in the nation, are visited by more than 20 million shoppers each year. Katy Mills Mall houses 200 retail outlets in 1.3 million square feet of space. Uptown Park is a European-style shopping center featuring unique wares. The largest market on the Texas Gulf Coast is Traders Village, a collection of 800 dealers sprawled over 105 acres each weekend. Early 2005 brought the grand opening of Market Square Market, an outdoor marketplace held each Saturday in historic Market Square Park. Antiques and collectibles shoppers seek out Antique World II, Trader Village-Houston, and the Houston Flea Market, while those seeking Western gear head to Stelzig of Texas and The Hat Store.

With more than 6,100 restaurants and 600 bars and nightclubs in the Houston area to choose from, diners can enjoy a great variety of menus and cuisines. Gulf seafood, such as oysters, shrimp, lobster, and fish, is a regional specialty; other regional specialties include Texas beef, barbecue, Southwestern mesquite-grilled food, Tex-Mex and Mexican fare, and traditional Southern dishes like catfish and chicken-fried steak. Ethnic and international establishments in the Houston area offer the cuisine of 35 countries, including France, Italy, Spain, Greece, Morocco, and India.

***Visitor Information:*** Greater Houston Convention & Visitors Bureau, 901 Bagby, Ste. 100, Houston, TX 77002; telephone (713)227-3100; toll-free; 800-4-HOUSTON

# Convention Facilities

The $165-million expansion of the George R. Brown Convention Center was completed in late 2003. Encompassing 1.8 million square feet in total, the center nearly doubled its exhibition space to 853,500 square feet and now features 105 meeting rooms. Adjacent to the Brown Convention Center is the new Hilton Americas-Houston. In addition to more than 1,200 guest rooms, this convention hotel offers 91,000 square feet of flexible meeting space, including 26,000- and 40,000-square foot ballrooms and 30 meeting rooms. Reliant Center, home to the Houston Texans, offers 1.4 million square feet of convention and meeting space.

***Convention Information:*** Greater Houston Convention & Visitors Bureau, 901 Bagby, Ste. 100, Houston, TX 77002; telephone (713)227-3100; toll-free; 800-4-HOUSTON

# Transportation

## Approaching the City

With two major airports and several regional air facilities, Houston ranks as a central transportation hub. Nearly 45 million passengers passed through the Houston Airport System in 2004. Passenger service is provided by all major domestic and international carriers at the George Bush Intercontinental Airport on the north side of the city, and by most major domestic carriers at the more centrally located William P. Hobby Airport about seven miles south of downtown. Ellington Field serves approximately 80,000 private and corporate passengers each year.

Houston is the crossroads for Interstate Highways 10 and 45. Other major highways serving Houston are I-610, US-59, US-290, US-90, SH-288, SH-225, Hardy Toll Road, Beltway 8, and SH-99. Amtrak passenger rail service to Houston is available on the Miami-Houston-Los Angeles routes. Greyhound and Kerrville Bus Company offer regular motor coach service. Visitors can now arrive in Houston via the ocean, as Norwegian Cruise Lines launched service from the Port of Houston in November 2003.

## Traveling in the City

Automobiles constitute one of Houston's principal transportation headaches, although an ambitious transit program offers the hope of unsnarling some of the major traffic problems. An extensive commuter bus system operated by the Metropolitan Transit Authority of Harris County (METRO) provides service in the inner city and most outlying areas with a fleet of 1,595 buses covering 1,285 square miles of service area; in 2001 approximately 120 million passengers rode these buses. In 2004 METRO began operating a light rail system. Initially the line runs a 7.5 mile route through downtown Houston, but is scheduled to expand to 20 miles by 2012 and to 80 miles by 2025.

# Communications

## Newspapers and Magazines

Houston's major daily, the *Houston Chronicle*, is joined by four smaller-circulation dailies and by the weeklies *Houston Business Journal* and *Houston Press,* an alternative paper. Campus newspapers include the *Houston Cougar* (University of Houston), the *Thresher* (Rice University), and the *UHCLidian* (University of Houston-Clear Lake).

## Television and Radio

Eight television stations broadcasting from Houston include five network affiliates, a public broadcasting affiliate that was the nation's first public broadcasting television station, and two independents. Cable television programming is also available in the Houston area. The city's 18 AM and FM radio stations broadcast programming ranging from news,

Spanish-language, and Christian talk shows to top-forty, polka, rhythm and blues, jazz, and country music, university, and public radio.

***Media Information:*** *Houston Chronicle,* 801 Texas Ave., Houston, TX 77002; telephone (713)220-7171

**Houston Online**

City of Houston Home Page. Available www.houstontx.gov

Greater Houston Convention & Visitors Bureau. Available www.visithoustontexas.com

Greater Houston Partnership. Available www.houston.org

Harris County Public Library. Available www.hcpl.lib.tx.us

The Heritage Society. Available www.heritagesociety.org

*Houston Chronicle.* Available www.chron.com

Houston Independent School District. Available www.houstonisd.org

Houston Public Library. Available www.houstonlibrary.org

NASA Johnson Space Center. Available www1.nasa.gov/centers/johnson

Texas Workforce Commission. Available www.twc.state.tx.us

## Selected Bibliography

James, Marquis, *The Raven: A Biography of Sam Houston* (Norwalk, Conn.: Easton Press, 1988)

Landphair, Ted, and Carol M. Highsmith, *Houston: Deep in the Heart* (Houston, TX: Houston International Protocol Alliance, 2000)

McMurtrey, Larry, *Terms of Endearment* (New York: Simon & Schuster, 1975)

Winningham, Geoff, and Alan Reinhart, *A Place of Dreams: Houston, An American City* (Houston, TX: Rice University, 1986)

# San Antonio

## *The City in Brief*

**Founded:** 1718 (incorporated 1809)

**Head Official:** Mayor Ed Garza (D) (since 2001)

**City Population**
   1980: 785,940
   1990: 976,514
   2000: 1,144,646
   2003 estimate: 1,214,725
   Percent change, 1990–2000: 17.2%
   U.S. rank in 1980: 11th
   U.S. rank in 1990: 10th (State rank: 3rd)
   U.S. rank in 2000: 13th (State rank: 3rd)

**Metropolitan Area Population**
   1980: 1,089,000
   1990: 1,325,000

   2000: 1,592,383
   Percent change, 1990–2000: 20.2%
   U.S. rank in 1980: 34th (MSA)
   U.S. rank in 1990: 30th (MSA)
   U.S. rank in 2000: 29th (MSA)

**Area:** 407.6 square miles (2000)
**Elevation:** Approximately 701 feet above sea level
**Average Annual Temperature:** 68.6° F
**Average Annual Precipitation:** 27.9 inches

**Major Economic Sectors:** services, wholesale and retail trade, government
**Unemployment rate:** 4.5% (December 2004)
**Per Capita Income:** $17,487 (2000)

**2002 FBI Crime Index Total:** 94,132

**Major Colleges and Universities:** University of Texas at San Antonio, St. Mary's University, San Antonio College

**Daily Newspaper:** *Express-News*

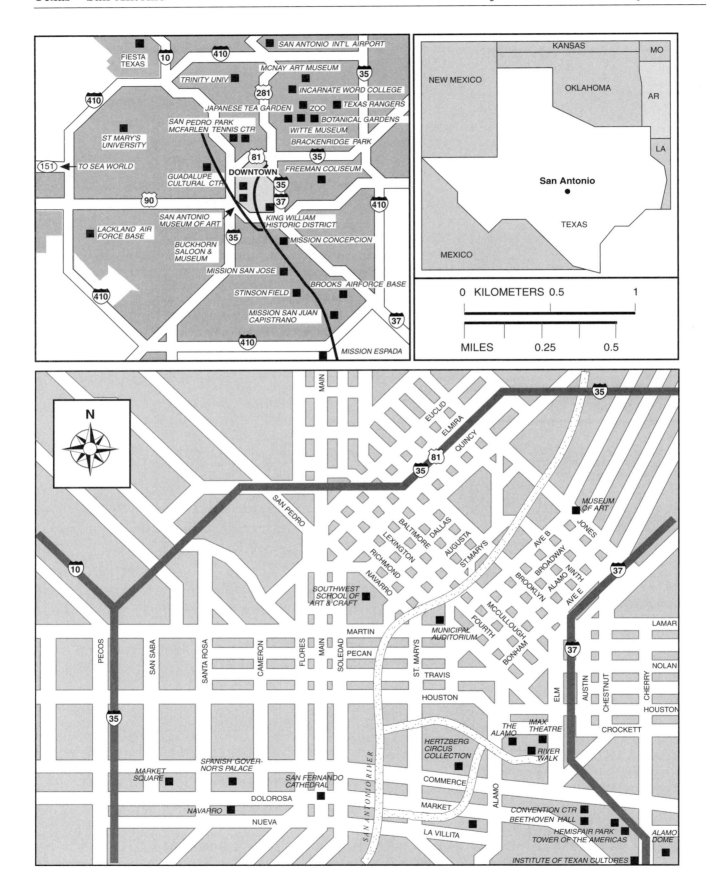

# Introduction

San Antonio, the Alamo City, is often regarded as the Heart of Texas, for its illustrious past and its cosmopolitan present have come to symbolize the rich heritage of the state. The oft-quoted humorist Will Rogers is said to have called San Antonio "one of America's four unique cities," and this Sun Belt metropolis takes pride in its reputation. As large in population as the bustling Dallas, San Antonio retains its small-town flavor while serving as the headquarters for five of the country's major military installations. Besides government, the city's third largest industry, trade, high-technology services, and tourism also profit the local economy. Visitors by the millions are drawn to the city's meandering River Walk, the eighteenth-century Spanish missions, and of course, the site where Davey Crockett, Jim Bowie, William Travis, and 185 others made their last stand in the name of freedom from Mexico. The coexistence of the old and new is one reason San Antonio is viewed as an attractive place to relocate or visit.

# Geography and Climate

Commonly known as "the place where the sunshine spends the winter," San Antonio is situated in south central Texas between the Edwards Plateau to the northwest and the Gulf Coastal Plains to the southeast. The city's gently rolling terrain is dotted with oak trees, mesquite, and cacti, which flourish under the clear or partly cloudy skies that prevail more than 60 percent of the time. Although San Antonio lies 140 miles from the Gulf of Mexico, the seat of Bexar County, pronounced "bear," is still close enough to experience the warm, muggy air of a semitropical climate. During the winter, temperatures drop below the freezing mark an average of only 20 days; precipitation is mostly in the form of light rain or drizzle. Annual rainfall is nearly 28 inches, enough for production of most crops. May and September see the most rainfall, building to thunderstorms with winds from the southeast. The city's proximity to the Gulf of Mexico, however, can bring San Antonio some severe tropical storms. Summers are hot; in fact, federal studies of weather patterns rank San Antonio as the fourth hottest city in the nation because of the average 111 days each year that temperatures reach 90 degrees or higher.

**Area:** 407.6 square miles (2000)

**Elevation:** Approximately 701 feet above sea level

**Average Temperatures:** January, 49.3° F; August, 84.9° F; annual average, 68.6° F

**Average Annual Precipitation:** 27.9 inches

# History

### Alamo Dominates Early History

Crossing six miles of city blocks, the San Antonio River is the focus of the city, just as it has been ever since the surrounding valley drew wandering Coahuitecan tribes seeking respite from the heat. Members of the Payaya tribe who camped on the river's banks named the region Yanaguana, or "Place of Restful Waters." But written records of these tribes' presence are minimal, and it was not until 1691 that the first visit to the river valley was made by a European. That year, on June 13, a day devoted to Saint Anthony of Padua on the Roman Catholic calendar, the river was christened by a Spanish official exploring the region. After he moved on, it was not until 1709 that a second party of Spaniards encountered the river while searching for a site for a new mission. They returned to the area in 1718 to found Mission San Antonio de Valero and Villa de Bexar, the outpost established to govern the Texas province. The mission eventually became the most famous of all Spanish missions established throughout the American Southwest. Although its crude huts were destroyed in 1724 by a hurricane, they were rebuilt on the site where its remains now stand. The mission's nickname became the Alamo; in Spanish, the word "alamo" means cottonwood, and writings by settlers of the period note the region's groves of trees, its water supply, and its mild climate reminiscent of their home country.

Six missions in all were founded around San Antonio, with a goal of converting the native population to Roman Catholicism. A presidio, or fort, was established near each mission, with soldiers to protect the missionaries and, when necessary, to add force to the missionary argument. The system was designed to create new Spanish subjects out of the natives, enabling Spain to hold onto the vast territories it claimed in North America. Historians blame the eventual failure of the mission system on epidemics that reduced the population, periodic raids by Apaches and Comanches, and cultural differences resulting in feuds among friars, soldiers, and colonists. Mission San Antonio was secularized (removed from Church control) in 1793, and the city was incorporated in 1809.

From 1810 to 1821, San Antonio, which served as the seat of the Spanish government in Texas, was the site of several major battles in Mexico's fight for independence from Spain. Anglo-American colonization began with 300 families brought to Texas by Stephen F. Austin, whose father envisioned a settlement with ties to neither Spain nor Mexico. By 1835, the settlers' resentment of Mexico had grown into an armed revolt. Mexico's first attempt to quell the rebellion was defeated. In revenge, Mexican dictator Antonio López de Santa Anna brought with him an army of 5,000 men to attack San Antonio's defenders, a force of fewer than

200 Texans fighting from inside the fortified Alamo. Among those within its walls who held off Santa Anna's troops for 13 days beginning in February 1836, were frontiersman Davey Crockett, soldier Jim Bowie, and Lieutenant Colonel William Travis, who vowed to neither surrender nor retreat.

## Statehood's Aftermath

The "Victory or Death" dedication of the Alamo's defenders, who ultimately perished when their call for reinforcements went unanswered, inspired other insurgents throughout Texas to take up arms against Mexico. Forty-six days after the Alamo fell—to the battle cry "Remember the Alamo!"—Sam Houston's Texans defeated Santa Anna at San Jacinto, and the Republic of Texas was established. The battles and uncertainties, however, did not end until 1845 when Texas became the twenty-eighth U.S. state. The ensuing period brought an influx of German settlers to San Antonio, which increased the population from about 800 to 8,000 people. Texas, aligned with the Confederacy in the Civil War, maintained its rough frontier atmosphere until 1877, when the railroad linked the isolated region with the rest of the nation.

## The City in the Twentieth Century

A regional cattle industry evolved, and San Antonio's progress was further enhanced with the advent of gas lights, telephones, and electricity. When the city entered the twentieth century, it was a melting pot of German and Hispanic influence, and its population swelled with newcomers from urban America. Between 1870 and 1920 San Antonio grew to 161,000 people, making it Texas's largest city. Shortly after the turn of the century, "Aeroplane No. 1," a Wright brothers-type aircraft, flew over Fort Sam Houston and marked the debut of military aviation as an economic force in the region. Downtown businesses flourished, and the coming of the automobile fed the growth of newer surrounding communities.

World War I solidified San Antonio's position as a military command center; 70,000 troops trained there in 1917 and 1918. The war also diminished the status of the city's German community, leading to the resurgence of the Hispanic population, which was growing due to the influx of hundreds of thousands of Mexicans into Texas. San Antonio's Great Flood of 1921 left destruction in its wake, but by 1929 the city's adobe structures were complemented by skyscrapers, the most notable being the Tower Life Building, at one time the tallest office building in the state. San Antonio's Conservation Society became a vigorous presence in the preservation of the city's historical treasures, including the river around which it is built.

The onset of World War II meant intensive military activity for San Antonio. Lackland Air Force Base, for instance,

trained more than one third of the war's air cadets. Expansion of the military complex led to tremendous postwar growth for the city and its environs. The 1968 HemisFair celebration placed an international spotlight on the city, attracting thousands of visitors, including some who decided to make the thriving Sun Belt community their home. By the 1970s the city's population numbered well over 700,000 people, of which more than half were Hispanic. Demand for more services and housing increased, yet language and cultural barriers had created pockets of poverty and ethnic tensions. Politics reflected the city's changing mood, and in 1975 Lila Cockrell became the first woman mayor of San Antonio. Eventually the Hispanic majority concentrated its new political force in the person of Councilman Henry Cisneros, elected in 1981 as the country's first Mexican-American mayor of a major city. San Antonio entered the 1980s as a national example of growing Latin influence in politics. The 1990 groundbreaking for the Alamodome, a $170 million domed stadium which served as the home to the NBA Spurs and was the city's first venue for major conventions and special events, marked the beginning of a progressive decade for the city. In recent years the city has seen further growth, with the completion of such projects as the expansion of the Henry B. Gonzalez Convention Center, which has helped bring the city's annual convention attendance to 500,000, and the completion of the SBC Center, a new home for the Spurs. The Mission Trails project, which will make the area's historic missions more easily accessible, is nearing completion. San Antonio's multifaceted allure currently brings nearly 8 million visitors to the city per year.

***Historical Information:*** San Antonio Conservation Society, 418 Villita Street, San Antonio, TX 78205; telephone (210)224-5711

# *Population Profile*

## Metropolitan Area Residents
*1980:* 1,089,000
*1990:* 1,324,749
*2000:* 1,592,383
*Percent change, 1990–2000:* 20.2%
*U.S. rank in 1980:* 34th (MSA)
*U.S. rank in 1990:* 30th (MSA)
*U.S. rank in 2000:* 29th (MSA)

## City Residents
*1980:* 785,940
*1990:* 976,514
*2000:* 1,144,646
*2003 estimate:* 1,214,725
*Percent change, 1990–2000:* 17.2%

*U.S. rank in 1980:* 11th

*U.S. rank in 1990:* 10th (State rank: 3rd)

*U.S. rank in 2000:* 13th (State rank: 3rd)

*Density:* 2,808.5 people per square mile (2000)

*Racial and ethnic characteristics* (2000)
   White: 774,708
   Black or African American: 78,120
   American Indian and Alaska Native: 9,584
   Asian: 17,934
   Native Hawaiian and Pacific Islander: 1,067
   Hispanic or Latino (may be of any race): 671,394
   Other: 263,233

*Percent of residents born in state:* 66.8% (2000)

*Age characteristics* (2000)
   Population under 5 years old: 92,446
   Population 5 to 9 years old: 91,849
   Population 10 to 14 years old: 89,113
   Population 15 to 19 years old: 88,951
   Population 20 to 24 years old: 87,684
   Population 25 to 34 years old: 177,842
   Population 35 to 44 years old: 174,810
   Population 45 to 54 years old: 138,880
   Population 55 to 59 years old: 46,898
   Population 60 to 64 years old: 36,811
   Population 65 to 74 years old: 64,108
   Population 75 to 84 years old: 41,707
   Population 85 years and older: 13,547
   Median age: 31.7 years

*Births* (2002)
   Total number: 23,169

*Deaths* (2002)
   Total number: 9,386 (of which, 168 were infants under
      the age of 1 year)

*Money income* (1999)
   Per capita income: $17,487
   Median household income: $36,214
   Total households: 405,887

*Number of households with income of . . .*
   less than $10,000: 46,058
   $10,000 to $14,999: 28,462
   $15,000 to $24,999: 61,545
   $25,000 to $34,999: 59,989
   $35,000 to $49,999: 69,799
   $50,000 to $74,999: 72,213
   $75,000 to $99,999: 32,724
   $100,000 to $149,999: 23,245
   $150,000 to $199,999: 5,942
   $200,000 or more: 5,910

*Percent of families below poverty level:* 14.0% (23.1% of
   which were female householder families with related
   children under 5 years)

*2002 FBI Crime Index Total:* 76,777

# Municipal Government

San Antonio, the Bexar County seat, is administered by a
council-manager form of city government. City council members are elected from 10 districts and the mayor is elected at-
large. The mayor and city council appoint the city manager.

**Head Officials:** Mayor Ed Garza (D) (since 2001; current
   term expires 2005); City Manager J. Rolando Bono

**Total Number of City Employees:** more than 12,000 (2004)

*City Information:* City of San Antonio, PO Box 839966,
San Antonio, TX 78283; telephone (210)207-7060; fax
(210)207-4077

# Economy

## Major Industries and Commercial Activity

As of February 2005, San Antonio has seen 13 consecutive
quarters of economic growth and has earned a top ranking
among large Texas cities. The largest employment sectors in
San Antonio are services, manufacturing, and government.
The large concentration of government workers is due mainly
to the location of four military bases in the area—three Air
Force bases (Brooks, Lackland, and Randolph) and one Army
post (Fort Sam Houston). From the days its first mission and
accompanying presidio military post were founded in 1718,
San Antonio has been regarded as an area of strategic importance. By the end of World War II, the city had become the
location for the nerve center of the nation's defense network,
and it remains the headquarters for the largest military establishment in the United States. The bases provide employment
to approximately 74,500 military and civilian personnel and
have an economic impact on the local community of $4.9
billion. In July of 2001, another of San Antonio's military
bases—Kelly—closed and was redeveloped as KellyUSA, a
commercial port. Comprised of an airport and rail-served
business park, KellyUSA employs 12,361 people (among
them, 7,221 Air Force employees) and has a $2.5 billion eco-
nomic impact on the San Antonio area.

The service sector is the largest and fastest growing sector of
the economy, largely because of increased demand for

health care and business services, and San Antonio's sound tourism industry. Medical and biomedical industries now account for the largest part of the city's economy, contributing approximately $11.9 billion to the area in 2003. San Antonio's highly regarded medical industry includes the 900-acre South Texas Medical Center, which employs approximately 25,000 people. Medical industry employees account for 14 percent of all employees in the San Antonio. In a 2003 survey by the Tourism Division of Texas, 5 of the top 10 tourist draws in the state were in San Antonio, with the Alamo and the River Walk in the number one and two spots, respectively. The attractions of the Alamo City, as San Antonio is known, appeal to tourists from across the country. Approximately 8 million people visit San Antonio per year, and the tourism industry has an estimated $4 billion impact on the city's economy.

Toyota Motor Corp. recently chose the San Antonio area as the location for one of its newest truck manufacturing plants. The plant, expected to generate approximately 2,500 jobs, will produce approximately 150,000 trucks annually. Production start-up is scheduled for 2006.

*Items and goods produced:* processed foods, airplane parts, storage batteries, steel forms, structural steel, food handling equipment, semiconductors, rolled aluminum sheet, cement

### Incentive Programs—New and Existing Companies

*Local programs*—The San Antonio Economic Development Foundation is a not-for-profit organization, founded and supported by the business community of San Antonio for the purpose of recruiting new manufacturing, office, research and development, warehousing, and distribution operations to San Antonio. The staff provides factual information on the community from which a business can make an informed decision on establishing or relocating a new facility in San Antonio. The City of San Antonio's Economic Development Department (EDD) helps relocating, expanding, and start-up businesses. EDD offers a variety of financial incentives to encourage business and residential development, including tax and fee incentives, financing, regulatory reductions, and workforce development assistance, and provides customized, one-on-one service.

*State programs*—Texas is a right-to-work state. Texas Economic Development is the state's leading economic development agency. It offers financial incentives through various programs: the Capital Access Fund supports businesses and nonprofits that fall outside the guidelines of conventional lending or otherwise face barriers in accessing capital; Linked Deposit Fund encourages lending to non-profits, childcare-providers, historically underutilized businesses, and/or small businesses; Leverage Fund is an "economic development bank" providing financing to Texas cities that have passed an

economic development sales tax; Industrial Revenue Bonds offers tax-exempt financing on land and property for eligible industrial or manufacturing projects; Defense Zone Program supports Texas's military presence; and Enterprise Zone Program encourages investment and job creation in areas or "zone"s of economic distress. San Antonio has five designated enterprise zones.

*Job training programs*—The Alamo Workforce Development Council will assist businesses in employee recruitment, screening, assessment, and customized training. Also, the State's Skills Development Fund has $25 million available to fund training programs designed by employers in partnership with local community colleges. The Texas Workforce Commission provides funds for training. In 2003 there were 32 grants, totaling $12 million.

### Development Projects

San Antonio is getting ready to welcome even more visitors with its expanded convention center, the new SBC Center sports arena (opened in October of 2002), and other new construction. In 2004, $2.2 billion worth of construction permits were issued; the city usually is in the $1.4 billion to $1.6 billion range. Projects underway as of 2005 include the building of a new Texas A&M campus, a new convention center hotel, the Toyota plant, and several retail centers. San Antonio's Henry B. Gonzalez Convention Center recently underwent a six-year, $218-million expansion that increased its square footage to 1.3 million. The convention center has more than 203,000 square feet of meeting space that is divisible in 67 ways, four exhibit halls offering a total of approximately 440,000 square feet of contiguous display space, and three ballrooms. The convention center complex also features the Lila Cockrell Theatre, a performance art theater offering seating for more than 2,500. The San Antonio Spurs share the SBC Center, a $175 million, 18,500-seat venue, with the San Antonio Livestock Exposition.

***Economic Development Information:*** San Antonio Economic Development Foundation, 602 East Commerce Street, San Antonio, TX 78205; telephone (210) 226-1394; fax (210)223-3386; email edf@dcci.com. City of San Antonio Economic Development Department, PO Box 839966, San Antonio, TX 78283-3966; telephone (210)207-8080; fax (210)207-8151

### Commercial Shipping

Positioned on airline, highway, and railroad routes to Mexico, San Antonio is also the center of a 47-county agribusiness market area for crops grown elsewhere in the state of Texas. San Antonio firms handle processing, packaging, and nationwide distribution of vegetables, pecans, watermelons, and citrus fruits. Livestock, poultry and poultry products, and dairy products also pass through San Antonio.

San Antonio's KellyUSA is a major logistics port. It has 300,000 square feet of warehouse space available and 11,500-foot heavy-duty runway. Kelly is directly linked by three interchanges with Interstate-90 to I-35, I-10, and I-37, and is located on two major rail lines. San Antonio International Airport provides direct and non-stop service to all major hubs. Dallas and Houston are 50 minutes away by air and Mexico City is one and one-half hours away. Stinson Municipal Airport handles general aviation traffic and acts as a reliever airpost for San Antonio International Airport. Two freight railroads serve the area, providing service to Mexico and linking San Antonio with St. Louis. The city of San Antonio operates a general purpose Foreign Trade Zone (FTZ) under the supervision of the U.S. Customs Service. Sometimes referred to as "free ports," FTZs are secured areas that officially fall outside U.S. Customs territory. FTZs help U.S.-based businesses cut costs, improve cash flow, and increase return on investment by deferring, reducing, or altogether eliminating duties and excise taxes if the final product is exported from the zone.

**Labor Force and Employment Outlook**

San Antonio's economy saw unprecedented growth in the 1990s and has remained strong in recent years. In 2004, Houston was the only Texas city to exceed San Antonio's job growth rate; that year, the San Antonio area added 12,000 new jobs. In 2005, an additional 18,500 new jobs are expected. A local economist theorizes that the remarkable strength of San Antonio's job market can be attributed to its economic diversity. Projected job growth between 2005 and 2009 is expected to be 87,340 new jobs, with the largest gains projected in the following sectors: services; trade; government; finance, insurance, and real estate; and construction.

The following is a summary of data regarding the San Antonio metropolitan area labor force, 2003 annual averages.

*Size of nonagricultural labor force:* 725,000

*Number of workers employed in . . .*
   *natural resources and mining:* 2,300
   *construction:* 39,900
   *manufacturing:* 45,400
   *trade, transportation and utilities:* 129,800
   *information:* 23,500
   *financial activities:* 59,200
   *professional and business services:* 85,800
   *educational and health services:* 96,500
   *leisure and hospitality:* 80,400
   *other services:* 27,200
   *government:* 135,000

*Average hourly earnings of workers employed in manufacturing:* $10.85

*Unemployment rate:* 4.5% (December 2004)

| Largest employers | Number of employees |
|---|---|
| United Service Automobile Assoc. (insurance) | 13,773 |
| H.E.B. Food Stores | 9,942 |
| H.B. Zachry Co. (contractors) | 8,000 |
| SBC Communications | 7,000 |
| Southwestern Bell | 4,589 |
| Frost National Bank | 3,290 |
| West Telemarketing | 3,087 |
| Taco Cabana | 3,000 |
| Ultramar Diamond Shamrock (oil refining) | 2,857 |
| QVC Network | 2,034 |

**Cost of Living**

San Antonio's cost of living is one of the lowest among large American cities. San Antonio's housing costs rank among the lowest of the 25 largest metropolitan areas.

The following is a summary of data regarding several key cost of living factors for the San Antonio area.

*2004 (3rd Quarter) ACCRA Average House Price:* $238,000

*2004 (3rd Quarter) ACCRA Cost of Living Index:* 95.2 (U.S. average = 100.0)

*State income tax rate:* None

*State sales tax rate:* 6.25% (groceries and medicines are exempt)

*Local income tax rate:* None

*Local sales tax rate:* 1.5% (groceries, medicines, rent, mortgage payments, and gasoline are exempt)

*Property tax rate:* $0.58 per $100 of assessed valuation (100% of market value) for real property; also hospital and school district, county and flood taxes (2003)

***Economic Information:*** San Antonio Economic Development Foundation, 602 East Commerce Street San Antonio, TX 78205; telephone (210) 226-1394; fax (210)223-3386. City of San Antonio, Economic Development Department, PO Box 839966, San Antonio, TX 78283; telephone (210)207-8080

# *Education and Research*

**Elementary and Secondary Schools**

Unlike many school systems elsewhere, the San Antonio area's 19 school districts (the largest of which—the Northside Independent School District—is the sixth largest in Texas) function as separate, independent entities. Each has its own superintendent, its own elected board of education, and its own taxing authority. The Texas Education Agency in Austin oversees all districts, but they function apart from city or county jurisdiction.

The public school system in San Antonio is supplemented by specialized high schools including the Business Careers High School, Jay Science & Engineering Academy High School, Communication Arts High School, and Health Careers High School, which provide curriculums focused on specific fields of study.

The following is a summary of data regarding the Northside Independent School District as of the 2003-2004 school year.

*Total enrollment:* 74,018

*Number of facilities*
  *elementary schools:* 54
  *middle schools:* 14
  *senior high schools:* 12
  *other:* 19

*Student/teacher ratio:* 15.6:1

*Teacher salaries*
  *minimum:* $35,020
  *maximum:* $59,051

*Funding per pupil:* $6,933

More than 100 parochial schools and private schools also operate in San Antonio.

***Public Schools Information:*** Northside Independent School District, 5900 Evers Road, San Antonio, TX 78238; telephone (210)397-8500

## Colleges and Universities

Variously offering associate, undergraduate, and graduate degrees in many disciplines, San Antonio's institutions of higher learning include the University of Texas at San Antonio (UTSA), is comprised of Colleges of Business, Education and Human Development, Engineering, Liberal and Fine Arts, Sciences, Public Policy, and Honors College; a school of Architecture; and Graduate School. UTSA offers 106 undergraduate and graduate degree programs and is the second largest University of Texas component after UT at Austin. At the University of Texas Health Science Center, students pursue degrees in medicine, dentistry, and nursing, and receive training at affiliated teaching hospitals. Trinity University, a private school founded by Presbyterians that offers its students degrees in the liberal arts and the sciences, has been repeatedly selected by *U.S. News and World Report* as one of the best colleges in the western U.S.; in 2005 Trinity ranked

1st overall among schools offering undergrad and master's programs in this region. St. Mary's University, a private Catholic institution, is particularly known for its law and business schools. University of the Incarnate Word, also a private Catholic school, is known for its nursing curriculum. Our Lady of the Lake University is a private Catholic institution that emphasizes minority programs, particularly for Hispanics. Oblate School of Theology is a private Catholic college serving men and women seeking graduate study in theology. San Antonio College, one of the major junior colleges in Texas, has an average enrollment of more than 22,000 students and is among the largest single-campus two-year colleges in the United States. St. Philip's College, a two-year public facility that focuses its curriculum on restaurant management, data processing, and health-related fields as well as arts and sciences, was founded in 1898 and is one of the oldest and most diverse community colleges in the country. San Antonio's Universidad Nacional Autonoma de Mexico (National Autonomous University of Mexico) offers Hispanic-oriented courses and is the only U.S. branch of UNAM's home campus in Mexico City, Mexico. Palo Alto College, a two-year college in San Antonio's south side, has recently added new programs in Academic Computing Technology, Aviation Management, Criminal Justice, Environmental Technology, Electrical Mechanical Technology, Health Professions, Logistics, Nursing, Teacher Assistant, and Turfgrass Management.

## Libraries and Research Centers

The San Antonio Public Library operates the San Antonio Central Library and 18 branch libraries across the city. The Central Library at 600 Soledad Street has received national attention for its unique design and color (''enchilada red''). The library was designed by Ricardo Legorreta Arquitectos of Mexico City. The library collection encompasses 1.8 million volumes. The Central Library houses the Texana/Genealogy and Latino reference collections, showcasing the history, culture, and art of the region. The Central Library also features an art gallery with exhibits that change periodically. The Central Library is six stories high plus a basement level; the entire third floor is devoted to children 3 and under. Children have their own ''KidsCat'' computer catalog and a spacious story and craft room.

San Antonio's numerous research centers include those supported by the University of Texas in the fields of archaeology, environmental resources, neuroscience, women's studies, biotechnology, culture and community, aging, music, bioengineering; UT's Health Science Center has many additional research centers, devoted to areas of the medical field. Others include the Texas Public Policy Foundation, the U.S. Army Institute of Surgical Research, and the Mexican-American Cultural Center, which seeks the harmonious integration of Hispanic and North American cultures in a manner consistent with democratic and Christian precepts. San Antonio's Southwest Research Institute occupies 1,200 acres and has a staff of 2,800 studying many topics such as automation, robotics, space sciences, and fuels and lubricants.

***Public Library Information:*** San Antonio Public Library, 600 Soledad Street, San Antonio, Texas 78205; telephone (210)207-2500

# Health Care

The 900-acre South Texas Medical Center (STMC) includes the prestigious University of Health Science Center at San Antonio, nine major hospitals including a veterans hospital, two physical rehabilitation centers, and two psychiatric hospitals. Approximately 25,000 people are employed at the facilities of STMC, which is recognized worldwide by medical and health care professionals for the impact of its advanced research, patient diagnosis, treatment and rehabilitation, degree programs, and state-of-the-art physical structures.

The San Antonio area also has numerous medical facilities outside the boundaries of the South Texas Medical Center, including over two dozen general hospitals, two state hospitals, two children's psychiatric hospitals, and two Department of Defense hospitals: Brooke Army Medical Center at Fort Sam Houston, one of the Army's largest and considered a premier burn treatment facility, and Wilford Hall Medical Center, the Air Force's largest medical facility, at Lackland Air Force Base.

***Health Care Information:*** Bexar County Medical Society, 6243 West Ih 10, Suite 600, San Antonio, TX 78201

# Recreation

### Sightseeing

San Antonio's most popular tourist destinations are the Alamo and the Paseo del Rio, or River Walk. The River Walk is a one and a half mile winding waterway of landscaped cobblestone paths and bridges set 20 feet below street level. The result of a downtown urban revitalization project, the River Walk is lined with cafes, shops, galleries, restaurants, and nightclubs. A visitor can sample the flavor of Mexico or relive the birth of Texas by simply enjoying the scenery, day or night. Tree-lined footpaths are lighted at night, creating a romantic ambience. For those who want

more than a waterside view, boats cruise the 21 blocks at 10-minute intervals.

Mission San Antonio de Valero, the Alamo, was the first of five missions established in San Antonio and dates back to 1718 and is located downtown near the river. The chapel's facade represents what is left of the site where nearly 200 Texans died in their fight for independence from Mexico. Nearby lies the Long Barracks Museum and Library. In October of 2005, the Museum will unveil a new exhibit that will incorporate recent interpretations of events that occurred at the Alamo, and the Alamo's place in history. The four other missions are all part of the San Antonio Missions National Park, a 10 mile long Mission Trail that begins at the Alamo, located at street level between Commerce and Houston Streets on Alamo Plaza.

A walking tour from the town's center will take in a number of other attractions. Among them are La Villita, the ''little town,'' adjacent to the River Walk on Alamo Street and across from the Convention Center, where former adobe houses along cobblestone walkways now contain shops, galleries, and a museum; Market Square with its Farmers Market and El Mercado area, with its specialty shops and weekend arts demonstrations; HemisFair Park, site of San Antonio's World's Fair in 1968 and now the center of downtown entertainment; and the King William Historic Area, a 25-block area that had been San Antonio's most elegant residential area, near downtown on the river's south banks.

Now a National Historic District, La Villita was the city's earliest settlement, evolving into a slum by the 1930s. After extensive renovation, it is now home to artists and craftspeople. Market Square is billed as the home of chili, and chili stands draw numerous visitors. The square is also host to a number of citywide festivals throughout the year. Each morning in the Farmers Market section of Market Square, fresh produce is sold directly to consumers. And in El Mercado, patterned after a Mexican market, there are 80 specialty shops. Inside the 92-acre HemisFair Plaza stands the Tower of the Americas, where an observation deck provides a panoramic view of the city from 500 feet up. The King William Historic Area serves as a reminder of the city's German heritage, and its stately mansions date to the 1800s. In the King William Historic Area, the Steves Homestead, an 1876 mansion with a slate mansard roof and 13-inch think limestone walls houses Victorian antiques and is open to the public.

The colorful flora and fauna of the Japanese Tea Gardens located at the northwestern edge of 343-acre Brackenridge Park offer a change of pace to visitors. The Sunken Garden Theatre here features Sunday afternoon concerts in the summertime. The main entrance to the park is about two miles from downtown. Inside the park are a bike trail, picnic area,

San Jose Mission is one of five missions established in San Antonio.

polo field, golf course, carousel, a miniature railroad, riding stables, and paddle boats. The San Antonio Zoo, where exotic animals roam in barless cages, is also located in Brackenridge Park. The 35-acre Zoo is particularly notable for its endangered animals, including snow leopards, Sumatran tigers, and white rhinos. The newest addition to the Zoo is its Kronkosky's Tiny Tot Nature Spot, designed to connect children aged five and younger with the natural world. Across from the zoo's main entrance is the Skyride, where cable cars afford a panoramic view of the city's skyline. Nearby is Splashtown waterpark, which features water slides and south Texas's largest wave pool.

The military bases of San Antonio are also tourist destinations, but public access can vary. Group tours are welcomed, but advance reservations are advised at all posts except Fort Sam Houston, which is open to the public without restriction. Established in 1876 at its present location, historic Fort Sam Houston was the site of the first military airplane flight. Located here are the Army Medical Department Museum, which traces the history of the U.S. Army medical department with its collection of U.S. Army uniforms, medical equipment, and POW memorabilia; the Fort Sam Houston Museum, which houses a collection of military memorabilia; and the Post Chapel, built in 1917 and dedicated by President Taft. Birds and small animals roam the quadrangle grounds, where the centerpiece is the clock tower. Brooks Air Force Base, now known as Brooks City Base, permits the public to tour the Hangar 9/Edward H. White Museum, the oldest in the Air Force, which contains capsules used by the first space monkeys. A History and Traditions Museum at Lackland Air Force Base contains combat aircraft parts. Randolph Air Force Base features the Taj Mahal offices of the 12th Flying Wing. The rotunda of the white structure displays aviation memorabilia.

The newest San Antonio attractions include Sea World San Antonio, the world's largest marine life showplace and home of The Steel Eel exhibit, the Southwest's only hypercoaster; and Six Flags Fiesta Texas, a $100 million showplace park with live musical productions and world-class rides, including the Rattler, the world's tallest, fastest, and steepest wooden roller coaster. Fiesta Texas added $30 million in new rides and attractions in 1999, including a million-gallon wave pool shaped like the state of Texas. Other sites of note in the San Antonio area include San Fernando Cathedral, where the remains of Alamo heroes are thought to be held in a marble coffin on display; Spanish Governor's Palace, called the "most beautiful building in San Antonio" by the National Geographic Society, a national historic landmark dating from 1749 that once served as offices for the Spanish Province of Texas; San Antonio Botanical Gardens, emphasizing native Texas vegetation and incorporating a biblical garden, a children's garden, and a conservatory featuring tropical and exotic plants; and Jose

Antonio Navarro State Historical Park, the former home of the prominent Texan who participated in the convention to ratify Texas as a state.

## Arts and Culture

When actress Sarah Bernhardt performed in San Antonio's Grand Opera House, built in 1886, she called the city "the art center of Texas." While San Antonio attracts well-known performers, it is perhaps better known for opening its cultural doors to the public through colorful festivals that celebrate the blending of its Anglo-Hispanic heritage. The San Antonio Performing Arts Association, founded in 1976, functions as the city's presenter agency.

The Majestic Performing Arts Center, a relic of the days of "movie palaces," has been restored and is home to the San Antonio Symphony, which enjoys a reputation as one of the best in the country. Its repertoire ranges from pops to classical. The Majestic Theater plays host to many of the city's premier events, ranging from traveling Broadway companies to ballet performances to classical music concerts. Not simply a theater or a museum, the Carver Community Cultural Center is a showcase for African American artists while also providing entertainment with broad cultural appeal. Music, literature, art, drama and dance, and a major film festival, all with a Hispanic flavor, are combined at the Guadalupe Cultural Arts Center, where local, national, and international presentations are offered. Grand Opera is performed by the San Antonio Opera Company. The Chamber Arts Ensemble and the Texas Bach Choir, the only one of its kind in the state, round out San Antonio's musical options.

Flamenco dancing is offered at the Arneson River Theatre, a unique venue spanning both sides of the river. The Mexican Cultural Institute showcases folkloric dance as well as theater.

Among the city's museums and galleries is the San Antonio Museum of Art, one of the largest museums in the Southwest and home to the Nelson A. Rockefeller Center for Latin American Art, featuring a 2,500-piece collection dating as far back as 500 B.C.; notable works include a portrait of a Mayan nobleman from A.D. 700-900. An expansion of the museum's Asian wing is underway and will add 9,000 square feet of new art gallery space for Asian art, as well as renovate the museum's current 6,000 square feet of Asian art space. Witte Museum, located at one of the Brackenridge Park entrances, presents local and natural history exhibits and special children's exhibits. Marion Koogler McNay Art Museum is a former private mansion that now houses modern art. The folk history of Texas unfolds through a multimedia exhibit using 36 screens at the Institute of Texan Cultures. Oddities and western memorabilia are the focus at the Buckhorn Saloon and Museum, housed in a renovated 1881 saloon.

Other special collections and contemporary and historical exhibits are on display at the Mexican Cultural Institute; HemisFair Plaza, featuring art from Mexico and South America; the Pioneer, Trail Drivers and Texas Rangers Memorial Museum; the Hertzberg Circus Collection, where Tom Thumb's carriage is among more than 20,000 items representing big top memorabilia; and the Buckhorn Museum containing curiosities such as a two headed calf and a lamb with eight legs. New attractions directly across from the Alamo are the Guinness World Records Museum; Ripley's Haunted Adventure, a multi-million dollar haunted house; and the Plaza Wax Museum. The San Antonio IMAX Theatre at Rivercenter shows a 48-minute docudrama depicting the famous battle at the Alamo. Images shown on a huge screen and magnetic surround sound makes viewers feel that they are there in the thick of battle.

### Festivals and Holidays

For ten days in mid-April, from dawn to well past dusk, San Antonio celebrates the Fiesta San Antonio. Featuring more than 150 events illustrative of the city's gastronomic, ethnic and western history, Fiesta starts out with an oyster bake and culminates in colorful spectacles. Along the way revelers enjoy the crowning of King Antonio, a giant block party known as A Night in Old Santonio, fireworks, musical productions, fashion shows, and the Battle of the Flowers parade, in which 7,000 participants honor the Queen of the Order of the Alamo and her court. Flickering torches light up the Fiesta Flambeau parade; other activities include street dancing, a carnival, and concerts. Fiesta events have multiplied over the years, and they now attract some 3.5 million people annually.

San Antonio hosts a number of other celebrations and festivals throughout the year. The San Antonio River takes the spotlight in January when River Walk Mud Festival revolves around the annual draining of the river for maintenance. Championship rodeo competitors display their skills during February's San Antonio Stock Show and Rodeo, a 16-day western roundup that begins with a downtown parade. In March the San Antonio River is renamed the River Shannon and is dyed green for the St. Patrick's Day celebration, when Irish music and entertainment prevail. The Starving Artists Show in early April brings professionals and amateurs to the River Walk to sell their creations. The Cinco de Mayo events during the weekend nearest May 5 celebrate one of Mexico's Independence Days through mariachi music, folkloric dancing, and parades. Tejano music, described as a mixture of Mexican and German, is celebrated and studied at the annual Tejano Conjunto Festival in May. The beat of Latin music and dance fills the air in the outdoor Arneson River Theatre in June, kicking off the Fiesta Noche del Rio, which runs on weekends through the summer. San Antonio's Contemporary Art Month, held in July, is the only month-long contemporary arts festival in the nation; it features more than 400 exhibitions and involves more than 50 venues. September's FotoSeptiembre USA is one of the three largest photography festivals in the country. Oktoberfest and the River Art Group Show by major state artists enliven the month of October. The Christmas season has a Mexican flair led by the four-day Fiestas Navidenas in Market Square and Las Posadas, a reenactment of the Holy Family's search for an inn during which children go door-to-door seeking shelter. The River Walk itself becomes a festival of lights known as the Fiesta de las Luminarias.

### Sports for the Spectator

The San Antonio Spurs of the National Basketball Association and he San Antonio Rampage of the American Hockey League play their home games at the SBC Center, opened in October of 2002. The Center is a state-of-the-art 18,500 seat arena. The facility is 730,000 square feet, with four concourses, 54 suites, a practice facility, and restaurants. San Antonio's baseball team, the Missions of the Texas League, play at the Municipal Stadium. Major league pari-mutuel live and televised horse racing are offered at Retama Park year-round.

### Sports for the Participant

The mild climate of San Antonio lends itself to a multitude of outdoor sport activities, many tied to the network of more than 100 parks administered by the city Department of Parks and Recreation. San Pedro Park, the city's oldest, includes the McFarlin Tennis Center. Brackenridge Park is San Antonio's showplace, with more than 300 acres of ballfields, horseback riding trails, bike paths, and scenic walkways through intricate gardens. Overnight camping is available at McAllister Park, an 850-acre facility with a number of playing fields. Outside of the city lies Friedrich Park, where wilderness trails offer a peaceful challenge to hikers. The city operates 21 public swimming pools throughout San Antonio, including a year-round indoor Natatorium where competitions take place. Some 100 tennis courts in various locations augment the Fairchild and McFarlin Tennis Centers.

Bordered by the Texas Hill Country, San Antonio provides ready access to a number of recreation areas where hunting and water sports are popular activities. Fifteen lakes are within 150 miles of the city, and the Guadalupe River north of San Antonio is a favorite spot for canoeing, tubing, and white water rafting. Lake McQueeney, 25 miles from the city, attracts weekenders for boating and swimming. Corpus Christi and other Gulf Coast towns provide seacoast attractions about 140 miles from San Antonio. Natural bridge Caverns are located nearby between San Antonio and New Braunfels, off I-35, exit 175. Here you can tour spectacular caverns, climb and ''zip'' from the tallest climbing tower in

Texas while the less adventurous pan for gems and minerals. Natural Bridge Wildlife Ranch, located in the same area, is a Texas style African safari with hundreds of Animals from all over the world roaming freely. The Vietnam War Memorial is located at Veterans Memorial Plaza. Also not to be missed and located at 3400 Fredericksburg Road is the marker for the Old Spanish Trail which linked cities of Spanish conquest and settlement.

Blessed with more than 300 days of sunshine each year, San Antonio is becoming a major golf destination. Thirty-five courses (including military and private) and a championship course at the Hyatt Regency Hill Country Resort are the lure. Citizens are also fond of bowling—more than 26 commercial and military bowling centers dot the city. It was a San Antonio firm, Columbia Industries, that introduced polyester resin into the manufacture of bowling balls in 1960.

### Shopping and Dining

The newest and most exciting shopping, dining, and entertainment venue in San Antonio is Sunset Station, housed in the restored 1902 South Pacific Railroad depot near the convention center. Market Square downtown houses a large specialty shopping area, as well as a Mexican-style market featuring crafts, apparel, pottery, and jewelry. La Villita has 26 arts and crafts shops and three restaurants. Southwest School of Art and Craft, on the grounds of a former cloistered convent, sells the works of local artists and operates a restaurant in a beautiful historic setting. Many other art galleries feature Latin American and Native American artworks. Souvenir shops offer the latest in Western wear, including hand-crafted leather boots and ten-gallon hats. Antique stores feature authentic and reproduction items, including miniature replica Civil War and Texas Revolution toy soldiers and fine furniture and jewelry that may once have belonged to turn-of-the-century settlers. For those who wish to make a day of it, many antique stores can be found along the main streets of nearby charming towns such as Comfort, Boerne, Fredericksburg, Castroville, New Braunfels, Gruene and Leon Springs. In addition, the San Antonio area has 16 retail shopping malls and two major outlet malls.

Downtown dining ranges from ethnic cuisine to barbecue. Many restaurants feature some Tex-Mex dishes on their menus, and a number of restaurants specialize in south-of-the-border food. An emerging style of cooking, called New Southwestern, incorporates local produce and game. Italian, Greek, and German restaurants are well represented, as are delicatessens.

*Visitor Information:* San Antonio Convention & Visitors Bureau, 121 Alamo Plaza, San Antonio, 78205, telephone (210)207-6700

# Convention Facilities

San Antonio's Henry B. Gonzalez Convention Center, in the heart of San Antonio's historic district along the riverwalk, is the city's largest convention facility. Built in 1968 as part of the HemisFair, it recently underwent a $218-million expansion that increased its square footage to 1.3 million. The convention center has more than 203,000 square feet of meeting space that is divisible in 67 ways, four exhibit halls offering a total of approximately 440,000 square feet of contiguous display space, and three ballrooms. The convention center complex also features the Lila Cockrell Theatre, a performance art theater offering seating for more than 2,500.

The Alamodome, a $186-million state-of-the-art facility that can be used to host large conventions as well as trade shows and other events, opened in 1993. Featuring a Southwestern color scheme, the Alamodome has 160,000 gross square feet of contiguous floor space and configurations for groups of up to 77,000 people. The Alamodome is within walking distance of the Henry B. Gonzalez Convention Center and HemisFair Park, the River Walk, the Alamo, and more than 9,000 hotel rooms.

San Antonio's alternate meeting facility is the Municipal Auditorium and Conference, an opulent structure dating to 1926 and lovingly restored with attention to historical detail after a 1979 fire. Its main auditorium offers seating for nearly 5,000. The lobby and two small wings on the main level and approximately 24,000 square feet on the lower level provide additional space for meetings, exhibits, and banquets.

*Convention Information:* San Antonio Convention and Visitors Bureau, 121 Alamo Plaza, San Antonio, TX 78205; telephone (210)207-6700

# Transportation

### Approaching the city

San Antonio International Airport, a modern facility located 13 miles from the downtown River Walk, is served by 14 major carriers flying domestic and international routes, including nonstop flights to 28 destinations. The airport has an average of 248 daily departures and arrivals. Primary domestic destinations include Dallas/Ft. Worth and Houston, New York, Chicago, Washington D.C., Las Vegas, Los Angeles, Atlanta, Baltimore, and Phoenix; primary international destinations include Mexico City, Monterrey, Cancun, and Cozumel. Its terminal was described as ''one of the most beautiful in years'' by the American Institute of

Architects. Traveling from the airport downtown by taxi takes about 15 minutes during normal traffic. Express limousine service runs to major hotels, and buses depart every half-hour. Stinson Field, also operated by the city Aviation Department, handles general aviation traffic. Amtrak carries rail passengers to San Antonio from points all around the country. Entering San Antonio by road is comparatively easy; the loop design of San Antonio freeways and their connecting highways enable a motorist to reach the central district from any direction.

## Traveling in the City

The centerpiece of San Antonio's transportation network is its VIA Metropolitan Transit Service. This service enables visitors to experience the major attractions without a car and commuters can enjoy a near perfect on-time record. VIA's buses cover 106 routes; special vehicles serve the handicapped and elderly. To ease the flow of cars into downtown, VIA operates a number of park-and-ride locations from which commuters can catch an express bus to the business area. There are also special schedules for major events. In the downtown area, VIA Streetcars with wooden slats and brass railings cover five routes and function as a shuttle to many major attraction and major stores.

San Antonio can be reached in 30 minutes or less by car from any point in Bexar County. The San Antonio's "hub and spoke" expressway arrangement, where all highways radiate from the central business district, makes all parts of the city easily accessible.

The Mission Trails Project, a $17.7 million transportation enhancement project, is well underway and parts of it will be completed and operational in 2005. Described as a project equal in importance to the city's famed River Walk, the Mission Trails Project is a hike and bike trail connecting the Alamo, Mission Concepcion, Mission San José, and Mission Espada along a 10-mile trail, and enhance the roadways leading to the missions.

# *Communications*

## Newspapers and Magazines

San Antonio's major daily (morning) newspaper is the *Express-News.* San Antonio has numerous community newspapers, among them the *San Antonio Register* which serves the African American community, and specialty papers such as *Go! 50+* for mature readers and *San Antonio Business Journal* for the business community. Several local newspapers, including *Brooks Discovery, Fort Sam Houston Newsleader, Kelly USA Observer, Lackland Tailspinner, Medical Patriot,* and *Randolph Wingspread,* serve the military community. Additionally, the official trade magazine of the U.S. Airforce, *Airman,* is published here. Eight medical newspapers and magazines are published in San Antonio, four magazines focus on cattle, and two magazines provide information on local events, entertainment, shopping, and dining.

## Television and Radio

Eight television stations broadcast from San Antonio: four network affiliates, one public, one independent broadcasting religious and educational programming, one station affiliated with Telemundo and another with Univision. Additional stations are available via cable. Radio stations number more than 20 and offer a wide variety of formats, including Spanish-language programming.

*Media Information: Express-News,* PO Box 2171, San Antonio, TX 78297; telephone: (210)250-3000

## San Antonio Online

City of San Antonio Home Page. Available www.ci.sat.tx.us

Greater San Antonio Chamber of Commerce. Available www.sachamber.org

San Antonio Convention & Visitors Bureau. Available www .sanantoniocvb.com

San Antonio Economic Development Foundation. Available saedf.dcci.com

*San Antonio Express-News.* Available www.expressnews .com

San Antonio Public Library. Available www.sat.lib.tx.us

## Selected Bibliography

Harrigan, Stephen, *The Gates of the Alamo* (New York: Alfred A. Knopf, 2000)

Scott, Bob and Robert Scott, *After the Alamo* (Plano, Tx.: Republic of Texas Press, 1999)

# VIRGINIA

# The State in Brief

**Nickname:** Old Dominion
**Motto:** *Sic semper tyrannis* (Thus always to tyrants)

**Flower:** Dogwood
**Bird:** Cardinal

**Area:** 42,774 square miles (2000; U.S. Rank: 35th)
**Elevation:** Ranges from sea level to 5,729 feet above sea level
**Climate:** Mild, cooler in mountains; rainfall evenly distributed throughout the year

**Admitted to Union:** June 25, 1788
**Capital:** Richmond
**Head Official:** Governor Mark Warner (D) (until 2006)

**Population**
    **1980:** 5,347,000
    **1990:** 6,187,358
    **2000:** 7,078,515
    **2004 estimate:** 7,459,827
    **Percent change, 1990–2000:** 14.4%
    **U.S. rank in 2004:** 12th
    **Percent of residents born in state:** 57.1% (2000)
    **Density:** 178.8 people per square mile (2000)
    **2002 FBI Crime Index Total:** 229,039

**Racial and Ethnic Characteristics** (2000)
    **White:** 5,120,110

**Black or African American:** 1,390,293
**American Indian and Alaska Native:** 21,172
**Asian:** 261,025
**Native Hawaiian and Pacific Islander:** 3,946
**Hispanic or Latino (may be of any race):** 329,540
**Other:** 138,900

**Age Characteristics** (2000)
    **Population under 5 years old:** 461,982
    **Population 5 to 19 years old:** 1,475,104
    **Percent of population 65 years and over:** 11.2%
    **Median age:** 35.7 years (2000)

**Vital Statistics**
    **Total number of births (2003):** 101,303
    **Total number of deaths (2003):** 58,264 (infant deaths, 758)
    **AIDS cases reported through 2003:** 7,735

**Economy**
    **Major industries:** Tobacco, agriculture, manufacturing, trade, tourism, services, government, electrical equipment, food, textiles, paper products
    **Unemployment rate:** 3.3% (December 2004)
    **Per capita personal income:** $33,651 (2003; U.S. rank: 10th)
    **Median household income:** $52,587 (3-year average, 2001-2003)
    **Percentage of persons below poverty level:** 9.3% (3-year average, 2001-2003)
    **Income tax rate:** Ranges from 2.0% to 5.75%
    **Sales tax rate:** 4.5%

# Norfolk

## *The City in Brief*

**Founded:** 1682 (incorporated 1705)

**Head Official:** Mayor Paul D. Fraim (I) (since 1994)

**City Population**
  **1980:** 266,979
  **1990:** 261,250
  **2000:** 234,403
  **2003 estimate:** 241,727
  **Percent change, 1990–2000:** − 10.2%
  **U.S. rank in 1990:** 75th (State rank: 2nd)
  **U.S. rank in 2000:** 72nd (State rank: 2nd)

**Metropolitan Area Population (MSA)**
  **1980:** 1,200,998
  **1990:** 1,430,974
  **2000:** 1,551,351

  **Percent change, 1990–2000:** 8.4%
  **U.S. rank in 1990:** 27th
  **U.S. rank in 2000:** 33rd

**Area:** 53.73 square miles (2000)
**Elevation:** 13 feet above sea level
**Average Annual Temperature:** 59.57° F;
**Average Annual Precipitation:** 43.89 inches total; 7.5 inches of snowfall

**Major Economic Sectors:** Services, trade, government
**Unemployment rate:** 4.0% (December 2004)
**Per Capita Income:** $17,372 (1999)

**2002 FBI Crime Index Total:** 15,476

**Major Colleges and Universities:** Old Dominion University, Norfolk State University, Virginia Wesleyan College, Eastern Virginia Medical School, Troy State University, Tidewater Community College

**Daily Newspaper:** *The Virginian-Pilot*

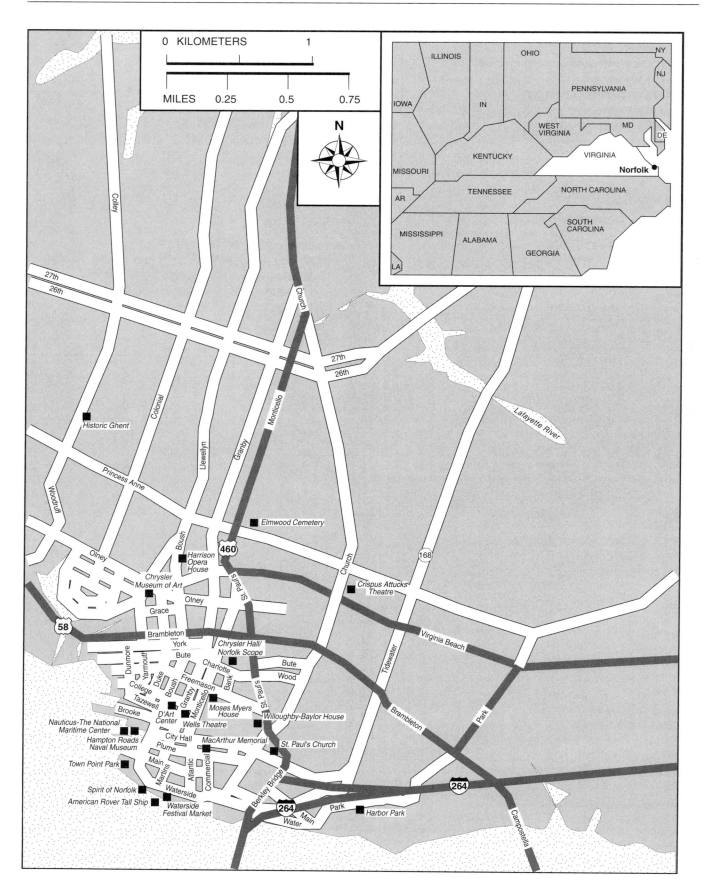

# Introduction

Norfolk, Virginia, one of the world's largest and busiest port cities, is the financial and legal center of southeastern Virginia. Water is central to the past, present and future of Norfolk, where the infamous *Merrimac* sea vessel was converted to the ironclad *Virginia* and where the National Maritime Center today recognizes the waterlogged character of this culturally and historically rich community.

# Geography and Climate

Norfolk, nearly surrounded by the waters of the Chesapeake Bay, is located near the southern border of Virginia, 18 miles west of the Atlantic Ocean and about 200 miles southeast of Washington, D.C. Immediately north is Chesapeake Bay and west is Hampton Roads, the natural channel through which the waters of the James River and its tributaries flow into the mouth of the Chesapeake Bay. Norfolk is situated at the mouth of the James, Elizabeth, and Nansemond rivers. Within the city the land is low and level.

Norfolk is fortunate in that it is south of the average path of storms originating in the higher latitudes. It is also north of the usual tracks of hurricanes and other tropical storms. The city usually has mild winters and sunny, warm autumns and springs. The long hot summers are often interrupted by cool periods as a result of the northeasterly winds off the Atlantic Ocean. Waves of extreme cold are rare, and often winters have no measurable snow. All in all, the National Weather Service has ranked Norfolk's climate as "one of the most desirable in the nation."

**Area:** 53.73 square miles of land; 42.58 square miles of water; 96.30 square miles total area (2000)

**Elevation:** 13 feet above sea level

**Average Temperatures:** January, 40° F; July, 79° F; annual average, 59.57° F;

**Average Annual Precipitation:** 43.89 inches total; 7.5 inches of snowfall

# History

### In the Beginning

Beginning in about 9500 B.C., the area that is now Norfolk was called Skicoak, and was ruled by the Chesipean Indians.

But by the time the first Europeans reached the area, the tribe members had been driven out or killed by Chief Powhatan, after one of his advisors told Powhatan that in a dream he had seen the Powhatan Confederacy destroyed by strangers from the East. Powhatan thought this was a sign he should destroy the Chesipeans, even though they were a peaceful people.

In the 1560s, settlers arrived from Spain, briefly living along the York River in a Jesuit community called Ajacan. Initially, the plan was to convert the Indians, but when the native people attacked the settlement in 1571, the Spanish abandoned Ajacan. The English were the next to test the area as a colony site, establishing Roanoke Settlement in 1585 under the guidance of Sir Walter Raleigh. The initial group of colonists abandoned Roanoke the next year and were followed by a second group in 1587; this second settlement disappeared without a trace by 1590 in one of the enduring mysteries of early recorded American history.

In 1624 Virginia became a Royal Colony when King James I of England granted 500 acres of land in what is now the Ocean View section of Norfolk to Thomas Willoughby. Twelve years later, King Charles I of England gave Willoughby 200 additional acres, and this also became part of the original town of Norfolk.

In 1670, the British government directed the "building of storehouses to receive imported merchandise. . .and tobacco for export." This marked the beginning of Norfolk's importance as a port city. In 1673 the Virginia House of Burgesses called for the construction of Half Moon fort at the site of what is now Town Point Park.

### City Prospers, Then Faces Destruction and Rebuilding

In 1682 England decreed that the "Towne of Lower Norfolk County" be established. The town was incorporated in 1705 and rechartered as a borough in 1736. For several decades the building of homes, farms, and businesses continued throughout the area, and Norfolk developed into a center for West Indies trade and the shipping of export products from the plantations of Virginia and the Carolinas. By 1775, Norfolk was known as the most prosperous city in Virginia.

The city served as a center for Tory forces during the American Revolution. On New Year's Day 1776, English ships under Royal Governor Lord Dunmore opened fire on the city, continuing their assault for eleven hours. High winds whipped up the flames and two-thirds of the city was destroyed by fire or cannonballs. By month's end the patriot colonists had torched the rest of the city to prevent the sheltering of Lord Dunmore and his forces. Every building in the city was destroyed by fire or cannonballs except Saint Paul's Church; a British cannonball remains in the wall of the church as testimony to the conflict. After the war, the citizens rallied and the city was rebuilt. In time it became a major shipbuilding and maritime center. In 1810, the U.S. government constructed a new fort at the site of dilapidated old Fort Norfolk. At that time the city's population stood at about 9,000 people.

## Ports, Forts and Exports

The nineteenth century brought more troubles for the city. A major fire in 1804 destroyed 300 houses, warehouses, and stores. The population, which had been growing steadily, actually declined from more than 9,000 people in 1810 to 8,478 people by 1820.

Conveniently situated on the water and philosophically allied with the agitating Confederate states, Norfolk in 1821 became the embarkation point for African and African American individuals being sent back to Africa. Norfolk native Joseph Jenkins Roberts went on to become the first president of the Republic of Liberia after being deported. Virginia seceded from the Union in 1861, with the Norfolk Navy Yard assuming a critical role as vessels docked there were burned or scuttled, including the famed *Merrimac*. It was in the Navy Yard that the *Merrimac* was rebuilt as an ironclad vessel renamed the *Virginia,* which went on to engage in the first ironclad battle against the *Monitor*. In May 1862, early in the Civil War, Norfolk was captured by Union forces. The troops ransacked the houses of the citizenry and forced passengers on local ferries to trample on the Confederate flag.

At the end of the Civil War, Norfolk buildings were in ruins and the city's foreign trade was nonexistent. At that time, the population stood at about 19,000 citizens. But within 20 years the city experienced a turnaround and three-story brick buildings lined the streets of Norfolk, which by then had thriving hotels and a large farmers' market. Steamships visited the port regularly and rail service connected it with other parts of the country. The 1880 population had grown to 21,966 residents.

## And the Pendulum Swings: Prosperity, Then Depression Times

In 1907, the Jamestown Exposition, held to celebrate the 300-year history of that nearby city, led to Norfolk's building several downtown hotels and office buildings. Visitors came from every state and dignitaries traveled from around the world to take part in the seven-month run of the event.

Norfolk's tremendous military growth began during World War I. In 1917, the land that was the site of the Jamestown Exposition became the U.S. Naval Operating Base and Training Station, which was later renamed Naval Station Norfolk. It was during this time that Norfolk was nationally recognized for leading the country in Navy recruitment. Between 1910 and 1920 the city's population grew from

around 67,000 people to nearly 116,000 people as the city also experienced an influx of workers at numerous new private manufacturing plants.

Prosperity declined after the heady war years, when Norfolk handled much of the coal that came by train from West Virginia to be shipped elsewhere. In 1922 Norfolk helped establish solid economic ground for itself by building a $5 million grain elevator and terminal. It also built a $500,000 farmers' market and annexed 27 square miles of nearby land, which included the Navy base area and the Ocean View resort district. Because of large-scale naval operations, the city did not suffer as much from the Great Depression as some others, and by 1940 the population stood at more than 144,000 residents.

## New Development Follows War Years

With the coming of World War II, Norfolk once again saw thousands of workers descend on the city and the region, where more than 100 ships and landing craft were built during the war. The war years saw a rapid increase in the development of individual residences and apartment buildings, and the city struggled to deal with overcrowding. Between 1940 and 1944, the population practically doubled. That period also saw the expansion of furniture manufacturing, fertilizer plants, and other industries.

In the years after World War II, Norfolk began a campaign to annex neighboring counties. Slums were cleared and public housing was constructed. In addition, hundreds of acres of land in the downtown were razed and rebuilt. Much of this redevelopment was spurred by the SCOPE Convention and Cultural Center. This facility includes the Chrysler Museum and Chrysler Hall, named in honor of automobile mogul Walter P. Chrysler, who donated his extensive art collection to the city.

In 1952 the Elizabeth River Tunnel between Norfolk and Portsmouth was completed, and a second tunnel followed 10 years later. By then the Hampton Roads Bridge-Tunnel linking Norfolk to the nearby city of Hampton was also built.

Virginia's third medical college, the Eastern Virginia Medical School, was built in Norfolk in 1973. During the next decade old buildings were razed and the Waterside Festival Marketplace, Town Point Park, and a number of condominiums were built along Norfolk's waterfront. Between 1950 and 1980 the population grew from 213,513 people to nearly 267,000 people. The 1980s saw development in the city that included th National Maritime Center, a new baseball stadium, and the construction of the Ghent Square neighborhood containing restored upscale residences.

In June 2000 the city was home to OpSail 2000, the largest tall ship and maritime event in history. Norfolk served as one of only six U.S. host ports for the events, which involved a fleet of 150 ships from more than 50 nations.

Today, Norfolk continues its long tradition of self-renewal with ambitious building projects in the downtown area strategically planned to continue through 2010, new residential developments along the water, and revitalization efforts within the abundance of varied historical neighborhoods. The Navy and the port continue to define Norfolk's character; the battleship U.S.S. *Wisconsin* is docked at Norfolk, with the National Maritime Center nearby on the waterfront. No matter what else changes in Norfolk, the sea stays at its core.

***Historical Information:*** Norfolk County Historical Society, PO Box 6367, Norfolk, VA 23508-0367

# Population Profile

## Metropolitan Area Residents
*1980:* 1,200,998
*1990:* 1,430,974
*2000:* 1,551,351
*2003 estimate:* 1,630,242
*Percent change, 1990–2000:* 8.4%
*U.S. rank in 1990:* 27th
*U.S. rank in 2000:* 33rd

## City Residents
*1980:* 266,979
*1990:* 261,250
*2000:* 234,403
*2003 estimate:* 241,727
*Percent change, 1990–2000:* − 10.2 %
*U.S. rank in 1990:* 75th (State rank: 2nd)
*U.S. rank in 2000:* 72nd (State rank: 2nd)

*Density:* 4,362.8 people per square mile (2000)

*Racial and ethnic characteristics* (2000)
　White: 113,358
　Black or African American: 103,387
　American Indian and Alaska Native: 1,071
　Asian: 6,593
　Native Hawaiian and Other Pacific Islander: 251
　Hispanic or Latino (may be of any race): 8,915
　Other: 3,923

*Percent of residents born in state:* 48.9% (2000)

*Age characteristics* (2000)
　Population under 5 years old: 16,546
　Population 5 to 9 years old: 16,508
　Population 10 to 14 years old: 15,072

Population 15 to 19 years old: 18,926
Population 20 to 24 years old: 31,983
Population 25 to 34 years old: 36,620
Population 35 to 44 years old: 33,569
Population 45 to 54 years old: 25,010
Population 55 to 59 years old: 8,143
Population 60 to 64 years old: 6,494
Population 65 to 74 years old: 12,979
Population 75 to 84 years old: 9,693
Population 85 years and over: 2,860
Median age: 29.6 years (2000)

*Births* (2003)
　Total number: 3,942

*Deaths* (2003)
　Total number: 2,729 (of which, 53 were infants under the age of 1 year)

*Money income* (1999)
　Per capita income: $17,372
　Median household income: $31,815
　Total households: 86,178

*Number of households with income of . . .*
　less than $10,000: 12,024
　$10,000 to $14,999: 6,883
　$15,000 to $24,999: 14,465
　$25,000 to $34,999: 13,470
　$35,000 to $49,999: 15,232
　$50,000 to $74,999: 13,402
　$75,000 to $99,999: 5,264
　$100,000 to $149,999: 3,318
　$150,000 to $199,999: 915
　$200,000 or more: 1,205

*Percent of families below poverty level:* 15.5% (30.5% of which were female householder families with related children under 5 years)

*2002 FBI Crime Index Total:* 15,476

# Municipal Government

Norfolk operates under a council-city manager form of government. It has seven city commissioners, one of whom is elected mayor by the council members. Council members serve for four years and the mayor's term is two years. The council appoints a city manager who oversees daily city business matters.

**Head Official:** Mayor Paul D. Fraim (I) (since 1994; current term expires 2006)

**Total Number of City Employees:** Approximately 6,000 (2005)

*City Information:* Mayor's Office, City of Norfolk, 810 Union St., Norfolk, VA 23510; telephone (757)664-4000

# Economy

## Major Industries and Commercial Activity

Norfolk serves as the business and financial center of the Hampton Roads region of Virginia. Shipbuilding and shipping are a vital part of Norfolk's economy, with the city's 45-foot-deep channel allowing it to accommodate very large ships. As a major seaport through which millions of tons of cargo pass each year, it handles such commodities as tobacco, cotton, timber, coal, truck crops, and grain.

With an ideal harbor and waterways, the city is the site of the Naval Base Norfolk, the largest naval base in the United States and the world. It also serves as home to the headquarters of the Fifth Naval District of the Atlantic Fleet and the Second Fleet, and it houses the district headquarters of the Coast Guard. In addition to the thousands of U.S. Navy personnel stationed in Norfolk, many local citizens also work in naval operations. The city is second only to San Diego, California, in the number of retired navy men and women who reside there.

Local industries include ship and light truck manufacturing, creation of law enforcement and military equipment, plastic production and communications. Between the rich local history and the presence of a plethora of seaside resorts, tourism is another important local industry. Local boats provide ferry service to nearby Portsmouth.

*Items and goods produced:* chemicals, fertilizer, textiles, automobiles, ships, military and law enforcement equipment, agricultural machinery, seafood, and peanut oil

## Incentive Programs—New and Existing Companies

*Local programs*—Through its Local Enterprise Zone Incentive Program, the city of Norfolk offers local tax and fee reductions on a five-year declining percentage ratio for business license and utility tax. In the first year of qualification a one-time-only 50 percent reduction is allowed on fees related to building, electrical, mechanical and plumbing permits. In the case of businesses that invest a minimum of $500,000 in the Local Enterprise Zone, the city agrees to complete complementary public improvements in the immediate vicinity. Additionally, the city offers security audits free of charge to businesses in the zone.

*State programs*—In its State Enterprise Zone Program, the State of Virginia offers tax incentives, property tax incentives, sales and use tax exemptions, and job grants. Among Virginia's tax credits are a General Income Tax Credit (up to 80 percent in the first year and 60 percent in years 2-10) and a Real Property Improvement Tax Credit (up to 30 percent, not to exceed $125,000 within a 5 year period).

*Job training programs*—In the Hampton Roads area, Opportunity, Inc., provides employers and job seekers with necessary networks and resources in an effort to achieve their mission of ''strengthening the localized talent pool of workers to match private sector investments in technology, capital, and product improvement.'' Acting under the auspices of the Hampton Roads Workforce Development Board and funded through the Workforce Investment Act, the agency offers workshops, links to online tools and access to a statewide collection of strategic partners.

The Hampton Roads Chamber of Commerce also supports the Workforce Focus program, which keeps local employers abreast of labor market trends, employment best practices and workforce resources.

## Development Projects

The Norfolk 2010 strategic plan calls for a menu of renovation and new construction in the downtown and outlying areas; new office space, retail trade facilities, entertainment enterprises, and hotels are currently being built in the revitalized city center. The Chesapeake Bay project began construction in 2003 and will eventually house 237 luxury condominiums along an attractive Harbor Walk. The development will be mixed use, presenting an urban feel to a beachfront area designed to encourage pedestrian usage. Additionally, Trader Publishing announced in August 2004 that it plans to bring its national headquarters to downtown Norfolk, which will bring 1,600 new jobs to the area.

On the former site of a brick and earthwork fort, the new Fort Norfolk has been taking shape as the bridge between the downtown area and the Hampton Roads major medical complex. Construction of a $30 million Public Health Center contributed a biotech incubator, in which bioelectric research and experimentation will be conducted. The facility is joined to the Eastern Virginia Medical School by a walkway and has also allowed for vast expansion of the medical school's Edward E. Brickell Medical Service Library. The city of Norfolk demonstrated considerable foresight in designating Plum Point as open space, a parcel of land that was donated by the Virginia Port Authority.

Further capitalizing on its layers of history and potential for increased tourist trade, the City of Norfolk is supporting the renovation of several historic structures in the Church Street district within the city center. The Attucks Theater, begun in 1919 and named after the African American man who was the first casualty of the American Revolution, is the oldest theater in the state and remains a landmark for African Americans throughout the U.S. The Crispus Attucks Cultural Center, Inc., will additionally receive its share of attention as the city continues to build on its history.

Old Dominion University and its Real Estate Foundation have partnered with the City of Norfolk in expanding and updating the campus, including office and research facilities, shopping areas, a convocation hall and other components of what is being called the University Village.

***Economic Development Information:*** Department of Development, City of Norfolk, 500 East Main St., Suite 1500, Norfolk, VA 23510; telephone (757)664-4338

## Commercial Shipping

In 2004, more than 14.7 million tons of cargo passed through the port of Virginia in Norfolk, a 6 percent increase from the previous year. Between the purchase of eight Suez-class cranes and a $280 million dollar renovation and expansion, the port is poised to compete for the number one spot as an East Coast container port. Exports of coal, food products, tobacco, and the majority of grain from the United States pass through the port of Norfolk.

Norfolk International Airport provides a cargo service in support of the city's 135 motor freight carriers. Railroad freight carriers include the Norfolk Southern, Norfolk & Portsmouth Belt Line, Norfolk & Western, Southern, Eastern Shore, and CSX railroads.

## Labor Force and Employment Outlook

The Chamber of Commerce notes that the local workforce is numerous but unprepared for the new employment opportunities offered by the community's companies. Efforts have been underway since at least 2003 to enlist the support of Hampton Roads employers in advocating for classes and degree programs that are tailored more closely to the needs of local industries; at the same time, the city continues to focus on attracting technological, medical and industrial companies that will entice graduates of the region's universities to stay and work locally.

The following is a summary of data regarding the Norfolk metropolitan area labor force as of 2003.

*Size of nonagricultural labor force:* 730,800

*Number of workers employed in . . .*
  *construction and mining:* 44,700
  *manufacturing:* 59,800
  *trade, transportation and public utilities:* 134,900
  *information:* 16,100
  *financial activities:* 38,000
  *professional and business services:* 98,800

  *educational and health services:* 78,100
  *leisure and hospitality:* 77,300
  *other services:* 33,500
  *government:* 149,800

*Average hourly earnings of production workers employed in manufacturing:* $18.42

*Unemployment rate:* 4.0% (December 2004)

| Largest employers | Number of employees |
|---|---|
| Sentara Health Care | 15,000 |
| City of Norfolk | 6,000 |
| Norfolk Public School District | 5,280 |
| Naval Station Norfolk | 4,000 |
| Old Dominion University | 1,600 |
| Norfolk Southern | 1,100 |

## Cost of Living

The following is a summary of data regarding several key cost of living factors for the Norfolk area.

*2004 (3rd Quarter) ACCRA Average House Price:* $266,775

*2004 (3rd quarter) ACCRA Cost of Living Index:* 102.1 (U.S. average = 100.0)

*State income tax rate:* 2.0% to 5.75% (corporate business tax rate: 6%)

*State sales tax rate:* 3.5%; 3.0% on food

*Local income tax rate:* None

*Local sales tax rate:* None

*Property tax rate:* Based on 100% of Fair Market Value × $1.40 per $100 of assessed valuation ($1.58 per $100.00 for the business district).

***Economic Information:*** Hampton Roads Chamber of Commerce, PO Box 327, Norfolk, VA 23501; telephone (757)622-2312

# *Education and Research*

## Elementary and Secondary Schools

The Norfolk Public School District is noted for its ethnic and racial diversity, largely as a result of the local military presence. Norfolk schools offer many special programs, such as gifted and special education programs and also utilize community-based education to reify the academic concepts being taught in classes. For example, Norfolk Public School District students have developed an artificial reef and grown their own oysters in conjunction with the Chesapeake Bay Foundation and its Oyster Restoration Program. The innovations and improvements in the district received statewide attention in May 2004 with the selection of the superintendent, Dr. John Simpson, as Virginia Superintendent of the Year.

The following is a summary of data regarding the Norfolk public school system as of the 2003–2004 school year.

*Total enrollment:* 36,724

*Number of facilities*
  *elementary schools:* 35
  *junior high/middle schools:* 8
  *senior high schools:* 5

*Student/teacher ratio:* 11:1

*Teacher salaries*
  *minimum:* $27,640
  *maximum:* $73,731

*Funding per pupil:* $7,403

The area is also host to a variety of specialized education programs, from private schools founded in a particular religion, to Headstart programs, to technical/vocational schools.

***Public Schools Information:*** Norfolk Public Schools, 800 E. City Hall Avenue, Norfolk, VA 23510; telephone (757)628-3843

## Colleges and Universities

Norfolk is home to a number of institutions of higher learning that span the spectrum of vocational specialty schools, community colleges, and colleges or universities. Old Dominion University is a public coeducational school and a sea- and space-grant institution with a combined undergraduate and graduate enrollment of about 20,802 students. From baccalaureate to doctoral programs, Old Dominion grants degrees in education, liberal arts, business and public administration, sciences, health sciences, engineering, and technology. The university capitalizes on its proximity to the naval base and the Virginia Space Flight Center on Wallops Island, creating fieldwork experiences that contribute to those industries.

Virginia Wesleyan College, with 1,400 students, is a private liberal arts college that emphasizes the value of gaining real-world experience through internships, field work, study abroad, and community service. The college offers baccalaureate degrees in various divisions of the humanities, natural sciences and mathematics, and the social sciences.

Norfolk State University is one of the largest predominantly African American institutions in the United States, with an enrollment approaching 8,000 students. It has undergraduate

schools in business, education, liberal arts, social work, and science and technology, as well as 18 graduate departments.

The Eastern Virginia Medical School is a public institution with its main campus at Norfolk's Eastern Virginia Medical Center. It has 2,565 students enrolled in a selection of medical degree programs that lead to careers as physician's assistants, nurses, doctors, and researchers. The school is supported by a teaching hospital, a model that the Norfolk General Hospital also employs.

At ITT Technical Institute, students are enrolled in baccalaureate and associate degree programs in information technology, electronics technology, drafting and design, business, and criminal justice.

## Libraries and Research Centers

The more than 100 year old Norfolk Public Library system contains nearly 1 million books and subscribes to more than 1,250 periodicals. It serves patrons through 12 branches and a bookmobile. The library has special sections on African-American literature, business, juvenile literature, and local history. Within the next 10 years, the Norfolk Public Library plans to upgrade neighborhood branch facilities, renovate or rebuild the main library, and increase its efforts in the area of child literacy.

The city's Chrysler Museum of Art houses the Jean Outland Chrysler Library, containing 80,000 books, with special emphasis on Western European and American painting, drawing, sculpture, Art Nouveau decorative arts, textiles, glass, art history, and photography. The library's archives are home to many treasures, not the least of which is Mark Twain's original typescript of a speech he delivered at the Tricentennial Exposition of 1907 in Jamestown.

MacArthur Memorial Library and Archives has special collections on the life of American General Douglas MacArthur, who is buried nearby, and on American wars in the first half of the twentieth century. The U.S. Navy's Submarine Force Library and Archives has 6,000 volumes focusing on submarine development, salvage and history. The Joint Forces Staff College Library, with 113,000 scholarly volumes and periodicals, is available only to military personnel.

There are also college libraries at Virginia Wesleyan College, Norfolk State University, and Old Dominion University. Medical libraries are found at the local hospitals, at Norfolk Psychiatric Center, and at Eastern Virginia Medical School. The Norfolk Law Library provides legal reference material to the public, lawyers and the courts.

Specialized research facilities include the Jones Institute for Reproductive Medicine, which focuses on the study of human reproduction, and Old Dominion University, which is home to a diverse collection of research facilities ranging from the Langley Full-Scale Wind Tunnel to the Center for Advanced Ship Repair and Maintenance. Old Dominion University's Office of Research acts as a clearing house for research efforts centralized at the university.

Marine and naval research facilities abound within Naval Station Norfolk, including a laboratory that focuses on specific medical issues related to service in a submarine.

***Public Library Information:*** Norfolk Public Library, 301 E. City Hall Avenue, Norfolk, VA 23510; telephone (757)664-4000

# Health Care

Norfolk is the site of Virginia's only free-standing, full-service pediatric hospital, Children's Hospital of the King's Daughters. The 186-bed facility serves more than 5,900 children as inpatients each year, with nearly 99,000 children receiving outpatient services. Staffed with educators, therapists and social workers in addition to pediatric medical specialists, the hospital specializes in the treatment of cancer, neonatal medicine, infectious diseases, orthopedics, and craniofacial and urological reconstructive surgery. The Sentara Norfolk General Hospital is a 664-bed tertiary care facility located on a large medical campus and serving the area with Level I Trauma services. It has gained recognition for its highly specialized care and facilities, which include cardiac services, a cancer institute, high-risk pregnancy center, in-vitro fertilization, a transplant program, microsurgery, and reconstructive surgery. The Sentara Leigh Hospital is a 250-bed hospital featuring private rooms and specializing in orthopedic, gynecological, general, and urological services. The hospital was honored in both 2001 and 2002 as one of the nation's top-performing hospitals, as reported by *100 Top Hospitals National Benchmarks for Success*; the hospital also has a Family Maternity Suite and a Breast Cancer Center with an all-female staff. Bon Secours DePaul Medical Center is a 366-bed acute care facility that includes a birthing center, diabetes center, cancer center, gerontology center and institute and additional programs for hearing/balance, sleep disorders, cardiac care, and joint/spine injuries. Lake Taylor Hospital is a 332-bed transitional care and chronic disease facility. Inpatient behavioral health and substance abuse services for adolescents are available through the Norfolk Psychiatric Center on Kempsville Road.

The Norfolk area and its major medical facilities are supported by dozens of specialized clinics, hundreds of private medical practitioners and a number of alternative treatment providers. The Naval Medical Center Portsmouth serves all branches of the U.S. military and their families.

# Recreation

### Sightseeing

Visitors to Norfolk can observe giant aircraft carriers and guided-missile cruisers juxtaposed with sailboats and pedestrian ferries in the city's busy harbor. As home to the world's largest naval base, Naval Station Norfolk, the port has many significant U.S. Marine, U.S. Coast Guard, and NATO facilities as well. The *Spirit of Norfolk* passenger ship offers lunch and dinner cruises along Norfolk's scenic and historic waterfront.

Sightseeing harbor cruises are also provided by the three-masted schooner *American Rover,* the Mississippi-style paddle-wheeler *Carrie B,* and the sleek ship *Spirit of Norfolk.* Trolley tours to the city's major historic and cultural attractions are offered daily from the Waterside complex. Tour buses also make trips to Naval Station Norfolk, home port to more than 100 ships of the Atlantic fleet.

Nauticus, the National Maritime Center, is a 120,000 square foot science center with a nautical theme that celebrates the region's rich maritime heritage. It offers interactive exhibits, a shark tank, a weather forecasting lab, a giant-screen theater, and hands-on displays for all ages, as well as traveling exhibits. Within Nauticus is the Hampton Roads Naval Museum, which introduces tourists to more than two centuries of naval history through ship models, works of art, and artifacts from sunken ships. Docked outside is the 1933 tugboat *Huntington,* which houses a tugboat museum that salutes the "Workhorses of the Waterways." The largest and last battleship ever built by the U.S. Navy is also moored next to Nauticus; visitors can take self-guided tours across the decks of the World War II vessel, the USS *Wisconsin.*

Strollers through Town Point Park can stop by the Armed Forces Memorial, which has on display descriptions of life during wartime taken from letters written home by U.S. service people who were killed in wars, from the American Revolution to the Persian Gulf War. The region's military history is further reflected in Fort Norfolk, with brick and earthwork buildings dating back to 1810. It is surrounded by a wall and ramparts built to protect the structure against invasion by the British.

Nearby is the picturesque Freemason district, Norfolk's oldest existing neighborhood. There visitors can walk along cobblestone streets, following the Cannonball Trail through 400 years of recorded history and past the Willoughby-Baylor House (a 1794 Federal townhouse that features period furnishings), Freemason Street Baptist Church, the cannonball-studded wall of St. Paul's Episcopal Church and the Confederate Memorial. Norfolk's Freemason District is also part of the Civil War Trails system, linking more than 200 Civil War sites around and beyond the city. Included in Norfolk is the Black Civil War Memorial, which stands as the only recognition of African American troops to date in the South.

The Ghent district, Norfolk's first planned community, is a combination of restored houses, galleries, boutiques, restaurants, and antique shops. The Hermitage Foundation Museum is housed in a wooded setting on the Lafayette River on a 12-acre estate. Within the splendid English Tudor home are displays of European ceramics and paintings, German hand-painted glass *objets d'art*, ivory carvings, Persian rugs, and ritual bronzes and ceramic tomb figures from China.

For more than a century the Virginia Zoological Park has provided a look into the lives of many kinds of animals, which now number more than 350 and range from white rhinos to red-ruffed lemurs. The most recent addition is a male African lion named Mramba; the lion is part of a long-term breeding and conservation effort at select zoos across the country. The zoo grounds are divided into habitats of animals from various continents in large enclosures that encourage natural behaviors. On a path that features interactive exhibits about African river deltas and other ecological zones, visitors encounter many interesting animals and sights, including a unique dismal swamp exhibit. The Norfolk Botanical Gardens encompasses 155 acres of colorful flower gardens; in 2005, a special exhibition titled ''Treasure Island'' will lead visitors to themed destinations and offer a variety of interactive, educational activities for children of all ages. Boat trips are available through the garden's waterways with their brilliant exotic blooms.

## Arts and Culture

The Chrysler Museum of Art contains a collection of 30,000 original works from many time periods and geographic areas. The American Painting and Sculpture collection contains a selection of colonial and folk art offerings along with examples of American Impressionism. The European Painting and Sculpture collection features Italian Renaissance, Baroque, Dutch, and French works from such masters as Rubens, de Clerck, and Renoir. The showpiece exhibit may be a magnificent 8,000-piece glass collection featuring wonderful Tiffany and Lalique displays.

The D'Art Center is comprised of 30 studios in which artists both create and sell their works; visitors can tour the studios to watch painters, sculptors, potters, and jewelry makers at work.

Military museums abound in Norfolk, including The National Maritime Center and the Hampton Roads Naval Museum. The latter incorporates 225 years of Hampton Roads naval history and operates the living history experience aboard the USS *Wisconsin*.

Downtown Norfolk provides a number of opportunities to see what life was like in the early days of the city, including the Hermitage Foundation Museum (a Tudor home from 1908) and the Hunter House Victorian Museum (built in 1894 by architect W.D. Wentworth).

Norfolk boasts the oldest theater designed, developed, financed, and operated entirely by African Americans—the Attucks Theatre, named for the African American man who fell as the first casualty of the American Revolution. The theater has recently been renovated after being closed in the mid 1950s, with the aim of again hosting luminaries of the caliber of Duke Ellington and Nat King Cole.

Norfolk's premiere performing arts center is Chrysler Hall, which annually stages the Broadway at Chrysler Hall series, touring productions of musicals and plays, and a star-studded roster of musical and spoken-word performers. Harrison Opera House is home to the well-respected Virginia Opera, which offers five productions annually in addition to other dance, music and theatrical works. The opera building also houses the Virginia Opera's Education and Outreach Program, sending resident artists into the public schools to awaken students to the joys, passions and tragedies that are opera. The Virginia Stage Company professional theater produces six major shows yearly, as well as smaller shows and children's theater activities at the historic and elegant Wells Theater. Several small, local theater groups also operate in the Norfolk region, including the Generic Theater (offbeat theater), the Little Theatre of Norfolk (one of the nation's oldest community theaters) and the Hurrah Players (family theater starring aspiring performers).

Hampton Roads' sole professional dance company is the Virginia Ballet Theatre, which is one of only two professional companies in the entire state of Virginia. The Ballet Theatre was created in 1961 to promote regional ballet, train young dancers, and provide a creative center for the performing arts.

The Virginia Symphony performs more than 140 concerts each year, from classical to pops. The group also offers young people's concerts. Under the current maestro, the Symphony has recorded five CDs for national release, performed ''Peter and the Wolf'' for airing on National Public Radio, and played the Kennedy Center in January 2000. The Virginia Symphony also lends orchestral support to the Virginia Opera.

The Virginia Chorale has, since 1984, been the commonwealth's only fully professional choral group, performing music from all time periods and particularly skilled in *a cappella* renditions. The Chorale offers Masters Classes and the Young Singers Project as part of their outreach and education endeavors.

The Governor's School for the Arts, at home in Norfolk, plays a pivotal role in keeping the arts alive in the Hampton

Roads area. Art education programs are offered in dance, vocal and instrumental music, theater, and visual arts, with a number of student productions performed to further develop the artists and showcase their burgeoning talents.

**Festivals and Holidays**

Norfolk enjoys a variety of events and festivals at different sites around the city. In September, Town Point Park is the site of three related events: the Virginia in Water Boat Expo, the Norfolk Seafood Sampler, and the Beach Music Festival. For cinema aficionados, the SOL Film Festival comes to downtown Norfolk in early October, with independent films competing for prizes. October breezes also bring the Great Chesapeake Bay Schooner race, a three-day race designed to increase awareness of the fragile ecosystem contained in the Bay. The race concludes at Town Point Park, where the racing vessels line up and create a backdrop for the Town Point Virginia Wine Festival. At this event, more than 25 Virginia wineries provide samplings; also featured are gourmet foods, specialty crafts, and live musical entertainment. The holidays are welcomed with the Grand Illumination Parade and its associated events that take place in downtown Norfolk and nearby Portsmouth, including a progressive dinner termed ''Wine and Dine.''

Norfolk celebrates St. Patrick's Day on March 17 with the Greening of Ghent, which includes a parade and party in the Ghent neighborhood. April's events include the International Azalea Festival at the Botanical Gardens, and the Virginia International Tattoo, a spectacle of music featuring drill teams, massed pipe and drum corps, gymnasts, and folk dancers. The Tattoo is part of Virginia's Arts Festival, a month-long celebration of the arts that includes classical music, jazz, and chamber music events, as well as dance and visual arts exhibitions that take place throughout the region.

May is the time for the Cinco de Mayo Celebration featuring Mexican food and music, the annual Town Point Jazz and Blues Festival, and the Afr'Am Fest, a weekend cultural celebration of ethnic music, dance, theater and exhibits. The Elizabeth Riverfront in Town Point Park is the site of numerous music, arts, and cultural festivals throughout the spring and summer months. In June the Norfolk Harborfest celebrates the region's rich nautical heritage. Independence Day brings the Great American Picnic and Celebration, which ends with a spectacular fireworks display. The last big event of the summer is the Norfolk Latino Festival in late August, celebrating the heat with spicy cuisine, smokin' music, and sizzling art.

**Sports for the Spectator**

Norfolk fans watch the puck drop to start the games of the Hampton Roads Admirals of the American Hockey League,

who play at Norfolk SCOPE. The Norfolk Tides baseball team, a minor league affiliate of the New York Mets, play at the Riverfront's Harbor Park. Rugby fans can enjoy Norfolk Blue rugby team matches; the highly successful club has been playing in the Norfolk area since 1978. Norfolk State University varsity teams compete in the Central Intercollegiate Athletic Association football league, while Old Dominion's men's and women's basketball teams are both Division I NCAA competitors. Other Old Dominion University sport offerings include baseball, soccer, women's field hockey, track and field events, and a variety of club sports. The Virginia Wesleyan Marlins play basketball in Division III of the NCAA and can entertain fans with a selection of varsity and club sports.

**Sports for the Participant**

Surrounded by all that water, it's natural that the Norfolk area entices avid rowers, sea kayakers, swimmers, jet skiers and windsurfers. Fishing can become a religion for some, with access to Chesapeake species such as speckled trout, flounder, bluefish, rockfish, and more. A number of private companies run charters out of the Chesapeake Bay area. The City of Norfolk Police Department coordinates the Police Athletic League, or PAL, which gives local youth a chance to participate in volleyball, boxing, basketball, football, girls' softball and track events. Golfers can go 18 holes on any of three public golf courses: Lake Wright Golf Course, Stumpy Lake Golf Course and Ocean View Golf Course. Nearby Virginia Beach is home to even more public and private courses. The Tidewater Tennis Center and Northside Park, where many local tournaments are held, are but two of more than a dozen tennis courts in the city.

Venturing outside of Norfolk, there are spectacular hikes in Shenandoah National Park in the Blue Ridge Mountains approximately 2.5 hours northwest of the Tidewater region. The Old Rag Summit Ridge Trail is often recommended, as is the section of the Appalachian Trail that meanders through the park.

**Shopping and Dining**

MacArthur Center, a regional shopping mecca, is within walking distance of the local convention center. The $300 million complex offers more than a million square feet of shops, restaurants and entertainment centers, with Nordstrom and Dillards as its anchor stores. The Selden Arcade downtown in the city's financial district offers clothing shops, bookstores, and jewelry shops. The upscale Ghent Shopping District is known for its home furnishings, boutiques, and clothing shops. Military Circle is a mega-mall that offers department stores and a cinema. JANAF Shopping Center offers bargains on clothing, sports equipment, and home furnishings. For an eclectic mix of retailers, restaurateurs and entertainers, the Waterside Festival Marketplace is the place to be; located right on the water, with ferries and boat tours departing from the premises, it's a one-stop-shop for food and fun.

Speaking of food, Norfolk's southern location means that diners can get quality soul food, including ribs, fried chicken, collard greens, biscuits, and other delectables. The community is home to an astonishing number of establishments serving Italian food, with northern Italian cuisine coming on strong at present. Southwestern and Mexican restaurants are also plentiful, with a couple of spots dedicated to the art of tapas. Diners can catch a taste of fresh seafood at a number of places along the waterfront and beyond. Being a port city with a constant international influence, Norfolk eateries cater to a broad variety of other tastes as well, including French, Mediterranean, Cajun/Creole, German, Caribbean, Indian, Greek, Irish, Chinese, Thai, Japanese, and American fare.

*Visitor Information:* Norfolk Convention and Visitors Bureau, 232 E. Main Street, Norfolk, VA 23510; telephone (757)664-6620; toll-free (800)368-3097

# Convention Facilities

Just blocks from Norfolk's waterfront is the SCOPE Cultural and Convention Center, which features the dome-shaped SCOPE Arena, Chrysler Hall, and a self-contained parking facility. SCOPE offers 85,000 square feet of contiguous meeting space, accommodates up to 11,300 delegates for a convention, and handles banquets for up to 3,650 people. It also features six meeting rooms with capacities from 10 to 400 people, and a 150-seat restaurant. The Waterside Convention Connection is a joint project of the Waterside Convention Center, the Waterside Festival Marketplace and the Sheraton, Marriott, and Radisson hotels. These combined entities offer 121,000 square feet of function space, 55 meeting rooms, 1,000 first-class rooms for lodging and a large exhibit hall that can accommodate up to 2,400 guests for a reception, 2,000 people in a theater set-up, and 1,400 for a banquet. Local theater buildings, attractions and dining establishments can also be reserved for meetings and conventions, creating a unique experience with a definite Norfolk flavor.

*Convention Information:* Norfolk Convention and Visitors Bureau, 232 E. Main Street, Norfolk, VA 23510; telephone (757)664-6620; toll-free (800)368-3097

# Transportation

**Approaching the City**

The city has easy access to Interstates 64 and 264. Greyhound provides bus service to the city and train travel is offered by Amtrak. The 17-mile-long Chesapeake Bay Bridge-Tunnel links the Norfolk region to the Delmarva Peninsula, and the Paddlewheel Ferry (a natural gas-powered pedestrian ferry) provides service between Norfolk's Waterside and Portsmouth. Pleasure craft can travel on the Atlantic Intracoastal Waterway from Norfolk all the way down to Miami, Florida, on a protected inland channel.

Norfolk International Airport, located eight miles northeast of the city's downtown area, is served by eight commercial airlines, including American, Continental, Delta, Northwest, TWA, United, and USAir. The airport handles more than 3 million passengers annually on more than 200 flights daily.

**Traveling in the City**

Interstates 64/564 run north and south through the city, and Interstate 264 runs east and west. State Highway 460, known locally as St. Paul's Boulevard, runs north and south through the downtown, while State Highway 58, known as Brambleton Avenue, runs east and west. Other main downtown streets running north-south are Boush Street, Church Street, and Tidewater Avenue. Waterside Drive and Water St. run east and west along the riverfront. Hampton Roads Transit provides public transportation regionally, connecting Norfolk with Virginia Beach, Newport News, Suffolk, Portsmouth, and Chesapeake. HRT also operates the Norfolk Electric Transit service (NET), which offers free service around the downtown area.

# Communications

**Newspapers and Magazines**

The *Virginian-Pilot* is Norfolk's daily newspaper. The city is also home to military newspapers *Flagship* and *Soundings*. *The Mace and Crown* is the newspaper of Old Dominion University.

**Television and Radio**

Norfolk is served by 3 network affiliates and a network station from nearby Portsmouth. Norfolk is home to 11 FM radio stations (4 classical, plus public, talk, and music format stations) and 4 AM stations with public, religious, and music formats.

*Media Information:* *Virginian-Pilot,* 150 W. Brambleton Avenue, Norfolk, VA 23510; telephone (757)446-2000

**Norfolk Online**

City of Norfolk. Available www.norfolk.gov

Hampton Roads Chamber of Commerce. Available www .hamptonroadschamber.com

Naval Station Norfolk. Available www.navstanorva.navy .mil

Norfolk Convention and Visitors Bureau. Available www .norfolkcvb.com/home

Norfolk Public Library system. Available www2.npl.lib.va .us

Norfolk Public Schools. Available www.nps.k12.va.us/ index.htm

*Virginian-Pilot* newspaper. Available www.hamptonroads .com/pilotonline

**Selected Bibliography**

Flanders, Alan B., *Bluejackets on the Elizabeth: A Maritime History of Portsmouth & Norfolk, Virginia from the Colonial Period to the Present* (Portsmouth, VA: Portsmouth Naval Shipyard Museum, 1998)

Lewis, Earl, *In Their Own Interests: Race, Class & Power in Twentieth-Century Norfolk, Virginia* (Los Angeles: University of California Press, 1993)

Parramore, Thomas C., Peter C. Stewart (Contributor), and Tommy L. Bogger (Contributor), *Norfolk: The First Four Centuries* (Charlottesville, VA: University Press of Virginia, 1994)

# Richmond

## *The City in Brief*

**Founded:** 1742 (incorporated, 1782)

**Head Official:** Mayor L. Douglas Wilder (D) (since 2004)

**City Population**
  **1980:** 219,214
  **1990:** 202,798
  **2000:** 197,790
  **2003 estimate:** 194,729
  **Percent change, 1990–2000:** − 2.5%
  **U.S. rank in 1980:** 64th
  **U.S. rank in 1990:** 76th (State rank: 3rd)
  **U.S. rank in 2000:** 105th (State rank: 4th)

**Metropolitan Area Population**
  **1980:** 761,000
  **1990:** 866,000
  **2000:** 1,096,957
  **Percent change, 1990–2000:** 26.6%

**U.S. rank in 1980:** 48th (MSA)
**U.S. rank in 1990:** 49th (MSA)
**U.S. rank in 2000:** 46th (MSA)

**Area:** 62.55 total square miles (2000)
**Elevation:** Ranges from 9 to approximately 312 feet above sea level
**Average Annual Temperature:** 57.7° F;
**Average Annual Precipitation:** 43.13 inches of rainfall; 16.9 inches of snowfall

**Major Economic Sectors:** government; education, health and social services, retail trade
**Unemployment rate:** 3.6% (December 2004)
**Per Capita Personal Income:** $20,337 (1999)

**2002 FBI Crime Index Total:** 18,002

**Major Colleges and Universities:** Virginia Commonwealth University, University of Richmond, Virginia Union University, J Sargeant Reynolds Community College, ECPI Technical College

**Daily Newspaper:** *Richmond Times-Dispatch*

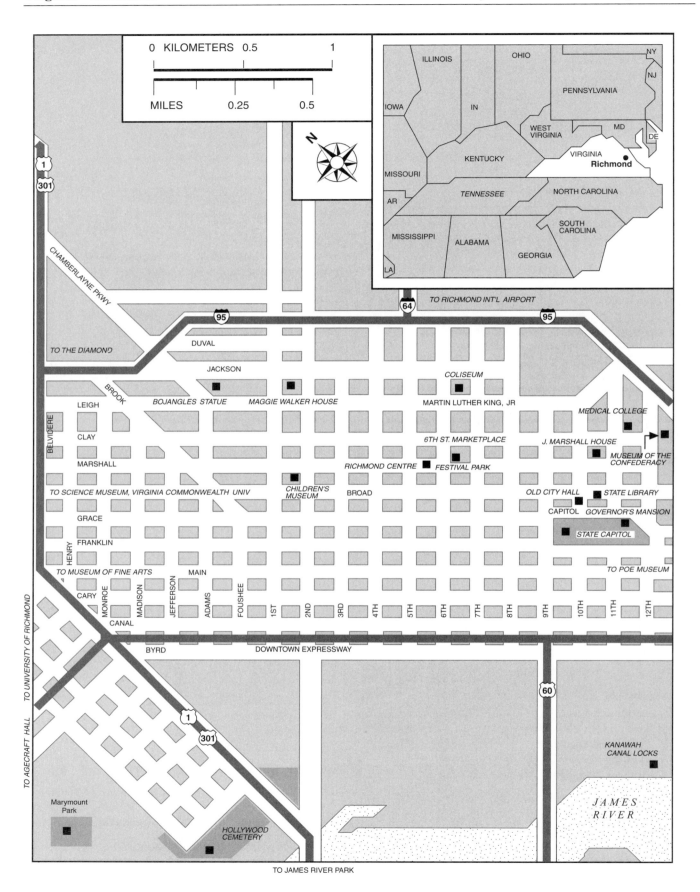

# Introduction

The capital of Virginia, Richmond is steeped in a history that spans nearly 400 years, dating back to 1607 when Jamestown colonists identified the site. During the Revolutionary War era, it was the locale of several important conventions at which such notables as Thomas Jefferson and Patrick Henry sounded the call for freedom and determined the course of a fledgling nation. Later, Richmond proudly served as the capital of the Confederate States of America.

Nowadays, Richmond and its booming metropolitan area (which also encompasses the counties of Chesterfield, Hanover, and Henrico) are regarded as a prime example of the ideal ''New South'' community—one that successfully blends its heritage with modern social and industrial development. The city's strategic location in the middle of the eastern seaboard puts it within 500 miles of nearly half the entire population of the United States and only 100 miles from the nation's capital. Combining this asset with a mild climate, gently rolling terrain, and a wealth of cultural and recreational attractions has made Richmond another Sun Belt city on the move, and all indications point to a promising future.

# Geography and Climate

Richmond is located at the head of the navigable part of the James River between Virginia's coastal plains and the Piedmont, beyond which are the Blue Ridge Mountains. The open waters of Chesapeake Bay and the Atlantic Ocean to the east and the mountain barrier to the west are responsible for the region's warm, humid summers and generally mild winters. Precipitation, mostly in the form of rain, is distributed fairly evenly throughout the year, though dry spells lasting several weeks are especially common in the fall. Snow usually accumulates in amounts of less than four inches and remains on the ground only one or two days.

The James River occasionally floods low-lying areas, but the Richmond flood wall, completed in the 1990s, goes a long way toward minimizing damage in those areas. Hurricanes have been the cause of most flooding during the summer and fall, particularly Hurricanes Connie and Diane in 1955, Hurricane Camille in August 1969, Hurricane Agnes in June 1972, and Hurricane Isabel in September 2003. On August 31, 2004, flooding instigated by Tropical Storm Gaston devastated the historic Shockoe Bottom District which lies along the James River.

**Area:** 62.55 square miles (2000)

**Elevation:** Ranges from a few feet above sea level along the James River to approximately 312 feet above sea level in the western parts of the city

**Average Temperatures:** January, 36.6° F; July, 77.9° F; annual average; 57.7° F;

**Average Annual Precipitation:** 43.13 inches of rainfall; 16.9 inches of snowfall

# History

## Conflicts Prevent Settlement

On May 21, 1607, a week after Captain John Smith and his party landed at Jamestown, a group led by Captain Christopher Newport set out from camp to explore the James River. Within a week, their travels took them to some falls and a small island where on May 27 they set up a cross. This marked the ''discovery'' of Richmond, though three decades would pass before another Englishman established a permanent post on the site; the area had already long been home to Powhatan tribes.

During their first few years in the New World, the English colonists devoted most of their energies to securing the stockade at Jamestown. Their arrival had displaced many of the Algonquin and other Native Americans in the region and, as a result, the newcomers often found themselves engaged in violent battles with the indigenous tribes. Temporary truces brought occasional respite from the hostilities, but it still proved difficult to entice settlers to homestead outside the stockade. Several attempts to colonize a site near the falls on the James River failed due to repeated conflicts with angry Algonquins.

## The Founding of Richmond

In 1637, however, Thomas Stegg set up a trading post at the spot where the river became navigable; he was later granted some additional land around the falls. After a sudden native uprising in 1644, some Jamestown settlers built a fort near Stegg's claim and offered freedom from taxation to anyone willing to establish a home there. Few people took the settlers up on their offer until after 1670 when, upon the death of Stegg's son, the family holdings (which had expanded to include property on both sides of the river) passed to William Byrd I, a nephew. Byrd received certain additional privileges in return for inducing able-bodied men to homestead in the area, and at last the post began to grow, eventually becoming a trading center for furs, tobacco, and other products.

The year 1737 marked the official laying out of the town of Richmond and its founding as the central marketplace for inland Virginia. Despite the fact that it served as host to three historic political conventions in the pre-Revolutionary War years, including the one at which Patrick Henry closed his impassioned speech with the memorable "Give me liberty or give me death," the town grew very slowly throughout most of the rest of the eighteenth century, even after it was named the capital of Virginia in 1779. Following the Revolutionary War, however, Richmond entered an era of rapid growth. In 1782, it was officially incorporated as a city. By 1790, it boasted a population of 3,761 people, up from only 684 people ten years earlier.

## City Made Confederate Capital

By the time of the Civil War, Richmond was one of the major commercial and industrial centers of the country. It prospered as a port city. In addition, America's first iron and brick supplies were manufactured in Richmond, and the first-discovered coal veins in America were mined in neighboring Chesterfield County. Tobacco processing and flour milling also emerged as regional industrial powers. Shortly after Virginia seceded from the Union in April 1861, Richmond was made the capital of the Confederacy in acknowledgment of its preeminent economic and political position.

The Civil War left the city in ruins. Besieged for nearly four years by Union troops but never taken in battle, Richmond was very nearly destroyed in April 1865 by Confederate troops who set fire to tobacco and cotton warehouses as they fled the city. After the war, Richmond began the slow task of rebuilding its bankrupt economy. The old industries, tobacco and iron in particular, once again surfaced as the dominant forces, remaining so throughout the early 1900s. Banking also emerged as an important factor on the local scene as Richmond became one of the South's leading financial centers.

## A City Divided and Finally United

Both world wars sparked industrial expansion in Richmond, leading to a diversification that has made the area prosperous for many years. Racial tensions surfaced during the 1950s with the development of a strategy of "massive resistance" during which Virginia politicians and leaders were encouraged to prevent desegregation of schools in the wake of the *Brown vs. the Board of Education* ruling. The NAACP filed numerous suits and the federal government ordered integration of a number of Virginia counties and municipalities; in response, the Virginia governor ordered many schools to close rather than comply. Richmond fought integration until 1970, when a district court judge devised a busing strategy to integrate the schools. Sixteen years later, the same judge approved a neighborhood schools system that effectively ended the city's struggles in regard to segregation.

The 1980s were marked by concerted efforts to foster cooperation and growth to benefit the entire metropolitan area. Those efforts are felt today, as Richmond is not only a manufacturing center of note, but also a hub for research, federal and state government, banking, transportation, trade, and health care. It is a city that is committed to preserving the best of its nearly 400-year past while carefully crafting a future that includes continued economic development. This synthesis is possibly reflected best in the development agency Richmond Renaissance, which acts as a bridge between the corporate, governmental, and African American communities as they work toward a common goal of a vital, thriving city in the "New South."

**Historical Information:** Library of Virginia, 800 E. Broad Street, Richmond, VA 23219; telephone (804)692-3500. Virginia Historical Society Library and Museum, 428 North Blvd., PO Box 7311, Richmond, VA 23221; telephone (804)358-4901

# Population Profile

## Metropolitan Area Residents
*1980:* 761,000
*1990:* 865,640
*2000:* 1,096,957
*Percent change, 1990–2000:* 13.7%
*U.S. rank in 1980:* 48th (MSA)
*U.S. rank in 1990:* 49th (MSA)
*U.S. rank in 2000:* 46th (MSA)

## City Residents
*1980:* 219,214
*1990:* 202,798
*2000:* 197,790
*2003 estimate:* 194,729
*Percent change, 1990–2000:* −2.5%
*U.S. rank in 1980:* 64th
*U.S. rank in 1990:* 76th (State rank: 3rd)
*U.S. rank in 2000:* 105th (State rank: 4th)

*Density:* 3,292.6 people per square mile (in 2000)

*Racial and ethnic characteristics* (2000)
    White: 75,744
    Black or African American: 113,108
    American Indian or Alaska Native: 479
    Asian: 2,471
    Native Hawaiian or Other Pacific Islander: 157
    Hispanic or Latino (may be of any race): 5,074
    Other: 2,948

*Percent of residents born in state:* 67.2% (2000)

*Age characteristics* (2000)
    Population under 5 years old: 12,376
    Population 5 to 9 years old: 12,765
    Population 10 to 14 years old: 11,713
    Population 15 to 19 years old: 13,870
    Population 20 to 24 years old: 18,386
    Population 25 to 34 years old: 32,871
    Population 35 to 44 years old: 29,841
    Population 45 to 54 years old: 24,985
    Population 55 to 59 years old: 8,208
    Population 60 to 64 years old: 6,646
    Population 65 to 74 years old: 12,843
    Population 75 to 84 years old: 9,764
    Population 85 years and older: 3,522
    Median age: 33.9 years (2000)

*Births* (2003)
    Total number: 3,069

*Deaths* (2003)
    Total number: 2,368 (of which, 44 were infants under
        the age of 1 year)

*Money income* (2000)
    Per capita income: $20,337
    Median household income: $31,121
    Total households: 84,549

*Number of households with income of . . .*
    less than $10,000: 13,492
    $10,000 to $14,999: 6,914
    $15,000 to $24,999: 13,688
    $25,000 to $34,999: 12,197
    $35,000 to $49,999: 13,317
    $50,000 to $74,999: 12,482
    $75,000 to $99,999: 5,465
    $100,000 to $149,999: 3,999
    $150,000 to $199,999: 1,253
    $200,000 or more: 1,759

*Percent of families below poverty level:* 17.1% (33.68%
    of which were female householder families with re-
    lated children under 5 years)

*2002 FBI Crime Index Total:* 18,002

# Municipal Government

The city of Richmond operates under the mayor-council
form of government, with council members serving two-
year terms and each representing one of nine districts in the
city. A mayor is elected by the general populace, and the
council elects a vice-mayor and assistant vice-mayor from

among its own ranks. The city was formerly governed by a
council-manager system and in 2004 elected its first mayor
in almost 60 years.

**Head Official:** Mayor L. Douglas Wilder (D) (since 2004;
    current term expires 2006)

**Total Number of City Employees:** 8,761 (2004)

*City Information:* City of Richmond, 900 East Broad Street,
Richmond, VA 23219; telephone (804) 646-7000

# Economy

## Major Industries and Commercial Activity

The Richmond area has a strong and diverse manufacturing
base that has helped the community remain resilient during
economic recessions and even the Great Depression. Other
factors that have contributed to this economic stability include the concentration of federal and state agencies, the
headquarters of major corporations and bank-holding companies, numerous health facilities, and the concentration of
educational institutions in the area. Services and government
together account for more than half of all jobs in Richmond.

Information technology and major semiconductor manufacturing firms have been attracted to Richmond throughout the
past 7 to 10 years. The increase in semiconductor firms in the
area has made the city a central point of the East Coast's
Silicon Dominion. Cutting edge technology makes Richmond
a hub for innovation and entrepreneurship. The Virginia Biotechnology Research Park, located in the heart of the East
Coast's pharmaceutical and biotechnology corridor, supports
research and development in drug development, medical diagnostics, biomedical engineering, forensics and environmental analysis. Located on 20 acres next to Virginia
Commonwealth University's (VCU) Medical College of Virginia, the facility is home to about 45 biotechnology, bioscience and other related companies and research institutions.

Richmond, as headquarters of the Fifth Federal Reserve
District, is a financial nerve center for an industrially strong
and diverse region that consists of Maryland, Virginia, West
Virginia, North Carolina, South Carolina, and the District of
Columbia. Banking has always been a significant employment factor in the Richmond area, and liberalization of
banking laws has increased the centralization of headquarters activity in the Richmond area by many of the state's
large and regionally oriented banks.

Insurance is also a strong, steady growth industry in the
Richmond area. Richmond is headquarters for GE Financial
Assurance (a unit of GE Capital Services), Anthem, Inc.,

Markel Corp., and LandAmerica Financial Group, as well as diversified financial service companies.

Philip Morris, which began in tobacco production, has been a part of Richmond's business community since 1929. Richmond's $200 million Philip Morris Manufacturing Center today is the largest and most modern facility of its kind in the world. Located on a 200-acre site, the 1.6-million-square-foot facility represents the largest single capital investment in Philip Morris history. Richmond has become a major East Coast distribution center and customer service center with the arrival of firms like Capital One, Hewlett Packard, Owens & Minor, Mazda, and Time-Life.

Other major companies with substantial capital investment in plants and operations in the Richmond area are DuPont, Allied Corporation, Kraft Foods, McKesson Corp., Alcoa and Smurfit-Stone Containers. Five *Fortune* 500 companies are headquartered in the region, including CSX, Dominion Resources, Circuit City Stores, Performance Food Group, and Pittston Company.

*Items and goods produced:* tobacco products, toiletries, processed foods, aluminum, chemicals, textiles, paper, printing, over-the-counter pharmaceuticals

## Incentive programs—New and Existing Companies

*Local programs*—In addition to the state's enterprise zone incentives, Richmond contributes local tax and financing incentives in designated Enterprise Zones. At the Richmond International Airport, Foreign Trade Zone #207 allows for imported goods to be held in the zone and exempted from U.S. Customs duties until they've crossed the zone barrier into use in the United States. The Greater Richmond Partnership, Inc., provides relocation services for personnel of new companies, and financing for small businesses is available through the James River Certified Development Corporation, the Crater Development Corporation and the Micro Enterprise Program with the City of Richmond. The City of Richmond also offers infrastructure improvement incentives.

*State programs*—Virginia is a right-to-work state. The State General Assembly has kept Virginia's taxes on industry very competitive by maintaining relatively moderate corporate income tax rates for nearly 30 years and by eliminating many tax irritants, resulting in very modest tax bills for business and industry. While this alone constitutes an attractive incentive for new and existing businesses, the State of Virginia further offers Governor's Opportunity Funds, which allows the Governor to secure business locations or expansion projects with matching funds from the local community; Virginia Investment Partnership Grant Funds, supporting large employers with businesses established for a minimum of five years in Virginia; property tax exemptions;

sales and use tax exemptions; enterprise zones; technology zones; and foreign trade zones.

*Job training programs*—The Virginia Workforce Development Services program, located in Richmond, is a cooperative effort of the Virginia Community College System with local businesses to cultivate a deep, skilled pool of workers who can benefit local industries and achieve their own career goals. Two community colleges, J. Sargeant Reynolds Community College and John Tyler Community College, have joined forces to create the Community College Workforce Alliance. The CCWA supports economic development and provides workforce development in both the private and public sectors. Employers can potentially receive a tax credit for sending their employees through professional development with CCWA. The Virginia Employment Commission offers job resources and assistance to workers and serves employers through applicant screening, labor market information reports, and unemployment insurance administration. The Capital Area Training Consortium, with an office in Richmond, is an official Employment and Training Agency providing career assessment, counseling, training, re-training and job search assistance. Community members with disabilities can access job training and support services via the Department of Rehabilitative Services, while older job seekers may find assistance through the Capital Area Agency on Aging.

## Development Projects

After Tropical Depression Gaston flooded the Shockoe Bottom District along the James River in 2004, local business owners and the City of Richmond were able to access Federal Emergency Management Agency support to bolster ongoing efforts to rebuild, renovate, and ultimately revitalize that historic area. Several loft and apartment residence projects have been recently completed or are underway, and the 40,000 square foot former site of Lady Byrd Hat Company is being developed into a multi-tenant site that will potentially incorporate entertainment, restaurant, and retail areas. In 2005 the Tredegar National Civil War Center will complete phase one of a museum that will eventually provide a holistic look at the Civil War from Union, Confederate and African American perspectives. Riverside on the James, a mixed-use development project along the Canal Walk, is expected to reach completion in 2005 and will add more than 275,000 square feet of retail, office and apartment space to the area. Dominion Virginia Power will add 1,200 jobs to the River District as it expands its headquarters.

In 2005, the Richmond Braves Triple-A baseball team pitched a concept for a $330 million ballpark to be built in the Shockoe Bottom District. The project was still in public hearing stages in the early part of the year, but the community reportedly supports the addition of an event-driven venue in an area that is increasingly busy and alive.

The Richmond Office of Economic Development reports that Richmond is in the middle of a scientific renaissance, in large part because of Richmond's Virginia Biotechnology Research Park and the Medical College of Virginia. Development at the Virginia Biotechnology Research Park began in 1997 and is only one-third completed at present; even so, it houses more than 45 biosciences entities, research institutes affiliated with Virginia Commonwealth University, and state and national medical laboratories. The Park isn't confined to the 34 acre downtown campus, having branches and partnerships in Henrico and Chesterfield counties.

An expansion of the Greater Richmond Convention Center was completed in 2003, bringing the facility up to 700,000 total square feet of space—180,000 square feet of exhibit space, 32 meeting rooms totaling 50,000 square feet, and a 30,550 square foot Grand Ballroom.

The Richmond Coliseum received a seven million dollar facelift. With new seats, lights, paint schemes, elevators, a kitchen, and floors in addition to renovated restrooms and an onsite professional chef, the updated building is more inviting and will ideally draw more ticket purchasers to big name musical concerts.

***Economic Development Information:*** Greater Richmond Partnership, 901 East Byrd Street, Suite 801, Richmond, VA 23219-4070; telephone (804)643-3227; toll-free (800)229-6332. City of Richmond Office of Economic Development, 501 E. Franklin St., Suite 800, Richmond, VA 23219; telephone (804)646-5633; fax (804)646-6793; email econdev @ci.richmond.va.us

## Commercial Shipping

Richmond has its own port, owned by the municipal government and offering direct container ship service to Europe, Mexico, the Mediterranean, the Caribbean, and South America. The Port of Richmond is located four miles south of Richmond's Central Business District and offers services such as stevedoring, supply chain services, export packaging and transfer, and warehouse and inland distribution services. The port is equipped for heavy lifting and can handle a range of cargo, from livestock to breakbulk.

Seven air cargo and cargo charter flights can be accessed at the Richmond International Airport, which is located 10 minutes from the downtown area. The airport is a Foreign Trade Zone with U.S. Customs inspection on-site and can hold cargo in 142,000 square feet of warehouse space. Six major passenger carriers provide service to cities across North America, with 180 daily flights.

Richmond is criss-crossed by north-south and east-west interstates and railroads, making it an ideal United Parcel Service (UPS) district hub and FedEx regional hub. More than 100 motor freight companies and brokers serve the area and can handle loads including heavy hauling, liquid bulk, dry bulk and oversize loads. The Richmond area is within a day's drive of 50 percent of the U.S. population, 55 percent of the nation's manufacturing facilities, and 60 percent of the country's corporate headquarters. A 750-mile radius encompasses almost three-fifths of the population and two-thirds of the nation's manufacturing facilities.

Two rail lines converge in Richmond: the Norfolk Southern and CSX, which is the nation's largest railroad and has its corporate headquarters in Richmond. CSX covers 23,000 miles across 23 states and extends its reach to Canada, Mexico, Europe, Asia, Latin America, Australia, Hong Kong, China and Russia. CSX provides service to and from the Port of Richmond along with international terminal services, domestic container shipping, domestic ocean-liner services, and more.

## Labor Force and Employment Outlook

Trends over the past ten years indicate that the number of manufacturing and federal government jobs is on the decline, while employment opportunities in services and finance (banking, insurance, real estate) have demonstrated a spike. The Richmond area has a higher percentage of white-collar professional, technical, sales and clerical workers than both the South Atlantic region and the United States as a whole. Blue-collar and service-worker totals are close to the national average. The percentage of women in the work force is higher in the Richmond region than in the United States as a whole.

Generally speaking, a positive labor-management relationship enhances the Richmond work ethic. As the northernmost right-to-work state, less than 10 percent of the work force is organized, and approximately 30 percent of workers in union shops choose not to join. Strikes are rare, and Richmond enjoys one of the lowest work-stoppage records in the nation.

The following is a summary of data regarding the Richmond-Petersburg metropolitan area labor force as of 2003.

*Size of nonagricultural labor force:* 564,100

*Number of workers employed in . . .*
  *construction and mining:* 38,500
  *manufacturing:* 45,300
  *trade, transportation and public utilities:* 107,400
  *information:* 11,600
  *financial activities:* 45,900
  *professional and business services:* 82,700
  *educational and health services:* 58,500
  *leisure and hospitality:* 44,500
  *other services:* 24,500
  *government:* 105,100

*Average hourly earnings of production workers employed in manufacturing:* $16.39

*Unemployment rate:* 3.6% (December 2004)

| Largest private employers | Number of employees |
|---|---|
| Capital One Financial Corp. | 9,018 |
| Philip Morris | 6,462 |
| HCA Inc | 6,454 |
| Virginia Commonwealth University Health | 6,216 |
| Wal-Mart Stores, Inc. | 5,449 |
| Wachovia Corp. | 4,521 |
| Bon Secours Richmond Health | 4,044 |

## Cost of Living

The following is a summary of data regarding key cost of living factors for the Richmond area.

*2004 (3rd Quarter) ACCRA Average House Price:* $263,334

*2004 (3rd Quarter) ACCRA Cost of Living Index:* 101.5 (U.S. average = 100.0)

*State income tax rate:* Ranges from 2.0% to 5.75%

*State sales tax rate:* 4% (2.5% on food after 4/1/01)

*Local income tax rate:* none

*Local sales tax rate:* 1.0%

*Property tax rate:* $3.70 per $100 assessed value

**Economic Information:** Greater Richmond Chamber of Commerce, 201 E. Franklin St., Richmond, VA 23219; telephone (804)648-1234

# Education and Research

## Elementary and Secondary Schools

The Richmond public schools, one of four major systems in the area, are garnering a growing share of excellent achievement results, and the system has earned a reputation for innovative and highly successful new programs. The Special Achievement for Academic and Creative Excellence, or SPACE, program provides accelerated challenges for elementary, middle and high school students. Richmond Community High School provides a focused curriculum to prepare gifted students for college; the school emphasizes outreach to economically and socially disadvantaged youth. The city also has a public military school, the first in the nation in a public school system. The Open High School offers academic strategies to reach alternative learners.

All four public school systems in the Richmond area have one joint educational venture, the Mathematics and Science Center located in Henrico County. It is believed to be the only such regional center in the country supported completely by local funds, and it is one of the early examples of regional cooperation in the Richmond area.

The following is a summary of data regarding Richmond's public schools as of the 2003–2004 school year.

*Total enrollment:* 25,000

*Number of facilities*
   *elementary schools:* 31
   *junior high/middle schools:* 9
   *senior high schools:* 8
   *other:* 17, including one military school and a gifted high school

*Student/teacher ratio:* K-1, 24:1; grades 2-5, 25:1; grades 6-12, 22:1

*Teacher salaries*
   *minimum:* $34,948
   *maximum:* $79,676

*Funding per pupil:* $7,969

More than 45 alternative institutions offer instruction to Richmond area students, including private college-preparatory schools and schools for exceptional children.

## Colleges and Universities

Metro Richmond is home to 11 institutions of higher learning. Virginia Commonwealth University (VCU) is the state's largest urban public university; it enrolls more than 24,000 students. VCU is the home of the Medical College of Virginia and additionally offers 162 baccalaureate, master's, doctoral and certificate degree programs in the Colleges of Humanities and Sciences, and schools of Allied Health Professions, Arts, Basic Health Sciences, Business, Community and International Programs, Dentistry, Education, Graduate Studies, School of Medicine, Nursing, Pharmacy, and Social Work. VCU has an entrepreneurship program for young women at its School of Business. In 1998, VCU added a $40 million School of Engineering facility that houses a Microelectronics Center with clean room technology for semiconductor research.

The University of Richmond is one of the largest private colleges in Virginia and one of the most academically challenging schools in the country. It began in 1830 as Richmond College, a college of liberal arts and sciences for men. Around this nucleus have been added the School of Arts and Sciences, the Jepson School of Leadership Studies (the first school of its kind in the nation), and the E. Claiborne Robins School of Business. The school opened the T.C. Williams School of Law in 1870, making it one of the oldest law schools in the state. The university offers its enrollment of 2,976 undergraduates a menu of baccalaureate degrees in 56 major areas of study, with 40 minors and 12 concentrations.

Virginia Union University was founded in 1865 by the Baptist Church to give educational opportunities to African Americans. Today it offers its diverse student body undergraduate liberal arts, sciences, education, and business courses, as well as graduate courses in theology. The liberal arts foundation is augmented by specialized programs, such as a dual-degree engineering program, offered in conjunction with the University of Michigan, the University of Iowa, and Howard University in Washington, D.C.

Union Theological Seminary is one of the top ten theological institutions in the nation. It is recognized for its rigorous academic program and its pioneering work in field education and student-in-ministry experiences. A seminary of the Presbyterian Church (USA), Union Theological offers doctor of ministry, master of divinity, master of theology, and doctor of philosophy degrees. The Presbyterian School of Christian Education, a graduate school, is the only one of eleven theological institutions of the Presbyterian Church to specialize solely in the discipline of Christian education.

J. Sargeant Reynolds Community College operates three campuses: one in downtown Richmond, another in Henrico County, and the western campus in Goochland County. It offers programs in liberal arts and sciences, engineering, education, and business administration as well as technical vocation training in a number of fields.

John Tyler Community College operates a main campus in Chesterfield County and two auxiliary campuses. Also offering higher educational opportunities in Metro Richmond are Randolph-Macon College, Virginia State University, and Richard Bland Community College.

### Libraries and Research Centers

Libraries abound in Richmond. There is the Library of Virginia, with 1,783,287 books, periodicals, government publications and microforms specializing in Virginiana, Southern and Confederate history, and genealogy. The Richmond Public Library system has a main library plus 9 branches containing more than 800,000 books, periodicals, and audio- and videocassettes. The county of Henrico library system has more than 550,000 books, videocassettes, periodicals, and art prints. Many other libraries are operated by area universities, colleges, and museums. The Virginia Department for the Blind and Vision Impaired is a member of the National Library Service for the Visually and Physically Handicapped, a Library of Congress network. As the seat of government in Virginia, Richmond is naturally home to the primary branch of the Virginia State Law Library, containing comprehensive legal materials for use by defendants, inmates, attorneys, the courts and the general public.

Virginia Commonwealth University is home to the third largest research library system in the state of Virginia, with more than 1.7 million print volumes. The Tompkins-McCaw Library at VCU contains the largest collection of medical materials in the state. In general, VCU is the headquarters of nearly a dozen research centers and programs, primarily in the biological and health sciences. Virginia Biotechnology Research Park is home to 45 biotechnology, bioscience, and other related companies and research institutions that are helping to make Virginia an East Coast technology leader. Also located in Richmond is the Hazardous Technical Information Services.

***Public Library Information:*** Richmond Public Library, 101 East Franklin Street, Richmond, VA 23219-2193; telephone (804)646-4867

# Health Care

Richmond has obvious credentials to support its claim as one of the best medical/health-service areas in the country. Eighteen general and specialized hospitals employ 2,000 physicians in the metropolitan area. The Columbia/HCA health system operates three hospitals in Greater Richmond: Chippenham and Johnston-Willis Hospitals have been merged to form CJW Medical Center, nationally recognized as a heart-bypass surgery center and also on the cutting edge of neuroscience; Henrico Doctors' Hospital, which performs organ transplants and is home of the Virginia Cancer Treatment Center; and Retreat Hospital, which offers mind-body medicine, wound healing, and geriatric care. Bon Secours Richmond Health System, a not-for-profit Catholic system, operates three hospitals and numerous outpatient service sites.

Largest among the area's major health-care institutions is the Virginia Commonwealth University Medical Center. The Medical Center provides a real-life laboratory for teaching, research, community service, and health-care delivery and is the centerpiece of the health sciences campus of Virginia Commonwealth University. The hospital has the area's only Level I Trauma Center and sees more than 30,000 admissions per year, with 500,000 outpatients seen annually.

# Recreation

### Sightseeing

Richmond boasts more than 100 attractions of interest to visitors. Among them are homes and other buildings from all eras of the city's history, as well as battlegrounds and

The Jefferson Davis Monument, located on Monument Avenue.

cemeteries. A great place to start is with the Canal Walk along the James River in downtown Richmond, where visitors can meander for 1.25 miles by foot or ride a tour boat past 22 historical markers, statues and points of interest. One of those points of interest is the Civil War Visitor Center along the Canal Walk. Housed in the former Tredegar Iron Works, the Civil War Visitor Center contains three floors of exhibits and interpretive displays recollecting Richmond's role in the Civil War, and provides an introduction to the National Battlefield Park in Richmond.

A convenient next stop along the Canal Walk is Brown's Island, a historic city park often used for outdoor concerts, picnics, biking, and Frisbee. Belle Isle is accessible via the footbridge under the Lee Bridge near the Tredegar Iron Works building. The site served as a camp for Union prisoners of war but is now a popular recreation spot for Richmond residents. More canal history is reflected by the Kanawha Canal Locks, where Reynolds Metals Company has preserved two locks that were built in 1854. The magnificent stone locks were part of the nation's first canal system, as originally planned by George Washington to carry river traffic around the falls.

The Floodwall along the James River, built to minimize damage from storm-induced rising waters, has become a work of art in its own right with the Floodwall Picture Gallery of murals. A walking tour can transition from the Floodwall into the Shockoe Bottom District, where a variety of historic structures remain and have been restored postflood. The focal point in Capital Square's 12-acre park-like setting is the Virginia State Capitol, which has served as the seat of state government since 1788. Thomas Jefferson designed the central portion of the classic building, the first of its kind in America. Inside, French sculptor Houdon's lifesize statute of George Washington stands in the Rotunda.

Visitors can find many examples of residential life in early Richmond, including Scotchtown, which was the Hanover County home that Patrick Henry occupied during the years of his Revolutionary War activities. The restored house and grounds are a national historic landmark. City-owned and recently restored as a museum, John Marshall's sturdy but unpretentious brick house (1790) honors the third Chief Justice of the U.S. Supreme Court who lived in Richmond. Built in 1813 and frequently remodeled (most recently in 1999 at a cost of $7.2 million), the Governor's Mansion is the oldest executive mansion in the United States in continuous use for its original purpose. It has been furnished with fine antiques by a Virginia citizens group. Dabbs House is a pre-Civil War dwelling that was used by General Robert E. Lee as headquarters during the "Seven Days Battle" in 1862. It is now Henrico eastern division police headquarters. This White House of the Confederacy served as the residence of Jefferson Davis during the Civil War. The Maggie

Walker House, now a museum, was the home of the African American woman who became the nation's first woman of any race to found a bank and become its president.

The late-Victorian estate Maymont, located in the heart of Richmond, has more than 100 acres featuring a Victorian home and decorative arts, formal Japanese and Italian gardens, a unique arboretum, a nature center with an outdoor wildlife habitat (native Virginia species), a demonstration farm, and a working carriage collection. Maymont opened the doors of its new Robins Nature and Visitors Center in late 1999; the center features a 20-foot waterfall and exhibits describing the history and power of the James River.

Agecroft Hall, a medieval manor house moved to Richmond from England during the 1920s, is perched above the James River much as it originally overlooked the Irwell River. The house was built in England about the time Columbus was planning his voyage in 1492 to the New World. It is now a museum house open to the public and features an Elizabethan Knot garden. Also shipped to Richmond from England during the 1920s were portions of the sixteenth-century English house, Warwick Priory. Situated in Windsor Farms, a fashionable residential area, it was originally a private home but is now a museum known as Virginia House.

Sightseers can visit several other kinds of historic buildings in Richmond. At Hanover Courthouse, a young Patrick Henry successfully argued his first major case. St. John's Church in Richmond's Church Hill district, built in 1741, is famous as the site of Henry's impassioned "Give me liberty or give me death" speech. Finally, the Egyptian Building, erected in 1845 and still in use, is the Medical College of Virginia's first building. Its Egyptian Revival architecture is regarded as the finest of its kind in the country. The Egyptian motif extends to the fence, which has posts shaped like mummy cases.

History buffs may also find places of interest elsewhere in and around the Richmond area. Flowerdew Hundred is the site of an excavated, seventeenth-century English settlement in Prince George County, location of the first windmill in English North America. A visitors center in the former plantation schoolhouse features films and archaeological exhibits. Chickahominy Bluff, Cold Harbor, Malvern Hill, Fort Harrison, and Drewry's Bluff have special interpretive facilities. Hollywood Cemetery (named for its holly trees) is the burial place of U.S. presidents James Monroe and John Tyler, Confederate president Jefferson Davis, General J.E.B. Stuart and 1,800 Confederate soldiers, along with members of prominent Richmond families. Illustrious Chief Justice John Marshall and the infamous Elizabeth Van Lew, a Yankee spy during the Civil War, are both buried at Shockoe Cemetery.

Atop the 22-story City Hall is a sky deck from which visitors can obtain a sweeping view of Richmond and its environs. A map is available to help identify the visible landmarks in a panorama that covers four centuries of the city's history.

Plantation homes dating from the seventeenth century fan out on all sides of Richmond. Of special interest are the elegant James River Plantations to the east. Other Richmond area plantations include Belle Air (c. 1670); Berkeley (ancestral home of two U.S. presidents and the site of the first Thanksgiving in 1619); Evelynton (ancestral home of the Ruffin family); Sherwood Forest (home of President John Tyler); Shirley (home of the Carter family since 1723); Tuckahoe Plantation (the most complete plantation layout in North America, dating from the eighteenth century); Westover (c. 1730; home of William Byrd II, founder of Richmond); and Wilton (built in 1750 by William Randolph II and moved to Richmond in 1933).

Self-guided automobile tours, bus tours, walking tours, individual tours, and riverboat paddlewheel cruises (as far downriver as Shirley Plantation) are also available. Philip Morris offers regular tours of its $200 million cigarette manufacturing center, which also houses a tobacco museum, shop, and visitors' gallery. Antique shopping is also a favorite pastime.

Visitors and residents alike find relaxation and meaning along the statue-studded length of Monument Avenue. Robert E. Lee, "Stonewall" Jackson, J.E.B. Stuart, Jefferson Davis, Bill "Mr. Bojangles" Robinson, Arthur Ashe, and Matthew Moury each command major focal points. One of the grand boulevards of the world, Monument Avenue provides a good site for an easy-paced stroll, and it is closed off once a year for one of the city's largest street festivals.

### Arts and Culture

A driving and energetic force in the Richmond arts and culture scene is the Arts Council of Richmond, Inc., which sponsors festivals and art exhibits throughout the year. The Arts Council has established partnerships with all Richmond Public Schools in an effort to extend the performing and visual art experience to students of all ages.

The Carpenter Center for the Performing Arts is housed in the renovated Loew's Theatre in downtown Richmond. The Carpenter Center is the home of the Richmond Symphony and offers local ballet and opera, as well as Broadway shows and other productions of national acclaim.

The Richmond Symphony and the Richmond Philharmonic remain dynamic musical entities in the area. The Richmond Symphony's Masterworks Series focuses on the classics and brings the world's great soloists to the city, while programs such as Kicked Back Classics and Family Concerts broaden the appeal of the traditional symphonic repertoire. The Richmond Philharmonic, a member-run orchestra, has entertained Richmond for more than 30 years and performs four or five concerts per season.

Richmond is also home to a number of community orchestras and choruses, school and university musical organizations, and a growing number of other musical groups. The Virginia Opera Association performs an expanded number of productions each season at the Landmark Theater, the Edythe C. and Stanley L. Harrison Opera House, and George Mason University's Center for the Arts. The opera company operates a nationally-recognized In-School Touring Program to bring opera to the students, then brings the students to the opera with special Student Nights and Student Matinees. The Richmond Pops/Great Big Band plays a winter series as well as a summer series. The Richmond Concert Band's annual Fourth of July performance in Dogwood Dell of Tchaikovsky's *1812 Overture* is a Richmond tradition. Other musical groups include the Greater Richmond Chapter of the Sweet Adelines, the Virginia Chorale, the Richmond Chamber Players, the Richmond Renaissance Singers, and many others. Outdoor performances are frequently presented at parks and public sites around the city.

Theater of all sorts is plentiful. Besides Carpenter Center, Richmond's Landmark Theater plays host to musical groups of national prominence in an opulent structure equipped with a magnificent Wurlitzer theater organ.

Theater IV is one of Richmond's most active theater companies. The company is based in the renovated Empire Theatre, the oldest theater still in use in Virginia. It offers a Broadway Series, an Off-Broadway Series, and a Family Playhouse, the nation's second largest children's theater. The Barksdale Theatre houses the oldest not-for-profit theater in the area and features professionally-staged productions throughout the year. For a more off-beat or contemporary theater experience, the Firehouse Theatre Project offers productions of off-Broadway and original works never before seen in the Richmond area. The Richmond Triangle Players push the envelope even more, in theater that explores alternative themes.

Theatre VCU, Virginia Commonwealth University's student theater group, performs dramas, comedies, and musicals in the university's Shafer Street Playhouse and in the Raymond Hodges Theatre in VCU's Performing Arts Center. The University Players at the University of Richmond perform four productions a year in the Camp Theater of the Modlin Fine Arts Center. Virginia Union University Players perform in the university's Wall Auditorium. The Randolph-Macon Drama Guild presents four plays a season in the college's old Chapel Theater. Other theater groups include Chamberlayne Actors Theatre, Fieldens Cabaret Theater, and the Henrico Theatre Company.

Richmond also has three ballet companies: the Richmond Ballet, the Concert Ballet of Virginia, and the Latin Ballet of Virginia. The Richmond Ballet's interpretation of *The Nutcracker* is an annual Christmas classic that has been playing to sold-out audiences for years. The Richmond Ballet is a professional ballet company, maintaining dancers on full-time seasonal contracts. Accompanied by the Richmond Symphony, it provides the best dance training in the state and attracts dancers from across the United States and abroad, with an impressive repertoire and touring schedule throughout the state and nation. The Concert Ballet of Virginia holds four repertoire programs per season featuring Virginia composers, choreographers, musicians, and dancers. The Latin Ballet of Richmond is a relatively recent addition, having formed as a non-profit in 1997. The company aims to fuse Latin dance styles with ballet in evoking the passionate cultures and histories of Spain and Latin America. The company educates and attracts diverse participants and audiences through its outreach activities and performances.

The Virginia Museum of Fine Arts has long had a national reputation for creative and innovative arts programming, dating back to its founding in 1936 as the nation's first state-supported art museum. The museum achieved an international reputation with the 1985 opening of the West Wing, which houses collections of nineteenth- and twentieth-century decorative arts, contemporary paintings and sculptures, and various eighteenth-, nineteenth-, and twentieth-century British, French, and American works of art. Further expansion is planned that will create more parking, improve the fire suppression system, and refine the sculpture garden. The museum houses more than 30 permanent galleries, as well as collections that are broad and varied: French Impressionists, Indian sculpture, medieval tapestries, French Romantics, American art of all periods, and the largest collection outside Russia of the Russian Imperial jewels crafted by Peter Carl Fabergé.

Another museum that has focused international attention on Richmond is the Science Museum of Virginia. The museum's $7 million Universe Planetarium/Space Theater is equipped with Digistar 1, the world's first computer graphics planetarium projection system. Information on the 6,772 stars visible from earth and the 55 known major objects in the solar system is programmed in the computer's memory. The 280-seat domed theater has the largest projection surface of any planetarium in the world, and the world's largest projector, the Omnimax, is used to present 70-millimeter film productions on the wraparound screen. The Science Museum also owns the Aviation Museum on the east side of Richmond and has plans to expand that facility with a new wing. Development at the Science Museum includes new exhibits on local industry and technology, as well as in-depth looks at ecosystems. The museum operates a Science-by-Van program that takes sciences out to the public schools.

Besides the Science Museum and the Virginia Museum of Fine Arts, there are many other Richmond-area museums, all distinctive in character. Among them is the Chesterfield County Museum, which houses murals and displays depicting the county's history through the Revolutionary and Civil wars and into modern times. Among its artifacts, the Museum of the Confederacy displays the sword and uniform worn by Lee when he surrendered at Appomattox. The uniform coat worn by J.E.B. Stuart when he was felled is displayed at the Virginia Historical Society Museum, visible bullet hole and all. The Fire and Police Museum, dating to the early 1800s, uses window bars, a possible gallows, and fire poles to tell the story of its history as a jail and a police station. Memorabilia of Edgar Allan Poe is displayed in the Poe Museum; the eighteenth-century stone structure is believed to be the oldest in the city. The Virginia E. Randolph Museum, a Henrico County cottage, is dedicated in memory of Virginia E. Randolph, an African American woman who was a pioneer educator and humanitarian. The Black History Museum and Cultural Center of Virginia was founded in 1981 to preserve the oral, visual, and written records that commemorate the lives and accomplishments of African Americans in Virginia and to serve as a cultural and educational center for exhibitions, performances, and displays.

The Valentine Richmond History Center is devoted to the life and history of Richmond. The Children's Museum, established in 1981, introduces young people to the arts and humanities through participation in exhibits, workshops, and special programs; a move is planned for the Children's Museum that will triple its size.

Galleries include the Virginia Museum of Fine Arts, Virginia Commonwealth University's Anderson Gallery, and the 1708 Gallery. The University of Richmond features exhibitions in Marsh Gallery in the Modlin Fine Arts Center. Nonprofit galleries include the Weinstein Jewish Community Center, the Last Stop (home of the Richmond Chapter of the National Conference of Artists, an African American arts and education group), the Richmond Public Library, the Westover Hills Branch Library, and many bank spaces and commercial galleries.

**Festivals and Holidays**

Richmond hosts several major celebrations throughout the year. Perhaps the biggest of all is The Big Gig, a 16-day-long music festival in early July that offers classical Jazz, New Age, African, folk, and popular music performances staged at locations all over town. Music is also the focus at Jumpin', a series of weekly concerts held in July at the Virginia Museum of Fine Arts Sculpture Garden, as well as the Midweek Mojo and Friday Cheers concert series.

Richmond's other special celebrations include the Strawberry Hill Horse Races in April; the Virginia State Fair, a 12-day event held in late September and early October; February's Maymont Flower and Garden Show; the Winston Cup Race weekend in March; Historic Garden week in April; Arts in the Park, the Greek Festival, and the Camptown Races, all in May; the Virginia State Horse show in August; the 2nd Street Festival, celebrating African American history in September; November's Richmond Marathon; and the Grand Illumination and Christmas Parade in December.

### Sports for the Spectator

Richmond's ball park, The Diamond, is home to the Richmond Braves, a Triple A affiliate of the National League Atlanta Braves. A new $330 million ballpark proposal is under consideration by the government and citizenry of Richmond. The Richmond Rhythm of the International Basketball League had their inaugural season in 1999 at the recently-renovated Richmond Coliseum, an air-conditioned dome that also hosts stage shows, concerts, college basketball, professional basketball and hockey games, ice shows, the circus, and professional wrestling matches. Professional hockey is the forte of the Richmond Renegades, who play in the East Coast Hockey League and take on opponents at the Freezer. The Richmond Speed play arena football, and the Richmond Kickers are the local soccer team to watch. Richmond also hosts the Round-Robin World's Largest Softball Tournament each Memorial Day weekend, with teams from across the U.S., Canada and Iceland participating. Virginia Commonwealth University supports both men's and women's NCAA Division I basketball teams. In football action, the Gold Bowl Classic is one of 21 college games scheduled in the Richmond area during the year.

The Richmond International Raceway is the only three-quarter-mile track of its kind on the NASCAR circuit. The raceway is host to two Grand National Series races and two Winston Cup Series races.

### Sports for the Participant

The Richmond Marathon was mentioned as America's friendliest marathon in the January 2005 issue of *Runner's World* magazine, with comfortable temperatures, a scenic route and an enthusiastic crowd along the entire 26.2 mile route.

When Richmond residents want to get out, the James River is the destination of choice. Kayaking and rafting instruction and trips are available, and fishing is also a popular pastime. Attractions along the James also include James River Park, one of the few wilderness parks in the United States that has an urban setting. The 450-acre James River Park is just a tiny segment of what may be the largest amount of park space in any urban area of the country with a total of 24,118 acres of local, state, and national park land in and around the Richmond metropolitan area. The Pony Pasture loop trail is recommended as an easy, one-hour hike that passes through wetlands and meadows. Pocahontas State Park and Forest,

south of the river in Chesterfield County, and several lakes surrounding the Richmond area offer myriad outdoor activities as well.

Golfers can haul their clubs to any of a vast array of local and area courses, including the 18-hole Belmont Golf Course and the 27 holes of family golfing at the Hollows Golf Club just west of Richmond. Private and public tennis facilities are also available, most notably the Arthur Ashe Center.

### Shopping and Dining

Richmond's downtown area offers shoppers a wide variety of stores from which to choose. Shockoe Slip, a cobble-stoned riverfront area that used to serve as a cotton and tobacco trading district, is now a focus for nightlife, restaurants, shops, offices, and apartments. The Carytown section of Richmond features several blocks of unique and colorful shops and restaurants. The "On the Avenues" shopping area at the juncture of Libbie and Grove Avenues is a collection of 45 specialty shops intermingled with Victorian residences and sidewalk cafes, creating a boutique shopping experience. The 300-year-old 17th Street Farmers' Market supplies regional and organic foods to locals and tourists, along with an open-air community experience of conversation and music with neighbors. A variety of more mainstream malls are sprinkled throughout Richmond, including The Shops at Willow Lawn, Regency Square Mall, River Road Shopping Center, and Chesterfield Towne Center. Just outside the city are outlet malls that attract numerous bargain-hunters, and Richmond is within easy distance of the renowned Williamsburg Pottery Factory.

Richmond has cultivated an increasingly international flavor as a city, and its varied menu of restaurants is evidence. Barbecue and soul food eateries have a strong presence, with Italian and seafood spots running a close second. Other restaurant specialties include Argentinean, steaks, British, cheese and wine, Chinese, continental, French, German, Greek, Indian, international, Irish-American, Japanese, Vietnamese, Mexican-American, organic, Polynesian, regional specialties, southern cooking, and tea rooms.

***Visitor Information:*** Richmond Visitors Center, 405 N. 3rd St., Richmond, VA 23219; telephone (804)783-7450; toll free (800)866-3705

## Convention Facilities

The Greater Richmond Convention Center (GRCC) is the most capacious meeting and exhibition space in town, with 700,000 total square feet of room. Adjacent to the Richmond

Marriott Hotel and close to sports venues, GRCC accommodations include 180,000 square feet of exhibit space, 32 meeting rooms and a Grand Ballroom that spans 30,550 square feet. Within a short walk or trolley ride are one-third of the area's hotel rooms. The center is just blocks off Interstate 95 and within easy access of the Richmond International Airport.

Other convention and meeting facilities include the recently-renovated Richmond Coliseum, which offers a total of 50,000 square feet of exhibition space under a giant circular dome and is capable of seating up to 13,359 persons; Richmond's Landmark Theater; the Fairgrounds; the Showplace, and the Carpenter Center for the Performing Arts. More than 40 hotels have extensive meeting facilities.

*Convention Information:* Richmond Region Visitors Center, c/o Greater Richmond Convention Center, 403 North 3rd Street, Richmond, VA 23219; telephone (804)783-7450

# Transportation

### Approaching the City

Six major carriers with nonstop and direct flights to more than 200 cities serve Richmond International Airport (RIA), which is located 10 minutes, via Interstate 64, from the center city. Airlines include American, Delta, US Airways, Continental, NWA and United. The airport offers complete executive and general aviation services. More than 2.7 million passengers are estimated to pass through RIA in any given year, spurring current expansion plans to add air carrier gates, new roadways and a terminal extension. As an alternative to the busier RIA, general and corporate aviation services are also available at the Chesterfield County Airport.

Crisscrossing the metropolitan area are major north-south and east-west interstates. Interstate-95 provides ready access to markets up and down the East Coast. I-64 is a major corridor from St. Louis to the port of Hampton Roads. I-295 connects with I-95 to the north and south of Richmond. Intercity bus service, freight shipments, and express shipments are provided by Greyhound.

Rail passenger service is provided by Amtrak, serving the East Coast and points west with six passenger trains daily, plus four additional trains on selected days. Amtrak opened a new downtown Main Street Station in fall 2003, restoring a train station that was originally opened in 1901. The new station integrates bus, trolley, airport shuttle, taxi, limousine and train services within a multi-modal transportation hub that returned passenger train service to downtown Richmond.

### Traveling in the City

The Richmond area is served by a well-planned and well-maintained network of expressways, cross-town arteries, and streets that make the use of private vehicles convenient. The Greater Richmond Transit Company (GRTC) operates a fleet of buses on a radial network of routes that include park-and-ride lots and express service during peak hours. GRTC offers specialized services such as CARE and C-Van to provide access to riders with mobility issues, while the Ridefinders program matches carpool and vanpool candidates. From June through November, a trolley system connects sites in the different areas of downtown.

# Communications

### Newspapers and Magazines

Richmond's daily newspaper is the morning *Richmond Times-Dispatch.* Of the nine other newspapers or tabloids published in Richmond, four are religious-oriented, several are related to business or the media, one is dedicated to Richmond nightlife, and one is aimed at the population over the age of 50. The local universities each publish their own collegiate newspaper. Several other magazines and journals are published in Richmond, including *Richmond Magazine,* a lifestyle magazine and *Virginia Business,* a comprehensive statewide business journal.

### Television and Radio

Six television stations broadcast from Richmond: four network affiliates and two public broadcasting channels. Richmond is served by two cable television companies. Ten AM and FM radio stations broadcast from Richmond, featuring public radio, adult contemporary, sports, and others.

***Media Information:*** *Richmond Times-Dispatch,* 300 E. Franklin Street, Richmond, VA 23219; telephone (804) 649-6000; toll-free (800) 468-3382

### Richmond Online

City of Richmond home page. Available www.ci.richmond .va.us/index.asp

Greater Richmond Chamber of Commerce. Available www .grcc.com

Richmond Convention & Visitors Bureau (Richmond.com). Available www.richmond.com/visitors

Richmond Public Library. Available www.richmondpublic library.org

Richmond Public Schools. Available www.richmond.k12 .va.us

Richmond Renaissance. Available www.richmond renaissance.org

*Richmond Times-Dispatch.* Available www.timesdispatch .com

Virginia Department of Education, Superintendent of Schools' Reports. Available www.pen.k12.va.us/VDOE/ Publications

## Selected Bibliography

Furguson, Ernest B., *Ashes of Glory: Richmond at War* (New York: Alfred A. Knopf, 1996)

# Virginia Beach

## *The City in Brief*

**Founded:** 1906 (city formed by merger with Princess Anne County, 1963)

**Head Official:** Mayor Meyera E. Oberndorf (since July 1988); City Manager James Spore (since November 1991)

**City Population**
  1980: 262,000
  1990: 393,089
  2000: 425,257
  2003 estimate: 439,467
  **Percent change, 1990–2000:** 8.2%
  **U.S. rank in 1980:** 56th
  **U.S. rank in 1990:** 37th (State rank: 1st)
  **U.S. rank in 2000:** 38th (State rank: 1st)

**Metropolitan Area Population**
  1980: 1,201,000
  1990: 1,445,000

2000: 1,569,541
**Percent change, 1990–2000:** 8.8%
**U.S. rank in 1980:** 31st (MSA)
**U.S. rank in 1990:** 28th (MSA)
**U.S. rank in 2000:** 33rd (MSA)

**Area:** 248 square miles (2000)
**Elevation:** Sea level to 12 feet above sea level
**Average Annual Temperature:** 59.6° F
**Average Annual Precipitation:** 45.74 inches

**Major Economic Sectors:** services, wholesale and retail trade, government
**Unemployment rate:** 4.0% (December 2004)
**Per Capita Personal Income:** $22,365 (2000)

**2002 FBI Crime Index Total:** 15,492

**Major Colleges and Universities:** Old Dominion University, Norfolk State University, ODU/NSU Virginia Beach Higher Education Center, Regent University, Virginia Wesleyan College, Tidewater Community College

**Daily Newspaper:** *The Virginian-Pilot*

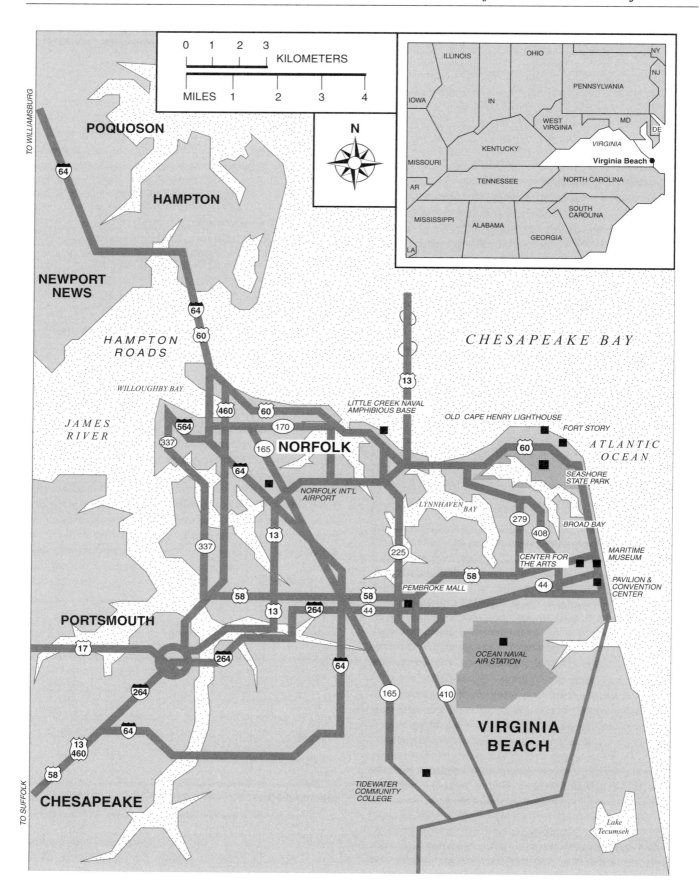

# Introduction

The city of Virginia Beach combines the elegance of a rich past with the energy of one of the most rapidly developing cities on the East Coast. Virginia Beach is part of a seven-city metropolitan area called Hampton Roads. Among the attractions of the city are 30 miles of shoreline with 28 miles of public beach, state-of-the-art medical facilities, and the ever-changing beauty of its four moderate seasons. Civic leaders, working together to ensure that growth is orderly and sensitive to environmental concerns, have formulated and implemented strategic plans for land use, economic development, and education. The city is home of ''The Golden Mile,'' a rapidly growing cluster of new high-technology firms.

The city's location, temperate climate, quality labor force, economic stability, competitive taxes, and good transportation system have attracted a growing number of national and international firms who have relocated their corporate headquarters to the area. The city's economy is strengthened by a strong tourist and convention industry, four major military bases, stable real estate, construction, retail and wholesale trade, and distribution. History buff, entrepreneur, culture-lover, or nature enthusiast, Virginia Beach offers something for everyone.

# Geography and Climate

Virginia Beach is located on the ocean in the mid-Atlantic region in the southeastern corner of Virginia, with the Atlantic Ocean on the east and the Chesapeake Bay on the north. It is part of the area known as Hampton Roads. In the early 1600s the world's largest natural harbor—where the Chesapeake Bay meets the James River—provided easy access to the colony of Virginia. An English nobleman named Henry Wriothesley, the third Earl of Southampton, financed early expeditions to Virginia. In his honor the harbor was named Earl of Southampton's Roadstead, roadstead meaning a sheltered anchorage. Eventually it was shortened to Hampton Roads. Today, a bridge-tunnel spans the great harbor linking the peninsula cities of Hampton, Newport News, and Williamsburg, the town of Poquoson, and the counties of Gloucester, James City, and York with the Southside cities of Virginia Beach, Chesapeake, Norfolk, Portsmouth, Suffolk, Franklin, and the counties of Isle of Wight and Southampton. The area experiences four moderate seasons without climactic extremes, in which the warm spring leads to hazy, hot summer days, and warm muggy nights that turn into the bright sunny days and cool crisp nights of autumn

and the colder days of winter. The area has an average snowfall of 8.9 inches annually.

**Area:** 248 square miles (2000)

**Elevation:** sea level to 12 feet above sea level

**Average Temperatures:** January, 40.1° F; July, 79.1° F; annual average, 59.6° F

**Average Annual Precipitation:** 45.74 inches

# History

### British Land at Cape Henry

In spring of 1607, Captain John Smith and his band of explorers landed at Cape Henry at the northern tip of what is now Virginia Beach. Around them they saw expanses of white sand, rolling dunes, and pine forests. A few days later, they sailed up the James River to establish the New World's first permanent settlement at Jamestown.

Cape Henry, where the Chesapeake Bay meets the Atlantic Ocean, soon became a pathway for British merchant ships that traversed the treacherous seas to reach America. In 1720, the governor of Virginia requested that a lighthouse be built to increase safety. The kings of England refused until 1774. The Revolutionary War halted construction of the lighthouse, and it was not completed until 1791. A new tower was erected in 1881, but the old one lived on to become Virginia Beach's official symbol in 1962. Cape Henry played a critical role in the Revolution, for it was there the French fleet, led by Admiral Compte De Grasse, stopped the British fleet.

### Resort Town Built on Rail Line

Virginia Beach's history as a resort town began in 1880 when a clubhouse was built on the ocean. In 1883, with the help of northern capitalists, a corporation was formed to build a railroad from the busy port of Norfolk to the ocean front. An elaborate hotel that occupied two ocean front blocks, the Princess Anne Hotel, marked the birth of Virginia Beach. The hotel had rail tracks running almost into the lobby for the unloading of steamer trunks. In addition to sunbathing and swimming in the ocean, visitors could soak in salt and freshwater tubs, and enjoy the casino, dance halls, and saltwater pools of nearby Seaside Park.

Two of Hampton Roads' oldest cities, Norfolk and Portsmouth, experienced two centuries of moderate growth following the colonization of the New World, and grew significantly during the twentieth century due to the massive military build-up in support of World War II. Until the 1980s, Norfolk was the most populated city in the region.

## Annexation Brings Tremendous Growth

The popularity of Virginia Beach's beach front, which according to the *Guinness Book of Records* is the largest pleasure beach in the world, extends to the present. Since the building of the boardwalk and the Cavalier Hotel in the late 1920s, the city has experienced tremendous growth both as a resort and as a center of industry for the East Coast. Before World War II, the total combined population of the city and county was fewer than 20,000 people. In 1963, by annexing adjacent Princess Anne County, a small resort community became a city of 125,000 people that had grown from an original 1,600 acres to 172,800 acres. With more land for development, Virginia Beach soon surpassed Norfolk as the region's most populated city. With a growth rate of nearly 50 percent between 1980 and 1990, Virginia Beach became the largest city in Virginia. While this explosive growth rate slowed the following decade, Virginia Beach remains the state's largest city. A diverse economy, downtown development projects, and a burgeoning tourism business make the city "a vibrant city where people live, learn, work and play," according to Mayor Oberndorf in a March 2005 state of the city address.

*Historical Information:* Princess Anne County-Virginia Beach Historical Society, 2040 Potters Road, Virginia Beach, VA 23454; telephone (804)491-0127; Hampton Roads History Center; telephone (804)727-0800

# Population Profile

## Metropolitan Area Residents
*1980:* 1,201,000 (MSA)
*1990:* 1,444,710 (MSA)
*2000:* 1,569,541(MSA)
*2003 estimate:* 1,637,251
*Percent change, 1990–2000:* 8.8%
*U.S. rank in 1980:* 31st (MSA)
*U.S. rank in 1990:* 28th (MSA)
*U.S. rank in 2000:* 33rd (MSA)

## City Residents
*1980:* 262,000
*1990:* 393,089
*2000:* 425,257
*2003 estimate:* 439,467
*Percent change, 1990–2000:* 8.2%
*U.S. rank in 1980:* 56th
*U.S. rank in 1990:* 37th (State rank: 1st)
*U.S. rank in 2000:* 38th (State rank: 1st)

*Density:* 1,712.7 people per square mile (2000)

*Racial and ethnic characteristics* (2000)
　White: 303,681
　Black: 80,593
　American Indian and Alaskan Native: 1,619
　Asian: 20,869
　Native Hawaiian and other Pacific Islander: 416
　Hispanic or Latino (may be of any race): 17,770
　Other: 6,402

*Percent of residents born in state:* 37.7 (2000)

*Age characteristics* (2000)
　Population under 5 years old: 30,616
　Population 5 to 9 years old: 33,523
　Population 10 to 14 years old: 33,749
　Population 15 to 19 years old: 30,239
　Population 20 to 24 years old: 31,313
　Population 25 to 34 years old: 69,842
　Population 35 to 44 years old: 75,897
　Population 45 to 54 years old: 53,798
　Population 55 to 59 years old: 17,465
　Population 60 to 64 years old: 12,882
　Population 65 to 74 years old: 20,735
　Population 75 to 84 years old: 11,649
　Population 85 years and older: 3,549
　Median age: 32.7 years

*Births* (2003)
　Total number: 6,370

*Deaths* (2003)
　Total number: 2,311 (of which, 19 were infants under the age of 1 year)

*Money income* (1999)
　Per capita income: $22,365 (1999)
　Median household income: $48,705
　Total households: 154,635

*Number of households with income of . . .*
　less than $10,000: 6,628
　$10,000 to $14,999: 5,344
　$15,000 to $24,999: 15,496
　$25,000 to $34,999: 21,204
　$35,000 to $49,999: 30,976
　$50,000 to $74,999: 37,918
　$75,000 to $99,999: 18,367
　$100,000 to $149,999: 12,620
　$150,000 to $199,999: 2,794
　$200,000 or more: 3,288

*Percent of families below poverty level:* 5.1% (55% of which were female householder families in poverty)

*2002 FBI Crime Index Total:* 15,492

# Municipal Government

An eleven-member city council and a city manager govern Virginia Beach. Seven council seats are filled by individuals who reside in the seven boroughs of the city, and there are no borough residency requirements for the remaining four seats. The mayor is elected by voters and occupies one of the ''at large'' seats.

**Head Officials:** Mayor Meyera E. Oberndorf (since July 1988; current term expires 2008); City Manager James Spore (since November 1991)

**Total Number of City Employees:** 6,000 (2005)

*City Information:* City of Virginia Beach, 1 Municipal Center, Virginia Beach, VA 23456; telephone (757) 427-4601

# Economy

## Major Industries and Commercial Activity

Virginia Beach has a diverse economy based on private enterprise, thriving tourism, and a strong military presence. In addition, many international corporations have established headquarters in the region. The growth in population (from 84,215 people in 1960 to an estimated 439,467 in 2003) has resulted in flourishing retail sales and has also provided a large labor pool and support services. Open land for industrial development and high-quality office space continue to attract new industry.

Agribusiness contributes substantially to the local economy. There are around 150 farms in the city. In 2002 the economic impact of the agricultural community was estimated at more than $59 million. Principal products included swine, soybeans, corn, horticultural specialties, wheat, vegetables, horse breeding, and dairy products.

Four military bases in Virginia Beach have a tremendous economic impact on the region, with the Department of Defense spending $11 billion in 2002, and increasing in following years due to the War with Iraq. The bases include Oceana Naval Air Station, the largest master jet base in the United States, employing 12,000; Little Creek Naval Amphibious Base, which employs 13,000; Fort Story, which conducts amphibious training operations and employs approximately 1,200 military and civilian personnel; and Dam Neck, a training base for combat direction and control systems, which employs 4,700 persons. Businesses serving soldiers, sailors, and their families employ even more area

residents. Military Exchanges and PX's accounted for $123.8 million in sales in 2002.

In 2002 over 3 million sun-loving visitors spent more than $700 million during their stays at the resort city for accommodations, meals, entertainment, and other services, resulting in about 11,000 new service jobs. The city received $29 million in net direct revenue from tourist activity.

About one-third of Virginia Beach's labor force is employed in retail and wholesale business. The city had more than 7,800 retail/wholesale businesses with total taxable sales of over $3.9 billion in 2002, an increase of 4.3 percent from the previous year. Distribution greatly benefits from the fact that Virginia Beach is within 750 miles of three-fourths of the country's industrial activity and two-thirds of its population. An integrated system of highway, air, rail, and sea services provides easy access to national and international markets.

*Items and goods produced:* power tools, furniture, coated abrasives, welding equipment, recreational products, machinery, agricultural products

## Incentive Programs—New and Existing Companies

*Local programs*—Virginia Beach offers several incentives to reduce the costs of relocating and expanding a facility within the city. The Virginia Beach Department of Economic Development (DED) prepares customized in-depth research packages for prospects, conducts tours of facilities, helps new industry begin operations and aids existing businesses in their growth, advises on the availability of Industrial Development Bonds and conventional funding, and assists in the development of office parks. DED also helps to expedite the permit process for developments under construction, and provides engineering and landscape assistance at no charge. The Department of Economic Development assists firms in identifying and securing conventional financing. The Virginia Beach Development Authority issues tax-exempt industrial development bonds covering the cost of land, buildings, machinery, and equipment to eligible manufacturing facilities. For non-manufacturers, the Virginia Business Financing Authority provides long-term fixed asset financing at rates below those of conventional sources for financing land, buildings and capital equipment. In order to attract new businesses, Virginia Beach has initiated an innovative program aimed at offering cost-saving benefits to employees of new and relocating businesses and industries. The program includes incentives, special offers, and discounts from Virginia Beach businesses including retail merchants, hotels/motels and apartment complexes, utility companies, mortgage companies, and real estate firms.

*State programs*—Virginia is a right-to-work state. The State General Assembly has kept Virginia's taxes on industry very competitive by enacting one of the best corporate income tax laws in the nation and by eliminating many tax irritants, resulting in very modest tax bills for business and industry. Consequently, property tax exemption or investment tax credits are not used to lure new companies into the state.

*Job training programs*—The Workforce Services Program of the Virginia Department of Economic Development prepares and coordinates business training programs tailored to meet the specific needs of new or expanding companies seeking to increase employment. Services provided at no cost to employers include recruiting prospective employees, analyzing job training requirements, developing and implementing employment programs, arranging for training facilities, and preparing instructional audiovisual materials. The Virginia Employment Commission will, at no cost, interview, pre-test, pre-screen, and refer selected applicants to an employer. The city of Virginia Beach has funds available through the federal Title II Job Training Partnership Act (JTPA) program to recruit prospective workers, and provide wage subsidies and customer training programs. The Southeastern Virginia Job Training Administration administers these funds.

### Development Projects

The Town Center of Virginia Beach is a massive, $350 million mixed-use development encompassing 17 blocks in the downtown area. It will consist of office towers, retail space, luxury residential buildings, hotels, restaurants, and a performing arts center, connected by pedestrian-friendly brick sidewalks, fountains, gardens and green areas. Parts of Phase I and II will open in 2005, and more phases are to be completed over the next few years. The Performing Arts Theater at Town Center, a 1,200 seat facility, will be completed in 2007.

Hotel building and expansions have been brisk in Virginia Beach to keep pace with increasing numbers of tourists. New projects being constructed in 2005 include a $62 million Hilton Resort and Conference Center to be built near the new Virginia Beach Convention Center, and a $40 million Embassy Suites being built near the Hampton Roads convention center.

***Economic Development Information:*** Department of Economic Development, City of Virginia Beach, One Columbus Center, Suite 300, Virginia Beach, VA 23462; telephone (757)437-6434; (800)989-4567; fax (757)499-9894; email ecdev@city.virgina-beach.va.us

### Commercial Shipping

Norfolk International Airport is located less than a mile from the Virginia Beach city limits. In addition to the nine commercial carriers that serve the area, cargo airlines and air

freight forwarders have offices in the airport complex. Also serving the Hampton Roads area is the Newport News/Williamsburg International Airport, less than an hour away. The nearby Norfolk International and Portsmouth Marine Terminals, part of the Port of Virginia system, handled 15 million tons of cargo in 2004 and has a channel depth to 50 feet. With the addition of 4 Suez class container cranes in 2004, Norfolk International has doubled its cargo handling capacity. There are 135 motor carriers and 50 common carrier terminals in the Virginia Beach region. Federal Express, UPS, Puralator Courier, Emery Worldwide, U.S. Mail Express, and a number of smaller couriers serve the area. Railroads serving Virginia Beach are Norfolk Southern Railway and Eastern Shore Railroad, with a connection to CSX Transportation.

***Economic Development Information:*** Virginia Beach Department of Economic Development, One Columbus Center, Suite 300, Virginia Beach, VA 23462; telephone (757)437-6434; (800)989-4567; fax (757)499-9894; email ecdev@city.virgina-beach.va.us

### Labor Force and Employment Outlook

In terms of major occupations, the Hampton Roads area population, including that of Virginia Beach, exhibits a balanced proportion of managerial, professional, technical, and support personnel in a variety of businesses and industries. Of the more than 7,500 annual high school graduates, nearly 70 percent attend either a two- or four-year college or university, while 15 percent continue their education at vocational or trade schools, or through an apprenticeship program.

The following is a summary of data regarding the Norfolk/Virginia Beach/Newport News metropolitan area labor force, 2003 annual averages.

*Size of nonagricultural labor force:* 730,800

*Number of workers employed in . . .*
   *construction and mining:* 44,700
   *manufacturing:* 59,800
   *trade, transportation and utilities:* 134,900
   *information:* 16,100
   *financial activities:* 38,000
   *professional and business services:* 98,800
   *educational and health services:* 78,100
   *leisure and hospitality:* 77,300
   *other services:* 33,500
   *government:* 149,800

*Average hourly earnings of production workers employed in manufacturing:* $18.27 (2003)

*Unemployment rate:* 4.0% (December 2004)

| *Largest private employers* | *Number of employees* |
|---|---|
| American Systems Engineering | 2,300 |
| Amerigroup | 2,300 |
| Manpower | 1,775 |
| Geico Direct | 1,743 |
| Gold Key Resorts | 1,600 |
| Stihl | 1,279 |
| Virginian-Pilot Production Plant | 977 |
| Christian Broadcasting Network | 941 |
| Lillian Vernon Corporation | 900 |
| MILCOM Systems | 800 |
| UPS | 750 |

## Cost of Living

The cost of living in the Virginia Beach area, including consumer goods and services, is slightly above the national average.

The following is a summary of data regarding several key cost of living factors for the Virginia Beach area.

*2004 (3rd Quarter) ACCRA Average House Price:* $288,851

*2004 (3rd Quarter) ACCRA Cost of Living Index:* 102.1 (U.S. average = 100.0)

*State income tax rate:* Ranges from 2.0% to 5.75%

*State sales tax rate:* 4%

*Local income tax rate:* None

*Local sales tax rate:* 1%

*Property tax rate:* $1.22 per $100 of assessed valuation (2002); assessment ratio = 100% for residential

*Economic Information:* Department of Economic Development, One Columbus Center, Suite 300, Virginia Beach, VA 23462; telephone (757)437-6434; toll-free (800)989-4567; fax (757)499-9894; email ecdev@city.virgina-beach.va.us

# Education and Research

## Elementary and Secondary Schools

The Virginia Beach City Public Schools is the second largest city school system in the Commonwealth of Virginia and the thirty-ninth largest in the country. Its motto, "Ahead of the Curve", conveys its dedication to being in the forefront of innovative educational programs. In 2004, it was recognized by the American School Board Journal for its student-mentor program, and for LEAD, a teacher education program. Among the specialized curricula it offers are math and science academies, a visual and performing arts academy, an Advanced Technology Center and an international baccalaureate

program. Virginia Beach students consistently score above the national average for all grade levels on achievement tests.

The following is a summary of data regarding Virginia Beach's public schools as of the 2004–2005 school year.

*Total enrollment:* 74,682

*Number of facilities*
  *elementary schools:* 55
  *junior high/middle schools:* 15
  *senior high schools:* 11
  *other:* 15 city-wide centers/schools

*Student/teacher ratio:* elementary, 15.3:1; secondary, 12:1

*Teacher salaries*
  *minimum:* $34,274
  *maximum:* $72,325

*Funding per pupil:* $7,414 (2002-2003)

There are 43 private, parochial and military schools in the city enrolling students from Pre-K to 12th grade.

*Public Schools Information:* Virginia Beach City Public Schools, 2512 George Mason Drive, Virginia Beach, VA 23456-0038; telephone (757)427-4585; email vbcpsweb @vbcps.k12.va.us

## Colleges and Universities

Old Dominion University (ODU) in Norfolk enrolls more than 20,000 students in 150 academic programs offering 67 undergraduate, 68 masters, 26 doctoral degrees, and two certificates of advanced study. The most popular recent majors have been psychology, finance/banking, education and nursing. Tidewater Community College's Virginia Beach campus, enrolling more than 19,000 students annually, is a participant in Virginia's Center for Innovative Technology with ODU.

Virginia Wesleyan College, a four-year liberal arts private college located on the Virginia Beach/Norfolk border, enrolls more than 1,400 students in 38 degree programs. Other institutions of higher education in the area are Eastern Virginia Medical School (900 students), Norfolk State University (8,900 students), Regent University (1,500 students), ODU/NSU Virginia Beach Education Center (5,800 students), and Hampton Roads Graduate Center, part of University of Virginia and Virginia Polytechnic Institute and State University, with 250 students.

## Libraries and Research Centers

The Virginia Beach Department of Public Libraries encompasses the central library and six area libraries with a Municipal Reference Library, Public Law Library, bookmobile, and a Library for the Blind and Physically Handicapped. The library system has almost than 800,000 books, plus the

Princess Anne (County) Historical Collection. The library publishes a bimonthly newsletter. Other libraries in the area include college- and church-affiliated libraries; the Edgar Cayce Foundation Library, specializing in metaphysical topics; the Virginia Marine Science's Museum Library; and the Mariner's Museum Library.

Research centers in Virginia Beach include the Association for Research and Enlightenment and the Virginia Institute of Marine Science, Eastern Shore Lab, which is affiliated with the College of William and Mary.

*Public Library Information:* Virginia Beach Central Library, 4100 Virginia Beach Blvd, Virginia Beach, VA 23452; telephone (757)431-3001

# Health Care

Sentara Healthcare, a not-for-profit health care provider in southeastern Virginia, operates nine hospitals in the Hampton Roads area, with two of them in Virginia Beach. Sentara Virginia Beach General Hospital is a 274-bed facility that houses the region's only Level 3 Trauma Center, plus a neonatal intensive care unit and a sleep disorder clinic. It also specializes in cardiac surgery, cancer care, women's health, oncology, and orthopedics. In the fall of 2005, a $29 million wing will open with the new Sentara Heart Center and 108 all-private rooms. Sentara Bayside Hospital has 158 beds and features a vascular lab, breast cancer center, and a gastrointestinal center.

Virginia Beach Psychiatric Center is a freestanding hospital that offers psychiatric and substance abuse services for children, adolescents, and adults. Virginia Beach also has five rehabilitation centers, several nursing homes, and a dialysis center.

# Recreation

### Sightseeing

Virginia Beach is home to many interesting historical landmarks and recreational areas. The First Landing Cross marks the spot where America's first permanent English settlers, the Jamestown colonists, reached the New World in 1607. The Old Cape Henry Lighthouse at Fort Story, built in 1791, is open for tours. The Old Coast Guard Station, one of the first life-saving stations in the United States, is one of several such stations along the East Coast that are still open to the public. Veterans are saluted by the Tidewater Veterans Memorial, complete with a flag display and waterfall. The

Norwegian Lady statue, a gift from the people of Moss, Norway, commemorates the wreck of the Norwegian bark *Dictator* off the city's coastline.

Local historical houses include the Adam Thoroughgood House, built in the mid-1600s, which may be the oldest remaining brick house in America; the Lynnhaven House, one of America's best-preserved eighteenth-century middle class dwellings; Francis Land House and Historic Site, built in 1732, which is the largest and finest gambrel-roofed house in Virginia; and Upper Wolfsnare, a beautifully restored 1759 house that is a Virginia Landmark Home. The Princess Anne Courthouse, built in 1824, and the beautifully landscaped Municipal Building are among the 28 major buildings that house the executive offices of the local government.

The Virginia Aquarium & Marine Science Center's more than 800,000 gallons of aquaria and over 300 hands-on exhibits offer visitors the opportunity to explore the depths of the Atlantic Ocean, walk under the waves of the Chesapeake Bay, view the life of a saltwater marsh, and stroll through a coastal plains river. A 3D IMAX theater, a nature trail, and traveling exhibits add to the fun. Located in a 1903 former Coast Guard Station, the Old Coast Guard Station displays photographs, nautical artifacts, scrimshaw, ship models, and other marine memorabilia about the Life-Saving Service. The Association for Research and Enlightenment Library and Conference Center documents the life work of Edgar Cayce, world-renowned psychic, through exhibits, lectures, and extrasensory perception testing. The center also has a meditation garden and labyrinth for peaceful contemplation. Family fun awaits visitors to Ocean Breeze Festival Park, home of a water park, a Formula One racing track, go-carts, bumper boats, miniature golf, batting cages and the new Skyscraper roller coaster. The Virginia Beach Farmer's Market, open every day of the year, offers 17,000 square feet of food stalls, craft items, and a country-style restaurant. In the warm months the Market has educational programs for students and Friday Night Hoedowns. Guided tours are available at the Christian Broadcasting Network Center, which includes Regent University and state-of-the-art broadcasting facilities where the popular religious program "The 700 Club" is taped.

Within one hour's drive of the city are many attractions for culture-lovers and history buffs alike. The Virginia Air & Space Center and Hampton Roads History Center, located in historic Hampton, are housed in a nine-story wonder of a building on the waterfront that combines supermodern and traditional architectural styles. Visitors can view vintage aircraft suspended from the ceiling, the Apollo 12 Command Module with a 3-billion-year-old moon rock, plus an authentic Chesapeake Bay deadrise workboat. Based on the theme, "From the Sea to the Stars," this $30 million building reviews Hampton Roads' seafood and shipbuilding history, and its role as a military defense post and pioneer in aviation

**Virginia Beach is popular for its 28 miles of shoreline, including a boardwalk and bike paths.**

and space exploration. The museum also features a 300-seat 3D IMAX theater, which shows aviation and space exploration films; and a restored 1920 merry-go-round.

Located between Virginia Beach and Williamsburg is the Mariner's Museum, which invites visitors to reflect on the lore of the sea and maritime exploration over the past 3,000 years. The museum's 11 galleries contain a unique collection of figureheads, paintings, small craft, ship models, and other marine artifacts. In addition, the museum offers demonstrations by costumed interpreters, films, and a 5-mile nature trail around picturesque Lake Murray. The nearby Peninsula Fine Arts Center provides changing monthly exhibits, a children's art center and adult classes, and the War Memorial Museum of Virginia traces U.S. military history from the Revolution to the first Gulf War.

Just one hour west of Virginia Beach, Williamsburg's Colonial Williamsburg helps tourists make the journey back to the early days of our nation. Visions of our colonial ancestors abound in the 173-acre Historic Area, which features over 30 buildings and craftsmen in eighteenth-century attire practicing industries of the era. Also in the area is Busch Gardens Williamsburg, where visitors can step back in time to life in old England, Scotland, Germany, Italy, and Ireland, while enjoying thrill rides, live shows, and animal attractions. The Williamsburg Pottery Factory has been offering bargain prices for over 60 years, and the water park Water Country USA contains one of the longest flume rides in the country. A trip to Yorktown allows one to look over the site of the 1781 battle that ended the Revolutionary War, and visitors to historic Jamestown can see full-sized replicas of three 1607 ships, re-creations of the colonist' fort, and a Powhatan village.

### Arts and Culture

The Virginia Center for Contemporary Art celebrates the work of both American artists and artists from around the world. The Artists At Work: Gallery and Studios is a working marketplace for the visual arts that provides views of the actual process of artistic creation. Many of the art works are for sale.

The Virginia Symphony Orchestra delights audiences with its classical music programs at Regent University Theater in Virginia Beach and at venues in Norfolk and Williamsburg. Concerts are also offered by Beach Events on the oceanfront. The Verizon Wireless Virginia Beach Amphitheater is a 20,000-seat venue hosting major musical acts from April through October. As a resort town, Virginia Beach also offers a wide range of jazz, blues, reggae, and rock at the many local nightclubs and dance halls. Virginia Opera performs in the Harrison Opera House and to thousands of school children every year. The Tidewater Winds, a concert band in the Souza tradition, performs all over the Hampton Roads area.

The Virginia Stage Company, the region's only professional troupe, brings its dramas and musicals to the Wells Theater in Norfolk. The Little Theatre of Virginia Beach is a community theater that produces five shows and a summer musical per year. Three full-scale musical comedies are presented at the Pavilion by the Virginia Musical Theater October through April.

### Festivals and Holidays

The Neptune Festival in September is the main festival of the year. It attracts more than 1 million spectators and features parades, an air show, a triathlon, art and crafts exhibits, wine tastings, live entertainment, a sand sculpting contest and more. In January the Pavilion plays host to the Virginia Flower & Garden Show. The Millennium Chess Festival draws players from all over to Virginia Beach in February, as does the Mid-Atlantic Sports & Boat Show. Dogs on Parade at the Associated Specialty Dog Show happens in March, as well as the Shamrock Marathon & SportsFest. The Virginia Beach and Princess Anne Garden Tours, the International Azalea Festival, the Atlantic Coast Kite Festival and the Mid-Atlantic Home & Garden Show happen in April. May brings in the Patriotic Festival, Big Flea Market, Strawberry Festival, and Beach Music Festival. June has the Annual Boardwalk Art Show and Latin Fest. July features a huge Fourth of July Celebration and the Mid-Atlantic Hermit Crab Challenge. The Soul Music Beach Fest is in August, as well as the American Folk Art Festival. Labor Day weekend brings the American Music Festival and the Rock 'n' Roll Half Marathon. October brings the city's Annual Historic Homes Tour and October Brewfest. The Countryside Christmas Craft Show and Hometown Holiday Parade happen in November; and December's Holiday Lights at the Beach, annual Nutcracker program, and New Year's Rock Around the Clock ends the year.

### Sports for the Spectator

September's Professional Golfer's Association Virginia Beach Open takes place at Tournament Players Club in April. National athletic stars come to the city for the Shamrock Marathon and SportsFest, which takes place each March. Rudee Inlet is the site every August of the East Coast Surfing Championship. Sports lovers in the Hampton Roads region attend the baseball games of the Triple A Norfolk Tides (affiliated with the N.Y. Mets) and the matches of the American Hockey League's Norfolk Admirals. The Virginia Beach Mariners soccer team plays at the Virginia Beach Sportsplex. NCAA teams from Old Dominion, Norfolk State and Virginia Wesleyan are also popular with students and locals. Professional and amateur surfers head to the East Coast Surfing Championship held in August, which is free for spectators.

### Sports for the Participant

Virginia Beach's greatest asset is the 28 miles of golden shoreline that has attracted visitors for more than a century.

The city's 3-mile-long boardwalk, with a parallel bike track, is enhanced with teak benches, lampposts, and colorful flags. The city's most popular beaches are the Resort Area, North End, Back Bay, Croatan, Sandbridge, and Chesapeake beaches. Mild weather year-round makes golf a tremendous draw for visitors. Nine private and two municipal 18-hole golf courses participate in the city's Golf Package Program, and many other courses dot the region.

The Virginia Beach Fishing Center offers half-day or full-day offshore sport fishing, as well as wreck fishing, and deep sea fishing is available from Lynnhaven Seafood & Marina. Freshwater fishing is enjoyed at Back Bay or Lake Smith, and pier fishing is possible at several sites around the city. Sightseeing, scuba diving and whale watching cruises can also be booked with the many charter boats at the Marina. Kayak rentals and tours of the area are offered by Back Bay Getaways and Kayak Nature Tours. Mount Trashmore is a mountain of compacted layers of soil and garbage within the city that has been transformed into a 162-acre park with bicycle trails, playgrounds, skateboard ramps, picnic facilities, and two lakes. A registered National Landmark, First Landing State Park offers more than 20 miles of hiking and biking trails through its 2,770 acres. Back Bay National Wildlife Refuge has 5,000 acres of beach, woodland, and marsh, where whistling swans, peregrine falcons, and bald eagles can be spotted in the wintertime. Hiking trails exist at First Landing and False Cape State Parks. Camping is permitted at False Cape State Park among the maritime forests and ocean dunes. Virginia Beach's jet observation parks permit spectators to watch the U.S. Navy's most advanced aircraft take off and land from Ocean Naval Air Station.

Virginia Beach boasts 194 public tennis courts, anchored by the Owl Creek Tennis Center. The resort area's other recreational offerings include boogie-boarding, windsurfing, jet skiing, para-sailing, miniature golf, volleyball, softball tournaments, bowling, and roller skating. Most recreational equipment, including bicycles, can be rented near the beach. The city's 208 parks, encompassing 4,000 acres, offer such features as playgrounds, ball fields, dog parks, and picnic areas.

### Shopping and Dining

Numerous off-price outlets, such as the great American Outlet Mall and Loehmann's Plaza, make Virginia Beach a shopper's delight. The new Town Center has shopping ranging from major department stores to small boutiques. There are traditional malls, such as Lynnhaven, one of the largest malls on the east coast; Pembroke Mall, with large department stores and specialty shops; the various Hilltop locations and La Promenade; as well as the boardwalk and resort area's souvenir shops, surf shops, boutiques, and craft shops. The Virginia Beach Farmers Market is open year round.

Seafood in a wide variety of forms is the star of the culinary show in Virginia Beach. The oyster and the blue crab are local delicacies, and flounder, scallops, and numerous other varieties of fish tempt the palate at local restaurants. Ethnic dishes run the gamut from fajitas, to sushi, to Cajun jambalaya or Fettuccine Alfredo. Oceanfront cafes offer scenic dining opportunities, and eating establishments range from elegant to casual. The new Town Center development is becoming a hub for restaurants as well, with large national chain restaurants like P.F. Chang's and The Cheesecake Factory moving in.

*Visitor Information:* Virginia Beach Department of Convention and Visitor Development, 2101 Parks Avenue, Virginia Beach, VA 23451; telephone (757)437-4700; toll-free (800)700-7702; fax (757)437-4747

## Convention Facilities

In the summer of 2005 a new $202 million Virginia Beach Convention Center is scheduled to open its first phase, and the Pavilion Convention Center will be demolished. When finally completed in 2007, the new 500,000 square foot center will have a 150,000 square feet of exhibition space, a 31,000 square foot banquet room, 29,000 square feet of meeting space, and 2,230 free parking spaces. Many other downtown hotels offer meeting and convention facilities.

*Convention Information:* Virginia Beach Department of Convention and Visitor Development, 2101 Parks Avenue, Virginia Beach, VA 23451; telephone (757)437-4700; toll-free (800)700-7702; fax (757)437-4747

## Transportation

### Approaching the City

Air travelers to the city arrive at Norfolk International Airport, located less than a mile from the city limits. The airport is served by 9 carriers that offer more than 200 daily flights connecting to all major hubs and many major cities in the U.S. and around the world. Interstate Highway 64, U.S. 460, and U.S. 58 approach the city from the west; from the north and south convenient routes are I-85 or I-95, U.S. 13 and U.S. 17. All these routes cross I-64, which circles the Hampton Roads region and links with Route 44, the Virginia Beach-Norfolk Expressway, which ends at the city's ocean-front resort area. The Chesapeake Bay Bridge-Tunnel connects Virginia Beach with Virginia's eastern shore. The Hampton Roads Bridge-

Tunnel links the southside of Hampton Roads with the peninsula cities of Newport News and Hampton. The Merrimac-Monitor Memorial Bridge Tunnel connects the south side and peninsula via the James River.

Bus service is provided by the Greyhound Bus Line and Amtrak provides rail service and connections to numerous Eastern and Southern points from nearby Newport News. Virginia Beach can be reached by water from the Atlantic Ocean or via the Intercoastal Waterway.

### Traveling in the City

The Wave, a three-route trolley system, services residents and visitors throughout the summertime, extending from the resort area to shopping malls to points of local cultural and historic importance. Hampton Roads Transit provides area bus transportation.

# Communications

### Newspapers and Magazines

Virginia Beach's daily newspaper, the morning *The Virginian-Pilot,* is published in Norfolk. *The Virginia Beach Sun* is the city's weekly community newspaper. *Beach: The Magazine of Virginia Beach* is a quarterly magazine produced by the city. Also published in Virginia Beach are *Senior Times,* a shopper; *The Shilling,* a journal focusing on ways to make money; *Tidewater Parent, Port Folio Weekly,* and *Tidewater Women.*

### Television and Radio

Virginia Beach is served by cable television and by stations broadcasting from the surrounding Hampton Roads area. Seven AM and FM radio stations provide music, talk shows, and religious programming.

***Media Information:*** *The Virginian-Pilot,* Landmark Communications, 150 W. Brambleton Avenue, Norfolk, VA 23510; telephone (757)446-9000; toll-free (800)446-2005; email vpquestions/comments@pilotonline.com

### Virginia Beach Online

City of Virginia Beach home page. Available www.vbgov .com

Virginia Beach City Public Schools. Available www.vbcps .k12.va.us

Virginia Beach Public Library. Available www.vbgov.com/ dept/library

Virginia Beach Tourist Information. Available www.vbfun .com

*Virginian Pilot.* Available www.pilotonline.com

### Selected Bibliography

Jackson, Katherine, *Walking Virginia Beach* (Helena, Mont.: Falcon Publishing Co., 1999)

# Washington, D.C.

## *The City in Brief*

**Founded:** 1790 (authorized by Congressional act)

**Head Official:** Mayor Anthony Williams (D) (since 1999)

**City Population**
  1980: 638,333
  1990: 607,000
  2000: 572,059
  2003 estimate: 563,384
  Percent change, 1990–2000: −5.7%
  U.S. rank in 1980: 15th
  U.S. rank in 1990: 19th
  U.S. rank in 2000: 21st

**Metropolitan Area Population**
  1980: 3,478,000
  1990: 4,223,000
  2000: 4,923,153

  Percent change, 1990–2000: 16.5%
  U.S. rank in 1980: 8th
  U.S. rank in 1990: 8th
  U.S. rank in 2000: 8th

**Area:** 68.3 square miles (2000)
**Elevation:** Ranges from 40 to 410 feet above sea level
**Average Annual Temperature:** 54.0° F
**Average Annual Precipitation:** 39.73 inches

**Major Economic Sectors:** services, government, wholesale and retail trade
**Unemployment rate:** 2.9% (December 2004)
**Per Capita Income:** $28,659 (1999)

**2002 FBI Crime Index Total:** 44,349

**Major Colleges and Universities:** Georgetown University, Howard University, American University, Catholic University of America, George Washington University

**Daily Newspaper:** *The Washington Post; The Washington Times*

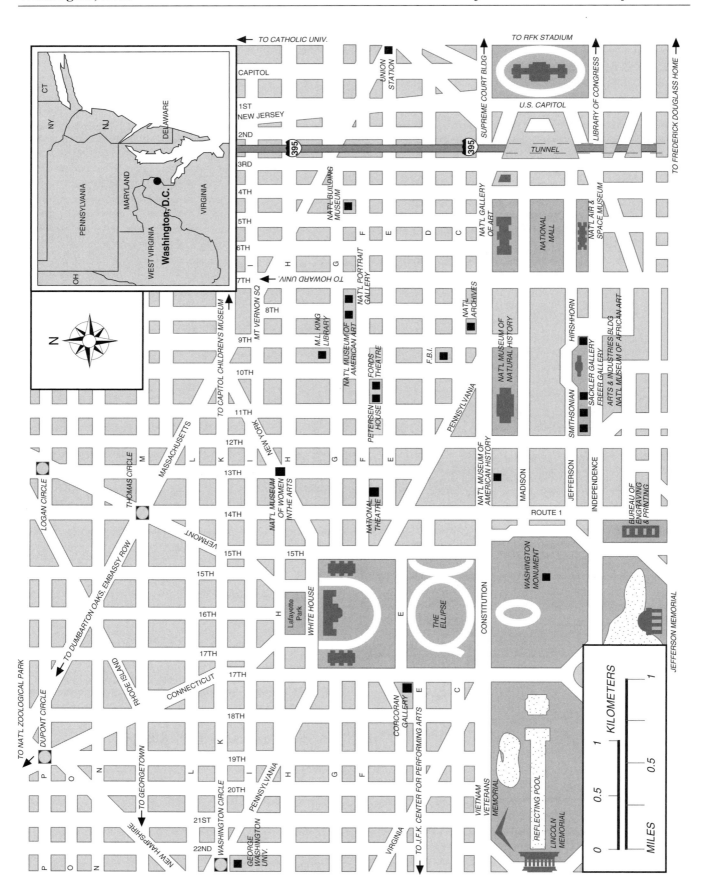

# Introduction

During the nineteenth century, Washington, D.C., the capital of the United States, was considered so unbearably warm and humid during the summer months that foreign diplomats received hardship pay for serving there. Now, the district holds a worldwide reputation as a cosmopolitan city rich in museums, monuments, and culture—and crackling with political power. From the hill where the U.S. Capitol sits, to Embassy Row, home to much of the foreign diplomatic corps in Washington, the wide avenues hum with the business of America. With more than 2,000 foreign diplomats posted to Washington, the city exudes an international flavor.

But heavy industry never took hold in the region and outside the downtown government district and the upscale northwest quarter of the city, poverty grips many residents. City officials have worked hard to change that. Downtown, once-seedy sections of Pennsylvania Avenue, embarrassingly close to the White House, were renovated in the early 1980s. The city's standing as the nation's capital has always attracted conventioneers, and in March 2003 the new granite and limestone Washington Convention Center further revitalized the downtown area with more than 700,000 square feet of prime exhibit space. Residents from the District and surrounding suburbs commute on a clean and efficient subway system that is still expanding. And in spite of all that growth, Washingtonians pride themselves on showing an almost southern-style hospitality. In the words of Frederick Douglass, "Wherever the American citizen may be a stranger, he is at home here."

Never was the nation's reverence for its capital city more reaffirmed than in the wake of the tragic September 11 terrorist attacks that shook New York and Washington D.C. One of several hijacked planes was crashed into the massive, fortress-like Pentagon Building, claiming the lives of more than 120 people. It is widely believed that another hijacked aircraft, which eventually was forced down by heroic passengers in Pennsylvania, was bound to crash into the Capitol Building. In the months following, an Anthrax scare ripped through the city when traces of the deadly agent were discovered in packages sent to various political offices around town. All these events served to remind the city's residents of its link to historic events and its prominence as the greatest seat of political power on the planet, all somewhat sobering even as the city was on the upsurge to begin a new century.

# Geography and Climate

Located on the Potomac River between the Blue Ridge Mountains and the Atlantic Ocean, Washington is known for its hot, humid summers, pleasant springs and autumns, and mild winters with seasonal snowfall averaging just over 17 inches. Carved from south-central Maryland, Washington is bordered on three sides by that state and sits across the Potomac River from Virginia on its fourth side. The District is also divided by the Anacostia River and Rock Creek. One fourth of the District is park land. The city is divided artificially into four quadrants: northeast, northwest, southeast, and southwest.

**Area:** 68.3 square miles (2000)

**Elevation:** Ranges from 40 to 410 feet above sea level

**Average Temperatures:** January, 36.0° F; August, 77.0° F; annual average, 54.0° F

**Average Annual Precipitation:** 39.73 inches (including 17.3 inches of snow)

# History

### George Washington Chooses Capital's Site

When the U.S. Congress sought a new capital for the young United States in the late eighteenth century, it chose an obscure piece of undeveloped swampland on the Potomac River. This unlikely location was a compromise. Southern politicians resisted placement of the capital too far north in New York or New England. For all representatives—northern and southern alike—Philadelphia, the capital in 1783, was deemed too close to potentially volatile constituents, especially one band of angry soldiers who had disrupted a Congressional session earlier that year to demand back pay. Determining the new capital's exact location was left to President George Washington, who had known the area since boyhood. The diamond-shaped district he carved out included parts of Maryland and Virginia. President Washington modestly referred to the city that came to bear his name as the Federal City.

### Early Days of Future Capital

In 1571 Pedro Menendez, a Spanish admiral who founded St. Augustine and was governor of Spain's Florida territories, was the first European to explore the future capital region. The area became a trading center for British settlers who dealt with regional Native American tribes. The Potomac River, one of the few native place names to survive colonialization, means "trading place" in the Algonquin language. Later, white landowners in the region made huge profits growing tobacco.

When the area was selected as the new capital site in 1790, Congress had almost no money to spend on its future home. Virginia and Maryland contributed small sums to erect public buildings, but President Washington was left to try to barter with the tobacco-growing landowners in the area for property. Meanwhile, the task of creating the look of a capital city worthy of the new nation fell to Pierre L'Enfant, a French architect and engineer also selected by President Washington, who eventually persuaded tobacco planters to sell their land cheaply. At the time, L'Enfant's vision of boulevards 400 feet wide and a mile long lined by great buildings seemed like a waste of real estate to the property owners. Nonetheless, the first temporary buildings of the new capital were ready in 1800 and in May of that year the government left Philadelphia. One year later, Thomas Jefferson was the first U.S. president to be inaugurated in Washington. But L'Enfant's vision of what Washington should be remained for decades just a vision. Today's grand Pennsylvania Avenue was an unpaved road from the U.S. Capitol to the White House and a muddy path on the other side of the White House during the first half of the nineteenth century. Americans and foreign diplomats assigned to the city dreaded its dull cultural life and oppressive summers. Few houses and plenty of open space separated official buildings.

**Wars Impact on the City**

The War of 1812 made life in Washington even more unpleasant, as British forces stormed the city in 1814, burning the President's House—later rebuilt, painted white, and forever after known as the White House—as well as the partially completed U.S. Capitol and other federal buildings. By the 1860s Washington's population had grown to 75,000 people. As the geographic border between the North and South, the District of Columbia acutely felt the mounting tension between factions at the approach of the Civil War. President Abraham Lincoln's 1861 inauguration was completed under a heavily armed phalanx of soldiers ready to repel an attack by the South. Washington was the headquarters for Northern troops during the four-year war, and several times during the bloody conflict Confederate troops nearly took the capital, defeated only by bad luck or faulty military intelligence.

**Government Buildings Proliferate**

Gradually, Washington architects filled in the blanks left by L'Enfant. The Mall—a vast tree-lined park stretching out from the U.S. Capitol—sprouted other government buildings and the Smithsonian museums. Tributes to some of the nation's great men were built: the Washington Monument, the Lincoln Memorial, and the Jefferson Memorial. The population of the city jumped during World War I as the civil service rapidly expanded, and again during the Great Depression of the 1930s when working for the government was the most secure kind of employment. Many of the current government buildings date from the 1930s when President Franklin D. Roosevelt's Works Progress Adminis-

tration erected offices for the Internal Revenue, Commerce, and other federal departments.

Washington during the 1960s reflected the social upheaval and turbulence experienced throughout the nation. The 1963 ''March on Washington for Jobs and Freedom'' showed America at its best and most righteous. It was there that Martin Luther King, Jr., delivered his inspirational ''I have a dream'' speech to 200,000 citizens. But when King was assassinated in Memphis, Tennessee, in 1968, violent riots rocked the capital. Recovering from the damage during the last half of the 1970s and into the 1980s, the capital enjoyed an economic rebirth with major commercial projects downtown and in some neighborhoods.

Behind the glitter and glamour attendant upon conducting one of the world's most powerful governments, though, lies a district plagued by many problems. Washington, D.C. suffered from virtual insolvency in the 1990s, a crumbling infrastructure, and significant population loss. Since 1995 Washington, D.C. has operated under a federal control board to control spending. The board stripped the local school board of most of its powers and eliminated thousands of jobs. Anthony Williams, who was appointed the city's first independent chief financial officer, managed to reverse years of fiscal mismanagement and turned a runaway budget deficit into a steadily growing surplus. He also hired highly qualified people and held them accountable and streamlined the agencies under his control. In 1999 Williams was elected mayor; by that time Washington, D.C. had come a long way toward reversing its decline. Williams continued to place emphasis on the city's economy, housing, health care, education, and public safety. Citizens came together in the aftermath of the September 11, 2001 terrorist attacked that rocked the country and especially Washington, D.C. and New York City. In 2004 Washington, D.C. was selected as the second best city to live in for African Americans by *Black Enterprise* magazine.

*Historical Information:* Historical Society of Washington, D.C., City Museum of Washington, D.C., 801 K Street, NW, Washington, D.C. 20001; telephone (202)383-1850

# *Population Profile*

**Metropolitan Area Residents**
*1980:* 3,478,000
*1990:* 4,223,000
*2000:* 4,923,153
*Percent change, 1990–2000:* 16.5%
*U.S. rank in 1980:* 8th (MSA)
*U.S. rank in 1990:* 8th (MSA)
*U.S. rank in 2000:* 8th (MSA)

**City Residents**

*1980:* 638,333

*1990:* 607,000

*2000:* 572,059

*2003 estimate:* 563,384

*Percent change, 1990–2000:* −5.7%

*U.S. rank in 1980:* 15th

*U.S. rank in 1990:* 19th

*U.S. rank in 2000:* 21st

*Density:* 9,316.4 people per square mile (based on 2000 land area)

*Racial and ethnic characteristics* (2000)

White: 176,101

Black or African American: 343,312

American Indian and Alaska Native: 1,713

Asian: 15,189

Native Hawaiian and Other Pacific Islander: 348

Hispanic or Latino (may be of any race): 44,953

Other: 21,950

*Percent of residents born in state:* 39.2% (2000)

*Age characteristics* (2000)

Population under 5 years old: 32,536

Population 5 to 9 years old: 35,385

Population 10 to 14 years old: 30,018

Population 15 to 19 years old: 37,867

Population 20 to 24 years old: 51,823

Population 25 to 34 years old: 101,762

Population 35 to 44 years old: 87,677

Population 45 to 54 years old: 75,310

Population 55 to 59 years old: 27,803

Population 60 to 64 years old: 21,980

Population 65 to 74 years old: 35,919

Population 75 to 84 years old: 25,004

Population 85 years and older: 8,975

Median age: 34.6 years (2000)

*Births* (2002)

Total number: 7,494

*Deaths* (2002)

Total number: 5,779 (of which, 86 were infants under the age of 1 year)

*Money income* (1999)

Per capita income: $28,659

Median household income: $40,127

Total households: 248,590

*Number of households with income of . . .*

less than $10,000: 36,939

$10,000 to $14,999: 14,954

$15,000 to $24,999: 28,443

$25,000 to $34,999: 30,592

$35,000 to $49,999: 35,311

$50,000 to $74,999: 39,533

$75,000 to $99,999: 22,437

$100,000 to $149,999: 20,790

$150,000 to $199,999: 8,292

$200,000 or more: 11,639

*Percent of families below poverty level:* 16.7% (47.7% of which were female householder families with related children under 5 years)

*2002 FBI Crime Index Total:* 44,349

# Municipal Government

Washington won the right to govern itself in 1975. Until then, Congress had complete jurisdiction over the District. Now Washington is led by a mayor and thirteen city council members, all of whom serve four-year terms. Eight city council members represent separate wards, while five are elected at large. District voters also elect a non-voting delegate to the U.S. Congress.

**Head Official:** Mayor Anthony Williams (D) (since 1999; current term expires January 1, 2007)

**Total Number of City Employees:** 34,000 (2005)

*City Information:* Council of the District of Columbia, 1350 Pennsylvania Avenue, NW, Washington, D.C. 20004; telephone (202)727-1000

# Economy

## Major Industries and Commercial Activity

A 2004 report by the D.C. Chamber of Commerce characterized the local economy as diversifying and growing, though still narrowly specialized and externally driven. The Washington area ranks first among all national metropolitan areas in federal procurement dollars. Taking advantage of that influx of capital, as well as the city's advantage as the center of all national capital functions, will be key to the D.C. area's future economic vitality and job growth. The Washington area is expected to achieve a 58 percent increase (inflation adjusted) in its economic activity between 2000 and 2015, with the job base growing 29 percent and the resident population increasing 21 percent. Key sectors driving the economy will continue to be the federal government, technology, construction, international business, and hospitality. Manufacturing has never been a strong suit; only 3.9 percent of area jobs were in manufacturing, and that figure is expected to fall to 2.8 percent by 2015.

Indeed, people often think of Washington, D.C. as a "company town" where most people work for the federal government. However, in the early twenty-first century, only one of six workers in the area was on the government payroll. That figure is down from one in four in 1977. By contrast, there has been a great deal of growth in the private service sector, which now accounts for one of every three jobs. Still, many of these employees work for companies who rely on government contracts. As the largest consumer of technological equipment and service in the world, the federal government stimulates business through purchases, research and development funding, and grant and loan programs. As a result, Washington is a magnet for growth industries, such as paper products, telecommunications, information and computer firms, and many service industries, especially tourism and hospitality firms. Nearly 50 of the major *Fortune* 500 companies have offices in the district, which is also the location of leading world, national, and regional financial institutions.

There are more than 500 publishing and printing companies in the district to produce the vast array of documents generated by the federal government. In addition, the city houses more than 1,000 national associations' headquarters and lobby groups who need a presence in the district to attempt to shape and influence the legislation process on their own behalf.

The Capital City has an inventory of nearly 100 million square feet of office space. A key to office development has been the growth of the Metrorail subway stations. Commercial projects have typically followed the opening of new subway stops. Many of the new buildings are connected directly to the stations through underground tunnels that also serve retail stores and restaurants. Major residential projects on Pennsylvania Avenue N.W. and at Market Square include residential housing units mixed with other types of retail, office, and commercial uses.

*Items and goods produced:* printed and published documents; telecommunications equipment

### Incentive Programs—New and Existing Companies

*Local programs*—Because of its recent economic resurgence, Washington, D.C. can offer numerous financial incentives to attract and retain businesses and associations. The New E-conomy Transformation Act of 2000 (NET 2000), effective January 1, 2001, provides certain credits, exemptions and other benefits for a Qualified High Technology Company. These incentives include resources to develop their workforce, secure affordable facilities for their business and benefit from reduced real estate, personal property, sales and income taxes.

*State programs*—Federal incentives designed to tap the investment and employment potential of the Enterprise Zone include three types of wage credits, an additional expensing allowance, a zero federal capital gains tax rate on certain investments and tax-exempt bond financing. The District's Revenue Bond Program offers below market interest rate loans to qualified private enterprises that are located in the Enterprise Zone as well as non-profit and manufacturing organizations citywide.

*Job training programs*—The D.C. Department of Employment Services contracts with private companies to provide customized training programs through the D.C. Private Industry Council, the federal Workforce Investment Act (WIA) (formerly Job Training Partnership Act), the Youth Employment Act, the Training and Retraining for Employment Program, the On-The-Job Training program, and through the One-Stop Career Center approach now in effect in several states and supported in part by the Department of Labor. Contracts have encompassed such areas as shop training, technical training, basic education areas, office skills, legal research, food service, tourism, art-related occupations, industrial maintenance, mail handling, bank tellering, health care, child care, truck driving, construction industry retraining, and brick and masonry training.

### Development Projects

The $650 million Washington Convention Center opened in 2004 to rave reviews for its design and state-of-the-art facilities. With more than 700,000 square feet of convention space, the Center had more than one million visitors in its first year and generated $426 million in local delegate spending. It was also named Best New Convention Center by *Meetings East* magazine. The new center also made way for further downtown development by making the older facility redundant—it was imploded in 2004. In Dec. 2004, D.C. and Major League Baseball agreed to a financing package for a $400 million publicly financed baseball stadium to allow the former Montreal Expos (now the Washington Nationals) to move to D.C. Play at the new stadium, to be located at South Capitol and N Streets, SE, is projected to begin in 2008. Until that time, the Nationals will play at existing RFK Stadium, former home of the Washington Redskins.

***Economic Development Information:*** Director, Washington, D.C. Marketing Center, D.C. Chamber of Commerce, 1710 H. Street, NW, 11th Floor, Washington, D.C. 20006; telephone (202)638-7333; fax (202)833-2693; email dchristian@dcchamber.org

### Commercial Shipping

Ronald Reagan Washington National Airport, Dulles International Airport, and Baltimore-Washington International Airport handle the bulk of air freight in the area. For shipping, Washington, D.C. has its own port at the Anacostia and Potomac Rivers but mainly utilizes larger port facilities in Baltimore, Maryland, and in both Alexandria and Norfolk, Virginia.

## Labor Force and Employment Outlook

The D.C. Department of Labor Services issued a report identifying high demand and emerging occupations for the years 2000-2010. Key white collar sectors included business management and financial services, lawyers, computer and technical specialists, and public relations. Blue collar and non-skilled growth areas include office clerks, secretaries, legal secretaries, laborers and movers, janitors and food service workers, and police officers. While government employment continues to shrink due to downsizing and streamlining, private-sector jobs have increased dramatically in the last decade, especially in the services sector. All sectors of the hospitality industry, the city's second strongest industry after the federal government, have reported strong growth due to the city's high number of tourists and travelers on government business. The new Convention Center, opened in 2004, will likely attract a vigorous convention business and stimulate new hotels, restaurants, and spending downtown.

The following is a summary of data regarding the Washington, D.C. metropolitan area labor force for December 2004 (annual average figures unavailable).

*Size of nonagricultural labor force:* 673,800

*Number of workers employed in . . .*
   *construction and mining:* 12,000
   *manufacturing:* 2,500
   *trade, transportation, and utilities:* 28,800
   *information:* 23,100
   *financial activities:* 30,400
   *professional and business services:* 143,800
   *educational and health services:* 93,700
   *leisure and hospitality:* 51,800
   *other services:* 59,200
   *government:* 230,900

*Average hourly earnings of production workers employed in manufacturing:* $16.73

*Unemployment rate:* 8.8% (December 2004)

***Largest employers ranked by number of employees (2002):*** George Washington University, Howard University, Washington Hospital Center, Georgetown University, Georgetown University Hospital, Children's National Medical Center, Fannie Mae, Howard University Hospital, American University.

## Cost of Living

A 2004 ACCRA study cited Washington, D.C. as the third highest metropolitan area in terms of cost of living in the United States, behind only New York and Los Angeles. Housing costs in Washington, D.C. are higher than U.S. averages due primarily to the fact that approximately two-thirds of all land is either owned or controlled by the federal government, foreign embassies, and other non-profit organizations, which renders that land and property tax-exempt. Housing prices range from $90,000 to well over $1 million. The cost of living for food and other essentials is more in line with nationwide standards. The city levies a 10 percent sales tax on restaurant meals, 14.5 percent tax on hotel rooms, and a 12 percent tax on motor vehicle parking in private garages.

The following is a summary of data regarding several key cost of living factors for the Washington, D.C. area.

*2004 (3rd Quarter) ACCRA Average House Price:*$505,428

*2004 (3rd Quarter) ACCRA Cost of Living Index:* 140.0 (U.S. average = 100.0)

*Local income tax rate:* Ranges from 5.0% to 9.5%

*Local sales tax rate:* 5.75%

*Property tax rate:* $0.96 per $100 of assessed valuation; assessed at 100% (2005)

***Economic Information:*** Washington, D.C. Marketing Center, D.C. Chamber of Commerce, 1710 H. Street, NW, 11th Floor, Washington, D.C. 20006; telephone (202)638-7333; fax (202)833-2693; email dchristian@dcchamber.org

# Education and Research

## Elementary and Secondary Schools

The District of Columbia's public school system is among the largest in the country, serving approximately 68,000 students at 167 schools. A 2003 *Newsweek* study ranked three D.C. high schools—Banneker, Wilson, and School Without Walls—among the nation's finest. Besides Head Start, Magnet Schools, and Alternative Education programs, the district offers a range of special programs to meet the needs of a diverse student body, including a youth orchestra, boys choir, substance abuse prevention education, and English-as-a-Second-Language program.

The following is a summary of data regarding Washington D.C.'s public schools as of the 2002–2003 school year.

*Total enrollment:* 67,522

*Number of facilities*
 *elementary schools:* 101
 *junior high/middle schools:* 9
 *senior high schools:* 20
 *other:* 6 educational centers; 20 special schools

*Student/teacher ratio:* 13.5: 1

*Teacher salaries*
 *average:* $53,194

*Funding per pupil:* $6,903

Dozens of private and parochial schools also operate in the district with varied curriculums. More than 60 major private schools, including several of national renown, operate as traditional, parochial, and alternative/arts schools.

*Public Schools Information:* Washington-District of Columbia Schools District, 415 Twelfth Street NW, Washington, D.C. 20004

### Colleges and Universities

Washington, D.C. is home to 12 universities and colleges. Georgetown University has the largest school of international affairs in the world and the second largest law school in the United States. Howard University, the alma mater of many prominent African Americans, enrolls the most foreign students in the country. Nearby in Baltimore, the Johns Hopkins University is the nation's oldest research university. Other major institutions are American, Catholic, Gallaudet, George Washington, Corcoran College of Art and Design, Mount Vernon and Trinity colleges, and University of the District of Columbia. More than 20 licensed trade and technical schools also operate in the district, including the American College of Computer and Information Sciences, the ITT Technical Institute, Kennedy-Western University, and the Harrison Center for Career Education.

### Libraries and Research Centers

The Library of Congress is the nation's oldest federal cultural institution and serves as the research arm of Congress. It is also the largest library in the world, with nearly 128 million items on approximately 530 miles of bookshelves. The collections include more than 29 million books and other printed materials, 2.7 million recordings, 12 million photographs, 4.8 million maps, and 57 million manuscripts. In December 2002, the U.S. Congress approved the Library's plan for a national digital information infrastructure and a program to preserve digital archives, a long-term project that will be a model for national programs seeking to organize the massive amounts of digital publishing taking place on the internet.

The District of Columbia Public Library system has 27 branches, the Martin Luther King Memorial Library, 1 kiosk, and a total of more than 2.4 million volumes. In 2004 four branch libraries were closed for major renovations. Among the several special collections is Washingtoniana, which specializes in local history and celebrated its 100th anniversary in 2005. In addition to public libraries, there are nearly 600 special libraries in the district, including those maintained by foreign embassies, colleges and universities, and the Smithsonian Institution.

*Public Library Information:* District of Columbia Public Library, Martin Luther King Memorial Library, 901 G Street NW, Washington, D.C. 20001; telephone (202)727-0321; Library of Congress, telephone (202)707-5000

# Health Care

The District of Columbia boasts one of the finest health care systems in the country. Its 14 hospitals, many of which are affiliated with major medical schools and research centers, include hospitals at Georgetown, Howard, and George Washington universities. The city offers state-of-the-art specialty hospitals for women, children, and veterans; world-renowned centers for neuroscientific research and the study of fertility, pregnancy, and development; and nationally recognized services for trauma, cancer, heart disease, and organ transplants. Also nearby is the Johns Hopkins Hospital and Health Systems, supported by the university's School of Medicine and one of the most renowned medical care and research facilities in the world. In 2003 the institution was named the nation's best hospital, second best medical college, and was the largest recipient of National Institutes of Health funding in America.

# Recreation

### Sightseeing

As a city with tremendous history as a worldwide capital, and also a place where news and historic events take place nearly every day, Washington, D.C. is one of America's most popular tourist destinations for American families, serious researchers, and foreign travelers. Visitors to Washington can choose from 40 museums and more than 150 historical sites—most of them free of charge. Any tour of Washington starts on the Mall, the long strip of open park land between Capitol Hill and the Lincoln Memorial. Tours of the U.S. Capitol building are given daily and visitors can receive admittance cards from their elected representatives to visit the House or Senate chambers, when in session. In the middle of the Mall, surrounded by American flags, stands the 555-foot-tall Washington Monument, completed

**Tours of the U.S. Capitol are given daily and visitors with passes may visit the House and Senate chambers.**

in 1888. An elevator ride to the top provides the best—and highest—view of the District of Columbia. The Washington Monument was closed temporarily in 2004 due to construction that would enhance security, but was scheduled to re-open in spring 2005. The president's residence, the White House, is the oldest public building in Washington and is open for tours Tuesdays through Saturdays. The majestic Lincoln Memorial, on the west end of the Mall, was finished in 1922. Here the 19-foot-high statue of Lincoln looks out over the Reflecting Pool, which mirrors the Washington Monument dramatically at dusk.

Just outside the Mall, the Jefferson Memorial, at the foot of the Tidal Basin, is a popular spot to view the city's famous cherry blossoms in the spring. The Vietnam Veteran's Memorial provides a moving experience for the millions of people who observe the names of the war dead with which it is inscribed. The Federal Bureau of Investigation in the J. Edgar Hoover Building offers tours that include a videotape history of the agency, photos of notorious crimes and criminals, and a firearm demonstration. The Bureau of Engraving and Printing shows how it provides the nation with currency and stamps. The National Archives displays copies of the Declaration of Independence, the U.S. Constitution, and the Bill of Rights, plus other key documents in U.S. history. The Library of Congress, besides being one of the nation's premier research facilities, also hosts concerts and literary programs. Sessions at the Supreme Court Building, near the U.S. Capitol, are always open to the public. Lafayette Park, across from the White House, is notable for frequent civil demonstrations on current issues, in addition to its statue honoring Andrew Jackson.

Elsewhere in central Washington, costumed guides at the Frederick Douglass Home explain the life of the former slave, statesman, and civil rights activist. Ford Theater, where Lincoln was shot, and the Peterson House, where he died, retain their 1860s style and are open to the public. The National Arboretum and Dumbarton Oaks on the edge of Georgetown display a breathtaking variety of plant life.

Sixteen miles outside the city, in Mount Vernon, Virginia, George Washington's Mount Vernon Estate and Gardens sits on 500 acres overlooking the Potomac River. Another of America's most revered monuments is the Arlington National Cemetary in nearby Arlington, Virginia. The 600 acre site bears thousands of simple white crosses to honor the nation's war dead, as well as the gravesites of other prominent citizens that include President John F. Kennedy, boxer Joe Louis, and the Tomb of the Unknowns.

## Arts and Culture

Washington, D.C. is a cultural as well as governmental center. It boasts a higher concentration of museums and art galleries than any other city in the nation. The District of

Columbia regularly attracts performers as diverse as touring Broadway shows and major rock and jazz acts to its opulent theaters and concert halls.

Much of Washington's cultural life is based in the John F. Kennedy Center for the Performing Arts, home of the National Symphony Orchestra and the Washington Opera, and host to almost-daily performances by world-famous artists. The Kennedy Center presents more than 3,300 performances a year before more than 2 million guests. Each December the Kennedy Center Honors is a national celebration of the arts that recognizes the talents and achievements of the world's greatest performing artists. The Arena Stage and the National Theater all offer major stage shows, including dramas and musicals. Other local theater groups include the Avalon, Shakespeare Theater, Theater J, Old Vat Theater, Source Theater, Wooly Mammoth Theatre Company, Studio Theatre, GALA Hispanic Theater, and scores more around the Washington, D.C. area. The Washington Ballet presents a varied repertoire and the District of Columbia's African Heritage Dancers and Drummers present special children's programs. Young audiences enjoy special performances presented at the Kennedy Center Lab. Children's theater is also offered by Picture Book Players, Summer Theatre Camp and special events for young people at the Washington, D.C. Armory. Many college-affiliated groups offer theatrical performances.

Washington, D.C.'s many museums and galleries provide a feast of viewing variety. The museums operated by the Smithsonian Institution, often called ''America's Attic,'' contain everything from a 50-foot section of the legendary American highway Route 66 to the original Kermit the Frog hand puppet, from Charles Lindbergh's historic trans-Atlantic solo plane, *The Spirit of St. Louis,* to Archie Bunker's armchair from the television series ''All in the Family.'' Smithsonian museums, which would take weeks to fully navigate, are mostly located on or just off the Mall and include the National Air and Space Museum (the most visited museum on earth), the Arts and Industries Building, the Freer Gallery of Art, the Hirshhorn Museum and Sculpture Garden (modern and contemporary art), the National Gallery of Art, the National Museum of Natural History, the National Portrait Gallery, the National Museum of American Art, the National Museum of American History, the Arthur M. Sackler Gallery of Asian Art, and the National Museum of African Art. In 2003 President George W. Bush signed legislation that will create the National Museum of African American History and Culture within the Smithsonian. The Smithsonian's National Zoological Park is set on 160 acres in Rock Creek Park.

Other museums in the city include the Pope John Paul II Cultural Museum, the International Spy Museum, the U.S. Marine Corps Museum, the United States Holocaust Memorial Museum, Corcoran Gallery of Art (specializing in American art), the Museum of Modern Art of Latin America, the National Museum of Women in the Arts, and the National Building Museum.

## Festivals and Holidays

Washington, D.C.'s biggest and best-known celebration is the Cherry Blossom Festival, held in early April to coincide with the blooming of the trees. Started in 1927 to mark the first planting of 3,000 Japanese cherry trees as a gift from the mayor of Tokyo in 1912, the festival now runs two weeks. Special events include a major parade, a Japanese lantern lighting ceremony and street festival with more than 80 exhibitors, and a Smithsonian Kite Festival held near the Washington Monument.

Other exciting annual events include the Washington Antiques Show in January; the Chinese New Year's celebration in February; the St. Patrick's Day Parade along Constitution Avenue in March; the White House Easter Egg Roll and the White House Spring Garden Tour in April, as well as the off-beat Gross National Product Parade on April Fool's Day; the Goodwill Embassy Tour—allowing the public into several foreign embassies in town—in May; the Potomac Riverfest and a National Barbecue Battle in June; the Smithsonian's Festival of American Folklife in late June through early July; a massive July Fourth celebration; the Kennedy Center Prelude Festival in September; the Marine Corps Marathon in October, the November Washington Craft Show; and the lighting of the national Christmas tree outside the White House in December.

## Sports for the Spectator

Plagued by controversy that almost squashed the deal, Washington D.C. was finally able to convince taxpayers and Major League Baseball that it was the right place for the new home of Major League Baseball's struggling Montreal Expos franchise. The Washington Nationals began play in 2005 and brought big-league baseball back to the city for the first time since the old Washington Senators left town some 30 years prior. Until a new $400 million ballpark can be constructed (estimated completion 2008), the team will play its games at the existing Robert F. Kennedy Stadium. Washington is home to four other major league professional sports teams. The Washington Redskins are the true sporting passion of Washingtonians and face National Football League opponents at the FedEx Stadium in Landover, Maryland. The Washington Capitals of the National Hockey League, the Washington Wizards of the National Basketball Association, and the Washington Mystics of the Women's National Basketball Association play at the MCI Center. The basketball team of Georgetown University has earned a national reputation for outstanding performance.

## Sports for the Participant

Washington, D.C. offers a wide selection of participant sports. The city's close approximation to rivers, bays, and the Atlantic Ocean make a variety of water sports within reach, particularly boating, sailing, fishing, canoeing, SCUBA diving, and windsurfing. A true oasis in the city and one of its most treasured resources is Rock Creek Park, operated by the National Park Service and featuring more than 25 miles of trails for hiking among 1,755 acres. In all the city maintains more than 800 acres of parkland, 300 parks, 75 playgrounds, 71 community recreation centers, 33 public swimming pools, and more than 150 basketball and tennis courts.

## Shopping and Dining

Avid shoppers can lose themselves in the proliferation of urban malls in downtown Washington, D.C. Perhaps the most legendary is Union Station, an historic urban shopping center with marble floors, upscale shopping at more than 130 shops, a full schedule of events and exhibitions, and more than 25 million visitors a year. At The Shops at National Place, 60 shops and a food hall serving all palates is convenient to the Metro Center subway stop. The glass-roofed Pavilion at the Old Post Office, once a working post office, is now home to retail concerns, restaurants, and offices and has been ranked as the 8th most popular destination in D.C. A different kind of shopping experience is found in Georgetown, where unique boutiques and specialty stores are housed in historic townhouses, mostly along Wisconsin Avenue and M Street; elegant shops abound at Georgetown Park Mall. Mazza Gallerie is a three-storied enclosed mall filled with elite shops, stylish boutiques, and a new state-of-the-art movie theater. Washington's Eastern Market, in the southeast section of the city, has been a farmer's market since 1873 with fresh fruit, vegetables, poultry, and sausage for sale Tuesday through Saturday.

Restaurants in Washington reflect the influence of the many foreign cultures present in the capital, and the last decade has seen an explosion of culinary creativity on the local restaurant scene. Many of the most interesting establishments are clustered in the Georgetown and Dupont Circle areas and in the urban malls downtown. In a 2005 online poll travelers to Washington, D.C. ranked the Italian restaurant Obelisk (Dupont Circle) as the city's best restaurant, followed by Sequoia (American contemporary; Georgetown), Café Atlantico (Caribbean and South American; downtown), Georgia Brown's (American; downtown), and Jaleo (Spanish; Seventh Street). Ann Cashion, chef at Cashion's Eat Place, was named one of James Beard's best chefs in America in 2004. Capital Grille, located between the White House and the Capitol Building, is one of the best places to spot high-powered politicos gathered for lunch, drinks, or dinner.

*Visitor Information:* Washington, D.C. Convention and Visitors Association, 1212 New York Avenue, N.W., Suite 600, Washington, D.C. 20005; telephone (202)789-7099; fax (202)789-7037

# Convention Facilities

In 2004 the city opened its all-new Washington Convention Center in the heart of downtown, with 2.3 million square feet total and 700,000 square feet of exhibit space covering 6 city blocks. With the addition of this state-of-the-art facility, along with the city's proximity to the nation's government, powerbase, and riches of cultural and tourist destinations, Washington D.C. should continue to be one of the great magnets for America's lucrative convention business well into the 21st century.

While the old convention center was razed in 2004 to make way for new development, The D.C. Armory Starplex, with 124,471 square feet of exhibit space, offers alternative space for smaller gatherings. The Washington area also provides more than 70,000 hotel rooms; and many hotels offer meeting space, such as the Sheraton Washington Hotel (115,000 square feet), the Shoreham Omni Hotel (85,134 square feet), the Capital Hilton (space for up 1,200 people), and the Grand Hyatt Washington (40,000 square feet of meeting space).

*Convention Information:* Washington, D.C. Convention and Visitors Association, 1212 New York Avenue, N.W., Suite 600, Washington, D.C. 20005; telephone (202)789-7000; fax (202)789-7037

# Transportation

## Approaching the City

Washington is served by three major international airports. The closest, Ronald Reagan Washington National—across the Potomac in Virginia—is minutes from downtown Washington by car or the Metro subway system. Dulles International is about 20 miles west of the District of Columbia in Virginia. Baltimore-Washington International is 20 miles northeast of the city in Maryland.

Travelers driving to Washington by car have to cross the Capital Beltway, also known as Interstate 495, which circles the city and connects it with Maryland and Virginia. Interstates 395 and 66 also run between the District of Columbia and surrounding areas.

Continuous daily trains connect New York's Pennsylvania Station to Washington's Union Station, which is in sight of the Capitol, and 50 daily trains connect Washington, D.C. with more than 500 cities around the U.S. Taxi fares are based on a zone system and cabs do not carry meters.

## Traveling in the City

Travel in the District of Columbia, second most congested area in the nation after Los Angeles, is made easier by the mass transportation system operated by the Washington Metropolitan Area Transit Authority, which runs the second largest rail transit system and fifth largest bus network in the United States. The award-winning Metrorail system includes 103 miles of track and 86 operating stations, including three new stations opened in 2004 extending the Blue and Red lines. The system has stations at Union Station and National Airport. In 2004 the Metrorail moved 190 million riders. The 1,460 vehicle Metrobus system has bus routes on all major streets in D.C. and nearly all primary roads in the region and carried 140 million riders in 2004.

More than 10,000 taxis cruise city streets charging inexpensive fares based on a simple zone system.

# Communications

## Newspapers and Magazines

The capital's major daily newspaper, and one of the most influential newspapers in the country, is the Pulitzer Prize-winning *Washington Post,* which is published in the morning. The Washington Post Company also publishes *The Washington Post Magazine,* a weekly covering Washington personalities and issues affecting the city, Virginia and Maryland suburbs, and the nation. A smaller newspaper, *The Washington Times* is the more conservative voice in the city. The national daily, *USA Today,* is another of the 40-plus newspapers published in the capital. The monthly *Washingtonian Magazine,* one of nearly 700 periodicals published in D.C., looks at local politics, lifestyles, culture, and dining.

## Television and Radio

Washington has 7 television stations broadcasting in the city; two cable systems are available. The capital is also served by 12 FM and AM radio stations in the city and many more in surrounding areas, including several public radio outlets.

*Media Information: Washington Post,* 1150 Fifteenth Street NW, Washington, D.C. 20071; telephone (202)334-6000;

*Washington Times,* 3600 New York Avenue, NE, Washington, D.C. 20002; telephone (202)6236 3028

**Washington, D.C. Online**

City of Washington, D.C. Home Page. Available www.dc .gov

Cultural Tourism D.C. Available www.culturaltourismdc.org

D.C. Chamber of Commerce. Available www.dcchamber.org

D.C. Marketing Center Available www.dcmarketingcenter .com

District of Columbia Public Library. Available www .dclibrary.org

Downtown D.C. Available www.downtowndc.org

*InTowner.* Available www.intowner.com

Library of Congress. Available at www.loc.gov

*Washington Business Journal.* Available www.amcity.com/ washington

*Washington City Paper.* Available www.washington citypaper.com

Washington, D.C. Convention and Visitors Association. Available www.washington.org

Washington, D.C. Historical Society. Available www.city museumdc.org

Washington D.C. top sites. Available dcpages.com/Top_ Sites/

*Washington Post.* Available www.washingtonpost.com

*Washington Times.* Available www.washtimes.com

*Washingtonian Magazine.* Available www.washingtonian .com

**Selected Bibliography**

Baldacci, David, *Saving Faith* (New York: Warner Books, 1999)

Fink, Michael, *Never Forget: An Oral History of September 11, 2001* (Regan Books, 2002)

Gottlieb, Steve *Washington, DC: Portrait of a City* (Taylor Trade Publishing, 2004)

Vidal, Gore, *Washington, D.C.,* (Boston: Little Brown, 1967)

Wright, Jim, *Balance of Power: Presidents and Congress From the Era of McCarthy to the Age of Gingrich* (Atlanta: Turner Publishing, 1996)

# WEST VIRGINIA

# The State in Brief

**Nickname:** Mountain State
**Motto:** *Montani semper liberi* (Mountaineers are always free)

**Flower:** Big rhododendron
**Bird:** Cardinal

**Area:** 24,230 square miles (2000; U.S. rank: 41st)
**Elevation:** Ranges from 240 feet to 4,861 feet above sea level
**Climate:** Continental; humid, with hot summers and cool winters, colder in mountains

**Admitted to Union:** June 20, 1863
**Capital:** Charleston
**Head Official:** Governor Joe Manchin (D) (until 2009)

## Population
**1980:** 1,950,000
**1990:** 1,793,477
**2000:** 1,808,344
**2004 estimate:** 1,815,354
**Percent change, 1990–2000:** 0.8%
**U.S. rank in 2004:** 37th
**Percent of residents born in state:** 74.2% (2000)
**Density:** 75.1 people per square mile (2000)
**2002 FBI Crime Index Total:** 45,320

## Racial and Ethnic Characteristics (2000)
**White:** 1,718,777
**Black or African American:** 57,232
**American Indian and Alaska Native:** 3,606
**Asian:** 9,434
**Native Hawaiian and Pacific Islander:** 400
**Hispanic or Latino (may be of any race):** 12,279
**Other:** 3,107

## Age Characteristics (2000)
**Population under 5 years old:** 101,805
**Population 5 to 19 years old:** 352,910
**Percent of population 65 years and over:** 15.3%
**Median age:** 38.9 years (2000)

## Vital Statistics
**Total number of births (2003):** 20,817
**Total number of deaths (2003):** 21,102 (infant deaths, 153)
**AIDS cases reported through 2003:** 645

## Economy
**Major industries:** Chemicals, mining, metals, timber, oil, coal, tourism
**Unemployment rate:** 4.9% (December 2004)
**Per capita income:** $24,672 (2003; U.S. rank: 49th)
**Median household income:** $31,210 (3-year average, 2001-2003)
**Percentage of persons below poverty level:** 16.9% (3-year average, 2001-2003)
**Income tax rate:** Ranges from 3.0% to 6.5%
**Sales tax rate:** 6.0%

# Charleston

## *The City in Brief*

**Founded:** 1794 (incorporated 1818)

**Head Official:** Mayor Danny Jones (since 2003)

**City Population**
   **1980:** 63,968
   **1990:** 57,287
   **2000:** 53,421
   **2003 estimate:** 51,394
   **Percent change, 1990–2000:** −7.4%
   **U.S. rank in 1980:** 310th
   **U.S. rank in 1990:** 415th (State rank: 1st)
   **U.S. rank in 2000:** 662nd

**Metropolitan Area Population**
   **1980:** 270,000
   **1990:** 250,000
   **2000:** 251,662
   **Percent change, 1990–2000:** .5%

**U.S. rank in 1980:** 118th (MSA)
**U.S. rank in 1990:** 134th (MSA)
**U.S. rank in 2000:** 141st (MSA)

**Area:** 32 square miles (2000)
**Elevation:** Ranges from 601 feet to approximately 1,100 feet above sea level
**Average Annual Temperature:** 56.2° F
**Average Annual Precipitation:** 44.05 inches

**Major Economic Sectors:** services, trade, government
**Unemployment rate:** 4.3% (December 2004)
**Per Capita Income:** $26,017 (1999)

**2002 FBI Crime Index Total:** 4,463

**Major Colleges and Universities:** West Virginia State University, West Virginia University Institute of Technology, University of Charleston, Marshall University Graduate College

**Daily Newspaper:** *Charleston Daily Mail; Charleston Gazette*

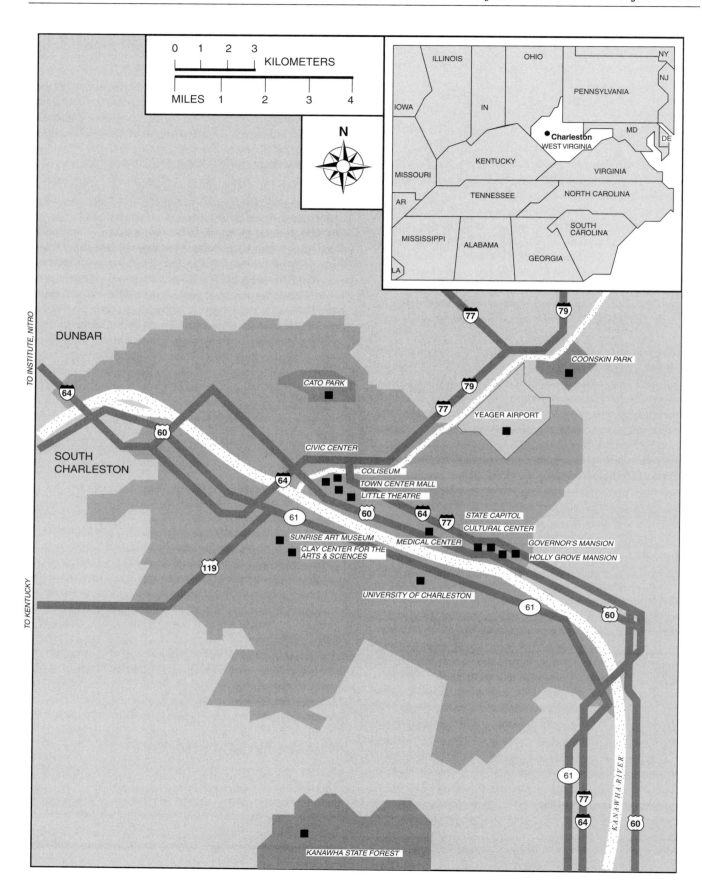

# Introduction

Charleston, the capital of West Virginia and seat of Kanawha County, is a regional hub for transportation, finance, retail trade, commerce, government, and health care, and acts as a lively center for the arts and recreation while also serving as West Virginia's state capital. A vital urban area, the city also projects a comfortable charm that invites visitors and residents alike; its downtown is active and filled with people in the evening. With its nineteenth-century style brick sidewalks and streets lit by antique reproduction light posts and dotted with wooden benches, the Village District stands as a monument to the modern thinking that has kept the city on track both financially and aesthetically for years.

# Geography and Climate

Charleston is located in a narrow valley in the western Appalachian Mountains at the junction of the Kanawha and Elk rivers. Framed with green hills, the city and neighboring towns have developed along the Kanawha to the east and west, though some residential areas can be found on the surrounding hills and in nearby valleys.

The region's weather is highly changeable, particularly during the winter months when Arctic air may alternate with tropical air. Consequently, sharp temperature contrasts are the rule—even on a day-to-day basis—and total annual snowfall ranges from less than 5 inches to more than 50. Spring temperatures warm rapidly, however, and summers can occasionally be hot, hazy, and humid. Most of Charleston's precipitation falls in the form of rain; the brief, sometimes heavy, thunderstorms of July make it the wettest month of the year. The terrain and air flow patterns combine to make Charleston one of the foggiest cities in the United States.

**Area:** 32 square miles (2000)

**Elevation:** Ranges from 601 feet in the downtown area to approximately 1,100 feet above sea level in the hilltops

**Average Temperatures:** January, 35.7° F; July, 75.9° F; annual average, 56.2° F

**Average Annual Precipitation:** 44.05 inches

# History

### Fort Leads to Founding of City

Centuries before the first white frontiersmen explored the area that is now Charleston, the Adena, a Native American tribe, inhabited the Kanawha Valley. The Adenas were mound builders, and one of West Virginia's largest examples of their unique earthworks is located in downtown South Charleston.

The influx of traders and land surveyors—most of whom were Virginians—into the Kanawha Valley region began in the mid-1760s. In 1773, Colonel Thomas Bullitt and a group of surveyors on their way to Kentucky briefly established a camp there. Bullitt again visited the valley in 1775 and, in return for his military service during the French and Indian War, he was allowed to stake a claim of more than 1,000 acres. Upon his death the claim went to his brother, Cuthbert Bullitt, who in turn sold the land to Colonel George Clendenin in 1787.

Just a few weeks after the deal was finalized, the governor of Virginia instructed Clendenin to organize a company of soldiers to protect the Kanawha Valley from native raiding parties. In 1788, the colonel erected a fort on a portion of his land that ran along the river. The completion of this stockade—known officially as Fort Lee but often referred to as Clendenin's Settlement—and the security it represented attracted a number of pioneers to the area in just a few years. So many people had settled there by 1794 that some of the other Clendenin land holdings were divided into lots, and the Virginia Assembly authorized the creation of a town, named Charles Town in honor of George Clendenin's father. (Common usage eventually shortened this to Charleston, the name of record on January 19, 1818, the day the town was officially established.) Drawn by reports of abundant game in the valley, Daniel Boone and his family were among Charleston's early residents, but the region grew so quickly that they soon left for the Kentucky wilderness.

### Economy Grows Around Natural Resources

Salt manufacturing was the first industry to gain a foothold in Charleston. In 1797, a salt furnace was constructed in nearby Malden, and by the mid-1800s Kanawha Valley salt was being shipped from Charleston to all parts of the country. Throughout the first half of the century the city also grew in importance as a transportation center, primarily as a point of transfer for east-west travelers who arrived by wagon or on horseback and continued their journey by boat.

The Civil War divided Charleston. Some citizens fought for the Confederacy, but most sided with the Union. The conflict also hastened the decline of the salt trade (which had already reached its peak around 1856) and forced the development of alternative industries, particularly those involving coal, oil, and gas. The city grew rapidly after the war, aided in part by the relocation of West Virginia's capital from Wheeling to Charleston in 1870. The coming of the railroad in 1873 and improved navigation on the Kanawha River opened up coal mining on an even larger scale, and Charleston prospered as a market and wholesale center.

Between 1885 and the beginning of World War I, Charleston grew slowly but steadily, its economy bolstered by increasing demand for the natural resources it processed and sold throughout the country. Around 1913, however, a new era in the city's development began when the first chemical company was established. Others soon followed and were eventually joined by glass manufacturers. With America's entry into the war, some of these new factories switched over to producing munitions, but coal and chemicals continued to attract the most foreign capital and new residents.

In the years since World War I, Charleston has come to rely more and more on the manufacture of synthetic materials as the basis of its industrial economy; during World War II, for example, the Kanawha Valley was a center for synthetic rubber production. Thus, as has been the case since its earliest days as a frontier town, the fortunes of the city are inextricably linked with the demand for the natural resources it has in such abundance.

Charleston, as well as most of West Virginia, was affected by recession in the early 1980s. Moderate growth followed, and between 1985 and 1990 personal income grew due to Charleston's industrial growth. According to former Mayor Jay Goldman: "The year 2000 marks a period of potential growth and rebirth for Charleston. Downtown revitalization has brought pride and enthusiasm back to those who live and work [in] Charleston while maintaining our small-town ambience." Today's Charleston prides itself on its friendliness to visitors. The city's commitment to revitalization is evident throughout beautification and quality of life projects throughout the early years of the 21st century.

**Historical Information:** West Virginia (State) Department of Education and the Arts, Division of Culture and History, Archives and History Library, 1900 Kanawha Blvd. E., Charleston, WV 25305; telephone (304)558-0230

# Population Profile

## Metropolitan Area Residents
*1980:* 270,000
*1990:* 250,454
*2000:* 251,662

*Percent change, 1990–2000:* .5%
*U.S. rank in 1980:* 118th (MSA)
*U.S. rank in 1990:* 134th (MSA)
*U.S. rank in 2000:* 141st

## City Residents
*1980:* 63,968
*1990:* 57,287
*2000:* 53,421
*2003 estimate:* 51,394
*Percent change, 1990–2000:* −7.4%
*U.S. rank in 1980:* 310th
*U.S. rank in 1990:* 415th (State rank: 1st)
*U.S. rank in 2000:* 662nd

*Density:* 1,690.4 people per square mile (2000)

*Racial and ethnic characteristics* (2000)
   White: 43,072
   Black or African American: 8,048
   American Indian and Alaska Native: 127
   Asian: 979
   Native Hawaiian and Pacific Islander: 16
   Hispanic or Latino (may be of any race): 432
   Other: 158

*Percent of residents born in state:* 74.8% (2000)

*Age characteristics* (2000)
   Population under 5 years old: 2,961
   Population 5 to 9 years old: 3,087
   Population 10 to 14 years old: 3,145
   Population 15 to 19 years old: 3,096
   Population 25 to 34 years old: 6,707
   Population 35 to 44 years old: 8220
   Population 45 to 54 years old: 8,345
   Population 55 to 59 years old: 2,791
   Population 60 to 64 years old: 2,381
   Population 65 to 74 years old: 4,564
   Population 75 to 84 years old: 3,545
   Population 85 years and older: 1,314
   Median age: 40.8 years

*Births* (2002, Kanawha County)
   Total number: 2,423

*Deaths* (2002, Kanawha County)
   Total number: 2,510 (of which, 20 were infants under the age of 1 year)

*Money income* (1999)
   Per capita income: $26,017
   Median household income: $34,009
   Total households: 24,522

*Number of households with income of . . .*
   less than $10,000: 3,956

$10,000 to $14,999: 1,883
$15,000 to $24,999: 3,658
$25,000 to $34,999: 3,015
$35,000 to $49,999: 3,457
$50,000 to $74,999: 3,448
$75,000 to $99,999: 1,898
$100,000 to $149,999: 1,720
$150,000 to $199,999: 537
$200,000 or more: 950

*Percent of families below poverty level:* 12.7% (64% of which were female householder families with related children under 5 years)

*2002 FBI Crime Index Total:* 4,463

# Municipal Government

Charleston, the capital of West Virginia and the Kanawha County seat, has a mayor-council form of government. The mayor and all 27 council members are elected every four years.

**Head Official:** Mayor Danny Jones (since 2003; current term expires 2007)

**Total Number of City Employees:** 850 (2005)

*City Information:* City of Charleston, 501 Virginia Street, E., Charleston, WV 25301

# Economy

## Major Industries and Commercial Activity

The Kanawha Valley owes much of its past and future prosperity to its reputation as a transportation and distribution hub. From river port to interstate hub, the sophisticated transportation routes have lured and kept industry in the region when other parts of West Virginia were troubled with the same economic doldrums that affected much of the nation. Insulated from the boom-or-bust coal industry, the Kanawha Valley has relied on its diversity of natural resources and its importance in the eastern and central states' waterways system, moving goods to the Gulf of Mexico via the Ohio and Mississippi rivers. Three interstate highways converging in downtown Charleston provide the extra transportation links that the rivers cannot provide. Moreover, the highways bring Charleston within 500 miles of more than 50 percent of the nation's major market areas and 50 percent of its entire population.

The valley's market proximity and transportation advantages are responsible for the economic diversity and health of the area. Further, the abundance of natural resources and the residents' ingenuity in using them have established the region as the state's center of finance, retail trade, government, industry, arts and culture, and health care. In recent years, growth in health services and the state banking industry has outpaced that of other sectors.

Since 1929, the chemical industry has been an economic force in the valley, providing a large, stable employment base for many years. Union Carbide Corporation, Monsanto, E. I. du Pont de Nemours, Clearon Corp., and FMC are among the companies with chemical-connected facilities in the Charleston area. Union Carbide also has its headquarters for research and development in the Tech Center complex in South Charleston. Valley residents have been very supportive of the chemical industry, acknowledging that the industry's first priority has always been safety. Likewise, local governments have been involved and have participated in safety and emergency planning. Other Kanawha Valley industries include heavy steel fabricating, glass manufacturing, and energy development. Columbia Gas Transmission Corporation, headquartered in Charleston, employs almost one-third of its workforce in the Charleston headquarters.

Today, Charleston enjoys a diverse economy. An abundant and well-educated workforce is employed in thriving chemical, automotive, telecommunications, healthcare, and professional services sectors. Retail trade and tourism are also thriving economic sectors.

*Items and goods produced:* chemicals, telecommunications products, publishing, mining equipment, fabricated metal products, automobile parts

### Incentive Programs — New and Existing Companies

*Local programs*—The Business and Industrial Development Corporation (BIDCO) is a non-profit economic development corporation serving Metropolitan Charleston. BIDCO offers a range of services to companies considering the area for new or expanded operations. Assistance is offered in worker training and education, financing, site selection, and with buildings. Both professional economic development and engineering services are free and confidential.

*State programs*—Charleston participates in a state-wide program presided over by the West Virginia Economic Development Authority (WVEDA) that provides low-interest financing for land, building, and equipment. In addition to its direct loan program, WVEDA offers a Capital Access Program and Loan Insurance Program. West Virginia has one of the nation's most liberal tax incentive programs, permitting significant recapture of principal taxes as well as capital investment. Additional credits are available for corporate headquarters relocation, research and development, and veterans employment.

*Job training programs*—The Governor's Guaranteed Work Force Program provides companies creating at least 10 new jobs $2,000 per employee, or the actual cost of training, whichever is less. Three vocational-technical schools and one adult career center offer industry and occupation-specific courses and degree programs designed to produce graduates who meet the demands of a global marketplace.

## Development Projects

The $80 million, 240,000 square foot Clay Center for the Arts and Sciences opened in 2003 and houses a variety of performing and visual arts and science facilities. The Clay Center's Maier Foundation Performance Hall is a 1,883 seat theater; the Walker Theater seats up to 200 people; the Avampato Discovery Museum offers science, art, and theater; the Juliet Museum of Art presents permanent and visiting collections; the ElectricSky Theater offers planetarium and laser shows; and a café and gift shop round out the center's offerings.

As part of a collaboration among the City of Charleston, the Charleston Convention and Visitors Bureau, and several other organizations, Charleston is making itself more visitor friendly with new, colorful signs pointing out specific destinations, sights, and tourist information spots. The $55,000 project was 8 years in development and began in September 2004. Once finished in 2005, there will be 200 signs pointing visitors to malls, parking, visitor info, and area tourist destinations.

*Economic Development Information:* BIDCO, 1116 Smith Street, Charleston, WV 25301; telephone (304)340-4253; fax (304)340-4275

## Commercial Shipping

The Kanawha Valley's transportation systems may be the region's biggest economic asset, since Charleston is the region's hub for air service, river commerce, and highways. The city is an important distribution center because of its extremely sophisticated transportation routes. Charleston was designated a port of entry by the U.S. Customs Office in 1973, and the business and industrial sectors take advantage of direct shipments from foreign countries. The customs office at Yeager Airport inspects air, barge, rail, and other freight shipments received at locations throughout the region. A fixed-base operator with complete maintenance shop and 24-hour service is located at Yeager.

West Virginia's two railway systems transport chemicals, minerals, ores, primary metals, coal, petroleum, stone, or glass. The state has 3,931 miles of track, most of it linking the Atlantic Coast to the Midwest.

The U.S. Army Corps of Engineers maintains a navigation channel 200 feet wide and nine feet deep in the Kanawha River—from the mouth at Point Pleasant on the West Virginia-Ohio border to a point 91 miles east at Deepwater, about 40 miles up river from Charleston. Waterborne commerce has tripled on the Kanawha River since the early 1950s. Charleston is served by more than 40 motor freight carriers.

## Labor Force and Employment Outlook

Due to the strong manufacturing base of Charleston's economy, the city boasts a workforce that is familiar with the machinery, equipment, and processes involved in technologically complex operations. But as the mining and manufacturing sectors shrink in response to national economic trends, services and retail trade are continuing to show significant growth. The area's extensive transportation network, stable workforce, and diverse economy combine to enable companies in the chemical, automotive, healthcare, telecommunications, and professional services sectors to thrive. Charleston and the surrounding region has seen steady economic growth with total employment increasing 21 percent over the past 10 years. Unemployment in the area is similar to the national average.

The following is a summary of data regarding the Charleston metropolitan area labor force, 2003 annual averages.

*Size of nonagricultural labor force:* 133,100

*Number of workers employed in . . .*
    *construction and mining:* 8,800
    *manufacturing:* 7,600
    *trade, transportation and utilities:* 26,500
    *information:* 3,400
    *financial activities:* 8,000
    *professional and business services:* 13,500
    *education and health services:* 18,500
    *leisure and hospitality:* 11,600
    *other services:* 10,400
    *government:* 24,800

*Average hourly earnings of production workers employed in manufacturing:* $16.05

*Unemployment rate:* 4.3% (December 2004)

| Largest employers | Number of employees |
|---|---|
| State Government | 12,400 |
| Charleston Area Medical Center | 5,000 |
| Kanawha County Schools | 5,000 |
| Federal Government | 2,700 |
| Verizon West Virginia | 1,500 |

## Cost of Living

The following is a summary of data regarding several key cost of living factors for the Charleston area.

*2004 (3rd Quarter) ACCRA Average House Price:* $224,900

*2004 (3rd Quarter) ACCRA Cost of Living Index:* 92.4 (U.S. average = 100.0)

*State income tax rate:* Ranges from 3.0% to 6.5%

*State sales tax rate:* 6.0%

*Local income tax rate:* None

*Local sales tax rate:* None

*Property tax rate:* $8.20 per $1.000 of assessed valuation; (assessed valuation = approximately 60% of market value)

***Economic Information:*** Charleston Regional Chamber of Commerce & Development, 1116 Smith Street, Charleston, WV 25301-2610; telephone (304)340-4253

# Education and Research

## Elementary and Secondary Schools

Public education in Charleston is provided by the Kanawha County Public Schools. The district is administered by a five-member board of education and a superintendent who follow policies established by the State Department of Education and the West Virginia Board of Education. Kanawha County Schools has been awarded the What Parents Want award at least three times from SchoolMatch, a national educational research and consulting firm. The system offers a unique program consisting of several Family Resource Centers (FRCs) and Parent/Educator Resource Centers (PERCs) in the public schools. The centers offer families, students, and educators a variety of services to help support students and families.

The following is a summary of data regarding the Kanawha County Public Schools as of the 2002–2003 school year.

*Total enrollment:* 28,417

*Number of facilities*
   *elementary schools:* 46
   *junior high/middle schools:* 13
   *senior high schools:* 8

*Student/teacher ratio:* 14:1

*Teacher salaries*
   *average:* $39,356

*Funding per pupil:* $7,704

Students in Charleston may also attend one of the valley's more than a dozen private Catholic, Christian, and non-denominational schools.

***Public Schools Information:*** Kanawha County School District, 200 Elizabeth Street, Charleston, WV 25311; telephone (304)348-7732; fax (304)348-1934

## Colleges and Universities

In the Kanawha Valley, there are two state-supported colleges, West Virginia State University and West Virginia University Institute of Technology; a state-supported graduate school, the West Virginia Graduate College of Marshall University; and a privately funded institution, the University of Charleston.

West Virginia State University, 8 miles west of Charleston on Interstate 64 in the town of Institute, is the second-largest public four-year college in the state. The college provides a broad spectrum of undergraduate degree programs, both baccalaureate and associate. In 2003, the former West Virginia State College became accredited as a university and began offering MS and MA degrees.

West Virginia University Institute of Technology, a regional campus of West Virginia University, offers engineering and other degree programs; its Center for Applied Business, Engineering and Technology includes a small business development center and an engineering consultant program.

Established in 1969 as the West Virginia Graduate College to aid degree-holders working in the valley in obtaining master's degrees without leaving the community, the West Virginia Graduate College of Marshall University offers graduate study in several degree programs. The 1998 merger of the Graduate College with Marshall University has increased the available resources and course offerings.

The University of Charleston, a privately endowed institution, has a beautiful campus that is situated on the Kanawha River across from the State Capitol. It offers undergraduate degrees as well as graduate programs that include a master of business administration degree program and master's degrees in human services. The Charleston Conservatory of Music offers instruction as part of the University of Charleston.

## Libraries and Research Centers

Housed in the former Federal Building in downtown Charleston, the Kanawha County Public Library is the largest public non-university library in West Virginia. In 10 branches in area communities and a bookmobile, the system maintains more than 60,000 volumes and holds special history and oral history collections plus government documents. The Cultural Center in the Capitol Complex houses state archives, a genealogical library, and a general reference library. There are several special libraries in Charleston, including the Columbia Gas Transmission/Law Library, the First Presbyterian Church of Charleston Library, and several law and medical firms holding library collections.

Union Carbide's South Charleston Technical Center provides research and development support for the company's other facilities in Charleston and throughout the world.

*Public Library Information:* Kanawha County Public Library, 123 Capitol Street, Charleston, WV 25301-2686; telephone (304)343-4646

# Health Care

Charleston is the hub of West Virginia's health-care system. The area's largest major hospital, the Charleston Area Medical Center with 913 beds, has three locations in the city and is a major teaching facility, serving as the Charleston base for West Virginia University's School of Medicine. St. Francis Hospital is a 200-bed acute care facility; Thomas Memorial Hospital is a 261-bed, not-for-profit hospital serving South Charleston.

# Recreation

### Sightseeing

Charleston's parks, museums, and music and cultural activities provide a variety of enjoyable and stimulating experiences. The state's Cultural Center at the Capitol Complex has a museum, performing arts, film and music festivals, and The Shop, which sells only West Virginia native crafts. The Capitol Complex also offers tours of the Governor's Mansion two days a week. On the State Capitol grounds is a memorial honoring Malden, West Virginia, native Booker T. Washington. Glass factories in the area provide tours to groups, and the museums at the Clay Center for the Arts and Sciences are a favorite of visitors. The Haddad Riverfront Park invites residents and visitors with its river views, evening concerts, and plays. The park offers paved paths for runners, walkers, and cyclists, as well as plenty of areas for picnicking, sunbathing, and relaxing.

A variety of historic homes from the late 1800s and early 1900s can be toured in Charleston. The Craik-Patton House,

built in 1834 in the Greek Revival style of architecture, is open mid-April through mid-October for tours. The East End Historical District features homes in a variety of architectural styles, including Queen Anne, Victorian, Richardson Romanesque, Georgian, Italianate, and others, mainly built between 1895 and 1925. Victorian Block on Capitol Street features some of the oldest structures on Capitol Street, with homes dating back to 1887. Shrewsbury Street acknowledges sites and buildings that are prominent in West Virginia's African American history.

Formerly the Daniel Boone Hotel, 405 Capitol Street was built in 1929 at a then-extravagant cost of more than $1.2 million. Renovated in the 1990s, the building now houses business offices and is known for its unique 10-story atrium. Also afforded new life in the city is the C & O Railroad Depot, built in 1905. Refurbished in 1987, the Beaux Arts-style brick and terra cotta trimmed depot houses offices and a restaurant.

Charleston is home port to the *P. A. Denny,* a beautiful excursion sternwheeler available for scenic rides on the Kanawha or for rental trips for private groups. In addition, many of the forests, parks and resorts in West Virginia's excellent park system are within a half-day's drive of Kanawha Valley.

### Arts and Culture

A well-respected symphony orchestra, a resident chamber-music string quartet, a youth orchestra and visiting chamber-music ensembles ensure a steady diet of live classical music in the Charleston area. The new Clay Center for the Arts and Sciences is home to the West Virginia Symphony Orchestra, which performs monthly concerts featuring guest artists from around the world. Municipal Auditorium hosts the Charleston Chamber Music Association, Broadway touring shows, and national recording artists. The West Virginia Youth Symphony Orchestra is one of Charleston's special cultural assets, and the group performs extensively in the Kanawha County school system and in schools throughout the state. The Charleston Light Opera Guild provides musical comedy and drama each season. Many community singers, actors, and actresses, such as the Charleston Civic Chorus, have formed a close-knit group of talented performers who act, sing, and dance their way through Broadway musicals each year.

The Civic Center in Charleston contains a 13,500-seat coliseum as well as the 750-seat Little Theatre, home for most of Charleston's community theater groups. Children's Theatre of Charleston introduces many youngsters to the stage. The group produces four plays annually and conducts a performing arts school for its aspiring young actors and actresses. The Kanawha Players—the oldest continuous community theater group in West Virginia—hosts a season of drama and comedy performances each year. From experimental

The West Virginia State Capitol building.

drama and dinner theater settings to more traditional offerings, the Kanawha Players has performed in Charleston since the 1920s and the group has been designated the official state theater of West Virginia. Using community directors and actors, the group plays to full houses season after season and performs at the workshops in Kanawha City and the Civic Center Little Theatre. Mountain Stage, a West Virginia Public Radio presentation that brings jazz, folk, blues, rock, and classical musicians from around the world to the city is broadcasted live to a national audience from the Cultural Center at the Capitol. Tickets to Sunday performances are available to the public.

Charleston is also home to the Charleston Ballet, which performs three to five ballets each season, and the West Virginia Dance theater and the Appalachian Youth Jazz Ballet.

For those with a penchant for the visual arts, the Avampato Discovery Museum at the Clay Center for the Arts and Sciences has a breathtaking gallery and provides art activities, programs, and workshops throughout the year.

*Arts and Culture Information:* Charleston Convention and Visitors Bureau, 200 Civic Center Drive, Charleston, WV 25301; telephone (304)344-5075; fax (304)344-1241.

## Festivals and Holidays

For sheer spectacle, few festivals match Charleston's Annual Sternwheel Regatta Festival. The festival began as a small Labor Day race for sternwheel boats operating on the Kanawha River. From that modest beginning, the event expanded to an entire weekend, then a week, and finally to its current 10 days, which are scheduled each year during the days leading up to and including Labor Day. While the Regatta Festival's concerts draw the most impressive crowds, its other events are just as exciting. The Grand Feature Parade kicks off the festival and features balloon figures similar to those in Macy's Thanksgiving Day Parade. The Olympia Brass Band visits each year to highlight the traditional New Orleans-style Funeral Parade, where the unusual and inventive take to the streets for a spectacle that has to be seen to be believed. The Regatta Festival's Taste of Charleston is a major gourmet food event that brings a number of Charleston restaurants together under one roof to offer house specialties and other tasty dishes to regatta-goers. Other festival events include arts and craft shows, river cruises, film festivals, street fairs, and an antique car show.

"Symphony Sunday," held each year in the spring, features an outdoor concert on the campus of the University of Charleston. Another annual event that has become a favorite of West Virginians and thousands of out-of-state visitors is May's Vandalia Festival. For this event, crowds flock to the Cultural Center and its grounds to see magnificent quilts, traditional folk dancers, and demonstrations of black-

smithing and toy making and to taste treats like corn roasted over open fires. But it is the traditional music that lures most spectators. Banjo pickers, fiddlers, and dulcimer players compete in good-natured contests, and "jam sessions" seem to be going on everywhere. The first Sunday of June the State Capital Complex features artisans, food, and music at the Rhododendron Art & Craft Show. The Capital City Art and Craft Show at the Civic Center, held the week prior to Thanksgiving, brings together craftspeople and music and craft events for an exhibition with a holiday theme.

## Sports for the Spectator

Charleston has the West Virginia Power, a single A South Atlantic League farm team of the Milwaukee Brewers, who play baseball at Appalachian Power Park. For fans of dog racing, the Tri-State Greyhound Park in Cross Lanes operates six days a week all year long.

## Sports for the Participant

In Charleston, recreation can be as simple as a riverside stroll down Kanawha Boulevard when the dogwoods are in bloom or chipping a golf ball around one of the four private or five public golf courses in the area. Cyclists, hikers, and runners appreciate the miles of wooded trails and paved paths available in nearby parks, and the paved riverfront path at Kanawha Boulevard downtown. The city and county support numerous recreational centers, parks, ballfields, and golf and tennis facilities. These—along with a number of private country clubs and sports and fitness facilities—can accommodate many recreational interests.

Charleston annually hosts the Charleston Distance Run, one of the oldest and rated one of the 10 best road runs in the United States. This rigorous course—set along 4 miles on the hills and 11 miles on the flatlands—has tested the mettle of world champions.

The Kanawha Parks and Recreation Commission operates seven recreational facilities in Kanawha County. The largest, Coonskin Park, has 1,200 wooded acres near Yeager Airport and offers picnic areas, shelters, tennis, swimming, golf, hiking, a modern amphitheater, soccer stadium, and wedding garden. Sandy Brae Golf Course, 20 minutes north of Charleston off Interstate 79, is an 18-hole championship course. Big Bend is a 6,000-yard golf course along the beautiful Coal River at Tornado.

Kanawha State Forest, adjacent to Charleston, is a sprawling, 9,300 acre unspoiled area ideal for picnicking, hiking, fishing, horseback riding, mountain biking and camping, and cross-country skiing in the winter. Some of the best whitewater rafting in the country is available just a short distance from Charleston on the Gauley and New rivers; the area attracts more than 100,000 rafters and kayakers each year.

## Shopping and Dining

Opportunities for pleasant shopping and dining experiences are abundant in Charleston. The Charleston Village District features specialty shops for clothing, books, photography, and other unique items in an architecturally interesting setting. The Village District also offers fine dining experiences. Town Center Mall has more than 130 shops and specialties, in addition to its three main anchor stores. Kanawha Mall, 10 minutes from downtown, features 40 stores and unique eateries. A number of hand production glass factories are in the area, where one may observe skilled craftspersons at work and purchase their wares. Quilts and furniture, handcrafted in West Virginia, are available at local specialty stores. Diners in Charleston will find options for casual and fine dining as well as ethnic flavors of Chinese, Greek, Japanese, Indian, Mediterranean, Italian, and Mexican specialties.

*Visitor Information:* Charleston Convention and Visitors Bureau, 200 Civic Center Drive, Charleston, WV 25301; telephone (304)344-5075; fax (304)344-1241.

# Convention Facilities

In total, Charleston offers more than 173,300 square feet of meeting space, more than 4,000 hotel rooms, and easy access to shopping, dining, and recreation for visitors. One of the city's main meeting locations, the Charleston Civic Center, has more than 100,000 square feet of exhibition space in its Grand Hall, North and South halls, and meeting rooms. Located only one block from the central business district, the modern Charleston Civic Center is available for large gatherings, events, and concerts. Adjacent to the Civic Center is the Coliseum, a multipurpose facility that offers unobstructed-view seating for 13,500 people for events ranging from concerts and circuses to athletic competitions and horse races. A brick walkway links the Charleston Town Center complex— which consists of the Civic Coliseum, a three-story enclosed mall, the four-star Marriott Hotel, and many restaurants and night clubs—with the renovated Village District. Just two blocks away is the Charleston Municipal Auditorium with seating for up to 3,500 people. The Haddad Riverfront Park is available for special events. The University of Charleston also has facilities for groups of varying size, and all downtown hotels have ample meeting space.

Many shops and restaurants are within walking distance of the downtown hotels, and a low crime rate further enhances the appeal of the area for visitors and conventioneers.

*Convention Information:* Charleston Convention and Visitors Bureau, 200 Civic Center Drive, Charleston, WV 25301; telephone (304)344-5075; fax (304)344-1241

# Transportation

## Approaching the City

Arriving in Charleston by air, travelers land at Yeager Airport—a facility located 10 minutes from downtown that is a remarkable feat of engineering named for an even more remarkable man. First known as the Kanawha Airport, it was built in the late 1940s by shearing off mountaintops and filling in adjacent valleys. In 1986, the terminal facilities were completely renovated, and the airport was renamed after General Charles S. ''Chuck'' Yeager, World War II flying ace and the first man to break the sound barrier. Yeager happens to be a native of Lincoln County, located about 30 miles southwest of Charleston. Yeager Airport provides service from six commercial air carriers, has private aviation facilities, and is home to the 130th Tactical Airlift Group of the West Virginia Air National Guard. In 2004 Yeager Airport announced the addition of Independence Air, offering low-cost service to Washington D.C.'s Dulles airport.

Arriving by car, visitors approach Charleston via three major interstates, 64, 77, and 79, which intersect near downtown. Charleston is one of 13 cities in the nation where three interstates merge. I-64 links the Midwest through Charleston to Virginia's eastern seaboard. I-77 links the Great Lakes area through Charleston to South Carolina and north to Cleveland. The West Virginia Turnpike, which originates in Charleston and ends at the Virginia border near Princeton, has been incorporated into the I-77 and I-64 systems. Interstate-79 runs from Erie, Pennsylvania, where it connects with the New York throughways, through Pittsburgh, and terminates in Charleston. Amtrak offers rail passenger service.

## Traveling in the City

Charleston and the Kanawha Valley have a reputation of being cosmopolitan and compact. For those who live and work in the city, it is 10 minutes to work from most neighborhoods and 15 minutes to the airport. A bus system provided by the Kanawha Valley Regional Transportation Authority serves the entire valley from the western end at Nitro to the eastern end as far as Montgomery, 26 miles east of Charleston. Buses in downtown Charleston are designed as replicas of old fashioned trolleys and shuttle passengers between major downtown sites.

# Communications

## Newspapers and Magazines

Charleston's two daily newspapers are the *Charleston Daily Mail* (evening) and the *Charleston Gazette* (morning). On

Sundays they combine efforts to produce the *Sunday Gazette-Mail.* Several magazines—most of them special-interest publications aimed at readers in the fields of business and health care—are also published in the city. *Wonderful West Virginia* is published monthly by the state Department of Natural Resources.

## Television and Radio

Cable television is available in Charleston, as are several television stations broadcasting from neighboring towns in West Virginia, Kentucky, and Ohio, providing viewers with a full range of options. Ten radio stations offer Charleston listeners a variety of formats, including country/western, talk radio, sports, adult contemporary, and public radio.

*Media Information: Charleston Daily Mail* and *Charleston Gazette;* 1001 Virginia Street East, Charleston, WV 25301; telephone (304)348-5140

## Charleston Online

BIDCO. Available www.charleston-wv.com

*Charleston Daily Mail.* Available www.dailymail.com

*Charleston Gazette.* Available www.wvgazette.com

Charleston West Virginia Convention & Visitors Bureau. Available www.charlestonwv.com

City of Charleston Home Page. Available www.cityof charleston.org

Kanawha County Public Library. Available http://kanawha .lib.wv.us/chas.html

Kanawha County Schools. Available http://kcs.kana.k12.wv .us

## Selected Bibliography

Bell, Quentin, Virginia Nicholson, and Alen MacWeeney, *Charleston: A Bloomsbury House and Garden* (London: Francis Lincoln, 1997)

# Huntington

## *The City in Brief*

**Founded:** 1871

**Head Official:** Mayor David Felinton (D) (since 2005)

**City Population**
 1980: 63,684
 1990: 54,844
 2000: 51,475
 **2003 estimate:** 49,533
 **Percent change, 1990–2000:** −6.2%
 **U.S. rank in 1980:** 314th
 **U.S. rank in 1990:** 450th (State rank: 2nd)
 **U.S. rank in 2000:** 696th (State rank: 2nd)

**Metropolitan Area Population**
 1980: 311,350
 1990: 312,529
 2000: 315,538

**Percent change, 1990–2000:** 0.2%
**U.S. rank in 1980:** 97th
**U.S. rank in 1990:** 114th
**U.S. rank in 2000:** 126th

**Area:** 16 square miles (2000)
**Elevation:** Averages 570 feet above sea level
**Average Annual Temperature:** 55.0° F
**Average Annual Precipitation:** 42.31 inches

**Major Economic Sectors:** services, manufacturing, transportation, wholesale and retail trade
**Unemployment rate:** 6.1% (January 2005)
**Per Capita Income:** $16,717 (2000)

**2002 FBI Crime Index Total:** 4,008

**Major Colleges and Universities:** Marshall University, Marshall Community and Technical College, Huntington Junior College

**Daily Newspaper:** *The Herald-Dispatch*

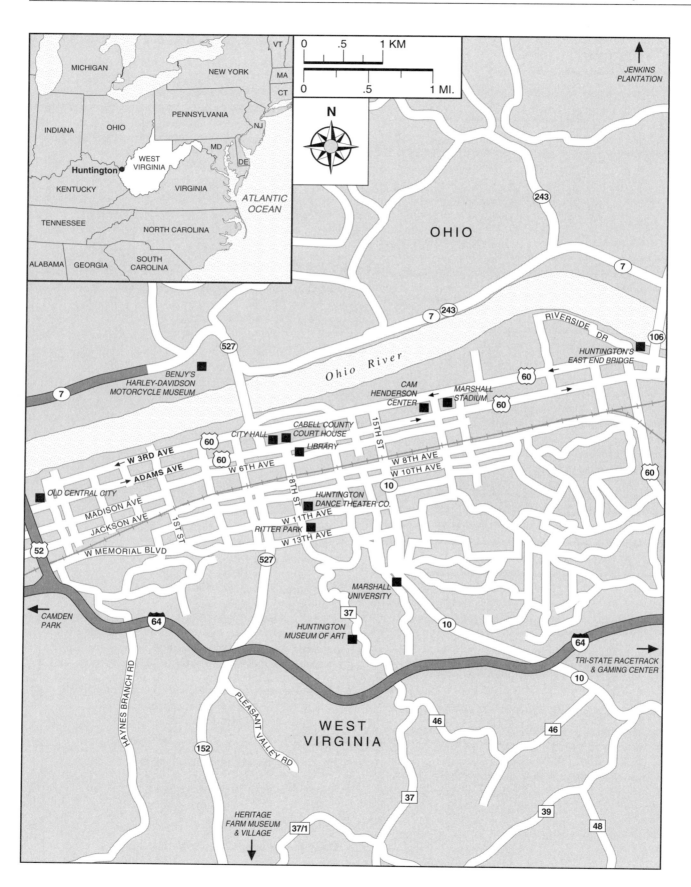

# Introduction

Huntington is the largest city in the Tri-State Region, being just across the Ohio River from Ohio and across the Big Sandy River from Kentucky. The city retains the charm of an earlier time, with century-old homes, historic districts, and nineteenth-century preserved villages. It also looks to the future by encouraging business creation in technology and biotechnology, with a world-class university vitalizing the city with a youth and art scene.

# Geography and Climate

Huntington is located on the flood plain of the Ohio River, which acts as its northern border, and also sits at the foothills of the Appalachian Mountains. It is the county seat of Cabell County, but parts of the city are also in Wayne County. Because of the proximity to the river, flooding has been a problem during heavy rains. Huntington is less than an hour away by car from Charleston, West Virginia's capital. The other two cities in the Tri-State area are Ashland, Kentucky, and Ironton, Ohio. Huntington is in a continental temperate zone, with warm and humid summers, and cold winters without arctic fronts.

**Area:** 16 square miles (2000)

**Elevation:** Averages 570 feet above sea level.

**Average Temperatures:** January, 32.7° F; August, 73.9° F; annual average, 55.0° F

**Average Annual Precipitation:** 42.31 inches

# History

### Native Tribes are First Inhabitants

The first known inhabitants of the Ohio River Valley were the Adena people, also known as the ''mound builders'' because of the artifact-laden mounds they built, some over 2000 years ago. Since the 1500s, different Native American tribes lived in the Ohio Valley and in the area now called Huntington, such as the Hurons, but the area was also used as hunting grounds by the larger Shawnee of Ohio and the Iroquois Confederacy from New York. There was much fighting in the region between the British and Native Americans in the 1760s and 1770s, resulting in battles and massacres of entire villages. As more settlers entered the region after the American Revolution, the Mingo and Shawnee tribes were forced to move further inland.

### War and Railroads

In 1837 Marshall Academy, the forerunner of Marshall University, was created in the town of Barboursville. Named after U.S. Supreme Court Chief Justice John Marshall, it started as a subscription school, and after being closed during the Civil War it reopened as the State Normal School of Marshall College to train teachers.

Inhabitants of Cabell County during the Civil War were divided about their allegiances. The Border Rangers were a local pro-South militia formed in 1860, but the county's representative to the Virginia secession convention of 1861 voted to remain in the Union. While Virginia seceded, Cabell County voted to stay in the Union, with the exception of the town of Guyandotte, now part of Huntington. The Battle at Barboursville in 1861 was the first battle in the county, won by the Confederacy. The town was eventually captured by Union forces, which then burned most of Guyandotte to the ground. It was due to the area's Union leanings that caused the State of West Virginia to be created in 1862.

Huntington, originally called Halderby's Landing, was named after Collis P. Huntington, a railroad baron who was a major partner in the Central Pacific Railroad, and who bought out the Chesapeake & Ohio Railway. In 1869 he began construction of the western terminus to the C & O, connecting the Ohio River and trains from the Midwest to the Atlantic Seaboard. The city was incorporated in 1871 by the West Virginia State Legislature. In 1873, the first locomotive arrived from Richmond to the celebration of the entire community. The railroad was the city's largest employer for a century, until eventually becoming part of CSX in the 1970s.

### A Glimpse of Modern Life

In 1884 the Ohio River overflowed its banks, flooding the city and causing major damage. Huntington became the seat of Cabell County in 1887, just after the first electric streetlights were installed. Electric streetcars became a fixture in the city soon afterwards. Just west of Huntington, Central City was incorporated in 1893. Central City started as just a few farms but grew as manufacturers, such as glass and chain factories, entered the area, and in 1909 Central City was annexed by Huntington. The same year, construction of Ritter Park was begun, which was completed in 1913, and the park continues to be a valued part of Huntington today.

Again in 1913 the river flooded Huntington, causing serious damage. However, it was not as bad as the flood to come. The ''Great Flood of 1937'' left 6,000 residents homeless and the region devastated. The disaster caused the U.S.

Army Corps of Engineers to build a 15-mile flood wall to protect the town, which it continues to do today.

Readily available raw materials, cheap coal power, and connections to major markets by the railroad caused Huntington to grow into the industrial hub of the area. Steel producers and fabricators blossomed along with manufacturers of railcars and railroad equipment. Huntington is still known for its glassworks and pigment production.

**Huntington Today**

In 1970, tragedy struck the city when a plane carrying 75 passengers, including the entire Marshall University football team, crashed in rain and fog on approach to Tri-State Airport. The crash was the worst aviation disaster in the country that year.

West Virginia's economy has had its ups and downs. At first, mechanization in mining increased the unemployment rate when fewer workers were needed. In the 1970s, when energy prices were high, the coal industry and state profited. When energy prices dropped in the 1980s it was a devastating blow to the entire state, affecting all the mining communities and all business sectors beyond. Huntington suffered from factory closures and a declining population.

Today's Huntington is still a center of manufacturing and shipping, especially of the region's coal. As Mayor David Felinton said in his 2004 State of the City Address, "West Virginia is experiencing a time of rebirth. We are on the edge of economic development with the potential for unprecedented growth and prosperity within the next five years. We can be confident that Huntington is on the right path for the future."

*Historical Information:* The City of Huntington, City Hall, 8th Street and 5th Avenue, Huntington, WV 25701; telephone: (304)696-5580

# Population Profile

**Metropolitan Area Residents**
*1980:* 311,350
*1990:* 312,529
*2000:* 315,538
*Percent change, 1990–2000:* 0.2%
*U.S. rank in 1980:* 97th
*U.S. rank in 1990:* 114th
*U.S. rank in 2000:* 126th

**City Residents**
*1980:* 63,684

*1990:* 54,844
*2000:* 51,475
*2003 estimate:* 49,533
*Percent change, 1990–2000:* −6.2%
*U.S. rank in 1980:* 314th
*U.S. rank in 1990:* 450th (State rank: 2nd)
*U.S. rank in 2000:* 574th (State rank: 2nd)

*Density:* 3,234.1 people per square mile (2000)

*Racial and ethnic characteristics* (2000)
White: 46,127
Black: 3,858
American Indian and Alaskan Native: 101
Asian: 422
Native Hawaiian and other Pacific Islander: 25
Hispanic or Latino (may be of any race): 437
Other: 155

*Percent of residents born in state:* 74.1% (2000)

*Age characteristics* (2000)
Population under 5 years old: 2,499
Population 5 to 9 years old: 2,539
Population 10 to 14 years old: 2,471
Population 15 to 19 years old: 4,237
Population 20 to 24 years old: 6,402
Population 25 to 34 years old: 6,539
Population 35 to 44 years old: 6,303
Population 45 to 54 years old: 6,565
Population 55 to 59 years old: 2,422
Population 60 to 64 years old: 2,226
Population 65 to 74 years old: 4,502
Population 75 to 84 years old: 3,611
Population 85 years and older: 1,159
Median age: 36.7 years

*Births* (2002)
Total number: 675

*Deaths* (2002)
Total number: 768 (of which, 4 were infants under the age of 1 year)

*Money income* (1999)
Per capita income: $16,717
Median household income: $23,234
Total households: 23,067

*Number of households with income of . . .*
less than $10,000: 5,276
$10,000 to $14,999: 2,783
$15,000 to $24,999: 3,995
$25,000 to $34,999: 2,995
$35,000 to $49,999: 3,051
$50,000 to $74,999: 2,848
$75,000 to $99,999: 1,065

$100,000 to $149,999: 576
$150,000 to $199,999: 182
$200,000 or more: 296

*Percent of families below poverty level:* 17.5% (59.5% of which were female householder families with related children under 5 years)

*2002 FBI Crime Index Total:* 4,008

# Municipal Government

The Huntington City Council has eleven members, one from each of the nine municipal election districts and two members elected at-large. The mayor and council members are elected for four-year terms in November, with primaries held in May.

**Head Official:** Mayor David Felinton (D) (since 2005; current term expires 2009)

**Total Number of City Employees:** 350 (2005)

*City Information:* City Huntington, 8th Street and 5th Avenue, Huntington, WV 25701; telephone (304)696-5580

# Economy

## Major Industries and Commercial Activity

Huntington and Cabell County have long been known for their strong manufacturing base, although now the service sector makes up the largest percentage of jobs. Steel and glass were industries that grew in the city's Industrial Revolution origins, as did the transportation sector, which created the town. New industries are being lured to the area with economic incentives. The health care industry in the area continues to grow, with health care organizations being among the area's top employers.

## Incentive Programs—New and Existing Companies

*Local programs—*A variety of incentive programs are available to companies who establish new businesses in the Huntington area, including free land programs, relocation grants, financing of equipment, rent breaks, and others.

*State programs—*West Virginia has a number of state tax exemption and incentive programs, such as the Warehouse Freeport Tax Exemption on goods traveling through the state, the Manufacturing Sales Tax Exemption on materials or equipment, and the Strategic R&D Credit program. Companies that relocate their corporate headquarters are eligible for the Corporate Headquarters Credit.

*Job training programs—*The Governor's Guaranteed Work Force Program offers one-stop service for all economic development-related job training in the Huntington area. The program provides funds for up to 100 percent of the cost for training new or existing employees in qualifying companies, up to a total of $2,000. The Cabell County Career Technology Center provides vocational and technology training, while the Robert C. Byrd Institute for Advanced Flexible Manufacturing helps small- and medium-sized manufacturers with technology and technical training. The Apprenticeship for Child Development Specialists Training Program offers on-the-job training to child care professionals. Area colleges also provide many job training programs.

## Development Projects

The Huntington Area Development Council (HADCO) has been an important factor in economic growth in recent years. Two major projects that have recently come to fruition are Kinetic Park and Pullman Square. Kinetic Park is a 95-acre technology and business park and retail center, which in 2005 will see its first occupants build and begin business activities. In 2004, after years of planning, Pullman Square opened, a $60 million open-air retail and entertainment complex that hopes to rejuvenate the downtown area. HADCO and Marshall University have joined forces to promote and develop the biotech industry in the area, and together will build the Velocity Center in Kinetic Park to encourage business growth. HADCO boasts that in 10 years the organization has brought 9,000 new jobs to Huntington; has brought in 30 new companies; and has leased, sold or built 1.7 million feet of building space. Other recent developments include the re-opening of a former glass bottle factory as a steel plant by Capresa, a Spanish steelmaker based in Barcelona, and two new call centers for Amazon.com and Global Contact Services.

*Items and goods produced:* steel, glass, railroad equipment

*Economic Development Information:* Huntington Area Development Council, 916 Fifth Avenue, Suite 400, Huntington, WV 25701; telephone (304)525-1161; fax (304)525-1163; email hadco@hadco.org. Huntington Regional Chamber of Commerce, 720 Fourth Ave., Huntington, WV 25701; telephone (304)525-5131

## Commercial Shipping

Huntington's central location in the heart of the Tri-State region of West Virginia, Ohio, and Kentucky affords it a convenient midway point between Pittsburgh, Pennsylvania, and Louisville, Kentucky. Products and people move through the Tri-State region's efficient transportation network that includes the Tri-State Airport; an interstate highway system that links the area to East Coast, Southern, and Midwestern markets; an advanced rail network; and the largest tonnage barge port on the Ohio River. In addition, Huntington is within a 24 hour drive of approximately 44 percent of the nation's industrial market, and 37 percent of the consumer market.

## Labor Force and Employment Outlook

The outlook for the Huntington area looks bright, despite the city's continuing decline in population. HADCO's development plans and joint ventures with Marshall University offer the promise of bringing new technology and biotech firms to the area. Higher energy prices in the mid-2000s could bring much needed capital into West Virginia, through the coal industry. In this case, investment in new business sectors and redevelopment of the old industrial base could provide a boom to the Tri-State region. Employment rates in Cabell County have remained fairly stable in the last few years, but there has also been a −0.7% decrease in population between 2000 and 2003. Since 2000, only 22.4% of the adult population over 25 have bachelor degrees; more education and training programs may be needed to keep technology-based jobs in the city.

The following is a summary of data regarding the Huntington metropolitan area labor force, 2003 annual averages.

*Size of nonagricultural labor force:* 121,400

*Number of workers employed in . . .*
  *construction and mining:* 6,800
  *manufacturing:* 10,600
  *trade, transportation and utilities:* 26,100
  *information:* 1,600
  *financial activities:* 5,300
  *business and professional services:* 11,000
  *educational and health services:* 20,300
  *leisure and hospitality:* 10,900
  *other services:* 8,100
  *government:* 20,700

*Average hourly earnings of production workers employed in manufacturing:* $15.48

*Unemployment rate:* 6.1% (January 2005)

| *Largest employers* | *Number of employees* |
| --- | --- |
| Marshall University | 2,000 |
| St. Mary's Hospital | 2,000 |
| Marathon Ashland Petroleum | 1,700 |
| Cabell-Huntington Hospital | 1,500 |
| AK Steel | 1,400 |
| CSX Huntington | 1,100 |

| *Largest employers* | *Number of employees* |
| --- | --- |
| Applied Card Systems | 1,000 |
| Alcon Surgical | 506 |
| U.S. Army Corps of Engineers | 450 |
| Client Logic | 400 |

## Cost of Living

The cost of living in Huntington is somewhat lower than comparable cities in the United States.

The following is a summary of data regarding several key cost of living factors for the Huntington area.

*2004 (3rd Quarter) ACCRA Average House Price:* $232,360

*2004 (3rd Quarter) ACCRA Cost of Living Index:* 96.7 (U.S. average = 100.0)

*State income tax rate:* Ranges from 3.0 to 6.5%

*State sales tax rate:* 6.0%

*Local income tax rate:* none

*Local sales tax rate:* none

*Property tax rate:* $.035088 per $100 of assessed valuation (calculated on 60% of market value)

**Economic Information:** Huntington Area Development Council, 916 Fifth Avenue, Suite 400, Huntington, WV 25701; telephone (304)525-1161; fax (304)525-1163

# Education and Research

## Elementary and Secondary Schools

Cabell County Schools experienced a period of change in the mid-2000s. In 2005 the Superintendent of Schools was replaced when his contract was bought out. The high school drop-out rate was 20 percent in 2003, up from an already-high 13 percent a decade earlier. However, new policies in the district are expected to create improvements. The county has a higher than national average percentage of children in pre-kindergarten programs. Elementary schools in the district have adopted a "balanced literacy" system with co-teachers in class that has over 80 percent of students reading at or above grade level. New curriculum standards were also recently put in place. Before-school enrichment classes are available at many schools, and in most schools, students meet or exceed standards on the SAT tests.

The following is a summary of data regarding Cabell County's public schools as of the 2004–2005 school year.

*Total enrollment:* 12,294

*Number of facilities*
  *elementary schools:* 20
  *middle schools:* 6
  *senior high schools:* 2
  *other:* 2

*Student/teacher ratio:* 14.5:1

*Teacher salaries*
  *average:* $38,240

*Funding per pupil:* $7,795 (2002–2003)

Seven private and parochial schools serve Huntington and Cabell County.

*Public Schools Information:* Cabell County Schools, 2850 Fifth Avenue, Huntington, WV 25702; telephone (304)528-5000; fax (304)528-5080

### Colleges and Universities

Huntington is home to three colleges and universities. Marshall University (MU) is the area's largest university, and is ranked by *U.S. News and World Report* as one of ''America's Best Buys'' in education. With enrollment at 17,000 students, it offers degree programs in business, education, journalism, medicine and health sciences, information and engineering, and the performing and fine arts.

Affiliated with MU is the Marshall Community and Technical College, a two-year institute offering associates degrees in allied health, business, information and manufacturing technologies, and its unique Railroad Conductor Training Program. Huntington Junior College is located in the downtown area and offers seven associates degree programs in the business and health professions.

### Libraries and Research Centers

The Cabell County Public Library system operates a main library in Huntington and seven branches in neighboring towns. Over 100 years old, it was the first library system in the state to have a computerized catalog and circulation system. The main branch is home to a local history and genealogy room, and three social services agencies: The Tri-State Literacy Council, the Adult Learning Center, and the Information and Referral Services.

Marshall University has several prominent research centers. The Center for Business and Economic Research investigates promoting regional economic growth. The Center for Environmental, Geotechnical and Applied Sciences researches environmental management and technology using geo-science. The Robert C. Byrd Center for Rural Health Resources runs rural health programs across the state, and the Center of Biomedical Research Excellence focuses on cancer research.

*Public Library Information:* Cabell County Public Library; 455 9th Street Plaza, Huntington, WV 25701; telephone (304)528-5700

# Health Care

The Tri-State area has seven hospitals that serve the community, with a total of 1,300 beds. The largest in the area, and second largest in the state, is St. Mary's Hospital. With 400 beds and centers in cardiac care, neuroscience, diabetes, and cancer treatment, St. Mary's is a teaching hospital for Marshall Univerity's School of Medicine and School of Nursing. Cabell Huntington Hospital, a 291-bed facility, opened the 50,000 square-foot Edwards Comprehensive Cancer Center in 2005. The hospital is also home to West Virginia's only Burn Intensive Care Unit, a Neonatal Intensive Care Unit, and a Joint Replacement unit that opened in 2004. The Huntington VA Medical Center serves veterans with a 50-bed acute care and surgical hospital and 4 outpatient clinics.

Valley Health operates 22 general health care centers and public health programs. Health South operates two centers in the area: the Rehabilitation Hospital of Huntington and the Cabell-Huntington Outpatient Surgery Center. The Prestera Center provides outpatient mental health services for adults, children, and families, and has inpatient substance abuse and psychiatric facilities. Mildred Mitchell-Bateman Hospital is an adult inpatient psychiatric facility, and River Park Hospital provides inpatient services for both adults and adolescents. Genesis HealthCare runs Heritage Center, an 189-bed eldercare and rehabilitation center.

# Recreation

### Sightseeing

Huntington has a range of attractions for the history buff, the arts lover, and families. A number of the city's historic buildings are open to the public and available for tours. The Jenkins Plantation Museum is a brick mansion built in 1835 and is part of the Civil War Discovery Trail. Featured are tours, reenactments and special events. In 2005, the museum is undergoing restoration to restore its original nineteenth-century appearance. The Madie Caroll House, run by the Huntington Park District, was floated into town on a barge in 1810 and survived an attack by federal troops in 1861. The building was home to the Caroll family, existed as an inn, and was the first house of Catholic worship in Cabell County. The Cabell County Courthouse was built in 1901 and is on the National Register of Historic Places. Heritage Village, across from Riverfront Park, consists of the restored original B & O Railway station and Huntington's first bank, reportedly robbed by Jesse James in 1875. On display are a period locomotive and Pullman car, and shops and restaurants draw visitors.

Heritage Farm Museum and Village displays Appalachian farm culture by preserving 16 buildings from the 1800s, including a schoolhouse, blacksmith shop, meeting hall, a mill, and barns. Collections of farm equipment, a petting zoo, a country store, and four bed and breakfasts are part of the attractions. The Rose Garden at Ritter Park has existed for over 70 years and features more than 2,000 rose bushes. Blenko Glass Company is home to artisans creating handmade glassware, which can be viewed from an observation area. Camden Park, West Virginia's only amusement park, has been in existence since 1903 but is still going strong with 18 major rides, a Kiddieland area with 9 rides, and a Midway full of games and food. The Tri-City Racetrack and Gaming Center is in nearby Cross Lanes, and features Greyhound racing, slot machines, and video gambling.

## Arts and Culture

The 5th Avenue Theater Company, a non-profit production company, specializes in musicals and theater for children and families. The company performs in the historic Jean Carlo Stephenson Auditorium in Huntington's City Hall. The Renaissance Theater at Marshall University hosts plays, films, musicians, dance companies, and other touring productions through the Marshall Artists Series. Students from Marshall's Department of Theater also put on productions at the University's venues. Huntington Outdoor Theater presents musicals every July in the Ritter Park Amphitheater. Free Spirit Productions presents classics and new plays at venues in the area, including Marshall University and the Huntington Museum of Art. Huntington Dance Theater performs and teaches ballet and modern dance. In nearby Ashland, Kentucky, the 1,400-seat Paramount Arts Center presents plays, music, and dance performances from national and local groups.

The Huntington Symphony Orchestra presents an average of six classical and three pops performances each season, with classical performances presented at Jean Carlo Stephenson Auditorium, and pops shows at Harris Riverfront Park in the summer. Marshall University's many ensembles showcase jazz, chamber, orchestral, and choral music. The Greater Huntington Park and Recreation District hosts music performances at Veteran's Memorial Field House and Ritter Amphitheater.

Huntington's several museums and galleries appeal to a wide variety of tastes. The Huntington Museum of Art has a broad collection of nineteenth- and twentieth-century paintings, drawings, sculpture, glass, silver, folk art, and firearms. Attached to the Museum of Art is the C. Fred Edwards Conservatory, West Virginia's only plant conservatory and home to sub-tropical native plants and seasonal displays. The Huntington Railroad Museum in Ritter Park is home to two locomotives and two cabooses; free tours are available by arrangement. The Birke Art Gallery at Marshall University displays student and professional art. The Museum of Radio and Technology features radios from the 1920s through the 1950s, military radio technology, and vintage computers. Benjy's Harley-Davidson Motorcycle Museum, located in a Harley dealership, shows off an amazing collection of antique and modern motorcycles.

## Festivals and Holidays

In March, Huntington's Park District holds a St. Patrick's Day Celebration with live music, Irish food, and fun for kids. At Easter time, an Egg Hunt goes on in Ritter Park. The Huntington Dogwood Arts and Crafts Festival takes place in April at the Big Sandy Superstore Arena. The city celebrates West Virginia Day, June 20th, with entertainment, food, and crafts. Also in June, Jazz-MU-Tazz, Marshall University's Marshall University jazz festival, features plenty of free music outdoors, and Old Central City Days has the area's streets busy with flea markets and historic tours. The Fourth of July brings fireworks and music to Riverfront Park. The Cabell County Fair takes place in July and August. Food is first billing in August's Ribfest and September's Chilifest. September also brings the Hilltop Festival to the Huntington Museum of Art and the Pilot Club of Huntington Antique Show and Sale. In October comes the Grecian Festival at St. George Greek Orthodox Church, the Harvest Festival, and the West Virginia Pumpkin Festival. Guyandotte Civil War Days in November brings re-enactors together to commemorate the raid on the town in 1861 with period music, history tours, and craft displays. The Lions Tri-State Arts and Crafts Festival happens in December at the Big Sandy Superstore Arena.

## Sports for the Spectator

Fans of Marshall University's Thundering Herd sports program enjoy watching football, baseball, and men's and women's basketball. Other sports at Marshall include volleyball, soccer, golf, tennis, and swimming. Regional college and local high school football and basketball are also enjoyed by residents.

## Sports for the Participant

The Greater Huntington Park District offers 11 parks with many sports facilities. The Ritter Park Tennis Center has 11 hard courts with 4 indoor courts and a pro shop. Veterans

Memorial Field House is home to indoor soccer, inline hockey, and basketball games. Softball fields, basketball courts, pools and other amenities serve the community. Huntington's YMCA provides many recreational activities, including an indoor pool. An 18-hole golf course is at the Esquire Country Club in nearby Barboursville. Hiking trails, camping, boating and fishing are available activities in the three nearby state parks: Virginia Point Park, East Lynn Lake and Dam, and Beach Fork Lake and State Park.

**Shopping and Dining**

Huntington's several shopping areas range from the historic to the modern. Old Central City features antique shops and is close to the Railroad Museum and Heritage Farm. Pullman Square, the new entertainment and retail complex opened in 2004, is attracting specialty shops and national chains. The Huntington Mall has more than 100 stores, including clothing, book, electronics and jewelry retailers.

Dining choices at local restaurants vary and are plentiful. For casual eating, Huntington is well-known for its hot dog/root beer stands and ''Huntington-style'' hot dogs, such as those offered at the Frostop Drive-In, Stewart's Original, Sam's, and Bowincal. The hot dog's sauce, of which Stewart's claims to have invented, makes the difference. Jim's Steak and and Spaghetti House is a Huntington institution, in business for over 60 years and still operated by the original owner. Buddy's Bar-B-Que's killer wings are famous on the Marshall University campus. For more refined dining, fine Italian, American, seafood, Indian, and Mexican food are available. Two restaurants in historic buildings are Savannah's, serving traditional southern food in a 1903 Victorian mansion, and Boston Beanery, at the old B & O Railroad station.

*Visitor Information:* Cabell-Huntington Convention and Visitor's Bureau, PO Box 327, Huntington, WV 25708; telephone (304)525-7333; toll-free (800)635-6329

# *Convention Facilities*

The Big Sandy Superstore Arena and Conference Center offers more than 100,000 square feet of exhibition, conference, meeting and ballroom facilities, and offers an on-site caterer and videoconferencing equipment. Marshall University's Memorial Student Center can be rented for conferences; its recital halls and the Joan C. Edwards Playhouse make interesting venues for meetings or conferences. The University can also provide housing at its Twin Towers Residence Hall. The Veteran's Memorial Field House, operated by the Greater Huntington Park and Recreation District, has 20,000 square feet of exhibition space, and has played host to concerts, rodeos, circuses, and sporting events.

Hotels: with exhibition and conference space include the Executive Inn and Suites, the downtown Radisson, and the StoneLodge Huntington.

*Convention Information:* Cabell-Huntington Convention and Visitor's Bureau; PO Box 347, Huntington, WV 25708; telephone (304)525-7333; toll-free (800)635-6329.

# *Transportation*

**Approaching the City**

The Tri-State Airport is located only nine miles from Huntington, and is served by U.S. Airways Express and Delta Connection, making connections to Charlotte, North Carolina, and Cincinnati, Ohio. In nearby Charleston, West Virginia, Yeager Airport has United, Delta, Continental, Northwest, U.S. Airways and Independence Air flights to larger cities.

Interstate 64 runs along the south side of Huntington, heading east to the capitol, Charleston, and west to Lexington, Kentucky. West Virginia route 60 runs right through Huntington's downtown.

Intercity passenger service to Huntington is available on Amtrak's Cardinal Line, running three days a week from New York City to Chicago, Illinois. Greyhound Bus Lines offers regular service to downtown.

**Traveling in the City**

The Tri-State Transit Authority (TTA) runs nine bus lines, all connected at the TTA Center on 4th Avenue. The TTA connects Huntington with Milton, Barboursville, Ceredo and Kenova. Yellow Cabs are available for hire, and Top Hat Pedal Cab has two bicycle-powered rickshaws that drive passengers around downtown Huntington.

# *Communications*

**Newspapers and Magazines**

Huntington's daily newspaper is the *The Herald-Dispatch.* *Huntington Quarterly* is a full-color magazine that features articles about the community and city.

**Television and Radio**

Huntington is home to five television stations, and also receives broadcasts from Charleston, West Virginia, Ashland, Kentucky, and Portsmouth, Ohio. Six FM and three

AM radio stations broadcast from Huntington proper, with 27 other stations in the surrounding communities.

***Media Information:*** *The Herald Dispatch,* 946 5th Ave., Huntington, WV 25701; telephone (304)526-4000; toll-free (800)955-6110

## Huntington Online

Cabell County Public Library. Available cabell.lib.wv.us

Cabell County Schools. Available www.boe.cabe.k12.wv.us .org

Cabell-Huntington Convention and Visitors Bureau. Available www.wvvisit.org

City of Huntington Home Page. Available www.cityof huntington.com

*The Herald-Dispatch.* Available www.herald-dispatch.com

Huntington Regional Chamber of Commerce. Available www.huntingtonchamber.org

## Selected Bibliography

Casto, James E., *Huntington: An Illustrated History* (Northridge, CA: Windsor Publications, Inc., 1985)

Rice, Otis K., *West Virginia: A History* (Lexington, KY: The University of Kentucky Press, 1985)

# Cumulative Index

The one hundred eighty-nine cities featured in *Cities of the United States,* Volume 1: *The South,* Volume 2: *The West,* Volume 3: *The Midwest,* and Volume 4: *The Northeast,* along with names of individuals, organizations, historical events, etc., are designated in this Cumulative Index by name of the appropriate regional volume, or volumes, followed by the page number(s) on which the term appears in that volume.

Cumulative Index